SOCIETY IN HISTORY: TIME LINES

A time line is a visual device that helps us understand historical change. The upper time line represents 5 billion years of the history of the planet Earth. This time line is divided into three sections, each of which is drawn to a different scale of time. The first section, **The Earth's Origins**, begins with the planet's origins 5 billion years before the present (B.P.) and indicates that another full billion years passed before the earliest forms of life appeared. The second section, **Our Human Origins**, shows that plants and animals continued to evolve for billions more years until, approximately 12 million years ago, our earliest human ancestors came onto the scene. In the third section of this time line, **Earliest Civilisation**, we see that what we term civilisation is relatively recent, indeed, with the first permanent settlements occurring in the Middle East a scant 12,000 years ago. But the written record of our species' existence extends back only half this long, to the time humans invented writing and first farmed with animal-driven ploughs some 5,000 years B.P.

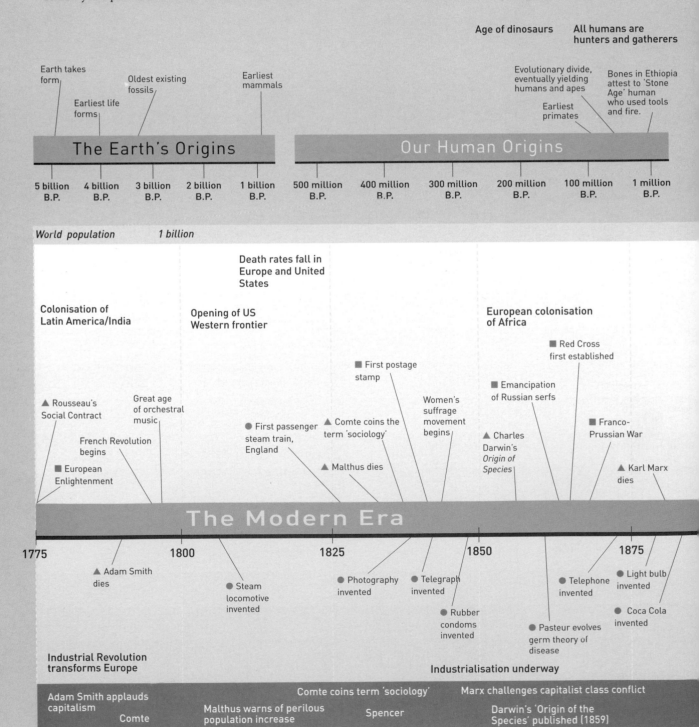

Age of dinosaurs

All humans are hunters and gatherers

Earth takes form

Earliest life forms

Oldest existing fossils

Earliest mammals

Evolutionary divide, eventually yielding humans and apes

Earliest primates

Bones in Ethiopia attest to 'Stone Age' human who used tools and fire.

The Earth's Origins

Our Human Origins

| 5 billion B.P. | 4 billion B.P. | 3 billion B.P. | 2 billion B.P. | 1 billion B.P. | 500 million B.P. | 400 million B.P. | 300 million B.P. | 200 million B.P. | 100 million B.P. | 1 million B.P. |

World population   1 billion

Death rates fall in Europe and United States

Colonisation of Latin America/India

Opening of US Western frontier

European colonisation of Africa

■ Red Cross first established

■ First postage stamp

▲ Rousseau's Social Contract

Great age of orchestral music

Women's suffrage movement begins

■ Emancipation of Russian serfs

■ Franco-Prussian War

● First passenger steam train, England

▲ Comte coins the term 'sociology'

French Revolution begins

▲ Charles Darwin's *Origin of Species*

▲ Karl Marx dies

■ European Enlightenment

▲ Malthus dies

The Modern Era

| 1775 | 1800 | 1825 | 1850 | 1875 |

▲ Adam Smith dies

● Steam locomotive invented

● Photography invented

● Telegraph invented

● Rubber condoms invented

● Telephone invented

● Light bulb invented

● Coca Cola invented

● Pasteur evolves germ theory of disease

Industrial Revolution transforms Europe

Industrialisation underway

Adam Smith applauds capitalism

Comte

Comte coins term 'sociology'

Malthus warns of perilous population increase

Spencer

Marx challenges capitalist class conflict

Darwin's 'Origin of the Species' published (1859)

Sociology came into being in the wake of the many changes to society wrought by the Industrial Revolution over the last few centuries – just the blink of an eye in evolutionary perspective. The lower time line provides a close-up look at the events and trends that have defined **The Modern Era**, most of which are discussed in this text.

Innovations in technology are charted in the panel below the line and provide a useful backdrop for viewing the milestones of social progress highlighted in the panel above the line. Major contributions to the development of sociological thought are traced along the very bottom of this time line.

Events are coded according to the broad themes as follows:

● Technology

■ National/global events and trends

▲ Sociology as a discipline

For Time Lines on the world wide web, see www.hyperhistory.com

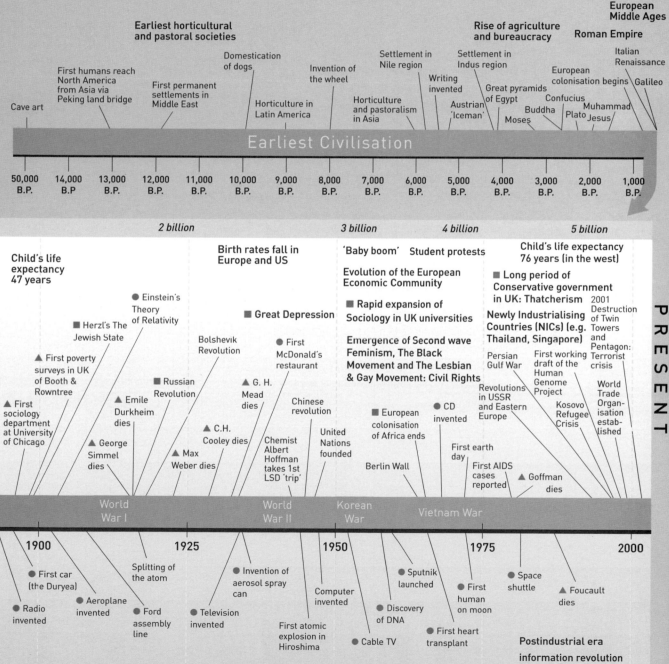

We work with leading authors to develop the strongest educational materials in sociology, bringing cutting-edge thinking and best learning practice to a global market.

Under a range of well-known imprints, including Prentice Hall, we craft high quality print and electronic publications which help readers to understand and apply their content, whether studying or at work.

To find out more about the complete range of our publishing, please visit us on the World Wide Web at: **www.pearsoneduc.com**

Visit the *Sociology, third edition* Companion Website at **www.pearsoned.co.uk/plummer** to find valuable student learning material including:

- Key concepts explored
- True/false questions to help test your learning
- Links to relevant sites on the web
- An online glossary to explain key terms
- Flashcards to test your knowledge of key terms and definitions

SOCIOLOGY

CANADA

UNITED STATES
OF AMERICA

ATLANTIC
OCEAN

MEXICO

WEST INDIES

BELIZE
GUATEMALA HONDURAS
EL SALVADOR   NICARAGUA
COSTA
RICA
PANAMA

VENEZUELA   GUYANA
SURINAME
FRENCH
GUIANA
(Fr.)
COLOMBIA

ECUADOR

PERU

BRAZIL

BOLIVIA

CHILE   PARAGUAY

URUGUAY

ARGENTINA

IRELAND   UNITED
KINGDOM

FRANC

PORTUGAL   SPAIN

MOROCCO

ALGERIA

WESTERN SAHARA

MAURITANIA   MALI

SENEGAL
GAMBIA   BURKINA
GUINEA-BISSAU   FASO
GUINEA

SIERRA LEONE   IVORY   GHANA   BENIN
COAST
LIBERIA   TOGO

SOCIOLOGY
A Global Introduction

John J. Macionis

Ken Plummer

Third edition

PEARSON
Prentice Hall

Harlow, England • London • New York • Boston • San Francisco • Toronto
Sydney • Tokyo • Singapore • Hong Kong • Seoul • Taipei • New Delhi
Cape Town • Madrid • Mexico City • Amsterdam • Munich • Paris • Milan

Pearson Education Limited
Edinburgh Gate
Harlow
Essex CM20 2JE

and associated Companies throughout the world

Visit us on the World Wide Web at:
www.pearsoneduc.com

First published 1997
Second edition published 2002
Third Edition published 2005

ISBN 0 131 28746 X

British Library Cataloguing-in-Publication Data
A catalogue record for this book is available from the British Library

10 9 8 7 6 5 4 3 2 1
09 08 07 06 05

Typeset in 9/12pt Giovanni by 30
Printed and bound by Mateu Cromo Artes Graficas, Spain

BRIEF CONTENTS

PART 1 INTRODUCING SOCIOLOGY

PART 2 THE FOUNDATIONS OF SOCIETY: FROM MACRO TO MICRO

PART 3 SOCIAL DIVISIONS AND SOCIAL INEQUALITIES

PART 4 SOCIAL STRUCTURES, SOCIAL PRACTICES AND SOCIAL INSTITUTIONS

PART 5 SOCIAL CHANGE

FULL CONTENTS

PART 1	INTRODUCING SOCIOLOGY

1 The Sociological Imagination   2

2 Thinking Sociologically, Thinking Globally   22

3 Doing Social Science: an Introduction to Method   42

PART 2	THE FOUNDATIONS OF SOCIETY: FROM MACRO TO MICRO

4 Societies   72

5 Culture   104

SOCIAL SHAPES OF THE WORLD

GUIDE TO BOXES

PROFILES

CONTROVERSY AND DEBATE

EUROPEAN EYE

GUIDE TO FIGURES AND TABLES

TABLES

PREFACE: HOW TO USE THIS BOOK

Welcome to the third edition

The book *Sociology: A Global Introduction* has fast become one of the more prominent sociology texts in many countries, and this *third edition* aims to consolidate some of its past achievements. Its key goals are:

- to introduce all the main areas of study, the key concepts, the historical debates and basic approaches to the discipline. It assumes you know nothing about sociology; and thus **it is not an advanced text**. It sets its goals as *opening up the field* of enquiry for the very first time. If you wish to go further, there are suggestions at the end of each chapter for doing this, as well as a website which has been designed to give you further links, readings, questions and food for thought.

- to tell a story about the parallel rise of sociology and the modern world and how its is persistently shaped by both technologies and inequalities. This is not a text which just summarises vast streams of sociological studies. It aims, rather, to tell a narrative which suggests how the modern world developed from more traditional ones, and how now in ther twenty first century it may well be moving into yet another new phase.

- to recognise that sociology these days must be global. Many textbooks focus upon one country. Whilst this textbook does often focus on UK, Europe and North America, it also takes its orbit to be the world. We suggest that increasingly it is impossible to understand one country in isolation from others. Indeed, a recurrent theme through this book is that the modern world is becoming progressively globalised.

- to introduce analyses of a number of newer topics that are not always included in introductory sociology textbooks. We have selected some issues that are becoming increasingly critical in the twenty-first century. These include the role of globalisation (Chapter 2); the new areas of body, emotions and identity (Chapter 7); the importance of age, children and the growing number of the elderly (Chapter 13); the importance of human rights regimes (Chapter 15); the rising (global) power of the mass media (Chapter 21); the significance of many countries outside the West that are facing poverty (Chapter 9); the importance of science, cyberspace and the new reproductive technologies (Chapter 22); the global significance of environmental hazards (Chapter 24); the sociological significance of AIDS (Chapter 20); and debates around postmodernity and the new kind of society that may be appearing in the twenty-first century (Chapters 2 and 25 in particular).

- and, finally, we aim to present all of this in a distinctly fresh and 'user friendly' way. We hope the book looks good with its crisp style, clean design and full colour. But even though we have tried to present it in a highly readable way, there is still a lot of material to digest, even in a book as introductory as this. So a number of tools have been provided to help study. We hope it is written in a lively style. We have tried to illustrate arguments with visuals, maps, debating boxes and charts which should stimulate discussions. Films and videos – and sometimes novels – are suggested to take you further in your thinking. For above all, sociology is about the lively and critical thinking about society. It is not in our view the learning of facts, theories or names of sociologists. It is driven by a passion to understand just what is going on in the modern world.

Some features of the text and how to use it

Sociology: A Global Introduction not only aims to provide a highly readable text, it also provides a number of special features that will help you to study. We hope that this is a 'user friendly' book pitched at **a very introductory level for those who have never studied sociology before**. Amongst the tools in the book that you should note and work with are the following:

1. **The boxes**. These are aimed at focusing you on specific issues. We believe, and hope you do too, that they provide handy tools for thinking and analysing. They come in six forms each identified by an icon.

   European Eye boxes highlight issues in Europe and the European Union.

   Voices boxes focus on multicultural issues and amplify the voices of people who are outside the mainstream of sociological analysis – such as women, gays and ethnic groups.

Profile boxes highlight Western sociologists who have shaped or are shaping the discipline of sociology, and provide a capsule guide to some of their ideas.

Controversy and debate boxes present different points of view on an issue of contemporary importance.

World Watch boxes focus on issues over a range of different countries and provide **Society Fact Files** detailing these countries.

Research in Action boxes which show sociological research actually being conducted.

Some miscellaneous boxes focus on a range of other issues that are of importance within sociology.

2. **Global and national maps.** These are aimed at helping you locate many of the issues discussed in the text through graphic illustration. They come in three forms:

   - **The Social Shapes of the World** global maps are sociological maps offering a comparative look at a range of sociological issues such as favoured languages and religions, permitted marriage forms, the degree of political freedom, the extent of the world's rain forests, and a host of other issues.

   - **National maps** focus on social diversity within a country or a group of countries.

   - **The World at a Glance** at the back of the book suggests very quickly some of the major regional divides in the world and can be used as a handy reference as you are studying the book.

3. **The Time Line.** This three-part time line found at the front of the book locates every era and important development mentioned in the text, and tracks the emergence of crucial trends.

4. **Glossary and Key Concepts.** A listing of key concepts with their definitions appears on the website, and a **complete glossary** is to be found at the end of the book.

5. Each chapter also contains a numbered **Summary** and some **Critical-Thinking Questions. You should note that there are more of these on the website.**

6. Each chapter ends with a short list of **Resources for Going Further**. This aims to provide

   - a short introductory reading list
   - a few videos or films of relevance
   - links to other chapters
   - a few key websites.

Again, you can take these further on the website.

7. A consolidated bibliography at the end of the book.

8. Websites. Included in the Resources for Going Further are a number of relevant website page addresses. Chapter 1 provides an appendix to introduce them.

In addition the book provides:

Images: a key opening image to each chapter as well as numerous photographs throughout.

Vignettes that begin each chapter. These openings hopefully will spark the interest of the reader as they introduce important themes.

Recognition of differences. Readers will encounter the diversity of societies. Although there is an emphasis on Europe and the USA in the book – the dominant Western cultures – there is also a concern with global issues and people from other cultures. There is also an inclusive focus on women and men. Beyond devoting a full chapter to the important concepts of sex and gender, the book mainstreams gender into most chapters, showing how the topic at hand affects women and men differently, and explaining how gender operates as a basic dimension of social organisation.

Theoretically clear and balanced presentation. The discipline's major theoretical approaches are introduced in Chapter 2. They are then systematically treated on the website and often reappear in later chapters. The text highlights not only the conflict, functional and action paradigms, but incorporates social-exchange analysis, ethnomethodology, cultural theory, sociobiology and developments in the newer postmodern theories where different voices can be heard.

Students are also provided with an easy-to-understand introduction to important social theorists before they encounter their work in later chapters. The ideas of Max Weber, Karl Marx and Emile Durkheim appear in distinct sections.

Emphasis on critical thinking. Critical-thinking skills include the ability to challenge common assumptions by formulating questions, identifying and weighing appropriate evidence, and reaching reasoned conclusions. This text not only teaches but encourages students to discover on their own recent sociological research.

A short note on currency

As currencies vary across all cultures and rates of exchange are constantly in a state of flux, the application of any particular unit of currency was a problem. However, the currencies used in our data sources were the pound sterling and the US dollar; for this reason these are the currencies adopted in this book.

Sociology, computers and websites

Computers and the new information technology are playing an increasingly prominent role in sociology. Currently, probably the most common uses for students are the following.

- Word processing (when you prepare your essays and projects)
- Research (when you need statistical techniques such as those discussed in Chapter 2)
- Searching various databases (the most common of which is probably your university library, when you retrieve information on books)
- Using electronic mail (e-mail) to talk to both lecturers and fellow students. Often this can be done via 'discussion groups' linking students and others with similar interests (such as wanting to find out more about postmodern culture, feminism or Marx), who then communicate via e-mail
- Linking to websites. The World Wide Web is a system that helps you gain systematic access to all the information housed in the vast worldwide network of computer networks known as the Internet. It connects you to libraries, businesses, research centres, voluntary organisations, etc., all over the world.

Problems with the Internet

The trouble with the Internet is that it contains millions of bits of disconnected data. In order to make sense of it and find what you want, you will need a web browser such as 'Netscape Navigator' or 'Internet Explorer' which enables you to be more systematic in your searches.

Every document on the Internet has a URL – a Uniform Resource Locator – or address. This is what you need to know when you start your search for sociology websites. Alternatively, you can search for relevant websites by entering one or more keywords on the home page of a 'search engine' such as Yahoo or Google. But once you are inside a web page, you can usually 'click' on a number of items, and you will find yourself rapidly transported to them. (Technically, this is called hypertext.) So many 'web searches' involve just jumping from one site to another.

A word of warning

There is a huge amount of sociological data on the Web, and although it can be very easy to access, it can also bring problems. Throughout this book, we will suggest websites, but we do so with some anxiety for the following reasons.

- Websites keep changing. There is no guarantee that a site will not be closed or its name changed. Even whilst preparing this book, we found a number that had 'vanished' and others that had opened for just a few weeks.
- The quality of websites is very variable: we have checked most of the sites listed in this book and they were 'good' at that time. But they change, and sometimes they can be the home page of one 'crank' who is really only listing his or her own private interests. So use carefully and critically.
- The usage of websites at key times can be very intensive. So a cardinal rule is to be patient!
- And, finally, note that accuracy matters. Do not change addresses from lower-case to capitals, or miss out slashes and points. The website address must be precise.

Organisation of this text

Part one introduces the foundations of sociology. Underlying the discipline is the sociological perspective, the focus of Chapter 1, which explains how this invigorating point of view brings the world to life in a new and instructive way. Chapter 2 spotlights some of the key sociological perspectives and suggests the importance of globalisation as an idea. Chapter 3 looks at some of the issues involved in the practice of sociology, and explains how to use the logic of science to study human society. It also provides a guide to planning research.

Part two targets the foundations of social life. It may be useful to see this section as layered: society, culture, groups, interactions and biographies constitute the matrix of the social worlds we live in. Chapter 4 looks at the concept of society, presenting three time-honoured models of social organisation developed by Emile Durkheim, Karl Marx and Max Weber. It also looks at societies of the past and societies of the present. Chapter 5 focuses on the central concept of culture, emphasising the cultural diversity that makes up our society and our world. Chapter 6 offers coverage of groups and organisations, two additional and vital elements of social structure. Chapter 7 provides a micro-level look at the patterns of social interaction that make up our everyday lives.

Part three offers a wide discussion of social inequality, beginning with three chapters devoted to social stratification. Chapter 8 introduces major concepts and presents theoretical explanations of social inequality. This chapter is rich with illustrations of how stratification has changed historically, and how it varies around the world today. Chapter 9 extends the analysis with a look at global stratification, revealing the extent of differences in wealth and power between rich and poor societies. Chapter 10 surveys social inequality in a number of Western countries, but mainly the UK, exploring our perceptions of inequality and assessing how well they square with research findings. Race and ethnicity, additional important dimensions of social inequality in both Europe and the rest of the world, are detailed in Chapter 11. The focus of Chapter 12, gender and sexuality, explains how societies transform the distinction of biological sex into systems of gender stratification, and looks at the ways sexuality is produced. Childhood and the ageing process are addressed in Chapter 13.

Part four includes a full chapter on major social institutions and the practices that accompany them. Chapter 14 leads off investigating the economy, consumption and work, because most sociologists recognise the economy as having the greatest impact on all other institutions. This chapter highlights the processes of industrialisation and postindustrialisation, explains the emergence of a global economy, and suggests what such transformations mean. Chapter 15 investigates the roots of social power and looks at the modern development of social movements. In addition, this chapter includes discussion of the threat of war, and the search for peace. Chapter 16 looks at the control process, as well as some of the theories that explain why crime and deviance appear in societies. Chapter 17, on families, examines the many changes taking place around our personal ways of living together in the modern world, looking at some of the diversity of family life. Chapter 18, on religion, addresses the human search for

ultimate meaning, surveys world religions, and explains how religious beliefs are linked to other dimensions of social life. Chapter 19, on education, traces the expansion of schooling in industrial societies. Here again, educational patterns in the United Kingdom are brought to life through contrasts with those of many other societies. Chapter 20, on health and medicine, shows how health is a social issue just as much as it is a matter of biological processes, and compares UK patterns to those found in other countries. It also considers a major case study: HIV/AIDS. Chapter 21, on mass media, looks at forms of communications in societies, focusing especially on the rise of the modern global media. Lastly, in Chapter 22, we look at the institution of 'science' and consider some of its most recent manifestations, including the Human Genome Project, the New Reproductive Technologies and the importance of computing and the World Wide Web.

Part five examines important dimensions of global social change. Chapter 23 focuses on the powerful impact of population growth and urbanisation in Europe and throughout the world. Chapter 24 presents issues of contemporary concern by highlighting the interplay of society and the natural environment. Chapter 25 concludes the text with an overview of social change that highlights traditional, modern and postmodern societies. This chapter rounds out the text by explaining how and why world societies change, and by critically analysing the benefits and liabilities of traditional, modern and postmodern ways of life.

A note on authorship

John J. Macionis wrote the original first full US text. Macionis and Plummer produced the first European edition. Here, Ken Plummer has revised it now through three editions, adding several new chapters, introducing many new sections and significantly modifying the original UK edition. Since sociology is a changing and conflictual discipline, neither author necessarily agrees with everything the other has written. But there is strong agreement that sociology is a lively and challenging discipline that should be presented in a lively and challenging way. We hope that this book succeeds in this aim.

ABOUT THE AUTHORS

John J. Macionis

is Professor of Sociology at Kenyon College in Gambier, Ohio, having graduated from Cornell University and the University of Pennsylvania. At Kenyon, he has chaired the Anthropology–Sociology Department, directed the multidisciplinary programme in Humane Studies and presided over the College's Faculty. He has also been active in academic programmes in many other countries.

His publications are wide-ranging, focusing on community life in the US, interpersonal intimacy in families, effective teaching, humour and the importance of global education. He is co-editor of *Seeing Ourselves: Classic, Contemporary and Cross-Cultural Readings in Sociology*, co-author of *Cities and Urban Life* and author of the concise introductory text, *Society: The Basics*.

Professor Macionis considers himself 'first and foremost … a teacher' who wishes to share his expertise and experience with students both in person and through his textbooks.

Ken Plummer

is Professor of Sociology at the University of Essex, and has been actively involved in teaching introductory sociology for the past thirty years. He has been a Senior Lecturer at Middlesex University, and a visiting Professor at the University of California (Santa Barbara) and the University of New York (Stony Brook), as well as giving lectures in many countries around the world.

Apart from an interest in introductory teaching, his major research interests lie in the fields of sexuality, stigma, methodology and symbolic interactionist theory. He is the author of *Sexual Stigma* (1975), *Telling Sexual Stories* (1995) and *Documents of Life-2* (2001) as well as the editor of *The Making of the Modern Homosexual* (1981), *Symbolic Interactionism* (1991, 2 vols), *Modern Homosexualities* (1992), *The Chicago School* (1997, 4 vols) and *Sexualities: Critical Assessments* (2001, 4 vols). He is also the editor of the journal *Sexualities*.

Believing sociology has a lot to contribute to the modern world, he thinks it should become more accessible and hopes this textbook will help towards this.

GUIDED TOUR

Vignettes introduce the key themes of each chapter.

Profile boxes highlight Western sociologists who have shaped or are shaping the discipline of sociology, and provide a capsule guide to some of their ideas.

European Eye boxes highlight issues in Europe and the European Union.

World Watch boxes focus on issues over a range of different countries and provide Society Fact Files detailing these countries.

Voices boxes focus on multicultural issues and amplify the voices of people who are outside the mainstream of sociological anlayisis – such as women, gays and ethnic groups.

Controversy and debate boxes present different points of view on an issue of contemporary importance.

Research in Action highlight important research studies.

GUIDED TOUR

Going further...

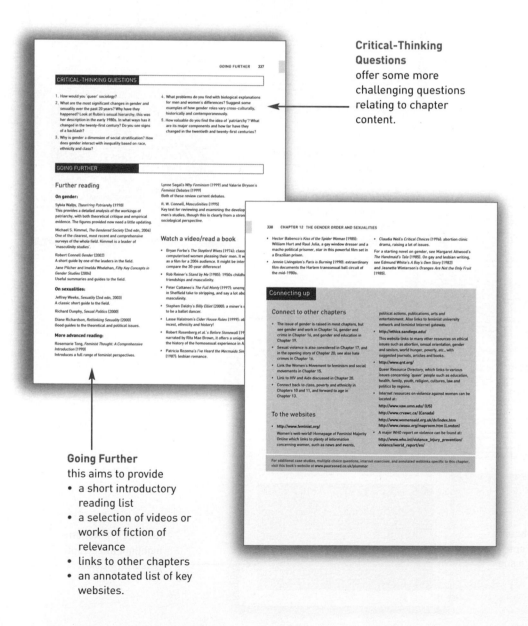

Critical-Thinking Questions offer some more challenging questions relating to chapter content.

Going Further this aims to provide
- a short introductory reading list
- a selection of videos or works of fiction of relevance
- links to other chapters
- an annotated list of key websites.

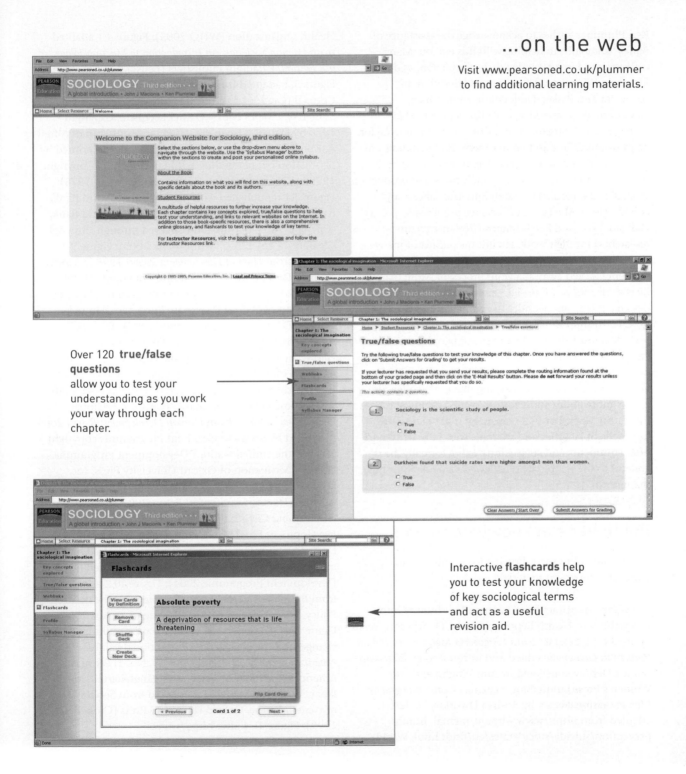

...on the web

Visit www.pearsoned.co.uk/plummer
to find additional learning materials.

Over 120 **true/false
questions**
allow you to test your
understanding as you work
your way through each
chapter.

Interactive **flashcards** help
you to test your knowledge
of key sociological terms
and act as a useful
revision aid.

ACKNOWLEDGEMENTS

Ken Plummer wishes to acknowledge the assistance of Agnes Skamballis in helping with this edition. Many colleagues at Essex provide much stimulation, as do friends in Wivenhoe. All at Pearson Education, in particular Tim Parker, Desk Editor, Paula Parish, Development Editor, Maggie Wells, Deputy Design Manager, Kay Holman, Project Controller, Andrew Taylor, Acquisitions Editor and Emma Travis, Editorial Assistant who all provided much support, enthusiasm and back-up for what in the end was an extremely pressured production schedule. Thanks also to Sarah Bury (freelance copy-editor), Helen MacFadyen (freelance proof-reader), Gary Hall (indexer) and Sue Williams (freelance picture researcher) for their work. Finally, my partner of many years, Everard Longland, had to endure a lot of time with me being locked away at a word processor. More than this, he is a cheerful proof reader, careful copy editor, wise design adviser, and wonderful companion. As usual his unreserved support has been invaluable.

John Macionis thanks the dozens of people whose efforts have resulted in Sociology, in particular members of the editorial, production and sales teams at Pearson Education. It goes without saying that every colleague knows more about some topics covered in this book than the author does. For that reason, he is grateful to the hundreds of faculties and students who have written to offer comments and suggestions. More formally, he is grateful to the people who reviewed some or all of this manuscript.

Publisher's acknowledgements

We are grateful to the following for permission to reproduce copyright material:

HMSO for an extract from Independent Inquiry into Inequalities in Health Report., 1998 by D. Acheson; Verso Limited for an extract from *I Rigoberta Menchu, An Indian Woman in Guatemala* edited and introduced by Elizabeth Burgos-Debray, translated by Ann Wright; and The Women's Press Limited for an extract from *Pornography: Men Possessing Women* by Andrea Dworkin; Table 1.1 adapted from http://www.who.int/mental_health/prevention/suicide/suiciderates/en/print.html, World Health Organization (WHO 2003); Figure 4.1 adapted from *Human Societies: An Introduction to Macrosociology, 9th Edition*, Paradigm Publishers (Lenski, G. *et al.* 2004); Figure 5.2 adapted from *The Future of English?*, The British Council (Graddol, D. 1997); Figure 7.2 adapted from *The Seasons of a Man's Life* by Daniel Levinson, copyright © 1978 by Daniel J. Levinson. Used by permission of Alfred A. Knopf, a division of Random House, Inc. Reprinted by permission of SLL/Sterling Lord Literistic, Inc. Copyright 1975 by Daniel Levinson (Levinson, D. J. *et al.* 1978); Figure 8.1 republished with permission of World Bank, from *World Development Indicators 2003* by World Bank, copyright 2003; permission conveyed through Copyright Clearance Center, Inc. (World Bank 2003); Figure 9.1 adapted from *Human Development Report 1998* by United Nations Development Programme, copyright © 1998 by the United Nations Development Programme. Used by permission of Oxford University Press, Inc. (United Nations Development Programme 1998); Table 9.1 republished with permission of World Bank, from *Global Poverty Monitoring* by World Bank, copyright 2002; permission conveyed through Copyright Clearance Center, Inc. (World Bank 2002); Figures 9.2 and 9.3 after 'Feature 2.1: Income Poverty Pie Chart', 'Feature 2.2: Global Disparities in HDI', from *Human Development Report 2003* by United Nations Development Programme, copyright © 2003 by the United Nations Development Programme. Used by permission of Oxford University Press, Inc. (United Nations Development Programme 2003); Table 9.2 from *Human Development Report 2004: Identity, Diversity and Globalization* by United Nations Development Programme, copyright © 2004 by the United Nations Development Programme. Used by permission of Oxford University Press, Inc. (United Nations Development Programme 2004); Figure 10.2 adapted from *Breadline Europe: The Measurement of Poverty*, The Policy Press (Gordon, D. and Townsend, P. eds, 2000); Figure 10.5 redrawn from Modernization, cultural change, and the persistence of traditional values, *American Sociological Review*, Vol. 65, No. 1, February, American Sociological Association (Inglehart, R. and Blake, W. 2000); Figure 11.2 adapted from *Social Change in Western Europe*, Oxford University Press (Crouch, C. 1999); Figure 11.4 after http://www.migrationinformation.org/globaldata/charts/3.1.shtml,

The Migration Information Source (www.migrationinfor-mation.org), Migration Policy Institute; Figure 12.1 republished with permission of World Bank, from *World Development Report 1995: Workers in an Integrating World* by World Bank, copyright 1995; permission conveyed though Copyright Clearance Center, Inc. (World Bank 1995); Figure 12.2 reproduced from *Pleasure and Danger: Exploring Female Sexuality* edited by Carol S. Vance, Pandora Press, London, 1989 (Rubin, G. 1989); Figure 13.2 adapted from Long-Range World Population projections on Ageing website, http://www.un.org/esa/socdev/ageing, United Nations; Figure 13.3 adapted from *Women and Men in Europe: A Statistical Portrait*, the European Communities (Eurostat 1995); Figure 14.2 adapted from *Global Shift: Transforming the World Economy, 1st Edition*, copyright © Peter Dicken, 1986, pub Paul Chapman Publishers, reprinted by permission of Sage Publications Ltd. (Dicken, P. 1986); Figure 14.4 redrawn from *Global Shift: Transforming the World Economy, 3rd Edition*, copyright © Peter Dicken, 1998, pub Paul Chapman Publishers, reprinted by permission of Sage Publications Ltd. (Dicken, P. 1998); Figure 15.1 adapted from *The Economist*, 31 July 1999, © The Economist Newspaper Limited, London, 31.7.99; Figure 15.2 redrawn from *The Guardian*, 15 June 2004, Copyright Guardian Newspapers Limited 2004; Table 15.2 from http://www.euractiv.com/Article?_lang =EN&tcmuri=tcm:29-117482-16&type=LinksDossier, reprinted by permission of EurActiv.com; Table 16.3 from *United Nations International Crime Survey of Victims*, United Nations (United Nations 2001); Table 16.4 compiled from World Prison Brief Online, www.prison-studies.org, International Centre for Prison Studies (ICPS) (ICPS 2004); Figure 18.1 redrawn from http://www.adherents.com/Religions_By_Adherents.html, © 2002 www.adherents.com, reprinted by permission of Preston Hunter; Figure 18.3 adapted from Religion by P. Brierley in A. H. Halsey *et al.* eds, *Twentieth Century British Social Trends, 3rd Edition*, 2000, pub Macmillan, reproduced with permission of Palgrave Macmillan (Brierley, P. 2000); Figure 20.8 redrawn from *New Internationalist*, 362, November 2003, reprinted by kind permission of New Internationalist. Copyright New Internationalist, www.newint.org; Figure 20.9 redrawn from *The Economist*, 13 December 2003, © The Economist Newspaper Limited, London, 13.12.03; Figure 20.11(a) adapted from *The Guardian*, 8 July 2000, Copyright Guardian Newspapers Limited 2000: Figure 20.11(b) adapted from *The Guardian*, 31 May 2001, Copyright Guardian Newspapers 2001; Figure 21.4 republished with permission of World Bank, from *World Development Report*, copyright 1997; permission conveyed through Copyright Clearance Center, Inc. (World Bank 1997); Figure 22.1 redrawn from http://www.glreach.com/globstats/index.php3, reprinted by permission of Global Reach http://www.global-reach.biz/globstats; Figure 23.4 adapted from *The Guardian*, 2 August 2001, Copyright Guardian Newspapers 2001; Figure 23.9 adapted from *World Urbanization Prospects: the 1999 revision*, United Nations (United Nations 1999); Figure 23.11 adapted from *The City*, published and reprinted by permission of The University of Chicago Press (Park, R. E. and Burgess, E. W. 1967, orig. 1925); Figures 24.1 and 24.2 adapted from Worldwatch Institute, *State of the World 2001*, copyright 2001, www.worldwatch.org (Brown, L. R. *et al.* eds, 2001); Figures 24.3 and 24.4 redrawn from *The Economist*, 20 March 2004, © The Economist Newspaper Limited, London, 20.3.04.

The publisher and authors are grateful to Myriad Editions Limited for permission to reproduce and adapt maps and figures on pages: p.404, Map 15.2; p.595, Figure 21.5; p.620, Figure 22.2 and pp.676-77, Figure 24.8.

Map 4.1 adapted from *Nomads and the Outside World*, Cambridge University Press (Khazanov, A. M. 1984); Map 5.3 adapted from *Culture Matters: How Values Shape Human Progress*, copyright © 2000 by Lawrence Harrison and Samuel Huntingdon, reprinted by permission of Basic Books, a member of Perseus Books, L.L.C. (Harrison, L. and Huntingdon, S. 2000); Map 11.1 adapted from *Bosnia: A Short History*, Macmillan, London, UK (Malcolm, N. 1994); Map 11.3 adapted from Ethnicity in *East Central Europe and the Former Soviet Union* edited by David Turnock, pub Arnold, copyright © 2001 Arnold, reproduced in adapted form by permission of Edward Arnold (Kocsis, K. 2001); Map 15.1 adapted from Map of Freedom 2003 from *Freedom House Annual Report 2003*, Freedom House, www.freedomhouse.org (Freedom House 2003); Map 15.3 adapted from Life after Communism: The facts, *New Internationalist*, 366, April 2004, reprinted by kind permission of New Internationalist. Copyright New Internationalist, www.newint.org; Map 20.2 adapted from www.who.int/statistics, World Health Organization (WHO 2000).

We are grateful to the Financial Times Limited for permission to reprint the following material:

Table 6.3 from Estimates of mobile phone ownership, 2001, © *Financial Times*, 14 June 2001.

We are grateful to the following for permission to reproduce photographic material:

p.2 Private Collection/Johnny Van Haeften Ltd., London / www.bridgeman.co.uk;
p.5 Images.com/Corbis. Creator Paul Schulenburg; p.6 Getty Photodisk; p.13 (a) Archivo Iconografico, S.A./Corbis, Creator: Emile Dreyer; (b) Bettmann/Corbis; (c) Hulton-Deutsch Collection/Corbis; (d) The Granger Collection, New York; p. 22 Motorola/Science Photo Library; p.32 (a) Homer Sykes/Network; (b) Eve Arnold/Magnum Photos; (c) Mike Goldwater/Network Photographers; (d) Abbas/Magnum Photos; p.33 Bettmann/Corbis; p.35 Luc Delahaye/Magnum Photos; p.42 National Galleries of Canada/ MGC/MBAC; p.44 G.Humer/Katz Gamma; p.48 (a) Steve McCurry/Magnum Photos; (b) Jenny Matthews/Network Photographers; p.60 photo from Balinese Character: A Photographic Analysis, Special Publications of the New York Academy of Sciences, Volume II, edited by Wilbur G. Valentine, reproduced by permission of New York Academy of Sciences (Bateson, G. and Mead, M. 1942); p.72 British Library, London/www.bridgeman.co.uk; p.74 Werner Nosko/Reuters/Corbis; p.77 Getty Photodisk; p.86 Katz Gamma; p.101 Robert Essel NYC/Corbis; p.118 (a) Dorothea Schmid/Network Photographers/Bildberg; (b) Network Photographers/Rapho - Jean-Erick Pasquier; (c) Chris Steele-Perkins/Magnum; (d) Chris Steele-Perkins/Magnum; p.120 Catherine Karnow/Corbis; p.122 Popperfoto; p.124 Eamonn McCabe; p.127 Popperfoto; p.132 Private collection/www.bridgeman.co.uk; p.133 McDonald Corporation; p.142 Popperfoto; p.145 Bernard Bisson/Corbis Sygma; p.150 Al Rod/Corbis; p.156 www.bridgeman.co.uk; p.162 Bettmann/Corbis; p.164 The Granger Collection, New York; p.170 American Sociological Association; p.180 Popperfoto; p.188 Alamy/Michael Dwyer; p.193 (a) Popperfoto, (b) David Orr/Corbis Sygma; p.196 Popperfoto; p.198 AntoingGyori/Corbis Sygma; p.212 (top) David Turnley/Corbis, (btm) Strauss/Curtis/Corbis; p.216 Johannesburg Art Gallery/www.bridgeman.co.uk. Courtesy of Gerard Sekoto Foundation; p.224 Chris Steele-Perkins/Magnum Photos; p.236 Adam Bernstein/Reuters/Corbis; p.244 The Art Archive; p.255 Ronald Grant Archive; p.257 (a) Doré: A London Pilgrimage, (b) Pat Benic/Bettmann/Corbis: p.272 Ron Waddams/www.bridgeman.co.uk; p.273 W Bocxe/JB Pictures/Network Photographers; p.274 Radu Sigheti/Reuters/Corbis; p.286 Bettmann/Corbis; p.288 (a) Faisal Mahmood/Reuters/Corbis, (b) Ed Kashi/Corbis; p.289 c Patrick Robert/Corbis, (d) Peter Turnley/Corbis; p.297 Commission for Racial Equality; p.301 Thomas Hoepker/Magnum Photos; p.302 Ian Hodgson/Reuters/Corbis; p.306 © Salvador Dali, Gali-Salvador Dali Foundation, DACS, London, 2000 / www.bridgeman.co.uk; p.308 © Leila Rupp and Verta Taylor, 2003; p.309 Bettmann/Corbis; p.310 Olivier Martel/Rapho/Network Photographers; p.316 Jeffrey L. Rotman/Corbis; p.323 Popperfoto; p.335 Associated Press/Gail Burton; p.340 Creator: Deirdre Scherer. Photographer: Jeff Baird; p.343 Mohammed Anwar/Impact Photos; p.354 (left) Popperfoto, (right) Rex Features; p.357 Antonio Olmos; p.364 Manchester Art Gallery/www.bridgeman.co.uk; p.375 Sophie Herxheimer; p.381 Associated Press/Richard Vogel; p.396 Novosti/www.bridgeman.co.uk; p.397 Christopher J. Morris/Corbis; p.410 (top) Reuters/Corbis/HO/Interpol, (btm) David Turnley/Corbis; p.411 Abbas/Magnum Photos; p.414 Popperfoto; p.419 Martin Godwin; p.420 Brooks Kraft/Corbis; p.426 Images.com/Corbis. Creator Alan E Cobe; p.435 Ronald Grant Archive; p.436 Carlos Friere/Rapho/Network Photographers; p.443 Mary Evans Picture Library; p.447 Jérome Sessini/In Visu/Corbis; p.448 M Ende/Bilderberg/Network Photographers; p.451 University of Chicago Press. Photographer Clifford R.S. Shaw. Design James Bradford Johnson; p.460 Swedish National Museum; p.469 Chris Steele-Perkins/Magnum Photos; p.479 Maggie Hallahan/Corbis; p.482 Illustrated London News; p.486 British Library, London/www.bridgeman.co.uk; p.488 Raghu Rai/ Magnum Photos; p.497 Popperfoto/Gieb Garanich/Reuters; p.499 (a) Abbas/Magnum Photos, (b) Abbas/Magnum Photos, (c) Popperfoto, (d) Popperfoto/Anuruddha Lokuhapuracahchi, (e) Gideon Mendel/Network Photographers; p.502 Popperfoto; p.506 Popperfoto/Dimitar Dilkoff/ Reuters; p.512 The Philadelphia Museum of Art/Corbis. Courtesy of the Jacob Lawrence Foundation; p.520 Bettmann/Corbis; p.524 Alain Nogues/Corbis Sygma; p.528 (a) Thorne Anderson/Corbis, (b) Alain Nogues/Corbis Sygma; p.533 Popperfoto/Rick T Wilking/Reuters; p.540 Modern Museum, Stockholm; p.541 Mariella Furrer/Saba/Network Photographers; p.545 Patrick Robert/Corbis Sygma; p.563 © 2004 The NAMES Project Foundation AIDS Memorial Quilt, Atlanta, GA. Paul Margolies, Photographer); p.568 Alamy/Jacky Chapman/Janine Weidel Photography; p.576 Private collection/www.bridgeman.co.uk; p.577 Witold Krassowski/Network Photographers; p582 © S.L. Hodkinson; p.589 Pascal Baril/Corbis Kipa; p.591 Getty Photodisk; p.597 Rex Features/Sipa; p.602 Scala, Florence; p.604 Peter Menzel/Science Photo Library; p.608 Science Photo Library (a) Sheila Terry, (b) Detlev

van Ravejswaay, (c) SPL, (d) A Barrington Brown; p.610 Corbis; p.612 Denis Scott/Corbis; p.616 Popperfoto/Rajesh Bhambi/Reuters; p.628 Yann Arthus-Bertrand/Corbis; p.647 Stephanie Maze/Corbis; p.652 (a) David Butow/Corbis Saba, (b) Douglas Kirkland/Corbis; p.658 Associated Press/Nick Ut; p.660 Popperfoto/Volodymr Repik/Reuters; p.662 Michael S. Yamashita/Corbis; p.677 P De Vallombreuse/Corbis

Sygma; p.686 Scottish Gallery of Modern Art /Marlborough Fine Art; p.690 (left) Bruno Barbey/Magnum Photos, (right) Susan Meiselas/Magnum Photos.

In some instances we have been unable to trace the owners of copyright material, and we would appreciate any information that would enable us to do so.

ABBREVIATIONS

AIDS	Acquired immunodeficiency syndrome
AS	Assisted conception
ASEAN	Association of Southeast Asian Nations
BHPS	British Household Panel Study
BSE	Bovine spongiform encephalopathy
CEE	Central Eastern Europe
CFC	Chlorofluorocarbon (used as a propellant in aerosol spray cans)
CIS	Commonwealth of Independent States
CJD	Creuzfeldt–Jakob Disease
EU	European Union
FAO	Food and Agriculture Organisation (United Nations)
G8	(formerly G7) The 'Group of Eight' advanced industrialised nations: Canada, France, Germany, Italy, Japan, Russia, UK and US
GATT	General Agreement on Tariffs and Trade (now the WTO)
GDP	Gross Domestic Product
GDI	Gender-related Development Index (a UN measurement)
GLF	Gay Liberation Front
GM	Genetically modified
GNP	Gross National Product
GSM	Global Social Movement
HDI	Human Development Index (a UN measuring index)
HFEA	Human Fertilisation and Embryology Authority
HIV	Human immunodeficiency virus
IGO	International governmental organisation

ILO	International Labour Organisation
IMF	International Monetary Fund
INGO	International non-governmental organisation
IVF	In-vitro fertilisation
NAFTA	North American Free Trade Agreement
NATO	North Atlantic Treaty Organisation
NGO	Non-governmental organisation
NIC	Newly industrialising country
NRM	New religious movement
NRT	New Reproductive Technologies
NSM	New social movement
OECD	Organisation for Economic Cooperation and Development
OPEC	Organisation of Petroleum Exporting Countries
PPP	Purchasing Power Parity
PSE	Poverty and Social Exclusion (Survey)
SARS	Severe acute respiratory syndrome
TNC	Transnational corporation
UN	United Nations
UNDP	United Nations Development Programme
UNEP	United Nations Environment Programme
UNESCO	United Nations Educational, Scientific and Cultural Organisation
UNHCR	United Nations High Commission for Refugees
UNICEF	United Nations Children's Fund
UNPFA	United Nations Fund for Population Activities
WFP	World Food Programme
WHO	World Health Organisation
WTO	World Trade Organisation (formerly GATT)

INTRODUCING SOCIOLOGY

CHAPTER 1   # THE SOCIOLOGICAL IMAGINATION

The first wisdom of sociology is this: things are not what they seem.

Peter Berger

IMAGE YOU WERE BORN SOME 300 YEARS AGO, IN THE YEAR 1700. Although this is very recent in terms of the billions of years of the existence of planet earth, you would still be living in a remarkably different world. You would probably be living in a very small community and you would not have travelled anywhere except perhaps to a nearby town. You would never have been to a shop, let alone a shopping centre. You would not have encountered the world of railways, cars, telephones, cameras, PCs, faxes, mobile phones, planes, videos, McDonald's, holiday tours, laptops or DVDs. And more than this, the idea of voting for your government, going to a university, choosing your religion, or even choosing your identity would all have been rare. Welcome to the modern world!

But imagine again: this time that you were born and living in the Republic of Sierra Leone, one of the poorest places in the world today. If you are a man, your life expectancy at birth would be no more than 36 years (if a woman, it would be slightly more at 39). By contrast, if you were born in the UK, your expectations would be double this. Indeed, in Sierra Leone, 316 children out of every thousand born die before they reach the age of five; in the UK, it is only six per thousand. Your chances of going on to further or higher education (tertiary education) would be only one in 50 (and there would be virtually no chance at all if you were a woman, as 82 per cent of women are still illiterate). In the UK, by contrast, almost every other person has some kind of further education. Likewise, media communications would be much rarer: in Sierra Leone, there are four telephone lines and 17 television sets per thousand people; in the UK, there are 528 telephone lines and 612 TV sets for the same number. As in most of Africa, personal computers are very rare.

But now have another leap of imagination: this time to a world that is yet to come – the world perhaps of your own grandchildren or great grandchildren. We cannot of course predict the future, but we can often see trends. For instance, we started to see 'babies in test tubes' being born at the end of the twentieth century, a trend that seems to be accelerating. This could mean that much of the future population will be born through new genetic engineering. It may even mean the start of 'designer babies'. We also saw the miniaturisation of electronics as new computers, cameras, mobile telephones etc. started to become pocket size and ubiquitous in the rich world. Could this mean that the future will see major conflicts between those who have access to these technologies and those who do not? Could it mean that the new technologies will be implanted into our bodies and our homes? Many think so. And we could give many more examples of a futuristic landscape.

The power of sociology is to demonstrate just how strong are the social forces that organise society in very different ways. Throughout this book, over and over again, you will see the variety of societies and the different opportunities that people have within them. Just where you were born – and when – has radically shaped much of what you know and what you can do. Having encountered sociology, you may never see the world with the same eyes again.

KEY THEMES
- The nature of sociology
- How sociological perspectives help in everyday life
- Some problems in doing sociology
- The development of sociology

(Left) Pieter Brueghel the younger: The Battle between Carnival and Lent

What is sociology?

We can start by saying that **sociology** is the *systematic study of human society*. At the heart of sociology we may say there is a distinctive point of view. It should be more than you find in a good documentary on a social issue. It is certainly more than listings of facts and figures about society. Instead it becomes *a form of consciousness, a way of thinking, a critical way of seeing the social*. It takes a while, sometimes years, for this 'consciousness' to become clear. In this section, and subsequently in the whole book, we ask what is distinctive about this way of seeing? The box below gives a few standard definitions which you may like to consider.

Seeing the general in the particular

Peter Berger's short book *Invitation to Sociology* (1963) has tempted several generations of students into seeing this perspective. In it he characterised the sociological perspective as *seeing the general in the particular*. He meant that sociologists can identify general patterns of social life by looking at concrete specific examples of social life. While acknowledging that each individual is unique, in other words, sociologists recognise that society acts differently on various *categories* of people (say, children compared to adults, women versus men,

the rich as opposed to the poor). We begin to think sociologically once we start to realise how the general categories into which we happen to fall shape our particular life experiences.

Each chapter of this book illustrates the general impact of society on the actions, thoughts and feelings of particular people. For instance, the differences that distinguish children from adults reflect not just biological maturity: by attaching meaning to age, society creates what we experience as distinct stages of life. Following these age-scripts, some societies expect children to be 'dependent' and adults to behave 'responsibly'. And, further along the life course, our society defines old age as a time of diminishing standing and withdrawal from earlier routines (see Chapter 13).

How do we know that society (and not simply biology) is at work here? Looking back in time or around the world today, we see that societies define the stages of life quite differently. Later chapters note that the Native American Hopi confer on children a surprising degree of independence, while in Abkhazia (part of the Russian Federation) elderly people enjoy the lion's share of social position and esteem.

A sociological look around us reveals the power of class position as well. Chapters 8 and 9 provide ample evidence that how we live – and, sometimes, whether we live at all – has a great deal to do with our ranking in the societal hierarchy.

SOME ATTEMPTS TO DEFINE SOCIOLOGY

The sociologist ... is someone concerned with understanding society in a disciplined way. The nature of this discipline is scientific. (Peter Berger, *Invitation to Sociology*, 1963: 27)

The term has two stems – the Latin *socius* (companionship) and the Greek *logos* (study of) – and literally means the study of the processes of companionship. In these terms, sociology may be defined as the study of the bases of social membership. More technically, sociology is the analysis of the structure of social relationships as constituted by social interaction, but no definition is entirely satisfactory because of the diversity of perspectives. (Nicholas Abercrombie, *Sociology*, 2004: 232)

The science or study of the origin, history & constitution of human society. (*Shorter Oxford English Dictionary*)

Defined in dictionaries as the science or study of society. The term was coined by Comte (1830), linking the Latin *socius* (originally a people, tribe or city allied to Rome, but later a society) to the Greek *logos* (reason or knowledge). The term spread rapidly and is now used in virtually all languages to denote any relatively rigorous, reasoned study of society. (Michael Mann, *Encyclopedia of Sociology*, 1983: 370)

A social science having as its main focus the study of the social institutions brought into being by the industrial transformations of the past two or three centuries . . . [It involves] an historical, an anthropological and a critical sensitivity. (Anthony Giddens, *Sociology: A Brief but Critical Introduction*, 2nd edn, 1989: 9 and 13)

Seeing the world sociologically also makes us aware of the importance of gender. As Chapter 12 points out, every society attaches meanings (though often different meanings) to being one gender or the other, giving women and men different kinds of work and family responsibilities. And as society changes, so do these meanings: the expectations around men and women now, at the start of the twenty-first century, are very different from what they were at the start of the twentieth. Individuals experience the workings of society as they encounter advantages and opportunities characteristic of each sex.

Figure 1.1 suggests that there are many factors that shape our lives.

Seeing the strange in the familiar

Especially at the beginning, using the sociological perspective amounts to *seeing the strange in the familiar*. As Peter Berger (1963: 34) says in his *Invitation to Sociology*, 'the first wisdom of sociology is this: things are not what they seem'. For instance, observing sociologically requires giving up the familiar idea that human behaviour is simply a matter of what people *decide* to do and accepting instead the initially strange notion that society guides our thoughts and deeds.

Learning to 'see' how society affects us may take a bit of practice. Asked why you 'chose' your particular college or university, you might offer any of the following personal reasons:

I wanted to stay close to home.
This college has the best women's rugby team.
A law degree from this university ensures a good job.
My girlfriend goes to university here.
I wasn't accepted by the university I really wanted to attend.

Such responses are certainly grounded in reality for the people expressing them. But do they tell the whole story? The sociological perspective provides deeper insights that may not be readily apparent.

Thinking sociologically about going on to further or higher education, we might first realise that, for most people throughout most of the world and for most of

Figure 1.1 **Society as a prison**
A key to sociological thinking is the basic idea that society guides our actions and life choices. In this diagram, human beings are located at the centre of numerous social forces. Think about the forces that have shaped your own life – and consider how your life would be very different if you were born into other languages, institutions or societies.
©Images.com/Corbis. Creator Paul Schulenburg

'Differences' around the world. The power of society over the individual can easily be grasped by looking at the world through different cultures. (a) Woman, Ivory coast, (b) teenage girl, Mali, (c) man, Egypt, (d) Muslim woman.
Source: Getty Photodisk

history, university is all but out of reach. Moreover, had we lived a century or two ago, the 'choice' to go to university was only an option for the smallest elite. But even in the here and now, a look around the classroom suggests that social forces still have much to do with whether or not one pursues higher education. Typically, college students are relatively young – generally between 18 and 24 years of age. Why? Because in our society going to university is associated with this period of life. But it needn't be – as the recent growth of 'mature students' starts to testify. Likewise, higher education is costly, so college students tend to come from families with above-average incomes. Young people lucky enough to belong to families from the service (middle) classes are some ten times more likely to go to university than are those from manual working-class families. There are also significant variations by ethnicity and gender.

So, at the broadest level, sociology sets out to show the patterns and processes by which society shapes what we do.

Individuality in social context

The sociological perspective often challenges common sense by revealing that human behaviour is not as individualistic as we may think. For most of us, daily living is very individual. It often carries a heavy load of personal responsibility, so that we pat ourselves on the back when we enjoy success and kick ourselves when things go wrong. Proud of our individuality, even in painful times, we resist the idea that we act in socially patterned ways.

But perhaps the most intriguing demonstration of how social forces affect human behaviour can be found in the study of suicide. Why? Because nothing seems a more personal 'choice' than the decision to take one's own life. This is why Emile Durkheim (1858–1917), a pioneer of sociology writing a century ago who will reappear in many chapters of this book, chose suicide as a topic of research. If he could show that an intensely individual act like suicide was socially shaped, then he would have made a strong case for sociology. And he did! He was able to demonstrate that social forces figure in the apparently isolated act of self-destruction.

Durkheim began by examining suicide records in and around his native France. The statistics clearly showed that some *categories of people* were more likely than others to choose to take their own lives. Specifically, Durkheim found that men, Protestants, wealthy people, and the unmarried each had significantly higher suicide rates compared to women, Roman Catholics and Jews, the poor, and married people, respectively. Durkheim

deduced that these differences corresponded to people's degree of *social integration*. Low suicide rates characterised categories of people with strong social ties; high suicide rates were found among those who were more socially isolated and individualistic.

In the male-dominated societies studied by Durkheim, men certainly had more autonomy than women. Whatever freedom's advantages for men, concluded Durkheim, autonomy means lower social integration, which contributes to a higher male suicide rate. Likewise, individualistic Protestants were more prone to suicide than Catholics and Jews, whose rituals fostered stronger social ties. The wealthy clearly have much more freedom of action than the poor but, once again, at the cost of a higher suicide rate. Finally, single people, with weaker social ties than married people, are also at greater risk of suicide.

A century later, Durkheim's analysis is still discussed. Table 1.1 shows suicide rates across the world. Thus, for example, in almost every country, men are more likely to commit suicide than women. Yet in China, this is not so. Statistics emerging from China on suicide suggest a very different pattern from the mainly Western one described by Durkheim. China, with 22 per cent of the world's people, accounts for some 40 per cent of suicides worldwide: a staggeringly higher rate. And whereas male suicides in the industrial West outnumber female suicides by roughly three or four to one, in China women's suicides outnumber men's. Likewise, whereas in the West suicide is linked to city life, in China it is three times higher in the countryside (*New Scientist*, 22 March 1997: 34–37). Sociologists, then, look at these statistics to detect broad social patterns that then need explaining.

But these patterns are not constant around the world. More recent figures suggest that:

- In the last half-century, suicide rates have increased by 60 per cent worldwide.

- In 2000, approximately *one million* people died of suicide – 16 per 100,000 or one every 40 seconds.

- This puts it among the three leading causes of death among those aged 15–44 (both sexes).

- Suicide attempts are up to 20 times more common than completed suicides.

In the United Kingdom:

- 75 per cent of suicides are by males.

- Suicide accounts for 18 per cent of all deaths of young people.

- Suicides by young men in England and Wales have risen by 172 per cent since 1985 (Befrienders International, www.befrienders.org/info/statistics.htm, 2000).

Table 1.1	Suicide rates around the world per 100,000 population by country and gender (as of May 2003)		
Country	**Year**	**Males**	**Females**
Argentina	1996	9.90	3.00
Australia	1999	21.20	5.10
Brazil	1995	6.60	1.80
Canada	1998	19.50	5.10
Chile	1994	10.20	1.40
China (selected rural and urban areas)	1999	13.00	**14.80**
China (Hong Kong SAR)	1999	16.70	9.80
Columbia	1994	5.50	1.50
Croatia	2000	32.90	10.30
Cuba	1996	24.50	12.00
Czech Republic	2000	26.00	6.70
Denmark	1998	20.90	8.10
Estonia	2000	45.80	11.90
Finland	2000	34.60	10.90
France	1999	26.10	9.40
Germany	1999	20.20	7.30
Greece	1999	5.70	1.60
Iceland	1997	19.10	5.20
India	1998	12.20	9.10
Ireland	1999	18.40	4.30
Italy	1999	11.10	3.40
Japan	1999	36.50	14.10
Kazakhstan	1999	46.40	8.60
Latvia	2000	56.60	11.90
Lithuania	2000	75.60	16.10
Norway	1999	19.50	6.80
Portugal	2000	8.50	2.00
Russian Federation	2000	70.60	11.90
Spain	1999	12.40	4.00
Sweden	1999	19.70	8.00
United Kingdom	1999	11.80	3.30
United States of America	1999	17.60	4.10

Suicide is usually seen as the most intensely personal act. Yet sociologists have long been interested in it, precisely because it shows definite social patterns. Consider what patterns are revealed. Why do you think there are these variations?

Source: adapted from World Health Organization (2003), http://www.who.int/mental_health/prevention/suicide/suiciderates/en/print.html

You may like to look at these figures, and consider both what they may say about social trends as well as the problems they pose for interpretation. Suicide rates reveal general social patterns in the most personal actions of particular individuals.

The sociological perspective in everyday life

Sociology and social marginality

Sociological thinking is especially common among social 'outsiders'. Social marginality is something we all experience from time to time. For some categories of people, however, being an outsider is part of daily living. The more acute people's social marginality, the more likely they are to be keenly aware of their surroundings and to embrace the sociological perspective.

No Turkish guest worker in Germany or Pakistani in England lives for long without learning how much 'race' affects personal experience. But white people, because they are the dominant majority in these countries, think about 'race' only occasionally and often take the attitude that race affects only people of colour rather than themselves as well.

Much the same is true of women, gays and lesbians, people with disabilities, the homeless and the very old. All those who can be relegated to the outskirts of social life typically become more aware of social patterns others take for granted. Turning the argument around, for any of us to develop a sociological perspective we must step back a bit from our familiar routines to look on our lives with a new awareness and curiosity. Sociology leads to a questioning of all that is taken for granted. Seeing the world through the eyes of others 'on the margins' can help us see the way the world works more clearly. And it raises challenging questions about how margins and boundaries come about.

Sociology and social crisis

Periods of massive social change or social crisis throw everyone a little off balance, and this, too, stimulates sociological vision. C. Wright Mills (1959), a noted US sociologist, illustrated this principle by recalling the Great Depression of the 1930s. As the unemployment rate in the United States soared to 25 per cent (as it did elsewhere – the depression was 'global'), people out of work could not help but see general social forces at work in their particular lives. Rather than personalising their plight by claiming 'Something is wrong with me. I can't find a job', they took a more sociological approach, observing: 'The economy has collapsed. There are no jobs to be found!'

Conversely, sociological thinking often fosters social change. The more we learn about the operation of 'the system', the more we may wish to change it in some way.

As women and men have confronted the power of gender, for example, many have actively tried to reduce the traditional differences that distinguish men and women.

In short, an introduction to sociology is an invitation to learn a new way of looking at familiar patterns of social life. At this point, we might well consider whether this invitation is worth accepting. In other words, what are the benefits of learning to use the sociological perspective?

Benefits of the sociological perspective

As we learn to use the sociological perspective, we can readily apply it to our daily lives. Doing so provides four general benefits.

1. *The sociological perspective becomes a way of thinking, a 'form of consciousness' that challenges familiar understandings of ourselves and of others, so that we can critically assess the truth of commonly held assumptions.* Thinking sociologically, in other words, we may realise that ideas we have taken for granted are not always true. As we have already seen, a good example of a widespread but misleading 'truth' is that Europe is populated with 'autonomous individuals'' who are personally responsible for their lives. Thinking this way, we are sometimes too quick to praise particularly successful people as superior to others whose more modest achievements mark them as personally deficient. A sociological approach becomes a way of thinking with an ingrained habit of asking awkward questions. It prompts us to ask whether these beliefs are actually true and, to the extent that they are not, why they are so widely held. Sociology challenges the 'taken for granted'.

2. *The sociological perspective enables us to assess both the opportunities and the constraints that characterise our lives.* Sociological thinking leads us to see that, for better or worse, our society operates in a particular way. It helps us to see the pattern and order that is found in all societies. Moreover, in the game of life, we may decide how to play our cards, but it is society that deals us the hand. The more we understand the game, then the more effective players we will be. Sociology helps us to understand what we are likely and unlikely to accomplish for ourselves and how we can pursue our goals most effectively.

3. *The sociological perspective empowers us to be active participants in our society.* Without an awareness of how society operates, we are likely to accept the status quo. We might just think that this is how all societies are, or how all people behave 'naturally'. But the greater our understanding of the operation of society, the

more we can take an active part in shaping social life. For some, this may mean embracing society as it is; others, however, may attempt nothing less than changing the entire world in some way. The discipline of sociology advocates no one particular political orientation, and sociologists themselves weigh in at many points across the political spectrum. But it does have a built-in 'critical' tendency. And evaluating any aspect of social life – whatever one's eventual goal – depends on the ability to identify social forces and to assess their consequences. Some 30 years ago, C. Wright Mills claimed that developing what he called the 'sociological imagination' would help people to become more active citizens. This major sociological thinker is highlighted in the Profile box on the next page. Other notable sociologists are featured in Profile boxes throughout this book.

4. *The sociological perspective helps us to recognise human differences and human suffering and to confront the challenges of living in a diverse world.* Sociological thinking highlights both the world's remarkable social variety and its sufferings, real and potential. 'The British', for example, represent only a small proportion of the world's population, and, as the remaining chapters of this book explain, many human beings live in dramatically different societies. People everywhere tend to define their own way of life as proper and 'natural', and to dismiss the lifestyles of those who differ. But the sociological perspective encourages us to think critically about the relative strengths and weaknesses of all ways of life – including our own. It also encourages us to see the many forms of suffering that occur – poverty, marital breakdown, illness, war and so on – and to see how such problems often arise because of the ways in which societies are organised.

Problems with the sociological perspective

While approaching the world sociologically brings many benefits, it also harbours some distinctive problems. Three can be mentioned.

1. *Sociology is part of a changing world.* One of the difficult things about studying sociology is that we are studying a moving object: society can change just as quickly as we study it! A 'finding' from one day may soon be proved wrong when situations and circumstances change. And, since it is a feature of the modern world that societies are changing extraordinarily rapidly, we can expect our knowledge about them to change rapidly too. For instance, many of the statistics you read in this book will be out of date by the time you read them.

C. WRIGHT MILLS: THE SOCIOLOGICAL IMAGINATION

Charles Wright Mills (1916–62) managed to cause a stir with almost everything he did. Even arriving for a class at New York's Columbia University – clad in a sweatshirt, jeans and boots, astride his motorcycle – he usually turned some heads. During the conservative 1950s, Mills not only dressed a bit out of the mainstream, he also produced a number of books that challenged most of the beliefs the majority of us take for granted. He was an American Marxist and, in the process, he acquired both adherents and adversaries.

As Mills saw it, sociology is not some dry enterprise detached from life. Rather, he held up sociology as an escape from the 'traps' of our lives because it can show us that society – not our own foibles or failings – is responsible for many of our problems. In this way, Mills maintained, sociology transforms personal problems into public and political issues. For Mills, 'The sociological imagination enables us to grasp history and biography and the relations between the two within society. That is its task and its promise . . .' (Mills, 1967: 4; orig. 1957).

In the following excerpts, Mills describes both the power of society to shape our individual lives, and the importance of connecting our lives (biographies) to history and society:

> When a society becomes industrialised, a peasant becomes a worker; a feudal lord is liquidated or becomes a businessman. When classes rise or fall, a man is employed or unemployed; when the rate of investment goes up or down, a man takes new heart or goes broke. When wars happen, an insurance salesman becomes a rocket launcher; a store clerk, a radar man; a wife lives alone; a child grows up without a father. Neither the life of an individual nor the history of a society can be understood without understanding both.
>
> Yet men do not usually define the troubles they endure in terms of historical change. . . . The well-being they enjoy, they do not usually impute to the big ups and downs of the society in which they live. Seldom aware of the intricate connection between the patterns of their own lives and the course of world history, ordinary men do not usually know what this connection means for the kind of men they are becoming and for the kinds of history-making in which they might take part. They do not possess the quality of mind essential to grasp the interplay of men and society, of biography and history, of self and world. . . .
>
> What they need . . . is a quality of mind that will help them to [see] . . . what is going on in the world and . . . what may be happening within themselves. It is this quality . . . that . . . may be called the sociological imagination. Always keep your eyes open to the image of man – the generic notion of his human nature – which by your work you are assuming and implying; and also to the image of history – your notion of how history is being made. In a word, continually work out and revise your views of the problems of history, the problems of biography, and the problems of a social structure in which biography and history intersect. Keep your eyes open to the varieties of individuality, and to the modes of epochal change. Use what you see and what you imagine as the clues to your study of the human variety . . . know that many personal troubles cannot be solved merely as troubles, but must be understood in terms of public issues – and in terms of the problems of history making. Know that the human meaning of public issues must be revealed by relating them to personal troubles and to the problems of individual life. Know that the problems of social science, when adequately formulated, must include both troubles and issues, both biography and history, and the range of their intricate relations. Within that range the life of the individual and the making of societies occur; and within that range the sociological imagination has its chance to make a difference in the quality of human life in our time. (Mills, 1967: 3–5, 225–6; orig. 1957).

This triple focus, on *biography*, *history and structure*, is sociology's heritage (see Bipul Kumar Bhadra, 1998).

(Notice that in this excerpt, Mills uses male pronouns to apply to all people. It is interesting – even ironic – that an outspoken critic of society like Mills reflected the conventional writing practices of his time as far as gender was concerned. But he was writing in the 1950s before gender became a key issue for sociology.)

2. *Sociologists are part of what they study.* 'I have seen society, and it is me.' As we are all part of society, we are all part of what we study. This cannot be otherwise, but it makes the tasks of a sociologist very difficult. Many other 'sciences' study objects that are separate from the human species, but sociologists do not. Since we are part of the very world we study, we may find it hard to distance ourselves from this world. A sociologist born in Europe may have all kinds of European assumptions which do not hold in Thailand or Brazil. With the best intentions in the world, much sociology remains *ethnocentric* – bound to a particular cultural view.

3. *Sociological knowledge becomes part of society.* The research and study that sociologists do – the books they write, the arguments they make – eventually become part of a society's knowledge about itself. Sociologists create ideas that can shape the ways in which societies work. Findings on crime – for example, that crime rates are soaring – can be reported in the media, and people then become more conscious of crime. As a result, even more crime is reported. Sociology has an impact on society.

Social change and the origins of sociology

Major historical events rarely just happen. They are typically products of powerful social forces that are always complex and only partly predictable. So it was with the emergence of sociology itself. Having described the discipline's distinctive perspective and surveyed some of its benefits, we can now consider how and why sociology emerged in the first place.

Although human beings have mused about society since the beginning of our history, sociology is of relatively recent origin. In many ways it was the product of the **Enlightenment**. The *French Philosophes* were the cornerstone of such thinking, a 'solid, respectable clan of revolutionaries' (Gay, 1970: 9) who included Montesquieu, Rousseau and Voltaire. Such thinking signposted the arrival of the 'modern world'. The sociologist Peter Hamilton has suggested ten hallmarks of the Enlightenment mind:

1. Reason became a key way of organising knowledge, but it was tempered with
2. Empiricism – facts that can be apprehended through the senses
3. Science – linked especially to experimental scientific revolution
4. Universalism – especially the search for general laws
5. Progress – the 'human condition' can be improved
6. Individualism – the starting point for all knowledge
7. Toleration – beliefs of other nations and groups are not inherently inferior to European Christianity
8. Freedom
9. Uniformity of Human Nature
10. Secularism – often opposed to the church
    (Hamilton, 1996)

However, only in 1838 did the French social thinker Auguste Comte (introduced in the Profile box below) coin the term *sociology* to describe a new way of looking at the world.

PROFILE

AUGUSTE COMTE: WEATHERING A STORM OF CHANGE

What sort of person would invent sociology? Certainly someone living in times of momentous change. Comte (1798–1857) grew up in the wake of the French Revolution, which brought a sweeping transformation to his country. And if that wasn't sufficient, another revolution was under way: factories were sprouting up across continental Europe, recasting the lives of the entire population. Just as people enduring a storm cannot help but think of the weather, so those living during Comte's turbulent era became keenly aware of the state of society.

Drawn from his small home town by the bustle of Paris, Comte was soon deeply involved in the exciting events of his time. More than anything else, he wanted to understand the human drama that was unfolding all around him. Once equipped with knowledge about how society operates, Comte believed, people would be able to build for themselves a better future. He divided his new discipline into two parts: how society is held together (which he called social statics), and how society changes (social dynamics). From the Greek and Latin words meaning 'the study of society', Comte came to describe his work as sociology.

Science and sociology

The nature of society was a major topic of enquiry for virtually all the brilliant thinkers of the ancient world, including the Chinese philosopher K'ung Futzu, also known as Confucius (551–479 BCE), and the Greek philosophers Plato (c. 427–347 BCE) and Aristotle (384–322 BCE).[1] Similarly, the medieval thinker St Thomas Aquinas (c. 1225–1274), the fourteenth-century Muslim Ibn Khaldun, and the French philosopher Montesquieu (1689–1755) all examined the state of human society.

There were many such social thinkers. Yet, as Emile Durkheim noted almost a century ago, none of these approached society from a truly sociological point of view.

> Looking back in history . . . we find that no philosophers ever viewed matters [with a sociological perspective] until quite recently. . . . It seemed to them sufficient to ascertain what the human will should strive for and what it should avoid in established societies. . . . Their aim was not to offer us as valid a description of nature as possible, but to present us with the idea of a perfect society, a model to be imitated.
>
> (Durkheim, 1972: 57; orig. 1918)

What sets sociology apart from earlier social thought? Prior to the birth of sociology, philosophers and theologians mostly focused on imagining the ideal society. None attempted to analyse society as it really was. Pioneers of the discipline such as Auguste Comte, Emile Durkheim and Ferdinand Toennies (see below) reversed these priorities. Although they were certainly concerned with how human society could be improved, their major goal was to understand how society actually operates.

The key to achieving this objective, according to Comte, was developing a scientific approach to society. Looking back in time, Comte sorted human efforts to comprehend the world into three distinct stages: theological, metaphysical and scientific (1975; orig. 1851–54). The earliest era, extending through to the medieval period in Europe, was the *theological stage*. At this point, thoughts about the world were guided by religion, so people regarded society as an expression of God's will – at least in so far as humans were capable of fulfilling a divine plan.

With the Renaissance, the theological approach to society gradually gave way to what Comte called the *metaphysical stage*. During this period, people came to understand society as a natural, rather than a

supernatural, phenomenon. Human nature figured heavily in metaphysical visions of society: Thomas Hobbes (1588–1679), for example, posited that society reflected not the perfection of God as much as the failings of a rather selfish human nature.

What Comte heralded as the final, *scientific stage* in the long quest to understand society was propelled by scientists such as Copernicus (1473–1543), Galileo[2] (1564–1642) and Isaac Newton (1642–1727). Comte's contribution came in applying this scientific approach – first used to study the physical world – to the study of society.

Comte was thus a proponent of **positivism**, defined as *a means to understand the world based on science*. As a positivist, Comte believed that society conforms to invariable laws, much as the physical world operates according to gravity and other laws of nature. Even today, most sociologists agree that science plays a crucial role in sociology. But, as Chapter 3 explains, we now realise both that human behaviour is often far more complex than natural phenomena and that science is itself more sophisticated than we thought before. Thus human beings are creatures with considerable imagination and spontaneity, so that our behaviour can never be fully explained by any rigid 'laws of society'. Likewise, the universe may be much more 'chaotic' and 'emergent' than we previously thought, making observations and laws much more difficult.

Change, transformation and sociology

Sociology was born out of the 'massive social transformation' of the past two centuries. Two great revolutions – the French Revolution of 1789 and the more general 'Industrial Revolution' traced to England in the eighteenth century – 'have all but totally dissolved the forms of social organisation in which humankind has lived for thousands of years of its previous history' (Giddens, 1986: 4). Striking transformations in eighteenth- and nineteenth-century Europe, then, drove

---

[1] Throughout this text, the abbreviation BCE designates 'before the common era'. We use this terminology in place of the traditional BC ('before Christ') in recognition of religious plurality. Similarly, in place of the traditional AD (*anno Domini*, or 'in the year of our Lord'), we employ the abbreviation CE ('common era'). See also the 'Time Lines' on the inside cover.

[2] Illustrating Comte's stages, the ancient Greeks and Romans viewed the planets as gods; Renaissance metaphysical thinkers saw them as astral influences (giving rise to astrology); by the time of Galileo, scientists understood planets as natural objects behaving in orderly ways.

(a)

(b)

(c)

(d)

Some shapers of a modern sociology. With the rise of industrial capitalism, the nineteenth and twentieth centuries saw an explosion of significant thinkers about society. Above are just four of them: (a) Karl Marx (see Chapters 2 and 4), (b) Emile Durkheim (see this chapter, and Chapters 2 and 4), (c) Herbert Spencer (see this chapter), and (d) Max Weber (See Chapters 2 and 4). What characteristics do they have in common?

Source: (a) © Archivo Iconografico, S.A./Corbis, Creator: Emile Dreyer; (b) © Bettmann/Corbis; (c) © Hulton-Deutsch Collection/Corbis; (d) © The Granger Collection, New York

the development of sociology. As the social ground trembled under their feet, people understandably focused their attention on society. Traditions were crumbling.

First came scientific discoveries and technological advances that produced a factory-based industrial economy. Second, factories drew millions of people from the countryside, causing an explosive growth of cities. Third, people in these burgeoning industrial cities soon entertained new ideas about democracy and political rights. Finally, the stable communities in which most people had lived for centuries started to decline. We shall briefly describe each of these four changes – though they all reappear for more detailed analysis during this book.

1. A new industrial economy: the growth of modern capitalism

During the European Middle Ages, most people tilled fields near their homes or engaged in small-scale *manufacturing* (a word derived from Latin words meaning 'to make by hand'). But, by the end of the eighteenth century, inventors had applied new sources of energy – first water power and then steam power – to the operation of large machines, which gave birth to factories. Now, instead of labouring at home, workers became part of a large and anonymous industrial workforce, toiling for strangers who owned the factories. This drastic change in the system of production weakened families and eroded traditions that had guided members of small communities for centuries. The development of modern capitalism will be considered in Chapter 4.

2. The growth of cities

Factories sprouting across much of Europe became magnets attracting people in need of work. This 'pull' of work in the new industrialised labour force was accentuated by an additional 'push' as landowners fenced off more and more ground, turning farms into grazing land for sheep – the source of wool for the thriving textile mills. This so-called 'enclosure movement' forced countless tenant farmers from the countryside towards cities in search of work in the new factories.

Many villages were soon abandoned; at the same time, however, factory towns swelled rapidly into large cities. Such urban growth dramatically changed people's lives. Cities churned with strangers, in numbers that overwhelmed available housing. Widespread social problems – including poverty, disease, pollution, crime

and homelessness – were the order of the day. Such social crises further stimulated development of the sociological perspective. We shall consider the rise of modern cities in Chapter 23.

3. Political change: control and democracy

During the Middle Ages, as Comte noted, most people thought of society as the expression of God's will. Royalty claimed to rule by 'divine right', and each person up and down the social hierarchy had some other part in the holy plan. Indeed, throughout history people have rarely seen themselves as being in control of their own lives. With economic development and the rapid growth of cities, changes in political thought were inevitable. Starting in the seventeenth century, every kind of tradition came under spirited attack. In the writings of Thomas Hobbes, John Locke (1632–1704) and Adam Smith (1723–90), we see a distinct shift in focus from people's moral obligations to remain loyal to their rulers to the idea that society is the product of individual self-interest. The key phrases in the new political climate, therefore, were *individual liberty* and *individual rights*. Echoing the thoughts of Locke, the American Declaration of Independence asserts that each individual has 'certain unalienable rights', including 'life, liberty, and the pursuit of happiness'.

The political revolution in France that began soon afterwards, in 1789, constituted an even more dramatic break with political and social traditions. As the French social analyst Alexis de Tocqueville (1805–59) surveyed his society after the French Revolution, he exaggerated only slightly when he asserted that the changes we have described amounted to 'nothing short of the regeneration of the whole human race' (1955: 13; orig. 1856). In this context, it is easy to see why Auguste Comte and other pioneers of sociology soon developed their new discipline. Sociology flowered in precisely those societies – France, Germany and England – where change was greatest.

4. The loss of *Gemeinschaft*: the eclipse of community

The German sociologist Ferdinand Toennies produced the theory of **Gemeinschaft** and **Gesellschaft** (see also Chapter 23). Toennies (1963; orig. 1887) saw the modern world as the progressive loss of *Gemeinschaft*, or human community. He argued that the Industrial Revolution had undermined the strong social fabric of family and tradition by fostering individualism and a businesslike emphasis on facts and efficiency. European and North American societies gradually became rootless and impersonal as people came to associate mostly on the basis of self-interest – the condition Toennies dubbed *Gesellschaft*. Toennies' thesis was that traditional societies, built on kinship and neighbourhood, nourished collective sentiments, virtue and honour. Modernisation washes across traditional society like an acid, eroding human community and unleashing rampant individualism.

Through much of the twentieth century, at least some areas of the Western world approximated Toennies' concept of *Gemeinschaft*. Families that had lived for generations in rural towns and villages were tightly integrated into a hard-working, slow-moving way of life. Before telephones (invented in 1876) and television (introduced in 1939, widespread after 1950), families and communities entertained themselves, communicating with distant members by letter. Before private cars became commonplace after the Second World War, many people viewed their home town as their entire world. Inevitable tensions and conflicts – sometimes based on race, ethnicity and religion – characterised past communities. According to Toennies, however, the traditional ties of *Gemeinschaft* bound people of a community together, 'essentially united in spite of all separating factors' (1963: 65; orig. 1887).

The modern world turned societies inside-out so that, as Toennies put it, people are 'essentially separated in spite of uniting factors' (1963: 65; orig. 1887). This is the world of *Gesellschaft* where, especially in large cities, most people live among strangers and ignore those they pass on the street. Trust is hard to come by in a mobile and anonymous society in which, according to researchers, people tend to put their personal needs ahead of group loyalty and a majority of adults claim that 'you can't be too careful' in dealing with people (Russell, 1993).

Toennies' work displays a deep distrust of the notion of 'progress', which he feared amounted to the steady loss of traditional morality. Toennies stopped short of claiming that modern society was 'worse' than societies of the past and he made a point of praising the spread of rational, scientific thinking. Nevertheless, the growing individualism and selfishness characteristic of modern societies troubled him. Knowing that there could be no return to the past, he looked to the future, hoping that new forms of social organisation would develop that would combine modern rationality with traditional collective responsibility.

Sociologists look to the future

Living through the momentous changes brought about by the French Revolution and the Industrial Revolution must have been both exciting and dangerous times. It is hard for the twenty-first-century person to grasp what it must have been like. But this was precisely the period that the earliest sociologists lived through and why they were driven to understand such changes and to consider where it may all have been heading. Sociology was born out of this firmament of change.

Yet sociologists reacted differently to the new social order then, just as they respond differently to society today. Some, including Auguste Comte and later Ferdinand Toennies, feared that people would be uprooted from long-established local communities and overpowered by change. So, in a conservative approach, Comte sought to shore up the family and traditional morality.

In contrast, Karl Marx (1818–83) worried little about the loss of tradition. But he could not condone the way industrial technology concentrated its great wealth in the hands of a small elite, while so many others faced hunger and misery. We examine his ideas at length in Chapter 4.

Clearly, Comte and Marx advanced radically different prescriptions for the problems of modernity. Yet they had in common the conviction that society rests on much more than individual choice. The sociological perspective animates the work of each, revealing that people's individual lives are framed by the broader society in which they live. This lesson, of course, remains as true today as it was a century ago.

Continuing change

Just as the changes brought by the nineteenth century were momentous, so too are the changes that are happening in the twenty-first century. This is an era which is being revolutionised by digital technologies, new media, new sciences such as the new reproductive technologies, and new global interconnections. It is an era when traditional families, religions, patterns of work and government are all being rethought. More and more, people are not given a clear blueprint on how to live their lives as they often were in the past. Instead they have to ask: what kind of life do I want to lead? They become more individualised, less committed to common standards, more prone to self-reflexivity. It is an era when divisions of class, ethnicity, age and gender have become more and more noticeable, and it is a world where significant new conflicts over religion and culture seem rife. All of these ideas will need defining, describing, analysing and explaining, and this is the continuing task for sociologists in the new century – as well as the task for this introductory book. Just as sociology was born of the Industrial Revolution, now it finds renewed excitement at the challenge of what we shall call the postmodern or information society.

In subsequent chapters of this book, then, we delve into some of these changes. We will look at the steady move to modernity and modern societies, and how these days this may be transforming into other kinds of society. We will discuss the major issues that concern contemporary sociologists. These pivotal social forces include culture, social class, race, ethnicity, gender, the economy and the family. They all involve ways in which individuals are guided, united and divided in the larger arena of society. Sociology is a challenging discipline, highly relevant to a world brimming with change. This book sets out to explore a little of this.

SUMMARY

1. Sociology is the systematic (and critical?) study of society.

2. The sociological perspective reveals 'the general in the particular' or the power of society to shape our lives. Because people in Western countries tend to think in terms of individual choice, recognising the impact of society on our lives initially seems like 'seeing the strange in the familiar'.

3. Socially marginal people are more likely than others to perceive the effects of society. For everyone, periods of social crisis foster sociological thinking.

4. There are four general benefits to using the sociological perspective. First, it challenges our familiar understandings of the world, helping us separate fact from fiction; second, it helps us appreciate the opportunities and constraints that frame our lives; third, it encourages more active participation in society; fourth, it increases our awareness of social diversity in the UK and in the world as a whole.

5. There are three problems in studying sociology. First, societies change very rapidly; second, we are part of the societies we study; and third, sociology itself becomes a part of society.

6. Auguste Comte gave sociology its name in 1838. Whereas previous social thought had focused on what society ought to be, Comte's new discipline of sociology used scientific methods to understand society as it is. Sociology emerged as a reaction to the rapid transformation of Europe during the eighteenth and nineteenth centuries.

7. Four dimensions of change – the rise of an industrial economy, the explosive growth of cities, the emergence of new political ideas, and the decline of community – helped focus people's attention on the operation of society.

8. A new kind of society might be appearing. Quite what it is to be called and what its features are will be raised throughout the book.

CRITICAL-THINKING QUESTIONS

1. Consider how sociology differs from economics, politics, psychology, history, literature and journalism. Using the box on page 4, try to define sociology and see what is distinctive about it.

2. In what ways does using the sociological perspective make us seem less in control of our lives? In what ways does it give us greater power over our surroundings?

3. Give a sociological explanation of why sociology developed where and when it did. Examine whether it had 'biases', and if so what they were.

4. Read or watch some science fiction then write a futuristic account of the society in which your grandchildren will live, based upon your current knowledge of any new social trends.

GOING FURTHER

Sociology has been an area of study for some 200 years, though it is only in the past 50 years that it has become really popular among students. The research and writing in sociology is now enormous and this book is meant only as an opening guide. Every topic discussed in the book could (and should) be taken further – much further! We hope that there will be many areas you would like to follow up. There are several ways to do this:

- At the end of each chapter, there is a short guide to ways you can pursue your thinking and study further. These sources – films, books, magazines – will also be of great help in writing essays, doing research or engaging in discussions.

- The book also links to a website which provides a mass of further detailed analyses along with links, further questions and bibliographies. Because links can so quickly go out of date, this book will provide only major website resources at the end of each chapter: many more can be found on the website.

Further reading

Classic introductions:

Peter Berger, *Invitation to Sociology* (1963)
The classic introduction, it is a very readable account and highlights sociology as a humanistic way of seeing the world.

C. Wright Mills, *The Sociological Imagination* (1959)
The classic introduced in the first Profile box.

Other short, readable introductions to sociology:

Nicholas Abercrombie, *Sociology* (2004)

Martin Albrow, *Sociology: The Basics* (1999)

Zygmunt Bauman and Tim May, *Thinking Sociologically* (rev. edn, 2001)

Steve Bruce, *Sociology: A Very Short Introduction* (1999)

Anthony Giddens, *Sociology: A Brief but Critical Introduction* (2nd edn, 1986)

Conrad L. Kanagy and Donald B. Kraybill, *The Riddles of Human Society* (1999)

Other introductions:

Pamela Abbott and Claire Wallace, *An Introduction to Sociology: Feminist Perspectives* (3rd edn, 2004)

An introductory text which provides a feminist perspective.

Steven P. Dandaneau, *Taking it Big: Developing Sociological Consciousness in Postmodern Times* (2001)
Aims to be the C. Wright Mills for the new century and is certainly a lively read.

Jon Gubbay, Chris Middleton and Chet Ballard, *The Student's Companion to Sociology* (1997)
A useful general reference source for sociology students.

Richard Osborne and Borin Van Loon, *Sociology for Beginners* (1996)
A 'cartoon style' introduction for beginners.

Kenneth Thompson, *Key Quotations in Sociology* (1996).
A guide to key quotations in sociology.

More information

Dictionaries:

There is a glossary of key concepts at the end of this book, but sometimes you will wish to explore the meanings of concepts more fully. For this, you will need a dictionary of sociology. There are many available. Amongst them are:

The Penguin Dictionary of Sociology (4th edn, 2000)

The Concise Oxford Dictionary of Sociology (3rd edn, 2005)

Tony Lawson and Joan Garrod, *The Complete A–Z Sociology Handbook* (3rd edn, 2003).

Magazines and journals:

Much useful reading is contained in magazines or journals which come out at regular intervals. In fact, academics are very dependent on these for the latest findings. Two very readable popular magazines for sociology students – even worth subscribing to – are:

- *Sociology Review*, from Philip Allan Publishers Ltd, Market Place, Deddington, Oxfordshire OX15 0SE. Published four times a year. Full of short, up-to-date articles on key issues in sociology and well illustrated. With a strong focus on the UK, this is a must for the budding sociologist.

- *New Internationalist*, from PO Box 79, Hertford SG14 1AQ. Published monthly. This takes a clear political stance and is packed full of valuable information on the 'global state' of the world.

Watch a video/Read a book

Each chapter will suggest a few films that may be worth a look. As an opener, you might like to look at three 'classic' films that hold very different views of what society is like:

- Fritz Lang's *Metropolis* (1926): a futuristic account;
- Frank Capra's *It's a Wonderful Life* (1946): a tale of small-town America;
- David Lynch's *Blue Velvet* (1986): another tale of small-town America but one that is very different and not for the weak-hearted or squeamish (be warned: this last film is strong stuff and not recommended for all).

A comparison of the three kinds of society depicted would make for an interesting discussion! Look also at:

- Harold Ramis's *Groundhog Day* (1993): in which everybody pretty much does the same thing every day. It is a good way of thinking about the ways in which everyday life is often routine and taken for granted.

A good start for thinking about Enlightenment thought is to read some classics of Enlightenment literature like Voltaire's *Candide* (1759) and Jonathan Swift's *Gulliver's Travels* (1726).

The Classic Collection

Some of the classic studies of English sociology have been disccussed on video. These studies are avaible from halovine and **mail@halovine.com**. They include:

Stanley Cohen on *Folk Devils and Moral Panics*
Paul Willis *Learning to Labour*
Jock Young *The Drug takers*
Peter Townsend *Poverty in the UK*
Anthony Giddens on *Capitalism and Modern Social Theory*
Michelle Stanworth *Gender and Schooling*
Eileen Barker *The Making of a Moonie*

Connecting up

Connect to other chapters

- For more on the positivist method, see Chapter 3.
- For more on explanations of social change, see Chapter 4.

For additional case studies, multiple choice questions, internet exercises, and annotated weblinks specific to this chapter, visit this book's website at
www.pearsoned.co.uk/plummer

APPENDIX

SURFING FOR SOCIOLOGY: AN ENTRANCE

There are now a large number of websites devoted to social science and to sociology. What follows is not meant to be a comprehensive listing but rather an 'entrance' for students and others who want to explore what is there. More sites are mentioned at the end of each chapter, and on the website itself. For a general introduction see Stuart Stein's *Sociology on the Web: A Student Guide* (2003).

General gateways to sociology

http://www.sociolog.com/
http://www.pscw.uva.nl/sociosite/
http://www.socioweb.com/~markbl/socioweb/
http://www.trinity.edu/~mkearl

These 'gateways' are very wide ranging. Not only are there links to a wide array of sociology sites and organisations, there are also links to key Sociology Associations and Sociology Departments throughout the world. They are very useful as first entries.

A-level links

Sociology Central: http://www.sociology.org.uk/

A useful site for A-level students. It takes you through key textbooks, tells you about up-and-coming conferences, and reviews university websites in the UK. Good, but not advanced.

Sociology OnLine: http://www.sociologyonline.co.uk/

A different kind of sociology site. It takes topical issues from the press and television and then makes connections and provides links to sociology. Good for starting out on popular research into current issues. Again, has an A-level flavour to it.

Statistics and databases

http://odwin.ucsd.edu/idata/

Excellent site produced from UC San Diego which contains main data from many archives around the world. Just type in what you are looking for and you are off . . .

A few key thinkers

A number of the general sites listed above provide the sites of many different sociologists. The following are a few entries to named sociologists.

Karl Marx: www.marxists.org/archive/marx

The site for Marx! Lots here.

Emile Durkheim:

http://www.utm.edu/research/iep/m/mead.htm

http://durkheim.itgo.com

George Herbert Mead: http://www.utm.edu/research/iep/m/mead.htm

A wonderful repository of Mead's work.

Max Weber: http://www.ne.jp/asahi/moriyuki/abukuma/

Offers some of Weber's work online.

Sigmund Freud:

http://plaza.interport.net/nypsan/freudarc.html

The Freud archive. Very useful in having a great many links to all manner of interesting things about Freud.

Symbolic interactionism: http://sun.soci.niu.edu/~sssi/

The home page of the Society for the Study of Symbolic Interaction. At last look, it had not been updated for a while.

Michel Foucault: http://www.csun.edu/~hfspc002/foucault.home.html

One of many Foucault sites: has some good links.

International data

United Nations: http://www.un.org/english

This home page can lead you to many discussions, facts and statements of rights.

World Bank: http://www.worldbank.org/

Another leading international home page which will lead to masses of information.

One World: http://www.oneworld.net/

Excellent 'alternative' home page for the charity One World which provides up-to-date information on rights, economic development, etc.

Amnesty International: http://www.amnesty.org/

Excellent site for human rights.

Human Rights Web: http://www.hrw.org/

A useful site, but it does not seem to have been updated lately.

European Union: http://www.europa.eu.int/index-en.htm

Useful on all formal aspects of the European Union.

Some special topics

Medical matters – Medscape:

http://www.medscape.com/px/urlinfo

Large and useful site for medical sources: good on HIV/AIDS, psychiatry, managed care and women's health.

Women's studies and feminism:

http://www.feminist.org

http://www.femarch.freeserve.co.uk/

http://www.voiceofwomen.com/

http://www.igc.org/index.html

http://eserver.org/feminism/index

There are many feminist and women's sites – the above is just the merest slight selection! For example, taking it further, on postmodernism and feminism, see:

http://www.cddc.vt.edu/feminism/law.html Pornography

Gay and Queer: http://www.qrd.org/qrd

Excellent links to all matters of Queer resources, though as with so many sites it looks as if it is getting out of date.

Subcultures: http://www.zearle.com/the_drug.htm; http://www.sociology.org.uk/carddev.htm

The first site is about drug taking and the other provides information on subcultures and deviant behaviour.

Criminology: http://www.crim.cam.ac.uk/

http://www.nicic.org

National Institute Corrections, an agency within the US Department of Justice.

http://www.law.cam.ac.uk/crim/CRIMLINK.HTM

From Edge Hill and the University of Cambridge, two very useful pages of links to criminology issues.

http://www.digeratiweb.com/sociorealm

Another criminology site, this time from Canada and the US.

http://www.aic.gov.au/index.html

Australian Institute for Criminology – has online publications on a variety of topics, including drugs.

Other interests and fields

Government documents:
http://www.open.gov.uk/index/topicindex.htm

Very useful source for all UK government materials – from law and justice to education.

Qualidata: http://www.essex.ac.uk/qualidata

The Essex Archive for Qualitative Data – called Qualidata. A lot of useful information about archiving and good links to many archives.

Methodology

General: http://www.soc.surrey.ac.uk/sru

Social research update from Surrey University.

Qualitative data:

http://www.ualberta.ca/~jrnorris/qual.html

http://maple.lemoyne.edu/~hevern/narpsych.html

The latter is a useful source for narrative theory.

Other libraries

http://www.bl.uk/index.shtml

Takes you into the British Library, where you can find, among many other things, the National Sound Archive. With the right browsers, you can listen to oral history tapes, for example.

(Readers are reminded that website addresses are subject to frequent changes. If any of the addresses listed in this book fail to give results, try links from other generic websites, or search using a good search engine such as Yahoo!, Google, Lycos or AltaVista.)

CHAPTER 2

THINKING SOCIOLOGICALLY, THINKING GLOBALLY

From now on, nothing that happens on our planet
is only a limited local event.

Ulrich Beck

IN THE MILLENNIUM YEAR OF 2000, the Earth was home to some six billion people who lived in the cities and countryside of nearly 200 nations. To grasp the social 'shape' of this world, imagine for a moment the planet's population reduced to a single settlement of 100 people. A visit to this 'global village' would reveal that more than half (61) of the inhabitants are from Asia, including 21 from the People's Republic of China and 17 from India. Next, in terms of numbers, we would find 13 from Africa, 12 from Europe, eight from South America, five from North America and one from Oceania.

A study of this settlement would reveal some startling conclusions. People believed in very different 'Gods': 32 were Christian, 19

KEY THEMES
- The classical ways of thinking about society
- The newer perspectives in sociology
- A global perspective in sociology
- Globalisation

Muslim, 13 Hindus, 12 practised folk religions (like shamanism), six were Buddhists, two belonged to other religions like Confucianism and the Bahai'i faith, one was Jewish and 15 were non-religious. There are some 6,000 languages but over half of the hundred spoke Chinese, nine spoke English, eight spoke Hindi, seven spoke Spanish, four spoke Arabic, four spoke Bengali, three spoke Portugese, and three spoke Russian.

The village is a rich place, with a vast array of goods and services for sale. Yet most people can do no more than dream of such treasures, because 80 per cent of the village's total income is earned by just 20 individuals.

Food is the greatest worry for the majority of the population. Every year, workers produce more than enough food to feed everyone; even so, half the village's people – including most of the children – go hungry. The worst-off 20 residents (who together have less money than the richest person in the village!) lack food, safe drinking water and secure shelter. They are weak and unable to work. Every day some of them fall ill with life-threatening diseases. Another 50 do not have a reliable source of food and are hungry much of the time.

Villagers talk of their community's many schools, including colleges and universities. Of 38 school-aged villagers, 31 attend school but few (7.5) reach university. Half of the village's people can neither read nor write.

The sociological perspective reminds us of the many differences of the world. Our life chances and our very experiences of social life will differ dramatically according to what kind of society we are born into. Human lives do not unfold according to sheer chance, nor do people live isolated lives relying solely on what philosophers call 'free will' in choosing every thought and action. On the contrary, while individuals make many important decisions every day, we do so within a larger arena called 'society' – a family, a university, a nation, an entire world. The essential wisdom of sociology is that the social world guides and constrains our actions and life choices just as the seasons influence our choices of activities and clothing. It sets the framework in which we make decisions about our lives. And, because sociologists know a great deal about how society works, they can analyse and predict with both insight and accuracy how we all behave. Many of the achievements we attribute to our personal abilities are products of the privileged position we occupy in the worldwide social system.[1]

[1] Global village scenario adapted from United Nations data. See also: Smith and Armstrong, 2003.

(Left) From space the Earth looks blue, as seen in this diagrammatic illustration which shows the Motorola iridium mobile phone satellites.
Source: Motorola/ SPL/PHOTO LIBRARY

What is the classical tradition of sociology? Starting a short tour of sociological theory

The task of weaving isolated observations into understanding brings us to another dimension of sociology: theory. Students are often put off by theory, believing it to be obscure and difficult. In fact, theory is what makes sociology different from, say, journalism or popular documentary television of social issues. For a **theory** is a *statement of how and why specific facts are related*. In a sense, we all theorise or generalise all the time. But sociology aims to do this more systematically (see Lee and Newby, 1983; Craib, 1992). Recall that Emile Durkheim observed that certain categories of people (men, Protestants, the wealthy and the unmarried) have higher suicide rates than others (women, Catholics and Jews, the poor and the married). He explained these observations by creating a theory: a high risk of suicide stems from a low level of social integration.

Of course, as Durkheim pondered the issue of suicide, he considered any number of possible theories. But merely linking facts together is no guarantee that a theory is correct. To evaluate a theory, as the next chapter explains, sociologists use critical and logical thinking along with an array of research tools to gather evidence. 'Facts', as we shall see, are always a bit of a problem – consider, for example, how the very idea of a suicide rate used by Durkheim brings problems. Just what does such a rate measure? Does it really record all the suicides? How can we really tell that a death has been a suicide? Nevertheless, sociologists do strive for 'facts', which often allow them to confirm some theories while rejecting or modifying others. As a sociologist, Durkheim was not content merely to identify a plausible cause of suicide; he set about collecting data to see precisely which categories of people committed suicide with the highest frequency. Poring over his data, Durkheim settled on a theory that best squared with all the available evidence.

In attempting to develop theories about human society, sociologists face a wide range of choices. What issues should we study? How should we link facts together to form theories? What assumptions might underpin our theories? In making sense of society, sociologists are guided by one or more theoretical 'road maps' or perspectives. A **theoretical perspective** can be seen as *a basic image that guides thinking and research*.

We noted earlier that two of sociology's founders – Auguste Comte and Karl Marx – made sense of the emerging modern society in strikingly different ways. Such differences persist today as some sociologists highlight how societies stay the same, while others focus on patterns of change. Similarly, some sociological theorists focus on what joins people together, while others investigate how society divides people according to gender, race, ethnicity or social class. Some sociologists seek to understand the operation of society as it is, while others actively promote what they view as desirable social change.

In short, sociologists often disagree about what the most interesting questions are; even when they agree on the questions, they may still differ over the answers. Nonetheless, the discipline of sociology is far from chaotic. Like many disciplines, it has built-in controversies and has multiple perspectives, containing *an array of basic images that guide thinking and research*. See Figure 2.1 for a summary of various positions. Over the past hundred years, sociologists have developed three major theoretical ways of thinking about society. We will introduce these next – and they will reappear at various points in the book. They may be called the **classical perspectives** that have shaped sociology in the past. But, like any growing discipline, these are constantly being refined and developed, while at the same time newer ones are appearing alongside them. After outlining these mainstream, or classical, stances, we will turn to some **emerging perspectives**.

Mainstream or 'classical' perspectives in sociology

Broadly, three perspectives have dominated sociological thinking until recently: functionalism, conflict and action theory. We will briefly describe each, and return to them throughout the book (they are also featured on the website which accompanies this book).

The functionalist perspective

Functionalism is *a framework for building theory that envisages society as a complex system whose parts work together to promote solidarity and stability*. This perspective begins by recognising that our lives are guided by **social structure**, meaning *relatively stable patterns of social behaviour*. Social structure is what gives shape to the family, directs people to exchange greetings on the street, or steers events in a university classroom. Second, this perspective leads us to understand social structure in terms of its **social functions**, or *consequences for the operation of society*. All social structure – from family life to a simple handshake – contributes to the operation of society, at least in its present form.

Functionalism owes much to the ideas of Auguste Comte who, as we have already explained, sought to promote social integration during a time of tumultuous change. A second architect of this theoretical approach, the influential English sociologist Herbert Spencer (1820–1903), is introduced in the box. Spencer was a student of both the human body and society, and he came to see that the two have much in common. The structural parts of the human body include the skeleton, muscles and various internal organs. These elements are interdependent, each contributing to the survival of the entire organism. In the same way, reasoned Spencer, various social structures are interdependent, working in concert to preserve society. The structural–functional perspective, then, organises sociological observations by identifying various structures of society and investigating the function of each one.

In France, several decades after Comte's death, Emile Durkheim continued the development of sociology. Durkheim did not share the social Darwinist thinking of his English colleague Spencer; rather, his work is primarily concerned with the issue of *social solidarity*, how societies 'hang together'. Because of the extent of Durkheim's influence on sociology, his work is detailed in Chapter 4.

As sociology developed in the United States, many of the ideas of Herbert Spencer and Emile Durkheim were carried forward by Talcott Parsons (1902–79). The major US proponent of the functional perspective, Parsons treated society as a system, identifying the basic tasks all societies must perform to survive and the ways they accomplish these tasks. All societies, he argued, need to be able to adapt, achieve their goals, maintain themselves and have members who are well socialised into their order. Without this, societies may begin to break down.

A contemporary of Parsons was US sociologist Robert K. Merton, who expanded our understanding of the concept of social function in novel ways. Merton (1968) explains, first, that the consequences of any social pattern are likely to differ for various members of a society. For example, conventional families may provide crucial

PROFILE

HERBERT SPENCER: THE SURVIVAL OF THE FITTEST

The most memorable idea of the English philosopher Herbert Spencer (1820–1903) was his assertion that the passing of time witnesses 'the survival of the fittest'. Many people associate this immortal phrase with the theory of species evolution developed by the natural scientist Charles Darwin (1809–82). The expression was actually Spencer's, however, and he used it to refer to society, not to living creatures. In it, we find not only an example of early structural–functional analysis, but a controversial theory that reflects the popular view in Spencer's day that society mirrored biology.

Spencer's ideas, which came to be known as social Darwinism, rested on the assertion that, if left to compete among themselves, the most intelligent, ambitious and productive people will inevitably win out. Spencer endorsed a world of fierce competition, thinking that as the 'fittest' survived, society would undergo steady improvements.

Society rewards its best members, Spencer continued, by allowing a free-market economy to function without government interference. Welfare, or other programmes aimed at redistributing money to benefit the poor, Spencer maintained, do just the opposite: they drag society down by elevating its weakest and least worthy members. For such opinions, nineteenth-century industrialists loudly applauded Spencer, and the rich saw in Spencer's analysis a scientific justification for big business to remain free of government regulation or social conscience. Indeed, John D. Rockefeller, who built a vast financial empire that included most of the US oil industry, often recited Spencer's 'social gospel' to young children in Sunday school, casting the growth of giant corporations as merely the naturally ordained 'survival of the fittest'.

But others objected to the idea that society amounted to little more than a jungle where self-interest reigned supreme. Gradually, social Darwinism fell out of favour among social scientists, though it still surfaces today as an influential element of conservative political thought. From a sociological point of view, Spencer's thinking is flawed because we now realise that ability only partly accounts for personal success, and favouring the rich and powerful does not necessarily benefit society as a whole. In addition, the heartlessness of Spencer's ideas strikes many people as cruel, with little room for human compassion.

For a positive appraisal of Spencer's work, see Jonathan Turner, *Herbert Spencer* (1985).

support for the development of children, but they also confer privileges on men while limiting the opportunities of women.

Second, Merton notes, people rarely perceive all the functions of a particular social structure. He described as **manifest functions** the *recognised and intended consequences of any social pattern*. By contrast, **latent functions** are *consequences that are largely unrecognised and unintended*. To illustrate, the obvious functions of higher education include providing people with the information and skills they need to perform jobs effectively. But perhaps just as important, although rarely acknowledged, is a university's function as a chance to meet potential partners. Another function may be to keep millions of young people out of a labour market where, presumably, many of them would not find jobs. And a third, less obvious function may well be to reinforce a system of prestige and inequality – by excluding those who do not go to universities from all sorts of work.

Merton makes a third point: not *all* the effects of any social structure turn out to be useful. Thus we designate as **social dysfunctions** *any social pattern's undesirable consequences for the operation of society*. And, to make matters still more complex, people may well disagree about what is useful or harmful. So some might argue that higher education promotes left-wing thinking that threatens traditional values. Others might dismiss such charges as trivial or simply wrong; higher education is dysfunctional for conferring further privileges on the wealthy (who disproportionately attend university) while poorer families find a university course beyond their financial reach.

Critical comment

The most salient characteristic of the functional perspective is its vision of society as a whole being comprehensible, orderly and stable. Sociologists typically couple this approach with scientific methods of research aimed at learning 'what makes society tick'.

Until the 1960s, the functional perspective dominated sociology. In recent decades, however, its influence has waned. How can we assume that society has a 'natural' order, critics ask, when social patterns vary from place to place and change over time? Further, by emphasising social integration, functionalism tends to gloss over inequality based on social class, race, ethnicity and gender – divisions that may generate considerable tension and conflict. This focus on stability at the expense of conflict and change can give the functional perspective a conservative character. In the main, functionalism is a theory that is much less discussed and used these days.

The conflict perspective

The **conflict perspective** is a *framework for building theory that envisages society as an arena of inequality that generates conflict and change*. This approach complements the functional perspective by highlighting not solidarity but division based on inequality. Guided by this perspective, sociologists investigate how factors such as social class, race, ethnicity, sex and age are linked to unequal distribution of money, power, education and social prestige. A conflict analysis points out that, rather than promoting the operation of society as a whole, social structure typically benefits some people while depriving others.

Working within the conflict perspective, sociologists spotlight ongoing conflict between dominant and disadvantaged categories of people – the rich in relation to the poor, white people as opposed to black, men versus women. Typically, those on top strive to protect their privileges; the disadvantaged counter by attempting to gain more resources for themselves.

To illustrate, a conflict analysis of our educational system might highlight how schooling perpetuates inequality by helping to reproduce the class structure in every new generation. The process may start in primary schools and continue as secondary schools stream students. From a functional point of view, this may benefit all of society because, ideally, students receive the training appropriate to their academic abilities. But conflict analysis counters that streaming often has less to do with talent than with a student's social background, as well-to-do students are placed in higher streams and poor students end up in the lower ones.

In this way, privileged families gain favoured treatment for their children from schools. And, with the best schooling behind them, these young people leave university to pursue occupations that confer both prestige and high income. By contrast, the children of poor families are less prepared for college. So, like their parents before them, these young people typically move straight from secondary school into low-paying jobs. In both cases, the social standing of one generation is passed on to another, with schools justifying the practice in terms not of privilege but of individual merit (Bowles and Gintis, 1976; and see Chapter 19).

Social conflict extends well beyond schools. Later chapters of this book highlight efforts by working people, women, racial, ethnic, gay and lesbian minorities to improve their lives. In each of these cases, the conflict perspective helps us to see how inequality and the conflict it generates are rooted in the organisation of society itself.

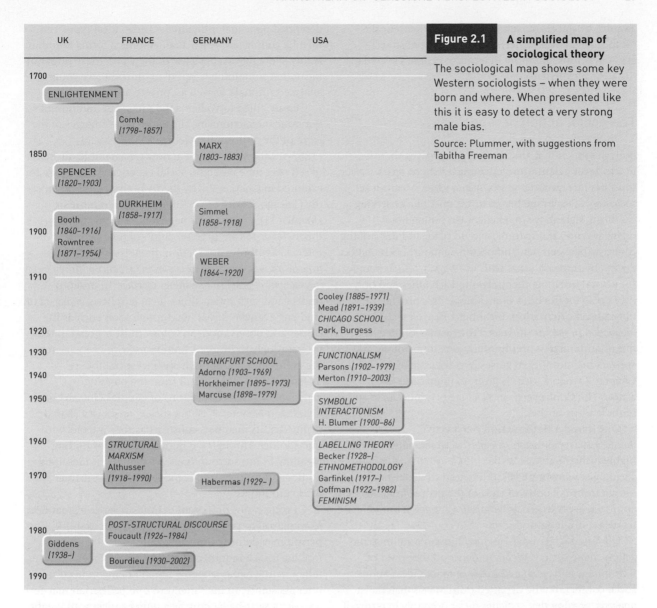

Figure 2.1   A simplified map of sociological theory

The sociological map shows some key Western sociologists – when they were born and where. When presented like this it is easy to detect a very strong male bias.

Source: Plummer, with suggestions from Tabitha Freeman

Finally, many sociologists who embrace the conflict perspective attempt not just to understand society but to reduce social inequality. This was the goal of Karl Marx, the social thinker whose ideas underlie the conflict perspective. Marx did not seek merely to understand how society works. In a well-known declaration (inscribed on his monument in London's Highgate Cemetery), Marx asserted: 'The philosophers have only interpreted the world, in various ways; the point, however, is to change it.'

Critical comment

The conflict perspective developed rapidly during the 1960s and the 1970s. Yet, like other approaches, it has come in for its share of criticism. Because this perspective highlights inequality and division, it glosses over how shared values or interdependence generate unity among members of a society. In addition, say critics, to the extent that the conflict approach explicitly pursues political goals, it can relinquish any claim to scientific objectivity. As the next chapter explains in detail, conflict theorists are uneasy with the notion that science can be 'objective'. They contend, on the contrary, that the conflict perspective as well as *all* theoretical approaches have political consequences, albeit different ones. Like functionalism, the language of conflict theory has gone more and more out of fashion in recent years.

One additional criticism, which applies equally to both the functional and conflict perspectives, is that they envisage society in very broad terms. 'Society' becomes a thing in itself, describing our lives as a composite of 'family', 'social class', and so on. A third theoretical perspective depicts society less in terms of abstract generalisations and more in terms of people's everyday, situational experiences.

The social action perspective

Both the functional and conflict perspectives share a **macro-level orientation**, meaning *a focus on broad social structures that characterise society as a whole*. Macro-level sociology takes in the big picture, rather like observing a city from high above in a helicopter, noting how highways carry traffic from place to place and the striking contrasts between rich and poor neighbourhoods. Action theory, by contrast, starts with the ways in which people (or actors) orientate themselves to each other and how they do so on the basis of meanings. This provides a **micro-level orientation**, meaning *a focus on social interaction in specific situations*. The distinction between macro and micro is an important one in sociology and it appears in a number of guises. We discuss it again in Chapter 7 when a focus is given to interaction and action. The Controversy and Debate box introduces some of these ideas further.

One founder of the **action perspective** – *a micro-theory that focuses on how actors assemble social meanings* – is the highly influential Max Weber (1864–1920), a German sociologist who emphasised the need to understand a setting from the point of view of the people in it. Weber's approach is presented at length in Chapter 4, but here a few ideas can be introduced.

His approach emphasises how human meanings and action shape society. Weber understood the power of technology, and he shared many of Marx's ideas about social conflict. But he departed from Marx's materialist analysis, arguing that societies differ primarily in terms of the ways in which their members think about the world. For Weber, ideas – especially beliefs and values – have transforming power. Thus he saw modern society as the product, not just of new technology and capitalism, but of a new way of thinking. This emphasis on ideas contrasts with Marx's focus on material production, leading scholars to describe Weber's work as 'a debate with the ghost of Karl Marx' (Cuff and Payne, 1979: 73–74).

In all his work, Weber contrasted social patterns in different times and places. To sharpen comparisons, he relied on the **ideal type**, *an abstract statement of the essential, though often exaggerated, characteristics of any social phenomenon*. He explored religion by contrasting the ideal 'Protestant' with the ideal 'Jew', 'Hindu' and 'Buddhist', knowing that these models precisely described no actual individuals. These 'ideal types' can then be contrasted with actual, empirical forms found in reality. Note that Weber's use of the word 'ideal' does not mean that something is 'good' or 'the best'; we could analyse 'criminals' as well as 'priests' as *ideal* types.

Closely allied to Weber is the American tradition of symbolic interactionism. The perspective emerges in the work of the philosopher George Herbert Mead (1863–1931), who looked at how we assemble our sense of self over time based on social experience. His ideas are explored in Chapter 7. The theory is also connected to the Chicago School of Sociology (explored more in Chapter 23), which examined city life in this way. The theory leads to careful observation of how people interact. **Symbolic interaction**, then, is *a theoretical framework that envisages society as the product of the everyday interactions of people doing things together*. In order to understand such interactions, great emphasis is placed on studying everyday social life through tools such as life stories and observation. Sociology must proceed in this view through an intimate familiarity with everyday real-life events and not through abstract social theory.

How does 'society' result from the ongoing experiences of tens of millions of people? One answer, detailed in Chapter 7, is that society arises as a shared reality that its members construct as they interact with one another. Through the human process of finding meaning in our surroundings, we define our identities, bodies and feelings, and come to 'socially construct' the world around us.

Of course, this process of definition varies a great deal from person to person. On a city street, for example, one person may define a homeless woman as 'a no-hoper looking for a handout' and ignore her. Another, however, might define her as a 'fellow human being in need' and offer assistance. In the same way, one pedestrian may feel a sense of security passing by a police officer walking the beat, while another may be seized by nervous anxiety. Sociologists guided by the symbolic-interaction approach, therefore, view society as a mosaic of subjective meanings and variable responses.

On this foundation, others have devised their own micro-level approaches to understanding social life. Chapter 7 presents the work of Erving Goffman (1922–82), whose *dramaturgical analysis* emphasises how we resemble actors on a stage as we play out our various roles before others. Other sociologists, including George Homans and Peter Blau, have developed *social-exchange analysis*. In their view, social interaction amounts to a negotiation in which individuals are guided by what they stand to gain and lose from others. In the ritual of courtship, for example, people typically seek mates

CONTROVERSY AND DEBATE

WHICH COMES FIRST? CHICKENS OR EGGS? ACTION OR STRUCTURE?

A classic problem for sociologists

Which comes first: the chicken or the egg? This classic conundrum has a parallel question for sociology which has persisted throughout the discipline's history. It can be put like this: which comes first – society or the individual? And like the chicken and egg problem, there is no simple solution. Indeed, what has to be recognised is that one does not come first – eggs cannot simply come before chickens, any more than chickens can simply come before eggs. *Both are needed*. And it is the interaction of the two that has to be seen. You cannot, in short, have one without the other. And the same is true for individuals and societies. What sociologists do is look at both individuals and societies, and at their best they look at them together through dialectical thinking which requires looking at two seeming opposites (like individual and society) and how a new form emerges through them.

Making it happen: individuals and action

One phase of sociological analysis is indeed to look at human beings. Not as a psychologist would – in terms of individual attributes like drives or personalities. Rather, the task is to look at the ways in which human beings are orientated towards action, to being world makers, creators of history and social life. Human beings make history, and sociology should look at the ways this happens. We are world makers.

For instance, if you want to understand how our current education system works, one task is to look at the ways in which people make it what it is. This means examining the ways in which legislators passed laws that provided the framework for schools, teaching, curriculum and exams. These did not just happen: they were made, and sociologists need to look at how they were made. Likewise, a pupil arrives in a class and, along with other students and teachers, sets about making the class happen. Sociologists like to get into the classrooms and observe this 'action' – to see just how human beings make the social world work.

Pattern and prison: social structures as maps

Yet people are also born into worlds that are not of their own making. Indeed, as the sociologist Peter Berger says, 'society is the walls of our imprisonment' (Berger, 1963: 109). We are born into families, communities and nations over which we have little immediate control; our lives are heavily shaped by the class, gender and ethnicity we are born into; indeed, even the very language we think with and talk with helps set a pattern to our life. And we had no initial choice over which language we plan to speak: it is given to us from early childhood. (It would be very odd, if you were born in England, if you were made to speak Swahili.) Thus, one moment of sociological analysis is to look at these broadest patterns of social organisation that shape our lives. Recurrent and habitual patterns of social life may be seen as structures. Think for a moment of the ways in which your own life is 'imprisoned'.

Putting 'action' and 'structure' together

So: a structural approach tends to map out society as a whole, while an *action* approach tends to examine the ways in which individuals and small groups come to make their social worlds. Of course, ideally both will be done. This is a task for more advanced social theory.

British sociologist Anthony Giddens, for example, has introduced the idea of **structuration** to focus on both simultaneously, to suggest a process whereby action and structure are always two sides of the same coin (Giddens, 1984). For him, people engage in social actions that create social structures, and it is through these social actions that the structures themselves are produced, maintained and eventually changed over time. Language is a good example of this. Language is a structure of rules, but people speak, write and act it in different ways, changing it as they go along. Without the rules, they would be incomprehensible, so the structures are needed. But just slavishly adhering to the structure would allow for no change, no creativity, no humanity. Looking at both individuals and structures at the same time is what is required. This is no easy task.

As you read this book, keep this puzzle in mind. And take the discussion further. ▶

CONTROVERSY AND DEBATE CONTINUED

CONTINUE THE DEBATE:

1. Do you see yourself as 'determined' by social structure? Look at Figure 1.1 again.
2. How much control do you have over your life? How far do you think you can change the world? Are you a world maker?
3. Look at attempts that have been made to resolve the problem between individual and society (see Craib, 1992).

who offer at least as much – in terms of physical attractiveness, intelligence and social background – as they provide in return.

Critical comment

The action perspective helps to correct a bias inherent in all macro-level approaches to understanding society. Without denying the usefulness of abstract social structures such as 'the family' and 'social class', we must bear in mind that society basically amounts to *people interacting*. Put another way, this micro-level approach

helps convey more of how individuals actually experience society and how they do things together (Becker, 1986).

The trouble is that by focusing on day-to-day interactions, these theorists can obscure larger social structures. Highlighting what is unique in each social scene risks overlooking the widespread effects of our culture, as well as factors such as class, gender and race.

Table 2.1 summarises the important characteristics of the functional, conflict and action perspectives. As we have explained, each perspective is partially helpful in answering particular kinds of question. By and large,

Table 2.1		Three traditional perspectives: a summary	
Theoretical perspective	**Orientation**	**Image of society**	**Core questions**
Functional	Macro-level	A system of interrelated parts that is relatively stable based on widespread consensus as to what is morally desirable; each part has functional consequences for the operation of society as a whole	• How is society integrated? • What are the major parts of society? • How are these parts interrelated? • What are the consequences of each one for the operation of society?
Conflict	Macro-level	A system characterised by social inequality; each part of society benefits some categories of people more than others; conflict-based social inequality promotes social change	• How is society divided? • What are the major patterns of social inequality? • How do some categories of people attempt to protect their privileges? • How do other categories of people challenge the status quo?
Symbolic-interaction	Micro-level	An ongoing process of social interaction in specific settings based on symbolic communications; individual perceptions of reality are variable and changing	• How is society experienced? • How do human beings interact to create, sustain and change social patterns? • How do individuals attempt to shape the reality perceived by others? • How does individual behaviour change from one situation to another?

however, the fullest understanding of society comes from linking the sociological perspective to all three. Sociologists examine the social world by looking at *functions and dysfunctions, conflicts and consensus, actions and meanings*. The three theoretical perspectives certainly offer different insights, but none is more correct than the others, and all three have become increasingly modified in the light of newer theories.

The newer perspectives in sociology: other voices and the postmodern

Although functionalism, conflict theory and action sociology are still common positions within sociology, many others have emerged over the past two decades. As we have seen, sociology is often seen as containing **multiple perspectives**, which means it *takes on many perspectives for looking at social life rather than just one*. It is the sign of a lively subject that as society changes so too do some of the approaches being adopted within it.

Some of them are really just further developments of the above theories. Thus, they may, for example, focus on different aspects of 'action' such as language and conversation (**conversational analysis** is an approach which does this: see Chapter 7). Or they may develop the idea that societies are structures through a focus either on the system of signs and languages that often organise them (as **semiotics** does: see Chapter 5) or on the way the state works (as in **Althusserian Marxism**: see Chapter 21). We will say a little more about these theories when we discuss the mass media later in the book (Chapter 21).

Other developments, however, are seen by some to go deeper than this. A number of critics of sociology suggest the discipline has now entered a stage of 'crisis' in which many of its older ideas and perspectives are seen as being too narrowly conceived. Broadly, the newer approaches highlight **different** *perspectives, standpoints, cultures* or *voices*: they are much more self-conscious that all of sociology has to come from a perspective, a position or a point of view. We can never grasp the 'full truth' of a society, a completely full picture of it, even though we should try. Hence we should be more open about the partial perspectives we adopt and understand where we stand in relation to these partial perspectives. Sociology will always be selective. Max Weber himself recognised this long ago when he said:

> There is no absolutely 'objective' scientific analysis of culture or . . . of 'social phenomena' independent of special and 'one-sided' viewpoints

according to which . . . they are selected, analysed and organised

> (Weber, 1949: 72).

This recognition of *perspectives, points of view, different cultures* or *standpoints* from which analysis proceeds has become more and more important for modern sociology. And this means that it helps to be explicit and open about the perspective we take. At its most critical, many of the new perspectives suggest that the major perspective of the past has been that of white, Western, Anglo-American, heterosexual men. This may sound a cliché, but as you read this book you should look for authors and sociologists who lie outside this tradition. They will, sadly, be somewhat hard to find. Whether the sociologist uses a functionalist, conflict or (inter)action perspective, they all shared common assumptions derived from their male and Western position.

In contrast, the newer perspectives generally see a range of other voices that have been missed out of sociology in the past. Taken together, they provide a lot more 'angles' from which to approach society as a whole. They help to enrich the openness of the discipline to the range of ways of seeing society. This does *not* mean that everything is relative and anything goes. Quite the opposite: it means by carefully and systematically unpacking different perspectives we can come to see societies more deeply and in a more rounded way. The aim of sociology is still to be 'objective' even if , as we shall see in Chapter 3, this is much harder than sociologists used to think and even if we can only ever approximate truth.

Many of these newer approaches are very critical of the dominant, earlier approaches – what we have called the classical perspectives above. At present, however, it may be most helpful to see them as complementing and challenging these earlier perspectives, but not entirely replacing them. They do disagree with these early theories whenever they suggest they are telling the whole story of society: only partial stories are now possible in this newer view. Some of these newer sociologies thus speak of the 'death of the metanarrative' – a term coined by the French philosopher Lyotard – as a way of rejecting any idea that there is one, and only one, 'Big Story of Sociology'.

What, then, are these new voices? They include women, racial and ethnic minorities, colonised peoples throughout the world, gays and lesbians, the elderly, disabled people and various other marginalised or overlooked groups. You may well belong to one or more of these many groups, and should read this book with this in mind.

(a)

(c)

(b)

(d)

A multicultural world. Sociology used to be the study of white Western men by white Western men. This is no longer always so. It has become far more multicultural and listens more attentively to the voices of a whole array of different groups: (a) lesbian couple in New York, (b) Navaho matriarch in Arizona, (c) Pataxou Indians in Brazil, (d) young people in Karoo Desert, South Africa.

Source: (a) © Homer Sykes; Magnum Photos (b) © Eve Arnold; Magnum Photos (c) © Abbas; Network (d) © Mike Goldwater; Network

Taken together, a number of criticisms of classical sociology can be briefly summarised as follows.

1. That sociology has mainly been by men for men and about men – and for men, read white and heterosexual and usually privileged and relatively affluent. As such it has had a persistently limited, even biased approach.

2. That areas of significance to other groups – 'racism' for ethnic groups, 'patriarchy' for women, 'homophobia' for gays, 'colonisation' for many non-Western groups, 'disablement' for disabled people – have often been overlooked. You may like to think what each of these terms means; they will be introduced later in this book.

3. That these areas of significance, when they have been included, have often been presented in a distorted fashion: often sociology has been sexist, racist, homophobic, etc.

Many voices have been missing in sociology, and they have led to a number of newer sociological stances that will be introduced throughout the book.

An example: the case of a feminist sociology and the missing voice of women

To illustrate: the most apparent absence until the 1970s was that of women's voices. Until then, sociology had mainly been by men, about men and for men. All this started to change with the development of a second wave of feminism (see Chapter 12) which helped to foster both a *feminist sociology* and a *feminist methodology*. Broadly, these place either women or gender at the centre of their specific analysis. They do this because they see the need for a more political role for sociologists in trying to reduce or eliminate women's subordination and oppression in societies across the world. Although you will find a chapter in this book that looks at gender specifically (Chapter 12), you will also find that gender as an issue will be considered in nearly every chapter. Bringing a feminist gender perspective to any analysis helps to widen and deepen understanding (see Abbott and Wallace, 1997).

Once we enter a feminist sociology, however, we will find that there is no one or unified voice here either! To put it bluntly, not all women are the same across the globe! When we start suggesting that women are all the same we start to engage in what has been called essentialist thinking – **essentialism** is *the belief in essences that are similar*. It is to suggest here that there is an 'essence' or pure core to what it is to be a woman. Yet we will find a plurality of women's stances too – ranging, as we shall see, from those who adopt conflict perspectives

In the early days of sociology, men dominated its concerns. Today, there has been the growth of a much more feminist-based sociology. Jane Addams is often seen as pioneer of sociology through her concern with city life in Chicago. Some have argued she is the true founder of the Chicago School (See Chapter 23).
Source: © Bellmann/Corbis

to those who focus more on action perspectives; from those who highlight post-colonialist perspectives to those who focus on 'black' perspectives. For example, the experiences of a black woman living in poverty in Sierra Leone are very different from those of most white women studying in European universities.

Some do try to bring all these different voices together. But to do this, there has to be a major recognition that voices are not unified but fragmentary and multi-situated. As you will start to sense, this is no easy task! (Harriet Bradley's book *Fractured Identities* (1996), discussed in Chapter 10, is a very good introduction to all this.)

And other voices: a postmodern drift

Following on from all this, then, there are many new developments in sociology and you will encounter these throughout this book. For instance, Chapter 5 introduces ideas around multiculturalism; Chapter 7 introduces ideas around social constructionism; Chapter 11 debates post-colonial theory; Chapter 12 will extend feminist theory and introduce Queer theory; Chapter 16 introduces ideas around Foucault's 'discourse theory'; Chapter 20 will introduce disablement theory; while Chapter 25 will further present some ideas around postmodern social theory. As in any introduction, we cannot take these newer ideas very far. But at least you will sense that sociology is a continuously growing and changing discipline of study that is always bringing new challenges to its students.

Some sociologists have started to suggest that in the twenty-first century a new generation of sociology is in the making, and that it is bringing what has sometimes been called a postmodern stance. Although sociology was born of the modern world – industrialisation, capitalism, the growth of big cities, the rise of democracies, the decline of traditional communities, etc. – it is now finding itself in a world where the features of modernity are accelerating: modernity is speeding up and going faster. It is what Giddens has called 'a runaway world' (Giddens, 1999). Over the past 30 years or so, there have been many rapid changes both within society and within our understanding of ways of approaching society. Sociology itself, therefore, has had to rethink some of its key ideas to at least accommodate these changes – which have been increasingly identified as 'postmodern' or a 'late modern turn' (see Giddens, 1992).

For some thinkers these changes have been so extreme as to question the very foundations of sociology. Two French thinkers, for example, have more or less proclaimed the death of sociology and suggested we have moved into a postmodern world. Thus Baudrillard writes that

> . . It has all been done. The extreme limit of . . . possibilities has been reached. It has destroyed itself. It has deconstructed its entire universe. So all that are left are pieces. All that remains to be done is play with the pieces. Playing with the pieces – that is post-modern.
>
> (Baudrillard, 1984: 24)

This is an extreme position which will not be adopted in this book. Rather, this textbook will tell the story of the shift from a traditional form of society, one which was usually authoritarian with strong religious commitments to an overarching belief system, towards what we might see as *a more provisional world – one that is altogether less sure of itself*. Modernity has brought many changes; and in the twenty-first century this modern world is an accelerating one where there is an increased sensitivity to diversities and differences. In this view the world becomes less dominated by generalities and 'master narratives', and there is a turn towards 'local

cultures' and their 'multiplicity of stories'. We could see postmodernism as

> . . . the liberation of differences, of local elements, of what could generally be called dialect. With the demise of the idea of a central rationality of history, the world of generalised communication explodes like a multiplicity of 'local' rationalities – ethnic, sexual, religious, cultural or aesthetic minorities – that finally speak up for themselves. They are no longer repressed and cowed into silence by the idea of a single pure form of humanity that must be realised irrespective of particularity and individual finitude, transience and contingency . . .
>
> (Vattimo, 1992: 8–9)

All this leads to a new approach to sociology, but not one that has to reject its past. Rob Stones suggests that a postmodern sociology has three concerns:

> Postmodernists argue . . . for respecting the existence of a plurality of perspectives, as against a notion that there is one single truth from a privileged perspective; local, contextual studies in place of grand narratives; an emphasis on disorder, flux and openness, as opposed to order, continuity and restraint.
>
> (Stones, 1996: 22)

Thinking globally: a global perspective in sociology

Part of this shift in voice and concern within sociology over recent years has been that of recognising the position of different, local voices around the world. In recent years, as even the furthest reaches of the earth have become more easily accessible through advances in technology, many academic disciplines have been forced to incorporate a **global perspective**, *the study of the larger world and each society's place in it*. Instead of the overwhelming dominance in sociology of Western voices, we can now pay attention to voices heard in all parts of the world – from various African states to those found in Latin American countries. They often see the world in radically different ways and it is important, if sociology is to develop, to take these voices seriously.

Many sociology textbooks in the recent past have tended to focus on one country only. While this certainly deepens understanding of *one* society, it is insular and limited. This book therefore tries to look outwards to a range of societies, while at the same time maintaining some kind of focus on Europe and the UK, the societies that will probably interest the readers of this book most.

How does a global perspective enhance sociology?

Global awareness is a logical extension of the sociological perspective. Sociology's basic insight is that where we are placed in a society profoundly affects individual experiences. The position of a society in the larger world system affects everyone. The opening story provided a brief sketch of our global village, indicating that people the world over are far from equal in their quality of life. Almost every chapter of this text will highlight life in the world beyond our own borders. Why? Here are three reasons to consider why global thinking should figure prominently in the sociological perspective.

1. *Societies the world over are increasingly interconnected.* A feature of the world over the past 300 years or so has been the ways in which countries have become more and more internationally connected, initially through 'the great explorers', then through colonialism, slavery and mass migrations, and nowadays through high finance, tourism and the electronic world. In recent times, the world has become linked as never before. Jet aircraft whisk people across continents in hours, while new electronic devices transmit pictures, sounds and written documents around the globe in seconds.

   One consequence of this new technology, as later chapters explain, is that people all over the world now share many tastes in music, clothing and food. With their economic strength, high-income nations cast a global shadow, influencing members of other societies who eagerly gobble up American hamburgers, dance to British 'pop music', and, more and more, speak the English language.

Commerce across national borders has also propelled a global economy. Large corporations manufacture and market goods worldwide, just as global financial markets linked by satellite communications now operate around the clock. Today, no stock trader in London dares to ignore what happens in the financial markets in Tokyo and Hong Kong, just as no fisherman in Scotland can afford to ignore the European common fishing policy! But as the West projects its way of life on to much of the world, the larger world also reacts back. All of this is linked to the process of **globalisation**, *the increasing interconnectedness of societies*. This process will be discussed further in the next section and in many parts of this book.

2. *A global perspective enables us to see that many human problems we face in Europe are far more serious elsewhere.* Poverty is certainly a serious problem in Europe, and especially Eastern Europe. But, as Chapter 9 explains, poverty is both more widespread and more severe throughout Latin America, Africa and Asia. Similarly, the social standing of women, children and the disabled is especially low in poor countries of the world. And, although racism may be pronounced in the UK, it has even harsher forms throughout many parts of the world. Ethnic cleansings in Bosnia, 'Islamophobia', and hostility to German 'guest workers' are three examples that will be considered later (Chapter 11). Then, too, many of the toughest problems we grapple with at home are global in scope. Environmental pollution is one example: as Chapter 24 demonstrates, the world is a single ecosystem in which the action (or inaction) of one nation has implications for all others.

One important reason to gain a global understanding is that, living in a high-income society such as the UK, we can scarcely appreciate the suffering that goes on in much of the world. The life of this Rwandan boy has been shredded by civil war. But even in more peaceful nations of Africa, children have less than a 50–50 chance to grow to adulthood. We discuss this in Chapters 4 and 9.
Source: Magnum Photos © Luc Delahaye

3. *Thinking globally is also an excellent way to learn more about ourselves.* We cannot walk the streets of a distant city without becoming keenly aware of what it means to live in Western Europe at the beginning of the twenty-first century. Making global comparisons also leads to unexpected lessons. For instance, Chapter 9 transports us to a squatter settlement in Madras, India. There we are surprised to find people thriving in the love and support of family members, despite a desperate lack of basic material comforts. Such discoveries prompt us to think about why poverty in Europe so often involves isolation and anger, and whether material things – so crucial to our definition of a 'rich' life – are the best way to gauge human well-being.

In sum, in an increasingly interconnected world, we can understand ourselves only to the extent that we comprehend others.

Globalisation and sociology

Since the 1990s, sociologists have increasingly used the term 'globalisation' and it has become one of the most influential of sociological ideas in the past decade. It is itself used across the globe: for the Germans it is *Globalisierung*; in Spain and Latin America it is *globalización*; and in France it is *mondialisation*! Yet even though it translates into many languages, its meaning is far from clear. It has become a 'buzz word' which brings many different meanings and controversies; and it will be raised at many points during this book. To start with, and simply, we can define it as *the increasing interconnectedness of societies*, but the box suggests a number of other definitions you may like to consider.

At the most basic, the term globalisation can be grasped through the imagery of worldwide multicultural companies such as *Coca-Cola*, *McDonald's* and *Nike*. These companies exist across the globe – and in a number of ways. They *produce* goods across many countries; they *market* goods across many countries; and they *present* their logos and images which travel the globe ahead of them. Think of how McDonald's can be found in many countries – even though it had its origins in the United States (see Chapter 5). Likewise, a Nike shoe – with its characteristic logo of the swoosh – is produced in many parts of the poorer world and yet sold everywhere. As we shall see, they are simultaneously loved by millions and hated by millions – as signs of convenience and the modern world, and as signs of corporate takeover of mass culture. We will have more to say on all this in later

GLOBALISATION: SOME DEFINITIONS

- Globalisation has something to do with the thesis that we all now live in one world . . . . (Anthony Giddens, 1999: 7)
- Globalisation is the widening, deepening and speeding up of worldwide interconnectedness in all aspects of contemporary life, from the cultural to the criminal, the financial to the spiritual. (David Held *et al.*, 1999: 14–16)
- Globalisation . . . denotes the processes through which sovereign national states are criss-crossed and undermined by transnational actors with varying prospects of power, orientations, identities and networks. (Ulrich Beck, 2000b: 11)
- The process of increasing interconnectedness between societies such that events in one part of the world more and more have effects on peoples

and societies far away. (John Baylis and Steve Smith, 1997: 7)
- Globalisation . . . refers both to the compression of the world and the intensification of consciousness of the world as a whole . . . [It] does not simply refer to the objectiveness of increasing interconnectedness. It also refers to cultural and subjective matter, namely, the scope and depth of consciousness of the world as a single place. (Roland Robertson, 1992: 8)
- The Global Age involves the supplanting of modernity with globality . . . [this includes] the global environmental consequences of aggregate human activities; the loss of security where weaponry has global destructiveness; the globality of communication systems; the rise of a global economy; and the reflexivity of globalism, where people and groups of all kinds refer to the globe as the frame for their beliefs. (Martin Albrow, 1996: 4)

chapters. They capture the economic, social and cultural impact of this process and simultaneously symbolise what may be good and bad about it. Globalisation is thus a controversial term. As we shall see (Chapter 15), major social movements have developed in the past few years to protest against it: in Seattle, in Prague, in London, in Genoa. For the time being we will just suggest a few of the key features of globalisation. We suggest that globalisation has:

1. *Shifted the borders of economic transactions* – bringing a marked change in the pace of economic development in the world. Business companies, banking and investment now cross more national borders than ever before. In many instances these huge companies (TNCs or *transnational corporations*) have incomes and expenditures which are bigger than those of whole countries! Many argue that this has led to growing inequalities across the world, both within countries and between them. We will consider this in Chapters 9 and 15.

2. *Expanded communications into global networks.* Television satellites, digital media, personal computers, mobile phones, and all the information technologies help to 'shrink the world'. This has led to a major rethinking of ideas of *space and time*. We now no longer think mainly in terms of very local places. Instead we have entered a world where telephones, jet planes, and now the Internet make communications with others all over the globe instantaneous and hence very different from the past. Think especially of the phenomenal growth in the use of the mobile phone – handies, cellphones, etc. – and how this makes communications so much less restricted to face-to-face relations. Of course, telephones are not new, but the idea of being able to keep a phone on one's body wherever you are does make for a different pattern of communication. For growing numbers of people the whole world can be accessed instantly. Whereas a few hundred years ago it would take years for people to know what was happening in other parts of the world, now ideas can be moved instantly. We will consider this further in Chapters 21 and 22.

3. *Fostered a new, widespread 'global culture'.* Many urban areas come to look like each other, and many television programmes, much music, film, and so on, travels easily around the world. MTV has become a global youth form. And if you go to your local record store, the chances are you will now find quite a large section on global music! Not only do we have Hollywood but we have Bollywood. We will consider all this in Chapters 5 and 21.

4. *Developed new forms of international governance.* Some suggest that globalisation means the weakening of the nation state. Though this is controversial, what is not in doubt is the growth of international agencies such as the United Nations, the European Court of Human Rights and the World Health Organisation. These enact programmes that are publicly committed to what has been called 'the democratisation of the world' – a growing belief that democracy as a political system will become dominant in the world. We will consider this in Chapter 15.

5. *Created a growing awareness of shared common world problems.* It is harder and harder to think of the world's problems as just the problems belonging to any one country. For instance, crime – as we shall see in Chapter 16 – has become increasingly global: drugs markets spread across continents, cyber-crimes push against the laws of any one country, international courts proclaim international justice. Likewise, the major impact of industrialisation on the environment becomes a compelling common problem in all countries (which will be discussed in Chapters 23 and 24). Meanwhile, world poverty studies highlight growing inequalities both between and within nations; while debates on migration, refugees, wars and terrorism bring an international focus.

6. *Fostered a growing sense of risk* – what the German sociologist Ulrich Beck (1992) has called the *World Risk Society*. New technologies are generating risks which are of a quite different order from those found throughout earlier human history. Of course, past societies were risky and dangerous places too – whole populations could be wiped out by major earthquakes, floods or plagues, for example. Life for most people throughout history has been nasty, brutish and short. Nature brought with it its own dangers and risks. But Beck argues that new kinds of risk appear with the industrial world which are not 'in nature' but 'manufactured'.

These risks are associated with the many new technologies which generate new dangers to lives and the planet itself. These are humanly produced, may have massively unforeseen consequences, and may take many, many thousands of years to reverse. These 'manufactured risks' are taking us to the edge of catastrophe: to 'threats to all forms of life on this planet', to 'the exponential growth of risks and the impossibility of escaping them'. Risk, then, is associated with a globalising world that tries to break away from tradition and the past, and where change and the future become more valued. All these changes – from the railway to the computer, from genetic engineering to nuclear weapons – have unforeseen consequences that we cannot easily predict. The list of examples of new risks could be quite long: the changes in work and family patterns, fallout from the atomic bomb, the spread of networks of cars and planes throughout the planet, the arrival of AIDS as a major world pandemic, the development of genetically modified crops, the cloning of animals (and people), the deforestation of the planet, 'designer children and surrogate mothering', the intensity of computer games and the new ways of relating (or not relating!) this might bring, and the arrival of new

CONTROVERSY AND DEBATE

THE GLOBALISATION OF SPORT

One example to help you sense the power and centrality of globalisation is to look at sport and its cultures. Almost anywhere on earth, one of the quickest ways to enter a particular society or culture is to look at its world of sports. Initially we can think of sport as a very local thing: your local college football team, your local gym. Yet, whereas in the past, most sports were local – a few friends kicking about a ball, the rivalry between schools – they have increasingly become embedded in worldwide dimensions. Sport has become part of the globalisation process. We can now see sports as matters of global finance, international superstars, teams and supporters who travel the world, the development of international mass media coverage, the creation of an array of new logos known worldwide, advertising and commercial products. Think of the Olympics, the World Cup, Wimbledon, European Football: sport is now part of the world economy, world media, world travel. The globalisation of sport has meant sport is becoming truly international – and a big business. It has meant:

- The commodification of sports: sports now means an aggressive merchandising of products, where multinationals sell replica team shirts, training shoes, wall posters. In the US alone, the retail sales of sporting goods reached $45.8billion in 2003. Globalisation also leads to branding: company logos go on sports shirts, their adverts dominate sports fields, their sponsorship hooks them into the media, their shops and outlets are closely connected to the various games. Companies with a major impact on global sport include Murdoch's empire (Fox, Sky, Star), Nike, TimeWarner, Kirch Group, Disney, Coca-Cola, ISL and NBC.
- The creation of sports cities. Cities bid for various world events not just because of the sporting activity but because of the ways in which this can rejuvenate their cities (in the 1984 games based at Los Angeles, a profit of $215 million was made for the city).
- Global superstars and global identities. Sporting events are now part of the global media world – sporting celebrities play a world role. From Tiger Woods and Michael Jordan (the sale of Nike shoes bearing his name totalled some $1.4 billion) to David Beckham, sports stars become worldwide super-heroes and can command enormous salaries – teams and regions foster an international rivalry. David Beckham, for example, is much more than a football player: he is a brand. Vodaphone and Pepsi each pay him at least £2 million a year, and his wider impact is to increase the sale of some commodities to over £1 billion. In 2003, David Beckham was bought by Real Madrid, for a transfer payment of £25 million to his original club (Manchester United, the richest soccer club in the world) in addition to the £4.2 million it paid Beckham. Real Madrid now starts to rival Man U as a brand!

And in addition, consider the ways in which:

- Global supporters become travellers and sports stars become sporting migrants.
- International scandals from bribery to drug taking become common place.
- Sports violence becomes a feature of some sports – as teams become 'national icons' and their winning or losing becomes a kind of neo-nationalism.
- Other groups – women, the disabled, gays – come to hold their own international games.

CONTINUE THE DEBATE:

Discuss the general issues around globalisation with the issues raised above about sport.

Sources: Armstrong and Giulianotti, 2001; Coakley and Dunning, 2002; Foer, 2004; Brownell, 2003: 86

forms of terrorism where suicide bombers are willing to fly into major buildings (such as happened at the World Trade Center on 11 September 2001), and on and on. All have consequences which may be far reaching and are at present unpredictable. In some of the chapters that follow, we will look at some of these main 'risks' and how they affect all countries and people. We consider this in many places, but especially in Chapters 22, 23 and 24.

7. *Led to the emergence of 'transnational global actors' who 'network'.* From Greenpeace to Disneyworld, from the United Nations to tourism, from the Moonies to the Women's Movement, there are more and more people who move in networks that are not just bound to a fixed spatial community. Instead, they connect across the globe, making the global their local. They are global citizens.

Taking stock and looking ahead

This chapter has aimed to introduce you to some of the perspectives needed to think about society. We have suggested some classical ways (looking at society as functions, as structures, as actions, as conflicts, as consensus) and some emerging ways (looking at societies as an array of competing perspectives: from feminism to the post-colonial). We have suggested that some of the classical ways are now being questioned by what might be seen as a postmodern perspective.

Perhaps the most significant development in all this has been to push for sociology not to focus on just one country, but to focus on many. Here we have suggested that sociologists should take a global perspective and a possibly helpful idea in doing this is globalisation. We shall return to all this throughout the book.

SUMMARY

1. Building theory involves linking insights to gain understanding. Various theoretical perspectives guide sociologists as they construct theories.

2. The functional perspective is a framework for exploring how social structures promote the stability and integration of society. This approach minimises the importance of social inequality, conflict and change, whereas the conflict perspective highlights these aspects. At the same time, the conflict approach downplays the extent of society's integration and stability. In contrast to these broad, macro-level approaches, the action perspective is a micro-level theoretical framework that focuses on face-to-face interaction in specific settings. Because each perspective spotlights different dimensions of any social issue, the richest sociological understanding is derived from applying all three. Sociological thinking involves the action–structure debate.

3. Newer developments in sociological theory have highlighted how all sociology must work from perspectives or different voices. Classically, sociology

has heard only the voices of white, Western, heterosexual men: other voices are now being heard. Feminist sociology is a prime example. Postmodernism suggests that a new social order is in the making that is accelerating social change and creating a more 'provisional' world. Postmodern sociology stresses the need to look at multiple perspectives, takes seriously the local elements, and tries to keep a provisional 'openness' in its ideas.

4. A global perspective enhances the sociological perspective because, first, societies of the world are becoming more and more interconnected; second, many social problems are most serious beyond the borders of European countries; and, third, recognising how others live helps us better understand ourselves. Globalisation is an emerging widespread process by which social relations acquire relatively distanceless and borderless qualities. Globalisation highlights the interconnectedness of business and TNCs, the development of global media, the emergence of global cultures, international governance and world citizens.

CRITICAL-THINKING QUESTIONS

1. Start keeping a map of sociologists you encounter throughout this book. Locate them historically, the name of the theory they are identified with, some examples of what they looked at and examined, and the key features and problems of their theories.

2. Guided by some of these theoretical perspectives, what kinds of questions might a sociologist ask about (a) television, (b) war, (c) sport, (d) colleges and universities, and (e) men and women?

3. Start keeping a 'sociological glossary' of key new words you find in sociology. Try to make sure you can say (a) what the word means, (b) what debates and research it is applied in, and (c) whether you find it helpful or not: does it enable you to see society more sharply or does it confuse and hinder?

4. Is 'globalisation' a new phenomenon and is it really such a different world from that of the past? Consider what the term means and draw out some illustrations of it. How has your own life been touched by globalisation?

GOING FURTHER

Further reading

Sociological theory:

Mike O'Donnell, *Classical and Contemporary Sociology* (2001)

E. C. Cuff, Wes Sharrock and D. Francis, *Perspectives in Sociology* (4th edn, 1997)
These both outline most of the major positions.

Rob Stones (ed.), *Key Sociological Thinkers* (1998)
Provides 21 short and readable essays on many of the key sociologists, past and present.

Ian Craib, *Classical Social Theory* (1997) and *Modern Social Theory* (2nd edn, 1992)
Are highly readable introductions both to the classics – Marx, Durkheim, Weber, Freud and Simmel – and to the more contemporary debates, especially around 'action' and 'structure'.

Charles Lemert (ed.), *Social Theory: The Multicultural and Classic Readings* (1993)
A major compendium of articles that debates the full range of sociological theories – classical and newer.
It is a very large volume! But for anyone very interested in the full range of sociological theory from the original authors it is an invaluable starting point.

George Ritzer, *Sociological Theory* (3rd edn, 1992)
A classic overview theory textbook.

Richard Appignanesi and Chris Garratt, *Postmodernism for Beginners* (1995)
A cartoon and fun book, but at the same time looks at the world of the 'postmodern' in some depth: a good opening introduction for 'would-be postmodernists'!

Short guides to the idea of globalisation:

Zygmunt Bauman, *Globalization: The Human Consequences* (1998)

Anthony Giddens, *Runaway World: How Globalization is Reshaping Our Lives* (1999)
Two short, readable guides to the idea of globalisation.

Jan Nederveen Pieterse, *Globalization and Culture* (2004)

Malcolm Waters, *Globalization* (2000)
Also short but more detailed and systematic treatments. A little more advanced.

David Held *et al.*, *Global Transformations* (1999)
An altogether more advanced, very detailed and long account of globalisation. A standard work.

Watch a video/Read a book

One way into issues of globalisation is through international film and video. Look at the films of other cultures across the world and see how they are interconnecting with your own. A good source for such films is **http://worldfilm. about.com/movies/worldfilm/mbody.htm** – a major site for world films. For some opening examples, try:

- Ang Lee's *The Wedding Banquet* (1993): a romantic comedy about a gay Asian man in the US who marries a Chinese girl to please his parents
- Carlos Saura's *Blood Wedding* (1981): a powerful dance movie based on a Garcia Lorca story, starring Antonio Gades and Christina Hoyos
- Bahman Ghobadi's *A Time for Drunken Horses* (2000: a film about the suffering and hard lot of Kurdish children
- Marziyeh Meshkini's *The Day I Became a Woman* (2001): a disturbing portrayal of the role of women in Iran.

You will get the idea of a post modern novel from reading: John Fowles' *The French Lieutenant's Woman*, Umberto Eco's *The Name of the Rose*, Brett Easton's *American Pyscho* (all are also films); and from examining Steven Connor's *Postmodern Culture* (1997).

Connecting up

Connect to other chapters

- For more on Marx, Durkheim and Weber, see Chapter 4.
- For more on action and interaction, see Chapter 7.
- For more on globalisation, see all chapters but especially Chapters 9 and 21–24.

To the websites

On sociologists in general, see:
http://www2.fmg.uva.nl.sociosite/topics/ sociologists.html

On Marx, see:
http://www.marxists.org/archive/marx/

On Durkheim, see:
http://durkheim.itgo.com/main.html

On Weber, see:
http://www.ne.jp/asahi/moriyuki/abukuma/ weber_texts.html

For additional case studies, multiple choice questions, internet exercises, and annotated weblinks specific to this chapter, visit this book's website at **www.pearsoned.co.uk/plummer**

CHAPTER 3

DOING SOCIAL SCIENCE: AN INTRODUCTION TO METHOD

I have striven not to laugh at human actions, not to weep at them, not to hate them, but to understand them.

Benedict Spinoza

A SMALL ALUMINIUM MOTORBOAT CHUGGED STEADILY ALONG THE MUDDY ORINOCO RIVER, deep within South America's vast tropical rainforest. Anthropologist Napoleon Chagnon was nearing the end of a three-day journey to the home territory of the Yanomami, one of the most isolated and seemingly violent societies on earth. Chagnon's heart pounded as the boat slid on to the riverbank near a Yanomami village. Sounds of activity came from nearby. Chagnon and his guide climbed from the boat and walked towards the village, stooping as they pushed their way through the dense undergrowth. Chagnon describes what happened next.

KEY THEMES

- The nature of sociological knowledge, evidence and 'truth'
- The tools of sociological research
- The major political and ethical issues in research

I looked up and gasped when I saw a dozen burly, naked, sweaty, hideous men staring at us down the shafts of their drawn arrows! Immense wads of green tobacco were stuck between their lower teeth and lips making them look even more hideous, and strands of dark green slime dripped or hung from their nostrils – strands so long that they clung to their [chests] or drizzled down their chins.

My next discovery was that there were a dozen or so vicious, underfed dogs snapping at my legs, circling me as if I were to be their next meal. I just stood there holding my notebook, helpless and pathetic. Then the stench of the decaying vegetation and filth hit me and I almost got sick. I was horrified. What kind of welcome was this for the person who came here to live with you and learn your way of life, to become friends with you? (1997: 11–12)

Fortunately for Chagnon, the Yanomami villagers recognised his guide and lowered their weapons. Reassured that he would survive at least the afternoon, Chagnon was still shaken by his inability to make any sense of the people surrounding him. And this was to be his home for a year and a half! He wondered why he had forsaken physics to study human culture in the first place.

In the 1960s and 1970s, Chagnon studied some of the 12,000 Yanomami who live in villages scattered along the border of Venezuela and Brazil. His research, recorded on film and in books, suggested a violent way of life. He called them 'The Fierce People' and his research made him one of the most famous anthropologists on earth.

But recently his work has come under scrutiny. He has been accused of errors of fact as well as faking data. He has been called a 'hit and run anthropologist who comes into villages with armloads of machetes to purchase co-operation for his research'. He has been charged with building dubious theories. Worst of all, critics suggest he has played a role in the destruction of a culture – even in genocide and murder. Chagnon was an anthropologist; but his work raises issues for us all.

(Chagnon, 1997; Tierney, 2000).

(Left) To Prince Edward Island © Alex Colville (1965)
Source: National Gallery of Canada, Ottawa © MGC/MBAC

Culture shock: confronting the Yanomami suggests a very different way of life to that in the 'West'.
Source: Frank Spooner/Gamma © G. Hunter/Gamma/Katz

Just how do social scientists get their data? The anthropologist Napoleon Chagnon went into the field and observed the daily life of the Yanomami. Others interview, survey, give out questionnaires, draw upon documents of all kinds, set up focus groups. Some even monitor their own conduct. Such research may then get written up as stories and narratives; other researchers turn them into statistical reports. The ways of doing social science are many and varied. In this chapter we provide a brief review of some of the issues involved in 'doing social science'.

As we have seen, sociology involves a way of thinking; but it also involves a way of doing. It is a practice that looks at problems and then digs out the best 'data', 'evidence' or 'facts' that it can. This chapter will look at some of the ways sociologists actually go about studying the social world. It will ask about the very nature of 'knowledge'. It will highlight the methods that sociologists use to conduct research, and suggest appropriate questions to raise in assessing the value of any particular sociological study or 'finding'. Along the way, we shall see that sociological research involves not just procedures for gathering information but also controversies about whether that research should strive to be objective or to offer a bolder prescription for social change. Can it be neutral or is it bound up with politics and values? Sociologists are divided on all these issues.

The issues this chapter raises should help you think about the adequacy of the methods used in the sociological studies you read about. It should also enable you to start thinking about how you could conduct your own research – the chapter ends with some basic guidelines for you to plan your own project.

The basics of sociological investigation

Sociological investigation begins with two simple requirements. The first was the focus of Chapters 1 and 2: *look at the world using the sociological perspective*. Suddenly, from this point of view, all around us we see curious patterns of social life that call out for further theoretical study. This brings us to the second requirement for sociological investigation: *be curious and critical by asking sociological questions*.

These two requirements – seeing the world sociologically and asking critical sociological questions – are fundamental to sociological investigation. Yet they are only the beginning. They draw us into the social world, stimulating our imagination. But then we face the challenging task of finding answers to our questions. To understand the kinds of insight sociology offers, it helps to divide the research process into the following three types of issue.

- *Theoretical/epistemological questions*. Here we ask about the *kind* of truth we are trying to produce. Do we, for example, want to produce a strong 'factual' scientific kind of truth with lots of evidence? Or do we wish to provide a wider theoretical understanding of what is going on? As we shall see, there are different versions of sociology and it helps to be clear which kind of sociology is being done.

- *Technical questions*. Here we ask questions about how to use tools and procedures which enable our 'findings' to be as good as they can be. There is the matter of the kinds of research tool to use – interviewing, observing, questionnaires, statistical calculations, for example; and then making sure they perform their tasks well and do not mislead us. We must always remember though that methods like this are a means to an end and should never be an end in themselves (sadly, a lot of social science forgets this and elevates the idea of methods to a fetish).

- *Ethical, political and policy questions.* Here we ask questions about the *point* of doing the research and consider what consequences it might have: for us, for our research subjects, and even for the wider world. All sociology is embroiled with politics and ethics: if it looks like it is being neutral, you may well want to be suspicious.

The discussion in this chapter will be framed by these questions. You can use them as a guide for thinking about your own research projects. But they are only a guide, and suggestions for taking them further will – as usual – be found at the end of the chapter.

What is a sociological 'truth'? Matters of epistemology

A key question to ask of social investigation is a very hard one: 'What kind of truth am I trying to produce?' This raises questions of **epistemology**, *that branch of philosophy that investigates the nature of knowledge and truth*. Our opening concern is to realise that there are different kinds of 'truth'.

People's 'truths' differ the world over, and we often encounter 'facts' at odds with our own. Imagine being a volunteer with Voluntary Service Overseas (VSO) and arriving in a small, traditional village in Africa. With the job of helping the local people to grow more food, you take to the fields, observing a curious practice: farmers carefully planting seeds and then placing a dead fish directly on top of each one. In response to your question, they reply that the fish is a gift to the god of the harvest. A local elder adds sternly that the harvest was poor one year when no fish were offered as gifts.

From that society's point of view, using fish as gifts to the harvest god makes sense. The people believe in it, their experts endorse it, and everyone seems to agree that the system works. But, with scientific training in agriculture, you have to shake your head and wonder. The scientific 'truth' in this situation is something entirely different: the decomposing fish fertilise the ground, producing a better crop.

Our VSO worker example does not mean, of course, that people in traditional villages ignore what their senses tell them, or that members of technologically advanced societies reject non-scientific ways of knowing. A medical researcher using science to seek an effective treatment for cancer, for example, may still practise her religion as a matter of faith; she may turn to experts when making financial decisions; and she may derive political opinions from family and friends. In short, we all embrace various kinds of truth at the same time.

But science represents a very distinctive way of knowing, and one that has come to dominate in the modern Western world.

Common sense versus scientific evidence

Scientific evidence sometimes challenges our common sense. Here are four statements that many people might assume to be 'true', even though each is at least partly contradicted by scientific research.

1. *Poor people are far more likely than rich people to break the law.* Watching a crime show on TV, one might well conclude that police arrest only people from 'bad' neighbourhoods. And, as Chapter 16 explains, poor people are arrested in disproportionate numbers. But research also reveals that police and prosecutors are more likely to treat apparent wrongdoing by well-to-do people more leniently. Further, some researchers argue that our society drafts laws in such a way as to reduce the risk that affluent people will be criminalised.

2. *We now live in a middle-class society in which most people are more or less equal.* Data presented in Chapter 9 show that a very small group of people throughout the world control wealth. If people are equal, then some are much 'more equal' than others.

3. *Differences in the behaviour of females and males reflect 'human nature'.* Much of what we call 'human nature' is created by the society in which we are raised, as Chapter 5 details. Further, as Chapter 12 argues, some societies define 'feminine' and 'masculine' very differently from the way we do.

4. *Most people marry because they are in love.* To members of our society, few statements are so self-evident. But surprising as it may seem, research shows that, in most societies, marriage has little to do with love. Chapter 17 explains why.

These examples confirm the old saying that 'It's not what we don't know that gets us into trouble as much as the things we *do* know that just aren't so'. We have all been brought up believing conventional truths, bombarded by expert advice, and pressured to accept the opinions of people around us. Sociology teaches us to evaluate critically what we see, read and hear. Like any way of knowing, sociology has limitations, as we shall see. But sociology gives us the tools to assess many kinds of information.

The two sociologies: positivist and humanistic sociologies

The trouble is that precisely what is meant even by 'science' is not agreed upon by philosophers of knowledge. Traditionally, they take one of two views: positivist or humanist (often called interpretivist).

Positivism is *a logical system that bases knowledge on direct, systematic observation*. It usually seeks out law-like statements of social life that can be tested. The work of Durkheim on suicide introduced in Chapter 1 would be an instance of this. Scientific knowledge rests on **empirical evidence** (for Durkheim, recall, these were suicide rates), meaning *information we can verify with our senses*. But even here there is controversy among philosophers over the true nature of science, as we shall soon see.

The second position is interpretivism or humanism. **Humanist epistemology** sees that studying the human world is very different from studying the physical, biological or material world. There is a focus on the human and the symbolic. As such, social science must produce a different kind of knowledge, one that seeks to understand meanings. Research in this tradition will look at the empirical world (as in positivism) but will highlight the importance of understanding and interpretation.

Below, we will look at these two basic positions in a little more detail.

The positivist baseline

Positivist sociologists apply science to the study of society in much the same way that natural scientists investigate the physical world. Whether they end up confirming a widely held opinion or revealing that it is completely groundless, sociologists use scientific techniques to gather empirical evidence. The following sections of this chapter introduce the major elements of positivist investigation.

The ideal of objectivity

Assume that ten writers who work for a magazine in Amsterdam are collaborating on a story about that city's best restaurants. With their editor paying, they head out on the town for a week of fine dining. Later, they get together to compare notes. Do you think one restaurant would be everyone's clear favourite? That hardly seems likely.

In scientific terms, each of the ten reporters probably operationalises the concept 'best restaurant' differently. For one, it might be a place that serves Indonesian food at reasonable prices; for another, the choice might turn on a superb view of the canals; for yet another, stunning decor and attentive service might be the deciding factor. Like so many other things in life, the best restaurant turns out to be mostly a matter of individual taste.

Personal values are fine when it comes to restaurants, but they pose a challenge to scientific research. On the one hand, every scientist has personal opinions about the world. On the other, science endorses the goal of **objectivity**, *a state of personal neutrality in conducting research*. Objectivity in research depends on carefully adhering to scientific procedures in order not to bias the results. Scientific objectivity is an ideal rather than a reality, of course, since complete impartiality is virtually impossible for any researcher to achieve. Even the subject a researcher selects to study and the framing of the questions are likely to grow out of personal interest. But scientists cultivate detachment and follow specific methods to lessen the chance that conscious or unconscious biases will distort their work. As an additional safeguard, researchers should try to identify and report their personal leanings to help readers evaluate their conclusions in the proper context.

The influential German sociologist Max Weber expected personal beliefs to play a part in a sociologist's selection of research topic. Why, after all, would one person study world hunger, another investigate the effects of racism, and still another examine one-parent families? But Weber (1958; orig. 1905) warned that even though sociologists select topics that are *value-relevant*, they should conduct research that is *value-free* in their pursuit of conclusions. Only by being dispassionate in their work (as we expect any professional to be) can researchers study the world *as it is* rather than telling others how they think *it should be*. In Weber's view, this detachment was a crucial element of science that sets it apart from politics. Politicians, in other words, are committed to a particular outcome; scientists try to maintain an open-minded readiness to accept the results of their investigations, whatever they may be.

By and large, sociologists accept Weber's argument, though most concede that we can never be completely value-free or even aware of all our biases. Moreover, sociologists are not 'average' people: most are white people who are highly educated and more politically liberal than the population as a whole (L. Wilson, 1979).

Sociologists need to remember that they, too, are affected by their own social backgrounds.

One strategy for limiting distortion caused by personal values is **replication**, *repetition of research by other investigators*. If other researchers repeat a study using the same procedures and obtain the same results, they gain confidence that the original research (as well as their own) was conducted objectively. The need for replication in scientific investigation is probably the reason why the search for knowledge is called *research* in the first place.

In any case, keep in mind that the logic and methodology of science hold out no guarantee that we will grasp objective, absolute truth. What science offers is an approach to knowledge that is *self-correcting* so that, in the long run, researchers stand the best chance to overcome their own biases and achieve greater understanding. Objectivity and truth, then, lie not in any particular research method, but in the scientific process itself.

Some limitations of scientific sociology

The first scientists probed the operation of the natural world. Many sociologists use science to study the social world; however, the scientific study of people has several important limitations.

1. *Human behaviour is too complex to allow sociologists to predict precisely any individual's actions*. Astronomers calculate the movement of planets with remarkable precision, announcing years in advance when a comet will next pass near the earth. But planets and comets are unthinking objects; humans, by contrast, have minds of their own. Because no two people react to any event in exactly the same way, the best that sociologists can do is to show that categories of people typically act in one way or another. This is no failing of sociology; it is simply consistent with the nature of our task: studying creative, spontaneous people.

2. *Because humans respond to their surroundings, the mere presence of a researcher may affect the behaviour being studied*. An astronomer gazing at the moon has no effect whatever on that celestial body. But people usually react to being observed. Some may become anxious, angry or defensive; others may try to 'help' by providing the answers or actions they think researchers expect of them.

3. *Social patterns change constantly; what is true in one time or place may not hold true in another*. The laws of physics apply tomorrow as well as today; they hold true all around the world. But human behaviour is too variable for us to set down immutable sociological

laws. In fact, some of the most interesting sociological research focuses on social diversity and social change.

4. *Because sociologists are part of the social world they study, being value-free when conducting social research can be difficult*. Barring a laboratory mishap, chemists are rarely personally affected by what goes on in test tubes. But sociologists live in their 'test tube' – the society they study. Therefore, social scientists face a greater challenge in controlling – or even recognising – personal values that may distort their work.

5. *Human behaviour differs from all other phenomena precisely because human beings are symbolic, subjective creatures*. Human beings – unlike planets or molecules – are always constructing meaning. And what marks us off from other animals is the elaborate symbolic systems we weave for ourselves. Therefore, sociologists cannot simply study societies from outside; they have to take on board ways of 'entering' these worlds of meaning.

The humanistic stance: the importance of subjective interpretation

As we have explained, scientists tend to think of 'subjectivity' as 'bias' – a source of error to be avoided as much as possible. But there is also a good side to subjectivity, since creative thinking is vital to sociological investigation in three key ways.

First, science is basically a series of rules that guide research, rather like a recipe for cooking. But just as more than a recipe is required to make a great chef, so scientific procedure does not, by itself, produce a great sociologist. Also needed is an inspired human imagination. After all, insight comes not from science itself but from the lively thinking of creative human beings (Nisbet, 1970). The genius of physicist Albert Einstein or sociologist Max Weber lay not only in their use of the scientific method but also in their curiosity and ingenuity.

Second, science cannot account for the vast and complex range of human motivations and feelings, including greed, love, pride and despair. Science certainly helps us gather facts about how people act, but it can never fully explain the complex meanings people attach to their behaviour (Berger and Kellner, 1981).

Third, we also do well to remember that scientific data never speak for themselves. After sociologists and other scientists 'collect the numbers', they face the ultimate task of *interpretation* – creating meaning from their observations. For this reason, good sociological investigation is as much art as science.

Being observed. A basic lesson of social research is that being observed affects how people behave. Researchers can never be certain precisely how this will occur; while some people resent public attention, others become highly animated when they think they have an audience.

Source: (Top) Magnum Photos Steve McCurry, (bottom) Network © Jenny Matthews, victory signs, Kosovo, 1993

Sociology and the humanities

The recognition of all these limitations leads many sociologists to adopt a somewhat different stance towards their study. They do not claim to be scientists as above, but instead try to make sociology a more humanistic discipline concerned with understanding. In his study of *Sociology as an Art Form*, Nisbet reflects 'How different things would be . . . if the social sciences at the time of their systematic formation in the nineteenth century had taken the arts in the same degree they took the physical science as models' (Nisbet, 1976: 16).

This corrective sociology may be called 'humanistic' and has at least four central criteria. It must pay tribute to *human subjectivity and creativity*, showing how individuals respond to social constraints and actively assemble social worlds. It must deal with concrete human experiences – talk, feelings, actions – through their *social, and especially economic, organisation* (and not just their inner, psychic or biological structuring). It must show a naturalistic *'intimate familiarity'* with such experiences – abstractions untempered by close involvement are ruled out. And there must be a self-awareness by the sociologist of the ultimate *moral and political role* in moving towards a social structure in which there is less exploitation, oppression and injustice and more creativity, diversity and equality. A list like this is open to detailed extension and revision, but it is hard to imagine a humanistic sociology which is not so minimally committed to these criteria.

Table 3.1 summarises some of the wide-ranging contrasts between the positivistic and humanistic approaches to sociological investigation.

Emergent epistemologies

The traditional debates in sociology over epistemology have been between the positivist stance and the humanist stance. Unfortunately, matters are not quite as simple as this, as there are a number of other positions that are important. We will look further at science in Chapter 22. But here we briefly raise five others: realism, critical stances, standpoints, Queer theory and postmodernism.

The realist stance: theorising science

Realism is *a theoretical system of concepts that are evolved to handle a particular problem* (like how the economy, our minds or even the solar system works). While it may also gather empirical evidence, this is not central to its research – since it argues that 'empirical evidence' is never straightforward. We can never be sure of 'facts'. What we need, therefore, are strong explanations – built up from theoretical tools that will help us do this. The work of Marx is usually seen as a realist theory. For him, the problem was how capitalism works. To explain this, he did not simply go out and talk with people or simply look at documents (although he did do both these things). Instead he developed the idea of the **mode of production**, *the way a society is organised to produce goods and services*. From this concept, he could start to evolve an understanding of how societies work and change.

Critical sociology

Critical sociology developed in reaction to positivist science, and is often inspired by Marx. It rejects the idea that society exists as a 'natural' system open to discovery. Critical sociologists suggest that not only should the social world be understood, it should ultimately be changed. They see the task of sociology to be avowedly political, tying knowledge to action. They look at *all knowledge as harbouring political interests and the task of sociology is critically to unmask what is actually going on.*

Table 3.1	A bridgeable divide? Humanistic and positivist research contrasted	
	Towards the humanities	**Towards the sciences**
Foci	Unique and idiographic Human-centred The inner: subjective, meaning, feeling, experience	General and nomothetic Structure-centred The outer: objective, 'things', events, facts
Epistemology	Phenomenalist Relational/relativist Perspectivist/pragmatist	Realist Absolutist/essentialist Logical positivist
Task	Interpret, understand Describe, observe Appreciate	Causal explanation Measure Theorise
Style	'Soft', 'warm' Imaginative Valid, 'real', 'rich' Personal research	'Hard', 'cold' Systematic Reliable, 'replicable' Large-scale funding
Theory	Inductive and grounded 'Story telling'	Deductive and abstract 'Operationalism'
Values	Ethically and politically committed Egalitarianism	Ethically and politically neutral 'Expertise and elites'

from Plummer, 2001a: 9

Thus, for example, much sociology may suggest that we are free-thinking rational agents with choices: critical sociology would take this as a problem and try to show how all of this is shaped by social institutions. It subverts societies dominant ideologies and beliefs. (For more on this, see Chapter 5, p. 123)

Standpoint theory/standpoint epistemologies

Linked to the 'voices' raised in Chapter 1, **standpoint epistemologies** suggest that knowledge always comes out of specific kinds of social experience. *All knowledge is grounded in standpoints and standpoint theory enables groups to analyse their situation (problems and oppressions) from within the context of their own experiences.* The standpoint for most of social science has routinely been that of white, heterosexual, middle-class and middle-aged men – conventionally the dominant group in studying society. They have made their own standpoint appear to be 'the truth'.

But there is a range of other standpoints in the world: just as we saw in Chapter 2, there may be a feminist standpoint, which arises from the experiences and situations of women; a black standpoint, which arises from the situation of black people; or a gay standpoint, which arises from the experiences of lesbians and gays. The starting point, then, of this kind of epistemology is with the experience of these varied groups. The point is that starting from the (many different) daily activities of, for instance, lesbians enables us to see things in the social world that might otherwise have been invisible to us, not just about those lives but about heterosexual women's lives and men's lives, straight as well as gay (Harding, 1991: 252).

But problems can soon arise. For in taking, say, a feminist standpoint, it soon becomes clear that there is not just one position or stand to take – there is no universal (or essential) women's view. Women in low-income societies will almost certainly have different standpoints from those of middle-class white feminists in high-income societies. As we have already seen (Chapter 2), to work from a position which suggests there is only one standpoint of women would be to engage in **essentialism** – *the belief that qualities are inherent (essential to) specific objects.* A non-essentialising stance has to be taken which recognises how standpoints interweave (Collins, 1990; Harding, 1991).

Queer theory

Queer theory argues that *most sociological theory still has a bias towards 'heterosexuality' and that non-heterosexual voices need to be heard.* Such theorists would argue that all the topics discussed in this book – from stratification and ethnicity, to religion and economy – would be greatly enhanced if the position of 'non-heterosexual voices' were placed at the centre. For example, it suggests that many religions have been organised around 'homophobic' persecutions; that a new form of economy is emerging that is based upon the spending power of young middle-class gay men – the pink economy; and that the experience of being lesbian or gay can differ significantly across different ethnic minority communities (Seidman, 1996). New insights can be provided for all the traditional concerns of sociology once we give a focus to a different group such as 'queers'. This is a position that is a little like standpoint theory. It is discussed further in Chapter 12.

Postmodern methodology

We could go on with other standpoints. As we have seen in Chapter 2, a number of different approaches have emerged within sociology over the past two decades which stress differing voices and an anti-essentialism. Most prominently, and most generally, there has been the arrival of what may be called postmodern methodology.

This suggests that any strong search for *the* truth (like the positivism discussed above) is part of the (now doomed) Enlightenment project of science. Postmodernists hold that this view of an absolute, scientific truth has now been discredited: truths are much more multiple, fluid, changing and fragmentary. Postmodern epistemology would highlight:

- the death of the meta-narrative, i.e. the end of any one big claim to truth;

- the need for local knowledges produced out of particular contexts, i.e. our truths must be located in specific situations;

- the need to be aware of the contexts which shape this knowledge. Part of this means a much greater self-awareness on the part of the researchers – knowing how they come to do this research and their involvement in it;

- the need to understand the ways in which this knowledge is then told – how it is represented through 'writing strategies'. This means an awareness of how knowledge is represented. Metaphors such as stories, discourses and narratives become part of this. Part may also be the visual turn – the importance given to film, video, cam-recording and the like as new tools for gathering data and new tools for presenting it;

- the need to know why this knowledge is being produced and how it will be used. Here sociological knowledge is rarely just 'knowledge for knowledge's sake': it is bound up with moral, political and ethical judgements. Sociology becomes a moral and political tale.

A caution

We have to be careful. Ever since its birth, sociology has been locked into controversy as to its true character. A lot of recent debates are not in the end that recent – they have often been voiced, slightly differently, at earlier moments. The work of C. Wright Mills, for example, introduced in Chapter 1, was an earlier version of some of these ideas. What is important for you to sense at this stage is that the character of sociological knowledge itself has always been discussed and has led to many battles. These still continue today.

Making sense of sociological data

Whichever epistemology is to be claimed, sociological research also always involves learning some 'tricks of the trade'. These are very practical matters – tools that are needed to make sure that you are doing the research as best you can.

Concepts, variables and measurement

A crucial element of all 'science' is the **concept**, *a mental construct that represents some part of the world, inevitably in a simplified form.* 'Society' is itself a concept, as are the structural parts of societies, including 'the family' and 'the economy'. Sociologists also use concepts to describe individuals, by noting, for example, their 'sex', 'race' or 'social class'.

A **variable** is *a concept whose value changes from case to case.* The familiar variable 'price', for example, changes from item to item in a supermarket. Similarly, people use the concept 'social class' to evaluate people as 'upper-class', 'middle-class', 'working-class' or 'lower-class'.

The use of variables depends on **measurement**, *the process of determining the value of a variable in a specific case.* Some variables are easy to measure, such as adding up income at tax time. But measuring many sociological variables can be far more difficult. For example, how would you measure a person's 'social class'? You might be tempted to look at clothing, listen to patterns of speech, or note a home address. Or, trying to be more precise, you might ask about someone's income, occupation and education.

Researchers know that almost any variable can be measured in more than one way. Having a very high income might qualify a person as 'upper-class'. But what if the income is derived from selling cars, an occupation most people think of as middle- or even working-class? And would leaving school at 16 make a person 'lower-class'? To resolve such a dilemma, sociologists sensibly (if somewhat arbitrarily) combine these three measures – income, occupation and education – into a single composite assessment of social class, called socio-economic status, which is described in Chapters 8 and 10.

Sociologists also face the challenge of describing thousands or even millions of people according to some variable of interest such as income. Reporting an interminable stream of numbers would carry little meaning and tell us nothing about the people as a whole. Hence sociologists use *statistical measures* to describe people efficiently and collectively. The box on the next page explains how.

Measurement is always a bit arbitrary because the value of any variable depends, in part, on how one defines it. **Operationalising a variable** means *specifying exactly what one is to measure in assigning a value to a variable.* If we were measuring people's social class, for example, we would have to decide whether we were going to measure income, occupational prestige, education or something else and, if we measure more than one of these, how we will combine the scores. When reporting their results, researchers should specify how they operationalised each variable, so that readers can evaluate the research and fully understand the conclusions.

Reliability and validity of measurement

Useful measurement involves two further considerations. **Reliability** is *the quality of consistent measurement.* For a measure to be reliable, in other words, repeating the process should yield the same result. But consistency is no guarantee of **validity**, which is *the quality of measuring precisely what one intends to measure.* Valid measurement, in other words, means more than getting the same result time and again – it means obtaining a *correct* measurement.

To illustrate the difficulty of valid measurement, say you want to investigate how religious people are. A reasonable strategy would be to ask how often they attend religious services. But, in trying to gauge *religiosity* in this way, what you are actually measuring is *attendance at services*, which may or may not amount to the same thing. Generally, religious people do attend services more frequently, but people also participate in religious rituals

'AVERAGES': THREE USEFUL (AND SIMPLE) STATISTICAL MEASURES

We all talk about 'averages': the average price of a litre of petrol or the average salary for graduates. Sociologists, too, are interested in averages, and they use three different statistical measures to describe what is typical.

Assume that we wish to describe the salaries paid to seven members of a company: £23,000, £28,500, £27,800, £28,000, £23,000, £52,000 and £23,000.

The simplest statistical measure is **the mode**, defined as *the value that occurs most often in a series of numbers*. In this example, the mode is £23,000 because that value occurs three times, while each of the others occurs only once. If all the values were to occur only once, there would be no mode; if two values occurred three times (or twice), there would be two modes. Although the mode is easy to identify, sociologists rarely make use of it because this statistic provides at best only a crude measure of the 'average'.

A more common statistical measure, **the mean**, refers to *the arithmetic average of a series of numbers*, and is calculated by adding all the values together and dividing by the number of cases. The sum of the seven incomes is £205,300; dividing by 7 yields a mean income of £29,329. But notice that the mean is actually higher than the income of six of the seven members. Because the mean is 'pulled' up or down by an especially high or low value (in this case, the £52,000 paid to one member who also serves as a director), it has the drawback of giving a distorted picture of any distribution with extreme scores.

The median is *the value that occurs midway in a series of numbers arranged in order of magnitude* or, simply, the middle case. Here the median income for the seven people is £27,800, because three incomes are higher and three are lower. (With an even number of cases, the median is halfway between the two middle cases.) Since a median is unaffected by an extreme score, it usually gives a more accurate picture of what is 'average' than the mean does.

out of habit or because of a sense of duty to someone else. Moreover, some devout believers shun organised religion altogether. Thus, even when a measurement yields consistent results (making it reliable), it can still miss the real, intended target (and lack validity). In sum, sociological research is no better than the quality of its measurement.

Relationships among variables

Once they achieve valid measurement, investigators can pursue the real payoff, which is determining how variables are related. The scientific ideal is **cause and effect**, *a relationship in which we know that change in one variable causes change in another*. A familiar cause-and-effect relationship occurs when a girl teases her brother until he becomes angry. *The variable that causes the change* (in this case, the teasing) is called the **independent variable**. *The variable that changes* (the behaviour of the brother) is known as the **dependent variable**. The value of one variable, in other words, is dependent on the value of another. Why is linking variables in terms of cause and effect important? Because doing so is the basis

of **prediction**, that is, *researchers using what they do know to predict what they don't know*.

Because science puts a premium on prediction, people may be tempted to think that a cause-and-effect relationship is present whenever variables change together. Consider, for instance, that the marriage rate in the United Kingdom falls to its lowest point in January, exactly the same month our national death rate peaks. This hardly means that people die because they fail to marry (or that they don't marry because they die). In fact, it is the dreary weather during January (and perhaps also the post-holiday blues) that causes both a low marriage rate and a high death rate. The converse holds as well: the warmer and sunnier summer months have the highest marriage rate as well as the lowest death rate. Thus, researchers often have to untangle cause-and-effect relationships that are not readily apparent.

To take a second case, sociologists have long recognised that juvenile delinquency is more common among young people who live in crowded housing. Say we operationalise the variable 'juvenile delinquency' as the number of times (if any) a person under the age of 18 has been arrested, and assess 'crowded housing' by looking at the total square footage of living space per person in a home. We would find the variables related; that is, delinquency rates are, indeed, high in densely populated neighbourhoods. But should we conclude that crowding in the home (the independent variable) is what causes delinquency (the dependent variable)?

Not necessarily. **Correlation** is *a relationship by which two (or more) variables change together*. We know that density and delinquency are correlated because they change together, as shown in Figure 3.1(a). This relationship *may* mean that crowding causes misconduct, but often some third factor is at work, causing change in both the variables under observation. To see how, think what kind of people live in crowded housing: people with less money, power and choice – the poor. Poor children are also more likely to end up with police records. Thus, crowded housing and juvenile delinquency are found together because *both* are caused by a third factor – poverty – as shown in Figure 3.1(b). In other words, the apparent connection between crowding and delinquency is 'explained away' by a third variable – low income – that causes them both to change. So our original connection turns out to be a **spurious correlation**, *an apparent, though false, association between two (or more) variables caused by some other variable*.

Unmasking a correlation as spurious requires a bit of detective work, assisted by a technique called **control**, *holding constant all relevant variables except one in order to clearly see its effect*. In the example above, we suspect that income level may be behind a spurious connection between housing density and delinquency. To check, we control for income (that is, we hold it constant) by using as research subjects only young people of the same income level and looking again for a correlation between density and delinquency. If, by doing this, a correlation between density and delinquency remains (that is, if young people living in more crowded housing show higher rates of delinquency than young people with the same family income in less crowded housing), we gain confidence that crowding does, in fact, cause delinquency. But if the relationship disappears when we control for income, as shown in Figure 3.1(c), we confirm that we have been dealing with a spurious correlation. Research has, in fact, shown that virtually all correlation between crowding and delinquency disappears if income is controlled (Fischer, 1984). So we have now sorted out the relationship among the three variables, as illustrated in Figure 3.1(d). Housing density and juvenile delinquency have a spurious correlation; evidence shows that both variables rise or fall according to people's income.

To sum up, correlation means only that two (or more) variables change together. Cause-and-effect rests on three conditions: (1) a demonstrated correlation, but also (2)

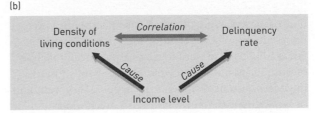

(a)

If two variables vary together, they are said to be correlated. In this example, density of living conditions and juvenile delinquency increase and decrease together.

(b)

Here we consider the effect of a third variable: income level. Low income level may cause both high-density living conditions and a high delinquency rate. In other words, as income level decreases, both density of living conditions and the delinquency rate increase.

(c)

If we control income level — that is, examine only cases with the same income level — do those with higher-density living conditions still have a higher delinquency rate? The answer is no. There is no longer a correlation between these two variables.

(d)

This finding leads us to conclude that income level is a cause of both density of living conditions and the delinquency rate. The original two variables (density of living conditions and delinquency rate) are thus correlated, but neither one causes the other. Their correlation is therefore spurious.

Figure 3.1   Correlation and cause: an example

that the independent (or causal) variable precedes the dependent variable in time, and (3) that no evidence suggests a third variable is responsible for a spurious correlation between the two.

Natural scientists identify cause-and-effect relationships more easily than social scientists because the laboratories used for study of the physical world allow control of many variables at one time. The sociologist, carrying out research in a workplace or on the streets, faces a considerably more difficult task. Often, sociologists must be satisfied with demonstrating only correlation. In every case, moreover, human behaviour is highly complex, involving dozens of causal variables at any one time.

Issues of sampling

One of the key issues of research is to know just how representative of a wider group are the people you study. For example, if you want to speak about the population of Australia as a whole, it would be sheer folly just to interview Australian students on campus. They would not be representative. You would need a much wider sampling frame – maybe a list of everybody who lives in Australia. But clearly, obtaining such a list would be very costly, and contacting everybody on it would be prohibitively expensive and time-consuming. Hence full-scale population surveys – the Census found in many countries – usually take place only every ten years or so. The United States Census for 2000 (which can be found on the website http://www.census.gov/) and the UK census for 2001 are the most recent of such censuses and are discussed in the Research Focus box opposite (see http://www.census.ac.uk/).

Much more commonly, social scientists engage in *sampling*. Usually, a researcher begins a survey by designating a **population**, *the people who are the focus of research*. For example, if you wanted a random sample of your college or university, you would initially need a sampling frame of everybody attending it. Researchers then collect data from a **sample**, *a part of a population that represents the whole*. The now familiar national

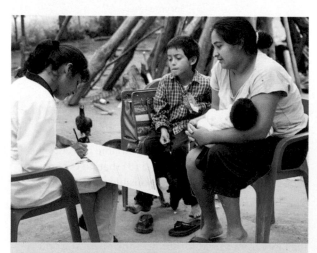

Argentine family answers questions during nationwide census

Source: Reuters/Corbis © Julio Pantoya

political surveys utilise a sample of some 1,500 people to gauge the political mood of the entire country. You use the logic of sampling all the time. If you look around a lecture room and notice five or six students nodding off, you might conclude that the class finds the day's lecture dull. Such a conclusion involves making an inference about *all* the people (the 'population') from observing *some* of the people (the 'sample'). But how do we know whether a sample actually represents the entire population? There are a number of different sampling strategies.

The main distinction in sampling theory is usually between probability sampling and non-probability (convenience) sampling. The former is more sophisticated, for each of the elements of the sample has the same probability of being included. This is the only approach for a truly representative sample. It usually comes in two forms – simple random samples (something like every tenth person), or stratified random samples (where the population is divided into known strata or groups in advance, such as gender or age). In *random sampling*, researchers draw a sample from the population in such a way that every element in the population has the same chance of ending up in the sample. If this is the case, the mathematical laws of probability dictate that the sample they select will, in the vast majority of cases, represent the population with a minimal amount of error. Experienced researchers use special computer programs to generate random samples. Novice researchers, however, sometimes make the mistake of assuming that 'randomly' walking up to people on the street produces a sample representative of an entire city. This is a serious error, for such a strategy does not give every person an equal chance to be included in the sample. For one thing, any street – whether in a rich or a poor neighbourhood or in a 'university city' – contains more of some kinds of people than others. For another, any researcher is apt to find some people more approachable than others, again introducing a bias.

Examples of non-probability samples include *quota samples* and *snowball samples*. A quota sample represents the group of people it wants to make statements about. Thus interviewers may be told how many respondents with particular kinds of characteristics are needed for the study: if we know that the population has equal numbers of men and women, then interviewers are asked to interview equal numbers of each. If we know that it is likely to be an older group, then we make sure the sample contains an appropriate mix of ages. This is not a random sample, but one that is purposely constructed with people in their correct proportions or ratios.

RESEARCH IN ACTION

THE POPULATION CENSUS

A **census** is *a count of everyone who lives in the country*. It is seen as crucial for broad planning and the shaping of policies. Most countries try to have one, but the problems it can pose are formidable.

In the UK, it has been held every ten years since 1801 (with the exception of 1841) when the population was 9 million. In 2001, when it was last published, it cost £255 million. In the UK it is run by the Office for National Statistics (ONS). It tries to count every person in the UK at the same moment. Although a lot of attention is given to the design of the questionnaire, by 2001 it had some 40 questions (compared with 30 in 1991). And for the first time it had to be posted back. (There was also to be a follow-up survey – some 4,000 professional interviewers conducting some 32,000 ten-minute interviews.)

It was becoming clear by 1991 that the scale of the census was heading towards trouble. Some statisticians often chose to ignore its data because it had only a 96 per cent return rate and was indeed much lower in some inner-city regions. Again, in 2001, the figures did not quite tally with earlier estimates. Indeed, there were some 900,000 people less than predicted – this was eventually put down to an increased emigration (possibly of young men). But there were other discrepancies. In Westminster, the population was revised downwards by a quarter, and in Manchester by a tenth. All this mattered because lower populations meant lower government grants.

Among the most commonly cited problems with the census are:

- Undercounting: some councils have complained that their populations are undercounted, and are suggesting a recount.
- Cost: as populations grow, the costs of a census can become prohibitive.
- Distribution: it is becoming harder both to get the forms to the right people and to get them to complete and return the forms.
- Immigration: there were more immigrants and some cannot read English.
- Civil liberties: there are suspicions about the nature of the questions in the Census and how they impinge on civil liberties.

There is now talk that the census may be discontinued. Identity cards may be the solution as these will keep a regular tag on the whole population.

Source: Graham Bowley, 'The last census?' *Prospect*, No. 92 (November 2003): 26–31.

For the census websites for the UK, the USA and for India, see:
http://www.statistics.gov.uk/census2001/default.asp;
http://www.census.gov/; http://www.censusindia.net/.

Snowball sampling also does not aim at real representativeness and is usually associated with case studies and qualitative research, often in areas of research where respondents are hard to find. The basic method relies upon searching out more respondents from the respondents you interview, and building up a network of contacts through each interview. In a research project on drug users or alcoholics, for example, it is impossible to find a full sampling frame which lists 'all drug users' from which you can draw a random sample. Instead, a more common method is to make contact with some drug users and then ask about their friends and acquaintances and subsequently interview them. Such a method, of course, can never provide a truly representative sample, but it is convenient.

Although good sampling is no simple task, it offers a considerable saving in time and expense. We are spared the tedious work of contacting everyone in a population, while obtaining useful results.

The tools of sociological research

A **research tool** is *a systematic technique for conducting research*. This section briefly introduces the most commonly used tools of sociological investigation. There are others. None is inherently better or worse than any other. Rather, in the same way that a carpenter selects a particular tool for a specific task, researchers choose a tool according to what they wish to learn. We will start by considering the four most common social science methods, before also considering a range of others.

1. The experiment

The logic of positivist science is most clearly expressed in the **experiment**, *a research method for investigating cause and effect under highly controlled conditions*. This is rarely used by sociologists, but more commonly by psychologists and social psychologists. However, it is a pure form of research: it is *explanatory*, and asks not just what happens but why. Typically, researchers turn to an experiment to test a specific **hypothesis**, *an unverified statement of a relationship between variables.*

Ideally, we evaluate a hypothesis in three steps. First, the experimenter measures the dependent variable (the 'effect'); second, the investigator exposes the dependent variable to the independent variable (the 'cause' or 'treatment'); and third, the researcher again measures the dependent variable to see if the predicted change took place. If the expected change did occur, the experiment lends support to the hypothesis; if not, the hypothesis is discounted.

2. The survey

A survey is *a research method in which subjects respond to a series of items in a questionnaire or an interview.* Surveys are particularly well suited to studying attitudes that investigators cannot observe directly, including political and religious beliefs or the subjective effects of racism. Although surveys can shed light on cause and effect, most often they yield *descriptive* findings, as researchers seek to paint a picture of subjects' views on some issue.

Questionnaires and interviews

A **questionnaire** is *a series of written questions a researcher supplies to subjects requesting their responses.* One type of questionnaire provides not only the questions but a series of fixed responses (similar to a multiple-choice examination). This *closed-ended format* makes the task of analysing the results relatively easy, yet narrows the range of responses in a way that might distort the findings. By contrast, a second type of questionnaire, using an open-ended format, allows subjects to respond freely, expressing various shades of opinion. The drawback of this approach is that the researcher later has to make sense out of what can be a bewildering array of answers.

An **interview** is *a series of questions a researcher addresses personally to respondents.* Interviews come in several forms. In a *closed-ended* interview, researchers would read a question or statement and then ask the subject to select a response from several alternatives. Generally, however, interviews are *open-ended* so that subjects can respond in whatever way they choose and researchers can probe with follow-up questions.

Closed-ended and open-ended interviews are both relatively formal. But there is another kind of informal conversational interview, which is more commonly used

in the qualitative field research described in the next section. With this mode of interviewing, the goal is to encourage the respondent to participate fully and equally in discussion with the interviewer. Certain key themes provide the shape for the discussion but there is no questionnaire as such, and the relationship between interviewer and respondent is much more casual, friendly and egalitarian. This mode of research is more suitable to gaining 'in-depth' understanding and for researching more sensitive topics. The 'conversations' are usually taped. This can lead to problems of a mass of data that is much less organised and accessible to analysis than the data found with more formal interviewing. See Table 3.2 for some key differences in interview forms.

3. Fieldwork, ethnography, participant observation

The most widely used strategy for humanistic field study is **participant observation**, *a method by which researchers systematically observe people while joining in their routine activities.* Researchers choose participant observation in order to gain an inside look at social life in settings ranging from nightclubs to religious seminaries. Cultural anthropologists commonly employ participant observation (which they call *fieldwork*) to study communities in other societies. They term their descriptions of unfamiliar cultures *ethnographies*; sociologists prefer to describe their accounts of people in particular settings as *case studies*.

At the outset of a field study, social scientists typically have just a vague idea of what they will encounter. Thus, most field research is *exploratory* and *descriptive*. Researchers might have hypotheses in mind, but it's just

Table 3.2	A continuum of interview forms	
Positivist		**Interpretative**
Interviews 'collect' data		Interviews 'construct' data
Standardised		Flexible
Mass		Formative
Focused		Open
Structured		Unstructured
Survey		Ethnographic
'Objective'		Phenomenological/'subjective'
Passive		Active
Short		Long

Source: Plummer (2001a)

as likely that they may not yet realise what the important questions will turn out to be.

As its name suggests, participant observation has two facets. On the one hand, gaining an 'insider's look' depends on becoming a participant in the setting – 'hanging out' with others, attempting to act, think and even feel the way they do. Compared to experiments and survey research, then, participant observation has fewer hard-and-fast rules. But it is precisely this flexibility that allows investigators to explore the unfamiliar and to adapt to the unexpected.

Unlike other research methods, participant observation requires a researcher to become immersed in the setting, not for a week or two, but for months or even years. For the duration of the study, however, the researcher must maintain some distance as an 'observer', mentally stepping back to record field notes and, eventually, to make sense of the action. The tension inherent in this method comes through in the name: 'playing the *participant*' gains for the researcher acceptance and access to people's lives; yet 'playing the *observer*' affords the distance and perspective needed for thoughtful analysis. The twin roles of 'insider' participant and 'outsider' observer, then, often come down to a series of careful compromises.

Most sociologists carry out participant observation alone, so they must remain mindful that results depend on the interpretations of a single individual.

An aside: qualitative and quantitative research

Participant observation is typically **qualitative research**, meaning *investigation by which a researcher gathers subjective, not numerical, data*. (The informal conversational interviews we encountered earlier are also part of this approach.) Unlike experiments or surveys, participant observation and informal interviews usually involve little **quantitative research**, *investigation by which a researcher collects numerical data*. Some scientists disparage a 'soft' method such as participant observation as lacking in scientific rigour. Yet, much qualitative research has become very rigorous in recent years, even to the point of having computer programs such as *The Ethnograph* and *NUDIST* to enable a rigorous analysis of 'soft' data. Further, its personal approach – relying so heavily on personal impressions – is also a strength: while a highly visible team of sociologists attempting to administer formal surveys would disrupt many social settings, a sensitive participant-observer can often gain considerable insight into people's natural day to day behaviour.

4. Secondary and historical analysis

Not all research requires investigators to collect their own data personally. In many cases, sociologists engage in **secondary analysis**, *a research method in which a researcher utilises data collected by others*.

The most widely used statistics in social science are gathered by government agencies. The Office for National Statistics in the UK continuously updates information about the UK population, and offers much of interest to sociologists. Comparable data on Europe is available via *Eurostat*, from the Office for Official Publications of the European Communities in Luxembourg. Global investigations benefit from various publications of the United Nations and the World Bank. And much of the data of previous research is housed in archives such as the Social Science Research Data Archive at the University of Essex, UK. In short, a wide range of data about the whole world is as close as the university library. And most of these data sets, these days, are available on CD-Rom or on the World Wide Web.

Clearly, using available data – whether government statistics or the findings of individuals – saves researchers time and money. Therefore, this approach holds special appeal to sociologists with low budgets. Just as important, the quality of government data is generally better than what even well-funded researchers could hope to obtain on their own.

Still, secondary analysis has inherent problems. For one thing, available data may not exist in precisely the form one might wish; further, there are always questions about the meaning and accuracy of work done by others. For example, in his classic study of suicide, Emile Durkheim realised that he could not be sure that a death classified as an 'accident' was not, in reality, a 'suicide' and vice versa. And he also knew that various agencies use different procedures and categories in collecting data, making comparisons difficult. In the end, then, using second-hand data is a little like shopping for a used car: bargains are plentiful, but you have to shop carefully to avoid being stuck with a 'lemon'.

Emerging research tools: from life stories to visual sociology

So far, we have described the four most common tools used by sociologists to dig out data and understand the world. They are compared in Table 3.3. But there are others that are becoming increasingly common: we call them *documents of life* (see Plummer, 2001). These are accounts of people's lives told by themselves – usually in

Table 3.3	Four classic research methods: a summary		
Method	**Application**	**Advantages**	**Limitations**
Experiment	For explanatory research that specifies relationships among variables; generates quantitative data	Provides greatest ability to specify cause-and-effect relationships; replication of research is relatively easy	Laboratory settings have artificial quality; unless research environment is carefully controlled, results may be biased
Survey	For gathering information about issues that cannot be directly observed, such as attitudes and values; useful for descriptive and explanatory research; generates quantitative or qualitative data	Sampling allows surveys of large populations using questionnaires; interviews provide in-depth responses	Questionnaires must be carefully prepared and may produce a low return rate; interviews are expensive and time consuming
Participant observation	For exploratory and descriptive study of people in a 'natural' setting; generates qualitative data	Allows study of 'natural' behaviour; usually inexpensive	Time consuming; replication of research is difficult; researcher must balance roles of participant and observer
Secondary analysis	For exploratory, descriptive or explanatory research whenever suitable data are available	Saves time and expense of data collection; makes historical research possible	Researcher has no control over possible bias in data; data may not be suitable for current research needs

words, but sometimes through other media such as video. The world is crammed full of these personal documents. People keep diaries, send letters, take photos, make their own video diaries, write memos, tell biographies, scrawl graffiti, publish their memoirs, write letters to the papers, leave suicide notes, inscribe memorials on tombstones, shoot films, paint pictures, make music and try to record their personal dreams. All of these expressions of personal life are hurled out into the world by the millions and can be of interest to anyone who cares to seek them out. They are all in the broadest sense 'documents of life', and are there to be gathered and analysed by sociologists. They come in a number of forms, which include the following.

1. Life stories

The life history method was established with the 300-page story of a Polish émigré to Chicago, Wladek Wisniewski, written in three months before the outbreak of the First World War. It was one volume of the massive study by W. I. Thomas and F. Znaniecki, *The Polish Peasant in Europe and America*, first published between 1918 and 1920. Wladek describes the early phases of his life in the Polish village of Lubotynborn as the son of a rural blacksmith, his early schooling, his entry to the baker's trade, his migration to Germany to seek work, and his ultimate arrival in Chicago and his plight there. Following the classic work, life histories became an important tool in the work of Chicago and Polish sociologists. The authors have claimed this to be the best form of sociological method.

> We are safe in saying that personal life records, as complete as possible, constitute the perfect type of sociological material, and that if social science has to use other materials at all it is only because of the practical difficulty of obtaining at the moment a sufficient number of such records to cover the totality of sociological problems, and of the enormous amount of work demanded for an adequate analysis of all the personal material necessary to characterise the life of a social group.
>
> (Thomas and Znaniecki, 1958: 1832–3)

2. Diaries

For Allport (1942: 95), the diary is the document of life *par excellence*, chronicling as it does the immediately contemporaneous flow of public and private events that are significant to the diarist. The word 'contemporary' is crucial here, for each diary entry – unlike life histories – is sedimented into a particular moment in time. In some recent research on sexual behaviour and AIDS, researchers have asked subjects to keep diaries of their sexual activities and they have then analysed them (Coxon, 1997).

3. 'Logs' and 'time budgets'

Sorokin pioneered this method when he asked informants to keep detailed 'time-budget schedules' showing just how they allocated their time during a day (Sorokin and Berger, 1938). The anthropologist Oscar Lewis's particular method focused on a few specific families in Mexico, and the analysis of a 'day' in each of their lives. Of course, his actual familiarity with each family was in no way limited to a day. He 'spent hundreds of hours with them in their homes, ate with them, joined in their fiestas and dances, listened to their troubles, and discussed with them the history of their lives' (Lewis, 1959: 5). But in the end he decided that it would be analytically more valuable, for

both humanistic and scientific purposes, to focus upon 'the day' as a unit of study. Thus each family – Martinez, Gomez, Gutierez, Sanchez and Castro – is first presented as a 'cast of characters' and then followed through one arbitrarily chosen but not untypical day of their life. Lewis believed that a study of a day had at least a threefold value: practically, it was small enough to allow for intensive observation; quantitatively, it permitted controlled comparisons across family units; and qualitatively, it encouraged a sensitivity to the subtlety, immediacy and wholeness of life.

4. Letters

Letters remain a relatively rare document of life in the social sciences. The most thoroughgoing use of letters is still to be found in Thomas and Znaniecki's *Polish Peasant*, where on discovering that there was extensive correspondence between Poles and Polish émigrés to America, an advertisement was placed in a Chicago journal offering to pay between 10 and 20 cents for each letter received. Through this method they were able to gain many hundreds of letters, 764 of which are printed in the first volume of their study, totalling some 800 pages and arranged in 50 family sequences. Each sequence is prefaced with a commentary that introduces the family members and the main concerns.

RESEARCH IN ACTION

ASKING QUESTIONS OF PHOTOGRAPHS

In a general study of photography Akeret (1973) coins the term 'photoanalysis' and suggests the following useful scheme of questions to be asked. We suggest you keep this question list to hand – and add some of your own – when you look at some of the photos in this book.

What is your immediate impression (of the photograph)? Who and what do you see? What is happening in the photo? Is the background against which the photo was taken of any significance, either real or symbolic? What feelings does it evoke in you? What do you notice about physical intimacy or distance? Are people touching physically? How are they touching? How do the people in the photo feel about their bodies? Are they using their bodies to show them off, to hide behind, to be seductive, are they

proud of their bodies, ashamed? What do you notice about the emotional state of each person? Is (s)he shy, compliant, aloof, proud, fearful, mad, suspicious, introspective, superior, confused, happy, anxious, angry, weak, pained, suffering, bright, curious, sexy, distant, etc.? Can you visualise how those emotions are expressed in facial dynamics and body movement? If there is more than one person in the photo what do you notice about the group mood? Is there harmony or chaos? How do people relate? Are they tense or relaxed? What are their messages towards each other? Who has the power, the grace? Do you see love present? What do you notice about the various parts of each person? Look carefully at the general body posture and then the hands, the legs, the arms, the face, the eyes, the mouth. What does each part tell you? Are the parts harmonious or are there inconsistencies? Pay particular attention to the face, always the most expressive part of the

RESEARCH IN ACTION CONTINUED

person. Learn to read any photo as you would read a book from left to right then downwards. Go over it again and again, each time trying to pick out something you have missed. Ask yourself more general questions, as many as you can think of. What is obvious and what is subtle? What is the sense of movement or is there any? What memories and experiences does the photo stir in you? How do you identify with the people in the photo? How are you alike, how different? What moves you most about the photo?

What do you find distasteful about it? Is there anything that disturbs you? Try to define the social and economic class of the people photographed. What is their cultural background? If it is a family, would you want to be a member of it? Would you want your children to play with theirs? If the photos are personal – of you, your family, friends or associates – try to remember the exact circumstances of the photo session. How have you changed since then? How have you remained the same? (Akeret, 1973: 35–36)

5. Visual sociology/Photography

Invented at approximately the same time as sociology, photography has only occasionally figured in sociological research. It is true that in the earliest days of the *American Journal of Sociology* photographs were a regular feature of its muck-raking, reformist articles: between 1896 and 1916 31 articles used 244 photographs. Likewise many early fieldwork studies were illustrated with photographs. Thrasher's *The Gang*, for example, contains nearly 40 photos of boys and boy gangs. The lead has primarily come from anthropologists, and in particular the pioneering work of Gregory Bateson and Margaret Mead (1942), who provided a volume devoted entirely to photographic images from the culture of the Balinese. The photo below is drawn from this book. Oddly one of the most frequent places to find

visuals is in sociology textbooks like this one. Indeed, throughout this book you will find many images: you may like to consider their value and use in sociology as you look at them (see Research In Action box).

In the main sociologists have not taken much interest in what should now be viewed as a major tool for investigation. Yet recently there has been growing interest in what has been called *visual sociology*. Images of all kinds may be taken as topics or resources. As topics, we ask questions about how the image came to be made, how it was assembled, what it tried to achieve. As a resource, we take it to be an illustration – an image that makes a point and helps clarify what is going on.

Perhaps the most obvious use to date is that of the photograph as documentation, when photographs can be used by social scientists as a resource for further explanations. Thus Thompson (1974) was able to interview respondents through photos of the My Lai massacre of the Vietnam War. Banish also used the technique of combining interview with photography in his work on *City Families* (1976). This researcher first visited selected families in order to take photographs of them as they wished to see themselves and then returned to talk about the photographs, to ask which was their favourite and to interview them about their hopes and aspirations in life. The study is composed of the preferred photographs on one page matched with the interviews and observations on the opposite page. Of added interest in this work is the range of families studied and the contrasts drawn between the families of two cities: London and Chicago.

From this comes one of the most obvious usages of photographs in social science: to ask the respondent for a look at their family albums (see Musello, 1979). In a most striking way, all manner of details about childhood relationships, friendship, family rituals and family

Balinese cockfighting
Source: Bateson and Mead (1942: 140)

history are highlighted. However, the sociologist who opts for this kind of approach needs to be attuned to the problems of reading photography.

6. Visual sociology/Film and video

The twentieth century has been called by Norman Denzin 'the cinematic century' (1995). Film, and later television, video and DVD, became prime modes for looking at social life. Yet few sociologists have seriously engaged with it as a tool for research.

It is the documentary film makers and anthropologists who have been most adept at exploiting this medium to date. At the start of the century, ethnographers started to film various tribal peoples engaged in social rituals. In 1901 Spencer filmed Australian aborigines in kangaroo dances and rain ceremonies, while in 1914 Curtis filmed the Kwakiutl Indians. But the birth of the documentary film is commonly agreed to be Robert Flaherty's *Nanook of the North* (1922) about 'Eskimo' life. Flaherty, a compassionate romantic appalled by the dehumanisation of modern technology, lived in 'Eskimo' country for 11 years, and shot his film under the most adverse conditions on the life of one specific individual – Nanook. In this film he reveals the constant struggle for life in a hostile environment. Sensitively, the power of the image is left behind.

One of Flaherty's most successful visual techniques was to follow an exotic act visually, showing it step by step as it developed, not explaining it in words. In one sequence we see Nanook tugging on a line leading into a hole in the ice. We are engaged in that act, and think about it. Eventually, the suspense is broken: our questions are answered when Nanook pulls out a seal. Flaherty creates the same visual involvement when Nanook makes the igloo, especially at the end of the sequence, when Nanook cuts a slab of ice for a window, sets it in place, and fixes a snow slab reflector along one side. For a time we are puzzled and, therefore, involved. But when Nanook steps back, finished, we understand (Heider, 1976: 24).

In the main sociologists have either ignored the medium or used the documentaries created by film makers like those of Frederick Wiseman. His films perhaps come closest to embodying sociological concerns: most deal directly with the ways in which individuals, in their social hierarchies, cope (or fail to cope) with the day-to-day pressures of social institutions. As he puts it:

> What I'm aiming at is a series on American institutions, using the word 'institutions' to cover a series of activities that take place in a limited geographical area with a more or less consistent group of people being involved. I want to use film technology to have a look at places like high schools, hospitals, prisons, and police, which seems to be very fresh material for film; I want to get away from the typical documentary where you follow one charming person or one Hollywood star around. I want to make films where the institutions will be the star but will also reflect larger issues in general society. (in Rosenthal, 1971: 69).

Hence Wiseman's 'documents' treat not 'lives' but 'institutions' – the police in *Law and Order* (1969), hospitals for the criminally insane in *The Titicut Follies* (1969), army life in *Basic Training* (1971) as well as films on *Welfare* (1975), *High School* (1968) and *Hospital* (1970).

Research methods on the Internet

Over the past decade or so, research within the social sciences has come to use the Internet more and more (Hewson *et al.*, 2003). Three uses will be briefly outlined here. The first can be found in using the Internet to gain relatively straightforward access to data on all manner of worldwide issues. By using a search engine (such as Google) and typing in key words, you will soon gain access to world maps, library catalogues, archived newspapers and journals, official government documents, social movement archives and all manner of cultural phenomena. In many ways this is a good starting point for almost any social research (Gauntlett, 2000), and sometimes it may prove to be all you need: data on the Web is like secondary data that is open to analysis (e.g. crime statistics).

A second use can be to deploy research tools on the Internet. The most obvious example here is email interviewing. Having found your sample or special subject (remember that those who use the Internet may well be a very selective group and are in no way a random sample!), questions can be asked by email and the respondent replies. This can lead to further and fuller questioning. Ultimately, the data gained this way can be handily saved on the computer in carefully designated folders and files (as well, of course, as being printed off).

A third approach is to investigate the nature of online life itself. Increasingly, we spend more of our time 'living online', so it becomes of sociological interest to see how people use the Internet. In a manner almost like participant observation, researchers have studied life in chat rooms (Markham, 2001; Turkle, 1996), or the use of the Internet to meet partners (Ben-Ze'ev, 2004).

The problem of validity – again

As researchers come to use websites more and more for their basic materials, they can come up with a huge amount of 'dross', that is websites that are unreliable and even useless for the purposes of accurate information. Anybody can make a website after all, and what is to stop people putting misinformation on the site – either deliberately or out of ignorance. The question then arises: how do we assess the accuracy of different websites? Stein (2003) suggests the need to look for authoritative documents and offers the following advice:

- First, think of the agenda behind the site. Most websites do indeed have an agenda, even those belonging to organisations (for example, to recruit students in the case of a university, or to act as a pressure group for change in the case of Greenpeace). This will give you some idea as to why the data is being presented in the way it is.

- Next, ask if the site gives information about the author of the page: if you cannot trace the author, be a little wary. The most reliable sites are probably those of high-profile organisations, such as the United Nations or Amnesty International, or those of organisations such as universities. Even so, these will always have agendas. The least reliable are likely to be those of individuals, although there are plenty of dedicated individuals out there who simply want to bring all the work of Marx or Mead into a public forum.

- Ask, too, if there is appropriate attribution and bibliography. Is the source of the material provided acknowledged?

- Finally, consider when the web page was assembled, and especially the page you are using. Good websites will show a date, and are kept up to date. If you have a very old date, it may be worth searching further to find a more recent update of the site.

Ethical, political and policy questions

As Max Weber observed long ago, a fine line separates politics from science. Most sociologists endorse Weber's goal of value-free research, but a growing number of researchers are challenging the notion that politics and science can – or should – be distinct.

Alvin Gouldner (1970a, 1970b) was among the first to claim that the ideal of 'value-free' research paints a 'storybook picture' of sociology. Every element of social life is political, he argues, in that it benefits some people more than others. If so, Gouldner reasoned, the topics sociologists choose to study and the conclusions they reach also have political consequences.

If sociologists have no choice about their work being political, Gouldner continues, they do have a choice about *which* positions are worthy of support. Moreover, as he sees it, sociologists have an obligation to endorse political objectives that will improve society. Although this viewpoint is not limited to sociologists of any one political orientation, it prevails among those with left-leaning politics, especially those guided by the ideas of Karl Marx. Recall Marx's (1972: 109; orig. 1845) claim that the point is not simply to understand the world but to change it.

Researchers must always remain respectful of subjects and mindful of their well-being. In part, this means that investigators must become familiar – well ahead of time – with the cultural patterns of those they wish to study.

Such thinking, colliding with the value-free approach, has carried many universities into a spirited debate over 'political correctness'. In simple terms, this controversy pits advocates of Weberian value-free teaching and research against proponents of Marx's view that, since all knowledge is political, sociologists should strive to promote positive societal change.

Feminist methodology: gender and research

One political dimension of research involves **gender**, *the social aspects of differences and hierarchies between female or male*. Sociologists have come to realise that gender often plays a significant part in their work. Margrit Eichler (1988) identifies the following five threats to sound research that relate to gender.

1. *Androcentricity*. Androcentricity (*andro* is the Greek word for 'male'; *centricity* means 'being centred on') refers to approaching an issue from a male perspective. Sometimes researchers enter a setting as if only the activities of men are important while ignoring what women do. For years, for example, researchers studying occupations focused on the paid work of men while overlooking the housework and child care traditionally performed by women (Counts, 1925; Hodge *et al.*, 1966). Clearly, research that seeks to understand human behaviour cannot ignore half of humanity.

   Eichler notes that the parallel situation of *gynocentricity* – seeing the world from a female perspective – is equally limiting to sociological investigation. However, in our male-dominated society, this narrowness of vision arises less frequently.

2. *Overgeneralising.* This problem occurs when researchers use data drawn from only people of one sex to support conclusions about both sexes. Historically, sociologists have studied men and then made sweeping claims about 'humanity' or 'society'. Gathering information about a community from a handful of public officials (typically, men) and then drawing conclusions about the entire community illustrates the problem of overgeneralising.

Here, again, the bias can occur in reverse. For example, in an investigation of child-rearing practices, collecting data only from women would allow researchers to draw conclusions about 'motherhood' but not about the more general issue of 'parenthood'.

3. *Gender blindness.* This refers to the failure of a researcher to consider the variable of gender at all. As we note throughout this book, the lives of men and women typically differ in virtually every setting. A study of growing old in Europe that overlooked the fact that most elderly men live with spouses while elderly women generally live alone would be weakened by its gender blindness.

4. *Double standards.* Researchers must be careful not to distort what they study by applying different standards to men and women. For example, a family researcher who labels a couple as 'man and wife' may define the man as the 'head of household' and treat him accordingly, while assuming that the woman simply engages in family 'support work'.

5. *Interference.* In this case, gender distorts a study because a subject reacts to the sex of the researcher in ways that interfere with the research operation. While studying a small community in Sicily, for instance, Maureen Giovannini (1992) found that many men responded to her as a woman rather than as a researcher, compromising her research efforts. Gender dynamics precluded her from certain activities, such as private conversations with men, that were deemed inappropriate for single women. In addition, local residents denied Giovannini access to places considered off-limits to members of her sex.

Of course, there is nothing wrong with focusing research on one sex or the other. But all sociologists, as well as people who read their work, should stay mindful about how gender can affect the process of sociological investigation.

Feminist research

Sociology's pervasive attention to men in the past has prompted some contemporary researchers to make special efforts to investigate the lives of women. Advocates of feminist research embrace two key tenets: (1) that their research should focus on the condition of women in society, and (2) that the research must be grounded in the assumption that women generally experience subordination. Thus feminist research rejects Weber's value-free orientation in favour of being overtly political – doing research in pursuit of gender equality.

Some proponents of feminist research advocate the use of conventional scientific techniques, including all those described in this chapter. Others maintain that feminist research must transform the essence of science, which they see as a masculine form of knowledge. Whereas scientific investigation traditionally has demanded detachment, feminists deliberately foster a sympathetic understanding between investigator and subject. Moreover, conventional scientists take charge of the research agenda by deciding in advance what issues to raise and how to study them. Feminist researchers, by contrast, favour a less structured approach to gathering information so that participants in research can offer their own ideas on their own terms (Stanley and Wise, 1983; Nielsen, 1990; Stanley, 1990; Reinharz, 1992).

Such alterations in research premises and methods have led more conventional sociologists to charge that feminist research is less science than simple political activism. Feminists respond that research and politics should not – indeed cannot – ever be distinct. Therefore, traditional notions that placed politics and science in separate spheres have now given way to some new thinking that merges these two dimensions.

Research ethics

Like all investigators, sociologists must be mindful that research can be harmful as well as helpful to subjects or communities. For this reason, the British Sociological Association – the major professional association of sociologists in the UK – has established formal guidelines for the conduct of research. (For addresses of sociological associations, see 'Going further' at the end of Chapter 1.)

The prime directive is that sociologists strive to be both technically competent and fair-minded in conducting their research. Sociologists must disclose all their findings, without omitting significant data. Further, they must point out various interpretations of data, and they are ethically bound to make their results available to other sociologists, some of whom may wish to replicate the study.

Whether social scientists need to inform people that they are the objects of study is a matter of continuing debate among sociologists. No one objects to studying public behaviour (say, observing how people interact in a gambling casino or a park) without announcing one's presence, but most sociologists agree that a researcher must not target specific individuals for study without their permission. Taking this debate one step further, should researchers employ deception in their work? Obviously, if researchers tell people exactly what they are looking for, they will not observe natural behaviour. On the other hand, misleading subjects may generate understandable resentment. Sociologists disagree about such ethical quandaries, but there is a trend towards greater sensitivity for the well-being of subjects in research.

Virtually everyone agrees, however, that researchers must strive to protect the safety of people involved in a research project. Sociologists have an obligation to terminate research, however promising it may seem, if they become aware of any danger to participants. And if research is likely to cause subjects substantial discomfort or inconvenience, sociologists must ensure in advance that all participants understand and accept any risks.

In addition, sociologists must include in their published results the sources of any and all financial support. They must never accept funding from any organisation that seeks to influence the research process for its own purposes.

Finally, there are also global dimensions to research ethics. Before beginning research in other countries, investigators must become familiar enough with the society to be studied to understand what people *there* are likely to perceive as a violation of privacy or a source of personal danger. In a multicultural society like ours, of course, the same rule applies to studying people whose cultural background differs from one's own.

The interplay of theory and method

There are, of course, some research tasks that remain unaffected by technological change. No matter how we gather data, sociologists must ultimately transform facts into meaning by building theory.

ISSUES OF ETHICS AND POLITICS IN SOCIOLOGY

Confidentiality. In most sociology, research subjects need to be guaranteed confidentiality. Thus names of people are changed, schools studied get 'pseudonyms'.

Informed consent. Respondents in research should know that they are involved in a research undertaking and roughly what this research is about.

Honesty. As in life, so in research, 'honesty' would seem to be a fairly basic requirement! So a minimal canon of 'science' might well be seen as suggesting that the researcher should be as accurate, painstaking and honest as possible.

Deception. A related form of dishonesty arises with deception. In sociology, the dilemma appears where the researcher conceals his or her identity and 'cons' his way into a new group – an issue that is often dubbed the overt/covert debate.

Exploitation. A subject is asked by a sociologist to give up hours – often hundreds of hours – of his or her life to tell their story. It might be very painful and involve a great deal of effort. And at the end of it all – for reasons of confidentiality – the subject must remain anonymous while the sociologist publishes.

And certainly there have been prosecutions over such alleged abuses: the mother of one 'case study' – that of Genie, a 'wild child' found at the age of 13 to be living in complete isolation and subsequently studied in detail by psychologists – filed a suit against the researchers on the grounds that private and confidential information had been disclosed for 'prestige and profit' and that Genie had been subjected to 'unreasonable and outrageous' testing.

Hurt and harm. A final worry is the *hurt and harm* that may befall the subjects through the researcher's activities. Social science has produced many instances where communities have been upset by community studies on them – feeling they have been misrepresented; or where individual people feel they have told a story in good faith only for it to result in a kind of damaging or sensational exposure.

As a village schoolmaster said to anthropologist Nancy Scheper-Hughes:

It's not your science I am questioning, but this: don't we have the right to lead unexamined lives, the right not to be analysed? Don't we have a right to hold on to an image of ourselves as different to be sure, but as innocent and unblemished all the same?

(quoted in Brettell, 1993: 13)

Actually, sociological investigators move back and forth between facts and theory. **Inductive logical thought** is *reasoning that transforms specific observations into general theory*. In this mode, a researcher's thinking runs from the specific to the general, something like this: 'I have some interesting data here; what are the data saying about human behaviour?'

A second type of logical thought works 'downwards' in the opposite direction. **Deductive logical thought** is *reasoning that transforms general theory into specific hypotheses suitable for scientific testing.* This time, the researcher's thinking goes from the general to the specific: 'I have this hunch about human behaviour; let's put it in a form we can test, collect some data, and see if it is correct.' Working deductively, the researcher first states the theory in the form of a hypothesis and then selects a method by which to test it. To the extent that the data support the hypothesis, we conclude that the theory is correct; data that refute the hypothesis alert the researcher that the theory should be revised or perhaps rejected entirely.

Just as researchers commonly employ several methods over the course of one study, they typically make use of *both* types of logical thought. Figure 3.2 illustrates the two phases of scientific thinking: inductively building theory from observations and deductively making observations to test our theory.

Finally, it is worth noting that statistics, too, play a key part in the process of turning facts into meaning. Commonly, sociological researchers provide quantitative data as part of their research results. And precisely how they present their numbers affects the conclusions their

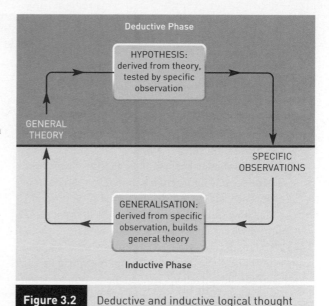

Figure 3.2   Deductive and inductive logical thought

readers draw. In other words, data presentation always provides the opportunity to 'spin' reality in one way or another.

Often, we conclude that an argument must be true simply because there are statistics to back it up. However, readers must use a cautious eye when encountering statistical data. After all, researchers choose what data to present, they offer interpretations of the statistics, and they may use tables or graphs to encourage others to reach particular conclusions. The final box in this chapter takes a closer look at these important issues.

CONTROVERSY AND DEBATE

HOW TO LIE WITH STATISTICS – AT LEAST SOME OF THE TIME!

The English politician Benjamin Disraeli once noted wryly: 'There are three kinds of lies: lies, damned lies, and statistics!' Every method of data collection is prone to error, and data do not speak for themselves. Throughout this book – as well as in much of the press – you will find statistical tables that aim to summarise much data. Indeed, we live in a world that bombards us with 'scientific facts' and 'official figures' and it is well worth pausing to consider what such 'statistical evidence' means.

As you find statistics in this book, ask yourself some of the questions below. You will soon learn that statistics should never be taken at simple face value and you will start to say that some seem more reasonable than others. Some of the questions you should ask of data include:

1. Are the statistics valid? Do they measure what they say they are trying to measure – like the 'suicide' rate, the 'crime' rate or 'human development'? If you simply think of the problems of just how 'suicide' (see Chapter 1), 'crime' (Chapter 16), 'class' (Chapter 10) or 'human development' (Chapter 4) can be defined (and indeed what they mean), you should soon see some of the problems. ▶

CONTROVERSY AND DEBATE CONTINUED

2. Are the statistics possible to disaggregate or break down into different parts? Thus statistics can conceal differences between groups – such as men and women, or young and old, or region to region. Is it possible to break the statistics down to see these differences at work?

3. Are the statistics consistently measured over time? Statistics may be produced at different times using different measuring devices. Again, you need to check how the statistics were made in order to see if they were measuring the same things.

4. Who created this statistic? There is always someone who made the statistic – from a big world agency like the United Nations to the smallest undergraduate survey. Knowing a bit about them may help you see possible sources of error and bias.

5. Why was this statistic created? What were the author(s) trying to achieve by making these statistics? For example, if it is a poverty statistic produced by campaigners against poverty, it is good to know this! And if it is a measure of church memberships produced by devout Christians, it is good to know this too!

6. How was this statistic actually created? Was it, for example, part of a multimillion pound bureaucratic enterprise involving the filling of many forms by many different people across the world? If it was bureaucratically produced, how did the various contributors play their role – what rules guided them?

7. How is the statistic being used? Was the statistic produced as part of a political campaign and is it being used perhaps to get more resources? How statistics are used may give clues as to hidden biases. There are usually plenty of statistics available for people on all sides of a political debate to use as ammunition to bolster their arguments. Watch out for over-use, under-use, misuse, political abuse, and oversimplification.

8. Why was this statistic selected to be presented? Often the data we confront are not wrong; they just do not tell the whole story.

9. How is the statistic being presented? Very often graphs and charts can be used to 'spin' the truth. The picture tells only part of the story. A graph of the crime rate over only the last several years, for example, would reveal a downward trend; shifting the time frame to include the last few decades, however, would show a sharp increase.

Above all, initially be suspicious of all statistics. Put them through some of the above tests, and then make your mind up about them.

CONTINUE THE DEBATE:

1. Look at some of the statistics in this book. Consider where they have come from, why they are being used and just what it is they purport to measure.

2. When would you trust a statistic?

3. Why do you think people are so quick to accept 'statistics' as true?

See Best (2001).

Putting it all together: planning a sociological project

Drawing together the elements of sociological investigation presented in this chapter, a typical project in sociology will include each of the following 14 steps. The emphasis here is upon planning the project well.

1. *Get yourself a research problem and define the topic of investigation.* Nothing is more important than getting yourself a good question. Being curious and looking at the world sociologically can generate ideas for social research anywhere. The issue you choose to study is likely to have some personal significance. But a social problem is not a sociological problem and you need to be clear how you can pose a sociological question.

2. *Start keeping a log and record files.* Keep a log of how you develop your research, how you change your views and problems, and how you make key decisions. This will be useful in helping you reflect, but it may also provide good source material for writing up the methodology chapter in your study – if you are to have one. Keep all your notes well organised, and plan this early.

3. *Find out what others have learned about the topic.* You are probably not the first person to develop an interest in a particular issue. Spend time in the library to see what theories and methods researchers have applied to your topic in the past. In reviewing existing research, note problems that may have come up before. Check on the findings.

4. *Assess the requirements for carrying out the research.* How much time and money will the research require? What special equipment or skills are necessary? Can you do the work yourself? What sources of funding are available to support the research? You should answer all these questions before beginning to design the research project.

5. *Specify the research questions.* Are you seeking to explore an unfamiliar social setting? To describe some category of people? Or to investigate cause and effect among variables? If your study is exploratory, identify general questions that will guide the work. If it is descriptive, specify the population and the variables of interest. If it is explanatory, state the hypothesis to be tested and carefully operationalise each variable. Make a long list of what puzzles you; and then work to narrow it to a firmer focus.

6. *Specify your theoretical orientation, and perhaps your disciplinary links.* You should try to locate your own research within certain traditions. For example, some research might be historical, some anthropological, and some more theoretical. And if it is to be theoretical, what kinds of theory will you use: to return to Chapter 1, would you find a functionalist, conflict or action approach most suitable?

7. *Consider ethical issues.* Not all research raises serious ethical issues, but you should be sensitive to this matter throughout your investigation. Could the research harm anyone? How might you design the study to minimise the chances of injury? Do you plan to promise anonymity to the subjects? If so, how will you ensure that anonymity will be maintained?

8. *Devise a research strategy.* Consider all major research strategies – as well as innovative combinations of approaches. Keep in mind that the appropriate method depends on the kinds of question you are asking as well as the resources available to support your research.

9. *Draw up a written research proposal in which you outline the above stages and say what you will be doing.* This is very valuable in providing a guide and checklist for doing the research.

10. *Gather and record the data.* The way you collect data depends on the research method you choose. Be sure to record accurately all information in a way that will make sense later (it may be some time before you actually write up the results of your work). Remain vigilant for any bias that may creep into the research. Bias may be inevitable, but you should be aware of it.

11. *Interpret the data.* Scrutinise the data in terms of the initial questions and decide what answers they suggest. If your study involves a specific hypothesis, you should be able to confirm, reject or modify the hypothesis based on the data. In writing up your research report, keep in mind that there may be several ways to interpret the results of your study, consistent with different theoretical paradigms, and you should consider them all.

12. *State your conclusions.* As you write your final report, specify conclusions supported by the data. Consider the significance of your work both to sociological theory and to improving research methods. Of what value is your research to people outside sociology? Finally, evaluate your own work, noting problems that arose and questions left unanswered. Note ways in which your own biases may have coloured your conclusions.

13. *Share your results.* Consider submitting your research paper to a campus newspaper or magazine, or making a presentation to a seminar, a meeting of any people you have been involved in studying, or perhaps a meeting of professional sociologists. The important point is to share what you have learned with others and to let others respond to your work.

14. *Where possible, store your data in an archive.* You never know! At some point some other researchers may want to see your data, or even reuse it. So it is always wise to think about ways of storing it or keeping it available for others to see and use.

SUMMARY

1. Two basic requirements for sociological investigation are (1) viewing the world from a sociological perspective, and (2) being curious and asking questions about society.

2. Sociological research involves asking questions about three issues: (1) epistemology, (2) technical tools, and (3) ethics and politics.

3. Two major approaches to epistemology are positivism and humanism. Others include realism, critical sociology, standpoint theory, Queer theory and postmodernism.

4. Measurement is the process of determining the value of a variable in any specific case. Sound measurement is both reliable and valid. A goal of science is discovering how variables are related. Correlation means that two or more variables change value together. Knowledge about cause-and-effect relationships is more powerful, however, because a researcher can use an independent variable to predict change in a dependent variable.

5. There are four major research tools. Experiments, which are performed under controlled conditions, attempt to specify causal relationships between two (or more) variables. Surveys, which gather people's responses to statements or questions, may employ questionnaires or interviews. Through participant observation, a form of field research, sociologists directly observe a social setting while participating in it for an extended period of time. Secondary analysis, or making use of available data, is often preferable to collecting one's own data; it is also essential in the study of historical questions. Other tools include 'documents of life' which are records of personal lives recorded by the subjects themselves. They help to gain an understanding of subjective experience, and include life histories, diaries and letters.

6. Visual sociology is a growing area of interest – as is the use of the personal computer in doing research.

7. Although investigators select topics according to their personal interests, the scientific ideal of objectivity demands that they try to suspend personal values and biases as they conduct research. Rejecting conventional ideas about scientific objectivity, some sociologists argue that research inevitably involves political values and that, with this in mind, research should be directed towards promoting desirable social change. Feminist methodologies take gender bias very seriously and aim to correct it.

8. Because sociological research has the potential to cause discomfort and harm to subjects, sociological investigators are bound by ethical guidelines.

CRITICAL-THINKING QUESTIONS

1. What does it mean to state that there are various kinds of truth? What is the basic rationale for relying on science as a way of knowing? Is sociology a science? Should it be? And if so, what kind? Identify several ways in which sociological research is similar to – and different from – research in the natural sciences.

2. What sorts of measure do scientists adopt as they strive for objectivity? Why do some sociologists consider objectivity an undesirable goal?

3. Dissect any one sociological study in order to evaluate its methodology.

4. If there can be a feminist methodology, can there also be an anti-racist methodology, or a gay/queer methodology?

Further reading

Basic texts:

Alan Bryman, *Social Research Methods* (2nd edn, 2004)
This has become a core standard text, though there are
many others.

Julia O'Connell Davidson and Derek Layder, *Methods, Sex
and Madness* (1994a)
Covers the whole field in an introductory, readable way –
but with an emphasis on research conducted into sexuality.

C. Wright Mills, *The Sociological Imagination* (1959)
This has already been introduced in Chapter 1. It has a very
useful appendix on how to do sociology and is strongly
recommended.

Judith Bell, *Doing Your Research Project: A Guide for First-
Time Researchers in Education and Social Science* (2nd edn,
1993)
One of a number of standard guides to understanding
research projects and how to do them.

Fiona Devine and Sue Heath, *Sociological Research Methods
in Context* (1999)
This introduces eight recent studies of sociology done in
the UK, and dissects their methodologies.

On different styles and tools of doing research:

Ken Plummer, *Documents of Life 2: An Invitation to a Critical
Humanism* (2001a)

Brian Roberts, *Biographical Research* (2002)
These have a major focus on life story interviewing and also
raise many of the problems in doing research.

Steiner Kvale, *Interviews: An Introduction to Qualitative
Research Interviewing* (1996)

This provides a tour of all the issues in qualitative
interviewing, with a number of useful study boxes on such
things as 'types of interviewer question' and 'seven stages
of an interview investigation'.

Robert Burgess, *In the Field* (1984)

Martin Hammersley and Paul Atkinson, *Ethnography:
Principles in Practice* (2nd edn, 1995)
Two useful guides to fieldwork in sociology.

Ruth Levitas and Will Guy (eds), *Interpreting Official Statistics*
(1996) and Joel Best, *Damned Lies and Statistics* (2001)
Two useful critiques of statistics.

Liz Stanley and Sue Wise, *Breaking Out Again: Feminist
Consciousness and Feminist Research* (2nd edn, 1993)
One of the founding statements for a feminist methodology,
here updated

Liz Wells (ed.), *Photography: A Critical Introduction* (2nd edn,
2003)

Elizabeth Chaplin, *Sociology and Visual Representation* (1994)
Good general introductory textbooks on photography and
visual sociology.

Ann Gray, *Research Practice for Cultural Studies* (2003)
A helpful guide to methods for cultural studies.

Hewson, Claire *et al. Internet Research Methods: A Practical
Guide* (2003)

Stuart, Stein, *Sociology on the Web* (2003)
Two accounts of how to make the most out of web research.

The Yanomami:

For some of the controversies linked to the Yanomami
discussed in the opening page, see Patrick Tierney,
*Darkness in El Dorado: How Scientists and Journalists
Devastated the Amazon* (2000).

Watch a video/Read a book

- Akira Kurosawa's *Rashomon* (1951): a much celebrated introduction to the idea of different perspectives capturing a common reality.

It will also be valuable now to watch some classic documentary films and consider whether they can offer more to understanding than conventional sociological research. For example, see:

- Robert Flaherty's *Nanook of the North* (1922: a classic early documentary about the Innu

- Leni Riefenstahl's *Triumph of the Will* (1935): a controversial documentary made at the start of Hitler's rule

- Tod Browning's *Freaks* (1932): a very disturbrng introduction to deviance, not really a documentary.

Several novels have tried to capture the life of a social researcher. See Alison Lurie's *Imaginary Friends* (1967) which looks at the researchers of a strange religious cult. And for one useful overview of documentary, see: Sharon R. Sherman, *Documenting Ourselves: Film, Video and Culture* (1998).

Connecting up

Connect to other chapters

- Inspect some of the tables and statistics throughout this book, and view them critically.

- See life stories in 'Voices' boxes. What problems do you find with such stories?

- For more on the growth of multiple voices and feminism, see Chapter 2.

To the websites

- http://www.nova.edu/ssss/QR/web.html

  An online journal which provides a major listing of qualitative research websites.

- http://odwin.ucsd.edu/idata/

  Based at the University of California at San Diego, this is a useful site for quantitative data. It houses some 850 sources for gathering data.

- National Statistics UK

  http://www.statistics.gov.uk

  The British government's website for all official statistics.

- Essex Data Archive

  http://www.data-archive.ac.uk

  This site, based at Essex University, is home for most of the major surveys and researches conducted in the UK.

For additional case studies, multiple choice questions, internet exercises, and annotated weblinks specific to this chapter, visit this book's website at **www.pearsoned.co.uk/plummer**

PART TWO

THE FOUNDATIONS OF SOCIETY:
FROM MACRO TO MICRO

CHAPTER 4

SOCIETIES

There is no such thing as society.

Margaret Thatcher

'I THOUGHT AT FIRST IT WAS A DOLL'S HEAD', said Helmut Simon, a German tourist who, in 1991, made one of the scientific finds of the century. Simon was hiking across a huge glacier in south-west Austria near the Italian border when he stumbled upon a familiar shape protruding from the melting ice. He soon realised that it

was not a doll but a human body: the so-called Iceman, who died some 5,300 years ago (before the construction of the Great Pyramids of Egypt), making him the oldest member of our species to be discovered essentially intact.

Experts from around the world soon were buzzing with excitement. They estimate that, at the time of his death, the Iceman was about 30 years of age, five feet two inches tall and weighed about 110 pounds. Scientists speculate that he was a shepherd, tending his flock high in the Alps in early autumn, when he

was overtaken by a cold storm that forced him to take refuge in a narrow ridge in the mountain. Tired from his ordeal, he lay down and fell asleep, and, as the temperature continued to drop, he froze to death. Deep snows and a wall of ice soon entombed his body in a massive glacier. There, at a flesh-preserving temperature of −6°C he remained for 53 centuries. Only an unusual melt of the glacier – and the luck of a sharp-eyed hiker – led to the Iceman's discovery.

Examining the Iceman's garments, scientists were astonished at how advanced this 'cave man's' society was. The Iceman's hair was neatly trimmed, and his body displayed numerous tattoos that probably symbolised his standing in his home community. He wore a skilfully stitched leather coat over which a woven grass cape provided greater protection from the elements. His shoes, also made of leather, were stuffed with grass for comfort and warmth. He carried with him an axe, a wood-handled knife, and a bow that shot feathered arrows with flint points. A primitive backpack held additional tools and personal items, including natural medicines made from plants.

(Rademaekers and Schoenthal, 1992).

KEY THEMES

- The different types of society throughout history
- The rise of modern industrial societies and Marx, Durkheim and Weber's approaches to these changes
- The broad shapes of contemporary world societies
- The emergence of a 'modern Europe'

(Left) A detail from an illustration from the Khamsa of Nizami by Aqa Mirak copied in Tabriz 1543 for Tahmasp1

As we saw in Chapter 1, sociology was born out of a concern with the rapidly changing character of this modern, industrial world: with where we have come from and where we are heading. New technologies, the advance of capitalism, the growth of cities, and the rise of democratic politics all ushered in this new world. This chapter both reaches back into the different kinds of society that existed before the arrival of the modern world and looks forward into the changing shape of the contemporary world. Along the way, it offers some major reasons for the changes that have happened and that are even now accelerating. The central concept of **society** refers to *people who interact in a defined space and share culture*. In this sense, both Europe, and specific countries such as Norway or England, may be seen as societies.

We shall start by describing the changing character of human society over the last 10,000 years. This is a very difficult task! The remainder of the chapter then analyses some of the main patterns of different kinds of society, and presents classic visions of society developed by three of sociology's founders, already introduced in earlier chapters. Karl Marx understood human history as a long and complex process of economic conflict. His concern was with the ways the economy generates *conflicts and inequalities* around the production of material goods in order to live (to eat and have shelter, for instance), and how these conflicts provided the motor force for change. Max Weber recognised the importance of productive forces as well, but he sought to demonstrate the power of *human ideas* (especially those found in religions) to animate society. Weber believed that rational thinking underlies modern society and promotes change. Finally, Emile Durkheim investigated patterns of *social solidarity*,

noting that the bonds uniting traditional societies are strikingly different from those uniting their modern counterparts. All of them were concerned with the momentous changes taking place in European societies in their times, and with how the future would develop. At the end of the chapter we will turn to just what the 200 or so societies in the world today look like, and how they may be characterised. But we will be returning to much of this later in the book.

Changing patterns of society

The Iceman, introduced at the opening of this chapter, was a member of a very early human society. He had already died before a great empire flourished in Egypt, before the flowering of culture in ancient Greece, and before any society in Europe could boast of a single city.

As people who take for granted rapid transportation and instant global communication, we look on this ancestor from our distant past with keen curiosity. But sociologists who study the past (working with archaeologists and anthropologists) have learned quite a bit about our human heritage. Gerhard Lenski and Jean Lenski have chronicled the great differences among societies that have flourished and declined throughout human history. Just as important, the work of these researchers helps us better understand how we live today. The Lenskis call the focus of their research **sociocultural evolution**, *the process of change that results from a society's gaining new information, particularly technology* (Lenski *et al.*, 1995). Rather like a biologist examining how a living species evolves over millennia, a sociologist employing

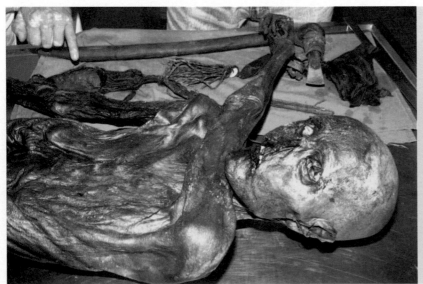

The world's oldest mummy, the Italian Iceman known as Otzi, is shown in this picture from September 25, 2000. Otzi, was defrosted to allow scientists to take samples which they hope will allow them to learn more about the man who roamed the Alps 5,300 years ago. The Iceman was found sticking out of a glacier by two climbers nine years earlier in Otztaker Alps on the Austro-Italian border. He had been freeze-dried 10,000 feet (3,000) meters above see level

Source: Reuters/Corbis © Werner Nosko

this approach observes how societies change over centuries as they gain a greater ability to manipulate their physical environments. It suggests that societies with rudimentary technology can support only a small number of people who enjoy few choices about how to live. Technologically complex societies – while not necessarily 'better' in any absolute sense – develop larger populations which are more likely to be characterised by diverse, highly specialised lives.

The greater the amount of technological information a society has in its grasp, the faster the rate at which it changes. Technologically less complex societies, then, change very slowly; in fact, some of the clothing worn by the Austrian Iceman differs only slightly from garments used by shepherds in the same area early in the twentieth century. By contrast, industrial, high-technology societies can start to change so quickly that people witness dramatic transformations in the span of their lifetimes. Again, consider some familiar elements of contemporary culture that would probably puzzle, delight, but most likely alarm people who lived just a few generations ago: fast food, faxes, mobile phones, computer 'cybersex', artificial hearts, laser surgery, test-tube babies, genetic engineering, computer-based virtual reality, fibre optics, smart bombs, the threat of nuclear holocaust, space shuttles, transsexual surgery, and 'tell-all' talk shows transmitted across the world to all countries! It is indeed a strange modern world we have arrived in – even when compared with the world of the recent past.

As a society extends its technological reach, the effects ripple through the cultural system, generating countless repercussions. When our ancestors first harnessed the power of the wind by using a sail, they set the stage for discovering kites, sailing ships, windmills and, eventually, aircraft. Consider, as more recent examples, the many ways modern life has been changed by atomic energy or the computer.

Drawing on the Lenskis' work, we will describe five general types of society distinguished by their technology: hunting and gathering societies; horticultural and pastoral societies; agrarian societies; industrial societies; and post-industrial societies. We could equally well describe societies as distinguished by the political systems, or their kinds of community.

1. Hunting and gathering societies

Hunting and gathering refers to *simple technology for hunting animals and gathering vegetation*. From the emergence of our species until about 12,000 years ago, all humans were hunters and gatherers. Hunting and gathering societies remained common several centuries ago, but today they are in sharp decline as they are more and more ravaged by the advance of industrial societies. Still, estimates suggest there may still be around 300 million **indigenous peoples:** *peoples with ties to the land, water and wildlife of their ancestral domain*. Many of these have been or still are hunter-gatherers. Today these include the Aka and Pygmies of central Africa, the Bushmen of south-western Africa, the Aborigines and Torres Strait Islanders of Australia, the Maori of New Zealand, the Kaska Indians of north-west Canada, and the Batek and Semai of Malaysia (Endicott, 1992; Hewlett, 1992: UN Commissioner on Human Rights Fact Sheets).

Most members of these societies looked continually for game and edible plants. Only in lush areas where food was plentiful would hunters and gatherers have much leisure time. Moreover, foraging for food demands a large amount of land, so hunting and gathering societies comprise small bands of a few dozen people living at some distance from one another. These groups were also nomadic, moving on as they depleted vegetation in one area or in pursuit of migratory animals. Although they periodically returned to favoured sites, they rarely formed permanent settlements.

Hunting and gathering societies are based on kinship. The family obtains and distributes food, protects its members, and teaches necessary skills to children. Most activities are common to everyone and centre on seeking the next meal; some specialisation, however, corresponds to age and sex. The very young and the very old contribute only what they can, while healthy adults secure most of the food. The gathering of vegetation – the more reliable food source – is typically the work of women, while men take on the less certain job of hunting. Although the two sexes have somewhat different responsibilities, then, most hunters and gatherers probably accorded men and women comparable social importance (Leacock, 1978).

Hunting and gathering societies have few formal leaders. Most recognise a shaman, or spiritual leader, who enjoys high prestige but receives no greater material rewards than other members of the society and must help procure food like everyone else. Other individuals who are especially skilful at obtaining food may also have high prestige; overall, however, the social organisation of hunters and gatherers is relatively simple and egalitarian.

Hunting and gathering societies rarely use their weapons – the spear, the bow and arrow, and stone knife – to wage war. Nonetheless, they are often ravaged by the forces of nature. Storms and droughts can easily destroy their food supply, and they stand vulnerable to accident and disease. Such risks encourage cooperation and sharing, a strategy that increases everyone's odds of survival. Even so, many die in childhood, and perhaps half perish before the age of 20 (Lenski *et al.*, 1995: 104; Brody, 2000).

During the twentieth century, technologically complex societies slowly closed in on the remaining hunters and gatherers, reducing their landholdings and depleting game and vegetation. Many of these 'indigenous' peoples, such as the Inuit in Canada and Alaska, are finding their cultures increasingly destroyed by the industrial West. In the first half of the twentieth century, Brazil alone lost some 87 tribes. They live under conditions where their human rights are abused and where they are under constant threat of extinction. Yet at the same time, there are signs that such cultures are also now fighting back to protect their own ways of life. There is also now a Charter of Rights of Indigenous Peoples drawn up by the United Nations.

Map 4.1 shows the remaining distribution of hunter-gatherer peoples throughout the world, together with that of pastoral nomadic tribes.

2. Horticultural and pastoral societies

Ten to twelve thousand years ago, a new technology began to change many hunting and gathering societies. **Horticulture** is *technology based on using hand tools to cultivate plants*. The most important tools of horticulturists are the hoe to work the soil and the digging stick to punch holes in the ground for seeds. Humans first used these tools in fertile regions of the Middle East and, later, in Latin America and Asia. Cultural diffusion spread knowledge of horticulture throughout most of the world by about 6,000 years ago.

Not all societies were quick to abandon hunting and gathering in favour of horticulture. Hunters and gatherers living amid plentiful vegetation and game probably saw little reason to embrace the new technology (Fisher, 1979). The Yanomami of the Brazilian rainforest illustrate the common practice of combining horticulture with more traditional hunting and gathering. They are the last large isolated group of indigenous peoples in the Americas (Chagnon, 1997).

SOCIAL SHAPES OF THE WORLD

| Map 4.1 | Main nomadic groups by region |

Source: adapted from A. M. Khazanov, *Nomads and the Outside World*. Cambridge: Cambridge University Press, 1984: 185

Then, too, people in particularly arid regions (such as the Middle East) or mountainous areas (such as in the Alps, where the Iceman lived) found horticulture to be of little value. Such people turned to a different strategy for survival, **pastoralism**, which is *technology based on the domestication of animals*. Still others combined horticulture and pastoralism to produce a variety of foods. Today, many horticultural–pastoral societies thrive in South America, Africa and Asia.

The domestication of plants and animals greatly increased food production, enabling societies to support not dozens but hundreds of people. Pastoralists remained nomadic, leading their herds to fresh grazing lands. Horticulturalists, by contrast, formed settlements, moving on only when they depleted the soil. These settlements, joined by trade, comprised multi-centred societies with overall populations often in the thousands.

Domesticating plants and animals generates a *material surplus* – more resources than are necessary to sustain day-to-day living. A surplus frees some people from the job of securing food, allowing them to create crafts, engage in trade, cut hair, apply tattoos or serve as priests. In comparison to hunting and gathering societies, then, horticultural and pastoral societies display more specialised and complex social arrangements.

Hunters and gatherers recognise numerous spirits inhabiting the world. Horticulturalists, however, practise ancestor worship and conceive of God as creator. Pastoral societies carry this belief further, viewing God as directly involved in the well-being of the entire world. This view of God ('The Lord is my shepherd', Psalm 23) is widespread among members of contemporary societies because Christianity, Islam and Judaism originated as Middle Eastern, pastoral religions.

Expanding productive technology also intensifies social inequality. As some families produce more food than others, they assume positions of relative power and privilege. Forging alliances with other elite families ensures that social advantages endure over generations, and a formal system of social inequality emerges. Along with social hierarchy, rudimentary government – backed by military force – is formed to shore up the power of elites. However, without the ability to communicate or to travel quickly, a ruler can control only a limited number of people, so empire-building proceeds on a small scale.

The domestication of plants and animals surely made simpler societies more productive. But advancing technology is never entirely beneficial. Compared to hunters and gatherers, horticulturists and pastoralists display more social inequality and, in many cases, engage in slavery, protracted warfare, and even cannibalism.

3. Agrarian societies

About 5,000 years ago – at about the time the Iceman roamed the earth – another technological revolution was under way in the Middle East that would eventually transform most of the world. This was the discovery of **agriculture**, *the technology of large-scale farming using ploughs harnessed to animals or more powerful sources of energy*. The social significance of the animal-drawn plough, along with other technological innovations of the period – including irrigation, the wheel, writing, numbers, and the expanding use of metals – clearly suggests the arrival of a new kind of society.

Of Egypt's 130 pyramids, the Great Pyramids at Giza are the largest. Each of the three major structures stands more than 40 storeys high and is composed of about 3 million massive stone blocks. Some 4,500 years ago, tens of thousands of people laboured to construct these pyramids so that one man, the pharaoh, might have a god-like monument for his tomb. Clearly social inequality in this agrarian society was extreme.

Source: Getty Photodisk

Farmers with animal-drawn ploughs cultivated fields vastly larger than the garden-sized plots worked by horticulturists. Ploughs have the additional advantage of turning, and thereby aerating, the soil to increase fertility. Such technology encouraged agrarian societies to farm the same land for decades, which in turn led to humanity's first permanent settlements. Large food surpluses, transported on animal-powered wagons, allowed agrarian societies to expand to unprecedented land area and population. As an extreme case, the Roman Empire at its height (about 100 CE) boasted a population of 70 million spread over some 2 million square miles (Stavrianos, 1983; Lenski *et al.*, 1995).

As always, increasing production meant greater specialisation. Tasks once performed by everyone, such as clearing land and securing food, became distinct occupations. Specialisation made the early barter system obsolete and prompted the invention of money as a common standard of exchange. The appearance of money facilitated trade, sparking the growth of cities as economic centres with populations soaring into the millions.

Agrarian societies exhibit dramatic social inequality. In many cases, peasants or slaves constitute a significant share of the population and labour for elites. Freed from manual work, elites can then devote their time to the study of philosophy, art and literature.

Among hunters and gatherers and also among horticulturists, women are the primary providers of food. The development of agriculture, however, appears to have propelled men into a position of social dominance (Boulding, 1976; Fisher, 1979). The box looks more closely at the declining position of women at this point in the course of sociocultural evolution.

Religion reinforces the power of agricultural elites. Religious doctrine typically propounds the idea that people are morally obligated to perform whatever tasks correspond to their place in the social order. Many of the 'wonders of the ancient world', such as the Great Wall of China and the Great Pyramids of Egypt, were possible because emperors and pharaohs wielded virtually absolute power to mobilise their people to endure a lifetime of labour without pay.

In agrarian societies, then, elites gain unparalleled power. To maintain control of large empires, leaders require the services of a wide range of administrators. Consequently, along with the growing economy, the political system becomes established as a distinct sphere of life.

Agrarian societies have greater specialisation and more social inequality. And, compared to horticultural and pastoral societies, agrarian societies differ more from one another because advancing technology can increase human control over the natural world.

VOICES

TECHNOLOGY AND THE CHANGING STATUS OF WOMEN

In technologically simple societies of the past, women produced more food than men did. Hunters and gatherers valued meat highly, but men's hunting was not a dependable source of nourishment. Thus vegetation gathered by women was the primary means of ensuring survival. Similarly, tools and seeds used in horticulture developed under the control of women, who already had primary responsibility for providing and preparing food. For their part, men engaged in trade and tended herds of animals. Only at harvest time did both sexes work together.

About 5,000 years ago, humans discovered how to mould metals. This technology spread by cultural diffusion, primarily along trade networks forged by men. Thus it was men who devised the metal plough

and, since they already managed animals, they soon thought to hitch the implement to a cow.

This great innovation propelled the transition from horticulture to agriculture and, for the first time, thrust men into a dominant position in the production of food. Elise Boulding explains how this technological breakthrough undermined the social standing of women:

The shift of the status of the woman farmer may have happened quite rapidly, once there were two male specialisations relating to agriculture: plowing and the care of cattle. This situation left women with all the many subsidiary tasks, including weeding and carrying water to the fields. The new fields were larger, so women had to work just as many hours as they did before, but now they worked at more secondary tasks. This would contribute further to the erosion of the status of women. (Boulding, 1976; Fisher, 1979)

4. Industrial societies

Industrialism is *technology that powers sophisticated machinery with advanced sources of energy.* Until the industrial era, the major source of energy was the muscle power of humans and other animals. At the dawning of the *Industrial Revolution*, about 1750, mills and factories relied on flowing water and later steam to power ever-larger and more efficient machinery.

Once this technology was at hand, societies began to change faster, as shown in Figure 4.1. Industrial societies transformed themselves more in a century than they had in thousands of years before. As explained in Chapter 1, this stunning change stimulated the birth of sociology itself. During the nineteenth century, railways and steamships revolutionised transportation, and steel-framed skyscrapers recast the urban landscape, dwarfing the cathedrals that symbolised an earlier age.

As the twentieth century opened, the internal combustion engine further reshaped Western societies, and electricity was fast becoming the basis for countless 'modern conveniences'. Electronic communication, including the telephone, radio and television, was mass-producing cultural patterns and gradually making a large world seem smaller and smaller. More recently, transportation technology has given humanity the capacity to fly faster than sound and even to break the bonds of earth. Nuclear power has also changed the world for ever. And, during the last generation, computers have ushered in the *Information Revolution*, dramatically increasing humanity's capacity to process words and numbers.

Work, too, has changed. In agrarian societies, most men and women work in the home and on the land. Industrialisation, however, creates factories near centralised machinery and energy sources. Lost in the process are close working relationships and strong kinship ties, as well as many of the traditional values, beliefs and customs that guide agrarian life.

Industrialism engenders societies of unparalleled prosperity. Although health in the industrial cities of Europe and North America was initially poor, a rising standard of living and advancing health-related technology gradually brought infectious diseases under control. Consequently, life expectancy increased, fuelling rapid population growth. Industrialisation also draws people from the countryside to the cities where the factories are built. So, while roughly one in ten members of agrarian societies lives in cities, three out of four people in industrial societies are urbanites.

Occupational specialisation, which expanded over the long course of sociocultural evolution, has become more pronounced than ever. Industrial people often size up one another in terms of their jobs, rather than according to their kinship ties as agrarian people do. Rapid change and movement from place to place also generate anonymity and cultural diversity, sparking the formation of numerous subcultures and countercultures, as described in Chapter 5.

Industrial technology recasts the family, too, diminishing its traditional significance as the centre of social life. No longer does the family serve as the primary setting for economic production, learning and religious worship. And, as Chapter 17 explains in detail, technological change also underlies the trend away from so-called traditional families to greater numbers of single people, divorced people, single-parent families, lesbian and gay couples and stepfamilies.

Early industrialisation concentrated the benefits of advancing technology on a small segment of the population, with the majority living in poverty. In time, however, the material benefits of industrial productivity spread more widely. Poverty remains a serious problem in industrial societies, but compared to the situation a century ago, the standard of living has risen fivefold, and economic, social and political inequality has declined.

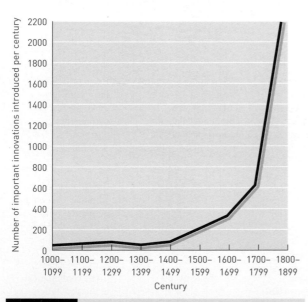

Figure 4.1   The increasing number of technological innovations

This figure illustrates the number of technological innovations in Western Europe after the beginning of the Industrial Revolution in the mid-eighteenth century. Technological innovation occurs at an accelerating rate because each innovation spins off existing cultural elements to produce many further innovations.

Source: adapted from Lenski, Nolan and Lenski (2004)

Some social levelling, detailed in Chapter 8, occurs because industrial societies demand a literate and skilled labour force. While most people in agrarian societies are illiterate, industrial societies provide state-funded schooling and confer numerous political rights on virtually everyone. Industrialisation, in fact, intensifies demands for political participation, as seen recently in South Korea, Taiwan, the People's Republic of China, the former Soviet Union, and the societies of Eastern Europe.

5. Post-industrial societies

Many industrial societies now appear to be entering yet another phase of technological development. In the early 1970s, Daniel Bell (1976) coined the term **post-industrialism** to refer to *computer-linked technology that supports an information-based economy*. While production in industrial societies focuses on factories and machinery that generate material goods, post-industrial production focuses on computers and other electronic devices that create, process, store and apply information. It is the information society. At the individual level, members of industrial societies concentrate on learning mechanical skills; people in post-industrial societies, however, work on honing information-based skills for work involving computers, facsimile machines, satellites and other forms of communication technology.

As this shift in key skills indicates, the emergence of post-industrialism dramatically changes a society's occupational structure. Chapter 14 examines this process in detail, explaining that a post-industrial society utilises

Table 4.1	Kinds of society: a summary			
Type of society	**Historical period**	**Productive technology**	**Population size**	**Settlement pattern**
Hunting and gathering societies	Only type of society until about 12,000 years ago; still common several centuries ago; the few examples remaining today are threatened with extinction	Primitive weapons	25–40 people	Often nomadic, but can be settled (Brody, 2000)
Horticultural and pastoral societies	From about 12,000 years ago, with decreasing numbers after about 3000 BCE	Horticultural societies use hand tools for cultivating plants; pastoral societies are based on the domestication of animals	Settlements of several hundred people, interconnected through trading ties to form societies of several thousand people	Horticulturalists form relatively small permanent settlements; pastoralists are nomadic
Agrarian societies	From about 5,000 years ago with large but decreasing numbers today	Animal-drawn plough	Millions of people	Cities become common, though they generally contain only a small proportion of the population
Industrial societies	From about 1750 to the present	Advanced sources of energy; mechanised production	Millions of people	Cities contain most of the population
Post-industrial societies	Emerging in recent decades	Computers that support an information-based economy	Millions of people	Population remains concentrated in cities

less and less of its labour force for industrial production. At the same time, the ranks of clerical workers, managers, and other people who process information (in fields ranging from academia and advertising to marketing and public relations) swell rapidly.

The Information Revolution is, of course, most pronounced in industrial, high-income societies, yet the reach of this new technology is so great that it is affecting the entire world. As explained in Chapters 6 and 22, the unprecedented worldwide flow of information originating in rich nations like our own has the predictable effect of tying far-flung societies together and fostering common patterns of global culture. This extends the process of globalisation. And as we saw in Chapter 2, this also brings a society that some speak of as being postmodern (**postmodernism** is *the ways of*

thinking which stress a plurality of perspectives as opposed to a unified, single core). It is a world where change is greatly speeding up, where classical boundaries across societies are breaking down, and a new sense of society is in the making.

At the same time, it is important to remember that all five of the different kinds of society we have outlined here still coexist. There are still societies which focus on agriculture, and the industrial world still tends to dominate. But as this book will show over and over again, there is a sense that as the twenty-first century continues to unfold, many changes will accelerate – making the world of 3001 (if it comes to exist!) a quite different order from that we live in now.

Table 4.1 summarises how technology helps shape societies at different stages of sociocultural evolution.

Social organisation	Examples
Family centred; specialisation limited to age and sex; little social inequality	Pygmies of central Africa Bushmen of south-western Africa Aborigines of Australia Semai of Malaysia Kaska Indians of Canada
Family centred; religious system begins to develop; moderate specialisation; increased social inequality	Middle-Eastern societies about 5000 BCE Various societies today in New Guinea and other Pacific islands Yanomami today in South America
Family loses significance as distinctive religious, political and economic systems emerge; extensive specialisation; increased social inequality	Egypt during construction of the Great Pyramids Medieval Europe Numerous non-industrial societies of the world today
Distinct religious, political, economic, educational and family systems; highly specialised; marked social inequality persists, diminishing somewhat over time	Most societies today in Europe and North America, Australia and Japan generate most of the world's industrial production
Similar to industrial societies with information processing and other service work gradually replacing industrial production	Industrial societies noted above are now entering post-industrial stage

Technological determinism: a cautious word

While different kinds of technology may well create preconditions for different kinds of society, there are four cautions that need to be given.

First, the technology does not *determine* societies. There is no automatic connection between the kinds of technology a society has available and the form of that society. It takes people to decide how to use technologies – and they may use them in very different ways, developing different skills and meanings. Under Nazi Germany, for example, the weight of modern technology was used to exterminate millions of people. The technologies of the Incas or the Egyptians were very sophisticated, but also involved systems of domination and slavery. As we will see later, modern information or computer societies need actions from people to use them – and they may be used for good or bad. Technology is neutral: it is people who shape technology.

Second, we must be very wary of saying these five societies *evolve* from one to the next, as if there is some kind of automatic progress. In fact, in the twenty-first century all of these societies may be said to coexist. Many indigenous peoples may have hunting, pastoral or agrarian societies with highly evolved technologies of their own. It is often a 'Eurocentric' view that wants to see them as prior to or more simple than European culture. We will return to some of these problems when we discuss multiculturalism in the next chapter.

Third, we must recognise *the limits of technology*. While technology remedies many human problems by raising productivity, by eliminating disease, and sometimes simply by relieving boredom, it provides no 'quick fix' for deeply rooted social problems. *Poverty* remains the plight of billions of people worldwide (see Chapter 9). Moreover, with the capacity to reshape the world, technology has created new problems that our ancestors hardly could have imagined. Industrial societies provide more personal freedom, often at the cost of the sense of community that characterised agrarian life. Further, although the most powerful societies of today's world infrequently engage in all-out warfare, *international conflict* now poses unimaginable horrors. Should nations ever unleash even a fraction of their present stockpiles of nuclear weapons, human society would almost certainly regress to a technologically primitive state if, indeed, we survived at all.

Finally, another stubborn social problem linked to technology involves humanity's relation to the *physical environment*. Each stage in sociocultural evolution has introduced more powerful sources of energy and accelerated our appetite for the earth's resources at a rate even faster than the population is growing. We now face an issue of vital concern – one that is the focus of Chapter 24: can humanity continue to pursue material prosperity without subjecting the planet to damage and strains from which it will never recover?

In some respects, then, technological advances have improved life and brought the world's people closer together within a 'global village'. Yet in technology's wake are daunting problems of establishing peace, ensuring justice, and sustaining a safe environment – problems that technology alone can never solve.

Explaining modern industrial society

There have been many attempts to explain how the modern industrial world was created. Sociology has its classic interpretations; and we saw at the start of this chapter three key visions of modern industrial society in the work of three of the key 'founders' of modern sociology: Karl Marx, Max Weber and Emile Durkheim. All three of their visions of society try to answer key questions:

- How do societies of the past and present differ from one another?
- How and why does a society change? What forces divide a society? What forces hold it together?
- Are societies getting better or worse?

The theorists profiled in this chapter all probed these questions, but they disagree on the answers. We shall highlight the similarities and differences in their views as we go along.

Karl Marx: capitalism and conflict

The first of our classic visions of society comes from Karl Marx (1818–83), who is introduced in the Profile box. Few observed the industrial transformation of Europe as keenly as he did. Marx spent most of his adult life in London, then the capital of the vast British Empire. He was awed by the productive power of the new factories; not only were European societies producing more goods than ever before, but a global system of commerce was funnelling resources from around the world through British factories at a dizzying rate.

Marx saw that industry's riches were increasingly concentrated in the hands of a few. A walk almost anywhere in London revealed dramatic extremes of splendid affluence and wretched squalor. A handful of aristocrats and industrialists lived in fabulous mansions, well staffed by servants, where they enjoyed luxury and privileges barely imaginable by the majority of their fellow Londoners. Most people laboured long hours for low wages, living in slums or even sleeping in the streets, where many eventually succumbed to poor nutrition and infectious disease.

Throughout his life, Marx wrestled with a basic contradiction: in a society so rich, how could so many be so poor? Just as important, Marx asked, how can this situation be changed? He was motivated by compassion for humanity, and sought to help a society already badly divided forge what he hoped would be a new and just social order.

The key to Marx's thinking is the idea of **social conflict**, *struggle between segments of society over valued resources*. Social conflict can, of course, take many forms: individuals may quarrel, some towns have long-standing rivalries, and nations sometimes go to war. For Marx, however, the most significant form of social conflict involved clashes between social classes that arise from the way a society produces material goods.

Society and production

Living in the nineteenth century, Marx observed the early stage of industrial capitalism in Europe. This economic system, Marx noted, transformed a small part of the population into **capitalists**, *people who own factories and other productive enterprises*. A capitalist's goal is profit, which results from selling a product for more than it costs to produce. Capitalism transforms most of the population into industrial workers, whom Marx called the **proletariat**, *people who provide labour necessary to operate factories and other productive enterprises*. Workers

PROFILE

KARL MARX: AN AGENDA FOR CHANGE

Few names evoke as strong a response as Karl Marx. Some consider him a genius and a prophet, while others see only evil in his ideas. Everyone agrees that Marx stands among the social thinkers with the greatest impact on the world's people. Today, more than one-fifth of all humanity live in societies that consider themselves Marxist.

Nor was Marx a stranger to controversy during his lifetime. Born in the German city of Trier, he earned a doctorate in 1841 and began working as a newspaper editor. But his relentless social criticism sparked clashes with government authorities, who managed to drive Marx from Germany to Paris. Soon controversy forced him to flee from France as well, and Marx spent the rest of his life in London.

Along with Max Weber and Emile Durkheim, Marx was a major figure in the development of sociology, as we saw in Chapter 1. However, sociologists in the United States paid relatively little attention to his ideas until the 1960s. Why? The answer lies in Marx's explicit criticism of industrial–capitalist society. Early sociologists often dismissed his ideas as mere 'politics' rather than serious scholarship. But for Marx, scholarship was politics. While most sociologists heeded Max Weber's call for value-free research by attempting to minimise or conceal their own values (see Chapter 3), Marx placed values at the centre of his thinking. Marx did not merely observe society; he offered a rousing prescription for profound social change. Now that we have come to recognise the extent to which values shape all ideas, Marx's social analysis has finally received the attention it deserves as a pivotal approach to sociology.

sell their labour for the wages they need to live. To Marx, an inevitable conflict between capitalists and workers has its roots in the productive process itself. To maximise profits, capitalists must minimise wages, generally their single greatest expense. Workers, however, want wages to be as high as possible. Since profits and wages come from the same pool of funds, ongoing conflict occurs. Marx argued that this conflict would end only when people abandoned the capitalist system.

All societies are composed of **social institutions**, defined as *the major spheres of social life, or society's subsystems, organised to meet basic human needs.* In his analysis of society, Marx contended that one specific institution – the economy – dominates all others when it comes to steering the direction of a society. Drawing on the philosophical doctrine of historical *materialism*, which asserts that how humans produce material goods shapes the rest of society, Marx claimed that all the other major social institutions – the political system, family, religion and education – operated under the influence of a society's economy. Marx argued that the economy is 'the real foundation. . . . The mode of production in

material life determines the general character of the social, political, and spiritual processes of life' (1959: 43; orig. 1859).

Marx therefore viewed the economic system as the base or social *infrastructure* (*infra* is Latin for 'below'). Other social institutions, including the family, the political system and religion, which are built on this foundation, form society's *superstructure* (*supra* meaning 'above' in Latin). These institutions extend economic principles into other areas of life, as illustrated in Figure 4.2. In practical terms, social institutions reinforce the domination of the capitalists, by legally protecting their wealth, for example, and by transferring property from one generation to the next through the family.

Generally speaking, members of industrial–capitalist societies do not view their legal or family systems as hotbeds of social conflict. On the contrary, individuals come to see their rights to private property as 'natural'. Many people find it easy to think that affluent people have earned their wealth, while those who are poor or out of work lack skills or motivation. Marx rejected this kind of reasoning as rooted in a capitalist preoccupation with the

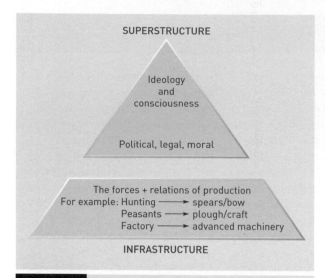

SUPERSTRUCTURE

Ideology
and
consciousness

Political, legal, moral

The forces + relations of production
For example: Hunting ⟶ spears/bow
Peasants ⟶ plough/craft
Factory ⟶ advanced machinery

INFRASTRUCTURE

Figure 4.2   Karl Marx's model of society

This diagram illustrates Marx's materialist view that the process of economic production underlies and shapes the entire society. Economic production involves both technology (industry, in the case of capitalism) and social relationships (for capitalism, the relationship between the capitalists, who control the process of economic production, and the workers, who are simply a source of labour). Upon this infrastructure, or foundation, are built the major social institutions as well as core cultural values and ideas. Taken together, these additional social elements represent the society's superstructure. Marx maintained that every part of a society operates in concert with the economic system.

'bottom line' that treats human well-being as a market commodity. Poverty and unemployment are not inevitable; as Marx saw it, grand wealth clashing with grinding poverty represents merely one set of human possibilities generated by capitalism (Cuff and Payne, 1979).

Marx rejected capitalist common sense, therefore, as **false consciousness**, *explanations of social problems grounded in the shortcomings of individuals rather than the flaws of society*. Marx was saying, in effect, that industrial capitalism itself is responsible for many of the social problems he saw all around him. False consciousness, he maintained, victimises people by obscuring the real cause of their problems.

Conflict in history

Marx studied how societies have changed throughout history, noting that they often evolve gradually, though they sometimes change in rapid, revolutionary fashion.

Marx observed that change is partly prompted by technological advance. But he steadfastly held that conflict between economic groups is the major engine of change.

Early hunters and gatherers formed primitive communist societies. The word 'communism' refers to a social system in which the production of food and other material goods is a common effort shared more or less equally by all members of society. Because the resources of nature were available to all hunters and gatherers (rather than privately owned), and because everyone performed similar work (rather than dividing work into highly specialised tasks), there was little possibility for social conflict.

Horticulture, Marx noted, introduced significant social inequality. Among horticultural, pastoral and early agrarian societies – which Marx lumped together as the 'ancient world' – the victors in frequent warfare forced their captives into servitude. A small elite (the 'masters') and their slaves were thus locked in an irreconcilable pattern of social conflict (Zeitlin, 1981).

Agriculture brought still more wealth to members of the elite, fuelling further social conflict. Agrarian serfs, occupying the lowest reaches of European feudalism from about the twelfth to the eighteenth centuries, were only slightly better off than slaves. In Marx's view, the power of both the church and the state defended feudal inequality by defining the existing social order as God's will. Thus, to Marx, feudalism amounted to little more than 'exploitation, veiled by religious and political illusions' (Marx and Engels, 1972: 337; orig. 1848).

Gradually, new productive forces undermined the feudal order. Commerce grew steadily throughout the Middle Ages as trade networks expanded and the power of guilds increased. Merchants and skilled crafts workers in the cities formed a new social category, the *bourgeoisie* (a French word meaning 'of the town'). Profits earned through expanding trade brought the bourgeoisie increasing wealth. After the mid-eighteenth century, with factories at their command, the bourgeoisie became true capitalists with power that soon rivalled that of the ancient, landed nobility. While the nobility regarded this upstart 'commercial' class with disdain, the latter's increasing wealth gradually shifted the control of European societies to the capitalists.

Industrialisation also fostered the development of the proletariat. English landowners converted fields once tilled by serfs into grazing land for sheep to secure wool for the prospering textile mills. Forced from the land, serfs migrated to cities to work in factories, where they joined the burgeoning industrial proletariat. Marx envisaged these workers one day joining hands across national boundaries to form a unified class, setting the stage for historic confrontation, this time between capitalists and the exploited workers.

Capitalism and class conflict

Much of Marx's analysis centres on destructive aspects of industrial capitalism – especially the ways in which it promotes class conflict and alienation. In examining his views on these topics, we will come to see why he advocated the overthrow of capitalist societies.

'The history of all hitherto existing society is the history of class struggles.' With this declaration, Marx and his collaborator Friedrich Engels began their best-known statement, the *Manifesto of the Communist Party* (1972: 335; orig. 1848). The idea of social class is at the heart of Marx's critique of capitalist society. Industrial capitalism, like earlier types of society, contains two major social classes – the dominant people and the oppressed – reflecting the two basic positions in the productive system. Capitalists and proletarians are the historical descendants of masters and slaves in the ancient world and of nobles and serfs in feudal systems. In each case, one class controls the other as productive property. Marx used the term **class conflict** (and sometimes *class struggle*) to refer to *antagonism between entire classes over the distribution of wealth and power in society*.

Class conflict, then, dates back to civilisations long gone (see Figure 4.3). What distinguishes the conflict in capitalist society, Marx pointed out, is how it has come out into the open. Agrarian nobles and serfs, for all their differences, were bound together by long-standing traditions and a host of mutual obligations. Industrial capitalism dissolved those ties so that pride and honour were replaced by 'naked self-interest' and the pursuit of profit in a blatant exercise of oppression. Marx believed that the proletariat, with no personal ties to the oppressors, had little reason to stand for its own subjugation.

But, though industrial capitalism brought class conflict out in the open, Marx realised that fundamental social change would not come easily. First, he claimed, workers must *become aware* of their shared oppression and see capitalism as its true cause. Second, they must *organise and act* to address their problems. This means workers must replace false consciousness with **class consciousness**, *the recognition by workers of their unity as a class in opposition to capitalists and, ultimately, to capitalism itself*. Because the inhumanity of early capitalism was plain for him to see, Marx concluded that industrial workers would inevitably rise up *en masse* to destroy industrial capitalism.

And what of the workers' adversaries, the capitalists? The capitalists' formidable wealth and power, protected by the institutions of society, might seem invulnerable.

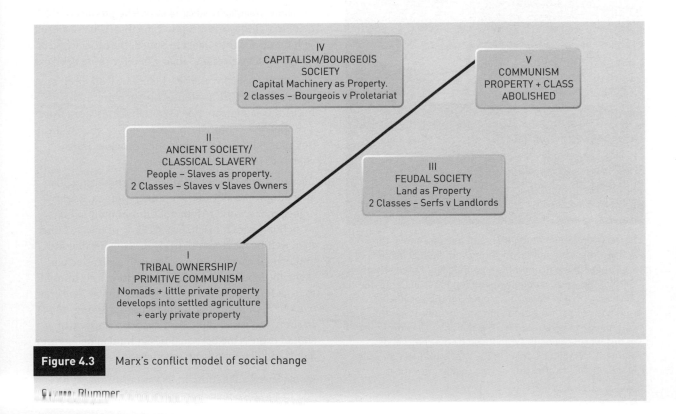

Figure 4.3   Marx's conflict model of social change

But Marx saw a weakness in the capitalist armour. Motivated by a desire for personal gain, capitalists fear the competition of other capitalists. Thus Marx thought that capitalists would be reluctant to band together, even though they too share common interests. Furthermore, he reasoned, capitalists keep employees' wages low in their drive to maximise profits. This strategy, in turn, bolsters the resolve of workers to forge an alliance against them. In the long run, Marx surmised, capitalists would only contribute to their own undoing.

In the twentieth century, Marxism became one of the world's most influential social movements: at its peak it was shaping the economic and political life of nearly a third of the world's people, including those of China, the Soviet Union and Eastern Europe. But the socialist regimes of Eastern Europe and the former Soviet Union collapsed in the late 1980s. The political transformation of this world region is symbolised by the removal of statues of Vladimir Lenin (1870–1924), architect of Soviet Marxism, in city after city during the last few years.

Source: Frank Spooner/Gamma

Capitalism and alienation

Marx also condemned capitalism for producing **alienation**, *the experience of isolation resulting from powerlessness*. Dominated by capitalists and dehumanised by their jobs (especially monotonous and repetitive factory work), proletarians find little satisfaction in, and feel individually powerless to improve, their situation. Herein lies another contradiction of capitalist society: as human beings devise technology to gain power over the world, the productive process increasingly assumes power over human beings.

Workers view themselves as merely a commodity, a source of labour, bought by capitalists and discarded when no longer needed. Marx cited four ways in which capitalism alienates workers.

1. *Alienation from the act of working.* Ideally, people work both to meet immediate needs and to develop their long-range personal potential. Capitalism, however, denies workers a say in what they produce or how they produce it. Furthermore, much work is tedious, involving countless repetitions of routine tasks. The modern-day replacement of human labour by machines would hardly have surprised Marx; as far as he was concerned, capitalism had turned human beings into machines long ago.

2. *Alienation from the products of work.* The product of work belongs not to workers but to capitalists, who dispose of it for profit. Thus, Marx reasoned, the more workers invest of themselves into their work, the more they lose.

3. *Alienation from other workers.* Marx saw work itself as the productive affirmation of human community. Industrial capitalism, however, transforms work from a cooperative venture into a competitive one. As the box illustrates, factory work often provides little chance for human companionship.

4. *Alienation from human potential.* Industrial capitalism alienates workers from their human potential. Marx argued that a worker 'does not fulfil himself in his work but denies himself, has a feeling of misery rather than well-being, does not freely develop his physical and mental energies, but is physically exhausted and mentally debased. The worker, therefore, feels himself to be at home only during his leisure time, whereas at work he feels homeless' (1964b: 124–125; orig. 1844). In short, industrial capitalism distorts an activity that should express the best qualities in human beings into a dull and dehumanising experience.

Marx viewed alienation, in its various forms, as a barrier to social change. But he hoped that industrial

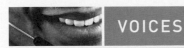 **VOICES**

THE ALIENATION OF WORK

In the 1970s, the oral historian Studs Terkel gathered many interviews of the experience of work. Many of these showed how dull, repetitive jobs can generate alienation for men and women.

Phil Stallings is a 27-year-old car worker in a Ford assembly plant in Chicago.

I start the automobile, the first welds. From there it goes to another line, where the floor's put on, the roof, the trunk, the hood, the doors. Then it's put on a frame. There is hundreds of lines. . . .

I stand in one spot, about two- or three-feet area, all night. The only time a person stops is when the line stops. We do about thirty-two jobs per car, per unit. Forty-eight units an hour, eight hours a day. Thirty-two times forty-eight times eight. Figure it out. That's how many times I push that button.

The noise, oh it's tremendous. You open your mouth and you're liable to get a mouthful of sparks. [Shows his arms.] That's a burn, these are burns. You don't compete against the noise. You go to yell and at the same time you're straining to manoeuvre the gun to where you have to weld.

You got some guys that are uptight, and they're not sociable. It's too rough. You pretty much stay to yourself. You get involved with yourself. You dream, you think of things you've done. I drift back continuously to when I was a kid and what me and my brothers did. The things you love most are what you drift back into.

It don't stop. It just goes and goes and goes. I bet there's men who have lived and died out there, never seen the end of the line. And they never will – because it's endless. It's like a serpent. It's just all body, no tail. It can do things to you . . . .
(Terkel, 1977: 151)

Twenty-four-year-old Sharon Atkins is a college graduate working as a telephone receptionist for a large midwestern business.

I don't have much contact with people. You can't see them. You don't know if they're laughing, if they're being satirical or being kind. So your conversations become very abrupt. I notice that in talking to people. My conversation would be very short and clipped, in short sentences, the way I talk to people all day on the telephone. . . .

You try to fill up your time with trying to think about other things: what you're going to do on the weekend or about your family. You have to use your imagination. If you don't have a very good one and you bore easily, you're in trouble. Just to fill in time, I write real bad poetry or letters to myself and to other people and never mail them. The letters are fantasies, sort of rambling, how I feel, how depressed I am.

. . . I never answer the phone at home.
(Terkel, 1977: 60)

More recently, Barbara Ehrenreich (2001) in the US and Polly Toynbee (2003) in the UK have experimented with going undercover in the world of low-pay women's work. They worked in cafés and fast-food restaurants, acted as cleaners and maids, as well as working in factories. Both were highly educated middle-class women, but on low incomes they did not fare well. They felt stigmatised; they had difficulty finding a place to live or ways of getting to work; and of course they worked long hours often with gruelling work. And there was more to the work than they thought. Barbara Ehrenreich remarks towards the end of her book:

How did I do as a low-wage worker? If I may begin with a brief round of applause: I didn't do half bad at the work itself, and I claim this as a considerable achievement. You might think that unskilled jobs would be a snap for someone who holds a Ph.D. and whose normal line of work requires learning entirely new things every couple of weeks. Not so. The first thing I discovered is that no job no matter how lowly, is truly 'unskilled.' Every one of the six jobs I entered into the course of this project required concentration, and most demanded that I master new terms, new tools, and new skills – from placing orders on restaurant computers to wielding the backpack vacuum cleaner. None of these things came as easily to me as I would have liked; no one ever said, 'Wow you're fast!' or 'Can you believe she just started?' Whatever my accomplishments in the rest of my life, in the low-wage work world I was a person of average ability – capable of learning the job and also capable of screwing up.
(Ehrenreich, 2001: 193–4)

workers eventually would overcome their alienation by uniting into a true social class, aware of the cause of their problems and galvanised to transform society.

Revolution

The only way out of the trap of capitalism, contended Marx, was deliberately to refashion society. He envisaged a more humane and egalitarian productive system, one that would enhance rather than undermine social ties. He called this system *socialism*. Marx knew well the obstacles to a socialist revolution; even so, he was disappointed that he never lived to see workers in England overthrow industrial capitalism. Still, convinced of the basic immorality of capitalist society, he was sure that in time the working majority would realise that they held the key to a better future in their own hands. This transformation would certainly be revolutionary, perhaps even violent. What emerged from the workers' revolution, however, would be a cooperative socialist society intended to meet the needs of all.

The discussion of social stratification in Chapter 8 reveals more about changes in industrial–capitalist societies since Marx's time and why the revolution he championed has not taken place. Later chapters also delve into why people in the societies of Eastern Europe recently revolted against established socialist governments. But, in his own time, Marx looked towards the future with hope (Marx and Engels 1972: 362; orig. 1848): 'The proletarians have nothing to lose but their chains. They have a world to win.'

Max Weber: the rationalisation of society and the disenchantment of the world

With a broad understanding of law, economics, religion and history, Max Weber (1864–1920), profiled in the box, produced what many regard as the greatest individual contribution to sociology. He generated ideas that were very wide-ranging, Here, we limit ourselves to his vision of how modern society differs from earlier types of social organisation.

As we saw in Chapter 1, Weber's sociology can be seen as an action theory. Weber understood the power of the economic and technological but he departed from Marx's materialist analysis. For him, ideas – especially beliefs and values – have transforming power. Thus he saw modern society as the product not just of new technology and capitalism, but of a new way of thinking. Growing

out of changes in religious belief, the modern world can be characterised as an increasingly rational world. We have seen too that Weber also used **ideal types**, contrasting the ideal 'Protestant' with the ideal 'Jew', 'Hindu' and 'Buddhist'. We have already compared 'hunting and gathering societies' and 'industrial societies' as well as 'capitalism' and 'socialism'. Much of Weber's analysis focused upon the ideal types of rationality.

Tradition and rationality

Rather than categorise societies in terms of technology or productive systems, Max Weber highlighted differences in the ways people view the world. In simple terms, Weber concluded that members of pre-industrial societies cling to *tradition*, while people in industrial–capitalist societies endorse *rationality*.

By **tradition**, Weber meant *sentiments and beliefs passed from generation to generation*. Thus traditional societies are guided by the past. Their members evaluate particular actions as right and proper precisely because these actions have been accepted for so long.

People in modern societies take a different view of the world, argued Weber, embracing **rationality**, *deliberate, matter-of-fact calculation of the most efficient means to accomplish a particular goal*. Sentiment has no place in a rational world-view, which treats tradition simply as one kind of information. Typically, modern people choose to think and act on the basis of present and future consequences, evaluating jobs, schooling and even relationships in terms of what we put into them and what we expect to receive in return.

Weber viewed both the Industrial Revolution and capitalism as evidence of a historical surge of rationality. He used the phrase **rationalisation of society** to denote *the historical change from tradition to rationality as the dominant mode of human thought*. Modern society, he concluded, has been 'disenchanted', as scientific thinking and technology have swept away sentimental ties to the past.

The willingness to adopt the latest technology, then, is one good indicator of how rationalised a society is.

Drawing on Weber's comparative perspective we deduce that various societies place different values on technological advancement. What one society might herald as a breakthrough, another might deem unimportant, and a third might strongly oppose as a threat to tradition. Inventors in ancient Greece, for instance, devised many surprisingly elaborate mechanical devices to perform household tasks. But since elites were well served by slaves, they viewed such inventions as

PROFILE

MAX WEBER: EXPANDING THE BOUNDARIES OF SOCIOLOGY

To be called merely a 'sociologist' would probably have offended Max Weber. Not that he disliked the study of society; in fact, he spent most of his life doing just that. But Weber's contribution to understanding humanity is so broad and rich that no single discipline can claim him.

Born to a prosperous German family, Weber completed law school and set off on a legal career. But he soon felt confined by the work of a lawyer. Continuing his studies, he became a college professor. With his curiosity racing across the entire human condition, he compiled an amazing legacy of scholarship.

The influence of Weber's parents stands out in his work. His mother's devout Calvinism probably encouraged Weber's study of world religions and his classic study of Calvinism and its impact on industrial capitalism, which we take up shortly. From his father, a notable politician, Weber clearly gained insights into the workings of political life and bureaucracy.

Weber flirted with politics, and his wife Marianne was a leading feminist of her time. But Weber found politics to be incompatible with scholarly work. The former, he claimed, demands action and personal conviction, while the latter requires impartiality and patient reflection. Weber tried to resolve this personal dilemma by urging his colleagues to become involved in politics outside the classroom while striving for scientific neutrality in their professional work.

For many reasons, Weber's life was far from happy. He did not get on well with his father, and soon after his father's death Weber began to suffer from psychological problems. Illness sharply limited his ability to work during the remainder of his life. Even so, the exceptional number of major studies he conducted has led many to regard him as the most brilliant sociologist in history.

mere entertainment. In Europe today, many small communities are guided by their traditions to staunchly oppose modern technology.

In Weber's view, then, technological innovation is promoted or hindered by the way people understand their world. He concluded that people in many societies discovered keys to technological change; however, only in the rational cultural climate of Western Europe did people exploit these discoveries to spark the Industrial Revolution (Weber, 1958; orig. 1905).

Rationality, Calvinism and industrial capitalism

Is industrial capitalism a rational economic system? Here again, Weber and Marx were in debate. Weber considered industrial capitalism as the essence of rationality, since capitalists pursue profit in eminently rational ways. Marx, however, was critical of capitalism, arguing that it was the antithesis of rationality, and claiming that it failed to meet the basic needs of most of the people (Gerth and Mills, 1946: 49).

But, to look more closely at Weber's analysis, how did industrial capitalism emerge in the first place? Weber contended that industrial capitalism was the legacy of Calvinism – a Christian religious movement spawned by the Protestant Reformation. Calvinists, Weber explained, approached life in a highly disciplined and rational way. Moreover, central to the religious doctrine of John Calvin (1509–64) was *predestination*, the idea that an all-knowing and all-powerful God has preordained some people for salvation and others for damnation. With everyone's fate set before birth, Calvinists believed that people could do nothing to alter their destiny. Nor could they even know what their future would be. Thus the lives of Calvinists were framed by hopeful visions of eternal salvation and anxious fears of unending damnation.

For such people, not knowing one's fate was intolerable. Calvinists gradually came to a resolution of sorts. Why shouldn't those chosen for glory in the next world, they reasoned, see signs of divine favour in *this* world? Such a conclusion prompted Calvinists to interpret worldly prosperity as a sign of God's grace. Anxious to acquire this reassurance, Calvinists threw themselves into a quest for success, applying rationality, discipline and hard work to their tasks. This pursuit of riches was not for its own sake, of course, since self-indulgently spending money was clearly sinful. Calvinists also were little moved to share their wealth with the poor, because they saw poverty as a sign of God's rejection. Their ever-present duty was to carry forward what they held to be their personal *calling* from God (see Figure 4.4).

As they reinvested their profits for greater success, Calvinists built the foundation of capitalism. They piously used wealth to generate more wealth, practised personal thrift, and eagerly embraced whatever technological advances would bolster their efforts.

These traits, Weber explained, distinguished Calvinism from other world religions. Catholicism, the traditional religion in most of Europe, gave rise to a passive, 'otherworldly' view of life with hope of greater reward in the life to come. For Catholics, material wealth had none of the spiritual significance that so motivated Calvinists. And so it was, Weber concluded, that industrial capitalism became established primarily in areas of Europe where Calvinism had a strong hold.

Weber's study of Calvinism provides striking evidence of the power of ideas to shape society (versus Marx's contention that ideas merely reflect the process of economic production). But always sceptical of simple explanations, Weber knew that industrial capitalism had many roots. In fact, one purpose of this research was to counter Marx's narrow explanation of modern society in strictly economic terms.

As religious fervour weakened among later generations of Calvinists, Weber concluded, success-seeking personal discipline remained strong. A *religious* or, more precisely, *Protestant ethic* became simply a '*work* ethic'. From this point of view, industrial capitalism emerged as 'disenchanted' religion, with wealth now valued for its own sake. It is revealing that 'accounting', which to early Calvinists meant keeping a daily record of moral deeds, now refers simply to keeping track of money.

Rational social organisation

Weber contended that, by unleashing the Industrial Revolution and sparking the development of capitalism, rationality had defined the character of modern society. Rational social organisation confers the following seven traits on today's social life.

1. *Distinctive social institutions.* Among hunters and gatherers, the family was the centre of virtually all activities. Gradually, however, other social institutions, including religious, political and economic systems, broke away from family life. In modern societies, institutions of education and health care have also appeared. The separation of social institutions – each detailed in a later chapter – is a rational strategy to address human needs more efficiently.

2. *Large-scale organisations.* Modern rationality is exemplified by a proliferation of large-scale organisations. As early as the horticultural era, political officials oversaw religious observances, public works and warfare. In medieval Europe, the Catholic Church grew larger still with thousands of officials. In modern, rational societies, the employees of national governments may number in the millions, and most people work for a large organisation.

3. *Specialised tasks.* Unlike members of traditional societies, individuals in modern societies pursue a wide range of specialised activities. The enormous breadth of occupations can be seen in any city's *Yellow Pages*, which typically runs to more than 1,000 pages.

4. *Personal discipline.* Modern society puts a premium on self-directed discipline. For early Calvinists, of course, such an approach to life was rooted in religious belief. Although now distanced from its religious origins, discipline is still encouraged by cultural values such as achievement, success and efficiency.

An elective affinity between		**Figure 4.4**	The Protestant Ethic and the spirit of capitalism
The Protestant Ethic	**The Spirit of Capitalism**		
Working hard as a sign of grace	Relentless profit and hard work		
The 'Calling' and Earthly Duties	Rationality		
Salvation and predestination via 'good works'	Time is money – invest for profit		
Self-monitoring and self-control	Hard work profit motive		
Sins of waste and idleness	Importance of hard work and saving		

5. *Awareness of time*. In traditional societies, people measure time according to the rhythm of sun and seasons. Modern people, by contrast, schedule events precisely by the hour and minute. Interestingly, clocks began appearing in European cities some 500 years ago, just as commerce was starting to expand; soon, people began to think (to borrow Benjamin Franklin's phrase) that 'time is money'.

6. *Technical competence*. Members of traditional societies evaluate one another largely on the basis of *who* they are – how they are joined to others in the web of kinship. Modern rationality, by contrast, prompts us to judge people according to *what* they are – that is, with an eye towards their skills and abilities.

7. *Impersonality*. Finally, in a rational society, technical competence takes priority over close relationships, rendering the world impersonal. Modern social life can be viewed as the interplay of specialists concerned with particular tasks, rather than people broadly concerned with one another. Weber explained that we tend to devalue personal feelings and emotions as 'irrational' because they are often difficult to control.

Rationality and bureaucracy

Although the medieval church grew large, Weber argued that it was never entirely rational because its goal was to preserve tradition. Truly rational organisations, with the principal focus on efficiency, appeared only in the last few centuries. The organisational type that Weber called *bureaucracy* became pronounced along with capitalism as an expression of rationality.

Chapter 6 explains that bureaucracy is the model for modern businesses, government agencies, trades unions and universities. For now, note that Weber considered this organisational form to be the clearest expression of a rational world-view because its chief elements – offices, duties and policies – are intended to achieve specific goals as efficiently as possible. By contrast, the inefficiency of traditional organisation is reflected in its hostility to change. In short, Weber asserted that bureaucracy transformed all of society in the same way that industrialisation transformed the economy.

Still, Weber emphasised that rational bureaucracy has a special affinity to capitalism. He wrote:

> Today, it is primarily the capitalist market economy which demands that the official business of public administration be discharged precisely, unambiguously, continuously, and with as much speed as possible. Normally, the very large capitalist enterprises are themselves unequalled models of strict bureaucratic organisation.
>
> (1978: 974; orig. 1921)

Rationality and alienation

Max Weber joined with Karl Marx in recognising the unparalleled efficiency of industrial capitalism. Weber also shared Marx's conclusion that modern society generates widespread alienation, though for different reasons. For Weber, the primary problem is not the economic inequality that so troubled Marx, but the stifling regulation and dehumanisation that comes with expanding bureaucracy. It leads to an increasing 'disenchantment with the world'.

Bureaucracies, Weber warned, treat people as a series of cases rather than as unique individuals. In addition, working for large organisations demands highly specialised and often tedious routines. In the end, Weber envisaged modern society as a vast and growing system of rules seeking to regulate everything and threatening to crush the human spirit.

An irony found in the work of Marx reappears in Weber's thinking: rather than serve humanity, modern society turns on its creators and enslaves them. In language reminiscent of Marx's description of the human toll of industrial capitalism, Weber portrayed the modern individual as 'only a small cog in a ceaselessly moving mechanism that prescribes to him an endlessly fixed routine of march' (1978: 988; orig. 1921). Thus, knowing well the advantages of modern society, Weber ended his life deeply pessimistic. He feared that the rationalisation of society would end up reducing people to robots.

Emile Durkheim: the bonds that tie us together: from mechanical to organic

'To love society is to love something beyond us and something in ourselves.' These are the words of Emile Durkheim (1858–1917), another architect of sociology, introduced in the Profile box. This curious phrase (1974: 55; orig. 1924) distils one more influential vision of human society.

EMILE DURKHEIM: UNMASKING THE POWER OF SOCIETY

Why would being a professor of sociology be controversial? Because there weren't any, at least not in France, until Emile Durkheim became the first one in 1887. Up to that time, the study of human behaviour was left to biologists and psychologists. But Durkheim made the assertion – widely disputed at the time – that one can understand people, not by looking at individuals, but only by examining their society.

Durkheim's investigation of suicide, detailed in Chapter 1, offers persuasive evidence of society's power to shape human behaviour. In this classic study, Durkheim showed that people's place within the social system – as women or men, rich or poor, Catholic, Jew or Protestant – affects even this most personal act.

Durkheim's work, like that of Marx and Weber, is discussed in many later chapters. His contributions to the understanding of crime figure prominently in Chapter 16. Durkheim also spent much of his life investigating religion, which he held to be a key foundation of social integration (see Chapter 18). Just as important, Durkheim is also one of the major architects of the structural–functional paradigm, which we refer to in almost every chapter that follows.

Structure: society beyond ourselves

First and foremost, Emile Durkheim recognised that society exists beyond ourselves. Society is more than the individuals who compose it; society has a life of its own that stretches beyond our personal experiences. It was here long before we were born, it makes claims on us while we are alive, and it will remain long after we are gone. Patterns of human behaviour, Durkheim explained, form established *structures*; they are *social facts* that have an objective reality beyond the lives and perceptions of particular individuals. Cultural norms, values, religious beliefs – all endure as social facts.

And because society looms larger than individual lives, it has the *power* to shape our thoughts and actions, Durkheim noted. So studying individuals alone (as psychologists or biologists do) can never capture the essence of human experience. Society is more than the sum of its parts; it exists as a complex organism rooted in our collective life. A reception class in a primary school, a family sharing a meal, people milling about a country auction – all are examples of the countless situations that set an organisation apart from any particular individual who has ever participated in them.

Once created by people, then, society takes on a momentum of its own, confronting its creators and demanding a measure of obedience. For our part, we experience society's influence as we come to see the order in our lives or as we face temptation and feel the tug of morality.

Function: society in action

Having established that society has structure, Durkheim turned to the concept of *function*. The significance of any social fact, he explained, extends beyond individuals to the operation of society itself.

To illustrate, consider crime. Most people think of lawbreaking as harmful acts that some individuals inflict on others. But, looking beyond individuals, Durkheim saw that crime has a vital function for the ongoing life of society itself. As Chapter 16 explains, only by recognising and responding to acts as criminal do people construct and defend morality, which gives necessary shape to our collective life. For this reason, Durkheim rejected the common view of crime as 'pathological'. On the contrary, he concluded, crime is quite 'normal' for the most basic of reasons: a society could not exist without it (1964a, orig. 1895; 1964b, orig. 1893).

Personality: society in ourselves

Durkheim contended that society is not only 'beyond ourselves', it is also 'in ourselves'. Each of us, in short, builds a personality by internalising social facts. How we act, think and feel – our essential humanity – is drawn from the society that nurtures us. Moreover, Durkheim explained, society regulates human beings through moral discipline. Durkheim held that human beings are naturally insatiable and in constant danger of being overpowered by our own desires: 'The more one has, the more one wants, since satisfactions received only stimulate instead of filling needs' (1966: 248; orig. 1897). Having given us life, then, society must also instil restraints in us.

Nowhere is the need for societal regulation better illustrated than in Durkheim's study of suicide (1966; orig. 1897), detailed in Chapter 1. Why is it that, over the years, rock stars have been so vulnerable to self-destruction? Durkheim had the answer long before anyone made electric music: it is the *least* regulated categories of people that suffer the *highest* rates of suicide. The greater licence afforded to those who are young, rich and famous exacts a high price in terms of the risk of suicide.

Modernity and anomie

Compared to traditional societies, modern societies impose fewer restrictions on everyone. Durkheim acknowledges the advantages of modern freedom, but he warned of a rise in **anomie**, *a condition in which society provides little moral guidance to individuals*. What so many celebrities describe as 'almost being destroyed by their fame' is one extreme example of the corrosive effects of anomie. Sudden fame tears people away from their families and familiar routines, disrupting society's support and regulation of an individual, sometimes with fatal results. Durkheim instructs us, therefore, that the desires of the individual must be balanced by the claims and guidance of society – a balance that has become precarious in the modern world.

Evolving societies: the division of labour

Like Marx and Weber, Durkheim witnessed at first hand the rapid social transformation of Europe during the nineteenth century. Analysing this change, Durkheim saw a sweeping evolution in the forms of social organisation.

In pre-industrial societies, explained Durkheim, strong tradition operates as the social cement that binds people together. In fact, what he termed the *collective conscience* is so strong that the community moves quickly to punish anyone who dares to challenge conventional ways of life. Durkheim called this system **mechanical solidarity**, meaning *social bonds, based on shared morality, that unite members of pre-industrial societies*. In practice, then, mechanical solidarity springs from *likeness*. Durkheim described these bonds as 'mechanical' because people feel a more or less automatic sense of belonging together.

Durkheim considered the decline of mechanical solidarity to be a defining trait of modern society. But this does not mean that society dissolves; rather, modernity generates a new type of solidarity that rushes into the void left by discarded traditions. Durkheim called this new social integration **organic solidarity**, defined as *social bonds, based on specialisation, that unite members of industrial societies*. In short, where solidarity was once rooted in likeness, it now flows from *differences* among people whose specialised pursuits make them rely on one another.

For Durkheim, then, the key dimension of change is a society's expanding **division of labour**, or *specialised economic activity*. As Max Weber explained, modern societies specialise in order to promote efficiency. Durkheim fills in the picture by showing us that members of modern societies count on the efforts of tens of thousands of others – most of them complete strangers – to secure the goods and services they need every day.

So modernity rests far less on *moral consensus* (the foundation of traditional societies) and far more on *functional interdependence*. That is, as members of modern societies, we depend more and more on people we trust less and less. Why, then, should we put our faith in people we hardly know and whose beliefs may differ radically from our own? Durkheim's answer: 'Because we can't live without them'. In a world in which morality sometimes seems like so much shifting sand, then, we confront what might be called 'Durkheim's dilemma': the technological power and expansive personal freedom of modern society come only at the cost of receding morality and the ever-present danger of anomie.

Like Marx and Weber, Durkheim had misgivings about the direction society was taking. But, of the three, Durkheim was the most optimistic. Confidence in the future sprang from his hope that we could enjoy greater freedom and privacy while creating for ourselves the social regulation that had once been forced on us by tradition.

Reviewing the theories

How have societies changed?

We started with a view – sociocultural evolution, furthest developed by the North American sociologists Gerhard and Jean Lenski (Lenski *et al.*, 1995) – in which societies differ primarily in terms of changing technology. Modern society stands out in this regard because of its enormous productive power. Karl Marx also stressed historical differences in productive systems, yet pointed to the persistence of social conflict throughout human history (except perhaps among simple hunters and gatherers). For Marx, modern society is capitalist, and is distinctive because it brings that conflict out in the open.

Max Weber looked at this question from another perspective, tracing evolving modes of thought. Pre-industrial societies, he claimed, are guided by tradition, while modern societies espouse a rational world-view. Bureaucracies take on a key role. Finally, for Emile Durkheim, traditional societies are characterised by mechanical solidarity based on moral consensus. In industrial societies, mechanical solidarity gives way to organic solidarity based on productive specialisation.

Why do societies change?

Marx's materialist approach pointed to the struggle between social classes as the 'engine of history', pushing societies towards revolutionary reorganisation. Weber's idealist view argues that modes of thought also contribute to social change. He demonstrated how rational Calvinism bolstered the Industrial Revolution, which in turn reshaped much of modern society. Finally, Durkheim pointed to an expanding division of labour as the key dimension of social change.

What holds societies together?

Marx spotlighted social division, not unity, treating class conflict as the hallmark of human societies throughout history. From his point of view, elites may force an uneasy peace between the classes, but true social unity would emerge only if production were to become a truly cooperative endeavour. To Weber, members of a society share a distinctive world-view. Just as traditional beliefs joined people together in the past, so modern societies have created rational, large-scale organisations with their own organisational cultures that fuse and guide people's lives. Finally, Durkheim made solidarity the focus of his work, contrasting the morality-based mechanical solidarity of pre-industrial societies with modern society's more practical organic solidarity.

Where are societies heading?

Finally, there is the question of where society may now be headed (see the Controversy and Debate box). For Marx, capitalism would generate the seeds of its own destruction: revolutionary change should bring about a new communist social order. In general, however, attempts to bring about a communist order during the twentieth century in the old Soviet Union and China were not successes. For Weber, there was a strong pessimistic streak: he saw the world as an Iron Cage, with growing rationality creating an ever-spreading 'disenchantment with the world'. Durkheim held out hope for new forms of association to emerge that would bind people together through their differences and resolve the problem of anomie. We will evaluate these views as we move through the book.

Like a kaleidoscope that shows us different patterns as we turn it, these approaches reveal an array of insights into society. Yet no one approach is, in an absolute sense, right or wrong. Society is exceedingly complex, and we gain the richest understanding from using all of these visions, as we do in the European Eye box (see also Table 4.3 on page 98).

CONTROVERSY AND DEBATE

IS OUR SOCIETY GETTING BETTER OR WORSE? THE PROBLEM OF PROGRESS

A major contrast between the USA and Europe is the former's sense of optimism. In Europe, generally, burdened by the sense of a long and troubled history, the fate of humankind is often looked upon with fore-boding. Much of its intellectual tradition highlights critique, disenchantment, cynicism, despair and pessimism. Weber, for instance, wrote of the 'disen-chantment of the world'. Freud, introduced in Chapter 7, saw civilisation as advancing at the cost of human happiness. And, perhaps most significant, the last 100 years have been the tragic century that witnessed two world wars and the Holocaust. In contrast, optimism has been a key trait of US society: as time goes on, life gets better.

Robert Nisbet (1989) has argued that one of the defining features of modernity has been a belief in progress, often in spite of problems. Indeed, Swedish sociologist Therborn also sees this as the key in dis-

CONTROVERSY AND DEBATE CONTINUED

tinguishing between premodernity, modernity and postmodernity. Progress is the definer of the modern world. He writes:

> Pre-modernity is looking back over its shoulder, to the past, to the latter's example of wisdom, beauty, glory, and to the experiences of the past. Modernity looks to the future, hopes for it, plans for it, constructs it, builds it. Post-modernity has lost or thrown away any sense of direction. . . . Modernity ends when words like progress, advance, development, emancipation, liberation, growth, accumulation, enlightenment, embetterment, avant-garde, lose their attraction and their function as guides to social action.
>
> (Therborn, 1995: 4)

So is there progress or has it come to an end as we move into the twenty-first century? Just what's going on here?

To begin, we can point to some good reasons for society's belief in progress. Since the beginning of the twentieth century, for example, the scope of education has expanded to an unprecedented level. Moreover, even taking account of inflation, average income and national productivity have grown significantly. In addition, back in 1900, it was a rare home that had a telephone and, outside large cities, none had access to electricity. No one had even heard of television, and cars were still on the drawing boards. Today, almost every Western home is served by a telephone, a host of electric appliances, one or more television sets, and a DVD player; many also are equipped with satellite or cable TV. Most important of all, people born in 1900 lived an average of just 47 years; children born today can look forward to 30 additional years of life.

But some trends, especially during the last 25 years, have been troubling. It is true that some countries seem to be enjoying higher standards of living, and so on, but is this at the expense of others? Contrasts of inequality are massive, as Chapters 8–10 will show. To give one figure from these chapters: 20 per cent of the world (some 1 billion people) lack the nutrition to work regularly, and 800 million are at risk for their lives. Add to this problems of cities, of pollution, of media, of environment, of risk, of crime, and so on. Rising crime rates have under-

mined people's sense of personal safety, even in their own homes. Our relative affluence, coupled with our capacity to move farther and faster than ever before, seems to have eroded our sense of responsibility for others, unleashing a wave of individualism that often comes across as unbridled selfishness. As a result, not only is pessimism on the rise, but many people have been losing confidence in the direction of society.

So, which is it? Is society getting better or worse?

The theorists whose ideas we have examined in this chapter shed some light on this question. It is easy to equate 'high tech' with 'progress'. But we should make such assumptions cautiously, the Lenskis maintain, because history shows us that, while advancing technology does offer real advantages, it is no guarantee of a 'better' life. Marx, Weber and Durkheim also acknowledged the growing affluence of societies over time; yet each offered a pointed criticism of modern society because of a dangerous tendency towards individualism. For Marx, capitalism is the culprit, elevating money to godlike status and fostering a culture of selfishness. Weber's analysis claims that the modern spirit of rationality wears away traditional ties of kinship and neighbourhood while expanding bureaucracy, which, he warned, both manipulates and isolates people. In Durkheim's view, functional interdependence joins members of modern societies, who are less and less able to establish a common moral framework within which to judge right and wrong.

In the end, what human societies gain through technological advances may be offset, to some extent, by the loss of human community.

CONTINUE THE DEBATE:

1. Draw up a balance sheet of 'progress' in the modern world. Do you think life in the modern world is getting better or worse? What evidence can you produce for your argument?

2. Is our society's increasing level of affluence good? What might Marx, Weber and Durkheim say?

3. Do you think people in low-income countries are aware of the 'advances' in Europe or the United States? Would they see them as advances?

WHAT IS EUROPEAN SOCIETY?

Marx, Weber and Durkheim – discussed in this chapter – were not just seeking to understand the nature of industrial societies; they were Europeans largely in search of understanding industrial Europe. But it is hard to know quite what 'Europe' is. Before going on, make a list of ways you might define Europe, and ponder what are its common elements and what are its differences.

In one sense it is hard to see Europe as anything coherent. There are over 40 countries, and even more languages. They are scattered over diverse climates – from Scandinavia to the Mediterranean – and diverse cultures – from 'Spanish' to 'Nordic'. There are diverse histories, rituals, politics, economic systems and religions. Northern Europe has more individualistic values than southern Europe and Ireland (where religious values are stronger). It is hard to see what the Nordic cultures of Denmark, Finland, Sweden and Norway have in common with the cultures of Spain, Italy or Portugal. And within each of these countries there are internal splits and differing ethnic groups (France has Algerians; Germany has guest workers; and the United Kingdom has Scots, Welsh and Irish alongside people of Asian and Afro-Caribbean descent). Most introductory UK textbooks ignore the diversity of this Europe and focus on the one voice of England (often with a diluted voice from North America). But clearly the English voice is not the French voice or

the Norwegian one. Yet despite this, people speak of a European society. What can be meant by this?

One way is to search for some common elements. A common history, common lands and geography and – perhaps – some broad common, cultural elements that could be seen as similar. It may indeed be what Benedict Anderson has called an 'imagined community', held together by a common sense of history and culture (Anderson, 1989). In part this may be because most of these cultures have deep values that link to being the first industrialising countries, the first modern democratic cultures and the first Christian cultures. As we will see, these values are pervasive. Taken together, it may be, as Agnes Heller argues, that 'European culture is modernity – cumulative knowledge and progress, technology and wealth – along with nation states and ideas of freedom and equality' (Wintle, 1996: 11).

Another way is to approach them as countries themselves seeking to be united. Since the Second World War (itself a curiously unifying factor), there have been persistent attempts to create a European Union. Starting with the Congress of Europe in 1948 at The Hague, the European Union has grown through many stages, as shown in Table 4.2. In 1951 Jean Monnet called the European Coal and Steel Community 'the first expression of the Europe that is being born'. But this involved only six countries: Belgium, France, Italy, West Germany, Luxembourg and The Netherlands. The chart and the map

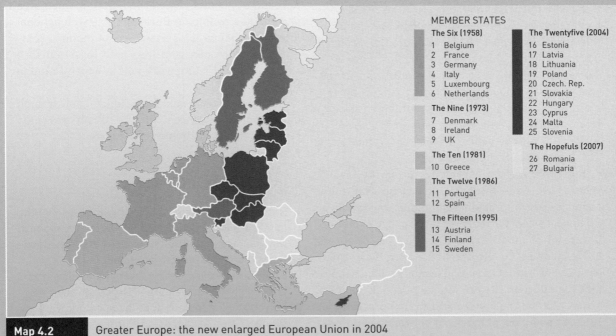

MEMBER STATES

The Six (1958)
1 Belgium
2 France
3 Germany
4 Italy
5 Luxembourg
6 Netherlands

The Nine (1973)
7 Denmark
8 Ireland
9 UK

The Ten (1981)
10 Greece

The Twelve (1986)
11 Portugal
12 Spain

The Fifteen (1995)
13 Austria
14 Finland
15 Sweden

The Twentyfive (2004)
16 Estonia
17 Latvia
18 Lithuania
19 Poland
20 Czech. Rep.
21 Slovakia
22 Hungary
23 Cyprus
24 Malta
25 Slovenia

The Hopefuls (2007)
26 Romania
27 Bulgaria

Map 4.2   Greater Europe: the new enlarged European Union in 2004
A geography of the European Union – a regional and economic perspective.

aim to give some sense of the European Union's growth in the past, and also the projected plans for the future.

To date, Britain has been an 'awkward partner' in Europe. Until the election of a Labour government on 1 May 1997, successive Conservative governments were the embodiment of 'euroscepticism'. Currently, the UK government adopts a generally more favourable stance, though at the time of writing, it has just announced that there will be a referendum on the European Constitution in 2006.

Table 4.2	Some landmarks in the making of the European Union

April 1951 Treaty of Paris establishes the European Coal and Steel Community (with France, West Germany, Italy, Belgium, The Netherlands and Luxembourg). Britain does not join

March 1957 Treaties of Rome, signed again by the above six, establish the European Economic Community and the European Atomic Energy Community. Also includes new parliament and new court and eliminates customs duties among member states

1 January 1958 Treaties of Rome become law. In effect, this is the start of the European Economic Community (EEC)

1964 Common agricultural policy established with uniform prices to start in 1967

22 January 1972 The United Kingdom, Denmark, Ireland and Norway admitted to membership from January 1973. Conservative government in the UK with Prime Minister Edward Heath takes Britain into the EEC, but a referendum in Norway rejects membership

June 1975 Labour government in UK wishes to withdraw and holds a referendum: 67% of voters decide they want to stay in

December 1975 Elected European Parliament planned to start in 1979. No powers to introduce legislation, but powers to advise

1978 Members agree to ECU (European Currency Unit)

1 January 1981 Greece becomes tenth member

January 1983 Common fishing policy

January 1985 First European passports issued. Jacques Delors is first president of European Commission

January 1986 Spain and Portugal join

February 1986 The Single Act; streamlining, with legalisation now passed by a majority

October 1990 Former East Germany becomes part of the Community

October 1991 European Free Trade Association (EFTA – Austria, Finland, Iceland, Liechtenstein, Norway, Sweden, Switzerland) agrees an extended cooperation project – the European Economic Area (EEA) – within the Community and EFTA, creating an integrated trade area

November 1991 Associations with Poland, Hungary and Czechoslovakia (but stopping short of full membership)

1992 The internal market

Maastricht: the Treaty on European Union established a single market with free movement of goods and capital, as well as a Charter of Social Rights

1 January 1995 Austria, Finland and Sweden join the EU, bringing membership to 15

June 1997 Treaty of Amsterdam concluded and launched in 1999

March 1998 EU opens negotiations with Cyprus, Czech Republic, Estonia, Hungary, Poland and Slovenia. New Agricultural policy – a ban on member states subsidising their own farmers

1 July 1998 European Central Bank inaugurated in Frankfurt

1 January 1999 Single monetary policy – the Euro; responsibility of European System of Central Banks. Launched by participating countries: all EU except Denmark, Sweden and the UK

March 1999 The Amsterdam Treaty: EU's new constitution

1 January 2000 Circulation of Euro banknotes and coins

Early 2002 Legal tender of national currencies withdrawn in most EU member states; the Euro becomes the currency. UK, Denmark and Sweden do not adopt Euro

1 May 2004 Enlargement of EU with ten new members, seven of which had lived under the Third Reich or Stalinist Communism. Estonia, Latvia and Lithuania were part of the former Soviet Union. Poland, Hungary, Slovakia and the Czech Republic were satellites under the Warsaw Pact. Slovenia had been part of socialist Yugoslavia. In addition, there are the islands of Malta and Cyprus

2007 Romania and Bulgaria set to join

http://europa.eu.int/abc/history/2003/ index-en.htm

Table 4.3	The classic theorists briefly contrasted		
	Marx	**Weber**	**Durkheim**
Type of society	Capitalism	Capitalism/rational bureaucratic	Organic solidarity
Source of change	Economic conflicts	Religion and ideas	Population density
The future	Revolutionary change – communism – optimistic	Iron Cage Disenchantment of the world – pessimistic	Breakdown and anomie, search for new guilds/ communities

The contemporary shape of world societies

We have looked at some of the range of world societies in the past and have considered some of the main explanations given for the rise of the modern industrial world. In this section, we now take a very quick tour of the contemporary world, introducing a few key themes before exploring them more fully in later chapters. You may also like to look at the map on the inside back cover, which suggests some of the major social regions of the world.

The world around 2005

The world population reached 6.4 billion in mid-2004 and is projected to peak at 9 billion in 2070. At the start of the twenty-first century, world societies could be divided in several ways.

Nation states

There are around 200 well-identified nation states (one indication of a society). There have been major shifts in power. The end of the 'Cold War', which dominated politics in the last half-century, led to the break-up of four multi-ethnic states: the USSR, Czechoslovakia, Yugoslavia and Ethiopia: over 20 new independent states emerged (Halliday, 2001: 9). But along with break-ups and fragmentations also came reunification: East Germany with West Germany, Hong Kong with the People's Republic of China, as well as the growth of a much more unified Europe through the European Union (see European Eye box p96–7).

Languages

There are up to 10,000 spoken languages. Since spoken languages indicate groups, it may be better to take the latter as an indicator of the range of societies functioning on planet earth. Thus, there are still a number of much smaller, usually indigenous, peoples who have maintained something of their own society. Thus, the languages of the native American Indians (numbering around 300), or of the Australian aboriginal peoples (about 250 are documented), help us sense something of the diversity of societies of the past and outside the 'nation state' systems of today (Crystal, 1997: 322–326).

First, Second and Third Worlds

There are a number of other ways of approaching world societies. After the Second World War, and until the collapse of the Soviet Union in 1991, it became a tradition to classify societies as 'First World' (the rich, industrialised countries), 'Second World' (less rich and often socialist) and 'Third World' (poor, 'developing'). Although widely used for decades, this 'three worlds' model has generally lost validity in recent years. It was a product of Cold War politics by which the capitalist West (the First World) confronted the socialist East (the Second World), while the rest of the world (the Third World) remained more or less on the sidelines. But the sweeping transformation of Eastern Europe and the former Soviet Union in the early 1990s meant that there no longer existed a distinctive Second World. Just as important, the superpower opposition that defined the Cold War has faded in recent years.

This model also lumped together in the Third World more than 100 countries at different levels of development. Some relatively better-off nations of the Third World (such as Chile in South America) have ten times the per-person productivity of the poorest countries of the world (including Ethiopia in eastern Africa). Most countries now also contain their own 'fourth worlds' – a term introduced by the World Bank in 1978 to refer to the very poorest of countries, and even the very poorest within wealthier countries.

Critics often see this characterisation as outmoded: too linked to the past conflicts of societies. They often prefer to refer to low-, medium- and high-income societies.

High-, medium- and low-income societies

Map 4.3(a) provides a visual guide to the relative economic development of the world's countries. The world's **high-income countries** are *industrialised nations in which most people enjoy material abundance.*[1] The largest and richest countries are known as the G8 ('group of eight') and embrace the USA, Japan, Germany, France, the UK, Italy, Canada and (more recently) Russia. They have been meeting since the 1970s to discuss the global economy. High-income countries include the United States and Canada, most of Western Europe, and Israel, Japan and Australia. Taken together, these 40 societies generate most of the world's goods and services and control most of the planet's wealth. On average, individuals in these countries live well, not because they are particularly bright or exceptionally hard-working, but because they had the good fortune to be born in an affluent region of the world.

A second category of societies comprises the world's **middle-income countries**, which are *nations characterised by limited industrialisation and moderate personal income.* Individuals living in any of the roughly 90 nations at this level of economic development – including some of the countries of Eastern Europe and most of Latin America – are more likely to live in rural areas than in cities, to walk or to ride bicycles, scooters or animals rather than to drive automobiles, and to receive only a few years of schooling. Most middle-income countries also have marked social inequality, so that while a few people are extremely rich (Hollywood superstars or sheiks of oil-producing nations in the Middle East, for example), many more lack safe housing and adequate nutrition.

Finally, about half of the world's people live in the 60 **low-income countries**, which are *nations with little industrialisation in which severe poverty is the rule.* As Map 4.3(a) shows, most of the poorest societies in the world are in Africa and Asia. Here again, a small number of

people in each of these nations are rich; but the majority barely get by with poor housing, unsafe water, too little food, little or no sanitation and, perhaps most seriously of all, little chance to improve their lives.

But the map is constantly changing, and one of the most significant recent developments is the emergence of **newly industrialising countries** (often called NICs), *lower-income countries that are fast becoming high-income ones.* A cluster of (mainly) Southeast Asian countries are making rapid economic progress. These countries include Hong Kong, Singapore, South Korea, Thailand and Taiwan. Some commentators have suggested that this new 'Asian Way' has been adopting different industrialisation patterns from those traditionally found in the West, and that they are indeed likely to become the trailblazers for the twenty-first century (Naisbitt, 1997).

The Human Development Index

An increasingly common way of looking at world societies is based on discussions around the Human Development Index (HDI). First used in 1990 by the United Nations Development Programme (and subsequently published annually in their *Human Development Report*), this is a composite figure bridging three main issues across all the countries for which relevant data are available. These are (a) **longevity** – life expectancy at birth; (b) **knowledge** – adult literacy rate and enrolment in schooling; and (c) **decent standards of living** – adjusted income per head. Of course, there are many critical problems in using such composite figures: statistics need very careful interpretation, especially across cultures. Map 4.3 (b) shows their regional distribution, and in Table 9.2 (Chapter 9) a listing of many countries on the Human Development Index scale in 2003 is provided. You may like to turn to this now so that some major preliminary points can be made:

- Of the 175 countries listed, 55 score high HDIs, 85 have medium HDIs and 34 have low HDIs.

- Norway, Iceland, Australia, Sweden and the Netherlands rank as the top five; Sierre Leone, Niger, Burundi, Burkina Faso and Mali are at the bottom. Turkey, Brazil, the Russian Federation, Iran, China, Egypt, India and South Africa are all medium countries.

- The United States is seventh; Japan is ninth; the United Kingdom is thirteenth; Italy and Spain are twenty-first and nineteenth respectively; and Ireland is twelfth.

- East Asia and the Pacific have made sustained advances in development over the past 30 years; but

---

[1] The text uses this terminology as opposed to the traditional, but outdated, terms 'First World', 'Second World' and 'Third World' for reasons described above. There are other classifications too, like **the North and the South.** In this classification, the North is usually identified with wealthier countries and the South with poorer ones. Or **the West and the East.** Again the West signifies the more prosperous, but also a major cultural difference since the East also incorporates much of Asia and hence a major cultural/religious difference, often discussed as 'Asian Values'.

SOCIAL SHAPES OF THE WORLD

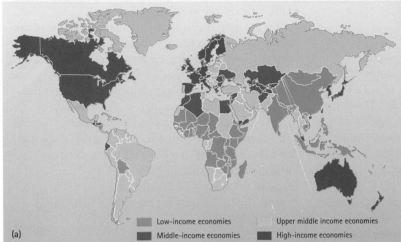

(a)

Low-income economies

Middle-income economies

Upper middle income economies

High-income economies

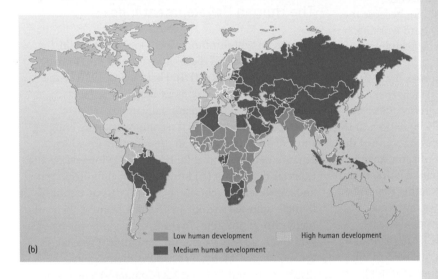

(b)

Low human development

Medium human development

High human development

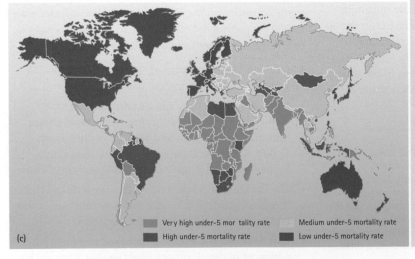

(c)

Very high under-5 mortality rate

High under-5 mortality rate

Medium under-5 mortality rate

Low under-5 mortality rate

Map 4.3   Three views of the world

(a) shows the world ranked by income (GNP per capita) and is discussed further in Chapter 9.

(b) shows the world according to the Human Development Index of the UN Development Programme.

(c) shows infant mortality rates and is relevant to Chapters 13 and 23. These maps are presented here to give a general impression and to stimulate discussion about world development.

Source: New Internationalist (2001/02), New Internationalist Publications, p. 43, compiled from data provided by (a) the World Bank, (b) the United Nations, and (c) UNICEF.

South Asia and sub-Saharan Africa lag far behind. In 1999, life expectancy in the latter was only 48.8 years, and the share of people living on less than one US dollar per day is around 46 per cent, whereas in East Asia, the Pacific and Latin America it is around 15 per cent.

- The Arab states also lag behind but have been making the most rapid progress. (UNDP, 2003)

Manuel Castells has commented that:

> for the population [of the world] as a whole, only the former Soviet Union (after the collapse of Stalinism) and Sub-Saharan Africa (after its marginalization from capitalism) have experienced a decline in living conditions.
>
> (Castells, 1989: 70–71)

At the same time, as we shall see in Chapter 9, the world has generally grown more polarised and more unequal.

The third map in the series, Map 4.3(c), shows countries ranked by the under-five infant mortality rate and is more relevant to Chapters 13, 20 and 23.

Classifying the approximately 200 nations on earth into any categories ignores pronounced differences in their ways of life. Countries have rich and varied histories, speak hundreds of languages and encompass diverse peoples, proud of their cultural distinctiveness.

Conclusion: Change and societies

This chapter has aimed to introduce you to a range of different kinds of society from both the past and the present and to suggest how they have come about and how they might be changing. For much of history, world societies have been dominated by hunting, gathering, horticultural and agrarian societies. What we have witnessed over the past few centuries has been a major shift into a capitalist, technological and 'modern' world. Such societies were the key focus of early sociologists such as Marx, Durkheim and Weber. Recently, many industrial societies seem to be entering yet another phase of society linked to computer technologies and globalisation.

As the book moves along, we shall try to appraise just what some of the more recent changes mean: whether indeed they do signpost a major new form of society in the making. The final chapter of this book will turn to a further assessment of this issue.

Aborigines with a laptop

Source: NYC/Corbis © Robert Essel

SUMMARY

1. In the work of the Lenskis, five kinds of society have been outlined as linked to sociocultural evolution and technology. The earliest *hunting and gathering* societies were composed of a small number of family-centred nomads. Horticulture began some 12,000 years ago as people devised hand tools for the cultivation of crops.

Pastoral societies domesticate animals and engage in extensive trade. *Agriculture*, about 5,000 years old, is large-scale cultivation traditionally using animal-drawn ploughs. This technology allows societies to grow into vast empires, making them more productive, more specialised and more unequal. *Industrial* societies began 250 years ago in Europe as people harnessed advanced energy sources to power sophisticated machinery. In *post-industrial, information* societies, enterprise shifts from the production of material things to the creation and dissemination of information; computers and other information-based technology replace the heavy machinery of the industrial era.

2. **Karl Marx**'s materialist analysis pointed to historical and contemporary conflict between social classes. Conflict in 'ancient' societies involved masters and slaves; in agrarian societies, it places nobles and serfs in opposition; in industrial–capitalist societies, capitalists confront the proletariat. Industrial capitalism alienates workers: from the act of working, from the products of work, from fellow workers, and from human potential. Once workers had overcome their own false consciousness, Marx believed they would overthrow capitalists and the industrial–capitalist system.

3. **Max Weber**'s idealist approach reveals that modes of thought have a powerful effect on society. Weber drew a sharp contrast between the tradition of pre-industrial societies and the rationality of modern, industrial societies. Weber feared that rationality, embodied in efficiency-conscious bureaucratic organisations, would stifle human creativity.

4. **Emile Durkheim** explained that society has an objective existence apart from individuals. His approach relates social elements to the larger society through their functions. Traditional societies are fused by mechanical solidarity based on moral consensus; modern societies depend on organic solidarity based on the division of labour or productive specialisation.

5. The contemporary world is composed of around 200 societies, which can be classified in various ways, including North and South, East and West, and low-, medium- and high-income societies.

6. The Human Development Index (HDI) has become one way of looking at world societies. This is a United Nations measurement which collates three issues: longevity, knowledge (or education) and standard of living.

CRITICAL-THINKING QUESTIONS

1. Draw up a balance sheet of the pros and cons of various technologies, and then discuss whether technological change amounts to 'progress'.

2. Examine the situation of any one contemporary indigenous people – such as the Innu. Is their way of life likely to survive into the future? (hint: see Samson, 2003).

3. Contrast the theories of Marx, Durkheim and Weber on the emergence of the modern world. Which do you find most helpful – and why?

4. Discuss some of the major features of contemporary world societies. What seem to be the major conflicts and issues for the twenty-first century?

GOING FURTHER

Further reading

On evolution:

Colin Tudge's, *The Day Before Yesterday: Five Million Years of Human History* (1995)
For the long historical view of the evolution of society – going back a mere five million years! – a highly readable account.

Michael Cook, *A Brief History of the Human Race* (2004)
An acclaimed book that throws much light on the emergence of different societies.

Hugh Brody, *The Other Side of Eden: Hunters, Farmers and the Shaping of the Modern World* (2000)
Provides a lively and affectionate account of the hunter-gatherer societies.

Barry Lopez, *Arctic Dreams* (1986)
An account of society in the Arctic which shows the high level of technological sophistication among Arctic people.

These last two books are useful correctives to any view that discounts 'traditional peoples'.

On modernity:

Krishan Kumar, *Prophecy and Progress: The Sociology of Industrial and Post-Industrial Society* (1978)
Takes further much of the discussion in this chapter.

Krishan Kumar, *From Post-Industrial to Post-Modern Society: New Theories of the Contemporary World* (1995)
Reviews current debates on the future of societies.

Gary Browning, Abigail Halci and Frank Webster (eds), *Understanding Contemporary Society: Theories of the Present* (2000)

Provides 33 short articles to introduce the reader to all the key aspects of modern and postmodern societies.

On the twentieth century:

Eric Hobsbawm, *Age of Extremes: The Short Twentieth Century*, 1914–1991 (1994)
This is a full account of the history of the world during the twentieth century, and leaves one at the very least being cautious about any simple view of progress.

Fred Halliday, *The World at 2000* (2001).
For a concise and stimulating review of world societies.

On Europe:

Goran Therborn, *European Modernity and Beyond: The Trajectory of European Societies, 1945–2000* (1995)
The most important sociological study of Europe to date is by a leading Swedish sociologist.

Colin Crouch, *Social Change in Western Europe* (1999)
A very valuable, if dense, guide to Western Europe.

Both of these books are quite hardgoing and not easy for beginners.

More information

The statistics profile of Europe can be found in Eurostat, *The Eurostat Yearbook* (annual), *and Demographic Statistics* (annual). Regular bulletins – *Employment Bulletin, Women of Europe*, etc. – are produced through the European Commission's offices in Brussels and Luxembourg.

Watch a video

- Ingmar Bergman's *The Seventh Seal* (1956–57): looks at the forces of life and death through a medieval knight returning from the crusades. See also his *Wild Strawberries* (1957) which examines the meanings of life in society
- Satyajit Ray's trilogy *The World of Apu* (1959) – *Pather Panchali, Aparajito* and *Apur Sansar*: examines the growth of a young Indian boy through childhood, rural youth and city adult life
- Luis Buñuel's surrealist films – especially *The Discreet Charm of the Bourgeoisie* (1972), *The Phantom of Liberty* (1974) and *That Obscure Object of Desire* (1977): turn many of the assumptions about society on their head
- Nicolas Roeg's *Walkabout* (1971): contrasts white and aboriginal children's world-views in the Australian outback.

Connecting up

Connect to other chapters

- The work of Marx, Durkheim and Weber is discussed in many chapters of the book and themed on the website.
- Discussion of low-, high- and medium-income societies is developed in Chapter 9.

To the websites

- Netwarriors
  http://www.hookele.com/non-hawaiians/draftdec.html
  provides the draft charter of rights of indigenous peoples.
- Indigenous Peoples:
  http://www.unhchr.ch/html/menu6/2/fs9.htm
  is a fact sheet on indigenous peoples.
- The Marx, Durkheim and Weber websites were introduced in Chapter 2.
- Europa:
  http://europa.eu.int/index-en.html
  Europa is the European Union's server to the Parliament, the Council, the Commission, the Court of Justice, the Council of Auditors and other EU bodies. This server offers news, simple answers to key questions, the history of the EU, information on policies and institutions, and links to Eurostat. Available in all EU languages.

For additional case studies, multiple choice questions, internet exercises, and annotated weblinks specific to this chapter, visit this book's website at **www.pearsoned.co.uk/plummer**

CHAPTER 5

CULTURE

There is no such thing as a human nature independent of culture. Men without culture ... would be unworkable monstrosities with very few useful instincts, fewer recognisable sentiments, and no intellect: mental basket cases.

Clifford Geertz

WE WERE FLYING INTO HONG KONG shortly before it was taken back into Chinese rule in 1997. The air stewardess welcomed us to the land, but with a cryptic message. She informed us that Hong Kong was the land where half the people had mobile phones but the other half believed in ghosts! And here, in a nutshell, is the clash of two cultures – a 'modernising' West touching a 'superstitious' East.

Everywhere one turns in Hong Kong the contrast is visible. The bustling, dirty old temples where women cry and wail at the altars of their ancestors, offering money to their gods; the glittering, elaborate shopping malls soaring to the skies – some of the largest in the world – where consumerist capitalism is at its most spectacular. Spirituality versus materialism. Or the Chinese schoolchildren elaborately dressed in their formal 'Western' school uniforms complete with satchels – clambering over the ill-equipped peasant boats in the harbour to their own overcrowded houseboat homes. Or the Bank of Hong Kong – a monument to modern architecture, but built with full regard to *feng shui* (pronounced 'fung shway', Chinese words that mean 'wind and water') and potential 'evil spirits' and designed to keep them at bay. Here are rich and vibrant cultures pushing against each other.

Or consider another example: New York real estate broker Barry Lewen, after six months of tough negotiations with a group of Taiwanese investors, is on the verge of signing what any broker would regard as a dream deal – the sale of a $14 million building on New York's Madison Avenue. But the investors soberly informed Lewen of 'one final concern'. Before any sale would go through, they explained, they would have to enlist the services of a master of *feng shui*. After flying to New York from Taiwan, this practitioner of the ancient Chinese art would inspect the building; only if he declared the structure to be acceptable would the sale be completed.

Several days later, a jet carrying the *feng shui* master landed at a New York airport and a car whisked him directly to the Madison Avenue building. A small crowd of anxious onlookers had assembled and they watched intently as he surveyed the setting, took account of the surrounding buildings, and, for 30 tense minutes, walked through the structure noting the shape and length of hallways, the location of doorways and lifts, and the presence of mirrors, fountains and even air conditioners. 'I can tell you there were a lot of sweaty palms', recounts Barry Lewen. In the end, the master turned to the apprehensive audience, smiled, and formally approved the building. A wave of relief broke over the group.

To the West's way of thinking, the merit of a building is a matter of its location, size, and the state of its plumbing and other systems. Such concerns are also of great importance to the Chinese. But, historically, members of Southeast Asian societies have also considered how physical space affects human feelings and emotions. From this point of view, a 'life force' or *qi* (pronounced 'chee') flows through all of nature – including buildings – so that the physical design of a home or office building will either help or hinder this flow. A 'good' building – that is, one that stands in harmony with nature – will enhance the luck, health and prosperity of the people living or working inside (Dunn, 1994). Understanding how such cultural differences work is a crucial part of sociology, and this chapter sets out to explore them.

KEY THEMES

- The meaning of 'culture', its development and its major components: language, symbols, values, norms and material cultures
- The diversities and changes that are found within cultures
- Ways of understanding cultures and youth cultures
- The rise of cultural studies

(Left) Mexican musicians at celebration.
Location Los Angeles, California, USA
Source: Corbis © Franklin McMahon

While the over six billion people on the earth today are members of a single biological species, *Homo sapiens*, we display remarkable differences. Some differences may be arbitrary matters of convention – the Chinese, for example, wear white at funerals while people in European countries prefer black. Similarly, Chinese people associate the number 4 with bad luck, in much the same way that people in England think of the number 13. Or take the practice of kissing: most people in Europe kiss in public, most Chinese kiss only in private; the French kiss publicly twice (once on each cheek), while Belgians kiss three times (starting on either cheek); for their part, most Nigerians don't kiss at all. At weddings, moreover, North American couples kiss, Koreans bow, and a Cambodian groom touches his nose to the bride's cheek! If you have travelled much, you will know that it really helps to be aware of these differences.

Other cultural differences, however, are more profound. The world over, people wear much or little clothing, have many or few children, venerate or shunt aside the elderly, are peaceful or warlike, embrace different religious beliefs, and enjoy different kinds of art, music, food and sport. In short, although we are all one biological species, human beings have developed strikingly different ideas about what is pleasant and repulsive, polite and rude, beautiful and ugly, right and wrong. This capacity for startling *difference* is a feature of our species: the expression of human culture.

What is culture?

Sociologists define **culture** as *'designs for living'*: *the values, beliefs, behaviour, practices and material objects that constitute a people's way of life*. Culture is a toolbox of solutions to everyday problems. It is a bridge to the past as well as a guide to the future. One classic account puts it like this:

> Believing, with Max Weber, that *man is an animal suspended in webs of significance he himself has spun*, I take *culture to be those webs*, and the analysis of it to be therefore not an experimental science in search of law but an interpretative one in search of meaning . . .
>
> (Geertz, 1995: 5, our italics)

To begin to understand what culture entails, it is helpful to distinguish between thoughts and things. What sociologists call **non-material culture** is *the intangible world of ideas created by members of a society* that span a wide range from altruism to zen. **Material culture**, on the other hand, constitutes *the tangible things created by members of a society*; here again, the range is vast, running

from armaments to zips, from mobile phones to pottery. They both involve cultural **practices** – *the practical logics by which we both act and think in a myriad of little encounters of daily life* (Bourdieu, 1990). Human beings make culture and it in turn 'makes us'. It becomes part of us – what we often (yet inaccurately) describe as 'human nature'. For sociologists, there is no such thing as human nature in itself: 'nature' is produced through our varying histories and cultures. This is often hard for students to grasp, but it is another example where common sense gets challenged by sociology.

No cultural trait is inherently 'natural' to humanity, even though most people around the world view their own way of life that way. What is crucial to our human species is the capacity to create culture in our collective lives. Every other form of life – from ants to zebras – behaves in more uniform, species-specific ways. But to a world traveller, the enormous diversity of human life stands out in contrast to the behaviour of cats and other creatures, which is more or less the same everywhere. Most living creatures are guided by instincts, a biological programming over which animals have no control. A few animals – notably chimpanzees and related primates – have the capacity for limited culture: researchers have observed them using tools and teaching simple skills to their offspring. But the creative power of humans far exceeds that of any other form of life; in short, *only humans generate and then rely on culture rather than instinct to ensure the survival of their kind*. To understand how this came to be, we must briefly review the history of our species on earth.

Culture, intelligence and the 'dance through time'

In a universe some 15 billion years old, our planet is a much younger 4.5 billion years of age. For a billion years after the earth was formed, no life at all appeared on our planet. Huge geological upheavals kept changing the earth's surface. Billions more years went by before dinosaurs ruled the earth and then disappeared. And then, some 65 million years ago, our history took a crucial turn with the appearance of the creatures we call primates.

What sets primates apart is their intelligence, based on the largest brains (relative to body size) of all living creatures. As primates evolved, the human line diverged from that of our closest relatives, the great apes, about 12 million years ago. But our common lineage shows through in the traits humans share with today's chimpanzees, gorillas and orangutans: great sociability, affectionate and long-lasting bonds for child-rearing and mutual protection, the ability to walk upright (normal in humans, less common among other primates), and hands that manipulate objects with great precision.

Studying fossil records, scientists conclude that, about 2 million years ago, our distant ancestors grasped cultural fundamentals such as the use of fire, tools and weapons, created simple shelters, and fashioned basic clothing. Although these Stone Age achievements may seem modest, they mark the point at which our ancestors embarked on a distinct evolutionary course, making culture the primary strategy for human survival.

To comprehend that human beings are wide-eyed infants in the larger scheme of things, Carl Sagan (1977) came up with the idea of superimposing the 15-billion-year history of our universe on a single calendar year. The life-giving atmosphere of the earth did not develop until the autumn, and the earliest beings who resembled humans did not appear until 31 December – the last day of the year – at 10.30 at night! Yet not until 250,000 years ago, which is mere minutes before the end of Sagan's 'year', did our own species finally emerge. These *Homo sapiens* (derived from Latin meaning 'thinking person') have continued to evolve so that, about 40,000 years ago, humans who looked more or less like we do roamed the earth. With larger brains, these 'modern' *Homo sapiens* produced culture at a rapid pace, as the wide range of tools and cave art from this period suggests.

Still, what we call 'civilisation', based on permanent settlements and specialised occupations, began in the Middle East (in what is today Iraq and Egypt) only about 12,000 years ago (Hamblin, 1973; Wenke, 1980). In terms of Sagan's 'year', this cultural flowering occurred during the final *seconds* before midnight on New Year's Eve. Our modern, industrial way of life, begun a mere 300 years ago, amounts to less than a second in Sagan's scheme. It is with this fraction of a second that most of this book is concerned. We are:

> latecomers to a global party that has been in progress for at least 3.5 billion years, since life began, and will continue till the death of the planet itself. It is a fabulous party, with billions of participants from all walks of life.
>
> (Tudge, 1995: 76)

Human culture, then, is very recent and was a long time in the making. As culture became a strategy for survival, our ancestors descended from the trees into the tall grasses of central Africa. There, walking upright, they discovered the advantages of hunting in groups. From this point on, the human brain grew larger, allowing for greater human capacity to create a way of life – as opposed to simply acting out biological imperatives.

Gradually, culture pushed aside the biological forces we call instincts so that humans gained the mental power *to fashion the natural environment for themselves*. Ever since, people have made and remade their worlds in countless ways, which explains today's extraordinary cultural diversity.

The major components of culture

Although the cultures found in all the world's nations differ in many ways, they all seem to be built on five major components: *symbols, language, values, norms and material culture*. In this section, we shall consider each in turn.

1. Symbols

Human beings not only sense the surrounding world as other creatures do, we build a reality of meaning. In doing so, humans transform elements of the world into **symbols**, *anything that carries a particular meaning recognised by people who share culture*. A whistle, a wall of graffiti, a flashing red light, and a fist raised in the air all serve as symbols. We can see the human capacity to create and manipulate symbols reflected in the very different meanings associated with the simple act of winking the eye. In some settings this action conveys interest; in others, understanding; in still others, insult.

We are so dependent on our culture's symbols that we take them for granted. But entering an unfamiliar society also reminds us of the power of symbols; culture shock is nothing more than the inability to 'read' meaning in one's surroundings. We feel lost and isolated, unsure of how to act, and sometimes frightened – a consequence of being outside the symbolic web of culture that joins individuals in meaningful social life.

Culture shock is a two-way process. On the one hand, it is something the traveller **experiences** when encountering people whose way of life is unfamiliar. On the other hand, it is also what the traveller **inflicts** on others by acting in ways that may well offend them. For example, because the English consider dogs to be beloved household pets, travellers to northern regions of the People's Republic of China might well be appalled to find people roasting dogs as a wintertime meal. On the other hand, visitors to England from much of Southeast Asia can be shocked to find how much alcohol they consume! Indeed, global travel provides almost endless opportunities for misunderstanding. When in an unfamiliar setting, we need to remember that even behaviour that seems innocent and quite normal to us may be anathema to others.

Symbolic meanings vary even within a single society. A fur coat, prized by one person as a luxurious symbol of success, may represent to another the inhumane treatment of animals. Cultural symbols also change over time. Jeans were created more than a century ago as sturdy and inexpensive clothing for workers. In the liberal political climate of the 1960s, this working-class aura made jeans popular among affluent students – many of whom wore them simply to look 'different' or perhaps to identify with working people. A decade later, 'designer jeans' emerged as high-priced 'status symbols' that conveyed quite a different message. In recent years, jeans remain as popular as ever; many people choose them as everyday clothing. Still others seek out designer labels to establish their difference from others. Jeans do not have a fixed symbolic meaning. In sum, symbols allow people to make sense of their lives, and without them human existence would be meaningless. Manipulating symbols correctly allows us to engage others readily within our own cultural system.

The *study of the symbols and signs* is called **semiotics**. Broadly, semiotics suggests that meanings are never inherent in objects but are constructed around them through a series of practices. The American pragmatist Peirce, the French language specialist de Saussure and the French philosopher Roland Barthes have made special studies of the ways in which any sign – a T-shirt, a flag, a pop song, a menu, a word – can be given different meanings. We return to this in Chapter 21.

2. Language

Language, the key to the world of culture, is *a system of symbols that allows members of a society to communicate with one another*. These symbols take the form of spoken and written words, which are culturally variable and composed of the various alphabets and ideograms used around the world. Even conventions for writing differ: in general, people in Western societies write from left to right, people in northern Africa and western Asia write from right to left, and people in eastern Asia write from top to bottom.

Figure 5.1 shows where in the world one finds the three most widely spoken languages. Chinese is the official language of 20 per cent of humanity (about 1.2 billion people). English is the mother tongue of about 10 per cent (600 million) of the world's people, with Spanish the official language of 6 per cent (350 million). While these are major languages, there are thousands of minor ones – estimates usually vary from 5,000 to 6,000.

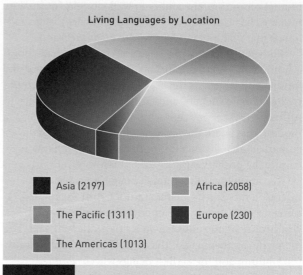

Living Languages by Location

- Asia (2197)
- Africa (2058)
- The Pacific (1311)
- Europe (230)
- The Americas (1013)

Figure 5.1   Living languages by location

A quarter of these languages have fewer than 1,000 speakers; half have fewer than 10,000; a few have only one speaker left! Many are dying out. Linguists predict that half of our 6,800 known living languages will die out during this century, and 80–90 per cent will die off in the next 200 years. Large languages dominate smaller ones. Figure 5.2 suggests some of the countries where 'the words won't be heard'. And yet there are small signs of this being resisted – as a number of language revivals that aim to rekindle interest in languages such as Welsh take place. (Crystal, 1997: 287; Bartholet, 2000; Nettle and Romaine, 2000).

Due to the worldwide influence of Britain over the past 200 years, and more recently of the United States, English is now becoming a global tongue that is a favoured second language in many of the world's nations. It is used as an official or semi-official language in over 60 countries, and is the main language of the World Wide Web, air traffic control, business conferences and pop music. But in many countries there is considerable concern about this. So much so that there is now a European Bureau of Lesser Used Languages which tries to promote and conserve these less-used languages (with a bulletin, *Contact*, published three times a year). And some countries, such as France and Wales, are trying hard to resist the weakening of their language by challenging English words. In any event, Chinese, remains the most popular language and is likely to triple its number of speakers by 2050. As Figure 5.3 suggests, by this time Hindi-Urdu, Spanish and Arabic are likely to have caught up with English.

The European Union itself is a Tower of Babel. The European Commission in Brussels employs 400 full-time

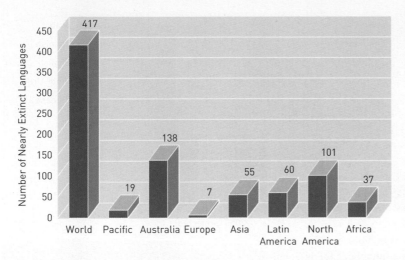

Figure 5.2   **Where the words won't be heard**

Thousands of languages may die out during the twenty-first century, and more than 420 are already characterised as 'nearly extinct' by Ethnologue, a catalogue of the world's tongues. They cover the globe.

Source: adapted from *Newsweek*, 19 June 2000 © 2000 Newsweek Inc. All rights reserved. Reprinted by permission.

staff to deal with translation problems. There are at present 11 official languages, although this could grow: the theoretically possible number is 30 (Crystal, 1997: 56).

Language and the ethnicity boom

From the mid-1960s onwards, North America and Western Europe experienced something of an 'ethnicity boom' – a widespread awareness of different ethnicities having their own languages. Thus, of 230 million people over the age of 5 in the United States, the 1990 Census reports that 32 million (14 per cent) typically speak a language other than English at home. Of these people, 54 per cent speak Spanish, 14 per cent use an Asian language, and the remaining 32 per cent employ some other tongue (the Census Bureau lists 25 languages, each of which is favoured by more than 100,000 people). In Europe, there are wide variations in language too, often generating conflicts. In Spain, Basque (Euskera) was banned during Franco's dictatorship from the mid-1930s: books written in it were publicly burnt. In the 1960s, policy changed, and by March 1980 the first Basque Parliament was elected and Euskera became its official language. In Britain, although English dominates, both Welsh and Gaelic are more widely spoken than many presume and given full support regionally, and there are speakers of Punjabi, Bengali, Urdu, Gujarati and Cantonese, not to mention German, Polish, Italian, Greek and Spanish. There is also 'Black English Vernacular' (BEV) linked to the use of a Creole English, used by the first blacks in America (Crystal, 1997: 36).

Language and cultural reproduction

For people everywhere, language is the major means of *cultural reproduction, the process by which one generation passes culture to the next.* Just as our bodies contain the genes of our ancestors, so our symbols carry our cultural heritage. Language gives us the power to gain access to centuries of accumulated wisdom.

Throughout human history, people have transmitted culture through speech, a process sociologists call the **oral cultural tradition**, *transmission of culture through speech.* Only as recently as 5,000 years ago did humans invent writing, and even then, just a favoured few ever learned to read and write. It was not until the twentieth century that nations (generally the industrial high-income countries) boasted of nearly universal literacy (see Chapter 21). Even so, in many industrial countries there are still a large number of people who are functionally illiterate – approximately one in five people in the UK have literacy and numeracy problems – an almost insurmountable barrier to opportunity in a society that increasingly demands symbolic skills. In low-income countries of the world, illiteracy rates range from 30 per cent (People's Republic of China) to as high as 80 per cent (Sierra Leone in Africa).

Language skills not only link us with others and with the past, they also set free the human imagination. Connecting symbols in new ways, we can conceive of an almost limitless range of future possibilities. Language – both spoken and written – distinguishes human beings as the only creatures who are self-conscious, mindful of our limitations and aware of our ultimate mortality. Yet our symbolic power also enables us to dream of a better world, and to work to bring that world into being.

Is language uniquely human?

Creatures great and small direct sounds, smells and gestures towards one another. In most cases, these signals are instinctive. But research shows that some animals

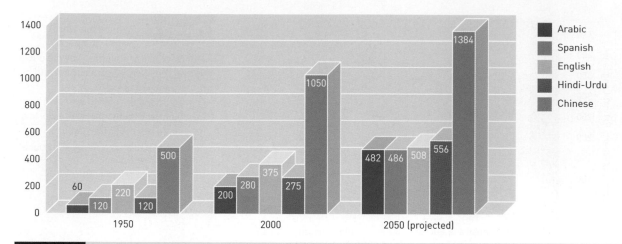

Figure 5.3   The world's leading primary languages (in millions)

Source: adapted from Graddol (1997)

have at least a rudimentary ability to use symbols to communicate with one another and with humans.

Consider the remarkable achievement of a 12-year-old pygmy chimp named Kanzi. Chimpanzees lack the physical ability to mimic human speech. But researcher E. Sue Savage-Rumbaugh discovered that Kanzi was able to learn language by listening and observing people. Under Savage-Rumbaugh's supervision, Kanzi has amassed a vocabulary of several hundred words, and has learned to 'speak' by pointing to pictures on a special keyboard. Kanzi has correctly responded to requests like 'Will you get a nappy for your sister?' and 'Put the melon in the potty'. More intriguing, Kanzi's abilities surpass mere rote learning because he can respond to requests he has not heard before. In short, this remarkable animal has the language ability of a human child aged two years six months (Linden, 1993).

Despite such accomplishments, the language skills of chimps, dolphins and a few other animals are limited. And even specially trained animals cannot, on their own, teach language skills to others of their kind. But the demonstrated language skills of Kanzi and others caution us against assuming that humans alone can lay claim to culture.

Does language shape reality?

Do the Chinese, who think using one set of symbols, actually experience the world differently from Swedes who think in Swedish or the English who think in English? The answer is yes, since each language has its own, distinct symbols that serve as the building blocks of reality.

Edward Sapir (1929, 1949) and Benjamin Whorf (1956; orig. 1941), two anthropologists who specialised in linguistic studies, noted that each language has words or expressions with no precise counterparts in other tongues. In addition, all languages fuse symbols with distinctive emotions. Thus, as multilingual people can attest, a single idea often 'feels' different if spoken in, say, German rather than in English or Chinese (Gerhard Falk, personal communication to J.J. Macionis, 1987).

Formally, then, what we now call the **Sapir–Whorf hypothesis** states that *people perceive the world through the cultural lens of language*. Using different symbolic systems, a Filipino, a Turk and a Brazilian actually experience 'distinct worlds, not merely the same world with different labels attached' (Sapir, 1949: 162). They combine two principles, **linguistic determinism**, which suggests that *language shapes the way we think*, and **linguistic relativity**, which states that *distinctions found in one language are not found in another*. Whorf's classic case studies involved the Hopis, who had only one word for everything that flies – insects, planes, pilots – except birds; and the Inuit, who had many different words for snow.

The capacity to create and manipulate language also gives humans everywhere the power to alter how they experience the world. For example, many African Americans hailed it as a step towards social equality with white people when the word 'negro' was replaced by the term 'black' and, more recently, by 'African American' or 'person of colour'. Likewise, homosexuals redefined themselves as 'gay' during the 1970s, creating a more forceful, positive self-definition.

In short, a system of language guides how we understand the world but does not limit how we do so.

3. Values and beliefs

Values are *the standards people have about what is good and bad*, which vary from culture to culture. They are prescriptive: statements about what ought to exist in a language of ethical and moral terms which are the broad principles that underlie **beliefs**, *specific statements that people hold to be true*. While values are abstract standards of goodness, beliefs are particular matters that individuals consider to be true or false.

Cultural values and beliefs not only colour how we perceive our surroundings, they also form the core of our moral world view. We learn from families, schools and religious organisations to think and act according to approved principles, to pursue worthy goals, and to believe a host of cultural truths while rejecting alternatives as false.

European values?

In a continent as large and diverse as Europe, of course, few cultural values and beliefs are shared by everyone. In fact, with a long history of immigration from the rest of the world, Europe may be seen as a cultural mosaic. Even so, there may be some broad shape to European life.

First, European values can be seen as the long accumulation of what might be called 'The Age of the Enlightenment' (Gay, 1970). That is, they hold broadly to the values of rationality, science and progress that came with the *philosophers* – the great writers and thinkers, mainly of the eighteenth century (for example, Voltaire, Hume, Diderot). This was a period marked by significant improvements in some lives due to reason, science and medicine. People started to sense they were the makers of their own futures, that they could exert some rational control over their world, that they could bring about change and make it a better place.

Second, Europe has been dominated by versions of the Judaeo-Christian religion, and its subsequent struggle with secularisation. Much of its heritage cannot be understood without grasping the long struggles between Catholic groups and emerging Protestant ones, and the more recent weakening of both. The very calendar year and most of its key holidays – Christmas, Easter – are bound up with Christian values, culture and identity: 'To be a European is to celebrate Christmas and Easter' (Therborn, 1995: 234). Thus core Christian values might suggest:

> You should love the Lord your God with all your heart, and with all your soul, and with all your mind. This is the first and great commandment. And a second is like it. You should love your neighbour

> as yourself. On these two commandments depend all the law and the prophets.
>
> (Matthew, 22: 37–40)

Third, European values have been structured by the development of nation states, and their belief in 'citizenship'. Here core values of rights and obligations can be laid out to suggest what a good citizen – a 'Spaniard', a 'German', a 'Scot' – is expected to do.

And finally, Europe may be seen as a culture that has generally highlighted a principle of hierarchy – that people should recognise their superiors and inferiors. Europe has deep roots in the values of a feudal and aristocratic system that turns into a class system (Therborn, 1995: 273).

European culture, then, in the broadest of strokes, is clearly different from Asian cultures. The box highlights some values, many of which may be taken more broadly to exemplify Western capitalist culture, and contrasts them with some non-Western cultures.

World values?

The political scientist Ronald Inglehart has produced an important, if somewhat controversial, body of evidence about the different kinds of values held across the six continents in some 60 different countries across the world over the past 20 years (Inglehart, 2000). He clusters societies on a number of different value dimensions, but two take prominence: what he calls traditional versus secular-rational, and survival versus self-expression.

- Traditional societies appeal to an authority rooted in the past – often via religion or through autocratic leaders. Secular-rational societies tend to be much less religious and can be seen to have values that are much more individualistic.
- The survival/self-expression dimension involves themes which link to the arrival of so-called post-modern or post-materialist societies.

Some cultures – usually what we have called low-income societies – emphasise '*survival values*'. For Inglehart, this means they report low levels of subjective well-being, relatively poor health, low interpersonal trust, relative intolerance towards outgroups, low support for gender equality, emphasis on materialist values, relatively high levels of faith in technology and science, relatively low concern with environmental activism, and relatively favourable attitudes to authoritarian government. '*Self-expression values*', by contrast, focus on the reverse of these.

In industrial societies, one of the main variations was found between age groups. Among the oldest, top priority was given to economic and physical security, but the younger birth cohort espouses what he calls a post-materialist view, where matters such as the environment and feminism become more important. Such younger groups give more importance to belonging and self-expression.

Post-materialist and postmodern values

Contemporary debates in the Western world centre on distinctions between post-materialist and postmodern values. Research on changing values has suggested that postmodern values are most likely to be found among the young and highly educated, and that they are on the rise in Western Europe at least – especially in The Netherlands and Sweden (Gibbins and Reimer, 1999: 103). Though post-materialists and postmodernists often have broadly similar concerns, such as feminism, the environment and lifestyle choice, the issues seem fixed and given for post-materialists, whereas postmodernists stress they are constantly changing – new issues keep appearing even as existing ones are being debated. Table 5.1 outlines the differences.

Some sources for understanding different cultural values are:

- *Eurobarometer*, conducted in the expanding European countries since 1973
- *Central and Eastern Eurobarometer*, conducted since 1989
- *World Values Study (WVS)*, conducted in 1981–, 1990–93, 1995–97 and 1999–2001 (see Map 5.1)
- More specific studies, such as *British Social Attitudes*.

Table 5.1	Changing values: post-material and postmodern
Post-materialist	**Postmodern**
Core values held	No core values; mix and match
Environmentalism, feminism, etc.	Agree but shifting forms and debates
Values for life	Values change and adapt with groups and individuals
Order and pattern	Loose knit, everyone should order for themselves
Specific	Mosaics
Unified	Image of the Internet, Web
Stable	Changing

Source: adapted from Gibbins and Reimer (1999) Ch. 6

Values: inconsistency and conflict

Cultural values can be inconsistent and even outright contradictory (Lynd, 1967; Bellah *et al.*, 1985). Living in Europe, we sometimes find ourselves torn between the 'me first' attitude of an individualistic way of life and the opposing need to belong and contribute to some larger community. Similarly, we affirm our belief in equality of opportunity, only to turn around and promote or degrade others because of their ethnicity, gender or sexual preference. Value inconsistency reflects the cultural diversity of society and the process of cultural change by which new trends supplant older traditions.

CONTROVERSY AND DEBATE

CULTURAL DIFFERENCE AND VALUES?

Many social scientists argue that culture is the key to understanding how societies grow and change. They explain the fact that some have become advanced industrialised nations and others have not by considering their core values. Core values are seen to shape society. We have already seen how Weber saw the rise of capitalism as having a strong affinity with Protestantism through the 'Protestant Ethic'.

Lawrence Harrison suggests that there are real cultural value differences between what he terms 'progressive' and 'static' societies. Progressive societies are the more industrialised societies; static ones are those which have not changed a great deal. Among the value differences he notes are:

1. *Education*: This is a key to progress for progressive cultures, but of marginal importance except for the elites in static cultures.
2. *Time orientation*: Progressives look to the future, statics look to the past or the present.

CONTROVERSY AND DEBATE CONTINUED

3. *Work*: Central for progressive societies, but often a burden in static cultures.
4. *Frugality*: A major value for progressive societies – leading to investment and financial security; often a threat to static cultures.
5. *Merit*: Central to advancement in progressive cultures; connections and family are what count in static cultures.
6. *Community*: In progressive cultures, community extends beyond the locality and the family; in static cultures, the family circumscribes community.
7. *Ethics*: More rigorous in advanced societies; corruption is greater in static societies.
8. *Justice and fair play*: Universal impersonal expectations in progressive cultures. In static societies, justice is often a function of who you know and how much you can pay.

9. *Authority*: Dispersed in progressive societies; concentrated in static societies.
10. *Secularism*: Progressive societies find religious influence on civic life dwindles. In static societies, religion has a substantial influence.

Source: Harrison and Huntingdon (2000: 299)

CONTINUE THE DEBATE:

1. What do you think progressive and static societies are? What are examples of them?

2. Do Lawrence's views suggest a moral split between the West and the rest of the world? How far do you think such a distinction does hold? Is he being ethnocentric?

3. How might culturalist explanations of change differ from materialist ones?

4. Norms

In China, people curious about how much money colleagues are paid readily ask about their salaries. In Europe, people consider such a question rude. Such patterns illustrate the operation of **norms**, *rules and expectations by which a society guides the behaviour of its members*. Some norms are *proscriptive*, mandating what we should not do, as when Chinese parents scold young lovers for holding hands in public. *Prescriptive* norms, on the other hand, spell out what we *should* do, as when some European schools teach practices of 'safe sex'.

Most important norms apply virtually anywhere and at any time. For example, parents expect obedience from children regardless of the setting. Many normative conventions, by contrast, are situation-specific. In Europe, we expect audience applause at the end of a musical performance; we discourage it when a priest or a rabbi finishes a sermon.

Mores and folkways

William Graham Sumner (1959; orig. 1906), an early US sociologist, recognised that some norms are more crucial to our lives than others. Sumner used the term **mores** to refer to *a society's standards of proper moral conduct*. Sumner counted among the mores all norms essential to maintaining a way of life; because of their importance, he contended that people develop an emotional attachment to mores and defend them publicly. In addition, mores apply to everyone, everywhere, all the time. Violation of mores – such as our society's prohibition against sexual relations between adults and children – typically brings a swift and strong reaction from others.

Sumner used the term **folkways** to designate *a society's customs for routine, casual interaction*. Folkways, which have less moral significance than mores, include notions about proper dress, appropriate greetings and common courtesy. In short, while mores distinguish between right and wrong, folkways draw a line between right and *rude*. Because they are less important than mores, societies afford individuals a measure of personal discretion in matters involving folkways, and punish infractions leniently. For example, a man who does not wear a tie to a formal dinner party is, at worst, guilty of a breach of etiquette. If, however, the man were to arrive at the dinner party wearing *only* a tie, he would be challenging the social mores and inviting more serious sanctions.

5. Material culture

In addition to intangible elements such as values and norms, every culture encompasses a wide range of tangible human creations that sociologists term *artefacts*. The Chinese eat with chopsticks rather than knives and forks, the Japanese place mats rather than rugs on the floor, and many men and women in India prefer flowing robes to the tighter clothing common in much of Europe. An unfamiliar people's material culture may seem as strange to us as their language, values and norms.

SOCIAL SHAPES OF THE WORLD

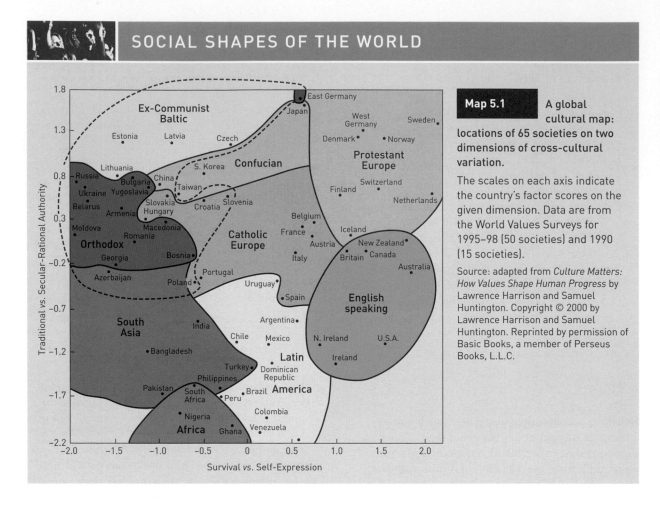

Map 5.1 A global cultural map: locations of 65 societies on two dimensions of cross-cultural variation.

The scales on each axis indicate the country's factor scores on the given dimension. Data are from the World Values Surveys for 1995–98 (50 societies) and 1990 (15 societies).

Source: adapted from *Culture Matters: How Values Shape Human Progress* by Lawrence Harrison and Samuel Huntington. Copyright © 2000 by Lawrence Harrison and Samuel Huntington. Reprinted by permission of Basic Books, a member of Perseus Books, L.L.C.

Cultural diversity: many ways of life in one world

When contractors and estate agents in New York take account of the Chinese art of *feng shui*, as noted in the opening to this chapter, we can see a nation of striking cultural diversity. In fact, between 1980 and 1990, the number of people in the United States with Chinese or other Asian ancestry more than doubled. Historical isolation makes Japan the most *monocultural* of all industrial nations; heavy immigration over centuries, by contrast, makes the United States the most *multicultural* of all industrial nations.

Between 1820 (when the US government began keeping track of immigration) and 2001, more than 67 million people travelled to the United States from other countries. At the end of the nineteenth century, as shown in Figure 5.4, most immigrants hailed from Europe; by the end of the twentieth century, a large majority of newcomers were arriving from Latin America and Asia.

Cultural variety has characterised most of the world, and not just the United States. We return to this in Chapter 11. In this section, we look at some ways of approaching these diversities and differences.

High culture and popular culture

Much cultural diversity is seen to have roots in social class. In fact, in everyday life, we often reserve the term 'culture' for sophisticated art forms such as classical literature, music, dance and painting. We praise some people as 'cultured', because they presumably appreciate the 'finer things in life'. The term 'culture' itself has the same Latin root as the word 'cultivate', suggesting that the 'cultured' individual has cultivated or refined tastes. By contrast, we speak less generously of ordinary people, assuming that everyday cultural patterns are somehow less worthy. In more concrete terms, Mozart is seen as 'more cultured' than Rap, French 'cuisine' as better than fish fingers, and polo as more polished than ping pong!

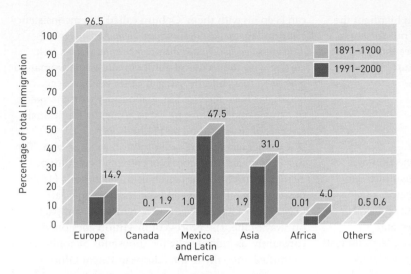

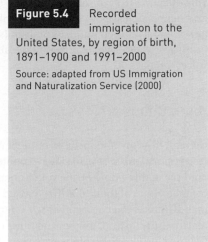

Figure 5.4 Recorded immigration to the United States, by region of birth, 1891–1900 and 1991–2000

Source: adapted from US Immigration and Naturalization Service (2000)

Such judgements imply that many cultural patterns are readily accessible to some but not all members of a society (Hall and Neitz, 1993). Sociologists use the shorthand term **high culture**[1] to refer to *cultural patterns that distinguish a society's elite*; **popular culture**, then, designates *cultural patterns that are widespread among a society's population*.

Common sense might suggest that high culture is superior to popular culture. After all, history chronicles the lives of elites much more than those of ordinary women and men. But sociologists are uneasy with such a sweeping evaluation: they generally use the term 'culture' to refer to *all elements of a society's way of life*. However, they do recognise too that culture is also used to define people's social standing – their tastes, their distinction. Indeed, the term **cultural capital** (invented by sociologist Pierre Bourdieu – see Profile in Chapter 19) is often used to designate *the practices where people can wield power and status because of their educational credentials, general cultural awareness and aesthetic preferences*. It is an idea which helps reinforce class distinctions – setting apart those who are 'cultured', who have 'travelled a lot', who know about their good wines and the latest 'art works'. 'Cultural' capital is distributed very unevenly in societies. Its acquisition starts in families and schools. But its impact continues through life as a major marker of distinction (Swartz, 1997: 76).

Subcultures and countercultures

Another set of differences are caught in the terms **subculture** (*cultural patterns that set apart some segment of a society's population*) and **counterculture** (*cultural patterns that strongly oppose those widely accepted within a society, contraculture*).

Rastafarians, young gays and lesbians, frequent-flyer executives, jazz musicians, old people in residential homes, homeless people, campus poets and offshore powerboat racers all display subcultural patterns. It is easy – but often inaccurate – to place people into subcultural categories. Almost everyone participates simultaneously in numerous subcultures, and we often have little commitment to many of them.

In some cases, however, important cultural traits such as ethnicity or religion do set off people from one another – sometimes with tragic results. Consider the former nation of Yugoslavia in southeast Europe. The turmoil there was fuelled by astounding cultural diversity. This *one* small country (which, before its break-up, was about half the size of England, with a population of 25 million) made use of *two* alphabets, professed *three* religions, spoke *four* languages, was home to *five* major nationalities, was divided into *six* political republics, and absorbed the cultural influences of *seven* surrounding countries. The cultural conflict that plunged this nation into civil war reveals that subcultures are a source not only of pleasing variety but also of tensions and outright violence (see Chapter 15 and Sekulic *et al.*, 1994).

Cultural diversity involves not just *variety* but also *hierarchy*. Too often, what we view as 'dominant' or 'highbrow' cultural patterns are those favoured by powerful segments of the population, while we relegate the lives of the disadvantaged to the realm of 'subculture'.

---

[1] The term 'high culture' is derived from the more popular term 'highbrow'. Influenced by phrenology, the bogus nineteenth-century theory that personality was determined by the shape of the human skull, people a century ago contrasted the praiseworthy tastes of those they termed 'highbrows' with the contemptible appetites of others they derided as 'lowbrows'.

This dilemma has led some researchers to highlight the experiences of less powerful members of our society in a new approach called multiculturalism (see the Controversy and Debate box 'Whose culture? Whose voice?' on page 127).

Youth Cultures?

Cultural diversity also includes outright rejection of conventional ideas or behaviour – countercultures. An example of this would be the youth-orientated counterculture of the 1960s that rejected the cultural mainstream as too competitive, self-centred and materialistic. Instead, hippies and other counterculturalists favoured a cooperative lifestyle in which 'being' took precedence over 'doing' and the capacity for personal growth – or 'expanded consciousness' – was prized over material possessions such as homes and cars. Such differences led some people at that time to 'drop out' of the larger society. Counterculture may involve not only distinctive values, but unconventional behaviour (including dress and forms of greeting) as well as music. Many members of the 1960s counterculture, for instance, drew personal identity from long hair, headbands and blue jeans; from displaying a peace sign rather than offering a handshake; and from drug use and the energy of ever-present rock-and-roll music.

Cultural change

A wise human axiom suggests that 'All things shall pass'. Even the dinosaurs, which thrived on this planet for some 160 million years, exist today only as fossils. Will humanity survive for millions of years to come? No one knows. All we can say with certainty is that, given our reliance on culture, for as long as we survive, the human record will be one of continuous change.

Change in one dimension of a culture usually accompanies other transformations as well. For example, women's rising participation in the labour force has paralleled changing family patterns, including later age at first marriage, a rising divorce rate, and a growing share of children being raised in households without fathers. Such connections illustrate the principle of **cultural integration**, *the close relationship among various elements of a cultural system.*

But all elements of a cultural system do not change at the same speed. William Ogburn (1964) observed that technology moves quickly, generating new elements of material culture (such as 'test-tube babies') faster than non-material culture (such as ideas about parenthood) can keep up with them. Ogburn called this inconsistency **cultural lag**, *the fact that cultural elements change at different rates, which may disrupt a cultural system.* In a culture with the technical ability to allow one woman to give birth to a child by using another woman's egg, which has been fertilised in a laboratory with the sperm of a total stranger, how are we to apply the traditional notions of motherhood and fatherhood?

Cultural changes are set in motion in three ways. The first is *invention*, the process of creating new cultural elements. Invention has given us the telephone (1876), powered aircraft (1903) and the aerosol spray can (1941), all of which have had a tremendous impact on our way of life. The process of invention goes on constantly, as indicated by the thousands of applications submitted annually to the European Patent Office.

Discovery, a second cause of cultural change, involves recognising and understanding something not fully understood before – from a distant star, to the foods of another culture, to the athletic prowess of US women. Many discoveries result from scientific research. Yet discovery can also happen quite by accident, as when Marie Curie left a rock on a piece of photographic paper in 1898 and serendipitously discovered radium.

The third cause of cultural change is *diffusion*, the spread of cultural traits from one society to another. The technological ability to send information around the globe in seconds – by means of radio, television, facsimile (fax) and computer – means that the level of cultural diffusion has never been greater than it is today.

Certainly, our own society has contributed many significant cultural elements to the world, ranging from computers to jazz music. But diffusion works the other way as well; for example, much of what we assume is inherently 'British' actually comes from other cultures. Ralph Linton (1937) explained that many commonplace elements of our way of life – most clothing and furniture, clocks, newspapers, money, and often the food we eat – are all derived from other cultures.

Ethnocentrism and cultural relativity

Western travellers are among the world's greatest shoppers. They delight in surveying hand-woven carpets in China or India, inspecting finely crafted metals in Turkey, or collecting beautifully coloured porcelain tiles in Morocco. And, of course, all these items are wonderful bargains. But one major reason for the low cost is unsettling: many products from low- and middle-income countries of the world are produced by children, many as young as 5 or 6 years old, who work long days for extremely low wages.

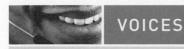

VOICES

YOUTH CULTURAL STYLES

The idea of 'culture' and all its linked concepts becomes clearer once we focus on a particular group. Young people are a good example. In many societies, new cultures spring from adolescence (Spates, 1976, 1983; Spates and Perkins, 1982). These have certainly not always been with us: most societies have no conception of a youth culture. Indeed, they only started to appear in very distinctive form in the period after the Second World War. Here was a period of relative affluence in the West, the extension of schooling, and the emergence of a pervasive consumer market. Relatively disconnected from the responsibilities of adult family life, young people were a noticeable consumer market. Many new products – from records and films, to sports gear and clothing styles – could be directed at them. From these 'material conditions', youth cultures started to appear with their own 'ways of life', their own 'webs of meaning'. In the United Kingdom, for instance, a string of cultural styles developed: Teddy Boys came first in the 1950s (in the wake of the first rock 'n' roll record and film – Bill Haley's *Rock around the Clock*); Mods and Rockers followed in the 1960s and adopted distinctive dress, music styles and values. These were followed by a whole gallery of youth types: skinheads, hippies, punks, rastas, grunge, goths, acid heads, new travellers and others. Some of these dominated for brief periods, but by the mid-1990s the situation was largely one of mixture – what some have called postmodern youth styles.

Sociologists in the cultural studies tradition (see the Profile box on page 124) have asked many questions about the nature and development of such cultures. At one level, these sociologists simply describe what's going on – they do participant observation and ethnographies which depict the symbols, languages, values and material cultures in which young people live. Style becomes important and often parodies the consumer culture they are part of: to put it generally, punks, bikers, goths, crusties, hippies dress down; mods, soul boys, home boys dress up!

At another level, sociologists try to show how these cultures work. During the 1980s they argued that such cultures 'express and resolve, albeit magically, the contradictions which remain hidden or unresolved in the parent culture' (Cohen, 1980: 82–83; orig. 1972).

Thus youth cultures were seen as active ways of dealing with the problems generated by both the wider culture (with all its pushes towards getting jobs, consuming goods, getting on in school, becoming men and women) and the immediate 'adult' culture of the parents. These were stressful times, and young people had to develop and negotiate their own responses. Youth styles came to be seen as forms of resistance, in which the young worked up their own cultures as a way of handling a string of problems.

A more recent wave of youth research suggests a more postmodern and fluid approach. The postmodern language of youth refuses to see any kind of unified coherence among the young. Indeed, it is now much less inclined to even talk of youth subcultures or contracultures which sounds much too uniform and fixed. Instead it sees tribes, neo-tribes, taste cultures, lifestyles and hybridity. Anoop Nayak uses the term 'youth scapes' (2003: 19) to indicate the potential diversity and movement of youth forms orbiting around different identities and values. Youth cultures are to be found moving through specifically geographical sites – there are a diverse array of 'geographies of youth': clubbing, local music scenes, urban landscapes, dance cultures, lifestyles, night time economies and 'cool places' (Skelton and Valentine, 1998). Boundaries are fluid and switchable. Nevertheless, there may be key themes. Paul Hodkinson's study of Goths (2002), for example, suggested four key indicators of the new youth movements: identity, commitment, consistent distictiveness and autonomy. All in all, youth cultures have been popular topics to study in sociology and in recent years there has been a major revival in ways of thinking about them.

These days, youth cultural styles are among the most global in the world. Partly because of a widely common youth language of pop music, cable and satellite TV, film and the like, much of youth culture depends on borrowing from many sources. Young people play around with the dominant culture, creating a collage of diverse bits in their own lives, mixing styles of fashion, music and consumption. The photographs capture some of the different dress styles of youth. Why do young people wear such clothes, and adopt values and languages to go with them?

Sources: Thornton (1995); Skelton and Valentine (1998); Hodkinson (2002); Nayak (2003); Muggleton and Weinzierl (2004)

(a)

(b)

(c)

(d)

Young people across the world like to differentiate themselves by the clothes they wear or the activities they perform as these examples show: (a) German skateboarders; (b) French hip hop culture; (c) Japanese fashion victims; (d) Saharan horse race followers.

Source: Network/Bildberg © D Schmid; Network/ Rapho © J-E Pasquier; Magnum © Chris Steele-Perkins (c and d)

We think of childhood as a time of innocence and freedom from adult burdens such as regular work. In poor countries throughout the world, however, families depend on income earned by children. So what people in one society think of as right and natural, people elsewhere find puzzling and even immoral. Perhaps the Chinese philosopher Confucius had it right when he noted that 'All people are the same; it's only their habits that are different'.

Just about every imaginable social habit is subject to at least some variation around the world, and such differences cause travellers excitement and distress in about equal measure. The tradition in Japan is to name road *junctions* rather than streets, a practice that regularly confuses Europeans, for example, who do the opposite; Egyptians move very close to others in conversation, irritating any foreign visitors who are used to maintaining several feet of 'personal space'; bathrooms have a water tap but lack toilet paper throughout much of Morocco, causing great agitation among Westerners unaccustomed to using one's left hand for bathroom hygiene!

Because a particular culture is the basis for everyone's reality, it is no wonder that people everywhere exhibit **ethnocentrism**, *the practice of judging another culture by the standards of one's own culture*. On one level, some ethnocentrism is inevitable if people are to be emotionally attached to a cultural system. On another level, however, ethnocentrism generates misunderstanding and sometimes conflict.

For example, take the seemingly trivial matter of people in Europe referring to China as the 'Far East'. Such a term, which has little meaning to the Chinese, is an ethnocentric expression for a region that is far east *of Europe*. For their part, the Chinese refer to their country with a word translated as 'Middle Kingdom', suggesting that, like us, they see their society as the centre of the world.

Is there an alternative to ethnocentrism? The logical alternative is to imagine unfamiliar cultural traits from the point of view of *them* rather than *us*. The casual observer of an Amish farmer in Pennsylvania tilling hundreds of hectares with a team of horses rather than a tractor might initially dismiss this practice as hopelessly backward and inefficient. But, from the Amish point of view, hard work is a foundation of religious discipline. The Amish are well aware of tractors; they simply believe that using such machinery would be their undoing.

This alternative approach, called **cultural relativism**, is *the practice of judging a culture by its own standards*. Cultural relativism is a difficult attitude to adopt because it requires that we not only understand the values and norms of another society but also suspend cultural standards we have known all our lives. But, as people of the world come into increasing contact with one another, so we confront the need to understand other cultures more fully.

The world may need greater cultural understanding, but cultural relativity introduces problems of its own. Virtually any kind of behaviour is practised somewhere in the world; does that mean that everything is equally right? Just because Indian and Moroccan families benefit from having their children work long hours, does that justify such child labour? It is hard to appreciate and understand other cultures and yet maybe maintain some sense of a universal standard. There are no simple answers to such dilemmas.

Resist making a snap judgement, so that you can observe unfamiliar cultural surroundings with an open mind. Try to imagine the issue from *their* point of view rather than *yours*. After careful thought, try to evaluate an unfamiliar custom. After all, there is no virtue in passively accepting every cultural practice. But, in reaching a judgement, bear in mind that – despite your efforts – you can never really experience the world as others do. Then turn the argument around and think about your own way of life as others might see it. What we gain most from studying others is insight into ourselves.

A global culture?

Today, more than ever before, we can observe many of the same cultural patterns the world over. Walking the streets of Seoul (South Korea), Kuala Lumpur (Malaysia), Chennai (India), Cairo (Egypt) and Casablanca (Morocco), we find familiar forms of dress, hear well-known pop music, and see advertising for many of the same products we use at home. Just as important, English is rapidly emerging as the preferred second language of most of the world. So are we witnessing the birth of a global culture?

Yet as we have seen, the world is still divided into around 200 nation-states and thousands of different cultural systems. Many of these are in deep conflict. As recent violence in the former Soviet Union, the former Yugoslavia, the Middle East, Sri Lanka and elsewhere attests, many people are intolerant of others whose cultures differ from their own. Yet, looking back through history, we might sense that societies around the world now have more contact with one another, and enjoy more cooperation, than ever before. These global connections involve the flow of goods, information and people.

1. *The global economy: the flow of goods*. The extent of international trade has never been greater. The global economy has introduced many of the same consumer goods (from cars to TV shows to T-shirts) the world over.

2. *Global communications: the flow of information*. A century ago, communication around the world depended on written messages delivered by boat, train, horse and wagon, or, occasionally, by telegraph wire. Today's satellite-based communication system enables people to experience sights and sounds of events taking place thousands of miles away – often as they happen.

3. *Global migration: the flow of people*. Knowledge about the rest of the world motivates people to move where they imagine life will be better. Moreover, today's transportation technology – especially air travel – makes relocating easier than ever before. As a result, most countries now contain significant numbers of people born elsewhere, and tourism has become one of the leading world industries.

Posters for Bollywood films, Bombay India

Source: Corbis © Catherine Karnow

These global links have partially made the cultures of the world more similar, at least in superficial respects. But they have also generated awareness of deep contrasts in world peoples. Some – usually poor and in low-income cultures – remain heavily restricted to a local world. But others have developed a much more flexible, global character. Ulf Hannerz describes this as a *cosmopolitan character*, who adopts:

> a stance towards diversity . . . towards the coexistence of cultures in the individual experience . . . a willingness to engage with the other . . . a stance of openness towards divergent cultural

experiences . . . a search for contrasts rather than towards uniformity . . . a state of readiness, a personal ability to make one's way into other cultures, through listening, looking, intuiting and reflecting . . .

(Hannerz, 1990: 239)

Sociologists also talk of the hybridisation of cultures. Just as in plant biology, a hybrid is a crossover between different species, so **cultural hybridisation** refers to *the ways in which parts of one culture (language, practices, symbols) get recombined with the cultures of another*. Dutch sociologist Jan Nederveen Pieterse puts this strikingly:

How do we come to terms with phenomena such as Thai boxing by Moroccan girls in Amsterdam, Asian rap in London, Irish bagels, Chinese tacos and Mardi Gras Indians in the United States, or Mexican schoolgirls dressed in Greek togas dancing in the style of Isadora Duncan? How do we interpret Peter Brook directing the Mahabharata, or Ariane Manouchkine staging a Shakespeare play in Japanese Kabuki style for a Paris audience in the Théatre Soleil?

(Pieterse, 1995: 53)

But there are three important limitations to the global culture thesis. First, the flow of goods, information and people has been uneven throughout the world. Generally speaking, urban areas (centres of commerce, communication and people) have stronger ties to one another, while rural villages remain more isolated. The greater economic and military power of North America and Western Europe means that these regions influence the rest of the world more than the other way around.

Second, the global culture thesis assumes that people everywhere are able to afford various new goods and services. The grinding poverty in much of the world deprives millions of even the basic necessities of a safe and secure life.

Third, although many cultural traits are now found throughout the world, we should not conclude that people everywhere attach the same meanings to them. Do teenagers in Tokyo understand rap music the way their counterparts in New York or Los Angeles do? Similarly, we mimic fashions from around the world with little knowledge of the lives of people who first came up with them. In short, people everywhere look at the world through their own cultural 'lenses' (Featherstone, 1990; Hall and Neitz, 1993). This process has been identified as **glocalisation**, *the ways in which global phenomena are responded to differently in local cultures*. Karaoke may have been sent round the world from Japan, but it takes on different meanings, songs and rituals when it is done in Thailand, London or San Francisco.

Understanding culture

Through culture, we make sense of ourselves and the surrounding world. Sociologists and anthropologists, however, have the special task of comprehending culture. They do so by using various theoretical paradigms.

The classic approach from anthropology: the functions of a culture

The reason for the stability of a cultural system, as functionalists see it, is that core values anchor its way of life (Parsons and Bales, 1955; Parsons, 1964; orig. 1951; Williams, 1970). The assertion that ideas (rather than, say, the system of material production) are the basis of human reality aligns functionalism with the philosophical doctrine of *idealism*. Core values give shape to most everyday activities, in the process binding together members of a society. New arrivals, of course, will not necessarily share a society's core orientations. But, according to the functionalist melting-pot scheme, immigrants learn to embrace such values over time.

Thinking functionally is also helpful in making sense of an unfamiliar way of life. Recall, for example, the Amish farmer ploughing hundreds of acres with a team of horses. This practice may violate the more widespread cultural value of efficiency; however, from the Amish point of view, hard work functions to generate discipline, which is crucial to Amish religious life. Long days of teamwork, along with family meals and recreation at home, not only make the Amish self-sufficient but unify families and local communities.

Of course, Amish practices have dysfunctions as well. Farm living is hard work, and some people find strict religious discipline too confining, ultimately choosing to leave the community. Then, too, different interpretations of religious principles have generated tensions and sometimes lasting divisions within the Amish world (Hostetler, 1980; Kraybill, 1989; Kraybill and Olshan, 1994).

Because cultures are strategies to meet human needs, we would expect that societies the world over would have some elements in common. The term **cultural universals** refers to *traits that are part of every known culture*. Comparing hundreds of cultures, George Murdock (1945) found dozens of traits common to them all. One cultural universal is the family, which functions everywhere to control sexual reproduction and to organise the care and upbringing of children. Funeral rites, too, are found everywhere, because all human communities cope with the reality of death. Jokes are also a cultural universal, acting as a relatively safe means of releasing social tensions.

Critical comment

The functional paradigm shows how culture operates as an integrated system for meeting human needs, yet by emphasising cultural stability, this approach downplays the extent to which societies change. Similarly, functionalism's assertion that cultural values are embraced by every member of a society overlooks the range of cultural diversity. Finally, the cultural patterns favoured by powerful people often dominate a society, while other ways of life are pushed to the margins. Thus, cultures typically generate more conflict than functional analysis leads us to believe.

OLD CULTURES AND NEW CULTURES IN EUROPE

However unified Europe may or may not seem, it is clear that it harbours many different cultures with different ways of life and ways of doing things. Think of the following:

- *Breakfasts*. While in the UK it is cereals or a fry-up, in France they have croissants and in The Netherlands, cheese and ham.
- *The working day*. While in the UK to have a 'siesta' would be looked upon as outrageously lazy, in most Mediterranean countries the whole system shuts down after lunch for a couple of hours. Workers in Spain or Italy tend to be very casual and relaxed, even chaotic; in Germany, everything is much more formal.
- *Consuming*. The English tend to form queues, but this is not so in many European Union (EU) countries. Further, the English tend to accept the prices of goods from street sellers; not so in most of Europe. In UK bars you order drinks at the bar, pay straight away and do not tip; in most of the EU, you are served, pay at the end and leave a tip.

Yet these cultural differences – many and small – are starting to change. Increasingly, for instance, breakfasts offered at hotels throughout Europe would give a choice of cereals, fry-ups, croissants, cheese and ham, and even Japanese noodles. Cultural differences are both recognised and are breaking down.

And the new cultures

Nowhere was this clearer than when Disney came to Paris. Disneylands all over the world have been a favourite topic of cultural studies (see Bryman, 1995: 81–82, for a listing). EuroDisney, covering about 1,500 acres 20 miles east of Paris and housing six themed hotels, opened on 12 April 1992. EuroDisney was derided by French intellectuals as a cultural Chernobyl, and the unions objected to an almost fascist concern with uniformity that is anathema to the French. 'No one on the Disney payroll is allowed to smoke, wear flashy jewellery, chew gum, tint their hair an unnatural shade, possess a visible tattoo, be fat or fail to subdue their sweat glands. Men must wear their hair short, and may not have a beard or a moustache' (B. Bryson, 1993: 17).

In its opening years it was a significant failure, losing as much as $60 million in one three-month period and raising fears of closure. Many reasons were put forward for this, including the high costs and the poor weather. But at the heart of the complaints was a fear that Disney had come to the wrong place. It was out of culture.

Thus, while the French value food, here it was all fast food. While the French have a lugubrious and nonchalant manner, here the workers had to be cheery and efficient. The French could not easily play the smiling hosts. There was a cultural resistance and cultural contagion. Slowly, EuroDisney has become more successful: there is a lot of money in it, after all. And traditional cultures look less and less stable in the light of McDisney Worlds . . .

Disneyland Paris
Source: Popperfoto

See Alan Bryman, *Disney and His Worlds* (London: Routledge, 1995) and Alan Bryman, *The Disneyization of Society* (London: Sage, 2004)

Culture, conflict and coercion

Cultures are usually unequal, and some traits may benefit some members of society at the expense of others. Why do certain values dominate a society in the first place, and what are the ways in which people come to create their own alternative 'cultures of resistance'? Sociologists, often influenced by Marx, argue that values reflect a society's system of economic production. 'It is not the consciousness of men that determines their existence', Marx proclaimed. 'It is their social existence that determines their consciousness' (1977: 4; orig. 1859).

The tradition of 'critical theory' was developed by the Frankfurt School in the 1930s. Theodor Adorno (1903–69), a leading proponent, suggested that the emerging 'mass culture' – of popular music and film, for example – weakened critical consciousness and manipulated the working masses. He studied the workings of the 'culture industry' and the ways in which it standardised culture, made people passive and served to make people uncritical. For Adorno, the 'culture industry perpetually cheats its consumers of what it perpetually promises' (Adorno and Horkheimer, 1972: 120–123).

Another Marxist tradition was spearheaded by the Italian Antonio Gramsci (1891–1937). A militant in the Italian Communist party, he spent ten years imprisoned by Mussolini. During this time he wrote his famous *Prison Notebooks* which developed the idea of **hegemony**, *the means by which a ruling/dominant group wins over a subordinate group through ideas.* 'Culture' in its many forms may thus serve as a mechanism for encouraging people to accept the existing social order uncritically – as a means of 'winning consent'. Through culture, coercive power may not be needed to maintain dominance. Watching a regular diet of soaps, daytime TV and sports programmes may be sufficient! This argument has been taken further by an English group of sociologists stimulated by the work of Stuart Hall (see Profile box).

From culture to cultural studies

Over the past 30 years, sociology has been challenged by a number of newer disciplines. One of these has been 'cultural studies'. In this section, we will briefly consider a number of routes into this.

The UK tradition: class and resistance

The UK tradition can be (roughly) dated from three important books written by socialist historians and literary critics. They differ from much of the discussion of this chapter, which focuses upon 'culture' as an anthropological and sociological term. Instead, each of these books switched attention to the study of the values, beliefs, behaviour and material culture of the working class in England. The three books are Richard Hoggart's *The Uses of Literacy* (1957), Raymond Williams's *Culture and Society* (1987; orig. 1958), and E. P. Thompson's *The Making of the English Working Class* (1963). What each of these books does is show that working-class culture is an intelligible, active, even coherent and vibrant culture that has historical roots. These authors highlighted the active nature of the working class – how they made their culture.

The Uses of Literacy looks at both traditional working-class culture (and Hoggart's own experiences in Leeds as a child) and the wider development of 1950s popular culture among the young – magazines, jukebox coffee bars – suggesting problems with the latter over the former as a new 'mass culture' emerged. *Culture and Society* formulated 'a theory of culture as the study of relationships in a whole way of life' (Williams, 1987; orig. 1958). *The Making of the English Working Class* traced 'the growth of class consciousness, especially through trade unions, friendly societies, educational and religious movements, political organisations and periodicals – working-class intellectual traditions, working-class community pattern, and a working-class structure of feeling' (Thompson, 1963). What this tradition highlighted, then, was the way in which working-class groups both created their own cultures and resisted other (dominant) ones. Cultures were active, and there was a worry that 'mass culture' was swamping this long-time 'active' nature.

This tradition was taken up and pushed further in the work of Stuart Hall. With Stuart Hall, 'cultural studies' comes into its own. Drawing from Hoggart and others, Hall makes culture a much more political idea. Indeed, as he says, popular culture is 'an arena of consent and resistance. It is partly where hegemony arises, and where it is secured. It is not a sphere where socialism, a socialist culture – already fully formed – might be simply expressed. But it is one of the places where socialism might be instituted. That is why "popular culture" matters' (Hall, in Storey, 1996: 3).

Postmodernism and the new culture

If modernism suggests the need to 'make it new', then postmodernism suggests it has all been done, and all we can do is 'play with the pieces'. In recent times, and despite its controversial nature, postmodernism has

STUART HALL: FROM CULTURE TO CULTURAL STUDIES

Stuart Hall (1932–)

Source: Eamonn McCabe

Born in Jamaica in 1932, Stuart Hall came to England in the early 1950s and eventually became director of the Birmingham Centre for Contemporary Cultural Studies (CCCS) and Professor of Sociology at the Open University. He retired in 1997. He has been one of the world's leading shapers of cultural studies, and has influenced a whole generation of young scholars studying class, race, gender and national cultures. We will see the impact of his work throughout this book, especially when we look at ethnicity, media, identity and class. His students have looked at the ways media 'represent' gender; how ethnic groups battle over their identities; and how dominant political forces – such as 'Thatcherism' – have been resisted through the creation of alternative cultures, rituals and identities. He was indeed a key intellectual to recognise the importance of '**Thatcherism'**, *a political belief grounded in economic individualism and the free market*, and showed how this political philosophy was part of an 'authoritarian populism' which gained wider support in the culture by appealing to materialist and individualist (populist) as well as traditional (Victorian) values. He produced a model of communication with four key moments: production, circulation, use (consumption) and reproduction (see Chapter 21).

His earliest work was explicitly drawn from Marx, but most of his later work does not look to the economy so much as culture. He sees always the importance of people's lived ideas, as they turn them into everyday cultures, though he always sees these cultures enmeshed in the wider workings of the state. Much of his earlier work draws from Althusser and Gramsci, and his more recent work from poststructuralism – again we introduce these terms later (but see the glossary at the end of the book now).

In one of his key books, *Policing the Crisis* (Hall, 1978), he and his colleagues looked at the crime of 'mugging' in England in the early 1970s (1972–73) and showed how black youth were scapegoated for such crimes as part of wider state responses to changes in the organisation of capitalism and the state. He was one of the first to suggest that the growth of new immigrant groups in the UK in the 1950s and 1960s, combined with the recession of the early 1970s, had hit immigrant groups hard. The attacks being made on them were part of a new kind of racist response, deflecting attention away from growing unemployment and declining wages.

One of his key themes has been the ways in which cultures are hybrids, which encourage a fusion of different forms. Hybrid cultures no longer have one form or one set of values, but are much more contradictory and complex. Likewise, people do not have one unitary identity or one sense of who they are. Rather, they speak from many positions, with ethnicity, gender, sexuality and class all coming into it. Globalisation has generated more extreme forms of racism as people try to defend their own national identity.

See Morley and Chen (1996), and Cashmore and Rojek (1999, Rojek (2002).

RESEARCH IN ACTION

CIRCUITS OF CULTURE: DOING CULTURAL STUDIES RESEARCH

In a celebrated discussion, Stuart Hall, Paul du Gay and others have suggested that any cultural item or object can be analysed through a circuit of culture which has five key features. Look at Figure 5.5, and then pick any cultural object that interests you. This can be a film like *Lord of the Rings*; a TV channel like MTV; a TV programme like *Big Brother*; an item of clothing like a *Nike* shoe; or even a technology like a mobile phone. Then think how you can present an analysis of it, following the questions below.

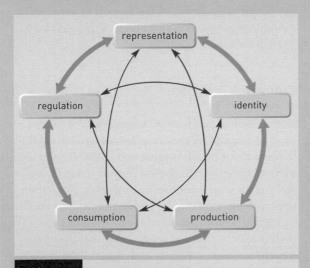

Figure 5.5   The circuit of culture

Circuit of culture

There are five moments in the process of the life of any cultural object – from fashion and food to houses and holidays. These five moments serve to establish:

- *Production*. How are raw materials, labour, time and technologies combined to create an object?

This may include the inventor and founder of the object, but also the economics of its making as well as the cultures of work, the organisation of businesses and so on that generate it.

- *Representation*. What are the ways in which meanings are presented around the object (for example, images in magazines, on television and film, though logos)? This may be through spoken and written words, but also through photographs, videos, drawing, music and painting – in fact any way of representing the 'object'. It now becomes a set of signs, open to interpretation and the creation of meanings.

- *Identities*. What are the roles or positions from which people are recruited to buy this object? Certain styles of fashion (or houses or food) appeal to certain kinds of people. Consuming certain items and not others may enhance style, create a sense of difference and allow for a new identity to be found.

- *Consumption*. What is involved in the exchange of services at the moment when objects are bought and consumed? It is very closely linked to production (but then, as we have shown, they are all linked), where we are concerned in part with marketing strategies, market research, advertising and design features. But the prime concern here is with the accumulation of material goods and the proliferation of spaces for consumption – shops, malls, mail order, emarkets, etc. It is linked with social differentiation (how different groups consume different items) and the ways that consumption may change people's consciousness and perceptions.

- *Regulation*. What are the ways in which the public and private spheres of life are linked in the governance and control of production and consumption? This means looking at the employment rules, any censorship rules, laws which may regulate the way it can be produced and consumed.

Source: Paul Du Gay, Stuart Hall, L. Janes, H. MacKay, and K. Negus (eds), *Doing Cultural Studies: The Story of the Sony Walkman* (Buckingham: Open University Press, 1997).

become a dominant world-view, and is heavily shaped by North America. Once again, a key to the postmodern is a sense of the fragments and the loss of any one unifying theme. Postmodern culture is usually seen to (a) celebrate the surface rather than depth; (b) be eclectic and pastiched; and (c) adopt ironic and even cynical tones.

Postmodern culture is usually seen to originate in the provinces of architecture and art. Thus, postmodern architecture borrows colourfully from past styles and is less concerned with obvious function. It is found in the work of Robert Venturi, Richard Rogers, I. M. Pei and Charles Moore. The Bonaventura Hotel in Los Angeles is perhaps the classic example. Here is a massive hotel in the heart of the downtown city area whose lobby seems to serve like a gigantic aircraft hanger *cum* shopping mall!

Postmodernism suggests a wide variety of pastiched and differing styles. In art it is often linked to new playful forms, such as video art, body art and 'art installations'. Many of the new art galleries, such as the Tate Modern in London, the Guggenheim at Bilbao and the new Getty in Los Angeles, are also seen as prime examples. In literature, postmodernism becomes what writer John Barth has called 'the literature of exhaustion': it is often indulgently self-reflective and is often linked to contradiction, permutation, discontinuity, randomness and excess (Lodge, 1977: 228). Likewise, postmodern films (found in the work of directors such as Jim Jarmusch and David Lynch) often engage with a radical reordering of what are seen as traditional narrative forms. And in postmodern music (John Cage, John Adams, Michael Nyman) the form is usually bare and minimalist yet with striking techno-sonic effects.

Looking ahead: culture and human freedom

Throughout this chapter, we have touched on the extent to which cultural creatures are free. Does culture bind us to each other and to the past? Or does culture enhance our capacity for individual thought and independent choices?

Culture as constraint

Over the long course of human evolution, culture became the human strategy for survival. Truly, we cannot live without culture. But the capacity for culture does have some drawbacks. We may be the only animals who name ourselves, yet, as symbolic beings, we are also the only creatures who experience alienation. Moreover, culture is largely a matter of habit, limiting our choices and driving us to repeat troubling patterns, such as racial prejudice, in each new generation. And, in an electronic age, we may wonder at the extent to which the news media and businesses manipulate people into believing they must see the latest films or wear the latest styles of clothing.

Moreover, while our society's insistence on competitive achievement urges us towards excellence, this same pattern also isolates us from one another. Material comforts improve our lives in many ways, yet our preoccupation with acquiring things distracts us from seeking the security and satisfaction of close relationships or cultivating spiritual strength. Our emphasis on personal freedom affords us privacy and autonomy, yet our culture often denies us the support of a human community in which to share life's problems (Slater, 1976; Bellah *et al.*, 1985).

Culture as freedom

Human beings may seem to be prisoners of culture, just as other animals are prisoners of biology. But careful thought about the ideas presented in this chapter reveals a crucial difference. Biological instinct operates in a ready-made world; culture, by contrast, gives us the responsibility to make and remake a world for ourselves.

Therefore, although culture seems at times to circumscribe our lives, it always embodies the human capacity for hope, creativity and choice. There is no better evidence of this than the fascinating cultural diversity of our own society and the far greater human variety of the larger world. Furthermore, far from being static, culture is ever-changing; it allows our imagination and inventiveness to come to the fore. The more we discover about the operation of our culture, the greater our capacity to use the freedom it offers us.

CONTROVERSY AND DEBATE

WHOSE CULTURE? WHOSE VOICE? EUROCENTRISM, MULTICULTURALISM AND POSTCOLONIALISM IN SOCIOLOGY

For some, Europe can be seen as the cradle of the modern world. Indeed, for the Swedish sociologist Goran Therborn:

'There is no doubt that Europe was the pioneer of modernity and the centre of it. Neither the Islamic, the Black African, the Hindu nor the East Asian Confucian world seems to have discovered the future as a new place, attainable but never visited before. . . Europe became the undisputed centre of modernity in terms of knowledge as well as in terms of power'.

(Therborn, 1995: 19)

It was the 'chief organiser' of this modern world. For Therborn, there are many features of this. Europe's 'modernity' brought new knowledge, new settlements around the world, new technologies and capital investment, as well as the development of all the 'isms' – socialism, communism, anarchism, liberalism, Protestantism, etc.

But 'a sense of Europe' can go back a long way. Some writers suggest that European culture can be defined by four elements that mark it off from the rest of the world:

- The Hellenistic and Roman Empires – rediscovered through the Renaissance – which helped establish a sense of art, politics and philosophy that shapes a characteristic 'humanistic' temper.
- Christianity, which for two millennia, and despite oppositions and internal schisms, has pervaded the European idea (and at times the very words 'Europe' and 'Christendom' were synonymous).
- The Enlightenment – the creation of a scientific, sceptical, creative intellectual climate helps to define it – as does the 'Europabild' literature.
- Industrialisation: while not alone, and these days overtaken by many other countries, it was the first region to foster the industrial world (Hay, 1968; Joll, 1969).

Yet there are serious problems with this commonly held 'Eurocentric' view. Taking a European view of the world often minimises the importance of other cultures: Asian, Latin American, African, etc. It also cultivates a view of Europe as an entity with a history of continuity, which on closer inspection is hard to sustain. Greek history, for example, is as much connected to the Middle East and the Orient. Indeed, the eminent historian Arnold Toynbee saw this continuity as a 'thoroughgoing misinterpretation of the history of Mankind' – a dangerous tendency that minimised the contribution of many other cultures. These days, this is recognised as the twin problem of 'multiculturalism' and 'postcolonialism'.

The European flag
Source: Popperfoto

Originally emerging as an education policy in the United States, **multiculturalism** *recognises past and present cultural diversity and promotes the equality of all cultural traditions*. This movement represents a sharp turn from the view where cultures are defined through their European links. **Post-colonialism** *recognises how many cultures have been made through oppressor–subject relationships and seeks to unpack these, showing how cultures are made*.

For more than two centuries, historians have highlighted people of English and other European ancestry and chronicled events from their point of view. In the process, little attention has been paid to the perspectives and accomplishments of other cultures. Multiculturalists condemn this pattern as **Eurocentrism**, *the dominance of European (particularly English) cultural patterns*. Molefi Kete Asante, a leading advocate of multiculturalism, draws a ▶

CONTROVERSY AND DEBATE CONTINUED

historical analogy. Like the fifteenth-century Europeans who could not let go of the idea that the earth was the centre of the universe, many today find it difficult not to view European culture as the centre of the social universe (Asante, 1988: 7).

Few deny that our culture has wide-ranging roots. But multiculturalism is controversial because it demands that we rethink the norms and values at the core of our society. Not surprisingly, battles are now raging over how to describe culture. To counter pervasive Eurocentrism, some multiculturalists are calling for **Afrocentrism,** *the dominance of African cultural patterns*, which they see as a corrective for centuries of minimising or altogether ignoring the cultural achievements of African societies.

And other cultures are making similar claims. Throughout much of history the world has been colonised by other countries and nations. Many countries have been invaded by others and had their cultures uprooted, transformed, even destroyed. And today, whenever we look at cultures, we tend to see them from the point of our own.

Frantz Fanon analysed the impact of white colonialism on blacks. He aimed through his writings to liberate the consciousness of the oppressed. In the first phase he sees how blacks may become assimilated to dominant white culture; a second phase sees the black writer disturbed; and a third sees the native writers turning themselves into awakeners of the people. But labels such as African, Muslim, American, 'Chinese' or, worse, 'Chineseness' are no more than starting points. The object then is to 'deconstruct' them – to take them apart and see what lies behind them.

Although multiculturalism and postcolonialism have found widespread favour in the last several years, they have provoked criticism as well. Opponents think they encourage divisiveness rather than unity by urging individuals to identify with their own category rather than with common elements. Similarly, rather than recognise any common standards of truth, say critics, multiculturalism maintains that we should evaluate ideas according to the race (and sex) of those who present them. Common humanity thus dissolves into an 'African voice', an 'Asian voice', and so on.

Critics say that multiculturalism and postcolonialism may not end up helping minorities, as proponents contend. They argue that multiculturalist initiatives (from African-American studies to all-black college accommodation) seem to demand precisely the kind of racial segregation we do not want. Then, too, an Asiacentric curriculum may well deny children a wide range of crucial knowledge and skills by forcing them to study only certain topics from a single point of view. Whose voices are to be heard?

Is there any common ground in this debate? Virtually everyone agrees that all people in Europe need to gain greater appreciation of the extent of cultural diversity. Eurocentric views distort an appreciation of the emergent global cultures, all with their differing languages, symbols, countercultures, etc. But precisely where the balance is to be struck is a burning issue for a new generation of sociologists.

CONTINUE THE DEBATE:

1. Do you think there is a truly distinctive 'European' culture with history and roots? What does it look like, and what is its history? Does it have a coherence, or does it conceal many voices?

2. How does the multiculturalism debate shape our views on school curricula and language learning? What are the pros and cons of different curricula and languages?

3. Whose voices are being heard once you adopt a 'postcolonial' voice?

Sources: Wintle (1996), Castles and Miller (1993)

SUMMARY

1. Cultures are 'designs for living' and refer to ways of life. They are partly material (tangible things like telephones or pottery), partly non-material (for example, ideas) and involve practices (the practical logics through which we act and think in everyday life). Several species display a limited capacity for culture, but only human beings rely on culture for survival.

2. As the human brain evolved, the first elements of culture appeared some 2 million years ago; the development of culture reached the point we call 'the birth of civilisation' approximately 12,000 years ago.

3. Humans build culture on *symbols* by attaching meaning to objects and action. *Language* is the symbolic system by which one generation transmits culture to the next. *Values* represent general orientations to the world around us; *beliefs* are statements that people who share a culture hold to be true. Cultural *norms* guide human behaviour: *mores* consist of norms of great moral significance; *folkways* guide everyday life and afford greater individual discretion. *Material culture* refers to tangible human creations.

4. High culture refers to patterns that distinguish a society's elites; popular culture includes patterns widespread in a society. Subculture refers to distinctive cultural patterns adopted by a segment of a population; counterculture means patterns strongly at odds with a conventional way of life.

5. Multiculturalism represents educational efforts to enhance awareness and appreciation of cultural diversity.

6. Invention, discovery and diffusion all generate cultural change. When parts of a cultural system change at different rates, this is called cultural lag.

7. Because we learn the standards of one culture, we evaluate other cultures ethnocentrically. An alternative to ethnocentrism, cultural relativism, means judging another culture according to its own standards. The conflict perspective envisages culture as a dynamic arena of inequality and conflict. Cultural patterns typically benefit some categories of people more than others.

8. Increasingly we live in global cultures that generated hybrids and cosmopolitan characters.

9. Cultures may be approached functionally (as a relatively stable system built on core values. Cultural traits function to maintain the overall system). They may also be approached conflictually as webs of inequality, mass culture and hegemony.

10. The past 20 years has seen the growth of cultural studies.

11. Multiculturalism and postcolonialism help us develop ways of thinking outside our own cultures.

12. Culture can constrain human needs and ambitions; yet, as cultural creatures, we have the capacity to shape and reshape the world to meet our needs and pursue our dreams.

CRITICAL-THINKING QUESTIONS

1. What is the cultural significance of a carefully manicured lawn in a highly mobile and largely anonymous society? What does a well-tended (or untended) front garden say about a person? Now consider what 'becoming a Goth' says about a person? Can all things be looked at this way?

2. Give instances of Eurocentrism found in this textbook (if you can find them!). Are there European values? Do you think European cultural values are changing? If so, how and why?

3. Using some of the key concepts developed in this chapter – language, values, material culture, etc. – present an analysis of any one cultural group you know (such as a religious culture, a sports culture, a youth culture or a 'deviant' culture). (*Hint*: look back at Chapter 3 on ways of doing research.)

4. Are we seeing the globalisation of youth? How far do you think young people in your own country have more in common with youth of other countries compared with older people in their own country? Discuss in relation to the idea of globalisation introduced in Chapter 2 and 'glocalisation' introduced in this chapter.

GOING FURTHER

Further reading

General:

Martin J. Gannon, *Understanding Global Cultures: Metaphorical Journeys through 23 Nations* (2nd edn, 2001) Provides a series of short case studies of different cultures through an organising image such as 'The Japanese Garden', 'The Brazilian Samba', American Football, the Spanish Bullfight and the Swedish *Stuga*.

The youth cultures debates:

Ken Gelder and Sarah Thornton (eds), *The Subcultures Reader* (1997) Provides a series of classic readings around subcultures and the different forms of youth cultures. It is essential reading for anyone interested in this field.

D. Muggleton and R. Weinzierl (eds), *The Post-Subcultures Reader* (2004) Provides a more up-to-date challenge to subcultural theories, raising many new concepts and ideas.

On cultural studies:

The new field of cultural studies should not be confused with 'culture', which generally has a much broader set of concerns.

Simon Duhring (ed.), *The Cultural Studies Reader* (1993) Includes articles by Adorno, Hall, Williams, Bourdieu and many others.

Ellis Cashmore, *Beckham* (2004) An interesting case study which looks at the famous footballer and his cultural implications.

Watch a video/Read a book

Wim Wender's much acclaimed film *Buona Vista Social Club* (1991) ostensibly looks at the making of music in Cuba, but conveys much more about culture. Watch some videos that display youth cultures and look for their language, values, symbols, etc. Have a look at Nicholas Ray's *Rebel without a Cause* (1955), Dennis Hopper's *Easy Rider* (1969), John Badham's *Saturday Night Fever* (1977), Michael Lehman's *Heathers* (1989) and Catherine Hardwicke's *Thirteen* (2004). These are just a few and span some 50 years. All are based on US culture and show the drifting cultural forms of youth cultures. Search for more and maybe think of drawing up a comparison.

Maybe also read some books on 'culture clash'. E. M. Forster's *A Passsage to India* (1924) (also a film by David Lean (1985)) and Henry James's *The Europeans* (1978 edn), also a Merchant-Ivory film (1978), would be interesting starts.

Connecting up

Connect to other chapters

- For more on semiology and how to do a mass media analysis, see Chapter 21.
- For more on cultural studies, see Bourdieu in Chapter 19.
- For links to media studies, see Chapter 21.

To the websites

- World Values Survey:
  http://wvs.isr.umich.edu/
- Eurobarometer:
  http://www.social-science-gesis.de/en/data_service/eurobarometer/ceeb/
  http://europa.eu.int/comm/dg10/epo/eb.html
- British Social Attitudes, conducted by the National Centre for Social Research each year with a random sample of around 3,500:
  http://www.natcen.ac.uk/
  A major listing of resources for cultural studies from Blackwell publishers:
  http://www.blackwellpublishers.co.uk/cultural/
- A good source of social theory for fans of popular culture:
  http://www.theory.org.uk
- Human Relations Area Files are a major resource on different cultures:
  http://www.yale.edu/hraf/
  Cultural Studies Central
  www.culturalstudies.net

For additional case studies, multiple choice questions, internet exercises, and annotated weblinks specific to this chapter, visit this book's website at **www.pearsoned.co.uk/plummer**

CHAPTER 6

GROUPS, ORGANISATIONS AND THE RISE OF THE NETWORK SOCIETY

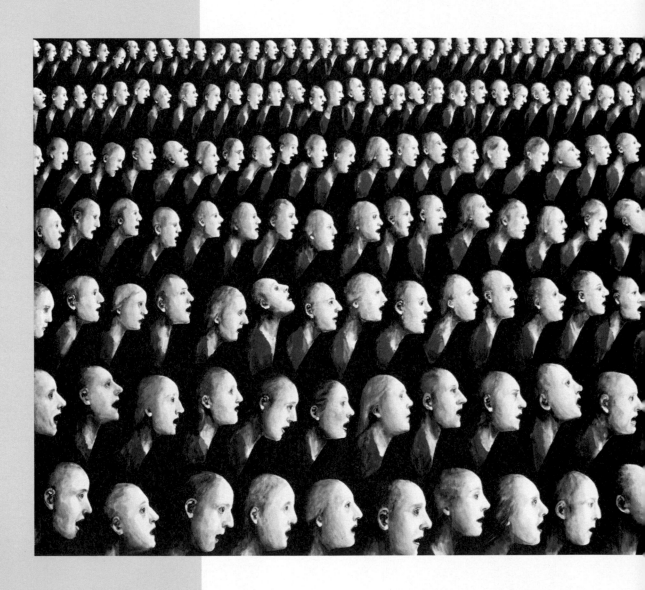

Life is a network.

David Wellman

SIXTY YEARS AGO, the opening of a new restaurant in Pasadena, California, attracted little attention from the local community and went unnoticed by the world as a whole. Yet this seemingly insignificant small business, owned and operated by Mac and Dick McDonald, would eventually spark a revolution in the restaurant industry and provide an organisational model that would be copied by countless other businesses and even schools and churches.

The basic formula the McDonald brothers put into place –'fast food' – was to serve food quickly and inexpensively to large numbers of people. They trained employees to perform highly specialised jobs, so that one person grilled hamburgers, while others 'dressed' them, made French fries, whipped up milkshakes, and presented the food to the customers in assembly-line fashion.

As the years went by, the McDonald brothers prospered, and they moved their single restaurant from Pasadena to San Bernardino. It was there, in 1954, that events took an unexpected turn when Ray Kroc, a travelling blender and mixer merchant, paid a visit to the McDonalds.

Kroc was fascinated by the brothers' efficient system, and, almost immediately, he saw the potential for a greatly expanded system of fast-food restaurants. Initially, Kroc launched his plans in partnership with the McDonald brothers. Soon, however, he bought out their interests and set out on his own to become one of the greatest success stories of all time. Today, 30,000 McDonald's restaurants serve 45 million meals a day across 121 countries of the world. One in 200 people across the world visit a McDonald's daily. In the UK, more than 2.5 million people eat at a McDonald's everyday. It is the best-known 'brand' in the world. It is also the biggest toy distributor, and 96 per cent of US children can identify Ronald McDonald by name ... second only to Santa Claus.

KEY THEMES

- The nature of social groups
- The workings of organisations
- The McDonaldisation thesis and its critics
- Network theory and the rise of the network society

(Left) Face to Face, 1994. (oil on canvas) Evelyn Williams. © Private collection/www.bridgeman.co.uk
Source: Bridgeman Art Library

(Above) Artist's impression of new McDonalds resturant in Des Moines
Source: McDonald Corporation

From a sociological point of view, the success of McDonald's reveals much more than the popularity of hamburgers. As this chapter will explain, the larger importance of this story lies in the extent to which the principles that guide the operation of McDonald's are coming to dominate much of social life in very many parts of the world. So much so, that sociologists have started to talk of the **McDonaldisation of society**, *a process by which the principles of the fast-food industry come to be applied to more and more features of social life.* Close intimate groups are giving way to fast, efficient but distant ones. At the same time, the way that people communicate and get close to others is changing. No longer living in stable or well-bounded groups and communities, as we like to think people did in the past, many people now live their lives increasingly through networks. Through standard phones, mobile phones, the car, the email, the fax, we can now develop close relations with a complex network of people scattered over a wide area, even the globe. Often people we have never seen can become our 'friends'!

In this chapter we will begin by examining one of the oldest ideas of sociology: that we live in *social groups*, the clusters of people with whom we associate in much of our daily lives. As we shall see, the scope of group life expanded greatly during the twentieth century. From a world built on kin and community – usually small, local, face-to-face and intense – the structure of many societies now turns on the operation of vast businesses, bureaucracies and formal organisations – usually large, impersonal and fleeting. And even more recently, we can 'log on' to our computer and surf the Net with a vast array of unknown individuals across the world. We now, as they say, 'network'. Understanding how this changing and expanding scale of life has come to dominate society, and what it means for us as individuals, are the chapter's key objectives.

Social groups

Virtually everyone moves through life with a sense of belonging; this is the experience of group life. A **social group** refers to *two or more people who identify and interact with one another.* Human beings continually come together to form couples, families, circles of friends, gangs, neighbourhoods, churches, businesses, clubs, communities, transnational corporations and numerous large organisations. Whatever the form, groups encompass people with shared experiences, loyalties and interests. In short, while maintaining their individuality, the members of social groups also think of themselves as

a special 'we'. In what follows, we shall introduce a few terms that help clarify our thinking about groups: primary and secondary groups, group conformity, reference groups and group size.

A basic distinction: primary and secondary groups

Acquaintances commonly greet one another with a smile and the simple phrase 'How are you?'. The response is usually a well-scripted 'Fine, thanks. How are you?'. This answer, of course, is often more formal than truthful. In most cases, providing a detailed account of how you are *really* doing would prompt the other person to beat a hasty and awkward exit.

Sociologists classify social groups by measuring them against two ideal types based on members' level of genuine personal concern. This variation is the key to distinguishing *primary* from *secondary* groups.

Charles Horton Cooley (1864–1929) was a pioneering North American sociologist. He is most famed for his idea of the *looking-glass self*, discussed in Chapter 7. According to Cooley, a **primary group** is a *small social group whose members share personal and enduring relationships.* Bound together by *primary relationships*, individuals in primary groups typically spend a great deal of time together, engage in a wide range of common activities and feel that they know one another well. Although not without periodic conflict, members of primary groups display sincere concern for each other's welfare. This is the world of family and friends. The strength of primary relationships gives people a comforting sense of security. In the familiar social circles of family or friends, people feel they can 'be themselves' without constantly worrying about the impressions they are making.

Members of primary groups generally provide one another with economic and other forms of assistance as well. But, as important as primary ties are, people generally think of a primary group as an end in itself rather than as a means to other ends. In other words, we prefer to think that kinship or friendship links people who 'belong together', rather than people who expect to benefit from each other. For this reason, we readily call on family members or close friends to help us move into a new apartment, without expecting to pay for their services. And we would do the same for them. A friend who never returns a favour, by contrast, is likely to leave us feeling 'used' and questioning the depth of the friendship.

Moreover, this personal orientation means that members of a primary group view each other as unique and irreplaceable. We typically do not care who cashes our cheque at the bank or takes our money at the supermarket checkout. Yet in the primary group – especially the family – we are bound to specific others by emotion and loyalty. So even though brothers and sisters do not always get along, they always remain siblings.

In contrast to the primary group, the **secondary group** is *a large and impersonal social group whose members pursue a specific interest or activity*. In most respects, secondary groups have precisely the opposite characteristics of primary groups. *Secondary relationships* usually involve weak emotional ties and little personal knowledge of one another. Secondary groups vary in duration, but they are frequently short-term, beginning and ending without particular significance. Students following a university course, for instance, who may not see one another after the term ends, exemplify the secondary group.

Weaker social ties permit secondary groups to include many more people than primary groups do. For example, dozens or even hundreds of people may work together in the same office, yet most of them pay only passing attention to one another. Sometimes the passing of time will transform a group from secondary to primary, as with co-workers who share an office for many years. Generally, however, the boundary separating members of a secondary group from non-members is far less clear than it is for primary groups.

Secondary groups lack strong loyalties and emotions because members look to one another only to achieve limited ends. So while members of primary groups display a *personal orientation*, people in secondary groups reveal a *goal orientation*. Secondary ties are not necessarily always aloof or cold, of course. Social interactions among students, co-workers and business associates are often quite pleasant, even if they are rather impersonal. The goal orientation of secondary groups encourages individuals to craft their behaviour carefully. In these roles, we remain characteristically impersonal and polite. The secondary relationship, therefore, is one in which the question 'How are you?' may be asked without really expecting a truthful answer.

In primary groups, members define each other according to *who* they are – that is, in terms of kinship or unique, personal qualities. Members of secondary groups, by contrast, look to one another for *what* they are or what they can do for each other. In secondary groups, in other words, we are always mindful of what we offer others and what we receive in return. This 'scorekeeping' comes through most clearly in business relationships. Likewise, the people next door typically expect that a neighbourly favour will be reciprocated. Table 6.1 summarises these characteristics. (Keep in mind that

these traits define two types of social group in ideal terms; actual group in our lives may well contain elements of both.) By placing these concepts as ends of a continuum, sociologists have devised a basic but useful scheme for describing and analysing group life.

A long-standing sociological view suggests that rural areas and small towns tend towards a greater emphasis on primary relationships while large cities are typically more secondary. While this holds some truth, some urban neighbourhoods – especially those populated by people of a single ethnicity, religion, or even sexual orientation – can be quite tightly knit. 'Jewish neighbourhoods', ' Polish communities' or 'gay communities' are usually strong in primary orientation, with local meeting places or bars to facilitate this.

Primary relationships may well predominate in low-income pre-industrial societies throughout Latin America, Africa and Asia, in which people's lives still often revolve around families and local villages. Especially in rural areas, strangers stand out in the social landscape. But even many of these countries now find more and more of their populations live in cities where secondary relations have become much more common. In high-income industrial societies, in which people assume highly specialised social roles, secondary ties usually take precedence. Most people in England, for example, routinely engage in impersonal, secondary contacts with virtual strangers – people about whom they know very little and whom they may never meet again.

Table 6.1	Primary groups and secondary groups: a summary	
	Primary group	**Secondary group**
Quality of relationships	Personal orientation	Goal orientation
Duration of relationships	Usually long-term	Variable; often short-term
Breadth of relationships	Broad; usually involving many activities	Narrow; usually involving few activities
Subjective perception of relationships	As ends in themselves	As means to an end
Typical examples	Families; circles of friends	Co-workers; political organisations

Group conformity

In most of the Western world, people do not like to think they are 'conformists', that they follow the group. Most people like to think they are unique individuals, that they in some way stand out from the crowd. But think for a minute of the main groups you belong to – at school, university, in sport, at home. Think of your peer group and how you want (or even need) to be accepted by them. Maybe you do stand out as a less conformist person, but many social psychological studies have shown that group conformity is very likely. This section looks at two classic yet still widely cited social psychological studies that suggest this. Social scientists confirm the power of group pressure to shape human behaviour and report that it remains strong in adulthood as well as in adolescence.

Asch's research

Solomon Asch (1952) conducted a classic investigation that revealed the power of group conformity. Asch recruited students for an alleged study of visual perception. Before the actual experiment, however, he revealed to all but one member in each small group that their real purpose was to impose group pressure on the remaining subject. Placing all the students around a table, Asch asked each, in turn, to note the length of a 'standard' line, as shown on Card 1 in Figure 6.1, and match it to one of three lines on Card 2.

Anyone with normal vision could easily see that the line marked 'A' on Card 2 was the correct choice. Initially, as planned, everyone made the matches correctly. But then Asch's secret accomplices began answering incorrectly, making the naive subject (seated at the table in order to answer next to last) bewildered and uncomfortable.

What happened? Asch found that one-third of all subjects placed in this situation chose to conform to the others by answering incorrectly. His investigation indicates that many people are willing to compromise their judgements to avoid the discomfort of being different from others, even from people they do not know. Think about yourself for a minute: do you think you would conform like this?

Milgram's research

In an equally famous (even notorious) set of experiments, Stanley Milgram – a former student of Solomon Asch – conducted conformity experiments that were even more surprising. In Milgram's initial study (Milgram, 1963, 1965; Miller, 1986), a researcher explained to male recruits that they were about to engage in a study of how punishment affects learning. One by one, he assigned them the role of 'teacher' and placed another individual – an insider to the study – in a connecting room as the 'learner'.

The teacher saw the learner sit down in an ominous contraption resembling an electric chair with an electrode attached to one arm. The researcher then had the teacher read aloud pairs of words. In the next step, the teacher repeated the first word of each pair and asked the learner to recall the corresponding second word.

As mistakes occurred, the researcher instructed the teacher to shock the learner using a 'shock generator', a bogus but forbidding-looking piece of equipment with a shock switch and a dial marked to regulate electric current from 15 volts (labelled 'mild shock') to 300 volts (marked 'intense shock') to 450 volts (marked 'Danger: Severe Shock' and 'XXX'). Beginning at the lowest level, the researcher told the teacher to increase the shock by 15 volts every time the learner made a mistake. The shocks, explained the researcher, would become painful but cause no permanent damage. And so it went. At 75, 90 and 105 volts, the teacher heard audible moans from the learner; at 120 volts, shouts of pain; at 270 volts, screams of agony; and, after 330 volts, deadly silence.

The results show just how readily authority figures can obtain compliance from ordinary people. None of 40 subjects assigned in the role of teacher during the initial research even questioned the procedure before 300 volts had been applied, and 26 of the subjects – almost two-thirds – went all the way to 450 volts.

Milgram (1964) then modified his research to see if Solomon Asch had documented such a high degree of group conformity only because the task of matching lines seemed trivial. What if groups pressured people to

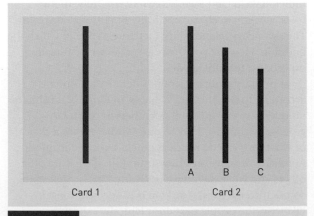

Figure 6.1   Cards used in Asch's experiment (Asch, 1952) in group conformity

administer electrical shocks? To investigate, he varied the experiment so that a group of three teachers, two of whom were his accomplices, made decisions jointly. Milgram's rule was that each of the three teachers would suggest a shock level when the learner made an error and they would then administer the lowest of the three suggestions. This arrangement gave the naive subject the power to lessen the shock level regardless of the other two teachers' recommendations.

The accomplices called for increasing the shock level with each error, placing group pressure on the third member to do the same. Responding to this group pressure, subjects applied voltages three to four times higher than in control conditions in which subjects acted alone. Thus Milgram's research suggests that people are surprisingly likely to follow the directions not only of 'legitimate authority figures', but also of groups of ordinary individuals.

Reference groups

How do we assess our own attitudes or behaviour? Frequently, we make use of a **reference group**, *a social group that serves as a point of reference in making evaluations or decisions*.

A young lad who imagines the response of his 'mates' to a girl he is going out with is using his friends as a reference group. Similarly, a banker who assesses her colleagues' reactions to a new loan policy is using her co-workers as a standard of reference. As these examples illustrate, reference groups can be primary or secondary. In each case, the motivation to conform to a group means that the attitudes of others can greatly affect us. We also use groups that we do *not* belong to for reference. People preparing for job interviews typically notice how those in the company they wish to join dress and act, adjusting their personal performances accordingly.

Stouffer's classic research

Samuel A. Stouffer (1949) and his associates conducted a classic study of reference group dynamics during the Second World War. In a survey, researchers asked soldiers to evaluate the chances of promotion for a competent soldier in their branch of the service. One might guess that soldiers serving in outfits with a high promotion rate would be optimistic about their future advancement. Yet survey results supported the opposite conclusion: soldiers in branches of the service with low promotion rates were actually more optimistic about their own chances to move ahead.

The key to this paradox lies in sorting out the groups against which the soldiers measured their progress. Those in branches with low promotion rates looked around them and saw people making no more headway than they were. That is, they had not been promoted, but neither had many others, so they did not feel unjustly deprived. Soldiers in service branches with high promotion rates, however, could easily think of people who had been promoted sooner or more often than they had. With such people in mind, even soldiers who had been promoted themselves were likely to feel short-changed. So these were the soldiers who voiced more negative attitudes in their evaluations.

Stouffer's research demonstrates that we do not make judgements about ourselves in isolation, nor do we compare ourselves with just anyone. Instead, we use specific social groups as standards in developing individual attitudes. Whatever our situation in *absolute* terms, then, we assess our well-being subjectively, *relative* to some specific reference group (Merton, 1968; Mirowsky, 1987).

Group size: form over content

If you are the first person to arrive at a party, you can observe some fascinating group dynamics. Until about six people enter the room, everyone generally shares a single conversation. But as more people arrive, the group divides into two or more smaller clusters. It is apparent that size plays a crucial role in how group members interact.

To understand why, consider the formal (and here, mathematical) connection between the number of people in a social group and the number of relationships among them. As Figure 6.2 shows, two people form a single relationship (a dyad); adding a third person generates three relationships (a triad); adding a fourth person yields six. Increasing the number of people one at a time, then, boosts the number of relationships much more rapidly, since every new individual can interact with everyone already there. Thus, five people produce ten relationships and, by the time six people join one conversation, 15 'channels' connect them. This leaves too many people unable to speak, which is why the group usually divides at this point.

The dyad

The German sociologist Georg Simmel (1858–1918), profiled in the box, built a sociology of forms in which he explored social dynamics in the smallest social groups. He used the term **dyad** to designate *a social group with two members*. Throughout the world, most love affairs, marriages and the closest friendships are dyadic.

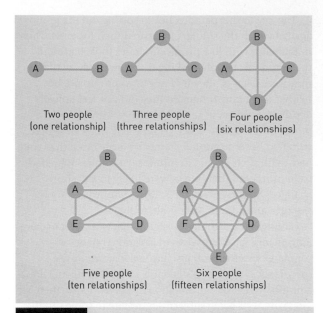

Figure 6.2	Group size and relationships

What makes the dyad a special relationship? First, explained Simmel, social interaction in a dyad is typically more intense than in larger groups since, in a one-to-one relationship, neither member shares the other's attention with anyone else. Thus dyads have the potential to be the most meaningful social bonds we ever experience.

Second, Simmel explains, like a stool with only two legs, dyads have a characteristic instability. Both members of a dyad must actively sustain the relationship; if either one withdraws, the group collapses. Because of the importance of marriage to society, the marital dyad is supported with legal, economic and often religious ties. By contrast, a large group such as a charity run by volunteers is inherently much more stable, as it can survive the loss of many members.

Marriage in our society is dyadic; ideally, we expect powerful emotional ties to unite husbands and wives. As we shall see in Chapter 17, however, marriage in other societies may involve more than two people. In that case, the household is usually more stable, though many of the marital relationships are weaker (Simmel, 1950; orig. 1902).

The triad

Simmel also probed the **triad**, *a social group with three members*. A triad encompasses three relationships, each uniting two of the three people. A triad is more stable than a dyad because, should the relationship between any two members become strained, the third can act as a

mediator to restore the group's vitality. This process of group dynamics helps explain why members of a dyad (say, a married couple) sometimes seek out a third person (a counsellor) to air tensions between them.

Nonetheless, two of the three can form a coalition to press their views on the third, or two may intensify their relationship, leaving the other feeling like a 'third wheel'. For example, two members of a triad who develop a romantic interest in each other will understand the old saying 'Two's company, three's a crowd'.

As groups grow beyond three members, they become progressively more stable because the loss of even several members does not threaten the group's existence. At the same time, increases in group size typically reduce the intense personal interaction possible only in the smallest groups. Larger groups are thus based less on personal attachments and more on formal rules and regulations. Such formality helps a large group persist over time, though the group is not immune to change. After all, their numerous members give large groups more contact with the outside world, opening the door to new attitudes and behaviour (Carley, 1991).

Does a social group have an ideal size? The answer depends on the group's purpose. A dyad offers unsurpassed emotional intensity, while a group of several dozen members is more stable, capable of accomplishing larger, more complex tasks, and is better able to assimilate new members or ideas. People typically find more *personal pleasure* in smaller groups, while deriving greater *task satisfaction* from accomplishments in larger organisations (Slater, 1958; Ridgeway, 1983; Carley, 1991).

Social diversity

Social diversity affects group dynamics, especially the likelihood that members will interact with someone of another group. Peter Blau (Blau, 1977; Blau *et al.*, 1982; South and Messner, 1986) points out four ways in which the composition of social groups affects intergroup association.

1. *Large groups turn inwards*. Extending Simmel's analysis of group size, Blau explains that the larger a group, the more likely its members are to maintain relationships exclusively among themselves. The smaller the group, by contrast, the more members will reach beyond their immediate social circle.

   To illustrate, consider the efforts of many universities to include a wider range of students from overseas. Increasing the number of international students may add important dimensions to a campus, but, as their

PROFILE

GEORG SIMMEL: A SOCIOLOGY OF FORMS

When students encounter sociology, they invariably hear of the three giants – Marx, Durkheim, Weber – who have already been introduced several times in this book. They may hear of a fourth 'founding theorist' – Simmel (1858–1918), but rarely will they ever consider him in any detail. Yet his influence has been very profound.

Simmel adopted a distinctive and wide-ranging approach to sociology, studying many things from money and gender to cities and 'strangers'. He viewed society as interaction, and believed the task of the sociologist was to study the interactive webs into which people entered. He was keen to depict the ways in which changing numbers and scales of interactions brought about profoundly different relationships. In the text, you see how he contrasted simple dyads with triads and the difference this makes.

But he also looked at how social relations changed as cities emerged and relationships became more and more impersonal. He provided a sociological portrait of people's changing consciousness under modernity, and especially cities. He saw there was a downside to this: people kept their distance from each other. But there was also an upside: people became more tolerant and even sophisticated (see Chapter 23).

Simmel invented a style of sociology known as formal sociology: a sociology which studies the underlying forms of interaction in society. To do this, he distinguished between content and form. Social life is about content in so far as it studies such things as marriage, war, education and drug-taking. But for sociology to be systematic it needed more than studies of little areas of social life and their contents: instead it also needed to piece together the underlying social processes that they have in common. Thus, for instance, one common process found in social life is conflict: you can look at marriages, wars, education and drug-taking and you will usually find elements of social interaction involving conflicts. Sociologists needed not just to study contents, then, but also forms.

A brilliant essayist, Simmel left his mark on much contemporary sociology which looks at forms of interaction.

For a short guide to Simmel's work, see David Frisby, *Georg Simmel* (London: Tavistock, 1984).

---

numbers rise, these students eventually are able to maintain their own distinctive social group. Thus intentional efforts to promote social diversity may well have the unintended effect of promoting separatism.

2. *Heterogeneous groups turn outwards.* The more internally heterogeneous a group is, the more likely its members are to interact with members of other groups. We would expect, for example, that campus groups that recruit members of both sexes and people of various ethnic and geographic backgrounds would promote more intergroup contact than those that choose members of only one social type.

3. *Social parity promotes contact.* An environment in which all groups have roughly equal standing encourages people of all social backgrounds to mingle and form social ties. Thus, whether groups insulate their members or not depends on whether the groups themselves form a social hierarchy.

4. *Physical boundaries foster social boundaries.* Blau contends that physical space affects the chances of contacts among groups. To the extent that a social group is physically segregated from others (by having its own accommodation or dining area, for example), its members are less apt to engage other people.

Organisations

Throughout human history, most people lived in small groups of family members and neighbours; this pattern was still widespread in Europe and the United States a century ago. Today, families and neighbourhoods persist, of course, but our lives revolve far more around **formal organisations**, *large, secondary groups that are organised to achieve their goals efficiently*.

Formal organisations, such as corporations and government agencies, differ significantly from families and neighbourhoods: their greater size renders social relationships less personal and fosters a planned, formal atmosphere. In other words, formal organisations operate to accomplish complex jobs rather than to meet personal needs.

When you think about it, organising a continent like Europe, with some 500 million members, is a remarkable feat. Countless tasks are involved, from collecting taxes and delivering the mail to the production and distribution of consumer goods. To meet most of these tasks, we rely on large, formal organisations. From national governments to private corporations, millions of people are employed in them. Such vast organisations develop lives and cultures of their own, so that as members come and go, the statuses they fill and the roles they perform remain unchanged over the years. Consider the following figures which give some indication of the numbers of major organisations that now *exist across the world*, that is, are global. (Even this excludes hundreds of others such as global religious organisations or global social movements.) There are:

- 60,000 major transnational corporations/companies (TNCs) such as Coca-Cola, Ford and Microsoft (with 500,000 affiliated organisations)
- 10,000 single-country non-governmental organisations (NGOs) such as Medecins sans Frontières (France) and Population Concern (UK)
- 250 intergovernmental organisations (IGOs) such as the United Nations, NATO and the European Union
- 4,800 international NGOs such as Amnesty International and the International Red Cross (Willetts, 2001: 357).

Types of formal organisation

There are a number of classifications of organisations. A classic one was presented by Amitai Etzioni (1975) who identified three types, distinguished by why people participate: utilitarian organisations, normative organisations and coercive organisations.

Just about everyone who works for income is a member of a *utilitarian organisation*, which provides material rewards for its members. Large business enterprises, for example, generate profits for their owners and income in the form of salaries and wages for their employees. Joining utilitarian organisations is usually a matter of individual choice, though most people must join one or another utilitarian organisation to make a living.

People join *normative organisations* not for income but to pursue goals they consider morally worthwhile. Sometimes called *voluntary associations*, these include community service groups (such as the Boy Scouts and Girl Guides or the Red Cross), political parties, religious organisations, and numerous other confederations concerned with specific social issues (such as Greenpeace or Liberty). In 1996, about 10 per cent of adults in Britain belonged to an environmental organisation or charity – the National Trust and the Royal Society for the Protection of Birds are the largest; Greenpeace comes a respectable third with 380,000 members (*Social Trends*).

In Etzioni's typology, *coercive organisations* are distinguished by involuntary membership. That is, people are forced to join the organisation as a form of punishment (prisons) or treatment (psychiatric hospitals). Coercive organisations have extraordinary physical features, such as locked doors and barred windows, and are supervised by security personnel (Goffman, 1961). These are settings that segregate people as 'inmates' or 'patients' for a period of time and sometimes radically alter their attitudes and behaviour. *Total institutions* transform a human being's overall sense of self.

From differing vantage points, any particular organisation may fall into *all* these categories. A psychiatric hospital, for example, serves as a coercive organisation for a patient, a utilitarian organisation for a psychiatrist and a normative organisation for a part-time hospital volunteer.

The nature of bureaucracy

Formal organisations date back thousands of years. Elites who governed early empires relied on government officials to extend their power over millions of people and vast geographical regions. Formal organisation allowed these rulers to collect taxes, undertake military campaigns and construct monumental structures such as the Great Wall of China and the pyramids of Egypt.

The power of these early organisations was limited, however, not because elites lacked grandiose ambition, but by the traditional character of pre-industrial societies. Typically, cultural patterns placed greater importance on preserving the past or carrying out 'God's will' than on organisational efficiency. Only in the last few centuries did there emerge what Max Weber called a 'rational world-view', as described in Chapter 4. In the wake of the Industrial Revolution, the organisational structure called *bureaucracy* became commonplace in Europe and North America.

Weber and bureaucracy

Bureaucracy is *an organisational model rationally designed to perform complex tasks efficiently.* In a bureaucratic business or government agency, officials deliberately enact and revise policy to make the organisation as efficient as possible. What specific traits promote organisational efficiency? Max Weber (1978; orig. 1921) identified six key elements of the ideal bureaucratic organisation.

1. *Specialisation.* Through most of human history, everyone pursued the basic goals of securing food and shelter. Bureaucracy, by contrast, assigns to individuals highly specialised duties.

2. *Hierarchy of offices.* Bureaucracies arrange personnel in a vertical hierarchy of offices. Each person is thus supervised by 'higher-ups' in the organisation while, in turn, supervising others in lower positions.

3. *Rules and regulations.* Cultural tradition holds scant sway in bureaucracy. Instead, operations are guided by rationally enacted rules and regulations. These rules control not only the organisation's own functioning but, as much as possible, its larger environment. Ideally, a bureaucracy seeks to operate in a completely predictable fashion.

4. *Technical competence.* A bureaucratic organisation expects officials to have the technical competence to carry out their official duties. Bureaucracies regularly monitor the performance of staff members. Such impersonal evaluation based on performance contrasts sharply with the custom, followed through most of human history, of favouring relatives – whatever their talents – over strangers.

5. *Impersonality.* In bureaucratic organisations, rules take precedence over personal whim. This impersonality encourages uniform treatment for each client as well as other workers. From this detached approach stems the notion of the 'faceless bureaucrat'.

6. *Formal, written communications.* An old adage states that the heart of bureaucracy is not people but paperwork. Rather than casual, verbal communication, bureaucracy relies on formal, written memos and reports. Over time, this correspondence accumulates into vast *files*. These files guide the subsequent operation of an organisation in roughly the same way that social background shapes the life of an individual.

These traits represent a clear contrast to the more personal character of small groups. Bureaucratic organisation promotes efficiency by carefully recruiting personnel and limiting the unpredictable effects of personal tastes and opinions. In smaller, informal groups, members allow one another considerable discretion in their behaviour; they respond to each other personally and regard everyone as more or less equal in rank. Table 6.2 summarises the differences between small social groups and large formal organisations.

Table 6.2	Small groups, formal organisations and networks: a comparison		
	Small groups	**Formal organisations**	**Networks**
Activities	Members typically engage in many of the same activities	Members typically engage in distinct, highly specialised activities	Members again have common focus
Hierarchy	Often informal or non-existent	Clearly defined, corresponding to offices	Largely non-existent – web-like
Norms	Informal application of general norms	Clearly defined rules and regulations	Emergent norms over time (e.g. 'netiquette')
Criteria for membership	Variable, often based on personal affection or kinship	Technical competence to carry out assigned tasks	Self-selecting
Relationships	Variable, typically primary	Typically secondary, with selective primary ties	Fragmented, focused
Communications	Typically casual and face-to-face	Typically formal and in writing	Digitalised
Focus	Person orientated	Task orientated	Communications

BUREAUCRACY'S DARKEST HOUR: KILLING 20 MILLION PEOPLE IN THE HOLOCAUST

One of the most significant events of twentieth-century history was Hitler's Final Solution: the mass extermination of over 20 million people – 6 million Jews, along with gypsies, gays, 'impure races' and others – throughout the Second World War. There have been many other genocides in history. The book *Century of Genocide* (Totten *et al.*, 1997) looks at eyewitness accounts of large numbers of people slaughtered during the twentieth century in Armenia, Bangladesh, Burundi, Cambodia, East Timor, Indonesia, Rwanda, South West Africa and Ukraine. Some have involved larger numbers of people – Rummel (1996) suggests that over 60 million people were killed in the Soviet Gulag state. But the Holocaust must be seen as unique because it involved the systematic, huge-scale extermination of large numbers of people through bureaucratic means in concentration camps such as Auschwitz in a mechanical way. People were 'rounded up'; trains took them to the death camps; there they were stripped, numbered, herded and led, finally, to the gas chambers or other execution.

Zygmunt Bauman, in his powerful sociological study *Modernity and the Holocaust* (1989), shows that 'we live in a type of society that made the Holocaust possible' (p. 88). For him, the modern world facilitated the mass exterminations. Drawing from Max Weber's analysis of bureaucracy and Durkheim's analysis of the division of labour, he suggests that these very characteristic features of modern society made the Holocaust possible. People could exterminate large numbers of others simply because they were distant links in a work chain, following the abstract rules that most jobs now dictate. There was an abrogation of personal responsibility, fostered by bureaucracy that made it all possible then – and indeed possible again now. People become dehumanised, and moral standards become irrelevant to the success of the technical operation.

When society seemed to be at its most advanced, and most civilised, the dark atrocities of mass extermination became a routine, bureaucratic commonplace. The challenge for sociology is to see this extreme horror – even 'evil' – as part of the routine workings of modern societies. The twentieth century was, in fact, a century of genocides.

See Bauman (1989); Rummel (1996); and Totten *et al.* (1997)

Belsen concentration camp, Second World War. Note the heap of shoes from those who have been killed in the gas chambers.

Source: Popperfoto

The informal side of bureaucracy

Weber's ideal bureaucracy deliberately regulates every activity. In actual organisations, however, human beings have the creativity (or the stubbornness) to resist conforming to bureaucratic blueprints. Sometimes informality helps to meet a legitimate need overlooked by formal regulations. In other situations informality may amount to simply cutting corners in one's job (Scott, 1981).

In principle, power resides in offices, not with the people who occupy them. Nonetheless, the personalities of officials greatly affect patterns of leadership. For example, studies of corporations document that the qualities and quirks of individuals – including personal charisma and interpersonal skills – have a tremendous impact on organisational outcomes.

Authoritarian, democratic and *laissez-faire* types of leadership also reflect individual personality as much as any organisational plan. Then, too, in the 'real world' of organisations, leaders and their cronies sometimes seek to benefit personally through the abuse of organisational power. And perhaps even more commonly, leaders take credit for the efforts of their subordinates. Many secretaries, for example, have far more authority and responsibility than their official job titles and salaries suggest.

Communication offers another example of how informality creeps into large organisations. Formally, memos and other written communications disseminate information through the hierarchy. Typically, however, individuals cultivate informal networks or 'grapevines' that spread information much faster, if not always accurately. Grapevines are particularly important to subordinates because high officials often attempt to conceal important information from them.

Throughout the hierarchy, employees modify or ignore rigid bureaucratic structures for a host of reasons. A classic study of the Western Electric factory in Chicago revealed that few employees reported fellow workers who violated rules, as the company required (Roethlisberger and Dickson, 1939). On the contrary, workers took action against those who *did* blow the whistle on their colleagues, shunning them as 'squealers'. Although the company formally set productivity standards, workers informally created their own definition of a fair day's work, criticising those who exceeded it as 'rate-busters' and those who fell short as 'chisellers'.

Such informal social structures suggest that people act to personalise rigidly defined social situations. This leads us to take a closer look at some of the problems of bureaucracy.

Problems of bureaucracy

Despite our reliance on bureaucracy to manage countless dimensions of everyday life, many members of our society are ambivalent about this organisational form. The following sections review several of the problems associated with bureaucracy, ranging from its tendency to dehumanise and alienate individuals to the threats it poses to personal privacy and political democracy.

1. Bureaucratic alienation

Max Weber saw that bureaucracy could be a model of productivity. Nonetheless, he was keenly aware of bureaucracy's potential to *dehumanise* those it purports to serve. That is, the same impersonality that fosters efficiency simultaneously denies officials and clients the ability to respond to each other's unique, personal needs. On the contrary, officials must treat each client impersonally as a standard 'case'.

The impersonal bureaucratic environment, then, gives rise to *alienation*. All too often, Weber contended, formal organisations reduce the human being to 'a small cog in a ceaselessly moving mechanism' (1978: 988; orig. 1921). The trend towards more and more formal organisation, therefore, left him deeply pessimistic about the future of humankind. Although formal organisations are designed to benefit humanity, he feared that humanity might well end up serving formal organisations.

2. Bureaucratic inefficiency and ritualism

Then there is the familiar problem of inefficiency, the failure of a bureaucratic organisation to carry out the work it was created to perform. Perhaps the greatest challenge to a large, formal organisation is responding to special needs or circumstances. Anyone who has ever tried to replace a lost driving licence, return defective merchandise to a discount store or change an address on a magazine subscription knows that bureaucracies sometimes can be maddeningly unresponsive.

The problem of inefficiency is captured in the concept of *red tape* (a phrase derived from the red tape used by eighteenth-century English administrators to wrap official parcels and records; Shipley, 1985). Red tape refers to a tedious preoccupation with organisational routines and procedures. Sociologist Robert Merton (1968) points out that red tape amounts to a new twist on the already familiar concept of group conformity. He coined the term **bureaucratic ritualism** to designate *a preoccupation with rules and regulations to the point of thwarting an organisation's goals*. Ritualism impedes individual and organisational performance as it stifles creativity and imagination. In part, ritualism emerges because organisations, which pay modest, fixed salaries, give officials little or no financial stake in performing efficiently. Then, too, bureaucratic ritualism stands as another expression of the alienation that Weber feared would arise from bureaucratic rigidity (Whyte, 1957; Merton, 1968; Coleman, 1990; Kiser and Schneider, 1994).

3. *Bureaucratic inertia*

If bureaucrats sometimes have little motivation to be efficient, they certainly have every reason to protect their jobs. Thus, officials typically strive to perpetuate their organisation even when its purpose has been fulfilled. As Weber put it, 'once fully established, bureaucracy is among the social structures which are hardest to destroy' (1978: 987; orig. 1921).

Bureaucratic inertia refers to *the tendency of bureaucratic organisations to perpetuate themselves*. Formal organisations, in other words, tend to take on a life of their own beyond their formal objectives. Occasionally, a formal organisation that meets its goals will simply disband; more commonly, an organisation stays in business by redefining its goals so it can continue to provide a livelihood for its members.

For example, consider the history of the US National Association for Infantile Paralysis, the sponsor of a fundraising campaign known as the March of Dimes (Sills, 1969). This organisation came into being as part of the drive to find a cure for polio. The goal was accomplished in the early 1950s when Dr Jonas Salk developed the polio vaccine. Subsequently, however, the March of Dimes did not close down; rather, it redirected its efforts towards other medical problems, such as birth defects, and continues to this day.

4. *Bureaucratic abuse of power: oligarchy*

Early in the twentieth century, Robert Michels (1876–1936) pointed out the link between bureaucracy and political **oligarchy**, *the rule of the many by the few* (1949; orig. 1911). According to what Michels called 'the iron law of oligarchy', the pyramid-like structure of bureaucracy places a few leaders in charge of vast and powerful government organisations.

Max Weber credited bureaucracy's strict hierarchy of responsibility with increasing organisational efficiency. By applying Weber's thesis to the organisation of government, Michels reveals that this hierarchical structure concentrates power and thus endangers democracy. While the public expects organisational officials to subordinate personal interests to organisational goals, people who occupy powerful positions can – and often do – use their access to

information and the media, plus numerous other advantages, to promote their personal interests. Furthermore, bureaucracy also insulates officials from public accountability, whether in the form of a corporate president who is 'unavailable for comment' to the local press or a national president seeking to control information by claiming 'executive privilege'. Oligarchy, then, thrives in the hierarchical structure of bureaucracy and undermines people's control over their elected leaders (Tolson, 1995).

The 'total institution' as a specific form of organisation

A specific form of organisation involves being confined – often against a person's will – in prisons or mental hospitals. These are specific forms of bureaucracies in that they are **total institutions**, *settings in which people are isolated from the rest of society and manipulated by an administrative staff*.

According to Erving Goffman (1961), total institutions have three distinctive characteristics. First, staff members supervise all spheres of daily life, including where residents ('inmates') eat, sleep and work. Second, a rigid system provides inmates with standardised food, sleeping quarters and activities. Third, formal rules and daily schedules dictate when, where and how inmates perform virtually every part of their daily routines.

Total institutions impose such regimentation often with the goal of a radical resocialisation, altering an inmate's personality through deliberate manipulation of the environment. The power of a total institution to resocialise is also enhanced by its forcible segregation of inmates from the 'outside' by means of physical barriers such as walls and fences topped with barbed wire and guard towers, barred windows and locked doors. Cut off in this way, the inmate's entire world can be manipulated by the administrative staff to produce lasting change – or at least immediate compliance – in the inmate.

Parkinson's Law and the Peter Principle

Finally, and on a lighter note, we acknowledge two additional insights concerning the limitations of bureaucratic organisations. The concerns of C. Northcote Parkinson and Laurence J. Peter are familiar to anyone who has ever been a part of a formal organisation.

Parkinson (1957) summed up his understanding of bureaucratic inefficiency with the assertion: *Work expands to fill the time available for its completion*. There is enough truth underlying this tongue-in-cheek assertion that it is known today as Parkinson's Law. To illustrate, assume that a bureaucrat working at the Driver and Vehicle

A 'total institution'?
Children with shaved heads and yellow uniforms sit in rows in a classroom of an orphanage for juvenile deliquents in Bucharest, Romania
Source: © Bernard Bisson/Corbis Sygma

Licensing Centre processes 50 driving licence applications in an average day. If one day this worker had only 25 applications to examine, how much time would the task require? The logical answer is half a day. But Parkinson's Law suggests that if a full day is available to complete the work, a full day is how long it will take.

Because organisational employees have little personal involvement in their jobs, few are likely to seek extra work to fill their spare time. Bureaucrats do strive to *appear* busy, however, and their apparent activity often prompts organisations to take on more employees. The added time and expense required to hire, train, supervise and evaluate a larger staff make everyone busier still, setting in motion a vicious cycle that results in *bureaucratic bloat*. Ironically, the larger organisation may accomplish no more real work than it did before.

In the same light-hearted spirit as Parkinson, Laurence J. Peter (Peter and Hull, 1969) devised the Peter Principle: *Bureaucrats rise to their level of incompetence*. The logic here is simple: employees competent at one level of the organisational hierarchy are likely to earn promotion to higher positions. Eventually, however, they will reach a position where they are in over their heads; there, they perform poorly and thus are no longer eligible for promotion.

Reaching their level of incompetence dooms officials to a future of inefficiency. Adding to the problem, after years in the office they have almost certainly learned how to avoid demotion by hiding behind rules and regulations and taking credit for work actually performed by their more competent subordinates.

Weber revisited: the 'McDonaldisation' of society

Weber's discussion of organisation was written in the early part of the twentieth century. Some 80 years on, the North American sociologist George Ritzer suggested the 'bureaucratisation of society' has proceeded further and deeper. He took the case of McDonald's restaurants as his illustration, but drew much wider implications.

Consider for a moment the nature of McDonald's, introduced at the start of this chapter. Have you ever eaten in one? Chances are the answer is 'yes'. Indeed, everywhere in the world your authors have travelled, they have not been far from a McDonald's! And sometimes in the most surprising of places. While visiting Hong Kong, both of us visited the former Portuguese colony of Macau – a little nub jutting from the Chinese coast. Few people here speak English, and life on the streets seems a world apart from the urban rhythms of London, Amsterdam or Los Angeles – where you would certainly expect to find a McDonald's. But strolling the old streets, we turn the corner and stand face to face with the famous McDonald's logo! But the most amazing thing is that the food – the burger, fries and drinks – looks, smells and tastes (almost!) the same as it does thousands of miles away in Sydney!

As noted in the opening to this chapter, McDonald's has enjoyed enormous success.[1] From a single store in the mid-1950s, McDonald's now operates nearly 29,000 restaurants throughout much of the world. There are more than 850 pairs of golden arches in Japan, for example, and the world's largest McDonald's opened for business in China's capital city of Beijing in April 1992, with some 700 seats, 29 cash registers, and 40,000 customers on its first day!

But while McDonald's may be everywhere and has become a symbol of the modern world, this is not Ritzer's point. For him, McDonaldisation suggests that the organisational principles that underlie McDonald's are steadily coming to dominate our entire society. Our culture is becoming 'McDonaldised' – a way of saying that we now model many aspects of life on the famous restaurant chain. Parents buy toys at worldwide chain stores such as Toys R Us; more vacations take the form of resort and tour packages; television presents news in the form of ten-second sound bites; sports become packaged into ever larger stadia and broadcasts; and religion is to be found in megachurches and cyberchurches. McDonaldisation has even had an impact on education: universities devise mass courses based on pre-packaged 'modules'; admissions officers size up students they have never met by glancing over their grades; lecturers assign ghost-written textbooks and evaluate students with tests mass-produced for them by publishing companies; and even sociology may start to become McDonaldised – as McSociology! (B. Smart, 1999). The list goes on and on.

McDonaldisation: four principles

What do all these developments have in common? According to George Ritzer, the 'McDonaldisation of society' involves four basic organisational principles.

1. *Efficiency*. Ray Kroc, the marketing genius behind the expansion of McDonald's, set out with the goal of serving a hamburger, French fries and a milkshake to a customer in 50 seconds. Today, one of the company's most popular items is the Egg McMuffin, an entire breakfast in a single sandwich. In the restaurant, customers clear their own trays or, better still, drive away from the pickup window taking the packaging and whatever mess they make with them.

Efficiency is now a value virtually without critics in our society. Almost everyone believes that anything that can be done quickly is, for that reason alone, good.

2. *Calculability*. The first McDonald's operating manual declared the weight of a regular raw hamburger to be 1.6 ounces, its size to be 3.875 inches across, and its fat content to be 19 per cent. A slice of cheese weighs exactly half an ounce. Fries are cut precisely nine-thirty-seconds of an inch thick.

   Think about how many objects around the home, the workplace or the university campus are designed and mass-produced uniformly according to a calculated plan. Not just our environment but our life experiences – from travelling on motorways to sitting at home watching television – are now more deliberately planned than ever before.

3. *Uniformity and predictability*. An individual can walk into a McDonald's restaurant anywhere and receive the same sandwiches, drinks and desserts prepared in precisely the same way. Predictability, of course, is the result of a highly rational system that specifies every course of action and leaves nothing to chance.

4. *Control through automation*. The most unreliable element in the McDonald's system is human beings. People, after all, have good and bad days, sometimes let their minds wander, or simply decide to try something a different way. To eliminate, as much as possible, the unpredictable human element, McDonald's has automated its equipment to cook food at fixed temperatures for set lengths of time. Even the cash register at a McDonald's is little more than pictures of the items so as to minimise the responsibility of the human being taking the customer's order.

The scope of McDonaldisation is expanding throughout the world. Automatic banking machines are replacing banks, highly automated bakeries now produce bread with scarcely any human intervention, and chickens and eggs (or is it eggs and chickens?) emerge from automated hatcheries. In supermarkets, laser scanners are phasing out (less reliable) human checkout operators. Much shopping now occurs in large precincts, in which everything from temperature and humidity to the kinds of store and product are subject to continuous control and supervision.

---

[1] This section draws on George Ritzer's (1993) book of the same name.

Can rationality be irrational?

No one would challenge the popularity or the efficiency of McDonald's and similar organisations (although there has been a lot of critical comment of late and their sales are falling in parts of the world). But there is another side to the story. Max Weber viewed the increasing rationalisation of the world with alarm, fearing that the expanding control of formal organisations would take away spontaneity and human creativity – crushing the human spirit. As he saw it, rational systems were efficient, but at the terrible cost of dehumanisation and disenchantment. Each of the four principles noted above depends on controlling human creativity, discretion and autonomy. George Ritzer contends that McDonald's food is not particularly good for people, nor is the company's extensive use of packaging good for the natural environment. Taking a broader perspective, Ritzer echoes Weber's concern, asserting that 'the ultimate irrationality of McDonaldization is that people could lose control over the system and it would come to control us' (1993: 145). In his book he therefore spends some time discussing ways in which people could resist the McDonalisation process. This includes avoiding daily routines as much as possible, avoiding classes where tests are short answer and graded by a computer, and eating in local, non-standardised restaurants.

Changing organisational forms

After the Second World War, most formal organisations in Europe were typically conventional bureaucracies, run from the top down according to a stern chain of command. Today, especially as businesses face growing global competition, rigid structures are breaking down. One important element of this trend is the increasing use of the *self-managed work team*. Members of these small groups have the skills necessary to carry out tasks with minimal supervision. By allowing employees to operate within autonomous groups, organisations enhance worker involvement in the job, generate a broader understanding of operations and raise employee morale. A few corporations (such as Procter & Gamble) have had autonomous work units since the 1960s. In recent years, many more are following suit.

Even though it is difficult to compare the performance of organisations with disparate goals and operations, research indicates that self-managed work teams do boost productivity while heading off some of the problems – including alienation – of the traditional bureaucratic model. In the business world, many companies have found that decentralising responsibility

in this way also raises product quality and lowers rates of employee absenteeism and turnover (Yeatts, 1991, 1995; Maddox, 1995).

Humanising bureaucracies

Humanising bureaucracy means *fostering a more democratic organisational atmosphere that recognises and encourages the contributions of everyone.* Research by Kanter (1977, 1983, 1989; Kanter and Stein, 1980) and others (Peters and Waterman, 1982) suggests that 'humanising' bureaucracy produces both happier employees and healthier profits. Based on the discussion so far, we can identify three paths to a more humane organisational structure.

1. *Social inclusiveness.* The social composition of the organisation should, ideally, make no one feel 'out of place' because of gender, race or ethnicity. The performance of all employees will improve to the extent that no one is subject to social exclusion.

2. *Sharing of responsibilities.* When organisations ease rigid organisational structures, they spread power and responsibility more widely. Managers cannot benefit from the ideas of employees who have no channels for expressing their opinions. Knowing that superiors are open to suggestions encourages all employees to think creatively, increasing organisational effectiveness.

3. *Expanding opportunities for advancement.* Expanding opportunity reduces the number of employees stuck in routine, dead-end jobs with little motivation to perform well. The organisation should give employees at all levels a chance to share ideas and try new approaches, defining everyone's job as the start of an upward career path.

Kanter's work takes a fresh look at the concept of bureaucracy and its application to business organisations. Rigid formality may have made sense in the past, when organisations hired unschooled workers primarily to perform physical labour. But today's educated workforce can contribute a wealth of ideas to bolster organisational efficiency – if the organisation encourages and rewards innovation.

There is broad support for the idea that loosening up rigid organisations improves performance. Moreover, companies that treat employees as a resource to be developed rather than as a group to be controlled stand out as more profitable. But some critics challenge Kanter's claim that social heterogeneity necessarily yields greater productivity. In controlled comparisons, they maintain, it is homogeneous work groups that typically produce more, while heterogeneous groups are better at generating a diversity of ideas and approaches. Optimal working groups, then, appear to be those that strike a balance: team members bring to the decision-making process a variety of backgrounds and perspectives, yet are similar enough in outlook and goals to effectively coordinate their efforts (Hackman, 1988).

The Japanese situation and the drift to post-modern organisations

We have described efforts to 'humanise' formal organisations. Interestingly, however, organisations in some countries have long been more personal than those in others. For instance, organisations in Japan, a nation that has had remarkable economic success, thrive within a culture of strong collective identity and solidarity. Unlike much of Europe and the United States, where individualism is a strong tradition, the Japanese maintain traditions of cooperation.

Because of Japan's social cohesiveness, formal organisations in that society approximate to very large primary groups. William Ouchi (1981) highlights five distinctions between formal organisations in Japan and their counterparts in industrial societies of the West. In each case, the Japanese organisation reflects that society's more collective orientation.

1. *Hiring and advancement.* Organisations in Europe hold out promotions and salary increases as prizes won through individual competition. In Japanese organisations, however, companies hire new graduates together, and all employees of a particular age cohort receive the same salary and responsibilities. Only after several years is anyone likely to be singled out for individual advancement.

2. *Lifetime security.* Employees in much of Europe expect to move from one company to another to advance their careers. Companies are also quick to lay off employees when economic setbacks strike. By contrast, most Japanese firms hire employees for life, fostering strong, mutual loyalties among members. Japanese companies avoid lay-offs by retraining expendable workers for new jobs in the organisation.

3. *Holistic involvement.* European workers tend to see the home and the workplace as distinct spheres. Japanese organisations take a different tack, playing a broad role in their employees' lives by providing home mortgages, sponsoring recreational activities and scheduling social events. Such interaction beyond the workplace strengthens collective identity and offers the respectful Japanese worker an opportunity to voice suggestions and criticisms informally.

4. *Non-specialised training.* Bureaucratic organisation in Europe is based on specialisation; many people spend

their entire working life at a single task. From the outset, a Japanese organisation trains employees in all phases of its operation, again with the idea that employees will remain with the organisation for life.

5. *Collective decision-making.* In Europe, important decisions fall to key executives. Although Japanese leaders also take responsibility for their organisation's performance, they involve workers in 'quality circles' that seek employee input in any decision that affects them. A closer working relationship is also encouraged by greater economic equality between management and workers. The salary differential between executives and lower-ranking employees is much less.

These characteristics give the Japanese a strong sense of organisational loyalty. The cultural emphasis on *individual* achievement in our society finds its parallel in Japanese *groupism*. By tying their personal interests to those of their company, workers realise their ambitions through the organisation.

Stuart Clegg (1990) has taken this argument further, suggesting that Japanese firms approximate to what he calls the postmodern firm. Such organisations are much more flexible and fluid than firms of the past. Strict demarcations are weakened, and they employ the 'Just in Time' (JIT) system of production. Here, goods are produced as required – there is no mass stocking of parts. And this in turn makes the system more adaptable and flexible.

'Social Networks' and the rise of the network society

Groups and organisations have proved to be very useful concepts for sociologists to develop. But as relationships change – from primary groups to secondary groups, from secondary groups to formal organisations, from formal organisations to postmodern organisations – so sociologists keep refining their language. Currently, more and more sociologists are finding the idea of 'network' an attractive one to use to understand shifts in society. Formally, a **social network** may be seen as *a web of social ties that links people who identify with one another*. Think of a network as a 'fuzzy' group that brings people into contact without a group's sense of boundaries and belonging. If we consider a group as a 'circle of friends', then we might describe a network as a 'social web' expanding outwards, often reaching great distances and including larger numbers of people. The most basic pattern of a network – between only two people, such as two people who are merely standing in the same room – can be represented as in Figure 6.3.

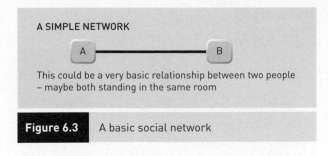

A SIMPLE NETWORK

This could be a very basic relationship between two people – maybe both standing in the same room

Figure 6.3   A basic social network

Social networks go beyond ideas of groups, or even organisations. Groups and organisations usually presume some kind of boundary, often with face-to-face interactions going on within them. Networks, by contrast, envisage a field of connections and relations: a set of *nodes* (key points) and a set of *ties* (or links) that connect some or all of these nodes. The nodes could be people, or groups, or even nation states. A more complex social network is represented in Figure 6.4. Here there are some central people – John, Rob, Lydia and Miriam – but they have different positions and access to different people (Kadushin, 2000).

Social network analysis, then, looks at underlying patterns and links that shape such social networks. For example, we could look at the *number* of ties, the *diversity* of ties, the *frequency* and *intensities* of interactional ties, the *directions* of interactional ties, the *content* of the ties, and the *quality* of ties. We could build up maps of

friendships which interconnect; see how bounded communities or families relate beyond themselves; or even locate patterns of people who have been part of the same network of sexual partners (an area of research that has been of value in studying AIDS: see Chapter 20).

Some such networks may then be seen as densely knit (most nodes are connected) and tightly bounded (most stay within the same subset of nodes). Or by contrast they may be seen as very thin and loose (Wellman, 1999). 'Contemporary Western communities rarely are tightly bounded, densely knit groups of broadly based ties. They usually are loosely bounded, sparsely knit, ramifying networks of specialised ties' (Wellman: 1999: 97). From this, we can now talk of network communities. Living in a specific geographical area or space no longer defines your community of personal interactions – instead now it is defined through phones, cars, the Internet, public transport systems and the like. These can connect you to a wide range of people. Living in a residential community may now mean that you are not really living in a specific, geographically bounded community but in an altogether wider network community! As you connect more and more through your network, so the older style of direct face-to-face communications ceases to have the same kind of meaning. And as a result of this, each of us may well come to live in our own network. We come to live with our own personal maps of the spaces we inhabit.

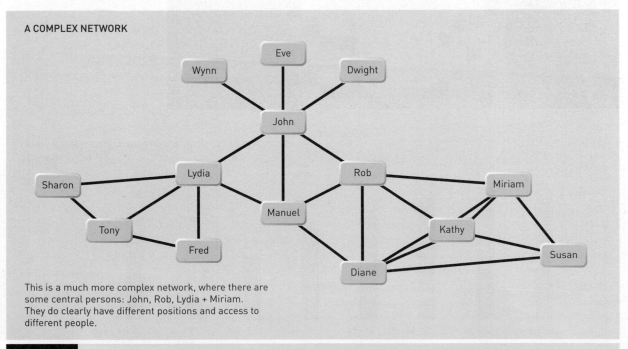

A COMPLEX NETWORK

This is a much more complex network, where there are some central persons: John, Rob, Lydia + Miriam. They do clearly have different positions and access to different people.

Figure 6.4   A more complex social network

An example: From telephones to mobile phones

Technologies have played one major role in the rise of networking. Consider the telephone. To appreciate networking, ponder that any one of the millions and millions of phones in the world can connect anybody, within seconds, to any other phone – in homes, businesses, automobiles, even in the middle of a football field. Such instant communication is beyond the imagination of those who lived in the ancient world. Of course, the telephone system depends on technological developments such as electricity, fibre optics and computers. But the system could not exist without the organisational capacity to keep track of every telephone call – noting which phone called which other phone, when and for how long – and presenting all this information to hundreds of millions of telephone users in the form of regular bills. So it is connected to bureaucracies too. But it starts to enable a very different

Table 6.3	Estimates of mobile phone ownership, 2001
Region	**Penetration rate (%)**
'Four tigers' (Hong Kong, Singapore, South Korea and Taiwan)	72.4
Western Europe	72.1
Japan	53.4
Australasia	49.6
North America	42.7
Latin America	15.6
Middle East	12.1
Central Europe	8.6
Rest of Asia	4.2
Africa	3.2

Source: *Financial Times*, 14 June, 2001: 26.

Mobile phones can be used anywhere – even in the mosl surprising places.
Source: © Al Rod/Corbis

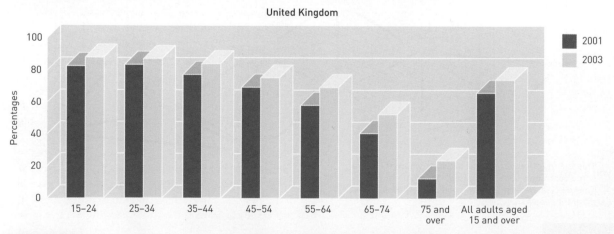

Figure 6.5	Adult mobile phone ownership by age in the UK, 2001 and 2003

mode of building up relations. Of course access to phones differs significantly in different parts of the world. In Europe and North America there are over 500 lines per hundred people; in Africa, often less than one (see Table 6.3).

Mobile phones make for even more complex networks. The spread of mobile phone use has been one of the most speedy and intensive developments of communication technologies. Within just a few years, many people have come to take them for granted. They are common in many countries and among all age groups (although there are differences outlined in Figure 6.5 and Table 6.3).

Northern Europe has some of the world's highest rates of mobile ownership. In 2003, Finland had the highest rate per head of population. In the UK, around 75 per cent of the population used 'mobiles'. As we might expect, the largest age group were the young and there was a steep decline among the 75 years old and over. However, in 2003, the older group showed the fastest rate of growth. It is estimated that nearly a third of people will own mobiles world wide by the end of 2005 (*Economist*, 2005: 111)

The new phones may well signify a shift in patterns of contact and communication. Of course it depends a great deal whether you carry the phone around with you all the time, and whether it is switched on or off. But when it is both these things (on and with you), we shift to a new mode of contact probably unique in our history: that of *perpetual contact*. Slowly, new rules for conducting phone calls are emerging. Just as you have access to all on the phones, so they have access to you. This means that several things have happened in networking contacts. First, there has been a breakdown of the old split between home and street, etc. – people can now talk anywhere. Second, it is intrusive – it can interrupt other streams of life. Thus going shopping, being in lectures, eating in a restaurant, or simply while talking with someone else, the mobile can ring or you can ring it and the network of interaction shifts (Katz and Aakhus, 2002).

Networks in the global village

Some network contacts are regular, as among college friends who years later stay in touch by mail and telephone. More commonly, however, a network includes people we *know of* – or who *know of us* – but with whom we interact infrequently, if at all. As one woman with a widespread reputation as a community organiser explains, 'I get calls at home, someone says, "Are you Roseann Navarro? Somebody told me to call you. I have this problem …" ' (quoted in Kaminer, 1984: 94). For this reason, social networks amount to 'clusters of weak ties' (Granovetter, 1973).

Network ties may be weak, but they serve as a significant resource. For example, many people rely on their networks to find jobs. Even the scientific genius

Albert Einstein needed a hand in landing his first job. After a year of unsuccessful interviewing, he obtained employment only when the father of one of his fellow students put him in touch with an office manager who hired him (Fischer, 1977: 19). This use of networks to one's advantage suggests that, as the saying goes, *who you know* is often just as important as *what you know*.

Networks are based on people's colleges and universities, clubs, local communities, political parties and informal cliques. Some networks encompass people with considerably more wealth, power and prestige than others do, which is the essence of describing someone as 'well connected'. And some people have denser networks than others – that is, they are connected to more people – which is also a valuable social resource. Typically, the most extensive social networks are maintained by people who are young, well educated and living in urban areas (Marsden, 1987; Kadushin, 1995).

Gender, too, shapes networks. Although the networks of men and women are typically the same size, women include more relatives in their networks, while those of men are filled out with more co-workers. Women's networks, therefore, may not carry quite the same clout as the 'old boy' networks do. Even so, research indicates that, as gender inequality lessens, this difference is diminishing over time (Moore, 1991, 1992).

The network society

New information technology has generated a global network of unprecedented size in the form of the Internet. Its origins seem right out of the 1960s Cold War film *Dr Strangelove*. Five decades ago, US government officials and scientists were trying to imagine how to run the country after an atomic attack, which, they assumed, would instantaneously eliminate telephones and television. The brilliant solution was to devise a communication system with no central headquarters, no one in charge and no main power switch – in short, an electronic web that would link the country in one vast network.

By 1985, the US federal government was installing high-speed data lines around the country and the Internet was about to be born. Today, thousands of government offices, as well as colleges and universities across the world, are joined by the Internet and share in the cost of its operation. Millions of other individuals connect their home computers to this 'information superhighway' through a telephone-line modem and a commercial 'gateway' such as America OnLine and British Telecom.

No one knows precisely how many people make use of the Internet. But a rough 2000 estimate put the total at 180 countries around the world, making it the largest network in history. And the numbers are increasing at unprecedented rates.

What is available on the Internet? Far more than anyone could ever list in a single directory. Popular activities include email (start a cyber-romance with a pen pal, write to your textbook author, or even send a message to the Prime Minister), participating in discussion groups or receiving newsletters on a wide range of topics, or searching libraries across the campus or around the world for books or other information. Because the Internet has no formal rules for its use, its potential defies the imagination.

Looking ahead: the network society

Spanish sociologist Manuel Castells (1989) uses the term 'network society' to capture the new kind of society we are moving into – one based on computers and information technologies, and characterised by new networks of relating.

Older patterns of group life and communication are being replaced by 'networking'. This brings with it a potential for self-expansion and a new logic of thinking

(think of how you read a book and how you search the Web to capture the different logics at work here). Castells argues that the new information technology brings five features:

- Information as the raw material to act on
- The pervasivness of information technologies
- The network logic of any system using them
- Flexibility
- Convergence of technologies (Vol. 1,1996: p. 21).

Power is no longer concentrated in institutions like the state but now diffuses through global networks. We shall return to this in more detail in later chapters (see Chapters 8, 14 and 22 especially).

All the themes touched upon in this book must now be placed alongside this new 'culture of virtuality' in a globalising world. Thus, we shall see in later chapters how this is shaping the economy, power, all forms of media, and even issues like class, gender and education. We will take stock of this idea of a 'network society' in the closing chapters of this book.

CONTROVERSY AND DEBATE

THE FUTURE OF POSTMODERN CYBER-RELATIONS

The intimate face-to-face relationships of the primary group have long been breaking down. We have all been familiar with the more impersonal and transitory relationships of the secondary group for a long time. Indeed, most of us have come to accept that, while there is a part of our life where the primary group matters most, for much of our daily activities, from work to shopping to entertainment, we depend more and more on secondary groups. The ways of relating in the world have changed.

But it may well be that this is about to change again! Indeed, many of the themes found in this text suggest that a new set of relationships are starting to happen. Some might even call them 'postmodern cyber-relations'. One way of thinking about these is to look at your relationships with the world of hi-tech gadgetry: faxes, videos, multimedia, mobile phones, video games, interactive websites and, most important of all, your personal computer. Now think about how much time you spend doing these things, usually away from face-to-face contact with people. For

many, this will be a lot of time. Indeed, we know many students who seem to spend 24 hours a day on their computer: they cannot be taken away from it! They do their work, their play, their shopping and their relationships all through it!

But think for a minute how this is changing our group involvement. Sociologist Sherry Turkle (1996) and social psychologist Ken Gergen (1991) have both been studying these changes. They see a new way of relating and a new way of life starting to appear. Consider some of the changes:

- Personal face-to-face talking relationships are replaced by distanced writing relationships on the screen: face-to-face contact ceases in this medium.
- Close primary groups and even secondary groups give way to global groups: providing you are connected up to the Web, you can talk with anybody in the world. Intimacy can now spread across the globe (and it does, literally, through computer sex lines – or cybersex).
- Straightforward linear thinking – as in most writing – becomes taken over by 'hypertext' where the reader jumps around, splices the text, moves in

CONTROVERSY AND DEBATE CONTINUED

and out of different 'MUDS' (multi-user domains). Ways of thinking start to shift.

- Identities are no longer given in face-to-face interaction (for example, as a man or a woman), but assembled through the machine. In a literal sense, you can make yourself anybody you wish.

This is just a preliminary list. You may like to continue it. But the big question becomes: What will happen when we all start to conduct our lives like this, as many argue we will?

There may be many downsides to this. What happens when people cannot afford a computer (and most of the world not only cannot afford it, but remain illiterate)? Might this divide the world into a new form of stratification – the cyberclasses and the non-cyberclasses?

There again, what happens when people can afford it? Some researchers are starting to suggest that there has been an increase in shyness and an inability to communicate with others since the com-

puter has arrived. We avoid primary groups and face-to-face relationships, and are only comfortable with machines and text talk.

So there are pluses and minuses to the arrival of this new technology.

CONTINUE THE DEBATE:

1. How might the new information technology change our relationships? Draw up a pros and cons list of the dangers and merits.

2. What is cybersex? How can people have sex with or on a computer? Is this the way ahead for all our sexual problems?

3. Does the new technology lead to a growing inequality?

Sources: Gergen (1991) and Turkle (1996).

SUMMARY

1. Social groups – important building blocks of societies – foster personal development and common identity as well as performing various tasks. Primary groups tend to be small and person-orientated; secondary groups are typically large and goal-orientated. The process of group conformity is well documented by researchers. Because members often seek consensus, work groups do not necessarily generate a wider range of ideas than do individuals working alone. Individuals use reference groups to form attitudes and make decisions.

2. Georg Simmel characterised the dyad relationship as intense but unstable; a triad, he noted, can easily dissolve into a dyad by excluding one member.

3. Peter Blau explored how the size, internal homogeneity, relative social parity and physical segregation of groups all affect members' behaviour. Formal organisations are large, secondary groups that seek to perform complex tasks efficiently. According to their members' reasons for joining, formal organisations are classified as utilitarian, normative or coercive. Bureaucratic organisation expands in modern societies to perform many complex tasks efficiently. Bureaucracy is based on specialisation, hierarchy, rules and regulations,

technical competence, impersonal interaction and formal, written communications. Ideal bureaucracy may promote efficiency, but bureaucracy also generates alienation and inefficiency, tends to perpetuate itself beyond the achievement of its goals and contributes to the contemporary erosion of privacy.

4. The trend towards the 'McDonaldisation of society' involves increasing automation and impersonality. It is defined by growing efficiency, predictability, calculability and control through automation.

5. Humanising bureaucracy means recognising people as an organisation's greatest resource. To develop human resources, organisations should spread responsibility and opportunity widely. One way to put this ideal into action is through self-managed work teams. Reflecting the collective spirit of Japanese culture, formal organisations in Japan are based on more personal ties than are their counterparts in the United States and Europe.

6. Social networks are relational webs that link people. The Internet is a vast electronic network linking millions of computers worldwide. Mobile phones are starting to change group relations.

CRITICAL-THINKING QUESTIONS

1. Identify various (a) primary and secondary groups, (b) formal and informal organisations, and (c) networks, in your own life. What do you like or dislike about each type of setting?

2. How can we resist the 'McDonaldisation of society'?

3. Draw up your own social network and contrast it with that of a friend.

4. Does the 'network society' suggest a really different way of relating to people than that found in the past? Consider how you use your mobile phone and computer and how this differs from interaction in the past?

GOING FURTHER

Further reading

Group studies:

George C. Homans, *The Human Group* (1992; orig. 1950) An early and enduring sociological investigation of the group, the setting for much of our lives.

The nature of McDonalidisation:

George Ritzer, *The McDonaldization of Society* (2nd edn, 1996)
A highly readable and lively account of the McDonald's phenomenon and how it provides a blueprint for contemporary organisational life. The book has spawned a number of linked books.

Barry Smart (ed.), *Resisting McDonaldization* (1999) A useful critical commentary on Ritzer.

Organisation theory:

Stuart R. Clegg, *Modern Organisations: Organisation Studies in the Postmodern World* (1990)
An important review of earlier studies of organisations which also suggests the postmodern organisation. There are some intriguing case studies too of the French bread industry the Italian fashion industry, and 'post-Confucian' Asian enterprises.

Network theory:

John Scott, *Social Network Analysis: A Handbook* (2nd edn, 2000a)

Reviews the whole field of network research.

Barry Wellman (ed.), *Networks in the Global Village* (1999)

Manuel Castells, *The Rise of the Network Society*, Vol. 1 of *The Information Age* (1996)
Important studies of networks at work.

Sherry Turkle, *Life on the Screen: Identity in the Age of the Internet* (1996)

James Katz and Mark Aakhus (eds), *Perpetual Contact: Mobile Communication*, *Private talk* , *Public Performance*. (2002)
Two good books that introduce changes in our relationships that are emerging as a consequence of the high-tech world (computers and mobile phones).

Watch a video

On McDonaldisation:

Morgan Spurlock's *Super Size Me* (2004): chronicles a month in the life of Morgan Spurlock, who eats nothing but McDonald's food and becomes dangerously ill as a result.

On aspects of organisational life:

Compare:

- Irwin Winkler's *The Net* (1995): life through cyber-relations at the end of the twentieth century
- Frank Darabont's *The Shawshank Redemption* (1994): life in a prison
- Nunally Johnson's *Man in a Grey Flannel Suit* (1957): life as an organisation man in the mid-1950s
- Walter Hill's *The Warriors* (1979): life in a gang in New York
- Steven Spielberg's *Schindler's List* (1993): life in the Holocaust.

Connecting up

Connect to other chapters

- For more on genocide, see Chapters 11 and 15.
- Cyberworlds are featured in Chapter 22.
- Goffman is discussed further in Chapter 7.

To the websites

The McDonaldisation website can be located at
http://www.mcdonaldization.com/main.shtml

For additional case studies, multiple choice questions,
internet exercises, and annotated weblinks specific to
this chapter, visit this book's website at
www.pearsoned.co.uk/plummer

CHAPTER 7   MICRO-SOCIOLOGY: THE SOCIAL CONSTRUCTION OF EVERYDAY LIFE

If we had a keen vision and feeling of all ordinary human life, it would
be like hearing the grass grow and the squirrel's heart beat, and we
should die at the roar which lies on the other side of silence.

George Eliot, *Middlemarch*, 1872

ON A COLD WINTER DAY IN 1938, a social worker walked anxiously to the door of a rural Pennsylvania farmhouse. Investigating a case of possible child abuse, the social worker soon discovered a five-year-old girl hidden in a second-floor storage room. The child, whose name was Anna, was wedged into

KEY THEMES

- Micro-sociology and the ways in which sociologists study everyday life
- How we become social and develop biographies across the life course
- How everyday life is constructed and negotiated
- How our identities, bodies and emotions are socially formed

an old chair with her arms tied above her head so that she could not move. She was dressed in filthy garments, and her arms and legs – looking like matchsticks – were so frail that she could not use them.

Anna's situation can only be described as tragic. She was born in 1932 to an unmarried and mentally impaired woman of 26

who lived with her father. Enraged by his daughter's 'illegitimate' motherhood, the grandfather did not even want the child in his house. Anna therefore spent her first six months in various institutions. But her mother was unable to pay for such care, so Anna returned to the hostile home of her grandfather.

At this point, her ordeal intensified. To lessen the grandfather's anger, Anna's mother moved the child to the attic room, where she received little attention and just enough milk to keep her alive. There she stayed – day after day, month after month, with essentially no human contact – for five long years.

Upon learning of the discovery of Anna, sociologist Kingsley Davis (1940) travelled immediately to see the child. He found her at a county home, where local authorities had taken her. Davis was appalled by Anna's condition. She was emaciated and feeble. Unable to laugh, smile, speak or even show anger, she was completely unresponsive, as if alone in an empty world.

(Left) Painting of a masked ball by Lincoln Seligman that features on a wall of the Berkley Hotel
Source: Bridgeman Art Library

This classic story of Anna is a sad but instructive case of a human being deprived of virtually all social contact. Although physically alive, Anna hardly seemed human. Her plight reveals that, isolated in this way, an individual develops scarcely any capacity for thought, emotion and meaningful behaviour. In short, without social experience, an individual is not a social human being.

This chapter explores what Anna was deprived of – the means by which we become fully human. It looks at how we become social; how our bodies and emotions become social; how identities are formed; and how we assemble our everyday lives. In doing this, we move to a different kind of problem and a different level of analysis from those encountered so far. Up till now our discussions have been looking at the big picture: of society, cultures and organisations, along with the broad changes that have been taking place in them as first industrialisation and more recently the information revolution have brought new forms of society. This is **macro-sociology** – *the study of large-scale society*.

By contrast, we now turn to what may be seen as the building blocks of a society – the human actions in little social worlds that enable social life to get done. We are interested here in everyday life – how people go shopping, make breakfasts, go to work, use mobile phones, make love, fight wars, lie, cheat and steal! All the wonders of daily life are here. This is **micro-sociology** – *the study of everyday life in social interactions*. We will start by seeing just how our everyday realities are 'socially constructed'. From this, we will look at the ways in which we come to assemble our sense of who we are through what can be called the socialisation process. We will then look at five key ideas that help organise our everyday lives: interaction, identity, bodies, emotion and biography.

The social construction of reality

Nearly 100 years ago, the Italian playwright Luigi Pirandello (1867–1936) skilfully applied the sociological perspective to social interaction. In *The Pleasure of Honesty*, Angelo Baldovino – a brilliant man with a chequered past – enters the fashionable home of the Renni family and introduces himself in a most peculiar way:

> Inevitably we construct ourselves. Let me explain. I enter this house and immediately I become what I have to become, what I can become: I construct myself. That is, I present myself to you in a form suitable to the relationship I wish to achieve with you. And, of course, you do the same with me.
>
> (Pirandello, 1962: 157–158)

This curious introduction suggests that each human being has some ability to shape what happens from moment to moment. 'Reality', in other words, is not as fixed as we may think.

The phrase **social construction of reality** was introduced by Peter Berger and Thomas Luckmann (1967) to identify *the process by which people creatively shape reality through social interaction*. Human worlds are socially produced, changed and modified. This idea stands at the foundation of the symbolic-interaction paradigm, as described in earlier chapters, and is the hallmark of what is now called the social constructionist perspective. As Angelo Baldovino's remark suggests, especially in an unfamiliar situation, quite a bit of 'reality' remains unclear in everyone's mind. So as Baldovino 'presents himself' in terms that suit his purposes, and as others do the same, a complex reality emerges, though few people are so 'up front' about their deliberate efforts to foster an impression.

Social interaction, then, amounts to negotiating reality. Most everyday situations involve at least some agreement about what's going on, but participants perceive events differently, to the extent that they are motivated by disparate interests and intentions.

Steering reality in this way is sometimes referred to as 'street smarts'. In his autobiography *Down These Mean Streets* (1967), Piri Thomas recalls moving to a new apartment in New York City's Spanish Harlem, which placed him squarely on the turf of the local street gang. Returning home one evening, young Piri found himself cut off by Waneko, the gang's leader, who was flanked by a dozen of his cohorts.

> 'Whatta ya say, Mr Johnny Gringo,' drawled Waneko.
> *Think man*, I told myself, *think your way out of a stomping. Make it good*. 'I hear you 104th street coolies are supposed to have heart,' I said. 'I don't know this for sure. You know there's a lot of streets where a whole "click" is made out of punks who can't fight one guy unless they all jump him for the stomp.' I hoped this would push Waneko into giving me a fair one. His expression didn't change.
> 'Maybe we don't look at it that way.'
> *Crazy, man*, I cheer inwardly, *the cabron is falling into my setup*. . . . 'I wasn't talking to you,' I said. 'Where I come from, the pres is president 'cause he got heart when it comes to dealing.'
> Waneko was starting to look uneasy. He had bit on my worm and felt like a sucker fish. His boys were now light on me. They were no longer so much interested in stomping me as seeing the outcome between Waneko and me. 'Yeah,' was his reply. . . .

I knew I'd won. Sure, I'd have to fight; but one guy, not ten or fifteen. If I lost, I might still get stomped, and if I won I might get stomped. I took care of this with my next sentence. 'I don't know you or your boys,' I said, 'but they look cool to me. They don't feature as punks.'

I had left him out purposely when I said 'they'. Now his boys were in a separate class. I had cut him off. He would have to fight me on his own, to prove his heart to himself, to his boys, and most important, to his turf. He got away from the stoop and asked, 'Fair one, Gringo?'

(Thomas, 1967: 56–57)

This situation reveals the drama – sometimes subtle, sometimes savage – by which human beings creatively build reality. There are limits, of course, to what even the most skilful and persuasive person can achieve. And, of course, not everyone enters a negotiation with equal standing. Should a police officer have come on the scene of the fight that ensued between Piri and Waneko, both young men might well have ended up in jail.

The Thomas theorem

By displaying his wits and boxing with Waneko until they both grew tired, Piri Thomas won acceptance that evening and became one of the group. W. I. Thomas (1966: 301; orig. 1931) succinctly expressed this insight in what has come to be known as the **Thomas theorem:** *situations we define as real become real in their consequences.*

Applied to social interaction, Thomas's insight means that, although reality is initially 'soft', as it is fashioned it can become 'hard' in its effects. In the case of Piri Thomas, having succeeded in defining himself as worthy, this young man became worthy in the eyes of his new comrades.

Becoming social: the process of socialisation

Just how did Anna and Piri come to inhabit the social worlds that they did? Sociologists suggest it is through a process of **socialisation**, *a lifelong social experience by which individuals construct their personal biography, assemble daily interactional rules and come to terms with the wider patterns of their culture.* Unlike other living species whose behaviour may be largely biologically set, human beings rely on social experience to learn the nuances of their culture in order to survive.

Questions for an account of socialisation

Socialisation theory can ask five broad questions, which may be summarised as follows:

1. *Who is being socialised?*
2. *By whom?*
3. *How?*
4. *Where?*
5. *When?*

The first question raises the issue of the nature of the person being socialised and ultimately asks about *'human nature'*. Is this something people are born with or are they the product of their environment? This is the classic 'nature/nurture' argument.

The second question looks at the role of *'agents of socialisation'*. This might start out with the formative role of mothers, fathers and siblings as *primary* socialisers, but it soon moves on to other agents such as friends, peers, teachers, significant others and indeed even the mass media (see Chapter 21).

The 'how' question asks about the processes through which people become socialised. *These are socialisation theories*, which look at the mechanisms through which we become human. Two major theories will be considered below – those of psychodynamicists and interactionists.

Finally, the last three questions aim to locate the life in time and place. We will briefly look at some of these questions in more detail below.

How do we develop – nature, nurture or both?

Virtually helpless at birth, the human infant depends on others for care and nourishment as well as learning. Although Anna's short life makes these facts very clear, most people mistakenly believe that human behaviour is the product of biological imperatives: for many, instincts, evolution and genes are seen as the core of human behaviour. 'It's genetic' is one of the most common claims made these days. But sociologists cast much doubt on the overstated power of the gene, as we shall see.

Initially it was Charles Darwin who argued, plausibly, that each species evolves over thousands of generations as genetic variations enhance survival and reproduction. Biologically rooted traits that enhance survival emerge as a species' 'nature'. As Darwin's fame grew, people assumed that humans, like other forms of life, had a fixed, instinctive 'nature' as well.

Such notions are still with us. People sometimes claim, for example, that our economic system is a reflection of 'instinctive human competitiveness', that some people are 'born criminals', or that women are more 'naturally' emotional while men are 'inherently' more rational. Indeed, almost anything social – from race differences to illness, from wealth to intelligence – is explained by some as genetic. We often describe familiar traits as *human nature*, as if people were born with them, just as we are born with five senses. More accurately, however, our human nature leads us to create and learn cultural traits, as we shall see.

People trying to understand cultural diversity also misconstrued Darwin's thinking. Centuries of world exploration and empire building taught Western Europeans that people around the world behaved quite differently from themselves. They attributed such contrasts to biology rather than culture. It was a simple – although terribly damaging – step to conclude that members of technologically simple societies were biologically less evolved and, therefore, less human. Such a self-serving and ethnocentric view helped justify colonial practices, including land seizures and slavery, since it is easier to exploit others if you are convinced that they are not truly human in the same sense that you are.

In the twentieth century, social scientists launched a broad attack on naturalistic explanations of human **behaviour**. Psychologist John B. Watson (1878–1958) devised a theory called **behaviourism**, which held that *specific behaviour patterns are not instinctive but learned*. Thus people the world over have the same claim to humanity Watson insisted; humans differ only in their cultural environment. In a classic observation, Watson remarked that 'human nature' was infinitely malleable:

> Give me a dozen healthy infants . . . and my own specified world to bring them up in, and I will guarantee to take any one at random and train him [or her] to become any type of specialist that I might select – doctor, lawyer, artist, merchant, chief, and yes, even beggar-man and thief – regardless of his [or her] talents, penchants, tendencies, abilities, vocations, and race of his [or her] ancestors.
>
> (Watson, 1930: 104)

Anthropologists weighed in on this debate as well, showing how variable the world's cultures are. An outspoken proponent of the 'nurture' view, anthropologist Margaret Mead summed up the evidence:

> The differences between individuals who are members of different cultures, like the differences between individuals within a culture, are almost entirely to be laid to differences in conditioning, especially during early childhood, and this conditioning is culturally determined.
>
> (Mead, 1963: 280; orig. 1935)

Today, social scientists (and many biologists who specialise in genetics too) are cautious about describing any type of behaviour as *simply* instinctive or genetic. Of course, this does not mean that biology plays *no* part in human behaviour. Human life, after all, depends on the functioning of the body. We also know that children share many biological traits with their parents, especially physical characteristics such as height, weight, hair and eye colour, and facial features. Intelligence and various personality characteristics (for example, how one reacts to stimulation or frustration) have some genetic component, as does the potential to excel in such activities as art and music. But whether a person develops an inherited potential depends on the opportunities associated with social position (Herrnstein, 1973; Plomin and Foch, 1980; Goldsmith, 1983).

Sociologists generally work from the assumption that nurture is far more important than nature in determining human behaviour. We should not think of nature as opposing nurture, though, since we express our human nature as we build culture. For humans, then, nature and nurture are inseparable.

Social isolation

For obvious ethical reasons, researchers cannot subject human beings to experimental isolation. Consequently, much of what we know about this issue comes from rare cases of abused children like Anna. Researchers have, however, studied the impact of social isolation on animals.

Effects of social isolation on non-human primates

Psychologists Harry and Margaret Harlow (1962) conducted a classic investigation of the effects of social isolation on non-human primates. They observed the consequences of various conditions of isolation on rhesus monkeys, whose behaviour is in some ways remarkably similar to that of humans.

The Harlows found that complete social isolation for even six months (with adequate nutrition) seriously disturbed the monkeys' development. When these monkeys subsequently returned to their group, they were anxious, passive and fearful.

The Harlows then isolated infant rhesus monkeys, but provided an artificial 'mother' made of wire mesh with a wooden head and the nipple of a feeding tube where the breast would be. These monkeys survived but they, too, subsequently displayed emotional damage.

But when the researchers covered the artificial 'mother' with soft terry cloth, the infant monkeys would cling to it, apparently deriving emotional benefit from the closeness. Subsequently, these monkeys revealed less emotional distress. The Harlows thus concluded that normal emotional development requires affectionate cradling as part of parent–infant interaction.

The Harlows made two other discoveries. First, as long as they were surrounded by other infants, monkeys were not adversely affected by the absence of a mother. This finding suggests that deprivation of social experience, rather than the absence of a specific parent, has devastating effects. Second, the Harlows found that lesser periods of social isolation – up to about three months – caused emotional distress, but only temporarily. The damage of short-term isolation, then, can be overcome; longer-term isolation, however, appears to inflict on monkeys irreversible emotional and behavioural damage.

Effects of social isolation on children

The case of Anna, described earlier, is the best-known instance of the extended social isolation of a human infant. After her discovery, Anna benefited from intense social contact and soon showed improvement. Visiting her in the county home after ten days, Kingsley Davis (1940) noted that she was more alert and even smiled with obvious pleasure. During the next year, Anna made slow but steady progress, showing greater interest in other people and gradually learned to walk. After a year and a half, she could feed herself and play with toys.

Consistent with the observations of the Harlows, however, it was becoming apparent that Anna's five years of social isolation had left her permanently damaged. At the age of eight her mental and social development was still less than that of a two-year-old. Not until she was almost ten did she begin to grasp language. Of course, since Anna's mother had learning difficulties, perhaps Anna was similarly disadvantaged. The riddle was never solved, because Anna died at the age of ten from a blood disorder, possibly related to her years of abuse (Davis, 1940, 1947).

A second, quite similar case involves another girl, found at about the same time as Anna and under strikingly similar circumstances. After more than six years of virtual isolation, this girl – known as Isabelle – displayed the same lack of human responsiveness as Anna. Unlike Anna, though, Isabelle benefited from a special learning programme directed by psychologists. Within a week, Isabelle was attempting to speak, and a year and a half later, her vocabulary included nearly 2,000 words. The psychologists concluded that intensive effort had propelled Isabelle through six years

of normal development in only two years. By the time she was 14, Isabelle was attending sixth-grade classes, apparently on her way to at least an approximately normal life (Davis, 1947).

A final case of childhood isolation involves a 13-year-old California girl victimised in a host of ways by her parents from the age of two (Curtiss, 1977; Pines, 1981; Rymer, 1994). Genie's ordeal included extended periods of being locked alone in a garage. Upon discovery, her condition mirrored that of Anna and Isabelle. Genie was emaciated (weighing only 59 pounds) and had the mental development of a one-year-old. She received intensive treatment by specialists and thrived physically. Yet even after years of care, her ability to use language remains that of a young child, and she lives today in a home for developmentally disabled adults.

All the evidence points to the crucial role of social experience in personal development. Human beings are resilient creatures, sometimes able to recover from even the crushing experience of abuse and isolation. But there is a point – precisely when is unclear from the limited number of cases – at which social isolation in infancy results in irreparable developmental damage.

Becoming biographies? Two theories of socialisation

Socialisation results in a personal **biography**, a *person's unique history of thinking, feeling and acting*. We build a biography through interacting with others throughout all our lives: as biography develops, we participate in a culture while remaining, in some respects, distinct individuals. But in the absence of social experience, as the case of Anna shows, a biography can hardly start to emerge at all.

Social experience is vital for society just as it is for individuals. Societies exist beyond the life span of any person, and thus each generation must teach something of its way of life to the next. Broadly speaking, then, socialisation amounts to the ongoing process of cultural transmission. Socialisation is a complex, lifelong process. In what follows, we highlight two major theories of human development. There are many others (which can be accessed via the website).

Sigmund Freud: the importance of the unconscious and emotional structuring

Sigmund Freud (1856–1939) lived in Vienna at a time when most Europeans considered human behaviour to be biologically fixed. Trained as a physician, Freud gradually turned to the study of personality and eventually developed the celebrated theory of psychoanalysis.

The cornerstone of this theory is the workings of the repressed **unconscious**: people's lives are partly shaped by emotional *experiences*, traumas and 'family romances' *which then become too difficult to confront and so become hidden from the surface workings of life, while still motivating our actions*. The unconscious goes deep: it is repressed and cannot be easily recovered. (Psychoanalysis and 'dream analysis' are two 'roads to the unconscious'.) In any event the unconscious often means that we really do not know why we do certain things.

Many aspects of Freud's work bear directly on our understanding of how we become social.

Life and death

Freud contended that biology is diffuse but plays an important part in social development, though not in terms of the simple instincts that guide other species. Humans, Freud theorised, respond to two general needs or drives. We have a basic need for pleasure and bonding, which Freud called the life instincts, or *eros* (from the Greek god of love). Second, opposing this need, are aggressive drives, which Freud termed the death instincts, or *thanatos* (from the Greek meaning 'death'). Freud postulated that these opposing forces, operating primarily at the level of the unconscious mind, generate deeply rooted inner tensions.

Sigmund Freud (1856–1936). Freud is the great theorist of the unconscious, but with a few exceptions (such as Parsons, the Frankfurt School and some feminisms) he has not had a major impact on sociology.

Source: Corbis

Id, ego, superego

These basic drives need to be controlled and Freud incorporated them and the influence of society into a model of personality with three parts: id, ego and superego. The **id** (Latin for 'that') represents *the human being's basic drives*, which are unconscious and demand immediate satisfaction. Rooted in our biology, the id is present at birth, making a newborn a bundle of needs demanding attention, touching and all kinds of nervous and sexual experience. They are a 'cauldron of seething excitation' and we seek the release of our desires. But society does not tolerate such a self-centred orientation, so the id's desires inevitably encounter resistance. Because of this cultural opposition, one of the first words a child comprehends is 'no'.

To avoid frustration, the child learns to approach the world realistically. This accomplishment forms the second component of the personality, the **ego** (Latin for 'I'), which is *a person's conscious efforts to balance innate, pleasure-seeking drives with the demands of society*. It is dominated by what Freud calls the reality principle. The ego arises as we gain awareness of our distinct existence; it reaches fruition as we come to understand that we cannot have everything we want. We start to adjust and adapt to the vagaries of everyday life.

Finally, the human personality develops the **superego** (Latin, meaning 'above' or 'beyond' the ego), which is the *operation of culture within the individual*. With the emergence of the superego, we can see *why* we cannot have everything we want. The superego consists of cultural values and norms – internalised in the form of conscience – that define moral limits. The superego begins to emerge as children recognise parental control; it matures as they learn that their own behaviour and that of their parents – in fact, everyone's behaviour – reflects a broader system of cultural demands. It is a conscience and it creates new tensions, generating guilt and guilty thoughts.

Personality development

The id-centred child first encounters the world as a bewildering array of physical sensations and need satisfactions. With the gradual development of the superego, however, the child's comprehension extends beyond pleasure and pain to include the moral concepts of right and wrong. Initially, in other words, children can feel good only in the physical sense; but, after three or four years, they feel good or bad as they evaluate their own behaviour according to cultural standards.

Conflict between id and superego is ongoing, but, in a well-adjusted person, these opposing forces are managed by the ego. Unresolved conflicts, especially during childhood, typically result in personality disorders later on.

As the source of superego, culture operates to control human drives, a process Freud termed *repression*. Some repression is inevitable, since any society must coerce people to look beyond themselves. Often the competing demands of self and society are resolved through compromise. This process, which Freud called *sublimation*, transforms fundamentally selfish drives into socially acceptable activities. Sexual urges, for example, may lead to marriage, just as aggression gives rise to competitive sports.

Freud and the Oedipus Complex

Central to Freud's thought, and to his theory of socialisation, is his concept of the Oedipus Complex: a metaphor for the emotional and psychic struggles and conflicts a young child experiences with its mother and father. The term is derived from the Greek tragedy in which Oedipus marries his mother and murders his father, and looks at the passionate 'little love affairs' that children have with their families in the earliest years of life.

Broadly, Freud suggests that newborn children initially feel a strong closeness and attachment to the mother, and that the father is experienced as something of a threat to this attachment. The child thus starts to harbour hostile feelings towards the father, for which it feels increasingly guilty. This little dilemma can be experienced very profoundly. Freud uses the term 'castration complex' to suggest a powerful threat to the child. And in order to resolve this threat, the child starts to identify with the father instead.

The Oedipus Complex is the key to getting the id and all its desires under control: the father becomes part of the superego as an authority figure. Freud is outlining a basic predicament in becoming social: how to cope with all our desires and become a socialised adult with a conscience. And he does this through seeing a struggle in emotional identification.

Critical comment

Freud's work sparked controversy in his own lifetime, and some of that controversy still smoulders today. The world he knew vigorously repressed human sexuality, so that few of his contemporaries were prepared to concede that sex is a basic human need. More recently, Freud has come under fire for his depictions of humanity in allegedly male terms, thereby devaluing the lives of women (Donovan and Littenberg, 1982). But Freud also provided a foundation that influenced virtually everyone who later studied the human personality. Of special

importance to sociology is his notion that we internalise social norms and that childhood experiences have a lasting impact on socialisation. More than this, in his book *Civilisation and its Discontents* (2004; orig. 1930), he saw a distinct parallel between social and individual developments. Just as human beings develop through instinctual repression, so civilisation as a whole advances through controls. Civilisation, then, depends upon repression but in the process it generates many problems.

George Herbert Mead and the social self

Our understanding of socialisation stems in large part from the life work of George Herbert Mead (1863–1931), who is introduced in the Profile box. Mead (1962; orig. 1934) described his approach as *social behaviourism*, calling to mind the behaviourism of psychologist John B. Watson described earlier. Both recognised the power of the environment to shape human behaviour. But Watson focused on outward behaviour, while Mead highlighted inward *thinking*, which he contended was humanity's defining trait.

The self

Mead's central concept is the **self**, *the human capacity to be reflexive and take the role of others*. Mead's genius lay in seeing that the self is inseparable from society, and bound up with communication. It is a connection explained in a series of steps.

First, Mead asserted, *the self emerges from social experience*. The self is not part of the body, and it does not exist at birth. But it is distinctly what makes us human. Mead rejected simple ideas about biological drives, and argued that the self develops *only* through social experience. In the absence of social interaction, as we saw above in the cases of isolated children, the body may grow but no self will emerge.

Second, Mead explained, *social experience involves communication and the exchange of symbols*. Using words, a wave of the hand or a smile, people create meaning, which is a distinctively human experience. We can use reward and punishment to train a dog, after all, but the dog attaches no meaning to these actions. Human beings, by contrast, make sense of actions by inferring people's underlying intentions. In short, a dog responds to *what you do*; a human responds to *what you have in mind* as you do it.

Return to our friendly dog for a moment. You can train a dog to walk to the porch and return with an umbrella. But the dog grasps no meaning in the act, no

PROFILE

GEORGE HERBERT MEAD: THE SELF IS BORN OF SOCIETY (1863–1933)

Source: © The Granger Collection, New York

George Herbert Mead was a leading US philosopher. Based at the University of Chicago, he has been identified as a leading pragmatist. His work *Mind, Self and Society* (1962; orig. 1934) was published after his death from notes taken by students and provides his major theory of the self.

Few people were surprised that Mead became a college professor. He was born to a Massachusetts family with a strong intellectual tradition, and both his parents were academics. His father was both a preacher and a teacher at a number of colleges, and his mother served for a decade as president of Mount Holyoke College.

But Mead also had a hand in shaping his own life, rebelling against the strongly religious atmosphere of his home and community. After completing college, he restlessly travelled throughout the Pacific Northwest, surveying for the railroad and reading voraciously. He gradually settled on the idea of studying philosophy, an academic endeavour he pursued at Harvard and in Europe.

Mead took a teaching position at the new University of Chicago. But his outlook still veered from the conventional. He rarely published, going against a long-standing tradition among academics. Mead's reputation and stature grew only after his death, when colleagues and former students collected and published his lecture notes. Mead drew together a wide range of ideas to help launch the new field of social psychology.

Never content with life as it was, Mead was an active social reformer. To him, the course of an entire society was as ongoing and changeable as the life of any individual. This insight follows from his basic contention: society may have the power to shape individuals, but people also have the capacity to mould their society.

Sources: based, in part, on Coser (1977) and Schellenberg (1978).

intention behind the command. Thus, if the dog cannot find the umbrella, it is incapable of the human response: to look for a raincoat instead.

Third, says Mead, *to understand intention, you must imagine the situation from another person's point of view.* Using symbols, we can imaginatively place ourselves in another person's shoes and thus see ourselves as that person does. This capacity allows us to anticipate how others will respond to us even before we act. A simple toss of a ball requires stepping outside ourselves to imagine how another will respond to our throw. Social interaction, then, involves seeing ourselves as others see us – a process that Mead called *taking the role of the other*. The self, then, is reflective and reflexive.

The looking-glass self

In social life, other people represent the mirror or looking glass in which we perceive ourselves. Charles Horton Cooley (1864–1929), one of Mead's colleagues, used the phrase **looking-glass self** to designate *the image people have of themselves based on how they believe others perceive them* (1964; orig. 1902). Whether we think of ourselves as clever or clumsy, worthy or worthless, depends in large measure on what we think others think of us. This insight goes a long way towards explaining Carol Gilligan's (1982) finding that young women lose self-confidence as they come of age in a society that discourages women from being too assertive.

The I and the Me

Our capacity to see ourselves through others implies that the self has two components. First, *the self is subject* as we initiate social action. Humans are innately active and spontaneous, Mead claimed, dubbing this subjective element of the self the *I* (the subjective form of the personal pronoun). But second, *the self is object* because, taking the role of another, we form impressions of ourselves. Mead called this objective element of the self the *Me* (the objective form of the personal pronoun). All social experience begins with someone initiating action (the I-phase of self) and then guiding the action (the Me-phase of self) by taking the role of the other. Social experience is thus the interplay of the I and the Me: our actions are spontaneous yet guided by how others respond to us.

Mead stressed that thinking itself constitutes a social experience. Our thoughts are partly creative (representing the I), but in thought we also become objects to ourselves (representing the Me) as we imagine how others will respond to our ideas. Table 7.1 draws out some of these contrasts.

Table 7.1	The Meadian 'I' and 'ME'
The I phase	**The ME phase**
Subject	Object
Impulsive	Determined
Knowing	Known
Acts in world	Attitudes of others
Social experience is the interplay of I and Me in process	

Development of the self

According to Mead, gaining a self amounts to learning to take the role of the other. Like Freud, Mead regarded early childhood as the crucial time for this task, but he did not link the development of the self to biological maturation. Mead maintained that the self emerges over time with increasing social experience.

Infants respond to others only in terms of *imitation*. They mimic behaviour without understanding underlying intentions. Unable to use symbols, Mead concluded, infants have no self.

Children first learn to use language and other symbols in the form of *play*, especially role playing. Initially, they model themselves on key people in their lives – such as parents – whom we call *significant others*. Playing 'mummy and daddy', for example, helps children imagine the world from their parents' point of view.

Gradually, children learn to take the roles of several others at once. This skill is the key to moving from simple play (say, playing catch) involving one other to complex *games* (like baseball) involving many others. Only by the age of seven or eight have most children acquired sufficient social experience to engage in team sports that demand taking the role of numerous others simultaneously.

Figure 7.1 shows the logical progression from imitation to play to games. But a final stage in the development of the self remains. A game involves taking the role of others in just one situation. But members of a society also need to see themselves as others in general might. In other words, we recognise that people in any situation in society share cultural norms and values, and we begin to incorporate these general patterns into the self. Mead used the term **generalised other** to refer to *widespread cultural norms and values we use as references in evaluating ourselves*.

Of course, the emergence of the self is not the end of socialisation. Quite the contrary: Mead claimed that socialisation continues as long as we have social experience, so that changing circumstances can reshape who we are. The self may change, for example, with divorce, disability or unexpected wealth. And we retain some control over this process as we respond to events and circumstances and thereby play a part in our own socialisation. Mead's theory was really the start of the perspective we introduced in Chapter 2: symbolic interactionism.

Critical comment

The strength of Mead's work lies in exploring the nature of social experience itself. He succeeded in explaining

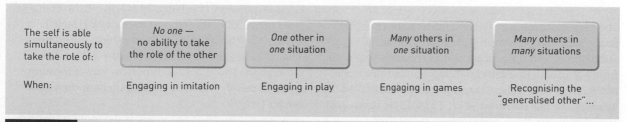

Figure 7.1   **Building on social experience**

George Herbert Mead described the development of the self as the process of gaining social experience. This is largely a matter of taking the role of the other with increasing sophistications, broadening out from specific others in greater complexity

how symbolic interaction is the foundation of both the self and society. Yet some critics disparage Mead's view as radically social because it acknowledges no biological element in the emergence of the self (in fact this is false criticism, as he certainly did highlight bodily processes and 'impulses'). Mead's concepts of the I and the Me are often confused with Freud's concepts of the id and the superego. But Freud rooted the id in the biological organism, while Mead saw the I as impulsive and the Me as regulative. Freud's concept of the superego and Mead's concept of the Me both reflect the power of society to shape personality. But for Freud, superego and id are locked in continual combat. Mead, however, held that the I and the Me work closely and cooperatively together, in a dialectical process (Meltzer, 1978).

The life course and generations

While both Freud and Mead focus on the earlier (or primary) socialisation stages of lives, 'life course' is a term that enables us to look right across the whole structure of a person's life – and the secondary socialisation that this usually involves. Although each stage of life is linked to the biological process of ageing, the life course itself is largely a social construction. People in different societies may experience a stage of life quite differently, or not at all. Yet each stage of any society's life course presents characteristic problems and transitions that involve learning something new and unlearning familiar routines. Note, too, that just because societies organise human experience according to age, this in no way negates the effects of other features of stratification we are examining, such as class, race, ethnicity and gender. Thus, the general patterns we have described are all subject to further modification as they apply to various categories of people.

Understanding life course development

The most basic feature of development is the changing sequencing and phasing of a life course. We are all familiar with *chronological age* and its common sequencing from babyhood, through childhood, youth, middle age, old age, and so on. These have commonly been called the 'seasons of a life' (Levinson *et al.*, 1978, 1996; Kortre and Hall, 1999). But these categories are themselves a problem – ageing, for example, is now quite frequently broken into a 'third age' (65–74) and a 'fourth age' (75+),

or into the younger elderly (65–75), the older elderly (75–85), and the very old (see Chapter 13). Indeed, as we find more and more people living longer and longer, the category of 'centenarian' will become more and more common. So we must note that age phase categories themselves change: 'childhood', 'middle age' and 'youth' are now seen by sociologists and historians to be recent historical inventions – they are certainly not found in all societies (for example, Shweder, 1998). We understand now that 'life phases' themselves change across history.

Lives also need to be located on a *'historical time line'* and through their demographic features. A life occurs within a definite historical time span. A line of key world events (a bit like the time line which opens this book) can be drawn which 'situates' a life firmly within its specific cultural history. South African lives, Australian lives and Peruvian lives will have a differing sense of key dates and experiences within their cultures. In Table 7.2, we have listed just a few Anglo-American themes: clearly a life that has been through two world wars (those born before 1914) has a different historical matrix from one that has not (those born after 1945).

From this we can locate *birth cohorts*: people born in the same year, or in a cluster of named years. A **cohort** is *a category of people with a common characteristic, usually their age*. Age cohorts are likely to have been influenced by the same economic and cultural trends so that members typically display similar attitudes and values (Riley *et al.*, 1988). The lives of women and men born early in the twentieth century, for example, were framed by an economic depression and two world wars – events unknown to their children or grandchildren. For their part, younger people today are living in a world where playstations, hi-tech information and websites have become taken for granted in their lives (in ways which older cohorts cannot really grasp). An *'age cohort generation'*, then, is a group of people born in a specified period of years, who are hence tied together through a particular shared historical time period. The most obvious examples would include the 'Children of the Great Depression' (see Elder, 1974), the 'Baby Boomers' (see Light, 1988), the 'Hippy Generation' (Hazlett, 1998), 'Thatcher's Children', 'Generation X' and the 'Digital Kids' (Rushkoff, 1999) and the 'Millennial Generation'. This is a most important way of locating a group of people – akin to locating them in class and gender (see Chapter 13).

A *'generation cohort perspective'* is the more subjective sense that people acquire of belonging to a particular age reference group through which they may make sense of

| Table 7.2 | **Mapping a life: life cohorts and life stages:** (a) life cohorts; (b) life stages; (c) Erikson's (1980) 'Eight Stages of Man' |

(a) Life cohorts

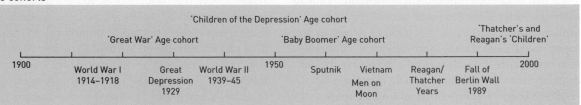

(b) Life stages

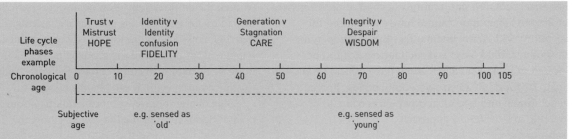

(c) 'Eight Stages of Man' – Erik Erikson

		1	2	3	4	5	6	7	8
Old Age	VIII								Integrity vs. Despair, disgust. WISDOM
Adulthood	VII							Generativity vs. Stagnation. CARE	
Young Adulthood	VI						Intimacy vs. Isolation. LOVE		
Adolescence	V					Identity vs. Identity confusion FIDELITY			
School Age	IV				Industry vs. Inferiority. COMPETENCE				
Play Age	III			Initiative vs. Guilt. PURPOSE					
Early Childhood	II		Autonomy vs. Shame, doubt. WILL						
Infancy	I	Basic trust vs. Basic mistrust. HOPE							

Source: adapted from Plummer (2001a: 126–127)

their 'memories' and 'identities' (they share a common perspective and say things like 'We all lived through the war together', 'In our days, feminism was more active', 'I was part of the Peace Movement in Vietnam', 'I am an older gay – part of the Stonewall Generation'). The former category is structural – it locates a person in the society overall; the latter is more subjective – it shows who people identify with over time. Both nevertheless take the researcher into an important awareness of historical time – and how different lives are shaped throughout by different historical baselines and different historical roots. To put it bluntly: a child of the Thatcher or Reagan Generation cannot have experienced the Second World War at first hand as their grandparents inevitably would have; and such factors need to be located in looking at a life. Often these critical locations are to be found in a person's 'youth' period. Shared generational and historical experiences come to play a key role in a *life history* approach.

All this is closely linked to mapping lives as a 'life trajectory' or as a 'life course' – 'a pathway defined by the ageing process or by movement across the age structure' (Elder, 1985). It is common here to see a tripartite life course, characterised by an early period of preparation, a middle part of work (including domestic work), and a final part for 'retirement'. We used to be able to think very straightforwardly of this – long periods of work were followed by retirement, punctuated by raising children, maturation and growth, followed by disengagement and decline. For men the emphasis was most on work; for women the emphasis most on raising children. But nowadays the shape of life courses is changing: heterogeneity, fragmentation and discontinuities have happened for many and the sequencing is no longer quite so clear. Not all cultures have the same 'shape' to this life course; again, it can change historically.

Some contemporary writers are talking about the postmodernisation of the life course – how the formal

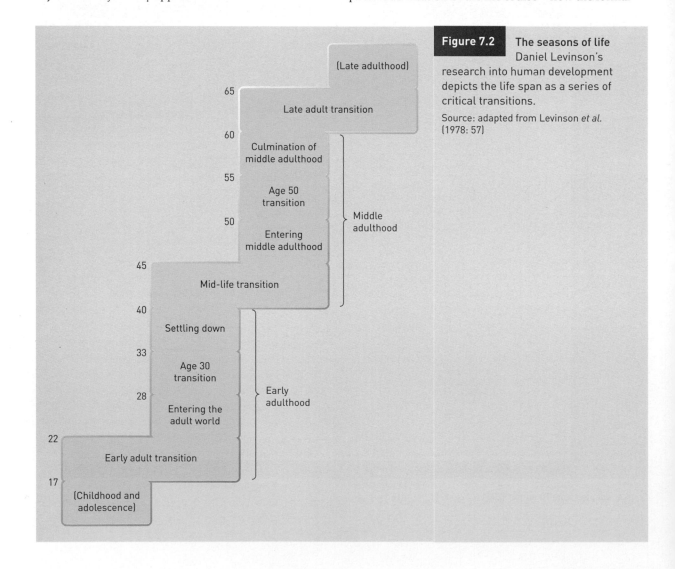

Figure 7.2 **The seasons of life**
Daniel Levinson's research into human development depicts the life span as a series of critical transitions.

Source: adapted from Levinson *et al.* (1978: 57)

patterns found in the past are breaking down, with people 'dipping in and out' of phases in a much less regularised and institutionalised fashion. We have what German sociologist Ulrich Beck refers to as the *'individualisation of the life course'*. As traditional industrial ways of life become destroyed, so individuals find they have to construct their own life plans and course: the routines and rituals of the past have gone too. As Beck says: 'individuals must produce, stage and cobble together their biographies themselves . . . the individual is actor, designer, juggler and stage director of his own biography, identity, social networks, commitment and convictions' (Beck, 1997: 95).

Within a life trajectory, we can then go on to identify *'critical life events'* and *life cycle crises*. These may range from major events such as death and divorce to less significant ones. There is a very substantial amount of writing and analysis of these themes, spearheaded by Erik Erikson's classic work on the Eight Stages of Man, but now developed in many directions. Again, though, we must distinguish between scientific accounts which try to capture some sense of an 'objective' series of phases lying, so to speak, within a life; and the more subjective awareness of subjects of their own sense of crises, their subjective identification with age, and the process of subjective reminiscences (see Table 7.2 and Figure 7.2).

Constructing situations: Erving Goffman and drama

Erving Goffman (1922–1982), profiled in the box, was the twentieth century's leading micro-sociologist. He studied what he called the **interaction order** – *what we do in the immediate presence of others* (Goffman, 1982: 2). One of the major ways he enhanced our understanding of everyday life was by noting that people routinely behave much like actors performing on a stage. By imagining ourselves as directors scrutinising what goes on in some situational 'theatre', we engage in what Goffman called **dramaturgical analysis**, *the investigation of social interaction in terms borrowed from theatrical performance.* Everyday social life becomes theatre. Dramaturgical analysis offers a fresh look at two now-familiar concepts. In theatrical terms, people come to play parts and roles as if in a play, and scripts emerge to supply dialogue and action for each of the characters. Moreover, in any setting, a person is both actor and audience. Goffman described each individual's 'performance' as the **presentation of self,** *an individual's effort to create specific impressions in the minds of others.* Presentation of self, or *impression management,*

contains several distinctive elements (Goffman, 1959, 1967). We can see daily life as a series of stagecraft rules.

Performances

As we present ourselves in everyday situations, we convey information – consciously and unconsciously – to others. An individual's performance includes dress (costume), any objects carried along (props) and tone of voice and particular gestures (manner). In addition, people craft their performance according to the setting (stage). We may joke loudly in the street, for example, but assume a more reverent manner upon entering a church. In addition, individuals design settings, such as a home or office, to enhance a performance by invoking the desired reactions in others.

Consider, for example, how a doctor's surgery conveys information to an audience of patients. Doctors enjoy prestige and power, a fact immediately grasped by patients upon entering the surgery or health centre. First, the doctor is nowhere to be seen. Instead, in what Goffman describes as the 'front region' of the setting, the patient encounters a receptionist who functions as a gatekeeper, deciding if and when the patient can meet the doctor. A simple survey of the waiting room, with patients (often impatiently) awaiting their call to the inner sanctum, leaves little doubt that the medical team controls events.

The doctor's private examination room or surgery constitutes the 'back region' of the setting. Here the patient confronts a wide range of props, such as medical books and framed degrees, which together reinforce the impression that the doctor has the specialised knowledge necessary to be in charge. In the surgery the doctor may remain seated behind a desk – the larger and grander the desk, the greater the statement of power – while the patient is provided with only a chair.

The doctor's appearance and manner convey still more information. The common hospital doctor's costume of white lab coat may have the practical function of keeping clothes from becoming soiled, but its social function is to let others know at a glance the doctor's status. A stethoscope around the neck or a black medical bag in hand has the same purpose. A doctor's highly technical terminology – frequently mystifying – also emphasises the hierarchy in the situation. The use of the title 'Doctor' by patients who, in turn, are frequently addressed only by their first names, also underscores the physician's dominant position. The overall message of a doctor's performance is clear: 'I will help you only if you allow me to take charge.'

PROFILE

THE DRAMATIC WORLD OF ERVING GOFFMAN (1922–1982)

Source: © American Sociological Association

Universal human nature is not a very human thing. By acquiring it, the person becomes a kind of construct, built up not from psychic propensities but from moral rules that are impressed from without . . .

Erving Goffman, *Interactional Ritual* (1967: 45)

Erving Goffman is generally considered to be the most influential of twentieth-century micro-sociologists and carved out a world of analysis that was distinctly his. A Canadian, he was trained at the University of Chicago and his first major field trip was to the Shetland Isles in Scotland for his PhD – for the book that eventually became his first classic, *The Presentation of Self in Everyday Life* (1959). Observing life closely on those islands, he started to develop a framework for seeing social life as a kind of drama. Just like people on a stage, people in everyday life could be seen as actors playing out roles and giving impressions to others that enabled the others to make sense of what was going on. This was the *dramaturgical* perspective.

Throughout his work – which often changed direction and was idiosyncratically written – his main concern was with *the interaction order*: what people do in the presence of others. He studied how behaviour in public places works – how people walk through doors and

down streets. He looked at how people develop 'interaction rituals': 'the world in truth is a wedding' is one of his famous lines, in which he suggests that much of the most routine everyday interaction has important ritual elements to it. He looked at the ways in which identities became spoilt – how some people became stigmatised and had to work hard to present themselves as 'normal'.

Along the way, Goffman literally produced a new language for thinking about the everyday. He produced an array of 'mini-concepts' which help us see how daily life is composed, terms such as 'face-work', 'cooling the mark', front and back regions, moral careers, information control, impression management, passing, own and wise, frames, keying, role distance, role playing, role attachments, civil inattention, situational adjustments, people as 'vehicular units', total institution, avoidance rituals, presentation rituals, tie signs.

In the light of this, and your reading of some of Goffman's work, you might like to write your own 'dramaturgical handbook'. Think about who are the key players in your life and where you interact with them, and map out some of your own ways of presenting yourself and making 'interaction rituals'. Is this a useful framework for thinking about how life is constructed? What are the problems with it?

Non-verbal communication

Novelist William Sansom describes a fictional Mr Preedy – an English holidaymaker on a beach in Spain:

He took care to avoid catching anyone's eye. First, he had to make it clear to those potential companions

of his holiday that they were of no concern to him whatsoever. He stared through them, round them, over them – eyes lost in space. The beach might have been empty. If by chance a ball was thrown his way, he looked surprised; then let a smile of amusement light his face (Kindly Preedy), looked around dazed to see that there were people on the beach, tossed it back with a smile to himself and not a smile at the people. . . .

. . . [He] then gathered together his beach-wrap and bag into a neat sand-resistant pile (Methodical and Sensible Preedy), rose slowly to stretch his huge frame (Big-Cat Preedy), and tossed aside his sandals (Carefree Preedy, after all).

(1956; quoted in Goffman, 1959: 4–5)

Through his conduct, Mr Preedy offers a great deal of information about himself to anyone caring to observe him. Notice that he does so without uttering a single word. This illustrates the process of **non-verbal communication**, *communication using body movements, gestures and facial expressions rather than speech.*

Virtually any part of the body can be used to generate *body language*, that is, to convey information to others. Facial expressions form the most significant element of non-verbal communication. Smiling and other facial gestures express basic emotions such as pleasure, surprise and anger the world over. Further, people project particular shades of meaning with their faces. We distinguish, for example, between the deliberate smile of Kindly Preedy on the beach, a spontaneous smile of joy at seeing a friend, a pained smile of embarrassment and a full, unrestrained smile of self-satisfaction that we often associate with the 'cat who ate the canary'.

Eye contact is another crucial element of non-verbal communication. Generally, we use eye contact to initiate social interaction. Someone across the room 'catches our eye', for example, sparking a conversation. Avoiding the eyes of another, on the other hand, discourages communication. Hands, too, speak for us. Common hand gestures in our culture convey, among other things, an insult, a request for a lift, an invitation for someone to join us, or a demand that others stop in their tracks. Gestures also supplement spoken words. Pointing in a menacing way at someone, for example, intensifies a word of warning, just as shrugging the shoulders adds an air of indifference to the phrase 'I don't know', and rapidly waving the arms lends urgency to the single word 'Hurry!'.

But, as any actor knows, the 'perfect performance' is an elusive goal. In everyday performances, some element of body language often contradicts our intended meaning. A teenage boy offers an explanation for getting home late, for example, but his mother doubts his words because he avoids looking her in the eye. The movie star on a television talk show claims that her recent flop at the box office is 'no big deal', but the nervous swing of her leg belies her casual denial. In practical terms, carefully observing non-verbal communication (most of

which is not easily controlled) provides clues to deception, in much the same way that a lie detector records tell-tale changes in breathing, pulse rate, perspiration and blood pressure.

Yet detecting lies is difficult, because no single bodily gesture directly indicates deceit in the way that, say, a smile indicates pleasure. Even so, because any performance involves so many expressions, few people can confidently lie without allowing some piece of contradictory information to slip through, arousing the suspicions of a careful observer. Therefore, the key to detecting deceit is to scan the whole performance with an eye for inconsistencies and discrepancies.

In sum, lies are detectable, but training is the key to noticing relevant clues. Another key to spotting deception is knowing the other person well, the reason that parents can usually pick up deceit in their children. Finally, almost anyone can unmask deception when the liar is trying to cover up strong emotions.

Gender and personal performances

Because women are socialised to be less assertive than men, they tend to be especially sensitive to non-verbal communication. In fact, gender is a central element in personal performances. Based on the work of Nancy Henley, Mykol Hamilton and Barrie Thorne (1992), we can extend the present discussion of personal performances to spotlight the importance of gender.

Demeanour

Demeanour – that is, general conduct or deportment – reflects a person's level of social power. Simply put, powerful people enjoy far greater personal discretion in how they act; subordinates act more formally and self-consciously. Off-colour remarks, swearing or casually removing shoes and putting feet up on the desk may be acceptable for the boss, but rarely for employees. Similarly, people in positions of dominance can interrupt the performances of others with impunity, while others are expected to display deference by remaining silent (Smith-Lovin and Brody, 1989; Henley *et al.*, 1992; Cathryn Johnson, 1994).

Since women generally occupy positions of lesser power, demeanour is a gender issue as well. As Chapter 12 explains, about half of all working women in Europe and the United States hold clerical or service jobs that place them under the control of supervisors who are usually men. Women, then, craft their personal performances more carefully than men and display a greater degree of deference in everyday interaction.

Use of space

How much space does a personal performance require? Here again, power plays a key role, since using more space conveys a non-verbal message of personal importance. According to Henley, *et al.* (1992), men typically command more space than women do, whether pacing back and forth before an audience or casually lounging on the beach. Why? Our culture traditionally has measured femininity by how *little* space women occupy (the standard of 'daintiness'), while gauging masculinity by how *much* territory a man controls (the standard of 'turf').

The concept of **personal space** refers to *the surrounding area to which an individual makes some claim to privacy*. In the United Kingdom, for example, people typically position themselves several feet apart when speaking; throughout the Middle East, by contrast, individuals interact within a much closer space.

Throughout the world, gender further modifies these patterns. In daily life, men commonly intrude on the personal space of women. A woman's encroachment into a man's personal space, however, is likely to be construed as a sexual overture. Here again, women have less power in everyday interaction than men do.

Staring, smiling and touching

Eye contact encourages interaction. Typically, women employ eye contact to sustain conversation more than men do. Men have their own distinctive brand of eye contact: staring. By making women the targets of stares, men are both making a claim of social dominance and defining women as sexual objects.

Although frequently signalling pleasure, *smiling* has a host of meanings. In a male-dominated world, women often smile to indicate appeasement or acceptance of submission. For this reason, Henley, Hamilton and Thorne maintain, women smile more than men; in extreme cases, smiling may reach the level of nervous habit.

Finally, *touching* constitutes an intriguing social pattern. Mutual touching conveys feelings of intimacy and caring. Apart from close relationships, however, touching is generally something men do to women (though rarely, in our culture, to other men). A male doctor touches the shoulder of his female nurse as they examine a report, a young man touches the back of his woman friend as he guides her across the street, or a male skiing instructor looks for opportunities to touch his female students. In these examples – as well as many others – touching may evoke little response, so common is it in everyday life. But it amounts to a subtle ritual by which men express their dominant position in an assumed hierarchy that subordinates women.

Idealisation

Complex motives underlie human behaviour. Even so, according to Goffman, we construct performances to *idealise* our intentions. That is, we try to convince others (and perhaps ourselves) that what we do reflects ideal cultural standards rather than more selfish motives.

Idealisation is easily illustrated by returning to the world of doctors and patients. In a hospital, consultants engage in a performance commonly described as 'making the rounds'. Approaching the patient, the doctor often stops at the foot of the bed and silently examines the patient's chart. Afterwards, doctor and patient converse briefly. In ideal terms, this routine involves a doctor making a personal visit to enquire about a patient's condition.

In reality, something less exemplary is usually going on. A doctor who sees several dozen patients a day may remember little about most of them. Reading the chart gives the doctor the opportunity to rediscover the patient's identity and medical problems. Openly revealing the actual impersonality of much medical care would undermine the culturally ideal perception of the doctor as deeply concerned about the welfare of others.

Idealisation is woven into the fabric of everyday life in countless ways. Doctors, university lecturers and other professionals typically idealise their motives for entering their chosen careers. They describe their work as 'making a contribution to science', 'helping others', 'answering a calling from God', or perhaps 'serving the community'. Rarely do such people concede the less honourable, though common, motives of seeking the income, power, prestige and leisure these occupations confer.

Taking a broader view, idealisation underlies social civility, since we smile and make polite remarks to people we do not like. Such small hypocrisies ease our way through social interactions. Even when we suspect that others are putting on an act, rarely do we openly challenge their performance, for reasons we shall explain next.

Embarrassment and tact

The eminent professor consistently mispronounces the dean's name; the visiting dignitary rises from the table to speak, unaware of the napkin that still hangs from her neck; the president becomes ill at a state dinner. As carefully as individuals may craft their performances, slip-ups of all kinds frequently occur. The result is *embarrassment*, which, in dramaturgical terms, means the discomfort that follows a spoiled performance. Goffman describes embarrassment simply as 'losing face'.

Embarrassment looms as an ever-present danger because, first, all performances typically contain some measure of deception and, second, most performances involve a complex array of elements, any one of which, in a thoughtless moment, may shatter the intended impression.

Interestingly, an audience usually overlooks flaws in a performance, thereby allowing an actor to avoid embarrassment. If we do point out a mis-step ('Excuse me, but do you know that your fly is open?'), we do it discreetly and only to help someone avoid even greater loss of face. In Hans Christian Andersen's classic fable *The Emperor's New Clothes*, the child who blurts out that the emperor is parading around naked is telling the truth, yet is scolded for being rude.

But members of an audience usually do more than ignore flaws in a performance, Goffman explains; typically, they help the performer recover from them. *Tact*, then, amounts to helping another person 'save face'. After hearing a supposed expert make an embarrassingly inaccurate remark, for example, people may tactfully ignore the comment as if it were never spoken at all. Alternatively, mild laughter may indicate that they wish to dismiss what they have heard as a joke. Or a listener may simply respond, 'I'm sure you didn't mean that',

acknowledging the statement but not allowing it to destroy the actor's performance.

Why is tact such a common response? Because embarrassment provokes discomfort not simply for one person but for *everyone*. Just as the entire audience feels uneasy when an actor forgets a line, people who observe awkward behaviour are reminded of how fragile their own performances often are. Socially constructed reality thus functions like a dam holding back a sea of chaotic possibility. Should one person's performance spring a leak, others tactfully assist in making repairs. Everyone, after all, jointly engages in building culture, and no one wants reality to be suddenly swept away.

In sum, Goffman's research shows that, while behaviour is spontaneous in some respects, it is more patterned than we like to think. Almost 400 years ago, William Shakespeare captured this idea in memorable lines that still ring true:

> All the world's a stage,
> And all the men and women merely players:
> They have their exits and their entrances;
> And one man in his time plays many parts. . . .

(*As You Like It*, II)

VOICES

DISABILITY, INTERACTION AND FACIAL DISFIGUREMENT

In 1961, the sociologist Fred Davis wrote a very influential article on the disabled. He indicated the ways in which the presence of disability had the ability to 'flood' interaction – to be overwhelmed by it and often to cause the interaction to breakdown. Disability violated the routine rules of physical ability and the norms of everyday looks. When confronted with the disabled, people may behave in strange ways (Davis, 1961).

In 2004, a television programme called *Celebrity Disfigurement*, arranged for two minor stars – a fashion star and a comedian – to have temporary facial disfigurement and then to go about their business for a couple of days (with a camera and recorder attached). Commentaries were made by people with real disfigurements (often of an extreme nature). They stood in the street trying to get people to sign a petition – and people avoided them. They went into a school and the students could hardly bring them-

selves to look at them. In a cosmetic shop, the assistants keep their eyes firmly on the job and away from eye contact with the disfigured person. At a bar, the barman repeatedly ignored requests for drinks. At a roller rink, no help was forthcoming for half an hour.

Several key interactional responses were noted:

- Avoidance in many forms – looking away, walking away, ignoring;
- The projection of anger – almost saying how dare you be here in my space
- The generalised spreading of fear;
- Sterotyping: the facial features were generalised to suggest that the person was mad or bad;
- In one case, the facial difference was seen to be an indication that the person had Down's Syndrome.

One person made it clear that he had two choices: (1) not to go out, and this would make him more and more passive and self-loathing, or (2) to go out and resist these responses. With practice one learned just to carry on.

Source: *Celebrity Disfigurement* (Channel 4), 18 May 2004

Ethnomethodology and conversational analysis

Rather than assume that reality is something 'out there', the symbolic-interaction paradigm posits that reality is created by people in everyday encounters. But how, exactly, do we define reality for ourselves? What is the logic through which we make sense of everyday life? Answering this question is the objective of other theoretical approaches: *ethnomethodology* and *conversational analysis*.

Ethnomethodology

The term itself has two parts: the Greek *ethno* refers to people and how they understand their surroundings; 'methodology' designates a set of methods or principles. Combining them makes **ethnomethodology**, *the study of the way people make sense of their everyday lives*. Ethnomethodology is largely the creation of the Californian-based sociologist Harold Garfinkel (1967), who challenged the then-dominant view of society as a broad, abstract 'system' (recall the approach of Emile Durkheim, described in Chapters 1, 2 and 4). Garfinkel wanted to explore how we make sense of countless familiar situations by looking at the practical reasoning we employ in everyday situations. On the surface, we engage in intentional speech or action; but these efforts rest on deeper assumptions about the world that we usually take for granted.

Think, for a moment, about what we assume in asking someone the simple question, 'How are you?' Do we mean physically? Mentally? Spiritually? Financially? Are we even looking for an answer, or are we 'just being polite'?

Ethnomethodology, then, delves into the sense-making process in any social encounter. Because so much of this process is ingrained, Garfinkel argues that one effective way to expose how we make sense of events is purposely to *break the rules*. Deliberately ignoring conventional rules and observing how people respond, he points out, allows us to tease out how people build a reality. Thus, Garfinkel (1967) directed his students to refuse to 'play the game' in a wide range of situations. Some students living with their parents started acting as if they were boarders rather than children. Others entered stores and insisted on bargaining for items. Some recruited people into simple games (like tic-tac-toe or noughts-and-crosses) only to intentionally flout the

rules. Still others initiated conversations while slowly moving closer and closer to the other person. It was a matter of making the everyday 'strange', of 'breaching' common-sense assumptions; and this was done to show just how everyday life depends upon our ongoing sense of 'trust' with each other. Life is fragile, yet it has a rule- and game-like quality which human beings daily recognise, produce and reproduce.

Conversational analysis

Taking this one step further, some sociologists argue that the guiding feature of everyday interaction is language (see Chapter 5). To understand society and the everyday life through which it is made, we need to look at language and the rules through which we speak. In a sense, societies are languages.

Conversational analysis provides *a rigorous set of techniques to technically record and then analyse what happens in everyday speech*. It sets about listening to and observing language, recording it, transcribing it, often videotaping it. Everywhere people are talking, conversational analysts are interested in understanding their talk. Thus they look everywhere – at courts, hospitals, street conversations, political speeches, suicide notes, statistic making, children's play, television – to see how people construct their daily talk. They see this talk and conversation as a *topic* to investigate in its own right: they are not interested in what people actually say in terms of its contents (which they call resource). Rather, they are interested in its forms and rules, which they see as the underlying feature of social interaction. Human realities are accomplished through talk.

As one example, conversational analysts are concerned with the '*sequencing*' of talk: sentences generally follow on from one another. 'Normal' interaction depends upon this, and everyday life can only really be accomplished if people are willing to follow certain 'sequencing rules'. One of these, for instance, is '*turn taking*': people bide their time, and take turns at being hearers and tellers to talk to others. Another is the 'adjacency pair' through which most greetings, openings and closings of conversations have an unstated rule that as one speaks a line, so another makes the most appropriate conventional response to it. Thus, for example, a standard opening line may be: how are you? And this requires a response, usually of the form: very well, thank you. Everyday life is in this way deeply regulated by social rules (Heritage, 1987).

Identity

Identity has become a key concept within contemporary sociology, although it is far from new. For Richard Jenkins, **social identity** is *'our understanding of who we are and of who other people are, and, reciprocally, other people's understanding of themselves and of others'* (Jenkins, 1996). As a sociological concept, it serves as a crucial bridge in social life between human beings and wider cultures. Identity refers to sameness (from Latin *idem*, the same; after the Latin *identitas*, and similar to the word 'identical'); the word entered the English language around 1570. It highlights the quality or condition of being the same; of oneness and continuity. As Jeffrey Weeks says:

> Identity is about belonging, about what you have in common with some people and what differentiates you from others. At its most basic it gives you a sense of personal location, the stable core to your individuality. But it is also about your social relationships, your complex involvement with others.
>
> (Weeks, 1991: 88)

Far from being a new idea, then, it implies a sense of meaning and a sense of categorisation and difference: we mark out our identity and sameness with some by highlighting the differences between ourselves and others. It implies a necessary 'other' who is not 'us'. Zygmunt Bauman, a leading contemporary theorist, puts this strikingly when he says:

> woman is the other of man, animal is the other of human, stranger is the other of native, abnormality the other of norm, deviation the other of law abiding, illness the other of health, insanity the other of reason, lay public the other of expert, foreigner the other of state subject, enemy the other of friend . . .
>
> (Bauman, 1991: 8)

Identity as a concept, then, looks both inwards and outwards. On the one hand, it speaks to the most microscopic of events – the inner world of how we feel about ourselves. (Freud may be our partial guide here.) It suggests that there is an inner flow of being that is social. On the other hand, it also looks outwards to the most macro of organisations – to the nation state and the global world. We can speak of Catholic identity through our identification with the Catholic Church, or Celtic identity through our identity with Ireland. Communities of many different kinds – Catholic, Celtic, Chinese – provide meanings from which we can come to fashion our sense of who we are and who we are not.

By its very terminology, then, identity theory implies some sense of sameness, commonality, continuity: if not actually present, the search is nevertheless at least on for an identity – a project of knowing who one is or what one's nation is. At the strongest extremes this is a jingoistic, brazen, self-assertive 'I am this: British, Black, Gay, or Male'. The category behind the identity is presumed and is often stridently clear. I am what I am. At the opposite extreme, the identity has so far dissolved that it is permanently unsettled, destabilised, under provisional construction, very much a project and never a thing. We are not quite sure who we are, or at any event who we are is open to frequent change. But even in this most extreme form it has to recognise the need for and the power of categories and boundaries in the organisation of the social: it is just that these continuities and sameness are much more pluralised, shifting and fragmented than they were previously thought to be. In what follows, we will look a little more at some of these key contrasts.

Changing meanings of identity

In the past, small, homogeneous and slowly changing societies provided a firm (if narrow) foundation for building meaningful identity. In many societies throughout history, the idea of identity has not really been a problem. In traditional worlds, 'pre-modern identities' may often be taken for granted. People know who they are, and often define themselves through traditions and religion. They find what seems to be 'a natural place' in the order of things. Identities are shared and communal, given as part of the world, the cosmos and nature. Such identities remain quite common today. For example, in the tight-knit Amish communities that flourish in parts of the United States (well depicted in the film *Witness*, 1985) young people are taught 'correct' ways to think and behave. Not everyone born into an Amish community can tolerate these demands for conformity, but most members establish an identity that is well integrated into the community (see Hostetler, 1980; Kraybill and Olshan, 1994).

As capitalism developed, there appeared an increased concern with human individuality, which starts to make the issue of individual identity more and more important. The modern (industrial, capitalist) period becomes a time of enormous self-reflection upon just who one is. An individual identity starts to emerge which seems a unified, singular and unique, integral individual, endowed with reason and a possible essential core of human beingness. This is what has been seen as the 'birth' of the modern human subject with a quest for personal self-understanding and identity.

THE 'WHO AM I?' TEST

Sociologists working in the 1950s devised the simplest of tools for measuring self and identity, what has been called the 'Who am I?' or 'Twenty Statements' test. The authors – Kuhn and McPartland (1954) – suggest to students that they should write the first 20 statements that come to mind in answer to the question 'Who am I?'. They stress there are no right and wrong answers. You might like to try it.

There are 20 numbered blanks in the table below. Please write 20 answers to the simple question: 'Who am I?' in the blanks. Just give 20 different answers to this question. Answer as if you were giving the answers to yourself, not to somebody else. Write the answers in the order they occur to you. Don't worry about logic or 'importance'. Go along fairly fast, for time is limited.

1	6	11	16
2	7	12	17
3	8	13	18
4	9	14	19
5	10	15	20

But modern societies, with their characteristic diversity and rapid change, offer only shifting sands on which to build a personal identity. Left to make our own life decisions, many of us – especially those with greater affluence – confront a bewildering array of options. Autonomy has little value without standards for making choices, and people may find one path no more compelling than the next. Not surprisingly, many people shuttle from one identity to another, changing their lifestyle, relationships and even religion in search of an elusive 'true self'. Beset by the widespread 'relativism' of modern societies, people without a moral compass have lost the security and certainty once provided by tradition.

To David Riesman (1970; orig. 1950), pre-industrial societies promote what he calls **tradition-directedness**, *rigid conformity to time-honoured ways of living*. Members of traditional societies model their lives on what has gone before, so that what is 'good' is equivalent to 'what has always been'. Tradition-directedness, then, carries to the level of individual experience Toennies' *Gemeinschaft* and Durkheim's mechanical solidarity (see Chapters 1 and 4). Culturally conservative, tradition-directed people think and act alike because everyone draws on the same solid cultural foundation. Amish people exemplify tradition-direction; in Amish culture, tradition ties everyone to ancestors and descendants in an unbroken chain of righteous living.

Many members of diverse and rapidly changing societies define a tradition-directed personality as deviant because it seems so rigid. Modern people, by and large, prize personal flexibility, the capacity to adapt and sensitivity to others. Riesman describes this type of social character as **other-directedness**, *a receptiveness to the latest trends and fashions, often expressed in the practice of imitating others*. Because their socialisation occurs within societies that are constantly in flux, other-directed people develop fluid identities marked by superficiality, inconsistency and change. They try on different 'selves', almost like so many pieces of new clothing, seek out 'role models' and engage in varied 'performances' as they move from setting to setting (Goffman, 1959). In a traditional society, such 'shiftiness' marks a person as untrustworthy, but in a changing, modern society, the chameleon-like ability to fit in virtually anywhere stands as a valued personal trait.

In societies that value the up-to-date rather than the traditional, people anxiously solicit the approval of others, looking to members of their own generation rather than to elders as significant role models. 'Peer pressure' can sometimes be irresistible to people with no enduring standards to guide them. Our society urges individuals to be true to themselves. But when social surroundings change so rapidly, how can people determine to which self they should be true? This problem lies at the root of the identity crisis so widespread in industrial societies today. 'Who am I?' is a nagging question that many of us struggle to answer. In truth, this problem is not so much psychological as sociological, reflecting the inherent instability of modern mass society.

Most recently, we have seen the arrival of postmodern identities. These are altogether less unified identities and much more fragmented. Identity now becomes **decentred**, *a process by which a centre, core or essence is destabilised and weakened*. This connects to many of the changes we have already identified – globalisation, feminism, proliferating new voices – and generates the search for 'new frameworks' of self-understanding. Giddens talks about all this as a reflexive self-identity:

> . . . because of the 'openness' of social life today, the pluralisation of contexts of action and the diversity of 'authorities', life style choice is increasingly important in the constitution of identity and daily activity. Reflexively organised life planning . . . becomes a central feature of the structuring of self-identity.

(Giddens, 1991: 5)

What we find is that the very idea of personal identity can be thrown into doubt.

As we shall see later (Chapters 21 and 22), the presence of the new information technologies and the new media also leads to what has been called a 'culture of simulation'. This is a kind of virtual reality through which we come to live increasingly in worlds of media images and cyberspaces. The question now being asked is in what way this might be leading to new kinds of 'simulated identity' and 'cyber identity', as even the modern boundaries get eroded. On the Net, it is suggested, people can – if only for a while – become whoever they wish.

Table 7.3 briefly charts some of these shifts in the meanings of identities.

Table 7.3	The shifting nature of identities	
Traditional	**Modern**	**Postmodern**
Given	Determined and structured	Chosen
Taken-for-granted	Polarised/dichotomous	Multiple/fragmenting
Powerful but hidden	Predictable	Chaotic
Essential	Essentialising	De-essentialising

The sociologies of the body and the emotions

A further way of thinking about day-to-day interaction is to consider our bodies and emotions, both new and interesting fields for sociologists to study.

Bodies

Bodies – perhaps more than anything else – seem to be straightforwardly biological, 'natural' and given. Indeed, at first sight, bodies do not seem to be the most obvious area for sociologists to study. After all, so the argument goes, bodies are biological and individual: sociologists are surely only interested in the cultural and the social. But if we think about our own bodies for a bit and use our newly discovered sociological imagination (see Chapter 1), we will soon discover that our bodies are indeed social (see Figure 7.3).

The social body

Traditionally we may look at bodies through what has been called a 'Cartesian dualism' that divides bodies from non-bodies and mind from matter. René Descartes (1591–1650) is often considered the founder of modern philosophy, and at the heart of his arguments was the conclusion that mind is a non-corporeal substance, distinct from a material or bodily substance. The taken-for-granted assumption is that of the 'natural body'. True, it may become weakened in all sorts of ways (and medicine is largely there to help repair it), but the body is 'natural'.

This view is no longer tenable for sociologists. The boundaries and borders of bodies with nature and technologies have significantly dissolved. We are instead, according to the sociologist Chris Shilling, involved in **body projects**, *the process of becoming and transforming a biological entity through social action*. We work on our bodies in myriad ways – from clothing, washing and hygiene to medical and fitness regimes.

The scaling and commodification of bodies – poor bodies/rich bodies

Bodies change across space and time, and much of this may also be linked to bodies in poor and rich countries. What we could call 'poor bodies' may be linked to dirt (sanitation), disease, death, danger and diet (or lack of it), while bodies in high-income countries ('rich bodies') engage with 'body projects' such as dieting, exercise, training, body modification – from tattoos and haircuts to plastic surgery, transgender surgery and on to cyborgs (Shilling, 2003). If intimacies are grounded in bodies, then the scaling of bodies give very different meanings and responses in rich and poor worlds.

Linked to globalisation is the growth of trafficking in body parts. Everything from skin, bone and blood to organs and genetic materials of 'the other' is now up for sale, and this global trafficking is almost invariably in one direction: from the poorest to the richest. Often justified in terms of 'choices', this is part of a process of bodily commodification. As two people remarked in seeming desperation:

> I am willing to sell any organ of my body that is not vital to my survival and which could help save another person's life in exchange for an amount of money that will allow me to feed my family.
>
> (Ad placed in the *Diaro de Pernambuyco*, Recife, Brazil, by Miguel Correira de Oliveira, age 30)

> Please, I need money to get dentures, and am a senior desparet [sic] for money. Want to sell a very good kidney. Am desparet for money for teeth. Am a senior citizen in excellent medical shape, but need $ for dentures. My husband and I have no dental plan.
>
> (Email from E.B., Oak Hills, California, cited in Scheper-Hughes and Wacquant, 2002: 42)

Nancy Scheper-Hughes has chronicled the rise in this process of bodily commodification and the sale of organs, and puts it dramatically:

> Continuous throughout these transactions across time and space is the division of society into two populations, one socially and medically included and the other excluded, one with and one utterly lacking the ability to draw on the beauty, strength, reproductive, sexual, or anatomical power of the other. … Commercialised transplant medicine has allowed global society to be divided into two decidedly unequal populations – organ givers and organ receivers. The former are an invisible and discredited collection of anonymous suppliers of spare parts; the latter are cherished patients, treated as moral and body parts of the poor, living and dead, are virtually unquestioned.
>
> (Scheper-Hughes and Wacquant, 2002: 4)

Open and closed bodies

Sociologist Deborah Lupton (1998: 72) has indeed suggested a movement from a body that was predominately 'open' in pre-modern times to one that has become increasingly 'closed' and regulated in modern times. Basically, what she means to capture with this idea is a major shift from societies where the body was ever present to one where we increasingly try to regulate and control it. In an analysis of medieval and early modern German culture, the historian Christel Roper describes how the body was seen as:

> a container for a series of processes: defecation, sexual pollution, vomiting. Fluids course about within the body, erupting out of it, leaving their mark on the outside world. The body is not so much a collection of joints and limbs, or a skeletal structure, as a container of fluids, bursting out in every direction to impact on the environment
>
> (Roper, 1994: 23)

This was a messy world of strange fluids, smells and diseases – the body an ever-present source of chaos.

But with the enlightenment (see Chapter 1), the sociologist Norbert Elias (see Profile box) suggests that we became increasingly preoccupied with taming and regulating our bodily functions and processes. They became increasingly civilised and under control. The most apparent examples of this today would be dieting, fitness regimes, medical regimes for the elderly and sick as well as plastic surgery. On this latter concern alone, Adele Clarke estimates that it is a $1.75 billion a year industry in the United States, with about 1.5 million people undergoing plastic surgery of some kind (Clarke, 1995: 147).

But there are more extreme examples which are becoming of interest. Thus, the Human Genome Project – discussed in Chapter 22 – raises the issue of genetics and the body. Basically, when every gene in the body has been identified, will this lead to radical transformations of our bodies as we undergo gene replacement?

Sociologists are also starting to discuss **cyborgs**, *creatures which connect human and biological properties to technological ones.* Anyone drugged to feel better, reprogrammed to resist disease or given an artificial organ or limb, is technically a cyborg. By this definition, currently some:

Figure 7.3	The Social Body From Classical Bodies to Postmodern Bodies

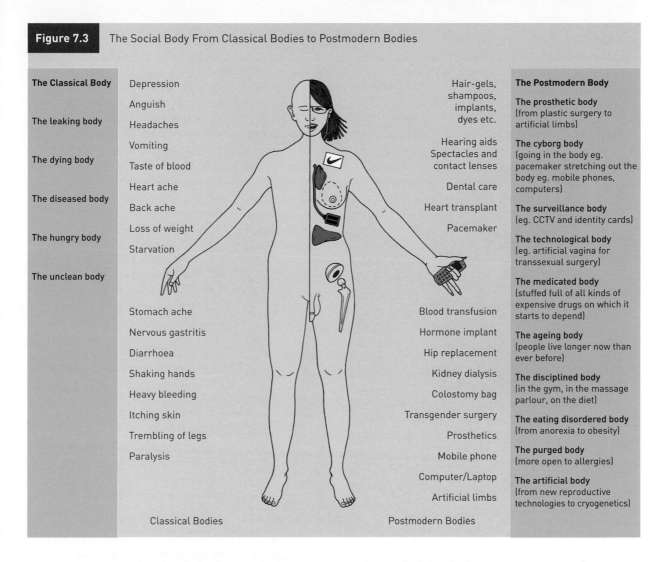

The Classical Body

The leaking body

The dying body

The diseased body

The hungry body

The unclean body

Depression
Anguish
Headaches
Vomiting
Taste of blood
Heart ache
Back ache
Loss of weight
Starvation

Stomach ache
Nervous gastritis
Diarrhoea
Shaking hands
Heavy bleeding
Itching skin
Trembling of legs
Paralysis

Hair-gels, shampoos, implants, dyes etc.

Hearing aids Spectacles and contact lenses

Dental care

Heart transplant

Pacemaker

Blood transfusion
Hormone implant
Hip replacement
Kidney dialysis
Colostomy bag
Transgender surgery
Prosthetics
Mobile phone
Computer/Laptop
Artificial limbs

The Postmodern Body

The prosthetic body
(from plastic surgery to artificial limbs)

The cyborg body
(going in the body eg. pacemaker stretching out the body eg. mobile phones, computers)

The surveillance body
(eg. CCTV and identity cards)

The technological body
(eg. artificial vagina for transsexual surgery)

The medicated body
(stuffed full of all kinds of expensive drugs on which it starts to depend)

The ageing body
(people live longer now than ever before)

The disciplined body
(in the gym, in the massage parlour, on the diet)

The eating disordered body
(from anorexia to obesity)

The purged body
(more open to allergies)

The artificial body
(from new reproductive technologies to cryogenetics)

Classical Bodies   Postmodern Bodies

10% of the US population are estimated to be cyborgs in the technical sense, including people with electronic pacemakers, artificial joints, drug implant systems, implanted corneal lenses and artificial skin. A much higher percentage participate in occupations that make them into metaphoric cyborgs, including the computer keyboard joined in cybernetic system with the screen, the neurosurgeon guided by fibre optic microscopy during an operation, and the teen game player in the local video arcade.

(Hayles, 1995: 321)

Health and illness

The sociology of health and illness – discussed more fully in Chapter 20 – may also be seen as looking at the way in which the body breaks down and needs to be socially repaired. Medical regimes are required to organise all this work around disease, decay and death. The final inability to repair the body results in death, and the need then is to find some socially organised way of dealing with dead bodies.

Sarah Nettleton has suggested a number of reasons for the growing sociological interest in the body. First has been the recent attempts by women to gain control over their bodies from male-dominated professionals (evidenced in the Boston Women's Health Book Collective, *Our Bodies, Ourselves* (1978; orig. 1971)). Second has been the growth of the new reproductive technologies (described in Chapter 17), which are shifting the meaning of foetus, birth and body. Third, the 'greying of the population' (highlighted in Chapter 13)

PROFILE

NORBERT ELIAS: THE CIVILISING OF BODIES AND SOCIETIES

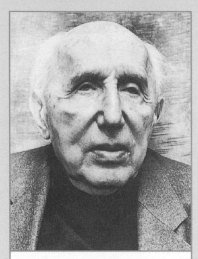

Norbert Elias (1897–1990)

Source: © Popperfoto

The German–English sociologist Norbert Elias (1897–1990) made important contributions to the study of both sociology and social change. A refugee from Hitler's Germany, his studies of *The Civilizing Process* (originally published in Germany in 1939!) suggest how from the Middle Ages onwards in most of Europe, people came to exert greater self-control over their behaviour and their bodies. Through a series of studies of ways of eating, sleeping, dressing, spitting, having sex, defecating, dying and eliminating, he charts the changing ways of life.

Medieval life was unpredictable, highly emotional, often chaotic and indulgent, and there were few codes around bodily functions. Court society slowly started to change all this, by bringing about etiquette for body management, locations for defecation, and sleeping. Restraint appeared in codes such as those managing table manners. The state developed side by side with a 'civilised' system of self-control.

The civilised society has self-discipline, self-control, higher shame and embarrassment, etc.

Chris Shilling (1993) summarises three key processes involved in civilising: socialisation, rationalisation and individualisation. People are taught to hide natural functions – like defecating and urinating; rationalisation makes us less emotional; individualisation suggests we come to see ourselves and our bodies as distinctively separate.

All of this is part of Elias's wider approach to sociology, developed in his *What is Sociology?* (1978b; orig. 1970), and known as 'figurational sociology'. Interactions between individuals and societies are his area of study: 'the network of interdependencies among human beings is what binds them together' (1978a: 261; orig. 1939).

Elias's work has been influential on a range of scholars who study everyday life processes. Stephen Mennell, for instance, has studied food.

Source: Elias (1978a; orig. 1939).

---

means that larger numbers of people will have to come to terms not only with the 'ageing body' but also the possibility of taking their own life. Fourth, consumer patterns (see Chapter 14) are increasingly concerned with body products: everything from 'the fitness industry' to the 'cosmetics industry'. Fifth, the arrival of AIDS in the early 1980s served to remind us of the limits of medical technology. And finally, ethical issues around the body – from abortion to research on embryos – are opening up debates about the boundaries between life and death (Nettleton, 1995: 102–103).

Emotions in everyday life

Emotions would seem to be another one of those topics that is far removed from sociological analysis. Emotions, after all, are something we feel within; they are personal, psychological, private. But think about it again. For in recent years, sociologists have turned their attentions to a full array of feelings, and suggested that there may indeed be social patterns to these too.

Think for a moment about your own emotions and those of your friends. Do you show them with ease, or do you perhaps try to conceal them? Do you talk about your feelings at all? And do you show different patterns of feeling from those of your friends? Maybe boys show aggression more than girls? There are surely moments when you are permitted to cry (at weddings and funerals) and moments when you may want to but know it is not appropriate (at job interviews or in gang conflicts!). There are places when it seems right to 'disclose' your feelings (to loved ones, in therapy groups) and other times when it would be clearly odd to do so (perhaps to shop assistants or public officials). There is once again a certain social pattern around our feelings, and it is this which sociologists look for.

Arlie Hochschild (1983) has been prominent in introducing an important way of thinking about emotions in sociology. One of her early studies was concerned with the everyday work of airline stewardesses. This is becoming an increasingly common job – and it requires working under great pressure. Global traffic, tight confinements, 'air rage passengers', 'waitressing' and the like make this quite a taxing job. But as Hochchild spends time observing the training of these flight attendants, she realises that they are being trained to do a different kind of job. She comments:

> The young trainee sitting next to me wrote on her notepad, 'Important to smile. Don't forget to smile'. The admonition came from the speaker in the front of the room, a crew-cut pilot in his early fifties, speaking in a Southern drawl: 'Now girls, I want you to go out there and really *smile*. Your smile is your biggest asset. I want you to go out there and use it. Smile, *really* smile. Really *lay it on*.'
>
> (Hochschild, 1983: 4)

A core of their training, she found, was that they should be 'nice to people'. This is one of many jobs which involve service work where a central task is to smile, be courteous, and to show your 'niceness' to others. Indeed, so basic is it that if a stewardess was not nice to you, she may well lose her job. (Unless, of course, there were very good reasons for this behaviour: for example, you had attacked her!) From this study, Hochschild introduces several key ideas. First, she shows how emotions are socially constructed and presented. In this she continues to draw upon the work of Goffman mentioned above. Here we are dealing not so much with self-management as with emotional management. But in any event, how you present your feelings also plays a role in forming and showing your self and identity. Second, she suggests that the task for a sociologist is to locate the *feeling rules* that are found in specific situations and that enable people to match their feelings with the expectations of a situation; feeling rules act as guides as to how to perform. Finally, she pioneered an important new concept: **emotional labour**, *the management of feeling to create a publicly observable facial and bodily display* (Hochschild, 1983: 7). In a way this is a new form of work involving more and more people. It involves the selling not of a skill or a craft, but of a particular emotional style. Emotion work is another form of emotional labour but it is done in private: caring, for example, within the home; or sometimes maybe during sex with a partner (Duncombe and Marsden, 1993).

In Duncombe and Marsden's (1993) study of love and intimacy in heterosexual coupledom, they stress the importance of emotional work inside relationships. From their findings, they report the unhappiness of women at men's general unwillingness to do the emotional work needed to sustain a relationship. The women felt 'pyschically deserted'. Rather pessimistically, they conclude that 'men's difficulties in expressing intimate emotions will emerge as a major source of the "private troubles" underlying the "public issues" of rising divorces and family breakdown, or the instability of cohabitation among couples who may often be parents' (Duncombe and Mardsen, 1993: 233).

CONTROVERSY AND DEBATE

THE PROBLEM WITH 'FREE INDIVIDUALS': CAN WE BE FREE WITHIN SOCIETY?

Throughout this chapter we have returned to one key theme: society shapes how we think, feel and act. But, if this is so, in what sense are we free?

Sociologists speak with many voices when addressing this question. One response, with politically liberal overtones, is that individuals are not free of society – in fact, as social creatures, we never can be. But if we are condemned to live in a society with power over us, it is important to do what we can to make our home as just as possible, that is, to lessen class differences and eliminate barriers to opportunity based on sex and race. Another approach, this one with conservative overtones, is that we are free because society can never control the aspirations or break the will of people committed to their dreams, whatever these may be.

We find both of these orientations in the work of George Herbert Mead, who made a crucial contribution to our understanding of socialisation. Mead recognised the power of society to make demands on us, sometimes setting itself before us as a barrier. But he also reminded us that human beings are spontaneous and creative, capable of continually acting back – individually or collectively – on society. Here is the dialectic between the I and the Me. Thus Mead acknowledged the power of society while still affirm-

ing the human capacity to evaluate, criticise and, ultimately, to choose and to change.

In the end, then, we may resemble puppets, but only superficially. A crucial difference – one that allows us to claim a significant measure of freedom – is that we have the power to stop, and peer upward at the 'strings' that animate much of our action, and perhaps even to jerk down on them defiantly (Berger, 1963: 176). If our pull is persistent and powerful enough, we may accomplish more than we might imagine.

CONTINUE THE DEBATE:

1. Return to the action–structure debate raised in Chapter 2, and see how far your understanding in this chapter helps you to see the 'action' more clearly. What are the structures of our everyday lives?

2. Given a sociological perspective, is freedom possible? What are its limits? How far is 'freedom' and the 'free individual' socially constructed? Might freedom differ for different groups?

3. Jump ahead to the next part of the book, skim it and think about how class, ethnicity, gender and age may well pattern these 'freedoms'.

4. Can an understanding of sociology enhance personal freedom?

Conclusion: micro-sociology

This chapter has served as only the briefest of introductions to a number of issues that are often termed micro-sociology, and that focus on everyday life and its social construction. We have suggested the importance of a lifelong socialisation process in helping to shape who

we become over our lives; and of the importance of situations in building up the social notions of identity, body and emotion. Even as we may like to think of ourselves as 'free individuals', micro-sociology shows us how, even in the smallest moments of everyday feelings and encounters, the social is present, helping to shape the outcomes.

SUMMARY

1. The phrase 'social construction of reality' conveys the important idea that we all build the social world through our interaction. The Thomas theorem states: 'Situations defined as real become real in their consequences'.

2. For individuals, socialisation is the process of building our humanity and particular identity through social experience. For society as a whole, socialisation is the means by which one generation transmits culture to the

next. The permanently damaging effects of social isolation reveal the importance of social experience to human development.

3. A century ago, people thought most human behaviour was guided by biological instinct. Today, the nature–nurture debate has tipped the other way as we understand human behaviour to be primarily a product of a social environment. So-called human nature is actually the capacity to create variable cultural patterns.

4. Sigmund Freud envisaged the human personality as composed of three parts. The id represents general human drives (the life and death instincts), which Freud claimed were innate. The superego embodies cultural values and norms internalised by individuals. Competition between the needs of the id and the restraints of the superego are mediated by the ego. To George Herbert Mead, socialisation is based on the emergence of the self, which he viewed as partly autonomous (the I) and partly guided by society (the Me). Mead contended that, beginning with imitative behaviour, the self develops through play and games and eventually recognises the 'generalised other'. Charles Horton Cooley used the term 'looking-glass self' to underscore that the self is influenced by how we think others respond to us.

5. Dramaturgical analysis studies how people construct personal performances. This approach casts everyday life in terms of theatrical performances, noting the settings of interaction, the use of body language and how performers often idealise their intentions. Ethnomethodology seeks to reveal the assumptions and understandings people have of their social world.

6. The life course itself is largely a social construction. People in different societies may experience a stage of life quite differently, or not at all. Lives can be located through such ideas as a 'historical time line' and birth cohorts. Life stages may be changing as the formal patterns found in the past are breaking down, with people 'dipping in and out' of phases in a much less regularised and institutionalised fashion.

7. Identity concerns our understanding of who we are. Identity refers to sameness and serves to link a sense of who we are to a wider culture. Identities change across time and space, from traditional societies where identities are shared and communal, given as part of the world, the cosmos and nature, to postmodern societies where identities are seriously questioned and challenged.

8. Bodies were predominately 'open' and ever present in pre-modern times, whereas they become increasingly 'closed' and regulated in modern times. The body is social and 'body projects' involve the process of becoming and transforming a biological entity through social action. We 'work on' our bodies in myriad ways – from clothing, washing and hygiene to medical and fitness regimes.

9. Emotions are also socially patterned. Emotional labour suggests ways in which feelings are managed to create a publicly observable facial and bodily display. Much work, from counselling to airline stewarding, involves more and more the sale of emotional labour.

CRITICAL-THINKING QUESTIONS

1. Using the questions raised about the socialisation process as your guide, consider your own life experiences of socialisation.

2. Take any social situation – a meeting with friends, a visit to the doctor, a shopping trip, a fight – and using ideas from this chapter, suggest how it is 'socially constructed'.

3. Consider the ways in which a physical disability can become an identity. How do people commonly characterise, say, a person with the physical disability cerebral palsy with regard to mental ability? With regard to sexuality? What interaction strategies may be employed by those with disabilities to smooth their interactions?

4. Starting with your hair, move down your body to your feet – considering each body part. How far is each of these body parts made 'social'?

5. Examine the ways in which the body is being changed by machines of all kinds.

6. Are men less emotional than women, or do they just construct their emotions in different ways?

GOING FURTHER

Further reading

Introducing social psychology:

Alfred R. Lindesmith, Anselm L. Strauss and Norman K. Denzin, *Social Psychology* (8th edn, 1999; orig. 1949)
A classic textbook to introduce this whole field, with strong links to symbolic interactionism.

John P. Hewitt, *Self and Society* (8th edn, 1999)
Provides an account of the symbolic-interactionist tradition on which much of this chapter is based. The most recent edition above has some useful pedagogic tables for clarification.

Conversational analysis:

Robin Woofitt and Ian Hutchley, *Conversational Analysis: Principles, Practices and Applications* (1998)

Celia Kitzinger, *Feminism and Conversational Analysis* (2003)
Two useful guides to CA with different emphases.

The work of Erving Goffman:

Erving Goffman, *The Presentation of Self in Everyday Life* (1959)
Goffman's first and best-known book.

Constructing social reality:

Peter L. Berger and Thomas Luckmann, *The Social Construction of Reality: A Treatise in the Sociology of Knowledge* (1967)
A more advanced study that elaborates on the argument that individuals generate meaning through their social interaction.

Identity:

Anthony Giddens, *Self Identity and Late Modernity* (1991)
An important study that suggests how socialisation processes are changing in the modern world.

The body:

Joanne Entwistle, *The Fashioned Body* (2000)
Looks at the way the body is adorned, and the way such dress helps define identity and gender.

Nancy Scheper-Hughes and Loic Wacquant (eds), *Commodifying Bodies* (2002)
A lively collection of essays which details the ways in which bodily parts and bodies are sold or turned into sellable commodities.

Emotions:

Simon Williams, *Emotion and Social Theory* (2001)
A comprehensive review of the links between sociology and emotion.

Watch a video/Read a book

Case studies of extremely deprived children:

- François Truffaut's *The Wild Boy of Aveyron* (1970): a delightful film about a the French 'wolf boy' Victor
- Werner Herzog's *The Enigma of Kasper Hauser* (1974): classic about a German boy
- The story of Helen Keller is told in her *The Story of My Life* (1902) and in Arthur Penn's film *The Miracle Worker* (1962) and in William Gibson's play *The Miracle Worker* (1962) (with Anne Bancroft and Patty Duke – both of whom won Oscars).

Interaction issues:

- Hal Ashby's *Being There* (1979): a comedy in which Peter Sellers plays an illiterate gardener, unable to present himself properly, eventually coming to be seen as some kind of hero
- Harold Ramis's *Groundhog Day* (1993): life lived over and over again in the same way. This really is an interaction ritual
- Woody Allen's *Zelig* (1983): like most of Woody Allen films this one raises the problems of human interaction. *Zelig* is good on multiple identities and the film is full of technical trickery to achieve this
- Read also Luke Rheinehart's *The Dice Man* (1971 reissued 2000) for an account of a man who creates his identity based upon the throw of a dice. The work of George Eliot, especially *Middlemarch* (1871–1872), conveys a great deal about emotion and interaction. See also Candace Clark's *Misery and Company: Sympathy in Everyday Life* (1977).

The body:

- David Cronenberg's *The Fly* (1986): a classic horror film remade to be even more gruesome, but interesting in thinking about the social body, as a man's body becomes that of a fly
- James Glickenhaus's *The Exterminator* (1970) and later spin-offs with Arnold Schwarzenegger were popular in the early 1990s and bring to the screen the issues of cyborgs, as does Fritz Lang's *Metropolis* (1926).

Connecting up

Connect to chapters

- Discussions on the body connect to many chapters, but see Chapter 12 on gender, Chapter 13 on ageing and Chapter 20 on health.
- Link the discussion of Mead to that of symbolic interactionism in Chapter 2.

To the websites

- http://plaza.interport.net/nypsan/freudarc.html
  There are many websites on Freud, but this one contains his biography, writings, photos, libraries and museums.
- http://sun.soci.niu.edu/~sssi/papers/papers,html
  The website of the Society for the Study of Symbolic Interaction. A good source for developing ideas about symbolic interactionism, but not always up to date.
- http://www.feralchildren.com/en/children.php
  The website feral children provides a detailed listing of all known feral children, including links to original documents.
  Ethno/CA News
  http://www2.fmg.uva.nl.emca/

For additional case studies, multiple choice questions, internet exercises, and annotated weblinks specific to this chapter, visit this book's website at **www.pearsoned.co.uk/plummer**

PART THREE

SOCIAL DIVISIONS AND SOCIAL INEQUALITIES

CHAPTER 8

SOCIAL DIVISIONS AND SOCIAL STRATIFICATION

All animals are equal, but
some are more equal than
others.

George Orwell, *Animal Farm*, 1945:
Ch. 10

ON 10 APRIL 1912, the ocean liner *Titanic* slipped away from Southampton docks on its maiden voyage across the North Atlantic to New York. A proud symbol of the new industrial age, the towering ship carried 2,300 passengers, some enjoying more luxury than most travellers today could imagine. By contrast, poor immigrants crowded the lower decks, journeying to what they hoped would be a better life in the USA.

Two days out, the crew received radio warnings of icebergs in the area but paid little notice. Then, near midnight, as the ship steamed swiftly and silently westwards, a lookout was stunned to see a massive shape rising out of the dark ocean directly ahead. Moments later, the *Titanic* collided with a huge iceberg, almost as tall as the ship itself, which split open its starboard side as if the grand vessel were nothing more than a giant tin can.

Sea water surged into the ship's lower levels, and within 25 minutes people were rushing for the lifeboats. By 2.00 am, the bow of the *Titanic* was submerged and the stern reared high above the water. Clinging to the deck, quietly observed by those in the lifeboats, hundreds of helpless passengers solemnly passed their final minutes before the ship disappeared into the frigid Atlantic (Lord, 1976).

The tragic loss of more than 1,600 lives made news around the world. Looking back dispassionately at this terrible accident with a sociological eye, however, we see that some categories of passengers had much better odds of survival than others. In an age of conventional gallantry, women and children boarded the boats first, so that 80 per cent of the casualties were men. Class, too, was at work. Of people holding first-class tickets, more than 60 per cent were saved, primarily because they were on the upper decks, where warnings were sounded first and lifeboats were accessible. Only 36 per cent of the second-class passengers survived, and of the third-class passengers on the lower decks, only 24 per cent escaped drowning. On board the *Titanic*, class turned out to mean much more than the quality of accommodation: it was truly a matter of life or death.

KEY THEMES

- The nature of social divisions and social stratification
- The way social divisions are patterned through economy, gender, sexuality, age, ethnicity, with slavery, caste and class as some of the main forms
- The prevalence and persistence of these divisions
- The future of inequalities – especially the digital divide

(Left) Two boys scavenge in view of the world's largest cathedral Notre Dame de la Paix Basilica in Yamoussoukro Ivory Coast

Source: © Alamy/Michael Dwyer

The fate of the *Titanic* dramatically illustrates the consequences of social inequality for the ways people live – and sometimes whether they live at all. Social diversity and differences are everywhere part of society. Indeed, group differentiation is a key organising feature of all societies. But when such differences start to become socially significant – as we can see on the *Titanic* – sociologists start to speak of **social divisions**: these happen when human *differences are rendered socially significant*. While differences may be found everywhere and can often be inconsequential (such as the differences between stamp collectors, sports people and cooks), *differences between people that are valorised, given strength and made significant start to play crucial roles in the shaping of a society*.

Most (and probably all) societies exist with systems of social division and social stratification, through which entire categories of people are elevated above others, providing one segment of the population with a disproportionate amount of money, power and prestige.

What is social stratification

Sociologists use both the concepts of social divison and **social stratification** to refer to *a system by which a society ranks categories of people in a hierarchy*. Five basic principles tend to organise them everywhere.

1. *Social stratification is a characteristic of society, not simply a reflection of individual differences*. It is a system which confers unequal access to resources. Members of industrial societies consider social standing as a reflection of personal talent and effort, though we typically exaggerate the extent to which people control their destinies. Did a higher percentage of the first-class passengers survive the sinking of the *Titanic* because they were smarter or better swimmers than the second- and third-class passengers? Hardly. They fared better because of their privileged position on the ship. Similarly, children born into wealthy families are more likely than those born into poverty to enjoy health, achieve academically, succeed in their life's work and live well into old age. Neither rich nor poor people are responsible for creating social stratification, yet this system shapes the lives of them all.

2. *Social stratification persists over generations*. To understand that stratification stems from society rather than individual differences, note how inequality persists over time. In all societies, parents confer their social positions on their children, so that patterns of inequality stay much the same from generation to generation.

Some individuals do experience **social mobility**, *change in one's position in a social hierarchy*. Social mobility may be upwards or downwards. Our society celebrates the achievements of a David Beckham or a Madonna, who rose to prominence from modest beginnings. But we also acknowledge that people move downward as a result of business setbacks, unemployment or illness. More often, people move *horizontally* when they exchange one occupation for another that is comparable. For most people, however, social standing remains much the same over a lifetime.

3. *Social stratification is universal but variable*. Social stratification seems to be found everywhere. At the same time, *what* is unequal and *how* unequal it is varies from one society to another. Among the members of technologically simple societies, social differentiation may be minimal and based mostly on age and sex (though these factors still matter in most societies today as well).

4. *Social stratification involves not just inequality but beliefs*. Any system of inequality not only gives some people more resources than others but defines certain arrangements as fair. Just as *what* is unequal differs from society to society, then so does the explanation of *why* people should be unequal. Sociologists have introduced ideas such as ideology and hegemony to help us understand this. Virtually everywhere, however, people with the greatest social privileges express the strongest support for their society's system of social stratification, while those with fewer social resources are more likely to seek change.

5. *Social stratification engenders shared identities* as belonging to a particular social category different from others. Identity serves to mark off one social division from another, often being closely linked to different kinds of culture as well. In all systems of social division, people have a sense of their location – and may accept, negotiate or even resist it. For Marx, for example, a sense of class consciousness was very significant; and class identities could have been harbingers of major social change (Payne, 2000; Braham and Janes, 2002).

For a long time, sociologists have focused primarily upon one major system of stratification: that which deals with social and economic positions. Broadly, this is how people are ranked in terms of their economic position, their power and their prestige. It included systems of slavery, caste and the modern class system. But more recently, sociologists have recognised that social divisions

The personal experience of poverty is captured in Sebastiao Salgado's haunting photograph, which stands as a universal portrait of human suffering. The essential sociological insight is that, however strongly individuals feel its effects, our social standing is largely a consequence of the way in which a society (or a world of societies) structures opportunity and reward. To the core of our being, then, we are all the products of social stratification.

Source: © Sebastiao Salgado/Network Photographers

- *Social and economic divisions*. Here a person's labour, wealth and income play a key role: see Chapters 9 and 10.

- *Gender and sexuality divisions*. Here a person's position as a man or as a woman plays a key role: see Chapter 12.

- *Ethnic and racialised divisions*. Here a person's race and ethnicity plays a key role: see Chapter 11.

- *Age divisions*. Here a person's age plays a key role: see Chapter 13.

There are others, too, including disabilities, language and dialect and nationalities, which you will encounter if you read further than this simple introduction. Within such divisions and stratification systems, Iris Marion Young has identified a number of key processes at work. These include:

- *Social exclusion and marginalisation*. A process by which 'a whole category of people is expelled from useful participation in social life' (Young, 1990: 53). Here, people are pushed from the mainstream of participation in society. We will see this when we talk about the idea of the exclusive and inclusive society in Chapter 10.

- *Exploitation*. A process by which there is 'the transfer of the results of the labour of one social group to benefit another' (Young, 1990: 49).

can be organised through other key social processes such as gender, ethnicity, sexuality, disability and age. Thus, there are hierarchies which can be introduced as:

RESEARCH IN ACTION

INTERVIEWS AND SUFFERING

Pierre Bourdieu was one of the leading French sociologists of the late twentieth century (he is discussed more fully later in Chapter 19). Although much of his research may be described as theoretical, one of his major books *The Weight of the World* (1999) (originally published 1993 as *La Misère du Monde*) is a remarkable instance of the sociological interview at work. The book contains around 70 interviews and commentaries with men and women who have confided 'their lives and the difficulties they have had in living those lives'. In general, they have been denied a socially respected and valuable existence – suffering from racism, or poverty, or marginalisation; and they have not been able to adjust to rapid changes around them. We could say they lead 'damaged lives' because of inequalities.

These are no ordinary social science interviews, which can be flat, dull and overly structured. Instead,

these interviews are more detailed and are often reproduced in the book as direct interviews with the interview questions included. They are placed side by side with interviews from people who hold different social positions – even though they live on the same housing estate or work at the same place. Each interview is also given an interpretation, in which the interview has been examined and listened to repeatedly by the researcher(s) in order to make sense of it.

Complex and multilayered representations, unlike those found in the press and much journalism, can often lead the reader to sense some kind of social explanation of the social sufferings many people experience. They also lead us to see the 'multiplicity of co-existing, and sometimes directly competing, points of view' (Bourdieu, *et al.*, 1999: 3). This study is a fine example of the interview at work in tracking the personal experience of inequalities.

- *Powerlessness.* A process by which people come to lack the authority, status and sense of self that many professionals tend to have (Young, 1990: 57).

- *Cultural imperialism.* Which is 'the universalization of a dominant group's experience and culture, and its establishment as the norm' (Young, 1990: 59). We will see this when we discuss ideas around the post-colonial in Chapter 11.

- *Violence.* Which is directed at members of a group simply because they belong to that group (Young, 1990: 62). Thus, we will discuss the violence against women and the homophobia against gays in Chapter 12.

Overview

This section of the book looks at aspects of these systems, gives examples of them and raises some debates around them. This chapter considers some contrasting patterns of social-economic stratification and ponders why it is so widespread. Chapter 9 then looks at the wider world, raising such issues as global poverty, widening inequalities and the uneven development of societies across the globe. Chapter 10 then examines how social and economic stratification works in specific 'high-income' countries such as the UK and the United States (where poverty, for example, curiously continues to exist on a massive scale). Chapter 11 turns to the ethnic stratification system and discusses matters of race and migration. While it will focus specifically on Europe, we will also see that 'race stratification' goes deep in all cultures of the world. Chapter 12 will draw ideas from feminist and Queer sociology to introduce the ideas of patriarchy and heterosexism to see how gender acts as a major system of stratification. Finally, Chapter 13 looks at age stratification, focusing especially on children as well as the social exclusion of those in later life. As populations skew to more and more older people, a major change is in the air.

Of course, one key problem with these varying systems of stratification is how they all interconnect. We will discuss this as we go along. But it is one of the major issues of current sociology to learn how to do this adequately.

Closed and open systems of stratification: slavery, caste, estate and class

In describing social stratification in particular societies, sociologists often stress the degree of social closure and mobility that is allowed in the society. 'Closed' systems allow little change in social position, while 'open' systems permit some mobility (Tumin, 1985).

Slavery

Slavery is *a form of social stratification in which people are owned by others as property.* Chattel slavery turns human beings into things to be bought or sold. Many early civilisations such as Egypt and Persia (now Iran), as well as the ancient Greeks and Romans, relied heavily on slave labour. Slaves could be worked to death in the building of huge pyramids or in massive public works such as irrigation systems.

But it was not just a pervasive feature of 'classical worlds'. Between the fifteenth and nineteenth centuries, there was a major slave trade into the New World. It has been estimated that the total population of the African continent in 1500 was 47 million. As S. I. Martin chronicles:

> Over the next 350 years, between 10 and 15 million Africans arrived in chains in the New World. Four to six million more are believed to have died during their capture or the rigours of the Atlantic crossing – a total of between 14 and 21 million people. This excludes the 17 million Africans thought to have been abducted as a result of the trans-Saharan slave trade. History has seen few disruptions on such a scale.
>
> (Martin, 1999: 21)

The forms that slavery has taken have been highly variable. The legal rights and autonomy of slaves varied. In classical Athens, for example, slaves could often hold positions of great responsibility even though they were owned by their masters. But the slaves who worked building pyramids, or excavating mines, or on plantations, were much more regulated and treated as less than human. People captured in warfare often became slaves.

Modern slavery

The British Empire abolished slavery in 1833, and the American Civil War brought slavery in the United States to an end in 1865. Although slavery no longer exists in its classical forms, it does still persist in a variety of forms in many parts of the world today. Although traditional slavery probably still exists (the United Nations investigated claims that some 100,000 people in Mauritania in West Africa were being kept in slavery), English social scientist Kevin Bales suggests that traditional and modern slavery differ. For him, one key

(a)

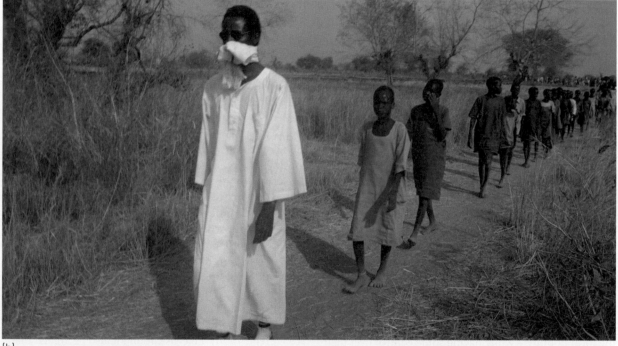

(b)

Slavery in Africa in the past, when people were rounded up and shipped off to work on plantations (a), is not very different from the slavery that some people still face at the present time. (b) Here it is the Dinka Slave trade in Sudan.

Source: (a) Popperfoto, (b) Corbis Sygma (David Orr)

difference is that modern slavery is not about direct ownership but about control through violence, usually with major elements of economic exploitation (Bales, 2000). With this is mind, he estimates that there are some 27 million people across the world in modern slavery. This could include:

- *forced labour*, where governments forcibly recruit labour. This often involves children who may be forced to leave home;

- *debt bondage*, where people labour to pay off a debt they will probably never be able to repay and which may be inherited by subsequent generations;

- *prostitution*, where women (and children) may move between countries in the hope of work only to find themselves part of the human chain of sex traffic from which it may be hard to escape;

- *servile marriage*, where women are given in marriage without the right to refuse.

As other forms of slavery appear through the selling of immigrants to other countries, and the selling of body parts – usually from the bodies found in poorer countries to those needing body parts in the richer countries (see Scheper-Hughes, 2000), so estimates of modern slavery are increasing. Indeed, some agencies working in this field suggest that numbers may well be much greater than Bales estimates – with suggestions of at least 200 million people in modern slavery. Sometimes slavery can appear in the most unlikely places: one estimate suggested that there are some 3,000 households in Paris holding slaves!

Usually, modern slaves are found among the poor, the uneducated, the low-status groups of a society: frequently, of course, these are women and children. In all cases, it is a closed system of stratification, robbing a life of much hope of control or change.

The estate system

Medieval Europe was a feudal system based on ideas of an **estate**, *a system based on a rigidly interlocking hierarchy of rights and obligations*. Estates were created politically and supplied an orderly chain of rights and obligations throughout society. Thus, usually a chain of obligations runs through three major groups – nobility, clergy and commoners. Land was controlled by powerful lords who enlisted the military to protect their land in return for rights over a part of it. Peasants were then dominated by the local nobility – while having some control over their own pieces of land. The tenants were vassals (dependants) of the lord; the lord was linked to the monarch, and so forth.

The caste system

The **caste system** has complex meanings (Sharma, 1999) but is usually seen as a form of *social stratification based on inherited status or ascription*. A pure caste system, in other words, is 'closed' so that birth alone determines one's social destiny with no opportunity for social mobility based on individual efforts. Caste systems rank categories of people in a rigid hierarchy. Some scholars believe that the concept can only really be applied to the system found in India – a system that is now under change. Others see it as a more widespread system, one which could embrace the Deep South in America in the post-slavery period, South Africa under apartheid, elements of the system of relationships in contemporary Thailand, and even the Gypsies in England.

The most frequently cited example of a caste system is that of India, or at least India's traditional Hindu villages in which most people still live. The Indian system of caste is usually discussed in terms of *varna*, a Sanskrit word that means 'colour'. It denotes four major categories: Brahmans (priests and writers) who claim the highest status, Kshatriyas (warriors and rulers), Vaishyas (the merchants and landowners) and Shurdas (artisans and servants). People outside the system become 'untouchables', who often have the most unpleasant work – handling sewage, burning corpses, scavenging. It is estimated that there are some 150 million untouchables in India (about 20 per cent of the population), whereas the Brahmans at the top make up just 3 per cent.

Each local community develops its own language and ways of building up what is, in effect, an endogamous (or closed) community which lays down a very broad system of positioning. This guides people into very clear rules about washing, eating or communicating with other people. It suggests ideas of ritual purity, pollution and exclusion. In the past it was largely a fixed system – no movement between castes was possible. The most controversial group (in Western eyes at any rate) were the 'untouchables' who performed polluted work.

It could be argued that race is often used as a tool for the caste system (though many disagree). In the southern plantations of the USA after slavery, for example, it has been argued that the division between 'blacks' and 'whites' into strictly segregated groups was so extreme that it amounted to a version of a caste system (Dollard, 1937; repr. 1998). Likewise, it might also be argued that caste played a key role in South Africa until recently. In this nation's former policy of apartheid, the 5 million South Africans of European ancestry enjoyed a commanding share of wealth and power, dominating some 30 million black South Africans. In a middle position were another 3 million mixed-race people, known as 'coloureds', and about 1 million Asians. The box details the problems of dismantling South Africa's racial caste system.

The nature of a caste system

In a caste system, birth determines the fundamental shape of people's lives in four crucial respects. First, traditional caste groups are linked to occupation, so that generations of a family perform the same type of work. In rural India, although some occupations (such as farming) are open to all, castes are identified with the work their members do (as priests, barbers, leather workers, street sweepers and so on). In South Africa, whites still hold most of the desirable jobs, with most blacks consigned to manual labour and other low-level service work.

No rigid social hierarchy could persist if people regularly married outside their own categories, as then most children would have uncertain rank. To maintain the hierarchy, then, a second trait of caste systems is mandating that people marry others of the same ranking. Sociologists call this pattern *endogamous* marriage (*endo* stems from Greek, meaning 'within'). Traditionally, Indian parents select their children's marriage partners, often before the children reach their teens. Until 1985, South Africa banned marriage and even sex between the races. Even now, interracial couples are rare since blacks and whites continue to live in separate areas.

Third, caste guides everyday life so that people remain in the company of 'their own kind'. Hindus in India enforce this segregation with the belief that a ritually 'pure' person of a higher caste will be 'polluted' by contact with someone of lower standing. Often this leads to 'caste feuds', with bitter attacks and murders usually on lower caste citizens. Apartheid in South Africa also led to much bitter conflict.

Finally, caste systems rest on powerful cultural beliefs. Indian culture is built on Hindu traditions that mandate accepting one's life work, whatever it may be, as a moral duty. Although apartheid is no longer a matter of law, South Africans still cling to notions distinguishing 'white jobs' from 'black jobs'.

Caste and agrarian life

Caste systems are typical of agrarian societies, because the lifelong routines of agriculture depend on a rigid sense of duty and discipline. Thus, caste still persists in rural India, half a century after being formally outlawed, even as its grip is easing in the nation's more industrial cities, where most people exercise greater choice about their work and marriage partners (Bahl, 1991). Similarly, the rapid industrialisation of South Africa elevated the importance of personal choice and individual rights, making the abolition of apartheid increasingly likely.

Note, however, that the erosion of caste does not signal the end of social stratification. On the contrary, it simply marks a change in its character, as the next sections explain ('Briefing: The Untouchables', *The Week*, May 15th, 2004: 13).

The class system

Agrarian life relies on the discipline wrought by caste systems; industrial societies, by contrast, depend on developing specialised talents. Industrialisation erodes caste in favour of **social class**, *social stratification resulting from the unequal distribution of wealth, power and prestige*. Unlike caste, estate and slavery, it is a system that claims to be more open and based on individual achievement. A class system is more 'open' so that people who gain schooling and skills may experience some social mobility in relation to their parents and siblings. Mobility, in turn, blurs class distinctions. Social boundaries also break down as people immigrate from abroad or move from the countryside to the city, lured by greater opportunity for education and better jobs (Lipset and Bendix, 1967). Typically, newcomers take low-paying jobs, thereby pushing others up the social ladder (Tyree *et al.*, 1979).

People in industrial societies come to think that everyone is entitled to 'rights', rather than just those of particular social standing. The principle of equal standing before the law steadily assumes a central place in the political culture of industrial class systems. Class systems are no different from caste systems in one basic respect: people remain unequal. But social stratification now rests less on the accident of birth. Careers become not a matter of moral duty but an issue of individual choice; likewise, class systems allow more individual freedom in the selection of marriage partners.

A note on status consistency

Status consistency refers to the degree of consistency of a person's social standing across various dimensions of social inequality. In a caste system, limited social mobility generates high status consistency so that the typical person has the same relative ranking with regard to wealth, power and prestige. By contrast, the greater mobility of class systems allows for lower status consistency. In industrial nations such as Sweden or Canada, then, a university professor with an advanced degree might enjoy high social prestige while receiving a modest income. Such low status consistency is a key reason that *classes* are less well defined than *castes*.

WORLD WATCH

RACE AS CASTE: A REPORT FROM SOUTH AFRICA

At the southern tip of the African continent lies South Africa. Long inhabited by black people, the region attracted white Dutch traders and farmers in the mid-seventeenth century. Early in the nineteenth century, a second wave of colonisation saw British immigrants push the Dutch inland. By the early 1900s, the British had taken over the country, proclaiming it the Union of South Africa. In 1961, the United Kingdom gave up control and recognised the independence of the Republic of South Africa.

But freedom was a reality for only the white minority. Years before, to ensure their political control over the black majority, whites had instituted a policy of apartheid, or racial separation. Apartheid was made law in 1948, denying blacks national citizenship, ownership of land and any formal voice in the government. In effect, black South Africans became lower caste, receiving little schooling and performing menial low-paid jobs. Under this system, even 'middle-class' white households had at least one black household servant. The prosperous white minority defended apartheid, claiming that blacks threatened their cultural traditions or, more simply, were inferior beings. But resistance to apartheid rose steadily, prompting whites to resort to brutal military repression to maintain their power.

Steady resistance – especially from younger blacks, impatient for a political voice and economic opportunity – gradually forced change. Adding to the pressure was criticism and boycotts from many nations. By the mid-1980s the tide began to turn as the South African government granted limited political rights to people of mixed race and Asian ancestry. Then came the right for all people to form labour unions, to enter occupations once restricted to whites, and to own property. Officials also began to dismantle the system of laws that separated the races in public places. The rate of change increased in 1990 with Nelson Mandela's release from prison. In 1994, the first national election open to all people of all races elected Mandela the president, ending centuries of white minority rule.

Nelson Mandela, leader of the African National Congress (ANC), who was imprisoned by the white apartheid government for 27 years, celebrates his election victory as South Africa's first black president.

Source: Popperfoto

The suffering of people under apartheid remains one of the twentieth century's epic stories of 'man's continuing inhumanity to man'. In order that these experiences should not be easily forgotten, a Truth and Reconciliation Commission was established which compiled the evidence of over 20,000 witnesses to the regime, breaking the silence that surrounded the many gross violations of human rights committed during those years.

Despite this awareness of its past and the current dramatic political change, however, social stratification in South Africa is still partially based on race. Even with the right to own property, one-third of

WORLD WATCH CONTINUED

COUNTRY FACT FILE

SOUTH AFRICA

Population	45,172,000 (2002)
Urban population	57.7% (2002)
Per capita GNP	$3,020 (2002)
Life expectancy	50.7 male; 51.4 female (2001)
Literacy	83% (1995)
Languages	11 official languages: Afrikaans, English, Ndebele, Sepedi, Sesotho, Swati, Xitsonga, Setswana, Tshivenda, Xhosa, Zulu
Religions	Mainly Christianity (83%); African religions also followed
Main cities	Pretoria: 1,590,000; Cape Town: 2,930,000; Johannesburg: 3,000,000; Durban: 2,391,000; Port Elizabeth: 1,000,000 (2000)
Human Development Index 2004	119th

Source: adapted from *The World Guide 2001*; Brittania Almanac, 2004

black South Africans have no jobs, and the majority remain poor. The worst-off are some 7 million *ukublelekka*, which means 'marginal people' in the Xhosa language. Soweto-by-the-Sea may sound like a summer getaway, but it is home to thousands of *ukublelekka* who live crammed into shacks made of packing cases, corrugated metal, cardboard and other discarded materials. There is no electricity for lights or refrigeration. Without plumbing, people use buckets to haul sewage, and women line up to take a turn at a single water tap that serves more than 3,000 people. Any job is hard to come by, and those who do find work are lucky to earn $200 a month. Crime has become a major problem. South Africa's new president, Thabo Mbeki, elected in 1999, leads a nation still twisted by centuries of racial caste.

Sources: Kenneth Christie, 2000; Truth and Reconciliation Commission, 2000; Howarth and Norval, 1998.

Some examples of stratification at work: Japan and Russia

An example: Japan

Social stratification in Japan mixes the traditional and the contemporary. Japan is at once the world's oldest, continuously operating monarchy and a modern society in which wealth follows individual achievement.

Feudal Japan

As early as the fifth century CE, Japan was an agrarian society with a rigid caste system composed of nobles and commoners and ruled by an 'imperial family'. Despite the

people's belief that the emperor ruled by divine right, limited government organisation forced the emperor to delegate much authority to a network of regional nobles or *shoguns*.

Below the nobility stood the *samurai*, or warrior caste. The word *samurai* means 'to serve', indicating that this second rank of Japanese society comprised soldiers who cultivated elaborate martial skills and pledged their loyalty to the nobility. To set themselves off from the rest of the commoners, the *samurai* dressed and behaved according to a traditional code of honour.

As in Great Britain, the majority of people in Japan at this time in history were commoners who laboured to eke out a bare subsistence. Unlike their European counterparts, however, Japanese commoners were not the lowest in rank. The *burakumin*, or 'outcasts', stood further down in that country's hierarchy, shunned by lord and commoner alike. Much like the lowest caste groups in India, 'outcasts' lived apart from others, engaged in the most distasteful occupations and, like everyone else, had no opportunity to change their standing.

Japan today

Important changes in nineteenth-century Japan – industrialisation, the growth of cities, and the opening of Japanese society to outside influences – combined to weaken the traditional caste structure. In 1871, the Japanese legally banned the social category of 'outcast', though even today people look down on women and men who trace their lineage to this rank. After Japan's defeat in the Second World War, the nobility, too, lost legal standing, and, as the years have passed, fewer and fewer Japanese accept the notion that their emperor rules by divine right.

Thus social stratification in contemporary Japan is a far cry from the rigid caste system in force centuries ago. Analysts describe the modern-day Japanese population in terms of social gradations, including 'upper', 'upper-middle', 'lower-middle' and 'lower'. But since classes have no firm boundaries, they disagree about what proportion of the population falls in each.

Today's Japanese class system also reveals this nation's fascinating ability to weave together tradition and modernity. Because many Japanese people revere the past, family background is never far from the surface in assessing someone's social standing. Therefore, despite legal reforms that assure that everyone is of equal standing before the law and a modern culture that stresses individual achievement, the Japanese continue to perceive each other through the centuries-old lens of caste.

This dynamic mix echoes from the university campus to the corporate boardroom. The most prestigious universities – now gateways to success in the industrial world – admit students with outstanding scores on rigorous entrance examinations. Even so, the highest achievers and business leaders in Japan are products of privilege, with noble or *samurai* background. At the other extreme, 'outcasts' continue to live in isolated communities cut off from opportunities to better themselves (Hiroshi, 1974; Norbeck, 1983).

Finally, traditional ideas about gender still shape Japanese society. Despite legal reforms that confer formal equality on the sexes, women are clearly subordinate to men in most important respects. Japanese parents are more likely to push sons than daughters towards university and the nation thus retains a significant 'gender gap' in education (Brinton, 1988). As a consequence, women predominate in lower-level support positions in the corporate world, only rarely assuming leadership roles. In this sense, too, individual achievement in Japan's modern class system operates in the shadow of centuries of traditional privileges.

Homeless children Sergei, 9, and Andrea, 12, asleep in the metro in Moscow, Russia

Source: © Gyori Antoine/Corbis Sygma

An example: the Russian Federation

The Russian Federation, which rivalled the USA as a superpower while it existed as the Soviet Union, was born out of revolution in 1917. The feudal estate system ruled by a hereditary nobility came to an abrupt end as the Russian revolution transferred most farms, factories and other productive property from private ownership to state control.

A classless society?

This transformation was guided by the ideas of Karl Marx, who argued that private ownership of productive property was the basis of social classes (see Chapter 4). As the state gained control of the economy, Soviet officials claimed that they had engineered a remarkable achievement: humanity's first classless society.

Analysts outside the Soviet Union were sceptical about this claim of classlessness (Lane, 1984). The occupations of the people in the former Soviet Union, they pointed out, clustered into a four-level hierarchy. At the top were high government officials, or *apparatchiks*. Next came the Soviet intelligentsia, including lower government officials, university lecturers, scientists, physicians and engineers. Below them stood the manual workers and, in the lowest stratum, the rural peasantry.

Since people in each of these categories enjoyed very different living standards, the former Soviet Union was never classless in the sense of having no social inequality. But one can say, more modestly, that placing factories, farms, colleges and hospitals under state control did rein in economic inequality (although not necessarily differences of power) compared to capitalist societies such as the members of the European Union.

The 1917 Russian revolution radically recast the society as prescribed by Karl Marx (and revolutionary Russian leader Vladimir Lenin). Then in the 1980s, the Soviet Union underwent another sweeping transformation. Economic reforms accelerated when Mikhail Gorbachev came on the scene in 1985. His economic programme, popularly known as *perestroika*, meaning 'restructuring', sought to solve a dire problem: while the Soviet system had succeeded in minimising economic inequality, everyone was relatively poor and living standards lagged far behind those of other industrial nations. Simply put, Gorbachev hoped to stimulate economic expansion by reducing inefficient centralised control of the economy.

Gorbachev's reforms soon escalated into one of the most dramatic social movements in history, as popular uprisings toppled one socialist government after another throughout Eastern Europe and, ultimately, brought down the Soviet system itself. In essence, people blamed their economic plight as well as their lack of basic freedoms on a repressive ruling class of Communist party officials.

From the Soviet Union's founding in 1917 until its demise in 1991, the Communist party retained a monopoly of power. Near the end, 18 million party members (6 per cent of the Soviet people) still made all the decisions about Soviet life while enjoying privileges such as vacation homes, chauffeured cars and access to prized consumer goods and elite education for their children (Zaslavsky, 1982; Shipler, 1984; Theen, 1984). The second Russian revolution, then, mirrors the first in that it was nothing less than the overthrow of the ruling class.

The transformation of the Soviet Union into the Russian Federation demonstrates that social inequality involves more than economic resources. Figure 8.1 confirms that Soviet society lacked the income disparity

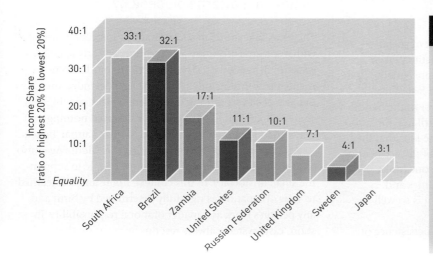

Figure 8.1   Economic inequality in selected countries, 1993–2001.

These data are the most recent available, representing income share for various years between 1993 and 2001.

Source: after *World Development Indicators 2003* by World Bank. Copyright 2003 by World Bank. Reproduced with permission of World Bank in the format Textbook via Copyright Clearance Center

typical of European states and the United States. But elite standing in the former Soviet Union was based on power rather than wealth. Thus, even though Mikhail Gorbachev and Boris Yeltsin earned far less than a US president, they wielded awesome power.

And what about social mobility in Russia? Evidence indicates that during the twentieth century there was more upward social mobility in the Soviet Union than in Great Britain, Japan or the United States. Why? For one thing, Soviet society lacked the concentrated wealth that families elsewhere pass from one generation to the next. Even more important, industrialisation and rapid bureaucratisation during the twentieth century pushed a large proportion of the working class and rural peasantry upwards to occupations in industry and government (Dobson, 1977; Lane, 1984; Shipler, 1984). Nevertheless, this pattern has begun to change as dynasties, sometimes linked with organised crime, have formed in Russia in the last few years.

Often, as the Russian experience attests, widespread societal changes affect people's individual social standing in a process sociologists call **structural social mobility**, *a shift in the social position of large numbers of people due more to changes in society itself than to individual efforts*. Half a century ago, industrialisation in the Soviet Union created a vast number of new factory jobs that drew rural people to cities. Similarly, the growth of bureaucracy propelled countless Soviet citizens from ploughing to paperwork. Now, with new laws sanctioning individual ownership of private property and business, some experts monitoring the changing Russian scene predict further structural social mobility along with greater economic inequality (Róna-Tas, 1994). But, equal or not, everyone hopes to enjoy a higher standard of living.

The role of ideology: stratification's 'staying power'

Looking around the world at the extent of social inequality, we might wonder how societies persist without distributing their resources more equally. Caste-like systems in Great Britain and Japan lasted for centuries, concentrating land and power in the hands of several hundred families. Even more striking, for 2,000 years most people in India accepted the idea that they should be privileged or poor because of the accident of birth. Many still do today. Everywhere one looks throughout the world, we find inequalities and stratification; and we have to ask why it is so well enshrined in societies.

One key reason for the remarkable persistence of social hierarchies is that they are built on **ideology**, *cultural beliefs that serve to legitimate key interests and hence justify social stratification*. Any beliefs – for example, the claim that the rich are clever while the poor are lazy – are ideological to the extent that they bolster the dominance of wealthy elites and suggest that poor people deserve their plight.

Plato and Marx on ideology

The ancient Greek philosopher Plato (427–347 BCE) defined justice as agreement about who should have what. Every society, Plato explained, teaches its members to view some stratification system as 'fair'. Karl Marx, too, understood this process, though he was far more critical of inequality than Plato was. Marx took capitalist societies to task for channelling wealth and power into the hands of a few, all the while defining the practice as simply 'a law of the marketplace'. Capitalist law, Marx continued, defines the right to own property as a bedrock principle. Then, laws of inheritance, which are tied to kinship, funnel money and privileges from one generation to the next. In short, Marx concluded, ideas as well as resources are controlled by a society's elite, which helps to explain why established hierarchies are so difficult to change.

Both Plato and Marx recognised that ideology is rarely a simple matter of privileged people conspiring together to propound self-serving ideas about social inequality. By contrast, ideology usually takes the form of cultural patterns that evolve over a long period of time. As people learn to embrace their society's conception of fairness, they may question the rightness of their own position but are unlikely to challenge the system itself.

Historical patterns of ideology

The ideas that shore up social stratification change along with a society's economy and technology. Early agrarian societies depended on slaves to perform burdensome manual labour. Aristotle (384–322 BCE) defended the practice of slavery among the ancient Greeks, arguing that some people with little intelligence deserved nothing better than life under the direction of their natural 'betters'.

Agrarian societies in Europe during the Middle Ages also required the daily farm labour of most people to support the small aristocracy. In this context, noble and serf learned to view occupation as rightfully determined by birth and any person's work as a matter of moral responsibility. In short, caste systems always rest on the assertion that social ranking is the product of a 'natural' order.

A millennium ago, a rigid estate system in Europe rested on Church teachings that such arrangements reflected the will of God. More specifically, the Church endorsed as divinely sanctioned a system by which most people laboured as serfs, driving the feudal economy with their muscles. According to the Church, nobility was charged with responsibility for defending the realm and maintaining public order. To question this system meant challenging the Church and, ultimately, defying God. The religious justification that supported the medieval estate system for centuries is expressed in the following stanza from the nineteenth-century English hymn 'All Things Bright and Beautiful':

> The rich man in his castle,
> The poor man at his gate,
> He made them high and lowly
> And ordered their estate.

The Industrial Revolution opened the way for newly rich industrialists to topple the feudal nobility. In the process, industrial culture advanced a new ideology. Capitalists mocked the centuries-old notion that social hierarchy should depend on the accident of birth. Under God's law, the new thinking went, the most talented and hard-working individuals should dominate society. The rise of industrial capitalism transformed wealth and power into prizes won by those who display the greatest talent and effort. Class systems celebrate individualism and achievement, so that social standing serves as a measure of personal worthiness. Thus poverty, which called for charity under feudalism, became under industrial capitalism a scorned state of personal inadequacy. The same thinking recast the poor from objects of charity into unworthy people lacking ability and ambition. The ideological shift from birth to individual achievement as the basis of social inequality was well established by the time early nineteenth-century German writer Johann Wolfgang von Goethe quipped:

> Really to own
> What you inherit,
> You first must earn it
> With your merit.

Clearly, medieval and modern justifications for inequality differ dramatically: what an earlier era viewed as fair, a later one rejected as wrong. Yet both cases illustrate the pivotal role of ideology – cultural beliefs that define a particular kind of hierarchy as fair and natural. Justifications for social stratification, then, are culturally variable across history and from place to place.

Ideology, gender and ethnicity

Throughout human history, most people have regarded social stratification as unshakeable. Especially as traditions weaken, however, people begin to question cultural 'truths' and unmask their political foundations and consequences. Historical notions of a 'woman's place' today seem far from natural and are losing their power to deprive women of opportunities. For the present, however, the contemporary class system still subjects women to caste-like expectations that they perform traditional tasks out of altruism while men are financially rewarded for their efforts. Most chefs are men who work for income while most household cooks are women who perform this role as a household duty.

Yet, while gender differences persist in Europe and elsewhere, there is little doubt that people are steadily becoming more equal in important respects. The continuing struggle for racial equality in South Africa also exemplifies widespread rejection of apartheid, which for decades shaped economic, political and educational life in that nation. Apartheid has never been widely accepted by blacks, and it has lost its support as a 'natural' system among whites who reject ideological racism (Friedrich, 1987; Contreras, 1992).

Explaining social stratification

Why are societies stratified at all? In the next few sections we look at major rival theories – one which suggests stratification may be functional; another which claims that societies work through exploitation and conflict; and a third – Weberian – which sees stratification as multidimensional.

Stratification as functional

One answer, consistent with the functional perspective, is that social inequality plays a vital part in the operation of all societies. It is, so to speak, 'needed'. Over 50 years ago, Kingsley Davis and Wilbert Moore (1945) set out such an argument by asserting that social stratification has beneficial consequences for the operation of a society. How else, asked Davis and Moore, can we explain the fact that some form of social stratification has been found everywhere? Davis and Moore described our society as a complex system involving hundreds of occupational positions of varying importance. Certain jobs, say, changing spark plugs in a car, are fairly easy and can be performed by almost anyone. Other jobs, such as transplanting a human organ, are quite difficult and demand the scarce talents of people who have received extensive (and expensive) education. Positions of high day-to-day responsibility that demand special abilities are the most functionally significant.

In general, Davis and Moore explained, the greater the functional importance of a position, the more rewards a society will attach to it. This strategy pays off, since rewarding important work with income, prestige, power and leisure encourages people to do these things. In effect, by distributing resources unequally, a society motivates each person to aspire to the most significant work possible, and to work better, harder and longer. The overall effect of a social system of unequal rewards – which is what social stratification amounts to – is a more productive society.

Davis and Moore conceded that every society could be egalitarian. But, they cautioned, rewards could be equal only to the extent that people were willing to let *anyone* perform *any* job. Equality also demands that someone who carries out a job poorly be rewarded on a par with another who performs well. Logic dictates that such a system offers little incentive for people to make their best efforts, and thereby reduces a society's productive efficiency.

Meritocracy

The Davis–Moore thesis implies that a productive society is a **meritocracy**, *a system of social stratification based on personal merit*. Such societies hold out rewards to develop the talents and encourage the efforts of everyone. In pursuit of meritocracy, a society promotes equality of opportunity while, at the same time, mandating inequality of rewards. In other words, a pure class system would be a meritocracy, rewarding everyone based on ability and effort. In addition, such a society would have extensive social mobility, blurring social categories as individuals move up or down in the social system depending on their performance.

For their part, caste societies can speak of 'merit' (from Latin, meaning 'worthy of praise') only in terms of persistence in low-skill labour such as farming. Caste systems, in short, offer honour to those who remain dutifully 'in their place'.

Although caste systems waste human potential, they are quite orderly. And herein lies a clue to an important question: why do modern industrial societies resist becoming pure meritocracies by retaining many caste-like qualities? Simply because, left unchecked, meritocracy erodes social structure such as kinship. No one, for example, evaluates family members solely on the basis of performance. Class systems in industrial societies, therefore, retain some caste elements to promote order and social cohesion.

Critical comment

The Davis–Moore thesis is a conservative one (as most functional arguments are). While Davis and Moore pointed out that *some* form of stratification exists everywhere, they could not explain why these systems can be so very different – from harsh and rigid ones, to much more flexible ones. Nor did Davis and Moore specify precisely what reward should be attached to any occupational position. They merely pointed out that positions a society deems crucial must yield sufficient rewards to draw talent away from less important work. Can we even measure functional importance? Surgeons may perform a valuable service in saving lives, but a related profession, nursing, is vastly less well paid. Many popular footballers, pop singers and 'stars' can earn more in a few nights than most primary school teachers and childminders earn in their working lives – and the latter are responsible for raising the next generation!

Further, the Davis–Moore thesis exaggerates social stratification's role in developing individual talent. Our society does reward individual achievement, but we also allow families to transfer wealth and power from generation to generation in caste-like fashion. Additionally, for women, ethnic groups, the disabled and others with limited opportunities, stratification still raises barriers to personal accomplishment. Social stratification functions to develop some people's abilities to the fullest while barring others from ever reaching their potential.

Third, by contending that social stratification benefits all of society, the Davis–Moore thesis ignores how social inequality promotes conflict and, sometimes, even outright revolution. This assertion leads us to the social-conflict paradigm, which provides a very different explanation for the persistence of social hierarchy (Tumin, 1953).

Marxist and neo-Marxist ideas on stratification and conflict

Conflict analysis argues that, rather than benefit society as a whole, social stratification provides major advantages to some people at the expense of others. This theoretical perspective draws heavily on the ideas of Karl Marx (whose approach to understanding social inequality was introduced in Chapter 4).

Writing (with Engels) in the original manifesto of the Communist party (1848), Marx identified two major social classes corresponding to the two basic relationships to the means of production: individuals either (1) own productive property or (2) labour for others. In medieval Europe, the nobility and the Church owned the productive land; peasants toiled as farmers. Similarly, in industrial class systems, the capitalists (or the *bourgeoisie*) own and operate factories, which utilise the labour of workers (the *proletariat*). Figure 8.2 on page 209 suggests these polarities occur throughout history.

Marx noted great differences in wealth and power arising from the industrial–capitalist productive system, which, he contended, made class conflict inevitable. In time, he believed, oppression and misery would drive the working majority to organise and, ultimately, to overthrow capitalism. A process would take place in which the poorer classes would become more pauperised, polarised and aware of their class position. This would lead to a class consciousness of their true economic exploitation.

Marx's analysis was grounded in his observations of capitalism in the nineteenth century, when great industrialists dominated the economic scene. In North America, for example, Andrew Carnegie, J. P. Morgan and John Jacob Astor (one of the few very rich passengers to perish on the *Titanic*) lived in fabulous mansions filled with priceless art and staffed by dozens of servants. According to Marx, the capitalist elite draws its strength from more than the operation of the economy. He noted that, through the family, opportunity and wealth are passed down from generation to generation. Moreover, the legal system defends this practice through inheritance law. Similarly, exclusive schools bring children of the elite together, encouraging informal social ties that will benefit them throughout their lives. Overall, from Marx's point of view, capitalist society *reproduces the class structure in each new generation*.

Critical comment

Exploring how the capitalist economic system generates conflict between classes, Marx's analysis of social stratification has had enormous influence on sociological thinking in recent decades. Because it is revolutionary – calling for the overthrow of capitalist society – Marxism is also highly controversial.

One of the strongest criticisms of the Marxist approach is that it denies one of the central tenets of the Davis–Moore thesis: that motivating people to perform various social roles requires some system of unequal rewards. Marx separated reward from performance, endorsing an egalitarian system based on the principle of 'from each according to ability; to each according to need' (1972: 388; orig. 1845). Critics argue that severing rewards from performance is precisely the flaw that generated the low productivity characteristic of the former Soviet Union and other socialist economies around the world.

Defenders of Marx rebut this line of attack by pointing to considerable evidence supporting Marx's general view of humanity as inherently social rather than unflinchingly selfish (Clark, 1991; Alan Fiske, 1991). They counter that we should not assume that individual rewards (much less monetary compensation alone) are the only way to motivate people to perform their social roles. Table 8.1 compares the functional and conflict paradigms.

Table 8.1	Two explanations of social stratification: a summary

Functional paradigm	Conflict paradigm
Social stratification keeps society operating. The linkage of greater rewards to more important social positions benefits society as a whole.	Social stratification is the result of social conflict. Differences in social resources serve the interests of some and harm the interests of others.
Social stratification encourages a matching of talents and abilities to appropriate positions. Social stratification is both useful and inevitable.	Social stratification ensures that much talent and ability within society will not be utilised at all. Social stratification is useful to only some people; it is not inevitable.
The values and beliefs that legitimise social inequality are widely shared throughout society.	Values and beliefs tend to be ideological; they reflect the interests of the more powerful members of society.
Because systems of social stratification are useful to society as a whole and are supported by cultural values and beliefs, they are usually stable over time.	Because systems of social stratification reflect the interests of only part of society, they are unlikely to remain stable over time.

Source: adapted in part from Stinchcombe, 1963: 808.

CONTROVERSY AND DEBATE

ARE THE RICH WORTH WHAT THEY EARN?

For an hour of work, a residential care worker in Southern England can earn about £4.25; a university teaching assistant can earn a little more at about £8; and a computer programmer earns between £12 and £30. These wages seem insignificant in comparison to the hundreds of thousands to millions earned annually by actors like Rowan Atkinson (Mr Bean), sports stars like Eric Cantona, and music chart toppers like Elton John or the Spice Girls. The Duchess of York paid off a personal debt in excess of £1 million (a debt greater than the lifetime earnings of many Britons) by writing children's stories and working the talk show and lecture circuits in the United States.

The Davis–Moore thesis states that rewards reflect an occupation's value to society. But are the antics of Mr Bean worth as much to our society as the work of all teachers in several primary schools? In short, do earnings really reflect people's social importance?

Salaries in industrial–capitalist societies such as the UK are a product of the market forces of supply and demand. In simple terms, if you can do something better than others, and people value it, you can command greater rewards. According to this view, movie stars, top athletes, skilled professionals and many business executives have rare talents that are much in demand; thus, they may earn many times more than the typical worker in the UK.

But critics claim that the market is really a poor evaluator of occupational importance. First, they claim, the British economy is dominated by a small proportion of people who manipulate the system for their own benefit. Corporate executives pay themselves multimillion pound salaries and bonuses even in years when their companies flounder. Japanese executives, by contrast, earn far less than their counterparts in this country, yet most Japanese corporations have comfortably outperformed their rivals in the UK.

A second problem with the idea that the market measures people's contributions to society is that many people who make clear and significant contributions receive surprisingly little money for their efforts. Hundreds of thousands of teachers, counsellors and health-care workers contribute daily to the welfare of others for very little salary.

Using social worth to justify income, then, is hazardous. Some defend the market as the most accurate measure of occupational worth; what, they ask, would be better? But others contend that what is lucrative may or may not be socially valuable. From this standpoint, a market system amounts to a closed game in which only a handful of people have the money to play.

CONTINUE THE DEBATE:

1. Track down the earnings of your favourite sports and media stars.

2. Look around you and consider how much cleaners and even teachers are likely to be earning.

3. Debate the significance of these disparities.

In addition, although few doubt that capitalist society does perpetuate poverty and privilege, as Marx asserted, the revolutionary developments he considered inevitable have failed to materialise. The next section explores why the socialist revolution Marx predicted and promoted has not occurred, at least in advanced capitalist societies.

Why no Marxist revolution?

Despite Marx's prediction, capitalism is still thriving. Why have workers in the UK and other industrial societies not overthrown capitalism? Some while ago, Ralf Dahrendorf (1959) pointed to four reasons.

1. *The fragmentation of the capitalist class.* The 120 years since Marx's death have witnessed the fragmentation of the capitalist class in Europe. A century ago, *single families* typically owned large companies; today, *numerous stockholders* fill that position. The diffusion of ownership has also stimulated the emergence of a managerial class, who may or may not be major stockholders (Wright, 1985; Wright *et al.*, 1992). We will find more evidence of this in the next chapter (see Scott, 1991).

2. *White-collar work and a rising standard of living.* A 'white-collar revolution' has transformed Marx's industrial proletariat. As Chapter 14 details, the

majority of workers in Marx's time laboured either on farms or in factories. They had **blue-collar or manual occupations**, *lower-prestige jobs involving mostly manual labour*. By contrast, most workers today hold **white-collar occupations**, *higher-prestige work involving mostly mental activity*. These occupations include positions in sales, management and other service work, frequently in large, bureaucratic organisations.

While many of today's white-collar workers perform repetitive tasks like the industrial workers known to Marx, evidence indicates that most do not think of themselves in those terms. Rather, most white-collar workers now perceive their social positions as higher than those of their blue-collar parents and grandparents. One key reason is that workers' overall standard of living in Europe rose fourfold over the course of the twentieth century, even as the working week decreased. As a result of a rising tide of social mobility, society seems less sharply divided between rich and poor than it did to people during Marx's lifetime (Edwards, 1979; Gagliani, 1981; Wright and Martin, 1987).

3. *More extensive worker organisation.* Employees have organisational strengths they lacked a century ago. Workers have won the right to organise into trades unions that can and do make demands of management backed by threats of 'working to rule' and strikes. Although union membership started to decline seriously in the 1980s, research suggests that well-established unions can still enhance the economic standing of the workers they represent (Rubin, 1986). Further, today's negotiations between labour and management are typically institutionalised and peaceful, a picture quite different from the often-violent confrontations common before the mid-twentieth century.

4. *More extensive legal protections.* Since Marx's death, the government has extended laws to protect workers' rights and has given workers greater access to the courts for redressing grievances. Government programmes such as National Insurance, disability protection and social security also provide workers with substantially greater financial resources than the capitalists of the nineteenth century were willing to grant them.

Taken together, these four developments mean that, despite persistent stratification, many societies have smoothed out some of capitalism's rough edges. Consequently, social conflict today may be less intense than it was a century ago.

We could also add that Marx's time was starting to see the growth of the mass press, but he could hardly have foreseen the major escalation in all media forms. As Chapter 21 will suggest, we increasingly live our lives in a 'mediated society' where the media infuses all we do. Of course, some of this adopts a critical and reflective stance. But the growth of pop music, mass film, television, gameboys, computer games and the like can mean that we have started to 'amuse ourselves to death' (Postman, 1986). As we have become media-saturated with entertainment, so many people have lost the critical edge for thinking about the nature of their class position.

A counterpoint

Many sociologists continue to find value in Marx's analysis, often in modified form (Miliband, 1969; Edwards, 1979; Giddens, 1982; Domhoff, 1983; Stephens, 1986; Boswell and Dixon, 1993; Hout *et al.*, 1993). They respond with their own set of five key points, defending Marx's analysis of capitalism.

1. *Wealth remains highly concentrated.* As Marx contended, wealth remains in the hands of the few. In Europe, about half of all privately controlled corporate stock is owned by just 1 per cent of individuals, who persist as a capitalist class.

2. *White-collar positions offer little to workers.* As defenders of Marx's thinking see it, the white-collar revolution has delivered little in the way of higher income or better working conditions compared to the factory jobs of a century ago. On the contrary, much white-collar work remains monotonous and routine, especially the low-level clerical jobs commonly held by women.

3. *Progress requires struggle.* Trades unions may have advanced the interests of the workers during the twentieth century, but regular negotiation between workers and management hardly signals the end of social conflict. In fact, many of the concessions won by workers came about precisely through the class conflict Marx described. Moreover, workers still strive to gain concessions from capitalists and struggle to hold on to the advances already achieved. As an example, half of all workers in the United States and much of Europe have no company-sponsored pension scheme.

4. *The law still favours the rich.* Workers have gained some legal protections over the course of the twentieth century. Even so, the law still defends the overall distribution of wealth in Europe. Just as important, 'average' people cannot use the legal system to the same advantage as the rich do.

5. *The global system of capitalism.* Tellingly, much of the production of goods in the twenty-first century has shifted from the high-income countries to low-income countries. As we will see in the next chapter, it is in these low-income countries that workers can be paid very little for their labour. Marx's model may still hold for societies once the global dimension is taken into consideration.

Max Weber: class, status and power

Max Weber, whose approach to social analysis is described in Chapter 4, agreed with Karl Marx that social stratification sparks social conflict, but differed from Marx in several important respects. Weber considered Marx's model of two social classes too simple. Instead, he viewed social stratification as a more complex interplay of three distinct dimensions. First is economic inequality – the issue so vital to Marx – which Weber termed *class* position. Weber's use of 'class' refers not to crude categories but to a continuum on which anyone can be ranked from high to low. A second continuum, *status*, measures social prestige. Finally, Weber noted the importance of *power* as a third dimension of social hierarchy.

The socio-economic status hierarchy

Marx believed that social prestige and power derived from economic position; thus he saw no reason to treat them as distinct dimensions of social inequality. Weber disagreed, recognising that stratification in industrial societies has characteristically low status consistency. An individual, Weber pointed out, might have high standing on one dimension of inequality but a lower position on another. For example, bureaucratic officials might wield considerable power yet have little wealth or social prestige.

So while Marx viewed inequality in terms of two clearly defined classes, Weber saw something more subtle at work in the stratification of industrial societies. Weber's key contribution in this area, then, lies in identifying the multidimensional nature of social rankings. Sociologists often use the term **socio-economic status** (SES) to refer to *a composite ranking based on various dimensions of social inequality*.

A population that varies widely in class, status and power – Weber's three dimensions of inequality – creates a virtually infinite array of social categories, all of which pursue their own interests. Thus, unlike Marx, who focused on conflict between two overarching classes, Weber considered social conflict as highly variable and complex.

Inequality in history

Weber also made a key historical observation, noting that each of his three dimensions of social inequality stands out at different points in the evolution of human societies. Agrarian societies, he maintained, emphasise status or social prestige, typically in the form of honour or symbolic purity. Members of these societies gain such status by conforming to cultural norms corresponding to their rank.

Industrialisation and the development of capitalism level traditional rankings based on birth, but generate striking material differences in the population. Thus, Weber argued, the crucial difference among people in industrial–capitalist societies lies in the economic dimension of class.

In time, industrial societies witness a surging growth of the bureaucratic state. This expansion of government, coupled with the proliferation of other types of formal organisation, brings power to the fore in the stratification system. Power is also central to the organisation of socialist societies, as we see in their extensive government regulation of many aspects of life. The elite members of such societies are mostly high-ranking officials rather than rich people.

This historical analysis underlies a final disagreement between Weber and Marx. Looking to the future, Marx believed that social stratification could be largely eliminated by abolishing private ownership of productive property. Weber doubted that overthrowing capitalism would significantly diminish social stratification in modern societies. While doing so might lessen economic disparity, Weber reasoned, the significance of power based on organisational position would only increase. In fact, Weber imagined, a socialist revolution might well *increase* social inequality by expanding government and concentrating power in the hands of a political elite. Recent popular uprisings against entrenched bureaucracies in Eastern Europe and the former Soviet Union lend support to Weber's argument.

Critical comment

Weber's multidimensional analysis of social stratification retains enormous influence among sociologists, especially in Europe. Some analysts (particularly those influenced by Marx's ideas) argue that while social class boundaries have blurred, striking patterns of social inequality persist in the industrial world.

As we shall see in Chapter 10, the enormous wealth of the most privileged members of our society contrasts sharply with the grinding poverty of millions who barely meet their day-to-day needs. Moreover, the upward social mobility that historically fuelled optimism in this country all but came to a halt in the 1970s, and evidence points to an increase in economic inequality during the 1980s. Against this backdrop of economic polarisation, the 1990s were marked by a renewed emphasis on 'classes' in conflict rather than on the subtle shadings of a 'multidimensional hierarchy'.

Stratification and technology in global perspective

We can weave together a number of observations made in this chapter by considering the relationship between a society's technology and its type of social stratification. Gerhard and Jean Lenski's model of sociocultural evolution, detailed in Chapter 4, puts social stratification in historical perspective and also helps us to understand the varying degrees of inequality found around the world today (Lenski, 1966; Lenski *et al.*, 1995).

CONTROVERSY AND DEBATE

THE BELL CURVE DEBATE: ARE RICH PEOPLE REALLY SMARTER?

It is rare that the publication of a new book in the social sciences captures the attention of the public at large. But *The Bell Curve: Intelligence and Class Structure in American Life* (1994) by Richard J. Herrnstein and Charles Murray did that and more, igniting a firestorm of controversy over why pronounced social stratification divides US society and, just as important, what to do about it. Although the book speaks specifically about the USA, its general argument has been made for many countries. In Europe, for instance, its main proponent has been the psychologist Hans Eysenck.

The Bell Curve is a long (800 page) book that addresses many critical issues and resists simple summary. But its basic thesis is captured in the following propositions:

1. Something we can describe as 'general intelligence' exists; people with more of it tend to be more successful in their careers than those with less.
2. At least half the variation in human intelligence (Herrnstein and Murray use figures of 60 to 70 per cent) is transmitted genetically from one generation to another; the remaining variability is due to environmental factors.
3. Over the course of the twentieth century – and especially since the 'information revolution' – intelligence has become more necessary to the performance of industrial societies' top occupational positions.
4. Simultaneously, the best US universities have shifted their admissions policies away from favour-

ing children of inherited wealth to admitting young people who perform best on standardised tests.
5. As a result of these changes in the workplace and higher education, US society is now coming to be dominated by a 'cognitive elite', who are, on average, not only better trained than most people but actually more intelligent.
6. Because more intelligent people are socially segregated on the university campus and in the workplace, it is no surprise that they tend to pair up, marry and have intelligent children, perpetuating the 'cognitive elite'.
7. Near the bottom of the social ladder, a similar process is at work. Increasingly, poor people are individuals with lower intelligence, who live segregated from others, and who tend to pass along their modest abilities to their children.

Resting on the validity of the seven assertions presented above, Herrnstein and Murray then offer, as an eighth point, a basic approach to public policy:

8. To the extent that membership in the affluent elite or the impoverished underclass is rooted in intelligence and determined mostly by genetic inheritance, programmes to assist underprivileged people will have few practical benefits.

The book has prompted considerable controversy. Critics first questioned exactly what is meant by 'intelligence', arguing that anyone's innate abilities can hardly be separated from the effects of socialisation. Of course, rich children perform better on intelligence tests, they explained: these people have had all the advantages! Some critics dismiss the concept of 'intelligence' outright as phony science.

CONTROVERSY AND DEBATE CONTINUED

Others take a more moderate view, claiming that we should not think of 'intelligence' as the sole cause of achievement, since recent research indicates that mental abilities and life experiences are interactive, each affecting the other.

In addition, while most researchers who study intelligence agree that genetics does play a part in transmitting intelligence, the consensus is that no more than 25–40 per cent is inherited – only about half what Herrnstein and Murray claim. Therefore, critics conclude, *The Bell Curve* misleads readers into thinking that social elitism is both natural and inevitable. In its assumptions and conclusions, moreover, *The Bell Curve* amounts to little more than a rehash of the social Darwinism popular a century ago, which heralded the success of industrial tycoons as merely 'the survival of the fittest'.

Perhaps, as one commentator noted, the more society seems like a jungle, the more people think of stratification as a matter of blood rather than upbringing. But, despite its flaws and exaggerations, the book's success suggests that *The Bell Curve* raises many issues we cannot easily ignore. Can a democratic system tolerate the 'dangerous knowledge' that elites (including not only rich people but also political leaders) may be just a little more intelligent than the rest of us? What of *The Bell Curve's*

description that elites are increasingly insulating themselves from social problems such as crime, homelessness and poor schools? As such problems have become worse in recent years, how do we counter the easy explanation that poor people are hobbled by their own limited ability? And, most basically, what should be done to ensure that all people have the opportunity to develop their abilities as fully as possible?

CONTINUE THE DEBATE:

1. Do you agree that 'general intelligence' exists? Why or why not?

2. In general, do you think that people of higher social position are more intelligent than those of low social position? If you think intelligence differs by social standing, which factor is cause and which is effect?

3. Do you think sociologists should study controversial issues such as differences in human intelligence? Why or why not? Is *The Bell Curve* ideology or science – and what is the difference?

Sources: Herrnstein and Murray (1994); Jacoby and Glauberman (1995).

Hunting and gathering societies

Simple technology limits the production of hunting and gathering societies to only what is necessary for day-to-day living. No doubt some individuals are more successful hunters or gatherers than others, but the group's survival depends on all sharing what they have. With little or no surplus, therefore, no categories of people emerge as better off than others. Thus social stratification among hunters and gatherers, based simply on age and sex, is less complex than among societies with more advanced technology.

Horticultural, pastoral and agrarian societies

Technological advances generate surplus production, while intensifying social inequality. In horticultural and

pastoral societies, a small elite controls most of the surplus. Agrarian technology based on large-scale farming generates even greater abundance, but marked inequality means various categories of people lead strikingly different lives. The social distance between the elite hereditary nobility and the common serfs who work the land looms as large as at any time in human history. In most cases, lords wield godlike power over the masses.

Industrial societies

Industrialisation reverses the historical trend, prompting some decrease in social inequality. The eclipse of tradition and the need to develop individual talents gradually erode caste rankings in favour of greater individual opportunity. Then, too, the increasing productivity of industrial technology steadily raises the living standards of the historically poor majority.

Specialised, technical work also demands the expansion of schooling, sharply reducing illiteracy. A literate population, in turn, tends to press for a greater voice in political decision-making, further diminishing social inequality. As already noted, continuing technological advances transform much blue-collar labour into higher-prestige white-collar work. All these social shifts help to explain why Marxist revolutions occurred in agrarian societies – such as Russia (1917), Cuba (1959) and Nicaragua (1979) – in which social inequality is most pronounced, rather than in industrial societies, as Marx predicted more than a century ago.

Initially, the great wealth generated by industrialisation is concentrated in the hands of a few – the pattern so troubling to Marx. In time, however, the share of all property in the hands of the very rich declines somewhat. According to estimates, the proportion of all wealth controlled by the richest 1 per cent of US families peaked at about 36 per cent just before the stock market crash in 1929; during the entrepreneurial 1980s, this economic elite owned one-third of all wealth (Williamson and Lindert, 1980; Beeghley, 1989).

Finally, industrialisation diminishes the domination of women by men, a pattern that is strongest in agrarian societies. The movement towards social parity for the sexes derives from the industrial economy's need to cultivate individual talent as well as a growing belief in basic human equality.

The Kuznets curve

The trend described above can be distilled into the following statement. *In human history, technological progress first sharply increases but then moderates the intensity of social stratification.* So if greater inequality is functional for agrarian societies, then industrial societies benefit from a more egalitarian climate. This historical shift, recognised by Nobel Prize-winning economist Simon Kuznets (1966), is illustrated by the Kuznets curve, shown in Figure 8.2.

Current patterns of social inequality around the world generally square with the Kuznets curve. As shown in Map 8.1, industrial societies have somewhat less income inequality – one important measure of social stratification – than nations that remain predominantly agrarian. Specifically, mature industrial societies, such as those in the European Union, Australia and the United States, exhibit less income inequality than the less industrialised countries of Latin America, Africa and Asia.

Yet income disparity reflects a host of factors beyond technology, especially political and economic priorities.

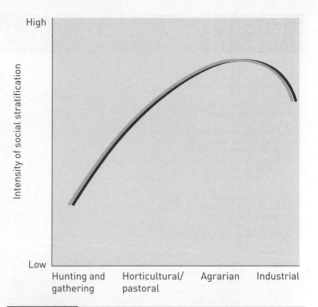

Figure 8.2   Social stratification and technological development: the Kuznets curve

The Kuznets curve reveals that greater technological sophistication is generally accompanied by more pronounced social stratification. The trend reverses itself, however, as industrial societies gradually become more egalitarian. Rigid caste-like distinctions are relaxed in favour of greater opportunity and equality under the law. Political rights are more widely extended, and there is even some levelling of economic differences. The Kuznets curve may also be usefully applied to the relative social standing of the two sexes.

Societies that have had socialist economic systems (including the People's Republic of China, the Russian Federation and the nations of Eastern Europe) display relatively little income inequality. Keep in mind, however, that an allegedly egalitarian society such as the People's Republic of China has an average income level that is quite low by world standards; further, on non-economic dimensions such as political power, China's society reveals pronounced inequality.

And what of the future? Although the global pattern described by the Kuznets curve may be valid, this analysis does not necessarily mean that industrial societies will gradually become less and less stratified. In the abstract, members of our society endorse the principle of equal opportunity for all; even so, this goal has not been and may never become a reality. The notion of social equality, like all concepts related to social stratification, is controversial, as the final section of this chapter explains.

SOCIAL SHAPES OF THE WORLD

The combined wealth of the world's 225 richest people is the same as the annual income of the poorer half of the world population.

The 20 percent of the world's population that live in the richest countries consume 16 times as much per person as the 20 percent living in the poorest countries.

The inequalities are lowest in terms of food. The richest populations consume 7 times as much fish and 11 times as much meat as the poorest. The richest also consume 17 times as much energy per person and almost 80 times as much paper. Measured in terms of cars, the consumption levels of the rich are 145 times higher than those of the poor.

Disparities of wealth are as great within countries as between them. In most of the rich countries more than 10 percent of the population live in poverty. Norway and Sweden are the exceptions.

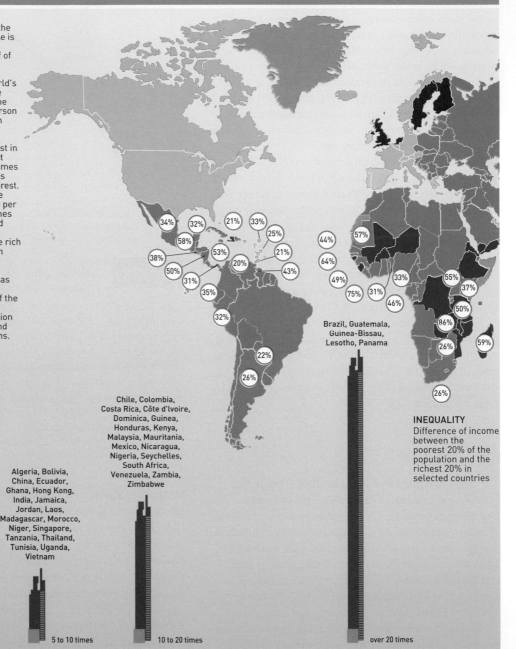

Brazil, Guatemala, Guinea-Bissau, Lesotho, Panama

INEQUALITY
Difference of income between the poorest 20% of the population and the richest 20% in selected countries

Chile, Colombia, Costa Rica, Côte d'Ivoire, Dominica, Guinea, Honduras, Kenya, Malaysia, Mauritania, Mexico, Nicaragua, Nigeria, Seychelles, South Africa, Venezuela, Zambia, Zimbabwe

Algeria, Bolivia, China, Ecuador, Ghana, Hong Kong, India, Jamaica, Jordan, Laos, Madagascar, Morocco, Niger, Singapore, Tanzania, Thailand, Tunisia, Uganda, Vietnam

Bangladesh, Egypt, Indonesia, Nepal, Pakistan, Sri Lanka

3 to 5 times   5 to 10 times   10 to 20 times   over 20 times

Map 8.1   Income disparity in global perspective

Societies throughout the world differ in the rigidity and intensity of social stratification as well as in overall standard of living. This map highlights income inequality. Generally speaking, countries that have had centralised, socialist economies (including the People's Republic of China, the former Soviet Union and Cuba) display the least income inequality, although their standard of living has been relatively low. Industrial societies with

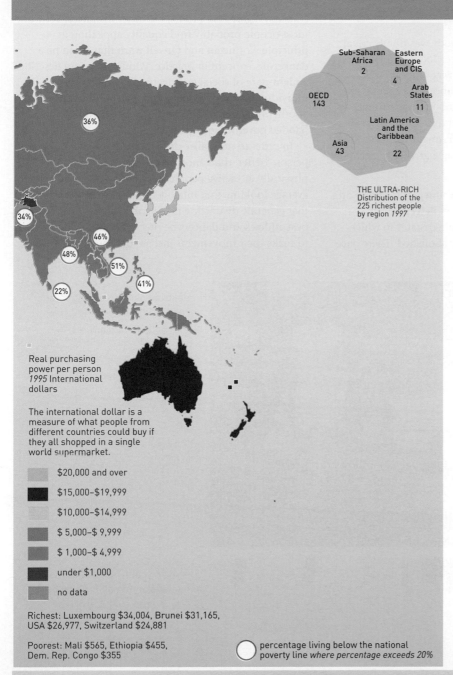

THE ULTRA-RICH
Distribution of the
225 richest people
by region *1997*

Sub-Saharan
Africa
2

Eastern
Europe
and CIS
4

Arab
States
11

OECD
143

Latin America
and the
Caribbean

Asia
43

22

Real purchasing
power per person
1995 International
dollars

The international dollar is a
measure of what people from
different countries could buy if
they all shopped in a single
world supermarket.

- $20,000 and over
- $15,000–$19,999
- $10,000–$14,999
- $ 5,000–$ 9,999
- $ 1,000–$ 4,999
- under $1,000
- no data

Richest: Luxembourg $34,004, Brunei $31,165,
USA $26,977, Switzerland $24,881

Poorest: Mali $565, Ethiopia $455,
Dem. Rep. Congo $355

◯ percentage living below the national
poverty line *where percentage exceeds 20%*

predominantly capitalist economies, including the United States and most of Western Europe, have higher overall living standards, accompanied by severe income disparity. The low-income countries of Latin America and Africa (including Mexico, Brazil and Zaïre) exhibit the most pronounced inequality of income.

Source: adapted from *The State of the World Atlas: New Edition for the 21st Century*, Dan Smith, 1999. Penguin Books Ltd.

How might social stratification change in the future?

The year was 2081 and everybody was finally equal. They weren't only equal before God and the law. They were equal every which way. Nobody was smarter than anybody else. Nobody was better looking than anybody else. Nobody was stronger or quicker than anybody else. All this equality was due to the 211th, 212th, and 213th Amendments to the Constitution and the unceasing vigilance of agents of the Handicapper General . . .

With these words, novelist Kurt Vonnegut, Jr (1968; orig. 1961) begins the story of 'Harrison Bergeron', an imaginary account of a future United States in which social inequality has been totally abolished. There have been many such 'utopian' novels of a much dreamed-of equality. George Orwell's *Animal Farm* (1946) and *Nineteen Eighty-Four* (1949) are other instances. Yet while most people probably find equality appealing in principle, Vonnegut and Orwell warn that it can be a dangerous concept in practice. Vonnegut's story describes a nightmare of social engineering in which every individual talent that makes one person different from another has been systematically neutralised by high-handed government agents.

In order to neutralise differences that make one person 'better' than another, the state mandates that physically attractive people wear masks that render them average looking, that intelligent people don earphones that generate distracting noise and that the legs of the best athletes and dancers be precisely fitted with weights to make their movements just as cumbersome as

Pedestrian passing a beggar and children, Durban, South Africa
Source: © David Turnley/Corbis

Everyday wealth? Man with mobile phone and laptop on tropical beach
Source: © Strauss/Curtis/ Corbis

everyone else's. In short, although we may imagine that social equality would liberate people to make the most of their talents, Vonnegut concludes that an egalitarian society would only succeed in reducing everyone to a lowest common denominator.

This chapter's explanations of social stratification also involve value judgements. The Davis–Moore thesis, which cites universal social stratification, interprets this pattern as evidence that inequality is a necessary element of social organisation. Class differences, then, reflect both variation in human abilities and the importance of occupational roles. From this point of view, the spectre of equality is a threat to a society of diverse people, since such uniformity could exist only as the product of the relentless and stifling efforts of officials like Vonnegut's fictitious 'Handicapper General'.

The conflict theory of Marx interprets universal social inequality in a very different way. Rejecting the notion that inequality is in any sense necessary, Marx condemned social hierarchy as a product of greed and exploitation. Guided by egalitarian values, he advocated social arrangements that would enable everyone to share all important resources equally. Rather than undermining the quality of life, Marx maintained that equality would enhance human well-being.

The 'bell curve' debate (see the box on page 207) addresses the link between intelligence and social class. This issue, also a mix of facts and values, is among the most troublesome in social science, partly because of the difficulty in defining and measuring 'intelligence', but also because the idea that elites are inherently 'better' than others challenges our democratic culture.

SUMMARY

1. Social stratification refers to categories of people ranked in a hierarchy. There are four major stratification systems: socio-economic, ethnic, gender and age. Stratification is (a) a characteristic of society, not something that merely arises from individual differences; (b) persistent over many generations; (c) universal, yet variable in form; and (d) supported by cultural beliefs.

2. Slavery, estate and caste are major forms of stratification. Slavery still exists today. Caste systems, typical of agrarian societies, are based on ascription and rest on strong moral beliefs, shaping a person's entire life, including occupation and marriage. Class systems, common to industrial societies, reflect a greater measure of individual achievement. Because the emphasis on achievement opens the way for social mobility, classes are less clearly defined than castes.

3. Historically, socialist societies have claimed to be classless, based on their public ownership of productive property. While such societies may exhibit far less economic inequality than their capitalist counterparts, they are notably stratified with regard to power.

4. Social stratification persists for two reasons – support from various social institutions and the power of ideology to define certain kinds of inequality as both natural and just.

5. The Davis–Moore thesis states that social stratification is universal because it contributes to the operation of society. In class systems, unequal rewards motivate people to aspire to the occupational roles most important to the functioning of society. Critics of the Davis–Moore thesis note that (a) it is difficult to assess objectively the functional importance of any occupational position; (b) stratification prevents many people from developing their abilities; and (c) social stratification often generates social conflict.

6. Marx recognised two major social classes in industrial societies. The capitalists, or bourgeoisie, own the means of production in pursuit of profits; the proletariat, by contrast, offer their labour in exchange for wages. The socialist revolution that Marx predicted has not occurred in industrial societies such as Germany or the United States. Some sociologists see this as evidence that Marx's anlysis was flawed; others, however, point out that our society is still marked by pronounced social inequality and substantial class conflict.

7. Max Weber identified three distinct dimensions of social inequality: economic class, social status or prestige, and power. Taken together, these three dimensions form a complex hierarchy of socio-economic standing.

8. Gerhard Lenski and Jean Lenski explained that, historically, technological advances have been associated with more pronounced social stratification. A limited reversal of this trend occurs in advanced industrial societies, as represented by the Kuznets curve.

9. Social stratification is a complex and controversial area of research because it deals not only with facts but with values that suggest how society should be organised. Two ideas of the twentieth century may help to reorganise stratification in the twenty-first century: cyberpower and human rights.

CRITICAL-THINKING QUESTIONS

1. How are social divisions and social stratification evident in your university or college? Locate your own position in the stratification system. Compare it with those of friends and family.

2. Consider the mix of class, ethnicity, gender, sexuality, disability and age as systems of stratification. Are they all equally important? Can they be usefully combined?

3. Compare some slavery systems from the past (like the plantation system of the USA) with those at work in the world today. (Hint: see Bales, 2000).

4. Discuss systems of stratification found in any two countries today.

5. In what respects have the predictions of Karl Marx failed to materialise? In what respects does his analysis ring true?

GOING FURTHER

Further reading

For general introductions to inequalities and social divisions:

Geoff Payne (ed.), *Social Divisions* (2000; 3rd edn 2005) Introduces the idea of social divisions and has major chapters on each kind, including some not discussed here.

Evelyn Kallen, *Social Inequality and Social Injustice* (2004) A very valuable account that looks at the links between inequalities and rights, and discusses a series of major cases like the rights of children, women's rights, lesbian and gay rights and aboriginal rights.

Jodi O'Brien and Judith Howard (eds), *Everyday Inequalities: Critical Inquiries* (1998) A useful collection of empirical readings which show how inequalities of gender, class and race permeate everyday life.

Peter Braham and Linda Janes (eds), *Social Differences and Divisions* (2002) Covers a wide range of divisions from class to ethnicity in a lively Open University text.

On specific patterns of inequality:

Kevin Bales, *Disposable People: New Slavery in the Global Economy* (2000) A major contemporary account of slavery: readable and also very disturbing to those who thought slavery was a thing of the past.

Ursula Sharma, *Caste* (1999) A critical appraisal of the concept of caste, which also provides a good introduction to empirical work in India.

John Scott, *Stratification and Power: Structures of Class, Status and Command* (1996) Addresses the current crisis in class theory, and provides a Weberian account of stratification.

More information

It will be helpful to look at the United Nations Development Programme's *Human Development Report* 2004 which contains a host of data on inequalities around the world.

For more on slavery, see Anti-Slavery International, Stableyard, Broomgrove Road, London SW9 9TL.

Watch a video

- Les Blair's *Jump the Gun* (1997): looks at the working class in Johannesburg
- Arthur Howes' *Nuba Conversations* (1999): looks at poverty, refugees and the Sudan
- Von Stroheim's silent classic *Greed* (1924): about lives ruined by the desire for money
- Srdjan Dragojevic's *The Wounds* (1999): portrays two of the most horrifically memorable under-age criminals amidst the devastating backdrop of the war in Bosnia.

Connecting up

Connect to other chapters

- Connect to Marx and Weber in Chapter 4.
- Connect to discussion of class in Chapter 10.
- Link Davis and Moore back to functionalism in Chapter 2.
- Link slavery to ideas on sexual slavery in Chapter 12.

To the websites

For more information on modern slavery, contact Anti-Slavery International:

http://www.anti-slavery.org

For additional case studies, multiple choice questions, internet exercises, and annotated weblinks specific to this chapter, visit this book's website at www.pearsoned.co.uk/plummer

CHAPTER 9

GLOBAL INEQUALITIES AND POVERTY

Poverty is an awful, eventually degrading thing and it is rare that anything good comes from it. We rise in spite of adversity, not because of it...

The letters of Thomas Wolfe

'Eradicating poverty is an ethical, social and economic imperative of mankind'.

Copenhagen Declaration, World Summit for Social Development, 1995

FED BY METHANE FROM THE DECOMPOSING GARBAGE, the fires never go out on Smokey Mountain, Manila's vast garbage dump. Manila – the capital of the Philippines – is the megalopolis of some 15 million souls; it produces some 9,000 tons of waste every day. The smoke envelops the hills of refuse like a thick fog. But Smokey organised by the local mafiosi to pick through the rubbish hills.

And all over Smokey Mountain are children – *children* – kids who must already sense the enormous odds against them. These are the lucky ones – they have work, and can get 20p for a kilo of recycled plastic! But what chance do they have, living in families that earn scarcely £100 a too. But, as we shall see, poverty in the poor countries of the world is not only more widespread, it is usually far more severe.

(*The Week*, 24 February 2001: 12)

PHILIPPINES

Population	80,000,000 (2002)
Urban population	60% (2002)
Per capita GNP	$1,040 (2000)
Life expectancy	70 years (2002)
Literacy	94.6% (1995)
Languages	Filipino, Cebuano, English
Religions	Majority Catholics with some Protestants; small number of Muslims, Anglipayen, Animists and Buddhists
Main cities	Manila: 1,581,082; Metropolitan Manila; 9,280,000; Quezon City: 2,173,831; Davao; 1, 147,116; Cebu: 718,821.
Human Development Index 2004	83rd

Source: The Week, *The World Guide*, 2001; Brittanica Almanac, 2004

KEY THEMES

- The scale of economic inequality across countries
- Whether such inequalities are growing across the globe
- The extent of poverty across the globe
- The key correlates of this inequality, such as technology, population growth and global power
- The ways such disparities can still exist in the twenty-first century
- Contrasting explanations for the 'under development of the world'

Mountain is more than a dump; it is home to thousands of people. The residents of Smokey Mountain are the poorest of the poor, and one is hard pressed to imagine a setting more hostile to human life. Amidst the smoke and the squalor, men and women walk deliberately about, doing what they can to survive, picking plastic bags from the garbage and washing them in the river, stacking flat cardboard boxes up the side of a family's plywood shack. They are the 'ecological operators' year? With barely any opportunity for schooling? Year after year, breathing this air? In July 2000, one of the dumps collapsed and some 2,000 child operators died.

Although they seem worlds away from the comfortable lives of many people in Europe, the residents of Manila's Smokey Mountain are far from unique. Their counterparts live throughout Latin America, Africa and Asia, and indeed in almost every country of the world. There is, of course, much poverty in Europe

(Left) Yellow houses: a street in Sophiatown, South Africa 1940.

Source: Gerard Sekoto (1913–1993). © Johannesburg Art Gallery/www.bridgeman.co.uk. Courtesy of the Gerard Sekoto Foundation.

What is global stratification?

The systems of social stratification we introduced in Chapter 8 are to be found in all countries across the world. There are pronounced economic inequalities. There are major gender divisions. There is social exclusion based on ethnicity and race which often results in displaced persons and refugees. There is an age stratification system at work by which both the young and the old can experience inequality more significantly. And there are processes of excluding all manner of people with difference and disability. These are the key components of global stratification and we touch on them all in the book. In this chapter the main focus will be on the poverty and economic inequalities found across the world, and why in the face of the great wealth in some countries, such discrepancies persist.

World poverty

A good starting point for thinking about all this is the issue of world poverty. Depending on how poverty is defined, somewhere between 1.3 billion and 3 billion people live in poverty – nearly half of the world's population. Table 9.1 shows the number of people living on less than $1 a day by region.

Further, although some countries are becoming wealthier, in general inequalities between countries seem to have been growing. Figure 9.1 divides the total global income by fifths of the population: the richest 20 per cent of the global population receives about 80 per cent of all income. At the other end of the social scale, the poorest 20 per cent of the world's people, by contrast, struggle to survive on just 1 per cent of global income.

Because global income is so concentrated, the average member of a rich society (such as most of Europe) lives extremely well by world standards. In fact, the living standard of most people below the poverty threshold far surpasses that of the majority of the earth's people.

GNP and GDP

Measuring a country's economic productvity is usually done through the GNP and the GDP. GDP or **gross domestic product** refers to *all the goods and services on record as produced by a country's economy in a given year*. Income earned outside the country by individuals or corporations is excluded from this measure; this is the key difference between GDP and **gross national product** (GNP), which *includes foreign earnings*. For countries that invest heavily abroad (Kuwait, for example), GDP is considerably less than GNP; for countries in which other nations invest heavily (such as Hong Kong), GDP is much higher than GNP. For countries that both invest heavily abroad and have considerable foreign investment at home (such as the United States), the two measures are roughly comparable. In what follows we will examine some of the striking differences in productivity of the various world economies. High, middle and low incomes are epitomised by, for example, Tokyo, Moscow and Bangladesh.

High-income countries

High-income countries are rich because theirs were the first economies to be transformed by the Industrial Revolution more than two centuries ago, increasing their productive capacity 100-fold. To grasp how this development enriched our own region of the world, consider that the typical European household may well spend more today just caring for their pets than the average European household did to meet all its needs during the Middle Ages.

A look back at Map 4.3(a) in Chapter 4 identifies the location of the 40 high-income countries of the world. They include most of the nations of Western Europe, including the UK, where industrialisation first took hold about 1750. Canada and the United States are also rich nations; in North America, the Industrial Revolution was well under way by 1850. In Asia, one of the world's leading economic powers is Japan; recent economic growth also places Hong Kong and Singapore in this favoured category. Finally, to the south of Asia in the global region known as Oceania, Australia and New Zealand also rank as industrial, high-income nations.

Taken together, countries with the most-developed economies cover roughly 25 per cent of the earth's land area – including parts of five continents – while lying mostly in the northern hemisphere. In mid-1996, the total population of these nations was 870 million, representing about 15 per cent of the earth's people. By global standards, rich nations are not densely populated; even so, some countries (such as Japan) are crowded, while others (such as Canada) are sparsely settled. Inside their borders, however, about three-quarters of the people in high-income countries congregate together in or near cities.

Table 9.1 Changes in the share and number of people living on very low income

	(a) Changes in Number and Percentage of People living on $1 Per Day			
Region	1990	1999	1990	1999
Sub-Saharan Africa	47.4	49.0	241	315
East Asia and the Pacific	30.5	15.6	486	279
Excluding China	24.2	10.6	110	57
South Asia	45.0	36.6	506	488
Latin American and the Caribbean	11.0	11.1	48	57
Central and Eastern Europe and the CIS[1]	6.8	20.3	31	97
Middle East and North Africa	2.1	2.2	5	6
Total[2]	29.6	23.2	1,292	1,169
Excluding China	28.5	25.0	917	945

	(b) Percentage of Population Living Below $1 Per Day							
	Poverty Rate (% below $1.08/day at 1993 PPP)							
	1981	1984	1987	1990	1993	1996	1999	2001
East Asia and the Pacific	57.7	38.9	28.0	29.6	24.9	16.6	15.7	14.9
China	63.8	41.0	28.5	33.0	28.4	17.4	17.8	16.6
Europe and Central Asia	0.7	0.5	0.4	0.5	3.7	4.2	6.3	3.7
Latin America and the Caribbean	9.7	11.8	10.9	11.3	11.3	10.7	10.5	9.5
Middle East and North Africa	5.1	3.8	3.2	2.3	1.6	2.0	2.6	2.4
South Asia	51.5	46.8	45.0	41.3	40.1	36.6	32.2	31.3
India	54.4	49.8	46.3	42.1	42.3	42.2	35.3	34.7
sub-Saharan Africa	41.6	46.3	46.8	44.6	44.0	45.6	45.7	46.9
Total	40.4	32.8	28.4	27.9	26.3	22.8	22.2	21.1

	(c) Percentage of Population Living Below $3 Per Day							
	Poverty Rate (% below $2.15/day at 1993 PPP)							
	1981	1984	1987	1990	1993	1996	1999	2001
East Asia and the Pacific	84.8	76.6	67.7	69.9	64.8	53.3	50.3	47.4
China	88.1	78.5	67.4	72.6	68.1	53.4	50.1	46.7
Europe and Central Asia	4.7	4.1	3.2	4.9	17.2	20.6	23.7	19.7
Latin America and the Caribbean	26.9	30.4	27.8	28.4	29.5	24.1	25.1	24.5
Middle East and North Africa	28.9	25.2	24.2	21.4	20.2	22.3	24.3	23.2
South Asia	89.1	87.2	86.7	85.5	84.5	81.7	78.1	77.2
India	89.6	88.2	87.3	86.1	85.7	85.2	80.6	79.9
sub-Saharan Africa	73.3	76.1	76.1	75.0	74.6	75.1	76.0	76.6
Total	66.7	63.7	60.1	60.8	60.1	55.5	54.4	52.9

[1] Changes measured using the $2 per day poverty line, which is considered a more appropriate extreme poverty line for Central and Eastern Europe and the CIS.
[2] Data are based on the $1 per day poverty line for all regions.

Source: *Global Poverty Monitoring* by World Bank. Copyright 2002 by World Bank. Reproduced with permission of World Bank in the format Textbook via Copyright Clearance Center

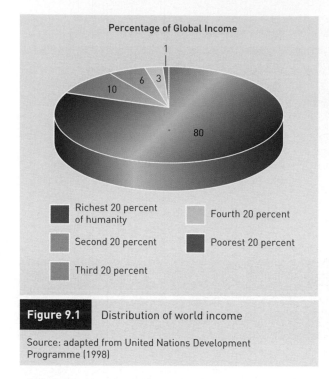

Percentage of Global Income

- Richest 20 percent of humanity
- Second 20 percent
- Third 20 percent
- Fourth 20 percent
- Poorest 20 percent

Figure 9.1   Distribution of world income

Source: adapted from United Nations Development Programme (1998)

High-income countries reveal significant cultural differences – the nations of Europe, for example, recognise more than 30 official languages. But these countries share an industrial capacity that generates, on average, a rich material life for their people. Per capita income in these societies ranges from about US $10,000 annually (in Portugal and Cyprus) to more than US $20,000 annually (in the United States and Switzerland).[1] This prosperity is so great that citizens of high-income countries enjoy more than half the world's total income. And many individuals enjoy personal wealth that is greater than many low-income societies. Thus in 2004, the two richest men in the world, William Gates III and Warren Buffett, were worth about $100 billion between them (Forbes lists, 2004).

Finally, just as people in a single society perform specialised work, so various regions form a global division of labour. Generally speaking, high-income countries dominate the world's scientific efforts and employ the most complex and productive technology. Production in rich societies is capital-intensive, meaning

high investments in factories and related machinery. High-income countries also stand at the forefront of new information technology; the majority of the largest corporations that design and market computers, for instance, are centred on rich societies. With the lion's share of wealth, high-income countries also control the world's financial markets: ups and downs on the financial exchanges of New York, London and Tokyo affect people throughout the world.

Middle-income countries

Middle-income countries are those with per capita income ranging between US $2,500 and $10,000, or roughly the median for the world's *nations* (but higher than that of the world's *people* since most people live in low-income countries). These nations have experienced limited industrialisation, primarily centred on cities. But about half their people still live in rural areas and engage in agricultural production. Especially in the countryside, schooling, medical care, adequate housing and even safe water are hard to come by, which represents a standard of living far below what members of high-income societies take for granted.

At the high end of this category, Barbados (Caribbean), Greece (Europe) and South Korea (Asia) provide people with about $5,000 in annual income. Ecuador (Latin America), Albania (Europe) and Sri Lanka (Asia) hover at the lower end of this category with roughly $1,750 annually in per capita income. Looking back at Map 4.3(a) shows that about 90 of the world's nations fall into this classification, and they are a very diverse lot.

One group of middle-income countries includes the former Soviet Union and the nations of Eastern Europe (in the past, also known as the Second World). The former Soviet Union's military strength rivalled that of the United States, giving it 'superpower' status. Its satellite states in Eastern Europe, including Poland, the German Democratic Republic (East Germany), Czechoslovakia, Hungary, Romania and Bulgaria, had predominantly socialist economies until popular revolts between 1989 and 1991 swept aside their governments. Since then, these nations have begun to introduce market systems. This process, detailed in Chapter 14, has yet to solve serious economic woes; on the contrary, in the short term at least, nations of the former Eastern Bloc are battling high inflation and some people enjoy fewer consumer goods than ever. A look at Table 9.1 shows that this bloc is rapidly becoming an area of low income.

In the second category of middle-income countries are most of the oil-producing nations of the Middle East (or,

---

[1] High-income countries have per capita annual income of at least US $10,000. For middle- and low-income countries, the comparable figures are $2,500 to £10,000 and below $2,500. All data reflect the United Nations' concept of 'purchasing power parities', which avoids distortion caused by exchange rates when converting all currencies to US dollars. Instead, the data represent the local purchasng power of each nation's currency.

less ethnocentrically, western Asia). These nations, including Saudi Arabia, Oman and Iran, are very rich, but their wealth is so concentrated that most people receive little benefit and remain poor. The third, and largest, category of middle-income countries can be found in Latin America and northern and western Africa. These nations (which might be termed the better-off countries of the Third World) include Argentina and Brazil in South America as well as Algeria and Botswana in Africa. Although South Africa's white minority lives as well as people in the United States, this country, too, must be considered middle-income because its majority black population scrapes by with far less income.

Taken together, middle-income countries span roughly 40 per cent of the earth's land area; and upwards of 2 billion people, or one-third of humanity, call these nations home. Compared to high-income countries, therefore, these nations are densely populated though, again, some countries in this category (such as El Salvador) are far more crowded than others (such as Russia).

Low-income countries

Low-income countries of the world, where most people are very poor, are primarily agrarian societies with little industry. These 60 nations, whose location is shown in Map 4.3(a), are found primarily in central and eastern Africa as well as in Asia. Low-income countries (or the poorest nations within the so-called Third World) represent about 35 per cent of the planet's land area but are home to half its people. Combining these facts, the population density for poor countries is generally high, though it is much higher in Asian countries (such as Bangladesh and India) than in more sparsely settled central African nations (such as Chad or Zaïre). Figure 9.2 shows the world distribution of people living in poverty in 1999.

In poor countries, barely 25 per cent of the people live in cities; most inhabit villages and farm as their families have done for centuries. In fact, half the world's people are peasants, and most of them live in the low-income countries. By and large, peasants are staunchly traditional, following the folkways of their ancestors. Living without industrial technology, peasants are not very productive – one reason many endure severe poverty. Hunger, minimal housing and frequent disease all frame the lives of the world's poorest people.

This broad overview of global economic development gives us a foundation for understanding the problem of global inequality. For people living in affluent nations, the scope of human want in much of the world is difficult to 𝔣𝔥𝔦𝔦𝔬. From time to time, televised scenes of famine in

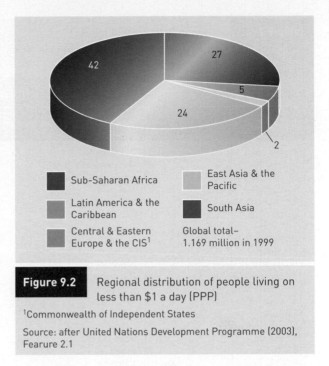

Sub-Saharan Africa	East Asia & the Pacific
Latin America & the Caribbean	South Asia
Central & Eastern Europe & the CIS[1]	Global total– 1.169 million in 1999

Figure 9.2   Regional distribution of people living on less than $1 a day (PPP)

[1]Commonwealth of Independent States

Source: after United Nations Development Programme (2003), Fearure 2.1

very poor countries such as Ethiopia and Bangladesh give us a shocking glimpse of the absolute poverty that makes every day a life-and-death struggle. Behind these images lie cultural, historical and economic forces that we shall explore in the remainder of this chapter.

Global wealth and poverty

To classify a country as 'low-income' does not mean that only poor people live there. On the contrary, the rich districts of Manila and Chennai (Madras) testify to the high living standards of some. Indeed, given the low wages paid to most urbanites in these countries, the typical well-to-do household is staffed by several servants and served by a gardener and chauffeur. But for the majority in the world's poor countries, poverty is the rule. Moreover, with incomes of only several hundred pounds a year, the burden of poverty is greater than it is among the poor in high-income societies.

Measurement and disparity in global poverty

Poverty in poor countries is more severe than it is in rich nations. The data in Table 9.2 suggest why. It is possible to measure poverty, per capita GDP in terms of what the United Nations Development Programme (UNDP) (2001) calls 'purchasing power parities', the value of people's income in terms of what it can buy in a local

Table 9.2	Human Development Index		

The HDI measures achievements in terms of life expectancy, educational attainment and adjusted real income.

HDI rank	HDI rank	HDI rank
High human development	**Medium human development**	**Low human development**
1 Norway	56 Bulgaria	101 Iran, Islamic Rep. of	142 Pakistan
2 Sweden	57 Russian Federation	102 Occupied Palestinian	143 Togo
3 Australia	58 Libyan Arab Jamahiriya	Territories	144 Congo
4 Canada	59 Malaysia	103 El Salvador	145 Lesotho
5 Netherlands	60 Macedonia,TFYR	104 Guyana	146 Uganda
6 Belgium	61 Panama	105 Cape Verde	147 Zimbabwe
7 Iceland	62 Belarus	106 Syrian Arab Republic	148 Kenya
8 United States	63 Tonga	107 Uzbekistan	149 Yemen
9 Japan	64 Mauritius	108 Algeria	150 Madagascar
10 Ireland	65 Albania	109 Equatorial Guinea	151 Nigeria
11 Switzerland	66 Bosnia and Herzegovina	110 Kyrgyzstan	152 Mauritania
12 United Kingdom	67 Suriname	111 Indonesia	153 Haiti
13 Finland	68 Venezuela	112 Viet Nam	154 Djibouti
14 Austria	69 Romania	113 Moldova, Rep. of	155 Gambia
15 Luxembourg	70 Ukraine	114 Bolivia	156 Eritrea
16 France	71 Saint Lucia	115 Honduras	157 Senegal
17 Denmark	72 Brazil	116 Tajikistan	158 Timor-Leste
18 New Zealand	73 Colombia	117 Mongolia	159 Rwanda
19 Germany	74 Oman	118 Nicaragua	160 Guinea
20 Spain	75 Samoa (Western)	119 South Africa	161 Benin
21 Italy	76 Thailand	120 Egypt	162 Tanzania, U. Rep. of
22 Israel	77 Saudi Arabia	121 Guatemala	163 Côte d'Ivoire
23 Hong Kong, China (SAR)	78 Kazakhstan	122 Gabon	164 Zambia
24 Greece	79 Jamaica	123 Sio Tome and Principe	165 Malawi
25 Singapore	80 Lebanon	124 Solomon Islands	166 Angola
26 Portugal	81 Fiji	125 Morocco	167 Chad
27 Slovenia	82 Armenia	126 Namibia	168 Congo, Dem. Rep. of the
28 Korea, Rep. of	83 Philippines	127 India	169 Central African Republic
29 Barbados	84 Maldives	128 Botswana	170 Ethiopia
30 Cyprus	85 Peru	129 Vanuatu	171 Mozambique
31 Malta	86 Turkmenistan	130 Cambodia	172 Guinea-Bissau
32 Czech Republic	87 St.Vincent & the Grenadines	131 Ghana	173 Burundi
33 Brunei Darussalam	88 Turkey	132 Myanmar	174 Mali
34 Argentina	89 Paraguay	133 Papua New Guinea	175 Burkina Faso
35 Seychelles	90 Jordan	134 Bhutan	176 Niger
36 Estonia	91 Azerbajan	135 Lao People's Dem. Rep.	177 Sierra Leone
37 Poland	92 Tunisia	136 Comoros	
38 Hungary	93 Grenada	137 Swaziland	
39 Saint Kitts and Nevis	94 China	138 Bangladesh	
40 Bahrain	95 Dominica	139 Sudan	
41 Lithuania	96 Sri Lanka	140 Nepal	
42 Slovakia	97 Georgia	141 Cameroon	
43 Chile	98 Dominican Republic		
44 Kuwait	99 Belize		
45 Costa Rica	100 Ecuador		
46 Uruguay			
47 Qatar			
48 Croatia			
49 United Arab Emirates			
50 Latvia			
51 Bahamas			
52 Cuba			
53 Mexico			
54 Trinidad and Tobago			
55 Antigua and Barbuda			

Source: adapted from United Nations Development Programme, 2004

economy. (Thus, living on $1 a day does not mean being able to afford what $1 would buy when converted into a local currency, but the equivalent of what $1 would buy in the United States, for example a newspaper, a local bus ride, a small bag of rice. (UNDP, 2003: 41). The resulting figures for rich countries such as Norway, Australia and Canada are very high – in the range of $24,000. Per capita GDP for middle-income countries, including Iran, China and Ukraine, is much lower – in the $4,000 range. And in the world's low-income countries, per capita annual income is no more than just a few hundred dollars (the average is $1,200). In the African nations of Zaïre or Ethiopia, for example, a typical person labours all year in order to earn what the average worker in the United States reaps in just several days.

But more and more, researchers try to go beyond the economic on its own. The Human Development Index (HDI) was introduced briefly in Chapter 4, but brings together income, education and life expectancy as a composite measure. Index values are decimals that fall

between hypothetical extremes of 1 (highest) and zero (lowest). By this calculation, Norwegians enjoy the highest quality of life (HDI value 0.944), with residents of Canada, Australia and Sweden close behind; at the other extreme, people in the African nations of Sierra Leone and Niger have the world's lowest quality of life (0.275 and 0.292 respectively). Figure 9.3 suggests some of the regional disparities in the Human Development Index with some idea of how they changed between 1975 and 2001.

A key reason for marked disparities in quality of life is that economic productivity is lowest in precisely the regions of the globe where population growth is highest. Figure 9.4 shows the division of global population and global income for countries at each level of economic development. High-income countries are by far the most advantaged with 55 per cent of global income supporting just 15 per cent of the world's people. Middle-income nations contain about 33 per cent of the global population; these people earn about 37 per cent of the world's income. This leaves more than half the planet's

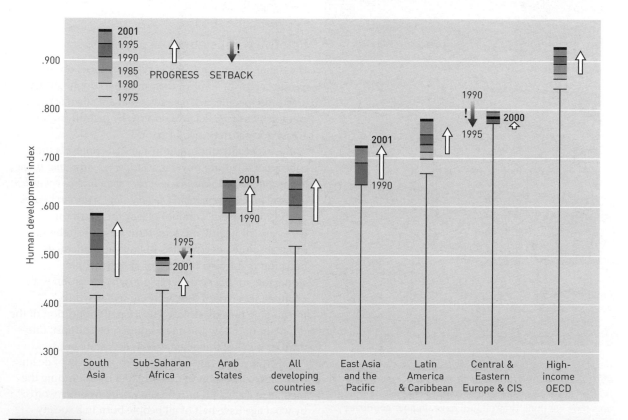

Figure 9.3   Global disparities in HDI

Source: after United Nations Development Programme (2003), Feature 2.2

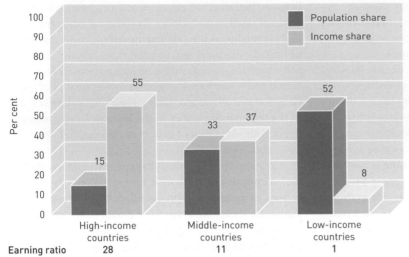

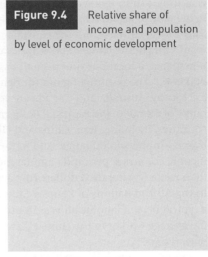

| Figure 9.4 | Relative share of income and population by level of economic development |

Earning ratio: High-income countries 28, Middle-income countries 11, Low-income countries 1

Relative or absolute poverty? By and large, rich nations such as the United Kingdom wrestle with the problem of *relative* poverty, meaning that poor people get by with less than we think they should have. In poor countries such as Somalia, *absolute* poverty means that people lack what they need to survive. Here people gather in Baidoa, Somalia to bury in a common grave family members who died from starvation.

Source: Magnum © Chris Steele-Perkins

population with a scant 8 per cent of total global income. Factoring together income and population, for every unit of currency received by individuals in the low-income countries, their counterparts in the high-income nations enjoy roughly 28 more!

Relative versus absolute poverty

The members of rich societies typically focus on the *relative poverty* of some of their members, highlighting how those people lack resources that are taken for granted by others. Relative poverty, by definition, cuts across every society, rich or poor.

But especially important in a global context is the concept of **absolute poverty**, *a lack of resources that is life threatening (often measured as a per capita income equivalent to less than one international dollar a day)*. Human beings in absolute poverty commonly lack the nutrition necessary for health and long-term survival. To be sure, some absolute poverty exists in Europe. Inadequate nutrition that leaves children or elderly people vulnerable to illness and even outright starvation is a reality in this nation. But such immediately life-threatening poverty strikes only a small proportion of the population. In low-income countries, by contrast, one-third or more of the people are in desperate need.

Since absolute poverty places people at risk of death, we can see the extent of this problem by examining the median age at death around the world. In other words, by what age have half of all people born in a society died? Map 9.1 shows that death in high-income countries, on average, occurs among the elderly beyond the age of 75. Death occurs somewhat earlier in middle-income nations, reflecting a lower standard of living. But in many low-income countries of Africa and western

Asia, the greater extent of absolute poverty is brought home by the fact that half of all deaths occur among children under the age of ten.

The measurement of world poverty

All of the above raises the problems around defining poverty. Frequently it is seen as a lack of income – and as we have seen, one quite common indicator is to suggest that people are poor if they earn less than $1 a day. (At least, this is one definition used by the United Nations at the Millennium Summit.)

For the Nobel Prize-winning economist Amartya Sen, however, 'poverty must be seen as the deprivation of basic capabilities rather than merely as lowness of incomes' (Sen, 1999: 20). This 'capabilities' approach suggests that if the people of a country are healthier,

better educated, and have access to public services without discrimination, that country is making progress in reducing poverty. Poverty is linked to a sense of entitlement (Sen, 1999: 162).

The extent of world poverty

Poverty in poor countries is more extensive than it is in rich nations. Poverty in Europe may well affect one in five of the population – the figure varies dramatically by country and region (see Chapter 10). But in low-income countries, most people live no better than the poor in the Western nations and many people are living close to the edge of survival. As the high death rates among children suggest, the extent of absolute poverty is greatest in Africa, where half the population is malnourished. At the turn of the millennium, in the world as a whole:

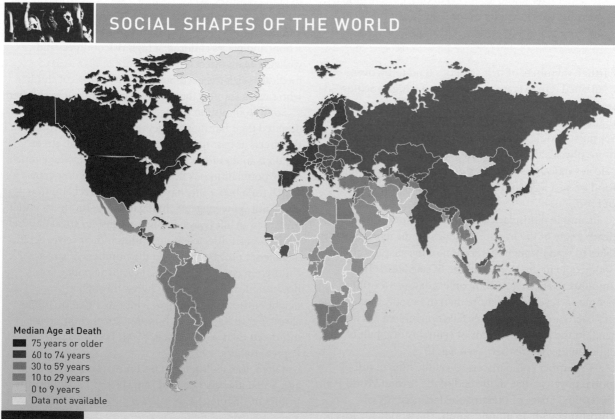

SOCIAL SHAPES OF THE WORLD

Median Age at Death
- ■ 75 years or older
- ■ 60 to 74 years
- ■ 30 to 59 years
- ■ 10 to 29 years
- □ 0 to 9 years
- □ Data not available

Map 9.1   **Median age at death in global perspective**

This map identifies the age below which half of all deaths occur in any year. In high-income countries, it is the elderly who face death – that is, people aged 75 or older. In middle-income countries, including most of Latin America, most people die years or even decades earlier. In low-income countries, especially in Africa and parts of Asia, it is children who die, with half of all lives ending before individuals reach 10 years of age.

Source: adapted from The World Bank (1993).

- Over 20 per cent of the people (about 1.2 billion) survive on less than $1 a day and lack the nutrition they need to work regularly. They are in absolute poverty.

- More than twice as many (2.8 billion) live on less than $2 a day.

- Each year, some 18 million die prematurely from poverty related causes.

- Some 800 million are at risk for their lives.

- Some 35,000 children die each day from preventable or easily treatable diseases (UNDP, 2003: 40; Bradshaw and Wallace, 1996: 15).

Meanwhile, as Thomas Pogge says:

> The average income of citizens in affluent countries is about 50 times greater in purchasing power and about 200 times greater in terms of market exchange rates than the global poor. 2.8 billion people together have about 1.2 per cent of aggregate global income, while the 903 million people of the 'high income economies' together have 79.7 per cent'.
>
> (Pogge, 2002: 2).

Further, members of rich societies tend to be over-nourished. On average, a member of a high-income society consumes about 3,500 calories daily, an excess that contributes to obesity and related health problems. Yet most people in low-income countries not only do more physical labour, but they consume less than 2,000 calories daily. In short, they do not consume enough food or, just as important, enough of the right kinds of food.

In simple terms, lack of necessary nutrition makes death a way of life in poor societies. In the ten minutes it takes to read through this section of the chapter, about 300 people in the world will die of starvation. This amounts to about 40,000 people a day, or 15 million people each year. Even more than in Europe, the burden of poverty in poor countries falls on children. As we have seen, in the poorest nations of central Africa, half of all children die before they reach age 10.

Two further comparisons reveal the human toll of global poverty. First, at the end of the Second World War, the United States obliterated the Japanese city of Hiroshima with an atomic bomb. The worldwide loss of life from starvation reaches the Hiroshima death toll *every three days*. Second, the annual loss of life stemming from poverty is ten times greater than that resulting from all the world's armed conflicts. Given the magnitude of this problem, easing world hunger is one of the most serious responsibilities facing the world today.

Who are the global poor?

In this section, we turn to some of the processes and people who become most vulnerable to poverty. Although there are others, our main focus will be on children, women and refugees.

Children and poverty

Poverty hits children hardest, and the extent and severity of child poverty are greatest in low-income countries. As we have already explained, death often comes early in poor societies, where families lack adequate food, safe water, secure housing and access to medical care. In many cases, too, children in poor countries leave their families because their chances to survive are better on the streets.

Organisations combating child poverty in the world estimate that poverty forces some 100 million city children in poor countries to beg, steal, sell sex or serve as couriers for drug gangs in order to provide income for their families. Such a life almost always means dropping out of school and places children at high risk of illness and violence. Many street girls, with little or no access to medical assistance, become pregnant – a case of children who cannot support themselves having still more children.

Some 100 million of the world's children have deserted their families altogether, sleeping and living on the streets as best they can. Roughly half of all street children are found in Latin America. Brazil, where much of the population has flocked to cities in a desperate search for a better life, has millions of street children – many not yet teenagers – living in makeshift huts, under bridges or in alleyways. Public response to street children is often anger directed at the children themselves. In Rio de Janeiro, police try to keep the numbers of street children in check. When this unrealistic policy fails, however, death squads may sweep through a neighbourhood, engaging in a bloody ritual of 'urban cleansing'. In Rio, several hundred street children are murdered each year (Larmer, 1992; US House of Representatives, 1992).

Often, too, children can become orphaned at an early age. Some may also be sold into slavery. We discuss this further in Chapter 13.

Women and poverty

Women in Sikandernagar, one of India's countless rural villages, begin work at 4.00 in the morning, lighting the fires, milking the buffalo, sweeping floors and walking to the well for water. They care for other family members as they rise. By 8.00, when many people in Europe are just beginning their day, these women move on to their 'second shift', working under the hot sun in the fields until 5.00 in the afternoon. Returning home, the women gather wood for their fires, all the time searching for whatever plants they can find to enrich the evening meal. The buffalo, too, are ready for a meal and the women tend to them. It is well past dark before their 18-hour day is over (Jacobson, 1993: 61).

In rich societies, the work women do is typically unrecognised, undervalued and underpaid; women receive less income for their efforts than men do. In low-income countries, this pattern is even more pronounced. Women do most of the work in poor societies, and families depend on women's work to provide income. At the same time, just as tradition keeps many women from school, it also accords them primary responsibility for child-rearing and maintaining the household. In poor societies, the United Nations estimates, men own 90 per

cent of the land, representing a far greater gender disparity in wealth than is found in industrial nations. Clearly, multilayered systems of tradition and law subordinate women in poor societies. Caught in a spiral of circumstance that promises little hope for change, women are disproportionately the poorest of the poor. More than 500 million of the world's 800 million people living in absolute poverty and at risk for their lives are women.

Women in poor countries have limited access to birth control (which raises the birth rate), and they typically give birth without the assistance of any trained health personnel. There is a stark contrast between high- and low-income countries in this regard. Overall, gender inequality is strongest in low-income societies, especially in Asia where cultural traditions overwhelmingly favour males. This pattern of denigrating women affects virtually every dimension of life and has produced a stunning lack of females in some regions of the world (Kishor, 1993) (see Chapter 13).

SOCIAL SHAPES OF THE WORLD

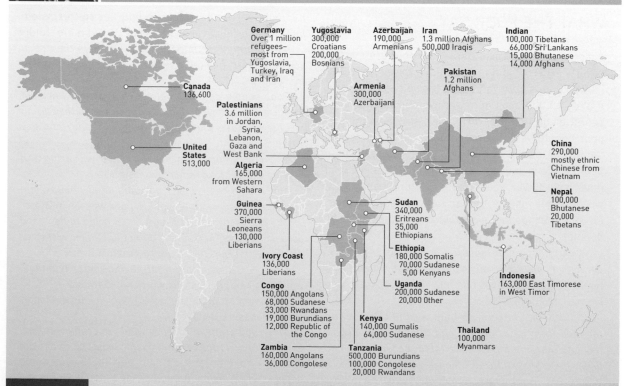

Map 9.2   **Major refugee populations worldwide, 1999**

This map identifies the major groupings of refugees in the world at the end of the twentieth century and provides an estimate of their numbers.

Source: adapted from UNHCR, *The State of the World's Refugees* (2000). Such estimates are always very provisional and tend to be underestimates, for more detailed and recent estimates, see the World Refugee Survey.

Refugees and the displaced

Refugees are people who '*flee their own country for political or economic reasons, or to avoid war and oppression*' (New Internationalist, 1998: 221). They usually experience a well-founded fear of persecution. In leaving their 'home', often with no choice, they leave behind most of their worldly possessions. At the end of 2000 there were estimated to be 14,544,000 refugees and asylum seekers worldwide. Over three and a half million were Afghans (who dispersed mainly to Pakistan and Iran) and nearly four million were Palestinians (who dispersed throughout the Middle East, but especially Jordan, the West Bank, the Gaza Strip, Syria and Lebanon). Map 9.2 shows the major refugee populations worldwide in 1999. Kushner and Knox, stressing how pervasive this phenomenon now is, have noted: 'Future historians will call the twentieth century the century of the refugee. Almost nobody at the end of the century is where they were at the beginning of it.

It has been an extraordinary period of movement and upheavals' (Kushner and Knox, 1999).

In contrast, **displaced peoples** are *those who often find themselves homeless in their own land*. This may be due to civil war, or to some environmental catastrophe through which they lose whatever home and possessions they may have had. An estimated 50 million people live off land that is rapidly deteriorating. After a time they will be unable to live or work off it, requiring them to move on (see Chapter 11).

Refugees are always politically controversial. On the one hand, they symbolise humanitarian need; and on the other, they raise in potent ways issues of racism and the symbolic boundaries of a nation state (see Chapter 11). Refugees test the willingness of governments and their people to provide asylum. They can also lead to human trafficking, where people are sold their illegal passage into a new country. Some have estimated this to be the largest industry in the world (see Chapter 15).

 **VOICES**

WHAT THE POOR SAY

According to the World Bank, 'the poor are the true poverty experts'. In a major study , *Voices of the Poor* (2000), Deepa Narayan heard the voices of approximately 60,000 poor men and women from over 60 countries around the world. With striking similarity, poor people describe repeatedly and in distressing detail the impact of poverty. The large majority of poor people included in *Voices* said they are worse off now, have fewer economic opportunities, and live with greater insecurity than in the past. Here are a few of the things they said (look at the website for full details):

Poverty is pain; it feels like a disease. It attacks a person not only materially but also morally. It eats away one's dignity and drives one into total despair. A poor woman, Moldova

Children are hungry, so they start to cry. They ask for food from their mother and their mother doesn't have it. Then the father is irritated, because the children are crying, and he takes it out on his wife. So hitting and disagreement break up the marriage. Poor people in Bosnia

A group of young men in Jamaica ranked lack of self-confidence as the second biggest impact of poverty: *Poverty means we don't believe in self, we hardly travel out of the community . . . so frustrated, just locked up in the house all day.*

My children were hungry and I told them the rice is cooking, until they fell asleep from hunger. An older man, Egypt

Poor people cannot improve their status because they live day by day, and if they get sick then they are in trouble because they have to borrow money and pay interest. Tra Vinh, Vietnam

Security is knowing what tomorrow will bring and how we will get food tomorrow. Bulgaria

There is no control over anything, at any hour a gun could go off, especially at night. A poor woman in Brazil

The rich is the one who says: 'I am going to do it' and does it. The poor, in contrast, do not fulfil their wishes or develop their capacities. A poor woman in Brazil

Poverty is like living in jail, living under bondage, waiting to be free. A young woman in Jamaica

It is neither leprosy nor poverty which kills the leper, but loneliness. Ghana

When you are poor, nobody wants to speak with you. Everyone's sorry for you and no one wants to drink with you. You have no self-esteem and that's why some people start drinking. A middle-aged man in Bulgaria

Now there are hungry children, and before it was not so evident. There are children that knock on your door and ask for bread, children without shoes. This one would never see before. La Matanza, Argentina

VOICES CONTINUED

If we knew that there would be an end to this crisis, we would endure it somehow. Be it for one year, or even for ten years. But now all we can do is sit and wait for the end to come. A woman from Entropole, Bulgaria

In slums in Malawi, the physical conditions were so bad and hopeless that the poor said *the only way we can get out of poverty is through death.*

The sewage runs in your front door, and when it rains, the water floods into the house and you need to lift the things . . . the waste brings some bugs, here we have rats, cockroaches, spiders, and even snakes and scorpions. A resident of Nova California, a slum in Brazil

In the Kyrgyz Republic, poor people said that they were forced to take many risks to survive, including stealing (with the risk of getting caught) or borrowing money (with the risk of becoming indebted). *The rich do not have to take this risk, they have money to protect themselves, and they also have power.*

You grow up in an environment full of diseases, violence and drugs . . . you don't have the right to education, work or leisure, and you are forced to 'eat in the hands of the government' . . . so you are easy prey for the rulers. You have to accept whatever they give you. A young woman, Padre Jordano, Brazil

Poor people describe four pervasive and systemic problems that affect their lives adversely almost everywhere: *corruption, violence, powerlessness* and *insecure livelihood.* Continue the comments on the website.

Source: http://www.worldbank.org/poverty/data/trends/poorsay.htm

---

The United Nations High Commission for Refugees (UNHCR) was established in 1950–51 to provide a major world structure for responding to the needs of refugees and to provide standards of protection under international law (Map 9.2 was produced through this organisation). Initially it focused on the displacement of Europeans caused by the Holocaust, the Second World War and the onset of the Cold War. It employed 33 staff and had a budget of $300,000. Over the years it has come to deal with the displacement of large groups of the world's population. It now has a budget of over $1 billion, employs 5,000 staff, has offices in 120 countries around the world and produces a major annual report (for example, UNHCR, 2000).

Global inequality: how is it to be explained?

Correlates of global poverty

What accounts for the severe and extensive poverty in low-income countries? The rest of this chapter weaves together explanations from the following facts about poor societies.

1. *Technology.* Almost two-thirds of people in low-income countries farm the land; the productive power of industrial technology is all but absent in these poorest nations. Energy from human muscles or ⏐ ᴜᴀᴏᴛᴏ ᴏᴘ ᴘᴜᴀᴛᴏᴏᴜ ᴏᴇᴌᴌᴄ ᴘᴀᴇ ᴄᴌᴜᴜᴇ ᴏᴘ ᴛᴜᴄ ᴘᴏᴇᴄᴄ unleashed

by steam, oil, gas or nuclear fuels – the power sources that propel complex machinery. Moreover, poor societies' focus on farming, rather than on specialised production, inhibits development of human skills and abilities.

2. *Population growth.* As Chapter 23 explains in detail, countries with the least-developed economies have the world's highest birth rates. Despite the death toll from poverty, the populations of poor countries in Africa, for example, double every 25 years. There, more than half the people have yet to enter their child-bearing years, so the wave of population growth will roll into the future. Even an expanding economy cannot support vast population surges. During 1993, for example, the population of Kenya swelled by 4 per cent; as a result, even with some economic development, living standards actually fell.

3. *Cultural patterns.* Poor societies are typically very traditional. Kinship groups pass folkways and mores from generation to generation. Adhering to long-established ways of life, people resist innovations – even those that promise a richer material life. The members of poor societies often accept their fate, although it may be bleak, in order to maintain family vitality and cultural heritage. Such attitudes bolster social bonds, but at the cost of discouraging development. The World Watch box on page 234 ('A different kind of poverty') explains why traditional people in India respond to their poverty differently than poor people in Europe commonly do.

4. *Social stratification*. While most societies distribute their wealth very unequally, in low-income societies the consequences are severe. In the farming regions of Bangladesh, for example, 10 per cent of the landowners own more than half the land area, while almost half of farming families hold title to little or no land of their own (Hartmann and Boyce, 1982). As another example, the richest 10 per cent of Central Americans control about three-quarters of that region's land.

5. *Gender inequality*. As we have already explained, poor societies subordinate women even more than industrial societies do. Moreover, women with few opportunities typically have many children and the needs of a growing population, in turn, restrain economic development. As a result, many analysts conclude that raising living standards in much of the world depends on improving the social standing of women.

6. *Global power relationships*. A final cause of global poverty lies in the relationships among the nations of the world. Historically, wealth flowed from poor societies to rich nations by means of **colonialism**, *the process by which some nations enrich themselves through political and economic control of other countries*. Historical patterns of trade, some analysts claim, spurred certain nations to prosper economically while others simultaneously were made poor. The societies of Western Europe colonised much of Latin America for more than 300 years and also controlled parts of Asia, notably India, for centuries. Africa, too, endured up to a century of colonisation, most of which ended in the 1960s.

During the twentieth century, about 130 former colonies gained their independence, leaving only a small number of countries as colonies today. As we shall see, however, a continuing pattern of domination has emerged. **Neo-colonialism** (*neos* is a Greek word for 'new') amounts to *a new form of global power relationship that involves not direct political control but economic exploitation by multinational corporations*. **Multinational corporations**, in turn, are *large corporations that operate in many different countries*. As Chapter 14 explains, the power of today's multinational corporations to dominate a poor nation often rivals that of colonial countries in centuries past.

Two rival theories

There are two classic explanations for the unequal distribution of the world's wealth and power – *modernisation theory* and *dependency theory*. Each of these approaches advances a thesis to explain why so many of the world's people are poor and why members of rich societies enjoy such relative advantages. The two explanations overlap to some extent. Both acknowledge the enormous inequality on our planet, and they agree that changes are needed to guarantee the future security of humanity, rich and poor alike. Yet, by emphasising different causes of global poverty, they reach differing conclusions as to what to do about this pressing problem.

Modernisation theory: the conservative view

Modernisation theory is *a model of economic and social development that explains global inequality in terms of differing levels of technological development among societies*. Modernisation theory emerged in the 1950s, a time when 'becoming modern' was a popular idea in the Western world generally, but also a period of hostility towards the United States (which symbolised it) in many poor societies. Socialist countries – especially the Soviet Union – were gaining influence among low-income nations by arguing that economic progress was impossible under the sway of rich, capitalist countries. In response, US policymakers framed a broad defence of rich nations' free-market economies that has shaped official foreign policy towards poor nations ever since.[2] Today, modernisation theory often moves under different names, but it is still a popular theory.

Historical perspective

Modernisation theorists point out that the entire world was poor as recently as several centuries ago. Because poverty has been the norm throughout human history, *affluence* – not deprivation – demands an explanation. Affluence came within reach of a small segment of humanity in Western Europe during the twilight of the Middle Ages as economic activity expanded. Initially, this economic growth was concentrated in and around cities. By the beginning of the sixteenth century, exploration of other parts of the world revealed vast commercial potential.

By 1750, Europeans were engaged in trade all over the world. But then an even greater economic force was unleashed as the Industrial Revolution began to transform Western Europe and, soon after, the United States. Industrial technology, coupled with the

---

[2] The following discussion of modernisation theory draws primarily on Rostow (1960, 1978), Bauer (1981) and Berger (1986).

innovations of countless entrepreneurs, created new wealth on a grand scale. At the outset, modernisation theorists concede, this new wealth benefited only a few. Yet industrial technology was so productive that gradually the standard of living of even the poorest people began to rise. Absolute poverty, which had cast a menacing shadow over humanity for its entire history, was finally being eliminated.

During the twentieth century, the standard of living in high-income countries, where the Industrial Revolution began, jumped at least fourfold. Many middle-income nations in Asia and Latin America are now industrialising, and they, too, are gaining greater wealth. But without industrial technology, low-income countries contend with the same meagre productivity they have endured throughout history.

The importance of culture

Why didn't the Industrial Revolution sweep away poverty the world over? Modernisation theory holds that not every society has been eager to seek out and use new technology. Indeed, depending on culture, some forward-looking societies have eagerly embraced technological innovation while other, more traditional peoples have sternly opposed it (see Chapter 5 on values and see Harrison and Huntington, 2000).

Modernisation theory identifies *tradition* as the greatest barrier to economic development. In societies that celebrate strong family networks and revere the past, ancient ways offer powerful guides to understanding the present and shaping the future. Predictably, tradition operates as a form of 'cultural inertia' that discourages the adoption of technological advances that would improve the standard of living. Even today, a host of peoples, including the Islamic people of Iran and the deeply traditional Semai of Malaysia, have battled against technological advances that threaten their strong family relationships, customs and religious beliefs.

Weber (1958; orig. 1905) explained that, at the end of the Middle Ages, Western Europe was quite another story: here was a cultural environment that distinctly favoured change. As detailed in Chapter 4, the Protestant Reformation reshaped traditional Catholicism to generate a progress-orientated culture. Material affluence – regarded with suspicion by the Roman Catholic church – became a personal virtue, and individualism steadily undermined the established emphasis on kinship and community. Taken together, these emerging cultural patterns nurtured the Industrial Revolution, which carried one segment of humanity from poverty to prosperity

Rostow's stages of modernisation

But, modernisation theory holds, the door to affluence remains open to all. Indeed, as technological advances diffuse around the world, all societies are gradually converging on one general form: the industrial model. According to W. W. Rostow (1960, 1978), the process of modernisation follows four overarching stages.

1. *Traditional stage*. Any society with long-standing and powerful traditions will resist technological innovation. Socialised to venerate the past, most people in traditional societies cannot even imagine how life can be very different from what they know. Traditionalists, therefore, build their lives around their families and neighbourhoods, grant little individual freedom to one another and, in so doing, inhibit change. Life in such communities is often spiritually rich but lacking in material abundance.

   A century ago, much of the world was at this initial stage of economic development. And, because nations such as Bangladesh, Niger and Somalia are still at the traditional stage, they remain impoverished to this day.

2. *Take-off stage*. As a society begins to shake off the grip of tradition, people start to use their talents and imagination, triggering economic growth. A market emerges as people produce goods not just for their own consumption but to trade with others for profit. The culture is marked by a developing spirit of individualism and a stronger achievement orientation, usually at the expense of family ties and long-standing norms and values. Great Britain reached take-off by about 1800, the United States by 1820. Thailand, a middle-income country in eastern Asia, is now at this stage. Such development typically depends on progressive influences from rich nations, including foreign aid, the availability of advanced technology and investment capital, and schooling abroad.

3. *Drive to technological maturity*. By this time, 'growth' has become a widely accepted concept, fuelling a society's full-scale pursuit of higher living standards. An active, diversified economy drives a population eager to enjoy the benefits of industrial technology. At the same time, however, people begin to realise (and sometimes lament) that industrialisation is eroding traditional family and community life. Great Britain reached this point by about 1840, the United States by 1860. Today, Mexico, the US territory of Puerto Rico and South Korea are among the nations driving to technological maturity.

   By this stage of economic development, absolute poverty has greatly declined. Cities swell with people who stream from the rural hinterland in search of economic opportunity, occupational specialisation renders relationships less personal, and heightened individualism sparks movements pressing for expanded political rights. Societies approaching technological maturity also provide basic schooling to all their people, with advanced training for some. Such people discard many traditions as 'backward', opening the door to further change. The social position of women steadily becomes more equal to that of men.

4. *High mass consumption*. Economic development driven by industrial technology steadily raises living standards. This rise occurs, Rostow explains, as mass production stimulates mass consumption. Simply put, people soon learn to 'need' the expanding array of goods that their society produces.

Much of Europe entered the era of high mass consumption around 1900. Other high-income countries were not far behind. Japan, for example, was sufficiently industrialised to become a military power early in the twentieth century. After recovering from the destruction of the Second World War, the Japanese entered an era of high mass consumption, and Japan's economic output is now second only to that of the United States. Now entering this level of economic development are two of the most prosperous small societies of eastern Asia, Hong Kong and Singapore.

The role of rich nations

Modernisation theory credits high-income countries with a crucial role in global economic development. More specifically, rich societies are the key to alleviating global inequality in the following ways:

1. *Assisting in population control*. We have already noted that population growth is greatest in the poorest societies of the world, where rising population easily overtakes economic advances and lowers the standard of living. As rich nations export birth control technology and promote its use, they help curb population growth, which is crucial to combating poverty. Integral to this process are programmes that advance the social standing of women. Once economic development is under way and women are earning more income, their lives are less centred on child-rearing, so birth rates begin to decline as they have in industrialised societies.

2. *Increasing food production*. Modernisation theory asserts that 'high-tech' farming methods, exported from rich to poor nations, raise agricultural yields. Such techniques, collectively referred to as the Green Revolution, involve the use of new hybrid seeds, modern irrigation methods, chemical fertilisers and pesticides.

3. *Introducing industrial technology*. Technological transfers go beyond agricultural innovations. Rich nations accelerate economic growth in poor societies by introducing machinery and information technology. Such cultural diffusion helps to shift the economies of low-income countries from a focus on agriculture to industrial and service work that raises productivity.

4. *Instituting programmes of foreign aid*. Investment capital from rich nations boosts the prospects of poor societies striving to reach the take-off stage. Developing countries can use this money to purchase fertilisers and high-technology irrigation projects that raise agricultural productivity, and also to build power plants and factories that improve industrial output.

Modernisation and women

In global perspective, gender inequality is most pronounced where people are poorest. Economic development may give women opportunities to attend school and to work outside the home, to reduce birth rates and to weaken traditional male domination, but along the way this process of modernisation often impedes women's progress. Investigating the lives of women in a poor, rural district of Bangladesh, Sultana Alam (1985) observed several hazards of development for women.

First, as economic opportunity draws men from rural areas to cities in search of work, women and children must fend for themselves. Some men sell their land and simply abandon their wives, who are left with nothing but their children. Second, the waning strength of the family and neighbourhood leaves women who are deserted in this way with little assistance. The same holds true for women who become single through divorce or the death of a spouse. In the past, Alam reports, kin or neighbours readily took in a Bangladeshi woman who found herself alone. Today, as Bangladesh struggles to advance economically, the number of poor households headed by women is increasing. Rather than enhance women's autonomy, Alam argues, a new spirit of individualism has actually eroded the social standing of women.

Third, economic development – as well as the growing influence of Western movies and mass media – undermines women's traditional roles as wives, sisters and mothers in favour of defining women as objects of men's sexual attention. The cultural emphasis on sexuality, familiar to most Westerners, now encourages men in poor countries to abandon ageing spouses for younger, more physically attractive partners. The same stress on sex contributes to the world's rising tide of prostitution, noted earlier in this chapter.

Modernisation, then, does not affect men and women in the same ways. In the long run, the evidence suggests, modernisation does give the sexes more equal standing. In the short run, however, the economic position of many women actually declines, as women are forced to contend with new problems that were virtually unknown in traditional societies (Alam, 1985; Mink, 1989).

Critical evaluation

Modernisation theory, a sweeping analysis of how industrialisation transforms social life, has influential supporters among social scientists (Parsons, 1966; Moore, 1977, 1979; Bauer, 1981; Berger, 1986). Moreover, in various guises, this model has guided the foreign policy of the United States and other rich nations for decades. Proponents point to rapid economic development in Asia as proof that the affluence created in Western Europe and North America is within reach of all regions of the world. With the assistance of rich countries, South Korea, Taiwan, and the former British colonies of Singapore and Hong Kong have significant records of economic achievement.

From the outset, however, modernisation theory has come under fire from socialist countries (and sympathetic analysts in the West) as a thinly veiled defence of capitalism. Its most serious flaw, according to critics, is that modernisation simply has not occurred in many of the world's poor societies. In fact, as we have seen, many low-income countries have seen their living standards fall, and the gap between rich and poor grow.

A second criticism lodged against modernisation theory concerns its assessment of the role of rich nations. Modernisation theorists contend that the presence of high-income countries ready and willing to offer various kinds of assistance makes economic development easier than ever. But many critics of modernisation theory see rich nations more as the cause of global poverty than its solution. Centuries ago, they argue, Europe and North America industrialised from a position of global *strength*; we should not expect low-income countries today to modernise from a position of global *weakness*.

Third, critics charge that modernisation theory treats rich and poor nations as worlds unto themselves, failing to see how international relations historically have affected the standing of all nations. It was colonisation, they maintain, that boosted the fortunes of Europe to begin with; further, this economic windfall came at the expense of countries in Latin America and Asia that are still reeling from the consequences.

Fourth, critics contend that modernisation theory holds up the world's high-income countries as the standard by which the rest of humanity should be judged, betraying an ethnocentric bias. As Chapter 24 explains, our Western conception of 'progress' has led us to degrade the physical environment throughout the world. Moreover, not every culture buys into our notions about competitive, materialistic living.

Finally, modernisation theory draws criticism for locating the causes of global poverty almost entirely in the poor societies themselves. Critics see this analysis as little more than 'blaming the victims' for their own plight. Instead, they argue, an analysis of global inequality should focus as much attention on the behaviour of *rich* nations as on that of poor nations (Wiarda, 1987).

From all these concerns has emerged a second major approach to understanding global inequality. This opposing view is called dependency theory. But again, it has more recent variants.

Dependency theory: the critical view

Dependency theory is *a model of economic and social development that explains global inequality in terms of the historical exploitation of poor societies by rich ones.* Dependency theory offers an analysis of global inequality dramatically different from modernisation theory, for it places primary responsibility for global poverty on rich nations. Dependency theory holds that high-income countries have systematically impoverished low-income countries, making poor societies *dependent* on rich ones. According to dependency theorists, this destructive process extends back for centuries and continues today.

Historical perspective

Everyone agrees that, before the Industrial Revolution, there was little of the affluence present in some parts of the world today. Dependency theory asserts, however, that many poor countries were actually better off economically in the past than they are now. André Gunder Frank (1975), a noted proponent of this approach, argues that the development of rich nations resulted from the same colonial ties that *underdeveloped* poor societies.

WORLD WATCH

A DIFFERENT KIND OF POVERTY: A REPORT FROM INDIA

Most Europeans know that India is one of the poorest societies of the world: per capita gross domestic product (GDP) in this low-income Asian nation is only slightly more than US $1,000 a year (look back at Table 9.1). Deprivation pervades this vast society, home to one-third of all the world's hungry people.

But Europeans do not readily comprehend the reality of poverty in India. Most of the country's 1,000 million people live in conditions far worse than those our society labels as 'poor'. A traveller's first experience of Indian life is sobering and sometimes shocking. Arriving in Chennai, one of India's largest cities with 7 million inhabitants, a visitor immediately recoils from the smell of human sewage that hangs over the city like a malodorous cloud. Untreated sewage also renders much of the region's water

COUNTRY FACT FILE

INDIA

Population	1,047,671,000 (2002)
Urban population	28.7% (2001)
Per capita GNP	$450 (2000)
Life expectancy	69.1 male; 63.1 female (2001)
Literacy	65.4% (2001)
Languages	18 official languages; Hindi most widely spoken
Religions	Mainly Hindu with Islam, Sikh, Christian and Buddhist minorities
Main cities	9,817,439 Delhi and New Delhi: 11,914.398 Greater Mumbai (formerly Bombay): 13,216,546 Calcutta
Human Development Index 2004	127th

Source: adapted from *The World Guide*, 2001; Brittanica Almanac 2004

unsafe to drink. The sights and sounds of Chennai are strange and intense – streets are choked by motor-bikes, trucks, carts pulled by oxen and waves of people. Along the roads, vendors sit on burlap cloth hawking fruits, vegetables and cooked food. Seemingly oblivious to the urban chaos all around them, people work, talk, bathe and even sleep in the streets. Tens of millions of homeless people fill the cities of India.

Chennai is also dotted by more than 1,000 shanty settlements, containing about half a million people, many of whom have converged on the city from rural villages in search of a better life.

Shanty towns are clusters of huts constructed of branches, leaves and discarded material. These dwellings offer little privacy and lack refrigeration, running water and bathrooms. The visitor from Europe or the United States understandably feels uneasy entering such a community, since the poorest sections of our inner cities seethe with frustration and often explode with violence.

But, here, again, India offers a sharp contrast because its people understand poverty differently from ourselves. No restless young men hang out at the corner, no drug dealers work the streets and there is surprisingly little danger. In the United States and much of Europe, poverty often means anger and isolation; in India, even shanty towns are built of strong families – children, parents and sometimes elderly grandparents – who extend a smile and a welcome.

In traditional societies like India, ways of life change slowly. To most Indians, life is shaped by *dharma*, the Hindu concept of duty and destiny, that encourages them to accept their fate, whatever it may be. Mother Teresa, who won praise for her work among the poorest of India's people, went to the heart of the cultural differences: 'Americans have angry poverty', she explained. 'In India, there is worse poverty, but it is a happy poverty.'

Perhaps we should not describe as 'happy' anyone who clings to the edge of survival. But the sting of poverty in India is eased by the strength and support of families and communities, a sense that existence has a purpose and a world-view that encourages each person to accept whatever life offers. As a result, the visitor comes away from a first encounter with Indian poverty in confusion: 'How can people be so desperately poor, and yet apparently content, vibrant and so alive?'

Source: based on Macionis's research in Chennai, India, November 1988.

Dependency theory hinges on the assertion that the economic positions of the rich and poor nations of the world are linked and cannot be understood correctly in isolation from one another. This analysis maintains that poor nations are not simply lagging behind rich ones on a linear 'path of progress'. Rather, the increasing prosperity of the high-income countries came largely at the expense of low-income societies. In short, then, some nations became rich only because other nations became poor. Both are products of the onset of global commerce that began half a millennium ago.

The importance of colonialism

Late in the fifteenth century, Europeans began surveying North America to the west, the massive continent of Africa to the south and the vast expanse of Asia to the east. Conventional history heralds great explorers such as Christopher Columbus, who sailed westward from Spain in 1492 in search of the Orient. But what Europeans celebrated as 'the discovery of the New World' might more correctly be described as the systematic conquest of one region of the world by another (Sale, 1990; Gray, 1991).

Colonisation brought vast wealth to European nations. By the nineteenth century, in fact, most of the world had come under the domination of European governments. Spain and Portugal colonised nearly all of Latin America from the sixteenth until the mid-nineteenth centuries. By the beginning of the twentieth century, Great Britain boasted that 'the sun never sets on the British Empire'. The United States, itself originally 13 small British colonies on the eastern seaboard, pushed across the continent, purchased Alaska, gained control of Haiti, Puerto Rico and part of Cuba, as well as Guam, the Philippines and the Hawaiian Islands.

Elsewhere, Europeans in collaboration with Africans initiated a brutal form of human exploitation – the slave trade, which persisted from about 1500 until 1850. But even as the world was rejecting the practice of slavery, Europeans rapidly seized control of Africa itself. As Map 9.3 shows, Europeans dominated most of the continent, and did so until the early 1960s.

During the last several decades, overt colonialism has largely disappeared from the world. However, according to dependency theory, *political* liberation has not translated into *economic* autonomy. Far from it. Poor societies maintain economic relationships with rich nations that reproduce the pattern of colonial exploitation. This neo-colonialism is fuelled by a capitalist world economy.

Wallerstein's capitalist world economy

Immanuel Wallerstein (1974, 1979, 1983, 1984) explains the origins of contemporary global inequality using a model of the 'capitalist world economy'.[3] Wallerstein's term *world economy* suggests that the productivity of all nations depends on the operation of a global economic network. He traces the roots of this global system to the economic expansion that began 500 years ago as rich nations cast their eyes on the wealth of the rest of the world. Centred on the high-income countries, then, the dominant character of the world economy is capitalist.

Wallerstein calls rich nations the *core* of the world economy. Colonialism enriched this core by funnelling raw materials from around the globe to Western Europe. Over the longer term, this wealth helped to ignite the Industrial Revolution. Formal colonialism may have ended, but multinational corporations still operate profitably around the world, drawing wealth to North America, Western Europe and Japan.

Low-income countries represent the *periphery* of the world economy. Originally drawn into this system by colonial exploitation, poor nations continue to support rich ones by providing inexpensive labour, easy access to raw materials and vast markets for industrial products. A remaining category of countries includes those on the

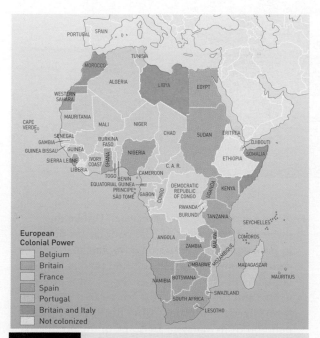

European Colonial Power

- Belgium
- Britain
- France
- Spain
- Portugal
- Britain and Italy
- Not colonized

Map 9.3   Africa's colonial history

---

[3] While based on Wallerstein's idea, this section also reflects the work of Frank (1980, 1981), Delacroix and Ragin (1981) and Bergesen (1983).

Children stand outside their small home in the impoverished El Pantonal neighbourhood in Tegucigalpa, Honduras, on October 11, 2001. United Nation figures show that 74% of the Honduran population live below the poverty line. Today, the world Bank officially approves a $75 million package that aims to reduce poverty by 25% over fifteen years in the Central American nation.

Source: © Adam Bernstein/Reuters/Corbis

semi-periphery of the world economy, including middle-income countries such as Portugal and South Korea that have closer ties to the global economic core.

According to Wallerstein, the world economy benefits rich societies (by generating profits) and harms the rest of the world (by perpetuating poverty). In short, the world economy imposes a state of dependency on poor nations, which remain under the control of rich ones. This dependency turns on the following three factors:

1. *Narrow, export-orientated economies*. Unlike the diversified economies of core nations, production in poor countries centres on a few raw materials or agricultural products that colonial powers forced labourers to extract or farmers to grow for export. Coffee and fruits from Latin American nations, oil from Nigeria, hardwoods from the Philippines and palm oil from Malaysia are some of the products central to the economies of these poor societies.

Multinational corporations maintain this pattern today by purchasing raw materials cheaply in poor societies and transporting them to core societies where factories process them for profitable sale. Corporations thus discourage production of food or goods needed by local people in poor nations. These corporations also own a great deal of land and have transformed traditional farmers into low-paid farm labourers. Overall, then, rich nations effectively prevent poor ones from developing industries of their own.

2. *Lack of industrial capacity*. Without an industrial base, poor societies face a double bind. Not only do they count on rich nations to buy their inexpensive raw materials but they also depend on rich nations to sell them whatever expensive manufactured goods they can afford.

   In a classic example of this double dependency, British colonialists allowed the people of India to raise cotton and then shipped Indian cotton back to the English textile mills in Birmingham and Manchester. There, English industrialists wove it into cloth and traders shipped the finished goods back for profitable sale in India.

   Dependency theorists also criticise aspects of the Green Revolution, widely praised by modernisation theorists. To promote agricultural productivity, poor countries end up buying expensive fertilisers, pesticides and mechanical equipment from core nations. Typically, rich countries profit more from 'high-tech' farming in poor societies than do the poor nations themselves.

3. *Foreign debt*. Such unequal trade patterns have plunged poor countries deeper and deeper into debt to industrialised societies. Collectively, the poor nations of the world owe rich countries more than US $2 trillion (Ransom, 1999: 10) – a debt of some $400 for every man, woman and child in the developing world, where average income for the very poorest is less than $1 a day! This staggering debt is a financial burden few poor societies can bear. Excessive debt, which drains the resources of any society, can destabilise a poor country's economy, making matters worse for nations already reeling from high unemployment and rampant inflation (Walton and Ragin, 1990).

   Moreover, the debt crisis requires continuous transfers of wealth from poor to rich societies – at least $50 billion annually (Baird, 1998) – further impoverishing peripheral societies and increasing their dependency on rich nations. This onerous debt, say dependency theorists, plays into the vicious cycle that makes rich nations richer and poor nations poorer.

Seeing no way out of the 'debt trap', some low-income countries have simply stopped making payments. Cuba, for example, refused to make further payments on its $7 billion foreign debt a decade ago. Because failure to repay loans threatens economic growth in rich countries, the United States and other rich nations strongly oppose such actions and have advanced various programmes to refinance these debts.

The role of rich nations

Nowhere is the difference between modernisation theory and dependency theory sharper than in the role each assigns to rich nations. In investigating the sources of global stratification, modernisation theory highlights the *production of wealth*. From this point of view, when rich societies create new wealth through technological innovation, this process does not harm other nations. On the contrary, as rich nations export productive technology and pro-growth attitudes, modernisation theorists assert, poor nations will benefit.

By contrast, dependency theory envisages global inequality in terms of the *distribution of wealth*. This approach contends that rich societies have unjustly seized the wealth of the world for their own purposes. That is, the *over*development of some parts of the globe is directly tied to the *under*development of the rest of it.

Dependency theorists dismiss the idea that strategies proposed by rich countries to control population or to boost agricultural and industrial output will help poor countries. They contend that, far from benefiting the vast majority of people in poor societies, such programmes provide profits to rich countries (through purchases of high technology), while rewarding not the poor majority but ruling elites who maintain a favourable 'business climate' for multinational corporations (Lappé *et al.*, 1981).

Hunger activists Frances Moore Lappé and Joseph Collins (1986) claim that the capitalist culture lulls people into thinking that absolute poverty is somehow inevitable. Following this line of reasoning, poverty results from 'natural' processes, including having too many children, and from natural disasters such as droughts. But they challenge this kind of thinking, pointing out that the world produces enough grain for every man, woman and child to consume 3,600 calories a day, sufficient to make everyone on the planet overweight! Even most of the poorest societies grow enough to feed their people. The problem, therefore, is not production but poverty: too many people cannot afford to buy available food. This skewed distribution of wealth – including food resources – means that millions in India suffer from malnutrition while their nation exports beef, wheat and rice. Similarly, millions of children go hungry in Africa, a vast continent whose agricultural abundance also makes it a net food exporter.

According to Lappé and Collins, the contradiction of poverty amid plenty stems from the policy of producing food for profits, not people. That is, corporations in rich nations collaborate with elites in poor countries to grow profitable crops for export. Thus, coffee is grown in much of Latin America instead of corn and beans, which are the staples for local consumption. Governments of poor societies often support the practice of growing for export rather than local consumption because food profits help to repay massive foreign debt. The problem is complex, but its core, according to Lappé and Collins, is the global capitalist economic system.

Critical evaluation

The central assertion of dependency theory is that the world's wealth and poverty both result from one interconnected system of global stratification. Citing Latin America and other poor regions of the world, dependency theorists claim that development simply cannot proceed under the constraints presently imposed by rich countries. Addressing global poverty, they conclude, demands more than change within poor societies. Rather, these theorists call for radical reform of the entire world economy so that it operates in the interests of the majority of people.

Critics of the dependency approach identify some important weaknesses in this analysis. First, they charge, dependency theory wrongly contends that the wealth of the high-income nations resulted from stealing resources from poor societies. Farmers, small business owners and industrialists can and do create new wealth through their imagination and drive. Put another way, wealth is not a zero-sum resource by which some gain only at the expense of others; the entire world's wealth has expanded fivefold since 1950, largely due to technological advances and other innovations.

Second, critics reason, if dependency theory were correct in condemning rich nations for creating global poverty, then nations with the strongest ties to rich societies would be among the poorest. However, some of the lowest-income countries of the world (such as Ethiopia) have had relatively little contact with rich countries. Similarly, critics continue, a long history of trade with rich countries has dramatically improved the economies of nations such as Singapore (a former British colony), South Korea, Japan and Hong Kong (since 1842 a British colony that reverted to the People's Republic of China in 1997). In addition, an increasing body of

evidence indicates that foreign investment by rich nations fosters economic growth, as modernisation theory claims, not economic decline, as dependency theorists assert (Vogel, 1991; Firebaugh, 1992).

Third, critics charge that dependency theory simplistically points the finger at a single factor – world capitalism – as the sole cause of global inequality (Worsley, 1990). By directing attention only to forces outside poor societies, dependency theory casts poor societies as innocent victims, ignoring factors *inside* these countries that contribute to their economic plight. Sociologists have long recognised the vital role of culture in shaping human behaviour. Cultural patterns vary greatly around the world; some societies embrace change readily while others staunchly resist economic development. As we noted earlier, for example, Iran's brand of Islamic fundamentalism has deliberately discouraged economic ties with other countries. Capitalist societies, then, hardly need accept the blame for Iran's economic stagnation.

Nor can rich societies be saddled with responsibility for the reckless behaviour of some foreign leaders. Members of poor societies have had to pick up the costs of far-reaching corruption and self-serving military campaigns that have marked the regimes of Ferdinand Marcos in the Philippines, François Duvalier in Haiti, Manuel Noriega in Panama, Mobutu Sese Seko in Zaïre and Saddam Hussein in Iraq. Governments have even withheld food supplies for leverage in internal political struggles, as we have seen in the African nations of Ethiopia, Sudan and Somalia. Other regimes throughout Latin America, Africa and Asia have failed to support programmes to improve the status of women and to control population growth.

Fourth, critics chide dependency theorists for downplaying the economic dependency fostered by the former Soviet Union. The Soviet army seized control of most of Eastern Europe during the Second World War and subsequently dominated the Eastern Bloc nations politically and economically. Many consider the uprisings between 1989 and 1991 against Soviet-installed leaders and the Soviet government itself as popular rejection of a vast Soviet colonial system.

A fifth criticism of dependency theory faults this approach for offering only vague prescriptions for remedying global poverty. Most dependency theorists urge poor societies to sever economic ties to rich countries and some call for nationalising foreign-owned industries. Dependency theory implies that the path to ending global poverty begins with the overthrow of international capitalism. At its core, say the critics, dependency theory advocates some sort of world socialism. In light of the failure of government-run socialist societies to meet the needs of their own people, critics ask, should we really expect such a system to lift the entire world towards prosperity?

Globalisation theory

Versions of modernisation and dependency theory have been discussed by sociologists for a long while now. The key differences are outlined in Table 9.3. In recent years, as ideas around globalisation – introduced in Chapter 2 – have grown, the debates have taken on a slightly different form (though there are clear echoes of the same positions). *Globalisers* argue that there is a growing global economy which is transcending nations and providing the motor force of change. They tend to be the new version of the 'modernisers'. They see the dynamic of international capitalism as a force for generating more and more wealth, from which more and more countries will be able to gain. By contrast, there are the *sceptics* who are critical of the globalisation thesis. They argue that there is much more economic independence by individual states than globalisers allow for. More, they also claim that there has been little real convergence of state policies across the globe. For them, real inequalities across countries can be shown to have actually grown. Sceptics often mirror a newer version of dependency theory (for example, Hirst and Thompson, 1996; Held *et al.*, 1999).

Global inequality: looking ahead

Among the most important trends of recent decades is the development of a global economy. While some see this as generating markets of increased wealth and productivity, others see it as simply exacerbating inequality around the world. Profitable investments, many of them in poor nations, and lucrative sales have brought greater affluence to those who already have substantial wealth. And increasing industrial production abroad has cut factory jobs, exerting downward pressure on wages. The net result: gradual economic polarisation.

It is true that in some regions of the world, such as the 'Pacific Rim' of eastern Asia, market forces are raising living standards rapidly and substantially. Many Latin American nations (such as Colombia and Chile) also have recorded strong economic growth in recent years. Meanwhile, however, other poor societies, especially in Africa, are experiencing economic turmoil that frustrates hopes for market-based development.

Table 9.3	Modernisation theory and dependency theory: a summary	
	Modernisation theory	**Dependency theory**
Historical pattern	The entire world was poor just two centuries ago; the Industrial Revolution brought affluence to high-income countries; as industrialisation gradually transforms poor societies, all nations are likely to become more equal and alike.	Global parity was disrupted by colonialism, which made some countries rich while simultaneously making other countries poor; barring radical change in the world capitalist system, rich nations will grow richer and poor nations will become poorer.
Primary causes of global poverty	Characteristics of poor societies cause their poverty, including lack of industrial technology, traditional cultural patterns that discourage innovation, and rapid population growth.	Global economic relations – historical colonialism and the operation of multinational corporations – have enriched high-income countries while placing low-income countries in a state of economic dependency.
Role of rich nations	Rich countries can and do assist poor nations through programmes of population control, technology transfers that increase food production and stimulate industrial development, and investment capital in the form of foreign aid.	Rich countries have concentrated global resources, conferring advantages on themselves while generating massive foreign debt in low-income countries; rich nations impede the economic development of poor nations.
Newer forms	The globalisers – advances through globalisation	The sceptics – critical of globalisation

The poor countries that have surged ahead economically have two factors in common. First, they are relatively small. Combined, the Asian nations of South Korea, Taiwan, Hong Kong, Singapore and Japan cover only about one-fifth of the land area and population of India. The economic problems smaller countries face are more manageable; consequently, small societies more effectively administer programmes of development. Second, these 'best-case' nations have cultural traits in common, especially traditions emphasising individual achievement and economic success.

In other areas of the world, where powerful cultural forces inhibit change and individualism, even smaller nations have failed to turn economic opportunities to their advantage. Social inequality is striking in this global context. The concentration of wealth among high-income countries, coupled with the grinding poverty typical of low-income nations, may well constitute the most important dilemma facing humanity in the twenty-first century. To some analysts, globalisation holds the keys to ending world poverty; to others, it is the cause of this tragic problem.

CONTROVERSY AND DEBATE

WILL THE WORLD STARVE?

Hunger casts its menacing shadow not only over regions of Asia, but also over much of Latin America, most of Africa, and even parts of North America. Throughout the world, hundreds of millions of adults do not consume enough food to enable them to work. And some 10 million of the world's children die each year because they do not get enough to eat. Meanwhile, in the Western world, many people suffer from obesity and spend their money on slimming aids!

At the start of a new century, what are the prospects for eradicating the wretched misery of so many human beings enduring daily hunger?

It is easy to be pessimistic. For one thing, the population of poor countries is currently increasing by 90 million people annually – equivalent to adding another Mexico to the world every year. Poor countries can scarcely feed the people they have now; looking ahead a generation to the future, how will they ever feed double their current populations?

In addition, as detailed in Chapter 24, hunger forces poor people to exploit the earth's resources by using short-term strategies for food production that will lead to long-term disaster. For example, to feed the swelling populations of poor tropical countries, farmers are cutting down rainforests in order to increase their farmland. But, without the protective canopy of trees, it is only a matter of time before much of this land turns to desert.

Taken together, rising populations and ecological approaches that borrow against the future raise the spectre of hunger and outright starvation escalating well beyond current levels. Regarded pessimistically, the world's future is bleak: unprecedented hunger, human misery and political calamity. But there are also some grounds for optimism. Thanks to the Green Revolution, food production the world over is up sharply over the last 50 years, even outpacing the growth in population. Taking a broader view, the world's economic productivity has risen steadily, so that the average person on the planet has more income now to purchase food and other necessities than ever before.

This growth has increased daily calorie intake as well as life expectancy, access to safe water and adult literacy, while infant mortality is going down. In fact, looking at these social indicators, we can see the gap between rich and poor countries actually narrowing. So what are the prospects for eradicating world hunger – especially in low-income nations? Overall, we see less hunger in both rich and poor countries; that is, a smaller share of the world's people faces starvation now than, say, in 1960. But as global population increases, with 90 per cent of children born in middle- and low-income countries, the number of lives at risk is as great today as ever before. Moreover, even though living standards are rising, there has not been any narrowing of the economic gap between rich and poor countries.

Also bear in mind that aggregate data mask different trends in various world regions. The 'best case' region of the world is eastern Asia, where incomes (controlled for inflation) have tripled over the last generation. It is to Asia that the 'optimists' in the global hunger debate typically turn for evidence that poor countries can and do raise living standards and reduce hunger. The 'worst case' region of the world is sub-Saharan Africa, where living standards have actually fallen over the last decade, and more and more people are pushed to the brink of starvation. It is here that high technology is least evident

CONTROVERSY AND DEBATE CONTINUED

and birth rates are highest. Pessimists typically look to Africa when they argue that poor countries are losing ground in the struggle to keep their people well nourished.

Television brings home the tragedy of hunger every year or so when news cameras focus on starving people in places such as Ethiopia, Somalia and Afghanistan. But hunger – and the early death from illness that it brings on – is the plight of millions all year round. The world does have the technical means to feed everyone; the question is do we have the moral determination to do so?

CONTINUE THE DEBATE:

1. In your opinion, what are the primary causes of global hunger?

2. Do you place responsibility for solving this problem on poor countries or rich ones? Why?

3. Do you expect the extent of global hunger to increase or decrease? Why?

Sources: Beckman (2001); United Nations Food and Agriculture Organisation (FAO) website.

SUMMARY

1. About 15 per cent of the world's people live in industrialised, high-income countries and take in 55 per cent of the earth's total income. Another one-third of humanity live in middle-income countries with limited industrialisation, receiving about 37 per cent of all income. Half the world's population live in low-income countries that have yet to industrialise; they earn only 8 per cent of global income.

2. While relative poverty is found everywhere, poor societies contend with widespread, absolute poverty. 2,800 million people live below the $2 a day purchasing parity measure of poverty. Over 1.2 billion live on less than $1. Three groups of world poor are given special attention: children, women and refugees.

3. The poverty found in much of the world is a complex problem reflecting limited industrial technology, rapid population growth, traditional cultural patterns, internal social stratification, male domination and global power relationships.

4. Modernisation theory maintains that successful development hinges on acquiring advanced productive technology and sees traditional cultural patterns as the key barrier. Rostow identifies four stages of development: traditional, take-off, drive to technological maturity and high mass consumption. He suggests that rich societies have the keys to creating wealth through bolstering population-control strategies, providing crop-enhancing

technologies, encouraging industrial development, and providing investment capital and other foreign aid. Critics of modernisation theory say this has produced limited economic development in the world, while ethnocentrically assuming that poor societies can follow the path to development taken by rich nations centuries ago.

5. Dependency theory claims that global wealth and poverty are directly linked to the historical operation of the capitalist world economy. The dependency of poor countries on rich ones is rooted in colonialism. Even though most poor countries have won political independence, dependency theorists argue, neo-colonialism persists as a form of exploitation carried out by multinational corporations. Wallerstein views the high-income countries as the privileged 'core' of the capitalist world economy; middle-income nations are the 'semi-periphery'; poor societies form the global 'periphery'. Three factors – export-orientated economies, a lack of industrial capacity and foreign debt – perpetuate poor countries' dependency on rich nations. Critics argue that this approach overlooks the success of many nations in creating new wealth. Total global wealth, they point out, has increased fivefold since 1950.

6. Both modernisation and dependency approaches offer useful insights into the development of global inequality. Some evidence supports each view. They have their more recent counterparts in debates over globalisation.

CRITICAL-THINKING QUESTIONS

1. For all the advances of globalisation and industralisation, it seems that poverty is still with us on a massive scale and inequalities still seem to be growing. Why do you think this is so? What could (or should) be done about it? Do you think that more economic aid from high-income societies will help low-income societies?

2. Do you think advertising (for coffee from Colombia or exotic vacations to Egypt or India) provides an accurate picture of life in low-income countries? Why or why not? Do you think most people in Europe have a realistic understanding of the extent and severity of poverty in the world?

3. Using website resources, chart the range of refugees and displaced people in the world, looking at the cause of their displacement, where (if anywhere) they have relocated, the problems they experience as 'asylum seekers', and what their future looks like.

4. Read the quotes in the Voices box 'What the poor say' (p. 228) and, if you can, watch one of the films listed below. Now engage in a *verstehen* exercise: try to understand the meanings and experiences of what it is like to be severely poor.

GOING FURTHER

Further reading

General guides to global poverty:

York W. Bradshaw and Michael Wallace, *Global Inequalities* (1996)
Discusses basic data region by region, as well as the major explanations of global inequalities.

Peter and Susan Calvert, *Politics and Society in the Third World* (2001)
A comprehensive tour.

United Nations, *Human Development Report* (yearly)
Each year the United Nations produces a themed volume on world development and poverty. This is detailed reading, but it always contains the latest available figures.

More personal accounts:

Jeremy Seabrook, *In the Cities of the South* (2nd edn, 2001)

Deepa Narayan, *Voices of the Poor: Can Anyone Hear Us?* (2000)
Highly readable introductions – brimming with personal experiences – of poverty and inequalities in low-income countries.

More advanced reading:

Thomas Pogge, *World Poverty and Human Rights* (2002)

Amartya Sen, *Development as Freedom* (1999)
Two important recent statements by economists about world poverty and what can be done about it.

More information

The following three annual publications provide a wide range of data on the comparative economic development of the world's nations: United Nations Development Programme, *Human Development Report 2004* (2004), The World Bank, *World Development Report 2004* (2004) and United Nations High Commission for Refugees (UNHCR), *The State of the World's Refugees: Fifty Years of Humanitarian Action* (2000).

The magazine *New Internationalist*, published in Oxford, provides a wealth of data on inequalities and the global situation. *The World* CD-Rom and book are also available from New Internationalist, along with the *The A to Z of World Development* – a very useful illustrated dictionary, compiled by Andy Crump and edited by Wayne Ellwood (New Internationalist, 1998).

Watch a video

- Jibril Diop Mambety's *Hyenas* (1992): classic allegory of international aid

- Soraya Mire's *Fire Eyes* (1993): a documentary about female genital mutilation

- Tsitsi Dangarembga's *Everyone's Child* (1996): film is a call for action on behalf of Africa's millions of parentless children

- Soulymane Cissé's *Yeelen* (1987): film about traditional African culture

- Miguel Littin's *The Promised Land* (1973: Chile), Hector Babenco's *Pixote* (1981: Brazil) and Victor Gaviria's *Rodrigo D: No Future* (1989: Medellin, Columbia) all vividly capture poverty.

Connecting up

Connect to other chapters

- Poverty is discussed further in Chapter 10.
- The discussion of refugees should also be linked to migration and racism in Chapter 11.
- Consider women's situation more fully in Chapter 12.
- More on children and poverty in Chapter 13.

To the websites

- http://www.worldbank.org/

  This is a major resource for looking at poverty. It is constantly updated with the latest figures, articles and plans for action, as well as a major section in which the poor speak for themselves. Strongly recommended. There is also a regular newsletter.

- On Africa and its neglect in cyberspace, see http://allafrica.com/ict

  (November 2000).

For additional case studies, multiple choice questions, internet exercises, and annotated weblinks specific to this chapter, visit this book's website at **www.pearsoned.co.uk/plummer**

CHAPTER 10

CLASS, POVERTY AND WELFARE

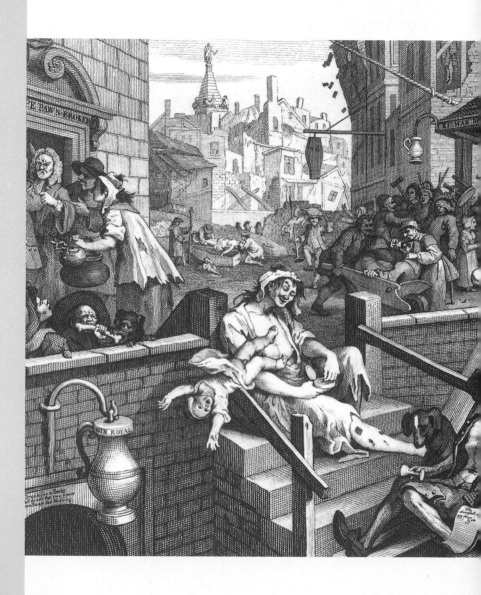

It's the rich what gets the pleasure,

It's the poor what gets the blame.

Ain't it all a bloody pity,

Ain't it all a bloody shame.

ALL CONTEMPORARY SOCIETIES HAVE CLASS STRUCTURES, though not every society treats class as an issue of premium social importance. In the United States, racial divides are often foremost in people's minds and people tend to see themselves as being much less class bound. Any visitor to the UK, by contrast, will soon hear people talk about class. Indeed they may soon see it: with elite educational institutions from public schools to Oxford and Cambridge universities, gentlemen's clubs, and the famous houses of the landed aristocracy. At the other extreme, the homeless sleeping in streets and slum housing can mark out 'the lower classes'. As Valerie Walkerdine and her colleagues (2001) suggest:

> Class is not something that is simply produced economically. It is performed, marked, written on minds and bodies. We can 'spot it a mile off' even in the midst of our wish for it no longer to be there.
>
> (cited in Roberts, 2001: 9)

In this chapter, we will examine the nature of classes, wealth and poverty in industrial capitalist societies, with a major focus on the UK. The chapter will ask how we can identify classes, present a brief 'portrait' of class life as it is lived in the UK, and examine poverty. Finally, we will consider the emergence of 'welfare states' as a means of dealing with some of the problems that inequalities generate.

KEY THEMES

- The nature of class and its measurement
- Looking at class structures in different countries
- Measuring poverty in the UK
- The nature of 'welfare states' and citizenship as a means of dealing with some of the problems that inequalities generate

(Left) William Hogarth's engraving *Gin Lane* shows the depravity of the poor of London when trying to forget their situation by turning to drink.

Source: The Art Archive

The nature of social class

In this chapter, many issues around class are raised and, to give it a firmer focus, the prime concern will be with the system of class found in the United Kingdom – after all it has long been considered one of the most class-ridden societies in the world, and it has been deeply studied by sociologists. As we shall see, modern class systems are dynamic, fluid, always changing. Yet there has been a tendency for contemporary sociologists broadly to take either a *Marxist view* which, as we would expect, emphasises the centrality of the economic, or a *Weberian view* which looks more at class, status and power and is hence multidimensional.

Marx: the economic position

Karl Marx defined class in terms of those who own the means of production and those who do not (with a residual class in between). Any Marxist definition of class must give a priority to the ownership of capital and patterns of work. Thus, the leading North American class theorist Erik Olin Wright (1985, 1992) elaborated on Marx's model by dividing ownership into three categories: those *controlling resource allocation*; those *controlling the means of production*; and those *controlling labour power*. Wright defines all low-level employees as working-class, and suggests that the rest in the middle occupy a contradictory position in which they may identify either with the capitalists or the working classes. Others break down Marx's original distinctions further into six (Warner and Lunt, 1941) or even seven (Coleman and Rainwater, 1978) categories. The separation of management and 'capital', and the failure of radical class consciousness to emerge among working people, have made such class definitions difficult to translate into numbers we can meaningfully measure and compare.

Weber: the multidimensional position

Other scholars endorse Max Weber's contention that, rather than clear-cut classes, people are ranked in a multidimensional status hierarchy. Those elaborating on Weber often examine socio-economic status (SES) as a composite measure of social position. This can involve class, status and power, embracing work, wealth and income, status dimensions (lifestyle), consciousness and identity as well as where a person stands politically.

This is clearly a complex equation; and such definitions run into many problems because of the relatively low level of status consistency in societies.

Especially around the middle of hierarchies, ranking on one dimension may often contradict one's position on another. A government official, for example, may have the power to administer a multimillion-pound budget, yet earn only a modest personal income. Similarly, members of the clergy typically enjoy ample prestige but only moderate power and low pay.

Perhaps most commonly, class these days is defined through people's *work situation* (their work tasks and the degree of control they have over their working timetables and methods) and *market situation* (people's life chances, which depend upon such things as their income and opportunity for promotion). John Scott (1997), for example, breaks down capitalist classes into three types: entrepreneurs, who own and control their own businesses; internal capitalists (top career managers); and finance capitalists, who own and manage big finance companies and big business (Scott, 1997).

Some dimensions of class and social inequality in the UK

Income

A first important dimension of inequality involves **income**, *occupational wages or salaries and earnings from investments*. In April 2003, the average gross weekly pay of full-time earners was £476, but there were huge discrepancies within this. Those involved in computing, software consultancy and radio and television earned between £690 and £770 per week, while those in the hotel industry earned an average of £288 per week (64 per cent earning less than £6 an hour). In 2003, women's hourly earnings were less – 82 per cent those of men (though in 1986 the hourly earnings were 74 per cent that of men, so there has been a change). If one had a degree, then average earnings were much higher. There were also regional differences. In the City of London pay averages were much higher than those found in parts of Wales, Scotland and Cornwall (*Social Trends*, 2004: 74–77). A national minimum wage came into being in April 1999, set initially at £3.60/70 for those aged 22 and over (£3.00/20 for those aged 18–21). It was raised to £4.10 in 2001, and to £4.85 and £4.10 in 2004 (www.lowpay.gov.uk/). Table 10.1 gives an idea of hourly pay rates in the UK.

At the same time, in 2000 there were some 200,000 millionaires in the UK (in 1997 there were 120,000 so this suggests significant growth!). This is one in every 480 people. What is suggested here is that as some people are getting significantly richer, many others are on very low wages and getting poorer. It is not just that actual incomes

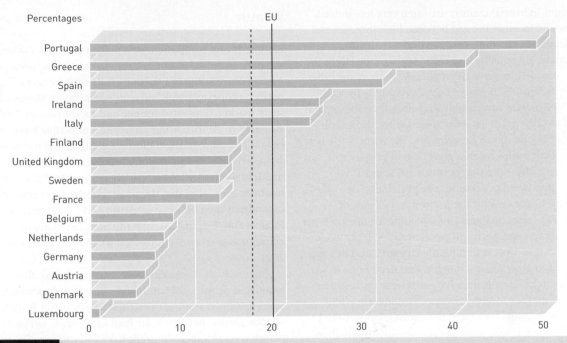

Percentages

EU

Portugal	
Greece	
Spain	
Ireland	
Italy	
Finland	
United Kingdom	
Sweden	
France	
Belgium	
Netherlands	
Germany	
Austria	
Denmark	
Luxembourg	

0   10   20   30   40   50

Figure 10.1   **Percentage of people with incomes[1] below 60 per cent of the median: EU comparison, 2000**

[1]Equivalised disposable income in each country.

Source: European Community Household Panel, Eurostat in *Social Trends*, 2004: 85

Table 10.1   Distribution of hourly earnings[1]: by industry, April 2003

Great Britain	Percentage				
	Less than £6	£6 but less than £8	£8 but less than £10	£10 but less than £12	£12 and over
Hotels and restaurants	64	18	8	4	6
Wholesale and retail trade	41	24	12	7	16
Agriculture, hunting, forestry and fishing	38	37	12	5	7
Health and social work	22	23	15	13	28
Real estate, renting and business activities	22	18	13	9	37
Construction	8	23	23	16	29
Education	20	18	13	9	39
Manufacturing	13	22	20	14	31
Transport, storage and communication	10	28	23	12	27
Public administration and defence	7	22	19	16	36
Financial intermediation	5	20	18	11	46
Mining, quarrying, electricity, gas and water supplies	4	15	17	19	44
Other services	28	23	15	9	25
All industries[2]	22	22	16	11	30

[1] Both full- and part-time employees on adult rates, including overtime payments, whose gross hourly earnings were less than £100 and whose pay for the survey period was unaffected by absence.

[2] Includes employees with no industry code.

Source: New Earnings Survey, Office for National Statistics

in a major industrial country are often very low indeed, but also the fact that the gap between high incomes and low incomes is growing. This gap bodes badly for concerns about equality and class. Again in the UK in the 1980s, inequalities were growing faster than in any other country in the OECD except New Zealand. By the early 1990s growth was more stable, but since then the gap has started to grow again. As we will see below, the Joseph Rowntree Foundation's Research and the work of the Low Income Unit both suggest a great deal of poverty still exists in the UK. Note that between 1979 and 1992, income *grew* by 36 per cent for the population as a whole, yet *fell* by 17 per cent for the poorest 10 per cent of people. Between 1983 and 1993, income for the top 5 per cent of earners *rose* nearly 50 per cent to £550 per week; for the bottom 5 per cent it hardly changed, and this gap continues to grow today. Note too that nearly one in ten households in Great Britain have no current account or investments. (See Joseph Rowntree Foundation, 1999; *Social Trends*, 2001; Low Income Commission website.)

While the UK may have less income inequality than, say, Venezuela, Kenya or Sri Lanka, income inequality in these countries is higher than in many other industrial societies. Figures 10.1 and 10.2 show some selected countries and the proportion living in poverty (see also Chapter 9).

Wealth

Income is one component of a person's **wealth**, *the total value of money and other assets, minus outstanding debts.* Assets contributing to wealth include such items as houses, property, jewels, cars, artworks, boats, shares in a stock market, deposited money and racehorses. As Table 10.2 shows, an increasing proportion of people have an expanding share of the national wealth. While the richest 1 per cent of Britons controlled 69 per cent of the national wealth in 1911, today they control 20 per cent. It has been estimated that the most wealthy 1 per cent of individuals own between one-fifth and a quarter of the total wealth. By contrast, half the population share between them 6 per cent of total wealth (*Social Trends*, 2001: 109).

Even though the wealth base has broadened, the wealthiest people still command considerable resources. Some examples among the richest 25 people in Britain include the former Beatle Sir Paul McCartney, whose personal wealth in 2004 exceeded £760 million; Sir Richard Branson (the entrepreneur who founded the various Virgin companies – his story is told in Branson, 1998), with a personal fortune estimated at between £2 billion and £3 billion; and the Duke of Westminster, wielding wealth of £5 billion. Such wealth gives the

Table 10.2	Distribution of wealth in the UK, spring 2001						
United Kingdom	Percentages						
	1976	1986	1991	1996	1999	2000	2001
Marketable wealth							
Percentage of wealth owned by[1]							
Most wealthy 1%	21	18	17	20	23	22	23
Most wealthy 5%	38	36	3	40	43	42	43
Most wealthy 10%	50	50	47	52	55	55	56
Most wealthy 25%	71	73	71	74	74	74	75
Most wealthy 50%	92	90	92	93	94	94	95
Total marketable wealth (£ billion)	280	955	1,711	2,092	2,842	3,093	3,363
Marketable wealth less value of dwellings							
Percentage of wealth owned by[1]							
Most wealthy 1%	29	25	29	26	34	32	33
Most wealthy 5%	47	46	51	49	59	58	58
Most wealthy 10%	57	58	64	63	72	72	72
Most wealthy 25%	73	75	80	81	86	88	86
Most wealthy 50%	88	89	93	94	98	98	97

[1] Adults aged 18 and over

Source: *Social Trends*, 2001: 109

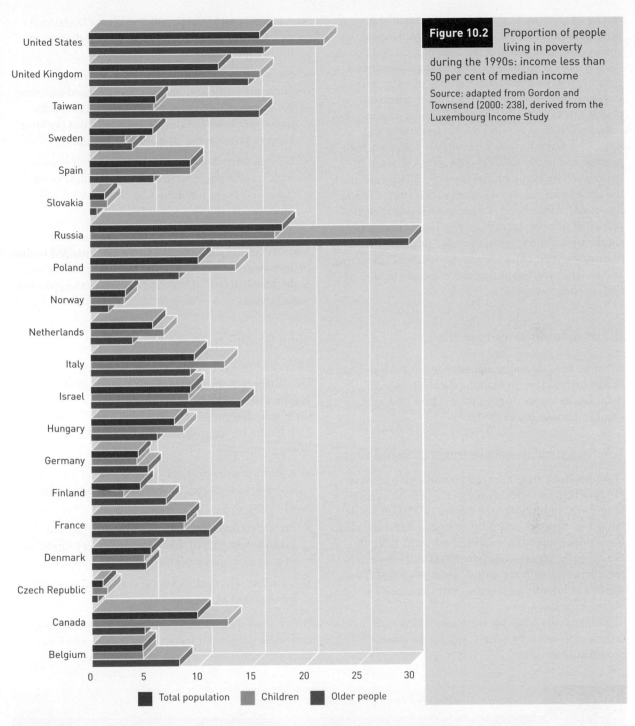

Figure 10.2 Proportion of people living in poverty during the 1990s: income less than 50 per cent of median income

Source: adapted from Gordon and Townsend (2000: 238), derived from the Luxembourg Income Study

■ Total population   ■ Children   ■ Older people

mega-rich considerable influence, from the field of national politics – in Italy, the media entrepreneur Silvio Berlusconi had amassed some £5.4 billion in 2004 and was also the Prime Minister (*Sunday Times* Rich List 2004) – to minor business transactions. The super-rich also tend to reinforce and protect each other's interests. As John Scott notes, the elite 0.1 per cent of industrial populations often share similar backgrounds, swap

directorships of high-performing companies, and are dominant shareholders in the leading businesses.

Prestige

For more than half a century, sociologists have assessed **prestige**, or *the value people in a society associate with* *various occupations.* In general, people attach high prestige to occupations such as medicine, law and engineering that also generate high income. But prestige reflects more than just pay, since favoured occupations typically require considerable ability and demand extensive education and training. By contrast, less prestigious work, such as that of a cleaner or porter, not only pays less but usually requires less ability and schooling. Nevertheless, as previously discussed, high prestige and high income do not always go hand in hand. Even so, occupational prestige rankings are much the same in all industrial societies (Ma, 1987; Lin and Xie, 1988). Almost everywhere, more highly ranked work that involves mental activity, free from extensive supervision, confers greater prestige than lower-class occupations that require supervised manual labour. In any society, privileged categories of people tend to fill high-prestige occupations.

Class measurements in the UK

So far we have looked at a number of variables and issues in identifying class. To examine the challenges of defining class more directly, we will now look at three classifications in use in the UK.

The Registrar General's Index of Social Class

This provided a straightforward classification of social classes which was widely used in the twentieth century. Originally introduced in the Census of 1911, this scale ranked occupations and skills of similar social standing, from 'professionals' to 'unskilled manuals'. Table 10.3 illustrates the six categories in this scale. It ceased to be used, however, with the arrival of the new NS-SEC scale which was introduced into the 2001 Census and which is discussed below.

Although the index has been very widely used, it does bring a great many problems. Among the most prominent have been:

- A huge chunk of the population is now in classes 3a and 3b, mainly because of occupational changes in the twentieth century.

- Pay scales and prestige within the same category are often quite different, or again have changed over time. For example, those in class 1 may earn £12,000 (a junior university lecturer) or £400,000 plus (a major lawyer). It makes the category nonsensical.

- Women were allocated class based on their nearest male relative (large numbers of women now work; there were fewer when the 1911 classification was introduced).

For these and other reasons, in the latter part of the twentieth century, sociologists in the UK struggled to find better measurements such as the Essex University Class Scale (Marshall *et al.*, 1988) and the Surrey Occupational Scale (1986).

John Goldthorpe's modification

John Goldthorpe, one of the most prominent of British class analysts of the late twentieth century, modified the Registrar General's scale. Goldthorpe groups workers into three main categories of work, and further subdivides each group. He suggests that there are the following broad groupings.

- A *service class* made up of (a) professional and managerial workers; (b) supervisors of non-manual workers.

- An *intermediate class* made up of (a) routine non-manual workers; (b) small proprietors; (c) supervisors of manual workers; (d) lower-grade technicians.

- A *working class* made up of (a) skilled; (b) semi-skilled; (c) unskilled manual workers.

Such a 'class scale' makes allowances for three factors that determine the general social power people gain from their occupation: prestige, income and wealth.

Table 10.3		The twentieth-century Registrar General scale categories	
Class	**Letter**	**Name of class**	**Examples**
1	A	Professional	Solicitors, accountants, surgeons, university lecturers
2	B	Managerial and technical	Managers, teachers, nurses
3a	C1	Skilled non-manual	Estate agents, secretaries, sales clerks
3b	C2	Skilled manual/craft	Bricklayers, electricians, drivers
4	D	Partly skilled manual	Postal carriers, pub/bar staff
5	E	Unskilled manual	Cleaners, labourers

THE PARADE OF CLASS

Imagine an hour-long parade of people with heights matched to income. What a parade it would be! For more than 25 minutes, all the toddlers and 'vertically challenged' would march by. Three-quarters of an hour would pass before we saw people of average height or taller. Suddenly, for the last minute we would be stunned to see people who would be 20 metres or so tall. Then in the final seconds, huge, colossal figures start to emerge, their heads lost in the clouds. Just a few massive people, and yet such vast numbers of small ones. One of the world's richest men, John Paul Getty, could stand as tall as 10 miles (Goodman *et al.*, 1997).

This is an example of the colourful language used in several recent reports on inequality. It makes a point. More prosaically, we can say that most Western societies are characterised by extremes of inequality: huge numbers with low incomes and a few with large incomes. But statistics conceal the experiences. At one end there is the life of luxury – a level of wealth that most of us can only imagine. But at the other extremes are what sociologist Richard Sennett has called 'the hidden injuries of class'. These are the deep scars often thrust upon a life because of no work or demeaning work over which one has little control; because of poor housing or no housing; because money is tight and there are no assets; and, maybe worst of all, a deep sense of being outside society, at the bottom of the heap.

The National Statistics Socio-Economic Classification (NS-SEC)

This is a more recent classification system. It was announced in December 1998 and was used for the first time in a major way in the UK Census in 2001.

It draws upon a number of features from the Goldthorpe scale above. Instead of just ranking occupations, it highlights (a) job security, (b) promotion opportunity, and (c) ability and opportunity to work on one's own and make decisions. It is shown in Table 10.4.

Table 10.4	Eight-, five- and three-class versions of the NS-SEC scale, and their nested relationship	
Eight classes	**Five classes**	**Three classes**
1 Higher managerial and professional occupations 1.1 Large employers and higher managerial occupations 1.2 Higher professional occupations 2 Lower managerial and professional occupations	1 Managerial and professional occupations	1 Higher occupations
3 Intermediate occupations 4 Small employers and own account workers	2 Intermediate occupations 3 Small employers and own account workers	2 Intermediate occupations
5 Lower supervisory and technical occupations 6 Semi-routine occupations 7 Routine occupations	4 Lower supervisory and technical occupations 5 Semi-routine and routine occupations	3 Lower occupations
8 Never worked and long-term unemployed	Never worked and long-term unemployed	Never worked and long-term unemployed

Note: The number of classes used depends upon both the analytical purposes at hand and the quality of available data.

Source: adapted from Office for National Statistics

Layers of social class in the UK

Goran Therborn has suggested that *social class is one of the key defining features of modern Europe*, as Europe was the first major arena of industrialisation. More than anywhere in the world, class is to be found here (1995: 68). Europe as a whole, he contends, first experienced the rise of a manual working class through the industrialisation period, followed much more recently by a decline in this section of the population. Nowadays, 'less than a third of the economically active population is engaged in industrial labour' (1995: 76), marking the shrinking size of the working-class population.

Yet, all main political parties in the UK, at least rhetorically, claim to want to create conditions for upward social mobility – a world where we all can 'make it'. Indeed, both of the last two Conservative Prime Ministers, John Major and Margaret Thatcher, came from 'humble' origins: he, the son of a circus acrobat and garden gnome salesman; she, the daughter of a grocer from Grantham.

There are various ways of visualising class patterns. Most conventionally, the class structure is seen as a ladder – here the steps suggest mobility as people move upwards. More often it is seen as a pyramid. Here the base would be a large working class, a smaller middle class, and a tiny upper class. But recent class studies suggest this is not an adequate image. It may be better to see it through the image of a rugby ball – with a large middle class in the centre and smaller working and upper classes at the ends. The middle class accounts for around 45–50 per cent of Western European societies – and has grown as traditional manual occupations decline (Edye and Lintner, 1996: 108): Figure 10.3 suggests this.

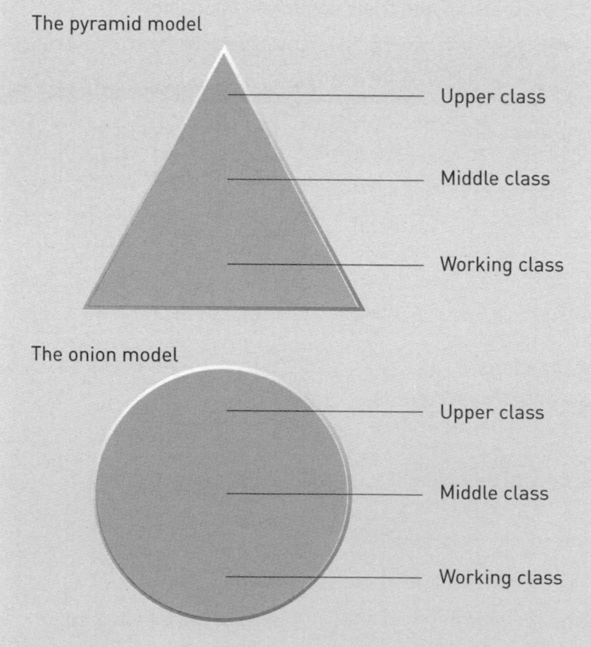

Europe remains highly stratified. Not only do the rich have controlling stakes in most businesses, they also benefit from the most schooling, enjoy the best health care, and consume the greatest share of almost all goods and services (Scott, 1991). Such privileges contrast sharply with unemployment throughout much of Europe, and the poverty of millions of people who struggle from day to day simply to buy food and keep a roof over their heads.

Sociologists have long debated just what social class is, and we have enountered some of these debates in Chapter 8. Some are very theoretical – building on the ideas of Marx and Weber developed in the last chapter. Some adopt the large-scale survey approach – attempting to measure 'classes'. Still others provide descriptive case studies. We will look at some of this research as we go along. In what follows, we will show some of the major ways class has been measured, discuss broad features of different classes and consider whether people are generally moving between classes. We will not, however, be concerned with the detailed complexities of the debates. It will be sufficient for our purposes to provide the broadest contours.

Runciman (1990) has produced such a map. He has documented that the approximate proportions of people at the different levels of the British class structure are as shown in Table 10.5. In the next sections, we will examine some of these distinctions and groups.

Figure 10.3   The shapes of class

Table 10.5	The possible shapes of class	
Upper class	0.2–0.1%	
Lower upper class	less than 10%	
	Upper class	
Upper middle and service class	15%	
Lower middle class	20%	Middle class
Skilled working class	20%	
Unskilled working class	30%	Working class
Underclass	5%	Underclass

Source: adapted from Runciman (1990)

The upper classes

In industrialised countries, the upper classes make up anything from 5 to 10 per cent of the populations, and include a small cadre of the super-rich (around 0.2 per cent). Traditionally, the upper classes have been linked to old aristocratic traditions and to significant ownership of property (especially land). But this 'old' money is increasingly being joined by 'new' money. We might distinguish two groups: the upper-uppers and the lower-uppers.

Upper-uppers

Membership of the upper-upper class is almost always the result of ascription or birth. In much of Europe, many large landed estates have passed from generation to generation for centuries. The British aristocracy owns 40 per cent of British land: with the monarch at the head, they include dukes, marquesses, earls and viscounts. These families possess enormous wealth, primarily inherited rather than earned. Most of them have *old money*. Set apart by their wealth, members of the upper-upper class live in a world of exclusive affiliations. Children typically attend private schools with others of similar background, completing their formal education at high-prestige colleges and universities.

Lower-uppers

Most upper-class people actually fall into the *lower-upper class*. From most people's point of view, this group is every bit as privileged as the upper-upper class. The major difference, however, is that lower-uppers are the 'working rich' who depend on earnings rather than inherited wealth as the primary source of their income. They include what we have come to call the 'fat cats', whose incomes often rise to extraordinary heights. The lower-upper class also includes 'the jet-set rich' – the very visible and very famous, such as the footballer who accepts a million-pound contract to play in the First Division; the computer whiz who designs a program that sets a standard for the industry; or the musician whose work tops the charts – these are the lucky and talented achievers who reach the level of the lower-upper class. Celebrities such as Elton John or Andrew Lloyd Webber are included here, but there are also the entrepreneurial rich, including such people as Richard Branson, the Guinness family (the brewers), the Sieff family (Marks & Spencers) and Anita Roddick of The Body Shop. Entrepreneurial capitalists, rentiers, executive and finance capitalists generally make the majority of their money through wise investments of stocks and bonds.

Especially in the eyes of members of 'society', the lower-upper class are merely the 'new rich' who can never savour the status enjoyed by those with rich and famous grandparents. Thus, while the new rich typically live in the biggest homes, they often find themselves excluded from the clubs and associations of old-money families.

The middle classes

The middle classes used to be the 'middle group' between poor and rich, who gained income through trade and manufacturing. Weber predicted its growth and Marx its demise. In fact, however, the middle classes have increasingly made up a larger and larger proportion of most of the class structure of Europe. Middle-class occupations have material and cultural advantages over working-class employment, generally offering more security, higher pay and higher prestige. The middle class encompasses far more racial and ethnic diversity than the upper class. While many upper-class people (especially upper-uppers) know each other personally, such exclusiveness and familiarity do not characterise the middle class. We can identify three general shades of middle class: the upper (or traditional) middle class, the service class and the lower middle class. It is a large and highly fragmented group, characterised by a great deal of lifestyle diversities (see Savage *et al.*, 1992).

The upper middle class

The more powerful end of this category, also dubbed the traditional middle class, earns above-average incomes. Family income may be even greater if both wife and husband work. High income allows upper middle-class families to gradually accumulate considerable property, a comfortable house in a fairly expensive area, several cars and investments. A majority of upper middle-class children receive university educations, and postgraduate degrees are common. Many go on to high-prestige occupations (as doctors, engineers, lawyers, accountants or business executives). Lacking the power of the upper class to influence national or international events, the upper middle class nonetheless often plays an important role in local political affairs.

The service class

The service class includes people who provide highly valued and well-paid services to employers, including middle-level bureaucrats, management of health, welfare and education services, technically trained secretaries and business consultants. This group also includes many people who work in media, teaching, fashion and therapy professions. Service-class people enjoy a lot of autonomy in their work, usually excercise and delegate authority, and tend to have secure careers (see Goldthorpe, 1982; Lash and Urry, 1987). David Lockwood (1992) further subdivides this group into professionals, who rely on cultural capital (knowledge); managers; and petty bourgeois (traders and small property owners). People in this class also tend to own property (though in less fashionable districts), to own vehicles (though less expensive models) and to have relatively high levels of education, though they are more likely to work to pull maximum advantage from state-sponsored education and to have attended second-tier colleges and universities.

The lower middle class

The rest of the middle class falls close to the centre of the class structure. People in the lower middle class typically

work in less prestigious white-collar occupations (such as bank clerks, middle managers or sales clerks) or in highly skilled blue-collar jobs (including electrical work and carpentry). Commonly, lower middle-class households earn incomes around the national average. Income at this level provides a secure, if modest, standard of living. Lower middle-class people generally accumulate some wealth over the course of their working lives, mostly in the form of a house. People in this class generally complete some post-secondary school qualifications, though not necessarily university degrees. They are sometimes seen as 'intermediate classes,' that is between the working and middle class.

The working classes

Two distinct phases have marked out the working class. What we might call *traditional* working-class life used to

VOICES

WHAT A DIFFERENCE A CLASS MAKES

Why do sociologists spend so much time talking about class? The answer is that there is little doubt that social stratification affects nearly every dimension of our lives. While class alone does not define our sense of place in society, class is one of the most significant influences on our lives. Our class status affects us objectively: that is, in our health, our education, our possessions and our lifestyle. But it also affects us *subjectively*: that is, in the way we see ourselves, our language, our values, our ideas, our 'cultural capital'. Here are a few examples of the impact of class on various aspects of life in the UK:

Infant mortality (see also Chapter 23)
Working-class children may be three times more likely to die in their first year of life than children of professional parents.

Health (see also Chapter 20)
Working-class people may be three times more likely to have long-term serious illness than people of the higher classes.

Death (see also Chapter 20 and 23)
A child of an unskilled manual worker may well die around seven years earlier than a counterpart born to professional parents.

Divorce (see Chapter 17)
The risk of divorce is four times higher among manuals than among professionals.

Education (see Chapter 19)
Just 1 per cent going to university come from the unskilled manual class, while some 78 per cent come from social class I.

Public safety (see Chapter 16)
Crime rates were lowest in affluent suburban and rural areas and highest in council estates and low-income areas.

Job security
There is much less job security for working-class occupations than for middle-class professions.

Unemployment
While around 14 per cent in social class V may be unemployed, it is much smaller in class I (around 3 per cent).

Home ownership
While some 90 per cent of professionals were owner-ocupiers, only around 40 per cent of unskilled manual workers were.

Note: The above is only a schematic and is meant only to provide a general sense that there are differences; the table does not specify years or detail. For further discussion, see the relevant chapters.

Sources: *Social Trends* (2004); Acheson (1998); Scott (2000b).

be defined in terms of strong identities based in communities associated with a particular field of labour, such as were found in traditional mining communities (Dennis *et al.*, 1956), steel communities (Beynon *et al.*, 1991), fishing communities, and so forth. But to name these communities is to sense their demise. In the UK the old coalfields around Durham or the steel furnaces blasting out around Middlesborough have gone and the fishing communities around the country are rapidly shrinking. With them went jobs, income, security and communities. After long periods of unemployment and demoralisation, some people benefit from new patterns of work that emerge. But these patterns are very different, often involving relocation and work that is much more fragmented. We have moved from work in the mine to work in McDonald's. And with that, traditional working-class communities are in steep decline.

But a new working class has also emerged. This is one that will own their own homes, live in suburbs and be more affluent, with cars and DVD players. It is even unlikely that they will see themselves as working class. Indeed, Beverley Skeggs' ethnographic research on young women from working-class backgrounds in a northern town suggests that being working class now carries a stigma and the concern is to be seen as respectable (Skeggs, 1997).

Working-class occupations generally yield a household income somewhat below the national average. Working-class families thus find themselves vulnerable to financial problems, especially when confronted by unemployment or illness. Besides generating less income, working-class jobs typically yield less personal satisfaction. Tasks tend to be routine, requiring discipline but rarely imagination, and workers are usually subject to continual supervision. Such jobs also provide fewer benefits, such as private medical insurance and pension schemes. About half of working-class families own their homes, usually in lower-cost districts.

Social exclusion and the idea of an underclass

Social exclusion

In recent years, an important new concept has entered the sociological language: that of social exclusion. The term probably has its origins in France, *'les exclus'* (the excluded) being those who fell though the net of social protection in the 1970s – lone parents, disabled, the uninsured unemployed (Burchard, 2000: 385). It is related in part to ideas of the underclass, as it highlights people being cut off from the mainstream of society. It has been used both in the United Nations (where it highlights a lack of access to the basic institutions of civil society, a lack of citizenship) and in Europe, where it has been widely adopted. In the UK, the Social Exclusion Unit (SEU) was set up under the 1997 Labour government and has focused on specific groups, such as street homeless and pregnant teenagers.

The novel *Angela's Ashes* depicts the harrowing childhood of Frank McCourt in the 1930s and 1940s in Limerick, Ireland. Later turned into a film, the starkness of poverty is dramatically conveyed – the overcrowded and basic housing, the lack of sanitation, the deprivation of food. Such stark poverty has often been depicted in literature.

Source: Ronald Grant Archive

There have been several attempts to chart the main indicators of social exclusion. The Rowntree/New Policy Institute has developed a substantial listing – embracing income, children, young adults, adults and the elderly, and whole communities (Gordon and Townsend, 2000: 367). The Institute for Public Policy Research (IPPR) highlights exclusion over four domains – income poverty, exclusion from the labour market, exclusion in education, and health. The Poverty and Social Exclusion (PSE) Survey distinguishes four dimensions of exclusion: impoverishment, or exclusion from adequate income or resources; labour market exclusion; service exclusion; and exclusion from social relations. Perhaps the tightest model is contained in Table 10.6, which clusters social exclusion under four main dimensions.

Table 10.6	Dimensions of social exclusion
Dimension	**Indicator**
Consumption	Low income
Production	Not engaged in valued activity, e.g. work, caring
Political engagement	Does not vote and not part of any organisation
Social interaction	Lacks emotional support

Source: adapted from Burchardt (2001: 391)

The underclass

The **underclass** is a more difficult term. For some sociologists, it comprises those people *'under the class structure', those who are economically, politically and socially marginalised and excluded*. Typically, these people live between unemployment and the labour market of casual and temporary work. They usually live on state benefits or charitable aid. Encompassing the frail pensioners, the single 'trapped' parents and the long-term unemployed, they are in a sense 'outside' the system of work and even class! In 1987, Dahrendorf estimated that about 5 per cent of the British population fell within the underclass – and that this percentage was growing rapidly.

The idea of an underclass has a long and controversial history. Marx spoke of the *lumpenproletariat* (the social scum of vagrants, misfits, dregs). Booth (1901–02),

Rowntree (1902) and Mayhew (1861) described the 'dangerous classes' of 'paupers, beggars and outcasts with a repugnance to regular labour'. There is a long history of distinguishing undeserving, disreputable poor from 'respectable' people trapped in a 'cycle of deprivation' (Morris, 1994). This is discussed in the Controversy and Debate box 'Blaming the poor' on page 263. All these writings point to a heavily stigmatised group at the bottom of the heap, excluded from work, living in dire poverty. The least generous observers suspect the underclass of turning to crime and, as we shall discuss more later, this view often associates racial and underclass issues.

The American sociologist Charles Murray has been a recent champion of the idea of 'underclass'. Looking at the United States, in his book *Losing Ground* (1984) he charted what he saw as the failure of welfare policies, where he argued that more and more people had become dependent on the state. In the late 1980s he brought these ideas to the UK and they became serialised in *The Sunday Times* (26 November 1989). For Murray, this underclass lived in a different world, raised its children differently and had different values. He pondered: 'How is a civilised society to take care of the deserving without encouraging people to become undeserving? How does it do good without engendering vice?'

In Europe, the problem of the underclass is often linked to problems of migration. Workers who cannot find work in their own countries want to go to others where work may be found. But in this process – as new arrivals, often with different ethnic backgrounds – all they can find is casual work. Algerians in France, Turks in Germany, Moroccans in Spain and Bangladeshis in the UK often confront both formal and informal barriers against their entering the regular labour market. People who have illegally joined family and friends in the European Union face an even more tenuous position, as they cannot even apply for benefits to meet basic needs. The drive for daily survival focuses the attention of underclass people more on the present. Without much prospect of work, people in the underclass live on the margins of society.

Although many people experience the conditions implied by the term 'underclass', the academic use of this term is problematic. 'Underclass' is often used as an abusive 'catch all' phrase that lumps together many different kinds of experience, and then proceeds to stigmatise them. It is the most recent term – in a long line – for blaming the poor for their poverty. So sociologists have to be very careful how they come to use it.

Poverty: the lower ends of inequality in capitalist society

Sociologists address the concept of poverty in two different ways. **Relative poverty** refers to *the deprivation of some people in relation to those who have more*. Relative poverty is universal and unavoidable; even a rich society has some members who live in relative poverty. It depends on the values and standards of living that a particular society sets; those falling below it are 'poor'. In contrast, absolute poverty is a deprivation of resources that is life threatening. It depends upon a universally agreed minimum for adequate nutrition and living. Much of the poverty we discussed in the previous chapter – the lives of perhaps 800 million people, one in seven of the earth's entire population – is like this.

Yet even in Europe, one of the most affluent regions in the whole world, as defined by its Gross Domestic Product (GDP), people still go hungry, become homeless, live in poor housing and endure poor health because of the wrenching reality of poverty.

Measuring poverty

Some of the earliest attempts to measure poverty were conducted in Britain in the latter part of the nineteenth century. Aware of the shocking conditions brought about through rapid industrialisation in major cities such as Manchester and London, the philanthropist and businessman Charles Booth set about a door-to-door survey in large areas of London, enumerating the numbers of people occupying each dwelling and measuring poverty in terms of their income. Poverty, for Booth, was taken to be absolute and objective: it was the amount of money people had to live on. If it fell below a certain breadline of nutritional needs, it meant that people were poor.

A little later, Seebohm Rowntree conducted three surveys between 1899 and 1951 in the city of York and concluded in the last study that poverty had more or less been eradicated in the UK by 1951. He defined absolute poverty in subsistence terms: 'nothing must be bought but that which is absolutely necessary for the maintenance of physical health and what is bought must

(a)

(b)

(a) Doré's London in Victorian times; (b) New York: keeping warm is always a problem to those living in the street and fashionable Fifth Avenue is no different. With her legs wrapped in newspaper, a woman enjoys the warmth from the grating. The fashions in the window have little meaning for her.

Source: (a) Plate from Dore: A London Pilgrimage; (b) © Pat Benic/Bettmann/Corbis

be of the plainest and most economical description'. Subsequent researchers developed more sophisticated modes of measurement (see Scott, 1994, for an excellent review of the work of Booth and Rowntree).

Since the mid-1950s, poverty in the UK has been studied by Peter Townsend, who defines it as 'the lack of the resources necessary to permit participation in the activities, customs and diets commonly approved by society' (Townsend, 1979: 81). After a major survey, using a national random sample, Townsend concluded that poverty and deprivation almost certainly begin to occur at a level which is over 50 per cent above the official government definition of poverty for means-tested social assistance rates. Social assistance rates are fixed by governments at minimum levels; Townsend and many subsequent researchers see this as far too low and basic, failing to take into account the relative need for 'participation' in a society.

A little later, Mack and Lansley took Townsend's ideas of relative poverty one step further. For a television series called *Breadline Britain*, they investigated the 'British standard of living' by conducting a public opinion poll. They asked people what they regarded were necessary for a good standard of living. Then, documenting the level of missing necessities experienced by a national quota sample of over 1,000 people (see Table 10.7), they defined the poor as those 'excluded from the way of life that most people take for granted' (Mack and Lansley, 1985: 15). They found that the number of poor people,

especially children, increased in Britain between 1983 and 1990.

The Mack and Lansley approach consistently moves the poverty line upwards over time, as expectations of living standards shift (Table 10.7). These days, for instance, students increasingly need computers for their work. You might ask yourself whether a student who is unable to afford to buy a computer is poor. This approach has recently been developed further and applied across Europe (Gordon and Townsend, 2000).

Given the complexities of these more sophisticated sociological approaches, it is most common, these days, for poverty to be measured relatively through income. Until 1987, poverty was measured as living below whatever was the government's current supplementary benefit level. (It moves under various names in various countries. Currently, in the UK it is the income support level.) Nowadays, below-average income is the most common measure.

The extent of poverty

The extent of poverty in the UK

Given the complexities of measuring poverty, estimates of it are notoriously variable. Indeed, the UK Conservative governments of 1979–97 more or less tried to ignore poverty by arguing that 'officially poverty does not exist in Britain. The government does not define a poverty

Table 10.7	Mack and Lansley's 'lack of necessities' as a poverty measure				
1983			**1990**		
Necessity		Percentage of households unable to afford	Necessity		Percentage of households unable to afford
1	Holiday	21	1	Regular savings	30
2	Two pairs of shoes	9	2	Holiday	20
3	Meat or fish every other day	8	3	Decent decoration	15
4	Hobby	7	4	Outing for children	14
4	Damp-free house	7	5	Insurance	10
4	Warm coat	7	5	Out-of-school activities	10
4	Weekly roast	7	7	Separate bedrooms	7
8	Leisure equipment for children	6	7	Hobby	7
8	New clothes	6	7	Telephone	7
8	Washing machines	6	10	Best outfit	8
			10	Entertaining of children's friends	8

Source: adapted from Frayman (1991: 6), reprinted in Scott (1994)

line. It argues that an objective definition is impossible, that any attempt to count the poor is doomed because it will depend on the subjective definitions of experts about what it is to be poor' (Frayman, 1991: 2). Disturbingly, this is the same period when most commentators argue that poverty, inequality and social exclusion soared in the UK (Walker and Walker, 1997).

Yet it is certainly true that 'poverty figures' can be quite wide-ranging. Rowntree in 1950 found only 1.5 per cent of York living in poverty, but he was applying very strict absolute standards. Under the more lenient relative standards of recent times, poverty is found to be anywhere between a tenth and a third of the population. Thus, Townsend's major study of 1969 (published in 1979) found that 21.8 per cent of the population were below 140 per cent of the Supplementary Benefit line, and 22.9 per cent below his deprivation standard. More recently, in 1993, the Low Pay Unit estimated that a third of the population lived in poverty; the OECD suggested there were 12 million poor in the UK (a quarter of Europe's 50 million living in poverty); and 10 per cent of people claimed income support (5.6 million people) (Skellington, 1996: 105–111).

When the Labour government came to power in 1997, it set itself a series of major targets to radically reduce relative poverty. By the end of 1999, the Rowntree study suggested that around a quarter (26 per cent) of the British population were living in poverty (as measured in terms of low income and multiple deprivation necessities). Table 10.8 shows the proportion of adults found to be lacking some basic necessities in 1999. Since that time, however, poverty in general has been slowly falling through such measures as a national minimum wage, working families tax credit, pension credit and winter fuel payments. In 2003, the Joseph Rowntree Foundation could declare:

Between 1996/7 and 2000/1 relative poverty fell, largely as a result of improvement in employment rates and in the level of some benefits. Overall, poverty fell by about one million, including about half a million fewer children in poverty. … The effect of policy changes introduced between 1997 and 2003/4 would [probably] reduce child poverty by about 1.3 million children, other things being equal. Pensioner poverty showed little change between 1996/7 and 2001, but a susbstantial reduction between 2001 and 2003/4.

(Joseph Rowntree Foundation, 2003: 1; Sutherland *et al.*, 2003)

Poverty in Europe

In the *European Union*, poverty and social exclusion has generally been rising, despite a series of programmes to combat it. In 1975, it was recorded at some 38 million, but by the 1990s it was being registered at some 50 million. It involves roughly 15 per cent of the European population. Usually, it is measured as those with per capita incomes below 50 per cent of the national average.

Poverty does not affect all European countries equally. Three clusters of countries have been identified:

- Higher levels of poverty: Greece, Ireland, Portugal, Spain and the UK
- Average levels of poverty: France, Italy
- Lower levels of poverty: Belgium, Denmark, Germany, The Netherlands (Bernt Schulte, in Funken and Cooper, 1995: 127).

A note on poverty in the United States

The *United States*, despite being one of the richest nations on earth, has a very high level of relative poverty. In 2001, the government counted 32.9 million men, women and

---

Table 10.8	Proportion of adults found to be lacking some basic necessities in 1999

- Roughly 9.5 million people in Britain lacked adequate housing conditions.
- About 8 million could not afford one or more essential household goods.
- Almost 7.5 million people were too poor to engage in common social activities considered necessary by the majority of the population.
- About 2 million British children went without at least two things they needed.
- About 6.5 million adults went without essential clothing.
- Around 4 million were not properly fed.
- Over 10.5 million suffered from financial insecurity.
- One in six people (17%) considered themselves and their families to be living in 'absolute poverty' as defined by the United Nations.

Source: adapted from Gordon and Townsend (2000) and Joseph Rowntree Foundation (1999)

children – 11.7 per cent of the population – as poor. The typical poor family had to get by on about $11,000 in 2001. Official poverty rates fell during the 1960s but have stayed much the same since then (US Bureau of the Census, 2002).

Who are the poor?

Although no single description covers all poor people, poverty is pronounced among certain categories of the population. In particular, it is likely to hit people who are disadvantaged in other ways: low-wage earners, the unemployed, disabled people. Here we will briefly focus on five groups: children, the elderly, ethnic groups, women and the disabled are all at high risk of being poor. Where these categories overlap, the problem of poverty is especially serious.

Age: children and the elderly

A generation ago, the elderly were at greatest risk of poverty. They still remain at risk, but studies now conclude that a 'new poverty' has emerged among the young and children. In the UK, the numbers of elderly needing assistance fell from 1.8 million in 1974 to 1.4 million in 1991. Today, the burden of poverty falls most heavily on children. Thus, numbers of children under 16 needing assistance in the UK rose from 800,000 in 1974 to 2.3 million in 1991. Ten per cent of children live below the poverty line (Funken and Cooper, 1995: 12).

The Rowntree study suggested that the poverty rates of children were higher among those:

- in households without any workers
- in lone-parent families
- with a larger number of siblings
- with household members suffering a long-standing illness
- of non-white ethnicity
- living in local authority housing
- in households in receipt of Job Seeker's Allowance or Income Support.

The same story is true in much of the rest of Europe (Figure 10.4). In the United States, it is even more extreme. In 2001, 16.3 per cent of people under the age of 18 were poor (11.7 million children). Thus, roughly four in ten of the US poor are children under the age of 18 (US Census Bureau, 2002).

Race and ethnicity

Studies also strongly suggest that 'mutiple deprivations' affect ethnic minorities, leading to significantly higher levels of poverty. The Joseph Rowntree Foundation's (1995) study of poverty in the UK was 'particularly concerned . . . at what is happening to the non-white population'. One in three of the non-white population was in the poorest fifth of the population. Most significant here were alarming rates of unemployment (worst of all among people of Pakistani and Bangladeshi

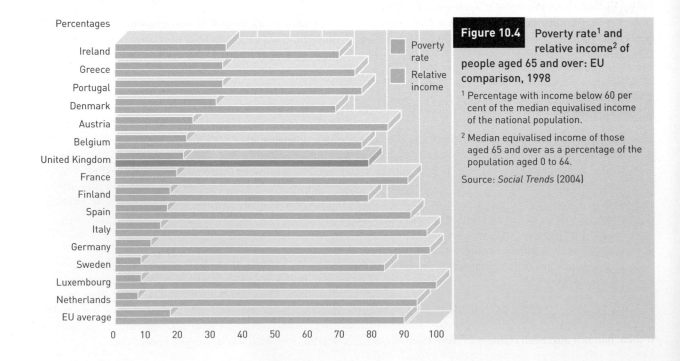

Figure 10.4 Poverty rate[1] and relative income[2] of people aged 65 and over: EU comparison, 1998

[1] Percentage with income below 60 per cent of the median equivalised income of the national population.

[2] Median equivalised income of those aged 65 and over as a percentage of the population aged 0 to 64.

Source: *Social Trends* (2004)

origin) and the difficulties of ethnic women and children, not least Afro-Caribbean single-parent families. Many of these groups were contributing to an emerging underclass (see above). Recent work by Lucinda Platt (2002) suggests little change.

Ethnicity is important across the world when looking at poverty. In the United States, for example, in absolute numbers, two-thirds of all poor people are white. But in relation to their overall numbers, African Americans are about three times as likely as white people to be poor. In 2001, 22.7 per cent of African Americans (8.1 million people) lived in poverty, compared to 21.4 per cent of Latinos (8 million), 10.2 per cent of Asians and Pacific Islanders (1.3 million), and 7.8 per cent of non-Hispanic white people (15.3 million). Thirty per cent of African American children are poor (US Census Bureau, 2002).

Gender and family patterns

The term **feminisation of poverty** describes *the trend by which women represent an increasing proportion of the poor*. Peter Townsend (1987) has identified four groups of women that make up the 'female poor':

- single (including divorced) women with children
- elderly women pensioners
- 'carers' who look after children or other dependents
- women with low earnings.

This *feminisation of poverty* is part of a larger change: the rapidly increasing number of households – at all class levels – headed by single women. This trend, coupled with the fact that households headed by women are at high risk of poverty, explains why women (and their children) represent an increasing share of the European poor. Black women appear in all these categories, and for them poverty becomes even more likely (see Glendenning and Millar, 1992).

Disablement

Disabled people may be severely affected by poverty. Often they have been excluded from the routine activities of everyday life – they may be less likely to have (well paid) employment. They usually have lower average income levels and in addition have to meet the 'extra costs' of impairment (Townsend, 1979; Barnes *et al.*, 1999: 134).

The 'Death of Class' debate

The past 50 years have seen so many changes in the socio-economic environment that it would be surprising if there had not also been changes in the nature of class.

Sociologists have for a long time disagreed about both its importance and how it should be studied. While some argue that 'class remains the sociological key to understanding the structure of society' (Scott, 1994: 19), others have contended that 'class as a concept is ceasing to do any useful work for sociology' (Pahl, 1989). Which is it?

The end of class?

Some sociologists argue that we have become more and more of a classless society and that the concept of class cannot incorporate the scope of the changes that are happening in the (post)modern world. It is not a question of whether inequalities persist – all agree that they do (and many suggest they are widening). But it is often more a matter of whether and how these inequalities can be traced back to class as *the* key issue.

For instance, as we have previously seen, in so much early sociology, women were excluded. Much of 'class theory' naively ignored gender, and much of it may well therefore be misconceived. Certainly, bringing women into the picture shifts the focus of class questions, such as how child-bearing, child-rearing, and 'domestic labour' and housework fit into the labour structure. Moreover, women as a group generally earn less than men – even at comparable levels of education and experience. While overt sex discrimination is illegal in the European Union (as well as in most other industrialised countries), women remain more likely to be 'ghettoised' into lower-paid occupations such as social work, auxiliary nursing, child care and routine secretarial roles (see Chapter 12 for further details). All this means, at the very least, that gender has to be an important factor in understanding inequality. And, as we shall see in the next chapter, the same can also be said of ethnicity.

One (ex?) Marxist, André Gortz (1982), significantly called his book *Farewell to the Working Class*. If class is seen as primarily economic, involving some sense of class awareness and consciousness, and if it is seen as an important force for bringing about social change, then critics argue it has clearly declined in significance. Thus, the power (or lack of it) linked to different groups and social movements – ethnic groups, the disabled, women, the elderly, etc. – has become much more prominent. Matters of consumption and lifestyle have become more and more important in people's lives. The role of new social movements in bringing about social change (see Chapter 15) also now seems more important generally than class in shaping change (Waters, 1997). Further, wider changes in society – the spread of share ownership, the growth of social mobility through education, the flexibility of what has been called post-Fordist production (see Chapter 14) – have all contributed to a reworking of the class order.

Perhaps the most widespread argument on the 'death of class' is that there has been a general 'levelling-up' of the classes. Traditional working-class communities such as those associated with mining or the steel industry have vanished and new working-class lives have become heavily shaped by home ownership and consumerism. The 'working class' no longer harbours the strong community that it once did. Indeed, there has been a clear failure of working-class-based action and a decline of working-class identity and trades unionism. During the Thatcher period, there was a major dealignment of politics, so that there is no longer even a clear working-class vote attached to the Labour party (Crewe, 1992).

The embourgeoisement thesis

One of the first major studies in the UK to examine the shifting nature of class was in the work of David Lockwood, John Goldthorpe, Frank Beckhoffer and Jennifer Platt, who looked at the changing nature of class among Luton car workers in the 1960s (Goldthorpe *et al.*, 1968). Their study was explicitly designed to examine the so-called 'embourgeoisement' thesis that 'we are all in the middle class now'. It was an early version of the theory of the decline of class: that the traditional 'proletarian' working class was losing its old identity, becoming more affluent and looking more and more like the middle classes. In the main, this study rejected such a thesis. True, it certainly showed major changes in class: the car factory workers were comparatively well paid, could spend money on major consumer goods, and were becoming home owners. But the middle class had advanced in line with this. Further, the car workers still usually voted Labour and did not really adopt middle-class lifestyles. They had become a new kind of working class – much more private and home-centred, seeing their work as a means to make money but with little sense of the job satisfaction found in middle-class work (Goldthorpe *et al.*, 1968). So the argument to be made here is not that class was weakening or vanishing, but that it was changing with the times.

This study, however, was conducted nearly 40 years ago. More recent studies have suggested that key divides now occur around consumption and lifestyles which cut across old class lines. Ray Pahl, looking at working-class households in Kent, saw the working class as becoming more and more divided – often between those in regular work and those drifting in and out of unemployment. Strikingly, he suggests that 'if the cathedral of the nineteenth century was the factory chimney, that of the twentieth century is the shopping mall' (Pahl, 1984; J. Pahl, 1989).

More important, perhaps, are the new divides between those who rely on the market and those who rely on the state; between those who own their houses and those who rent them; between those who work and those who are unemployed; between 'work-rich' and 'work-poor' households. Classes now need to be linked to the 'texture' of cultures and the key role of (largely middle-class) social movements, such as the Green Movement.

In this view, then, class analysis has become so complicated that the nature of what we are studying ceases to be clear! A myriad of variables are important to studying inequality, and 'class' as a concept can no longer handle this range. 'Class' is being replaced by 'lifestyle', 'differences' and all sorts of other inequality linked to ethnicity and gender (see Chapters 11 and 12). The failure of class analysis to seriously incorporate these concerns has made it weaker and weaker: an area of academic study restricted to a few ivory tower academics!

The continuing importance of class

But another group of sociologists, like John Scott, still take class as the central feature of societies. The nature of class may be changing, but it is still the central organising feature of industrial countries. Class here is not in dispute, but its changing character may be. These class theorists often point to a number of key changes, including the following.

1. The decreasing importance of the manual/non-manual labour distinction as manual work declines.

2. The collapse of a very traditional working class (for example, around mining communities).

3. The growth and diversity of the middle class, including the expansion of the service sector.

4. The identification of an underclass who are largely outside the class system and, indeed, society.

5. The introduction of both gender and ethnicity into various class schemas as a complicating factor.

Critics of social class would agree with all these too. But while these sociologists do try to incorporate many of the issues raised by those who have suggested the end of class, they concluded that class is still the most important factor. Class, and class analysis, are far from dead. Indeed, this chapter should have clearly shown that although class patterns are changing, they are deep and widespread. 'Classlessness' may have been exaggerated, for there remains a very clear, powerful and strong upper class. People still strongly identify with class groups; and new divisions and polarisations continue to appear.

Fractured identities

In an important discussion, Harriet Bradley (1996) has taken a conciliatory role between older theories of class and newer accounts. She is sympathetic to postmodernism, and hence suggests that the idea of any one overarching 'truth' is now unlikely. Older theorists of class sometimes placed a belief in the importance of class that may have made it too central, restricting their vision. But she is also very aware of the lived social divisions found in contemporary society. For Bradley, and for others such as Beverley Skeggs (1997), the way ahead lies in the idea of recognising that we all now inhabit fractured identities – identities that are not unitary or essential, but variable and changing and plural (see Chapter 5 for a previous discussion of this). People's sense of social location in social worlds is no longer simply a matter of class: their lives are bound into all the variations of inequality that this section of the book is discussing – class, yes, but also ethnicity, gender, age, and other factors such as disability or sexuality. Bradley suggests that identities around class are now highly fractured.

Class, then, remains an important area of sociological analysis. Recent analyses and research, however, suggest that it continues to change its forms, and must be considered alongside a whole array of new identities and social changes.

CONTROVERSY AND DEBATE

BLAMING THE POOR: WHO IS TO BLAME?

That the richest regions on earth – Europe and North America – are home to tens of millions of poor people raises serious questions. It is true, as some analysts remind us, that many of the people counted among the officially poor in industrialised countries are better off than the poor in other countries – 40 per cent of poor families in the United States, for instance, own their home and 60 per cent own a car (H. Jenkins, 1992). But it is also the case, as noted earlier, that malnutrition and outright hunger are quite widespread, along with violence, illness and a host of other problems that accompany economic deprivation. We now examine more closely the arguments underlying each of these two approaches to the problem of poverty. Together, they frame a lively and pressing political debate, as captured in Figure 10.5.

Blaming the poor: cycles of deprivation and cultures of poverty

One side of the issue is based on the following view: *The poor are primarily responsible for their own poverty.* Since the creation of the English Poor Laws, some thinkers in industrial nations have drawn distinctions between the 'deserving' and the 'undeserving' poor. Believing that social standing primarily reflects talent and individual effort, these people contend that industrial societies offer considerable opportunities to anyone able and willing to take advantage of them. The poor, then, are those who cannot or will not work, people with fewer skills, less schooling or simply lower motivation. While some people (historically, widows, orphans and the disabled) command our compassion as 'worthy poor', this line of reasoning leads us to condemn many people as, in one way or another, responsible for their own fate, and hence undeserving.

Some researchers have offered a different view, suggesting that a *culture of poverty* holds down the poor, fostering resignation to poverty as a matter of fate. Anthropologist Oscar Lewis (1961), who investigated the poor *barrios* of Latin American cities, is one of the early proponents of this view. Although Lewis doubted that most poor people could do much about their plight, he did not blame them individually for their poverty. Instead, he claimed that the *barrio* environment socialised children to believe that there is little point in aspiring to a better life. The result is a self-perpetuating cycle of poverty, as one generation transmits its way of life to the next. In the UK, this has been a widely influential model too.

Research in the United States led Charles Murray (1984) to much the same conclusion. Especially in areas of intense poverty such as the inner cities, claims Murray, a lower-class subculture has taken hold, eroding personal ambition and achievement. One element of this subculture, as he sees it, is a present-time orientation that encourages living for the moment. While a future orientation guides most better-off people to study, plan, work hard and save, Murray saw poor people as failing to look beyond the moment. In living for the present, he concluded, the poor perpetuate their own poverty and, therefore, reap what they deserve.

▶

Blaming society: social exclusion and structural divisions

The other side of the issue can be summed up as follows: *Society is primarily responsible for poverty*. This alternative position, argued by William Ryan (1976), holds that social structures – not people themselves – distribute the resources unequally and are, therefore, responsible for poverty. Looking at societies around the world from this point of view, we see that those that distribute wealth very unequally (such as the United Kingdom) also have high levels of relative poverty, while societies that strive for more economic equality (such as Sweden and Japan) lack such extremes of social stratification.

Poverty, Ryan insists, is not inevitable. Low income, not personal deficiencies, cause the problem. Ryan interprets any lack of ambition on the part of poor people as a consequence rather than a cause of their lack of opportunity. He therefore dismisses Lewis's analysis as little more than 'blaming the victims' for their own suffering. In Ryan's view, social policies that empower the poor would give them real economic opportunity and yield more economic equality.

Weighing the evidence

Each of these explanations of poverty has won its share of public support, and each has advocates among policymakers. As Murray sees it, society should pursue equality of opportunity, especially for the young, but otherwise people should take responsibility for themselves, and their success will correspond to their talents and interests.

Ryan takes a more activist approach, asserting that public policy should reduce poverty through more equitable redistribution of income. Programmes such as comprehensive child care, for example, could help poor mothers gain job skills; indeed, the living standard of every poor person could be raised by a tax-funded, guaranteed minimum income for every family.

Certainly, both of these views could be put into practice, and many societies periodically lean towards one or the other. Typically, conservative policies are sympathetic towards the first, while left-leaning and liberal strategies are usually more in tune with the second.

CONTINUE THE DEBATE:

1. What are the major groups in the communities of poor people? Is it reasonable to divide some of them into 'deserving' and some into 'undeserving' categories?

2. Why do you think poverty in Europe seems to be constantly on the increase?

3. Discuss strategies for reducing poverty.

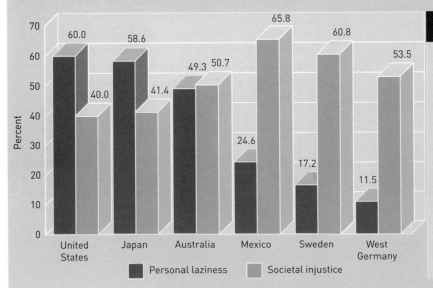

Figure 10.5 Assessing the causes of poverty

Survey question: 'Why are there people in this country who live in need?' Percentages reflect respondents' identification of either 'personal laziness' or 'societal injustice' as the primary cause of poverty. Percentages for each country do not add up to 100 because less frequently identified causes of poverty were omitted from this figure.

Source: adapted from *World Values Survey*, from Inglehart and Blake, (2000)

Citizenship and the rise of welfare states

An important development of modern, industrial capitalist societies has been the evolution of welfare states. A narrow definition of this would be 'the involvement of the state in social security and social services' (Cochrane and Clarke, 1993: 4). More broadly, some definitions of the welfare state include a commitment to full employment and a whole arena of welfare polices to do with education, health and families. Welfare states are therefore very much bound up with improving the quality of life for a society's citizens and reducing the problems generated through inequalities.

Most modern industrialised nations are welfare states – they increasingly have to deal with public problems and deal with them through public expenditure. In Britain, in 1981, 56.3 per cent of the government's budget was spent on welfare; in 1993, it was 64.1 per cent. This was despite an anti-welfare government for much of this time! (Much of the rise, though, was due to costs of increased unemployment, etc.)

Some industrial societies, such as Sweden, have highly developed welfare states, while others, such as the United States, have only minimal ones. Nevertheless, it is a characteristic feature of modern societies that they have to devote large sums to welfare.

A central question in understanding the workings of welfare states concerns the extent to which they are run by governments or through markets (see Chapter 14). When the market dominates, we often talk of the **marketisation** of the welfare state – here it is run by *an economic system based on the principles of the market, including supply, demand, choice and competition.* Thatcherism (discussed in Chapter 15) attempted to bring marketisation into all spheres of life, including much of the welfare state. Thus, as we shall see, both education (Chapter 19) and health (Chapter 20) were to move to the principles of the market. Even prisons, as we shall see in Chapter 16, have moved towards markets and privatisation.

The citizenship approach

The growth of state involvement with the 'welfare' of its citizens parallels the growth of industrial societies. In the optimistic version, this is a story of growing 'citizenship rights'. The key thinker in this area is the British sociologist T. S. Marshall (1893–1981), who argued that with industrialisation, citizenship emerged in three ways.

These were:

1. *Civil*: the rights necessary for individual freedom – liberty of the person, freedom of speech, thought and faith, the right to own property and to conclude valid contracts, and the right to justice. The key institutions to implement this would be the civil and criminal courts of justice.

2. *Political*: the right to participate in the exercise of political power, as a member of a body invested with political authority or as an elector of such a body. This included such institutions as parliament and local elective bodies, along with the extension of political suffrage.

3. *Social*: the whole range from the right to a modicum of economic welfare and security to the right to share to the full in the social heritage and to live the life of a civilised being according to the standards prevailing in the society. The educational and social welfare institutions are the key here.

For Marshall, each of these sets of rights appears in distinct periods. In the Middle Ages, they were 'wound together' but weak. Civil rights emerged most clearly in the eighteenth century, political rights in the nineteenth and social rights in the twentieth century.[1] Many do not agree with the precise periodisation and remark that Marshall's model was developed through one case study only – that of the UK. When applied to other countries it does not fit so well. Bryan Turner (1990), for example, has suggested that the foundations of citizenship differ for France, Germany and Sweden. Marshall's model does raise a series of key issues about the emerging rights and responsibilities in modern societies.

A Marxist approach

Marxists see the welfare state differently: instead of seeing it as a benign set of institutions that foster security and equality, they argue that it helps contribute to the smooth running of the capitalist order. In order for capitalism to work, it needs a well-trained labour force that is reasonably healthy and secure. The welfare state ensures this. Marxists suggest advanced capitalism needs welfare to 'buy off' working-class dissent and maintain social order with a secure workforce (Piven and Cloward, 1972).

---

[1] There is talk, at the beginning of the twenty-first century, of the emergence of a fourth cluster of citizen rights centred around 'intimate citizenship' (Plummer, 2003).

THE SOCIAL CHARTER: SOCIAL POLICIES IN THE EUROPEAN UNION

In May 1989, the European Community Charter of the Fundamental Social Rights of Workers – commonly known as The Social Charter – was approved. It was subsequently incorporated as the 'Social Chapter' into the Maastricht Treaty in 1991 (see Chapter 4). The Charter's main provisions included the following rights and guarantees of workers who hold citizenship in EU countries.

The rights were:

- to work in the EU country of one's choice
- to a fair wage
- to continuing improvements in living and working conditions
- to adequate social protection and social security
- to belong to a trade union (or professional body) and to be represented in collective bargaining
- to satisfactory health care and safe working conditions.

The guarantees were:

- equal treatment for men and women in the workplace, and 'enabling men and women to reconcile their occupational and family obligations'
- consultation between employers and workers
- protection of children and adolescents; with a minimum working age of 15, fair pay and reasonable hours
- minimum decent standard of living for the elderly
- changes to make it easier for the disabled to become part of the workforce.

Until 1997, the UK opted out of the Chapter. In practice, the UK did recognise many of the conditions, but the former Conservative government objected to the regulations of maximum hours and minimum wages, as well as to fathers being given a statutory three months' unpaid leave after the birth of a child. The Conservatives argued that these provisions would increase industrial costs to a level that would make the UK less competitive with the United States, Japan and the newly industrialising countries. The Labour government elected in 1997 rejected these arguments and signed up to the Social Chapter.

Like most such mission statements, these ideal goals are not always followed in practice. Although there is a clear statement that men and women should be treated equally, in practice there remain significant pay and opportunity differentials. Additionally, the charter does not always allow for consistent enforcement. Some issues, including a 48-hour maximum working week and a common retirement age for men and women, are laid down centrally, but other matters, including the power to set the age of retirement, remain at the discretion of national governments.

Through the Social Protection in Europe Directive (1993), all EU countries must provide a basic level of support in unemployment benefits, pensions, cover for work accidents, health cover and maternity benefits. A predictable pattern emerges: a high level of protection in Sweden, as is the case for Luxembourg and The Netherlands; a low level of protection in Spain, Portugal, Ireland, Greece and the UK; and middle levels of support in France, Germany, Finland, Denmark, Belgium and Austria.

The three worlds of welfare capitalism

In 1990, Costa Esping-Andersen published a much-discussed study of different kinds of welfare regime. For him, 'The welfare system is not just a mechanism that intervenes in ... inequality; it is, in its own right, a system of stratification' (1990: 23). He argued that there were three major kinds of welfare system, though they are a little like ideal types (see Chapter 1). They can be evaluated as systems of **decommodification**, whereby the focus is on *the degree to which welfare services are free from the market*. (Commodification, by contrast, turns welfare issues into sellable things and needs markets.) The three main 'worlds' he locates are:

1. *Social democratic*. This argues for universal rights, equality and a kind of 'universal solidarity' in favour of the welfare state. It is largely anti-market. It takes on many family responsiblities and is a universalist model. Scandinavian countries largely adopt this approach.

2. *Corporatist/'Bismarck'*. Here, welfare is mainly organised through work itself, through business, tradition, Church and existing powers. This approach does not enourage redistribution. While the state may deliver welfare, its aim is the maintenance of traditional families. This is a conservative model, found in Austria, France, Germany and Italy.

3. *Liberal*. This intervenes in the market as little as possible and gives benefits that are subject to strict entitlement rules. It is a basic safety-net approach, showing a direct line of inheritance from the old Poor Laws. It leads to market-based insurance for the

wealthy and means testing for the poor. Private schemes are encouraged. Examples are the United States, Australia and Canada. The UK used to be close to the social democratic model, but under Thatcherism moved closer and closer to the market/liberal model.

Esping-Andersen derived this classification from his own research into pensions, unemployment insurance and sickness benefits. He examined levels of benefit, protection against risks and strictness of rules that govern access across a number of countries. It was on this basis that he could classify societies thus:

- Lowest scores for welfare – liberal: USA and UK
- Intermediate scores for welfare – corporatist: France, Germany, Italy, Switzerland
- Highest scores for welfare – social democratic: Scandinavia, Belgium, The Netherlands.

More recently, Leibfried (2001) has added a fourth group – the 'Latin Rim countries' – Spain, Greece, Portugal, southern Italy and part of France, which have 'rudimentary welfare states'.

The welfare state in the UK

The UK is quite close to the liberal model but is, at least historically, a bit of a mixture of all three. Its roots go back to the Poor Law in Elizabethan and Tudor England, where government started to impose an elementary framework on what had previously been the task of churches and charities. But this rudimentary care of the sick broke down with mass industrialisation and the arrival of capitalism. In 1834 the Poor Law Amendment Act set up a national Poor Law Commission to oversee the development of a system with links eventually growing to state education and health care. All this shapes the 'state' links to a society's population, and especially its 'poor' and 'working class'.

Bit by bit, a system that was heavily *laissez-faire* gave way to a system that is more central and state-controlled. By the start of the twentieth century, legislation such as the Pensions Act of 1908 and National Insurance Act of 1911 provided cover for sickness and unemployment for some workers, introducing the 'insurance principle' into British social security.

The period 1945–75 may be seen as the years of the 'classic welfare state'. It was spearheaded by the work of William Beveridge in several major reports. Waging war on the 'five great evils' of 'Want, Disease, Ignorance, Squalor and Idleness', his plan for social security was to abolish Want – but only if the others could simultaneously be abolished (Beveridge, 1942: paragraph 8). This was a time when there was a commitment to a mixed economy, to full employment and to a welfare state that would provide universal rights. At this stage, the welfare state in the UK was closest to the social democratic model described above. In education, health, child care and welfare provisions, the UK seemed to be moving towards this social democratic welfare state. There were 'means tested' systems, but the broad principles stressed universality.

This was also the period when the National Health Service came into existence – a time very different from our own, when most people rented their houses, nobody had televisions but instead listened to the wireless, few had overseas holidays, only a minority had telephones, nobody had computers, and few had cars so most were dependent upon public transport. Social democratic thinkers believed the welfare state would create citizenship for all and would combat inequality. But by the mid-1970s – as unemployment surged forward and huge economic changes were in the offing – it was clear that it had not been especially successful in redistribution. Indeed, a number of commentators saw most of the benefits of the system going to the middle classes (Le Grand, 1982).

A new period was ushered in from the mid-1970s onwards. Most notably, from 1979 there emerged a much more 'anti-welfare state' approach. It was, as Prime Minister Margaret Thatcher bluntly put it, a rejection of the Nanny State. Monetarist theory (to be outlined in Chapter 14) was put into practice and at the same time the 'classic' welfare state began to be 'marketised'.

When the New Labour government was elected in 1997 with a landslide majority, many believed that they would reverse the marketisation policies of the Thatcher years. While they set up a Social Exclusion Unit which aimed to target specific groups in need (such as the homeless) and to provide integrated services for them, in the main they continued with a policy in which the market was given a major focus.

Looking ahead: class in the twenty-first century

This chapter has raised many problems about class and its role in modern industrial societies. We have seen there are many problems involved in knowing just what it is; and at the same time we have heard both from sociologists who regard it as the key feature of modern societies and from others who see it as a factor in decline.

For the authors of this book, it seems impossible to deny the continuing role that class plays in social life. It is tangibly present through poverty, low incomes, extremes of wealth, prestige systems and status, and differing degrees of control over work and life. However, it is changing and new patterns of class are in the making.

At the same time, one of the most important lessons of recent times is that class on its own is a weak concept. It needs to be placed in specific circumstances and connected to other key issues such as social exclusion, gender, ethnicity and age: it is these which the subsequent chapters will examine.

SUMMARY

1. Social inequality involves disparities in a host of variables, including income, wealth and power. Marxists would adopt an approach to measuring class that focuses upon the ownership of the means of production, while Weberians tend to focus on a range of variables, including work and market situation.

2. Occupation is a common way in which class is measured. The Registrar General's classification is the most commonly used such classification in the UK. This has recently been updated to the National Statistics Socio-Economic Scale (NS-SES). Income and wealth are other ways in which social class is often measured.

3. The upper class, which is small (about 5 per cent), includes the richest and most powerful families. Members of the upper-upper class, or the old rich, derive their wealth through inheritance over several generations; those in the lower-upper class, or the new rich, depend on earned income as their primary source of wealth. The middle class includes 40–45 per cent of the population. The upper middle class may be distinguished from the rest of the middle class on the basis of higher income, higher-prestige occupations and more schooling. The working class, sometimes called the lower middle

class, includes about one-third of the UK population. With below-average income, working-class families have less financial security than those in the middle class. Only one-third of working-class children reach college and most eventually work in blue-collar or lower-prestige white-collar jobs. There is a growing 'underclass' – people outside society and the class system.

4. Social class affects nearly all aspects of life, beginning with health and survival in infancy and encompassing a wide range of attitudes and patterns of family living.

5. Since the early 1970s, changes in the economy have reduced the standard of living for low- and moderate-income families. One important contemporary trend is a decline in manufacturing industries, paralleling growth in low-paying, service-sector jobs.

6. Oscar Lewis and Charles Murray advanced the *culture of poverty* thesis, which holds that poverty is perpetuated by the social patterns of the poor themselves. Opposing this view, William Ryan argues that poverty is caused by a society's unequal distribution of wealth.

7. An important development of modern capitalist societies has been the development of welfare states alongside the idea of 'citizenship'.

CRITICAL-THINKING QUESTIONS

1. Assess your own social class. Does your family have consistent standing on various dimensions of social stratification? Why do most people find talking about their own social position awkward? Identify some of the effects of social stratification on health, values, politics and family patterns.

2. Is class dead? If so, why?

3. What categories of people are at high risk of poverty in Europe? Does any evidence support the assertion that the poor are responsible for their situation? Does any evidence suggest that society is primarily responsible for poverty?

4. Compare three 'welfare states'. Why is public assistance for the poor more controversial in some countries than in others?

Further reading

General sociology texts on class:

Ken Roberts, *Class in Modern Britain* (2001)
A readable and comprehensive introduction to the UK class system, following the traditional debates.

Harriet Bradley, *Fractured Identities: Changing Patterns of Inequality* (1996)
Engages head-on with the recent critiques of class from postmodernist and other angles and provides a more forward-looking approach to the study of class.

Fiona Devine and Mary C. Waters, *Social Inequalities in Comparative Perspective* (2004)
Valuable recent series of essays on class systems in a range of (mainly Western) countries.

For discussions on poverty:

Lucinda Platt, 'Poverty' in Geoff Payne (ed.) (2000; 3rd edn, 2005) *Social Divisions*
A succinct and up-to-date summary of key issues around poverty in the UK.

John Scott, *Poverty and Wealth* (1994)
Packs a great deal of information into a short book.

David Gordon and Peter Townsend (eds), *Breadline Europe: The Measurement of Poverty* (2000) details a more up-to-date European situation.

See also:

P. Alcock, *Understanding Poverty* (2nd edn, 1997)

M. Howard, *et al.*, *Poverty: The Facts* (4th edn, 2001)

L. Platt, *Parallel Lives? Poverty among Ethnic Minority Groups in Britain* (2002)

On issues of exclusion and inclusion and welfare states:

Ruth Levitas, *The Inclusive Society? Social Exclusion and New Labour* (1998)
Is good on social exclusion.

C. Esping-Andersen, *The Three Worlds of Welfare Capitalism* (1990)
Is the now classic study of modern welfare which distinguishes three types (and clearly favours the Scandinavian model).

On social policy in general:

Gail Lewis, Sharon Gewirtz and John Clarke, *Rethinking Social Policy* (2000)
A series of short, critical and forward-looking commentaries on social policy in the UK.

Watch a video/Read a book

- Alan Parker's *Angela's Ashes* (2000): the compelling novel by Frank McCourt about grinding poverty in early twentieth-century Ireland is also a vivid and striking film depiction of poverty.

- Daryll Zanuck's *The Grapes of Wrath* (1940): John Steinbeck's classic novel of the Depression was turned into a major, moving and classic film.

- *Down and Out in Paris and London* (1933): George Orwell's classic account of tramps and derelicts working in kitchens and out of them. In a way, it is an early example of a kind of participant observation study.

Connecting up

Connect to other chapters

- Link discussion of poverty and its measurement back to Chapter 9.
- Think about links to ethnicity, gender and age to be discussed in Chapters 11–13.
- Return to Marx and Weber in Chapters 2 and 4 and think of how this links to class.
- Think about issues of method. See Chapter 3 and ask: How do you know you are measuring class and poverty in a valid and reliable way?
- Link class to issues of identity, as discussed in Chapter 7.

To the websites

- The Joseph Rowntree Foundation is very good for detailed reports on poverty:

  http://www.jrf.org.uk
- The Sunday Times Rich List is to be found on:

  http://www.wsws.org/articles/2001/apr2001/rich-a30.shtml
- The Social Exclusion Unit is at:

  http://www.socialexclusionunit.gov.uk
- The Low Pay Commission is at:

  http://www.lowpay.gov.uk/

  This will provide the most recent figures, especially on the minimum wage.
- Policylibrary.com is a useful guide to social policy issues:

  http://www.policylibrary.com/welfare

For additional case studies, multiple choice questions, internet exercises, and annotated weblinks specific to this chapter, visit this book's website at www.pearsoned.co.uk/plummer

CHAPTER 11

RACISM, ETHNICITIES AND MIGRATION

Race, as a meaningful criterion within the biological sciences, has long been recognised to be a fiction. When we speak of 'the white race' or 'the black race', 'the Jewish race' or 'the Aryan race', we speak in biological misnomers and, more generally, in metaphors . . .

Henry Louis Gates, Jr.

KEY THEMES

- The meanings of race, ethnicity and racialisation
- The problem of prejudice and racism
- Patterns and problems around migration and the links to ethnicity and racism
- The ethnic situation in the UK
- Future patterns

(Left) We the Peoples..., 1984 (acrylic on board), Ron Waddams. © Private Collection/www.bridgeman.co.uk
Source: Bridgeman Art Library

(Above) Serbs leave their homes in Sarajevo in 1992 so they do not have to live under Muslim rule.
Source: Network/JB Pictures © W Bocxe

BOSNIA, A FEDERAL STATE OF THE FORMER YUGOSLAVIA, is a country marked by multicultural and ethnic differences. Its chronicler, Noel Malcolm, has said: 'There is no such thing as a typical Bosnian face: there are fair-haired and dark-haired Bosnians, olive-skinned and freckled, big-boned and wiry-limbed. The genes of innumerable people have contributed to this human mosaic' (1996: 1). In its 1,000-year history it has been touched by all the great empires of the European past: Rome, Charlemagne, the Ottomans and the Austro-Hungarians. It has harboured most of the major faiths: Western Christianity, Eastern Christianity, Judaism and Islam. And it has been home to migrants from all over Europe bringing their own languages and culture. It has long been home to Slavs (who arrived 1,000 years ago), and Muslims and Croats whose own states bordered it (Croatia and Serbia). In 1991, the three main groups were Muslims (44 per cent), Serbs (31 per cent) and Croats (17 per cent).

Yet 1992 marked Bosnia's destruction. A bloody civil war erupted between the Serbs (Orthodox Christians), the Croatians (Catholics) and the Bosnian Muslims. Estimated to have cost the lives of some 500,000, unleashing some three and a half million refugees, it also involved the systematic rape of thousands of Muslim women, the destruction of much of the country's infrastructure, and the desecration of its great ancient mosques and churches. Whole cities were destroyed, as each group claimed its territories and aimed to 'cleanse' other ethnic groups. The biggest and most hideous ethnic cleansing was of the Bosnian Muslims, attacked by the Serbs. Only in 1995, after much humanitarian intervention, was a settlement reached (known as the Dayton Agreement).

Although it was a 'local war', it provoked international intervention. But even this could not prevent a large and devastating civil war. It was a modern 'ethnic' war complete with horrendous atrocities. Today, most wars are not between nation states. They are tribal conflicts between different ethnic groupings. Between 1989 and 1992 there were 80 armed conflicts – but only three of them were between countries. The rest were *within* countries – internal wars. It may be, then, that the days of the big wars are over. What we have seen growing at the end of the twentieth century is a proliferation of civil wars and 'tribal conflicts'. Currently there are some 30 civil wars taking place all over the world.

(Malcolm, 1996)

Globally, the pattern of inequality and conflict based on colour, ethnicity and culture becomes ever more pronounced. The extermination of Jews and other minorities, such as gypsies and homosexuals, in the Holocaust may mark the twentieth century's extreme low point (see Chapter 8), but ethnic strife still continues. Indeed, with the collapse of the former Soviet empire, Ukrainians, Moldavians, Azerbaijanis and a host of other ethnic peoples in Eastern Europe are struggling to recover their cultural identity after decades of Soviet subjugation. In the Middle East, deep-rooted friction divides Arabs and Jews, while blacks and whites strive to establish a just society in South Africa. In Turkey there is conflict between the government and Kurdish nationalists; in Sudan between north Muslim Arabs and southern blacks,

both Christian and animist – going on since the 1950s; in Sri Lanka between Hindu Tamils and Buddhist Sinhalese; in Rwanda between Hutus and Tutsis; in Iraq between Kurds and Marsh Arabs. And, of course, in Israel between Jews and Palestinians. The list goes on and on.

In the African nations, the Asian countries, in the Balkans, in Northern Ireland and elsewhere in the world, racial and ethnic rifts frequently flare into violent confrontation. In the United States, ethnic tensions exist

Map 11.2 The 1995 Dayton Agreement for Bosnia and Herzegovina

Map 11.1 Post-1945 Yugoslavia: republics, autonomous provinces, historic regions and cities

Source: adapted from Malcolm (1994)

Genocide survivors, Rwanda
Source: © Radu Sigheti/Reuters/Corbis

in most large, urban cities, exploding intermittently as with the Los Angeles 'riots' of 1992. And migration of displaced peoples everywhere across the globe nearly always generates cultural conflicts. Across the globe, ethnic antagonisms remain, fomenting hatred and violence and propelling violence and war.

This chapter examines the meaning of racism and ethnicity, explains how these social constructs have shaped our history and suggests why they continue to play such a central part – for better or worse – in the world today.

The social significance of race and ethnicities

What's in a name? Problems of terminology

People frequently use the terms 'race' and 'ethnicity' imprecisely and interchangeably. Using the 'correct' language in the study of race and ethnicity can be very difficult. Some commentators prefer the language used by different ethnic groups themselves: the word 'black' (in the UK) or 'people of colour' (in the United States). The trouble here is that there is no agreement within these groups: some, often more political, people prefer one word, others may prefer another. For example, 'Asian' black feminist Kum-Kum Bhavnani suggests that 'black' is used in Britain as a political category for racialised groups – all those non-white groups who experience racism. This would include Pakistani, Bangladeshi and Indian groups. The word would become a unifying force for a 'black movement'. But others do not agree. Tariq Modood argues that 'black' is not suitable for Asians in the UK because it generates a false sense of essential unity and is itself used inconsistently (it sometimes means only people of African descent). Indeed, he argues that most Asians do not use the term, and that what is really needed is a language of Asian pride with its own historical and cultural roots (Bhavnani, 1993; Modood, 1994).

Race and racialisation

'Race' is a very muddled (even dangerous) concept. The idea of **race** came into use between the latter part of the eighteenth century and the mid-nineteenth: it is thus a modern idea. It usually refers to *a category of people who share biologically transmitted traits that members of society deem socially significant.* People may classify each other into races based on different physical characteristics such as skin colour, facial features, hair texture and body shape. Such differences are superficial; individuals of all races are members of a single biological species. People the world over display a bewildering array of racial traits. This variety is the product of migration and intermarriage over the course of human history, so that many genetic characteristics once common to a single place are now evident throughout the world. The most striking racial variation appears in the Middle East (that is, western Asia), which has long served as a 'crossroads' of human migration. Striking racial uniformity, by contrast, characterises more isolated peoples such as the island-dwelling Japanese. But no society lacks genetic mixture, and increasing contact among the world's people will ensure that racial blending will accelerate in the future.

Nineteenth-century thinkers, such as A. de Gobineau (1816–1882) in his *Essay on the Inequality of the Human Races* (1915; orig. 1853), developed a three-part scheme of racial classification. Labelling people with relatively light skin and fine hair as *Caucasian*, those with darker skin and coarser, curlier hair *Negroid*, and those with yellow or brown skin and distinctive folds on the eyelids *Mongoloid*, a 'race science' was established, in which, for example, Caucasians were seen as people of greater intelligence and higher morality! Sociologists consider such theories and categories not just as very misleading (since we now know that no society is composed of biologically pure individuals) but also politically dangerous (in fuelling the fires of racism). Indeed, this has led most sociologists to reject the very idea of race and to look elsewhere for better concepts to understand these issues.

Nevertheless, people around the world do seem quick to classify each other racially. This *process of ranking people on the basis of their presumed race* sociologists now call **racialisation**: it is at the heart of this system of inequality and social exclusion. As will be explained later, people may also defend racial hierarchy with assertions that one category is inherently 'better' or more intelligent than another, though no sound scientific research supports such beliefs. But, because so much is at stake, it is no wonder that societies strive to make racial labelling much clearer than the 'facts' permit. Earlier in the twentieth century, for example, many southern states in the United States legally defined as 'coloured' anyone who had as little as one-thirty-second African ancestry (that is, one African-American great-great-great-grandparent). Today, with less of a caste distinction in the United States, the law enables parents to declare the race of a child, if they wish to do so at all.

hostility. Because attitudes are rooted in culture, everyone has at least some measure of prejudice. Most people recognise that white people commonly hold prejudiced views of minorities, but minorities, too, harbour prejudices, sometimes of whites and often of other minorities.

Stereotypes

Prejudices combine to form a **stereotype** (*stereo* is derived from Greek meaning 'hard' or 'solid'), described as *a prejudicial, exaggerated description applied to every person in a category of people*. Because many stereotypes involve emotions such as love and loyalty (generally towards members of in-groups) or hate and fear (towards out-groups), they are exaggerated images that are hard to change even in the face of contradictory evidence. For example, some people have a stereotypical understanding of the poor as lazy and irresponsible spongers who would rather rely on welfare than support themselves (Waxman, 1983; NORC, 1994). As Chapter 10 explained, however, this stereotype distorts reality because most poor people tend to be children, women, working adults or elderly people.

Stereotypes have been devised for virtually every racial and ethnic minority, and such attitudes may become deeply rooted in a society's culture. In the United States, for example, half of white people stereotype African-Americans as lacking motivation to improve their own lives (NORC, 1994: 236). Such attitudes assume that social disadvantage is a matter of personal deficiency, which, in most cases, it is not. Moreover, stereotypes of this kind ignore the fact that most poor people in the United States are white and that most African-Americans work as hard as anyone else and are not poor. In this case the bit of truth in the stereotype is that black people are more likely than white people to be poor (and slightly more likely, if poor, to receive welfare assistance). But by building a rigid attitude out of a few selected facts, stereotypes grossly distort reality.

Racism

A powerful and destructive form of prejudice, **racism** refers to *the belief that one racial category is innately superior or inferior to another*. Racism has pervaded world history. The ancient Greeks, the peoples of India and the Chinese – despite their many notable achievements – were all quick to view 'others' as inferior. Racism has also been widespread in our own history: indeed, it is probably found in every society in the world today. Thus in

Australia, targeted groups include aboriginals, Pacific Islanders and Chinese, while in Denmark the Somalians and other refugee groups are objects of racism. It is hard to find cultures that do not have some form of race tension or conflict.

Racism and social domination

Historically, the assertion that one specific category of people is innately inferior to another has served as a powerful justification for subjecting the targets of these taunts to *social* inferiority. By the end of the nineteenth century, European nations and the United States had forged vast empires, often ruthlessly and brutally subjugating foreign peoples with the callous claim that they were somehow less human than the explorers who enslaved them.

In the twentieth century, racism was central to the Nazi proclamation that a so-called Aryan super-race of blond-haired, blue-eyed Germans was destined to rule the world. Such racist ideology encouraged the systematic slaughter of anyone deemed inferior, including some 6 million European Jews and millions of Poles, gypsies, homosexuals and people with physical and mental disabilities.

More recently, racial conflict has intensified in Western Europe with the immigration of people from former colonies as well as from Eastern Europe seeking a higher standard of living. In Germany, France, Britain and elsewhere, growing public intolerance of immigrants has fuelled a resurgence of Nazi-style rhetoric and tactics. The United States, too, is experiencing increasing racial tensions in cities and on college campuses. Racism – in thought and deed – remains a serious social problem everywhere as people still contend that some racial and ethnic categories are 'better' than others.

Explaining racism

If prejudice does not represent a rational assessment of facts, what are its origins? Social scientists have come up with various answers to this vexing question, citing the importance of frustration, personality, culture and social conflict.

Scapegoat theory of prejudice

Scapegoat theory holds that prejudice springs from frustration. Such attitudes, therefore, are common among people who are themselves disadvantaged (Dollard *et al.*,

PROFILE

W. E. B. DU BOIS: RACE AND CONFLICT

One of sociology's pioneers, who has not received the attention he deserves, is William Edward Burghardt Du Bois (1868–1963). Born to a poor Massachusetts family, Du Bois showed extraordinary aptitude as a student. After graduating from high school, he went to college, one of only a handful of the young people in his small town (and the only person of African descent) to do so. After graduating from Fisk University in Nashville, Tennessee, Du Bois realised a childhood ambition and enrolled at Harvard, repeating his junior and senior years and then beginning graduate study. He earned the first doctorate awarded by Harvard to a person of colour.

Du Bois believed sociologists should direct their efforts to contemporary problems, and for him the vexing issue of race was the paramount social concern. Although he was accepted in the intellectual circles of his day, Du Bois believed that US society consigned African-Americans as a whole to an exis-

tence separate and apart. Unlike white people, who can make their way in the world simply as 'Americans', Du Bois pointed out, African-Americans have a 'double consciousness', reflecting their status as Americans who are never able to escape identification based on colour.

Politically speaking, his opposition to racial separation led Du Bois to serve as a founding member of the National Association for the Advancement of Colored People (NAACP). Du Bois maintained that his research, too, should attempt to address pressing racial problems. Later in his life, Du Bois reflected (1940: 51):

I was determined to put science into sociology through a study of the condition of my own group. I was going to study the facts, any and all facts, concerning the American Negro and his plight.

After taking a position at the University of Pennsylvania in Philadelphia, Du Bois set out to conduct the research that produced a sociological classic, *The Philadelphia Negro: A Social Study* (1967; orig.

1899). In this systematic investigation of Philadelphia's African-American community at the turn of the century, Du Bois chronicled both the strengths and weaknesses of people wrestling with overwhelming social problems. Running against the intellectual current of the times (especially Spencer's social Darwinism), Du Bois rejected the widespread notion of black inferiority, attributing the problems of African-Americans to white prejudice. But his criticism extended also to successful people of colour, whom he scolded for being so eager to win white acceptance that they abandoned all ties with those still in need. 'The first impulse of the best, the wisest and the richest', he lamented, 'is to segregate themselves from the mass' (1967: 317; orig. 1899).

At the time *The Philadelphia Negro* was published, Du Bois was optimistic about overcoming racial divisions. By the end of his life, however, he had grown bitter, believing that little had changed. At the age of 93, Du Bois left the United States for Ghana, where he died two years later.

Sources: based, in part, on Baltzell (1967; orig. 1899) and Du Bois (1967; orig. 1899).

1939). Take the case of a white woman frustrated at the low wages she earns working in a textile factory. Directing hostility at the powerful people who operate the factory carries obvious risks; therefore, she may well attribute her low pay to the presence of minority co-workers. Prejudice of this kind may not go far towards improving the woman's situation, but it serves as a relatively safe way to vent anger and it may give her the comforting feeling that at least she is superior to someone.

A **scapegoat**, then, is *a person or category of people, typically with little power, whom people unfairly blame for their own troubles*. Because they are often 'safe targets', minorities are easily used as scapegoats. The Nazis blamed the Jewish minority for all of Germany's ills 60

years ago. And today some Europeans attribute troubles at home to the presence of Turkish, Pakistani or other immigrants from abroad.

Authoritarian personality theory

Theodore W. Adorno and his colleagues (1950) claimed that extreme prejudice was a personality trait of particular individuals. They based this conclusion on research showing that people who displayed strong prejudice towards one minority were usually intolerant of all minorities. Such people exhibit *authoritarian personalities*, rigidly conforming to conventional cultural values, envisaging moral issues as clear-cut matters of right and wrong and advocating strongly ethnocentric views. People with authoritarian personalities also look upon society as naturally competitive and hierarchical, with 'better' people (such as themselves) inevitably dominating those who are weaker.

By contrast, Adorno found, people tolerant towards one minority were likely to be accepting of all. They tend to be more flexible in their moral judgements and believe that, ideally, society should be relatively egalitarian. They feel uncomfortable in any situation in which some people exercise excessive and damaging power over others.

According to these researchers, authoritarian personalities tend to develop in people with little education and harsh and demanding parents. Raised by cold and insistent authority figures, they theorised, children may become angry and anxious people who seek out scapegoats whom they come to define as their social inferiors.

Cultural theory of prejudice

A third approach holds that, while extreme prejudice may be characteristic of certain people, some prejudice is common to everyone because such attitudes are embedded in culture. As noted in Chapter 5, the social superiority of some categories of people is a core value of US culture. Recent multicultural research echoes this idea and calls for educational programmes to help people in the United States move beyond their traditionally Eurocentric attitudes to gain an appreciation of the culture and contributions of those of non-European descent (Asante, 1987, 1988).

For more than 40 years, Emory Bogardus (1968) studied the effects of culturally rooted prejudices on interpersonal relationships. He devised the concept of *social distance* to gauge how close or distant people feel in relation to members of various racial and ethnic categories. Interestingly, his research shows that people throughout the United States share similar views in this regard, leading Bogardus to conclude that such attitudes are culturally normative.

Bogardus found that members of US society regarded most positively people of English, Canadian and Scottish background, welcoming close relationships with and even marriage to them. There was somewhat less of a premium on interactions with people of French, German, Swedish and Dutch descent. The most negative prejudices, Bogardus discovered, targeted people of African and Asian descent.

If prejudice is widespread, can we dismiss intolerance as merely a trait of a handful of abnormal people, as Adorno asserted? A more all-encompassing approach recognises some bigotry is within us all as we become well adjusted to a 'culture of prejudice'.

Oppression of minorities

A fourth view claims that powerful people utilise prejudice as a strategy to oppress minorities. To the extent that the public looks down on Turkish guest workers in Germany, illegal Latino immigrants in the southwest United States, or refugees in the UK, employers are able to pay these people low wages for hard work. Similarly, elites benefit from prejudice that divides workers along racial and ethnic lines and discourages them from working together to advance their common interests (Geschwender, 1978; Olzak, 1989).

The post-colonial plight and the new racism

While older forms of 'scientific' racism (with their focus on biological races as inferior) still continue, an important theory to have an impact upon race thinking recently has been **post-colonial theory**. This refers to *the wide critiques of (usually 'white') Western cultures that are made from people who have been colonised in the past.* As is well known, from the sixteenth century onwards (but especially during the nineteenth century) European colonial empires such as those of the British, Portuguese, Spanish, French, Belgian and Dutch were established all over the world. The indigenous peoples of Asia, Africa and the Americas became subject to cultural conquest – often enslavement and genocide, too. But in an even wider sense, post-colonialism can bring an understanding of the wider world historical process by which people have invaded other cultures throughout history. It is a feature of many societies that as one culture invades another, so it attempts to settle its own values and beliefs over them – from the Incas, the Ottomans and the Chinese through to the British in North America with the native Indian tribes. It is a major world process that leads to the blurring and fragmentation of different groups across the world, each of which generally creates its own sense of the threatening 'other' within its midst.

Post-colonialism challenges the superiority of 'white' or dominant thinking and listens to the voices of peoples who have been hidden from sight through this

CONTROVERSY AND DEBATE

DANGEROUS EXTREMISTS: ISLAMIC FUNDAMENTALISTS OR ISLAMOPHOBES?

Islam is the dominant faith in some 40 states throughout the world, and is seen by many to be the fastest-growing religion. (In Chapter 18, we discuss its features in more detail.) In the UK, there has been a growth from 0.1 per cent to 0.6 per cent over the past 25 years. This is small in absolute numbers, but very significant in its expansion. It is estimated that there are now about 1 million Muslims in the UK and 3 million in France. Overall, Muslims account for some 3 per cent of European faith.

Islam has come to symbolise key questions about ethnicity, prejudice and tolerance. This can be seen from the prominence given to the debate over the Salman Rushdie affair and the Iranian *fatwah* (death threat) imposed upon him (see the opening vignette to Chapter 18). It is also seen in the Gulf Wars waged against Iraq in 1992 and 2003. Some have even claimed that this is a new Holy War between East and West, where the traditional forces of the anti-Western, anti-rational and anti-modern Islamic religions are in spiritual and moral combat with the modernising but decadent West. Benjamin Barber (1995), for one, sees this as a clash of civilisations, a conflict between the *Jihad* (Holy War) and the materialism symbolised by McDonaldisation (see Chapters 5, 6 and 18). It is a conflict which may also be linked to ethnicity and some see it as the major world conflict in the twenty-first century. Indeed, in the aftermath of the World Trade Center bombings in 2001, such tensions have become more and more acute.

On the one hand, some Westerners argue that Islam is a dangerous force in the world. It is seen as a fundamentalist religion (see Chapter 18) holding strongly to traditionalist views, emphasising religious texts and looking back to its past to affirm its puritan vision. It is seen to hold particular prejudices against many modern concerns of the West: the liberation of women, the 'open and free society', the decline of religion, the acceptance of diversity such as homosexuality and 'sexual freedom'. And it is seen to favour an absolutist religious state where nothing can exist outside the religion. Indeed, of the 40 or so states where Islam is dominant, few can be called democratic. All of this clashes with the modern values of the Western state.

Such claims certainly do have some basis in fact, but the critics argue that such statements are extreme: the Islamic faith actually comes in a number of varieties, and many of its supporters do not adopt these extreme positions. Just as Christianity has a number of its own divides, so too do the Muslims. Most are not extreme. Indeed, a key divide lies between Shi'ism and the Shi'ites (who hold more traditional and rigid views) and the Sunnis (who accept more diversity and change). In the UK, for instance, the majority of Muslims must be distinguished from small extreme groups like Al-Muhajiroun which calls for Islamic government in the UK (*Khilafah*).

It is the more extreme views which get reported most often, and it is these ideas which form the basis of a new form of prejudice called '**Islamophobia**' – *a hatred of all things Muslim*. Where once the Jews or blacks or 'Asians' were prime objects of attack, increasingly Muslims have become the new objects of prejudice and discrimination. Not only is the incidence of violent attacks against Muslims increasing, but prejudicial views are being widely held. No one, for example, blames the Catholics for IRA bombings in Ireland: the IRA is recognised as a more extreme group. So why blame Muslims for much of what is in fact only an extreme edge? In the UK, Muslims are generally among the most economically successful of new migrant groups, and this success may well be one basis for the prejudice.

In 1996, the Runnymede Trust – a major organisation which promotes and researches a multicultural society in the UK – announced a commission to look into what they considered as the most rapidly growing form of prejudice. They were concerned to look at such things as anti-Islamic and anti-Muslim attitudes; the relations between Islam and secular outlooks and other world faiths; the treatment of Islam and Muslim concerns in the media; and the contributions of British Muslims to government

▶

CONTROVERSY AND DEBATE CONTINUED

and society. The Trust has highlighted a major emerging form of prejudice in Western societies, one that is likely to become more and more recognised.

These divides raise serious issues around prejudice and discrimination. How far can a multicultural society which claims to accept religious and ethnic diversity pursue such outright attacks upon different religions? At the same time, how far can a religious strand which rejects tolerance and diversity be allowed to propagate its views? This is a classical dilemma of freedom for those who may advocate unlimited freedom.

CONTINUE THE DEBATE:

1. Consider some possible scenarios of what might happen in Europe and the West in the future. Will more and more Muslims be co-opted into Western secular individualism?

2. Will more and more Muslims stay with their own faith, while accepting multicultural values?

3. Or will a strong defence of Islamic fundamentalism lead to growing ethnic conflicts?

Source: Runnymede Trust (1997); Barber (1995).

---

process of colonialisation. These are people who, in effect, have 'lost their voice' (see Chapter 2). At the heart of this critical position is the recognition of just how much 'the West' (in this case, principally Western Europe and the United States) came to dominate the world throughout the nineteenth and early twentieth centuries. As Edward Said, a leading figure in the post-colonial movements, has commented:

> By 1914, . . . Europe held a grand total of roughly 85% of the earth as colonies, protectorates, dependencies, dominions and commonwealths. No other set of colonies in history was as large, none so totally dominated, none so unequal in power to the Western metropolis.
>
> (Said, 1993: 3)

Such colonisation has left its mark on the world.

What these newer ideas highlight are the ways in which ethnicities depend upon different senses of collectivity and belonging among groups. They stress the ways in which boundaries – often defined as 'the nation' or 'us' – are created, maintained, challenged and transformed between different ethnic groups (Jenkins, 1997: 16–24). State policies (for example, on immigration) are often closely connected to identifying these groupings, which are frequently identified through 'race' and 'colour', and then made the source of boundary definition. Nationalism often takes on an importance in such discussions: just what does 'being British', 'being German', 'being Scandinavian' or even 'being European' mean?

The categories are far from simple. Take the case of 'being British'. Although claims may be made by some about the purity of the category, sociologist Stuart Hall

has suggested it is very much a 'mongrel category': 'Our mongrel selves and most cultures are inextricably multicultural – mixed ethically, religiously, culturally and linguistically' (Hall, 1992a). Thus, 'being British' – historically encompassing descent from many waves of European immigrants as well as peoples of the 'Celtic fringe' of Scotland, Ireland and Wales – must at the every least engage with major migrations from Asia, the West Indies, etc., with the history of the Commonwealth, and with many countries across the world that have some legacy of colonisation. To quote Paul Gilroy, a leading sociologist of ethnicity and race:

> We increasingly face a racism which avoids being recognized as such because it is able to line up 'race' with nationhood, patriotism, and nationalism. A racism which has taken a necessary distance from crude ideas of biological inferiority now seeks to present an imaginary definition of the nation as a unified cultural community. It constructs and defends an image of national culture – homogeneous in its whiteness yet precarious and perpetually vulnerable to attack from enemies within and without.
>
> (Gilroy, 1987: 87)

Discrimination

Closely related to prejudice is the concept of **discrimination**, *any action that involves treating various categories of people unequally*. While prejudice refers to attitudes, discrimination is a matter of behaviour. Like prejudice, discrimination can be either positive (providing special advantages) or negative (placing obstacles in front of particular categories of people). Discrimination also varies in intensity, ranging from subtle to blatant.

Prejudice and discrimination often – but not always – occur together. A personnel manager prejudiced against members of a particular minority may refuse to employ them. Robert Merton (1976) describes such a person as an *active bigot*. Fearing legal action, however, another prejudiced personnel manager may not discriminate, thereby becoming a *timid bigot*. What Merton calls *fair-weather liberals* may be generally tolerant of minorities yet discriminate when it is expedient to do so, such as when a superior demands it. Finally, Merton's *all-weather liberal* is free of both prejudice and discrimination.

Not all kinds of discrimination are wrong. Individuals discriminate all the time, preferring the personalities, favouring the looks or admiring the talents of particular people. Discriminating in this basic sense of *making distinctions* is necessary to everyday life and rarely causes problems. But discriminating on the basis of race or ethnicity is another matter.

All societies praise some forms of discrimination, in other words, while condemning others. Universities, for example, systematically favour applicants with greater abilities over those with less aptitude. This kind of discrimination is entirely consistent with our culture-based expectation that the greatest rewards go to people with more ability or those who work harder.

But what if a university were to favour one category of people (Christians, say) over another (Jews) regardless of individual talent? Unless the university had a religious mission (making a specific religion directly relevant to performance in school), such a policy would discriminate in a manner both morally wrong and against the law.

In historical terms, principles of fair play change along with economic development. In low-income countries, people routinely favour members of their families, clans, religious groups and villages. Traditional people typically recognise a moral duty to 'look after their own'. In high-income industrial societies, by contrast, cultural norms elevate the individual over the group, so that achievement rather than ascription guides our code of fairness. Many organisations, therefore, seek out the most qualified applicant while forbidding 'nepotism' or 'conflict of interest' by which employees would favour a relative or reject someone based on race or sex.

Institutional discrimination

We typically think of prejudice and discrimination as the hateful ideas or actions of specific individuals. But far greater harm results from **institutional discrimination**, which refers to *bias in attitudes or action inherent in the operation of society's institutions*, including schools, hospitals, the police and the workplace. Until the US Supreme Court's *Brown* decision in 1954, the principle of 'separate but equal' legally justified the institutional discrimination by which black and white children in the United States attended different schools. In effect, the law before *Brown* upheld institutional racism in the form of an educational caste system. Institutional discrimination remains one of US society's most intractable problems. Despite the *Brown* decision, relatively little has changed since 1954: while no US schools remain officially 'black' or 'white', most students still attend schools in which one race or the other predominates overwhelmingly. Indeed, in 1991, a court decision recognised that neighbourhood schools would never provide equal education as long as the US population was divided into racially segregated neighbourhoods, with most African Americans living in city centres and most white people (and Asian Americans) living in geographically and politically separate suburbs.

In the UK, the Report by Sir William Macpherson into the murder of Stephen Lawrence suggested that police conduct during the case had been seriously lacking and that institutional racism was at work in the British police. On 22 April 1993, a young black man, Stephen Lawrence, was murdered by a gang of white youths as he waited at a bus stop. After the murder, there were complaints from the family that the murder had not been properly investigated and that indeed the police had behaved in a racist fashion. The Macpherson Report was a detailed investigation of the events around the crime, and concluded that although individual police officers may not have been deliberately prejudiced, the Metropolitan Police Service itself was 'institutionally racist'. Macpherson defined this as:

> The collective failure of an organisation to provide an appropriate and professional service to people because of their colour, culture, or ethnic origin. It can be seen or detected in processes, attitudes and behaviours which amount to the discrimination through unwitting prejudice, ignorance, thoughtlessness and racist stereotyping which disadvantage minority ethnic people.
>
> (Macpherson, 1999: 6.43)

The report has been influential in generating public debate on police policy and racism in the UK.

Prejudice and discrimination: the vicious cycle

Prejudice and discrimination frequently reinforce each other. W. I. Thomas offered a simple explanation of this fact, noted in Chapter 7. The Thomas theorem states: *if situations are defined as real, they are real in their consequences* (1966: 301; orig. 1931). Because people socially construct reality, stereotypes become real to those who believe them and sometimes even to those who are victimised by them. Power also plays a role here, since some categories of people have the ability to enforce their prejudices to the detriment of others.

Prejudice by whites against people of colour, for example, does not produce *innate* inferiority but it can produce *social* inferiority, consigning minorities to poverty, low-prestige occupations and poor housing in racially segregated neighbourhoods. If white people interpret social disadvantage as evidence that minorities do not measure up to their standards, they unleash a new round of prejudice and discrimination, giving rise to a *vicious cycle* whereby each perpetuates the other, as illustrated in Figure 11.1, even from generation to generation.

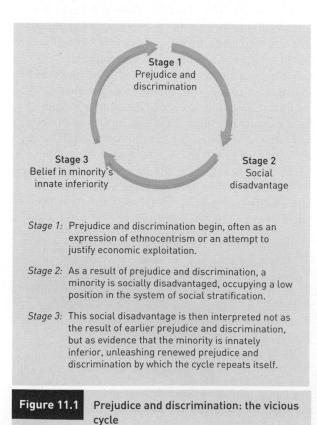

Stage 1: Prejudice and discrimination begin, often as an expression of ethnocentrism or an attempt to justify economic exploitation.

Stage 2: As a result of prejudice and discrimination, a minority is socially disadvantaged, occupying a low position in the system of social stratification.

Stage 3: This social disadvantage is then interpreted not as the result of earlier prejudice and discrimination, but as evidence that the minority is innately inferior, unleashing renewed prejudice and discrimination by which the cycle repeats itself.

Figure 11.1   Prejudice and discrimination: the vicious cycle

Majority and minority: patterns of interaction

Social scientists describe patterns of interaction among racial and ethnic categories in terms of four models: pluralism, assimilation, segregation and genocide.

Pluralism

Pluralism is *a state in which racial and ethnic minorities are distinct but have social parity*. In a pluralist society, categories of people are socially different, but they share basic social resources more or less equally. Most Western societies are – to differing degrees – pluralistic in several respects. They provide schooling and other services to all categories of people, and generally promise them equal standing before the law. Moreover, large cities contain dozens of 'ethnic villages' where people proudly display the cultural traditions of their immigrant ancestors. In London there are Arab, Chinese, Maltese, Greek, Italian, Jewish, 'West Indian' and, of course, differing Asian communities. In New York these include Spanish Harlem, Little Italy and Chinatown; in Philadelphia, Italian 'South Philly'; in Miami, 'Little Havana'; in Chicago, 'Little Saigon'; as well as Latino East Los Angeles.

Pluralism – living with difference – is one goal of the recent trend towards multiculturalism. As described earlier in Chapter 5, this scholarly and political initiative seeks to promote an ability to live with difference and to accept as equal the many cultural traditions that make up our national life.

But, in other respects, much of the West remains far from pluralistic. In the United States, for instance, while most people appreciate and value their cultural heritage, only a small proportion of minorities want to live and interact only and exclusively with their 'own kind' (NORC, 1994). Further, in many cases, racial and ethnic identity is forced on people by others who shun them as undesirable. For example, people in many communities in the Appalachian Mountains of the eastern United States remain culturally distinctive because others snub them as 'hillbillies'. And worse: in recent years, rising levels of immigration have stretched many people's tolerance for social diversity. One reaction against the new immigrants has been a social movement seeking to establish English as the official language of the United States – hardly a strategy to bolster pluralism.

Switzerland presents a much sharper example of pluralism. In this European nation of almost 7 million people, German, French and Italian cultural traditions run deep. The Swiss have been relatively successful in maintaining pluralism (albeit, but critically, involving little difference in colour), officially recognising all three languages. Just as important, the three categories have roughly the same economic standing (Simpson and Yinger, 1972).

Assimilation

Assimilation is *the process by which minorities gradually adopt patterns of the dominant culture*. Assimilation involves changing modes of dress, values, religion, language or friends. This is the so-called 'melting pot' model in which various nationalities have fused into an entirely new way of life. At the turn of the last century, one immigrant expressed this perception in these words:

> America is God's Crucible, the great melting-pot where all races of Europe are melting and reforming. Here you stand, good folks, think I, when I see them at Ellis Island [historical entry point for many immigrants in New York], here you stand with your fifty groups, with your fifty languages and histories, and your fifty blood-hatreds and rivalries. But you won't be long like that, brothers, for these are the fires of God . . . Germans and Frenchmen, Irishmen and Englishmen, Jews and Russians, into the Crucible with you all! God is making an American!
> (Zangwill, 1921: 33; orig. 1909)

The melting-pot image is misleading as a matter of historical fact. Rather than everyone 'melting' into some new cultural pattern, minorities typically adopt the traits (the dress, accent and sometimes even the names) of the dominant culture established by the earliest settlers.

Not surprisingly, elites tend to favour the assimilation model, since it holds them up as the standard to which others should aspire. Many immigrants, too, have been quick to pursue assimilation in the hope that it will free them from the prejudice and discrimination directed against distinctive foreigners and encourage upward social mobility (Newman, 1973). But multiculturalists find fault with the assimilation model because it tends to paint minorities as 'the problem' and define them (rather than the elites) as the ones who need to do all the changing.

Certainly some assimilation has occurred. In the UK, while Afro-Caribbean and Asian cultures may be strong, they have also taken on many key features of British society. In the United States, as fast as some urban 'ethnic villages' disappear, new ones emerge, the product of a steady and substantial stream of immigrants. Almost 30 per cent of today's New Yorkers are foreign born – the highest percentage in 50 years. No wonder some analysts argue that race and ethnicity endure as

basic building blocks of US society (Glazer and Moynihan, 1970; Alba, 1985).

As a cultural process, assimilation involves changes in ethnicity but not in race. For example, many Americans of Japanese descent have discarded their traditional way of life but still maintain their racial identity. However, racial traits do diminish over generations as the result of **miscegenation**, *biological reproduction by partners of different racial categories*. Miscegenation (typically outside marriage) has occurred throughout US history despite cultural and even legal prohibitions. Norms against miscegenation are now eroding and, while the share of officially recorded interracial births in the United States is still just 4 per cent, it is rising steadily.

Segregation

Segregation refers to *the physical and social separation of categories of people*. Some minorities, especially religious orders like the Amish of Pennsylvania, have voluntarily segregated themselves. Mostly, however, majorities segregate minorities involuntarily by excluding them. Various degrees of segregation characterise residential districts, schools, occupations, hospitals and even cemeteries. While pluralism fosters distinctiveness without disadvantage, segregation enforces separation to the detriment of a minority.

South Africa's system of apartheid (described in Chapter 8) illustrates racial segregation that has been both rigid and pervasive. Apartheid was created by the European minority it served, and white South Africans historically enforced this system through the use of brutal power. All this is changing dramatically, as the World Watch box in Chapter 8 indicated. Likewise, in the United States, racial segregation has a long history. Centuries of slavery gave way to racially separated lodging, schooling and transportation. Decisions such as the 1954 *Brown* case have reduced overt and *de jure* (Latin meaning 'by law') discrimination in the United States. However, *de facto* ('in fact') segregation continues.

In the 1960s, Karl and Alma Taeuber (1965) assessed the residential segregation of black people and white people in more than 200 cities in the United States. On a numerical scale ranging from zero (a mixing of races in all neighbourhoods) to 100 (racial mixing in no neighbourhoods), they calculated an *average* segregation score of 86.2. Subsequent research has shown that segregation has decreased since then, but only slightly; even African Americans with high incomes continue to find that their colour closes off opportunities for housing (Wilson, 1991; NORC, 1994).

Only a full century after the abolition of slavery did the US government take action to dismantle the 'Jim Crow' laws that continued to separate people of European and African ancestry. Until the early 1960s, these laws formally segregated hotels, restaurants, parks, buses and even drinking fountains. More than three decades later, de facto racial segregation in housing and schooling remains a reality for millions of people of colour in the United States.

Source: Corbis

We associate segregation with housing but, as Douglas Massey and Nancy Denton (1989) point out, racial separation involves a host of life experiences beyond neighbourhood composition. Many African Americans living in inner cities, these researchers concluded, have little social contact of any kind with the outside world. Such *hypersegregation* affects about one-fifth of all African Americans but only a small fraction of comparably poor whites (Jagarowsky and Bane, 1990).

In short, segregation generally means second-class citizenship for a minority. For this reason, many minority men and women have struggled valiantly against such exclusiveness. Sometimes the action of a single person can make a difference. On 1 December 1955, Rosa Parks boarded a bus in Montgomery, Alabama, and sat in a section designated by law for black people. When a crowd of white passengers boarded the bus, the driver asked Parks and three other African Americans to give up their seats. The three did so, but Rosa Parks refused. The driver left the bus and returned with police, who arrested her for violating the racial segregation laws. A court later convicted Parks and fined her $14. Her stand (or sitting) for justice sparked the African-American community of Montgomery to boycott city buses, ultimately bringing this form of legal segregation to an end (King, 1969).

Genocide

Genocide is *the systematic annihilation of one category of people by another*. A more recent term for this is **ethnic cleansing**, a term used especially in the Bosnian conflict described at the start of this chapter. This racist and ethnocentric brutality violates nearly every recognised moral standard; nonetheless, it has occurred time and again in the human record.

Genocide figured prominently in centuries of contact between Europeans and the original inhabitants of the Americas. From the sixteenth century on, the Spanish, Portuguese, English, French and Dutch forcefully colonised vast empires. These efforts decimated the native populations of North and South America, allowing Europeans to gain control of the continent's wealth. Some native people fell victim to calculated killing sprees; most succumbed to diseases carried by Europeans, to which native peoples had no natural defences (Cottrell, 1979; Butterworth and Chance, 1981; Matthiessen, 1984; Sale, 1990).

R. J. Rummel, in his book *Death by Government* (1996), has coined the concept of **democide** to capture *the mass murders by governments*. He argues that 'democracies commit less democide than other regimes' but shows how during the twentieth century some 169 million people have been the victims of state murders. He suggests that the Soviet Gulag state murdered the most – some 61 million, closely followed by the Communist Chinese (35 million), the Nazi genocide state (21 million) and the Chinese Nationalist regime (some 10 million). Unimaginable horrors befell large numbers of outcast people. But Rummel's calculations do not stop here. He suggests 5 million were murdered by Japan's military; 2 million were slaughtered by Pol Pot in Cambodia between 1975 and 1980: a quarter of the population perished in the Cambodian 'killing fields' (Shawcross, 1979); nearly 2 million were murdered in Turkey; and many more in Vietnam, Poland, Pakistan, North Korea and Mexico.

Migration, ethnicity and race

We live in a world of 100 million immigrants – 19 million of them refugees (Sowell, 1996). Migration patterns – the movements of people in and out of societies – offer crucial clues to the workings of societies. Not only do they help in understanding demographic patterns (discussed in Chapter 23), they focus sharp attention upon the dynamics of different groups in a society. Often these 'migratory' groups become singled out for the processes of racialisation and discrimination described above. And indeed it is hard to find any society where some outsider ethnic groups do not exist.

There have always been migratory movements: sometimes voluntary, sometimes planned, sometimes forced. 'Deportation and evacuations, exile and forcible repatriation, compulsory transfers and panic-stricken flight are an essential part of European history' (Stola, in Sowell, 1996: 2). In the past, the distances travelled were often short, but with new modes of travel, vast distances have often been covered. Sometimes there have been enforced geographical dispersals of a people (for example, Jews). These are the **diasporas**. Sometimes peoples have been assimilated and absorbed into a host culture. Sometimes there is a refusal to have permanent settlers.

There are four main identifiable patterns of modern migration.

- The classical model, which fits the United States, Canada and Australia. Generally such countries encourage migration and see immigrants as future citizens.

- The colonial model, which fits France, The Netherlands and the UK. Generally, migration to these countries has been heavily skewed to their colonies, giving them a kind of privileged position in as much as immigrants have potential citizenship rights.

- The 'guest worker' model, which fits Germany and Belgium. Generally, migration here is temporary and without potential citizen rights. As with the other models, migration is usually for work – but in this case, conditions of employment and potential security of work are much weaker.

- The 'illegal' models. Most countries have some illegal migration. It is characterised especially by people living outside the official society – and often, therefore, being forced to take the lowest paid, most temporary and demanding work.

Sociologists have suggested various phases through which migrants may pass. These phases of migration hold best for the classical pattern outlined above, but they are common in the others too.

In phase 1 there is temporary labour migration of young workers who send their earnings back home, and have a strong feeling that they still belong to the homeland. In phase 2 there is often a prolonging of stay and the development of some new social networks. In phase 3 there is often a family reunion – issues of long-term settlement can now start to appear, along with the development of new ethnic communities. And in phase 4 (and depending on government policies) there is permanent settlement (Castles and Miller, 1993: 25). This model is only an ideal type: it is much less relevant to certain groups of migrants, such as refugees or the highly skilled.

European patterns of migration

The history of Europe is the history of its migratory peoples. These migratory peoples may rapidly become outsider ethnic groups. So it is as well to remember that people originating from places as far flung as Africa, India and the Caribbean have lived in Europe for hundreds of years.

During this century, the European pattern may be seen as occurring in three main waves. Wave 1 was the 'European Exodus'. In the decades surrounding the turn of the nineteenth and twentieth centuries, it is estimated that 'around 52 million Europeans left their countries and 72% of them settled in North America' (Soysal, 1994: 17).

Wave 2 was the 'European Inflow', shortly after the Second World War, which saw a large number of immigrants in Europe. There were two main kinds of recruitment: one was of colonial workers – the inflow from former colonies – usually for work. This was true of the UK (with immigrants coming from Ireland, the West Indies and parts of Southern Asia and East Africa). France experienced migration from former Southern colonies: by 1970, there were 90,000 Tunisians, 140,000 Moroccans and over 600,000 Algerians. In The Netherlands, some 300,000 Indonesians (formerly the Dutch East Indies) resettled (Castles and Miller, 1993: 72). The second kind of flow was from guest workers – they are 'guests', temporarily visiting and not, strictly speaking, immigrants seeking to become permanent citizens able to make the country their home. They were expected to leave when their work came to an end and they had no political or economic rights: they were not citizens. Migrant workers constituted large portions of the manual working population in many European countries.

(a)

(b)

Refugees and Migration in Crisis

Throughout the world, through wars, genocides, conflicts and disasters, people are compelled to leave their homes. Sometimes this leads to refugee settlements, and sometimes long journeys to find a 'new home' – at least for a while. The photos above and opposite indicate some of the most recent humanitarian crises.

Afghanistan has a population of around 28 million – with several million living in refugee camps in Pakistan and Iran. From the 1930s to the 1970s it had a stable monarchy. This was overthrown by Marxist rebels and the USSR in the 1970s, which in turn were overthrown in 1992 through the establishing of an Islamic Republic. In 1996, this was overthrown by the Taliban – a fundamentalist faction of Islam. The events of September 11th 2001 identified the Taliban as protecting Osama Bin Laden and a bombing campaign was started by US and British forces. By late 2004, it was starting to look as though democratic elections could take place.

Sudan has a population of 38 million and is the largest country in Africa. The majority of its population

(c)

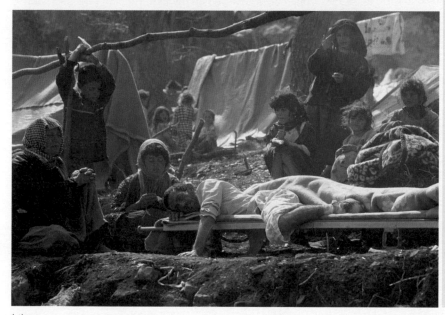

(d)

are Arab Muslims (22 million–over 50%) and are in the North; by contrast groups in the South (rich in oil) (and rival groups included the Dinka (11.5%), the Nuba (8. 1%) the Zande and the Nuer) tend to be Christian or Animist. From 1898 to 1956, the British colonised much of the area. Since that time there has been constant strife/war between the non-Muslim 'black' population of the South in rebellion against the Arab Muslim controlled government of the north. 30,000 are believed to have died in the war, and several million from the south are now homeless. In 2004, it was considered to be one of the worst humanitarian crises the world has seen.

Rwanda is quite a small country (population: 7 million) tucked away in East central Africa (bordered by Uganda, Tanzania, Burundi and the Congo). It has a life expectancy of around 38.5. It was originally inhabited by the Twa, and became home to the Hutu. The Tutsi appeared in the 14th century and came to rule in the fifteenth. There is a long history of periodic rules first by Hutu and then by Tutsi. In 1962 the Hutu took rule again, and waged wars and genocide, massacring over 500,000 Tutsi. And then as the Tutsi fought back, it left some 2 million refugees mainly Hutu to flee to neighboring countries...

LIVING THROUGH ETHNIC CLEANSING

Stevan Weine spent many years talking wih Bosnians who had witnessed ethnic cleansing. Below is one of the testimonies he gathered.

'For the first ten days they didn't give us any food. Then they fed us once a day at 6.00. They gave us three minutes to come from our building to the kitchen. Some of us were more than 50 metres away, and we had no chance to reach the kitchen. Those who came had three minutes to eat. Those who did not had no food. The guards formed a line that we had to run through to get to the kitchen. As we ran they beat us with guns, wheels, and tools.

After eleven days I asked them to let me go to the washroom just to wash my face. When I got there I didn't see that two men from Koĭarac also came inside along with some soldiers from special units. The soldiers started to beat them. When they saw me they took me to a place with a big sink and started to beat me. They told me to lick the floor of this washroom for 20,000 people which was dirty with urine and sewage. They broke my ribs. I vomited for one month. I vomited blood.

Sometimes they put us in a 4 x 4 meter room – 700 people. They told us to lie down and they closed the windows and the doors. It was summer. We lay like sardines in a can. Those on top were in the best position. Every morning, some on the bottom were dead. Every morning a guard came with a list and called people's names. Those they brought out never came back.

One day they came at 3 a.m. and they brought out 174 people. I was one of them. They lined us up behind a building they called the White House. Ten soldiers came with automatic weapons and they started to shoot us. Only three of us survived.

The worst event was when I watched one young man as they castrated him. Right now I can hear his cry and his prayers to be killed. And every night it wakes me. He was a nice young man. His executioner was his friend from school. He cut his body and he licked his blood. He asked him just to kill and to stop all that suffering. All day and all night we heard his prayers and his crying until he died. This is something that I cannot forget. It gives me nightmares and makes sleep almost impossible. I can't remember the people who were the executioners. For me all of them in those uniforms were the same. I can't remember who was who.

At the end of our first meeting, H. said I am all tears. When I speak about that even though my eyes are open I see all those images in front of me.

The second meeting begins tentatively, with H. saying, it is difficult to talk about anything when all the days were similar. So we review the last meeting's testimony with him and ask some questions to restart the dialogue.

Here in my neighborhood there is a man who was with me in the camp. He was a prisoner, like me, but he had the duty to beat us in order to save his own skin. And he did that very well. He wasn't alone. I know many examples of people like him. They had to do that just to survive. But I preferred it when he beat me. I always stayed on my feet. He didn't beat as hard as the others. I remember also one other man. He was a Muslim. He was very violent. He killed many prisoners. Finally we prisoners killed him by our own hands.

'You were there when that happened?'

Yes I was there. They moved him from our camp but then after some time they brought him back. And they pushed him inside a crowd of prisoners because they knew what would happen. All of us participated in that. One thousand people. And nobody could say 'I killed him' because all of us did. I didn't directly participate in the killing. But I was in the same room. I do not feel guilty. I wished to be in that group – the execution group – and I wished to participate in killing him. But I was really very weak.

I have to say something about the first prisoner who beat us and any other person who had to do the same job he did. Some people came to my house in Chicago to ask me to sign a note condemning him. I didn't do that because I do not think he is guilty. He helped many people. He didn't beat us like the Serbs did. He saved many, many lives. He needed to do that to save his own life.

Our region had very rich soil, and we had many farm animals. Day after day the Serbs brought our animals, and Muslim butchers had to slaughter them and put them in freezer trucks. Every day for two and a half months freezer trucks took that meat somewhere. Almost everything went into Serbia. The Serbs passed through our region especially to find gold and money. If someone wished to take all your property, he came and asked you to sign a paper that was something like a will, and you left

VOICES

him everything you had – car, truck, house, and everything inside. And for that he gave you a piece of bread. But if he went to your house and he couldn't find everything you signed over to him, he would then kill your family and come back into the camp and kill you.

I want to tell you something else. We had a special platoon. About a hundred prisoners had the duty of taking the bodies of murdered people, putting them in trucks, and bringing them to a special place with pits to dispose of them. They knew where they put all the Muslim bodies. One day before our camp was closed, before the Red Cross came, the soldiers killed all of them. Serbs killed all one hundred Muslims just to wipe out all witnesses. I was not in that group because I was too weak and too thin.'

Source: Weine (1999: 35–36).

These workers may be seen as an **industrial reserve army** – *a disadvantaged section of labour that can be supplied cheaply when there is a sudden extra demand*. Throughout much of Europe, such migrant workers were brought in to swell the labour force and were central to the reconstruction of Europe (see Gortz, 1961).

Wave 3 came after 1973, when there was a marked decline in migration to Europe. In the UK, for instance, new legislation started to restrict migration. Currently, about 15 million migrants in Europe are 'foreigners' – that is, they have no formal citizenship status (Soysal,

1994: 22). Foreign workers vary greatly: in 1990, they made up 2 per cent of the labour force in Denmark but 18 per cent in Switzerland. The Swedish have classically lacked much migration. In 1975, a new policy emerged that stressed equality between immigrants and Swedes, freedom of cultural choice for immigrants and cooperation between the native Swedish majority and various ethnic minorities (Soysal, 1994: 47). Figure 11.2 shows the balance of home, foreign and ethnic minority populations in 13 European countries.

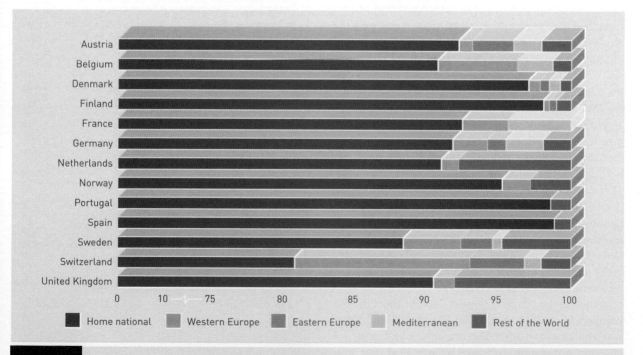

Figure 11.2   Minority populations in 13 countries in Europe

Source: adapted from Crouch 1999, *Social Change in Western Europe*, p.303. By permission of Oxford Universtiy Press

Future trends of migration

Castles and Miller suggest that migration is rapidly changing its forms at the end of the twentieth century. They predict four key features (1993: 8–9):

- The globalisation of migration: more and more countries will be affected.

- The acceleration of migration: growing in numbers in all major regions.

- The differentiation of migration: a whole array of types – refugees, labour migrants, permanent settlers all at the same time.

- The feminisation of migration: many more women are playing a much larger role (until recently, it was mainly men who migrated in the first instance).

This growth is likely to result in many cultures confronting more and more ethnic diversity. And as ethnic diversification grows, we may find an increase in levels of racism.

North America: the land of migration – and the coming majority?

Although Europe may be seen as a continent of migration, the figures of ethnic groups present here are small when compared with those found in the United States, truly the modern land of migration. Table 11.2 shows just how many groups have settled in the United States, and any visit to Ellis Island off New York – the place where most of the migrating people first arrived – would soon confirm the enormity of this migration pattern.

With such a vast pattern of migration, the argument is now made that 'white' groupings are about to become a minority. During the 1980s, Manhattan, the central borough of New York City, gained a minority-majority. This means that people of African, Asian and Latino descent, together with other racial and ethnic minorities, became a majority of the population. The same transformation has taken place in 186 counties across the United States (some 6 per cent of the total). As early as 2050, according to some projections, minorities will represent a majority of the country.

A look at the US 2000 Census data confirms the prospect of a minority-majority. Figure 11.3 shows that between 1990 and 2000, the 'majority' white, non-Hispanic population decreased by over 5 per cent whereas the numbers of Asians, Blacks and Latinos all increased. This population growth is highly concentrated, however, with more than half the increase

taking place in just three states: California, Florida and Texas.

Table 11.2	Racial and ethnic categories in the United States, 2000

Racial or ethnic classification[1]	Approximate US population	Percentage of total population
Hispanic descent	35,305,818	12.5
Mexican	20,640,711	7.3
Puerto Rican	3,406,178	1.2
Cuban	1,241,685	0.4
other Hispanic	10,017,244	3.6
African descent	34,658,190	12.3
Nigerian	165,481	0.1
Ethiopian	86,918	<
Cape Verdean	77,103	<
Ghanaian	49,944	<
South African	45,569	<
Native American descent	2,475,956	0.9
American Indian	1,815,653	0.6
Inuit (Eskimo)	45,919	<
Other Native American	614,384	0.2
Asian or pacific island descent	10,641,833	3.8
Chinese	2,432,585	0.9
Filipino	1,850,314	0.7
Asian Indian	1,678,765	0.6
Vietnamese	1,122,528	0.4
Korean	1,076,872	0.4
Japanese	796,700	0.3
Cambodian	171,937	<
Hmong	169,428	<
Laotian	168,707	<
Other Asian or Pacific Islander	1,173,997	0.4
West Indian descent	1,869,504	0.7
Arab descent	1,202,871	0.4
Non-Hispanic European descent	194,552,774	70.9
German	42,885,162	15.2
Irish	30,528,492	10.8
English	24,515,138	8.7
Italian	15,723,555	5.6
Polish	8,977,444	3.2
French	8,309,908	3.0
Scottish	4,890,581	1.7
Dutch	4,542,494	1.6
Norwegain	4,477,725	1.6
Two or more races	6,826,228	2.4

[1] People of Hispanic descent may be of any race. Many people also identify with more than one ethnic category. Therefore, figures total more than 100 per cent. < indicates less than 1/10 of 1 per cent.

Sources: US Census Bureau (2001, 2002, 2003)

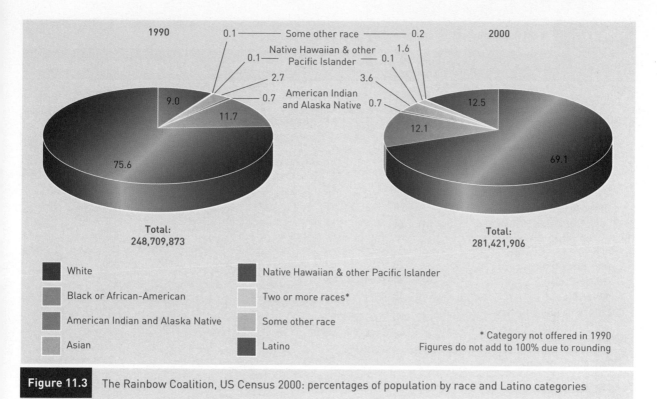

Figure 11.3 The Rainbow Coalition, US Census 2000: percentages of population by race and Latino categories

Source: adapted from US Bureau of the Census (2000)

Not everyone accepts the conclusion that the United States will have a minority-majority in the foreseeable future. Stephan Thernstrom (1998) points out that such a projection rests on two questionable assumptions. It assumes the US immigration rate must remain at its current high level despite government projections of a coming downturn. And it assumes that the high birth rates that characterise many immigrant minorities today must continue. But as the years pass, many immigrants typically begin to behave more or less like everyone else.

Ethnicity in the UK

So far, we have drawn a rather broad map, suggesting that racism is a continuing feature across the world. We will now consider the specific case of the UK. Table 11.3 presents the broad sweep of racial and ethnic diversity in the UK, as recorded by the 2001 Census.

History: ethnicity and migration

Since the Anglo-Saxon invaders of the sixth and seventh centuries drove Celtic-speaking Britons into Wales, Cornwall and the Scottish highlands, England has been more ethnically homogeneous than most of the rest of Europe. Nevertheless, there have been 'blacks' in England for hundreds of years (as many as 20,000 in the eighteenth century), who were often sailors or servants of white masters. Black communities often grew around seaports such as Liverpool (see Gerzina, 1995). In the nineteenth century, migrants to the cities were from the less wealthy or developing areas of the UK such as Ireland, Wales and Scotland. London, Manchester, Liverpool and Glasgow had large settlements from Ireland (by 1851, half a million Irish had settled in England and Wales). Jews started migrating in significant numbers around the time of the First World War and there was an acceleration during the 1930s. Nearly all the major migration during this latter period came from West European countries.

In modern times, the critical period for migration to the UK was the period following the Second World War. This was a part of massive immigration into Europe from all over the world – estimated to be around 30 million people (Castles *et al.*, 1984). At this time, after the war, there was a marked labour shortage which made many countries seek new reserves of labour. It was also a time when the colonies – so critical at an earlier period – were coming to an end. In England, the new Commonwealth (India, Pakistan and the West Indies)

Table 11.3	UK population, by ethnicity and age, 2001			
	Under 16	16–64	65 and over	All people (=100%) (thousands)
White	19	64	17	52,481
Mixed	50	47	3	674
Asian or Asian British				
Indian	23	71	7	1,052
Pakistani	35	61	4	747
Bangladeshi	38	58	3	283
Other Asian	24	71	5	247
All Asian or Asian British	29	66	5	2,329
Black or Black British				
Afro-Caribbean	20	69	11	566
Black African	30	68	2	485
Other Black	38	59	3	97
All Black or Black British	26	68	6	1,148
Chinese	19	76	5	243
Other ethnic groups	19	78	3	229
All ethnic groups	20	64	16	57,104

Source: *Social Trends* (2004: 18)

was important and provided a major recruiting base for migration and labour.

Initially, the largest post-war immigrant group coming to Britain were the Irish – nearly 900,000 (P. Johnson, 1994: 412). New Commonwealth immigrants came independently during the 1950s. Often, their arrival in England was a shock: the 'Mother Country' was grey and dreary. And very, very cold! Added to this was an unexpected turn towards racism, as UK society encountered, for the first time in its modern history, a 'mass' migration of 'black' workers. Famously, in 1948, the first of many ships, the *Empire Windrush*, carrying many Commonwealth immigrants, arrived in Britain. Many others followed. London Transport had directly recruited large numbers of these new immigrants. Many immigrants subsequently followed from Pakistan and India. From this time on, racism became a much more visible feature of the English landscape, with debates about the colour bar and the need to ban migrants from certain jobs. From the 1960s onwards, starting with the Commonwealth Immigrants Act of 1962, much stricter controls were introduced to regulate immigrant entry.

Minority ethnic populations

In the UK, the number of people from ethnic minorities has grown from a few tens of thousands in 1950 to more than three million now. Between 1992–94 and 1997–99, the ethnic community grew by over 15 per cent, from 3.2 million to 3.7 million, and in 2001 represented overall some 7.1 per cent of the UK population (*Population Trends*, September 2001). In London, the proportion is much higher, about 40 per cent. Indeed, by 2010, whites living in London could become a minority. Table 11.3 shows the UK population by ethnic origin, with half of the minority population being of South Asian (Indian, Pakistani or Bangladeshi) origin and over one-fifth of West Indian origin. The Asian population continues to grow, but the West Indians are declining in number. This is linked to changes in family structure (see Chapter 17). They are typically young: almost twice as many are under age five compared to the white population; most of the children were born in the UK (Skellington, 1996: 45–47).

Ethnic diversity is the key. The ethnic groups can be roughly divided into such groups as 'South Asian',

'Caribbean' or 'Irish', but within these groupings there are many sub-groupings of class, age (usually younger), gender and sexual orientation. Some ethnic groupings develop strong communities; others do not.

Ethnicity and class

In general, those of Caribbean, Pakistani and Bangladeshi descent tend to occupy the lowest position in the labour market and to experience the highest levels of unemployment (Mason, 2000a: 106).

We have seen that, although there is no official poverty line in the UK (Chapter 10), something like 15–25 per cent of the population may well be living in poverty! There are few specific data on ethnicity, but one commentator has remarked that:

> Every indicator of poverty shows that black people and other ethnic minorities are more at risk of high unemployment, low pay, shift work and poor social security rights. Their poverty is caused by immigration policies which have often excluded people from abroad from access to welfare, employment patterns which have marginalised black people and other ethnic groups into low paid manual work, direct and indirect discrimination in social security and the broader experience of racism in society as a whole.
>
> (Oppenheim, 1993: 130)

Ethnicity and age

A Joseph Rowntree Foundation report of 1995 (see Chapter 10) was alarmed at the disparities that were appearing between ethnic youth and others. In the late 1980s, while 12 per cent of young whites were unemployed, the figure was higher for young ethnic groups: 25 per cent of Afro-Caribbeans, 16 per cent of Indians, 27 per cent of Pakistanis and Bangladeshis (aged 16–24) (Skellington, 1996: 102).

Ethnicity and gender

If stratification systems appear across race, class and gender lines – which this book suggests they do – then black women are more likely to be at the centre of all three systems of stratification (if age is added, then elderly black women may be the most vulnerable of all).

There has been a growing amount of research on black women in the UK in recent years, which suggests among other things that black women:

- make up something like a quarter of the minority labour force (Phizacklea, 1995)

- are often heavily concentrated in the worst work: poorly paid, bad conditions, temporary, hard work, long hours, often unregistered home work, often subject to unemployment (Allen and Walkowitz, 1987)
- are often unpaid workers in family businesses (Anthias and Yuval Davis, 1993)
- are often in single households – over 30 per cent of British West Indian households are single parents (Anthias and Yuval Davis, 1993: 117)
- may perform well in school and university only to find they have less access to work and are less well paid
- are overrepresented in the prison population.

White feminism is often critical of the family, and the subordination of women within it. This can mean an implicit attack on Muslim women, whose lives are often circumscribed by the family, and on Afro-Caribbean women, who are often seen to be lone single-parent mothers. This has resulted in a significant debate between black women, who sometimes feel they have become the objects of white feminism, which is critical of their family life and their subordination to it.

Cultures of ethnicity

Ethnic groupings bring elements of their culture of origin to a hybrid arrangement of other cultures. This is a growing, and crucial, feature of modern global societies which mix and transform earlier cultural elements with newer ones. There are now a great many studies that document diverse aspects of these cultures. Below we discuss a few of these.

South Asian cultures

South Asian communities may be seen in many parts of the UK, but they are often structured by their roots in religion. As we will see in Chapter 18, most Bangladeshis and Pakistanis are Muslim; Indians may be Sikh, Hindu or Muslim.

Roger and Catherine Ballard (1982) looked at Sikhs in Leeds and the Jullunder Doab region of the Punjab. They saw various phases of development (much as in the migration model outlined above). A pioneer phase sees a small number of early migrants arriving and establishing small South Asian communities. Despite the major culture shock from the confrontation with UK culture, the old culture is maintained. From this there follows a phase of mass migration, where the diverse cultural patterns from home are imported and

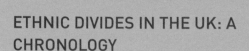

ETHNIC DIVIDES IN THE UK: A CHRONOLOGY

Prior to the 1950s

1066 Norman invasion of Britain from Northern France

1362 English language legally recognised

1707 Union of Scotland and England

1807 Slave trade abolished in the British Empire

1834–38 Slavery abolished in the British Empire

1892 Dadabhai Naoroji is the first Asian elected to the House of Commons

1919 Anti-black riots in Liverpool

1921 Anglo-Irish Treaty established Eire, and six northern counties with a Protestant majority to remain as part of the UK

1930-40s Around 60,000 Jews come to Britain to escape Nazis and the war

The modern period: from the 1950s

1948 British Nationality Act 1948 – distinguished British subjects who were citizens of the UK, and those from the Commonwealth and colonies. Both groups could enter and work in the UK; the arrival of the ship *Empire Windrush* with 492 West Indians on board

1955 Churchill wanted slogan 'Keep Britain white'

1958 First 'race riots' in Notting Hill, London

1962 Commonwealth Immigrants Act – withdrew right of entry to Commonwealth immigrants under most considerations; Enoch Powell's 'Rivers of Blood' speech

1965 Race Relations Act (under the Labour government) – an early attempt to ban discrimination in public places, or to incite racial hatred; Race Relations Board set up

1968 'Troubles' start in Northern Ireland; the Provisional Irish Republican Army (IRA) formed. Commonwealth Immigrants Act; Race Relations Act – the 1965 Act extended to employment and housing, but not to police

1971 Immigration Act – aliens could now enter only with a work permit; aliens could apply for citizenship after four years; distinctions between patrials and non-patrials

1976 Race Relations Act – Commission for Racial Equality formed and indirect discrimination (e.g. via advertising) made illegal; Anti-Nazi League formed

1981 British Nationality Act – British citizenship could pass to children only if their parents were born in the UK

1980s Inner-city 'race conflicts' at Brixton, Merseyside, Hackney; Lord Scarman reports on these conflicts in 1982, identifying key tension between police and local black youth; police relations with young black people were identified as significant

1983 Black sections in Labour Party

1988 Immigration Act – dependants of men who settled before 1973 could no longer join them, unless evidence of non-dependency

1991 Census questions on ethnicity (3 million people, 5.5% of population identified)

1993 Asylum and Immigration Act – certain countries to be refused asylum automatically

1999 Macpherson Report in the wake of the inquiry into Stephen Lawrence who was murdered in 1995

2000 The Race Relations (Amendment) Act – strengthens duty to promote race and equality

2000–01 More race tensions in Bradford, Burnley, Oldham

Source: Commission for Racial Equality

developed. Family, religious codes and dress all play a key solidifying role. There follows a major phase of family reunion, with a substantial second generation being born into the community. Throughout, there is a tension between the old culture and the new. New divisions start to appear: Sikhs from one region (such as Jullunder Doab) with Muslims from another (such as Mirpur district in Kashmir).

Afro-Caribbean cultures

Again, there is a mix of elements. Religion plays a strong role, but so too do elements of recovering an earlier culture. At the same time, much of this is mixed with elements from the dominant cultures. There are several notable strands, including Pentecostal culture and Rastafarianism.

Pentecostal culture has its roots in the Caribbean and the United States, and grew in England from the 1950s onwards. The first assemblies were in 1954 in Wolverhampton (Calley, 1965). There is a strong regard for the British way of life, while at the same time a strong moral system is imposed that is slightly at odds with much of the contemporary culture. Pentecostalists are not allowed to drink, swear, have any kind of sex outside marriage or even wear jewellery.

Rastafarian culture has its origins in Jamaica in the early 1930s after the demise of Marcus Garvey, who suggested 'Africa for the Africans'. 'Rastas' adopted Haile Selassie, one-time Emperor of Ethiopia, as the messiah and argued that Babylon was the system of European colonialism that enslaved Africans. There was a conspiracy to keep blacks suppressed. The culture surfaced in the UK in the 1970s and is easily distinguished by its dreadlocks hairstyle; many white youths copied the style during the 1970s and 1980s.

In practice, there is a diversity of culture. In a now classic study of male youth in the St Paul's area of Bristol, the late Ken Pryce (1986; orig. 1979) looked at six lifestyles, with a mix of Afro-Caribbean and UK culture. This was a participant observation that indicated, above all, the range of male youth forms that were developing. Broadly, he distinguished between those who held an expressive-disreputable orientation and those who valued a stable, law-abiding orientation.

Six types were identified at that time. In the first groupings were:

- Hustlers: males, marginal and hedonistic (Yardies are a more recent and tougher version)
- Teenyboppers: delinquents and/or Rastafarians.

In the second (more law-abiding) grouping were:

- Proletarian respectables: those who adopt more conventional lifestyles

- Saints: the Pentecostals as defined above

- Mainliners: white-collar black people

- In-betweeners: an older, law-abiding group, who also have a passion about their 'black culture'.

This brief excursion should make clear that to talk of any one ethnic culture is clearly a mistake. Ethnic cultures criss-cross class, gender and age. They have one foot in their 'culture of origin' and another foot in 'diverse British cultures' (also crossed by class, gender and age). They are dynamic in the sense that they are always on the move: each generation pushes its culture on in different ways and, as young generations become older generations, so the culture moves again.

Racism and ethnic antagonism in Europe

Racism, of various kinds, has been found throughout history. We have examined some of its complex roots above. It is not really suprising, then, that racism is found throughout Europe. As Map 11.3 and Figure 11.2 show, Europe is a culture in which there are many ethnic diversities. And much of this diversity makes for distinct antagonism. There are five features to note.

First, racism is generally on the increase. Nearly all countries in the European Union (EU) report increased

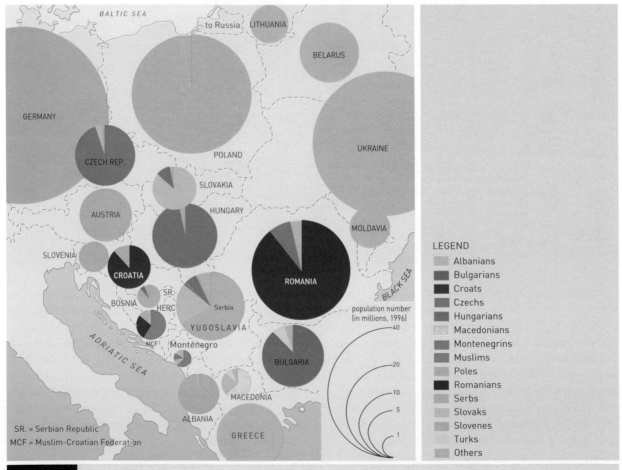

Map 11.3   Ethnic map of Eastern Europe, 1996

Source: adapted from Kocsis (2001: 89)

numbers of racist incidents and attacks on foreigners and individuals belonging to ethnic, racial or linguistic minorities. In France, this has involved numerous attacks on people of North African origin, as well as anti-Semitism. In Germany, the objects have mainly been Turkish, as well as gypsies (the Sinti and Roma). There also appears to be a worrying resurgence of anti-Semitism and 'Holocaust denial' spearheaded by new skinhead gangs. In part, the latter is explained through the growing tensions arising from the reunification with East Germany. Further, European football matches regularly produce concern about the levels of racist violence. And each year there are many deaths across Europe that are caused by racism (see the box on skinheads and Roma).

Second, problems of displaced people throughout Europe have led to many issues around 'asylum seekers' (see Figure 11.4). Leaving their home countries because of intolerable social, economic and political conditions, such asylum seekers may then find themselves confronting further racism and discrimination in the country of destination. Often, they are placed in camps that resemble prisons, and find themselves without family, support or funds. Governments, which are cautious of the political implications of allowing too many asylum seekers in their countries, often deploy subtle and tacit racist selection procedures.

A third development is the extremes of ethnic purging and cleansing that have been taking place across Eastern Europe. The horrors of the events of Bosnia (which were told at the start of this chapter) are but one of many such conflicts which have been taking place over religions and borders as the old cultures of Russia and Yugoslavia break down. In Europe we now have 'The Serbian Question', 'The Albanian Question', 'The Macedonian Question', 'The Hungarian Question', and the 'Roma Question' (see the European Eye box) (Kocsis, 2001).

A fourth development is the emergence of a more sophisticated kind of racism, one which Martin Barker called the 'new racism' in 1981. This new racism no longer makes the old arguments (usually about biological inferiority) but highlights *cultural* differences as those that really matter. Just how incompatible this 'different culture' is with the dominant one becomes a key issue.

Finally, there is an emerging mentality that is specific to Europe. In England, it takes the form of 'little England'; in Europe more generally, it is 'Fortress Europe'. There is a growing concern to exclude the poorer countries on the fringe of Europe, which includes some of the Eastern European countries, as well as those in Africa and Eastern Asia. And there has been a growing

intolerance of migrating groups – especially what have become known as 'bogus asylum seekers'.

Ethnic antagonisms in the UK

> Britain is now two entirely different worlds, and the one you inherit is determined by the colour of your skin.
>
> (Salman Rushdie, 1982: 418)

There has been a long history of ethnic antagonisms in the UK, but several main issues can be highlighted.

First, *public conflicts* – even riots. In the 1950s, shortly after the arrival of a major wave of West Indians, there were the Notting Hill Riots – in this case, with whites attacking blacks. But by the 1980s the rioting and conflicts had changed. Now it was the blacks themselves who protested, in a series of riots throughout the 1980s, mainly involving young people against the police – in Brixton (April 1981), St Paul's in Bristol, Handsworth, and Toxteth in Liverpool. They were considered serious enough for a committee of inquiry, chaired by Lord Scarman. In an influential report, he located the problems of black inner-city youth whose lives had become marginalised. He noted the tension between black youth and the police, the plight of inner-city living, and the exclusion experienced by black youth. Troubles erupted again in the summer of 2001, when further conflicts broke out in the North of England – at Bradford, Oldham, Leeds and Burnley. As usual, these conflicts primarily involved young men, but this time they flared up mainly in poor Muslim communities where there was also a menacing threat from right-wing campaigners such as the National Front.

Second, *racial attacks*. There is a long history of violence directed towards 'blacks' – what will be described in Chapter 16 as **hate crimes**. Many instances of these crimes have involved young people again, and the police. The Runnymede Trust estimated that between January 1970 and November 1989, some 74 people died as a result of racial attacks (Skellington, 1996: 83). During the 1980s and 1990s, the level of violence appears to have escalated – a Home Office survey suggested a growth of 80 per cent between 1983 and 1993. In 1993, there were 3,550 incidents recorded in London alone – with one-tenth of all incidents nationally being in the East End of London. (Note that recorded incidents may well seriously underestimate the true total. The British Crime Survey suggests they probably constitute only 10 per cent of the true number.)

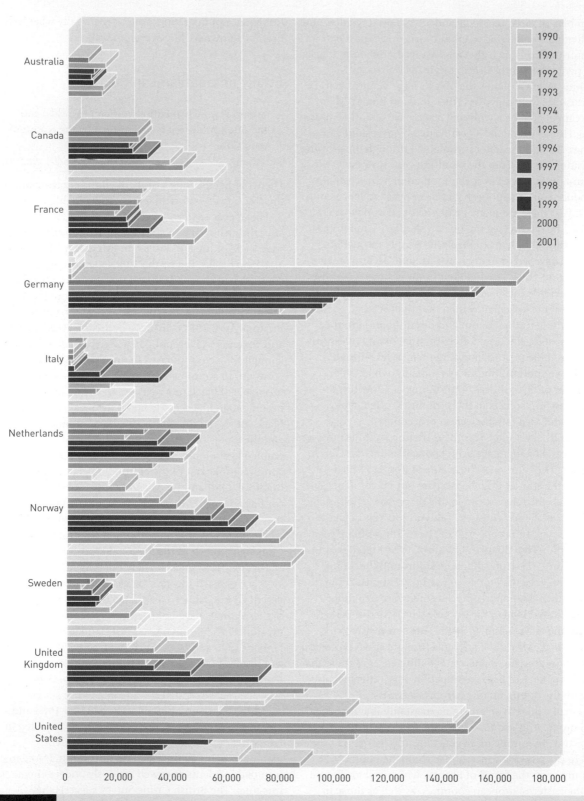

Figure 11.4   Asylum applications, selected countries, 1990–2001

Source: after Migration Policy Institute, http://www.migrationinformation.org/globaldata/charts/3.1.shtml

THE ROMA AND THE SKINHEADS

Upwards of 6 million gypsies or Roma live in Europe. They are largely scattered in small communities throughout the former communist societies and around the Mediterranean. For example, in Slovakia they make up as much as 10 per cent of the population; in Hungary and the Czech Republic it is estimated they comprise around 3 per cent; and in Romania they number some 2 million people – the largest national population in the world.

The terms used to describe them are often hard to define: 'pikeys', 'travellers', 'Gypsies', 'Roma', 'Bohemians', 'Manush', and 'Burugoti' can be used, though they do not all mean the same thing. One thing they have in common is that wherever they are found, they are usually badly treated. They also figure low on most social indicators – usually among the very poorest of a society, under-educated, short-lived, dependent on welfare, segregated, in poor health, and removed from political life. They are also among the most imprisoned. They are hugely discriminated against – from where they can live, to life in school, to being the victims of neo-Nazi thugs.

In one major incident, a Romani teenager, Mario Goral, was attacked by a group of skinheads in the central town of Slovakia, Ziar nad Hronom. Some 30 skinheads attacked a pub frequented by Roma with Molotov cocktails, crowbars and knives. They doused Mario with gasoline and polystyrene and set him on fire. He died a few days later. Only after the death did the Slovak government condemn the attack. And writing anonymously in the Presov evening newspapers, the skinheads explained who they were to the general public:

The skinheads want to protect Presov against Gypsies – Roma. Who else but the Gypsies create a mess in the city, steal, and participate in the black market? Now you can think that we are very racist. But you can hardly find a man who would not be ashamed of a Gypsy. . . . We want Slovaks to live in Presov, in Slovakia. We want a white Slovakia, because if nothing changes, then it will be a catastrophe for Presov and for Slovakia.

Sources: *The Economist*, 12 May 2001: 29-32; European Roma Rights Centre, 1997, updates from: http:/errc.org/publications/reports/slovakia.pdf

Gypsies or Romanies by a fire on a vacant lot near Berlin's Eastern Station.
Source: Magnum © Thomas Hoepker

Asian shopkeepers are a notable target of attack. But it is not just in inner-city areas where violence is rife; in rural areas, isolated black families may be especially vulnerable to attack. Police clear-up rates are generally low (of the order of 20 per cent).

Third, has been the widespread existence of *racial discrimination*. A number of surveys have found discrimination in the work situation. Studies from the Policy Studies Institute (formerly Political and Economic Planning (PEP)) have regularly documented high levels of discrimination (see Daniel, 1968; Modood *et al.*, 1997). Often, the studies show blatant discrimination – with white and black stooges applying for similar jobs, only to find that the black population is more discriminated against.

There have been attempts to criminalise racial violence, but so far they have all failed. For instance, the Racial Hatred and Violence Bill 1984 – seeking extra penalties for crimes with racial motivations and a new crime of 'racial harassment' – was talked out at its second reading (Skellington, 1996: 91).

All of the above signals a long-term and growing series of complex problems. Migration and ethnic diversity can bring fears, prejudice, racism – and the possibilities of more and more ethnic conflict and ethnic cleansing, even ethnic war. Stuart Hall (1992b: 308–309) has suggested three main responses to ethnic divides in a multicultural society. These are:

- A defensive strengthening of local/dominant cultural identities. People feel threatened and resolve this through a reassertion of absolute values. In the UK, this can mean an 'aggressive little Englandism'.

- A defensive strengthening of the minority culture identities. With the experience of racism and exclusion, the culture of origin is used to construct a strong counter-identity. This can be found in the UK as Rastafarianism (reasserting 'Africa' and the Caribbean) and the revival of Muslim Fundamentalism (in the Pakistani community).

- The creation of new 'mixed' identities – a possible consequence of globalisation, giving a broader sense of identity. In the UK, the identity 'black' can be used by both Afro-Caribbean and Asian communities. Paul Gilroy (1994) talks of 'the Black Atlantic' as a cultural network spanning many countries (Africa, the Caribbean, the Americas, the UK) where people may have African descent even though they have come to greatly modify it in new cultures.

Ann Barrow, the landlady of the "Live and Let Live" public house, surveys the damage caused to her pub, May 27, 2001, during overnight riots between police and youths in Oldham
Source: © Ian Hodgson/Reuters/Corbis

The future of ethnic relations

This chapter started by reviewing a number of major explanations of prejudice and discrimination. Often, such prejudices are seen as the individual quirks of a few people in prejudiced cultures. But this chapter has tried to show that these processes are at work across all (or most) cultures, and are based upon patterns of ethnic migration. Each culture comes to identify some people as different and outside the culture. Often connected to economic problems, these 'others' come to serve major scapegoating functions. They can be used to reassert the importance and dominance of majority populations. Ethnic divides seem wide and deep. As we saw in the opening story of Bosnia, many contemporary wars are connected to such divides. An understanding of the social processes at work in the construction of these hostilities seems ever more urgent.

SUMMARY

1. Race involves a presumed cluster of biological traits. A century ago, scientists identified three broad, overarching racial categories: Caucasians, Mongoloids and Negroids. However, there are no pure races and these categories are in disrepute. Ethnicity is a matter not of biology but of shared cultural heritage. Racialisation is the process of naming different races. Minorities, including those of certain races and ethnicities, are categories of people who are socially distinctive and who have a subordinate social position.

2. A prejudice is an inflexible and distorted generalisation about a category of people. Racism, a powerful type of prejudice, is any assertion that one race is innately superior or inferior to another. Discrimination is a pattern of action by which a person treats various categories of people unequally. Institutional discrimination refers to the fact that the law and other social institutions, in contrast to individuals, can treat different categories of people unequally. Pluralism refers to a state in which racial and ethnic categories, although distinct, have equal social standing. Assimilation is a process by which minorities gradually adopt the patterns of the dominant culture. Segregation means the physical and social separation of categories of people. Genocide involves the extermination of a category of people.

3. Migration patterns have played a significant role in shaping most cultures. Future patterns of migration are likely to be more global, and involve more women.

4. The main ethnic groups in the UK number about 7 per cent of the population. They are an ethnically heterogeneous group but include South Asians (from India, Bangladesh, Pakistan) and Afro-Caribbeans. Forty-eight per cent are under the age of 24.

5. Ethnic antagonisms are widespread and increasing in Europe. Attacks, harassment and discrimination are features of minority ethnic living in Europe.

CRITICAL-THINKING QUESTIONS

1. Discuss patterns of ethnic inequality in any one European culture.

2. What is meant by racialisation? How does it connect to the idea of 'race'?

3. What are the major patterns of migration in post-war Europe? Should there be limits on immigration?

4. Examine what is meant by the 'new racism'? Give examples.

GOING FURTHER

Further reading

David Mason, *Race and Ethnicity in Modern Britain* (2nd edn, 2000a)
A short, clear introduction to the whole field.

Sir W. Macpherson, *The Stephen Lawrence Inquiry* (The Macpherson Report) (1999)
Raises the issues of institutional racism in the UK. Although this details one tragic case, its implications are wide-ranging.

Mohan Lutra, *Britain's Black Population* (1997)
An accessible and comprehensive overview.

Tariq Modood *et al.*, Ethnic Minorities in Britain (4th edn, 1997)
An ongoing survey of ethnic minorities in the UK.

Patricia Hill Collins, *Black Feminist Thought* (1990)
An important statement of issues concerning black feminism.

Stephen Castles and Mark J. Miller, *The Age of Migration: International Population Movements in the Modern World* (3rd edn, 2003)
Discusses migration movements on a global level, and shows how they lead to ethnic minorities.

More information

Internationally, the Minority Rights Group publishes the *World Directory of Minorities*, which details 1,000 minorities (and their various persecutions). *The International Migration Review* (Center for Migration Studies, New York) is a regular and valuable source of information on migration patterns. R. Skellington, *'Race' in Britain Today* (2nd edn, 1996) is a useful reference book of facts and figures. *Race Today*, *Ethnic and Race Relations*, and *Race and Class* are all journals that highlight matters of race; the first is the most accessible to students. For up-to-date 'briefing papers' on issues of concern to the multi-ethnic society in the UK, look at The Runnymede Trust's website (see below).

Watch a video/Read a book

- Udayan Prasad's *My Son the Fanatic* (1997): a father is confronted by his Islamic fundamentalist son in Bradford.
- Tony Gatlif's *Gadjo Dilo* (1999): gives an ethnographer's eye on gypsy life and racism in Romania.
- Robert Mulligan's *To Kill a Mockingbird* (1962): racism in the deep South of the United States.
- Stephen Frear's *My Beautiful Launderette* (1985): Asian community in the UK meets gay life in a launderette.
- Damien O'Donnell's *East is East*: very funny look at discrimination within Asian communities in the UK.
- John Singleton's classic *Boyz N the Hood* (1991): about surviving the pressures of family and street life in south central Los Angeles
- Wayne Wang's *Chan is Missing* (1982): a 1982 film of two taxi drivers searching the streets of San Francisco. Something of a cult film.

Four good classic US novels on race and racism are Ralph Ellison's *Invisible Man*, (1999) Maya Angelou's *I Know Why the Caged Bird Sings* (1993); James Baldwin's *Giovanni's Room* (1956); and Alice Walker's *The Colour Purple* (1982).

Connecting up

Connect to other chapters

- For links to culture and language, see Chapter 5.
- For links to world poverty, see Chapter 9 .

To the websites

- Minority Rights International:

  http://www.minorityrights.org/

  An international NGO, based in London, which promotes the rights of ethnic, religious and other minorities. Contains a great deal of information.

Websites on race and racism:

- Commission for Racial Equality:

  http://www.cre.gov.uk

- Institute of Race Relations:

  http://www.irr.org.uk/

- The Runnymede Trust:

  http://www.runnymedetrust.org/

Websites on migration:

- Migration Information Sources :

  http://www.migrationinformation.org

- International Organisation for Information:

  http://www.iom.int/

- Immigration Index:

  http://www.immigrationindex.org/

All are major resources for information on racism, discrimination and asylum seekers.

For additional case studies, multiple choice questions, internet exercises, and annotated weblinks specific to this chapter, visit this book's website at www.pearsoned.co.uk/plummer

CHAPTER 12

THE GENDER ORDER AND SEXUALITIES

He is the Subject, he is the
Absolute – she is the Other.
Simone de Beauvoir, *The Second Sex*,
1997 introduction

IN THE NEW GUINEA SOCIETY OF THE SAMBIA, boys aged 7 to 10 are taken from their mothers to a special place outside the village. Here they experience powerful homosexual fellatio activities. For a number of years, they daily fellate, for some years as fellator and then later as fellated. Elders teach that semen is absolutely vital; that it should be consumed daily since it is the basis of biological maleness; and that their very masculinity depends on it! At the same time, they must avoid women who are seen to be contaminating. When they are young men, they are returned to society, where they settle down and marry women. With fatherhood, their homosexuality ceases. But then the cycle starts all over again when the men steer their own young sons into this erotic pattern. 'Homoeroticism is the royal road to Sambia manliness.' This is a ritualised form of homosexuality, and for the Sambia it is absolutely essential that men engage in these fellating activities in order to establish both their masculinity and, ultimately, their heterosexuality. Masculinity, here, is the outcome of a regime of ritualised homosexuality leading into manhood.

Some may find such research a little unsettling. Masculinity is often said to be the very opposite of homosexuality. Life among boys and men in the Sambia is clearly not like life among boys and men in modern Europe. In Europe, there is no ritualised homosexuality among all young boys in order for them to become men. Quite the opposite. If boys are found to be involved in sex with other boys, they are often presumed to be passing through a brief homosexual phase, or they are seen as being effeminate and queer. It is certainly not seen as 'manly'.

This is just one of many interesting researches that the field of gender studies has been developing for the past 25 years, and it has come up with all kinds of interesting research findings and theories. Once again we find that gender is not an automatically biological thing, but a phenomenon that involves a great deal of social activity. This chapter provides an introductory exploration of this area.

(Herdt, 1981)

KEY THEMES

- The distinction between sex, gender, sexism, patriarchy and gender stratification
- How we become gendered and learning gender identities
- The nature of the Women's Movement in challenging gender stratification
- The sociological approaches to sexuality
- The stratification of sexualities
- What lesbian and gay life/Queer theory is about

(Left) Gala Contemplating the Mediterranean Sea Which at Eighteen Metres Becomes the Portrait of Abraham Lincoln, (Homage to Rothko), 1976 (oil on photograhic paper), Salvador Dali (1904–89).

Source: © Salvador Dali, Gali-Salvador Foundation, DACS, London 2005/Museo Dali, Figueras, Spain/www.bridgeman.co.uk

life' (UNFPA, 2000: 25). Figures vary across countries and for differing kinds of abuse, but that such abuse is both widespread and frequently condoned makes it a crucial area for understanding patriarchy.

 SOCIAL SHAPES OF THE WORLD

PATRIARCHY 'AT WORK'

Although many women work throughout the world, their economic contributions are often undercounted because they are often in the informal sector. In some countries women are still unable to work, because of religious prohibitions which restrict their movements. Where women do work, they usually are paid much less than men, have lower-status jobs and find themselves unavailable to reach the higher levels of work. Patriarchy can be seen 'at work'.

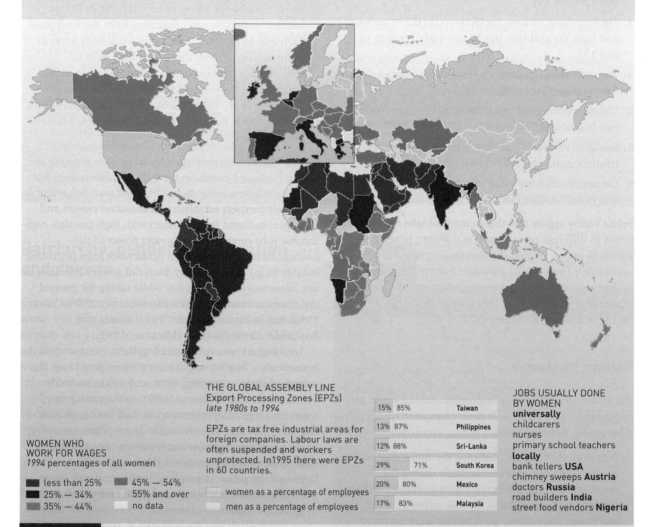

WOMEN WHO
WORK FOR WAGES
1994 percentages of all women

- ■ less than 25%
- ■ 25% — 34%
- ■ 35% — 44%
- ▦ 45% — 54%
- ▨ 55% and over
- ▢ no data

THE GLOBAL ASSEMBLY LINE
Export Processing Zones (EPZs)
late 1980s to 1994

EPZs are tax free industrial areas for foreign companies. Labour laws are often suspended and workers unprotected. In1995 there were EPZs in 60 countries.

▢ women as a percentage of employees
▢ men as a percentage of employees

15%	85%	Taiwan
13%	87%	Philippines
12%	88%	Sri-Lanka
29%	71%	South Korea
20%	80%	Mexico
17%	83%	Malaysia

JOBS USUALLY DONE
BY WOMEN
universally
childcarers
nurses
primary school teachers
locally
bank tellers **USA**
chimney sweeps **Austria**
doctors **Russia**
road builders **India**
street food vendors **Nigeria**

Map 12.1   Women's paid employment in global perspective

Throughout the industrialised world, at least one-third of the paid workforce is made up of women, though their work tends to be lower-paid and lower-status than men's. In poorer societies, women often work harder but are less likely to be paid for their efforts. In Latin America, for example, women represent only about 15 per cent of the paid workforce; in Islamic societies of North Africa and the Middle East, perhaps more for cultural than for economic reasons, the proportion is even lower.

Source: adapted from *Joni Seager, The State of Women in the World Atlas*, Penguin, p. 68.

WORLD WATCH

PATRIARCHY BREAKING DOWN: A REPORT FROM BOTSWANA

As the judge handed down the decision, Unity Dow beamed a smile towards the friends sitting all around her; people in the courtroom joined together in hugs and handshakes. Dow, then a 32-year-old lawyer and citizen of the southern African nation of Botswana, had won the first round in her efforts to overturn the laws by which, she maintains, her country defines women as second-class citizens.

The law that sparked Unity Dow's recent suit against her government specifies the citizenship rights of children. Botswana is traditionally patrilineal, meaning that people trace family membership through males, making children part of their father's – but not their mother's – family line.

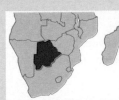

COUNTRY FACT FILE	
BOTSWANA	
Population	1,679,000 (2002)
Per capita GNP	$3,300
Life expectancy	36,8 male 37,5 female (2001)
Literacy	around 75% (2000)
Languages	Setswana (national) and English (official)
Religions	Some are Catholic or Protestant, while the rest practise African religions
Main cities	Gaborone: 185,891; Francistown: 84,406; Selebi-Pikwe: 50,012 (2001)
Human Development Index 2004	128th

Source: adapted from *The World Guide 2001*; Brittanica Almanac, 2004

Under the law, a child of a Botswanan man and a woman of another nationality is a citizen of Botswana, since in that country legal standing passes through the father. But the child of a Botswanan woman and a man from another nation has no rights of citizenship. Because she married a man from the United States, Unity Dow's children had no citizen's rights in the country where they were born.

The Dow case attracted broad attention because its significance extends far beyond citizenship to the overall legal standing of women and men. In rendering the decision in Dow's favour, High Court Judge Martin Horwitz declared, 'The time that women were treated as chattels or were there to obey the whims and wishes of males is long past'. In support of his decision, Horwitz pointed to the constitution of Botswana, which guarantees fundamental rights and freedoms to both women and men. Arguing for the government against Dow, Ian Kirby, a deputy attorney general, conceded that the constitution confers equal rights on the two sexes, but he claimed that the law can and should take account of sex where such patterns are deeply rooted in Botswanan male-dominated culture. To challenge such traditions in the name of Western feminism, he continued, amounts to cultural imperialism by which some people seek to subvert an established way of life by advancing foreign notions that are popular elsewhere.

Women from many African nations attended the Dow court case, sensing that a historic change was at hand. And, indeed, this has proven to be the case. As a result of the Dow ruling, the constitution of Botswana was amended to extend citizenship to children such as her own. Symbolically, this transformation greatly enhances the social standing of that nation's women.

To many people in Europe, the Dow case may seem strange, since the notion that men and women are entitled to equal rights and privileges is widely endorsed throughout the European Union.

The Declaration on the Elimination of Violence Against Women, adopted by the United Nations General Assembly in 1993, defines violence against women as 'any act of gender-based violence that results in, or is likely to result in, physical, sexual, or psychological harm or suffering to women, including threats of such acts, coercion or arbitrary deprivation of liberty, whether occurring in public or private life'. It encompasses, but is not limited to:

WORLD WATCH

SEX TOURISM AND THE SEX TRADE IN THAILAND

Another dimension of gender bias is the exploding growth of sexual slavery involving young women, which has spread rapidly across Southeast Asia. Bangkok is emerging as the sex-tourism capital of the

COUNTRY FACT FILE

THAILAND

Population	63,430,000 (2002)
Per capita GNP	$2,000 (2000)
Life expectancy	52 years (2001)
Literacy	around 93% (1995)
Religions	Buddhism
Main city	Bangkok 5,680,380 (2000)
Human Development Index 2004	76th

Source: adapted from *The World Guide 2001*; Brittanica Almanac, 2004

world; prostitution in Thailand currently claims over 1 million females, half under the age of 18. In some cases, parents sell female infants to agents who pay others to raise them, then 'harvest their crop' when the girls approach their teenage years and are old enough to work the sex trade. In other cases, girls who see little future in a rural village make their own way to the city, only to fall into the hands of pimps who soon have them working in brothels, soliciting in bars or performing in sex shows. Pimps provide girls with clothes and housing, but at a price that exceeds the girls' salaries. The result is a system of debt bondage that keeps women virtual prisoners of their unscrupulous employers. Those who run away are pursued by agents and forced to return.

The numbers involved are rapidly mounting: Thailand alone now has 1–2 million prostitutes (perhaps 8 per cent of the country's female population); about half of these are under the age of 18. The future for these girls and women is bleak. Most suffer from a host of diseases brought on by abuse and neglect, and 40 per cent are now infected with the virus that causes AIDS.

Source: Kempadoo and Doezema (1998); O'Connell Davidson (1998).

'Sex trafficking' is now a major industry all around the world. Here sex workers sit on steps in India awaiting trade.

Source: © Jeffery L. Rotman/Corbis

physical, sexual and psychological violence occurring in the family, including battering, sexual abuse of female children in the household, dowry-related violence, marital rape, female genital mutilation and other traditional practices harmful to women, non-spousal violence and violence related to exploitation; physical, sexual and psychological violence occurring within the general community, including rape, sexual abuse, sexual harassment and intimidation at work, in educational institutions and elsewhere; trafficking in women and forced prostitution; and physical, sexual and psychological violence perpetrated or condoned by the state, wherever it occurs.

(UNFPA, 2000: 25–6)

Taking this, the report concludes:

- In the United States, a woman is battered, usually by her intimate partner, every 15 seconds.

- Across the world, at least one in every three women has been beaten, coerced into sex or abused, usually by someone she knows.

- As many as 5,000 women and girls are killed annually in so-called 'honour' killings (many of them for the dishonour of being raped!).

- An estimated 4 million women and girls are bought and sold worldwide each year, into either marriage, prostitution or slavery.

- Rape in war is a common practice (Allen, 1996).

- Worldwide, some 130 million girls and young women have undergone female genital mutilation (FGM).

- Each year women undergo an estimated 50 million abortions, 20 million of which are unsafe; some 78,000 women die and millions suffer (UNFPA, 2000: 4–5; Chapter 3).

Such figures are often hard to interpret, but it is nevertheless clear that there is a major issue of violence against women across the world. The core of understanding these issues is not to see them as 'women's issues' but to see them as part of a gender regime in which patriarchy plays a key organising role. We need to see women and men through their relationships with each other: beatings and sexual violence are often just woven into the texture of a man and a woman's relationship.

Is patriarchy inevitable?

Technologically simple societies have little control over biological forces. Thus, men's greater physical strength, as well as women's common experience of pregnancy, combine to bolster patriarchy. Technological advances, however, give members of industrial societies a wider range of choices about gender. Industrial machinery has diminished the primacy of muscle power in everyday life, just as contraception has given women control over pregnancy. Today, then, biological differences provide little justification for patriarchy.

Categorical social inequality – whether based on race, ethnicity or sex – also comes under attack in the more egalitarian culture of industrial societies. In many industrial nations, law mandates equal employment opportunities for women and men and equal pay for comparable efforts. Nonetheless, in all industrial societies, the two sexes continue to hold different jobs and receive unequal pay, as we will explain presently. So does the persistence of patriarchy mean that it is inevitable? Some sociologists contend that biological factors underlie sex-based differences – especially a greater level of aggressiveness on the part of males. If this is so, of course, the eradication of patriarchy would be difficult and perhaps even impossible (Goldberg, 1974, 1993; Rossi, 1985; Popenoe, 1993). However, most sociologists believe that gender is primarily a social construction, subject to change. Simply because no society has yet eliminated patriarchy, then, does not mean that we must remain prisoners of the past.

To understand why patriarchy has persisted throughout human history, we need to see how gender is rooted and reproduced in society, a process that begins with the way we learn to think of ourselves as children and continues through the work we perform as adults.

Becoming gendered: the case of gender socialisation

The first question people usually ask about a newborn (and nowadays a pre-born too!) – 'Is it a boy or a girl?' – looms large because the answer involves not just sex but the likely direction of the child's entire life. In fact, gender is at work even before the birth of a child, since in many parts of the world parents generally hope to have a boy rather than a girl. As we noted in Chapter 11, in China, India and other strongly patriarchal societies, female embryos are at risk because parents may abort them, hoping later to produce a boy, whose social value is greater.

There is a huge amount of research and theorising on gender development, but three broad traditions can be briefly distinguished.

1. *Social learning theories.* These suggest that differences in gender behaviour are learnt, in the same way as all behaviours, through a mixture of rewards, reinforcements and punishments. From its earliest day the baby boy is rewarded for behaving in 'boyish' ways and punished for being 'girl-like'. Often, this theory suggests how boys come to model themselves upon or imitate the behaviour of other men and boys, as this will be most highly praised and rewarded. The boy, in effect, thinks 'I want rewards. I am rewarded for doing boy things, therefore I want to be a boy.' It is a very widely held theory, and a very simple one.

2. *Cognitive theories.* These suggest that differences in gender emerge through a categorisation process in which boys come to place themselves in a 'masculine' category and proceed to organise their experiences around it. Here the boy, in effect, says 'I am a boy, therefore I want to do boy things'. Some of these theories suggest that there may be preformed stages at which such identifications can take place, while others suggest that the identities emerge out of social contexts. Kohlberg (1981) is a major proponent of this view.

3. *Psychodynamic theories.* These, derived from Freud (introduced in Chapter 7), suggest that differences in gender emerge out of emotional struggles between the infant and its caretakers in the earliest years of life. Most classically, a boy's emotional structure emerges from the conflict between the love of his mother and the fear of his father which, if resolved successfully, will eventually lead the boy to identify strongly with his father and hence with masculinity. Psychodynamic theorists disagree with each other over the nature of this conflict and its timing, but it is basic to this theory that gender is structured 'unconsciously' into a deep emotional form in early childhood.

Each of these theories has many variants, is very widely held and has spawned a massive research and analytical literature. In general, the virtues of one theory are the weaknesses of the others, and each theory has its own emphasis, behaviour, cognition or emotion. It is far beyond the scope of this book to review all this material, but here we will focus on the Freudian tradition.

Nancy Chodorow and the reproduction of mothering

How do little girls grow up to become mothers? Why don't boys? Chodorow (1978) starts her analysis by criticising some of the most popular explanations of gender differences – those that stress biology, social learning and role learning. Although such theories may be partially correct, they all fail to deal adequately with the way in which gender differences are organised into the deep psychic structuring of individuals. She prefers to use a Freudian theory (introduced in Chapter 7). For her, masculinity and femininity are rooted in strong emotional structures established very early in life and are very hard to transform. Men in Anglo-Saxon culture tend, on the whole, to become more emotionally restricted yet more independent, and more work- and achievement-orientated than women, who seem to 'connect better'. Men often lack a 'connectedness' to relate to loved ones, while girls tend to develop stronger attachments and reproduce this in mothering. Of course, these are generalisations. (They are not that dissimilar to Talcott Parsons's distinctions between expressive and instrumental roles, discussed below.)

Chodorow (1978) argues that in order to understand the development of these strong emotional structures, we have to go back to the intense connections between child and mother in which both baby boy and baby girl are overwhelmingly dependent upon the mother. (Note that this is true of Western culture; it is by no means true of all.) From the beginning of life there is a process of forming strong attachments and dependencies with the mother, and an accompanying sense of anxiety and fear when she is absent. There is a massive identification of both boy and girl with the 'mother' – the primary caregiver who suckles, shelters and comforts the baby. The image of the mother is incorporated and internalised by the child.

So far, the description holds for both boys and girls. Bit by bit, the child has to break away from the strong identification with the carer, to test its competence against the outside world. Although both the baby girl and baby boy are primarily attached to the mother, the girl remains attached while the boy breaks away. The little girl does not outgrow her dependency, she does not develop a strong sense of separateness and boundaries, and this leads her ultimately to identify with the needs of others more than boys. In later life this asserts itself as the need for mothering. 'The basic feminine sense of self is connected to the world, the basic masculine sense of self is separate' (Chodorow, 1978: 169).

While the little girl stays in close identification with the mother and ultimately attains a less separate, more connected sense of identity, the little boy is pushed into a sharper, stronger and earlier separation. This rupture may be experienced as an abandonment and generate lifelong anxieties around rejection. For many boys, so the story goes, this leads to a turning to the outer world (especially of hitherto relatively insignificant fathers) and the establishment of a separate, autonomous identity – one fearful of connecting in case of abandonment, and often open to rage against the long-lost love object, the mother. In one swoop male autonomy, male inexpressiveness and male hostility towards women are explained!

Critical comment

Although this theory is influential, critics have worried that the evidence for it is inadequate: it depends on a few clinical cases for generalisations. Feminist critics have also accused the theory of 'blaming the victim', of ultimately blaming mothers for the reproduction of male power in their sons (see Trebilcot, 1984). Other critics also see the theory as presenting a model of development that is too unchangeable. These days, for example, we see many 'modern' 'new' men who are very seriously involved in 'mothering' – or 'parenting' as it is increasingly called. Chodorow responds by saying that although gender identity is established in early lives, it is only a provisional structure and one that is open to change in later life. Indeed, she advocates fathers being much more involved in raising children, so that it breaks the cycle of motherhood and both boys and girls find nurturance in fathers as well as mothers (Chodorow, 1978).

Gender across the life cycle

Chodorow's theory needs supplementing by looking at both wider influences on the child (peer group, school, workplace), and transformations over the life cycle. There is, for instance, a considerable body of research that suggests that childhood worlds are highly segregated by gender and that this segregation works to structure gender identity. Likewise, there is research on the male life cycle that suggests that as men become older they often change into more emotionally responsive and less powerfully autonomous people than was evidenced in their youth and childhood. Gender emerges over the entire life cycle through a series of ever-changing encounters in which meaning is built up, modified and transformed. Gender is not something fixed at any time, but is a process constantly open to historical changes in the wider world, local changes in situation and biographical shifts over the life cycle.

Gender and work

Andrew Tolson in what was the first major English study of masculinity, *The Limits of Masculinity* (1977),

suggested that in addition to early family experiences there are three major sites for boys and men in which gender is formed and structured: the peer group, the school and the workplace. He is particularly keen to emphasise the importance of the workplace in reinforcing male identity. Just as adult female lives often become swamped by thinking about 'their children', so male lives become overwhelmed by 'their work' – seeking success in it, dealing with boredom from it, finding alternatives to it, being humiliated by lack of it. In many ways this concern with work as a key to male identity simply reflects the earlier experiences of childhood – the quest for power, autonomy and the concomitant anxiety about failure and rejection.

Gender and the mass media

When it first captured the public imagination in the 1950s, television placed the dominant segment of the population – white males – at centre stage. Racial and ethnic minorities were all but absent from television until the early 1970s; only in the last two decades have programmes featured women in prominent roles. Even when both sexes appeared on camera, men generally played the brilliant detectives, fearless explorers and skilled surgeons. Women, by contrast, continued to be cast as the less capable characters, often prized primarily for their sexual attractiveness.

Change came most slowly to advertising, which sells products by conforming to widely established cultural norms. Advertising thus presented the two sexes, more often than not, in stereotypical ways. Historically, advertisements showed women in the home, happily using cleaning products, serving foods, modelling clothing and trying out new appliances. Men, on the other hand, predominated in ads for cars, travel, banking services, industrial companies and alcoholic beverages.

The beauty myth

Although gender biases in advertising are now very much weaker, advertising still actively perpetuates what Naomi Wolf calls 'the beauty myth'. She argues that society teaches women to measure personal importance, accomplishment and satisfaction largely in terms of physical appearance (Backman and Adams, 1991). Curiously, however, this myth also sets up unattainable standards of beauty for most women (such as the *Playboy* centrefold or the skinny Paris fashion model), making the quest for beauty ultimately self-defeating. It should not be surprising, argues Wolf, that the beauty myth surfaced in our culture during the 1890s, the 1920s and the 1980s – all times of anxiety and heightened debate about the social standing of women.

The beauty myth society teaches women to prize relationships with men, whom, presumably, they attract with their beauty. The relentless pursuit of beauty not only drives women towards being highly disciplined, but it also forces them to be keenly attuned and responsive to men. Beauty-minded women, in short, strive to please men and avoid challenging male power. More, through this myth men learn to want to possess women who embody beauty. In other words, our concept of beauty both reduces women to objects and motivates men to possess them as if they were dolls rather than human beings.

In short, Wolf argues, beauty is as much about behaviour as appearance. The myth holds that the key to women's personal happiness lies in beauty (or, for men, in possessing a beautiful woman). In fact, however, beauty amounts to an elaborate system – which this chapter explores – through which society teaches both women and men to embrace specific roles and attitudes that place them in a social hierarchy. The equation runs something like this: by embracing traditional notions of femininity and masculinity, we raise our prospects for personal and professional success. Thus, advertising commands masculine men to drive the 'right' car and feminine women to use beauty aids that will help them look younger and more attractive to men.

Understanding gender

Although they come to differing conclusions, the functional and conflict paradigms can again help us here: each points up the importance of gender to social organisation.

Functional analysis

As Chapter 4 suggested, members of hunting and gathering societies had little power over the forces of biology. Lacking effective birth control, women experienced frequent pregnancies, and the responsibilities of child care kept them close to home. Likewise, to take advantage of greater male strength, norms guided men towards the pursuit of game and other tasks away from the home. Over many generations, this sexual division of labour became institutionalised and largely taken for granted (Lengermann and Wallace, 1985).

Industrial technology opens up a vastly greater range of cultural possibilities. Human muscle power no longer serves as a vital source of energy, so the physical strength of men loses much of its earlier significance. At the same time, the ability to control reproduction gives women greater choice in shaping their lives. Modern societies come to see that traditional gender roles waste an enormous amount of human talent; yet change comes slowly, because gender is deeply embedded in social mores.

Talcott Parsons: gender and complementarity

In addition, as Talcott Parsons (1942, 1964; orig. 1951, 1964; orig. 1954) explained, gender differences help to integrate society – at least in its traditional form. Gender, Parsons noted, forms a *complementary* set of roles that links men and women together into family units that carry out various functions vital to the operation of society. Women take charge of family life, assuming primary responsibility for managing the household and raising children. Men, by contrast, connect the family to the larger world, primarily by participating in the labour force.

Parsons further argued that distinctive socialisation teaches the two sexes their appropriate gender identity and skills needed for adult life. Thus society teaches boys – presumably destined for the labour force – to be rational, self-assured and competitive. This complex of traits Parsons termed *instrumental*. To prepare girls for child-rearing, their socialisation stresses what Parsons called *expressive* qualities, such as emotional responsiveness and sensitivity to others.

Society, explains Parsons, promotes gender-linked behaviour through various schemes of social control. People incorporate cultural definitions about gender into their own identities, so that failing to be appropriately feminine or masculine produces guilt and fear of rejection by members of the opposite sex. In simple terms, women learn to view non-masculine men as sexually unattractive, while men learn to avoid unfeminine women.

Critical comment

Functionalism advances a theory of complementarity by which gender integrates society both structurally (in terms of what people do) and morally (in terms of what they believe). Although influential in the mid-twentieth century, this approach is rarely used today by researchers exploring the impact of gender.

For one thing, this analysis assumes a singular vision of society that is not shared by everyone. Poor women, for example, have always worked outside the home as a matter of economic necessity; today, more and more women at all social levels are entering the labour force for various reasons. A second problem, say the critics, is that Parsons' analysis minimises the personal strains and social costs produced by rigid, traditional gender roles (Giele, 1988). Third, and finally, to those whose goals include sexual equality, what Parsons describes as gender complementarity amounts to little more than male domination. As is often the case, we find that functionalist analysis has a conservative cast.

Conflict analysis

It is a different story from a conflict point of view: gender now involves not just differences in behaviour but disparities in power. Conventional ideas about gender have historically benefited men while subjecting women to prejudice, discrimination and sometimes outright violence, in a striking parallel to the treatment of racial and ethnic minorities (Hacker, 1951, 1974; Collins, 1971; Lengermann and Wallace, 1985). Thus, conflict theorists claim, conventional ideas about gender promote not cohesion but tension and conflict, with men seeking to protect their privileges while women challenge the status quo.

As earlier chapters noted, the conflict paradigm draws heavily on the ideas of Karl Marx. Yet Marx was a product of his time in so far as his writings focused almost exclusively on men. His friend and collaborator Friedrich Engels, however, did explore the link between gender and social class (1902; orig. 1884).

Friedrich Engels: gender and class

Looking back through history, Engels noted that in hunting and gathering societies the activities of women and men, though different, had comparable importance. A successful hunt may have brought men great prestige, but the vegetation gathered by women constituted most of a society's food supply (Leacock, 1978). As technological advances led to a productive surplus, however, social equality and communal sharing gave way to private property and, ultimately, a class hierarchy. At this point, men gained pronounced power over women. With surplus wealth to pass on to heirs, upper-class men took a keen interest in their children. The desire to control property, then, prompted the creation of monogamous marriage and the family. Ideally, men could be certain of paternity – especially who their sons were – and the law ensured that wealth passed to them. The same logic explains why women were taught to remain virgins until marriage, to remain faithful to their husbands thereafter and to build their lives around bearing and raising children.

According to Engels, capitalism intensifies this male domination. First, capitalism creates more wealth, which confers greater power on men as wage earners as well as owners and heirs of property. Second, an expanding capitalist economy depends on defining people – especially women – as consumers and convincing them that personal fulfilment derives from owning and using products. Third, to allow men to work, society assigns women the task of maintaining the home. The double exploitation of capitalism, as Engels saw it, lies in paying low wages for male labour and no wages for female work (Eisenstein, 1979; Barry, 1983; Jagger, 1983; Vogel, 1983).

Critical comment

Conflict analysis highlights how society places the two sexes in unequal positions of wealth, power and privilege. As a result, the conflict approach is decidedly critical of conventional ideas about gender, claiming that society would be better off if we minimised or even eliminated this dimension of social structure.

But conflict analysis, too, has its limitations. One problem, critics suggest, is that this approach casts conventional families – defended by traditionalists as morally positive – as a social evil. Second, from a more practical standpoint, conflict analysis minimises the extent to which women and men live together cooperatively and often quite happily. A third problem with this approach, for some critics, is its assertion that capitalism stands at the root of gender stratification. Agrarian countries, in fact, are typically more patriarchal than industrial–capitalist nations. And socialist societies, too – including the People's Republic of China – remain strongly patriarchal (Moore, 1992).

Resisting patriarchy: the Women's Movement and feminism

Feminism is *the advocacy of social equality for the sexes, in opposition to patriarchy and sexism*. With roots in the English Revolution and the French Revolution – each with their concern over equality – the 'first wave' of the feminist movement was initiated with Mary Wollstonecraft's *A Vindication of the Rights of Woman* (1992; orig. 1792) and continued with the liberal classic by John Stuart Mill and Harriet Taylor Mill, *The Subjection of Women* (1869). They argued against women's perceived (biologically) inferior status and argued for improved education and equality before the law. Many of the initial

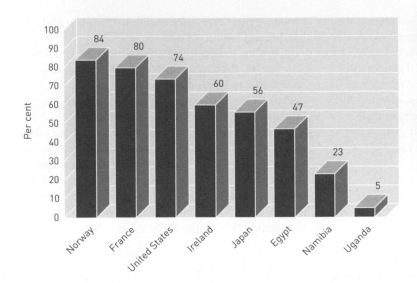

Figure 12.1 Use of contraception by married women of childbearing age

The Women's Movement has made a major issue over women's reproductive rights and the right to control their own bodies. Without this, feminists claim, women cannot gain autonomy.

Source: adapted from *World Development Report 1995: Workers in an Integrating World* (paper) by World Bank. Copyright 1995 by World Bank. Reproduced with permission of World Bank in the format Textbook via Copyright Clearence Center

campaigns centred on morality and sexuality, and an end to slavery. Perhaps the primary objective of the early Women's Movement was securing the right to vote, which British women first exercised in the general election on 14 December 1918 (O. Banks, 1981; Rowbottom, 1997). But other disadvantages persisted and a 'second wave' of feminism arose in the 1960s. More recently, some suggest a third – maybe postmodern – wave has arrived.

Basic feminist ideas

Although people who consider themselves feminists disagree about many things, most would probably support five general principles:

1. *The importance of change*. Feminist thinking is decidedly political; it links ideas to action. Feminism is critical of the status quo, advocating social equality for women and men.

2. *Expanding human choice*. Feminists maintain that cultural conceptions of gender divide the full range of human qualities into two opposing and limited spheres: the female world of emotion and cooperation and the male world of rationality and competition. As an alternative, feminists pursue a 'reintegration of humanity' by which each person develops *all* human traits (French, 1985).

3. *Eliminating gender stratification*. Feminism opposes laws and cultural norms that limit the education, income and job opportunities of women.

4. *Ending sexual violence*. A major objective of today's women's movement is eliminating sexual violence. Feminists argue that patriarchy distorts the

relationships between women and men and encourages violence against women in the form of rape, domestic abuse, sexual harassment and pornography (Millet, 1970; Dworkin, 1987; L. Kelly, 1988).

5. *Promoting sexual autonomy*. Finally, feminism advocates women's control of their sexuality and reproduction. Feminists support the free availability of birth control information. Figure 12.1 shows use of contraception in a range of countries, with Norway (and other Scandinavian countries) leading in use. In addition, most feminists support a woman's right to choose whether to bear children or to terminate a pregnancy, rather than allowing men – as husbands, doctors and legislators – to regulate sexuality. Many feminists also align with the gay and lesbian movement to overcome homophobia and heterosexism (which will be discussed later) (Vance, 1984; Segal, 1997).

Variations within feminism

As one would expect, feminism is not cut from one cloth. Indeed, it has many internal conflicts and much variety. We consider a few below.

Variations by country

One way in which feminism varies is simply by country. While 'North American feminism' has probably become the most organised, public and vocal in the world, it has also bred what might be called a 'superstar feminism' whereby a number of women become very prominent through their writing and media work (for example, Betty Friedan, Susan Brownmiller, Susan Faludi, Naomi Wolf).

In Europe, feminists are less likely to be so media-focused, and each country develops its own 'style' and set of conflicts. Angela Glasner has observed that:

Feminism in Europe exhibits a wide variety of forms . . . the political context has . . . been important in determining the specific form, and indeed in prescribing or proscribing feminism altogether. In Italy, Holland, Denmark and Norway, the second wave has been strongly influenced by left wing politics and has been predominantly led by middle class women. In France, the movement has been largely contained within the academic community, and in Germany it has been significantly diluted by conservatism.

(Glasner, 1992: 76–77)

We can also say that in Italy, Britain, Holland, Denmark and Norway it has been a more broadly based movement with alliances to the left. In Sweden the initiatives for change came much earlier: as a result, a strong collectivist culture emerged with women as a notable presence. Hence, there was little second-wave feminism as such. In the new democracies, by contrast (Spain, Portugal), hindered by both past authoritarianism and by the Roman Catholic background, the Women's Movement has been slower to develop.

Divisions in ideology

People pursue the goal of eliminating gender inequality in different ways. Classically, three major distinctions have been found within feminism, though recently many others have been noticed. Although the distinctions among them are far from clear-cut, each describes the problem of patriarchy in somewhat different terms and calls for correspondingly distinctive strategies for social change (O. Banks, 1981; Barry, 1983; Jagger, 1983; Stacey, 1983; Vogel, 1983).

1. Liberal feminism

Liberal feminism is grounded in classic liberal thinking that individuals should be free to develop their own talents and pursue their own interests. Liberal feminists accept the basic organisation of our society but seek to expand the rights and opportunities of women. Liberal feminists support equal rights and oppose prejudice and discrimination that block the aspirations of women.

Liberal feminists also endorse reproductive freedom for all women. Some respect aspects of the family as a social institution, calling for widely available maternity leave and child care for women who wish to work. Others are critical of the way in which the family

The London suffragettes demonstrate and are arrested, 1910.

Source: Popperfoto

reproduces gender and argue that freedom is not possible for women until families are dramatically changed (Okin, 1989).

With their strong belief in the rights of individuals, liberal feminists do not think that all women need to march in step towards any political goal. Both women and men, working individually, would be able to improve their lives if society simply ended legal and cultural barriers rooted in gender.

2. Socialist feminism

Socialist feminism evolved from Marxist conflict theory, in part as a response to how little attention Marx paid to gender, in part as a strategy to challenge both patriarchy and capitalism. Engels claimed that patriarchy (like class oppression) has its roots in private property; thus, capitalism intensifies patriarchy by concentrating wealth and power in the hands of a small number of men.

Socialist feminists view the reforms sought by liberal feminism as inadequate. The bourgeois family must be restructured, they argue, to end 'domestic slavery' in favour of some collective means of carrying out housework and child care. The key to this goal, in turn, is a socialist revolution that creates a state-centred economy operating to meet the needs of all. Such a basic transformation of society requires that women and men pursue their personal liberation together, rather than

example, much of Islam); others less so. There are those who are positive about it, and those who are extremely sex-negative (Davis, 1983).

The hierarchy of sex

Closely linked to the above, Gayle Rubin (1984) talks of the ways in which societies come to classify and sort their different patterns of sexuality, such that some are valued, others are not. Figure 12.2 shows Rubin's sex hierarchy and provides a striking visual image of these evaluations. Rubin devised this hierarchy in the early 1980s and it is interesting to consider whether the items on it have shifted over the past 20 years.

The institutions and identities of heterosexuality

Heterosexuality is usually seen as the 'natural' foundation of society, but once again sociologists often approach this as a social construction of power in which men are forceful, driven by sex, and active, while women are usually believed to be more passive. Heterosexuality helps structure inequalities between the sexes and undermines a gender hierarchy – of what it is to be a man and a woman – along with a series of assumptions about what it means to 'have sex'. As an institution, heterosexuality fosters cultural forms such as heterosexual courtship and romance, and generates what is called a binary way of thinking: the world gets divided into heterosexual and homosexual. It also frequently

embraces what has traditionally been called a 'double standard', where boys and men are seen as naturally more sexually active ('driven by drives') and girls and women less so. Indeed, once girls and women do become more sexually active, they are often labelled by the boys and men as 'slags' and 'tarts' (Lees, 1993; Holland *et al.*, 1998). The term 'compulsory heterosexuality' was introduced by the poet Adrienne Rich. Stevi Jackson is one of the UK's leading feminist sociologists to write about sexuality. She brings together key themes around heterosexuality, patriarchy and power. Her work has recently been brought together in *Heterosexuality in Question* (Jackson, 1999).

The continuum of violence

Central to much feminist thinking (as we have already seen and will see further below) are the ways in which many women's lives are engulfed in violence perpetrated by men. Much of this is sexualised. Think of the sheer range of sexual experiences that can affect women – from the little wolf-whistles in the street and the pornographic photograph hanging in the office, from flashing and obscene phone calls, to stalking and on to harassment, assault and pressurised sex. Liz Kelly speaks of 'pressurised sex' – when the woman (it could sometimes be a man) is expected to have sex even when they do not really want to: no direct force is involved. More apparent is coercive sex and, at the most extreme, rape, murder and genocide. These all exist alongside major systems of exclusion: class, race and gender.

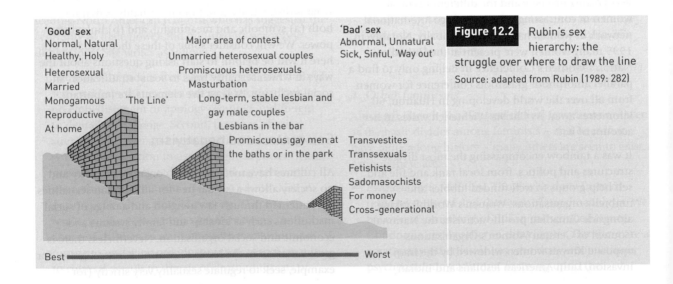

'Good' sex
Normal, Natural
Healthy, Holy
Heterosexual
Married
Monogamous   'The Line'
Reproductive
At home

Major area of contest
Unmarried heterosexual couples
Promiscuous heterosexuals
Masturbation
Long-term, stable lesbian and
gay male couples
Lesbians in the bar
Promiscuous gay men at
the baths or in the park

'Bad' sex
Abnormal, Unnatural
Sick, Sinful, 'Way out'

Transvestites
Transsexuals
Fetishists
Sadomasochists
For money
Cross-generational

Best ◄════════════════════════════► Worst

Figure 12.2 Rubin's sex hierarchy: the struggle over where to draw the line
Source: adapted from Rubin (1989: 282)

Heterosexism and homophobia

Heterosexism – like racism and sexism – describes an ideology that categorises and then unjustly dismisses as inferior a whole group of fellow citizens; in the case of heterosexism, the group are people who are not heterosexual. It has been institutionalised in laws, education, religions and language across the world. Attempts to enforce heterosexuality are as much a violation of human rights as racism and sexism, and are now increasingly challenged with equal determination.

Homophobia is the fear of and resulting contempt for homosexuals. The term **homophobia** was coined in the early 1970s by an American psychiatrist George Weinberg, who defined it as *the dread of being in close quarters with homosexuals* (Weinberg, 1973). Table 12.2 lists a number of questions Weinberg introduces in his book in order to construct what he called the standard homophobia scale. A number of researchers have suggested that people intolerant of homosexuals are likely to be more authoritarian, more dogmatic, more cognitively rigid, more intolerant of ambiguity, more status-conscious, more sexually rigid, more guilty and negative about their sexual impulses, and less accepting of others in general (Morin and Garfinkle, 1978).

Even a major organisation for human rights such as Amnesty International came to recognise the problem of homophobia only in the last decade of the twentieth century (previously refusing to see it as a problem). Nevertheless, in a recent report, they showed that there are more than 70 countries with laws that criminalise homosexual acts, and that a few of these – including Iran, Afghanistan, Saudi Arabia and Chechnya – have the death penalty for gay sex. Torture is common to extract confessions of 'deviance', gays are raped to 'cure them of it', and they are sometimes killed by death squads (Amnesty International, 2001).

Theories of sexuality

As we saw in Chapter 5, language, symbols and communications are vital to human beings: it is through these that we become distinctively social beings. It should not therefore be surprising to find that this is what sociologists highlight.

It may be an interesting exercise to think about all the ways in which human sexuality differs from animal sexuality. Being firmly embedded in language and communication, we become the 'talking' and 'thinking' sex. Animals do not. Further, we often tend to use sex for social ends, not just biological goals such as reproduction. Far from sex being just biological, we come to use it for many reasons: as an expression of love, as a means to establish bonding, as a way of being clear about our manliness or womanliness, or indeed our maturity. It can be used to show our aggression (as in rape) or to fill up our boredom or as a kind of hobby. It can be used as play, as performance, as power and as a form of work (for example, prostitution).

Table 12.2	Questions for Weinberg's standard homophobia scale	Yes	No
Homosexuals should be locked up to protect society		☐	☐
It would be upsetting for me to find out I was alone with a homosexual		☐	☐
Homosexuals should not be allowed to hold government positions		☐	☐
I would not want to be a member of an organisation which had any homosexuals in its membership		☐	☐
I find the thought of homosexual acts disgusting		☐	☐
If laws against homosexuality were eliminated, the proportion of homosexuals in the population would probably remain about the same		☐	☐
A homosexual could be a good President of the United States		☐	☐
I would be afraid for a child of mine to have a teacher who was homosexual		☐	☐
If a homosexual sat next to me on the bus I would get nervous		☐	☐

Source: adapted from Weinberg (1973)

Constructionism and scripting theory

Drawing on this, William Simon and John Gagnon were the founders of what has now become commonly known as the 'social constructionist' approach to sexuality. Both worked at the Kinsey Institute for Sexual Behavior in the 1960s, collecting and unearthing mounds of empirical data. And yet in the midst of this, both felt the need to look at what was happening in a more sociological way. To do this, they suggested that the metaphor of *script* was much more useful in understanding sexuality for humans than was biology (Gagnon and Simon, 1973). In scripting theory, human sexualities are best seen as drama. In Chapter 7, we saw how Erving Goffman viewed social life as drama. This idea can also be applied to sexuality. An elaborate set of stagecraft rules and performance guides our sexualities and brings them into action. Sex, for human beings, is not a matter of automatic sexual release; instead sexuality must have life breathed into it through drama. **Sexual scripts**, then, are guidelines *that help define the who, what, where, when and even why we have sex.*

Think for a minute of any sexual act, from that of 'a man and wife engaged in coitus inside marriage' to 'a woman engaged in prostitution' to 'a gay man meeting another in a gay bar'. In all cases, what has to be distinctive about these encounters is that they do not just happen 'out of the blue'. They depend upon rituals, signs and symbols to make sense of it all. In each case, certain people are defined as appropriate partners (the *who*). The activities can take place only in certain places (the *where*) – they cannot take place anywhere: places are limited. They define more or less what can be done – prostitutes set agreements and limits, partners know what is expected and do not usually go beyond boundaries (the *what*). Likewise, we cannot just do sex whenever we wish to – it is bounded into certain times (the *when*). And finally, when we come to talk about it – or just privately reflect on it – we start to tell ourselves the reasons why we did these things (the *why*).

Gagnon and Simon suggest that sexual scripts are crucial to human sexualities and they outline three major forms they can take. *Personal scripts* are those within our heads – telling us, for instance, what turns us on. *Interactive scripts* are those which emerge between partners or groups, telling what each person is expected to do. *Historical–cultural scripts* are those scripts which exist in the wider culture and which tell us what is expected of us sexually. Fieldwork studies have been conducted of sexual encounters, ranging from situations of rape and striptease to those of homosexual 'cruising' and 'sadomasochism', which attempt to unravel these scripts.

Discourse and sexualities

Closely linked is the 'discourse' approach to sexuality. Following on from the work of Michel Foucault (introduced in Chapter 16), many sociologists see sexuality as being located within an elaborate language structure that organises power relations. They are concerned with seeing the ways in which language shapes the way we see sex. A language approach to sex might, for instance, look at the ways in which 'chat shows' like *Oprah* let people talk about sex on television, and how this has some influences in the wider society. Or it may look at the ways in which new categories of sexual problems – sex addiction, AIDS, child sex abuse – come to be constructed and how they develop a language of their own. Much of our sexual life is lived through these discourses, and sociologists have increasingly turned their attention to them.

Foucault's study, *The History of Sexuality* (1979; orig. 1976), provides a major entrance to this way of thinking about sex and has been very influential. He suggests that the nineteenth century was not a time when sex was silenced and repressed, as was once commonly thought. On the contrary, he argues that it was a time when people were encouraged to talk more and more about it – usually in very negative ways. There was what he called 'an incitement to discourse' – people were encouraged to talk. Thus it was a time when scientists started to study sex (the psychiatrists and the sexologists); a time when new categories of sexuality came into being (like 'the hysterical woman', the 'masturbating child', 'the pervert' and the Malthusian Couple); and a time when sexualities became reorganised through all this talk into new forms of power relationships (Foucault, 1979; orig. 1976).

Feminist theories of sexuality

A third important impetus for the sociological study of sexuality has come from feminists, though as we might expect from the different positions outlined above there has been little agreement on a common approach. We will look briefly at two: the radical feminists and the libertarian socialists.

Radical feminism

In the radical feminist version, sexuality is seen to be one of the key mechanisms through which men have regulated women's lives. The nineteenth-century feminists recognised this when they waged war on prostitution, venereal disease, the low age of consent and immorality of all forms. They saw this as generated by men: as Frances Swiney wrote: 'women's redemption from sex slavery can only be achieved through man's redemption from sex-obsession'. The solution to the problem was 'votes for women and chastity for men' (see Jeffreys, 1987). Through establishing anti-vice organisations, their aim was to stop men's debauchery.

Late twentieth-century radical feminists have taken these arguments even further. They characterise the central features of sexuality as being male. Thus sexuality is centred on the penis, is aggressive, takes place devoid of emotional sensitivity and is often extremely fixated and fetishistic. It is men who rape, abuse and harass. It is men who buy and use pornography and pay sex workers. It is men who become serial sex offenders and sex killers.

Radical feminists argue that it is through men's sexuality exerting control over women's bodies that women are subordinated. Rape is the clear symbol here: it is not about sexual release, so much as about male power and violence. It is a mechanism through which 'all men keep all women in a constant state of fear'. Out of this wing of the Women's Movement have grown the campaigns over pornography, the battles against child sex abuse and over violence against women in the home, and the development of new arguments about rape and the setting up of rape crisis centres. Two of these will be briefly considered below.

The case of sexual harassment

Sexual harassment refers to *comments, gestures or physical contact of a sexual nature that are deliberate, repeated and unwelcome*. During the 1990s, sexual harassment became an issue of national importance that has already significantly redefined the rules for workplace interaction between the sexes.

Most victims of sexual harassment are women. This is because, first, our culture encourages men to be sexually assertive and to perceive women in sexual terms; social interaction in the workplace, on campus and elsewhere, then, can readily take on sexual overtones. Second, most individuals in positions of power – including business executives, doctors, assembly-line supervisors, university lecturers and military officers – are men who oversee the work of women. Surveys carried out in widely different work settings confirm that half of women respondents report receiving unwanted sexual attention (Loy and Stewart, 1984; Paul, 1991).

Sexual harassment is sometimes blatant and direct, as when a supervisor solicits sexual favours from a subordinate, coupled with the threat of reprisals if the advances are refused. Behaviour of this kind, which not only undermines the dignity of an individual but prevents her from earning a living, is widely condemned. Courts have declared such *quid pro quo* sexual harassment (the Latin phrase means 'one thing in return for another') to be an illegal violation of civil rights.

However, the problem of unwelcome sexual attention often involves subtle behaviour – sexual teasing, off-colour jokes, pin-ups displayed in the workplace – none of which any individual may *intend* as harassing to another person. But, using the *effect* standard favoured by many feminists, such actions add up to creating a *hostile environment* (Cohen, 1991; Paul, 1991). Incidents of this kind are far more complex because they involve very different perceptions of the same behaviour. For example, a man may think that showing romantic interest in a co-worker is paying the woman a compliment; she, on the other hand, may deem his behaviour offensive and a hindrance to her job performance.

Women's entry into the workplace does not in itself ensure that everyone is treated equally and with respect. Untangling precisely what constitutes a hostile working environment, however, demands clearer standards of conduct than exist at present. Creating such guidelines – and educating the public about them – is likely to take some time (Cohen, 1991; Majka, 1991). In the end, courts (and, ultimately, the court of public opinion) will draw the line between what amounts to 'reasonable friendliness' and behaviour that is 'unwarranted harassment'.

Rape and date rape

Another important area of action is that of rape. For a long time, the academic study of rape was mainly the province of male criminologists who saw rape through two main lenses. The first argued that rapists were pathological people and few and far between. The second suggested that many women said no to sex when they actually wished to participate; further, it was often precipitated by them.

Such arguments have been roundly condemned by feminists over the past 30 years, and through their campaigns they have brought about change. Critical here has been the growth of rape crisis centres, offering both support to rape victims and campaign materials that have worked to change police and court practice, as well as the law.

Libertarian and socialist perspectives

As the Controversy and Debate box indicates, not all feminists agree on the analysis of sexuality and men

WORLD WATCH

SEXUALITY IN JAPAN

Modern Japan seems lodged in two worlds. The first is a classic traditional one where body and sexuality are 'wrapped' (Hendry, 1993) in fine etiquette and rules and where traditional gender roles are firmly maintained. It is not, however, an anti-sex world (as the Anglo-American one largely is). For it is a world where the geisha can provide an ideal of female companionship for men which includes the explicitly erotic, and the samurai can provide an ideal of homo-erotic passion. It is a structured world of genteel sex (for men, that is!).

And yet while Japan clearly still has a classical culture, it also has long been at the forefront of a modern industrialising zeal. In Nicholas Bornhoff's *Pink Samurai* (1992), a growing preoccupation with sex in all its guises appears.

• *The comic strip book, or Manga*, is everywhere in Japan (and now widely exported). White has estimated that of 1.9 billion comic books produced in 1989, 474 million were explicitly sexual (White, 1993: 176). These are read by adults and children alike; and as one commentator remarks, 'Many comics are wild: scenes of violence, unnatural sex, and scatology are common, even in comics for children . . .' (Schodt, 1986: 16). With titles like 'No Panty Angels', 'Teach Me Love', 'Hunt of the Sex Maniac' (and drawings to match), they leave little to the imagination!

• *Japanese men are taking to virtual reality games around sex. Exciting Memory*, for example, a virtual reality game, offers love, friendship and nudity, and has been purchased by 600,000 men in the 16–35 age range. In these virtual worlds men can assemble romantic and erotic little worlds in which they can once again establish their control over women, a control that has become increasingly lost (*Guardian*, 8 April 1996: 9).

• *The existence of 'love hotels'* (*Rabu Hoteru*) is a widespread and common phenomenon in Japan: a mode of having sex outside the home for both the young and the older. Often garish in form and likened to Disneyland in their curious combination of childishness, innocence yet commercialism, in 1984 there were estimated to be 35,000 nationwide and 4,000 in Tokyo. Bornhoff's account remarks: 'The scope of fantasy is large: tatami matting and

plastic cherry trees for a classic Japanese touch, Hawaiian tropical, medieval Western torture chambers, heated swimming pools . . . in one instance the bed is like an island anchored in the middle of the pool, in another the bed suggests a 1950s Cadillac sitting complete . . . in the middle of what looks like an ornate Chinese restaurant' . . . (Bornhoff, 1992: 46–47).

• *There is a fascination with an array of 'sexualities'*, often in fantasy only such as roricon (The Lolita Complex) or paedophilia, or an interest in younger girls and 'cute' boys too, and 'panties' (see Bornhoff, 1992: 119–122).

This last interest has led to reports of speciality shops and even vending machines selling girls' used underwear (and shoes) – at the height of this craze in 1993, it has been estimated some 6,000–10,000 girls sold their underpants along with a photo of themselves in Tokyo for as much as US $50 (5,000 yen) (*Newsweek*, 23 December 1996: 28).

• *The growth of a teenage girl sex industry* – replete with erotic dancers, sex video catalogues and the phenomenon of telephone clubs. Here, men rent out booths showing soft porn, equipped with

COUNTRY FACT FILE

JAPAN

Population	127,347,000 (2002)
Urban population	78.4%
Per capita GNP	$35,620 (2000)
Life expectancy	77.5 male; 84 female (2000)
Literacy	100% (1990/96)
Languages	Japanese
Religions	(Official: none) Buddhism and Shintoism
Main cities	Tokyo: 11,771,819; Yokohama: 3,307,408; Osaka: 2,602,352; Nagoya: 2,153,293; Kyoto: 1,436,601
Human Development Index 2004	9th

Source: adapted from *The World Guide 2001*, Brittanica Almanac, 2004

WORLD WATCH CONTINUED

telephones where girls can ring them up (*Guardian*, 'Teenage kicks', 30 October 1996: 4).

- *The emergence of more and more couples who seem to be abstaining from sex*, and are 'sexless' (*Newsweek*, 23 December 1996: 30).

- *The emergence of a new kind of family structure* in which men have become increasingly absent, often through work but often through staying late at bars at night. Women seeking more egalitarian relations are leaving these men in growing numbers. 'Singlehood . . . has become partially recognised as a possible life style' (Yoshizumi, 1995: 96).

- *The emergence of a brand of comic that treats young gay male love romantically* – dreamlike, kissing in clouds – but that is marketed for teenage hetero-sexual girls, such as Kizuna by female illustrator Kazuma Kodoka (though they are also marketed in the United States for a gay audience, which often finds the romantic attraction between men to be very different from the erotic emphasis in US pub-lications) (*4Front*, 22 January 1997, citing the analysis of New York Design Critic, Abby Denson).

Sources: Bornhoff (1992); White (1993).

---

provided by radical feminists. These feminists – who count liberals and socialists in their number – charge that radical feminism is too extreme and too fixed in its conceptions of what male sexuality is, and ultimately adopts a position that makes heterosexuality impossible. It is also too sex-negative. Many feminists are trying to develop an account of sexuality that recognises that, while there is often *danger* in (male) sex, there can also be *pleasure* (Vance, 1984). Of course, acts of rape and coercive degradation remain unacceptable to all feminists, but they argue there should also be explorations about what it is that women desire, how women can have sexual relations with men that are not degrading, and how new patterns of positive sexuality can be developed (see Segal, 1994).

CONTROVERSY AND DEBATE

FEMINISM AND THE POLITICS OF PORNOGRAPHY

Pornography may be taken as a major symbol of our time because it condenses many of our fears and anx-ieties concerning sexuality and gender. For the past two decades, there has been an ongoing debate from many different positions about the role of pornogra-phy in society. One of the most telling debates has come not from the traditional conservatives and sexual radicals, but from within feminism itself. One group of feminists have made strong attacks on pornography and have tried to have it outlawed. Other feminists have been very critical of such actions.

On one side, radical feminists and others argue that pornography should be a major issue because it strikes at the core of gender and sexuality. Indeed, it shows you the very nature of what men desire and what male sexuality is. They argue that pornography is really a power issue because it fosters the notion that men should control both sexuality and women.

Catharine MacKinnon (1987) has branded pornog-raphy as one foundation of male dominance in the United States because it portrays women in dehu-manising fashion as the subservient playthings of men. Worth noting, in this context, is that the term 'pornography' is derived from the Greek word *porne*, meaning a harlot who acts as a man's sexual slave.

A related charge is that pornography promotes violence against women. Certainly, anyone who has viewed more recent 'hard-core' videos finds this assertion plausible. Yet demonstrating a scientific cause-and-effect relationship between what people watch and how they act is difficult. Research does support the contention, however, that pornography gives men licence to think of women as objects rather than as people.

- Pornography – like most of male sexuality – degrades and abuses women. It is violent, voyeuristic, objectificatory, dehumanising, and designed to satisfy the male's concern with masturbation.

CONTROVERSY AND DEBATE CONTINUED

- Pornography is about male power. It shows how men seek to control women, both in the porn itself – the male eye takes the woman over, the woman is represented as being there for the man – but also in the making of the porn: here women have often been turned into abuse objects and actually become prostitutes and whores for men.
- Pornography is an ideology that promotes sexual violence in society. By encouraging an objectificatory and abusive approach to women, it actually encourages rape and sexual violence. In the words of the famous epigram: 'pornography is the theory, rape is the practice'.

Many feminists do not agree with these arguments (and have set up movements to challenge the above). They argue:

- The pornography issue gives too much weight to sexuality as a source of women's oppression and deflects attention from other more important sources such as their weak position in the labour market, how racism compounds their problems, exploitation at home in the domestic labour market, and so on.
- The pornography issue encourages censorship, and this works against women's interests. Indeed, in some places where porn has been banned, so have all kinds of women's publications, especially those for lesbians.

- The pornography issue side-steps the issue of women's sexuality and their growing desire for their own erotica. Women make pornography for themselves; it is not all male. And anti-porn feminists make women seem to be passive, asexual victims of male desire. They are not.
- Finally, the representations of pornography do not have one clear meaning. They have different meanings to different groups and, while they can be about male power and violence, this is certainly not their only meaning.

Anti-porn feminists argue back that many of the above arguments either misrepresent their position or are themselves weak. What do you think?

CONTINUE THE DEBATE:

1. Do you think sexuality is largely defined by men for their own needs? What might a non-male sexuality look like?

2. What kinds of image in pornography would not be sexist, and would not subordinate women?

3. Where do we draw boundaries? Is there never a case for censorship?

Key elements of sexual stratification: gay and lesbian relations

Although same-sex erotic experiences exist across cultures and throughout history with varying degrees of acceptability and frequency, it was not until the nineteenth century in Europe and America that homosexuality was invented as an object of scientific investigation. The term itself was introduced by a sympathetic Hungarian doctor, Benkert, in 1869 amidst a flurry of attempts at classifying sexuality. From this time until the 1970s, the dominant mode of thinking about homosexuality was clinical – it was primarily viewed through a medical framework as a pathology, its causes were located in biological degeneracy or family pathology, and treatments ranging from castration to psychoanalysis were advocated. Although such an

approach still continues among a few, since 1973 the American Psychiatric Association has officially removed homosexuality from its clinical listing of pathologies, seeing it as non-pathological in itself. Ironically, some of the leading clinicians, and notably Freud, had never viewed it as a pathology: in 1935 Freud could write in a famous 'letter to a mother' that 'whilst homosexuality is assuredly no advantage, it is nothing to be classified as an illness; we consider it to be a variation of the sexual development'.

While the nineteenth century saw the ascendancy of the clinical model of homosexuality, it also saw the growth of writing and campaigning that challenged the orthodox heterosexual assumptions. Thus Magnus Hirschfield established the Scientific Humanitarian Committee and the Institute for Sexual Science in Germany in 1897 and campaigned through scientific research for the acceptance of homosexuality up until the 1930s, when the Nazi movement stopped such advocacy and started a policy of extermination instead. Others, such as Edward Carpenter in England and André Gide in France, pursued a more literary defence. It was not, however, until the period after the Second World War that a substantial body of published research suggested the ubiquity and normality of homosexual experience. Pivotal to this enterprise was the publication of the Kinsey Report in 1948 and 1953, which contained the findings of interviews with well over 12,000 American men and women. Among the men, Kinsey found that 37 per cent had experienced some post-adolescent homosexual orgasm and 4 per cent had a preponderance of such experience; among the women, the figures were around 13 per cent and 3 per cent respectively. When Kinsey added that such responses were to be found among all social groups and in all walks of life, he created a social bombshell. He concluded that homosexual behaviour was neither unnatural nor neurotic in itself but an 'inherent physiologic capacity'.

Throughout this period, however, homosexuality was strongly condemned by law in most European countries and in all American states. It was not until the 1960s, and a decade or so after proposals for change made in the British Wolfenden report and the American New Model Code, that the legal situation changed. Despite the progressive growth of organised groups during the 1950s, it is the New York 'Stonewall Riots' of 1969 that are generally taken to symbolise the birth of the modern international 'Gay Movement' (Weeks, 1977). The scientifically imposed term 'homosexual' was shifted to the self-created term 'gay'; medical rhetoric was converted to political language; organisations for gays became widespread in most large cities, and millions of gay men and women started to 'come out' and positively identify with the term 'gay'. The 1970s therefore started to demonstrate a real change in gay experiences in most high-income societies.

Queer theory

As lesbians, gays and bisexuals have 'come out', and become both more visible and more accepted within the mainstream of many Western societies, so their voices have increasingly entered sociology and social science debates. There has been a growth of lesbian and gay studies, which have been especially influential in the sociological study of sexualities (Plummer, 1992).

Nevertheless, **Queer theory** argues that *most sociological theory still has a bias towards 'heterosexuality' and that non-heterosexual voices need to be heard.* Such theorists would argue that all the topics discussed in this book – from stratification and ethnicity, to religion and economy –

would be greatly enhanced if the position of 'non-heterosexual voices' were placed at the centre. For example, it suggests that many religions have been organised around 'homophobic' persecutions; that a new form of economy is emerging that is based upon the spending power of young middle-class gay men – the pink economy; and that the experience of being lesbian or gay can differ significantly across different ethnic minority communities (Seidman, 1996). New insights can be provided for all the traditional concerns of sociology once we give a focus to a different group such as 'queers'. Queer theory started to emerge around the mid to late 1980s. The roots of Queer theory are usually seen to lie in the work of Eve Kasofsky Sedgwick, who argued that:

> many of the major nodes of thought and knowledge in twentieth-century Western culture as a whole are structured – indeed fractured – by a chronic, now endemic crisis of homo/heterosexual definition, indicatively male, dating from the end of the nineteenth century. … An understanding of any aspect of modern Western culture must be, not merely incomplete, but damaged in its central substance to the degree that it does not incorporate a critical analysis of modern homo/heterosexual definition.
>
> (Sedgwick, 1990: 1)

Judith Butler's work has also suggested there can be no kind of claim to any essential gender: it is all 'performative', slippery, unfixed. She sees gender as never essential, not innate, never natural but always constructed through performativity – as a 'stylized repetition of acts' (Butler, 1990: 141). Much of the interest in Queer theory has been concerned with playing around with gender. Initially fascinated by drag, transgender and transsexualism, with divas, drag kings, and key cross genderists such as Del LaGrace Volcano and Kate Bornstein (1995), some of it has functioned almost as a kind of subversive terrorist drag. It arouses curious, unknown queered desires, emancipating people from the constraints of the gendered tyranny of the presumed 'normal body' (Volcano *et al.*, 1999). Others have moved out to consider a wide array of playing with genders, from 'faeries' and 'bears', leather scenes and the Mardi Gras, and on to the more commercialised /normalised drag for mass consumption: RuPaul, Lily Savage, Graham Norton.

If there is a heart to Queer theory, then it must be seen as a radical stance around sexuality and gender that denies any fixed categories and seeks to subvert any tendencies towards normality within its study. Certain key themes are worth highlighting. Queer theory is a stance in which:

RESEARCH IN ACTION

QUEER ETHNOGRAPHY

Using Queer theory, Sasho Lambevski (1999), for instance, attempts to write 'an insider, critical and experiential ethnography of the multitude of social locations (class, gender, ethnicity, religion) from which 'gays' in Macedonia are positioned, governed, controlled and silenced as subaltern people' (1999: 301). As a 'gay' Macedonian (the terms must be a problem in this context?) who had spent time studying HIV in Australia, he looks at the sexual conflicts generated between the gay Macedonians and gay Albanians (never mind the Australian connection). Lambevski looks at the old cruising scenes in Skopje, known to him from before, that now take on multiple and different meanings bound up with sexualities, ethnicities, gender playing, clashing cultures. Cruising for sex here is no straightforward matter. He describes how in approaching and recognising a potential sex partner as an Albanian (in an old cruising haunt), he feels paralysed. Both bodies are flooded with ethnic meaning, not simply sexual ones, and ethnicities reek of power. He writes: 'I obeyed by putting the (discursive) mask of my Macedonicity

over my body'. In another time and place he may have reacted very differently.

Lambevski is overtly critical of much ethnography and wishes to write a Queer experiential ethnography, not a confessional one (1999: 298). He refuses to commit himself to what he calls 'a textual lie', which 'continues to persist in much of what is considered a real ethnographic text'. Here bodies, feelings, sexualities, ethnicities, religions can all be easily left out. Nor, he claims, can ethnography simply depend on site observation or one-off interviewing. There is a great chain of connection: 'the gay scene is inextricably linked to the Macedonian school system, the structuring of Macedonian and Albanian families and kinship relations, the Macedonian state and its political history, the Macedonian medical system with its power to mark and segregate "abnormality" (homosexuality)' (1999: 299). There is a chain of social sites; and at the same time his own life is an integral part of this (Macedonian queer, Australian gay). Few researchers have been so honest as to the tensions that infuse their lives and the wider chains of connectedness that shape their work.

- the polarised splits between both the heterosexual and the homosexual and the sex and gender are challenged

- identity – a sense of who one is – is no longer seen as stable or fixed

- all sexual categories are open and fluid (which means modern lesbian, gay identities, bisexual and transgender identities are fractured along with all heterosexual ones)

- its most frequent interests include a variety of sexual fetishes, drag kings and drag queens, gender and sexual playfulness, cybersexualities, polyarmoury, sadomasochism and all the social worlds of the so-called radical sexual fringe.

Social change and sexuality

AIDS and the gay movement are but one instance of major changes taking place in sexuality. The English sociologist Anthony Giddens, in his book *The*

Transformation of Intimacy (1992), talks about a number of other recent changes. Most important here is the arrival of 'plastic sexuality' and the 'pure relationship'. By the former he means that modern sexuality has broken away from its long historical connection to reproduction and has opened up into a much wider array of ways of doing sex. This is closely connected, of course, to the widespread availability and acceptability of contraceptive techniques. He also sees this 'plastic sex' as closely linked to the idea of the 'pure relationship', by which communication is enhanced between men and women and greater equality happens around sexual and emotional experiences. Giddens recognises that there is also room for danger in contemporary developments. For as women gain more and more equality, so some men feel more and more threatened. Modern times thus bring a growing potential for both an increasing democratisation of personal relationships and at the same time a growing potential for a gender war between men and women. We return to this thorny issue in Chapter 17, when we consider changes in the family.

This billboard shows the way that the action group Campaign For Our Children, Inc is getting their message across to young people that you do not have to follow the crowd into sexual activity at an early age, you can wait.

Source: Associated Press © Gail Burton

Looking ahead: gender and sexuality in the twenty-first century

On the surface, recent changes in the gender and sexuality spheres have been remarkable. Two centuries ago, women in the West occupied a position that was clearly and strikingly subordinate. Husbands controlled property in marriage, laws barred women from most jobs, women were excluded from holding political office and even from voting. Although women today often do remain in subordinate positions, especially when linked to class or ethnicity, the movement towards equality has brought many changes. Further, homosexuality was against the law and decried as a sickness. Today, in most Western countries, being gay, lesbian or queer has become a lifestyle choice and, as we shall see in Chapter 17 on families, the key debates now centre on the rights to have gay families and raise children. There are also other significant changes in sexuality: the growth of a general openness, the possibility of more democratic relationships between men and women, the more ready acceptance of birth control.

And yet, in a world context, the position of women and sexual minorities remains poor. As many chapters in this book suggest, women are more likely to experience poverty, to experience violence and sexual violence, to be forced into early marriages, to encounter genital mutilation and be forced to work for very low incomes in sweatshop conditions. A worldwide women's movement is challenging much of this, but there is also much

resistance. Likewise, in many countries throughout the world, lesbians and gays are persecuted and may even be executed. Again, an international gay movement attempts to bring about changes in these areas.

But in the West, too, a clear 'backlash' against feminism and Queer politics persists. Traditionalists argue that gender still forms an important foundation of personal identity and family life and that it is deeply woven into the moral fabric of our society. They see feminism as a threat to social stability. Traditionalists have also been arguing for a more conservative return to sexual values of the recent past, such as virginity and chastity (see photo above). For example, in the United States, new organisations such as the Silver Ring Thing have been set up to counter the twin problems of teenage pregnancy and sexually transmitted disease among teenagers. Opposing sex education, they attempt to attract the young to Christianity, encouraging teens to pay $15 for a bible, a silver (chastity) ring and to make a chastity pledge. By contrast, in Sweden and Holland, which have low rates of teen pregnancy, thorough programmes of sex education are championed (*The Week*, 22 May 2004).

But others recognise the variability of genders throughout cultures and history and sense that there are now many ways of being men and many ways of being women. Still others argue even more radically for the need to transcend all gender boundaries. On balance, however, changes across the boundaries of sexuality and gender seem likely to continue.

SUMMARY

1. Sex is a biological concept; a human foetus is female or male from the moment of conception. Hermaphrodites represent rare cases of people who combine the biological traits of both sexes. Transsexuals are people who feel they are one sex when biologically they are the other.

2. Heterosexuality is the dominant sexual orientation in virtually every society in the world, though people with a bisexual or exclusively homosexual orientation make up a small percentage of the population everywhere.

3. Gender involves how cultures assign human traits and power to each sex. Gender varies historically and across cultures. Some degree of patriarchy, however, exists in every society.

4. Through the socialisation process, people link gender with personality (gender identity) and actions (gender roles). Three theories dominate socialisation theory: behavioural learning, cognitive learning and psychodynamic learning. Learning to mother is an important part of this socialisation process. The major agents of socialisation – the family, peer groups, schools and the mass media – reinforce cultural definitions of what is feminine and masculine.

5. Gender stratification entails numerous social disadvantages for women. Although most women are now in the paid labour force, a majority of working women hold low-paying clerical or service jobs. Unpaid housework also remains predominantly a task performed by women.

6. Women earn less than men do. This disparity stems from differences in jobs and family responsibilities as well as discrimination.

7. Women now earn a slight majority of all bachelor's and master's degrees. Men still receive a majority of all doctorates and professional degrees.

8. The number of women in politics has increased sharply in recent decades. Still, the vast majority of people elected are men.

9. Minority women encounter greater social disadvantages than white women.

10. Violence against women is a widespread problem in the UK. Our society is also grappling with the issues of sexual harassment and pornography.

11. Functional analysis holds that pre-industrial societies benefit from distinctive roles for males and females, reflecting biological differences between the sexes. In industrial societies, marked gender inequality becomes dysfunctional and slowly decreases. Talcott Parsons claimed that complementary gender roles promote the social integration of families and society as a whole.

12. Conflict analysis views gender as a dimension of social inequality and conflict. Friedrich Engels tied gender stratification to the development of private property. He claimed that capitalism devalues women and housework.

13. Feminism endorses the social equality of the sexes and actively opposes patriarchy and sexism. Feminism also strives to eliminate violence against women, and to give women control over their sexuality.

14. There are three variants of feminist thinking. Liberal feminism seeks equal opportunity for both sexes within current social arrangements; socialist feminism advocates abolishing private property as the means to social equality; radical feminism aims to create a gender-free society.

15. There are three central approaches to the sociological study of sexuality: social constructionism, which highlights scripts, languages and symbols; discourse theory, which emphasises language structures and power; and feminism, which highlights power and gender and has two major variants – radical feminist and libertarian socialist.

16. Same-sex relations – gay and lesbian relationships – have undergone profound changes in the last 100 years.

17. Queer theory suggests the need to deconstruct or abolish the binary gender systems of male and female, gay and straight.

18. 'Plastic sex' and 'pure relationships' may be future patterns of sexuality. They both indicate a growing flexibility, openness and potential equality in relationships.

CRITICAL-THINKING QUESTIONS

1. How would you 'queer' sociology?

2. What are the most significant changes in gender and sexuality over the past 20 years? Why have they happened? Look at Rubin's sexual hierarchy; this was her description in the early 1980s. In what ways has it changed in the twenty-first century? Do you see signs of a backlash?

3. Why is gender a dimension of social stratification? How does gender interact with inequality based on race, ethnicity and class?

4. What problems do you find with biological explanations for men and women's differences? Suggest some examples of how gender roles vary cross-culturally, historically and contemporaneously.

5. How valuable do you find the idea of 'patriarchy'? What are its major components and how far have they changed in the twentieth and twenty-first centuries?

GOING FURTHER

Further reading

On gender:

Sylvia Walby, *Theorizing Patriarchy* (1990)
This provides a detailed analysis of the workings of patriarchy, with both theoretical critique and empirical evidence. The figures provided now need a little updating.

Michael S. Kimmel, *The Gendered Society* (2nd edn, 2004)
One of the clearest, most recent and comprehensive surveys of the whole field. Kimmel is a leader of 'masculinity studies'.

Robert Connell *Gender* (2002)
A short guide by one of the leaders in the field.

Jane Pilcher and Imelda Whelehan, *Fifty Key Concepts in Gender Studies* (2004)
Useful summaries and guides to the field.

On sexualities:

Jeffrey Weeks, *Sexuality* (2nd edn, 2003)
A classic short guide to the field.

Richard Dunphy, *Sexual Politics* (2000)

Diane Richardson, *Rethinking Sexuality* (2000)
Good guides to the theoretical and political issues.

More advanced reading:

Rosemarie Tong, *Feminist Thought: A Comprehensive Introduction* (1990)
Introduces a full range of feminist perspectives.

Lynne Segal's *Why Feminism* (1999) and Valerie Bryson's *Feminist Debates* (1999)
Both of these review current debates.

R. W. Connell, *Masculinities* (1995)
Key text for reviewing and examining the developing field of men's studies, though this is clearly from a strong sociological perspective.

Watch a video/read a book

- Bryan Forbe's *The Stepford Wives* (1974): classic story of computerised women pleasing their men. It was remade as a film for a 2004 audience. It might be interesting to compare the 30-year difference!

- Rob Reiner's *Stand by Me* (1985): 1950s childhood, friendships and masculinity.

- Peter Cattaneo's *The Full Monty* (1997): unemployed men in Sheffield take to stripping, and say a lot about their masculinity.

- Stephen Daldry's *Billy Elliot* (2000): a miner's son wants to be a ballet dancer.

- Lasse Halstrom's *Cider House Rules* (1999): abortion, incest, ethnicity and history!

- Robert Rosenberg *et al.*'s *Before Stonewall* (1985): narrated by Rita Mae Brown, it offers a unique portrait of the history of the homosexual experience in America.

- Patricia Rozema's *I've Heard the Mermaids Singing* (1987): lesbian romance.

- Hector Babenco's *Kiss of the Spider Woman* (1985): William Hurt and Raul Julia, a gay window dresser and a macho political prisoner, star in this powerful film set in a Brazilian prison.

- Jennie Livingston's *Paris is Burning* (1990): extraordinary film documents the Harlem transsexual ball circuit of the mid-1980s.

- Claudia Weil's *Critical Choices* (1996): abortion clinic drama, raising a lot of issues.

For a starting novel on gender, see Margaret Attwood's *The Handmaid's Tale* (1985). On gay and lesbian writing, see Edmund White's *A Boy's Own Story* (1982) and Jeanette Winterson's *Oranges Are Not the Only Fruit* (1985).

Connecting up

Connect to other chapters

- The issue of gender is raised in most chapters, but see gender and work in Chapter 14, gender and crime in Chapter 16, and gender and education in Chapter 19.

- Sexual violence is also considered in Chapter 17, and in the opening story of Chapter 20; see also hate crimes in Chapter 16.

- Link the Women's Movement to feminism and social movements in Chapter 15.

- Link to HIV and Aids discussed in Chapter 20.

- Connect back to class, poverty and ethnicity in Chapters 10 and 11, and forward to age in Chapter 13.

To the websites

- http://www.feminist.org/

  Women's web world! Homepage of Feminist Majority Online which links to plenty of information concerning women, such as news and events, political actions, publications, arts and entertainment. Also links to feminist university network and feminist Internet gateway.

- http://ethics.sandiego.edu/

  This website links to many other resources on ethical issues such as abortion, sexual orientation, gender and sexism, world hunger, poverty, etc., with suggested journals, articles and books.

- http://www.qrd.org/

  Queer Resource Directory, which links to various issues concerning 'queer' people such as education, health, family, youth, religion, cultures, law and politics by regions.

- Internet resources on violence against women can be located at:

  http://www.vaw.umn.edu/ (US)

  http://www.crvawc.ca/ (Canada)

  http://www.womensaid.org.uk/dv/index.htm
  http://www.cwasu.org/maproom.htm (London)

- A major WHO report on violence can be found at:

  http://www.who.int/violence_injury_prevention/
  violence/world_report/en/

For additional case studies, multiple choice questions, internet exercises, and annotated weblinks specific to this chapter, visit this book's website at www.pearsoned.co.uk/plummer

CHAPTER 13

AGE STRATIFICATION CHILDREN AND LATER LIFE

Ah, but I was so much older then,
I'm younger than that now.
Bob Dylan: *My Back Pages*, 1964

THERE IS A TENDENCY TO THINK of 'age' as something 'wired into our bodies'. It is biological. Yet, as you will be aware by now, the sociologist is always looking for the social patterns – for the more social side of life, of how everything gets socially organised. So it is also true that how we create and respond to age categories are also social events.

KEY THEMES

- The nature of age stratification
- The position of children in the world
- The changing pattern of youth cultures
- The problems of 'growing older' and the 'greying of the world'
- The implications of an older population

First, consider two small societies. The Sherpas are a Tibetan-speaking, Buddhist people in Nepal. In this society, there is almost an idealisation of old age. Old people here usually live in their own homes, and most are in good health. The old here are held in esteem and valued. By contrast, the Fulani of Africa move older people to the very edge of their communities and families – indeed, very near to their future graves. They may already be seen as socially dead and are held in low regard. Social expectations towards the elderly differ widely across societies (Schaefer, 2001: 319).

(Left) 'Gifts', © 1996 Deirdre Scherer – fabric and thread picture, 32" × 54", installed in the lobby of St Mary's Hospital in Rochester, New York, USA.
Source: Deirdre Scherer, photographer Jeff Baird

Now consider some of those growing older in the contemporary West. We now have rock stars like Sir Mick Jagger (of the Rolling Stones), Sir Paul McCartney (of the Beatles) or even Sir Cliff Richard 'growing old'. Yet in a curious way they are resisting what a few decades ago would have been seen as 'old age'. They are really part of the 'young growing older' – despite their chronological age, they do not see it as anything to do with being old. They are indeed not old in the ways people were at their age some 50 years ago.

And they are not alone. Think of the millions who now follow new consumption patterns for those growing old. In the UK, they go on Saga Holidays, winter retreats to the Costa del Sol (O'Reilly, 2000), join the University for the Third Age. Across the Western world we see the growth of retirement colonies, surgical reconstructions for the ailing body, new political movements – the so-called 'Grey Power Movement'. Growing old is not what it used to be. It has become a 'lifestyle enclave' (Bellah et al., 1985).

We also have a new group who are living longer and longer: the centenarians. Nellie Bruton is 104. Her husband died about 30 years ago and she has one son. Her two brothers died young: one from meningitis as a baby, the other was killed in the First World War. She remembers Queen Victoria coming to review local troops returning from the Boer War, and also recalls a memorial service in her local church after the Queen's death. For much of her working life she was the village postmistress; her husband was an agricultural worker.

Mrs Bruton has lived in the same Somerset house since she retired in the 1950s. She lives on her own, but is supported by friends, her church and 'meals on wheels'. She walks to church every week and still sings in the church choir, in which she has been a member since 1916! She recalls the time when the village baker came round, when milk was delivered by the bucket, and there was a grocer, butcher and a post office. None now remains. For Mrs Bruton, the secret of her long life has been 'Good plain living – not beef burgers like it is now. And a drop of sherry every morning. I've come to like it.'

Mrs Bruton is one of a rapidly growing group of centenarians. By the year 2030, there may well be 30,000 people living beyond their 100th birthday in Britain. In 1951, there were only 271, but by the 1991 Census, this number had risen to 4,400. Projections suggest there are about 8,000 centenarians living today. By the year 2050, the United Nations predicts that across the world the number of centenarians will increase fifteen-fold from approximately 210,000 to 3.2 million. An unprecedented 'expansion in life' is on the way.

(Blaikie,1999; Bellah et el., 1985; O'Reilly, 2000; DGAA Homelife, 1997)

Age divisions are found across all societies as a major means of differentiating peoples. Although all societies have systems of **age stratification**, whereby there is *an unequal distribution of wealth, power and privileges among people at different stages in the life course*, the nature of this varies across societies and history. And our twenty-first century is no exception. The historian Peter Laslett has recently suggested that we need *A Fresh Map of Life* (1989), to be approached through Four Ages. The First Age coincides broadly with childhood, and the second with adulthood and learning. A Third Age has grown in recent years and marks the period bounded between the end of work and the arrival of the Fourth Age of 'dependence, decrepitude and death' (Laslett, 1989: 90).

Others, more controversially, suggest that the postmodern world is seeing a breakdown of clear age bands, that chronological age patterns are becoming less crucial to people's lives. Social divisions around age are different from other divisions in so far as we are all likely to move through them: today's children are tomorrow's pensioners. But attached to each age band comes a series of socially produced assumptions about what it should be like to be in that age group. In this chapter we will look briefly at children (and the emerging new field known as the sociology of children) and in more detail at the increasing numbers of people who are 'growing older'. We touch on youth and adolescence elsewhere.

A sociology of children

There is a lot of evidence that ideas about children have changed remarkably over the centuries, and that indeed the experience of children across the world today can be very different indeed. Charles Dickens' classic novel *Oliver Twist* is set in London early in the nineteenth century, when the Industrial Revolution was rapidly transforming English society. Oliver's mother died in childbirth and, barely surviving himself, he began life as an indigent orphan, 'buffeted through the world, despised by all, and pitied by none' (Dickens, 1886: 36; orig. 1837–39). As was typical for a poor child of his time, Oliver Twist was soon facing the toil and drudgery of a workhouse, labouring long hours to pay for filthy shelter and meagre food.

But today, we think of *childhood* – roughly, the first 12 years of life – very differently: it is supposed to be a time of freedom from the burdens of the adult world. But until about a century ago, as *Oliver Twist* testifies, children in Europe and North America shouldered most of the burdens of adults. According to historian Philippe Ariès (1965), once children were able to survive without constant care, medieval Europeans expected them to take their place in the world as working adults. Likewise, as we look at the world's population of children in different countries today, we find that many of them

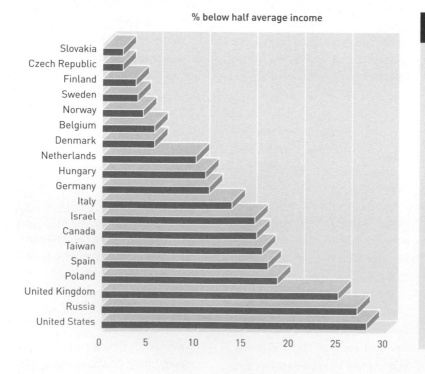

% below half average income

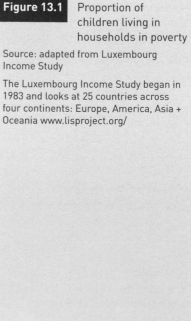

Figure 13.1 Proportion of children living in households in poverty

Source: adapted from Luxembourg Income Study

The Luxembourg Income Study began in 1983 and looks at 25 countries across four continents: Europe, America, Asia + Oceania www.lisproject.org/

take on responsibilities and concerns we associate with adult life. 'Being a child' is a very different experience across cultures (and indeed even within one culture according to the class, gender and ethnicity of the child). Consider just four dimensions: work, marriage, war and death. The most obvious feature of contemporary Western childhoods is to say that most children are 'protected' from most of these most of the time. But this is far from true of most children across the world today, as we briefly discuss below.

Child labour

'Child labour', often scorned in high-income countries, is a fact of daily life in many poorer societies today, especially in Africa and Asia. There are some 400 million working children (61 per cent in Asia, 32 per cent in Africa and 7 per cent in Latin America).

With our 'Western assumptions' we might be shocked by the notion of young children working long hours, because 'common sense' tells us that youngsters are very different from adults – physically immature and inexperienced in the ways of the world. But this difference is rooted in culture, where adults define how children should live their lives.

High-income societies are rich enough that many people – including children – do not need to work. In addition, societies with sophisticated technology extend childhood, so young people have time to learn the many complex skills required for adult activities. Thus, we construct the life course so that 'irresponsible' children are looked after by 'responsible' adults (Benedict, 1938).

Recently, some social scientists have declared that our conception of childhood is changing yet again. In an age of high divorce rates, mothers and fathers in the workforce, and an increasing level of 'adult' programming on television, they point out that children are no longer 'protected' from grown-up concerns as in the past. Rather, we are seeing the development of a 'hurried child' syndrome, meaning that children have to grapple with sex, drugs and violence as well as fend more and more for themselves (Elkind, 1981; Winn, 1983). Critics of this view, however, counter that there is no convincing evidence of any dramatic shift in our society's conception of childhood. Further, they note, the 'hurried child' thesis overlooks the fact that children in the lower class have always assumed adult responsibilities sooner than their middle- and upper-class counterparts (Lynott and Logue, 1993).

Child labour
Source: © Mohammed Anwar Impact Photos

Child marriage

As with work, so with marriage: many children across the world get 'married' – often for economic reasons. Early marriages are pervasive in parts of Africa and South Asia. In some countries over half of all girls are married by the time they reach age 18 (United Nations Children's Fund, March 2001: press release). The figure is 74 per cent in the Democratic Republic of the Congo, 70 per cent in Niger, and around 50 per cent in Bangladesh and Afghanistan.

Poverty is one of the major factors underpinning child marriage. In Bangladesh, for example, poverty-stricken parents may be persuaded to part with their daughters through a promise of marriage, or by false marriages, which are used to lure girls into prostitution abroad. There can be serious downsides to all this. Child marriage may serve as a major life restriction and can have a serious impact on health. It can cut off educational opportunities and for girls in particular (and the rate of child marriage is very much higher for girls) it will almost certainly mean premature pregnancy – with higher rates of maternal mortality and a lifetime of domestic and sexual subservience. According to a UNICEF report on child spouses, domestic violence is common and causes some girls to run away in desperation. 'Those who do so,' the report says, 'and those who choose a marriage partner against the wishes of their parents, may be punished, or even killed by their families. These girls run the risk of 'honour killings' that occur in Bangladesh, Egypt, Jordan, Lebanon, Pakistan, Turkey and elsewhere' (*Early Marriages, Child Spouses*: UNICEF Report, March 2001:13). Child prostitution is closely linked to this, with a current estimate that at least a million of the earth's children are forced into it.

Children and wars

Children across the world make up about a half of war refugees, while millions die and are often the main targets in war (being seen as the next generation of 'enemies'). Many are used as mine sweepers or spies and for kamikaze attacks. And many others are recruited or coerced into being soldiers: some 300,000 minors are recruited as active combatants by rebel groups and armies in some 41 countries, especially in Asia and Africa (New Internationalist, 2001: 40; Coalition to Stop the Use of Child Soldiers, www.hrw.org/reports/2004/childsoldiers0104/1.htm, 2004).

Child illness and mortality

For many children around the world, the early years of life are times of sickness and morbidity. As we shall see in later chapters, low-income societies are frequently societies with high infant mortality and morbidity.

Take the issues of AIDS, to be discussed more in Chapter 20. Of the 21.8 million people who had died from AIDS by 2000, 4.3 million were aged under 15 years old. Approximately 50 per cent of all new infections are occurring among young people. In Botswana and South Africa, it is estimated that one half of today's

VOICES

THE VOICES OF CHILD SOLDIERS

The army was a nightmare. We suffered greatly from the cruel treatment we received. We were being constantly beaten, mostly for no reason at all, just to keep us in a state of terror. I still have a scar on my lip and sharp pains in my stomach from being brutally kicked by the older soldiers. The food was scarce and they made us walk with heavy loads, much too heavy for our small and malnourished bodies. They forced me to learn how to fight the enemy in a war that I didn't understand why was being fought.

(Emilio, recruited by the Guatemalan army at the age of 14)

One boy tried to escape [from the rebels], but he was caught. His hands were tied, and then they made us, the other new captives, kill him with a stick. I felt sick. I knew this boy from before. We were from the same village. I refused to kill him and they told me they would shoot me. They pointed a gun at me, so I had to do it. The boy was asking me: 'Why are you doing this?' I said I had no choice. After we killed him, they made us smear his blood on our arms. … They said we had to do this so we would not fear death and so we would not try to escape.

(Susan, abducted by the Lord's Resistance Army in Uganda)

In May 2000, the United Nations established a new protocol for stopping the use of child soldiers. By April 2004, 115 countries had signed it and 71 countries had ratified it. The protocol argued that governments must ensure that nobody under the age of 18 should take part in hostilities or be conscripted into armies.

Source: Human Rights Watch on Children's Rights, www.hrw.org/

15-year-olds will die of AIDS. But more than this, many of the children in sub-Saharan Africa find their parents dying of HIV/AIDS and this makes for large numbers of what have been called 'AIDS orphans'.

Thinking about children

Traditionally children have been seen as either 'little innocents' (whose innocence needs protecting), as 'little devils' (whose naughtiness needs taming) or as adults in the making (what has often been called the child development approach, as children move through stages on their way to adulthood). Sociologists have recently come to reject all these views and have started to approach children as actively creating and living in their own complex worlds (see. James *et al.*, 1998). They have argued that seeing 'childhood as a natural state' works to subordinate children and place them in worlds 'protected' by adult worlds; it robs the child of what might be called his or her 'agency', and it obscures the power and dependency relations created by adults over children. Childhood may be seen as another socially constructed social division.

Allison James, Chris Jenks and Alan Prout have suggested four key ways in which sociologists can approach children. The first is *the socially constructed approach*. Here childhood does not exist in a fixed or essential form: instead we have to show how it is built up in specific groups and societies. It simply does not mean the same thing at different times. Thus, for instance, it may be thought of as exploitation to our minds to hear about children having to work; for much of history and in many societies today, it is simply considered the normal thing to do to help the family survive. Likewise, if we described a mixed family of children all huddled up in the same bed, we would probably consider this to be a form of child abuse and call in the welfare! But again, in many societies today and of the past, the separate spaces for children that Western societies now consider natural for children were in fact unknown.

A second approach is that of *the tribal child*. Here children's own worlds are seen as 'real places and provinces of meaning in their own right' (James *et al.*, 1998: 28). Their own worlds are honoured, whether this is a world of play in the schoolyard, the club, the gang or even computer games. This approach is mainly an ethnographic project of mapping what the child's actual worlds are like to live in for them, and not as seen through the eyes of adults.

A third approach sees the child as part of a *'minority group'*. This is a political form of analysis which looks at the ways in which power works in children's lives. It senses that often the child is one of the least equal members of a social group; that children are often excluded from adult activities and treated in ways that minimise their agency and autonomy. It is a position which can have a lot in common with children's rights arguments. Thus, in 1989 almost all countries in the world signed the United Nations Convention of the Rights of the Child. According to this, all children across the world should have the right to be protected by laws which would aim for their survival and development, as well as protection against harmful influences and exploitation. The laws urge full participation in family, cultural and social life, as well as access to health care, education, and services for children. Within this view, child labour, marriage and violence are all forms of childhood oppression to be overcome.

Finally, a fourth approach sees the child as *structural*. Here childhood is seen as part of the life course (see Chapter 7) and the lives of children share common characteristics which are worth describing and explaining. Thus their relationships to other children, to families, to work and education all need examining.

Growing older: the greying of the Western world

We turn now to the main topic of this chapter – growing older. A quiet but powerful revolution is reshaping the Western world: the number of people growing older is dramatically increasing. With this comes new concerns. Figure 13.2 shows the percentage increase of the world's older people from 1900, and then shows a United Nations projection for a massive increase by 2100. Whereas currently most of the world has an ageing population that is relatively small, the United Nations predicts that most of the world will soon have an ageing population well above 20 per cent, and for about a third of the world it will be well over 30 per cent. This shift in the age structure of a population will have marked implications for the organisation of society. After all, for most of history we have had 'young populations'.

WORLD WATCH

THE KILLING OF THE CHILDREN: INFANTICIDE IN INDIA

Rani, a young woman living in a remote Indian village, returned home from the hospital after delivering a baby girl. There was no joy in the family. On the contrary, upon learning of the birth, the men sombrely filed out of the mud house. Rani and her mother-in-law then set about the gruesome task of mashing oleander seeds into several drops of oil to make a poisonous paste, which they forced down the baby's throat. The day came to an end as Rani returned from a nearby field where she had buried the child.

As she walked home, Rani felt not sadness at losing her daughter but bitterness at not bearing a son. Members of her village, like poor people throughout the world (and especially Asia), favour boys while defining girls as an economic liability. Why? Because, in poor societies, most power and wealth falls into the hands of men. Parents recognise that boys are a better investment of their meagre resources, since males who survive to adulthood will provide for the family. Then, too, custom dictates that parents of a girl offer a dowry to the family of her prospective husband. In short, given the existing social structure, families are better off with boys and without girls.

One consequence of this double standard is the high rate of sex-selective abortion throughout rural India, China and other Asian nations. Curiously, in India, even villages that lack running water typically have a doctor who performs high-tech amniocentesis or ultrasound to determine the sex of a foetus. The woman's typical response, upon hearing the results of the test, is either elation at carrying a boy or resolve to terminate the pregnancy quickly so that she may 'try again'. Although there are no precise counts of abortion and female infanticide, analysts point out that, in some rural regions of Asia, men outnumber women by as many as ten to one.

For girls who manage to survive infancy, gender bias presents overwhelming barriers. Generally speaking, parents provide girls with less food, schooling and medical care than they give to boys. In times of drought or other crisis, families may leave girls to die while they channel what little resources they have towards the survival of a son.

Female infanticide was outlawed in India more than a century ago, but it still continues, and local authorities often collude in the slaughter of girls. 'It is just not possible not to notice that perhaps up to four out of ten baby girls are being killed soon after birth: it shows in the sex ratio of the children in their villages' (Calvert and Calvert, 2001: 242).

Look for a moment at the case of Britain. In 1880 fewer than 5 per cent of the population was *over 65*; in 2001, this was roughly 16 per cent, with 5.5 per cent over 75, and nearly 2 per cent over 85 (*Social Trends*, 2004). As 'baby boomers' reach their sixties around 2007, the elderly will rise even more steeply – perhaps to 19 per cent by 2035. Looking at absolute numbers, the elderly population jumped from 1.52 million in 1901 to 7.27 million in 1981. Projections suggest that by 2016, the number of people aged 65 and over will exceed those aged 16 and under (Social Trends, 2001: 31–32).

Similar change is occurring right across the rest of Europe, as Table 13.1 suggests. Within the EU, the average percentage of people over 65 rose from 10.6 per cent in 1960 to 14 per cent in 1991, and is predicted to rise to approximately 30 per cent by 2020. But there are differences across countries, with Ireland having the youngest population of EU countries and Sweden having the oldest (followed closely by Germany, France and the UK). Italy has the highest proportion of the elderly in the world – in 2000, out of a population of 57 million, nearly 10 million were over 65, 17.6 per cent of their population (Drake, 1994: 70; Walker and Maltby, 1997: 11).

Women outnumber men in the elderly population (due to their greater longevity) and the discrepancy increases with advancing age: at ages 70–74 there are roughly four women for every three men; at 80–84 there are two women for every man; and by 95, the ratio becomes three to one (Walker and Maltby, 1997: 11). However, the ratio of men to women is growing – what has been called the 'diminishing feminisation of later life'. (*Social Trends*, 2004: 3). We can soon expect to see many more men in old age.

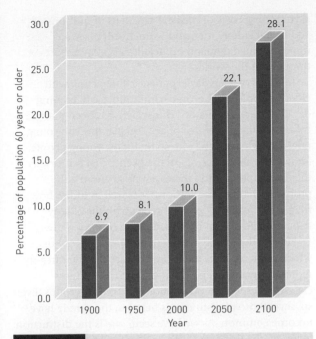

Figure 13.2 The greying of society: three centuries of world population ageing

Source: adapted from Long-Range World Population projections on Ageing website, http://www.un.org/esa/socdev/aging. The United Nations is the author of the orginal material

The dependency ratio

This greying of society characterises all industrial countries. Typically, rich nations have low birth rates, coupled with increasing longevity. This is sometimes called the 'demographic time bomb' and it highlights the **dependency ratio**: *the numbers of dependent children and retired persons relative to productive age groups* (Coleman and Salt, 1992: 542). This has been hovering around 58 and 53 over the past 25 years. Recently, because of falling fertility and family size it has been declining; it is not a problem yet. But changes predicted for this century suggest a growth in the dependency ratio – there will be fewer and fewer people of working age, and more and more will be dependants.

The past two centuries have witnessed a remarkable increase in life expectancy. Neither men nor women born in England and Wales in 1841 had a life expectancy of much more than 40. Today, most women born today can look forward to 80 years of life; and men to just over 75 years (*Social Trends*, 2001: 127). This represents an increase of roughly 100 per cent in less than two centuries. Since 1971, the proportion of the population aged 65 and over has increased from 15.9 per cent to 18.0 per cent for women and from 10.5 per cent to

Table 13.1 Percentage of the population aged 65 and over: EU comparison

	Percentages				
	1960	1970	1981	1991	1999[1]
Italy	9.3	10.8	13.2	15.1	17.6
Sweden	11.7	13.6	16.4	17.8	17.2
Greece	9.4	11.1	13.1	13.9	16.8
Belgium	12.0	13.3	14.2	15.0	16.5
Spain	8.2	9.5	11.2	13.8	16.4
France	11.6	12.8	13.8	14.1	15.8
United Kingdom	11.7	13.0	15.0	15.7	15.7
Germany	11.5	13.5	15.5	14.9	15.7
Austria	12.1	14.0	15.3	15.0	15.3
Portugal	8.0	9.7	11.4	13.6	15.2
Denmark	10.5	12.2	14.5	15.6	14.8
Finland	7.2	9.0	12.1	13.5	14.6
Luxembourg	10.8	12.5	13.6	13.4	14.3
Netherlands	8.9	10.1	11.6	12.9	13.6
Irish republic	11.1	11.1	10.7	11.4	11.6
EU average	10.6	12.1	13.9	14.7	16.0

[1] Population at 1 January 1999.

Source: adapted from Social Trends, 2001: 31

13.7 per cent for men (though it should be noted that this is a much slower rater of increase than in many other countries) (*Social Trends*, 2004: 1).

Underlying this gain in life span are medical advances that have virtually eliminated infectious diseases such as smallpox, diphtheria and measles, which killed many infants and young people in the past, as well as more recent medical strides which fend off cancer and heart disease, afflictions common in the elderly. Looking beyond the elderly population, a rising standard of living during the twentieth century has promoted the health of people of all ages.

We can only begin to imagine the consequences of this massive increase in the elderly population. As elderly people steadily retire from the labour force, the proportion of non-working adults will generate ever-greater demands for social resources and programmes. Indeed, as the ratio of elderly people to working-age adults, which analysts call the *old-age dependency ratio*, almost doubles in the next 50 years (rising from 20 to 37 elderly people per 100 people aged 18 to 64), this could shift the tax burden to the young, who will not be able to afford it. Some suggest that this may well lead to a major conflict between the generations (Kotlikoff and Burns, 2004). For instance, one key area of concern is the health-care system because the elderly today account for a quarter of all medical expenditures. With the

skyrocketing costs of medical care, tens of millions of additional elderly men and women will place an unprecedented demand on health-care systems throughout the world.

In terms of everyday experience, interacting with elderly people will become commonplace in coming decades. In recent history, our society has been marked by a considerable degree of age segregation. The young rarely mingle with the old, so that most young people know little about ageing. In the twenty-first century, as the elderly population increases, this pattern will probably change. But, tomorrow as well as today, how frequently younger people interact with the elderly depends a great deal on where in the country we live.

Finally, the elderly represent an open category in which all of us, if we are lucky, end up. But the category represents great diversity, representing all cultures, classes, sexes, sexual orientations and ethnic groups. Even so, several broad distinctions between the elderly have become common. As we have seen, one is the distinction between 'the **third age**' (50–74) – *a period of life often free from parenting and paid work when a more active, independent life is achieved* – and a '**fourth age**' – *an age of eventual dependence* (Laslett, 1996). Another distinction is between a very large group – the 'younger elderly' (65–75) – who enjoy good health and financial security, are typically autonomous and are likely to be living as

Table 13.2	Issues and implications of the greying of the world: a summary
Issue	**Implication**
Disabilities	Growing need for heath services and finance to support
Retirement	Changing shape of life course New patterns of both 'work' and leisure in later life Changing incomes of elderly
Poverty	Greater strain on finances for some groups in old age – living longer
Family	New roles: the young old look after the old old! Assisted conception means older people may have children
Psycho-social	Problems of isolation through bereavement, etc. Need for new meanings of later life and communities of support New identities for the ageing?
Politics	The rise of the 'grey vote'; a new politics of ageing
Culture	Shifting images of ageing as more and more people fit the category, and hence more facilities become available
Community	New retirement colonies for different groups, e.g. lesbian and gay communities in Palm Springs

couples, and the 'older elderly' (75–85) who become increasingly dependent on others because of both health and money problems. Finally, there is a growing group of 'very old'. Both these ways of grouping the elderly suggest a move from periods of increased activity and autonomy to one of growing dependency.

The social implications of ageing

Personal adjustment and quality of life

Although physical decline in old age is often less serious than most younger people think, this change can cause emotional stress. Older people can endure more pain, become resigned to limited activities, adjust to greater dependence on others and see in the death of friends or relatives frequent reminders of their own mortality. Moreover, because our culture places such a premium on youth, ageing may spark frustration, fear and self-doubt (Hamel, 1990). Psychiatrist Erik Erikson (1963, 1980), whose work has looked at the life cycle (see Chapter 7), suggests that in the final stages of life elderly people must resolve a tension that springs from 'integrity versus despair'. No matter how much they still may be learning and achieving, older people recognise that their lives are nearing an end. Thus the elderly spend much time reflecting on their past accomplishments and disappointments. To retain their personal integrity, Erikson explains, older women and men must face up to past mistakes as well as savour their successes. Otherwise, this stage of life may turn into a time of despair – a dead end with little positive meaning.

Despite these worries, research indicates that most people cope fairly well with the challenges of growing old. In a classic study of people in their seventies, Bernice Neugarten (1971) acknowledged that some people develop *disintegrated and disorganised personalities* because they find it nearly impossible to come to terms with old age. Despair is the common thread in these lives, sometimes to the point of making them passive residents of hospitals or nursing homes.

Another segment of Neugarten's subjects, those with *passive-dependent personalities*, were only slightly better off. They had little confidence in their abilities to cope with daily events, sometimes seeking help even if they do not actually need it. Always in danger of social withdrawal, their level of life satisfaction remained relatively low.

A third category of people had *defended personalities*, living independently but fearful of advancing age. Such people tried to shield themselves from the reality of old age by valiantly fighting to stay youthful and physically fit. While concerns about health are certainly positive, setting unrealistic standards for oneself can only breed stress and disappointment.

Most of Neugarten's subjects, however, fared far better, displaying what she called *integrated personalities*. As she sees it, the key to successful ageing lies in maintaining one's dignity, self-confidence and optimism while accepting the inevitability of growing old. This seems by far the most common pattern.

Given the youth orientation of most European societies, it may be easy to imagine that the elderly are generally unhappy. But research suggests that, while personal adjustments and problems are inevitable, the experience of growing old may also provide positive experiences – many old people do not even see themselves as old. As they say, 'I don't feel old' (Thompson *et al.*, 1990). Indeed, a European survey of the elderly found that only one in five were not satisfied with their lives, while two out of three reported they were very busy or leading full lives (Walker and Maltby, 1997: 23, 122). More recent research in the UK has looked at the quality of life and concluded that:

> 'most men and women rated their quality of life as good in varying degrees, as opposed to just alright or bad. Quality of life deteriorated with older age, but almost three quarters of the group aged 65–69 rated their lives overall as 'so good it could not be better' or 'very good' compared to a third to a half of those in older groups. It concluded the main drivers of quality of life in older age were: people's standards of comparison; their sense of optimism; good health and physical functioning; engaging on a large number of social activities; feeling supported; and living in safe communities with good community facilities and services.
>
> (Dean, 2004: 7)

Retirement

The transition from working life to retirement has been romanticised in European cultures, but retirement poses some problems for many older people. As the pattern of work changes in industrial societies, so there is a pronounced tendency for people to retire at earlier and earlier ages – sometimes by choice, sometimes through compulsory redundancies. Although the idea of retirement is familiar to us, it is actually a recent creation, becoming commonplace only in industrial societies during the nineteenth century (Atchley, 1983). The German Chancellor Otto von Bismarck first introduced retirement pensions in 1899, setting the age then at 70 (in 1916, it was lowered to 65).

GROWING (VERY) OLD: A REPORT FROM SARDINIA

Giovanni Frau sits quietly, shaded from the afternoon sun, in the piazza (village square) of Orroli, a small town on the Mediterranean island of Sardinia, lying to the east of Italy. Frau attracts little attention from the people passing by, but he is something of a celebrity. At the age of 111 he may well be the oldest person alive.

Frau is not the only one growing very old on Sardinia. His friend Vincenza Orgiana, who lives down the road, just turned 106, and during the past year, five others in the town had celebrated their 100th birthdays. All this in a town of only 2,748 people. In fact, records indicate that 220 Sardinians are at least 100 years old, twice the number found in nearby countries with much larger populations.

Several places in the world have an unusual number of people who have lived remarkably long lives. Sardinia is one, the Caucacaus region to the north is another, as is the Japanese island of Okinawa to the east.

How do we explain such longevity? The answer certainly is not advanced medical technology, so important to people in the United States; many residents of Orroli have never seen a physician or entered a hospital. One theory is biological: all these regions are isolated, with limited genetic mix that may play a part in long life. But the most important factor is probably cultural, including diet and pattern of physical activity. Rural Sardinians eat none of the fatty and processed foods that are so popular in the United States. They eat great amounts of local fruits and home-grown vegetables, consume almost no sugar, and enjoy a small daily ration of local wine. (Sardinians often raise their glasses and say, 'May you live to be 100.') Without television or other mass media, and little money for fancy appliances or power equipment, villagers of all ages lead active lives based on regular physical work.

Perhaps most important, a strong sense of tradition and community give everyone a clear sense of purpose and a strong sense of belonging. The elderly – the word 'elders' is more accurate – are at the centre of social life, in marked contrast to our own society's practice of pushing old people to the margins. Elders are indispensable guardians of a way of life and preside at all ceremonial occasions, where they transmit their knowledge to the young. Elders feel needed because, in their own minds and everyone else's, they are.

Sources: Based on Israely (2002) and also Benet (1971) and Spenser (1998).

Advancing technology reduces the need for everyone to work, as well as placing a premium on up-to-date skills. Retirement permits younger workers, who presumably have the most current knowledge and training, to predominate in the labour force. Some of the lowering of retirement ages may be linked to the growth of unemployment – stimulating early retirement policies in many countries. The establishment of private and public pension schemes provided the economic foundation for retirement. In poor societies that depend on the labour of everyone, and where no pension schemes exist, most people work until they become incapacitated.

Work provides not only earnings, it also figures prominently in our personal identity. Hence, retirement from paid work usually brings a significant reduction in income and sometimes entails a diminished status and even a loss of purpose in life (Chown, 1977).

Class differences are often important in retirement. Working-class retirement may often lack 'an active concept of retirement', whereas middle-class retirement – with better resources – has led to an expanding consumer market and culture (Fennell *et al.*, 1988: 83; Blaikie, 1999). For many older people, fresh activities and new interests minimise the personal disruption and loss of prestige brought on by retirement. They join 'the third age' – a time of active leisure. Volunteer work can be personally rewarding, allowing individuals to apply their career skills to new challenges and opportunities. But for others, and especially older women, this might be little more than a 'bourgeois option, unavailable to those who have low incomes and poor health' (Arber and Ginn, 1995: 8).

Around the world, there is little agreement as to when (or even if) a person should retire from paid work. In the light of such variability, one might wonder if a society should formally designate any specific age for retirement. Vast differences in the interests and capacities of older people make the notion of a fixed retirement age controversial. In the United States, as a result, Congress began phasing out mandatory retirement policies in the

1970s and virtually ended the practice by 1987. The United States is one of the few countries that have legislated against age discrimination – France, Spain, Canada, New Zealand and Australia being others (Walker and Maltby, 1997: 80).

In Europe, men more than women have faced the transition of retirement. Elderly women who spend their lives as homemakers do not retire *per se*, though the departure of the last child from home serves as a rough parallel. As the proportion of women in the labour force continues to rise, of course, both women and men will experience the changes brought on by retirement (Laczo and Phillipson, 1991).

Social isolation

Elderly people are also more likely than the whole population to experience social isolation, poverty and abuse. One of the most apparent concerns of the elderly is being 'old and alone' (Tunstall, 1966): there is a problem of both potential isolation and loneliness. Retirement may cut the old off from friends and workmates; the death of a spouse may leave the old on their own; and illness may bring limited mobility and a reduced chance to meet others. In Europe, '15% of those aged 60–4 live alone. This percentage doubles for those 70–4 and is almost 48% for those aged over 80' (Walker and Maltby, 1997: 13). This is much more likely to happen in the northern countries (the UK, The Netherlands, France, Belgium) and less likely in the southern (Greece, Portugal and Spain). But living alone is not the same as feeling lonely. Indeed, in the European survey, loneliness almost runs in reverse to living alone (Table 13.3). The elderly in Portugal and Greece are more likely to feel lonely, and those living in Germany, the UK and Denmark are least likely (Walker and Maltby, 1997: 26). One recent UK study suggested only a minority of older people were lonely (7 per cent) and a relatively small group (11–17 per cent) felt isolated (Dean, 2004: 13). While many do live alone, most old people seem to keep regular contact with their children – either by phone or by living near them. This has been called 'intimacy at a distance'.

One of the greatest causes of social isolation is the inevitable death of significant others. Few human experiences affect people as profoundly as the death of a spouse or family member. Widows and widowers must rebuild their lives in the glaring absence of people with whom, in many instances, they spent most of their adult lives. Some survivors choose not to live at all. One study of elderly men noted a sharp increase in mortality,

Table 13.3	Old and lonely: proportion of older people who often feel lonely by country (percentages)
Percentage feeling lonely often	**Country**
below 5	Denmark
5–9	Germany, The Netherlands, UK
10–14	Belgium, France, Ireland, Luxembourg, Spain
15–19	Italy
20 or more	Portugal, Greece (36%)

Source: adapted from Walker and Maltby (1997)

sometimes by suicide, in the months following the death of their wives (Benjamin and Wallis, 1963).

But there are other problems of isolation. Modern societies have often made going out very difficult for the elderly. There is, for instance, a growing concern about 'crime' among the elderly, often associated with a 'fear of crime'. This often means they become housebound. In The Netherlands, more than half those aged 65 or over no longer go out after dark; in Denmark, two-fifths of women aged 60 or over are afraid of being exposed to violence in the evening. Large numbers of old people are thus becoming stranded in their own homes.

The problem of social isolation falls most heavily on women, who typically outlive their husbands. Over 40 per cent of older women (especially the 'older elderly') live alone, compared to 16 per cent of older men. As with everything to do with old age, it is strongly structured by gender (Arber and Ginn, 1995).

Abuse of the elderly

Problems of family violence became increasingly recognised in Europe during the 1970s and 1980s. First came 'wife battering', then 'child abuse' (see Chapter 17). Most recently, an increasing number of researchers have noticed the phenomenon of 'granny battering' – or elder abuse. Abuse of older people takes many forms, from passive neglect to active torment, and includes verbal, emotional, financial and physical harm. Research suggests that between 3 and 4 per cent of elderly people (mainly women) suffer serious maltreatment each year, and three times as many sustain abuse at some point. Like family violence against children or women, it is difficult to determine how widespread abuse of the elderly is because victims are understandably reluctant to talk about their plight. But as the proportion of elderly people rises, so does the incidence of abuse (Bruno, 1985; Clark, 1986; Pillemer, 1988; Glendenning, 1993; Holmstrom, 1994). Nevertheless, most elderly people suffer from none of these things, and it has been suggested that these figures may be very unreliable (Whittaker, 1997).

What motivates people to abuse the elderly? Often the cause lies in the stress of caring – financially and emotionally – for ageing parents. Today's middle-aged adults represent a 'sandwich generation' who may well spend as much time caring for their ageing parents as for their own children. This care-giving responsibility is especially pronounced among adult women who not only look after parents and children but hold down jobs as well.

Even in Japan – where tradition demands that adult children care for ageing parents at home – more and more people find themselves unable to cope with the care-giving role. Abuse appears to be most common where the stresses are greatest: in families with a very old person suffering from serious health problems. Here, family life may be grossly distorted by demands and tensions that care-givers simply cannot endure, even if their intentions are good (Douglass, 1983; Gelman, 1985; Yates, 1986).

Poverty and inequalities

For most people in Europe, retirement leads to a significant decline in income. While some of the elderly are quite affluent (a new category – 'woopies', well-off older persons – has started to appear!), many lack sufficient savings or pension benefits to be self-supporting. John A. Vincent has argued that:

> The inequalities in the rest of society are reproduced in old age, and appear to be amplified. After retirement, the inequalities resulting from low pay, unemployment, disability, ill health, sex discrimination and racial discrimination are carried through into old age. The decline in the value of savings and pensions . . . means the worst off are the very old.
>
> (Vincent, 1996: 23–24)

He argues that the elderly are the most disadvantaged in society, and yet they are often excluded from mainstream studies of class and inequality. Simple matters such as income invariably decrease. There is a systematic curve that shows that income starts low in early life, increases until middle age and then declines through later years. Citing evidence from the General Household Survey, Vincent shows that the income of men over age 74 in the UK may drop by an average of £80 per week, while a woman's may drop nearly £60 (Vincent, 1996: 22). More of their income has to be spent on the 'bare necessities' of life: food, fuel, housing. And the older one gets, the poorer one becomes.

Throughout Europe a major source of income for the elderly is the pension. Generally, this is a two-tier system: public and private (usually an occupational pension). The latter is much more available to men, once again reinforcing the weaker position of women in old age. The value of this often decreases over time, so the elderly become relatively poorer. Only Denmark, Finland and Sweden have a universal flat-rate pension as a right of citizenship with no distinctions based on age or gender built into it (Walker and Maltby, 1997: 45), though at the time of writing the Swedish system is undergoing radical reform.

Poverty rates also rise significantly as people enter old age, making an increasing gap between the wealthy elderly and the poor elderly. The UK stands out in this polarisation of groups (Walker and Maltby, 1997: 48), and it has been much studied since the pioneering work of Peter Townsend (1957). Looking at Europe generally, the European Observatory on Ageing has concluded that although the living standards of older people have generally been rising in recent years, there are wide differences across countries. In general, there are low poverty rates in Denmark, Germany, Ireland and Luxembourg; medium poverty rates in Belgium, France, Italy and The Netherlands; and the countries with the highest poverty rates are Greece, Portugal, Spain and the UK. This said, however, when compared with the poverty rates found in the United States, all these levels are relatively low. One study ranking poverty levels gives Norway an index of 4.8 (low), the UK an index of 8.8 (middling) and the United States an index of 16.9 (high) (Vincent, 1996: 28).

In Europe, then, although many elderly are faring better than ever before, growing old (especially among women and other minorities) still means a growing risk of poverty, one that is feminised (more women experience it) and polarised (there is a sharp divide between the poor old and the wealthy old). What is distinctive about the deprivation of the elderly, however, is that it is often hidden from view. Because of personal pride and a desire to maintain the dignity of independent living, many elderly people conceal financial problems, even from their own families. It is often difficult for people who have supported their children for years to admit that they can no longer provide for themselves, even though it may be through no fault of their own.

Ageism and discrimination

Finally, as popular culture enshrines the value of youth, the elderly encounter discrimination and ageism. In earlier chapters, we explained how ideology – including racism and sexism – seeks to justify the social disadvantages of minorities. Sociologists use the parallel term **ageism** to designate *prejudice and discrimination against the elderly*. Like racism and sexism, ageism can be blatant (as when individuals deny elderly women or men a job simply because of their age) or subtle (as when people speak to the elderly with a condescending tone, as if they were children) (Kalish, 1979). Also, like racism and sexism, ageism builds physical traits into stereotypes; in the case of the elderly, people consider greying hair, wrinkled skin and stooped posture as signs of personal incompetence. Negative stereotypes picture the aged as helpless, confused, resistant to change and generally unhappy (Butler, 1975). Even sentimental notions of sweet little old ladies and charmingly eccentric old gentlemen gloss over older people's individuality, their distinct personalities and their long years of experience and accomplishment (Bytheway, 1995).

Ageism, like other expressions of prejudice, may have some foundation in reality. Statistically speaking, old people are more likely than young people to be mentally and physically impaired. But we slip into ageism when we make unwarranted generalisations about an entire category of people, most of whom do not conform to the stereotypes. Recently Betty Friedan, a pioneer of the contemporary feminist movement, asserted that ageism is central to our culture. The Voices box takes a closer look at this issue.

The elderly: a minority?

As a category of people in this country, the elderly do face social disadvantages. But sociologists disagree as to whether the aged form a minority in the same way as, say, Asian Europeans or people with disabilities do. Leonard Breen (1960) was the first to pronounce the elderly a minority, noting that older people have a clear social identity based on their age and, as a category, are subject to prejudice and discrimination. Yet, Gordon Streib (1968) countered, minority status is usually both permanent and exclusive. That is, a person is an Asian or a woman *for life* and cannot become part of the

dominant category of white males. Being elderly, Streib continued, is an *open* status because, first, people are elderly for only part of their lives and, second, everyone who has the good fortune to live long enough eventually grows old.

Streib made a further point. The social disadvantages faced by the elderly are less substantial than those experienced by the minorities described in earlier chapters. For example, old people have never been deprived of the right to own property, to vote or to hold office, as Asian Europeans and women have. Some elderly people, of course, do suffer economic disadvantages, but these do not stem primarily from old age. Instead, most of the aged poor also happen to fall into categories of people likely to be poor at any age. To Streib, the truth is that 'the poor grow old', not that 'the old grow poor'.

In light of this reasoning, and the rising economic fortunes of the elderly, it seems reasonable to conclude that old people are not a minority in the same sense as, say, Asian Europeans and women are. Perhaps the best way to describe the elderly is simply as a distinctive segment of our population with characteristic pleasures and challenges. In sum, growing old involves numerous problems and transitions. Some are brought on by physical decline. But others – including social isolation, adjustment to retirement, risk of poverty, abuse by family members and ageism – are social problems. In the next section, we will delve into various theoretical perspectives on how society shapes the lives of the elderly.

Researching ageing

Each of sociology's major theoretical paradigms sheds light on the process of ageing in Europe. We examine each in turn.

Functional analysis: ageing and disengagement

One of the earliest accounts came in the 1960s from Cumming and Henry (1961), borrowing some ideas from the leading functionalist Talcott Parsons. They argued that as ageing threatens society with disruption as physical decline and death take their toll, society's response is to *disengage* the elderly – to gradually transfer statuses and roles from the old to the young so that tasks are performed with minimal interruption.

VOICES

THE FOUNTAIN OF AGEING

In 1953, the French philosopher Simone de Beauvoir published a best-selling book, *The Second Sex* (orig. 1949 in France) in which she argued that women were defined in and through men as 'the other'. Ten years later, American author Betty Friedan argued in *The Feminine Mystique* (1963) that Western societies defined women only in sexual relation to men – as wives, mothers or sex objects. Thirty years later, having long established their feminist voices, both Friedan and de Beauvoir issued another call for change, this time in the way we view the elderly.

Surveying the mass media, Friedan concluded that elderly people are still conspicuous by their absence; only a small percentage of television shows, for example, feature central characters who are over 60. In addition, when members of many Western societies do think about older people, it is in negative terms: the elderly lack jobs, have lost their vitality and look back to their youth. In short, the 'ageing mystique' is that we define being old as little more

than a disease, marked by decline and deterioration, for which there is no cure.

This culture-based ageism is as widespread as it is powerful. Why do we still equate being old with living in an institution? Why do social service agencies foster dependency in older people rather than encouraging them to live – actively and independently – in society's mainstream?

Responding to this pervasive pessimism, Friedan claims that it is time we started seeking the 'fountain of ageing' by highlighting the potential and possibilities of this stage of life. All over North America and Europe, older people are discovering that they have more to contribute than others give them credit for. Playing in orchestras, assisting small business owners, designing housing for the poor, teaching children to read – there are countless ways in which older people can enhance their own lives by engaging people around them. The bottom line, concludes Friedan, is that people do not stop living when they grow old; they grow old when they stop living.

Source: based on Friedan (1963, 1993).
See also de Beauvoir (1997) and Bytheway (1995: 33–36).

Simone de Beauvoir, April 1983, aged 78.
Source: Popperfoto © Emile Pavaney

Betty Friedan (1921–)
Source: Rex Features

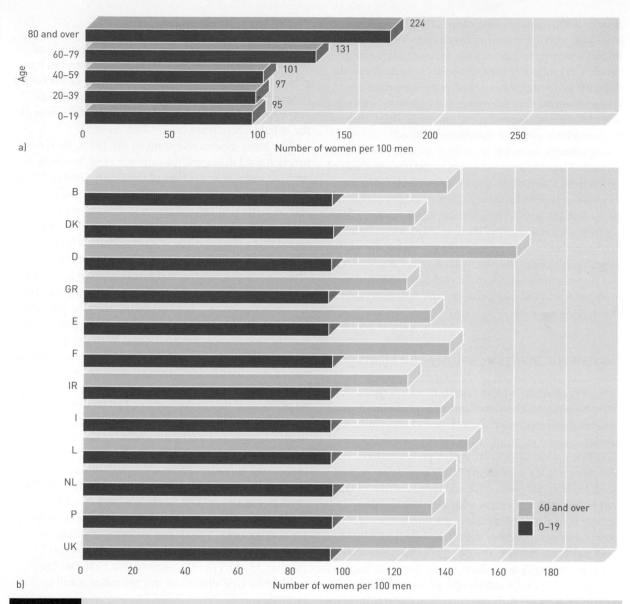

Figure 13.3 Number of women per 100 men in the EUR 12 countries, 1992: (a) by age range; (b) by country for 0–19 and 60+ age groups

Source: adapted from Eurostat, *Women and Men in Europe: A Statistical Portrait* (1995b: 13)

Thus, disengagement promotes the orderly functioning of society by removing ageing people from productive roles while they are still able to perform them. It is functional for them as ageing individuals with diminishing capacities can presumably look forward to relinquishing some of the pressures of their jobs in favour of new pursuits of their own choosing. Society also grants older people greater freedom, so that unusual behaviour on their part is construed as harmless eccentricity rather than dangerous deviance.

Such disengagement has an added benefit in a rapidly changing society because young workers typically have the most up-to-date skills and training. Formally, then, **disengagement theory** is *the proposition that society enhances its orderly operation by disengaging people from positions of responsibility as they reach old age*.

Although this is an old theory, it is still widely cited because some see it as explaining why rapidly changing, industrial societies typically define their oldest members as socially marginal. But it is largely rejected, and for four reasons. First, many workers cannot readily disengage from paid work because they do not have sufficient financial security to fall back on. Second, many elderly people – regardless of their financial circumstances – do not wish to disengage from their productive roles. Disengagement, after all, comes at a high price, including loss of social prestige and social isolation. Third, there is no compelling evidence that the benefits of disengagement outweigh its costs to society, which range from the loss of human resources to the increased care of people who might otherwise be able to fend better for themselves. Indeed, as the numbers of elderly people swell, devising ways to help seniors remain independent is a high national priority. Then, too, any useful system of disengagement would have to take account of the widely differing abilities of the elderly themselves. But fourth, and perhaps most significant, it makes the elderly appear too passive and too much like victims. And many studies show this is not true.

Humanistic analysis: activity and biography

This latter criticism is picked up from within symbolic interactionism and becomes almost a mirror image. Instead of disengagement (which would undermine the satisfaction and meaning many elderly people find in their lives), what we find are ageing people actively reconstructing the meanings of their lives. What seniors need, in short, are productive and recreational activities that imbue their retirement with meaning and joy. Activity theory proposes that, to the extent that elderly people do disengage, they substitute 'new lives' for the ones they leave behind. The elderly pursue active lives as much as the young do. Indeed, study after study suggests the importance to the elderly of following their interests, remaining engaged with daily activities and relationships, etc. (Havighurst *et al.*, 1968; Neugarten, 1977; Palmore, 1979a). Activity theory thus shifts the focus of analysis from the needs of society (as stated in disengagement theory) to the needs of the elderly themselves. This second approach also highlights social diversity among elderly people.

Functionalists might say this tends to exaggerate the well-being and competence of the elderly and even ask if we really want elderly people actively serving in crucial roles, say, as physicians or airline pilots. From another perspective, activity theory falls short by overlooking the fact that many of the problems that beset older people have more to do with how society, not any individual, operates.

The biographical approach

An important part of this activity theory is the role of telling the story of our lives. Of growing interest to both gerontologists and sociologists in recent times has been a biographical approach to ageing. This is a humanistic approach that aims to listen to the stories of the lives of the elderly. Three types can be distinguished.

First is the *reminiscence* story. In the 1960s, Butler and others started to suggest the importance of 'reminiscence' and 'life reviews' in the lives of the elderly (Butler, 1963). The act of purposely remembering can play a significant role in helping to create a coherent and unitary self (see, for example, Meyerhoff, 1992). Gerontologists have found that a characteristic of many elderly is their desire to tell, and tell again, some key highlights of their life. These can perform important functions both practically for the researcher, in providing key jumping-off points for further questions, but also therapeutically, since the telling of these stories is often an important part of the elderly person's adjustment process. With the 'greying of the population' and the growing tendency of the elderly to end their lives inside nursing homes, getting their life stories told can perform many valuable functions. The recognition of this has recently had something of the momentum of a social movement. A pioneer in this field, Joanna Bornat, has traced the origins of this movement in the UK to three sources: the academic growth of oral history; the spread of community publishing – such as the Centerprise Publishing Project in Hackney, London (with books such as Dot Steran's *When I Was a Child*, published in 1973); and the development of ideas in psychology around recall and memory, enabling almost everyone to become an oral historian of some kind (Bornat, 1994). (The UK organisation Help the Aged produced a type slide show in 1981 called Recall to facilitate this.)

Second is the *oral history*. Here the life is told in order to throw light on the times of the elderly person. Stories of the Second – or First – World War; stories of the Depression; stories of illegitimate children and the problem this led to. All this and more help the oral historian to fill out the portraits of the historical past (see Thompson *et al.*, 1990). Closely allied to this is the gathering of a family history. (These days, many bookshops provide rather elaborate 'family history' albums that facilitate this.)

Third is the *sociological life history*. Here the life is told through a series of stages and themes which help us understand the workings of a life over the life course. Does the life, for instance, fit into the stages discussed in

Chapter 7 of this book? What might be the life's major organising themes – possibly linked to power, intimacy, work, play and love? Does it, in the end, achieve some kind of coherence around the life? Jaber Gubrium, for instance, while listening to the life stories of elderly people in 'Florida Manor', can sense, tellingly, that many lives never achieve a coherence – that many 'elderly faces' may reveal the fragments of stories past while being unable to find connections with the (often diseased) present. As Gubrium says at the close of his book of life stories:

> There is little overall evidence that affairs are ultimately settled, sundered ties finally repaired, transgressions at last righted or accounted for, or preparations of the future or the afterlife completed.
>
> (Gubrium, 1993: 188)

Critical gerontology . . . ageing and inequality

Conflict theories highlight how different age categories compete for scarce social resources, a fact that contributes to age stratification. By and large, middle-aged people in Europe enjoy the greatest social privileges, while the elderly (as well as children) contend with less power and prestige and face a higher risk of poverty. Employers often shunt elderly workers aside in favour of younger men and women as a means of keeping down wages. As a consequence, conflict theorists note, older people become second-class citizens (Phillipson, 1982; Atchley, 1983).

To conflict theorists, age-based hierarchy is inherent in industrial–capitalist society. Capitalist culture has an overriding concern with profit, and hence facilitates the devaluation of those categories of people who are economically unproductive. Viewed as mildly deviant because they are less productive than their younger counterparts, the elderly are destined to be marginal members of a society consumed by material gain. In recent years, a cluster of British sociologists – Townsend, Walker, Phillipson and Vincent – have all highlighted the links between old age, dependency, divisions of labour and structures of inequality. The key to their work is the idea of **structured dependency**, *the process by which some people in society receive an unequal share in the results of social production* (Vincent, 1996: 186). Originally, in the work of Townsend and Walker, this referred to material dependency and focused upon the ways the elderly were structured out of work and into low incomes and poverty, and how this was reflected in welfare, health and care policies generally. More recently, it has become concerned with interpersonal dependence; with the ways the elderly are often infantilised into a form of helplessness, and how they may become segregated not only in institutions but also in the growing practices of keeping the elderly 'off the streets'. New dependencies can exclude the old from an autonomous 'normal' life.

Conflict analysis also draws attention to social diversity in the elderly population. Differences of class,

A sign of the future? Two centenarians.

Source: © Antonio Olmos

ethnicity and gender splinter older people as they do everyone else. Those in higher social classes have far more economic security, greater access to top-flight medical care and more options for personal satisfaction in old age than others do. Likewise, elderly WASPs (white, anglo-saxon protestants) typically enjoy a host of advantages denied to older minorities. For ethnic groups, ageing is confounded by 'triple jeopardy': because they are old, usually poor and also black. And throughout this chapter we have seen how women, who represent an increasing majority of the elderly population with advancing age (see Figure 13.3), experience the social and economic disadvantages of both ageism and sexism (Arber and Ginn, 1995).

Critical comment

Social conflict theory adds to our understanding of the ageing process by underscoring age-based inequality and explaining how capitalism devalues elderly people who are less productive. The implication of this analysis is that the aged fare better in non-capitalist societies, a view that has some support in research (Treas, 1979).

One shortcoming of this approach goes right to its core contention: rather than blame *capitalism* for the lower social standing of elderly people, critics hold that *industrialisation* is the true culprit. Thus, they claim, socialism does little to lessen age stratification. Furthermore, the notion that capitalism dooms the elderly to economic distress is challenged by the steady rise in the income of the elderly population in recent decades.

Looking ahead: ageing in the twenty-first century

This chapter has explored a remarkable trend: the 'greying' of the Western world. We can predict with confidence that the ranks of the elderly will swell dramatically in the decades to come. As this chapter has shown, not only will numbers increase, so too will those living to older and older ages. It will not be uncommon to find centenarians. Within the next 50 years society's oldest members will gain unprecedented visibility and perhaps influence in our everyday lives. As this prediction is realised, gerontology, the study of the elderly, will also

grow in stature as part of an expansion of research in all fields directed towards ageing and the elderly.

The reshaping of the age structure of our society raises many serious concerns. With more people living to an advanced age (and living longer once they reach old age), will the support services they need be available? As the elderly make more demands on services, the population will comprise proportionately fewer younger people to meet their needs. And what about the spiralling health-care costs of an ageing society? As the baby boomers enter old age, some analysts paint a doomsday picture of the modern world as a 'twenty-first century Calcutta', with desperate and dying elderly people everywhere (Longino, 1994: 13). For many the future will be bleak, as they face problems of poverty, lack of integration, fear of crime and the like.

But not all the signs are so ominous. For one thing, the health of tomorrow's elderly people (that is, today's young and middle-aged adults) is better than ever: smoking is down and the consumption of healthy foods is up. Such trends probably mean that the elderly of the end of this 21st century will be more vigorous and independent than their counterparts are today. Moreover, many of tomorrow's old people will enjoy the benefits of steadily advancing medical technology, though the elderly can prove costly in these areas.

Another positive sign may be the financial strength of the elderly. Costs of living are certain to rise, but tomorrow's elderly will confront them with unprecedented affluence. Note, too, that the baby boomers will be the first cohort of the elderly in which the vast majority of women have been in the labour force, a fact reflected in their more substantial savings and pensions.

On balance, there are reasons for both concern and optimism as we look ahead. But there can be no doubt that younger adults will face a mounting responsibility to care for ageing parents. Indeed, as the birth rate drops and the elderly population grows, our society is likely to experience a retargeting of care-giving from the very young to the very old.

Finally, an ageing population will almost certainly bring change to the way we view death. In all likelihood, death will become less of a social taboo and more a natural part of the life course, as it was in centuries past. Should this come to pass, both young and old alike may benefit.

THE ELDERLY AND SOCIAL POLICY IN EUROPE

Today, issues relating to ageing and the elderly command the attention of policymakers as never before. In some respects, growing old in industrialised countries has never been better: people live longer, have better health care than in the past, retire earlier and earlier, and experience less poverty than earlier generations. There is even talk of a positive, active 'third age' (Laslett, 1989). But stubborn problems persist. Many older people confront living alone and poverty, for example, and have to grapple with prejudice and discrimination. Many are afraid to leave their homes at night. That there is a significantly higher proportion of elderly women creates particular problems for them. Thus, as unprecedented numbers of women and men enter old age, new problems loom on the horizon.

The year 1993 was the European Union's first 'European Year of Older People and Solidarity between the Generations'. During this year, data on the elderly were collected in most EU countries and policies for the future suggested. The EU Observatory on Ageing and Older People, based on French *observatoires*, established a forum of independent experts from all the member states whose task, in this case, was to gather, synthesise and disseminate as much information as they could about the situation of the elderly in Europe. In addition, the Eurobarometer survey (which regularly conducts public opinion polls in each of the member states) looked at the attitudes of the general population towards the elderly and the attitudes of the elderly themselves. A major problem emerged: most countries felt that 'their government does not do enough for older people' (more if they were in Denmark, France, Luxembourg and The Netherlands; less in eastern Germany and Portugal). There are significant problems in comparing data across member states, but the studies produced a great deal of valuable data for the shaping of European policies towards the elderly.

The various reports found that there remains a good deal of social integration of the elderly in all the countries, but they nevertheless identified four key barriers. In many ways, these are the key issues to be debated over the coming years to assist and develop policies for the elderly. They are:

1. *Incomes*. It remains the case that the less income, the less your level of participation in the community. Consumption is restricted, travel is limited, life is hard. But there are marked variations: in Denmark, fewer than 10 per cent experienced isolation because of low income, while in Greece, Spain and Portugal more than 50 per cent experienced isolation.
2. *Age discrimination*. Having to retire early – or worse, being forced to retire early – remains a major source of isolation.
3. *Health and social care*. Older disabled people have higher levels of need, and services for them are rarely provided with a strong eye on their social integration.
4. *Fear*. Old people fear crime out of all proportion to the likelihood of their being victims. But this 'fear of crime' restricts their mobility and integration: many of the elderly in Europe become housebound at night (and a growing number are even becoming housebound by day).

From these problems, policies are recommended. These should provide adequate income for all older people, but especially older women. The Maastricht Treaty already stipulates that 'every worker of the EU must, at the time of retirement, be able to enjoy resources affording him or her a decent standard of living' (paragraph 24). Age discrimination in the labour market should be combated. There should be an increase in home care facilities that assist integration. and action on crime prevention would begin to remove fears of crime. Finally, the EU should move towards a policy of *productive ageing* – creating new, more active images and roles for older citizens in order to tap the massive resources of talent in the third and fourth ages.

Source: Walker and Maltby (1997).

SUMMARY

1. All societies have systems of *age stratification*, whereby there is an unequal distribution of wealth, power and privileges among people at different stages in the life course. This varies across societies and history.

2. Childhoods are socially constructed and organised differently across cultures and throughout history. To consider how children are linked to work, marriage, war and death in both high-income and low-income societies reveals these differences. The most obvious feature of contemporary Western childhoods is to say that most children are 'protected' from most of these for most of the time. But this is far from true of most children across the world today,

3. The proportion of elderly people in Europe has risen from 4 per cent in 1900 to over 12 per cent today. By the middle of the twenty-first century, 20 per cent of our society will be elderly.

4. Gerontology, the study of ageing and the elderly, focuses on biological and psychological changes in old age, as well as on cultural definitions of ageing.

5. Growing old is accompanied by a rising incidence of disease and disability. Younger people, however, commonly exaggerate the extent of disability among the elderly.

6. The age at which people are defined as old has varied through history. Until several centuries ago, old age began as early as age 30. In poor societies today, in which life expectancy is substantially lower than in Europe, people become old at 50 or even 40.

7. In global perspective, industrialisation fosters a decline in the social standing of elderly people.

8. As people age, they commonly experience social isolation brought on by retirement, physical disability and the death of friends or spouse. Even so, most elderly people look to family members for social support.

9. Since 1960, poverty among the elderly has dropped sharply. The aged poor are categories of people, including single women and people of colour, who are likely to be poor regardless of age.

10. Ageism – prejudice and discrimination against old people – serves to justify age stratification.

11. Although many seniors are socially disadvantaged, the elderly encompass people of both sexes, and all races, ethnicities and social classes. Thus older people do not qualify as a minority.

12. Disengagement theory, based on structural functional analysis, holds that the elderly disengage from positions of social responsibility before the onset of disability or death. In this way, a society accomplishes the orderly transfer of statuses and roles from an older to a younger generation.

13. Activity theory, based on symbolic-interaction analysis, claims that a high level of activity affords people personal satisfaction in old age.

14. Age stratification is a focus of social conflict analysis. The emphasis on economic output in capitalist societies leads to a devaluing of those who are less productive, including the elderly.

15. Modern society has set death apart from everyday life, prompting a cultural denial of human mortality. In part, this attitude is related to the fact that most people now die after reaching old age. Recent trends suggest that people are confronting death more directly and seeking control over the process of dying.

CRITICAL-THINKING QUESTIONS

1. Compare the experiences of children in a high-income society and a low-income society. How does this reveal the social construction of age?

2. Why are the populations of industrial societies getting older? What are some of the likely consequences of this demographic shift?

3. Start with common phrases such as 'little old lady' and 'dirty old man' and identify ways in which our culture devalues old people. From this explore the problems of 'ageism'.

4. Make a list of contrasting ageing experiences through ethnicity, class, gender, sexual orientation and disability. Consider what they have in common and how they may differ.

GOING FURTHER

Further reading

On children:

Allison James, Chris Jenks and Alan Prout, *Theorizing Childhood* (1998)

Chris Jenks, *Childhood* (1996)

Nick Lee, *Childhood and Society* (2001)
Key texts in shaping the new sociology of childhood.

Introductions to issues of ageing:

Andrew Blaikie, *Ageing and Popular Culture* (1999)

Bill Bytheway, *Ageism* (1995)

Graham Fennell, Chris Phillipson and Helen Evers, *The Sociology of Old Age* (1988)
Three very well-written and highly readable textbooks on ageing that guide the reader through the entire field in an engaging way.

Alan Walker and Tony Maltby, *Ageing Europe* (1997)
Uses research from the EU's 'Observatory on Ageing and Older People' and Eurobarometer surveys of both attitudes to the elderly in Europe and the attitudes of the elderly, to present a review of the situation of the elderly across the EU.

Growing Older Programme:

This was a major UK research initiative in the early 2000s (directed by Alan Walker) which produced an array of papers on many aspects of growing older. See www.shef.ac.uk/uni/projects/gop/

See also the discussion by Malcolm Dean, *Growing Older in the Twenty-First Century* (2004).

On global issues of ageing:

The World Bank, *Averting the Old Age Crisis: Policies to Protect the Old and Promote Growth* (1994) provides world figures and world analysis of the impending problems.

On aspects of social policy and old age:

Chris Phillipson, *Reconstructing Old Age: New Agendas in Social Theory and Practice* (1998)
An important statement of critical gerontology.

Sara Arber and Jay Ginn (eds), *Connecting Gender and Ageing: A Sociological Approach* (1995)
Looks at the different social effects of ageing on women's and men's roles, relationships and identity.

John A. Vincent, *Inequality and Old Age* (1996)
Focuses sharply on the elderly as a major, but neglected, pattern of inequality and provides both theory and evidence to support this claim.

On life stories and the elderly:

Joanna Bornat, *Reminiscence Reviewed* (1994)

Peter Coleman, *Ageing and Reminiscence Processes* (1986)

James Birren et al. (eds), *Ageing and Biography* (1996)
Three books that look at the stories of older people and the issue of reminiscence.

Barbara Meyerhoff, *Remembered Lives: The Work of Ritual, Storytelling and Growing Older* (1992)

Paul Thompson et al., *I Don't Feel Old: The Experience of Later Life* (1990)

Jaber F. Gubrium's *Speaking of Life: Horizons of Meaning for Nursing Home Residents* (1993)
G.M. Kenyon, *Re-storying Our Lives: Personal Growth through Autobiographical Reflection* (1997)

Focus on the process of story telling, with lots of examples from ageing people.

Watch a video/Read a book

On children:

- Jan Sverak's *Kolya* (1997): film of a five-year-old boy set against the Prague revolution
- Nicolas Roeg's *Walkabout* (1971): classic set in the Australian outback
- Tsitsi Dangarembga's *Everyone's Child* (2000): a call for action on behalf of Africa's millions of parentless children
- Iguel Arteta's *Chuck and Buck* (2000): an unnerving film about childhood friendships and perpetual 'childishness'.
- Read also William Golding's *Lord of the Flies* (1954) and Mark Twain's *The Adventures of Tom Sawyer* (1876) and *The Adventures of Huckleberry Finn* (1884).

On ageing, see:

- Ron Howard's *Cocoon* (1985), Bruce Beresford's *Driving Miss Daisy* (1989), Mark Rydell's *On Golden Pond* (1981) and Peter Marteson's *Trip to Bountiful* (1985): all Hollywood films that feature issues around people growing older

- James Ivory's *Roseland* (1977): a New York dance hall hosts the elderly ballroom dancers and tells their stories
- *The Alan Bennett Collection*: Bennett's observations on the old are always insightful.

Connecting up

Connect to other chapters

- Link to Chapter 4 on the shapes of society.
- For more on women and poverty, see Chapter 12 and on children and the elderly and poverty, see Chapter 10.
- For more on demographic trends, see Chapter 23.

To the websites

- http://www.unicef.org/sowc96/contents.htm

  This is the UNICEF 'State of the World's Children' site, and provides information and statistics on children around the world.
- http://www.bc.edu/bc_org/avp/wfnetwork/berkeley/

  This is the website for the Center for Working Families. It produces an excellent guide to reading in children.
- UN Programme on Ageing: Towards a Society for All Ages:

  http://www.un.org/esa/socdev/ageing/
- The National Council on Ageing, 1268 London Road, London SW16 4ER; phone 0208 679 8000; fax 0208 679 6069:

  http://www.ace.org.uk/

This agency works to improve the quality of life for older people in the UK, publishing books and research on the elderly via the Age Concern Institute of Gerontology at King's College London.

- The Centre for Policy on Ageing, at 25–31 Ironmonger Row, London EC1V 3QP, has a 'state of the art' database, held on CD-Rom; phone 0207 253 1787:

  http://www.cpa.org.uk/
- Research into ageing:

  http://research.helptheaged.org.uk/_research/default.htm
- *Age and Ageing* (the journal):

  http://ageing.oupjournals.org/
- National Institute of Ageing (US):

  http://www.nia.nih.gov/
- National Council on the Ageing:

  http://www.ncoa.org/
- American Society on Ageing:

  http://www.asaging.org/
- Retirement world:

  http://www.retirenet.com

For additional case studies, multiple choice questions, internet exercises, and annotated weblinks specific to this chapter, visit this book's website at **www.pearsoned.co.uk/plummer**

PART FOUR

SOCIAL STRUCTURES, SOCIAL PRACTICES AND SOCIAL INSTITUTIONS

CHAPTER 14   ECONOMIES, WORK AND CONSUMPTION

Global capitalism affects whatever it touches, and it touches virtually everything . . .
Arlie Hochschild

ON A HOT SUMMER'S DAY IN 2000, a large sealed container lorry arrived at Dover in the UK. As the lorry door was opened by immigration inspectors, it was clear that something terrible had happened. For a start there was no chilled air – which would have been usual for a lorry full of food. Indeed, there seemed to be no air at all. And there was a very strange smell. Soon the worst was uncovered: the lorry contained 58 dead young illegal Chinese migrants. Only two had survived the journey.

Kei Su Di, aged 20, was one of the two survivors. He had left his family in China 11 days earlier, having paid the first installment of a £20,000 fee. Travelling in groups, he and his hopeful companions flew from Beijing to Belgrade, and eventually reached Rotterdam where they were all packed tightly into a lorry for the concealed and illegal journey to the UK. Tomato racks were placed at the front to conceal the illegal travellers. Each person had no more space than the size of a newspaper; they had no food or water; there were little bags for excrement; and the ventilation was off so that any noise from within the lorry could not be heard. In the end, their silenced screams as they suffocated to death are hard to imagine.

Of the 58 dead found in the container lorry, 23 came from one county (Changle) in China, and the rest from neighbouring counties. In search of a better life, they had found the equivalent of 10 years' pay to give to organised criminals (the 'Snakeheads') to 'export' them to a land of opportunity. Full of hope, their families had waved them goodbye . . .

On a cold winter's night in 2004, a group of illegal Chinese immigrants trawled the wild and unruly beach at Morecambe (near Blackpool) in search of cockles to be sold on the market. They worked nine hours for a pound in the bitter cold. The beach was notoriously dangerous – even experienced fishermen would not use it. Suddenly, they found themselves engulfed by the incoming tide and 19 of them were drowned in the darkness – not knowing which way to run or turn, or how to escape. It was subsequently found that they were living 40 to a house in the most squalid conditions.

Here are two tragic incidents involving crime and illegal migration. But odd as this may seem, this is also now part of the economy. Behind both tragedies there appears to have been a gang – The Snakeheads (named after the sliding movement of a snake) – that preys on poor migrants. In the case of the illegal lorry, they charged migrants around £20,000 each to transport them across Russia to Europe, and in 2000 it was estimated they netted some £4 billion. This is human trafficking on a large scale. It has become a hugely profitable industry, probably worth US$30 billion each year. Europe may well account for some 6–7 million illegal immigrants each year. Likewise, the migrant cockle workers were desperate for some money and, although they earned very little and they put their lives at great risk, they seemed to have no other options. Here is the rough side of our economy at work (see guardian.co.uk/refugees).

(*The Guardian*, 19 June 2000, 6 April 2001; *The Week*, 1 July 2000; *The Sunday Telegraph*, 8 February 2004)

KEY THEMES

- The changing nature of the economy
- The different kinds of economic system
- The experience of work in the post-industrial economy
- The organisation of business and corporations
- The role of consumption in the modern economy
- The future of the economy of the twenty-first century?

(Left) Ford Maddox Brown – *Work*, a detail. This painting shows a whole range of people from various social strata going about their daily work.

Source: Manchester City Art Galleries/Bridgeman Art Library, London

It may seem odd to start a chapter on economies with two curious accounts of the death of Chinese illegal immigrants. But economies, for sociologists, are not simply about economics. For while **economies** may comprise of *social institutions that organise the production, distribution and consumption of goods and services,* such goods and services are diverse (such as here, the illegal sale of immigration) and connected to all the other social institutions (such as families who raised money for the migrants to travel and then had to cope with their deaths), politics (where governments restrict migration and the flow of peoples), crime (where illegal immigrants were forced to work £1 for nine hours for gang leaders) and media (which turned the deaths into a major issue). They are all interconnected. Economies are never just economies.

Hence in this chapter, we will explore the social significance and workings of economies, investigating the changing character of work in today's world, showing how economies are interdependent with other features of societies, and suggesting that they are now more closely interconnected internationally than ever before.

The great economic transformations: a brief overview

All societies have to deal with the social production, distribution and consumption of goods (such as food, clothing and shelter) and services (such as the work of religious leaders, doctors, police officers and telephone operators). As Chapter 4 explained, members of the earliest human societies relied on hunting and gathering to live off the land. In these societies, production, distribution and consumption of goods were all usually primarily dimensions of family life.

The Agricultural Revolution

The development of agriculture about 5,000 years ago brought change to these societies. Agriculture emerged as people harnessed animals to ploughs, increasing the productive power of hunting and gathering more than tenfold. The resulting surplus freed some people in society from the demands of food production. Individuals began to adopt specialised economic roles: forging crafts, designing tools, raising animals and constructing dwellings. A division of labour started to become more and more important as size increased.

With the development of agriculture under way, towns emerged, soon to be linked by networks of traders dealing in food, animals and other goods (Jacobs, 1970). These four factors – agricultural technology, productive specialisation and division of labour, permanent settlements and trade – were the keys to an expansion of the economy.

In the process, the world of work became less obviously bound up with families, though production still occurred close to home. In medieval Europe, for instance, most people farmed nearby fields. Both country and city dwellers often laboured in their homes – a pattern called *cottage industry* – producing goods sold in frequent outdoor 'flea markets' (a term suggesting that not everything was of high quality).

The Industrial Revolution

By the middle of the eighteenth century, a second technological revolution was proceeding apace, first in England and soon afterwards elsewhere in Europe and North America. The development of industry was to transform social life even more than agriculture had done thousands of years before. Industrialisation introduced five notable changes to the economies of Western societies.

1. *New forms of energy.* Throughout history, people derived energy from their own muscles or those of animals. Then, in 1765, James Watt pioneered the development of the steam engine. Surpassing muscle power 100 times over, steam engines soon operated large machinery with unprecedented efficiency.

2. *The centralisation of work in factories.* Steam-powered machinery soon rendered cottage industries obsolete. Factories – centralised and impersonal workplaces separate from the home – proliferated. Work moved from the private sphere to the public sphere – that is, people 'went out to work'.

3. *Manufacturing and mass production.* Before the Industrial Revolution, most work involved cultivating and gathering raw materials, such as crops, wood and wool. The industrial economy shifted most jobs into manufacturing that turned raw materials into a wide range of saleable products. For example, factories mass-produced timber into furniture and transformed wool into clothing.

4. *Division of labour and specialisation.* Typically, a single skilled worker in a cottage industry fashioned a product from beginning to end. Factory work, by contrast, demands division of labour and specialisation so that a labourer repeats a single task over and over again, making only a small contribution to the finished product. Thus as factories

raised productivity, they also lowered the skill level of the average worker (Warner and Low, 1947). Despoiling occurred.

5. *Wage labour*. Instead of working for themselves or joining together as households, industrial workers entered factories as wage labourers. They sold their labour to strangers who often cared less for them than for the machines they operated. Supervision became routine and intense. Incomes were usually pitifully low and workers were hence subject to great exploitation.

The impact of the Industrial Revolution gradually rippled outwards from the factories to transform all of society. While working conditions were very poor for many, greater productivity steadily raised the standard of living as countless new products and services filled an expanding marketplace. The benefits of industrial technology were shared very unequally. Some factory owners made vast fortunes, while the majority of industrial workers hovered perilously close to poverty. Children, too, worked in factories or deep in coal mines for pennies a day. Women factory workers, among the lowest paid, endured special hardships.

The Information Revolution and the post-industrial society

In Europe and North America, workers gradually formed trade unions to represent their collective interests in negotiations with factory owners. From the late nineteenth century onwards, governments in the West were forced to outlaw child labour, push wages upwards, improve workplace safety and extend schooling and political rights to a larger segment of the population.

The nature of production itself also started to change. By the middle of the twentieth century, many Western countries were being transformed. Automated machinery reduced the role of human labour in production, while bureaucracy simultaneously expanded the ranks of clerical workers and managers. Service industries – such as public relations, health care, education, media, advertising, banking and sales – start to employ the bulk of workers. Distinguishing the post-industrial era, then, is a shift from industrial work to service jobs.

Driving this economic change is a third technological transformation: the development of the computer. The *Information Revolution* in Europe, the United States, much of newly industrialising Asia and elsewhere starts to generate new kinds of information and new forms of communication, changing the character of work just as factories did two centuries ago. This Information Revolution unleashed three key changes.

1. *Tangible products to ideas*. The industrial era was defined by the production of goods; in the post-industrial era, more and more work revolves around creating and manipulating symbols. Computer programmers, writers, financial analysts, advertising executives, architects and all sorts of consultants represent the workers of the Information Age.

2. *Mechanical skills to literacy skills*. Just as the Industrial Revolution offered opportunities to those who learned a mechanical trade, the Information Revolution demands that workers have literacy skills – the ability to speak, write and use computer technology. People who can communicate effectively enjoy new opportunities; those who cannot face declining prospects.

3. *Decentralisation of work away from factories*. Just as industrial technology (steam power driving massive machines) drew workers together into factories, computer technology now permits many people to work almost anywhere. Indeed, laptop computers and facsimile (fax) machines linked to telephone lines now make the home, a car or even a plane a 'virtual office'. New information technology, in short, is reversing the industrial trend and bringing about a return of home-based 'cottage industries'. The virtual workplace and 'telecommuting' is becoming a reality for many.

The need for face-to-face communication as well as the availability of supplies and information still keep most workers in the office. On the other hand, today's more educated and creative labour force no longer requires – and often resists – the close supervision that marked yesterday's factories.

Post-Fordism and disorganised capitalism

Capitalism is a dynamic economic system and keeps changing its form – even in different countries. One major trend, starting in the 1960s, has been characterised as a shift in the flexibility of production: from Fordism to post-Fordism. Fordism is associated with the American car manufacturer Henry Ford, who, at the start of the twentieth century, developed the assembly line to produce cheap cars that could be purchased by the masses. **Fordism** is *an economic system based on mass assembly-line production, mass consumption and standardised commodities*. It depends upon dedicated machinery and tools producing identical components; centralised unskilled labour used intensively on specific tasks; and low-cost production of vast quantities of goods. Workers do repetitive work over long periods: the work is usually of mind-blowing tedium. They are paid reasonably well and this increases their consumer spending. Fordism is technically limited and not very flexible. A classic study by Huw Beynon looked at the Ford motor plant in Liverpool in the late 1960s and documented this moving assembly line where about 16,000 different components had to be 'screwed, stuck or spot welded' as the car moved and slipped down the line (Beynon, 1973: 105). The relentless pressure is more amusingly documented in Charlie Chaplin's classic silent film *Modern Times*.

While Fordist production techniques continued through much of the twentieth century, newer and more flexible ones emerged alongside them (especially in Japan and Southeast Asia). This newer process has involved the following:

- Shifts in production: more flexible systems of production

- More flexible time: part-time, temporary and self-employed workers

- Decentralisation of labour into smaller, less hierarchical units

- The 'casualisation of labour' where work becomes less stable and secure

- 'Just-in time' (that is, last-minute) rapid production

- Movement from standardised goods to goods including options

- Gradual replacement of 'mass marketing and advertising' by 'niche marketing', targeted at specific 'style' groups

- Globalisation, with a new international division of labour.

Often called **post-Fordism**, this *new economic system is based on flexibility (rather than standardisation), specialisation and tailor-made goods* (see Table 14.1 for comparison). We have already seen some of this at work

in organisational forms in Chapter 6 (where they were identified as 'postmodern'). These modes are not just to be found in work practices, but in consumption in the home as well. As we shall see, much of this new pattern has meant a system which is much more casual in its employment of workers (Beck, 2000a).

Sectors of the economy

The three 'revolutions' just described also reflect a shifting balance among the three sectors of a society's economy. The **primary sector** *generates raw materials directly from the natural environment* and includes agriculture, animal husbandry, fishing, forestry and mining. It predominates in pre-industrial societies. The **secondary sector** *transforms raw materials into manufactured goods* and includes the refining of petroleum and the use of metals to manufacture tools and automobiles. It grows quickly as societies industrialise. The **tertiary sector** *generates services rather than goods* and includes teachers, shop assistants, cleaners, solicitors, IT experts and media workers. Accounting for just 38 per cent of economic output in low-income countries, the tertiary sector grows with industrialisation and dominates the economies of high-income nations as they enter the post-industrial era. This marks one of the most significant change in modern economies.

Figure 14.1 shows these differences strikingly. Here we see that in low-income countries 23 per cent of the workforce is engaged in the primary sector, compared to just 2 per cent in high-income societies. When it comes to the tertiary sector of services, some 68 per cent of the labour force is 'in service' in high-income societies, but only 38 per cent in much poorer ones. Old economic patterns of agriculture and even manufacturing are giving way to an increasingly service and information-based economy (UNDP, 2000; World Bank, 2000b).

Table 14.1	A comparison of ideal types of production system: from Fordist to 'post-Fordist'	
	Fordist	**Post-Fordist**
Product	Standardised – all the same	Specialised – better quality?
Labour	Fragmented	Integrated
	Few tasks	Many tasks
	Little discretion	Flexible
Management	Centralised	Decentralised
Technology	Fixed machines	Multi-purpose/electronic
Contracts	Relatively secure	For most: insecure

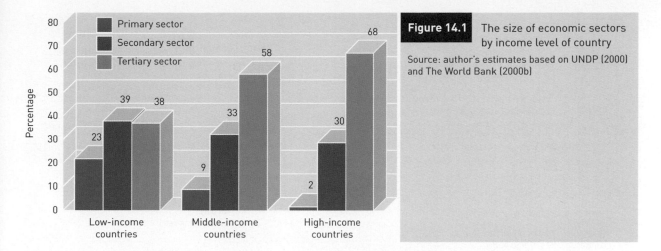

Figure 14.1 The size of economic sectors by income level of country

Source: author's estimates based on UNDP (2000) and The World Bank (2000b)

The global revolution: the global economy

As technology draws people around the world closer together, another important economic transformation seems to be taking place. As we saw in Chapter 2, globalisation has become a key feature of the late modern world: we have witnessed the emergence of a **global economy**, *economic activity spanning many nations of the world with little regard for national borders*. The development of a global economy has five main consequences.

First, we are seeing a global division of labour by which each region of the world specialises in particular kinds of economic activity. Agriculture occupies more than 70 per cent of the workforce in low-income countries while industrial production is concentrated in the middle- and high-income nations of the world. The economies of the richest nations, including Europe, now specialise in service-sector activity.

Second, we are seeing workers in the poorer countries working long hours for little pay in what have been called 'the sweatshops of the world'. They produce goods that can be sold in high-income countries. In a single day workers may produce hundreds of garments in poor work conditions. Just one garment sold back to high-income societies would sell for the equivalent of their wages for five days (Klein, 2000: 353)! Often, too, these workers are compelled to travel long distances, leaving families behind, in order even to find such opportunities for work. Note, too, that very frequently this labour is that of children. The International Labour Organisation suggests that some 250 million children work in low-income societies, a number that excludes child work

hidden from the statisticians, such as domestic labour (often by girls). This brings the total nearer 500 million, and this does not include the children who work in high-income societies.

Third, an increasing number of products pass through the economies of more than one nation. Consider, for instance, that workers in Taiwan may manufacture shoes, which a Hong Kong distributor sends to Italy, where they receive the stamp of an Italian designer; another distributor in Rome forwards the shoes to New York, where they are sold in a department store owned by a firm with its headquarters in Tokyo. As Figure 14.2 shows, it takes many countries to produce a car.

A fourth consequence of the global economy is that national governments no longer control the economic activity that takes place within their borders. In fact, governments cannot even regulate the value of their national currencies, since money is now traded around the clock in the financial centres of Tokyo, London and New York. Global markets are one consequence of satellite communications that forge information links among the world's major cities. Indeed, this gives rise to *global cities* (see Chapter 23).

The fifth consequence of the global economy is that a small number of businesses, operating internationally, now control a vast share of the world's economic activity. One estimate concludes that the 600 largest multinational companies account for fully half of the earth's entire total economic output (Kidron and Segal, 1991). The world is still divided into approximately 200 politically distinct nations. But, in light of the proliferation of international economic activity, 'nationhood' has lost much of its former significance.

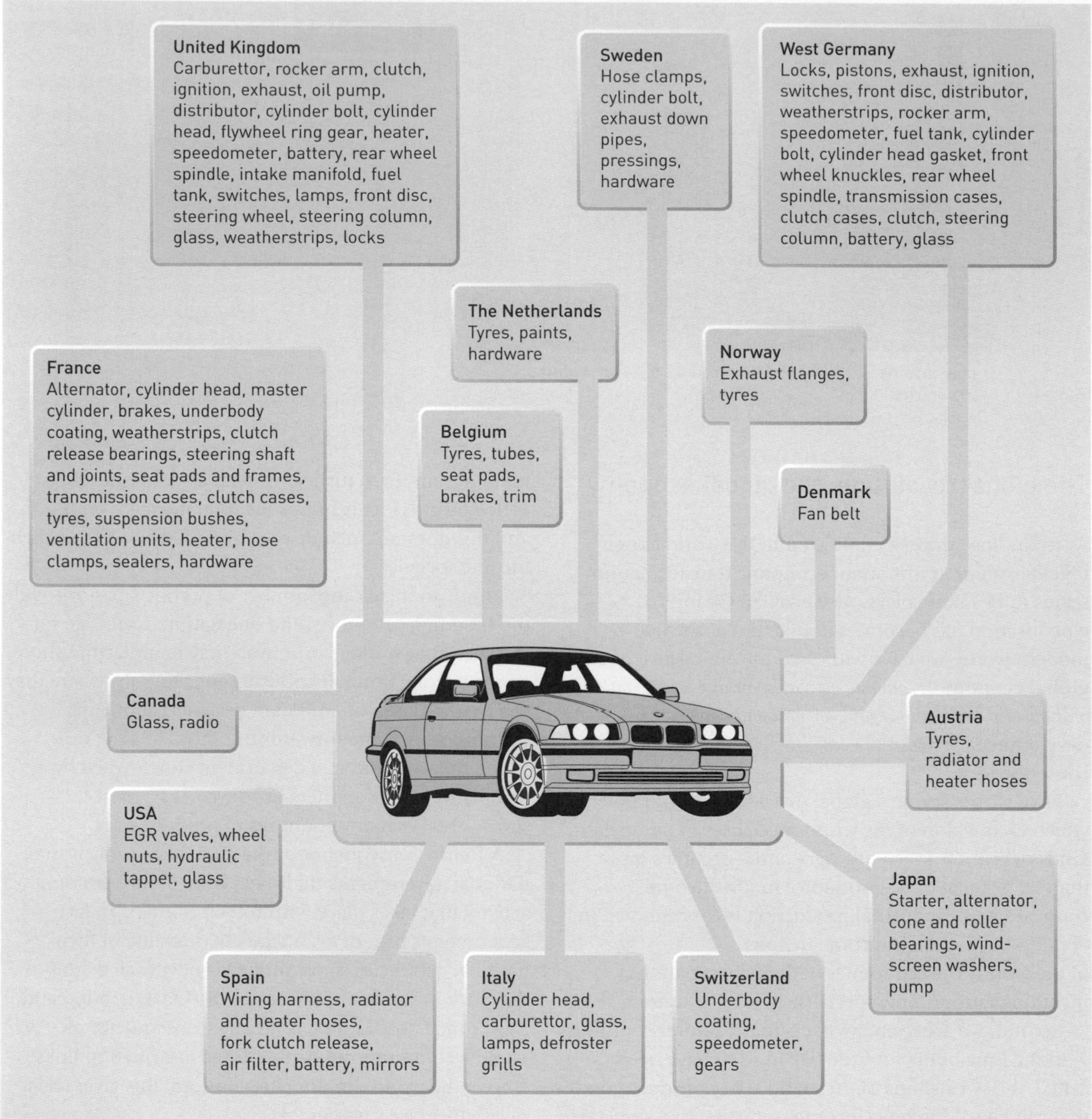

United Kingdom
Carburettor, rocker arm, clutch, ignition, exhaust, oil pump, distributor, cylinder bolt, cylinder head, flywheel ring gear, heater, speedometer, battery, rear wheel spindle, intake manifold, fuel tank, switches, lamps, front disc, steering wheel, steering column, glass, weatherstrips, locks

Sweden
Hose clamps, cylinder bolt, exhaust down pipes, pressings, hardware

West Germany
Locks, pistons, exhaust, ignition, switches, front disc, distributor, weatherstrips, rocker arm, speedometer, fuel tank, cylinder bolt, cylinder head gasket, front wheel knuckles, rear wheel spindle, transmission cases, clutch cases, clutch, steering column, battery, glass

The Netherlands
Tyres, paints, hardware

Norway
Exhaust flanges, tyres

France
Alternator, cylinder head, master cylinder, brakes, underbody coating, weatherstrips, clutch release bearings, steering shaft and joints, seat pads and frames, transmission cases, clutch cases, tyres, suspension bushes, ventilation units, heater, hose clamps, sealers, hardware

Belgium
Tyres, tubes, seat pads, brakes, trim

Denmark
Fan belt

Canada
Glass, radio

Austria
Tyres, radiator and heater hoses

USA
EGR valves, wheel nuts, hydraulic tappet, glass

Japan
Starter, alternator, cone and roller bearings, wind-screen washers, pump

Spain
Wiring harness, radiator and heater hoses, fork clutch release, air filter, battery, mirrors

Italy
Cylinder head, carburettor, glass, lamps, defroster grills

Switzerland
Underbody coating, speedometer, gears

Figure 14.2 **Global manufacturing: the component network for the European model of Ford Escort**
This image is derived from the first edition of Dicken's influential book, *Global shift* (1986). It captures the idea of global production well. However, it must be noted that in 2005 the details of this particular production process have changed considerably.
Source: adapted from Dicken (1986: 304)

SOCIOLOGY AND COMMODITIES: THE FOOD CHAIN

Think about what you have eaten in the last few days. Hamburgers, curries, apples, orange juice, coffee, tea, coke, beans, bread, chocolates, cod, chips, chicken, muesli, a Chinese take-away? Do you know where each item was produced? The chances are that many minimally processed products you may have eaten, such as fresh fruit and vegetables, were imported from countries on the other side of the globe. More heavily processed products, from chocolates to frozen meals, probably included ingredients produced and processed by many groups of people from many different countries, some of whom have prospered by selling the product you ate and some of whom themselves are worrying when they may get their next meal. If you were to trace the processes of producing each of the items you consumed in your last meal, Harvey reflects, you would discover:

> a relation of dependence upon a whole world of social labour conducted in many different places under very different relations and conditions of production. That dependency expands even further when we consider the materials and goods used in the production of goods we directly consume. Yet we can in practice consume our meal without the slightest knowledge of the intricate geography of production and the myriad social relationships that puts it upon our table.
> (Harvey, 1990)

For better or worse, the products we use each day have become part of a cycle of international exchange which is reshaping the way people around the world live and work.

Source: for a series of special issues on 'foods', see *New Internationalist* (1998): on coffee, 271; on cocoa, 304; on bananas, 317; on fish, 325.

Economies: differing kinds

Contemporary economies of the world can be analysed in terms of two abstract models – *capitalism* and *socialism*. Few societies have economies that are purely one or the other: most European countries have degrees of '*mixed economies*'. Sweden and the other Scandinavian countries are generally seen as a version of a more socialist approach – interventionist, corporatist and planned. But they are in the process of being pulled towards the German model, which is more inclined towards a social market. The system in the UK was mixed until the advent of Thatcherism in 1979, since when it has moved more and more towards a privatised market system (often called neo-liberalism). In effect, the New Labour government of 1997 has also followed this model, while introducing a language of the Third Way (to be discussed in Chapter 15). In short, in Europe 'there has been considerable convergence around the German social market model' (Edye and Lintner, 1996: 183).

Capitalism

Capitalism refers to *an economic system in which resources and the means of producing goods and services are privately owned*. There are many kinds of capitalist economy, but commonly there will be three distinctive features.

1. *Private ownership of property.* A capitalist economy supports the right of individuals to own almost anything. The more capitalist an economy is, the more private ownership there is of wealth-producing property such as factories or land. The downside of this can be a mass accumulation of profits by relatively few people, which can generate polarisation and cleavages between groups – the 'haves' and the 'have nots'. A potential for conflict is generated.

2. *Pursuit of personal profit.* A capitalist society encourages the accumulation of private property and defines a profit-minded orientation as natural and simply a matter of 'doing business'. The classical Scottish economist Adam Smith (1723–90) claimed that the

individual pursuit of self-interest helps an entire society prosper (1937: 508; orig. 1776). Others argue that it leads to the exploitation of the mass by the few, and consolidates a class system.

3. *Free competition, consumer sovereignty and markets.* A purely capitalist economy would operate with no government interference, sometimes called a *laissez-faire* approach. Adam Smith contended that a freely competitive economy regulates itself by the 'invisible hand' of the laws of supply and demand.

The market

Adam Smith maintained that the market system is dominated by consumers who select goods and services that offer the greatest value. Producers compete with one another by providing the highest-quality goods and services at the lowest possible price. Thus, while entrepreneurs are motivated by personal gain, everyone benefits from more efficient production and ever-increasing value. In Smith's time-honoured phrase, from narrow self-interest comes the 'greatest good for the greatest number of people'. Government control of an economy would inevitably upset the complex market system, reducing producer motivation, diminishing the quantity and quality of goods produced, and short-changing consumers.

Pure, ideal capitalism is non-existent. The United States may have the purest form – private markets are more extensive than in Europe – yet even there the guiding hand of government does play a role in economic affairs. Through taxation and various regulatory agencies, the government influences what companies produce, the quality and costs of merchandise, the products businesses import and export, and the consumption and conservation of natural resources. The federal government also owns and operates a host of businesses, including the US Postal Service, the Amtrak railway system and the Nuclear Regulatory Commission (which conducts atomic research and produces nuclear materials). The entire US military is also government-operated. Federal officials may step in to prevent the collapse of businesses, as in the 'bailout' of the savings and loan industry. Further, government policies mandate minimum wage levels, enforce workplace safety standards, regulate corporate mergers, provide farm price supports, and funnel income in the form of social security, public assistance, student loans and veterans' benefits to a majority of people.

Capitalism comes in many forms: Japan and the United States, for instance, work very differently. Generally, modern capitalism has moved through three phases. The first was a *liberal capitalism*, which dominated Britain and the United States in the early and middle nineteenth century and involved a free market, a 'facilitative' state and a legal framework which helps to maintain capitalism. Second was an *organised capitalism*, which involved an administered market and a more 'directive state'. There was, for example, in the UK between 1946 and 1979 much more 'state' intervention as governments often shaped economic policies. More recently a *disorganised/post-Fordist capitalism* has emerged, which involves an increase in the service sector, more global and dispersed operations and a decline of nation states (Lash and Urry, 1987; and see above).

Socialism

Socialism is *an economic system in which natural resources and the means of producing goods and services are collectively owned.* In its ideal form, a socialist economy opposes each of the three characteristics of capitalism just described.

1. *Collective ownership of property.* An economy is socialist to the extent that it limits the right to private property, especially property used in producing goods and services. Laws prohibiting private ownership of property are designed to make housing and other goods available to all, not just to those with the most money. Karl Marx asserted that private ownership of productive property spawns social classes as it generates an economic elite. Socialism, then, seeks to lessen economic inequality while forging a classless society.

2. *Pursuit of collective goals.* The individualistic pursuit of profit also stands at odds with the collective orientation of socialism. Socialist values and norms condemn what capitalists celebrate as the entrepreneurial spirit. For this reason, private trading is branded as illegal 'black market' activity.

3. *Government control of the economy.* Socialism rejects the idea that a free-market economy regulates itself. Instead of a *laissez-faire* approach, socialist governments oversee a *centrally controlled* or *command economy*. Socialism also rejects the idea that consumers guide capitalist production. From this point of view, consumers lack the information necessary to evaluate products and are manipulated by advertising to buy what is profitable for factory owners rather than what they, as consumers, genuinely need. Commercial advertising thus plays little role in socialist economies.

The People's Republic of China and a number of nations in Asia, Africa and Latin America – some two dozen in all – model their economies on socialism, placing almost all wealth-generating property under state control (McColm *et al.*, 1991). The extent of world socialism has declined in recent years, however, as societies in Eastern Europe and the former Soviet Union have forged new economic systems increasing the sway of market forces.

Socialism and communism

Some people equate the terms *socialism* and *communism*. More precisely, as the ideal spirit of socialism, **communism** is *an economic and political system in which all members of a society are socially equal*. Karl Marx viewed socialism as a transitory stage on the path towards the ideal of a communist society that had abolished all class divisions. In many socialist societies today, the dominant political party describes itself as communist, but nowhere has the pure communist goal been achieved.

Why? For one thing, social stratification involves differences of power as well as wealth. Socialist societies have generally succeeded in reducing disparities in wealth only through expanding government bureaucracies and subjecting the population to extensive regulation. In the process, government has not 'withered away' as Karl Marx imagined. On the contrary, socialist political elites have usually gained enormous power and privilege. Marx would probably have agreed that such a society is a *utopia* (from Greek words meaning 'not a place'). Yet Marx considered communism a worthy goal and might well have disparaged reputedly 'Marxist' societies such as North Korea, the former Soviet Union, the People's Republic of China and Cuba for falling far short of his ideal.

Democratic socialism and state capitalism

A limited measure of socialism, however, does not stifle democracy. In fact, some of the nations of Western Europe – including Sweden and Italy – have merged socialist economic policies with a democratic political system. Analysts call this **democratic socialism**, *an economic and political system that combines significant government control of the economy with free elections*.

Under democratic socialism, the government owns some of the largest industries and services, such as transportation, the mass media and health care. In Sweden and Italy, about 12 per cent of economic production is state controlled or 'nationalised'. That leaves most industry in private hands, but subject to extensive government regulation. High taxation (aimed especially at the rich) funds various social welfare programmes, transferring wealth to less-advantaged members of society.

Yet another blend of capitalism and socialism is **state capitalism**, *an economic and political system in which companies are privately owned though they cooperate closely with the government*. Systems of state capitalism are common in the rapidly developing Asian countries along the Pacific Rim. Japan, South Korea and Singapore, for example, are all capitalist nations, but their governments work closely with large companies, supplying financial assistance or controlling imports of foreign products to help businesses function as competitively as possible in world markets. Countries in East Asia and Western Europe illustrate that there are many ways in which governments and companies can work cooperatively (Gerlach, 1992).

The Third Way

During the 1990s, an approach called the **Third Way** was advocated. This has been the basis of the UK government under New Labour's Prime Minister Tony Blair (1997–) and to some extent in the United States under Democratic President Bill Clinton (1992–2000). Anthony Giddens suggests it is a *framework that adapts politics to a changed world, transcending old-style democracy and neo-liberalism* (Giddens, 1998: 26). As it may be more of a political system than an economic one, we will leave our discussion of this to Chapter 15.

Capitalism and socialism: relative advantages

Which economic system works best? In practice, most societies now work from a mix of capitalism and socialism to different degrees, although capitalism has become stronger and stronger. In 1989 and 1990, the nations of Eastern Europe (seized by the Soviet Union after the Second World War) rejected their socialist regimes. And today, China is also moving towards a market economy. But what was it like before these dramatic changes? We can look at this through three dimensions: economic productivity (or GDP), economic equality and civil liberties.

Economic productivity

Important elements of GDP, such as the proportion of the international export market a country controls, varied dramatically among capitalist countries. As a group, however, capitalist countries generated more goods and services than socialist countries. Averaging the economic output of industrialised nations at the end of the 1980s yielded a per capita GDP of about US $13,500. The comparable figure for the former Soviet Union and the nations of Eastern Europe was about US $5,000. This means that capitalist countries outproduced socialist nations by a ratio of 2.7 to 1 (UNDP, 1990).

Economic equality

How resources are distributed within a society stands as a second crucial issue. A comparative study completed in the mid-1970s calculated income ratios by comparing the earnings of the richest 5 per cent of the population and the poorest 5 per cent (Wiles, 1977). This research found that societies with predominantly capitalist economies had an income ratio of about 10 to 1; the corresponding figure for socialist countries was 5 to 1. This comparison of economic performance reveals that *capitalist economies produced a higher overall standard of living but also generated greater income disparity*. Or, put otherwise, *socialist economies created less income disparity but offered a lower overall standard of living*.

Civil liberties and personal freedom

A third issue to consider in evaluating socialism and capitalism is the personal freedom and civil liberties each offers its citizen. Capitalism emphasises *freedom to* pursue one's self-interest. It depends on the freedom of producers and consumers to interact in a free market, with minumum interference by the state. By contrast, socialist societies emphasise *freedom from* basic wants. Equality is the goal which requires state intervention in the economy, and this in turn limits some of the choices of citizens. There are then major tensions between freedom from and freedom to, between freedom and equality.

This tension has not been resolved between the two systems. In the capitalist West, many freedoms are ostensibly guaranteed, but are these freedoms worth as much to a poor person as a rich one? On the other hand, in Cuba or North Korea – two of the last remaining socialist states – economic equality is bought at the expense of the rights of people to express themselves freely.

Changes in socialist countries: Eastern Europe

As the old socialist regimes of Eastern Europe started to fall in the late 1980s (including the German Democratic Republic (GDR), Czechoslovakia, Hungary, Romania and Bulgaria), they started to move towards market-led or capitalist systems. In 1992, the Soviet Union itself dissolved. Ten years later, three fourths of state enterprises were partly or entirely under private ownership (Montaigne, 2001).

There were many reasons for these sweeping changes. In part, socialist economies underproduced compared to capitalist societies and often living standards were very low. And while members were formally equal, they often experienced large restrictions on freedom and heavy-handed states which regulated the media. New elites based on power usually appeared.

So far the market reforms in Eastern Europe are uneven. Some countries (Slovakia, Poland, the Czech Republic) are faring well; others (such as the Russian Federation itself) have brought out many of the weakest points of capitalism, with growing poverty and inequality, high competitiveness and social decline (Buraway, 1997).

The changing nature of work

The story of Rigoberta Menchú, told in the Voices box, suggests a world of work that is very common in low-income countries but which is increasingly disappearing in high-income societies. In this section, we look at work in Europe and the UK, and consider what changes seem to be taking place.

Work in Europe

In 1999, the active labour force aged 16–64 in the European Union was around 68 per cent of the population (78 per cent men, 59 per cent women). Some 155 million EU citizens were in work at that time, with a working week of around 40 hours. There were 16.2 million unemployed – around 10 per cent. By March 2001, however, this had fallen sharply to 11.5 million – an average of 7.8 per cent, with the lowest rates in The Netherlands (2.5 per cent) and Luxembourg (2.3 per cent). US unemployment stood at around 4.3 per cent and Japanese at 4.8 per cent (Eurostat, 2001).

In the UK, in 2003, there were some 28.1 million in employment – the highest number of people in employment on record. Unemployment peaked in 1993 (at 3 million) – and recently it has hovered at the one and a half million mark (in Spring 2003 it was 1.48 million). Contrary to a popular stereotype, the number of hours worked per week has been going up in recent years – we are not becoming a 'leisure society'. Looking at Europe, people working full time in Italy worked 37 hours per week (the lowest in the EU); whilst those in the UK worked 42 hours (one hour less than the countries with the highest) (*Social Trends*, 2004: Ch 4 & 5).

VOICES

THE STORY OF AN EIGHT-YEAR-OLD AGRICULTURAL WORKER IN GUATEMALA

The story of Rigoberta Menchú has become a famous life story in social science. She tells the story of her life in her book 'I, Rigoberta Menchú' – the life of a Guatemalan peasant who experiences revolutionary change. After the success of her book, she went on to become a leading political figure. In the short extract below, she talks of her early work experiences in the family and on the fields.

I worked from when I was very small, but I didn't earn anything. I was really helping my mother because she always had to carry a baby, my little brother on her back as she picked coffee. It made me very sad to see my mother's face covered in sweat as she tried to finish her load, and I wanted to help her. But my work wasn't paid, it just contributed to my mother's work. I either picked coffee with her or looked after my little brother, so that she could work faster. My brother was two at the time. ... I remember that, at the time, my mother's work was making food for forty workers. She ground maize, made tortillas, and put the nixtamal on the fire and cooked beans for the workers' food. That's a difficult job. ... All the dough made in the morning has to be finished the same morning because it goes bad. My mother had to make the number of tortillas the workers would eat. She was very appreciated by the workers because the food she gave them was fresh.

I was five when she was doing this work and I looked after my little brother. I wasn't earning yet. I used to watch my mother, who often had the food ready at three o'clock in the morning for the workers who started work early, and at eleven she had the food for the midday meal ready. At seven in the evening she had to run around again making food for her group. In between times, she worked picking coffee to supplement what she earned. Watching her made me feel useless and weak because I couldn't do anything to help her except look after my brother. That's when my consciousness was born. It's true. My mother didn't like the idea of me working, of earning my own money, but I did. I wanted to work, more than anything to help her, both economically and physically. The thing was that my mother was very brave and stood up to everything well, but there were times when one of my brothers or sisters was ill – if it wasn't one of them it was another – and everything she earned went on medicine for them. This made me very sad as well. ...

When I turned eight, I started to earn money on the finca. I set myself the task of picking 35 pounds of coffee a day ... my brothers and sisters finished work at about seven or eight in the evening and sometimes offered to help me, but I said: 'No, I have to learn because if I don't learn myself, who's going to teach me?' I had to finish my workload myself. Sometimes I picked barely 28 pounds because I got tired, especially when it was very hot. It gave me a headache. I'd fall asleep under a coffee bush, when suddenly I'd hear my brothers and sisters coming to look for me.

In the mornings we'd take turns to go off into the scrub to do our business. There are no toilets in the finca. There was only this place up in the hills where everyone went. There were about 400 of us living there and everyone went to this same place. It was the toilet for all those people. We had to take it in turns. When one lot of people came back, another lot would go. There were a lot of flies on all that filth up there and everyone went to this same place. There was only one tap in the shed where we lived, not even enough for us to wash our hands.

Source: Menchú (1984); see also Menchú (1998)

Rigoberta Menchú

Source: I. *Rigoberta Menchú: An Indian Woman in Guatemala* Verso, New Left Books, designed, illustrated and reprinted by permission of Sophie Herxheimer

Age clearly affects labour force participation. Typically, both women and men join the workforce in their teens and early twenties. During their child-bearing years, however, women's participation lags behind that of men. After about the age of 45, the working profiles now differ, with women more likely to continue in work and men less likely. There is a marked withdrawal from the labour force as people approach age 65. After that point in life, only a small proportion of each sex continues to perform steady income-producing work.

The decline of agricultural work

When the twentieth century began, about 40 per cent of the industrial world's labour force were engaged in farming. By its end, the figure was nearer 2 per cent, and many agricultural workers worked part-time. France, Germany, Spain, Ireland and the UK have the largest agricultural areas in Europe. Total income from agriculture in the EU fell by 34 per cent between 1973–75 and 1990–92, an average drop of 2.4 per cent each year, with the steepest falls in Denmark, the UK and Germany (Eurostat, 1995: 255).

Even though today's agriculture involves fewer people, it is often more productive. A century ago, a typical farmer grew food for five people; today, one farmer feeds 75. This dramatic rise in productivity also reflects new types of crop, pesticides that increase yields, more efficient machinery and other advances in farming technology. While, in southern Europe, holdings remain small (4 to 7 hectares in Greece, Portugal and Italy), in the north, the holdings are much larger (in the UK, the average is 68 hectares).

This process signals the eclipse of 'family farms', which are declining in number and produce only a small part of our agricultural yield, in favour of large *corporate agribusinesses*. But, more productive or not, this transformation has wrought painful adjustments for farming communities across the country, as a way of life is lost.

From factory work to service work

Industrialisation swelled the ranks of factory workers during the nineteenth century, but by 1911 more than 45 per cent of the United Kingdom workforce had service jobs (with 40 per cent in industry and some 15 per cent in agriculture) (Coleman and Salt, 1992: 375). Jobs in the service industries have continued to increase: between 1978 and 2000 by 36 per cent, from 15.6 million in 1978 to 21.2 million (and those in manufacturing industry fell by 39 per cent from 7.0 million to 4.2 million). Overwhelmingly, then, jobs in the industrialised world have moved to the service sector.

Table 14.2	Economic activity by gender and employment status in the UK, 1988 and 2003[1]					
United Kingdom						Millions
	1988			**2003**		
	Males	Females	All	Males	Females	All
Economically active						
In employment						
Full-time employees	11.4	5.8	17.2	11.5	6.7	18.3
Part-time employees	0.6	4.3	4.8	1.2	5.1	6.3
Self-employed	2.4	0.8	3.2	2.4	0.9	3.3
Other in employment[2]	0.3	0.2	0.6	0.1	0.1	0.2
All in employment	14.7	11.1	25.8	15.2	12.9	28.1
Unemployed	1.5	1.0	2.5	0.9	0.6	1.5
All economically active	16.2	12.1	28.3	16.1	13.5	29.6
Economically inactive	5.2	11.1	16.2	6.5	10.8	17.3

[1]At spring each year. Data are seasonally adjusted and have been adjusted to take account of the Census 2001 results.
[2]Those on government-supported training and employment programmes, and, for 2003, also unpaid family workers.

Source: Labour Force Survey, Office for National Statistics

A major new form of work in the service industry involves 'teleworking'. Well established in the US, it is now a major growth area in the UK. Between 1997 and 2002, the number of such workers grew by 70 per cent and in Spring 2001 there were 2.2 million teleworkers (equivalent to 7.4 per cent of the total UK workforce). Some of these work mainly in their own home in their main job or in various locations in their main job using home as a base. But others work at 'call centres'.

Not surprisingly, workers are often young and female, and the conditions in such call centres can be the modern equivalent of the old steel mills, with 'customer service representatives' (CSR) being expected to take as many as 20 calls an hour, or even two calls a minute. It is a new service industry that is relentless. And as with so much work in high-income countries, much of this work is farmed out to low-income countries such as India (*Economist*, 28 April 2001: 32–34).

In addition, note the growth of the new IT sector. In spring 2000 there were 855,000 people working in IT-linked occupations in the UK – an increase of 45 per cent in five years (*Social Trends*, 2001: Chapter 4). This trend towards a 'knowledge society' signposts a real shift in patterns of work. In 1995, Goran Therborn, a leading Swedish sociologist, could comment that so far 'Sweden is the only country in the world that has gone from being an industrial society to a 'knowledge and information society', having more 'professional, technical and related workers' than production and related workers, including labourers' (Therborn, 1995: 76). Many other countries are now following.

The growth of service occupations is one reason for the widespread description of Europe as a middle-class society. Nevertheless, as explained in Chapter 10, much service work – including sales positions, secretarial work and jobs in fast-food restaurants – yields little of the income and prestige of professional white-collar occupations, and often provides fewer rewards than factory work. In short, more and more jobs in this post-industrial era provide only a modest standard of living. This is illustrated in Table 14.3.

The dual labour market

The change from factory work to service jobs represents a shifting balance between two categories of work (Edwards, 1979). The **primary labour market** includes *occupations that provide extensive benefits to workers*. This favoured segment of the labour market contains the traditional white-collar professions and high

Table 14.3	Highest- and lowest-paid occupations, and average gross weekly pay (£) for Great Britain, April 2003

Highest paid
1. Directors and chief executives of major organisations	2,301.2
2. Medical practitioners	1,186.4
3. Financial managers and chartered secretaries	1,124.2
4. Solicitors and lawyers, judges and coroners	925.8
5. Marketing and sales managers	888.6
6. Information and communication technology managers	872.4
7. Management consultants, actuaries, economists and statisticians	863.1
8. Police officers (inspectors and above)	863.1
9. IT strategy and planning professionals	844.4
10. Financial and accounting technicians	838.1

Lowest paid
1. Retail cashiers and check-out operators	207.6
2. Launderers, dry cleaners, pressers	217.6
3. Bar staff	217.9
4. Waiters, waitresses	218.2
5. Kitchen and catering staff	228.4
6. Hotel porters	229.9
7. Hairdressers, barbers	231.8
8. Animal care occupations	232.3
9. Sewing machinists	239.8
10. Shelf fillers	241.5

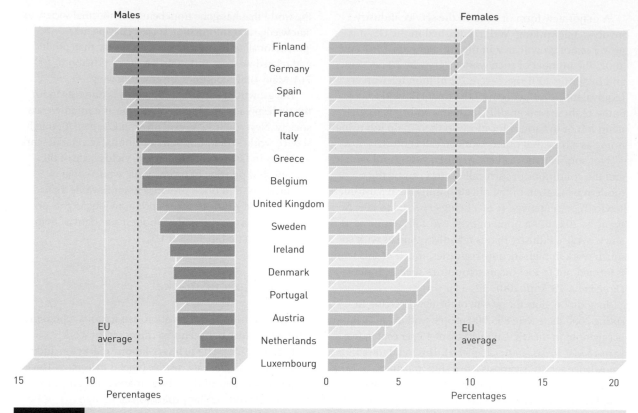

Figure 14.3   Unemployment rates[1]: by sex, EU comparison, 2002

[1] People aged 15 to 64, except for the United Kingdom where data refer to those aged 16 to 64.

Source: *Social Trends* (2004)

management positions. These are jobs that people think of as *careers*. Work in the primary labour market provides high income and job security and is also personally challenging and intrinsically satisfying. Such occupations require a broad education rather than specialised training and offer solid opportunity for advancement.

But few of these advantages apply to work in the **secondary labour market**, *jobs providing minimal benefits to workers*. This segment of the labour force is employed in the low-skilled, blue-collar type of work found in routine assembly-line operations, and in low-level service-sector jobs, including clerical positions. The secondary labour market offers workers much lower income, demands a longer working week and affords less job security and opportunity to advance. Not surprisingly, then, workers in the secondary labour market are most likely to experience alienation and dissatisfaction with their jobs. These problems most commonly beset women and other minorities, who are overly represented in this segment of the labour force (Kohn and Schooler, 1982). In spring 1996, only 8 per

cent of male employees worked part-time, while some 45 per cent of women did (*Social Trends*, 1997: 71).

Most new jobs in our post-industrial economy fall within the secondary labour market, and they involve the same kind of unchallenging tasks, low wages and poor working conditions characteristic of jobs in factories a century ago (Gruenberg, 1980). Moreover, job insecurity is on the rise as the economy shuttles an unprecedented share of workers from one temporary position to another.

Gender, women and work

One of the most striking features of the modern world is that more and more women are working across the world, accounting for around 36–40 per cent of the world's labour force. Men, by contrast, become increasingly unemployed, both when young and as they get older.

In the UK, for example, since the mid-1960s, employment rates for men have gradually fallen to reach

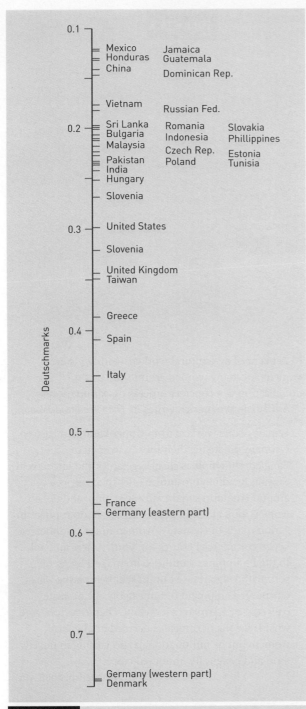

per cent in 1945 to 45 per cent by the end of the twentieth century. Over the last 30 years the numbers have grown from 10 million (in 1971) to 13 million in 1999, and projections say it will grow by another million or so by 2011 (*Social Trends*, 2001: 77).

The characteristics of women's work are often very different from those of men:

- They work more often for wages (as opposed to salaries)
- They are usually paid less than men
- Often their work has less status
- Job insecurity is greater
- They are more likely to become unemployed in many countries
- Advances into administrative and managerial positions are often blocked by what has been called 'the glass ceiling'.

Further, a process of **occupational gender segregation** *works to concentrate men and women in different types of job.* For instance, in the UK in 2000, 25 per cent of women's work was in clerical and secretarial occupations, while only 8 per cent of men's work was in that area (*Social Trends*, 2001: 81). Women's work is also often characterised by what Arlie Hochschild has called a **'second shift'** (maybe even more precisely a triple shift). After a day's work in the factory or the office, the woman usually returns home to do the domestic work, raise the children and cook the meals (we consider this in Chapters 12 and 17). All this is unpaid work (see Table 14.2).

'Doing the dirty work'

This unpaid and often hidden work – domestic labour – has another aspect. There is also a significant amount which is paid and visible: largely that which enables middle-class men and women to employ other women. Such work is often disproportionately performed by racialised groups and migrant workers (see Figure 14.4).

Bridget Anderson (2000), in her study of migrant domestic workers in five European cities (Athens, Barcelona, Bologna, Berlin and Paris in the mid-1990s), found that such work not only brought low pay and long hours, it could amount to a kind of 'slavery'. Women from poor countries would be asked to do impossible lists of work tasks; to care for children and families; to have very little time away from the home where they worked; and to be treated in subservient ways. Often they found it difficult to break away from the middle-class family that 'bought' them.

Figure 14.4 Labour costs per standard minute in the clothing industry

Source: after Dicken (1998: 296)

79 per cent of the working-age population in 1999, whereas among women they have risen to 69 per cent in 1999 (*Social Trends*, 2001: 73). There has been a steady growth of women in the labour market from roughly 30

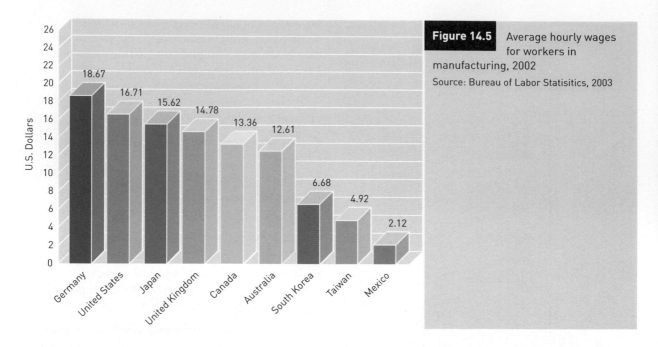

Figure 14.5 Average hourly wages for workers in manufacturing, 2002
Source: Bureau of Labor Statisitics, 2003

The sweatshops of the world

This global labour goes further. In lower-income countries, women are often compelled to work in the 'sweatshops of the world'. This term 'sweatshop' was introduced around the 1880s during the Industrial Revolution to describe the subcontracting system of labour. Miriam Ching Yoon Louie comments:

> Sweatshop workers toil at the bottom of a pyramid of labour exploitation and profit generation. Workers' immediate bosses are subcontractors, often men of their own ethnicity. Manufacturers and retailers sit at the top of the pyramid over the contractors who act as buffers, shock absorbers and shields. ... Like the ninteenth-century sweatshop middle-men, many of today's subcontractors survive the competition by 'sweating' their workers out of wages, hours, benefits and safety rights.
>
> (Louie 2001: 4)

Such sweatshops are especially common in the garment industry. With exceptionally low incomes (much less than a pound a day), work conditions are subject to little or no regulation, are casual and temporary, and are often hazardous. Much of women's work here is uncounted, so official figures can mean very little. These women are also 'on the move', migrating to where the work is. For example, each year about 100,000 women leave Asia's developing countries to work in newly industrialising economies. Although the world's agricultural force is shrinking rapidly, it is also becoming feminised – some

40 per cent of agricultural workers worldwide are women. For many women around the world, globalisation is a concrete process of exploitation.

As Christa Wichterich writes in *The Globalized Woman*:

> Female textile-workers from Upper Lusatia in Eastern Germany are losing their jobs to women in Bangladesh; Filipinas clean vegetables and kitchens in Kuwait; Brazilian prostitutes offer their services around Frankfurt's main railway station; and Polish women look after old people at rock-bottom prices in various parts of Germany. Women in the Caribbean key in commercial entries for North American banks. In the Philippines, families who make a living by sorting through refuse cannot sell their plastic wares whenever a shipment of unbeatably cheap waste, collected by Germany's recycling scheme, arrives. And what is for the next meal is decided not by local women, but by multinationals specialising in novelty food and genetically modified crops.
>
> (Wichterich, 2000: viii)

Business Process Outsourcing

A rapidly growing sector of work has been the spreading of industries from high-income societies to lower-income societies: we have already seen this in the manufacturing of many commodities above, but we also find it now in the re-routing of telephone calls to call centres set up in poorer parts of the world where educated workers can be

In the poorer countries all over the world workers are exploited to produce goods for the richer nations, as in this Korean enterprise where many Burmese work on textile production.

Source: © Associated Press/Richard Vogel

paid much less. In India, Business Process Outsourcing (BPO) has grown by 60 per cent a year since 2000 and employs over a million people. It employs graduates for long hours, having trained them in English to answer calls. Workers make about £140 in a month, way below the UK or US salaries for equivalent work, but more than a farm worker in India would make in six months (*The Guardian*, 6 February 2004: 18).

The spread of part-time and flexible work

Over the past decade, part-time work has become more common – especially for women. In the UK in 2000, there were some 5.7 million part-time jobs, of which 4.7 million were done by women. One consequence of this can be the undermining of job security. Several decades ago, workers could confidently assume that hard work and playing by the rules all but guaranteed that their jobs would be there until they were ready to retire. This is no longer the case. As one analyst puts it:

> The rise of the knowledge economy means a change, in less than twenty years, from an overbuilt system of large, slow-moving economic units to an array of small, widely dispersed economic centres, some as small as an individual boss. In the new economy, geography dissolves, the highways are electronic. Even Wall Street no longer has a reason to be on Wall Street. Companies become concepts . . . and jobs are almost as susceptible as electrons to vanishing into thin air.
>
> (Morrow, 1993: 41)

In the short run, at least, the dislocation for workers is tremendous. Companies scrambling to 'remain competitive' in the global economy are 'downsizing' and decentralising to gain 'flexibility'. These trends mean not only cutting the number of people on the payroll – managers as well as secretaries – but also replacing long-term employees with temporary workers. By hiring 'temps', companies no longer have to worry about providing insurance, paid vacations or pensions. And, if next month workers are no longer needed, they can be released without further cost.

In the UK, between 1986 and 1996, the number of women in part-time work increased by 18 per cent – to 5.3 million. Among men, the number doubled – but the total was only 1.2 million. Many who have these jobs say they do not want full-time work (8 in 10 women; but only 4 in 10 men) (*Social Trends*, 1997: 76). In the EU as a whole, some 10 per cent of all employment is part-time; and in some countries the figures soar: it is nearly 35 per cent of all employees in The Netherlands, and 22.5 per cent of employees in Denmark.

Self-employment

Self-employment – *earning a living without working for a large organisation* – was once commonplace in Europe. Families owned and operated farms, and self-employed urban workers owned shops and other small businesses or sold their skills on the open market. With the onset of the Industrial Revolution, however, the economy became more centralised so that self-employment diminished. But more recently this has been changing. The number of self-employed people in the UK increased throughout the 1980s to peak at 3.6 million in 1990. In spring 1996 there were 3.3 million, three-quarters of whom were men.

Most self-employed workers work in agriculture, fishing and construction, and are more likely to perform blue-collar than white-collar work. Society has always painted an appealing picture of working independently: no time clocks to punch, no one looking over your shoulder. For minorities who have long been excluded from particular kinds of work, self-employment has been an effective strategy for broadening economic opportunity (Evans, 1989). Further, self-employment holds the potential – though it is rarely realised – of earning a great deal of money. But for all its advantages, self-employment is vulnerable to fluctuations in the economy, one reason that only one-fifth of small businesses survive for more than ten years. Another common problem is that the self-employed generally lack pension and health-care benefits provided for employees by large organisations.

The underground economy

Running parallel with the economic activity monitored and regulated by governments is the **underground economy**, *economic activity generating income that is unreported to the government as required by law*. On a small scale, most people participate in the underground economy on a regular basis. One family makes extra money from a car boot sale; another allows its teenage children to baby-sit for the neighbours without reporting the income received. Taken in total, such activities amount to millions of pounds in lost taxes annually. But much of the underground economy (or 'black economy') is attributable to criminal activity which can run into billions of pounds. We opened with the story of 'people-trafficking', which may well be a hidden economy of many billions of pounds, but to this we can add the sale of illegal drugs and weapons, trafficking of stolen goods, bribery, extortion, illegal gambling and money-laundering. Some countries, including parts of the Russian Federation and parts of Latin America, face larger problems with illicit activity than others. But the dimensions of this form of work are also clearly global: there is a globalised underground economy.

Non-work

In 2000, in the UK, there were 36.3 million people of working age, of whom 27 million were in employment. This means that there were nearly 10 million people of working age who were not in work. Of these some 70 per cent were not looking for a job. These fell into four broad groups:

- Those looking after family and home (mainly women) – 22 per cent
- The long-term sick and disabled – 18 per cent
- Students, a significant group and growing – 14 per cent
- Others – 14 per cent.

There are still substantial numbers of 'workless households': around 16 per cent of working-age households were workless in spring 2000 (*Social Trends*, 2001: 80). Some sociologists have started to suggest that a future trend may well be the rise of the workless society, but others suggest a main trend is rather towards increasingly fragmented and casual work patterns.

Recent trends are undoing workplace bonds with remarkable speed and at all levels of the labour force. Like workers at the dawn of the industrial era centuries ago, many of today's secretaries, engineers, bank staff and even corporate executives are finding their job security vanishing before their eyes. For the foreseeable future, there is probably no going back to the traditional notion of lifetime employment with one company (Castro, 1993; Morrow, 1993).

Changes in trade unions

The changing economy has been accompanied by a declining role for **trade unions**, *organisations of workers* *collectively seeking to improve wages and working conditions through various strategies, including negotiations and strikes.* Membership in trade unions increased rapidly in Europe through the earlier part of the twentieth century, peaking at 13 million people in the UK in 1979 (around 55 per cent). But by the mid-1990s it had dropped to 9 million (around 35 per cent); by 2000 it had fallen to 29 per cent. In autumn 2002, there were 7.3 million trade union members in the UK, a decrease of 0.8 million since 1995 (*Social Trends*, 2003: 66).

During the 1980s, the British government under Margaret Thatcher was firmly committed to weakening the power of trade unions. Blaming unions for strikes and industrial unrest, the Thatcher government introduced much legislation (like the 1980 Employment Act and the 1984 Trade Union Act) which made secret ballots on industrial action compulsory, prohibited 'secondary picketing' by restricting union members to picket only at their own place of work, and which made industrial action in support of workers employed elsewhere illegal. The Thatcher government also reduced consultation with union officials. Symbolically, too, this was the time of the 1985 Miners' Strike, in which pit closures became a key issue and which was used by Thatcher as a key defining moment to bring the unions down. Add to this the increases in unemployment during this period, it is clear that the unions' strengths were considerably undermined. Hyman sees all this as a process of 'coercive pacification' in which employers and government suppress and weaken union activities (Hyman, 1989a).

But the decline of unions is not an isolated British phenomenon. In the United States, in absolute numbers, union membership peaked during the 1970s at almost 25 million people. Since then, it has steadily declined to about 16 per cent of non-farm workers, or about 18 million men and women.

While a similar trend has emerged throughout Europe, in a few countries, particularly Denmark, trade union membership has actually increased. Roughly 80 per cent of workers in the Scandinavian countries belong to unions, and employer–union cooperation is high. In Europe as a whole about 40 per cent belong to unions, while in Canada and Japan the proportion is about one-third (Western, 1993, 1995).

The relative decline of unions stems from a number of trends already noted. First, industrial countries have lost tens of thousands of jobs in the highly unionised factories as industrial jobs are 'exported' overseas. Many plant managers have succeeded in forcing concessions from workers, including, in some cases, the dissolution of trade unions. Moreover, most of the new service-sector jobs being created today are not unionised, and hardly any temporary workers belong to a trade union. Young people are much less likely to be unionised than older workers.

Falling job security may well make union membership a higher priority for workers in the years to come. But to expand their membership, unions will also have to adapt to the new global economy. Instead of seeing foreign workers as a threat to their interests, in short, union leadership will have to forge new international alliances (Mabry, 1992; Church, 1994).

Unemployment

Every industrial society has some unemployment. Much of it is temporary. Few young people entering the labour force find a job right away; some workers temporarily leave the labour force while seeking a new job, to have children or because of a strike; others suffer from long-term illnesses; still others may lack skills to work.

But the economy itself also generates unemployment, often called structural unemployment. Jobs disappear as occupations become obsolete, as businesses close in the face of foreign competition and as recessions force layoffs and bankruptcies. Since 1980, for example, the 'downsizing' of US businesses has eliminated some 5 million jobs – a quarter of the total – in that country's 500 largest corporations.

Unemployment rates vary over time as they do from country to country. In March 2001 the unemployment rate in the 15 countries of the European Union was 11.5 million – an average of 7.8 per cent, US unemployment stood at around 4.3 per cent and in Japan it was 4.8 per cent (Eurostat, 2001).

Unemployment in Europe

Unemployment rates and experiences both differ and fluctuate greatly across Europe, as Tables 14.4 and 14.5 show. In absolute terms, Russia had the largest number of unemployed in 1998, with some 9 million people, while Norway had a much more modest 75,000. In general, unemployment has been falling in most of the old European Union, Spain having the highest rates, and France, Germany and Italy also being quite high (around 10 per cent)(Table 14.4). The UK and Nordic countries are generally quite low – and much lower than they were during most of the 1980s and 1990s. Figure 14.3 shows the greater likelihood of women to be unemployed. Finally, by stark contrast with the old European Union, countries in Eastern and Central Europe have rates as high as 40 per cent (Table 14.5).

Table 14.4	Some unemployment rates in the old European Union, estimated 2002					
Austria	4.8%	Germany	9.8%	Spain	11.3%
Belgium	7.2%	Ireland	4.3%	Sweden	4%
Denmark	5.1%	Italy	9.1%	UK	5.2%
Finland	8.5%	Netherlands	3.0%		
France	9.1%	Portugal	4.7%		

Source: to be supplied

Table 14.5	Some unemployment rates in the wider Europe, estimated 2002					
Bosnia	40%	Macedonia	37%	Serbia	32%
Croatia	21.7%	Poland	18.1%	Bulgaria	18%
Slovakia	17.2%	Albania	17–30%	Lithuania	12.5%
Estonia	12.4%	Slovenia	11%	Greece	2.3%

Source: www.nationmaster.com 6.704

Unemployment in the UK

From the late 1940s to the 1970s in the UK, it was generally assumed that unemployment should never rise above 1 million. But since that time there have been quite dramatic swings: 3 million by 1985, down again to 1.5 million by the early 1990s, up again to 2.5 million people (8.5 per cent of the workforce) in 1994, and in 2001 the Blair government formally announced that it had fallen below the symbolic figure of 1 million. This figure crept up again so that in spring 2003 there were 1.48 million unemployed. Of course, this unemployment rate reflected large regional differences, with the lowest rate in the southeast and southwest (around 3.8 per cent) and the highest in the north of England (around 6.5 per cent) and Greater London (7 per cent) (*Social Trends*, 2003: 63).

Who are the unemployed?

Writing of the UK (but the data are probably generalisable across Europe), Adrian Sinfield (1981) suggests that five major groups are more likely to become or remain unemployed:

- Those who experience redundancies due to economic change
- Unskilled youth trying to make the transition from school to work
- Older workers who face enforced retirement

- Unemployed women
- The long-term unemployed.

Experiencing unemployment

Unemployment can wreak havoc on lives and families. Many studies have suggested that there is an initial shock, followed for a short while by denial and optimism (in which there may be a sense of being on holiday for a little while), but this is soon followed by distress and anxiety. If the unemployment continues for a long time, it may lead to resignation and adjustment. It has also been linked to 'ill health, premature death, attempted and actual suicide, marriage breakdown, child battering, racial conflicts and football hooliganism'. A subculture of despair can emerge, sometimes linked to the development of an underclass (see Chapter 10). For women who see work as an escape from the home, unemployment can be especially harsh (Jahoda *et al.*, 1972; orig 1933; Fagin and Little, 1984). Generally, unemployment affects those with least resources most.

Problems of measuring unemployment

Measuring unemployment is no easy task. Although there are official figures, they can conceal the difficulties in recording practices and the major differences within countries. In many countries, but especially lower-income ones, it can be almost impossible to count the numbers out of work.

Government unemployment statistics, based on monthly national surveys, generally understate unemployment for three reasons. First, to be counted among the unemployed, a person must be actively seeking work; 'discouraged workers', those who have given up looking for a job, are omitted from the statistics. Second, many people unable to find jobs for which they are qualified settle, at least for a while, for 'lesser' employment: a secretary works as a 'temp' several days a week or a former university lecturer drives a taxi while seeking a new teaching position. Such people are counted among the employed, though they might better be described as *under*employed. Third, changes in policies towards the unemployed or in the procedures for measuring unemployment can conceal and distort the 'true picture'. In the UK, for instance, between 1982 and 1996 there were at least 14 changes that tended towards lowering the figures. For example, since 1982, only those eligible for benefits are included in the unemployment figures; and since 1988, most people in the UK under the age of 18 became ineligible for benefits (income support), resulting in 90,000 being taken off the register. Dan Finn suggests that a lot of the youth training schemes were designed to conceal unemployment by taking young people out of the unemployment statistics (Finn, 1987). On the other hand, statistics also overlook the fact that many people officially out of work receive income 'under the table' from odd jobs or even from illegal activity. But, even considering off-the-books income, the actual level of unemployment is probably several percentage points above the official figure.

The world of corporations

At the core of today's capitalist economy lies the market which is composed centrally of **corporations**, *organisations with a legal existence, including rights and liabilities, apart from those of their members*. By incorporation, an organisation becomes an entity unto itself, able to enter into contracts and own property. More and more these corporations transcend nation states: as we have seen, they are transnational corporations (or TNCs) and they are the primary 'movers and shapers' of the world economy. A **transnational corporation** is *a firm which has the power to coordinate and control operations in more than one country, even if it does not own them* (Dicken, 1998: 177).

The practice of legal incorporation accelerated with the rise of large businesses a century ago because it offered company owners two advantages. First, incorporation shields them from the legal liabilities of their businesses,

protecting personal wealth from lawsuits arising from business debts or harm to consumers. Second, profits earned by corporations receive favourable treatment under the tax laws of Europe. The largest corporations are typically owned not by single families but by millions of stockholders, including other corporations. This dispersion of corporate ownership has spread wealth to some extent, making more people small-scale capitalists. Moreover, day-to-day operation of a corporation falls to white-collar executives, who may or may not be major stockholders themselves. Typically, however, a great deal of corporate stock is owned by a small number of the corporation's top executives and directors (Dicken, 1998).

Capitalist markets

Capitalist economies can vary greatly in their approach to the market. In the purest form, the market is simply a situation where there is private ownership of companies competing freely and equally with other companies. But as many commentators have noted, such a fully free system is rare. There are many reasons for this. Among these are the facts that governments often intervene in markets; some companies can become so large that they dominate certain markets; and companies can become heavily bureaucratic so that they are not open to quick adjustment to market situations. Table 14.6 suggests both a pure market form and ways in which it can be modified.

Economic concentration

While many companies are small, with assets worth less than £750,000, the largest corporations dominate the global economy (see Table 14.7). In 2001, for example, the largest world corporation was car maker General Motors (GM), with more than £175 billion in revenue (*Fortune*, 2001) (see Table 14.8). GM's sales during a single year can easily equal the tax revenue of smaller European countries.

Conglomerates and corporate linkages

Economic concentration has spawned **conglomerates**, *giant corporations composed of many smaller corporations.* Throughout much of the twentieth century, small companies were gobbled up by larger ones. Some industries, such as tobacco, came to be dominated by three or four major firms. Since the 1980s, however, there has been some shift in this process, as some companies decide to downsize and shift some of their functions to other firms.

Table 14.6	Crouch's characteristics of capitalist economies – from pure to modified

Pure market form	Modified market opposites
Ai Small firm, many in market	Large firm, few in market
Aii External labour market	Internal labour market
Bi Minimal economic role for state	State involvement
Bii No state regulation	Extensive state regulation
Ci Low membership of formal associations	High membership of formal associations
Di All relationships on pure contract	Reciprocity – interpersonal and community involvement
Dii Short-term financial arrangements	Close institutional relations with sources of finance

Source: derived from Crouch (1999: 170)

Table 14.7	Britain's top ten leading companies

Stock Market value in 1997	By sales value in 2000
1. BP	BP Amoco plc
2. Glaxo Wellcome	AXA Investment Managers
3. BT	Uniliver plc
4. Lloyds TSB	Tesco plc
5. SmithKline Beecham	BP International
6. Marks & Spencer	Cross Channel Catering
7. NatWest Bank	British Telecommunications
8. Grand Metropolitan	J. Sainsbury
9. GEC	Tesco Stores Ltd
10. BTR	Lloyds TSB group

Source: Financial Times and **http://www.top1000.co.uk/**

Table 14.8	The *Fortune* list of top world corporations by revenue

Global 500 rank	Company	Revenues ($million)
1	General Motors	176,558.0
2	Wal-Mart Stores	166,809.0
3	Exxon Mobil	163,381.0
4	Ford Motor	162,558.0
5	Daimler Chrysler	159,985.7
6	Mitsui	118,555.2
7	Mitsubishi	117,765.6
8	Toyota Motor	115,670.0
9	General Electric	111,630.0
10	Itochu	109,068.0
A sample of the positioning of a few others:		
11	Royal Dutch/Shell	105,366.0
16	IBM	87,548.0
23	Hitachi	71,858.5
28	AT&T	62,391.0
56	Prudential Insurance	42,220.3

Source: adapted from *FORTUNE Global 500* © 2001 Time Inc. All rights reserved.

Conglomerates emerge as corporations, enter new markets, spin off new companies or carry out take-overs of existing companies. Forging a conglomerate is also a strategy to diversify a company, so that new products can provide a hedge against declining profits in the original market. Faced with declining sales of tobacco products, for example, R. J. Reynolds merged with Nabisco foods, forming a conglomerate called RJR–Nabisco. Coca-Cola's soft drinks market is still growing, but this company now produces fruit drinks, coffee and bottled water, as well as movies and television programmes. Besides conglomerates, corporations are also linked through mutual ownership, since these giant organisations own each other's stock. In today's global economy, many companies have invested heavily in other corporations commonly regarded as their competitors. Chapter 21 looks a little more at how big media corporations such as Disney or TimeWarner link and diversify.

One more type of linkage among corporations is the *interlocking directorate*, a social network of people serving simultaneously on the boards of directors of many corporations. These connections give corporations access to valuable information about each other's products and marketing strategies. Laws forbid linkages of this kind among corporations that compete directly with one another. Yet beneficial linkages persist among non-competing corporations with common interests – for example, a corporation building tractors may share directors with one that manufactures tyres. Indirect linkages also occur when, for example, a member of General Motors' board of directors and a director of Ford both sit on the board of Exxon/Esso (Herman, 1981; Scott and Griff, 1985; Weidenbaum, 1995).

Corporate linkages do not necessarily run counter to the public interest, but they certainly concentrate power and they may encourage illegal activity. Price fixing, for example, is legal in much of the world (the Organisation of Petroleum Exporting Countries (OPEC) meets regularly to try to set oil prices), but not in Europe. By their nature, however, corporate linkages invite price fixing, especially when only a few corporations control an entire market.

Corporations and competition

The capitalist model assumes that businesses operate independently in a competitive market. But while smaller businesses and self-employed people may represent a competitive sector, they are usually at considerable disadvantage since the corporate core is largely non-competitive. Large corporations are not truly competitive because, first, their extensive linkages mean that they do not operate independently and, second, a small number of corporations come to dominate many large markets.

With the exception of some public utility providers (in the UK this used to include water), no large company can establish an actual **monopoly**, *domination of a market by a single producer*. The law does permit lesser economic concentration called **oligopoly**, *domination of a market by a few producers*. Oligopoly results from the vast investment needed to enter a new market such as the car industry. Certainly, the successful entry of foreign-owned corporations into the European car markets shows that new companies can successfully challenge the biggest corporations. But all large businesses strive to limit competition simply because it places profits at risk.

Although capitalism favours minimal government intervention in the economy, corporate power is now so great – and competition among corporations sometimes

so limited – that government regulation may be the only way to protect the public interest. Yet, governments are also the corporate world's single biggest customer, and national governments frequently intervene to bolster struggling corporations. In short, corporations and governments typically work together to make the entire economy more stable and profitable (Madsen, 1980).

Corporations and the global economy

Corporations have grown in size and power so fast that they are now responsible for most of the world's economic output. In the process, the largest corporations – centred in Europe, Japan and the United States – have spilled across national borders and now view the entire world as one vast marketplace. As noted in Chapter 9, multinationals are large corporations that produce and market products in many different nations.

Corporations become multinational in order to make more money, since most of the planet's resources and three-quarters of the world's people are found in less-developed countries. Worldwide operations, then, offer access to plentiful materials and vast markets. In addition, labour costs are far lower in poor countries of the world. A manufacturing worker in Taiwan labours all week to earn what a German worker earns in a single day or less.

The impact of multinationals on poor societies is controversial, as Chapter 9 explained in detail. On one side of the argument, modernisation theorists argue that multinationals unleash the great productivity of the capitalist economic system, which will boost economic development (Rostow, 1978; Madsen, 1980; Berger, 1986; Firebaugh and Beck, 1994). Cadbury-Schweppes alone, for example, far out-produces any one of the least-productive nations in the world. Corporations offer poor societies tax revenues, capital investment, new jobs and advanced technology – taken together, what modernisation theorists call a certain recipe for economic growth.

On the other side of the argument, dependency theorists who favour a socialist economy claim that multinationals only intensify global inequality (Vaughan, 1978; Wallerstein, 1979; Delacroix and Ragin, 1981; Bergesen, 1983; Walton and Ragin, 1990). Multinational investment, as they see it, may create a few jobs in poor countries but it also stifles the development of local industries, which are a better source of employment. Further, critics charge, multinationals generally push developing countries to produce expensive consumer goods for export to rich nations rather than food and other necessities that would bolster the standard of living in local communities. From this standpoint, multinationals establish a system of neo-colonialism, making poor societies poorer and increasingly reliant on rich, capitalist societies.

While modernisation theory hails the virtues of an unregulated market as the key to a future of progress and affluence for all the world's people, advocates of dependency theory call for the replacement of market systems by government regulation of economic affairs. The box on page 391 takes a closer look at the issue of market versus governmental economies.

Consumption in modern economies

Until very recently the dominant approach to the economy taken by sociologists has been around the production of goods, with a focus on either businesses or workers and work. So far this has been the main focus of this chapter. But sociologists have increasingly come to recognise the importance of not just what we produce, but what – and how – we consume. Indeed, as there has been a growing move in society *from production to consumption*, so there has been the growth of *a sociology of consumption*. Shopping and consuming has now become a major social practice of everyday life; and in some markets – such as the 'youth market' – it has become almost the number one social activity. 'Going shopping', 'Born to shop', 'Shop till you drop', 'I am what I consume' are common slogans.

Throughout most of history, the shop has been the 'open air market'. In Hong Kong or in Thailand's busy street markets today, there is a sense of historical continuity, of the bustle of the market. But with the arrival of the huge department store and the rise of advertising in the nineteenth century, new worlds of conspicuous consumption were slowly created. Goods move from being merely functional commodities such as food to eat, and become instead major markers of lifestyles and identities. The question now posed concerns whether consumers are sovereigns or dupes – *are we driven to consume through our needs and choices, or are we perhaps driven to consume through the mainpulation of our needs?*

The branding of commodities

The modern capitalist world is dominated by internationally known brand names such as Nike, Starbucks, Mitsubishi, Shell, Wal-Mart, Virgin, McDonald's, Calvin Klein, Sony, IBM, Coca-Cola, Toshiba. What we find here is that brands, not products,

become more and more central. Thus people no longer ask for a soft drink, they want a Coke; they do not want trainers but Nikes; they do not want underwear but Calvin Kleins. This branding depends on promotion and advertising: the growth in global advertising spending now outpaces the growth of the world economy by one-third (Klein, 2000: 9, 11). New markets are constantly being generated – Baby Gap for Kids, for example. Overall, however, many are strongly linked to the youth market, creating what has been called 'The Global Teen':

> Despite different cultures, middle class youth all over the world seem to live their lives as if in a parallel universe. They get up in the morning, put on their Levis and Nikes, grab their caps, backpacks and Sony personal CD players, and head for school.
>
> (Klein, 2000: 119)

The Branded World is organised through style, logos and image. Thus 'Tommy Hilfiger pioneered a clothing style that transforms its faithful adherents into walking, talking, lifesized Tommy dolls, mummified into fully branded Tommy worlds' (Klein, 2000: 28). Brands start to have their own superstores and sometimes even their own city space and 'branded villages' (Disney's Celebration Town in Florida). They sponsor sports, arts, music, education – each time getting their brand identified with the culture. And 'stars' are paid large sums to lend their names to the goods: Tiger Woods (with a $90 million contract with Nike over five years), Michael Jordan, Puff Daddy, Martha Stewart, Austin Powers, or Michael Jackson.

There are major downsides to all this. Commodities become very predictable – it is a world of 'theme park shopping', and a kind of self-censorship creeps in to stop diversity. Major companies are merged till they regulate the markets, and goods are produced largely in the sweatshops of low-income countries. Here the labour force has no unions and is utterly temporary: lines of young women hunched over their hard work for a dollar a day and with no job security. There is a floating workforce where 'temps' develop an odd kind of loyalty to their 'brand'.

Further, our identities – who we are – come to be shaped by everything we buy: designer clothes (or otherwise), the 'latest' film and music band (or 'golden oldies'), the 'coolest' (or plain) food, the holiday, the car and so on. We are what we buy. And this has fuelled the worlds of logos. For some people, logos matter more than the quality of the goods (see the discussion of 'Nike culture' in Goldman and Papson, 1998). Advertising, logos and consumption serve up images of the good life to which we start to aspire.

'Born to shop': the growth of consumer societies

Many suggest, then, that Western societies are cultivating 'consumer societies'. Indeed, shopping has become the second most popular leisure activity in Britain, after watching television (*Social Trends*, 2000). Think of your own life and how purchases – from buying clothes, CDs, tickets to sporting events and so forth – may play a part in it. Consider the following:

- *The massive growth of shopping malls* with 'megastores' such as Virgin Records, hypermarkets like Tescos, chain stores such as Argos, retail parks and the endless proliferation of DIY stores across the country. Each Tesco store in Britain had a minimum area of 10,670 square metres in the 1990s (compared with 3,048 in the 1970s). In some parts of Eastern Europe, such as Poland, there has been a massive expansion of 'hyper malls'.

- *The arrival of shopping not as a merely functional activity (for example, to buy the necessary food for a meal) but as a major leisure form in itself.* Malls and shopping centres are key public spaces to 'hang around' in, and shops are designed for us to wander voyeuristically, looking and enjoying the sights. Many people often go just to look, not to purchase, and can spend hours and hours doing this.

- *The growth of more and newer forms of commodities.* We now 'need' commodities that we could not even imagine some 50 years ago: sports clothes geared to every sport; new bathroom commodities such as shower gels, foot creams and electric toothbrushes; new electronic gadgets ranging from computer toys and video games to mobile phones and multimedia computers; new forms of entertainment such as multiplex cinemas and leisure complexes; new modes of eating out, from fast-food to up-market dining; holidays that take us to theme parks, on world cruises and to 'resort hotels'; and the rise in individual car ownership.

- *The attachment of our identities to our shopping.* Especially in the major 'youth markets', our identities can be constructed around the kinds of shop we go to and the sorts of commodity we buy. Caught in early phrases such as 'conspicuous consumption' and in more recent phrases such as 'I shop, therefore I am', much consumption heralds the types of people we are.

- *The spread of credit cards.* In the UK, at least one third of all consumption is based on credit; there were 25 million credit cards in the UK by 1998 and, in 2002, purchases of around £100 billion were made through credit cards. The figures are higher for many other countries, especially the United States (Ritzer, 1995; *Social Trends*, 2004: 93).

- *Teleshopping and netshopping.* After buying a digital television set-top box decoder, or a modem for your computer, an array of armchair services become available – from shopping and banking to travel and public services. Hundreds of channels with interactive shopping services come on stream through the television and the Internet, and all are purchasable through credit cards.

Mass consumption, cultural dopes and a shallow world

The rise of so much consumption has given sociologists much to discuss. In the first place, some argue that the 'consumerist' culture is having a deleterious effect on the quality of life. Socialist critic Jeremy Seabrook (1996) sees consumerism accelerating since 1945, and destroying traditional cultures and solidarities. The 'loads-a-money' culture promotes self-gratification, and with the market dominating, leads to a general flattening of life – destroying differences and communities. This is seen to lead to the weakening of creativity, the decline of participatory communities as people now go to the impersonal shopping mall and not 'the corner shop', and it generates a crass materialism. We have seen something of all this in our earlier discussion of George Ritzer's

Rank	Country	International Tourist Arrivals (thousands)	Market Share% of World Total
1	France	61,500	10.39
2	United States	44,791	7.57
3	Spain	41,295	6.98
4	Italy	35,500	6.00
5	China	26,055	4.40
6	United Kingdom	25,800	4.36
7	Mexico	21,732	3.67
8	Hungary	20,670	3.39
9	Poland	19,420	3.28
10	Canada	17,342	2.93

Figure 14.6   **The world's top ten tourism destinations**
One of the most striking new forms of consumption has been tourism.

Source: adapted from New Internationalist, *The A to Z of World Development*, 1998: 251

McDonaldisation thesis (Ritzer, 1993, and see Chapter 6). Indeed, in a later book, Ritzer has discussed more fully the dangers of what he calls 'cathedrals of consumption' (Ritzer, 2004a).

We have also seen the dangers inherent in what we could call the 'brand name society', where what is on sale is not so much a commodity as a logo. The importance of the sign – the Nike swoosh, the Virgin 'V', the Tommy Hilfiger colours – turns shoppers into walking advertising systems.

Consumption: a sovereign world of choice, distinctiveness and creativity?

Others, by contrast, argue that the new consumerism has been a major advance for most. It has become the means for a higher standard of living, as well as a chance not to deaden culture but to enhance it. Goods and brands may spread through the world, but they are used differently and become different things. With the packaging of CDs in vast megastores, for instance, global music has developed – and the sheer range of music available now has dramatically increased. The same is true of food, with supermarkets now making available ingredients and recipes unheard of 20 years ago. Far from flattening culture, consumerism has enriched it, giving us a greater choice and a better control of our lives. There has been a growing mass participation in creative activities, from DIY to music to cooking to reading to painting to all kinds of 'hobby'.

Inequalities and consumption

Many years ago the sociologist Thorstein Veblen recognised what he called conspicuous consumption, through which people (usually elites) can enhance their status through commodities, from clothes and houses to cars and other material symbols of wealth (Veblen, 1953; orig. 1899). Consumption and its display are not available to all and thus can become a marker of inequality.

In Veblen's view, consumption patterns lead to three ways of excluding people. The first is through money: many people simply cannot afford to purchase new or high-quality goods and services, and suffer 'economic exclusion' as a result. Others may be excluded spatially; without a car or good public transport they cannot easily get to shopping centres and other places of consumption. Often, indeed, if restricted to using small local shops, they will find they pay more and have less choice. Finally, some people will be excluded because they lack the knowledge and skills to consume. Being a skilful consumer these days may well require knowledge of the metric system, computing or international food, for example.

Of course, many people resist these pervasive forms of consumption: they do not want to be part of a high-consumption world and may actively prefer to support local shops, while being indifferent, or in some cases even hostile, towards international brand names. To some extent, this is what the new worldwide 'anti-globalism' protests are about (for example, Klein, 2000). Still, for some, not being able to shop and consume in this way can be experienced as a form of social exclusion.

The new consumption patterns may make life difficult for many. Elderly people, for instance, may find small local shops closing, while the new megastores – should they want to use them – are inaccessible. The elderly are less likely to drive and their state of health may make time and travel hard; and even the design of stores, with high shelves, big trolleys, masses of people and constant commotion, makes them seem very inhospitable places.

Disneyisation

One recent and useful lens into understanding the way contemporary consumption works has been provided through an analysis of the marketing strategies of Walt Disney. Most people have some idea of what a Disney theme park is like, and indeed large numbers of people have visited one! Alan Bryman, taking his lead from Ritzer's discussion of McDonaldisation (see Chapter 6), has suggested that **Disneyisation** is *the process by which the principle of the Disney theme parks are coming to dominate more and more sectors of American society as well as the rest of the world* (Bryman, 2004: 1).

Bryman suggests that four main principles lie behind Disneyisation, and that these can be found increasingly in our patterns of consumption. These are:

- *Theming*, putting the sales object into a story line with which it is not necessarily related. Thus a restaurant takes on the theme of Rock Music (for example, Hard Rock Café) or movies (Planet Hollywood), a hotel takes on the theme of a place (New York, Venice, Ancient Rome or Egypt in Las Vegas) or shopping takes on a historical theme (Liverpool's Albert Docks, London's Tobacco Dock, and Barcelona's Port Vaill).

- *Hybrid consumption*, in which one type of shopping becomes linked in with another very different kind, making them increasingly hard to distinguish. Airports and sports stadia, for example, become shopping malls too.

- *Merchandising*, the promotion and sale of goods which bear copyrighted images and logos. Thus films such as Toy Story, Star Wars or Jurassic Park also generate not just DVDs, CDs and videos but T shirts, greeting cards, toys, books, video games and tie-ins with food and clothing markets. Often the merchandise makes much more money than the original product.

- *Performative or emotional labour*, in which the frontline service industry is seen less as a job and more as a performance. Often this involves 'dressing up' and performing a role in line with the attire; usually it involves smiling and being friendly – acting as if the tasks being done are fun and friendly and not really work at all.

Looking ahead

This chapter has suggested that although industrial capitalism may have become the dominant economic form throughout most of the world, it continues to change. The chapter has looked at the rise of fragmentation in both work and production (post-Fordism); at the flow of companies across the world (globalisation); at the increasing use of women's labour; at the changing patterns of service work; and at the rise of major markets of mass consumption which seem to be generating ever-increasing demand for consumer goods.

Sociologists are not fortune-tellers and cannot predict the future. It would have been hard for them to predict, in the late eighteenth century, the rise of the new informational economy that appears to be emerging in the early twenty-first. But this chapter does at least suggest that just as capitalism has been flexible in the past, so it may well continue to adjust to the changes of the future.

CONTROVERSY AND DEBATE

THATCHERISM, PRIVATISATION AND MARKETS: DOES 'THE MARKET' SERVE THE PUBLIC INTEREST?

When Margaret Thatcher came to power in the UK in 1979, she started to revolutionise the way in which both the economy and the government were to be run. So influential was she that a whole ideology – **Thatcherism** – was named after her. Broadly, this is *a system of political beliefs based on free markets and economic individualism*. What she achieved was to radically shift the grounds of debate to a focus on the importance of market mechanisms. Before 1979, for example, very few people discussed health or education provision through market models. But it is a sign of her deep influence that the New Labour government of 1997 has actually continued to stress the importance of markets in many areas of life.

The debate is not a new one, however. Thatcher just 'modernised' it for the UK. Historically, most European societies have had a mix of market and government intervention – hence, mixed economies. From 1946 to 1979, the British government regularly

intervened in the economy, both through the welfare state and through its extensive programme of nation-alisation. The Scandinavian countries also had a pronounced 'welfare' and interventionist background. By contrast, US society has relied on 'the market' for most economic decisions: the market sets prices, as potential buyers and sellers bid for goods and serv-ices upwards or downwards in a changing balance of supply and demand.

With the rise of Thatcherism, the UK followed the US model – though even more intensely. It privatised all the nationalised industries (including telephones, water, gas, electricity and rail), and embarked on a programme to introduce internal markets into the welfare state (especially in health care and schools).

Defenders praise the market for encouraging choice, diversity and flexibility: in so doing, the market coordinates the efforts of countless people, each of whom – to return to Adam Smith's crucial insight – is motivated only by self-interest. The econ-omists Milton and Rose Friedman (1980) note that a more or less freely operating market system has pro-vided many members of capitalist societies with an unprecedented economic standard of living. ▶

CONTROVERSY AND DEBATE CONTINUED

But others celebrate the role of government in the operation of European economies. At one level, government steps in to accomplish some tasks that no one would do for profit. Even Adam Smith looked to government to defend the country against external enemies. Government also has a key role in constructing and maintaining public projects such as roads, utilities and schools, and in some countries the involvement of government goes much further – the Scandinavian countries probably take intervention further than in most other democratic, capitalist systems.

Free-marketers such as the Friedmans counter that virtually any task government undertakes, it performs inefficiently. They claim that the products we enjoy – such as computers, household appliances and the myriad offerings of supermarkets and shopping centres – are primarily products of the market. By contrast, the least-satisfying goods and services available today, and the Friedmans place schools, public transport and health services among these, are those operated by governments. Thus, while some government presence in the economy is necessary, supporters of free markets maintain that an economy that operates with minimal state regulation serves the public interest well.

Conservative government and privatisation

Other analysts, however, all but dismiss the market as a negative force. For one thing, critics point out, the market has little incentive to produce goods and services that generate little profit, which include just about everything consumed by poor people. Government-directed public housing, for example, stands as a vital resource that no profit-seeking developer would offer independently. Second, critics look to government to curb what they see as the market system's self-destructive tendencies. The formation of economic monopolies, for example, can threaten the public interest. Government can perform a host of regulatory functions, intervening in the market to control inflation, to enhance the well-being of workers (by imposing workplace safety standards) and to benefit con-

sumers (through product quality controls). Indeed, the power of global corporations is so great, conclude the critics, that even government cannot effectively defend the public interest. And as we shall see in Chapter 24, with increasing environmental degradation being heaped upon the planet, often through self-interested corporations, surely there is a need for international governments to provide some regulation?

Third, critics support government's role in curbing what they see as another market flaw: magnifying social stratification. As we have seen, capitalist economies characteristically concentrate income and wealth; a government system of taxation (typically applying higher rates to the rich) counters this tendency in the name of social justice. For a number of reasons, then, the market operating alone does not serve the public interest.

Does the market's 'invisible hand' feed us well or pick our pockets? Although many – perhaps most – people in Europe view the market as good, they also support some government role in economic life to benefit the public. Indeed, government assists not only citizens but business itself by providing investment capital, constructing roads and other infrastructure and shielding companies from foreign competition. Yet the precise balance struck between market forces and government decision-making continues to underlie much of the political debate in Europe and around the world.

CONTINUE THE DEBATE:

1. Why do defenders of the free market assert that 'the government that governs best is the government that governs least'?

2. Does a market system meet the needs of European countries? Does it serve some better than others?

3. What is your impression of the successes and failures of Thatcherism? Compare it with socialist economic systems.

Sources: Friedman and Friedman (1980), Hall and Jacques (1989).

SUMMARY

1. The economy is the major social institution by which a society produces, distributes and consumes goods and services. It is not just economic, but social.

2. In technologically simple societies, the economy is subsumed within the family. In agrarian societies, most economic activity takes place outside the home. Industrialisation sparks significant economic expansion built around new energy sources, large factories, mass production and worker specialisation. The post-industrial economy is characterised by a productive shift from tangible goods to services. Just as the technology of the Industrial Revolution propelled the industrial economy of the past, the Information Revolution is now advancing the post-industrial economy.

3. The primary sector of the economy generates raw materials; the secondary sector manufactures various goods; the tertiary sector focuses on providing services. In pre-industrial societies, the primary sector predominates; the secondary sector is of greatest importance in industrial societies; the tertiary sector prevails in post-industrial societies.

4. Social scientists describe the economies of today's industrial and post-industrial societies in terms of two models. Capitalism is based on private ownership of productive property and the pursuit of personal profit in a competitive marketplace. Socialism is based on collective ownership of productive property and the pursuit of collective well-being through government control of the economy. Although most European economies are predominantly capitalist, the European community and national governments are broadly involved in economic life. Governments play an even greater role in the 'democratic socialist' economies of some Western European nations and the 'state capitalism' of Japan. The Russian Federation has gradually introduced some market elements into its formerly centralised economy; the nations of Eastern Europe are making similar changes.

5. The emergence of a global economy means that nations no longer produce and consume products and services within national boundaries. Moreover, the 600 largest corporations, operating internationally, now account for most of the earth's economic output.

6. The nature of work is changing. Agricultural work is generally in decline and there is a move from factory work to service work. There is a spread of part-time and flexible work, a relative decline in trade union activity, and the growth of international labour markets which bring about 'sweatshop' labour. New forms of work such as 'teleworking' are growing rapidly.

7. Unemployment has many causes, including the operation of the economy itself. The European unemployment rate is generally at least 5 per cent.

8. Transnational corporations (TNCs) form the core of the world's economies. They produce and distribute products in most nations of the world, though the distribution of wealth resulting from this activity is hugely unequal.

9. The consumer society has become crucial to the working of modern capitalism. The Western world is increasingly buying goods and services in large, centralised establishments, a pattern that has sapped the strength of small, local-based industries.

10. Disneyisation suggests four principles that help shape this: theming, hybrid consumption, mechandising and performative labour.

CRITICAL-THINKING QUESTIONS

1. Make a critical analysis of your last 'shopping expedition'. Drawing from ideas in this chapter, discuss what you bought, the processes by which those items were produced, the people and agencies that benefited from your purchases, and why you felt motivated to purchase those goods and services. Consider whether you were involved in the process described in the chapter as 'Disneyisation' and, if so, in what ways.

2. Look at the people who work on your campus. What are their official designations – cleaners, teaching assistants, secretaries, professors, etc? From the tables in the text, guess how much they earn? What sort of contracts do they have? How much autonomy do they have over their working day?

3. Identify several ways in which the Industrial Revolution reshaped the economies of Europe. How is the Information Revolution transforming these economies once again?

4. What key characteristics distinguish capitalism, socialism and democratic socialism? Compare these systems in terms of productivity, economic inequality and support for civil liberties.

GOING FURTHER

Further reading

General reading:

Keith Grint, *The Sociology of Work: An Introduction* (2nd edn,1998)

Rosemary Crompton, *Women and Work in Modern Britain* (1997)
Two useful short guides.

Globalisation and the economy:

Peter Dicken, *Global Shift: Transforming of the World Economy* (4th edn, 2003)
A major study of the world economy, now in its fourth edition. It is stuffed full of diagrams and charts and is very comprehensive, although not an easy or introductory read!

Naomi Klein, *No Logo* (2000)
A popular and very lively read on the ways in which modern economies depend upon brand names. Her book is the 'bible' of the anti-capitalist movement.

Ulrich Beck, *The Brave New World of Work* (2000a)
This comes from one of the world's leading contemporary sociologists and is a polemic about where work may be heading in the future.

Consumption and the consumer society:

Daniel Miller (ed.), *Acknowledging Consumption* (1995)

George Ritzer, *Cathedrals of Consumption* (2004a)
Two useful books on consumption.

Watch a video

- Park Kwang-Su's *A Single Spark* (1998): tale of trying to improve working conditions in South Korea's garment shops, with powerful images of the sweatshops (world distribution: Fortisimo Films, Rotterdam)
- Charlie Chaplin's *Modern Times* (1936): classic silent comedy, which shows the Fordist production line.
- Joseph Santley's *Rosie the Riveter* (1944): five women who work during the Second World War

- Ken Loach's *Bread and Roses* (2001): illegal immigrant, Hispanic janitors work in Los Angeles to send money back home. On very low incomes and poor work conditions, they unionise. Strong stuff.

Connecting up

Connect to other chapters

- For more on the Third Way, see Chapter 15.
- For more on women and work, see gender in Chapter 12 and families in Chapter 17.
- For more on consumption and identity, see Chapter 5.

To the websites

- *Institute for Economic Affairs:*
  http://www.iea.org.uk/
- *International Labour Organisation:*
  http://www.ilo.org
- *Fortune Magazine:*
  http://www.fortune.com/fortune

One of the world's leading business magazines. Among many other things, you can access lists of the top companies, lists of some of the best companies to work for, and a list of the 40 richest under-40s in the United States.

- *Interbrand*
  http://www.interbrand.com/books_papers.asp
  A website devoted to discussion and details on brand names.
- Jobs exported to India
  www.bpoindia.org/companies

For additional case studies, multiple choice questions, internet exercises, and annotated weblinks specific to this chapter, visit this book's website at **www.pearsoned.co.uk/plummer**

CHAPTER 15

POWER, GOVERNANCE AND SOCIAL MOVEMENTS

(Above) Lenin addresses the workers to encourage them to support him.

Source: Novosti/Bridgeman Art Library, London

(Right) Demonstrators gather to protest the World Trade Organization (WTO) during their 1999 conference in Seattle. What started out as a peaceful protest turned into a violent clash between demonstrators and riot police, with many injuries, over 500 arrests, and major damage to the downtown area.

Source: © Christopher J. Morris/Corbis

Man is a political animal.

Aristotle

KEY THEMES

- Different kinds of power
- The nature of democracies and other global systems of power
- The distribution of power in democratic societies
- Revolutions, war and terrorism
- The significance of social movements
- The changing politics of the twenty-first century
- The significance of human rights regimes

THE PEOPLE CALLED IT 'The Battle of Seattle'. It started in early December 1999 on the streets of Seattle, which was for a short while to be the home of a major political conflict over world finance. The World Trade Organisation (WTO) had come to town for a major international conference, and the people were not happy with it. The WTO came into being in 1995 (originally set up under GATT) and claims to be the only 'global international organisation dealing with the rules of trade between nations'. 'The goal is to help producers of goods and services, exporters, and importers conduct their business. ... Its main function is to ensure that trade flows as smoothly, predictably, and freely as possible.' Based in Geneva, it now has around 500 staff, a budget of some $83 million, and over 130 nation members accounting for 90 per cent of world trade.

But the people said it was 'undemocratic': it had been formed from the powerful, global financial elite and did not represent the people of the world. Accused of neglecting the environment, poorer countries, child labour and exploitation, while championing free trade, it came to symbolise the new global world of high finance and transnational corporations. And the people protested. Some 30,000 protestors took to the streets. At its heart was a political attack on capitalism and the widespread global influence of corporations. There was a sense of global awareness that much of what the 'First World' consumes makes for the tragedies of the 'Third World'. But it was wider than this: in a sense it was a coming together of all the 'causes' of the late twentieth century: the Greens, animal rights, anti-slavery, disarmament and non-violence, the New Age, lifestyle politics, eco-feminism, labour rights, civil rights, human rights. As Vandana Shiva said:

> When labour joins hands with environmentalists, when farmers from the North and farmers from the South make a common commitment to say 'no' to genetically engineered crops,

they are not acting as special interest. They are defending the common interests and rights of all people everywhere. The divide and rule policy which has attempted to pit consumers against farmers, the North against the South, labour against environmentalists, has failed.

(quoted in Brecher *et al.*, 2000: 15)

But it was the same old story. Among thousands of peaceful protesters, there was some more violent protest. Hundreds of very visible Army National Guard troops were on the streets, along with active duty military personnel, including a small number of Special Forces troops sent by the Defense Department for the meeting. Police fired tear gas, curfews were imposed, some 500 people were arrested, the city was under siege and turned into 'an armed camp'. President Bill Clinton condemned the violent protesters but said demonstrators who came peacefully should be allowed to make their point. The president later called on the WTO to include the concerns of the demonstrators who had besieged the WTO meeting.

This has been called 'globalisation from below'. Of course, protests of this kind are far from new. But they are now seen across the globe and, with the help of websites, a common focus is being found. In Prague a year later, some 15,000 protesters from at least 30 countries gathered to disrupt a three-day meeting of the International Monetary Fund (IMF) and the World Bank. In London, May Day has become the time for similar scenes. In 2001 Genoa experienced mass violence and arrests. Loose groupings of political activists going under names such as 'Critical Mass', the 'Wombles' and 'Class War' take to the streets (and the websites) against a background of police and media reaction.

Sources: J. Thomas (2000); http://www.wto.org/index.htm; http://www.wtowatch.org/

Wanted by Interpol
BIN LADEN, Usama

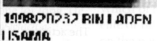

Pictures of Saudi-born Osama Bin Laden are posted on Interpol's wanted list, September 15, 2001
Source: © Reuters/Corbis/HO/Interpol

Terroists suicide bombings, New York City, September 11 2001
Source: © David Turnley/Corbis

VIOLENCE BEYOND THE RULES: A REPORT FROM THE FORMER YUGOSLAVIA

The conflicts and wars within and around Yugoslavia during the 1990s have led to a number of new, highly unstable mini-states and groupings. We have already seen what this has meant in Bosnia (see the chapter opening and the Voices box 'Living through ethnic cleansing' in Chapter 11). In many ways the extent of destruction and displacement of peoples reached catastrophic levels during this period. This is a deeply troubled region, and Serbs, Croats and Muslims have all committed war crimes – tens of thousands of deaths, rapes and serious injuries, plus an incalculable loss of property.

War is violent, but it also has rules. Many of the current norms of warfare emerged from the ashes of the Second World War, when German and Japanese military officials were brought to trial for war crimes. Subsequently, the United Nations has added to the broad principles of fair play in war that have become known as the 'Geneva Conventions' (the first of which dates back to 1864). One of the most important principles of the rules of war is that, whatever violence soldiers inflict upon each other, they cannot imprison, torture, rape or murder civilians; nor can they deliberately destroy civilian property or wantonly bomb or shell cities to foster widespread terror. Even so, a growing body of evidence reveals that all these crimes have occurred as part of the protracted and bloody civil war in the former Yugoslavia. And they have gone 'beyond the rules'.

The United Nations and the future of interventions
Late in 1993, therefore, a United Nations tribunal convened in The Netherlands to assess the evidence and consider possible responses. After the Second World War, the Allies successfully prosecuted (and, in several cases, executed) German officers for their crimes against humanity based on evidence culled from extensive Nazi records. This time, however, the task of punishing offenders is proving to be far more difficult.

For one thing, there appear to be no written records of the Balkan conflict; for another, United Nations officials fear that arrests may upset the delicate diplomatic efforts at bringing peace to the region.

Even so, since beginning their investigations in 1993, the United Nations has indicted more than 50 military officers on all sides of the conflict for war crimes. And in 2000, the former Yugoslavian president Slobodan Milosevic was arrested, and charged at the International Tribunal in The Hague with atrocities committed by troops under his command in Kosovo, and by others that link him with atrocities in the Croatian War of 1991, and the Bosnian conflict of 1992–95.

But many observers suspect that – despite a staggering toll in civilian deaths – very few of those responsible will ever be convicted.

Sources: adapted from Nelan (1993) and various news reports

Civil wars, such as the conflict in the former Yugoslavia, are among the most tragic forms of bloodshed because a large proportion of casualties are not soldiers but civilians who find themselves in harm's way. Dozens of people died in the conflict in Albania. Here people go about their daily lives amid the destruction with a makeshift market set up in the ruins of Albanian shops set afire by Serbs before leaving the city.

Source: Magnum © Abbas

Second, Johnson continues, terrorism is a tactic employed not only by groups but also by governments against their own people. **State terrorism** refers to *the use of violence, generally without the support of law, against individuals or groups by a government or its agents.* While contrary to democratic political principles, state terrorism figures prominently in authoritarian and totalitarian societies, which survive by inciting fear and intimidation. From the left-wing regimes in North Korea and the former Soviet Union to the extreme right-wing regimes in Nazi Germany and Zaïre, states have routinely employed terror against their own citizens. More recently, Saddam Hussein has ruled Iraq in the same manner.

Third, although democratic societies reject terrorism in principle, democracies are especially vulnerable to terrorists because they afford extensive civil liberties to their people and have minimal police networks. This susceptibility helps to explain the tendency of democratic governments to suspend civil liberties if officials perceive themselves to be under attack. Hostage taking and outright killing provoke widespread anger, but devising an effective response to such acts poses several thorny problems. Because most terrorist groups are shadowy organisations with no formal connection to any established state, targeting reprisals may be impossible. Yet the failure to respond can encourage other terrorist groups. Then, too, a forcible military reaction to terrorism may broaden the scope of violence, increasing the risk of confrontation with other governments.

Finally, terrorism is always a matter of definition. Governments claim the right to maintain order, even by force, and may brand opponents who use violence as 'terrorists'. Similarly, political differences may explain why one person's 'terrorist' is another's 'freedom fighter'.

The new terrorism

Since 11 September 2001, terrorism has taken a new pattern. It is seen to have four features:

1. *Organisational decentralisation*. Terrorist organisations no longer organise themelves in pyramidic, hierarchical structures. They are much more likely to take the form of loose clusterings organised through chains, hub-and-spoke networks, or through a series of contact points.

2. *Operational asymmetry*. The acts of violence become unanticipated and unconventional. Objects are attacked which may, on the surface, seem to have little relevance and attacks may happen quite unpredictably.

3. *Religious centrality*. Struggles are seen as between forces of good and evil, with religious belief and religious extremism as a core motivating factor.

4. *Weapons of mass destruction*. The stakes are raised with the new terrorism: high-yield weapons come to be employed and deaths can potentially be catastrophically large. These weapons include biological, chemical, radiological and nuclear agents (Martin, 2004).

War

Perhaps the most critical political issue is war. War is as old as humanity. In recorded history, since 3600 BCE, it has been estimated that some 14,500 major wars have been waged, killing some four billion people. In the twentieth century alone, it has been estimated that well over 100 million people died as a result of war. Many people think of war as extraordinary, yet it is periods of peace that are actually rare (*New Internationalist*, 1999: 18; Roxborough, 2004).

Mary Kaldor (1999), Martin Shaw (2003) and others have distinguished between different types of war over history. In the past, wars were usually waged with mercenary or conscript armies using weapons from swords to (more recently) firearms. Many of the twentieth-century wars were not like this. Funded on a large scale through the mobilisation of the whole economy, mass armies deployed massive firepower, tanks and aircraft. The two world wars of the twentieth century were sites of major destruction, including the dropping of the atomic bombs on Nagasaki and Hiroshima. A key feature of late twentieth-century warfare, then, was the potential destructiveness of today's nuclear arsenals and the ways in which more and more civilians come to be killed. Table 15.4 suggests ways in which these 'old wars' evolved.

At present over 30 wars are being waged across the earth with millions of casualties. Most of these armed conflicts of recent times tend to take place within states rather than between them. The Bosnia–Herzegovina war described at the start of Chapter 11 is a major example of what have been called 'new wars'. They are mixtures of war, organised crime and mass violations of human rights with civilian deaths, and do not follow any obvious rules of modern warfare. Indeed, they seem almost anarchic – attacking people and property at local, private levels. Rape and genocide become commonplace. Kaldor argues that these new wars require rethinking at an international, global level. They bring in the need for international intervention and regulations for their resolution, which she calls a 'cosmopolitan approach' (Kaldor, 1999). Martin Shaw sees them as **degenerate wars** –whereby there is '*a deliberate and systematic extension of war against an organized armed enemy to war against a largely unarmed civilian population*' (Shaw, 2003: 5). Such is typical of more and more modern wars.

The costs of war

The costs of armed conflicts extend far beyond battlefield casualties. Together, the world's nations spend some £3.5 trillion annually for military purposes. Such expenditures, of course, divert resources from the desperate struggle for survival by millions of poor people throughout the world. Moreover, a large proportion of the world's top scientists concentrate on military research; this resource, too, is siphoned away from other work that might benefit humanity.

In recent years, defence has been the largest single expenditure of most governments. The average proportion of GDP that the world spends on defence is around 3 per cent, but many countries spend more than that. In the United States, for example, defence accounts for 18 per cent of all federal spending, or $348 billion in 2002. The 'war on terrorism' has only pushed this number higher. The United States now stands as the world's single superpower, with more military might than the next nine countries combined (Gergen, 2002).

The United States became a superpower as it emerged victorious from the Second World War with newly developed nuclear weapons. The atomic bomb was first used in war by US forces to crush Japan in 1945. But the Soviet Union countered by exploding a nuclear bomb of its own in 1949, unleashing the 'Cold War', by which leaders of each superpower became convinced that their counterparts were committed to military superiority. Ironically, for the next 40 years, both sides pursued a policy of escalating military expenditures that neither nation wanted or could afford.

With the collapse of the Soviet Union in 1991, much of the Cold War dissipated. Yet US military expenditures remain high. Some analysts have argued that, all along, the US economy has relied on militarism to generate corporate profits (Marullo, 1987). This approach, closely allied to power elite theory, maintains that the United States is dominated by a **military–industrial complex**, *the close association among the federal government, the military and defence industries*. The roots of militarism, then, lie not just in external threats to US security; they also grow from within the institutional structures of US society.

Another reason for persistent militarism in the post-Cold War world is regional conflict. Since the collapse of the Soviet Union, for example, localised wars have broken out in Bosnia, Chechnya and Rwanda, and tensions still run high in a host of other countries, including Iraq and a divided Korea. Even wars of limited scope have the potential to escalate, involving other countries, and the danger of regional conflicts is growing as more and more nations gain access to nuclear weapons.

Nuclear weapons

Despite the easing of superpower tensions, the world still contains almost 25,000 nuclear warheads perched on missiles or ready to be carried by aircraft. This arsenal represents destructive power that one can barely imagine: five tons of TNT for every person on the planet. Should even a small fraction of this stockpile be detonated in war, life as we know it would cease on much of the earth. Albert Einstein, whose genius contributed to the development of nuclear weapons, reflected: 'The unleashed power of the atom has changed everything save our modes of thinking, and we thus drift toward unparalleled catastrophe.' In short, nuclear weapons have rendered unrestrained war unthinkable in a world not yet capable of peace.

Table 15.4	The evolution of 'old wars'			
	17th and 18th centuries	**19th century**	**Early 20th century**	**Late 20th century**
Type of polity	Absolutist state	Nation state	Coalitions of states; multinational states; empires	Blocs
Goals of war	Reasons of state; dynastic conflict; consolidation of borders	National conflict	National and ideological conflict	Ideological conflict
Type of army	Mercenary/professional	Professional/conscription	Mass armies	Scientific–military elite/professional armies
Military technique	Use of firearms, defensive manoeuvres, sieges	Railways and telegraph, rapid mobilisation	Massive firepower; tanks and aircraft	Nuclear weapons
War economy	Regularisation of taxation and borrowing	Expansion of administration and bureaucracy	Mobilisation economy	Military–industrial complex

Source: adapted from Kaldor (1999: 14)

CONTROVERSY AND DEBATE

BEYOND LEFT AND RIGHT: THE POLITICS OF DIFFERENCE

Industrialisation, the emergence of modern nation states and revolutionary movements on behalf of democracy have brought people to join together under the labels 'left' or 'right' for the past 200 years. (The terms originated in the French revolutionary assembly of the 1790s where the left were radicals and the right were moderates.) For most of the twentieth century, the political divides have been very sharply drawn on these lines: capitalism versus communism, right versus left, the East versus the West. The demise of the Cold War between the United States and what Reagan called the 'evil empire' of the USSR (dominated by Russia) was spectacularly symbolised at the end of the 1980s by the fall of the Berlin Wall. At the time there was much jubilation. But the problem now – in the twenty-first century – is where is all this heading? For many of the old communist countries a kind of chaos has been reached. For much of the old West, a kind of directionlessness has happened. If the old divides are crumbling, what is politics about in the twenty-first century?

One response was to see the end of these conflicts as the end of history. The fall of the Berlin Wall symbolised the final victory of capitalist democracy: this was the way of the world from now on. Francis Fukuyama (1989) sees 'the end of history' as nothing less than the worldwide triumph of modernity, capitalism and liberal democracy. The ideological battles are now over, and there are no alternatives. Fukuyama sees the 'universalisation of Western democracy as the final form of human government' (1989): monarchism, fascism and communism have been rendered indefensible for all but a few extreme groups. Even the old left has died: Britain's New Labour, for instance, now champions policies that sound suspiciously like the old Conservative party. Similar moves are happening around the world.

But not all agree with Fukuyama. Many new 'politics' are being suggested. For instance, in Chapter 24 we will document the degradation of our environment; here many argue for the worldwide development of a green politics. Others, such as the English social theorist Anthony Giddens, are arguing for a 'democratic life politics' – a global politics which rethinks how we are to live and how we are to revitalise democracy through dialogue in a world which is changing globally at an accelerating rate. Arguing that both 'socialism and conservatism have disintegrated' (1994: 9), Giddens champions a 'dialogic democracy' where importance is given to dialogues and the many different voices arguing for different ways to live. He seeks a radical rethinking of democracy – in opposition to fundamentalism of all kinds (see the Profile box on page 419).

Others see these 'fundamentalisms' as the very basis of conflicts in the future. Benjamin Barber (1995) argues that the world is no longer divided between left and right. Instead the divide has shifted globally to one between consumerist capitalism (symbolised by a global McDonald's, or McWorld) and religious and tribal fundamentalisms (symbolised by the Islamic *jihad*). The former saw rapidly dissolving nation states and political boundaries, leading to the triumph of individualism and the marketplace all over the world. At the same time, the latter is forcing ethnic, religious and tribal conflicts into politics everywhere. This tension may be seen as one which goes to the heart of global modernity, and its manifestations in 'tribal warfare' have become increasingly apparent. Indeed, after the Twin Tower attacks in New York in September 2001, many argue that such conflicts and wars are now well under way.

Jubilation at the fall of the Berlin Wall.
Source: Popperfoto

CONTROVERSY AND DEBATE CONTINUED

This is an important debate for contemporary sociology. Some argue that the old left and right positions of the twentieth century need a clear reasserting: they are still relevant. Others argue that we have reached 'the end of history' and we are now, more or less, stuck with capitalist liberal democracies which in the twenty-first century will rule the world. Still others see distinct dangers emerging in the continuing clashes between ethnic and religious fundamentalism and the free-for-all marketplace of consumer capitalism – the clash of civilisations. And still more are looking to the creation of new political forms with social movements and new issues – green politics, lifestyles politics, differences – at the forefront. There is a new political scene in the making at the start of the twenty-first century which is far removed from the Cold War of the twentieth.

CONTINUE THE DEBATE:

1. Have we really reached 'the end of history' and the triumph of liberal capitalism?

2. If fundamentalism is on the increase, will this not result in more and more bloody wars and conflicts?

3. How might sociological analyses of power, ethnicity (see Chapter 11) and religion (see Chapter 18) assist in understanding the war between the United States and its allies and 'terrorism'?

4. Is not a politics based on lifestyle just an indulgence of the over-rich West?

5. How central do you think social movements around 'green politics' will become in the twenty-first century?

Sources: Fukuyama (1989); Giddens (1994); Barber (1995).

Despite the easing of the superpower tensions of the Cold War, the world is again 'on alert' since the war on terrorism was declared by Bush in 2001. The world contains some 20,000 nuclear warheads. Even if only a small fraction of this stockpile was to be detonated, life as we know it would cease on much of the earth. At present, although the UK, France and China all have substantial nuclear capability, the vast majority of nuclear weapons are based in the United States and the Russian Federation. Other countries – Israel, India, Pakistan, North Korea – also possess some nuclear weapons, while others (including Iran) may be in process of developing them. Some nations have stopped the development of such weapons, including Argentina, Brazil and South Africa. Nevertheless, it is estimated that by 2010, as many as 50 nations could have the ability to fight a nuclear war (Shaw, 2003; Roxborough, 2004).

Information warfare

As earlier chapters have explained, the Information Revolution is changing almost every dimension of social life. Currently, military strategists envisage future conflict played out not with rumbling tanks and screaming aircraft but with electronic 'smart bombs' that would greatly reduce an enemy country's ability to transmit information. In such 'virtual wars', soldiers seated at workstation monitors would dispatch computer viruses to shut down an aggressor's communication lines, causing telephones to fall silent, air traffic control and railway switching systems to fail, computer systems to feed phoney orders to field officers, and televisions to broadcast 'morphed' news bulletins, prompting people to turn against their leaders.

Like the venom of a poisonous snake, the weapons of 'information warfare' can quickly paralyse an adversary, perhaps triggering a conventional military engagement. Another, more hopeful, possibility is that new information technology might not just precede conventional fighting but prevent it entirely. Yet so-called 'infowar' also poses new dangers, since, presumably, a few highly skilled operators with sophisticated electronic equipment could also wreak havoc on communications in Europe and the rest of the world.

A new politics in the twenty-first century? The new social movements

Politics is always on the move: things change. At the start of the twenty-first century, some are suggesting a new politics is in the making. We have already seen signs of this in this chapter: the partial break-up of nation states, globalised politics, the creation of major new political units such as the European Union, the arrival of 'new wars', and, as the Controversy and Debate box suggests, the collapse of traditional divides between left and right.

In addition, we could consider the seeming growth of political apathy and voter discontent (Norris, 1999); the embracing by some of what has been called 'post-materialist values'; and the potential for digital democracies, whereby voting systems are modified through the widespread use of computers (Alexander and Pal, 1998). Some sociologists, such as Ulrich Beck, now believe we have entered a period of '*sub-politics*', where the world of major political institutions built up in modernity is increasingly under question through a politics that takes place in everyday life. Formal politics becomes less and less effective as sub-politics develops (Beck, 1997). One feature of this may be the rise and proliferation of new social movements (NSMs), which are far more common today than in the past and take on a different form.

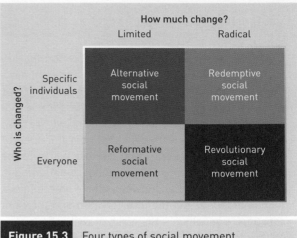

| **Figure 15.3** | Four types of social movement |

Source: based on Aberle (1966)

New social movements

Alan Touraine, Alberto Melucci, Klauss Offe and others suggest that the new post-industrial or information societies are fostering a growing awareness of differences through subcultures and counter-cultures, and that these are generating new social movements around a wide range of public issues. In recent decades, for example, gays, lesbians, bisexuals and transgendered people have organised to combat oppression and discrimination. A Green Movement has emerged to challenge environmental destruction. Disability alliances have been formed to champion the rights of the disabled. There has been a powerful Women's Movement, a men's movement, an age-activist movement, AIDS and various health movements. More recently, as the opening story told, there has been a worldwide anti-capitalist movement bridging many different groups, from the respectable lobbying groups to out-and-out anarchists. Like any social movement that challenges convention, they often spark counter-movements as others try to block their goals. In contemporary societies, almost every significant public issue gives rise to both a social movement favouring change and an opposing counter-movement to resist change and reinforce the status quo.

Classically, sociologists have grouped social movements according to several other criteria (Aberle, 1966; Cameron, 1966; Blumer, 1969). One variable asks *who is changed*, since some movements target selected people while others try to change everyone. A second variable looks at *how much change*; some movements attempt to foster only *superficial changes* in how we live, while others pursue a *radical transformation* of society. Combining these variables, we can identify four types of social movement, shown in Figure 15.3.

Alternative social movements are the least threatening to the established social order, seeking limited change only in a segment of the population. They are less avowedly political. The New Age Movement is a good example of this. It senses that with the 'Age of Aquarius', a new age is being born of self-spirituality. Encompassing a wide and global network of different groupings who may be involved, for example, in therapy, vegetarianism, counter-cultures, spirituality, meditation, crystals, 'angels', 'channelling', communes, naturalism, and spiritual healing, these groups all affirm a self ethic, rejecting any external authority and believing 'I am my own authority' (Heelas, 1996).

Redemptive social movements also have a selective focus, but they attempt to induce radical change in those they engage. Examples include fundamentalist Christian organisations that seek to win new members through conversion. The resulting transformation is sometimes so great that converts describe their experience as being 'born again'.

Reformative social movements aim for only limited social change but target everyone. The multiculturalism movement, described in Chapter 5, is an educational and political initiative that advocates working towards social parity for all racial and ethnic categories of people. Reformative social movements generally work inside the existing political system. They can be progressive (promoting a new social pattern) or reactionary (counter-movements trying to preserve the status quo or to reinstate past social mores). Just as multiculturalists are pushing for greater racial equality, for example, so do various white supremacist organisations persist in their efforts to maintain the historical dominance of one racial category.

Revolutionary social movements have the most severe and far-reaching consequences of all, striving for basic transformation of a society. Sometimes pursuing specific goals, sometimes spinning utopian dreams, followers of these social movements reject established social institutions as inherently flawed while favouring radically new alternatives. Many environmental movements seek to radically change how we use and distribute resources in order to protect the planet.

New politics – new movements – new identities

Although social movements have been around for a long time, the so-called 'new social movements' (or NSMs) generally broaden the range of what is considered political. They are much less concerned with the traditional issues of politics such as class and work (and the old trade unions and class movements). Their membership tends to be younger. Organisationally they tend to be much more informal, more fragmented, less hierarchical, with little interest in formal power. They employ a wider range of tactics for change – often illegal and direct. They do not usually pursue mainstream or conventional values, but are part of what we have already noted as 'post-materialist values' where the issue is much more the quality of life (see Chapter 5 on post-materialist cultural values). They are part of what Giddens has called the new politics of lifestyles (1990: 158).

Today's most notable social movements are concerned with global ecology, the social standing of women and gays, reducing the risks of war, animal rights, and the rejection of a worldwide global capitalism. One feature of these movements is their national and international scope. The power of the state continues to expand in post-industrial societies. Not surprisingly, then, as global political connections multiply, social movements respond by becoming international in scope. One clear strength of NSMs is their growing recognition of the global scale of response needed to deal with the development of a global economic and political system, and to spotlight the power of the mass media to unite people around the world in pursuit of political goals.

Critics argue that this approach exaggerates differences between past and present social movements. The Women's Movement, for example, focuses on many of the same issues, including workplace conditions and pay, that consumed the energies of labour organisations for decades.

Stages in social movements

Researchers have identified four phases in the life of the typical social movement (shown in Figure 15.4): emergence, coalescence, bureaucratisation and decline (Blumer, 1969; Mauss, 1975; Tilly, 1978). In Stage 1, emergence, social movements build on the perception that all is not well. Some, such as the gay and lesbian rights movement and the Women's Movement, are born

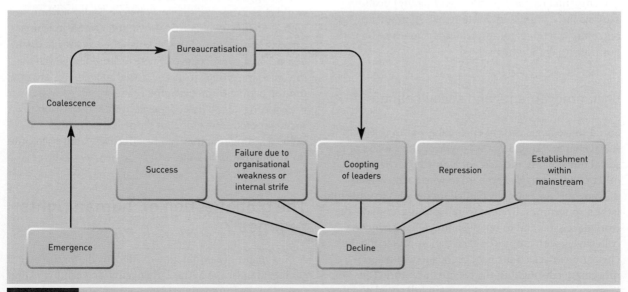

Figure 15.4   Stages in the life of social movements

of widespread dissatisfaction. Others emerge only as a small vanguard group, which increases public awareness of some issue.

By the second stage, coalescence, the movement must define itself and develop a strategy for 'going public'. Leaders must determine policies, decide on tactics, build morale and recruit new members. At this stage, the movement may engage in collective action such as rallies or demonstrations to attract media attention in the hope of capturing public notice. Additionally, the movement may form alliances with other organisations to gain necessary resources.

To become an established political force, a social movement must bureaucratise, that is develop formal structures (Stage 3). As procedures become formal, the movement depends less on the charisma and talents of a few leaders and relies more on a capable staff. Social movements which avoid this stage, such as the campaigns organised to prod legislation against 'dangerous dogs' and handgun ownership in Britain, have short lives, fading when leaders lose energy or even die. Bureaucratisation can also weaken a movement by blunting the radical and innovative edge. On the other hand, the well-established Greenpeace, despite its changing leadership, offers a steady voice on behalf of environmentalists.

Social movements are inherently dynamic, so a decline (Stage 4) need not signal a demise. Eventually, however, most social movements do wither. This may occur when members achieve their primary goals, or because of organisational factors, such as poor leadership or exhaustion of resources, or because hostile public or governmental reaction (sometimes literally) beats activists into submission. 'Selling out' is another possible outcome, when organisational leaders may use their positions to enrich themselves.

Social movements and social change

Social movements exist to encourage – or to resist – social change. Sometimes we overlook the success of past social movements and take for granted the changes that other people struggled so hard to win. Early workers' movements, for example, battled for decades to end child labour in factories, to limit working hours, to make the workplace safer and to establish the right to bargain collectively with employers. Legislation protecting the environment is also the product of successful social movements throughout the twentieth century. The Women's Movement has yet to attain full social equality for the sexes, but it has significantly extended the legal

rights and economic opportunities of women. In fact, younger people can be surprised to learn that, earlier in the twentieth century, few women worked for income and none were permitted to vote.

Past social movements have shaped society in ways that people now take for granted. Just as movements produce change, so change itself sparks social movements. New social movements have been shaped by widespread dissatisfaction with the existing political system and debates. They bring new issues (especially issues linked to the environment, gender, peace, sexuality, race, world development) and a broader conception of participatory politics, and often dissolve the clear distinction between public and private (see Chapter 21). As leading German sociologist Klauss Offe says, 'the conflicts and contradictions of advanced industrial society can no longer be resolved by the state or by increasing bureaucracy' (Offe, 1985). New social movements are seen as the answer.

This broad view leads to one overarching conclusion: we can draw a direct link between social movements and change. In one direction, social transformations, such as the Industrial Revolution and the rise of capitalism, sparked the emergence of various social movements. Going the other way, the efforts of workers, women, racial and ethnic minorities and gay people have sent ripples of change throughout industrial societies. Thus social change is both the cause and the consequence of social movements.

Social movements have become a growing feature of globalised post-industrial life. The scope of social movements is likely to grow, for two reasons. First, the technology of the Information Revolution has drawn the world closer together than ever before. Today anyone with a satellite dish, personal computer or fax machine can stay abreast of political events, often as they happen. Second, as a consequence of new technology as well as the emerging global economy, social movements are now uniting people throughout the entire world. As we saw in the opening tale to this chapter, with the realisation that many problems are global in scope has come the understanding that they can be effectively addressed only on an international scale.

The globalisation of 'human rights regimes'?

A final major development we will consider in the political landscape of the early twenty-first century is the arrival of the international language of 'human rights'. Increasingly, after the horrors of the Holocaust and other

PROFILE

ANTHONY GIDDENS: THE POLITICS OF 'LIFE CHOICE' AND THE 'THIRD WAY'

Anthony Giddens (1938–)
Source: © Martin Godwin

Anthony Giddens is one of the UK's leading sociologists. In his many early books he examined the classical social theories of sociologists (Marx, Durkheim and Weber), and ultimately produced his own theory of the link between action and structure – a theory known as structuration theory and briefly introduced in Chapter 1. In his later books, starting around the late 1980s, he becomes more concerned with the arrival of what he calls 'late modern society'. This is a society where the pace and scope of change deepens and accelerates – we break free from traditions, our sense of time and space gets reordered, and globalisation becomes a central process. Social life is lifted out ('disembedded') from local traditional contexts and becomes more open and fluid. In 1999 he summarised his major ideas for a worldwide audience in a series of talks he gave as the Reith Lectures (the BBC's most prominent annual lecture series). They were published in a short book, *Runaway World* (1999).

Giddens senses that contemporary identities are changing as we become more aware of having to choose who we are. Traditional institutions such as the family are also changing as relations between members become more equal, open and democratised. Above all he senses a major change in the political order. What was ushered in with modernity was an *'emancipatory politics'* – its main focus was on justice, freedom and equality. It was embodied in the ideals of the French Revolution and the American War of Independence. These political values remain to this day, but now they are not new but widespread. They will continue. But in addition a new set of concerns have arrived which make politics more concerned with questions about how we should live our lives in a late modern world. This is what he calls *'the politics of life choice'*, and it is this new politics which is becoming more prominent. He espouses a *utopian realism* in which new models of life and participation are to be evolved in helping us live in a new kind of social order (Giddens, 1990).

Giddens suggests that the old social democratic 'welfare consensus' that was found in many industrial countries till the late 1970s has collapsed. The classic distinctions of 'left' and 'right' have broken down. The changes have come about partly because of the rise of free-market philosophies associated with Thatcherism and Reaganism – capitalist neo-liberalism (identified in the previous chapter and often seen as uncaring and inadequate) along with the fall of the old Soviet Union and what some claim to be 'the death of socialism' (Giddens, 1998: 3).

The Third Way

Giddens talks of this new politics as the **Third Way** – *a framework that adapts politics to a changed world, transcending old-style social democracy and neo-liberalism.* He identifies a number of dilemmas of the late modern world and suggests that:

> The overall aim of third way politics should be to help citizens pilot their way through the major revolutions of our time: globalization, transformations in personal life and our relationships to nature . . . third way politics should preserve a core concern with social justice.

> (Giddens, 1998: 64)

He outlines the new 'Third Way Values' in a series of slogans: 'Equity', 'Protection of the vulnerable', 'Freedom as autonomy', 'No rights without responsibilities', 'No authority without democracy', 'Cosmopolitan pluralism' and 'Philosophic conservatism' (1998: 66). He suggests a Third Way programme which would involve a radical centre, a new democratic state, an active civil society, a democratic family, a new mixed economy, equality as inclusion, positive welfare, the social investment state, the cosmopolitan nation, and cosmopolitan democracy (1998: 70). These ideas are said to have had a major influence on the Blair government in the UK since its election in 1997. Most recently, Giddens has become concerned about the turn to the right in politics and indeed the growth of far right parties. In his latest writings, he suggests that the third way was a major source of change in the 1990s, but today we must go beyond this – beyond left and right.

Sources: Giddens (1990, 1991, 1998, 1999, 2004).

atrocities, a major trend in world politics has been towards 'rights'. Yet such a language is far from new. Three waves of human rights in recent history have been distinguished (Klug, 2000).

Wave one started in the late eighteenth century in the West against a background of totalitarianism and a lack of religious freedom: the search was on for liberty, justice and equality before the law. The 1789 French Declaration of the Rights of Man and Citizen spoke of 'the natural, inalienable and sacred rights of man', while the 1776 US Declaration of Independence from the colonial power of Britain claimed that:

> We hold these truths to be self evident, that all men are created equal; that they are endowed by their creator with certain inalienable Rights; that among these are life, liberty and the pursuit of happiness.

The prime task of this wave of rights was freedom from state tyranny and religious persecution and it led to the American Bill of Rights and the French Declaration of Rights.

Wave two started around the Second World War and an evolving United Nations (UN). International human rights treaties and declarations came to be enacted and enforced by international courts and monitoring bodies. Rights talk here focused especially on dignity, equality and community. It is enshrined in what most would consider the central document of human rights of our times – the Universal Declaration of Human Rights (UDHR), which is built into the UN Charter. 'Human Dignity' is the core value behind such rights. The Declaration established a potentially universal language of freedom and equal rights – even to those many countries like South Africa which were not able to achieve it at that time. Each of the main covenants has been ratified by some 140 out of 190 states, and the numbers are growing.

Wave three started to appear at the end of the Cold War (early 1990s) against a background of increasing globalisation and a new millennium looking for common values. It champions mutuality and participation. Here, more and more countries establish

U.S. President George W. Bush addresses the 57th session of the United Nations General assembly at UN Headquarters, New York

Source: © Brooks Kraft/Corbis

their own rights programmes and 'human rights regimes' begin to seem part of a major international political network. There are now, for instance, over 200 human rights NGOs in the United States, and a similar number in the UK and Europe. They are growing fast. Political scientist Benjamin Barber (1995) can now talk of a 'world of citizens without frontiers'. Most countries – even when they are riddled with the denial and corruption of human rights – still make claims to use versions of this language (which should of course alert us to some of the major problems with such a language: it can and does mean all things to all people!).

British sociologist Martin Albrow, in *The Global Age*, talks of a new kind of citizenship – *Global Citizenship* – which 'begins in people's daily lives, is realized in everyday practices and results in collective action up to the level of the globe' (Albrow, 1996: 177). He sees the

model for this as the international working-class movement in the nineteenth century, but now sees many roots into this through citizens who are, as he puts it, 'performing the state'. Here are global actions at the local level. Many of these claims now come conspicuously from new social movements – the Green movement of eco-warriors, the gay/lesbian/Queer/transgender movement, the Women's Movement – and they are epitomised in what has come to be called the Battle of Seattle, introduced in the opening to this chapter. These may not reinforce national systems of governance and may indeed even run counter to them. They challenge government to recognise key issues – often linked to how people can gain control over their (personal) lives in a 'runaway world'. They organise global conferences that establish worldwide agendas of rights. Human rights systems now appear across the world.

Map 15.3   Life After Communism

When communism collapsed in the late 1980s, a new hope and optimism appeared for the people of the former Soviet Union and Eastern Europe. They hoped for freedom, an expanding economy and an end of corruption. None of this has happened. GDP growth has declined in every country but Poland (with Russia, Georgia, Moldova, Ukraine, and Tajikistan the worst). Most countries have become poorer (poverty rose from 14 million in 1989 to 147 million in 1998) – indeed the increase in people living on less than a dollar a day has grown faster in the former Soviet Republics than anywhere else in the world. There are differences: Slovakia is one of the most equal countries in the world; Russia and Armenia are amongst the least equal. Map 15.3 charts some of the issues.

Source: adapted from 'Life after Communism: The facts', *New Internationalist*, 366, April 2004

THE HUMAN RIGHTS ACT, 1998

This came into force in the UK on 2 October 2000. It was the first time that the UK had enforceable official human rights protection. Drawing from the European Convention on Human Rights, the Act now means that old common law in the UK will have to change if it does not respect the rights enshrined in the convention, and that all legislation must now comply with these rights. The main rights are as follows.

ARTICLE

2. The right to life*
3. Freedom from torture, inhuman and degrading treatment
4. Freedom from slavery
5. Freedom from arbitrary arrest and detention
6. The right to a fair trial
7. Freedom from retrospective penalties
8. Right to privacy and family life
9. Freedom of religion
10. Freedom of expression
11. Freedom of assembly and association
12. The right to marry and found a family
14. Prohibition of discrimination
16. Restrictions on political activity of aliens
17. Prohibition of abuse of rights
18. Limitation on use of restrictions on rights.

In addition, the Act stipulates, among other things:

- The right to peaceful enjoyment of property
- The right to education
- The right to free elections
- Abolition of the death penalty
- Preservation of the death penalty in times of war.

The full text can be downloaded from http://www.hmso.gov.uk/acts/acts1998/19980042.htm

* Article 1 is missing as it does not list a right.

The trouble with rights

Although we can find talk of 'citizens and rights' everywhere in contemporary politics, a number of problems have been identified with it.

First is the claim to universalism. When the classic Universal Declaration of Human Rights was adopted, most Third World or low-income societies were still under colonial rule, and even today many remain suspicious of it. 'Human rights' can easily become a euphemism for Western intervention in other countries. It is often a universality of the privileged. Many of the rights claims just do not ring true in many parts of the world. The right to a paid vacation, for instance, makes no sense in most of the world where sweatshop labour conditions apply; and women's rights become a serious problem when there are major clashes of cultural and religious expectation around family and gender.

Second, even if there could be agreement, many of the rights claims are almost completely unenforceable pragmatically. There is evidence from international organisations such as Amnesty International and Human Rights Watch that these 'rights' are incessantly violated around the world. In wars of liberation, for example, one finds gross violations both by the oppressors as well as by the liberators. Rights regimes are often so private that they become unenforceable even with goodwill.

Finally, much rights talk is too individually based. There is a focus on individual rights as opposed to group rights. Collective human rights differ from individual rights. Human rights theory traditionally has focused on the rights of the individual, independent of social groupings, and advocates for individual human rights seek redress mainly through the nation state system or through intergovernmental structures, such as the United Nations. The focus of collective human rights, on the other hand, is on the rights of social groups, and proponents seek to create an innovative framework independent of nation states to enhance and protect these rights.

SUMMARY

1. Politics is the major social institution by which a society distributes power and organises decision-making. Max Weber explained that there are three ways to transform coercive power into legitimate authority: through tradition, through rationally enacted rules and regulations, and through the personal charisma of a leader.

2. Four clusters of government can be roughly outlined. Monarchy is based on traditional authority and is common in pre-industrial societies. Although constitutional monarchies persist in some industrial nations, industrialisation favours democracy based on rational–legal authority and extensive bureaucracy. Authoritarian political regimes deny popular participation in government. Totalitarian political systems go even further, tightly regulating people's everyday lives.

3. The world remains divided into between 190 and 200 politically independent nation states; one dimension of an emerging global political system, however, is the growing wealth and power of multinational corporations. Additionally, new technology associated with the Information Revolution means that national governments can no longer control the flow of information across national boundaries.

4. The dramatic growth of democratic governments in much of Europe during the past two centuries goes far beyond mere population increase; it reflects wider government involvement in the economy and all of society.

5. The traditional left (socialists) and right (conservatives) take different positions on economic and social issues. The left calls for government regulation of the economy and action to ensure economic equality; conservatives believe the government should not interfere in these arenas. Conservatives, however, do support government regulation of moral issues such as abortion, while the left, along with liberals, argue that government should not interfere in matters of conscience.

6. The pluralist model holds that political power is widely dispersed; the power elite model takes an opposing view, arguing that power is concentrated in the hands of a small, wealthy segment of the population. The Marxist or ruling class model argues that this elite is in fact an economic class.

7. Revolution, terrorism and war take power outside the normal workings of a political order. Revolution aims to radically transform a political system. Terrorism uses violence in pursuit of political goals. States as well as individuals engage in terrorism. War is armed conflict directed by governments. The development and proliferation of nuclear weapons have increased the threat of global catastrophe. Enhancing world peace ultimately depends on resolving the tensions and conflicts that fuel militarism.

8. A social movement entails deliberate activity intended to promote or discourage change. Social movements vary in the range of people they seek to engage and the extent to which they strive to change society. A typical social movement proceeds through consecutive stages: emergence (defining the public issue), coalescence (entering the public arena), bureaucratisation (becoming formally organised) and decline (brought on by failure or, sometimes, success).

9. At the start of the twenty-first century, the issue of global 'human rights' has been placed firmly on the political agenda.

CRITICAL-THINKING QUESTIONS

1. What is the Third Way? What are the main problems with such a position?

2. How is politics changing in the twenty-first century? What are the problems posed by the developing arguments around 'human rights'?

3. In what respects do some recent social movements (those concerned with the environment or animal rights) differ from older crusades (focus on, say, civil rights and gender equality)?

4. Do you think that the dangers of war in the world are greater or less than in past generations? In what ways has war changed? Are there 'new wars'?

GOING FURTHER

Further reading

Introductions to politics:

John Baylis and Steve Smith (eds), *The Globalization of World Politics* (1st edn, 1997; 2nd edn, 2000)
This is a wide-ranging textbook with a firm focus on the global processes of power in a wide range of areas from ecology and the Women's Movement to nationalism and the United Nations.

Anthony Giddens, *The Third Way: The Reward of Social Democracy* (1998)
A short, controversial and readable guide to some of the contemporary issues of world politics. It is meant to be a manifesto for this position which Giddens proposes and some politicians such as Tony Blair endorse.

On power in the UK:

John Scott, *Who Rules Britain?* (1991)
A clear account of the elites and power groups in British society.

Anthony Sampson, *Who Runs This Place? The Anatomy of Britain in the Twenty-first Century* (2004)
An update of a classic that reveals the political workings of key British institutions from business to the judiciary.

On wars:

Martin Shaw, *War and Genocide: Organized Killing in Modern Society* (2003)
Very readable and important text. It is also linked to Shaw's website.

Mary Kaldor, *New and Old Wars: Organized Violence in a Global Era* (1999)
Also looks at how wars have changed, and what the new era of globalised warfare may look like.

On terrorism:

Michael Ignatieff, *The Lesser Evil: Political Ethics in an Age of Terror* (2004)
Looks at forms of terrorism and ways in which it can be resisted through democracy.

More information

For recent political data on the UK, see *The Guardian Political Almanac* (annually).

Key magazines include: *New Statesman* (UK) and *Foreign Policy* (US).

See also the student magazine *Politics* (Blackwell publishers).

Watch a video

- Michael Moore's satire *Fahrenheit 9/11* (2004) received much praise as a critique of the Bush administration and the Iraq invasion.

- The Greek director Costa-Gravas made a reputation for himself in the 1970s with a series of probing political films, such as *Z* (1969), *The Confession* (1970) and *State of Siege* (1972). His *Missing* (1981) dealt with Allende's Chile and is a powerful moral and political drama.

- Stanley Kubrick's *Dr Strangelove: Or How I Learned to Stop Worrying and Love the Bomb* (1964), Gillo Pontecorvo's *The Battle of Algiers* (1965), Alan Parker's *Midnight Express* (1978), which deals with drugs and prison in Turkey, and Oliver Stone's *JFK* (1991) are all worth looking at.

- Classic films dealing with war include: Lewis Milestone's *All Quiet on the Western Front* (1930), Stanley Kubrick's *Paths of Glory* (1975), Michael Climino's *The Deer Hunter* (1977), Oliver Stone's *Born on the Fourth of July* (1989), and Steven Spielberg's *Schindler's List* (1993) and *Saving Private Ryan* (1998).

Connecting up

Connect to other chapters

- Link back to Marx and Weber in Chapter 3, and clarify how their theories of power link to social change.
- For more on gencocide, see Chapter 11.
- For more on wars and conflicts to science and the risk society, see Chapter 22.
- Consider how gender may be linked to power – see Chapter 12.
- To see how the ideas of the surveillance society and the work of Foucault are relevant to a discussion of power, refer to Chapter 16.

To the websites

- Freedom House charts the state of the world's democracies in its annual volume *Freedom in the World*, and their results are available on their website at

  http://www.freedomhouse.org/
- For the latest European political parties and parliamentary groups in the European Union, see:

  http://www.parties-and-elections.de/index.html
- There are a huge number of social movement sites. Look at

  http:www2.fmg.uva.nl/sociosite/topics/activism.html

- A good guide to US Social Movements can be found on

  http://www.wsu.edu:8080/~amerstu/smc/smcframe.html
- On Human Rights, some of the key documents from the *United Nations Universal Declaration of Human Rights* (1948) to the *Beijing Declaration on Women's Global Rights* (1995) have been usefully gathered in Ishay's *The Human Rights Reader* (1997).The American Bill of Rights and the French Declaration of Rights are available on websites at:

  http://www.yale.edu/lawweb/avalon/rightsof.htm and http://www.yale.edu/lawweb/avalon/rights1.htm
- Websites for the American Indian movement, animal rights, anti-semitism movement, civil rights movement, environmental concerns, eugenics movement, gay rights, and global justice can all be found at:

  http://psychology.about.com/od/socialmvmtag/
- Sites for human rights, hunger worldwide, individual rights, labour movement and peace movement, can all be found at:

  http://psychology.about.com/od/socialmvmthq/
- Rainforest conservation, religious, reproductive choice, temperance and prohibition, and women's issues can be found at:

  http://psychology.about.com/od/socialmvmtrz/

For additional case studies, multiple choice questions, internet exercises, and annotated weblinks specific to this chapter, visit this book's website at **www.pearsoned.co.uk/plummer**

CHAPTER 16

CONTROL, CRIME AND DEVIANCE

Crime is necessary, it is linked to the fundamental conditions of all social life and because of that it is useful; for those conditions to which it is bound are themselves indispensable to the normal evolution of morality.

Emile Durkheim

THE FILM *TRAFFIC*, which won several Oscars in 2001, tells a number of stories concerning drug use. A young girl from a wealthy background, whose father is a 'drug tsar', descends to the low life of an urban ghetto, selling her body for drugs, but finally is saved (we think) by a rehabilitation programme. A businessman, who made his billions through international drug trafficking, is taken to court but through the global world of organised crime manages to hire an assassin to kill the key witness. A policeman in Tijuana, Mexico, trying to stop the huge drug passages across the border of Mexico (via plane and lorry), finds the military, the government and his own boss are fully implicated in the trafficking. The lively and harrowing film tells many stories, but it is only fiction.

Real life is often stranger than fiction. Drug trafficking is now seen as the number one multibillion dollar industry in the black economy. The demand from richer countries, such as the United States, generates lucrative markets in the poorer countries. It touches most lives – even if only indirectly. The poorest peasant finds it simpler to grow coca, opium, marijuana or poppies from which the drugs can be made; other crops might get destroyed more easily and there is no real market for them anyway. International gangsters, usually working in cartels and syndicates, can organise the production of the drugs and their distribution across the globe. Drugs generate multibillion profits, and at the same time fuel organised crime across the world. Desperately poor countries, such as Afghanistan and Columbia, and governments whose gross national product is so much less than that of many international businesses become 'Narco States'. Here the state actually becomes dependent upon the drug market for its survival, and all the consumers throughout the world, along with their families and friends, fuel their supply. This is a major worldwide issue, and older ideas of crime and control seem pretty weak in approaching it. In the early 1990s, Americans spent a staggering $110,000 million a year on drugs, with huge profits for drug barons and dealers.

Sources: Jordan (1999); Cohen and Kennedy (2000: 161)

KEY THEMES

- Social and global patterns of crime
- The growth of globalised crime
- The changing character of social control
- The causes of crime

Dark artist's vision of life in prison

The 'drug debate' is just one of the very many issues of crime control facing almost every country in the world today. Crimes of all sorts are seen to be on the increase. And many of our concerns – like drug trafficking and control – stretch across the globe. Anxieties and fears about crime are up; our changing penal responses to crime are becoming more and more repressive. Nowadays, most governments make 'crime control' one of their central political arguments in elections, and the message is to 'get tough on crime'. Everywhere in the world it seems to be a growing issue.

In this chapter we open up some of the many questions dealing with control, crime and deviance. We start by trying to get a sense of just what the crime and deviance issues look like across the globe. We will look, too, at the changing shapes of the social control process, which seems to be expanding considerably across modern and late-modern society. We will also look at some of the reasons behind the growth of crime, by asking what indeed causes it. Table 16.1 suggests some of the major theories and positions within the study of crime. Although we do not have space to consider them all in this chapter, you may like to review them after you have read it, and see which ones you can identify.

Table 16.1	A timeline of criminology
Early modern period	Demonism, witchcraft
Late 18th century onwards	The Classical School and Beccaria
1870s	The Italian or Positivist School
1920s	Psycho-analytic theories
1920s	Life-story research
1910 onwards	Functionalist criminology
1930s onwards	Anomie theory
1920s/1930s	The Chicago tradition
1930s/1940s	Differential association
1960s/1970s	Subcultural theory
1960s/1970s	Labelling theory
1960s onwards	Control theory
1970s onwards	Moral panic theory
1973	New criminology
1970s	Critical criminology
1970s	Birmingham School BCCCS
1970s	The political economy of crime
1976	Just deserts/the justice model
1970s onwards	Feminist criminology
Late 1970s onwards	Black and anti-racist criminology
Late 1970s onwards	Focauldian genealogies and governance
1980s	Left Realism – square of crime
1980s	Resurgence of radical right
1990s	Cultural criminology and the seductions of crime/ postmodern criminology
2000s	Globalisation of crime
2000s	Human rights

Source: adapted from Carrabine *et al.* (2004)

Some opening definitions

Societies may be seen as layered by norms which guide virtually all human activities, and deviance is the violation of these norms along with the recognition and labelling of such violations. **Deviance** then involves *the recognised violation of cultural norms*. There are many kinds of norm: health norms, sexual norms, religious norms. People who violate such norms are ill (health norms), perverts (sex norms) or heretics (religious norms). One distinctive category of deviance is **crime**, *the violation of norms a society formally enacts into criminal law*. Criminal deviance is extensive, ranging from very minor traffic violations to serious offences such as murder and rape.

Some instances of deviance barely raise eyebrows; other cases command a swift and severe response. Members of our society pay little notice to mild non-conformity such as left-handedness or boastfulness; we usually take a dimmer view of drunken driving or vandalism; and we call the police in response to a burglary. There is a continuum of responses to crime, and we do not all respond in the same ways.

Not all deviance involves action or even choice. For some categories of individuals, just *existing* may be sufficient to provoke condemnation from others. To some older people, young people may symbolise trouble; to some whites, the mere presence of 'blacks' may cause suspicion. What deviant actions or attitudes have in common is some evaluation of *difference* that prompts us to regard another person as an 'outsider' (Becker, 1966). Deviance or crime is much more than a matter of individual choice or personal failing. *How* a society defines deviance, *whom* individuals brand as deviant and *what* people decide to do about non-conformity are all issues of social organisation.

The social and global shapes of crime

All societies have crime and deviance: sociologists generally agree that there is no such thing as a crime-free society. Indeed, crime may be a necessary price to pay for a certain social freedom (and hence non-conformity). It may serve as a means of bringing about change – the political criminals of one generation can become the leaders of another – and it may mark out the moral boundaries of society – if we had no 'bad', could we have any 'good'? A society with no crime or deviance would probably have to be a very rigid and very controlled society. At the same time, societies may have very different levels or rates of crime – too much 'freedom', for example, may lead to very high levels of crime. Not all societies have the same 'social shape' of crime.

Crime rates

In the UK, roughly 100,000 offences were recorded annually between 1876 and 1920, growing to half a million by 1950, two and a half million in 1980, and nearly six million in 2002–03. In the United States, the crime rate is also extremely high: during the 1990s, police have tallied some 8 million serious crimes annually. Crime rates, then, escalated throughout most of the twentieth century. In Europe generally, results from victim studies suggest that The Netherlands is the most criminal environment, followed closely by England and Wales, Switzerland, Scotland, France, Sweden, Finland and Austria, and with Northern Ireland the most law abiding (Levi and Maguire, 1998: 181)! Yet just how hard such data is to interpret is made clear when we learn that much of the Dutch experience – a bicycle-riding culture – is linked with reporting the theft of bicycles!

A declining crime rate?

At the turn of the twenty-first century, however, an interesting change was taking place. From roughly 1995, across 35 Western countries, including the United States, crime rates actually started to fall (Blumstein and Wallman, 2000; British Crime Survey, 2003–04; *Social Trends*, 2004; 134). In England and Wales in 2002–03, the number of crimes against adults living in private households fell by 2 per cent and was only slightly above the level of 1983. So talk of constantly rising crime rates is no longer true. However, as we shall see below, there are real problems in knowing exactly what criminal statistics such as these mean. For example, violent crime is still comparatively rare, but crimes involving firearms have doubled since 1997–98 (*Social Trends*, 2004: 136).

Types of crime in the UK

From reading the newspapers you could easily believe that sexual and violent crimes were everywhere. In fact, 93 per cent of all recorded crimes in England and Wales are property offences – often linked to theft of or from cars. While killings attract much attention, they account for around 600 or 700 offences a year, and well over half of these take place in the home, that is they are 'domestic'. Sex crimes, which probably attract most attention, are among the crimes with the lowest rates of all (T. Thomas, 2000). Looking at criminal statistics, the following generalisations may be made:

* In 2002, over 481,000 people were found guilty of or were cautioned for an indictable offence in England and Wales (see Table 16.2)
* Well over four-fifths were men (Figure 16.1)
* Young people offended the most, peaking at 19 for males and 15 for girls
* Households in inner cities are most likely to be victims of burglaries (twice as likely as elsewhere)
* Most offenders have already been convicted of an offence previously (seven out of ten males in 1994)
* A small proportion of offenders are responsible for a large proportion of offences.

Problems of measuring crime

Criminologists and sociologists usually turn to several key sources when they want to see the patterns of crime in a society. In the UK, for instance, the key sources are the statistics gathered by the Home Office and published annually as *Criminal Statistics in England and Wales*. Most industrial societies have comparable reports, but in low-income societies these figures are much less reliable and much harder to obtain.

The crime statistics presented above – like all statistics – must be read with extreme caution. One way of understanding the construction of crime statistics is to see them like a flow, through which smaller and smaller numbers of offences get counted. We start with a very large pool of actual offences where the numbers are unknown and unknowable. There is then a sharp drop in numbers at each stage. It seems likely that as few as two in 100 offences result in a conviction. This is the hidden figure of crime.

Table 16.2	Offenders found guilty of or cautioned for indictable offences: by gender, type of offence and age, 2002				
	10–15	16–24	25–34	35 and over	All aged 10 and over (thousands)
Males					
Theft and handling stolen goods	86	183	104	17	131.5
Drug offences	18	159	62	9	84.1
Violence against the person	31	77	32	9	51.8
Burglary	29	49	21	2	30.4
Criminal damage	13	18	7	2	12.5
Robbery	6	14	4	0	7.2
Sexual offences	3	4	3	2	5.0
Other indictable offences	11	102	59	12	69.0
All indictable offences	196	606	292	53	391.5
Females					
Theft and handling stolen goods	51	67	32	6	50.1
Drug offences	2	15	9	1	9.8
Violence against the person	11	12	5	1	9.5
Burglary	3	3	1	0	2.1
Criminal damage	2	2	1	0	1.6
Robbery	1	1	0	0	0.9
Sexual offences	0	0	0	0	0.1
Other indictable offences	3	20	13	2	14.4
All indictable offences	74	119	61	12	88.6

Source: adapted from *Social Trends* (2004: 140)

Official statistics of 'recorded crimes' include only crimes reported to the police. (But they may not include all the crimes reported – some, for instance, may not be crimes or may be very trivial.) So getting crimes reported is the first key issue in statistic construction and, quite clearly, not all crimes are reported, though this differs with offence. The police learn about almost all killings, but assaults – especially among acquaintances – are far less likely to be reported. The police record an even smaller proportion of property crimes, especially when losses are small. Some victims may not realise that a crime has occurred, or they may assume they have little chance of recovering their property even if they notify the police. Reports of rape, although rising over time, still grossly understate the extent of this crime.

The majority of crimes come to police attention by being reported by the public (about 90 per cent). The public's responsiveness is shaped by such issues as:

- tolerance of certain kinds of crime (such as vandalism)
- seriousness of offence (such as very minor thefts or brawls)

- confidence in the police ('nothing can be done')
- crimes without victims (such as drug offences)
- awareness that it is a crime (for example, some fraud).

The official criminal statistics are not the only way of recording crime. There are alternative ways. One is through a *victimisation survey*, in which a researcher asks a representative sample of people about their experience of crime. People do not always respond fully or truthfully to such surveys, experts acknowledge, but the results of these surveys indicate that actual criminality occurs at a rate two or three times higher than official reports suggest.

In England, since 1982, there has been a regular major victim survey of crime: the *British Crime Surveys*. Here a random sample of about 5,000 adults are asked questions about being victims of crime, whether they reported the crimes or not, and their fear of crime. These studies raise further doubts about the value of crime statistics, as they have persistently shown both much higher rates and significant discrepancies for different kinds of crime. At the same time, these figures also suggest that the overall growth of crime may have been exaggerated, since crime statistics are so dependent on the vagaries of reporting. Indeed, on the basis of these studies, 'the risk of becoming a victim of any form of crime is still historically low at 27 per cent, around the samel level as 1981, and one-third lower than the risk in 1995 (when it was 40 per cent) (*Social Trends*, 2004: 139).

A second way of measuring crime is through *self-reporting* studies. Here a sample of people are asked about the crimes they have committed and whether these were reported or not. Thus, for example, The Youth Lifestyles Survey (YLS) conducted in the UK in 1992–93 suggested that offending is much more widespread among young people. One in four males aged 18–21, and one in eight females aged 14–17, admitted to a theft or burglary (*Social Trends*, 1997: 159). Those with a single parent or step-families were more likely to commit crimes.

Globalisation and crime

Because it is impossible to be accurate about measuring crime in any one society such as the UK, it becomes even harder to compare crimes across cultures. In many low-income countries, the data are significantly flawed anyway. Despite these problems, crime rates do appear to differ throughout the world (Table 16.3).

Thus, although violent crime is prevalent in many countries of Western Europe, the violent crime rate in the United States generally emerges as about five times greater; and the rate of property crime is twice as high. With differences as great as this, it seems reasonable to conclude that crime is more frequent in the United States than in Western Europe. On the other hand, there are parts of Eastern Europe where it is very hard to measure what is actually going on. Indeed, it has been suggested that some of these countries have become increasingly 'gangsterised', with very high levels of crime. Since the fall of communism in these countries, market economies have appeared which have been ill-prepared to cope with changing demands. As a result, a kind of criminal wasteland has appeared in certain areas (Castells, 1998: 180–190). All this may contrast greatly with many nations of Asia, including India and Japan, where rates of violent and property crime seem to be among the lowest in the world. Likewise, in Iran and many other Muslim countries, rates of crime are generally thought to be low.

There again, in some of the largest cities of the world, such as Manila in the Philippines and São Paulo in Brazil, crime rates do appear to be soaring. These are the cities that have rapid population growth and millions of desperately poor people (see Chapter 23). By and large, however, the traditional character of less economically developed societies and their strong family structure allow local communities to control crime informally (Clinard and Abbott, 1973; *Der Spiegel*, 1989).

As noted in earlier chapters, we are experiencing 'globalisation' on many fronts, and crime is no exception. Some types of crime have always been multinational, including terrorism, espionage and arms dealing (Martin and Romano, 1992). But newer ones are appearing as crimes travel through countries and know no borders. Manuel Castells (1998: Chapter 3) has written about the 'Global Criminal Economy' and, following the United Nations Conference on Transnational Crime in 1994, has identified at least six main forms it is taking across the world:

1. Arms and weapons trafficking – a multibillion dollar industry in which states or guerilla groups are provided with weapons they should not have.

2. Trafficking of nuclear materials – smuggling nuclear weapons materials.

3. Smuggling of illegal immigrants – one estimate suggests that Chinese criminal gangs (triads) make $2.5 billion a year in trafficking migrants, often with disastrous consequences (see Cohen and Kennedy, 2000: 154). For instance, in 2000, 58 Chinese immigrants being smuggled into the UK were found dead on arrival: they had been packed into a lorry with the air vent closed. The driver was sent to prison for 14 years (see Chapter 14, opening story).

4. Trafficking in women and children (see Chapter 13).

5. Trafficking in body parts – a huge industry involving the sale of organs usually from poor people to the rich (see Chapter 7 on the body).

6. Money laundering – complex financial arrangements in which monies get banked, lost and then reworked into the formal system. It depends on offshore banks, secrecy and confidentiality. Money earned in illicit markets has to get back into the legitimate economy.

Global crime and Russia

When the Soviet Union became a market economy, it became the target of much organised crime. Many new private businesses became enmeshed in vast networks of crime and protection rackets sprouted. Indeed, by 1997, it was estimated that 41,000 companies, 50 per cent of banks and 80 per cent of joint ventures had criminal connections. In addition, in 1995, some 450 contract killings were identified (only 60 of which were solved by the police). Castells describes the situation vividly:

Table 16.3   World victims of crime (percentage of total population)

	Year	11 crimes[1]	Car theft	Theft from car	Car vandalism	Motocycle theft	Bicycle theft	Burglary	Attempted burglary	Robbery	Personal theft[2]	Sexual incidents[3]	Assaults & threats
Australia	1989	26.1	2.3	6.9	8.8	0.3	1.9	4.4	3.8	0.9	5.0	7.3	5.2
	1992	28.6	3.1	6.6	9.5	0.3	2.1	3.7	3.8	1.3	6.5	3.5	4.7
	2000	30.0	1.9	6.8	9.2	0.1	2.0	3.9	3.3	1.2	6.5	4.0	6.4
Austria	1996	18.8	0.1	1.6	6.7	0.0	3.3	0.9	0.5	0.2	5.0	3.8	2.1
Belgium	1989	17.7	0.8	2.7	6.6	0.4	2.7	2.3	2.3	1.0	4.0	1.3	2.1
	1992	19.3	1.0	3.9	6.1	1.1	2.8	2.1	1.6	1.0	3.1	1.4	1.8
	2000	21.4	0.7	3.6	6.1	0.3	3.5	2.0	2.8	1.0	4.1	1.1	3.2
Canada	1989	28.1	0.8	7.2	9.8	0.4	3.4	3.0	2.7	1.1	5.5	4.0	3.9
	1992	28.4	1.3	7.3	8.5	0.2	3.7	3.4	2.7	1.2	5.5	3.8	4.8
	1996	25.2	1.5	6.2	6.2	0.1	3.3	3.4	2.8	1.2	5.7	2.7	4.0
	2000	23.8	1.4	5.4	5.5	0.1	3.5	2.3	2.3	0.9	4.7	2.1	5.3
Catalonia (Spain)	2000	19.0	0.4	5.3	7.7	0.6	0.4	1.3	0.6	0.9	3.0	0.8	1.5
Denmark	2000	23.0	1.1	3.4	3.8	0.7	6.7	3.1	1.5	0.7	4.1	2.5	3.6
England and Wales	1989	19.4	1.8	5.6	6.8	0.1	1.0	2.1	1.7	0.7	3.1	1.1	1.9
	1992	30.2	3.7	8.6	10.6	0.4	3.0	3.0	2.9	1.1	4.2	2.1	3.8
	1996	30.9	2.5	8.1	10.4	0.2	3.5	3.0	3.4	1.4	5.0	2.0	5.9
	2000	26.4	2.1	6.4	8.8	0.4	2.4	2.8	2.8	1.2	4.6	2.7	6.1
Finland	1989	15.9	0.4	2.7	4.0	0.0	3.1	0.6	0.4	0.7	4.3	0.5	2.9
	1992	21.2	0.7	2.9	5.6	0.3	5.0	0.6	0.6	1.0	3.4	3.7	4.4
	1996	18.9	0.4	2.9	3.7	0.1	4.9	0.3	1.0	0.6	3.3	3.7	4.2
	2000	19.1	0.4	2.9	3.7	0.1	4.9	0.3	1.0	0.6	3.3	3.7	4.2
France	1989	19.4	2.4	6.0	6.4	0.6	1.4	2.4	2.3	0.4	3.6	1.1	2.0
	1996	25.3	1.6	7.2	8.3	0.8	2.8	2.3	2.2	1.0	4.0	0.9	3.9
	2000	21.4	1.7	5.5	8.2	0.3	1.8	1.0	1.3	1.1	3.0	1.1	4.2
German (West)	1989	21.9	0.4	4.7	8.7	0.2	3.3	1.3	1.8	0.8	4.0	2.8	3.1
Italy	1992	24.6	2.7	7.0	7.6	1.5	2.3	2.4	1.7	1.3	3.6	1.7	0.8
Japan[4]	1989	8.5	0.2	0.7	2.5	0.2	3.5	0.7	0.2	na	0.2	1.0	0.7
	1992	na	1.1	2.3	na	3.2	9.6	1.1	na	na	1.3	1.8	0.5
	2000	15.2	0.1	1.6	4.4	1.0	6.6	1.1	0.8	0.1	0.5	1.2	0.4
Netherlands	1989	26.8	0.3	5.2	8.2	0.4	7.5	2.4	2.6	0.8	4.4	2.6	3.3
	1992	31.3	0.5	6.8	9.6	1.0	10.0	2.0	3.0	1.0	4.6	2.2	4.0
	1996	31.5	0.4	5.4	9.9	0.7	9.5	2.6	3.3	0.6	6.8	3.6	4.0
	2000	25.2	0.4	3.9	8.9	0.6	7.0	1.9	2.7	0.8	4.7	3.0	3.4

Table 16.3   continued

	Year	11 crimes[1]	Car theft	Theft from car	Car vandalism	Motocycle theft	Bicycle theft	Burglary	Attempted burglary	Robbery	Personal theft[2]	Sexual incidents[3]	Assaults & threats
New Zealand	1992	29.4	2.7	6.9	7.9	0.3	4.4	4.3	3.6	0.7	5.3	2.7	5.7
Northern Ireland	1989	14.9	1.6	4.0	4.4	0.1	1.6	1.1	0.9	0.5	2.2	1.9	1.8
	1996	16.8	1.6	3.1	6.7	0.0	1.2	1.5	1.1	0.5	2.5	1.2	1.7
	2000	15.0	1.2	2.7	4.5	0.0	1.4	1.7	0.9	0.1	2.2	0.6	3.0
Norway	1989	16.4	1.1	2.8	4.6	0.3	2.8	0.7	0.4	0.5	3.2	2.2	3.0
Poland	1992	27.0	0.7	5.3	4.7	1.0	4.2	2.1	2.3	1.7	8.1	3.6	4.2
	1996	22.9	0.9	5.7	5.4	0.3	3.2	2.0	1.8	1.8	5.6	1.5	3.7
	2000	22.7	1.0	5.5	7.0	0.1	3.6	2.0	1.3	1.8	5.3	0.5	2.8
Portugal	2000	15.5	0.9	4.9	6.3	0.3	0.8	1.4	1.2	1.1	1.9	0.6	0.9
Scotland	1989	18.6	0.8	5.4	6.5	0.3	1.0	2.0	2.1	0.5	2.6	1.2	1.8
	1996	25.6	1.7	6.6	9.8	0.1	1.9	1.5	2.4	0.8	4.5	1.3	4.2
	2000	23.2	0.7	4.2	9.0	0.1	2.0	1.5	1.9	0.7	4.6	1.1	6.1
Spain	1989	24.8	1.4	9.6	6.6	0.8	1.1	1.6	2.1	3.1	5.2	2.3	3.1
Sweden	1992	21.5	1.7	3.9	4.5	0.6	7.0	1.4	0.8	0.3	4.2	0.9	2.7
	1996	24.0	1.2	4.9	4.6	0.5	8.8	1.3	1.1	0.5	4.6	2.9	4.5
	2000	24.7	1.3	5.3	4.6	0.4	7.2	1.7	0.7	0.9	5.8	2.6	3.8
Switzerland	1989	15.6	0.0	1.9	4.1	1.2	3.2	1.0	0.2	0.5	4.5	1.7	1.2
	1996	26.7	0.1	3.0	7.1	1.4	7.0	1.3	1.1	0.9	5.7	4.6	3.1
	2000	18.2	0.3	1.7	3.9	0.2	4.7	1.1	1.8	0.7	4.4	2.1	2.4
USA	1989	28.9	2.1	9.2	8.9	0.1	3.0	3.8	5.4	1.9	4.5	4.5	5.4
	1992	26.1	2.6	7.0	8.0	0.4	2.9	3.1	3.9	1.5	5.3	2.3	4.7
	1996	24.2	1.9	7.5	6.7	0.2	3.3	2.6	3.0	1.3	3.9	2.5	5.7
	2000	21.1	0.5	6.4	7.2	0.3	2.1	1.8	2.7	0.6	4.9	1.5	3.4
All countries[5]	1989	20.2	1.1	5.0	6.5	0.4	2.7	2.0	1.9	0.9	3.5	2.4	2.8
	1992	22.1	1.8	5.4	6.4	1.0	5.1	2.3	2.1	0.9	4.3	2.4	3.3
	1996	24.2	1.2	5.2	7.2	0.4	4.4	1.9	2.0	0.9	4.7	2.4	3.9
	2000	21.3	1.0	4.6	6.6	0.3	3.2	1.8	1.8	0.8	3.9	1.7	3.

1 Based on eleven crimes standard across sweeps.
2 Theft of personal property.
3 Asked of women only, but asked of men in Australia and Canada in 2000, omitted in this table.
4 Some results for Japan are not available.
5 Averages are based on all countries taking part in each sweep. As countries included vary across sweeps, comparisons should be made cautiously.

Source: United Nations (2001), *United Nations International Crime Survey of Victims*, Appendix 4, Table 1. The United Nations is the author of the original material

Smuggling of everything from everywhere to everywhere, including radio-active material, human organs and illegal immigrants; prostitution; gambling; loan sharking; kidnapping; racketeering and extortion; counterfeiting of goods, banknotes, financial documents, credit cards, fake identity cards; killers for hire; traffic of sensitive information, technology or art objects; international sales of stolen goods; or even dumping garbage illegally from one country into another.

(Castells, 1998: 167)

Money laundering is at the heart of the system. Globalisation has created a superhighway of movements where networking is the logic of crime. It is a huge system: even as early as 1993 estimates suggested it was costing 'US$trillion a year' – about the same as the US Federal budget at that time (Castells, 1998: 169). And why? It is part of a wider response to the collapse of the Soviet system, and subverts the wider institutions of the economy and state. The collapse of the Soviet Union created a kind of power vacuum, and ruthless actors rushed in to earn substantial profits. The change of regime in the 1990s inflicted a massive trauma on Russia – impoverishment and major disorientation came to much of the population. Wealth-grabbing in all its forms became the preoccupation of a small elite. Picking up common practices that are widely tolerated, and even nurtured under capitalism, it helps people survive in a world where wages are low, the rule of law is unclear,

where corruption has long been endemic, and where the corruption of the police force is well known

International trafficking in drugs

Trafficking in illegal commodities, especially drugs, accounts for billions of pounds and may well be the world's largest industry. The illegal drug trade is found all over the world: cocaine in Colombia and the Andes, opium/heroin from the Southeast Asian Golden Triangle, all along the Mexican border, Turkey, the Balkans, Afghanistan and Central Asia (Castells, 1998: 169). In part, the proliferation of illegal drugs in the United States and Europe stems from 'demand': there is a very profitable market for cocaine and other drugs, as well as many young people willing to risk arrest or even violent death by engaging in the lucrative drug trade. But the 'supply' side of the issue also propels drug trafficking. In the South American nation of Colombia, at least 20 per cent of the people depend on cocaine production for their livelihood. Furthermore, not only is cocaine Colombia's most profitable export, but it outsells all other exports combined (including coffee). Clearly, then, understanding crimes such as drug dealing requires analysing social conditions both in the country of consumption and around the world. More and more, the comprehension of crime and deviance requires moving beyond the borders of one country to look at a host of international connections.

Over 20 : 1	Sexual offences	75 : 1	
	Taking and driving away motor vehicles	33 : 1	
	Burglary	23 : 1	
	Motoring offences (indictable)	20.6 : 1	
5–20 : 1	Offences under the Public Order Act 1986	17 : 1	
	Criminal damage (summary/less than £2000)	16.5 : 1	
	Drunkenness	16.5 : 1	
	Robbery	13.5 : 1	
	Criminal damage (indictable over £2000)	9.4 : 1	
	Drug offences	9.4 : 1	
	Common assault (summary)	7.0 : 1	
	Violence against the person (indictable)	5.7 : 1	
	Assault on constable	5.5 : 1	
Under 5 : 1	Theft and handling stolen goods	2.8 : 1	
	Fraud and forgery	2.8 : 1	
Under 1 : 1 (women form majority)	TV licence evasion	1 : 2	
	Offence by prostitute	1 : 100	
	(After Coleman and Moynihan 1996: 95–6)		

Figure 16.1 Ratio of male to female offenders found guilty or cautioned for selected offence groupings in the UK

Source: after Coleman and Moynihan (1996: 95–96)

Anthony Burgess's futuristic novel *A Clockwork Orange* (1962) looks at the story of 15-year-old Alex and his three 'droog' delinquent friends living a life of violence and crime. Alex tells his story in 'nadstat', a teenage slang of a not too distant future. Unfortunately for Alex, he is caught and is subjected to 'Ludovico's Technique', a new form of social control involving 'brain therapy'. In 1971, Stanley Kubrick turned the novel into a highly controversial and chilling film – banned subsequently by Kubrick himself for 30 years. Malcolm McDowell is pictured above as Alex.

Source: Ronald Grant Archive

Changes in social control

Because societies have rules, members target each other with efforts at social control. Cases of more serious deviance may provoke a response from a formal **social control system** which involves *planned and programmed responses to expected deviance* (S. Cohen, 1985: 2). At the most visible level, this involves a **criminal justice system**, *a societal reaction to alleged violations of law utilising police, courts and prison officials* using various punishments and corrections, from prisons to probation. The criminal justice system is a society's formal response to crime. In some countries, military police keep a tight rein on people's behaviour; in others, officials have more limited powers to respond to specific violations of criminal law. But there are also less visible networks of control: from the informal networks of families and friends, through the monitoring done by social workers and psychiatrists, and on to the closed-circuit surveillance in shops and shopping centres, the development of electronic tagging

and the rise of private policing. Some of these will be discussed below.

Most of the key features of the modern Western control system – often called 'penality' – emerged at the end of the eighteenth century. Although, for instance, jails existed prior to this time, they were not the large-scale places with individual cells and strict rules that exist now. Instead, they were smaller and local and held crowds of people who were undifferentiated by crime and offence. Often they were just 'holding places' on the way to the gallows (Ignatieff, 1978). Likewise, policing was organised on a local basis. Only in 1829 was the Metropolitan Police force established in England.

But, with industrialisation and the emergence of the modern world, all this changed. *Control processes became subject to bureaucratisation, professionalisation and state funding.* Thus, control became organised through bureaucratic, rule-bound organisations run by new trained professionals such as prison officers and policemen, and central government started to play a significant role in legislation and in the funding of control. In 1999–2000, around £12 billion was spent on the criminal justice system in the UK (more than doubling between 1977 and 1997). Some 124,000 people were employed by the police (as well as 53,000 civilians) (*Social Trends*, 2001: 172). This scale is mirrored in most other industrial countries: everywhere social control today is a large part of public/state spending.

In his classic book *Discipline and Punish: The Birth of the Prison* (1977; orig.1975) Foucault (profiled in the box) depicts this change dramatically. In the striking opening pages – well worth a read! – he compares the earlier forms of brutal and chaotic punishment on the body with the more recent forms of surveillance and imprisonment which are intensely rule governed. As he says, it is the difference between the spectacle of a *public execution* and a *timetable*. The former leads to the following normal event in 1757:

> . . . on a scaffold that will be erected (at the Place de Grève), the flesh will be torn from his breasts, arms, thighs and calves with red hot pincer, his right hand . . . burnt with sulphur, and, on those places where the flesh will be torn away, poured molten lead, boiling oil, burning resin, wax and sulphur melted together and then his body drawn and quartered by four horses and his limbs and body consumed by fire, reduced to ashes and thrown to the winds . . .

> (Foucault, 1977; orig. 1975: 3)

PROFILE

MICHEL FOUCAULT: POWER AND SURVEILLANCE

Michel Foucault (1926–84)
Source: Network © Carlos Friere

The French philosopher Michel Foucault (1926–84) was one of the twentieth century's most influential thinkers. He examined a number of major changes that marked out the distinctive ways in which we think in 'the modern world' when compared with the past, and he developed an important theory of power, knowledge and discourse.

Always a radical and critical thinker, he saw dramatic ruptures with the past and suggested that these modern developments were not signs of simple 'enlightened' progress, but rather were evidence of extending power and increasing surveillance. For Foucault, power is everywhere and works its way through **discourses** – *bodies of ideas and language often backed up by institutions*. Thus, criminology is a discourse that invents or produces its own set of ideas and languages about the criminal as an object to be studied, backed up by many institutions such as the prison and the courts. Power works its way distinctly through this discourse to help shape the whole society's view of crime. 'Knowledge' in this view may act as a way of keeping people under control.

Foucault's work looks at such changes as (1) the appearance of the modern prison along with the rise of criminology; (2) the 'birth of the clinic' as a distinctly modern way of handling health; (3) the development of the psychiatric discourse and modern approaches to madness, through grasping the appearance of a very distinctive modern way of reasoning; and (4) the development of our modern languages around sexuality. Very wide-ranging, he even asks questions about the very idea of what it means to be an 'individual' human being in Western societies.

Many of Foucault's ideas challenge common sense. He argued, for instance, that 'sexuality' has not always existed: it is a creation of the modern world. And he suggested that prisons, far from solving the crime problem, actually extend it. His most accessible book is *Discipline and Punish* (1977; orig. 1975), in which he traced the development of the modern prison system. A brief extract from this is given in the text.

His ideas are controversial and much discussed. Some say he was one of the most brilliant figures of twentieth-century thought. Others feel that his difficult writing and complexity have detracted from engagement with what is happening in the world (for an introduction to Foucault's work, see Smart, 1985).

while the latter leads, 80 years on, to:

Art. 17. The prisoners' day will begin at six in the morning in winter and at five in the summer . . . they will work for nine hours a day. . . .

Art 18. Rising. At the first drum-roll, the prisoners must rise and dress in silence . . . at the second drum-roll, they must be dressed and make their beds. At the third, they must line up and proceed to the chapel for morning prayer . . .

Art 19. The prayers are conducted by the chaplain and followed by a moral or religious reading. This exercise must not last more than half an hour . . .

(Foucault, 1977; orig. 1975: 6)

The differences in systems of control are clearly illustrated.

HOW TO CONTROL DRUGS:
CASE STUDIES FROM SWEDEN
AND THE NETHERLANDS

The Swedish case

Sweden once had an image throughout the world as a permissive society. It had a free and open approach compared with most societies. In matters of sexuality, for example, it was the society of 'free love', tolerance and civility. And it had a much more radical approach to the roles of men, women and children outside traditional family forms. During the 'swinging sixties' Sweden also had quite a reputation for drug smoking among hippies – second only, perhaps, to those in Haight Ashbury, San Francisco. These were the fun-loving, beautiful people who smoked pot quite openly. Cannabis may have been officially illegal, but it was accepted everywhere.

All that has changed. While it remains liberal on matters of welfare and sexuality, Sweden today may have one of the most repressive drug policies in the world. The 1970s brought an end to this open and tolerant scene; and largely through the crusading work of the RNS (Riksorbundet Narkotikafritt Samhalle – National Union for a Narcotics Free Society), new policies have been adopted that have made the approach to drug use more and more severe.

Sweden now has one of the toughest drug policies and laws in Europe, criminalising drug use as well as possession. Passing a joint is trafficking and carries a compulsory prison sentence. Drugs generally are now invisible. The use of drugs has been driven underground.

There has been so strong an opposition to drug use that it is very hard to find people who will speak out in any kind of liberal way in favour of drug use. The term for people who favour the liberalisation of laws, *drogliberal*, has become a term of abuse! People are regarded with suspicion as 'drug legalisers' and excluded from public debate. And the media has a strong consensus of disapproval.

But there is little evidence that the 'war against drugs' in Sweden is working. On the contrary, despite harsh penalties, some 20 per cent of young Swedes in the larger cities use drugs (mainly cannabis), organised crime has grown, and there has been an escalation in many drug-related crimes. Adult crime in Stockholm has risen by some 80 per cent since 1975.

The Dutch case

Amsterdam is known as 'Europe's drugs capital'. Since 1976 it has operated a policy of 'decriminalisation' for soft drugs, making it a misdemeanour and not a crime. Individuals can own up to 30 grams of marijuana or hashish, which can be purchased in coffee shops (which are not allowed to deal in any kind of hard drug) and grown at home. The aim of this highly liberal and pragmatic policy (to be contrasted with the one described at the start of this chapter) is prevention and harm reduction: reducing the dangers to both community and the individual.

The key distinction in this policy is that between hard and soft drugs. Hard drugs are seen as very harmful and must be prohibited; soft drugs are much less harmful and may even be less harmful than currently permitted 'drugs' such as cigarettes (nicotine) and drink (alcohol). They are only a danger for specific groups (such as children) and are not likely to lead to escalation. Indeed, there are an estimated 675,000 people in The Netherlands who smoke soft drugs; but only 25,000 are involved with cocaine. By contrast, rates of use are much higher in most of Europe where the 'addict rate' is 2.7 people per thousand. In The Netherlands, it is 1.6 and there are few signs of pot leading to harder drugs.

At various times the Dutch government has argued that it would like soft drugs to be completely legal so that prices would fall and criminal connections would be disconnected. Soft drugs, it is argued, only need the kinds of control that have been routinely applied to alcohol (such restrictions as age limits, driving restrictions and advertising restrictions).

Most other countries condemn the Dutch policy on drugs, not least because it has an impact upon them. They argue that it weakens international prohibitions; that it encourages drugs tourism (people crossing borders seeking 'better-class drugs', which are more accessible and cheaper); that it makes too simple a distinction between hard and soft drugs; and, ultimately, that it does not drive out organised criminal networks. The mounting criticisms, and a concern about its international reputation, has recently made The Netherlands start to reconsider its policies.

Sources: Yates (1996); Maris (1996)

Control in the twenty-first century

The modern control system may be characterised in three ways. First, the old system of public control (financed by the state) of prisons and policing laid down during the nineteenth century has continued to expand. New prisons are being built and in some countries prison populations have increased dramatically. Second, and starting in the period after the Second World War, a new and largely informal system of control has been grafted on to this. This brings an ever-increasing number and wider range of people into the control network. Third, starting in the early 1980s, the system overall has expanded greatly to include a wide range of newer surveillance techniques, and many of these are privately sponsored and funded.

The growth of prisons

Prisons seem to be expanding and growing in nearly all countries. Nils Christie (2000) calls this the 'Prison Industrial Complex'. There has been a massive expansion in numbers going to prison, as well as numbers of prisons (see Table 16.4).

More than 8.75 million people are held in prisons throughout the world – about half of these in the United States (1.96 million), Russia (0.92 million) and China (1.43 million). The United States is frequently cited as the country with the highest prison population in the world – some 715 per 100,000 people. Japan has a conspicuously low rate of prisoners. In Europe, the trend may not be quite so developed. Indeed, some countries such as Sweden, Norway and The Netherlands have long been seen as having the most humane and contained prison systems in the world. But even here, in recent years, there have been significant changes. Prison use is on the increase and the treatment of prisoners is getting worse. For instance, in The Netherlands in 1975, there were 2,356 prison cells and the rate of imprisonment was 17 per 100,000. At the start of 2004, there were around 16,000 prisoners and a rate of 100 per 100,000. The UK had the second largest prison population in Europe, around 139 per 100,000 and is above the mid-point in the world list with a prison population of over 85,000. Portugal had the largest European prison population overall (Walmsley, 2003).

Imprisonment has become a huge industry and a system in crisis in the early twenty-first century. Part of this may be due to new policies such as the 'three strikes' policy (first introduced in Washington in 1992) which produces a mandatory life sentence after three offences. Part of this may also be due to a decisive penal shift in many countries

Table 16.4	Prison populations and rates for selected countries	
Country	Total population	Rate per 100, 000
United States	2,078,570	715
Russian Federation	846,967	584
South Africa	180,952	402
Turkmenistan	c. 22,000	c. 489
Singapore	16,310	388
Estonia	4,571	339
UK England and Wales	75,233	142
UK Scotland	6,858	134
UK Northern Ireland	1,263	72
New Zealand	6,403	161
Australia	22,507	114
Spain	58,299	142
Mexico	175,253	169
Portugal	13,670	130
China	1,549,000	119
India	313,635	29
Cuba	c. 55,000	c. 487
Poland	80,093	210
Brazil	308,304	169
Ukraine	198,900	417
France	56,957	95
Germany	79,153	96
Japan	69,502	54
Sweden	6,755	75
Netherlands	16,239	100
Norway	2,914	64
Denmark	3,908	72

Source: www.prisonstudies.org (last updated January 2004)

to be 'tough on crime and tough on the causes of crime'. There has been a clear shift from policies of rehabilitation to policies of punishment over the past decade.

Privatising prisons

Since the late twentieth century, there has been a turn away from state investment in prisons towards privatisation. Although private arrangements for running prisons can be traced back for some time (for instance, to early arrangements of labour leasing – the chain gangs), since the early 1990s more and more countries have come to see privatisation as one fruitful way of handling the 'penal crisis'.

Initially, privatisation was applied in the United States to the 'soft end' of the control process – to small facilities for juveniles, low-security prisons and women's prisons. The first contracted-out house for juveniles was established in 1975 in Pennsylvania. A little later, Corrections Corporation of America (CCA) and Wakenhut started to get contracts for adult prisons.

Those in favour of private prisons argued that they were more economic, more flexible and more efficient – they provided new and better facilities and costs were reduced in both prison building and operations. Critics suggested that it was 'punishment for profit'. It was an area where markets and profits could be made against the public and individual good.

The system has grown throughout the world. It has been taken up in Australia, but most European countries take it seriously too. France has had one of the strongest involvements, with at least 17 private institutions accommodating over 10,000 prisoners. Privatisation is also found in Germany, The Netherlands and the UK (see James *et al.*, 1997).

Spreading the net: informal control

This massive growth of prisons has ironically been accompanied by the spread of what have been called 'alternatives to prison'. They are clearly *not* 'alternatives' but exist side by side with prison expansion, bringing an ever-increasing number of people into the control network. Young offenders, for instance, who were once cautioned may now be placed on a community care order or required to attend some form of therapy group. The British criminologist Anthony Bottoms has called these developments the *bifurcation* of the system: 'put crudely, this bifurcation is between, on the one hand, the so-called 'really serious offender' for whom very tough

measures are typically advocated; and on the other hand, the 'ordinary offender' for whom we can afford to take a much more lenient line' (Bottoms, 1988).

The rise of the surveillance society

The penal system overall has expanded greatly to include a wide range of surveillance techniques, and many of these are privately sponsored and funded. Although surveillance has been around for a long time, its intensity has grown in the modern world so much that we can start to talk of a **surveillance society**, *a society dependent on communication and information technologies for adminstrative and control processes and which result in the close monitoring of everyday life* (Lyon, 2001).

In non-industrial societies, surveillance operates in an informal manner, often through primary groups (see Chapter 6). But larger organisations require much more complex monitoring of events. Since the rise of the industrial society, more and more energy has been given over to collecting records on the lives of citizens and monitoring their behaviour. Most noticeable here has been the dramatic increase in closed-circuit television (CCTV) in recent years. In shops, on motorways and in all kinds of public places, surveillance can now take place 24 hours a day, 365 days a year. Crime detection is no longer dependent upon the police being called; now they can systematically monitor and video-record crimes, sending appropriate squads to deal with them.

New digital technologies can also put faces into an electronic file of suspects so that previous shoplifters in stores can be identified as soon as they enter the shop! Developing systems are also going to be able to electronically identify people through the unique iris patterns in their eyes or through their unique voices. This could mean, for example, that passports or credit cards will become things of the past, as features of our body are digitally scanned as a unique identifying personal bar code!

CONTROVERSY AND DEBATE

THE EVER-PRESENT GAZE: CCTV SURVEILLANCE IN BRITAIN

Below is a fictional account by Norris and Armstrong (1999) of Thomas Kearn's day as he encounters various forms of surveillance. As you read it, spot the

different kinds of surveillance technique at work (they are numbered). When you have finished, chart your own day and see if it looks at all like this.

'Thomas Kearn's day starts as usual. At 7.15 am the sounds of BBC Radio Four, emanating from his clock radio, penetrate his slumbering consciousness.

CONTROVERSY AND DEBATE CONTINUED

He wakes quickly, showers and dresses in his best suit, which flatters his 38-year-old frame. His ten-year-old son and four-year-old daughter are washed and dressed by the time he joins them for breakfast. At 8.15 he kisses his wife goodbye and shuts the front door of his apartment behind him, children in tow, to dispatch them to school and nursery, before embarking on another office day. They head towards the lift along the concrete walkways and are captured on a covert video surveillance operation, set up by the local authority, aimed at identifying residents who are dealing in drugs from their premises (1). ... As they wait for the lift, their presence is monitored on the concierge's video system 12 floors below, as is their descent, for there is also a camera in the lift and their predictable daily routine is preserved on tape to be stored for 28 days, or longer if necessary (2). As they walk from the lobby of their apartment block to the car, it is not only the concierge who monitors the Kearns' departure, but Mr Adams on the fifteenth floor, who has tuned his television to receive output from the Housing Estate's cameras (3).

Thomas drives out of the estate on to the dual-carriageway and, although vaguely aware of the sign that declares 'reduce your speed now – video cameras in operation', still drives at 10 miles an hour over the speed limit and trips the automatic speed cameras (4). By 8.30 he has dropped his daughter off at the CCTV-monitored nursery (5) and is heading towards his son's school. He stops at a red light, which is as well because had he jumped it, another picture would have been taken to be used as evidence in his prosecution (6). As they wait in the playground for the buzzer to signal the start of school, they are filmed by a covert camera secreted in the building opposite to monitor the playground for signs of drug dealing (7) and their goodbye kiss is also captured on the school's internal CCTV system which monitors every entrance and exit (8). Noticing that his fuel tank is nearly empty, he drives to the petrol station and fills up. He knows that he is being filmed as a large sign at the cash desk declares: 'These premises are under 24-hour video surveillance' (9).

He leaves the garage and approaches the station, and quietly curses as he is stopped by the barriers at the railway crossing. His location is caught on one of the four Railtrack cameras monitoring the crossing specifically to ensure that the intersection of road and track is clear when the train crosses (10). A few minutes later he is parked in the car park opposite the station under the watchful eye of another set of cameras (11).

As usual, Thomas buys a newspaper at the newsagents, and is filmed by their in-store security cameras as he does so. No one is monitoring the images from the two cameras but they are taped on a multiplex video recorder which records the images from both cameras on one tape and enables any incident to be reviewed should it be necessary (12). Before buying his ticket, he makes a telephone call from the public box on the station forecourt to remind his wife that he will be late home. Unbeknown to him he is filmed by a covert camera installed by British Telecom to try to catch those who vandalise their telephone boxes and hoax callers to the emergency services (13). His call made, he buys his ticket, walks to the platform and waits for his train, all of which has been recorded and monitored by the 32 cameras operating at the station (14). On arrival at his destination, he walks the short distance to his office and smiles at the camera monitoring the reception area (15). He is, however, unaware that his movements are being recorded by a number of covert cameras hidden in the smoke detector housings as he walks along the corridor towards his office (16).

The story continues and leads us to consider residential surveillance, school surveillance, road traffic surveillance, telephone and cash machine surveillance, railway surveillance, retail and commercial surveillance, hospital surveillance, football stadia surveillance and police surveillance.

CONTINUE THE DEBATE:

1. Consider whether the rapid rise of CCTV is valuable. What are its chief advantages? What problems does it bring?

2. Is this the face of the future? Where might the limits of CCTV lie? Can it be checked now?

3. Read Orwell's *Nineteen Eighty-Four* and consider whether Orwell's reality has now become a commonplace part of everyday life in the UK.

Sources: Norris and Armstrong (1999: 40–42); Lyon (2001).

But not all surveillance operates so formally. Another interesting development has been the informal operation of *Neighbourhood Watch Schemes*. Starting in 1983, there has been an enormous growth in the numbers of people who want to watch over their communities. By 1996, it was estimated that there were some 143,000 such schemes in the UK (Morgan and Newburn, 1997: 62). Likewise, systems of electronic tagging – a system of home confinement aimed at monitoring, controlling and modifying the behaviour of defendants or offenders – have been introduced since the mid-1980s in a number of countries, including Canada, the United States, the UK, Sweden, Norway and Denmark. Here, the offender wears an electronic bracelet or anklet and is monitored for 24 hours a day. Public opinion was initially against the idea, and some governments, such as that in the UK, found it difficult to implement initially (not least because of the technical problems). But with adequate liaison with probation committees, it is slowly becoming one more pathway open to the penal system. It is much cheaper than imprisonment and has a moderate success rate. The main reasons for failure seem to be linked to alcohol and drug misuse.

The downside of all this, of course, is a civil liberties concern: we may never quite know who is watching us, when or where. George Orwell's nightmare world of *Nineteen Eighty-Four* may finally be upon us.

In sum, there has been a major expansion in social control and surveillance in modern societies. Boundaries of control are being blurred and many new deviants are being 'created' through this system.

Perpetuating the death penalty

As newer forms of control appear in the twenty-first century, so older ones might disappear. While the death penalty has a long history as a response to all kinds of crime, it has now been abolished in some 111 countries (in 76 countries for all crimes whereas other countries have kept it for exceptional crimes such as war crimes, or still have it as a law but have an established practice of not enforcing it). At the same time, countries such as the United States, China and many African states still enforce the death penalty (Map 16.1).

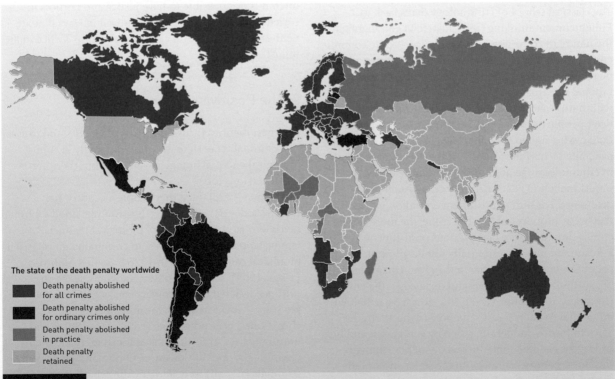

The state of the death penalty worldwide

- Death penalty abolished for all crimes
- Death penalty abolished for ordinary crimes only
- Death penalty abolished in practice
- Death penalty retained

Map 16.1   The Death Penalty in Global Perspective

This map shows the extent to which different degrees of the death penalty are still allowed in various parts of the world. Abolition of the death penalty has often been seen as the hallmark of a 'civilised' society. If this is so, what does this map suggest about the state of the world?

Among the advanced industrial societies, the United States retains the death penalty (it also has an oddly high homicide rate when compared with similar societies). Since 1976, when the death penalty was restored, roughly 912 people have been executed. Of these, 311 were black, 522 were white, and 57 were Hispanic. At the start of 2004, there were some 3,500 people (99 per cent of them are men) still awaiting execution in Death Row.

Explaining crime and deviance

We have so far shown how crime has definite social patterns, and we have examined some of the ways in which society responds to the criminal. Now we are ready for the question that haunts most people: just what makes people criminal or deviant? How can we explain this? Too often, though, this is the only question that people ask: why do people do it, and how can we stop them? What sociologists try to make clear is that crime is bound up with the very conditions of a society.

1. The classical school

The classical school of criminology dates back to Enlightenment thinking (see Chapter 1) and highlights the nature of crime as a rational choice. People commit crimes when they can (a) maximise their gains and (b) be relatively sure of not being punished. Crime is a rational act. This means that a great deal of emphasis within this school turns to adjusting the penal system to deter people from committing crimes. Cesare Beccaria, an Italian who argued for major penal reform in 1974, is generally seen as the founder of the 'Classical tradition' in criminology. He questioned the nature of severe punishment and advocated instead a system of deterrence. For him, punishments could only deter if they were 'proportional' to the crime: the more serious crimes should receive more serious punishments. Punishment must be essentially public, prompt, necessary, the least possible in the given circumstances, proportionate to the crimes and dictated by the laws (Beccama, 1963, orig. 1764). His ideas have remained influential. What is a just sentence? In the 1970s the 'Back to Justice' model suggested by von Hirsch and his colleagues claimed that 'the severity of punishment should be commensurate with the seriousness of the wrong' (von Hirsch, 1976: 66). They argued that:

- The degree of likelihood that the offender might return to crime should be irrelevant to the choice of sentence. He should be sentenced on what he has done.

- Indeterminate sentences should be abolished. Particular crimes merits particular punishments, and offenders should know what they will get.

- Sentencing discretion should be sharply reduced. A system of standardised penalties should be introduced.

- Imprisonment should be limited to serious offences – usually for crimes of serious harm.

- Milder penalties should not claim to rehabilitate, but simply be less severe punishments. (von Hirsch, 1976)

The problems with the classical model

Critics have suggested a number of problems with these classical ideas. First, they argue, it suggests that crime is a free choice and, as we shall see, many accounts of crime argue that it is determined in some way (from poor family background to unemployment). If this is so, simple deterrence will not work. Secondly, it assumes that people are rational, free and self-interested. If they can see they will be punished, they will be deterred; if they think they can get away with crime, they will. But not all human activity is like this. Finally, the theory assumes that societies work in fair and just ways, whereas often it is not possible to have justice and fairness in societies that are themselves organised in ways that are neither just nor fair. You cannot easily have 'justice in an unjust society'.

2. The Positivist school

Positivist theories focus on the characteristics and causes of a criminal type. Here we will look briefly at some biological and psychological versions (but there are social versions too).

Chapter 7 explained that people a century ago understood – or, more correctly, misunderstood – human behaviour as an expression of biological instincts. Understandably, early interest in criminality emphasised biological causes as well. In 1876 Caesare Lombroso (1835–1909), an Italian physician who worked in prisons, declared that criminals have a distinctive physique – low foreheads, prominent jaws and cheekbones, protruding ears, excessive hairiness and unusually long arms that, taken together, made them resemble the ape-like ancestors of human beings. Many criminals (not all) were atavistic throwbacks to an earlier form of species on the evolutionary scale (Lombroso 1970, 1911: 68).

But Lombroso's work was flawed. Had he looked beyond prison walls, he would have realised that the physical features he attributed exclusively to prisoners actually were found throughout the entire population. We now know that no physical attributes, of the kind described by Lombroso, distinguish criminals from non-criminals (Goring, 1972; orig. 1913).

In the middle of the twentieth century, William Sheldon and colleagues (1949) took a different tack, positing that body structure might predict criminality. Sheldon categorised hundreds of young men in terms of body type and, checking for any criminal history, concluded that delinquency occurred most frequently among boys with muscular, athletic builds. Sheldon Glueck and Eleanor Glueck (1950) confirmed Sheldon's conclusion, but cautioned that a powerful build does not necessarily cause or even predict criminality. The Gluecks postulated that parents treat powerfully built males with greater emotional distance so that they, in turn, grow up to display less sensitivity towards others. Moreover, in a self-fulfilling prophecy, people who expect muscular boys to act like bullies may provoke such aggressive behaviour.

Recent genetics research and the Human Genome Project (see Chapter 22) continue to seek possible links

C. LOMBROSO — *L'homme criminel*.   Pl. XXXVII.

FOUS CRIMINELS.

An example from Lombroso's study that claimed to relate physiognomy to criminal nature. This plate shows a variety of 'typical' criminals. Lombroso, 'L'homme criminel' plate xxxvii, 1895.

Source: © Mary Evans Picture Library

between biology and crime. To date, no conclusive evidence connects criminality to any *specific* genetic flaw. Yet people's overall genetic composition, in combination with social influences, may account for some variation in criminality (Rowe and Osgood, 1984; Wilson and Herrnstein, 1985; Jencks, 1987).

The key features of positivism

Despite differences, what most biological or psychological theories have in common is a particular approach or paradigm towards crime. This paradigm has been called *positivistic criminology* by the sociologist David Matza (1964) and it has three major characteristics.

First, it always focuses upon *the criminal as a specific type of person*. Thus criminology started to draw up long classification systems of different kinds of offender. Lombroso, for example, identified not just the born criminal, but also the emotional criminal, the morally insane criminal and the masked epileptic criminal.

Second, it looks for the *ways in which criminals differ from others*. The focus is upon finding the different characteristics, which may range from body parts (for example, size and weight of skulls) or body types or personality types. Long lists of ways in which offenders differ from non-offenders can be drawn up. This was advanced greatly by new technologies such as photography in the nineteenth century (which could record bodily and facial features) and fingerprint testing in the twentieth century. Most recently, chromosome typing (the XYY chromosome is said to be linked to violent offences) and DNA testing have become the focus of attention. The police now make regular use of 'criminal profiling'.

Third, positivism *seeks out explanations for criminal conduct as being in some way out of control* of the criminal who perpetrates criminal acts. Thus, crime is caused by 'feeble-mindedness', 'atavistic regression', 'unsuccessful socialisation' or 'XYY chromosomes'. Crime, says Matza, is not a free choice but is determined. Positivism is a deterministic theory.

Although this general account of crime is called positivistic criminology, it should not be confused with positivism introduced in Chapter 2, although it does have many similarities. Common to both is the belief in science. But as we have seen (Chapter 3) and shall see further (Chapter 22), science is not itself a straightforward idea.

Critical comment

At best, biological theories that trace crime to specific physical traits explain only a small proportion of all crimes. At this point, we know too little about the links between genes and human behaviour to draw any firm conclusions (Daly and Wilson, 1988). Likewise, although psychologists have demonstrated that personality patterns have some connection to delinquency and other types of deviance, the value of this approach is limited by one key fact: the vast majority of serious crimes are committed by people whose psychological profiles are *normal*.

The positivist approach to crime spotlights criminals as people; it offers no insight into how some kinds of behaviour come to be defined as deviant in the first place. Both biological and psychological approaches view deviance as an individual attribute without exploring how conceptions of right and wrong initially arise, why people define some rule breakers but not others as deviant, or the role of social power in shaping a society's system of social control.

3. Functionalism and the social foundations of deviance

Although we tend to think of deviance in terms of the free choice or personal failings of individuals, all behaviour – deviance as well as conformity – is shaped by society. There are three social foundations of deviance, identified below.

1. *Deviance varies according to cultural norms*. No thought or action is inherently deviant; it becomes deviant only in relation to particular norms. The life patterns of rural Icelanders, urban Californians and Welsh mining communities differ in significant ways; for this reason, what people in each area prize or scorn varies as well. Laws, too, differ from place to place. In Amsterdam, as we have seen in the European Eye box on page 436, the use of soft drugs is permitted, and there are even shops for their sale. In the rest of Europe, marijuana is outlawed.

2. *People become deviant as others define them that way*. Each of us violates cultural norms regularly, occasionally to the extent of breaking the law. For example, most of us have at some time walked around talking to ourselves or have 'borrowed' supplies, such as pens and paper, from the workplace. Whether such activities are sufficient to define us as mentally ill or criminal depends on how others perceive, define and respond to any given situation.

3. *Both rule making and rule breaking involve social power*. The law, Karl Marx asserted, amounts to little more than a strategy by which powerful people protect their interests. For example, the owners of an unprofitable

factory have a legal right to close their business, even if doing so throws thousands of people out of work. But if workers commit an act of vandalism that closes the same factory for a single day, the workers are subject to criminal prosecution. Similarly, a homeless person who stands on a street corner denouncing the city government risks arrest for disturbing the peace; a politician during an election campaign does exactly the same thing while receiving extensive police protection. In short, norms and their application are linked to social inequality.

The functions of crime

Functionalist theory teaches us a great paradox about crime and deviance: that far from always being disruptive, it may contribute to a social system and underlie the operation of society. In his pioneering study of deviance, Emile Durkheim (1964a; orig. 1895; 1964b; orig. 1893) made the remarkable assertion that there is nothing abnormal about deviance; in fact, it performs four functions that are essential to society.

1. *Deviance affirms cultural values and norms.* Culture involves moral choices. Unless our lives dissolve into chaos, people prefer some attitudes and behaviours to others. But any conception of virtue rests upon an opposing notion of vice. Just as there can be no good without evil, then, there can be no justice without crime. Deviance, in short, is indispensable to the process of generating and sustaining morality.

2. *Responding to deviance clarifies moral boundaries.* By defining some individuals as deviant, people draw a social boundary between right and wrong. For example, a university marks the line between academic honesty and cheating by disciplining those who commit plagiarism.

3. *Responding to deviance promotes social unity.* People typically react to serious deviance with collective outrage. In doing so, Durkheim explained, they reaffirm the moral ties that bind them. For example, most US citizens joined together in a chorus of condemnation after suicide bombers hijacked several planes and crashed them into the Pentagon and the twin towers of the World Trade Center on 11 September 2001.

4. *Deviance encourages social change.* Deviant people, Durkheim claimed, push a society's moral boundaries, suggesting alternatives to the status quo and encouraging change. Moreover, he declared, today's deviance sometimes becomes tomorrow's morality (1964a; orig. 1895: 71). In the 1950s, for example, many people denounced rock-and-roll music as a threat to the morals of youth and an affront to traditional musical tastes. Since then, however, rock and roll has been swept up in the musical mainstream, becoming a multibillion-dollar industry.

4. Strain theories

Merton's strain theory

While deviance is inevitable in all societies, Robert Merton (1938, 1968) argues that excessive violations arise from particular social arrangements. Specifically, the scope and character of deviance depend on how well a society makes cultural *goals* (such as financial success) accessible by providing the institutionalised *means* (such as schooling and job opportunities) to achieve them. This tension or norm breakdown he called *anomie*. We have seen this term before in the writings of Durkheim (see Chapter 4).

Writing originally about North American society in the 1930s, Merton argued that the path to *conformity* was to be found in pursuing conventional goals by approved means. The true 'success story', in other words, is someone who gains wealth and prestige through talent and hard work. But not everyone who desires conventional success has the opportunity to attain it. Children raised in poverty, for example, may see little hope of becoming successful if they 'play by the rules'. As a result, they may seek wealth through one or another kind of crime – say, by dealing in cocaine. Merton called this type of deviance *innovation* – the attempt to achieve a culturally approved goal (wealth) by unconventional means (drug sales).

According to Merton, the 'strain' between a culture's emphasis on wealth and the limited opportunity to get rich gives rise, especially among the poor, to theft, the selling of illegal drugs or other forms of street hustling. In some respects, at least, a 'notorious gangster' such as Al Capone was quite conventional – he pursued the fame and fortune at the heart of the 'American dream'. But, like many minorities who find the doors to success closed, this bright and enterprising man blazed his own trail to the top. As one analyst of the criminal world put it:

> The typical criminal of the Capone era was a boy who had . . . seen what was rated as success in the society he had been thrust into – the Cadillac, the big bankroll, the elegant apartment. How could he acquire that kind of recognisable status? He was almost always a boy of outstanding initiative, imagination, and ability; he was the kind of boy who, under different conditions, would have been a captain of industry or a key political figure of his time. But he

hadn't the opportunity of going to Yale and becoming a banker or broker; there was no passage for him to a law degree from Harvard. There was, however, a relatively easy way of acquiring these goods that he was incessantly told were available to him as an American citizen, and without which he had begun to feel he could not properly count himself as an American citizen. He could become a gangster.

(Allsop, 1961: 236)

The inability to become successful by normative means may also prompt another type of deviance that Merton calls *ritualism* (see Table 16.5). Ritualists resolve the strain of limited success by abandoning cultural goals in favour of almost compulsive efforts to live 'respectably'. In essence, they embrace the rules to the point where they lose sight of their larger goals. Lower-level bureaucrats, Merton suggests, often succumb to ritualism as a way of maintaining respectability.

A third response to the inability to succeed is *retreatism* – the rejection of both cultural goals and means so that one, in effect, 'drops out'. Retreatists include some alcoholics and drug addicts, and some of the street people found in cities. The deviance of retreatists lies in unconventional living and, perhaps more seriously, in accepting this situation. The fourth response to failure is *rebellion*. Like retreatists, rebels reject both the cultural definition of success and the normative means of achieving it. Rebels, however, go one step further by advocating radical alternatives to the existing social order. Typically, they call for a political or religious transformation of society, and often join a counterculture.

Table 16.5	Merton's theory of anomie and its adaptations	
Mode	**Institutionalised means (hard work)**	**Societal goal (acquisition of wealth)**
Non-deviant		
Conformity	+	+
Deviant		
Innovation	–	+
Ritualism	+	–
Retreatism	–	–
Rebellion	±	±

Note: + indicates acceptance; – indicates rejection; ± indicates replacement with new means and goals

Source: adapted from Merton (1968: 1940)

What is important in this kind of explanation is that it looks at society as a whole and finds stresses and strains within the system that seem to generate 'weak spots' – crime is induced through a system which has potential for contradiction and conflict. Merton's theory has been extremely influential in the development of 'delinquent gang theory', as we shall see.

Youthful deviant subcultures

Albert Cohen's (1971; orig. 1955) study of delinquent boys pioneered the idea of boys becoming delinquent because of what he termed '**status frustration**', *the process by which people feel thwarted when they aspire to a certain status*. In schools especially, Cohen noted that boys from more deprived backgrounds often found school life an alienating and frustrating experience. They wanted to be successes initially, but found that they had not developed the skills to do this in their family and community life. For example, reading books was alien, and being polite and well spoken hard. Their cultural differences had poorly equipped them for school life. Frustrated, Cohen suggests they invert the values of the school – achievement, hard work and planning for the future – and develop instead what can be called a contraculture: where values of non-achievement, playing around and not thinking of the future become deliberately, almost perversely, their goals. Cohen asserts that delinquency is most pronounced among lower-class youths because it is they who contend with the least opportunity to achieve success in conventional ways. Sometimes those whom society neglects seek self-respect by building a deviant subculture that 'defines as meritorious the characteristics they *do* possess, the kinds of conduct of which they *are* capable' (Cohen, 1971; orig. 1955: 66). Having a notorious street reputation, for example, may win no points with society as a whole, but it may satisfy a youth's gnawing desire to 'be somebody'.

Walter Miller (1970; orig. 1958) agrees that deviant subcultures typically develop among lower-class youths who contend with the least legitimate opportunity. He spotlights six focal concerns of these deviant subcultures: (1) *trouble*, arising from frequent conflict with teachers and police; (2) *toughness*, the value placed on physical size, strength and athletic skills, especially among males; (3) *smartness* (or 'street smarts'), the ability to out-think or 'con' others, and to avoid being similarly taken advantage of; (4) *excitement*, the search for thrills, risk or danger to escape from a daily routine that is predictable and unsatisfying; (5) a preoccupation with *fate*, derived from the lack of control these youths feel over their own lives; and (6) *autonomy*, a desire for freedom often expressed as resentment towards figures of authority.

Four girls from 'Gang 18', Secca, Sleepy, La Gata and La Diabla, make the symbol 18 with their hands. San Salvador, El Salvador

Source: © Jérome Sessini/In Visu/Corbis

Richard Cloward and Lloyd Ohlin (1966) also extended Merton's theory in their investigation of delinquent youth. They maintain that criminal deviance results not simply from limited legitimate opportunity but also from available illegitimate opportunity. In short, deviance or conformity grows out of the *relative opportunity structure* that frames young people's lives.

Consider, once again, the life of Al Capone. An ambitious individual denied legitimate opportunity, he organised a criminal empire to take advantage of the demand for alcohol in the United States during Prohibition (1920–33). As Capone's life shows, illegal opportunities foster the development of *criminal subcultures* that offer the knowledge, skills and other resources people need to succeed in unconventional ways. Indeed, gangs may specialise in one or another form of criminality according to available opportunities and resources (Sheley *et al.*, 1995).

But some poor and highly transient neighbourhoods may lack almost any form of opportunity – legal or illegal. Here, delinquency often surfaces in the form of *conflict subcultures* where violence is ignited by frustration and a desire for fame or respect. Alternatively, those who fail to achieve success, even by criminal means, may sink into *retreatist subcultures*, dropping out through abuse of alcohol or other drugs.

Critical comment

Derived from Durkheim's analysis, Merton's strain theory has also come under criticism for explaining some kinds of deviance (theft, for example) far better than others (such as crimes of passion or mental illness). In addition, not everyone seeks success in conventional terms of wealth, as strain theory implies. As we noted in Chapter 5, members of our society embrace many different cultural values and are motivated by various notions of personal success.

The general argument of Cloward and Ohlin, Cohen, and Miller points in interesting directions, but it falls short by assuming that everyone shares the same cultural standards for judging right and wrong. Moreover, we must be careful not to define deviance in ways that unfairly focus attention on poor people. If crime is defined to include stock fraud as well as street theft, offenders are more likely to include affluent individuals. Finally, all structural–functional theories imply that everyone who violates conventional cultural standards will be branded as deviant. Becoming deviant, however, is actually a highly complex process, as the next section explains.

5. Learning theories

Sutherland's differential association theory

Learning any social patterns – whether conventional or deviant – is a process that takes place in groups. According to Edwin Sutherland (1940), any person's tendency towards conformity or deviance depends on the relative frequency of association with others who encourage conventional behaviour or norm violation. This is Sutherland's theory of *differential association*.

6. Labelling theory

Labelling theory claims that *deviance and conformity result not so much from what people do as from how others respond to those actions; it highlights social responses to crime and deviance*. Consider these situations. An office worker

No social class stands apart from others as being either criminal or free from criminality. According to various sociologists, however, people with less stake in society and their own future typically exhibit less resistance to some kinds of deviance. Here in Sao Paulo we see a drug addict prostitute with a client.

Source: Network/Bilderberg © M Ende

'borrows' a computer from the office; a married man at a convention in a distant city has sex with a prostitute; a Member of Parliament drives home drunk after a party. In each case, 'reality' depends on the response of others. Is the first situation a matter of borrowing or is it theft? The consequences of the second case depend largely on whether news of the man's behaviour follows him back home. In the third situation, is the official an active socialite or a dangerous drunk? The social construction of reality, then, is a highly variable process of detection, definition and response. Because 'reality' is relative to time and place, one society's conventions may constitute another's deviance.

In its narrowest version, labelling theory asks what happens to criminals after they have been labelled, and suggests that crime may be heightened by criminal sanctions. Thus, sending an offender to prison may actually work to criminalise him or her further, and stigmatising minor infractions at too early an age may lead a young offender into a criminal career. In a broadest version, the theory suggests that criminology has given too much attention to criminals as types of people and insufficient attention to the panoply of social control responses – from the law and the police to media and public reactions – which help to give crime its shape.

Although the elementary understanding of the way in which criminal responses may shape crime goes back a long way – caught in popular phrases like 'give a dog a

bad name', etc. – the twentieth-century origins of the theory are usually seen to lie with Frank Tannenbaum in his classic study *Crime and the Community* (1938). Here he argued that:

> The process of making the criminal, therefore, is a process of tagging, defining, identifying, segregating, describing, emphasizing, evoking the very traits that are complained of. ... The person becomes the thing he is described as being. ... The way out is a refusal to dramatize the evil.
>
> (Tannenbaum, 1938: 19–20)

The theory also connects to the sociological ideas of Durkheim, G. H. Mead, the Chicago School, symbolic interactionism and conflict theory, and draws upon both the idea of a 'self-fulfilling prophecy' and the dictum of W. I. Thomas that 'when people define situations as real they become real in their consequences' (W.I. Thomas and D.S. Thomas, 1928).

It was not really until the period between the early 1960s and the late 1970s that labelling theory became a dominant sociological theory of crime, influential in challenging orthodox positivist criminology. During this heyday the key labelling theorists were usually seen to be the North American sociologists Howard S. Becker and Edwin Lemert.

Becker, whose own work focused on marijuana use and its control, outlined the broad problem of labelling when he asked: 'We [should] direct our attention in research and theory building to the questions: who applied the label of deviant to whom? What consequences does the application of a label have for the person so labelled? Under what circumstances is the label of a deviant successfully applied?' (Becker, 1963: 3). In what became the canonical statement of labelling theory, he announced that:

> Social groups create deviance by making the rules whose infraction constitutes deviance, and by applying those rules to particular people and labeling them as outsiders. ... Deviance is *not* a quality of the act the person commits, but rather a consequence of the application by others of rules and sanctions to an 'offender'. The deviant is one to whom that label has successfully been applied: deviant behaviour is behaviour that people so label.
>
> (Becker, 1963: 9)

Primary and secondary deviance

Edwin Lemert (1951, 1972) notes that many episodes of norm violation – say, truancy or under-age drinking – provoke little reaction from others and have little effect on a person's self-concept. Lemert calls such passing episodes *primary deviance*.

But what happens if other people take notice of someone's deviance and make something of it? If, for example, people begin to describe a young man as a 'boozer' and push him out of their social circle, he may become embittered, drink even more and seek the company of others who condone his behaviour. So the response to initial deviance can set in motion *secondary deviance*, by which an individual engages in repeated norm violations and begins to take on a deviant identity. The development of secondary deviance is one application of the Thomas theorem, which states: 'Situations defined as real become real in their consequences' (Thomas 1928).

The terms *primary and secondary deviance* capture the distinction between original and effective causes of deviance: primary deviance arises from many sources but 'has only marginal implications for the status and psychic structure of the person concerned', whereas secondary deviance refers to the ways in which stigma and punishment can actually make the crime or deviance 'become central facts of existence for those experiencing them, altering psychic structure, producing specialised organisation of social roles and self regarding attitudes' (Lemert, 1972: 40–41). Deviant ascription became a pivotal or master status. It was Lemert who argued that rather than seeing crime as leading to control, it may be more fruitful to see the process as one in which control agencies structured and even generated crime.

Stigma

The onset of secondary deviance marks the emergence of what Erving Goffman (1963) called a *deviant career*. As individuals develop a strong commitment to deviant behaviour, they typically acquire a **stigma**, *a powerfully negative social label that radically changes a person's self-concept and social identity.*

Stigma operates as a master status (see Chapter 7), overpowering other dimensions of social identity so that an individual is diminished and discounted in the minds of others and, consequently, socially isolated. Sometimes an entire community formally stigmatises individuals through what Harold Garfinkel (1956) calls a *degradation ceremony*. A criminal prosecution is one example, operating much like a university graduation except that people stand before the community to be labelled in a negative rather than a positive way.

Retrospective labelling

Once people have stigmatised a person, they may engage in **retrospective labelling**, *the interpretation of someone's past consistent with present deviance* (Scheff, 1984; orig.

1966). For example, after discovering that a priest has sexually molested a child, others may rethink his past, perhaps musing, 'He always did want to be around young children'. Retrospective labelling distorts a person's biography in a highly selective and prejudicial way, guided more by the present stigma than by any attempt to be fair. This process often deepens a person's deviant identity.

Labelling and mental illness

Is a woman who believes that Jesus rides the bus to work with her every day seriously deluded or merely expressing her religious faith in a highly graphic way? If a man refuses to bathe, much to the dismay of his family, is he insane or simply unconventional? Is a homeless woman who refuses to allow police to take her to a city shelter on a cold night mentally ill or simply trying to live independently?

Psychiatrist Thomas Szasz, a maverick among mental health professionals, charges that people apply the label of insanity to what is only 'difference'; therefore, he concludes, the notion of mental illness should be abandoned (1961, 1970, 1994, 1995). Illness, Szasz argues, is physical and afflicts only the body; mental illness, then, is a myth. The world is full of people whose 'differences' in thought or action may irritate us, but difference is no grounds on which to define someone as sick. To do so, Szasz claims, simply enforces conformity to the standards of people powerful enough to impose their will on others.

Many of Szasz's colleagues reject the notion that all mental illness is a fiction. But some have hailed his work for pointing out the danger of abusing medical practice in the interest of promoting conformity. Most of us, after all, experience periods of extreme stress or other mental disability from time to time. Such episodes, although upsetting, are usually of passing importance. If, however, others respond with labelling that forms the basis of a social stigma, the long-term result may be further deviance as a self-fulfilling prophecy (Scheff, 1984; orig. 1966).

The medicalisation of deviance

Labelling theory, particularly the ideas of Szasz and Goffman, helps to explain an important shift in the way our society understands deviance. Over the last 50 years, the growing influence of psychiatry and medicine has prompted the **medicalisation of deviance**, *the transformation of moral and legal issues into medical matters.*

In essence, medicalisation amounts to swapping one set of labels for another. In moral terms, we evaluate people or their behaviour as 'bad' or 'good'. However, the scientific objectivity of modern medicine passes no moral judgement, utilising instead clinical diagnoses such as 'sick' and 'well'.

To illustrate, until the middle of the twentieth century, people generally viewed alcoholics as weak and morally deficient people, easily tempted by the pleasure of drink. Gradually, however, medical specialists redefined alcoholism so that most people now consider alcoholism a disease, rendering individuals 'sick' rather than 'bad'. Similarly, obesity, drug addiction, child abuse, promiscuity and other behaviours that used to be moral matters are today widely defined as illnesses for which people need help rather than punishment.

The significance of labels

Whether we define deviance as a moral or medical issue has three profound consequences. First, it affects *who responds* to deviance. An offence against common morality typically provokes a reaction by ordinary people or the police. Applying medical labels, however, places the situation under the control of clinical specialists, including counsellors, psychiatrists and physicians.

A second difference is *how people respond* to deviance. A moral approach defines the deviant as an 'offender' subject to punishment. Medically, however, 'patients' need treatment (for their own good, of course). Therefore, while punishment is designed to fit the crime, treatment programmes are tailored to the patient and may involve virtually any therapy that a specialist thinks will prevent future deviance (von Hirsch, 1976).

Third, and most important, the two labels differ on the issue of *the personal competence of the deviant person*. Morally speaking, people take responsibility for their behaviour, whether right or wrong. If we are sick, however, we lose the capacity to control (or even comprehend) our behaviour. Defined as incompetent, the deviant person becomes vulnerable to intense, often involuntary, treatment. For this reason alone, attempts to define deviance in medical terms should be made only with extreme caution.

Critical comment

The various symbolic-interaction theories share a focus on deviance as process. Labelling theory links deviance not to *action* but to the *reaction* of others. Thus some people come to be defined as deviant while others who think or behave in the same way are not. The concepts of stigma, secondary deviance and deviant career demonstrate how people can incorporate the label of deviance into a lasting self-concept.

The labelling perspective brought political analysis into deviancy study. It recognised that labelling was a political act and that 'what rules are to be enforced, what behaviour regarded as deviant and which people labelled as outsiders must . . . be regarded as political questions' (Becker, 1963: 7). From this it went on to produce a series of empirical studies concerning the origins of deviancy definitions through political actions (in such areas as drug legislation, temperance legislation, delinquency definitions, homosexuality, prostitution and pornography) as well as the political bias in the apprehension and adjudication of deviants.

Closely allied to this political analysis was the view of deviance as a form of resistance: people did not simply accept the labels of deviance that others placed upon them. Instead, they employed a series of secondary adjustments – rebelling, retreating, rejecting, rationalising. Here were studies of the crafting of the deviant identity, where self-labelling, deviance avowal and deviance neutralisation took place.

Yet labelling theory has several limitations. First, because this theory takes a highly relative view of deviance, it glosses over how some kinds of behaviour, such as murder, are condemned virtually everywhere. Labelling theory is thus most usefully applied to less serious deviance, such as teenage misconduct or mental illness.

Second, the consequences of deviant labelling are unclear. Research is inconclusive as to whether deviant labelling produces subsequent deviance or discourages further violations (Sherman and Smith, 1992). The deterrent theory of crime, for instance, would actually see sanctions as inhibiting crime rather than amplifying it.

Third, the theory is seen as bringing political implications. Those on the political right often object to the theory on the ground that it seems to sympathise with the criminal and say 'hands off, leave the criminals alone'. Those on the political left, while acknowledging the theory brings power into the analysis, suggest that it fails to look at the wider *conflictual* workings of the society. It is to these latter theories we now turn.

7. Conflict criminologies

Conflict theory demonstrates how deviance reflects inequalities and power. This approach holds that the causes of crime may be linked to inequalities – of class, race and gender – and that who or what is labelled as deviant depends on the relative power of categories of people.

Conflict theory links deviance to power in three ways. First, the norms – and especially the laws – of any society generally bolster the interests of the rich and powerful.

VOICES

THE JACK-ROLLER AND CRIMINOLOGICAL LIFE STORIES

The gathering of life stories has been especially popular in the work of sociologists who study crime. Some of the earliest work of Henry Mayhew, for example, on the life and labour of the London poor provides rich life stories of the criminals of the Victorian underworld. Most famously, the Chicago School of Sociology gathered a great many rich life stories of delinquents in the 1920s and 1930s. The stories often follow a particular narrative convention which suggests:

- The importance of early childhood in the causes of crime
- Some key stages and sequences in criminal careers
- A major epiphany or turning point initiating a life of crime
- A role in integrating the life into a story.

In this short extract, Stanley – the Jack-Roller, interviewed by Clifford Shaw in the early 1930s – speaks. In the book he tells his full story from about the age of four, when he first gets into trouble, on to the age of 16. Here he captures some of the ideas of labelling theory discussed in the text.

Mingling in high society

'The guard led me, along with other prisoners, to the receiving and discharging department, where I was stripped of my civilian clothes and ordered to take a bath. Then I was given my prison uniform and led to the Bertillon Room, where my photographs and measurements were taken, and identification marks recorded. After having my hair shaved off, given a number for a name, and a large tablespoon to eat with, I was assigned to a cell.

The cell was bare, hard, and drab. As I sat on my bunk thinking, a great wave of feeling shook me, which I shall always remember, because of the great impression it made on me. There, for the first time in my life, I realised that I was a criminal. Before, I had been a mischievous lad, a poor city waif, a petty thief, a habitual runaway; but now, as I sat in my cell of stone and iron, dressed in a gray uniform, with my head shaved, small skull cap, like all the other hardened criminals around me, some strange feeling came over me. Never before had I realised that I was a criminal. I really became one as I sat there and brooded. At first I was almost afraid of myself, being like a stranger to my own self. It was hard for me to think of myself in my new surroundings. That night I tried to sleep, but instead I only tossed on my bunk, disturbed by my new life. Not one minute was I able to sleep.'

This brief passage is very suggestive. What do you sense from it and how does it link to a wider understanding of crime?

Why Stanley is especially interesting as a life story is that he was re-interviewed in his seventies by the criminologist Jon Snodgrass. He had moved from Chicago to Los Angeles, married and got divorced, and by and large lived an adult life free of crime. He had, however, been the victim of a mugging himself (see Snodgrass (1982); on life stories and crime in general, see Bennett (1981), Messerschmidt (2000).

THE JACK-ROLLER

A DELINQUENT BOY'S OWN STORY
By Clifford R. Shaw

with a new Introduction by HOWARD S. BECKER

'The Jack-Roller'

Source: *The Jack-Roller: A Delinquent Boy's Own Story.* Photo of the cover Shaw, Clifford. R.S. (1966; orig. 1930), with an introduction by Howard S. Becker, cover design by James Bradford Johnson (University of Chicago Press)

People who threaten the wealthy, either by seizing their property or by advocating a more egalitarian society, come to be tagged as 'common thieves' or 'political radicals'. As noted in Chapter 4, Karl Marx argued that the law (together with all social institutions) tends to support the interests of the rich. Echoing Marx, Richard Quinney makes the point succinctly: 'Capitalist justice is by the capitalist class, for the capitalist class, and against the working class' (1977: 3).

Second, even if their behaviour is called into question, the powerful have the resources to resist deviant labels. Corporate executives who order the dumping of hazardous wastes are rarely held personally accountable for these acts. And, as the O. J. Simpson trial in the United States made clear, even when charged with violent crimes, the rich have the resources to vigorously resist being labelled as criminal (although this particular case – and the main reason for so much interest in it – was complicated by race: O. J. Simpson was not just wealthy, but black).

Third, the widespread belief that norms and laws are natural and good masks their political character. For this reason, we may condemn the unequal application of the law but give little thought to whether the *laws themselves* are inherently fair (Quinney, 1977).

The new criminology

Although there is a long history of conflict theories of crime (from at least Marx onwards), since the 1970s there has been a significant revitalisation of interest. A key book here was by the British sociologists of crime, Ian Taylor, Paul Walton and Jock Young, called *The New Criminology* (1973). This was a substantial critique of all the theories outlined above, and more. Broadly, they argued that most existing theories of crime had not looked at a wide enough range of questions (to take in the wider structural explanations of control as well as of crime, for instance), and had often ignored wider material conflicts at the root of much of the criminal process. At the time of writing, all the authors were Marxists.

Spitzer (1980), also following the Marxist tradition, argues that deviant labels are applied to people who impede the operation of capitalism. First, because capitalism is based on private ownership of wealth, people who threaten the property of others – especially the poor who steal from the rich – are prime candidates for labelling as deviants. Conversely, the rich who exploit the poor rarely are called into question. Landlords, for example, who charge poor tenants high rents and evict those who cannot pay are not considered a threat to society; they are simply 'doing business'.

Second, because capitalism depends on productive labour, those who cannot or will not work risk deviant labelling. Many members of our society think of people out of work – even if through no fault of their own – as deviant.

Third, capitalism depends on respect for figures of authority, so people who resist authority are labelled as deviant. Examples are children who play truant or talk back to parents and teachers; adults who do not cooperate with employers or police; and anyone who opposes 'the system'.

Fourth, anyone who directly challenges the capitalist status quo is likely to be defined as deviant. Into this category fall anti-war activists, environmentalists and labour organisers.

To turn the argument around, society offers positive labels to whomever enhances the operation of capitalism. Winning athletes, for example, have celebrity status because they express the values of individual achievement and competition vital to capitalism.

Additionally, Spitzer notes, we condemn using drugs of escape (marijuana, psychedelics, heroin and crack) as deviant, while espousing the use of drugs that promote adjustment to the status quo (such as alcohol and caffeine).

The capitalist system also strives to control threatening categories of people. Those who are a 'costly yet relatively harmless burden' on society, says Spitzer, include Robert Merton's retreatists (for example, those addicted to alcohol or other drugs), the elderly and people with mental and/or physical disabilities. All are subject to control by social welfare agencies. But those who challenge the very underpinnings of the capitalist system, including the inner-city 'underclass' and revolutionaries – Merton's innovators and rebels – come under the purview of the criminal justice system and, in times of crisis, military forces such as the US National Guard.

Note that both the social welfare and criminal justice systems apply labels that blame individuals and not the system for the control they exert over people's lives. Welfare recipients are deemed unworthy freeloaders; poor people who vent rage at their powerlessness are labelled rioters; anyone who actively challenges the government is branded a radical or a communist; and those who attempt to gain illegally what they cannot otherwise acquire are called common thieves.

Critical comment

Like other analyses of deviance, however, conflict theory has its critics. First, this approach implies that laws and other cultural norms are created directly by and exclusively for the rich and powerful. At the very least, this assumption is an oversimplification, since many segments of our society influence, and benefit from, the political process. Laws also protect workers, consumers and the environment, sometimes in opposition to the interests of the rich.

Second, conflict analysis implies that criminality springs up only to the extent that a society treats its members unequally. However, as Durkheim noted, all societies generate deviance, whatever their economic system.

8. Recent developments

The emergence of left realism

Since the mid-1980s a new debate has appeared. One group of criminologists – from a conflict, Marxist background – have introduced the idea of left realism (Jock Young, Roger Matthews and John Lea, all based at Middlesex University in the UK). Seeing crime as a serious problem, especially in inner-city areas, that has grown in recent years, they analyse what they call 'the square' of crime – the state, society and the public at large, offenders and victims (Figure 16.2). All four factors need to be looked at for all types of crime.

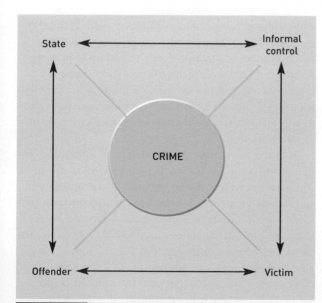

Figure 16.2 The 'square of crime' has become the organising framework for those theorists who call themselves the Left Realists.
Source: adapted from Jock Young

In their argument, a crucial fact is that the victims of crime are overwhelmingly the poor, working-class and often ethnically deprived groups – for example, unskilled workers are twice as likely to be burgled as other workers. *Much crime, then, is largely done by the working class on the working class.* They argue that the causes of crime need to be looked for in deep structural inequalities (see Chapter 10). Crime is produced by **relative deprivation**, *a perceived disadvantage arising from a specific comparison*, and **marginalisation**, where *people live on the edge of society and outside the mainstream with little stake in society overall.*

All this calls for the pursuit of justice at a wide level. The left realists argue for policies of fundamental shifts in economic situations, enlightened prison policies, environmental design and accountable police.

Crime in context

The claims made by left realists are to avoid over-generalised accounts of crime, and to see 'crime in context'. The specific shapes of crime, its causes and the way criminals are controlled, change across the world as society changes. New causes of crime and new patterns of crime appear worldwide. Ian Taylor, for example, argues that the strong shift to a 'market society' since the time of Thatcher and Reagan (discussed in Chapter 14) has not just tended to promote more 'ugly' crime, but has also brought more 'brutish' penal responses (Taylor, 1999). He sees a number of transitions that need to be dealt with in understanding current crime, including:

- *The job crisis.* New forms of work, as described in Chapter 14, have brought much less stable working conditions, under-employment and low pay. This provides a context for many young men especially to find better opportunities for a living in crime than in ordinary employment.

- *The crisis of material poverty and social inequality.* As we saw in Chapters 9 and 10, while most countries across the globe are experiencing some levels of prosperity, inequalities are widening. The marginalisation of whole groups of people makes crime an easier option.

- *The fear of crime and 'the other'.* The world appears to have become a dangerous place to live; there is a 'fear of crime' and a 'fortress mentality'. The heightened sense of insecurity makes many unable to deal reasonably with the problem of crime.

- *Other factors* include the crisis in the family and the wider culture.

The rise of a feminist and gendered criminology

It is an odd irony that conflict analyses of crime discussed above long neglected the importance of gender, despite its focus on social inequality. If, as conflict theory suggests, economic disadvantage is a primary cause of crime, why do women (whose economic position is generally much worse than that of men) commit far fewer crimes than men do?

Until the 1970s, the study of crime and deviance was very much a male province. But the influential work of British sociologist Carol Smart has changed all that. In her book *Women, Crime and Criminology*, published in 1977, she documented the ways in which women had been neglected in the study of crime and deviance. But she also showed that, when they had been included, the approach had usually been highly sexist or blatantly misogynist. For instance, in one notorious case, a criminologist, Otto Pollak, proposed that women are in fact more criminal than men: it is just that they are also more devious and cunning and hence can 'cover up their crimes' better (Pollock 1950)!

How does gender figure in some of the theories we have already examined? It is clear that Robert Merton's strain theory has a very masculine cast in that it defines cultural goals in terms of financial success. Traditionally, at least, this goal has had more to do with the lives of men, while women have been socialised to view success in terms of relationships, particularly marriage and motherhood (Leonard, 1982). A more woman-focused theory might point up the 'strain' caused by the cultural ideals of equality clashing with the reality of gender-based inequality. It could help us see that different forms of deviance may emerge for women: those that are linked to marriage and motherhood. Indeed, women who do not marry ('spinsters') and who do not have children ('childless') are often seen as 'problems' (see Hutter and Williams, 1981; Smart, 1984; Richardson, 1993).

Labelling theory offers greater insight into ways in which gender influences how we define deviance. To the extent that we judge the behaviour of females and males by different standards, the very process of labelling involves sex-linked biases. Further, because society generally places men in positions of power over women, men often escape direct responsibility for actions that victimise women. In the past, at least, men engaging in sexual harassment or other assaults against women have been tagged with only mildly deviant labels, if they have been punished at all.

But feminist criminologists have gone much further than reappraising past theories. They have opened up a whole field of new questions and issues. Among the issues have been the importance of the fear of crime in women's, and especially older women's, lives (see Chapter 13); the gendering of sexual violence, and especially the growth of domestic violence, rape and incest (see Chapter 17); and the gendering of social control.

This last topic concerns the ways in which women are handled differently by police, courts and prisons – often through a code of chivalry or through a mechanism by which women are pathologised and rendered as having medical problems. The classic debate here suggested that while men became criminals, women went mad! Feminist criminologies have thrown critical thought over such statements (see Busfield, 1997).

One further contribution of feminist criminology has been to raise the issue of men, violence and masculinity. They have suggested that since more men are involved in violent crimes, and more young men are involved in 'yob culture', there may be a link between forms of masculinity and forms of crime.

Masculinity and crime

And when you think about it, crime does seem to be a male preserve. Statistics repeatedly show that many more men than women commit crimes. Indeed, as Richard Collier notes, 'most crimes would remain unimaginable without the presence of men' (Collier, 1998: 2; see also Jefferson, 1997). Men are also more likely to come before courts and are more likely to end up in prison. Although there are women's prisons, they are greatly outnumbered by those for men. Figure 16.1 documents some of this. Given all this, then, it might seem obvious that in the past criminology should have focused upon the study of men.

But these facts alone should alert us to something very interesting going on. If there is such a skew towards men, could this mean that the whole process of crime is connected to gender? (Gender is more fully discussed in Chapter 12.) It must be a strong probability. We are not, of course, saying that all men are criminal and all women are not, but we are suggesting that there is something about 'masculinity' – or at least certain forms of it – that makes it more probable that men will commit crimes. We need, for instance, to explain why it is that men commit more crimes and women fewer. And indeed, once we start to raise these issues a whole new field of questions and problems arises.

For instance, in virtually every society in the world there would seem to be more stringent controls on women than men. Historically, our society has restricted the role of women to the home. Even in much of Europe today, many women find limited opportunities in the workplace, in politics and in the military. In many bars of Europe, women remain decidedly unwelcome: these places are men's domains. Moreover, women on their own in public places may be looked upon with some suspicion. And elsewhere in the world, the normative constraints placed on women are often greater still. In Saudi Arabia, women cannot vote or legally operate motor vehicles; in Iran, women who dare to expose their hair or wear make-up in public can be whipped.

James Messerschmidt (1993) in the United States, Tony Jefferson (1993) in the UK and others have started to analyse the roots of crime in masculinity.

The importance of race and ethnicity

Race and ethnicity have been correlated both to crime victimisation and to crime rates. In the UK, for instance, ethnic minorities are more likely to be victims of crime than the white population: some 26 per cent of all black households are likely to be a victim of theft compared to 20 per cent of white households. The figures are 22 per cent for those of Indian origin, and 25 per cent for those of Pakistani/Bangladeshi origin (Morgan and Newburn, 1997: 27).

Looking at crime rates in the UK, in 1995 people of Afro-Caribbean origin made up around 1.5 per cent of the total population, but 11 per cent of males in prison. For women, the figure was of greater disparity – some 20 per cent of women in prisons are Afro-Caribbean. For other ethnic groups in the UK, the figures are different: thus South Asians account for 2.7 per cent of the population and about 3 per cent of the prison population.

In the United States, the figures are even more striking – and more alarming. Official statistics indicate that 68 per cent of arrests for crimes in 1998 involved white people. However, arrests of African Americans were higher than for whites in proportion to their numbers: black people represent 12.7 per cent of the population and 31.9 per cent of arrests for property crimes (versus 65.3 per cent for whites) and 40.2 per cent of arrests for violent crimes (57.7 per cent for whites) (US Federal Bureau of Investigation, 1999).

What accounts for the disproportionate level of arrests among Afro-Caribbeans and African Americans? Several factors stand out. To the degree that prejudice related to colour or class prompts white police to arrest black people more readily and leads citizens more willingly to report 'blacks' to police as suspected offenders, people of colour are overly criminalised (Holmes *et al.*, 1993). In the UK, a 'stop and search' policy shows that in 1994–95, 22 per cent of people from ethnic minorities (compared with 5 per cent of the population) were stopped and searched: the figure in London was 37 per cent. This certainly suggests that 'blacks' are more likely to be placed under suspicion (ISTD Factsheet, 1997).

Second, race is closely linked to inequalities (see Chapter 11) and, as we have seen above, many of the categories of crime suggest that crime is linked to inequality. Criminality is promoted by the sting of being poor in the midst of affluence as poor people come to perceive society as unjust. Looking only at the US figures, unemployment among African American adults is double the rate among whites, two-thirds of black children are born to single mothers (in contrast to one in five white children), and almost half of black children grow up in poverty (as opposed to about one in six white children). With these patterns of inequality, no one should be too surprised at proportionately higher crime rates for African Americans (Sampson, 1987). And the broad pattern also holds for the UK.

Third, remember that the official crime index excludes arrests for offences ranging from drunk driving to white-collar violations. Clearly, this omission contributes to the view of the typical criminal as a person of colour. If we broaden our definition of crime to include driving while intoxicated, insider stock trading, embezzlement and cheating on income tax returns, the proportion of white criminals rises dramatically.

Finally, some categories of the population have unusually low rates of arrest. People of South Asian descent, who account for about 4 per cent of the population, figure in only 1.1 per cent of all arrests. As Chapter 11 documents, South Asians enjoy higher than average incomes and have established a more successful record of educational achievement, which enhances job opportunities. Moreover, the cultural patterns that characterise Asian communities emphasise family solidarity and discipline, both of which inhibit criminality.

CONTROVERSY AND DEBATE

IS CRIME REALLY INCREASING?

Durkheim suggests that crime has always existed, and indeed it is hard to find societies where no crime exists. At the same time, the rate of crime, the fear of crime and the general awareness of crime does differ sharply across different cultures, groups and historical period. So although there is clear evidence of crime going back a long way in British society, we could still argue that it is significantly on the increase. There again, if we are to take seriously recent crime statistics, it would look as if crime is actually on the decrease.

It would be interesting to consider some of the following recent social changes to assess the likelihood of them having an impact upon crime or not.

- As girls become more equal, they may also become more prone to being aggressive and assertive.

- As mass consumerism increases, so the desires for commodities are increased. We may see an escalation in credit card use with a potential increase in fraud.

- As labour markets become more casual and insecure, and as more people enter the informal or underground economy, so people may start to look for alternative ways to survive. Crime, especially in the informal economy, may be one of these.

- As families become less 'traditional', so older styles of parental controls on behaviour become weakened (Morgan, 1978; Dennis and Erdos, 1993).

- As shifts take place in city life (brought about by cars, suburbs, commuting, gated communities, etc.), we now see the development of a 'night-time economy', and all manner of crimes that are facilitated by movement.

- As we witness the massive growth of the new information technologies, so we find new patterns of crime, from cybercrimes to mobile phone theft.

- As young people become a separate and often unsupervised age group, so their criminal activities and drug-using propensities increase.

- As the population becomes older, so there may be a growth of both crimes among the elderly and the elderly as victims of crime (at present they figure relatively low on both counts) (Rothman *et al.*, 2000).

- As we experience changes in social ecology, so all manner of new crimes come into being connected to the environment. Some writers have called these green crimes (see Chapter 24).

- As the electronic mass media such as film and television produce more and more images of crime and violence, so people find such lives more and more plausible.

CONTINUE THE DEBATE

1. What is the evidence for the growth or decline in crime rates? Are some crimes growing more than others? What kind of evidence do you need to support your arguments?

2. Discuss each of the above propositions about social change and crime. Attempt to find evidence for or against them.

Looking ahead

The study of crime and deviance is generally one of the most popular areas that students study in sociology. In part this replicates the wider interests in crime found in society at large (witness the popularity of crime shows of all kinds on television). But often students approach this topic with a distinctly non-sociological approach: they want to explain what makes people murder, take drugs or engage in violence. For sociologists the questions are different.

Sociologists seek to show how crime and deviance are 'normal' and found in all societies. They look at the ways in which control systems grow, change and shape crime and deviance. They examine the crucial role that social inequalities play in structuring crime. And they are concerned with global dimensions: just how different crimes become more prevalent in some cultures than others, and how increasingly globalisation means that criminal worlds stretch across countries and continents. This chapter has opened up some of these topics.

SUMMARY

1. Deviance refers to the labelling of normative violations ranging from mild breaches of etiquette to serious violence.

2. Official statistics are not reliable and reflect a number of social processes. Alternatives to these statistics include victim surveys such as the British Crime Survey.

3. Social control has seen three major developments: the old system expands; a new one is grafted on; and surveillance increases. Modern societies are surveillance societies. There has been a significant expansion of prison populations throughout the world, along with the introduction of the privatisation of prisons.

4. Deviance has societal rather than individual roots because it (a) exists in relation to cultural norms, (b) results from a process of social definition, and (c) is shaped by the distribution of social power. Durkheim asserted that responding to deviance affirms values and norms, clarifies moral boundaries, promotes social unity and encourages social change.

5. Positivistic theories focus upon the characteristics and causes of a criminal type. Biological investigation, from Caesare Lombroso's nineteenth-century observations of convicts to recent research in human genetics, has yet to offer much insight into the causes of crime.

6. Labelling theory holds that deviance arises in the reaction of others to a person's behaviour. Acquiring a stigma of deviance can lead to secondary deviance and the onset of a deviant career.

7. Social conflict theories hold that laws and other norms reflect the interests of powerful members of society. Social conflict theory also spotlights white-collar crimes, which cause extensive social harm even though the offenders are rarely branded as criminals.

8. The square of crime suggests four dimensions that need to be considered: the state, informal control, the offender and the victim.

9. Feminist criminology has grown as a response to a neglect of gender issues in the study of crime. It has led to many new developments, including the study of masculinity and its link to criminality, and the gendering of social control processes.

CRITICAL-THINKING QUESTIONS

1. Look at your own life and consider how far you have become part of the surveillance society.

2. Why do you think crime rates are lower in some countries than in others? The portrait drawn of globalisation and crime by some commentators such as Manuel Castells makes crime problems in particular societies such as the UK fade by comparison. Do you think the globalisation of crime is a serious issue? In what ways? With drugs as an example, consider what might be done to alleviate the situation.

3. Examine the ideas of Michel Foucault on crime and prisons. Do you agree with his implicit view that our so-called 'humane treatment' of prisoners is in fact a controlling and corroding use of power?

4. Trace the emergence of the modern control system. Does it work?

GOING FURTHER

Further reading

Useful introductions to different areas of study in crime:

Eamonn Carrabine, Maggy Lee, Paul Iganski, Ken Plummer and Nigel South, *Criminology: A Sociological Introduction* (2004)
Provides a broad introduction to all the sociological fields of crime and deviance. A lively textbook.

Roger Hopkins Burke, *An Introduction to Criminological Theory* (2001).
A good introduction to the different theories and approaches to crime.

Malcolm Davies, Hazel Croall and Jane Tyrer, *Criminal Justice: An Introduction to the Criminal Justice System in England and Wales* (1995).
Especially good at introducing aspects of the criminal justice system in the UK.

Eugene McLaughlin and John Muncie, *The Sage Dictionary of Criminology* (2001)
A useful set of short essays on key terms and aspects of criminology.

On specific issues raised in the chapter:

Sandra Walkgate, *Gender and Crime: An Introduction* (1995)
A good guide to feminist criminology and gender concerns.

Clive Coleman and Jenny Moynihan, *Understanding Crime Data* (1996)
A clear introductory statement on crime figures and their limits.

Ian Taylor, *Crime in Context* (1999) and Jock Young, *The Exclusive Society* (2000)
Two lively studies that examine the crime problem from a critical perspective.

Stanley Cohen, *Visions of Social Control* (1985),
An important – if now a little outdated – study of changes in social control in the contemporary world.

A major overview of the field:

Mike Maguire *et al.*, *The Oxford Handbook of Criminology* (3nd edn, 2003). This is the key comprehensive text, with very extensive coverage of all the issues. It is a 'big book' and it is quite expensive.

More information

Organisations that can provide useful briefing sheets and background data include:

- *The Institute for the Study and Treatment of Delinquency (ISTD)*, King's College London, Strand, London WC2R 2LS, which produces a regular and very readable magazine on crime called *Criminal Justice Matters* (CJM), as well as the *British Journal of Criminology*.

- *NACRO (the National Association for the Care and Resettlement of Offenders)*, which also provides regular study sheets and bulletins.

- *Penal Reform International*, Unit 450, The Bon Marche Centre, 241-251 Ferndale Road, London, SW9 8BJ and the *Prison Reform Trust*, 15 Northburgh Street, London EC1V 0JR, which are especially concerned with prisons.

Watch a Video

Crime and deviance is one of the most popular genres of both film and writing. This list could be very extensive. Just think of some of the films you have seen recently. Note, too, some classics:

- William Friedkin's *The French Connection* (1971): the first major film – semi-documentary in style – about drug trafficking.

- Steven Sodenbergh's *Traffic* (2000): the film discussed in the opening to this chapter.

- François Truffaut's *Quatre Cents Coups* (*The Four Hundred Blows*) (1959): a classic film on delinquency by the celebrated French film maker Truffaut in which a young boy in Paris finds himself in a detention centre.

- Stanley Kubrick's *A Clockwork Orange* (1970): banned for nearly 30 years, a classic tale of 'modernity and control'.

- Louis J. Gassnier's *Reefer Madness* (1938): seemingly a warning film about the dangers of marijuana to America's youth, it now looks as if it has to be a spoof. But is it? (Also known as *Tell Your Children*.)

- Sydney Lumet's *Twelve Angry Men* (1957): the classic courtroom drama.

- Frederick Wiseman's *Law and Order* (1969): classic documentary – now there are many – on crime.

Connecting up

Connect to other chapters

- Link crime to gender debates in Chapter 12.
- Link problems of measuring crime to discussion of methods in Chapter 3.
- Link crime to groups, organisations and socialisation through Chapters 6 and 7.
- For the development of human rights and worldwide crime, see Chapter 15.

To the websites

- A useful timeline of major criminologists and their work:

  www. crimetheory.com
- A good website on penal matters in the UK, and through it you can enter the Prison Reform Trust:

  www.prisonreformtrust.org.uk/
- International Crime Statistics:

  http://www.crime.org/links
- The International Centre for Prison Studies:

  http://www.prisonstudies.org/

See also the very useful listing found in the webliography of Carrabine *et al.*, *Criminology: A Sociological Introduction* (2004).

For additional case studies, multiple choice questions, internet exercises, and annotated weblinks specific to this chapter, visit this book's website at **www.pearsoned.co.uk/plummer**

CHAPTER 17

FAMILIES AND HOUSEHOLDS

There is no such thing as *the* family – only families.

Diana Gittins (1993: 8)

IN 1980, CHINA BEGAN implementing a strict birth control policy of one child per couple. The government argued that its policy would avoid a population explosion, and indeed it has prevented some 250 million births. The policy has also resulted in a skewed age structure (it is getting older) and gender structure (many more boys have been born as girls have been aborted). There has also been a proliferation of forced abortions and sterilisations; newborn children have been abandoned or killed. Along with this, a hidden population of children, whose birth had to be concealed for fear of reprisals, has appeared. The average size of Chinese families has dropped from 3.96 people to 3.44 people. Recently, some flexibility has been brought into the system (parents outside the cities are often allowed to have a second child if the first-born was a girl).

Meanwhile, in Japan, women are simply not having children – not enough, at least, to replace adults of child-bearing age. Since 1950, in fact, the average number of children born to a Japanese woman during her lifetime has tumbled from 3.65 to 1.38. This precipitous decline is no indication that the Japanese have lost their love for children. Quite the contrary. Virtually all young Japanese couples claim to want children, and even screaming babies on a bus or train elicit smiles and sympathy from fellow travellers. The reason for the declining birth rate is that Japanese women display unprecedented reluctance to marry. Back in 1970, only 20 per cent of Japanese women reaching the age of 30 had yet to wed; today, that share has doubled to 40 per cent.

Why the second thoughts about marriage? For one thing, Japanese culture defines motherhood as a full-time responsibility, which precludes a career. Just as important, the typical Japanese husband works long hours – half are away from home at least 12 hours a day. When he is at home, moreover, the typical Japanese man performs almost no housework and spends little time with his children. To young women in Japan, therefore, marriage commonly amounts to a daily round of housework, doting on youngsters and shuttling older children to special 'cram' schools where they prepare for all-important college entrance examinations. Faced with such prospects, more women are opting to stay single, live with parents, work and enjoy plenty of free time and spending money. Business and governments are alarmed by this. New laws are being made to encourage women to have more children and some businesses are offering up to £6,000 to employees to have children.

Sources: Scharping, 2000; *The Economist*, 1994; *The Guardian*, 31 May 2000

KEY THEMES

- The definition and nature of families
- The main theories of families
- Families and differences in the UK
- Personal cultures and postmodern families

(Left) Carl Larsson – *My Loved Ones*
Source: National Museum, Stockholm
Photo: Sven Nilsson

The state of the family is a 'hot topic' all around the world, not just in Japan and China, where policies on families are very different. In the UK fewer than one in four households now conform to the traditional image of a married or cohabiting couple with children. Indeed, the often presumed model of the traditional nuclear family is now more likely to be found in the UK among households in Bangladeshi and Pakistani communities. In the United States the situation has developed further: one sociologist has suggested that even by 1986 'only 7% of households conformed to the 'modern' pattern of breadwinning father, homemaking mother and one to four children under the age of eighteen' (Stacey, 1996:133). In many countries, especially the Nordic countries and The Netherlands, there are new laws and key debates emerging around same-sex registered partnerships. And 'assisted conception', which ranges from 'test-tube babies' to 'surrogate motherhood' and 'baby selling' on the Internet (to be discussed in Chapter 22), brings new issues (Becker, 2000). All taken together, an important point is made: families are changing dramatically.

This chapter highlights some important recent changes in family life and offers some insights to explain these trends. Yet, as we shall also point out, changing family patterns are nothing new. Nearly two centuries ago, for example, as the Industrial Revolution propelled people from farms to factories, there was much concern over the decline of the family. Today, of course, many of the same concerns surround the rising share of women working, whose careers draw them away from home. In short, changes in other social institutions, especially the economy, keep shaping ways of living together, including marriage and family life.

What are 'families'?

For a long while in sociology, the **family** has been seen as *a social institution, found in all societies, that unites individuals into cooperative groups that oversee the bearing and raising of children*. Most families are built on **kinship**, *a social bond, based on blood, marriage or adoption, that joins individuals into families*. Although all societies contain families, just who is included under the umbrella of kinship has varied through history, and varies today from one culture to another. During the twentieth century, most members of society regarded a **family unit** as *a social group of two or more people, related by blood, marriage or adoption, who usually live together*. Initially, individuals

are born into a family composed of parents and siblings (a *family of orientation* central to socialisation) and in adulthood, people have or adopt children of their own (a *family of procreation*).

Throughout the world, families form around **marriage**, *a legally sanctioned relationship, involving economic cooperation as well as normative sexual activity and child-bearing, that people expect to be enduring*. Embedded in our language is evidence of a cultural belief that marriage alone is the appropriate context for procreation: traditionally, people have attached the label of *illegitimacy* to children born out of wedlock; moreover, *matrimony*, in Latin, means 'the condition of motherhood'. This link between child-bearing and marriage has weakened, however, as the proportion of children born to single women has increased (noted to be nearing one in four).

Many now object to defining as 'families' only married couples and children because that implies that everyone should embrace a single standard. As more and more people forge the non-traditional family ties, which we will discuss later, many are now thinking of kinship in terms of *families of affinity* or **families of choice** (Weston, 1991), *people with or without legal or blood ties who feel they belong together and wish to define themselves as a family*. What does or does not constitute a family, then, is a moral and political matter that lies at the heart of the contemporary 'family values' debate, raised in the European Eye box.

Sociologist Christopher Carrington, however, puts this somewhat differently: 'I understand family as consisting of people who love and care for one another' (Carrington, 1999: 5). Carrington's own family research was not with conventional kin, but involved conducting participant observation research within lesbian and gay families in California. He does not approach the family through ideas of kinship or institutions (which implies something too static) but instead as a series of activities: 'People', he says, '"do" family'. The chapters of his book reflect this as he looks at just how families are achieved through various forms of work: *feeding work* (who cooks, shops, plans); *house work* (who cleans, washes, looks after plants and pets, does the household repairs); *kin work* (looking after the children, visiting parents, etc.); *consumption work* (including the watching of TV, the arranging of holidays, the purchasing of clothes and household goods); and what we might also call *care work*, (looking after partners, children and others). All of this implies some continuing divisions of labour within the family and we shall return to this later in the chapter.

A LESS CENTRAL FAMILY? A REPORT FROM SWEDEN

Sweden is burdened with few of the social problems that are often identified with modern capitalism: in urban Sweden, there is little of the violent crime, drug abuse and grinding poverty that have blighted many other places. This Scandinavian nation seems to fulfil the promise of the modern welfare state, with an extensive and professional government bureaucracy that sees to virtually all human needs.

But Sweden also has very different kinds of family. Because people look to the government – not to spouses – for economic assistance, Swedes are less likely to marry than members of any other industrialised society. For the same reason, Sweden also has a high share of adults living alone (more than 20 per cent). Moreover, a large proportion of couples live together outside marriage (25 per cent) and half of all Swedish children (compared to about one in three in Europe) are born to unmarried parents. Average household size in Sweden is also the smallest in the world (2.2 persons). Finally, Swedish couples (whether married or not) are more likely to break up than partners in any other country. US sociologist David Popenoe sums up by claiming that the family 'has probably become weaker in Sweden than anywhere else – certainly among advanced Western nations. Individual family members are the most autonomous and least bound by the group' (Popenoe, 1991: 69).

Popenoe contends that a growing culture of individualism and self-fulfilment, coupled with the declining influence of religion, began to 'erode' Swedish families back in the 1960s. The movement of women into the labour force also plays a part. Sweden has the lowest proportion of women who are homemakers (10 per cent versus about 25 per cent in Europe) and the highest percentage of women in the labour force (77 per cent versus 59 per cent in Europe).

But, most important, according to Popenoe, is the expansion of the Swedish welfare state, one of the most far-reaching schemes of its kind. The Swedish government offers citizens a lifetime of services – and high taxes. Swedes can count on the government to give them jobs, sustain their income, deliver and educate their children, provide comprehensive health care and, when the time comes, pay for their funeral.

Many Swedes supported this welfare programme, Popenoe explains, thinking it would strengthen families. But with the benefit of hindsight, he concludes, we see that proliferating government programmes actually have been replacing families. Take the case of child care. The Swedish government operates public child-care centres open to all. As officials see it, this system puts care in the hands of professionals, and makes this service equally accessible regardless of parents' income. At the same time, however, the government offers no subsidy for parents who want to care for children in their own home. In effect, then, government has taken over much of the traditional family function of child-rearing.

If this system has solved so many social problems, why should anyone care about the erosion of traditional family life? For two reasons, says Popenoe. First, government can do only at great cost what families used to do for themselves. Recently, Swedes voted to cut back on their burgeoning welfare system because of skyrocketing costs.

Second, can government employees in large child-care centres provide children with the level of love and emotional security they would receive from two parents living as a family? Unlikely, claims Popenoe, noting that small, intimate groups can accomplish some human tasks much better than formal organisations can.

David Popenoe uses the case of Sweden as part of his claim for a return to traditional families. We return to this issue in the concluding box of this chapter.

Sources: Popenoe (1991, 1994) and Herrstrom (1990).

Family and history

When we look at the debate among historians and sociologists over just how the family has changed over time, one thing is clear. The notion of an 'ideal' nuclear family of two parents and two children has, historically, been rare. Throughout history, there have been all kinds of combination – shaped by age cycles, class, region, ethnicity and the like – which have made families very varied and complex. And at any one historical period,

we would not expect families to be all the same. Jean-Louis Flandrin (1979) has shown how, for example, a whole array of family types existed at the same time in different parts of France. And British historian Peter Laslett (1972) studied parish records of English country villages from 1564 to 1821 and found that extended families were rare because of late marriage and shorter lives. But there were also large households – where the richer would take in the poorer as labourers and domestic servants.

MARRIAGE PATTERNS

Cultural norms, as well as laws, identify people as desirable or unsuitable marriage partners. Some marital norms promote **endogamy**, *marriage between people of the same social category.* Endogamy limits marriage prospects to others of the same age, race, religion or social class. By contrast, **exogamy** mandates *marriage between people of different social categories.* In rural India, for example, young people are expected to marry someone of the same caste (endogamy), but from a different village (exogamy).

Throughout the world, societies pressure people to marry someone of the same social background but of the other sex. The logic of endogamy is simple: people of similar social position pass along their standing to offspring, thereby maintaining traditional social patterns. Exogamy, by contrast, helps to forge useful alliances and promotes cultural diffusion.

In industrial societies today, laws prescribe **monogamy** (from Greek meaning 'one union'), *a form of marriage joining two partners.* The high level of divorce and remarriage, however, suggests that serial monogamy is a more accurate description of UK marital practice. While monogamy is the rule throughout the Americas and in Europe, many preindustrial societies – especially in Africa and southern Asia – prescribe **polygamy** (from Greek meaning 'many unions'), *a form of marriage uniting three or more people.* There are two types of polygamy. By far the more common is **polygyny** (from Greek meaning 'many women'), *a form of marriage uniting one male and two or more females.* Islamic societies in Africa and southern Asia, for example, permit men up to four wives. In these societies, however, most families are still monogamous because few men have the wealth needed to support several wives and even more children. **Polyandry** (from Greek meaning 'many men' or 'many husbands') is *a form of marriage joining one female with two or more males.* This pattern appears only rarely. One example can be seen in Tibet where agriculture is difficult. There, polyandry discourages the division of land into parcels too small to support a family and divides the work of farming among many men. Polyandry has also been linked to female infanticide – the aborting of female foetuses or killing of female infants – because a decline in the female population forces men to share women.

Historically, most world societies have permitted more than one marital pattern; even so, most actual marriages have been monogamous (Murdock, 1965; orig. 1949). This cultural preference for monogamy reflects two key facts of life: the heavy financial burden of supporting multiple spouses and children and the rough numerical parity of the sexes, which limit the possibility of polygamy.

Lawrence Stone, in a classic study, has charted three phases of the family in Western Europe between 1500 and 1800: the first was 'Open Lineage' and involved a lack of close relations and lack of privacy, but extensive kin. The second was 'Restricted Patriarchy' (1530–1640) where there were increased loyalties to state and church and less to kin and community. The final stage of 'Closed Domesticated' families highlights privacy, bonds between children and parents and 'affective individualism'. It was 'an open ended, low keyed, unemotional, authoritarian institution' (Stone, 1977).

The English sociologists Michael Young and Peter Willmott have traced the changing form of families in modern Britain. In the 1950s they studied the very strong traditional family ties in 'traditional' Bethnal Green in East London and traced how they weakened as the families moved out to new housing estates such as Greenleigh in outer London (Young and Willmott, 1957). The three-generation (grandparents, parents and child) and larger family is replaced with a smaller nuclear pattern where the relationship between husband and wife becomes more intense. In a later study, Young and Willmott (1973) suggested that these newer families were becoming more 'symmetrical'. That is, the relationships were becoming increasingly equal with husband and wife spending more and more time together. These kinds of change have become a common theme in much of the writing on the family – one expects to find shifts from an extended and often patriarchal form of family to a more nuclear and symmetrical form. However, it must be remembered that this is only one pattern – a largely traditional, working-class one. Families vary and change with class and environment.

Thinking about families: theories and ideas

As in earlier chapters, several theoretical approaches offer a range of insights about the family.

The classic approach – the functions of the family

As we would expect, functionalism suggests we look for the functions of the family. Social scientists have produced long lists of functions, and then debated how they have changed over time. You may like to try to create your own list – what are the tasks of families? – before moving on. Below is a fairly standard listing.

1. *Socialisation*. As explained in Chapter 6, the family is the first and most influential setting for socialisation. Ideally, parents teach children to be well-integrated and contributing members of society (Parsons and Bales, 1955). Of course, family socialisation continues throughout the life cycle. Adults change within marriage, and, as any parent knows, mothers and fathers learn as much from raising their children as their children learn from them.

2. *Regulation of sexual activity*. Every culture regulates sexual activity in the interest of maintaining kinship organisation and property rights. One universal regulation is the **incest taboo**, *a cultural norm forbidding sexual relations or marriage between certain kin*. Precisely which kin fall within the incest taboo varies from one culture to another. The matrilineal Navajo, for example, forbid marrying any relative of one's mother. Our bilateral society applies the incest taboo to both sides of the family but limits it to close relatives, including parents, grandparents, siblings, aunts and uncles. But even brother–sister marriages found approval among the Ancient Egyptian, Incan and Hawaiian nobility (Murdock, 1965; orig. 1949). Reproduction between close relatives can adversely affect the mental and physical health of offspring. But this biological fact does not explain why, among all species of life, only human beings observe an incest taboo. The key reasons to control incest, then, are social. Why? First, the incest taboo minimises sexual competition within families by restricting legitimate sexuality to spouses. Second, it forces people to marry outside their immediate families, forging broader alliances. Third, since kinship defines people's rights and obligations towards each other, forbidding reproduction among close relatives protects kinship from collapsing into chaos.

3. *Social placement*. Families are not *biologically* necessary for people to reproduce, but they do provide for the *social* placement of children. Social identity based on race, ethnicity, religion and social class is ascribed at birth through the family. This fact explains the long-standing preference for so-called legitimate birth. Especially when parents are of similar social position, families clarify inheritance rights and allow for the stable transmission of social standing from parents to children.

4. *Material and emotional security*. People have long viewed the family as a 'haven in a heartless world', looking to kin for physical protection, emotional support and financial assistance. To a greater or lesser extent, most families do provide all these things, although not without periodic conflict.

When all these functions are taken together, families are often seen as 'the backbone of society'.

Critical comment

Functionalism identifies a number of the family's major functions. From this point of view, it is easy to see that society as we know it could not exist without families. But this approach overlooks the great diversity in ways people can live together in the modern world. Children are being socialised outside the traditional family; most people now have sexual relations outside the family; and there is a lot of evidence of abuse and violence within the family that makes it seem a very dysfunctional place. Moreover, functionalism pays little attention to how other social institutions (say, government) could meet at least some of the same human needs. Finally, it minimises the problems of family life. Established family forms reinforce patriarchy and incorporate a surprising amount of violence, with the dysfunctional effect of undermining individual self-confidence, health and well-being, especially of women and children.

Inequality and the family: conflict theory

Rather than concentrating on ways that kinship benefits society, other theorists investigate how families may perpetuate social inequality. The role of families in the social reproduction of inequality takes several forms.

1. *Property and inheritance*. As noted in Chapter 12, Friedrich Engels (1902; orig. 1884) traced the origin of the family to the need to identify heirs so that men (especially in the higher classes) could transmit property to their sons. Families thus support the concentration of wealth and reproduce the class structure in each succeeding generation (Mare, 1991).

2. *Patriarchy.* Engels also emphasised how the family promotes patriarchy. The only way men can know who their heirs are is to control the sexuality of women. Thus, Engels continued, families transform women into the sexual and economic property of men. A century ago in Europe, most wives' earnings belonged to their husbands. Although this practice is no longer lawful, men still exert power over women. Despite moving rapidly into the paid workforce, women continue to be paid less, work in more marginal occupations and still have to bear major responsibility for child-rearing and housework (Fuchs, 1986; Hochschild, 1989; Presser, 1993; Keith and Schafer, 1994; Benokraitis and Feagin, 1995). As we shall see from the work of Delphy and Leonard below, patriarchal families offer considerable benefits to men. They also deprive men of the chance to share in the personal satisfaction and growth derived from close interaction with children.

3. *Race and ethnicity.* Racial and ethnic categories will persist over generations only to the degree that people marry others like themselves. Thus endogamous marriage also shores up the racial and ethnic hierarchy.

A radical feminist approach to the family

Many of the arguments above have been significantly developed by many feminists who see the family as the central location of women's oppression. They argue that men generally benefit greatly from families while women often do not. Until recently, men have nearly always been head of the household and made the key decisions about the family allocating rewards (often payment in kind, such as holidays): even when women work, they often have little decision-making autonomy.

Christine Delphy and Diana Leonard, in their influential book *Familiar Exploitation* (1992), argue that the family is an economic system, where men benefit from the work of women (and in many countries the work of children too). This is not just the work in the labour market (of which they do increasing amounts), but also the work they do at home. Family members work for the head of the household. As they say, it is 'the work women do, the uses to which our bodies can be put, which constitutes the reason for our oppression'.

Many studies suggest that women still do more housework than men, still spend more time looking after the children (especially in the more mundane and humdrum ways) and are much more likely to have to look after the sick and the elderly (Finch, 1989;

Hochschild, 1989). They are also much more likely to have to give moral support to men (who often make little contribution to their wife's work).

These feminist arguments are strong claims and a careful evaluation of the evidence is needed to make sense of this. For instance, in modern families, there are now many single-parent households where women are alone; further, women increasingly are choosing not to marry, to get divorced once married and not to have children. Twenty per cent of women remain childless, by choice.

Critical comment

Some sociologists show how family life maintains social inequalities. During his era, Engels condemned the family as part and parcel of capitalism. Yet non-capitalist societies have families (and family problems) all the same. Kinship and social inequality are deeply intertwined, as Engels argued, but the family appears to carry out various societal functions that are not easily accomplished by other means. And the arguments produced by radical feminists usually fail to take into account the growing trends towards equality in decision-making between men and women.

The micro-sociology of the family

We saw in Chapter 7 how some sociology works not just at the grand macro-level but at the level of the situation. Micro-sociology would explore how individuals shape and experience family life. Seen from the inside, family life amounts to individuals engaging one another in a changing collage of meanings and work. People construct family life, building a reality that differs from case to case and from day to day. As we saw in Christopher Carrington's (1999) work on lesbian and gay families above, 'people do families'. It is work – caring work, feeding work, kin work and so on (Carrington, 1999: 6).

Family living also offers an opportunity for intimacy, a word with Latin roots meaning 'sharing fears'. That is, as a result of sharing a wide range of activities over a long period of time, members of families forge emotional bonds. Of course, the fact that parents act as authority figures often inhibits their communication with younger children. But, as young people reach adulthood, kinship ties typically 'open up' as family members recognise that they share concern for one another's welfare. They also engage in emotional work (see Chapter 7 and Hochschild, 1983; Macionis, 1978a).

Social-exchange analysis

Social-exchange analysis is also a micro-level approach. It depicts courtship and marriage as forms of negotiation (Blau, 1964). In the case of courtship, dating allows each person the chance to assess the likely advantages and disadvantages of taking the other as a spouse, always keeping in mind the value of what one has to offer in return. In essence, exchange analysts contend, individuals seek to make the best 'deal' they can in selecting a partner. Physical attractiveness is one critical dimension of social exchange. In patriarchal societies around the world, beauty has long been a commodity offered by women on the marriage market. The high value assigned to beauty explains women's traditional concern with physical appearance and their sensitivity about revealing their age. For their part, men have traditionally been assessed according to the financial resources they command. Recently, however, because increasing numbers of women are joining the labour force, they are less dependent on men to support them and their children. Thus, the terms of exchange have been converging for men and women.

Critical comments

Micro-level analysis offers a useful counterpoint to functionalist and conflict visions of the family as an institutional system. Adopting an interactional or exchange viewpoint, we gain a better sense of the individual's experience of family life and appreciate how people creatively shape this reality for themselves.

Using this approach, however, we run the risk of missing the bigger picture, namely, that family life is similar for people affected by any common set of economic and cultural forces. UK families vary in some predictable ways according to social class and ethnicity, and, as the next section explains, they typically evolve through stages linked to the life course.

New developments: 'doing families', 'family practices' and personal cultures

More recently, there have been a number of new ways of thinking about families and we will consider some of these here. First, the English sociologist David Morgan has suggested that families can be analysed as a set of 'practices'. At the start of the twenty-first century, most people no longer follow fixed paths for living in families. Like Carrington, he suggests that people are *doing family* rather than simply being in one. Family has come to signify a sense of intimate connections, and much less the formal legal ties of marriage. We are talking now about the multiple ways of doing families. But all this fluidity is not really random: people live their life through a regular set of practices. Rather than simply viewing the family as a fixed 'thing', it is now seen as a set of relationships built around such things as housework, caring, being a mother, being a child, or having sex. These practices highlight:

- *The doing of families* – what actually goes on and gets done in families. This is an active image of activities.
- *The everyday life of families* – we are more concerned with the relatively routine and trivial. David Morgan writes: 'what you had for breakfast today and how you consumed your breakfast may tell the observer as much about your routine understandings of family living as the more dramatic (rituals) such as weddings and funerals' (Morgan, 1999: 17).
- *The processes and fluidity of family life* – practices ebb and flow into each other and one set of practices mixes and merges with others.
- *Regularities* – even if active, people develop patterns, such as 'breakfasting', 'watching television', 'washing baby' or 'having sex'.
- *Interplay of biography and history* – lives are woven together and develop a sense of the past.
- *Interplay of positions* – there are many ways of viewing from the family: children, mothers, fathers, grandparents, visitors, friends, etc. (Morgan, 1999: 17–18).

Family differences in the UK: class, ethnicity and gender

Dimensions of inequality – social class, ethnicity and race, and gender – are powerful forces that shape marriage and family life. While this section addresses each factor separately, they overlap. The focus here is primarily on the UK, but such factors work in all families throughout the world.

Social class

Families can vary enormously across social class (see Chapter 10). Not only does class shape a family's financial security and range of opportunities, it can also affect the family size and shape. For instance, in the UK, families are still likely to be larger among the working class, who also have higher rates of divorce.

In an influential North American study, Lillian Rubin (1976) found that working-class wives deemed a good husband to be one who refrained from violence and excessive drinking and held a steady job. Rubin's middle-class informants, by contrast, never mentioned such things; these women simply *assumed* a husband would provide a safe and secure home. Their ideal husband was a man with whom they could communicate easily and share feelings and experiences.

Such differences reflect the fact that people with higher social standing have more schooling, and most have jobs that emphasise verbal skills. In addition, middle-class couples share a wider range of activities, while working-class life is more sharply divided along gender lines. Conventionally masculine ideas of self-control, Rubin explains, can stifle emotional expressiveness on the part of working-class men, prompting women to turn to each other as confidantes.

Clearly, what women (and men) can hope for in marriage – and what they end up with – are linked to their social class. Much the same holds true for children in families; boys and girls lucky enough to be born into more affluent families enjoy better mental and physical health, develop higher self-confidence, and go on to greater achievement than poor children do (Komarovsky, 1967; Bott, 1971; Rubin, 1976; Fitzpatrick, 1988; McLeod and Shanahan, 1993).

Ethnic minorities and family diversity

As Chapter 11 indicates, ethnicity and race are powerful social forces. The effects of both surface in family life. We must beware of stereotyping: just as there is enormous diversity behind the label 'white families', so there is great variety among ethnic families. But some differences do seem striking. Ethnic family forms in the UK have been subject to change over the past 40 years: in the early days of mass migration (1950–70), there was often a severe dislocation of family life, as patterns found in the former homes were disrupted. But subsequently new forms of stability emerged.

Asian families

The Asian population across the world generally has a very strong family system (Fukuyama, 1995). The first contact by Asians with UK culture after migration therefore often came as a culture shock. In the main, Asian culture has continued to assert the importance of family life.

The village model of India was for a while transferred to the UK, with a complex network of kin and responsibilities. In some ways this is the classic 'extended family' model. On arrival initially in the UK, these traditional family structures were disrupted: there were

smaller houses, there was less support and women became more isolated from other women. (Chain migration eventually restored this as families were reunited.) English families were often seen as 'morally bankrupt' (Elliot, 1996: 52).

In Asian families there are usually more people per household than in white families: three-quarters of Pakistani and Bangladeshi households have an average of five members, and three-fifths of Indian households contain four or more people, compared with a quarter of white households (Skellington, 1996: 62, 49).

An ideal type would suggest a value that places family before individual self-interest, and one that is patrilineal, patrilocal and with a strong gender hierarchy. Marriage is a contract between two families, not two individuals.

It is important to recognise again major differences between Asian communities (see Chapter 11). These can be compounded by gender. For instance, while East African and Indian women often work, taking them out of the house, Bangladeshi and Pakistani women's lives – more restricted by Islamic rules which do not permit women to be in close proximity to non-family men – lead to a much stronger home-based commitment, including 'homework'. Likewise, Muslims can marry close kin but this is not permitted for Sikhs and Hindus. *Purdah* is strong in Islam and restricts Islamic women more.

Sallie Westwood and Parminder Bhachu (1988) nevertheless see these traditions as evoking changes. Again, families do not remain static, but respond to current changes. Some become more nuclear and a diversity of Asian families starts to appear.

Afro-Caribbean families

These account for less than 1 per cent of all families in the UK (Skellington, 1996: 50). Thirty-seven per cent were headed by a female (compared with 9 per cent of white families). Marriage is often weaker, women-headed households are more common, and the husband/father role is likely to be less strong. In a curious fashion, there is a resemblance to the United States situation where African American families are also like this. Jocelyn Barrow explains this form of family by linking it to Caribbean society. Originally, while marriage is much valued in Caribbean societies, other patterns of sexual union were possible. There were common-law family households with unmarried cohabitation, as well as women-headed households (Barrow 1982).

In the main, extended kin units have not reappeared among Afro-Caribbean families in the UK. One study suggested that fewer than 1 per cent of children are cared for by grandmothers as the 'grandmother family' disappears. The families often tend to be matrifocal, even though Afro-Caribbean women are more likely to be working and have less support than in the Caribbean. Men often become marginal to family life.

Lone-parent families are highest among West Indian families (43 per cent in the 1991 Census) but lowest for Asian: the figures were 6 per cent for Indian and Pakistani, 5 per cent for Bangladeshi and 11 per cent for white families (Skellington, 1996: 50, 60).

Gender

Among all races, Jessie Bernard (1982) asserts, every marriage is actually two different relationships: a woman's marriage and a man's marriage. Although the extent of patriarchy has diminished with time, even today few marriages are composed of two equal partners. Studies in the UK suggest that although there have been some moves towards equality, and that families do come in many forms, it remains the case that men still make most of the major decisions, and that wives generally are economically dependent upon

husbands and are more likely to take responsibility for child care and the housework within the family (Pahl, 1989; Devine, 1992).

Practices of family life

Practising care

One of the key 'practices' of families is 'caring': caring for partners, caring for children and caring for parents. This is a three- or four-generational span of care. And there is an important distinction to be made here between *caring about*, which is about love, feelings and emotions, and *caring for*, which is an active form of work – a 'labour of love' which involves looking after someone (Ungerson, 1987). They may, of course, be deeply interwoven, but they need not be. Overwhelmingly, this latter care process falls upon the women in the family, although it is usually invisible. Although there are signs that some men are playing a small role in it, feminist research has generally shown that the caring process is closely linked in modern societies to what it means to be a woman. Recall in

A family in crisis. In Nairobi, Kenya, HIV positive wife with her children and husband at home in Langata slum 1998.
Source: Magnum Photos © Chris Steele-Perkins

Chapter 12 how Nancy Chodorow suggested that the social process of becoming a woman was closely linked to the social process of becoming a mother. It is the extension of this 'social mothering' that makes women more prone to look after the array of people within the family – and also outside it.

There has been quite a lot of research on 'care'. It suggests these commitments are rarely straightforward and always negotiated – often over long periods of time and implicitly. Sometimes there is an unwillingness to engage in care. Often the array of family members that will be carers is narrowly defined: usually from spouse, to daughter, to daughter-in-law and son. There is a hierarchy of care: sons and daughters define their care duties primarily to their own children and partners, only secondarily to their parents. Older people usually do not want to give up their independence – and so are looked after 'at a distance' ('intimacy at a distance'). Nevertheless, research strongly suggests that there is a great deal of care taking place among families today. But when governments cut back on public care, this can hit many families very hard, as they are already engaged in a great deal of unpaid care (Finch and Groves, 1983; Finch, 1989; Graham, 1991; Elliot, 1996: 122–140).

Doing violence

The ideal family may serve as a haven from the dangers of the outside world; the reality is that many families are exceedingly dangerous places. From the biblical story of Cain killing his brother Abel to the recent O. J. Simpson case, we see that the disturbing reality of many homes has been **family violence**, *emotional, physical or sexual abuse of one family member by another*. Sociologist Richard J. Gelles points to a chilling fact:

> The family is the most violent group in society with the exception of the police and the military. You are more likely to get killed, injured or physically attacked in your home by someone you are related to than in any other social context.
>
> (quoted in Roesch, 1984: 75)

Violence against women

During the 1970s a seemingly new 'family problem' was discovered: men's violence against women. The Women's Movement responded by actively establishing women's refuges throughout the country and also through a critical analysis of men's violence towards women (that often connected it to the rape and power debate discussed in Chapter 12).

Erin Pizzey set up the first Women's Refuge in Chiswick in 1972 (Pizzey, 1974), and today almost every large town in the UK has some such scheme (though usually, to avoid male harassers, they are kept fairly anonymous). A study by Jayne Mooney (2000) in North London found that about half of all women surveyed had experienced threats of violence or actual violence, although many of these women had not told anybody.

The problem is even greater in the United States. As elsewhere, family brutality usually goes unreported to police, but the US Bureau of Justice (1998) estimates that at least 840,000 women are victims of domestic violence each year. Women's activists say the figure may be as high as 8 million. Researchers note that men initiate most family violence and that women suffer most of the injuries (Straus and Gelles, 1986; Schwartz, 1987; Shupe *et al.*, 1987).

US government statistics show that almost 30 per cent of women who are murdered – as opposed to 3 per cent of men – are killed by partners or ex-partners. In the United States the death toll from family violence is 1,300 women each year. Overall, women are more likely to be injured by a family member than to be mugged or raped by a stranger or hurt in a car accident.

Not long ago, US law declared wives to be the property of their husbands, so that no man could be charged with raping his wife. By 1995, however, 40 states had passed marital rape laws, although in some cases such a charge can be made only under specific circumstances, such as after a legal separation (Russell, 1982). Although the law against rape in marriage has now also changed in most European countries, in 2001 only 30 countries worldwide recognised what is increasingly called non-consensual sex in marriage (NCSM).

People who hear about a case of abuse often shake their heads and wonder, 'Why didn't she just leave?' The answer is that most physically and emotionally abused women – especially those with children and without much money – have few options. Most wives are also committed to their marriages and believe (however unrealistically) that they can help abusive husbands to change. Some, unable to understand their husbands' violence, blame themselves. Others, raised in violent families, have learned to view assault as part of everyday family life.

In the past, the law regarded domestic violence as a private, family matter. Now, even without separation or divorce, a woman can obtain court protection from an abusive spouse. Anti-stalking laws (which prohibit people from following or threatening ex-partners), such as the 1997 Harassment Act in the UK, are now found in many countries. Finally, communities across Europe have established shelters that provide counselling as well as temporary housing for women and children driven from their homes by domestic violence.

The analysis has shifted from being based on individuals, to one based on the power relations – patriarchy – between men and women (see Chapter 12).

Violence against children

Family violence also victimises children. In the United States upwards of 3 million children – roughly 4 per cent of all youngsters – suffer abuse each year, including several thousand who die as a result. Child abuse entails more than physical injury because abusive adults misuse power and trust to undermine a child's emotional well-being. Child abuse is most common among the youngest and most vulnerable children (Straus and Gelles, 1986; Van Biema, 1994).

In the UK several noticeable cases have galvanised action and thinking. In 1973, the seven-year-old Maria Colwell was beaten to death by her stepfather after social workers had allowed her to return to her family from foster care. It led both to a moral panic (see Chapter 21) and to the development of a public awareness of abuse. Later, in 1985, the death of Jasmine Beckford also served to highlight the continuing problem. As a consequence of such cases, social work intervention increased, and registers of children at risk were created. In 2000, some 30,300 children were registered in the UK, of whom nearly 40 per cent were under the age of five (Department of Health website). Still, the plight of abused children continues: many suffer in silence, believing during their formative years that they are to blame for their own victimisation. The initial abuse, compounded by years of guilt, can leave lasting emotional scars that prevent people abused as children from forming healthy relationships as adults.

About 90 per cent of child abusers are men, but they conform to no simple stereotype. As one man who entered a therapy group reported, 'I kept waiting for all the guys with raincoats and greasy hair to show up. But everyone looked like regular middle-class people' (quoted in Lubenow, 1984). Most abusers, however, share one trait: they were abused themselves as children. Researchers have discovered that violent behaviour in close relationships is learned. In families, then, violence begets violence (Gwartney-Gibbs et al., 1987).

Towards the postmodern family?

At the start of the twenty-first century, families and relationships seem to be undergoing very significant changes. True, many of the older patterns persist, but there are certainly some new ones in the making. We have seen in Chapter 12 the emergence of a new, flexible, highly individualistic, sexually 'plastic', 'pure relationship' where partners are mutually interdependent (Cancian, 1987; Giddens, 1991; Beck and Beck-Gernsheim, 1995). The suggestion is that for some (and it *may* be a blue-print for the future), relationships are emerging where men and women are more interdependent and equal; where their child-rearing is altogether part of a more egalitarian and democratic system; where sexuality and love become more 'plastic', diffuse, open. This is a relationship of choice, closely allied to individualism.

The changes we outline have been taken by many to herald a new form of family relationship. American family sociologist Judith Stacey has argued that we may be discovering the postmodern family. She writes

> The postmodern family condition is not a new model of family life equivalent to that of the modern family; it is not the next stage in an orderly progression of stages in family history; rather the postmodern family condition signals the moment in history when our belief in a logical progression of stages has broken down. . . . The postmodern family condition incorporates both experimental and nostalgic dimensions as it lurches forward and backward into an uncertain future.
>
> (Stacey, 1996: 8)

In what follows, we shall look in more detail at some of the changes.

Household size

Increasingly, sociologists focus on 'households', looking at their shape and size. In the UK, the average household size has almost halved since the start of the century – to 2.4 people per household. With this has come a decline in the traditional household of two parents and dependent children – from about a third in 1971 to around a fifth in spring 2003. Over the same period, lone parent households doubled, accounting for 5 per cent. There were more households with couples and no children than households with children. One in four households had a single person living alone. The proportion of one-person households increased from 18 per cent in 1991 to 29 per cent in 2003, with the most significant growth being with men under age 65 (which grew three times the proportion in 1971) (*Social Trends*, 2004: 27–28). Table 17.1 shows households by family type for the UK.

WHAT'S GOING ON IN THE FAMILY IN THE UK?

Marriages

In 1971, 71 per cent of men and 65 per cent of women were married; by 2000, this had fallen to 54 per cent of men and 52 per cent of women (*Social Trends*, 2003: 45). More than 40 per cent of marriages are remarriages, compared with 21 per cent in 1971. People are also marrying later in life: the average age in the EU in 1993 was 28.5 for men and 26.1 for women. Sweden has the lowest marriage rate.

Cohabitation

This has risen significantly. The proportion of all non-married women aged 18–40 cohabiting has doubled since 1981 to 25 per cent. A quarter of non-married adults aged 16–59 were cohabiting in 2000–01 (*Social Trends*, 2003: 45). Cohabitation is often found among the divorced and often ends through remarriage.

Divorces

The peak period for divorce was in the 1970s. It is now more stable, at around 160,000 a year. Since 1971, marriages have fallen one-fifth and divorces have doubled. Almost half of marriages end in divorce, and most are sought by women (7 out of 10 petitions), while men are more likely to remarry. Roughly a quarter of children can now expect to find their original parents divorced by the time they are 16. The UK has the highest divorce rate in the European Union but it is not as high as it is in the United States.

Stepfamilies

In 2000–01 stepfamilies accounted for 8 per cent of families with dependent children.

Gay families of choice

Although figures are hard to come by, according to sociologist Michael Kimmel, in the United States there are an 'estimated 1.5 million to 5 million lesbian mothers and between 1 million and 3 million gay fathers. Currently, between 6 million and 14 million children (about 5% of all US children) are being raised by at least one gay parent' (Kimmel, 2000: 144). Despite hotly contested debates all over the world, gay marriages or registered partnerships now exist in many countries. In all the Scandinavian countries and most of Europe, such partnerships are now law. Registered partnerships became law in the UK in 2005.

Home alone

More people are now living alone. In the UK in 2002, 6.2 million adults were living alone. A quarter of all households are now one-person households. This is double what it was in 1971 (when it was 3 million). In addition, household size fell from 3.09 in 1961 to 2.46 in 1990. Many of these are elderly households (in 2000, 10 per cent of these belonged to elderly women and half of all women over 75 years live alone). A new trend is for younger men to live on their own (3 per cent in 1971; 10 per cent in 2000; predicted to be 14 per cent by 2021) (*Social Trends*, 2003: 43).

Lone parents

Almost one in five families with dependent children are lone-parent families. It has nearly trebled in 25 years from 1 million to 2.8 million. A large part is due to divorce. Ten per cent of lone-parent families are headed by lone fathers and 90 per cent by lone mothers (*Social Trends*, 2003: 44). Denmark and Sweden have the highest numbers of lone parents in Europe (52 per cent as the result of divorce or separation; about one-third of this amount are single mothers and 42 per cent of them have incomes below £100 per week (Figure 17.3).

Older people

The 2001 Census reports that 336,000 people are aged 90 or over.

Children

In 1901, 34.6 per cent of the population in the UK were under 16; in 1981 it was 22.3 per cent. The average number of children in a family was 1.8 (including adopted and stepchildren). The birth rate is 1.73 per woman. Most children still live in traditional families headed by a couple (78 per cent in spring 2002) (*Social Trends*, 2003: 43).

The generational gap

There is a large difference in attitude towards 'family' between those born before 1930 and those born since 1950. Older cohorts are firmly against living together before marriage (well over 60%) whereas younger cohorts born since 1950 strongly favour living together before marriage (*British Social Attitudes*, 2004).

Sexuality

The pill remains the most popular form of contraception with a quarter of all women aged 16–49 using it. In 1971, 21 per cent of births were conceived out of marriage; by 2000, it was over half. There has also been a dramatic decline in the age of first intercourse: the median for young men and women (born between 1966 and 1975) was 17 years. Gay and lesbian sexualities are more accepted.

Life expectancy
The twentieth century has seen 25 years added to human life expectancy, shifting the shape of the life cycle.

Births outside of marriage
In the UK, about one-third of all live births occur outside marriage and in nearly all European countries it has doubled in the last 30 years. Yet most occur in stable relationships outside marriage (in 1992, 75 per cent of registered births included both parents as opposed to 45 per cent in 1971). Birth rate outside marriage is highest in Sweden and lowest in Greece.

Women remaining childless
While most women do have children, the number who do not has been growing (20 per cent of those born in 1954 and 25 per cent of those born in 1979 remain childless) and women are having children later in the life cycle.

Adoption
The adoption rate has sharply fallen. There were 21,500 adoptions in 1971 and just under 6,000 in 2001.

Source: *Social Trends*, 2004 (also available on the web).

Table 17.1	Households by family type in the UK, 2003				
	Percentages				
	1971	1981	1991	2001[1]	2003[1]
One person					
Under state pension age	6	8	11	14	15
Over state pension age	12	14	16	15	14
Two or more unrelated adults	4	5	3	8	8
One family households					
Couple[2]					
No children	27	26	28	28	28
1–2 dependent children[3]	26	25	20	19	18
3 or more dependent children[3]	9	6	5	4	4
Non-dependent children only	8	8	8	6	6
Lone parent[2]					
Dependent children[3]	3	5	6	5	5
Non-dependent children only	4	4	4	3	3
Multi-family households	1	1	1	1	1
All households (=100%) (millions)	18.6	20.2	22.4	24.2	24.5

[1] At spring. These estimates are not seasonally adjusted and have not been adjusted to take account of the 2001 Census results.

[2] Other individuals who were not family members may also be included.

[3] May also include non-dependent children.

Source: *Social Trends* (2004: 26)

Marriage and divorce

One of the most striking features of modern societies has been the decline in first marriage and the rapid growth of divorce. There were 40 per cent fewer first marriages in the UK in 1994 than there were in 1971 – a steep drop. In 2001, around half of adults in the UK population were married. The age of marriage has also increased – in 2001, it was around 30.6 for men and 28.4 for women (in 1971 it was 24.6 and 22.6 respectively). By contrast, the number of divorces has more than doubled in the same period – a steep rise. There is also a general drift towards marrying at older ages.

These are trends found throughout Europe and other industrialising societies. Most countries in the European Union have seen a decline in marriage rates, with Sweden

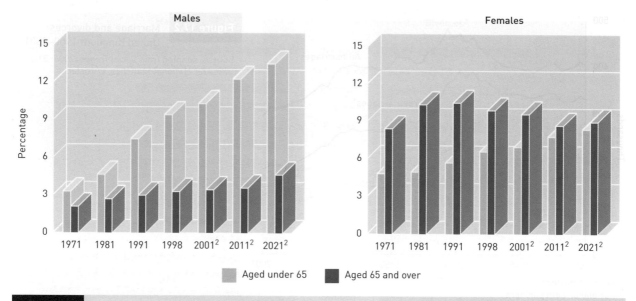

Figure 17.3   One-parent households[1]: by gender and whether aged under 65 or aged 65 and over

[1] Percentage of heads of household that were living alone as a percentage of all households
[2] 1996-based household projections

Source: Department of the Environment, Transport and Regions; National Assembly for Wales. Adapted from *Social Trends*, 2001, Fig. 2.16, p. 51, Office of National Statistics.

- *Prior marriage*: men and women who divorce once are more likely to divorce again, presumably because problems follow them from one marriage to another.

Finally, couples who have known their partners for short periods of time before marriage, those who marry in response to an unexpected pregnancy, and people who are not religious divorce more readily than other couples (Booth and White, 1980; Yoder and Nichols, 1980; Glenn and Shelton, 1985; 1980; Burgoyne *et al.*, 1987; Coleman and Salt, 1992).

The experience of divorce

A series of recent studies in the UK have looked at divorce and step-parenting and have persistently found that the decisions taken in these areas are not taken lightly and bring with them major moral concerns. Thus, for instance, the research of Carol Smart and Bren Neal (1999) examines relationships of parenting that are negotiated and renegotiated following a divorce, and are especially concerned with the influence this has on the children. Through their work a complex set of 'post-divorce' relationships, processes, phases and 'practices' come into view. They sense how new roles start to appear: solo parenting, co-parenting, custodial parenting. They find how a complex flow between parenting roles and those of 'others' (grandparents, step-siblings, etc.) surrounds it.

And they show new possibilities of 'step-grandparents' emerging. Firmly against the moral traditionalist position – for example, of Patricia Morgan (1995), who is cited as saying the divorce law 'allies' itself with the spouses who want to break up marriages, and in doing so, rewards selfishness, egoism and destructiveness over altruistic commitment – their focus is much more on the daily moral struggles which are encountered through divorce.

Likewise, Jane Ribbens McCarthy and others, in their studies of step-parenting (McCarthy et al., 2000), find an overwhelming sense that all their 'adults must take responsibility for children in their care, and therefore must seek the needs of the children first'. 'This', they say, 'is such a strong moral imperative that it seems to have been impossible for anyone to disagree with it in the accounts we have heard' (McCarthy *et al.*, 2000: 16) What we see here, then, is that divorce and step-parenting may lead to a heightened sense of moral decision-making in families. It may be a long process of negotiation, but there are elements of sharedness.

Some writers are starting to suggest that what we are seeing here in families is the emergence of a postmodern morality which is not to be handed down from on high by moralists but which is instead the very stuff of many people's everyday lives. Children may well now be exposed to a more complex set of relations from an earlier time than perhaps they were in the past. But none of this necessarily means they are open to neglect and indifference.

Custody residence and parenting

More than half of all divorcing couples must resolve the issue of child custody. Society's conventional practice is still to award custody of children to mothers, based on the notion that women are better parents than men. A recent trend, however, is towards joint custody, whereby children divide their time between the new homes of their two parents. Joint custody is difficult if divorced parents live far apart or do not get along, but it has the advantage of keeping children in regular contact with both parents.

Because mothers usually gain custody of children but fathers typically earn more income, the well-being of children often depends on fathers making court-ordered child-support payments.

Financial support

In 1991 the UK's Conservative government of the day set up the Child Support Agency (CSA) which aimed to make absent parents (mainly fathers) contribute to their children's upbringing. An agency was set up to administer it and collect money from absent fathers, focusing especially in the first instance on low-income fathers who were easier to locate (through social security offices). It led to considerable controversy and a campaign against the CSA (APART, Absent Parents Asking for Reasonable Treatment). Partly, this was because it did not take into account the obligations a parent may have to a second family, but in addition, it was retrospective, overturning earlier court agreements. Further, if the parent with the child was already on income support, everything collected was recouped by the Benefits Agency. In recent times, the CSA has come under much attack for inefficiency and waste.

Remarriage

Despite the rising divorce rate, marriage – and remarriage – remain as popular as ever. In the UK over one-third of all marriages each year are second marriages. Most people remarry within three to five years. Men, who derive greater benefits from wedlock, are more likely to remarry than women are.

Remarriage often creates *blended families*, composed of children and some combination of biological parents and step-parents. Members of blended families thus have to define precisely who is part of the child's nuclear family (Furstenberg, 1984). Blended families also require children to reorientate themselves; an only child,

for example, may suddenly find she has two older brothers. And, as already noted, the risk of divorce is high for partners in such families. But blended families also offer both young and old the opportunity to relax rigid family roles.

Lone-parent families

Lone parents headed some 23 per cent of all families with dependent children (and 12 per cent of all households) in the UK in 2003 (well over one in ten of all households with children) – three times the proportion in 1971 (Figure 17.4). Lone-parent families, over 90 per cent of which are headed by a single mother, may result from divorce, separation, death or the choice of an unmarried woman to have a child. Until the mid-1980s, most of the increase was due to divorce, but, since then, the proportion of divorced mothers has remained stable, while that of single never-married mothers has doubled (Family Policy Studies Centre, 1995: 2). There are at least five types of lone-parent family (Haskey, 1992):

Single lone mothers	35 per cent
Divorced lone mothers	31 per cent
Separated lone mothers	21 per cent
Widowed mothers	4 per cent
Lone fathers	9 per cent

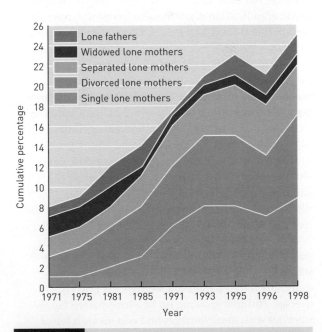

Figure 17.4 Lone-parent families by marital status in the UK, 1971–2000

Source: adapted from http://www.statistics.gov.uk

| Table 17.2 | Percentage of dependent children living in different family types in the UK |

	Percentages				
	1972	1981	1992	2001[1]	2003[1]
Couple families					
1 child	16	18	18	17	17
2 children	35	41	39	38	37
3 or more children	41	29	27	25	24
Lone mother families					
1 child	2	3	4	6	6
2 child	2	4	5	7	8
3 or more children	2	3	4	5	6
Lone father families					
1 child	–	1	1	1	2
2 or more children	1	1	1	1	1
All children[2]	100	100	100	100	100

[1] At spring. These estimates are not seasonally adjusted and have not been adjusted to take account of the Census 2001 results.

[2] Excludes cases where the dependent child is a family unit, for example, a foster child.

Source: *Social Trends* (2004: 27)

Across Europe the percentage of births outside marriage has been significantly rising. The rate is highest in the Scandinavian countries and lowest in Greece. In the UK it is around 32 per cent, compared with 8 per cent in 1971.

Entering the labour force has bolstered women's financial capacity to be single mothers. But lone parenthood – especially when the parent is a woman – greatly increases the risks of poverty, as it can limit the woman's ability to work and to further her education. Many women in Europe now become pregnant as unmarried teenagers, and many decide to raise their children on their own. These young women with children – especially if they have the additional disadvantage of being minorities – form the core of the rising problem of child poverty in Europe.

Some research suggests that growing up in a lone-parent family can disadvantage children. The most serious problem among families with one parent – especially if that parent is a woman – is poverty. On average, children growing up in a lone-parent family start out with disadvantages and end up with lesser educational achievement and lower incomes, and face a greater chance of forming lone-parent families themselves.

Cohabitation

Cohabitation is *the sharing of a household by an unmarried couple*. A generation ago, widespread use of terms like 'living in sin' and 'premarital sex' indicated disapproval of both cohabitation and sex outside marriage. But all this has changed. Attitude surveys find a generational difference, with older people often disapproving of cohabitation, but younger people overwhelmingly in favour of it (*Social Trends*, 2003: 33). Since 1981, the proportion of all non-married women aged 18–49 who were cohabiting doubled – to over a quarter (28 per cent) of all couplings. Divorced women and younger women in their twenties were the most likely to cohabit. Cohabitation rarely lasts more than two years, and frequently leads to marriage. In a sense, it has become the new form of 'engagement'.

Cohabitation is common in Europe as a whole. It is most pronounced in Sweden and other Scandinavian societies as a long-term form of family life, with or without children. By contrast, this family form is much rarer in more traditional (and Roman Catholic) nations such as Italy.

Step-parenting

In 1991 there were around half a million step-families and around 1 million children (step-children and natural children) living in such families. There were three times as many step-fathers as step-mothers, as children are more likely to stay with their natural mothers (*Social Trends*, 1997: 44). Step-families are growing fast: in 2000, there were some 2.5 million children in step-families, accounting for about 6 per cent of all families in the UK.

Gay and lesbian couples: 'families of choice', registered partnerships and marriage

Since the 1980s there has been increasing interest in gay and lesbian marriages and partnerships. Kath Weston suggests that these are 'families of choice' as opposed to the more conventional 'families of blood' (Weston, 1991). In 1989, Denmark became the first country to formally recognise homosexual marriages, thereby extending some social legitimacy to gay and lesbian couples as well as conferring legal advantages for inheritance, taxation and joint property ownership. A registered partnership gives two people of the same sex

Laura Marshall and Rosemary Rodgers receive their marriage certificate from San Francisco City Hall on Valentines Day. After living together for six years, they can now say they are wife and wife. In a controversial challenge to both legal and social convention, San Francisco officials began issuing same-sex licenses and officiating at City Hall marriages on February 12, 2004. The city has gone out of its way to provide the services. Volunteers worked through the entire weekend.

Source: © Maggie Hallahan/Corbis

the equivalent rights to heterosexual marriages except for the rights of adoption or a church marriage.

Versions of registered partnerships are becoming increasingly common throughout many countries of the world: Denmark (1989), Norway (1993), Sweden (1995), Iceland and Finland (1996). Other European countries have followed: France and Germany have passed legislation that will permit registered partnerships, while The Netherlands has made gay marriages legal. In the UK, a registered partnership law has gone through Parliament, and in other countries, such as South Africa, Mexico, and a few states of the United States, laws are being enacted.

Most gay and lesbian couples in households including children raise the offspring of previous, heterosexual unions and some couples have adopted children. But many gay parents are quiet about their sexuality, not wishing to draw unwelcome attention to their children. In several widely publicised cases in recent years, courts have removed children from homosexual couples, claiming to represent the best interests of the children (Weeks *et al.*, 2001)

In the United States, while gay people cannot legally marry (although they can adopt children), some cities (including San Francisco and New York) allow 'registered partnerships' that confer some of the legal benefits of marriage. However, it has been estimated that in the United States there are as many as 1 million gay and lesbian couples who are now raising one or more children.

While this pattern challenges many traditional notions about families in Europe, it also indicates that many gay and lesbian couples perceive the same rewards in child-rearing that 'straight' couples do. There is an irony in all this. As gays and lesbians establish the legal basis for 'marriage' around the world, more and more heterosexuals are running away from it as marriage becomes less popular and divorce increases.

Singlehood

Living alone is becoming more common in Europe. By 1999, nearly one-third of all households in the UK housed just one person living alone (about half of these were pensioners). Elderly widows have always represented a large share of single people. But a new group of men under the age of 65 have become the second biggest group to live alone: there were two and half times the number of men living alone in 1996 than in 1971. And it is projected that this group will continue to rise. In the United States, though, the story is somewhat different. Here it is younger women who are staying single. In 1960, 28 per cent of US women aged 20–24 were single; by 1994 the proportion had soared to two-thirds. Underlying this trend is women's greater participation in the labour force: women who are economically secure view a husband as a matter of choice rather than a financial necessity.

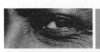

FAMILY TIME

In 1961 women comprised only a quarter of the work-force; now they make up at least half. Domestic work has fallen substantially. For example, in 1961 it took up, on average, 117 minutes per day in food preparation; by the mid-1990s this was down to 65 minutes. Working women have also reduced domestic work (from an average of 110 minutes a day in 1961 to 90 in the mid-1990s). (Men have increased domestic work from 15 minutes per day in 1961 to 45 minutes in 1995.)

But what is really important is that housework has been displaced for other things, such as shopping, travel and the children. Child-care time has doubled. As Gershuny says: 'Full time-employed women with children in 1995 appear to devote more time to child care than even non-employed did in 1961' (1997: 57).

Two factors may account especially for this. First, there is growing alarm about abuse and traffic danger, so parents are not letting their children roam too far. Second, there are all sorts of new services – sports, educational, leisure – which require parents to take children there. Families are also going out more.

FAMILY VALUES: HAVE CHANGES IN THE FAMILY GONE TOO FAR?

Are 'traditional families' vital to our way of life? Or are they a barrier to progress? To begin, people typically use the term 'traditional family' to mean a married couple who, at some point in their lives, raise children. But the term is more than simply descriptive – it is also a moral and political statement. That is, support for the traditional family implies that people place a high value on getting and staying married, that parents should place more importance on raising children than on pursuing their own careers, and that society should accord special respect to two-parent families rather than various 'alternative lifestyles'.

On one side of the debate, Patricia Morgan, from a conservative view, and Norman Dennis and George Erdos from an ethical socialist view, argue that there has been a serious erosion of the traditional family since 1960. And this is not hard to see from the figures in the European Eye box on page 472. There are fewer marriages, fewer children, more divorce, more singlehood, more single parents. Indeed, the number of children born out of wedlock has grown 'from one in ten in the late 1970s to over three in ten in the early 1990s' (Morgan, 1995: 4). And, because of both divorce and increasing numbers of children born out of wedlock, the share of youngsters living with a single parent at some time before age 18 has quadrupled since 1960 to half of all children. Combining the last two facts, just one in four of today's children will grow up with two parents and go on to maintain a stable marriage of their own.

In the light of such data, serious consequences follow. These include the rise of delinquency, the growth of incivility, the huge welfare burden. The family is not just changing, it is heading towards total collapse, and it does not look good for the future of society.

Patricia Morgan suggests that the traditional family of man–wife–children is being replaced by the mother–child state. She deplores the rise of lone-parent families, especially children born out of wedlock, and is very concerned about the growth of 'welfare dependency' for many of these poor lone-parent families. Norman Dennis, with similar arguments, is most concerned with the ways in which a new family without fatherhood has been created. It is this lack of a father to be an adequate role model for children which has created many problems. In sum, and drawing from research, he suggests that 'on average the life-long socially certified monogamous family of the pre-1960s pattern was better for children than any one of a variety of alternatives' (Dennis and Erdos, 1993: 34).

The same debate is found in the United States. There David Popenoe (1993) describes this breakdown as a fundamental shift from a 'culture of marriage' to a 'culture of divorce'. Traditional vows of marital commitment – 'till death us do part' – now amount to little more than 'as long as I am happy'. The negative consequences of the cultural trend towards weaker families, Popenoe continues, are obvious everywhere: as we pay less and less attention to children, the crime rate goes up along with a host of other problematic behaviours, including smoking, drinking and premarital sex.

As Popenoe sees it, then, we must work hard and quickly to reverse current trends. Government cannot be the solution (and may even be part of the problem): since 1960, as US government spending on social programmes has soared fivefold, the tradi-

CONTROVERSY AND DEBATE CONTINUED

tional family has grown weaker and weaker. The alternative, Popenoe reasons, is a cultural turn-around by which people will question and ultimately reject the recently popular 'me-first' view of our lives in favour of greater commitment to a spouse and children. (We have seen such a turnaround in the case of cigarette smoking.) Popenoe concludes that we should save the traditional family, and that means we need to affirm publicly the value of marital per-manence as well as endorse the two-parent family as best for the well-being of children.

On the other side of the debate, many sociologists argue that the recent changes in the family have mainly been for the good. They are really simply reflections of changes in the wider social world. As people's desire for choice, individuality, freedom, etc., has grown, so has their desire for more control over their personal life. The traditional families desired by the traditionalists are described in too romantic and nostalgic terms. Families of the past often meant that wives were stuck with vio-lent husbands and large families of children lived in abject poverty. Equality was minimal, as was choice.

Instead of returning to a mythical past, a goal now is to achieve democracy in the personal sphere. Equality and choice become key features of modern families. In any event, it is no longer possible to have only one ideal family form – even if we should want it. The world has grown too complex. As Beck and Beck-Gernsheim argue in *The Normal Chaos of Love* (1995), society has become individualised and with that 'It is no longer possible to pronounce in some binding way what family, marriage, parenthood, sexuality or love mean, what they should be or could be; rather they vary in sub-stance, exceptions, norms and morality from individual to individual and from relationships to relationships' (Beck and Beck-Gernsheim, 1995: 5). The traditional-ists are looking back to a world that has now gone, and cannot be returned to. They do not paint a rosy picture. They recognise that we are in a transition period, one in which there is likely to be 'a long and bitter battle – a war between men and women' (1995: 5).

Most of our current institutions were designed at a time when there was a sharp division between women in the home and men at work. Now this is changing: work situations, laws, town planning, school curricula all have to be changed.

For Judith Stacey, the traditional family is more problem than solution. Striking to the heart of the matter, Stacey writes (1990: 269): 'The family is not here to stay. Nor should we wish it were. On the con-trary, I believe that all democratic people, whatever their kinship preferences, should work to hasten its demise.' The main reason for rejecting the traditional

family, Stacey explains, is that it perpetuates and enhances various kinds of social inequality. Families play a key role in maintaining the class hierarchy, transferring wealth as well as 'cultural capital' from one generation to another. Moreover, feminists charge that the traditional family is built on patriarchy, which subjects women to their husbands' authority as well as saddling them with most of the responsibility for housework and child care. And from a gay-rights per-spective, she adds, a society that values traditional families inevitably denies homosexual men and women equal dignity and participation in social life.

Stacey thus applauds the breakdown of the family as a measure of social progress. Indeed, she views the family not as a basic social institution but as a political construction that serves to elevate one cate-gory of people, which she identifies as affluent white males, at the expense of women, homosexuals and poor people who lack the resources to maintain middle-class respectability.

Moreover, Stacey continues, the concept of 'tradi-tional family' is increasingly irrelevant to a diverse society in which people reject singular models of correct behaviour and in which both men and women must work for income. What society needs, Stacey concludes, is not a return to some golden age of the family but political and economic changes (including income parity for women, universal health care, programmes to reduce unemployment and expanded sex education in the schools) that will provide tangible support for children as well as ensure that people in diverse family forms receive the respect and dignity everyone deserves.

CONTINUE THE DEBATE:

1. To strengthen families, Popenoe urges parents to put children ahead of their own careers by limiting their joint working week to 60 hours. Do you agree? Why or why not?

2. Judith Stacey urges greater choice and equality in relationships and this means more diverse families. Do you agree?

3. What policies or programmes would you support to enhance the well-being of children?

4. Can you mount a 'defence of single parents', looking at evidence for their 'successes' and 'failures'?

Sources: Stacey (1990, 1993); Abbot and Wallace (1992); Dennis and Erdos (1993); Popenoe (1993); Beck and Beck-Gernsheim (1995); Council on Families in America (1995); Morgan (1995).

Looking ahead: families in the twenty-first century

In recent decades, transformation in family life throughout much of the world has generated controversy, with advocates of 'traditional family values' locked in debate with supporters of new family forms and greater personal choice. Whatever position one takes on the merits of current family trends, change is certain to continue into the coming century. Based on current evidence, we can make five predictions about the future of family life.

First, divorce rates are likely to remain high, even in the face of evidence that divorce can harm children. There may be some erosion of support for easy dissolution of marriage, yet several generations of high divorce rates have seriously weakened the idea that marriage is a lifetime commitment. Looking back through history, marital relationships are about as durable today as they were a century ago, when many marriages were cut short by death (Kain, 1990). But more couples now *choose* to end marriages that fail to live up to their expectations. Therefore, although the divorce rate has stabilised recently, it is unlikely that marriage will regain the durability characteristic of the 1950s. One major reason is that increasing numbers of women are able to support themselves, and traditional marriages appeal to fewer of them. Men, as well, are seeking more satisfying relationships. Perhaps we should view the recent trend towards higher divorce rates less as a threat to families than as a sign of change in family form. After all, most divorces still lead to remarriage, casting doubt on the notion that marriage itself is becoming obsolete. It is possible, too, that this trend may spread throughout parts of the non-Western world.

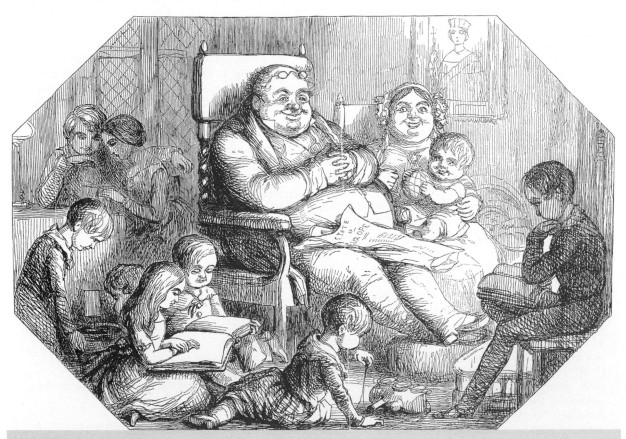

Mid Victorian image of the family from the Illustrated London News

Source: Illustrated London News, 1849

Second, family life in the twenty-first century will be highly variable. It may become increasingly 'postmodern'. We have noted an increasing number of cohabiting couples, lone-parent families, gay and lesbian families and blended families. Most families may still be based on marriage and most married couples still have children. But, taken together, the variety of family forms observed today represents a new conception of family life as a matter of choice.

Third, men are likely to play changing roles in child-rearing. For much of the nineteenth century and early twentieth century, men played limited roles in the raising of children. In the 1950s, a decade many people nostalgically recall as the 'golden age' of families, men began to withdraw from active parenting (Snell, 1990; Stacey, 1990). Since then, the share of children growing up in homes without their fathers has passed 25 per cent and is continuing to rise. A countertrend is emerging as some fathers – older, on average, and more established in their careers – eagerly jump into parenting. There has

also been the rise of the 'new man' highly involved in child-rearing. But, on balance, the high UK divorce rate and a surge in single motherhood point to more children growing up with weaker ties to fathers than ever before.

Fourth, economic changes will continue to reform marriage and the family. In many families, both household partners must work to ensure the family's financial security. As Arlie Hochschild (1989) points out, the economy is responsible for most of the change in society, but people *feel* these changes in the family. Marriage today is often the interaction of weary men and women: adults try their best to attend to children, yet often this can become minimal parenting. There are signs, however, that parents are giving increasing attention to their children in the UK (Gershuny, 1997).

Finally, the importance of new reproductive technologies will increase. While ethical concerns will surely slow these developments, new methods of reproduction will continue to alter the traditional meanings of parenthood.

SUMMARY

1. All societies are built on kinship, although family forms vary considerably across cultures and over time.

2. In industrial societies such as Europe, marriage is monogamous. Many pre-industrial societies, however, permit polygamy, of which there are two types: polygyny and polyandry.

3. In global perspective, patrilocality is most common, while industrial societies favour neolocality and a few societies have matrilocal residence. Industrial societies embrace bilateral descent; pre-industrial societies tend to be either patrilineal or matrilineal.

4. Families in the past were varied, and indeed varied in the same historical period. There is no such thing as one family form.

5. Functionalist analysis identifies major family functions: socialising the young, regulating sexual activity, transmitting social placement and providing material and emotional support.

6. Conflict theories explore how the family perpetuates social inequality by strengthening divisions based on class, ethnicity, race and gender.

7. Micro-level analysis highlights the variable nature of family life both over time and as experienced by individual family members.

8. Families differ according to class position, race and ethnicity.

9. Gender affects family dynamics since husbands play a dominant role in the vast majority of families. Research suggests that marriage provides more benefits to men than to women.

10. Today's divorce rate is much higher than a century ago; four in ten current marriages will end in divorce. Most people who divorce – especially men – remarry, often forming blended families that include children from previous marriages.

11. Family violence, victimising both women and children, is far more common than official records indicate. Adults who abuse family members most often suffered abuse themselves as children.

12. Society's family life is becoming more varied. Lone-parent families, cohabitation, gay and lesbian couples and singlehood have proliferated in recent years across the world.

13. Although ethically controversial, new reproductive technology is altering conventional notions of parenthood.

CRITICAL-THINKING QUESTIONS

1. How has the emerging post-industrial economy affected family life? What other factors are changing the family?

2. Why do some analysts describe the family as the 'backbone of society'? How do families perpetuate social inequality?

3. Do you think that lone-parent households do as good a job as two-parent households in raising children? Why or why not?

4. On balance, are families in Europe becoming 'postmodern'? What evidence supports your contention? When you take the world picture of families, would you also find evidence of major family changes?

5. What do you understand by David Morgan's idea of 'family practices'? Keep a diary on your own 'family practices' for a week.

GOING FURTHER

Further reading

Texts on the family:

Faith Robertson Elliot, *Gender, Family and Society* (1996)

Graham Allan and Graham Crow, *Families, Households and Society* (2001)
Reviews current issues and debates, mainly in the UK.

David Morgan, *Family Connections: An Introduction to Family Studies* (1996)
The key book for studying the family as a series of family practices.

Current theories of intimacy and change:

Ulrich Beck and Elisabeth Beck-Gernsheim, *The Normal Chaos of Love* (1995), translated by Mark Ritter and Jane Wiebel and originally published in German as *Das ganz normale Chaos der Liebe* (1990)
An account of changes in family and relationships at century's end by leading German sociologists.

Lynn Jamieson, *Intimacy: Personal Relationships in Modern Societies* (1998)
Helps establish this as a major new area of enquiry

Anthony Giddens, *The Transformation of Intimacy* (1992)
Written in a more accessible way and examines the major changes between men and women.

On gay and lesbian partnerships:

Jeffrey Weeks, Brian Heaphy and Catherine Donovan, *Same Sex Intimacies: Families of Choice and Other Life Experiments* (2001)
Provides original UK data on these 'experiments in living'.

Kath Weston, *Families We Choose: Lesbians, Gays, Kinship* (1991)
The first study of lesbian and gay families and coined the term ' families of choice'.

Watch a video

- Martin Scorsese's *Alice Doesn't Live Here Anymore* (1974) was one of the first 'single mum' films which, for its time, raised a lot of issues.

- There are many Hollywood treatments of classic issues, though they usually deserve very critical viewing. They include Robert Benton's Oscar-winning *Kramer vs Kramer* (1979) on divorce, Robert Redford's *Ordinary People* (1980) on neurotic mothers, and John Lithgow's *Terms of Endearment* (1983) on the importance of family bonds. They make an interesting comparison with films made nearly two decades later, such as Ang Lee's *The Ice Storm* (1997).

- In contrast with many Hollywood films, the films of Mike Leigh in the UK depict family life in tragi-comic tones: see his *Secrets and Lies* (1996), *Life is Sweet* (1990), and *Bleak Moments* (1971).

Connecting up

Connect to other chapters

- An important development – the new reproductive technologies – is discussed in Chapter 22.
- See Chapter 12 for linked discussions of both sexual violence and homosexuality.

To the websites

- http://singleparents.about.com/
  A US website which contains streams of information for single parents.
- http://www.buddybuddy.com
  A US website with resources for gay and lesbian couples.
- Institute of Economic Research at the University of Essex
  http://www.iser.essex.ac.uk/
- Center for Research on Family, Kinship and Childhood at the University of Leeds
  http://ww.leeds.ac.uk/family/

For additional case studies, multiple choice questions, internet exercises, and annotated weblinks specific to this chapter, visit this book's website at **www.pearsoned.co.uk/plummer**

CHAPTER 18   # RELIGION AND BELIEF

There is only one religion, though there are a hundred versions of it.

George Bernard Shaw: *Plays Pleasant and Unpleasant* (1898), vol. 2 preface

If God did not exist it would be necessary to invent him.

Voltaire

IN 1989 SALMAN RUSHDIE published his controversial novel *The Satanic Verses* in Britain. One character in the book, the Prophet Mahound, appears as a figure of debauchery, foul language and obscenity. Sensing that this was a thinly disguised, blasphemous attack on Mohammed and the Islamic faith, British Muslims soon expressed their anger and requested a publisher's apology for misrepresenting the Islamic faith. Matters rapidly escalated: the book was ritually burned in Bolton and Bradford; the media accused the Muslims of intolerance; voices were raised against Rushdie in India and Pakistan. On Valentine's Day 1989, the Iranian leader Ayatollah Khomeini issued his *fatwa* – or official call for execution – against Rushdie. Although initially a British affair, *The Satanic Verses* scandal escalated into an international one, symbolising battles between religious institutions and secular cultures, and accompanied by a resurgence of anti-Islamic feeling in the West. Fearing for his life, Rushdie went into hiding, where he stayed for over ten years.

In March 1995, a small group of terrorists released a poisonous gas in Tokyo's underground system, killing 12 but blinding many more and causing complete pandemonium. But this was no ordinary act of terrorism. It was conducted by Aum Shinriyko, a religious sect that claimed 10,000 Japanese members and 20,000 in Russia. Its leader Shoko Asahara had actually created a stockpile of weapons to kill around 10 million people.

In March 1997, Marshall Applewhite led 39 of his followers to commit suicide as part of the cult Heaven's Gate. Their dead bodies laid out neatly in bunk beds were found in Rancho Santa Fe, California. The cult was a distinctly modern group – they wore sneakers and were computer geeks – yet they looked for signs of religious meaning on their computers. They attached enormous significance to the Hale-Bopp comet as a sign that their time to go to heaven had arrived. And when it appeared, they were all led by their cult leader to drink a curious mix of vodka and barbiturates so that their 'earthly vessels' could rise to the Heavens.

And on 11 September 2001, in by far the most devastating terrorist action up to that date, four civil airliners were hijacked by suicide bombers and targeted at major US buildings. Two demolished the twin towers of the World Trade Center in New York, the third destroyed part of the Pentagon in Washington, and the fourth crashed in Pennsylvania. These were rapidly identified with terrorist attacks, and especially with Osama Bin Laden and his al-Qaeda international terrorist network. Bin Laden is on record as saying he is conducting a religious war – an Islamic jihad – against America.

It is often argued that religion is in decline in the modern world – in the face of rising rationality and science. And it is true that in many European countries, church going and even Christian beliefs are becoming less common. But, as the cases above well illustrate, in the contemporary world religion may play as powerful a role as it always has.

Sources: Appignanesi and Maitland (1989); Parekh (1989); Galanter (1999)

KEY THEMES

- Ways of understanding religion
- The organisation of religions
- The variety of global religions
- Religion in modern society and the problem of secularisation
- New developments in religion

(Left) *The ascent of the Prophet Mohammed to Heaven* by Aqa Mirak, 16th-century Persian manuscript.
Source: British Library, London/Bridgeman Art Library

SOCIAL SHAPES OF THE WORLD

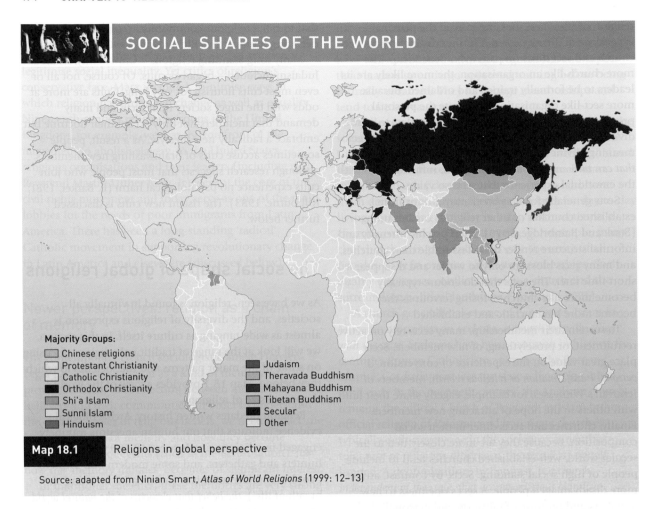

Majority Groups:

- ☐ Chinese religions
- ☐ Protestant Christianity
- ☐ Catholic Christianity
- ■ Orthodox Christianity
- ▦ Shi'a Islam
- ☐ Sunni Islam
- ▦ Hinduism
- ■ Judaism
- ☐ Theravada Buddhism
- ■ Mahayana Buddhism
- ▦ Tibetan Buddhism
- ■ Secular
- ☐ Other

Map 18.1   Religions in global perspective

Source: adapted from Ninian Smart, *Atlas of World Religions* (1999: 12–13)

contrast, span large areas and often have millions of adherents. We shall briefly describe six of the major world religions, which together claim as adherents some 4 billion people – almost three-quarters of humanity.

1. Christianity

Christianity is the most widespread religion, with nearly 2 billion followers, who constitute roughly one-third of humanity. Most Christians live in Europe or the Americas; more than 85 per cent of the people in the United States and Canada identify with Christianity. Moreover, people who are at least nominally Christian represent a significant share of the population in many other world regions, with the notable exceptions of northern Africa and Asia. The diffusion stems from the European colonisation of much of the world during the last 500 years. This dominance of Christianity in the West can be seen in the practice of numbering years on the calendar beginning with the birth of Christ.

Christianity originated as a cult, incorporating elements of its much older predecessor Judaism. Like many cults, Christianity was propelled by the personal charisma of a leader, Jesus of Nazareth, who preached a message of personal salvation. Jesus did not directly challenge the political powers of his day, calling on his followers to 'Render therefore to Caesar things that are Caesar's' (Matthew, xxii: 21). But his message was revolutionary, nonetheless, promising that faith and love would lead to triumph over sin and death.

Christianity is one example of **monotheism**, *belief in a single divine power*. This new religion broke with the Roman Empire's traditional **polytheism**, *belief in many gods*. Yet Christianity has a unique version of the Supreme Being as a sacred Trinity: God the Creator; Jesus Christ, Son of God and Redeemer; and the Holy Spirit, a Christian's personal experience of God's presence. The claim that Jesus was divine rests on accounts of his final days on earth. Tried and sentenced to death in Jerusalem on charges that he was a threat to established political leaders, Jesus endured a cruel execution by crucifixion,

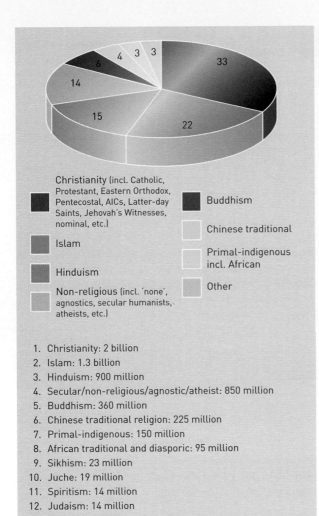

Christianity (incl. Catholic, Protestant, Eastern Orthodox, Pentecostal, AICs, Latter-day Saints, Jehovah's Witnesses, nominal, etc.)

Islam

Hinduism

Non-religious (incl. 'none', agnostics, secular humanists, atheists, etc.)

Buddhism

Chinese traditional

Primal-indigenous incl. African

Other

1. Christianity: 2 billion
2. Islam: 1.3 billion
3. Hinduism: 900 million
4. Secular/non-religious/agnostic/atheist: 850 million
5. Buddhism: 360 million
6. Chinese traditional religion: 225 million
7. Primal-indigenous: 150 million
8. African traditional and diasporic: 95 million
9. Sikhism: 23 million
10. Juche: 19 million
11. Spiritism: 14 million
12. Judaism: 14 million
13. Baha'i: 6 million
14. Jainism: 4 million
15. Shinto: 4 million
16. Cao Dai: 3 million
17. Tenrikyo: 2.4 million
18. Neo-Paganism: 1 million
19. Unitarian-Universalism: 800,000
20. Rastafarianism: 700,000
21. Scientology: 600,000
22. Zoroastrianism: 150,000

Figure 18.1   Major religions of the world ranked by number of adherents

Source: after http://www.adherents.com/Religions_By_Adherents.html, © 2002 www.adherents.com

which transformed the cross into a sacred Christian symbol. According to Christian belief, Jesus was resurrected – that is, he rose from the dead – showing that he was the Son of God.

The apostles of Jesus spread Christianity widely throughout the Mediterranean region. Although the Roman Empire initially persecuted Christians, by the fourth century Christianity had become an ecclesia – the official religion of what later came to be known as the Holy Roman Empire. What had begun as a cult four centuries before was by then an established church.

Christianity took various forms, including the Roman Catholic church and the Orthodox church, centred in Constantinople (now Istanbul, Turkey). Further division occurred towards the end of the Middle Ages, when the Protestant Reformation in Europe sparked the formation of hundreds of denominations. Dozens of these denominations now command sizeable followings in Britain (see Figure 18.2).

2. Islam

Islam has some 1.1 billion followers (19 per cent of humanity), called Muslims. Like all religions, it is not uniform but made of many Schisms – Sunnis, for example, are the more mystical branch of the Muslims. A majority of people in the Middle East are Muslims, which explains our tendency to associate Islam with Arabs in that region of the world. But most Muslims are *not* Arabs. Map 18.1 shows that a majority of people across northern Africa and western Asia are also Muslims. Moreover, significant concentrations of Muslims are found in Pakistan, India, Bangladesh, Indonesia and the southern republics of the former Soviet Union.

Islam is the second largest faith in Europe, with estimates of 6 million (3 per cent of most West European populations). If Eastern Europe were added in, the numbers would be significantly greater. Estimates place the number of British Muslims at 1,200,000 – most concentrated in the Midlands, London, Bradford, Strathclyde, Yorkshire and Lancashire. British Muslims are predominantly Sunni, with only around 25,000 Shi'as (Storry and Childs, 1997).

Islam is the word of God as revealed to the prophet Mohammed, who was born in the city of Mecca (now in Saudi Arabia) around the year 570 CE. To Muslims, Mohammed, like Jesus, is a prophet, but not a divine being (as Christians define Jesus). The Qur'an (Koran), sacred to Muslims, is the word of God (in Arabic 'Allah') as transmitted through Mohammed, God's messenger. In Arabic, the word 'Islam' means both 'submission' and 'peace', and the Qur'an urges submission to Allah as the path to inner peace. Muslims express this personal devotion in a daily ritual of five prayers.

Islam spread rapidly after the death of Mohammed, although divisions arose. All Muslims, however, accept the Five Pillars of Islam: (1) recognising Allah as the one, true God, and Mohammed as God's Messenger; (2) ritual prayer; (3) giving alms to the poor; (4) fasting during the

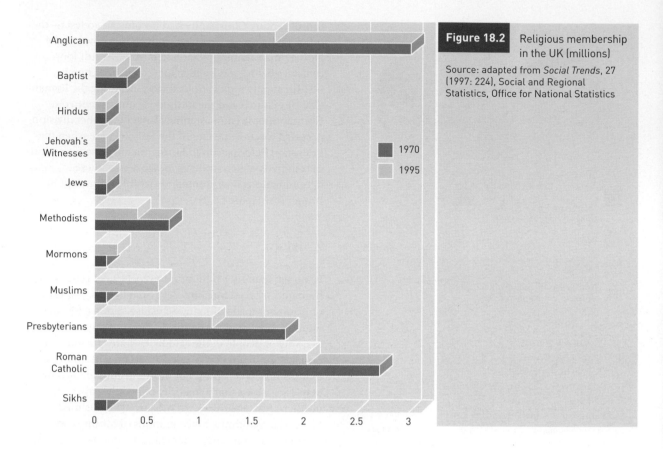

Figure 18.2 Religious membership in the UK (millions)

Source: adapted from *Social Trends*, 27 (1997: 224), Social and Regional Statistics, Office for National Statistics

month of Ramadan; and (5) making a pilgrimage at least once in a lifetime to the Sacred House of Allah in Mecca. Like Christianity, Islam holds people accountable to God for their deeds on earth. Those who live obediently will be rewarded in heaven, while evil-doers will suffer unending punishment.

Muslims are also obligated to defend their faith. Sometimes this tenet has justified holy wars against non-believers (in roughly the same way that medieval Christians joined the Crusades to recapture the Holy Land from the Muslims). Recently, in Algeria, Egypt, Iran and elsewhere, some Muslims have sought to rid their society of Western influences they regard as morally corrupting (Martin, 1982; Arjomand, 1988).

Many Westerners view Muslim women as among the most socially oppressed people on earth. Muslim women do lack many of the personal freedoms enjoyed by Muslim men, yet most accept the mandates of their religion. Moreover, patriarchy was well established in the Middle East before the birth of Mohammed. Some defenders of Islam's treatment of women argue that Islam actually improved the social position of women by demanding that husbands deal justly with their wives. Further, although Islam permits a man to have up to four wives, it admonishes men to have only one wife if having more than one would encourage him to treat women unjustly (Qur'an, 'The Women', v. 3).

3. Judaism

Speaking purely in numerical terms, Judaism, with only 15 million adherents worldwide, is among the smallest of the world's religions. Only in Israel do Jews represent a national majority. But Judaism has significance in many countries. The United States has the largest concentration of Jews (6 million people), and the largest European communities are found in France (500,000–600,000) and Britain (300,000) (Davie, 1994: 225).

Jews look to the past as a source of guidance in the present and for the future. Judaism has deep historical roots that extend back some 4,000 years before the birth of Christ to the ancient cultures of Mesopotamia. At this time, Jews were animistic, but this belief was to change after Jacob – grandson of Abraham, the earliest great ancestor – led his people to Egypt. Under Egyptian rule, Jews endured centuries of slavery. In the thirteenth century BCE, a turning point came as Moses, the adopted son of an Egyptian princess, was called by God to lead the Jews from bondage. This exodus (this word's Latin and Greek roots mean 'a marching out') from Egypt is commemorated by Jews today in the annual ritual of Passover. As a result of the Jews' liberation from bondage, Judaism became monotheistic, recognising a single, all-powerful God.

A distinctive concept of Judaism is the *covenant*, a special relationship with God by which Jews became a 'chosen people'. The covenant also implies a duty to observe God's law, especially the Ten Commandments as revealed to Moses on Mount Sinai. Jews regard the Bible (or, in Christian terms, The Old Testament) as both a record of their history and a statement of the obligations of Jewish life. Of special importance are the first five books of the Bible (Genesis, Exodus, Leviticus, Numbers and Deuteronomy), designated as the Torah (a word roughly meaning 'teaching' and 'law'). In contrast to Christianity's concern with personal salvation, Judaism emphasises moral behaviour in this world.

Judaism is composed of the three main denominations. Orthodox Jews hold strictly to traditional beliefs and practices, maintaining historical forms of dress, segregating men and women at religious services and consuming only kosher foods. Such traditional practices set off Orthodox Jews as the most sect-like. Hasidism is the most messianic and fosters a strong spiritual devotion to Judaism. In the mid-nineteenth century, many Jews sought greater accommodation to the larger society, leading to the formation of more church-like Reform Judaism. More recently, a third segment – Conservative Judaism – has established a middle ground between the other two denominations.

All Jews, however, share a keen awareness of their cultural history, which has included battling against considerable prejudice and discrimination. A collective

Two Jewish boys read the Talmud, the Jewish sacred book.
Source: Popperfoto © Gleb Garanich/Reuters

memory of centuries of slavery in Egypt, conquest by Rome and persecution in Europe has shaped Jewish identity. A militant Catholic church instigated a strong separation of Christian and Jew during the Crusades. Interestingly, the urban ghetto (derived from the Italian word *borghetto*, meaning 'settlement outside the city walls') was first home to Jews in Italy, and this form of residential segregation soon spread to other parts of Europe (Sowell, 1996: Chapter 6). Substantial numbers of Jews have lived in Eastern Europe since medieval times (with Poland often being the 'capital').

Around 120,000 Jews came to England as refugees from the pogroms of Russia between 1875 and 1914. Many settled in East London (Castles and Miller, 1993: 55). As larger numbers entered the country during the final decades of the nineteenth century, anti-Semitism increased. During the Second World War, anti-Semitism reached a vicious peak when Jews experienced the most horrific persecution in modern times as the Nazi regime in Germany systematically annihilated approximately 6 million Jews. The history of Judaism is a grim reminder of a tragic dimension of the human record – the extent to which religious minorities have been the target of hatred and even slaughter (Bedell *et al.*, 1975; Holm, 1977; Schmidt, 1980; Wilson, 1982; Eisen, 1983).

4. Hinduism

Hinduism is the oldest of all the world religions, originating in the Indus River Valley approximately 4,500 years ago. Hindus number some 775 million (14 per cent of humanity). Map 18.1 shows that Hinduism remains an eastern religion, the predominant creed of India today, although it does have a significant presence in a few societies of southern Africa as well as Indonesia.

Hinduism differs from most other religions because it did not spring from the life of any single person. Hinduism also has no sacred writings comparable to the Bible or the Qur'an. Nor does Hinduism even envisage God as a specific entity. For this reason, Hinduism – like other Eastern religions – is sometimes thought of as an 'ethical religion'. Hindu beliefs and practices vary widely, but all Hindus recognise a moral force in the universe that imposes on everyone responsibilities known as *dharma*. One traditional example of *dharma* is the need to act in concert with the traditional caste system, described in Chapter 8.

A second Hindu principle, *karma*, refers to the belief in the spiritual progress of the human soul. To a Hindu, all actions have spiritual consequences and proper living contributes to moral development. Karma works through *reincarnation*, a cycle of new birth following death, so that individuals are reborn into a spiritual state corresponding to the moral quality of their previous life. Unlike Christianity and Islam, Hinduism proclaims no ultimate judgement at the hands of a supreme god, although in the cycle of rebirth, each person reaps exactly what the individual has sown. The sublime state of *nirvana* represents spiritual perfection: when a soul reaches this rarefied plateau, it exits the cycle of rebirth.

Looking at Hinduism, we see also that not all religions can be neatly labelled monotheistic or polytheistic. Hinduism may be described as monotheistic because it envisages the universe as a single moral system; yet Hindus perceive this moral order in every element of nature. Rituals, which are central to a Hindu's life, are performed in a variety of ways. Most Hindus practise private devotions, including, for example, ritual cleansing following contact with a person of a lower caste. Many also participate in public rituals, such as *Kumbh Mela*, during which pilgrims flock to the sacred River Ganges in India to bathe in its purifying waters. This ritual, which occurs every 12 years, attracts 15 to 20 million people (Pitt, 1955: Sen, 1961; Kaufman, 1976; Schmidt, 1980).

5. Buddhism

Some 2,500 years ago, the rich culture of India also gave rise to Buddhism. Today more than 350 million people (6 per cent of humanity) embrace Buddhism, and almost all are Asians. As shown in Map 18.1, adherents of Buddhism are concentrated in parts of Southeast Asia – notably Myanmar (Burma), Thailand, Cambodia and Japan. Buddhism is also widespread in India and the People's Republic of China. Of the world religions considered so far, Buddhism most resembles Hinduism in doctrine, but, like Christianity, its inspiration springs from the life of one individual.

Siddhartha Gautama was born to a high-caste family in Nepal about 563 bce. As a young man, he was preoccupied with spiritual matters. At the age of 29, he underwent a radical personal transformation, setting off for years of travel and meditation. His path ended when he achieved what Buddhists describe as *bodhi*, or enlightenment. Understanding the essence of life, Gautama became a Buddha. During the third century BCE, the ruler of India joined the ranks of Buddhists, subsequently sending missionaries throughout Asia and elevating Buddhism to the status of a world religion.

Energised by the Buddha's personal charisma, followers spread his teachings, the *dhamma*, across India. The Buddhist ethics are found in the five Precepts: do not kill; do not steal; do not lie; do not be unchaste; do not drink intoxicants. Central to Buddhist belief is the notion that human existence involves suffering. The pleasures of the world are real, of course, but Buddhists see such experiences as transitory. This doctrine is rooted in the Buddha's own travels throughout a society rife with poverty. But the Buddha rejected wealth as a solution to suffering; on the contrary, he warned that materialism inhibits spiritual development. Buddhism's answer to world problems is for individuals to pursue personal, spiritual transformation.

Buddhism closely parallels Hinduism in recognising no god of judgement; rather, it finds spiritual consequences in each daily action. Another similarity lies in its belief in reincarnation. Here, again, only full enlightenment ends the cycle of death and rebirth, thereby liberating a person from the suffering of the world (Schumann, 1974).

6. Chinese religions and 'Confucianism'

From about 200 BCE until the beginning of the twentieth century, Confucianism was an ecclesia – the official religion of China. Following the 1949 Revolution, religion was suppressed by the communist government of the new People's Republic of China. Although officials provide little in the way of data to establish precise numbers, hundreds of millions of Chinese are still influenced by Confucianism. While almost all adherents to Confucianism live in China, Chinese immigration has introduced this religion to other societies in Southeast Asia.

Confucius or, properly, K'ung-Fu-tzu, lived between 551 and 479 BCE. He shared with Buddha a deep concern for the problems and suffering in the world. The Buddha's response was a sect-like withdrawal from the world; Confucius, by contrast, instructed his followers to engage in the world according to a strict code of moral conduct. Thus it was that Confucianism became fused with the traditional culture of China. Here we see a second example of what might be called a 'national religion'. As Hinduism has remained largely synonymous with Indian culture, Confucianism is enshrined in the Chinese way of life.

A central concept of Confucianism is *jen*, meaning humanness. In practice, this means that we must always subordinate our self-interest to moral principle. In the family, the individual must display loyalty and consideration for others. Likewise, families must remain mindful of their duties to the larger community. In this way, layer upon layer of moral obligation integrates society as a whole. Most of all, Confucianism stands out as lacking a clear sense of the sacred. We could view Confucianism, recalling Durkheim's analysis, as the celebration of society itself as sacred. Alternatively, we

(a)

(b)

(c)

(d)

(e)

When Western people perform religious rituals, they typically do so collectively and formally as members of specific congregations. Eastern people, by contrast, visit shrines individually and informally, without joining a specific congregation. (a) Filipino house maids at mass in Jaffa, Israel; (b) Children at Pentecostal Gospel Church in Seoul, South Korea; (c) Moonie wedding, South Korea; (d) Buddhist monks in Colombo protesting against the war; (e) Kumbh Mela festival in India

Source: (a) Magnum © Abbas, (b) Magnum © Abbas, (c) Popperfoto, (d) Popperfoto © Anuruddha Lokuhapuracahchi, (e) Network Photos © Gideon Mendel

might argue that Confucianism is less a religion than a model of disciplined living. Certainly the historical dominance of Confucianism helps to explain why Chinese culture has long taken a sceptical attitude towards the supernatural. If we conclude that Confucianism is best thought of as a disciplined way of life, we must also recognise that it shares with religion a body of beliefs and practices that have as their goal goodness, concern for others and the promotion of social harmony (Kaufman, 1976; Schmidt, 1980).

Religion: East and West

This brief overview of world religions points up two general differences between the belief systems that predominate in Eastern and Western societies. First, Western religions (Christianity, Judaism and Islam) are typically deity-based, with a clear focus on God. Eastern religions (Hinduism, Buddhism, Confucianism) tend to be more like ethical codes that make a less clear-cut distinction between the sacred and secular. Second, the operational unit of Western religious organisations is the congregation. That is, people attend a specific place of worship with others, most of whom are members. Eastern religious organisations, by contrast, are more broadly tied into culture itself. For this reason, for example, a visitor finds a Thai or Hong Kong temple awash with people – tourists and worshippers alike – who come and go on their own schedule, paying little attention to those around them.

These two distinctions do not overshadow the common element of all religions: having a conception of a higher moral force or purpose that transcends the concerns of everyday life. In all these religious beliefs, people of the world find guidance and a sense of purpose for their lives.

Religion in Europe

Christianity is one of the foundations of European societies. For much of the past two millennia, Christianity has defined life in Europe, dignifying all major actions, from birth and baptism through marriage to death and burial. It has held out the hope of 'salvation'. In pre-Reformation feudal society, the church was unitary – supported by royalty and the entire population. Hamilton says:

> The medieval world was Christian in the sense that everybody shared a common understanding of the world in which they lived based on Christian

premises. Only the very learned had full and detailed knowledge of the whole world picture, but everybody understood some part of it.
>
> (Hamilton, 1996: 87)

Yet, while all the countries of Europe make some claim to be Christian and to have Christian values, there are significant religious divides both within and across countries. A potted history would have to include:

- The early combats with Judaism in the struggle to establish a dominant religion.

- The fourth-century split of the European Christian Church into Roman Catholicism in the West and Greek Orthodoxy in the East. While Roman Catholicism spread to the Americas, the Eastern Orthodox lost ground in central Europe and Asia to Islam during the eleventh century.

- The long struggles between empires and the papacy. Pope Innocent III (1198–1216) finally established a papal state in central Italy.

- The conflicts within the church itself: the heretical struggles and executions of witches, etc., along with a rather dissolute clergy with an eye on wealth.

- The continuing conflicts with other religions, with high periodic violence (the Spanish Inquisition, the Crusades and the Nazi Holocaust).

- The Reformation: it started in Germany with Martin Luther (1483–1546) when reformists renounced allegiances to Rome in 1520. By 1570, Protestants had established a presence in many places – especially Scandinavia, Britain and 'Baltic Europe', moving later into The Netherlands, France, Spain and even Italy. Calvinism (formed by John Calvin, 1509–64) emerged in France, The Netherlands and Scotland.

- Migration and missionary missions to colonies in the Americas and Africa.

- The rise of science, with its claims for rationality, as a serious challenge to Christianity during the Enlightenment and the Industrial Revolution.

- The denial of religion throughout Eastern Europe during its communist period, with its attendant struggles from within. (In some countries, such as Poland, religion became a major instigator of change.) Subsequently, there have been major changes: the number of active churches in Moscow, for instance, grew from 50 in 1988 to 250 in 1993.

Today, in Europe, divides and schisms continue, often based on these past conflicts and issues. Indeed, Yugoslavia, torn by divisions between Christians as well as between Christianity and Islam, has dramatically revealed the sharper edge of the continuing conflicts. There are also deep-seated conflicts between Protestants and Catholics (as in Northern Ireland) and between religion and humanism (as in The Netherlands). The Christian Democratic Parties in many European governments partly base their platforms on Christian principles. In the UK, the Queen is head of both Church and state and the two are interconnected. In Germany, the government collects church taxes (*Kirchensteuer*) on behalf of churches and uses it for social services. Abortion issues continue to preoccupy those countries with a strong Catholic base.

The most obvious divide lies between the more religious, Catholic countries of southern Europe (Italy, Spain, Greece and Portugal) and the less religious Protestant north. But there are divergences: France and Ireland are predominantly Catholic, Belgium, The Netherlands, Britain and the Nordic countries are generally less religious.

There are three main minority faiths in Europe. Islam now constitutes the second largest faith in Europe, claiming 6 million faithful – 3 per cent of most European populations. If Eastern Europe were added in, the numbers would be significantly greater. Estimates place the number of British Muslims at 1,200,000.

There are possibly around 1 million Jews in post-Holocaust Western Europe, concentrated mainly in France (500,000–600,000) and Britain (300,000).

And as we shall see later, there has been a substantial increase in what we can call the new religious movements (NRMs) (Clarke, 1988; Davie, 2000: 13–14).

Religion in the UK

In contrast with the United States, where 90 per cent of adults voice a religious preference (NORC, 1994: 114), but in line with much of Europe, Britain is becoming a relatively non-religious country. Only 21 per cent of the British population say they have no doubts about the existence of God, whereas 26 per cent either do not believe in God or do not know whether God exists (*Social Trends*, 1997: 13.23). Trinitarian churches have seen a fall in membership from 9.1 million adults in 1970 to 6.4 million in 1995 (*Social Trends*, 1997: 13.23). There has been a major decline of support, as seen by attendance at religious services in recent years. Nearly half of the population either never or hardly ever attend (*Social Trends*, 2001: Table 23).

In Britain, the Churches of England and Wales are formally tied to both Parliament and the monarchy, though the Church of England has shed its image as the 'Tory Party at prayer'. Indeed, during the long period of Conservative government from 1979 to 1997, the Church of England regularly provided reports which implicitly criticised the policies of the government, particularly *Faith in the City* (ACUPA, 1985) which highlighted the plight of the poor who had not benefited from free-market Thatcherism.

Membership in established, 'mainstream' churches has dwindled. Figure 18.1 demonstrates that support for the Anglican, Roman Catholic, Presbyterian and Baptist churches has declined significantly in recent years. Nominally, there are around 27 million Anglicans (nearly two-thirds claimed to associate with the Church of England), but only 2 million have officially registered. There are some 5 million Catholics, who are much more likely to attend church (Liverpool is Britain's only mainly Catholic city). Nevertheless, the churches remain heavily involved in the cultural life of the UK, through such activities as playgroups, jumble sales, youth clubs, care for the elderly and community centres. Christianity may now be more of a cultural force than a spiritual one.

As the established churches lose members, however, other religious organisations are showing surprising strength. As Figure 18.1 suggests, the UK now has substantial populations of Muslims, Sikhs, Hindus and Jews, which, in contrast to the Christian faiths, have generally grown significantly in recent years. Immigration initially underpinned the numbers of Muslims, Sikhs and Hindus, but now many of the 1,200,000 Muslims, who have established large communities to be found in London, the Midlands, West Yorkshire and Strathclyde, were born in the UK. Britain has the second-largest Jewish community in Europe.

Despite these general observations, measuring religious involvement in any country can be quite a difficult exercise. Peter Brierley (2000), who has studied this in the UK in some detail, suggests there are three major ways to measure it. First, there is *involvement in religious community*: this would involve anyone associated with religion – through baptism, for example. Second, there is *religious membership* – those who actually join a religious organisation. Finally, there is *religious attendance* – those who actually go to religious services. Figure 18.3 attempts to estimate the religious structure of the UK population on the basis of these measurements. Although this is not up to date, it does show the structures that need measuring to assess religious involvement. Table 18.1 shows the level of these affiliations as measured at the 2001 Census (not all answered it though). It suggests that just over three quarters of the population reported having a religion,

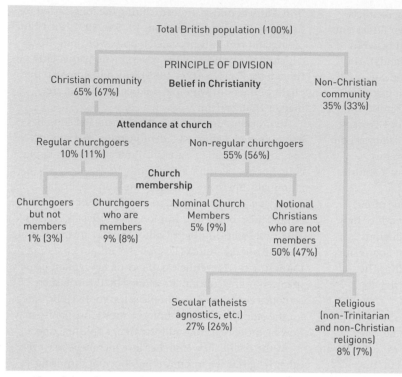

Total British population (100%)

PRINCIPLE OF DIVISION
Belief in Christianity

Christian community
65% (67%)

Non-Christian
community
35% (33%)

Attendance at church

Regular churchgoers
10% (11%)

Non-regular churchgoers
55% (56%)

Church membership

Churchgoers
but not
members
1% (3%)

Churchgoers
who are
members
9% (8%)

Nominal Church
Members
5% (9%)

Notional
Christians
who are not
members
50% (47%)

Secular (atheists
agnostics, etc.)
27% (26%)

Religious
(non-Trinitarian
and non-Christian
religions)
8% (7%)

Figure 18.3   Estimates of the religious structure of the population of Great Britain, 1980 and 1990

Figures in brackets give 1980 percentages. 'Normal' are people who are church members but who do not attend the church at least once a month; 'notional' are people who say they are Christian but are neither church members nor regular attendees.

Source: adapted from Brierley (2000: 661)

Table 18.1	UK population by religious identification	
	Thousands	**%**
Christian	42079	71.6
Buddhist	152	0.3
Hindu	559	1.0
Jewish	267	0.5
Muslim	1591	2.7
Sikh	336	0.6
Other religion	179	0.3
All religions	*45163*	*76.8*
No religion	9104	15.5
Not stated	4289	7.3
All no religion/not stated[1]	13626	23.2
Base	58789	100

Source: *Social Trends*, 2004

Muslim Leaders in front of Britain's oldest mosque, at Earlsfield.

Source: Popperfoto

and about 16 per cent reported they had no religion. This included agnostics, atheists, heathens and those who wrote Jedi Knight as a response to the question! (0.7 per cent!). In the end it shows that very few attend and very few are members but that a larger number may well affiliate with religions on particular occasions.

Religion in the twenty-first century

The twentieth century was predicted to be the age when 'the death of God' would be proclaimed. Yet at the start of the twenty-first century this is clearly not so. Indeed, some commentators have suggested that we are entering a new era where religion is alive and well all over the world, even though it is undergoing a number of quite significant changes.

In this section we will detect four major trends at work. These are:

1. Limited, partial secularisation.
2. The growth of fundamentalisms alongside 'the clash of civilisations'.
3. The arrival of new religious movements and the 'New Age'.
4. The development of new institutional (maybe postmodern?) forms of religion like cyber-churches and mega-churches.

Limited and partial secularisation

The first trend regularly discussed among sociologists is **secularisation**, *the historical decline in the importance of the supernatural and the sacred*. For society as a whole, secularisation points to the waning influence of religion in everyday life: we have just seen this in the description of religion in the UK above. And as religious organisations become more secular, they direct attention less to other-worldly issues (such as life after death) and more to worldly affairs (such as sheltering the homeless, feeding the hungry and raising funds). In addition, secularisation means that functions once performed mostly by the church (such as charity) are now primarily the responsibility of businesses and government. More, it means that people are less likely to view the world in spiritual terms and are more likely to see it in terms of material goods and consumption – a trend detected in Chapter 14.

Secularisation, with Latin roots meaning 'the present age', is commonly associated with modern, technologically advanced societies (Cox, 1971). Jose Casanova has suggested that the term itself can lead to confusion, as it contains three different strands that need clarifying. The first is 'secularisation as decline of religious beliefs and practices'. This is perhaps the most popular meaning, but it conceals other hidden and deeper meanings. Thus the second is 'secularisation as

differentiation of the secular spheres from religious institutions'. It is in Europe that one can find the least differentiation between state and the church. And finally, secularisation may be seen as 'marginalisation of religion to a privatised sphere' (Casanova, 1994: 211). Here, while religion may still be honoured in public, it plays less of a role in the private life of individuals.

Secularisation is often seen as one result of the increasing importance of science in understanding human affairs. Science takes over from religion. In broader terms, people perceive birth, illness and death less as the work of a divine power than as natural stages in the life course. Such events are now more likely to occur in the presence of physicians (scientific specialists) than religious leaders (whose knowledge is based on faith). With the rise of science, religion's sphere of influence has diminished. Theologian Harvey Cox elaborates:

> The world looks less and less to religious rules and rituals for its morality or its meanings. For some, religion provides a hobby, for others a mark of national or ethnic identification, for still others an aesthetic delight. For fewer and fewer does it provide an inclusive and commanding system of personal and cosmic values and explanations.
>
> (Cox, 1971: 3)

If Cox is correct, should we expect that religion will disappear completely some day? Is there a decline in religion? The consensus among sociologists is 'no' (Hammond, 1985; Berger, 1999), for two reasons. First, if the world is looked at globally, then religion is still an overwhelming and dominant force. It is true that religion holds less sway in Europe (and particularly the Scandinavian countries). It is also true that secular views are common among what may be identified as an international subculture of humanists among academics, whose views do have global significance and influence. But everywhere else, religious fervour is clearly rising. Peter Berger says: 'the world today, with some exceptions, is as furiously religious as it ever was, and in some places more so than ever' (1997: 32).

Second, even as traditional religious forms flourish, modernity and postmodernity – with their growing disenchantment with the world – create an ongoing requirement for something beyond itself, looking for new forms of meaning (Davie, 1998). We may see this as generating three forms of religious revival: (1) fundamentalisms; (2) the rise of new religious movements (NRMs); and (3) new forms of religion, including civil religion. We will consider each of these below.

Religious fundamentalisms and the 'clash of civilisations'

The most extreme version of this change is the apparent growth of **fundamentalism**, *a conservative religious doctrine that opposes intellectualism and worldly accommodation in favour of restoring traditional, other-worldly spirituality.* Although it is a bit of a rag-bag word – meaning all things to all people – it generally suggests belief in a timeless and absolute value given to sacred writings in all times and places. It is applied to a wide variety of groups: from the 'Moral Majority' in the United States, to Orthodox Jews in Israel and the Islamic government in Iran. In response to what they see as the growing influence of science and the erosion of the conventional family, religious fundamentalists defend their version of traditional values. From this point of view, the liberal churches are simply too tolerant of religious pluralism and too open to change. The enemy of fundamentalism is the 'Great Satan of Modernity' (Bruce, 2000).

A number of features distinguish religious fundamentalists of various stripes.

1. *They interpret 'infallible' sacred texts literally.* Fundamentalists, who see sacred texts as infallible blueprints for life, insist on literal interpretations of the sacred texts as a means of countering what they see as excessive intellectualism among more liberal and revisionist organisations.

2. *They reject religious pluralism.* Fundamentalists maintain that tolerance and relativism water down personal faith, and harshly judge most modern faiths as illegitimate.

3. *They find a personal experience of God's presence.* Fundamentalists seek to propagate spiritual revival. They define all areas of life as sacred. For example, fundamentalist Christians seek to be 'born again' to establish a personal relationship with Jesus that will shape a person's everyday life.

4. *They oppose secularisation and modernity.* Fundamentalists believe that modernity undermines religious conviction. Secular humanism leads to profane moral corruption.

5. *They promote conservative beliefs, including patriarchal ones.* Fundamentalists argue that God intends humans to live in heterosexual families ruled by men. They blame feminist and gay rights movements for contributing to moral decline. In particular, fundamentalists condemn abortion and decry lesbian and gay relations (Viguerie, 1981; Hunter, 1983; Speer, 1984; Ellison and Sherkat, 1993; Green, 1993).

6. *They emerge in response to social inequality or a perceived social crisis.* Fundamentalists attract members by offering solutions to desperate, worried or dejected people.

Taken together, these traits have given fundamentalism a backward and self-righteous reputation. At the same time, this brief sketch also helps us to understand why adherents find such religions an appealing alternative to the more intellectual, tolerant and worldly 'mainstream' denominations.

Fundamentalist religions in the UK and across Europe have recently gained strength, but we must use the term with care. While conservative branches of many religions have turned fundamentalist, the term is often used pejoratively to dismiss religious movements which question the status quo. In particular, as Chapter 11 noted, there has been the development of 'Islamophobia', whereby the label 'fundamentalist' is often used in the West to dismiss the claims of a range of Islamic movements. Even in cases where Islam has evolved into an extreme form, fundamentalist extremism often emerges in response to the capitalist version of modernity that has favoured the West while leaving extreme poverty elsewhere (Esposito, 1992: 14). As we have seen in Chapter 11, it is likely that issues of fundamentalism will become more and more central in the twenty-first century.

Moreover, we should not see fundamentalism as necessarily new. Steven Bruce indeed suggests that:

> There is nothing at all unusual in people taking religion very seriously. What we now regard as religious 'extremism' was commonplace 200 years ago in the Western world and is still commonplace in most parts of the globe. It is not the dogmatic believer who insists that the sacred texts are divinely inspired and true, who tries to model his life on the ethical requirements of those texts, and who seeks to impose these requirements on the entire society who is unusual. The liberal who supposes that his sacred texts are actually human constructions of differing moral worth, whose religion makes little difference to his life, and who is not quite happy to accept that what his God requires of him is not binding on other members of his society: this is the strange and remarkable creature.
>
> (Bruce, 2000: 116–117).

The clash of civilisations

It is precisely this religious conviction that has been behind many historical wars. Yet one of the more dramatic potentials that arise from the spread of fundamentalism may be the increasing risk of major international conflicts based upon religion. Samuel P. Huntington, for instance, sees new fault lines of world conflict arising from religious resurgence across the world in all faiths: 'The unsecularisation of the world is one of the dominant social facts in the late twentieth century' (Huntington, 1996: 96, citing George Wigel). He sees localised '*fault line*' wars breaking out all over the world, especially between Muslims and non-Muslims. At the same time, '*core state*' conflicts are also appearing between the major states of civilisations. A major issue here may be between the Christian West and the Muslim world. In any event, since the breakdown of the Cold War between East and West, the major issues of conflict have returned to all those religious schisms that dominated much of earlier history too.

The emergence of new religious movements (NRMs) and the 'New Age'

While membership in established, 'mainstream' churches may have plummeted, affiliation with other religious organisations (including Seventh-Day Adventists and Christian sects) has risen just as dramatically. Indeed, secularisation itself may be self-limiting. As church-like organisations become more worldly, some people within a religious 'marketplace' may simply abandon them in favour of more sect-like religious communities that better address their spiritual concerns and whose members seem to exhibit greater religious commitment (Stark and Bainbridge, 1981; Roof and McKinney, 1987; Jacquet and Jones, 1991; Warner, 1993; Iannaccone, 1994). Thus, in the face of secularisation and the seeming decline in religion, many so-called NRMs have appeared. Indeed, one of the most striking developments of recent years has been the proliferation of NRMs. It is estimated that there may now be as many as 20,000 new religious groupings in Europe alone.

One way of thinking about these movements is to see their affinities with the traditional mainstream religions described above. Thus, some are linked to Hinduism (Hari Krishnas and the disciples of Bhagwan Rajneesh); others to Buddhism (various Zen groups); and others to Christianity (the Children of God). Some NRMs are eclectic (The Unification Church), while others have links with the Human Potential Movement (which advocates therapies to liberate human potential, such as transcendental meditation). Roy Wallis (1976) has proposed a typology of these growing groups. He suggests three main kinds of NRM: world affirming, world rejecting and world accommodating.

The *world affirming* groups are usually individualistic, life-positive and aim to release 'human potentials'. They encourage an active participation in society. Research suggests that these are more common among middle-aged, middle-class groups who are often disillusioned and disenchanted with material values and in search of new positive meanings. These groups generally lack a church, ritual worship or strong ethical systems. They are often more akin to 'therapy groups' than traditional religions.

A major example of this is the Church of Scientology, founded by L. Ron Hubbard. Hubbard developed the philosophy of 'dianetics', which stresses the importance of 'unblocking the mind' and leading it to becoming 'clear'. Hubbard believed in a rebirthing. His church spread throughout the world (with a base in California) and generated courses (usually expensive) and books galore (see Wallis, 1976).

A second example is Transcendental Meditation (TM). Brought to the West by the Hindu Mahareshi Mahesh Yogi in the early 1950s, it focuses upon building a personal mantra which is then dwelt upon for periods each day. Again, the focus is upon a good world – not an evil one – and a way of 'finding oneself' through positive thinking. Much of this mode of thinking has helped generate a major new linked movement: that of 'New Age'.

'*New Age*' is a hybrid mix and match of religions, therapies and astrologies, and has become increasingly important since the 1970s. It is part of what might be seen as the globalisation of modern religion – mixing as it does elements from both Eastern and Western traditions, along with the wider concerns of environment and ecology. Bruce (1996: 197) suggests these are largely 'audience' or 'client cults'. The former has led to a major market of 'self-help therapy' books with mass distribution; the latter has led to the proliferation of new 'therapists' (from astrological to colour therapists), establishing new relationships between a consumer and a seller. Among the practices involved are tarot readings, crystals, reflexology, channelling and I Ching. Currently, many bookshops devote more shelf space to these sorts of book than to books on Christianity. The fascination with television programmes such as *The X Files* may also be seen as part of this. It brings a new science, a new ecology, a new psychology and a new spirituality. 'New Agers make the monistic assumption that the Self is sacred' (Heelas, 1996: 140).

The *world rejecting* groups are like the sects described above. In some ways they are quite like conventional religions in that they may require prayer and the study of key religious texts, and they have strong ethical codes. They are always highly critical of the outside (material evil) world and they demand change of their members through strong communal activities. They are exclusive,

Bulgarian Hare Krishna parade through the streets of Sofia, August 1996.

Source: Popperfoto © Dimitar Dilkoff/Reuters

share possessions and seek to submerge identities to the greater whole. They are often millenarian – expecting God's intervention to change the world and inspiring activism to make this come about ('millenarian' is derived from the millennium, the 1,000-year reign of Christ). Researchers have suggested that it may well be people who live on the margins who are most attracted to these groups.

Perhaps the most widely cited example is the Unification Church (popularly known as the Moonies), founded in Korea by the Reverend Sun Myung Moon in 1954. It appeared in California in the early 1960s where it was studied by the sociologist John Lofland in his book *Doomsday Cult* (2nd edn, 1977). Later Eileen Barker (1981, 1984) studied it in England. The Unification Church rejects the mundane secular world as evil and has strict moral rules: monogamous heterosexual sex, no smoking, no drinking, etc.

Another example is the Hare Krishna (Children of God, or ISKON – the International Society for Krishna Consciousness). The members are distinguished by their shaved heads, pigtails and flowing gowns; Hare Krishnas repeat a mantra 16 times a day.

These sects are the movements that have come under most public scrutiny in recent years, largely because of the fear of indoctrination and the problems of severe control and even mass suicide. There is a growing list of extreme examples – the mass suicide by Jim Jones's People Temple in Jonestown, Guyana (Hall, 1987); the Aum Supreme Truth (run by Shoko Ashara) which detonated poisonous gas canisters in the Tokyo underground in 1995, leaving 12 dead and 5,000 sick; the more recent suicidal death of the 39 members of Heaven's Gate in California when they sighted the Hale-Bopp comet. Heaven's Gate programmers posted a message on their website saying: 'We are happily prepared to leave this world.' While these new religious forms mirror the means and powers that other religions have continued to employ, they are seen by the press and public as deviant, and hence attract more attention.

World accommodating religions are more orthodox. They maintain some connections with mainstream religion, but give a high premium to the inner religious life. In England, the Neo-Pentecostals are a good example. The Holy Spirit 'speaks' through them, giving the gift of 'speaking in tongues'. Such religions are usually dismayed at both the state of the world and the state of organised mainstream religions. They seek to establish both older certainties and faith, while giving them a new vitality.

The arrival of new religious forms and organisations

One dimension of secularisation is the rise of what Robert Bellah (1975) has called **civil religion**, *a quasi-religious loyalty binding individuals in a basically secular society*. In other words, even if some traditional dimensions of religiosity are weakening, new religious qualities may be found in such things as patriotism, membership in associations, good citizenship and even sports meetings which can retain religious qualities. He conducted research in the United States, where, he argues, religious qualities appear in a range of rituals, from rising to sing the US national anthem at sporting events, to Presidential inauguration ceremonies, to sitting down to watch televised public parades several times a year. In England, ceremonies linked to the royal family (coronations, royal weddings, etc.), as well as village fêtes, town parades and similar gatherings, all may serve these same functions.

The enormous outpouring of grief around the death of Diana Princess of Wales could be taken as further evidence of civil religion. Immediately after her death in Paris on 31 August 1997, hundreds of thousands of people publicly showed their grief by sending flowers, attending the funeral and signing 'commemoration books'. These people came from all walks of life and religions, but created a strong sense of group belonging and national – even international – grief.

The electronic, 'cyber' and 'mega-church'

In contrast to the small village congregations of years past, some religious organisations – especially fundamentalists – have become electronic churches dominated by 'prime-time preachers' (Hadden and Swain, 1981). Electronic religion has been especially strong in the United States and has propelled charismatic preachers such as Oral Roberts, Pat Robertson, Robert Schuller and others to greater prominence than all but a few clergy have ever enjoyed in the past. About 5 per cent of the US television audience (around 10 million people) regularly tune into religious television, while perhaps 20 per cent (around 40 million) watch some religious programming every week (Martin, 1981; Gallup, 1982; NORC, 1994).

During the 1980s, regular solicitation of contributions brought a financial windfall to some religious organisations. Seen on 3,200 stations in half the countries in the world, for example, Jimmy Swaggart received as much as $180 million annually in donations. But some media-based ministries were corrupted by the power of money. In 1989, Jim Bakker (who began his television career in 1965 hosting a children's puppet show with his wife Tammy Faye) was jailed following a conviction for defrauding contributors. Such cases, although few in number, attracted enormous international attention and undermined public support as people began to wonder whether television preachers were more interested in raising moral standards or private cash.

Along with the electronic church, we can also find the growth of the 'cyber-church' and the 'mega-church'. The former is easy to find on a website (all major world religions now have a proliferation of websites) but so too do the multitude of smaller new religious movements. It is a prime force for information giving, but it is also an arena for membership recruitment.

'Mega-churches' are very large worship centres – often only loosely affiliated with existing denominations, and more likely to be identified with 'born-again' religions or charismatic Christians. In the United States and all over the world they can be found in shopping malls and parking lots. Characteristically, they are very large: they house as many as 1,000- 3,000 worshippers or more. The Yoido Full Gospel Church in Seoul, South Korea, has six daily services in a facility with 13,000 seats! It has some 700,000 members and reaches 30,000 other worshippers via closed-circuit television. There are 11 choirs and a 24-piece orchestra. In the United States, the largest mega-church is the Lakewood Church, Houston, with 25,060 total weekend attenders in 2003. In 1970, there were just ten such churches; by 2003 there were 740. Many of them function like businesses with their own media (contemporary music, television) technologies and massive budgets (upwards of US $12 million).

CONTROVERSY AND DEBATE

IS THE WORLD BECOMING DESECULARISED?

For years now, philosophers have proclaimed 'the death of God' and sociologists have talked about the ways in which the modern world is becoming increasingly secularised. After all, as science and rationality become more and more central to the ways in which the modern world works, so the mysteries of the universe, which religion so often had to explain, now become demystified. And yet, increasingly sociologists point to the weakness of this secularisation thesis and suggest that far from becoming less and less religious, the trends actually suggest we are becoming more and more religious. It is not secularisation that is the issue but desecularisation.

We are talking globally. It is clearly the case that much of northern Europe is becoming less and less religious. But it seems that everywhere else in the world this is not so. Peter Berger suggests that 'on the international religious scene, it is conservative or orthodox or traditionalist movements that are on the rise almost everywhere' (1999: 6). He suggests this is so partly because they are opposed to what they see as developments in the modern world, but

also because religion itself is the status quo: it has always been around, and it will continue to be so. What we are witnessing now is both an 'Islamic upsurge' alongside a Christian 'Evangelical upsurge'. The Catholic impact can be found from Manila to Krakow, and from Santiago to Seoul (Berger, 1999: 19). With over 1 billion adherents, it is to be found in almost every country, served by some 4,300 bishops and some 404,500 priests. Religion is fanning wars and civil wars on the Indian subcontinent, in the Balkans, in the Middle East and in Africa. There are disputes in Latin America, problems in Northern Ireland. But almost everywhere, religion is on the rise.

CONTINUE THE DEBATE:

1. What evidence is there for desecularisation? For secularisation?

2. Do you believe that the modern and postmodern worlds are showing a decline in religion? Why? Why not?

3. Are the new religious revivals a response to the crises of the modern world?

Taking stock and looking ahead

The pace of social change is accelerating. As the world becomes more complex, rapid change often seems to outstrip our capacity to make sense of it all. While technological advances undermine religiosity in some people, for others, religious guidance and religious communities offer the key for coping with change. Science alone seems unable to address the most central human needs and questions. Moreover, new technology confronts us with vexing moral dilemmas – when and whether to use genetically modified organs in animals or aborted human foetal tissue in transplants, how to ethically regulate cloning, and many others.

As we have seen, two contradictory processes are happening at the start of the twenty-first century. On the

one hand, the process of 'secularisation', a growing disenchantment with the spiritual and the supernatural and, for some, a turn to rationality and science, has gained increasing support with many. It has spread across much of Europe and other Western cultures, with the partial exception of the United States, but remains relatively weak in the rest of the world, where traditional religions hold stronger sway. On the other hand, the growth of religious fundamentalism, the continuing adherence of billions to the 'mainstream' religions, the continuing clash of civilisations over their passionate commitment to their faiths (as in the war in Afghanistan), and the development of more and more 'new religions' all suggest that multiple religions, with all their potential for conflicts, wars and human suffering, will remain a central element of modern society for many years to come.

SUMMARY

1. Religion is a major social institution based on distinguishing the sacred from the profane. Religion is a matter of faith, not scientific evidence, which people express through various rituals. Sociology analyses the social consequences and correlates of religion, but no scientific research can make claims about the ultimate truth or falsity of any religious belief.

2. **Emile Durkheim** argued that individuals experience the power of their society through religion. His structural–functional analysis suggests that religion promotes social cohesion and conformity by conferring meaning and purpose on life. Using the symbolic-interaction paradigm, **Peter Berger** explains that religious beliefs are socially constructed as a means of responding to life's uncertainties and disruptions. Using the social conflict paradigm, **Karl Marx** charged that religion promotes social inequality. Historically, however, religious ideals have both supported hierarchy and motivated people to seek greater equality. **Max Weber's** analysis of Calvinism's contribution to the rise of industrial capitalism demonstrates religion's power to promote social change. More recently, **Hervieu-Leger** has come to see religion as 'chain of memory'. Societies have memories, and as this weakens, so too does religion.

3. Churches, which are religious organisations well integrated into their society, fall into two categories – ecclesias and denominations. Sects, the result of religious division, are marked by suspicion of the larger society as well as charismatic leadership. Cults are religious organisations that embrace new and unconventional beliefs and practices.

4. Many hunter-gatherer societies are and have been generally animistic, with religious life just one facet of family life; in more complex societies, religion emerges as a distinct social institution. Followers of six world religions – Christianity, Islam, Judaism, Hinduism, Buddhism and Confucianism – represent three-quarters of all humanity.

5. Four main issues are appearing in contemporary debates over religion: secularisation, the growth of fundamentalism, the rise of new religious movements, and the development of new religious forms.

6. Secularisation refers to the diminishing importance of the supernatural and the sacred.

7. Fundamentalists oppose secularisation, religious pluralism and the breakdown of heterosexual patriarchy, which they see as the only moral structure of human society. Fundamentalists advocate literal interpretation of sacred texts and pursue the personal experience of God's presence. Many such movements arise in response to a crisis or extreme social inequality. Huntington sees the spread of fundamentalisms as connecting to a 'clash of civilisations'.

8. New religious movements (NRMs) may be world-affirming, world-rejecting or world-accommodating. Civil religion is a quasi-religious belief by which people profess loyalty to their society, often in the form of patriotism.

9. Recent developments include the growth of electronic, cyber and mega-churches which are often run like businesses and can attract huge followings.

CRITICAL-THINKING QUESTIONS

1. You can use the website to look at all of the world's major religions as outlined in the text. It is important to note that these 'traditional' religions are using the most up-to-date technologies to spread their word. Consider how modernist tools can be used to bring out traditional ideas of the sacred. What contradictions does this raise?

2. Using the website, track down the sites of some major new religious movements and inspect what they have to say. Why are there so many such sites? Does this indicate that religion really is not in decline?

3. Using the web, look for evidence which points to a decline in religion in Europe. In what ways does religion seem to be getting stronger?

GOING FURTHER

Further reading

For general introductions:

Steven Bruce, *Religion in the Modern World: From Cathedrals to Cults* (1996)

Grace Davie, *Religion in Modern Europe: A Memory Mutates* (2000)
Discuss the diversity of religion in Western Europe and follow the theory that religion is a form of collective memory.

On globalisation and religion:

Lester Kurtz, *Gods in the Global Village: The World's Religions in Sociological Perspective* (1995)
Provides a detailed account of all the world's major religions and an analysis of how they are changing under the impact of globalisation and multiculturalism.

On politics:

Steven Bruce, *Politics and Religion* (2003)
An important study of the ways in which religion connects to empires, nations, political parties and social protest.

On recent developments:

Peter Berger, *The Desecularization of the World* (1999)
Provides a major refutation of the secularisation thesis.

Steven Bruce, *Fundamentalism* (2000)
Looks at the rise of fundamentalism in the face of modernity, which fundamentalists see as the 'Great Satan'.

Marc Galanter, *Cults: Faith, Healing and Coercion* (2nd edn, 1999)
Looks at charismatic cults in the United States through plenty of case materials.

More information

Ninian Smart's *Atlas of the World's Religions* (1999) is a beautifully illustrated history and guide to the major world's religions. Paul Weller's *Religions in the UK: Directory 2001–03* (3rd edn, 2003) is a comprehensive guide to the UK's faith communities.

Watch a video

- Antonia Bird's *Priest* (1994): a young gay priest confronts his religion.

- Richard Brook's *Elmer Gantry* (1960): charlatanism and evangelism in a classic story.

- Stanley Kramer's *Inherit the Wind* (1960): based on the Scopes 'Monkey' trial – science versus religion.

- There is also an online *Journal of Film and Religion* produced from the University of Nebraska, http://www.unomaha.edu/~wwwjrf/.

Connecting up

Connect to other chapters

- For more on the theories of Marx, Durkheim and Weber, see Chapter 4.
- New religious movements express some of the themes of new social movements which are discussed in Chapter 15.

To the websites

Major world religion websites:

- World Council of Churches:
  http://www.wcc-coe.org/
- Islam at a glance:
  http://www.islam-guide.com/
- Jewish culture and history:
  http://www.igc.apc.org/ddickerson/judaica.html
- Hinduism Today:
  http://www.himalayanacademy.com/

- Zen Buddhism:
  http://www.dharmanet.org/infowebz.html
- Sociosite:
  http://www2.fmg.uva.nl/sociosite/topics/religion.html
  This major sociology site has an extensive page of links to all the major religions.
- New Religious Movements database:
  http://religiousmovements.lib.virginia.edu/
  Details more than 200 sites of new religions.
- Cult Information Centre:
  http://www.cultinformation.org.uk
  Details of the work of the centre, based at the London School of Economics.

Adherents.com

http://www.adherents.com/largecom/

Details some of the largest religious communities of all kinds to be found in the world.

For additional case studies, multiple choice questions, internet exercises, and annotated weblinks specific to this chapter, visit this book's website at **www.pearsoned.co.uk/plummer**

CHAPTER 19

EDUCATION

I have never let my schooling interfere with my education.
Mark Twain

Give a man a fish and you feed him for a day.
Teach a man to fish and you feed him for a lifetime.
Chinese proverb

COLIN SAMSON IS A SOCIAL RESEARCHER who spent years living with the Innu in Labrador in Northern Canada. For most of their history, the Innu were a nomadic people, living by hunting. They were independent, self-reliant and had a strong sense of their purpose in the world. When the Canadian government introduced a policy of assimilation, which extinguished their unique identity and their right to the land, their way of life came under severe threat. Samson documents how the changes left the Innu ashamed and confused, and precipitated high rates of suicide, gas sniffing, widespread alcoholism and child abuse. There was a failure to recognise the distinctiveness of formal lessons, abstractions, and all were alien to them. The school worked to transform them into *Akaneshaut* (white children). As some Innu commented:

> It made me 'think English' and gave me 'white thoughts'. ... I lost part of my life...

> The only thing that kids are able to learn in school is to be embarrassed by our culture...

> I am ashamed to say that I went to the school at all. ... I wasted my years in school...

> Kids now talk back to their parents. That comes from the school. They don't pay attention at all. They don't listen to parents because in school they get a lot of English. They are gradually losing their language. Kids are starting to talk to each other in English.

> (Samson, 2003: 199–201)

KEY THEMES
- Global education and literacy
- Schooling around the world
- Understanding education
- Social divisions and education
- Current issues being debated in the sociology of education

---

the group and its values and history, and in attempting to assimilate them, a crisis developed.

One part of this crisis was to be found in schooling, which the Canadian authorities insisted upon. In a sense the goal was to take on a new generation of Innu and help in the transformation of their culture into a more Western European one. In the West, we tend to see formal schooling as a necessity – for the transmission of culture and knowledge, and indeed the preservation of social solidarity, values and order. Education is also one of the major determinants of a person's life chances. But for the Innu, they found this experience of formal schooling an alienating one. It made them apprehensive and worried. They found that schools did not tell the truth about who the Innu were, and did not speak to their values or way of life. Instead they got linear timetables, school discipline,

Far from providing values and maintaining a way of life, the schools were seen to erode Innu values among the young. School is remembered as a kind of culture shock. Whereas their education before came from living with nature, the landscape, animals and their values from the persistent need to survive, now they found themselves confronted with abstractions and formalities. More used to lived experience in the past, the abstracted education of the West made them less competent in the world. The values they are now taught are often in terms of money and success – not in terms of spirituality, the hunting way of life and animals.

Source: Samson (2003)

(Left) Jacob Lawrence: The Libraries are appreciated

Source: Philadelphia Museum of Art/The Louis E. Stern Collection. Jacob Lawrence, Gwendolyn Knight Lawrence, courtesy of the Jacob Gwendolyn Lawrence Foundation. Image © Corbis Images/Geoffrey Clements

All societies pay attention to ways of transmitiing their cultures and values, and in the modern world these have increasingly become housed in schools and the broader educational process. This chapter spotlights **education**, *the social institution guiding the transmission of knowledge, job skills, cultural norms and values*. In industrial societies, as we shall see, much education is a matter of **schooling**, *formal instruction under the direction of specially trained teachers*.

Global education and literacy

Most people in the Western world spend much of their first 20 years in various kinds of school: nursery, primary, secondary and tertiary. Until recently, formal schooling in all societies was a privilege restricted to a small elite, and so it remains in many poorer societies today.

In hunter-gatherer and small agrarian societies, people's survival depended on learning as much as they could about the plants, animals and landscape in their environment. The Innu were not unusual. Elders devoted much time to passing on both cultural beliefs and knowledge of the natural world to the younger generations. As agrarian societies grew in size and complexity, people needed to learn only specialised knowledge for their field of work, rather than general knowledge. The majority of people in such systems spent most of their time performing physical labour which required little training, while a minority with the greatest wealth and power enjoyed the spare time to study literature, art, history and science. Indeed, the English word 'school' comes from the Greek word for 'leisure'.

We find marked diversity in schooling throughout the world today. In some developing regions, including much of central Asia and central America, religious organisations play a major role in providing education to children. In other regions, particularly East Asia, Europe, the United States, Canada, Australia and New Zealand, the state formally coordinates and regulates the majority of schools. In most high-income societies, a growing number of young people are awarded first degrees: this is much less common in low-income societies (see Figure 19.1).

All low-income countries have one trait in common: limited access to formal schooling. In the poorest nations, only half of all primary-aged children are in school. Nevertheless, the total number of children enrolled in primary school in the world has more than trebled over the past 50 years: from 206 million in 1950 to 411 million in 1970, 599 million in 1990 and 881 million in 1998. Low-income countries as a whole have achieved a net enrolment in primary education in excess

of 80 per cent – higher in East Asia and Latin America, lower in Africa. Likewise, enrolment in secondary education worldwide has expanded tenfold over the past 50 years (from 40 million in 1950 to more than 400 million today), and tertiary education has grown fourteen-fold from 6.5 million in 1950 to 88.2 million in 1997 (UNESCO, 2000: 13). Nevertheless, across the globe it is still the case that some 121 million children are denied any access to education (UNICEF, 2004b).

The illiteracy question

Despite the world growth in education, illiteracy remains a major issue. A person can be said to be literate 'who can, with understanding, both read and write a short simple statement on his or her everyday life' (UNESCO, 2000: 23). Although the number of literate adults worldwide has doubled from 1.5 billion in 1970 to 3.4 billion in 2000 (see Table 19.1), this still leaves a huge proportion of the world's population as illiterate. Indeed, at the end of the twentieth century there were some 1.5 billion illiterates, of whom two-thirds were women. As a consequence, illiteracy disadvantages many.

Even among some high-income countries, illiteracy remains a problem. While the United States opened educational opportunities to all citizens long before most other industrialised countries, some 25 million adults read and write at no more than a fourth-grade level and another 25 million have only eighth-grade language skills. This means that one in four adults in the United States is functionally illiterate, and the proportion is higher among the elderly and minorities. The problem of illiteracy in the United States is most serious among

Table 19.1	Literacy rates[1] across the world, 2000		
		Male	**Female**
Sub-Saharan Africa		69	53
Middle East and North Africa		74	52
South Asia		66	42
East Asia and Pacific		93	81
Latin America		90	88
CEE/CIS[2] and Baltic States		99	96
World		84	74

[1] Defined as percentage of persons aged 15 and over who can read and write
[2] Central Eastern Europe/Commonwealth of Independent States

Source: UNICEF (2004b: 121)

Women   Men

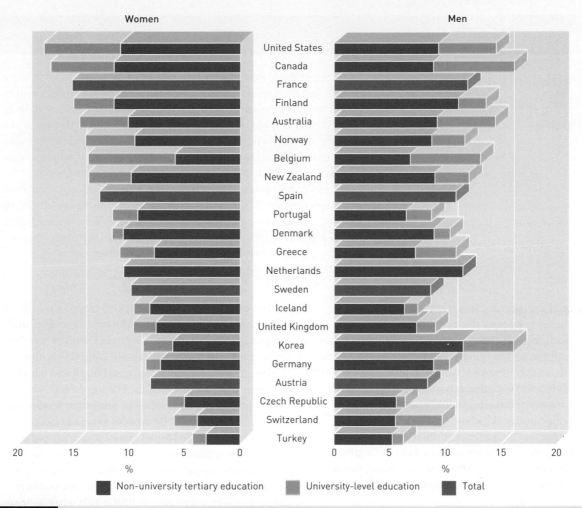

| United States |
| Canada |
| France |
| Finland |
| Australia |
| Norway |
| Belgium |
| New Zealand |
| Spain |
| Portugal |
| Denmark |
| Greece |
| Netherlands |
| Sweden |
| Iceland |
| United Kingdom |
| Korea |
| Germany |
| Austria |
| Czech Republic |
| Switzerland |
| Turkey |

20   15   10   5   0   0   5   10   15   20
%   %

■ Non-university tertiary education   ■ University-level education   ■ Total

Figure 19.1 Net enrolment in tertiary education in selected countries for persons aged 17–34 by tertiary level and gender

Source: adapted from OECD (1997)

Latinos. In part this is due to a drop-out rate among 14–24 year-olds of almost 30 per cent, which is three times the rate among whites or African Americans. The broader issue is that schools fail to teach many Spanish-speaking people to read and write *any* language very well (Kozol, 1980, 1985a, 1985b).

The new illiteracy

Even this conceals the real nature of what has been called the 'new illiteracy'. As societies develop and expand their information technologies, so illiteracy will increasingly come to mean the inability to use computers, word processing, email and websites. Although these skills are rapidly expanding across the world, they are still highly

selective. The United States has more computers than the rest of the world put together, while South Asia – with 23 per cent of the world's population – has hardly 1 per cent of the world's users (New Internationalist, 2001: 29). In 2001, there was effectively no take-up of the Internet in 70 countries. While there was only one Internet user per 100,000 in countries in sub-Saharan Africa and South Asia, there were 37 per 100,000 in the 'industralised countries' (UNICEF, 2004b: 121).

Resolving illiteracy

Observers such as Ivan Illich (1973) argue that the answer to widespread illiteracy is not to transpose Western-style schools into the rest of the world. Instead

PAULO FREIRE: EMPOWERING THE POOR

The Brazilian educator Paulo Freire (1921–97) used literacy programmes for the poor to enable them to take control of their own lives. He argued that formal education often enabled elites to impose their values on 'developing' peoples. In 1963 he pioneered a literacy project across Brazil for 5 million people, and was supported by a left-wing government. Later, however, he fell out of favour when a new right-wing government came to power. Freire was jailed, before going into exile in Bolivia and Chile. His key book was *Pedagogy of the Oppressed* (1972), and his key idea was **conscientisation**, where *education becomes a tool to transform the social order*. Ultimately, education struggles for liberation from all kinds of oppression. His work also became part of Liberation Theology in Latin America.

of formal degrees on paper, they suggest, people in developing areas need the practical knowledge and skills to provide for their basic life needs in a changing natural environment and to build small businesses that can generate wealth in ways sensitive to local cultural norms. In high-income societies, schooling for everyone serves as the means of training people to participate in democratic political life and apply the economic knowledge and technological skills increasingly important in the modern world. At the same time, however, schooling can also serve as a major mechanism for reproducing the social inequalities.

Schooling around the world

In this section, we make a quick tour of some school systems to provide a sense of their variety.

Schooling in the United States

The United States promoted mass education before most European countries. By 1850 about half the young people between the ages of five and 19 were enrolled in school. Today, four out of five have a secondary education, and more than one in five have a university degree. Both the national and state governments have striven to promote social mobility by funding state schools to offer *equal opportunity*, that is, the opportunity for all bright and motivated students to succeed in spite of the educational and economic background of their parents. The US educational system has also stressed the value of *practical* learning, that is, knowledge that has a direct bearing on people's work and interests.

Nevertheless, education has also played a role in maintaining social divisions. The top universities and secondary schools formally excluded women and people from most ethnic minorities until early this century. Indeed, the US formally segregated black and white students until 1954, when the US Supreme Court ruled that segregation had resulted in minorities receiving an inferior education. While schools generally have improved across the United States, young people in poor inner cities attend schools with increasingly larger class sizes, limited books and technological resources and decaying buildings. While many of the best teachers move to the more prosperous suburban schools, inner-city schools face growing problems from drug use and violence among students.

Schooling in India

The wealthy in India enjoy high-quality early schooling and many pursue university degrees. The majority of people in India cannot afford such privilege. Most people do now receive some primary education, typically in crowded schoolrooms where one teacher attends to upwards of 60 children. Children in the poorest families often begin full-time work at an early age to help supplement the family income. Fewer than half of Indians pursue secondary education. Pronounced patriarchy also shapes Indian education; 45 per cent of boys but only 30 per cent of girls attend secondary school. While just over one-third of the Indian population is illiterate, two-thirds of women lack basic literary skills. A large majority of the children working in Indian factories are girls (UNHDP, 1995).

Schooling in Japan

Before industrialisation brought mandatory education to this country in 1872, only a privileged few enrolled in school. Today, Japan's educational system produces some of the highest achievers in maths and sciences (Brinton, 1988; Simons, 1989). Early grades concentrate on transmitting Japanese traditions, especially obligation to family. By their early teens, students encounter Japan's system of rigorous and competitive examinations. The Japanese government invests heavily in the education of students who perform well in these exams, while students performing poorly are pushed out of the system. Understandably, then, around half of Japanese students attend 'cram schools' to supplement their standard education and prepare for the exams. Japanese women, most of whom are not in the labour force, often devote themselves to their children's success in school.

Schooling in Europe

While all countries in the European Union agree that schooling is highly important, each takes a different approach to education, as Figure 19.2 shows. Luxembourg requires children to attend pre-school. In The Netherlands, primary school begins at four. While the UK introduced compulsory education in 1870, Italy and Greece did not follow suit until the 1950s, and Spain waited until the 1960s. Portugal introduced six years of compulsory elementary schooling in 1968, and did not fully implement this requirement until 1986 (Chisholm, 1998: 139). EU countries also require different minimum periods of study. Portugal, Spain and Italy require only eight years of schooling; Ireland, Greece, Luxembourg and Denmark require nine years; France, The Netherlands and Germany ten years, the United Kingdom 11 years, and Belgium 12 years.

Many European countries have a multi-track secondary education system which channels some students towards university and others towards various levels of vocational training. In Germany, for example, students undertake general secondary education for two years from age 12, then split into the university (*Gymnasium*), basic vocational (*Hauptschule*) and higher vocational (*Realschule*) groups. Some countries encourage greater educational specialisation from the secondary level onwards than others. Secondary students in Italy and Germany have more subjects to study at the post-16 level than students in the UK. As with the previous examples, European educational structures also help maintain the social power structures, as we shall now see by looking more closely at the UK.

Schooling in the UK

During the Middle Ages, schooling was a privilege of the British nobility, who studied classical subjects since they had little need for the practical skills related to earning a living. As the Industrial Revolution created a need for an educated labour force, a rising share of the population entered the classroom. In 1891, the Education Act made elementary education free to all citizens. Three major Acts have shaped British education during the twentieth century. These are:

- *The Balfour Act in 1902*, which established Local Education Authorities (LEAs), and gave these bodies powers over secondary and higher education.

- *The Butler Act of 1944*, which established a Ministry of Education and set up the tripartite system of three different kinds of school – grammar, technical and secondary modern – to cater to the supposed differing intellectual abilities of students. The Act made education from five to 15 free for all people, improved equality of opportunity in education, and offered support services to students from poor families, including free milk, dental check-ups and health care.

- *The Baker Act of 1988*. Following the recommendations of the previous year's Black Report, the British government enacted a series of sweeping and controversial changes in the Education Act 1988. These included:

1. The introduction of the National Curriculum, with achievement targets for students at the ages of 7, 11, 14 and 16.

2. The right for schools to 'opt out' of the Local Education Authority system if a majority of parents voting in a secret ballot wanted to do so.

3. Devolution of the financial management of schools from LEAs to boards of governors.

4. The introduction of City Technology Colleges (15 in 1994).

Traditional social distinctions persist in British education. Many wealthy families send their children to *public schools*. Such elite schools not only teach academic subjects, they also convey to children from wealthy families the distinctive patterns of speech, mannerisms and social graces of the British upper class. These schools are far too expensive for most students. Until the 1970s another major divide in British education was between the grammar schools and secondary schools, with the former being both more middle-class and more successful. The Labour party in power at this time largely abolished grammar schools and introduced a

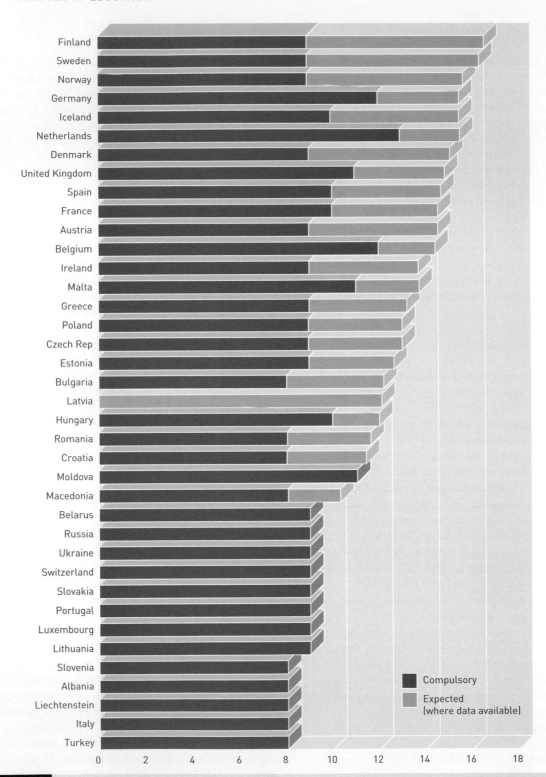

'comprehensive' system – ostensibly providing equality of education for all. In practice, some grammar schools remained and comprehensive schools became stratified into 'good' and 'bad'. Further, many prominent members of the Labour government in 1997 sent their own children to grant-maintained schools rather than comprehensives, recognising the continuing difference in the standards of education at each level. Moreover, graduates from Oxford and Cambridge, or 'Oxbridge', often enter the core of the British power elite. More than two-thirds of the top members of the civil service and successive British governments have 'Oxbridge' degrees, although there are many signs that this may now be changing (Sampson, 2004: 114).

Understanding education in the modern world

The previous brief comparisons illustrate that education is shaped by other institutions and social forces. Education transmits cultural values and can also contribute to social divisions. We will now look at several sociological approaches to studying education.

Classroom interaction: the micro-sociology of schools

One approach to studying education looks at what goes on inside the classroom. Researchers, often applying symbolic interactionism (see Chapters 2 and 7) and the method of participant observation (Chapter 3), have documented the *perspectives* of teachers and students, the *processes* through which classes are constructed and negotiated, the different student *roles* and *cultures* which emerge within these classrooms, and the impact of *social divisions* (gender, class, disability and race) on these interactions.

Apart from formal learning, an 'invisible pedagogy' (Bernstein, 1977), or hidden ranking system, in school culture shapes academic performance, and the long-term life chances of students. Early studies of classroom interaction in the UK suggest that while teachers may strive to be impartial, they are culturally conditioned to assess their students' ability by ranking them on a scale of other characteristics, such as appearance, personality, enthusiasm and conformity, which bear little relation to actual ability (Hargreaves, 1975). Teachers often favoured boys over girls (Stanworth, 1983) and white boys over Afro-Caribbean boys, by tacitly giving them much more attention and opportunities to speak. Likewise, Asian girls were also more likely to be stereotyped as 'passive' (Brah and Minhas, 1988). Labelling pupils in certain ways (as 'slow learners' or 'trouble') can bring about **self-fulfilling** prophecies whereby *children defined as low achievers at school actually become low achievers*. It is a matter of expectations.

More recent studies have suggested changes. For instance, the achievement of girls at all levels of education has overtaken that of boys, though it is often subject-linked. Thus, for example, in 1970–71 males outnumbered females in higher education by at least 2:1; by 1996–97 females outnumbered males (*Social Trends*, 1999). How this shift can be explained is an interesting question. Some suggest it is to do with the rising expectations placed on girls and women (in turn partly linked to the growth of the feminist ideals: see Chapter 12). Others suggest it may have much to do with 'the crisis of boys and men' whereby falling expectations are placed on some boys as they become part of a 'lads culture'. We discuss this further below (Weiner and Arnot, 1997; O'Donnell and Sharpe, 2000).

The social background of the students also plays a role in how they experience education. Paul Willis (1977) looked at a small group of working-class boys and studied their transition from school to work. He found that they generated an anti-school culture heavily focused upon their masculinity. They had little time for the middle-class school values and for posh qualifications, seeing them as boring, effeminate and a waste of time. They castigated other boys who followed the rules as 'ear'oles' and saw them as sissies. Similar studies found such boys associating good grades with femininity and, to keep face in the eyes of their mates, boys may hand in work that is poor and disorganised. For these 'lads', 'having a laff' was especially important, and it is a value they then take to their workplace. For instance, in class there may be 'a continuous scraping of chairs, a bad tempered 'tut-tutting' at the simplest request, and a continuous fidgeting which explores every permutation of sitting or lying on a chair'. They then carry this 'anti-authority', 'anti-achievement' culture to their place of work.

More recently, Mairtin Mac an Ghaill (1994) has looked at the construction of gender in classrooms, focusing on a hierarchy of dominant and subordinate masculinities. He observes four major types (there was also a small sub-group of gay male students):

- The '*Macho Lads*' – white, working-class boys who are defiant of the school and disdainful of student achievers.

- The '*Academic Achievers*' – boys whose male identities are built out of seeing themselves as future professionals: they take their work and school seriously, even though they are seen as effeminate 'dickheads' by the Macho Lads.

- The '*New Enterprisers*' – these are less keen on conventional A-levels, but do find a space for work in skills that interest them, such as computer sciences.

- The '*Real Englishmen*' – these saw themselves as superior to the teachers, and think they are capable of effortless academic achievement.

VOICES

A SELF-FULFILLING PROPHECY: FROM THE AUTOBIOGRAPHY OF MALCOLM X

Malcolm, a black American, went to school in Lansing, Michigan in the 1940s. He became leader of the Black Muslims and a spokesperson for many black Americans in the 1960s and was assassinated in 1965. This is an extract from his autobiography in which he illustrates the self-fulfilling prophecy at work in his school: think of the power of telling someone 'you're good with your hands'! (See also the film of his life by Spike Lee – Malcolm X (1992) with Denzil Washington in the lead role.)

One day something happened which was to become the first major turning point of my life. Somehow, I happened to be alone in the classroom with Mr. Ostrowski, my English teacher. He was a tall,

Malcolm X (1925–1965)
Source: Corbis

rather reddish white man and he had a thick mustachio. I had gotten some of my best marks under him, and he had always made me feel that he liked me.

I know that he probably meant well in what he happened to advise me that day. I doubt that he meant any harm. It was just in his nature as an American white man. I was one of his top students, one of the school's top students – but all he could see for me was the kind of future 'in your place' that almost all white people see for black people.

He told me, 'Malcolm, you ought to be thinking about a career. Have you been giving it thought?' The truth is, I hadn't. I never have figured out why I told him, 'Well, yes sir, I've been thinking I'd like to be a lawyer.' Lansing certainly had no black lawyers – or doctors either – in those days, to hold up an image I might have aspired to. All I really knew for certain was that a lawyer didn't wash dishes, as I was doing.

Mr. Ostrowski looked surprised, I remember, and leaned back in his chair and clasped his hands behind his head. He kind of half smiled and said, 'Malcolm, one of life's first needs is for us to be realistic. Don't misunderstand me, now. We all of us like you, you know that. But you've got to be realistic about being a nigger. You need to think about something you can be. You're good with your hands – making things. Everybody admires your carpentry shop work. Why don't you plan on carpentry? People like you as a person – you'd get all kinds of work.'

The more I thought afterwards about what he said, the more uneasy it made me. It just kept treading around in my mind.

What made it really begin to disturb me was Mr. Ostrowski's advice to others in my class – all of them white. They reported that Mr. Ostrowski had encouraged what they had wanted. Yet nearly none of them had earned marks equal to mine.

It was then that I began to change – inside.

I drew away from white people, I came to class, and I answered when called upon. It became a physical strain simply to sit in Mr. Ostrowski's class.

Adapted from Malcolm X, *The Autobiography of Malcolm X* (1966: 35–37).

Critical comment

Focusing on classroom interactions is valuable, but it does tend to under-emphasise the relations between the activities within schools and the wider working of society as a whole, as we shall see by looking at a different, more macro approach.

Education and social divisions

Another major approach to studying education is through social divisions and social conflict. Education – at all levels – becomes a means for the reproduction of society's inequalities: it can act as a means of social control, reinforcing acceptance of the status quo. In various, sometimes subtle, ways schools operate to reproduce the status hierarchy.

Thus a number of sociologists have suggested that the origins of the UK system in the nineteenth century lay in class issues and control. The public schools came very early for the elite; then in the nineteenth century came the rather limited Sunday schools to provide a basic education for the working classes – often moral education. There was a continuous fear of an insurgent working class rising up once it had too much education.

Samuel Bowles and Herbert Gintis (1976) point out that the clamour for public education in the late nineteenth century arose precisely when capitalists were seeking a literate, docile and disciplined workforce. In many countries with immigrants, but notably the United States, mandatory education laws ensured that schools would teach immigrants the dominant national language as well as cultural values supportive of capitalism. Compliance, punctuality and discipline were – and still are – part of what conflict theorists call the **hidden curriculum**, the *subtle presentation of political or cultural ideas in the classroom*. It teaches young people 'to know

their place and sit still in it' and 'reproduces inequality by justifying privilege and attributing poverty to personal failure' (Bowles and Gintis, 1976: 114). In the next section, we will look at just how some of these social divisions work in more detail.

Social divisions and schooling

Class divisions

Conflict theorists argue that schools routinely tailor education according to students' social background, thereby perpetuating social inequality. Indeed, out of all major Western cultures, it has been argued that 'only The Netherlands and Sweden show persistent trends of equalising access to education in the course of the twentieth century' (Therborn, 1995: 257). By contrast, education in countries such as the UK has reflected stratification in quality of provision both for individuals and for people of different social classes (Mackinnon *et al.*, 1996: 173).

Tables 19.2 and 19.3 show the differential performance of children at school from different class backgrounds. There is no doubt that children from working-class homes consistently under-achieve at every level of the educational system when compared to middle-class and upper-class children. Why should this be?

Some, like Charles Murray, have contended that genetic intellectual potential determines performance in school (Herrnstein and Murray, 1994). Indeed, the tripartite system in Britain gave prominence to the results of IQ tests given to children at age 11 in helping divide students into their supposedly appropriate schools. The implication of this explanation, however, is that lower-class people generally have lower genetic intellectual

Table 19.2	Education and qualifications in the UK, 2002		
Socio-economic group	Percentage with higher qualifications	Percentage with no qualifications	Percentage at private school
1	78	3	26
2	35	17	12
3	30	19	6
4	9	40	1
5	5	56	1
6	1	74	1

Source: based on General Household Survey

Table 19.3	GCSE attainment[1]: by parents' socio-economic classification, 2002					
	5 or more GCSE grades A*–C	1–4 GCSE grades A*–C[2]	5 or more GCSE grades D–G	1–4 GCSE grades D–G	None reported	All
Higher professional	77	13	6	–	3	100
Lower professional	64	21	11	2	2	100
Intermediate	52	25	17	2	4	100
Lower supervisory	35	30	27	4	4	100
Routine	32	32	25	5	6	100
Other	32	29	26	4	9	100

[1] For pupils in year 11. Includes equivalent GNVQ qualifications achieved in year 11.

[2] Consists of those with 1–4 GCSE grades A*–C and any number of other grades.

Source: *Social Trends* (2004: 42)

abilities. Thus lower-class people could be said to deserve their status because they lack the intellectual ability to compete with people from higher classes.

Many others reject this explanation, however, pointing out that governments have tended not to invest as heavily in the schools attended by the poorest people, and that the less well off also tend to experience greater health problems, which in turn affect their performance at school. Moreover, poorer families cannot afford to send their children to nursery pre-school training and later to cram schools, to hire private tutors, or to purchase items such as books or personal computers, which give children from more affluent backgrounds an advantage. Additionally, as the Willis (1977) study discovered, poorer children often grow up in environments where people see little hope of upward social mobility and rebel against the system rather than try to conform with

it. In such an environment, adults often discourage rather than encourage success at school. To make matters worse, people in different communities within a country often develop distinct dialects and colloquial vocabularies (Bernstein, 1977). While groups across the class divides do this, the dialects and words associated with richer and middle-class communities gain status, while those associated with lower-class communities get judged as 'uneducated'. In consequence, poor children are more likely to be more regularly criticised in school for 'weak' language skills and thus to develop lower educational confidence. These many factors, which have no relation to biological potential, have contributed to the educational class divide in countries such as the UK (see Halsey *et al.*, 1961; Jackson and Marsden, 1963; Douglas, 1964) (Figure 19.3). See also the profile box on Bourdieu.

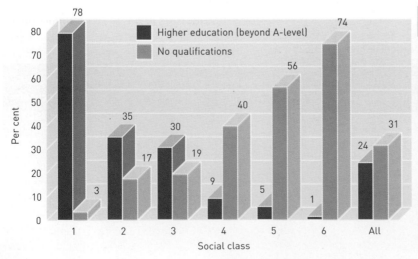

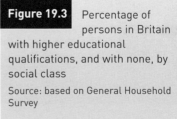

Figure 19.3 Percentage of persons in Britain with higher educational qualifications, and with none, by social class

Source: based on General Household Survey

Disability divisions

Historically, children with all kinds of disability have been socialised into low expectations of success in both education and work. In the UK system for many years, this took place largely through a process of exclusion in 'special schools' with an ideology of 'special educational needs'. There were schools for the 'deaf', schools for the 'blind' and schools for the 'physically handicapped' (all terms that are now often questioned). The 1944 Education Act encouraged disabled children to be educated in mainstream schools, but in practice local education authorities made separate provision. Although some say special schools are needed – how can the deaf learn British Sign Language, and how can they develop positive identities without special schools? – others suggest special schools actually perpetuate the disabling process. The education experience may remain inferior: disabled students come to have narrower curricula; teachers often have lower expectations; courses are taught in specialist training in life skills rather than academic knowledge. In a climate of 'league tables' introduced recently into British schools the disabled seem even less likely to succeed (Tomlinson, 1982).

Ethnic differences

Not every country has adopted the extreme policy of racial segregation in classrooms once practised in the United States and South Africa, but racial differences in educational achievement appear in many countries, and these differences often coincide with social status differences between ethnic groups. Studies in the UK, such as the report of the Swann Committee (Swann, 1985), for example, found that in general West Indian children perform less well than Asian children, and in both cases boys do less well than girls. Asian girls may often do better than white boys; but black boys regularly come out at the bottom of the heap. This pattern continues through higher education. Drawing on the work of David Gilborn (1995), Mairtin Mac an Ghaill (1994) and others, Gail Lewis (2000) has summarised a number of key studies and concluded that:

- Racial distinctions are applied to pupils of both African-Caribbean and Asian descent but in different ways, leading to divergent expectations of each group . . .

- Such racial distinctions are often based on racial stereotypes of Caribbean and Asian family structures and relationships as, equally but differently, pathological or dysfunctional . . .

- Pupils of Asian descent are characterised as academically able and diligent, if also quiet and docile; and African-Caribbean descent pupils are characterised as academically poor and lazy . . .

- Boys of African-Caribbean descent are assumed to be disorderly and thus to present teachers with behavioural problems.

- There is a high level of conflict between white teachers and African-Caribbean descent pupils . . .

- Teachers and schools themselves often play an active, though unintended part in the creation of this conflict . . .

- There is constant over-representation in school exclusions of black pupils . . . of both sexes . . .

- Levels of academic success may be achieved by pupils despite – rather than because of – teacher/school support . . . (Lewis, 2000: 269–270)

Some part of all this may be accounted for through links to class – Afro-Caribbean children are more likely to have parents in manual work. Another feature may well be the workings of a self-fulfilling prophecy (described in the Voices box on page 520). Another contributory factor must also be some forms of racism and racialisation at work (see Chapter 11). In addition, part of the explanation may lie in what Smith and Tomlinson (1989) term 'the school effect'. While these authors argue that 'what school a child goes to makes far more difference than which ethnic group he or she belongs to' (1989: 281), they also note that people from ethnic minorities are more likely to be clustered into particular areas, and that their children's educational fate rests in the hands of the schools near where they live. For groups more likely to be poor, or immigrants clustered in poor sections of central cities to cut costs as they adjust to a new culture, this can be bad news.

Since schools tend to reinforce the dominant culture in a society, students from minority communities often face a confusing problem when trying to reconcile differences between their own original culture and that of the larger society in which they live. Children may not feel inclined to sever their roots with their cultural origins, and wish to keep their own language or religion, for example. Often this can initially spark conflict within schools, as schools expect that children should be fully assimilated into the values of the dominant society. With this approach there has often been tacit ethnic discrimination, to which a major response was the promotion of anti-racism strategies in schools whereby discriminatory practices were more overtly condemned. More recently, multiculturalism is often promoted in the

PROFILE

PIERRE BOURDIEU: REPRODUCING CLASS

Pierre Bourdieu (1930–2002)
Source: Corbis

Pierre Bourdieu (1930–2002), a French sociologist, has made important contributions to the study of education, culture and class. Bourdieu has observed underlying patterns of class domination in education, art and 'culture' generally. He suggests that the primary roles of education are **social reproduction**, *the maintenance of power and privilege between social classes from one generation to the next*, and **cultural reproduction**, *the process by which a society transmits dominant knowledge from one generation to another.*

In his book Distinction (using large-scale questionnaires on consumer activities), Bourdieu (1984) captures the profound sense of social difference and distance we often feel when faced with different cultures, some of which may even offend our own sensitivies. He is concerned with our tastes for particular music (whether Blur or Mozart), foods (burgers or tofu), art and so forth, and with the ways items may move in and out of our scale of tastes. These can all be seen as ways of maintaining social distance and reproducing class relations.

Each family teaches its children a certain cultural capital and a certain ethos. Starting in the pre-school years, children have different access to cultural capital. For instance, children taken by parents around the world have experiences of many different cultures with their different languages, manners, foods, arts and etiquettes. They build up experiences of travel, diversity and languages which other children may never know. Cultural capital, then, is much more than formal education; it is found often in personalities who 'know things' – about art or food or films or history – who have a stock of cultural knowledge.

Cultural reproduction, Bourdieu notes, does not involve the reproduction of the culture of all segments of society, only that of the dominant classes. People in each class transmit a distinctive 'habitus' (classifications, perceptions, ways of talking, moving and generally carrying oneself) down the generations, but schools pick up only on the habitus of the most powerful classes. He argues that the educational system has systematic biases against working-class knowledge and skills.

Source: for an introductory guide to Bourdieu, see Jenkins (1992).

curriculum, allowing the diversity of cultures to be taken more seriously (see Giroux, 1992).

Gender differences

Peer groups socialise their members according to normative conceptions of gender. A series of feminist researchers in the UK – the late Sue Lees, Christine Griffin and Angela McRobbie among them – have interviewed girls and discovered the ways in which their 'femininity' is shaped from early years. Likewise, some male sociologists – Paul Willis, Mike O'Donnell and Mairtin Mac an Ghaill among them – have studied boys. Reading their studies, it is not hard to sense the overwhelming pressures placed on young boys and girls to conform to gender stereotypes, and to sense the sanctions they will experience if they step out of these roles.

Many of the world's societies have considered schooling more important for boys than for girls. Although the education gender gap has narrowed in Western countries in recent decades, many women still study traditionally feminine subjects such as literature, while men pursue mathematics and engineering. By stressing the experiences of people in traditionally masculine professions, such as the military, while ignoring the lives of other, largely female work forces, such as domestic workers, schools reinforce male dominance in society.

During the 1970s, sociologists discovered how girls were usually disadvantaged at school. Rosemary Deem demonstrated that education for girls in the past largely centred upon how it would prepare them for the family. Dale Spender found curricula riddled with 'sexism' and Sue Sharpe observed that schools steered girls towards 'feminine' subjects. Michelle Stanworth looked at a mixed group of students, finding that teachers gave more attention to boys than to girls. As a result of such experiences, girls learned to lack faith in their abilities (Deem, 1980; Spender, 1982; Stanworth, 1983; Sharpe, 1994).

More recently, however, boys seem to be doing less well and girls doing better (Figure 19.4). Partly this is a consequence of a shift in educational policies. The National Curriculum in the UK, for example, insists that all boys have to take a language and all girls have to take a science subject; and almost all schools and universities now have equal opportunities policies. Girls in the 1990s also became less family-focused, attaching more importance to education and work (Sharpe, 1994). At the same time, the continuing development of what is commonly called a 'lads culture' and a culture of under-achievement has grown among boys (Willis, 1977; Mac an Ghaill, 1994).

Although girls' education may have improved, women are still seriously disadvantaged. Only 8 per cent of British professors are women. Although at some newer universities, such as South Bank, the proportion is as high as 30 per cent, in others it is as low as 3 per cent. Women also earn less than their male counterparts in the education professions (*Times Higher Education Supplement*, 6 June 1997: 19). These issues are also highlighted by Carol Gilligan, profiled overleaf.

Sexuality, gender and the school

Gender segregation, while not total, is a common feature of children's and young people's lives. Playgrounds, classrooms, clubs and street life are all conspicuous for their spatial divisions into boys' worlds and girls' worlds. Here, in these segregated worlds, further divisions in gender identity are fashioned, particularly around sexuality. Especially among boys, calling each other queer or sissy, or using other homophobic insults, is a regular practice to isolate marginal children (Thorne and Luria, 1985). Such events make life particularly difficult for boys and girls who discover that they are gay.

Julian Wood (1984) found that not only is there a general, highly charged, sexual atmosphere in schools – a point that few commentators seem to have noticed before – but that there is also a massive amount of sexism among the boys. Boys tended to deride women as collections of vital body parts or members of limited, sexually defined categories, and such an atmosphere not only generated negative perceptions of women, but also denied space to explore identity for boys who did not sexually identify with women. The Controversy and Debate box highlights how 'homosexuality' appears – or rather does not appear – in this context.

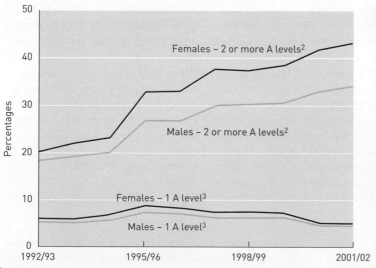

Figure 19.4 Achievement at GCE A level[1] or equivalent in the UK

Source: *Social Trends* (2004: 45)

[1] 2 AS levels count as 1 A level pass. Data from 2001/01 are not on the same basis as earlier years, and data prior to 1995/96 refer to school pupils only.
[2] Equivalent to 3 or more Scottish Highers.
[3] Equivalent to 1 or 2 Scottish Highers. Includes those with 1.5 A levels.

PROFILE

CAROL GILLIGAN: IN A DIFFERENT VOICE

Carol Gilligan, an educational psychologist at Harvard University, studies human development. In her early work she was disturbed to find that mainstream research had overlooked girls. This narrow focus, as she sees it, is typical of much social science, which uses the behaviour of males as the norm for how everyone should act.

Initially, she attempted to correct a research bias by which others had investigated only boys. Therefore Gilligan (1982, 1990) set out systematically to compare the moral development of females and males. Simply put, her conclusion is that the two sexes make moral judgements in different ways. Males, she contends, have a *justice perspective*, relying on formal rules and abstract principles to define right and wrong. Girls, on the other hand, have a *care and responsibility perspective*, judging a situation with an eye towards personal relationships and loyalties. Stealing, as boys see it, is wrong because it breaks the law and violates common moral sentiments. Girls, however, are more likely to wonder why someone would steal, looking less severely upon an individual who did so with the intention of helping another person.

Gilligan points out that the impersonal application of rules has long dominated men's lives in the workplace. Concern for attachments, by contrast, has been more relevant to women's lives as wives, mothers and caregivers. But, Gilligan asks, should we set up male standards as the norms by which we evaluate everyone? As her work progressed, Gilligan discovered that boys and girls employ distinctive standards in making moral decisions.

Gilligan's more recent work targets the issue of self-esteem. Her research team interviewed more than 2,000 girls, ranging from six to 18 years of age, over a five-year period. Their responses point up a clear pattern: young girls start out with considerable confidence and self-esteem, only to find these vital resources slipping away as they pass through adolescence.

Why? Gilligan claims that the answer lies in culture. Our way of life, she argues, still defines the ideal woman as calm, controlled and eager to please. Then, too, as girls move from the elementary grades to secondary school, they encounter fewer women teachers and find that most authority figures are men. So by their late teens, women are struggling to regain much of the personal strength they had a decade before.

Illustrating this trend, Gilligan and her colleagues returned to a girls' school – one site of their research – to present their findings. Most younger girls who had been interviewed were eager to have their names appear in the forthcoming book; the older girls, by contrast, were hesitant: many were fearful that they would be talked about.

Sources: Gilligan (1982, 1990),
Winkler (1990).

Ability or merit? Streaming and teaching

Despite continuing controversy over standardised tests, most schools use them as the basis for **streaming**, *the assignment of students to different types of educational* *programme*. Streaming, or tracking, is a common practice in many industrial societies, including the UK, the United States, France and Japan. The educational justification for tracking is to give students the kind of schooling appropriate to their individual aptitude. For a variety of reasons, including innate ability and level of motivation, some students are capable of more challenging work than others are. Young people also differ in their interests, with some drawn to, say, the study of languages, while others seek training in art or science. Given this diversity of talent and focus, no single programme for all students would serve any of them well.

But critics see streaming as a thinly veiled strategy to perpetuate privilege. The basis of this argument is research indicating that social background has as much to do with streaming as personal aptitude does. Students from affluent families generally do well on standardised, 'scientific' tests and so are placed in

university-bound streams, while schools assign those from modest backgrounds (including a disproportionate share of the poor) to programmes that curb their aspirations and teach technical trades. Streaming, therefore, effectively segregates students both academically and socially.

Most schools reserve their best teachers for students in favoured streams. Thus high-stream boys and girls find that their teachers put more effort into classes, show more respect towards students and expect more from them. By contrast, teachers of low-stream students concentrate on memorisation, classroom drill and other unstimulating techniques. Such classrooms also

CONTROVERSY AND DEBATE

STRUCTURING HOMOSEXUALITY OUT OF EDUCATION

What is it like to grow up gay in Europe? Many young people between 14 and 21, who generally seem to know they are gay quite early in life, find their experiences and feelings more or less completely overlooked while they are at school. Sociologists have suggested four ways in which schools make the situation of young gays and lesbians more difficult.

The first is through the hidden curriculum, which not only reproduces conventional gender roles in the classroom, but also reinforces heterosexuality. There have been attempts by some schools to introduce gay texts, but these attempts have caused much controversy.

A second mechanism concerns the absence of lesbian and gay role models in schools. Authorities have objected to teachers being 'known about' or openly discussing the issue of being gay. Yet it is precisely the quality of 'being out' that is required in schools if gay teenagers are to have the heterosexual assumption at least punctured and, more practically, if they are to have access to adults who may help them discuss their gay feelings.

A third mechanism, the social operation of youth peer groups, 'structures out' homosexuality. Adolescent culture after the age of ten places much importance on going out with the opposite sex – a key way of validating one's normality.

And there is a fourth and final mechanism that comes into force if all else fails. This entails a direct

homophobic response, through the harassment of gay youth by both teachers and other children. In a London survey, for example, about half of the respondents had been beaten up, teased, verbally abused or ostracised while at school. One boy, Peter, noted:

> The biggest shock came when I went to a secondary school and discovered words like 'queer', 'poof', etc., and realised that I was one of these vile, disgusting perverts and as far as I knew the only one.
>
> (Burbidge and Walters, 1981: 52).

As with each of the other mechanisms for making homosexuality invisible, this sort of direct homophobic response occurs in every setting a young person encounters. From mockery and abuse to physical violence, from being rejected by parents to losing one's job, from psychiatric treatment to imprisonment – all these remain distinct possibilities for those who dare to breach the heterosexual assumption.

CONTINUE THE DEBATE:

1. Briefly consider your own school experience. Did homosexuality get mentioned at all? If it was mentioned, was this a negative mention or a positive one?

2. Did you know any gays or lesbians when you were at school? If so, how did you respond to them?

Source: Plummer, in Herdt (1989).

emphasise regimentation, punctuality and respect for authority figures.

In light of these criticisms, schools are now cautious about making streaming assignments and allow greater mobility between streams. Some have even moved away from the practice entirely. While some streaming seems necessary to match instruction with abilities, rigid streaming has a powerful impact on students' learning and self-concept. Young people who spend years in higher streams tend to see themselves as bright and able, whereas those in lower streams develop lower ambition and self-esteem (Rosenbaum, 1980; Oakes, 1982, 1985; Hallinan and Williams, 1989; Kilgore, 1991; Gamoran, 1992).

Just as students are treated differently within schools, schools themselves differ in fundamental ways. One key distinction separates state and public schools in the UK. State schools often have larger class sizes, insufficient libraries and fewer science labs. But money alone does not magically bolster academic quality. Even more important are the cooperative efforts and enthusiasm of teachers, parents and students themselves. In other words,

even if school funding were exactly the same everywhere, the students whose families value and encourage education would still learn more than others (Jencks *et al.*, 1972). In short, we should not expect schools alone to overcome the effects of marked social inequality.

Yet, schools certainly reflect privilege and disadvantage. As educational critic Jonathan Kozol (1992) concludes, 'savage inequalities' in our school system alert young children to the reality that our society has already defined them as winners or losers. And, Kozol continues, all too often the children go on to fulfil this labelling.

Finally, a key theme of conflict analysis deserves to be highlighted: *schooling transforms social privilege into personal merit.* Attending university, in effect, is a rite of passage for people from well-to-do families. People are more likely to interpret university degrees as 'badges of ability' rather than as symbols of family affluence (Sennett and Cobb, 1973). At the same time, people tend to transform social disadvantage into personal deficiency when they criticise school leavers.

(a) Girls attend lessons in reading and writing at the Zarghona Ana school in Kandahar. After years of being excluded from public education, girls have now returned to schools in Afghanistan. (b) Four schoolboys represent the 'racial scale' in South Africa: black, Indian, half-caste, and white.

Source: (a) © Thorne Anderson/Corbis (b) © Alain Nogues/Corbis Sygma

THE POLITICS OF CURRICULUM

The 1988 Education Act in England and Wales established for the first time a 'national curriculum'. Established by a committee of central government, it laid out what should be taught to children between 5 and 16 in state-sponsored (but not independent) schools. All pupils must study religion, English, maths, science, history, geography, design and technology, music, art, physical education and a modern language. Students are assessed at four key stages (between 5 and 7; between 7 and 11; between 11 and 14; and between 14 and 16). Schools have to train pupils to reach target scores on these assessments. Much of the national curriculum was seen to be controversial at the time, and creating new precedents.

But it was not at all new. A national curriculum has been standard practice for a long time in much of Europe. In some countries – Portugal, Greece, France – there is a centralised system of regulation. In other countries, variations occur across regions or even schools. In Germany, for instance, the curriculum is controlled by each of 16 separate provinces, while in Belgium and The Netherlands the curriculum reflects compromises between antagonistic religious and language groups. In Denmark, there are national guidelines but schools can make their own decisions. In any event, versions of national curricula are very common throughout Europe. England and Wales came in later.

But when it came, it came with a vengeance. The UK system introduced tighter centralised control of both what is taught and how it is taught. There are strict guidelines for assessment, and a rigorous new set of procedures for monitoring the skills of teachers was introduced. Unlike most other European countries, the curriculum was not built out of a consensus: it was imposed. For a government supposed to be committed to free markets and choice, the UK government of the day took an unusually centralist approach, rejecting the advice of official curriculum committees and having their own say on what should or should not go in the curriculum.

Martin McLean, an English educationalist, has distinguished two approaches to the curricula across Europe. One, centralist, looks to a European-wide core curriculum; the other, centrifugalist, looks to the diversity of cultures across the European continent and seeks to incorporate these wide-ranging elements in the curriculum (McLean, 1993). (This is similar to the debates around multiculturalism introduced in Chapter 5.)

Centralists are strongly identified with Maastricht, the need for a 'harmonisation' of curricula across Europe, and a federal, unified Europe. This policy is largely supported in Germany and largely opposed in Denmark, France and southern Europe. Centrifugalists look for more diverse curricula. Pierre Bourdieu and François Gros have outlined six key principles:

- The need for constant revisions to meet the needs of changing societies
- Teaching to focus on strengths rather than weaknesses
- Coherence through interdisciplinary team teaching
- Absolute standards to be tempered by questions about skills and knowledge and the best way to transmit them
- Greater diversity of teaching methods
- Excellence may be universal in science yet relative in historical and cultural areas.

The trouble is that the UK curriculum fits neither of these positions. It has been structured as an 'increasingly authoritarian and monolithic national curriculum'. Its focus is on neither the unity of Europe nor its diversity. While the idea of a national curriculum may be common now across Europe, in the UK its suitability remains controversial.

Source: adapted from Martin McLean (1993).

Critical comment

This kind of analysis – allied to conflict theory – points up the connection between formal education and social inequality and shows how schooling transforms privilege into personal worthiness, and social disadvantage into personal deficiency. Critics claim that the approach minimises the extent to which schooling has met the intellectual and personal needs of students, propelling the upward social mobility of many young people in the process. Further, especially in recent years, 'politically correct' educational curricula, closely tied to conflict theory, are challenging the status quo on many fronts.

Some current issues in education

Most Western cultures now place a high premium upon their educational systems. Education debates figure prominently at election times. Perhaps because we expect our educational institutions to do so much – pass on culture and knowledge, equalise opportunity, instil discipline, stimulate individual imagination, provide a labour force, conduct pathbreaking research – education has remained at the centre of controversy for a number of years. In this section, we look at a few recent issues.

Funding crises, market forces and centralisation

All this significant increase in education – at primary, secondary and tertiary levels – has led to the need for more and more funding. So much so, it is reasonable to talk of a 'funding crisis' in education across the world. Just how is it all to be paid for?

The United States model suggests the importance of market structures, competition and profit. Unlike the UK and most of Europe, for instance, it has a clear two-tier university system – with the most prestigious colleges and universities (the Ivy League, etc.) being in the private sector, and the rest being run by the public sectors (such as the State of California). In the UK, the Blair government has not suggested the privatisation of universities but has introduced a system of student loans, replacing the previous system of grants.

The Education Act 1988 introduced the devolution of the financial management of schools from LEAs to boards of governors and gave schools the right to 'opt out' of the Local Education Authority system. Any school with over 300 students could vote to 'opt out' of the LEA and become 'grant maintained' – in effect, becoming a business funded from central government. In 1994, 592 of 3,773 secondary schools and 334 of 18,828 primary schools exercised this option.

The main thrust of the 1988 changes was to introduce market forces (supply, demand, competition and choice) into all levels of the education system. By more heavily assessing schools and publishing the results of assessments in 'league tables', the government of the time believed it would instil competition between schools and enable parents and students to make informed choices about where to study.

While the Labour government reversed some aspects of the 1988 policy in 1997, it largely continued the process of marketisation in higher education, introducing student loans and fees in the name of making students more keen consumers (and saving public money), and also promoting the repackaging of knowledge into short, non-cumulative 'modules' – often with mass-marketed textbooks, such as this one.

Yet while there is a concern with free markets at one level, at another level there has been increasing central state intervention in matters linked to the syllabus and assessment. A 1992 Education (Schools) Act introduced new centralised arrangements for school inspection (the Office for Standards in Education, OFSTED). Textbooks geared to mass education and new standard curricula

RESEARCH IN ACTION

ETHICS IN EDUCATIONAL FIELDWORK AND LIFE STORIES

Harry Wolcott researches in the field of education. In his book, *Sneaky Kid and Its Aftermath* (2002), he looks at the experience of educational failure, especially how there is so little support for those who are failed by our educational systems. He does this through the life story of Brad, a troubled 19 year old. The life story is organised by themes, taking us through issues like 'I don't have to steal, but…', 'a new life', and 'Being sneaky'. Intriguingly, the book also presents a short dramatic version of the story (with a heavy rock score!) which has been performed in some universities. Ever since its publication, it has been controversial. What is not told in the original story are the background details of how Wolcott met Brad, how Brad lived on his property, how Wolcott had sex regularly with him. All this happened before he got him to tell his life story. The original story then continues and tells how Brad develops schizophrenia and returns to Wolcott's house and burns it down in an attempt to kill him. Brad is screaming 'You fucker. I'm going to kill you. I'm going to kill you. I'm going to tie you up and leave you in the house and set the house on fire' (Wolcott, 2002: 74). Luckily, Harry escapes, unluckily, his house does not. It goes up entirely in flames, with all his and his partner's belongings. There is a serious court case, where despite Brad's guilt, Wolcott is himself scrutinised for his relationship with Brad. Brad's family is especially unhappy about the relationship with Wolcott, but so are many academics. Ultimately, Brad is institutionalised.

This life story raises a lot of issues. Most apparently, can there ever be a justification for having sex

RESEARCH IN ACTION CONTINUED

with a (vulnerable) research subject? It is true that the sex came before the research, but there will also be many who worry about the age difference. Wolcott, himself takes a strident tone against his critics. Almost in anger against those who morally preach at him, he says: '...one can be ethical or one can conduct social research, but one cannot be both ethical and a researcher in such settings. I'll opt for the label of researcher. I'm prepared to take my bumps' (Wolcott, 2002: 145).

This certainly goes against the current tide of work on the need for more ethics in research, not less. All of social life is ethical. There is no getting away from how people treat people, and often one makes a mess of it. What Wolcott seems to say is that the mess is one thing and the research is another. Yet, surely, the minute you start meddling around in other people's lives, you develop responsibilities. We have responsibilities as teachers, as friends, as sociologists. We cannot simply shunt them aside, as Wolcott seems to want to do.

In the final chapter, Wolcott reviews ethics and ethics boards. Once again, he does not mince his words. He has no time for them. These Institutional Review Boards are another example of the bureaucratisation of research. Above a simple risk analysis done by the researcher, there is no need for them. As he says:

> Some awfully petty personnel find comfort in enforcing some awfully petty rules, which takes up the valuable time of others from completely closing down the discovery-oriented approach qualitative researchers follow.
>
> (Wolcott, 2002: 148)

In our view, there should be some checks on students. Research training should include ethical dimensions, but so should economics, business studies, social work, psychology. There is no need to separate out social research. We should all become ingrained to take seriously how we conduct our work. What do you think of this case and the issues it raises?

---

may mean much less flexibility. The European Eye box (above) also shows how central government has played a role in the construction of national curricula.

'Excellence and quality': the culture of auditing

In many nations, concern has arisen about the standard of education. Some people in many industrialised nations fear that schools have done an increasingly poor job of motivating and training students, allowing general intellectual and performance standards to slip. Others, however, argue that the increasing focus on market forces in some countries is itself undermining standards.

Likewise, UK politicians of many colours have expressed alarm that 40 per cent of 11 year olds and 30 per cent of 14 year olds were not meeting national numeracy and literacy standards – well below international averages (see Figure 19.5). The Labour government which swept to power in the UK in 1997 claimed in its first White Paper, *Excellence in Schools*, that its main priorities were 'education, education and education'. Following on from the preceding government, Labour has striven to expand monitoring of schools,

through an improved Office for Standards in Education. Ministers have proposed testing children from the moment they start school, requiring primary schools to provide an hour a day on literacy and numeracy; weeding out the ranks of so-called incompetent teachers; and setting performance targets for each school, with those that fail to meet targets facing closure.

Some critics of both the former Conservative and the Labour governments have suggested that the language of concern over decline has scapegoated teachers and LEAs for all the wider problems with education. Without a workforce able to feel confidence in itself, they claim, teachers can hardly encourage confidence among children. Some academics at the university level reject Labour's marketisation push as undermining the authority of 'pure knowledge' (Coffey, 2001).

The culture of auditing

Debates over standards have become part of a wider movement of auditing, accountability and measuring 'outcomes'. We see it in:

- The creation of targets and tiers: education now has set syllabi, 'key stages' and 'bench marking' for

TIMSS, 1995, '13 year-olds', selected countries ranked by per cent correct index numbers. England = 10.

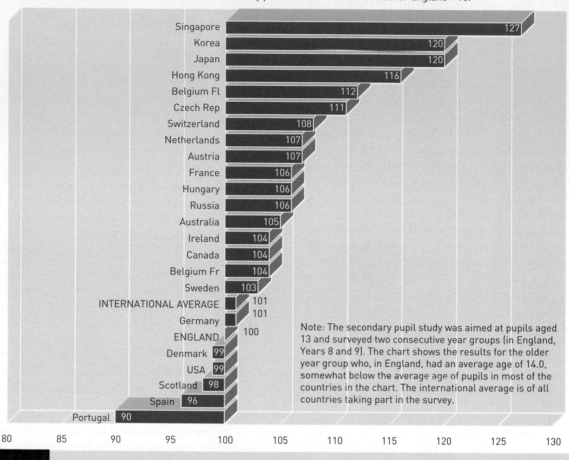

Note: The secondary pupil study was aimed at pupils aged 13 and surveyed two consecutive year groups (in England, Years 8 and 9). The chart shows the results for the older year group who, in England, had an average age of 14.0, somewhat below the average age of pupils in most of the countries in the chart. The international average is of all countries taking part in the survey.

| **Figure 19.5** | National scores in mathematics: secondary pupils |

Source: adapted from Department for Education and Employment, *Excellence in Schools* (1997)

measuring successful outcomes. In universities, the creation of the Research Assessment exercise in 1985 more or less suggests that every tutor should produce at least four good publications in the assessed period, and these are then evaluated by peer review.

- The surveillance of schools and inspection of teachers, largely through OFSTED.

- The creation of published league tables for all stages of education – primary, secondary and tertiary.

All this not only has the outcome of identifying the 'best' schools, it also leads to the phenomenon of the 'failing school'. At their extremes, such schools can be closed down, taken out of the hands of the local authority, and new 'super heads' can be brought in. Such schools seem to intensively encourage a labelling process. As teachers become more and more demoralised, hurt and angry, so

children start to find their own experiences now invalidated even more. A blame culture weakens both pupils and staff, lowering self-respect and self-esteem, and destroying confidence. This usually means a complete disruption and discontinuity of schooling, as old teachers leave and new ones are brought in. The schools, in practice, tend to be ones in inner-city areas or areas of significant deprivation.

Dangerous schools

In recent years, there has been growing concern about levels of violence and misconduct in schools. Thus, for instance, in a few notorious cases in the United States there have been prominent shootings at schools, which have necessitated high-security policing around school

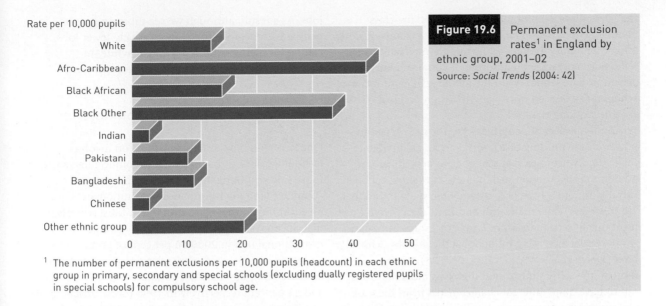

Figure 19.6 Permanent exclusion rates[1] in England by ethnic group, 2001–02

Source: *Social Trends* (2004: 42)

Rate per 10,000 pupils

White
Afro-Caribbean
Black African
Black Other
Indian
Pakistani
Bangladeshi
Chinese
Other ethnic group

0   10   20   30   40   50

[1] The number of permanent exclusions per 10,000 pupils (headcount) in each ethnic group in primary, secondary and special schools (excluding dually registered pupils in special schools) for compulsory school age.

buildings. In the most infamous case, at Columbine High School, two boys killed a teacher, 12 students and themselves. Although such killings are very rare, they almost always achieve much publicity and fuel the idea of 'dangerous and violent schools' (*Newsweek*, 23 August 1999). Such shootings have been much less prominent in the UK, though it has been estimated that there are something like three cases of arson per week in UK schools (*Guardian Education*, 30 October 2001, p.2). More and more teachers worry about their working conditions when some of their pupils are willing to abuse, fight or even stab them. This seems to be one of the major reasons cited by teachers for leaving the profession.

Linked to this, many children now find themselves outside the educational system, as schools say they cannot cope with 'problem children'. In 2001/2 some 10,000 children were permanently excluded from schools – 4% higher than the previous year, but lower than in 1996/7 (when 13,000 were excluded). Boys outnumbered girls by nearly five to one; and were highest among some ethnic groupings (Black Caribbean) (see Figure 19.6). As may be expected, the age group where exclusions were most common was those aged 13 and 14 (*Social Trends*, 2004: 42).

The ideology of parentocracy

Education in England and Wales (Scotland and Northern Ireland operate separate education systems) has gone through three phases: a concern for imparting basic information to the working classes, followed by a shift to a meritocratic ideology, followed by a new phase labelled **parentocracy**, *a system where a child's education is increasingly dependent upon the wealth and wishes of parents, rather than the ability and efforts of pupils* (P. Brown, 1990).

In part, the emphasis on parental choice in primary schools has fuelled this shift. One study of parents exercising choice over their children's schooling found

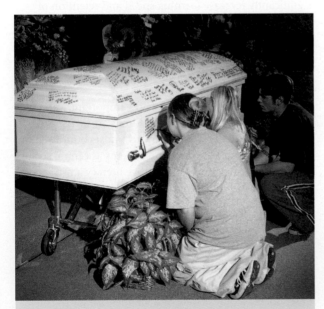

The massacre of 12 school children and one teacher at Columbine High School brought their friends together to consider their emotional and spiritual response to their deaths.

Source: Popperfoto © Rick T Wilking/Reuters

that class plays a major influence. For working-class parents, school had to be fitted into the demands of work and other family matters, while middle-class parents tended to reorganise their household arrangements to accommodate school. With the ideology of parentocracy, schools may be seen once again to disadvantage the less flexible working classes.

Another aspect of parentocracy is the rise of 'parent power' in the running of schools. Parents are invited to make their voices heard at school governors' meetings and, in the UK, vote on such matters as whether schools should 'opt out' of the LEA system. One study found that 'middle-class white males still dominate the powerful positions in secondary schools governorship', although women have increasing influence at the primary school level (Deem *et al.*, 1995; Deem, 1997: 28). Worryingly, though, the same study found that 'governors may turn out to have quite different characteristics from those of the pupils who attend the school they govern and to have much less interest in social justice than might be thought appropriate for those overseeing a public education service' (Deem, 1997: 31).

Credentialism

Randall Collins (1979) coined the term *credential society* for societies where people view diplomas and degrees as evidence of ability to perform specialised occupational roles. As modern societies have become more technologically complex, culturally diverse and socially mobile, a CV or résumé often says more about 'who you are' than family background does.

Credentialism, then, is *evaluating a person on the basis of educational qualifications*. Functional analysis views credentialism as simply the way our modern society goes about ensuring that important jobs are filled by well-trained people. But Collins points out that credentials often bear little relation to the responsibilities of a specific job, and maintains that degrees serve as a shorthand way to sort out the people with the manners and attitudes sought by many employers. In short, credentialism operates much like family background as a gatekeeping strategy that restricts prestigious occupations to a small segment of the population. Finally, this emphasis on credentials can encourage *over-education*, by which many workers have more schooling than they need to perform their

jobs. As a result, although we see more and more people with degrees, there are relatively fewer jobs calling for highly educated workers, while the proportion of low-skill service jobs is expanding.

Education and the Information Revolution

One key trend now reshaping education involves technology. Just as the Industrial Revolution had a major impact on schooling in the nineteenth century, computers and the Information Revolution are transforming formal education today. Most schools in high-income societies now have many computers for instructional use: in 2000 86 per cent of primary schools and 98 per cent of secondary schools in England had access to computer facilities compared with 17 per cent and 83 per cent respectively in 1998 (*Social Trends*, 2001: 61). The promise of new information technology goes beyond helping students learn basic skills to improving the overall quality of learning. Interacting with computers prompts students to be more active learners and has the added benefit of allowing them to progress at their own pace. For students with disabilities who cannot write with a pen or pencil, computers permit easier self-expression. The introduction of computers into schools at all levels of education appears to significantly increase learning speed and retention of information (see Fantini, 1986).

Looking ahead

This chapter has suggested just how important – and how full of problems – educational systems are across the world. Since the nineteenth century, most countries have seen the provision of education systems as central social institutions. Education can improve literacy, raise general standards of knowledge and awareness, and provide a better-trained workforce. But at the same time it may work to reproduce social divisions across class, gender and ethnicity.

In many low-income countries, children have few opportunities to pursue education beyond a basic level, while in richer countries students are often processed in school via a bureaucratic system, increasingly organised through credentialism, league tables and the 'audit culture'. In all countries there are major problems of funding.

CONTROVERSY AND DEBATE

THE DUMBING DOWN OF EDUCATION: THE CASE OF MASS HIGHER EDUCATION

There has been a marked expansion in numbers going to universities and other institutions of higher education across the world, but especially in the industrialised world. In one sense 'schooling' has now been extended for many young people to over 20 years of age. It has almost become compulsory for middle-class groups. In the UK alone, some 35 per cent of those aged 18 to 30 now attend university, and the New Labour government of 2001 was elected with a pledge to increase this to 50 per cent by 2010 (*The Economist*, 30 June 2001: 34). Figure 19.7 shows graduation rates from first university degrees for EU countries. The UK has the third highest place, behind Denmark and Finland.

This change has meant a shift from an *elite system* of higher education (where a very select few went to university who then automatically got the 'best jobs') to a *mass system* (where a much larger – if still selected – group go to university). Over the past cen-

tury, the UK has seen a shift from something like 1 per cent to 30 per cent of young people attending university, and a government goal is that some 50 per cent should eventually attain this. In the United States, such a system has existed for a long time, and it is now starting to appear everywhere.

There are many strands of the modern university which we can see as being shaped by some of the themes already discussed in this book. Universities have become large bureaucracies. Standardisation has become the norm for courses and assessments. There has been a *McDonaldisation of the university* as mass textbooks and PowerPoint slides take over from library searching and creative lecturing. Universities have become part of the *market*. They are now much more vocational and tied into market forces. Indeed, even within the universities the market dominates so that students now become 'customers'. There is an upside to this in so far as students may now have their immediate demands satisfied: 'We are paying after all!', they say. But there is also a downside: concern over long-term thinking and the values of university life may now have to recede as they are not part of market values.

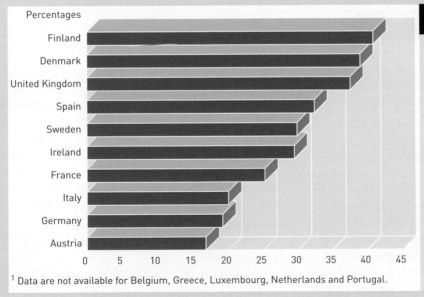

Percentages

Figure 19.7 Graduation rates from first university degrees: EU comparison[1], 2001

Source: *Social Trends* (2004: 46)

[1] Data are not available for Belgium, Greece, Luxembourg, Netherlands and Portugal.

CONTROVERSY AND DEBATE CONTINUED

Academics too may come to have more concern over patenting and intellectual property rights than with the search for truth. Instead of the classics of a culture being studied, new courses such as cultural studies, tourism and even golf course studies have appeared in the new curriculum. And the universities have become more and more involved in commercial practices. Contemporary changes in higher education may be closely linked to changes in the work situation. Post-Fordism (discussed in Chapter 14) may now be found in universities. Just as the work system has to become more flexible and adaptable (and this brings growing uncertainty), so too modern university systems need to do this.

Some argue that we are entering the phase of the *Postmodern University*. Frank Webster suggests that the idea of 'differences' is central to this. Universities may once have been elite institutions where a common background led to a common search for a common knowledge provided through tutors and libraries. All this has now gone. We have, as Webster says, differences in 'courses, students, purposes, academics and disciplines' (2000: 319). There seem to

be very few common traits that now bind the universities together. Along with this, they have declined in general standing: getting a degree now has become a commonplace, and it no longer has a major role in gaining employment or status in society. Elite universities prided themselves on their autonomy and freedom, but mass universities have become much more restrained by business and governments: they have become much more accountable. At the same time, universities have moved from being closed to open – expert knowledge was limited and now there is much more openness.

CONTINUE THE DEBATE:

1. Just what is happening to universities today? How have they changed? What do you see as their major problems?

2. Has 'more' meant 'worse'?

Sources: Scott (1995); Smith and Webster (1997); Webster (2000).

SUMMARY

1. Education is the major social institution for transmitting knowledge and skills, as well as teaching cultural norms and values.

2. Symbolic interactionists have observed that relations between teachers and students play a role in maintaining social structures outside schools. Conflict analysis points out how differences in class, race, gender and sexuality promote unequal opportunities for schooling. Formal education also serves as a means of generating conformity to produce compliant adult workers. When children get labelled as achievers or as failures at school, they learn to become the type of person which the label suggests they are.

3. Streaming, in theory, groups students of similar needs to maximise the appropriateness of teaching materials

and the pace of learning. Critics maintain that schools stream students according to their social background, thereby providing privileged youngsters with a richer and more challenging education.

4. The UK government has introduced market forces into the education system. Some believe that the market will improve services and choice, but others suggest that market forces are increasing inequalities and undermining the traditional principles of education.

5. Many education systems encourage people to get credentials which are not necessarily related to the available jobs.

6. Contemporary issues facing education include funding, auditing, parentocracy, credentialism and the information revolution.

CRITICAL-THINKING QUESTIONS

1. Why did widespread schooling develop in Europe only after the Industrial Revolution?

2. Referring to various countries, including the UK, describe ways in which schooling is shaped by economic, political or cultural factors.

3. How valuable do you find classroom interaction studies? Do one of your own, looking around your campus and class. Do the themes outlined in the text still apply?

4. Examine the controversy over why girls seem to be achieving more than boys in UK schools. Consider also how girls 'achieve' in low-income societies. Discuss how cultures may shape such achievement.

GOING FURTHER

Further reading

General issues:

Amanda Coffey, *Education and Social Change* (2001)
A lively discussion of the major issues facing education in the contemporary UK (and much of it is relevant to other Western cultures too).

A. H. Halsey, Hugh Lauder, Phillip Brown and Amy Stuart Wells, *Education: Culture, Economy and Society* (1997)
A very valuable collection of up-to-date readings which mark out the field of the contemporary sociology of education.

On gender and schooling:

Paul Willis, *Learning to Labour* (1977)
The classic UK ethnography: a study of a small group of working-class boys moving from school to work. Its fame may, however, be curiously misplaced: it studies only 12 boys and overlays the observation with a rather dense theoretical Marxism.

Mairtin Mac an Ghaill, *The Making of Men: Masculinities, Sexualities and Schooling* (1994)
A vivid study of gender, class and ethnicity in a secondary school.

Sue Sharpe, *Just like a Girl: How Girls Learn to Become Women* (2nd edn, 1994)
Updates her original 1976 study and finds that girls have changed.

On university and higher education:

Peter Scott, *The Meanings of Mass Higher Education* (1995) and Anthony Smith and Frank Webster (eds), *The Postmodern University? Contested Voices of Higher Education in Society* (1997)
Both useful discussions of the modern university.

More information

Donald Mackinnon, June Statham and Margaret Hales, *Education in the UK: Facts and Figures* (3rd edn, 1999) is one of a number of valuable overviews of the whole educational scene in the UK. It looks at its history, the main reports, legislation, the organisation and working of the system, and reviews matters linked to curriculum, preparation for employment and youth training. Not sociological as such, but helpful with facts, figures and information.

Watch a video

- Ken Loach's *Kes* (1969): a classic film set in the 1960s, it is one of the most remarkable films about education and the working classes.
- John Singleton's *Higher Learning* (1994): study of US campus life in the mid-1990s.
- Peter Weir's *Dead Poet's Society* (1989): Robin Williams in US elite school challenging his students.
- Mike Newell's *Mona Lisa Smile* (2003): Julia Roberts does the same as the above for girls, but not as well.

Connecting up

Connect to other chapters

- To link labelling processes to labelling theory, see Chapter 16.
- To link education to social class, see Chapter 10.
- To link education to gender and ethnicity, see Chapters 11 and 12.

To the websites

- The UNESCO website

  http://portal.unesco.org/en/

  A useful starting point for world analyses of education.

- Departmnent for Education and Skills (UK)

  http://www.dfes.gov.uk

  For UK government policy and information on funding.

For additional case studies, multiple choice questions, internet exercises, and annotated weblinks specific to this chapter, visit this book's website at **www.pearsoned.co.uk/plummer**

CHAPTER 20

HEALTH AND MEDICINE

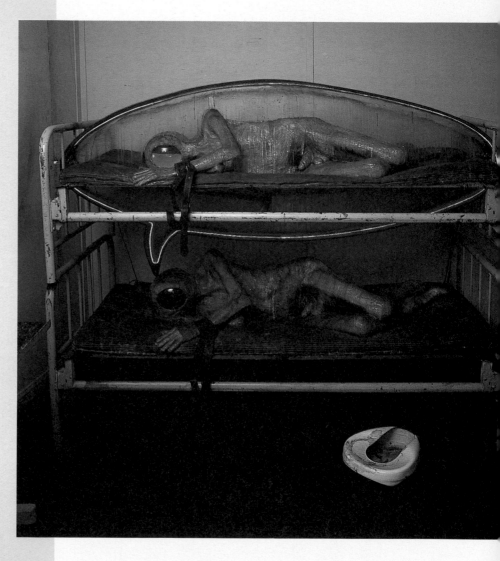

Men make use of their illnesses at least as much as they are made use of by them.

Aldous Huxley: *Collected Essays*

How well I should be if it were not for all those people shouting that I am ill!

André Gide: *Pretexts*

KEY THEMES

- Health as a sociological issue
- Health differences and inequalities across the world
- The social causes of illness and how are they linked to inequalities
- The different kinds of health system
- The main approaches to the study of health
- The sociological lessons to be learnt from three case studies: obesity, AIDS and death.

(Above) Female genital mutilation in Kenya: when medicine is politics
Source: Network/Saba © Mariella Furrer

(Left) Edward Keinholtz: *The State Hospital*. A chilling invented view of patients in a mental hospital.
Source: Moderna Museet, Stockholm

IN 1993, MESERAK RAMSEY, a woman born in Ethiopia who now works as a nurse in California, paid a visit to a friend's home. The friend's little girl – 18 months old – was huddled in the corner of a room in obvious distress. Ramsey was shocked to learn that the girl had recently undergone a clitoridectomy, or female circumcision, whereby the clitoris is surgically removed. This painful procedure is commonly performed by midwives, tribal practitioners or doctors, typically without anaesthetic, on young girls in Nigeria, Togo, Somalia, Egypt and three dozen other nations in Africa and the Middle East.

According to the patriarchal traditions of these societies, husbands demand that their wives be virgins at marriage and remain sexually faithful thereafter. The point of genital mutilation is to eliminate sexual sensation, thereby making the girl less likely to violate sexual mores. In the process, she becomes more desirable to men. In perhaps a fifth of all cases, a more severe procedure called infibulation is performed, removing the entire external genital area and stitching the surfaces together leaving only a small hole for urination. At marriage, in such cases, a husband can reopen the wound and ensure himself of his bride's virginity.

Throughout the world, millions of women have endured Female Genital Mutilation (FGM). It can quite frequently result in death. Western feminists have rallied against this practice for several decades; yet some feminists in countries where it is practised can also recognise that it is part of a culture's heritage and it brings with it enormous ritual significance. A woman's identity and life can be destroyed if she does not submit to the practice. It cannot therefore be easily changed. So although the United Nations has led efforts against it, outlawing it in some 15 of the 28 countries where it existed, the practice often still continues. It is too deep-rooted.

Medically, the consequences of genital mutilation are more than loss of sexual pleasure. Pain is excruciating and may persist, along with the danger of infection, infertility and even death. Meserak Ramsey herself underwent genital mutilation as a young girl, and since then she has been lucky to have had few medical problems. This is a system that distorts medicine into a brutal form of political and sexual control.

Sources: based on Crossette (1995); *Newsweek*, 5 July 1999

We tend to think of illness and disease as matters for doctors and biologists. But what this chapter will show is that disease is also very much a matter for sociologists. The story of Meserak Ramsey brings home strikingly that what happens to our bodies is very much a product of the kind of society we live in. Moreover, looking after our bodies has necessitated a major set of social institutions around medicine. In this chapter, we will start an exploration of all this.

What is health?

Billions of people around the planet face major health problems, and some are in a position to cope more successfully than others. The World Health Organisation famously defined **health** in 1946 as *a state of complete physical, mental and social well-being* (1946: 3). This definition underscores the major theme of this chapter: *health is as much a social as a biological issue*. And it provides major clues as to how a society or nation works. Societies with a lot of sickness and early deaths are likely to be socially organised very differently from those where people live longer lives and experience less illness.

Health and society

The health of any population is shaped by traits of the surrounding society. Key aspects of health include the following:

1. *People judge their health relative to others*. Standards of health vary from society to society. Earlier this century, the contagious skin disease, yaws, was so common in sub-Saharan Africa that people there considered it normal (Dubos, 1980; orig. 1965). Health is sometimes a matter of having the same diseases as one's neighbours.

2. *People often equate 'health' with morality*. In some cultures, for instance, the disabled may themselves be seen as in some way to blame – albinos, dwarfs and hydrocephalic children may be seen as supernatural (Barnes *et al.*, 1999: 14); and those who contract a sexually linked disease may be looked upon as morally suspect. Indeed, some countries require potential immigrants to take HIV and syphilis tests before they are given visas. In short, ideas about good health constitute a type of social control that encourages conformity to cultural norms.

3. *Cultural standards of health change over time*. In the nineteenth century masturbation (or onanism) was denounced as a threat to health. Today, such notions are rejected (and some therapists view masturbation very positively). Conversely, few people 60 years ago spoke of the dangers of cigarette smoking, a practice that is now widely regarded as a threat to health.

4. *Health and living standards are interrelated*. Poor societies routinely contend with malnutrition and poor sanitation, which promote high levels of infectious disease. Industrial development, taking little account of people's health, likewise has often lowered living standards.

5. *Health relates to social inequality*. Every society distributes resources unequally. The physical, mental and social health of the wealthy is far better than that of poor people. This pattern starts at birth, with infant mortality highest among the poor. Affluent people enjoy a greater chance of recovering from major illnesses and accidents than poor people.

Health and the body

As we saw in Chapter 7, sociologists have taken an increasing interest in the ways in which our bodies are social. And the sociology of health and illness can be seen as looking at the way in which the body breaks down in society and needs to be socially repaired. Medical regimes are then required to organise all this work around birth, disease, decay and death. From the moment the foetus is identified to the final inability to repair the body resulting in death, social organisation is needed to deal with these 'bodies'. And as we shall see later, the size of our bodies – from thin and anorexic to fat and obese – is linked to our wider health.

Health: a global survey

Because health is an important dimension of social life, we find pronounced change in human well-being over time. Historians of disease have identified three phases in human health. In a pre-agricultural phase, people lived short but healthy lives with few infectious diseases. The Agricultural Revolution improved food security, but the accompanying increases in social inequality allowed elites to enjoy better health, while peasants and slaves often laboured for long hours and lived in crowded, insanitary shelters. In the cities of medieval Europe, human waste and other refuse fuelled infectious diseases, including plagues that periodically wiped out entire towns (Mumford, 1961).

By the industrial era, people started to learn how to control many infectious diseases, but suffered from a range of diseases linked to environment, pollution and stress (such as cancers, strokes and heart disease). Contemporary ailments are more often helped by a change in lifestyle rather than by medication. Hence, as we shall see, medical work is increasingly preventive rather than curative (McKeown, 1976).

Health in low-income countries

Figures 20.1, 20.2 and 20.3 suggest some of the striking differences in health which distinguish societies of the world today. The World Health Organisation (WHO) reports that in 2002, life expectancy at birth reached 78 years for women in developed countries, it fell back to less than 46 years for men in sub-Saharan Africa (Map 20.2). Further, *1 billion people around the world suffer from serious illness linked to poverty*. Poor sanitation and malnutrition kill people of all ages, especially children. A high infant mortality rate is very common in poor countries. Indeed, 10 per cent of the world's children die before the age of one. In most parts of the world, once you survive childhood, there is a good chance of living as long as most people do in the richer countries (Calvert and Calvert, 2001: 58).

Health is compromised not just by having too little to eat, but also by being restricted to consuming only one kind of food, as the World Watch box explains. In impoverished countries, sanitary drinking water may be as scarce as the chance for a balanced diet. Contaminated water breeds many of the infectious diseases that imperil both adults and children. The leading causes of death in Europe a century ago, including influenza, pneumonia and tuberculosis, remain widespread killers in poor societies. Thus largely preventable diseases are still common:

- 1.5 million children under age five die annually from measles
- 400 million suffer from malaria
- 225 million have hookworm
- 200 million are sick with schistosomiasis (blood flukes)
- 20 million suffer from sleeping sickness (Calvert and Calvert, 2001: 60).

In addition, poor societies are further plagued by a shortage of doctors and other medical personnel, along with a lack of funding for medicines.

Illness and poverty form a vicious cycle in much of the world – poverty breeds disease, which, in turn, undermines people's ability to earn income. Moreover, when medical technology does curb infectious disease, the populations of poor nations soar. Without resources to ensure the well-being of the people they have now, poor societies can ill afford surging population growth. At present, the WHO reports that things are getting worse. Over 35 per cent of Africa's children are at higher risk of death than they were ten years ago. Every hour more than 500 African mothers lose a small child (WHO, 2003: 1). Thus, efforts to lower death rates in poor countries will ultimately succeed only if they simultaneously reduce birth rates as well. The damage this causes is vast: for example, there are some 11 million

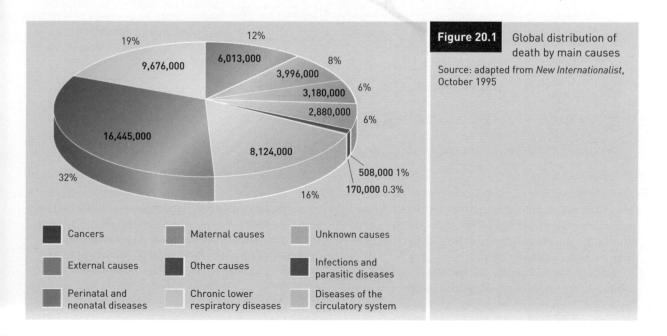

Figure 20.1 Global distribution of death by main causes

Source: adapted from *New Internationalist*, October 1995

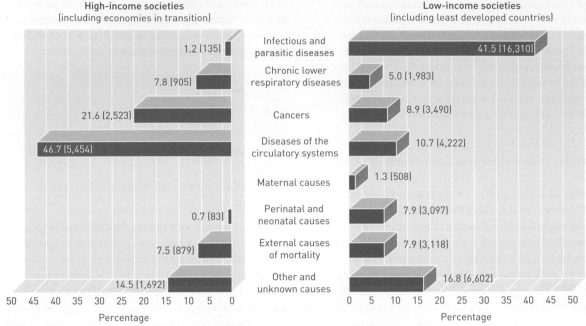

High-income societies (including economies in transition)		**Low-income societies** (including least developed countries)

1.2 (135) / Infectious and parasitic diseases / 41.5 (16,310)

7.8 (905) / Chronic lower respiratory diseases / 5.0 (1,983)

21.6 (2,523) / Cancers / 8.9 (3,490)

46.7 (5,454) / Diseases of the circulatory systems / 10.7 (4,222)

Maternal causes / 1.3 (508)

0.7 (83) / Perinatal and neonatal causes / 7.9 (3,097)

7.5 (879) / External causes of mortality / 7.9 (3,118)

14.5 (1,692) / Other and unknown causes / 16.8 (6,602)

50 45 40 35 30 25 20 15 10 5 0 — Percentage

0 5 10 15 20 25 30 35 40 45 50 — Percentage

(Figures in brackets refer to the actual number of deaths in thousands)

Figure 20.2   Causes of death, 1993

Source: adapted from *New Internationalist*, October 1995

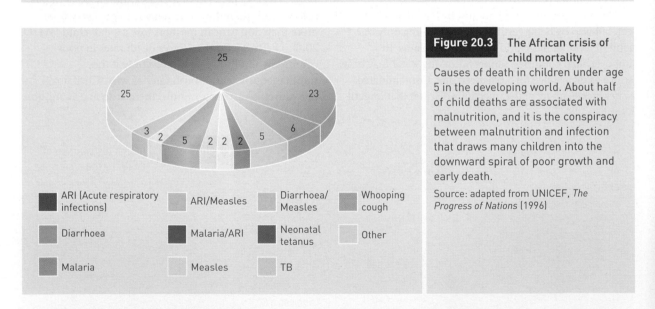

Figure 20.3   **The African crisis of child mortality**

Causes of death in children under age 5 in the developing world. About half of child deaths are associated with malnutrition, and it is the conspiracy between malnutrition and infection that draws many children into the downward spiral of poor growth and early death.

Source: adapted from UNICEF, *The Progress of Nations* (1996)

Pie chart values: 25, 23, 6, 5, 2, 2, 2, 5, 3, 25

Legend:
- ARI (Acute respiratory infections)
- Diarrhoea
- Malaria
- ARI/Measles
- Malaria/ARI
- Measles
- Diarrhoea/Measles
- Neonatal tetanus
- TB
- Whooping cough
- Other

'Aids Orphans' in sub-Saharan Africa – children whose parents have died from HIV/AIDS. Older brothers and sisters (and sometimes grandparents) are left to raise large families (UNICEF, 2004b).

Although 'death' is a clear and simple measure for combating the health of populations, recently a new useful measurement of disability-adjusted life years (DALYs) has been introduced. This measures the lost years of 'healthy' life. DALYs combine years of life lost (YLLs) through premature death with years lived with disability (YLDs).

Health as a human right

The 'Global Strategy' of *Health for All* by 2000, adopted by the WHO in 1982, saw health as a basic human right. It argued that 'all the people in all the countries should have at least such a level of health that they are capable of working productively and participating actively in the social life of the community in which they live'. The WHO aimed at ensuring all peoples have adequate access to safe water, sanitary facilities, immunisation against major infections and availability of local health care. 2000 was set as the target year for 'health for all' but it soon became clear that this would not be achieved (WHO, 2000; World Bank, 2000).

In some low-income countries such as Sri Lanka, People's Republic of China and Costa Rica, there have been successes: life expectancy is generally more than 65 years. Four factors have been suggested to assist this process: an ideological commitment to equity in social matters; equitable access to and distribution of public health care provision; equitable access to and distribution of public education; and adequate nutrition at all levels of society (Calvert and Calvert, 2001: 57). Where these factors are present, health becomes more available for all (Map 20.1).

Health in high-income countries

Industrialisation dramatically changed patterns of human health in Europe, though at first not for the better. By 1800, as the Industrial Revolution was taking

WORLD WATCH

KILLER POVERTY: A REPORT FROM AFRICA

Periodic famine in Africa brings home to people in the affluent West the horror of starving children. Some of the children portrayed by the mass media appear bloated, while others seem to have shrivelled to little more than skin drawn tightly over bones. Both of these deadly conditions, explains Susan George (1977), are direct consequences of poverty.

Children with bloated bodies are suffering from protein deficiency. In West Africa this condition is known as kwashiorkor, literally 'one-two'. The term derives from the common practice among mothers of abruptly weaning a first child upon the birth of a second. Deprived of mother's milk, a baby may receive virtually no protein at all.

Children with shrivelled bodies lack both protein and calories. This deficiency is the result of eating little food of any kind.

In either case, children usually do not die of starvation, strictly speaking. Their weakened condition makes them vulnerable to stomach ailments such as gastroenteritis or diseases such as measles. The death rate from measles, for example, is 1,000 times greater in parts of Africa than in North America. Depending on a single food also undermines nutrition, causing a deficiency of protein, vitamins and minerals. Millions of people in low-income countries suffer from goitre, a debilitating, diet-related disease of the thyroid gland. Pellagra, a disease common to people who consume mostly corn, is equally serious, frequently leading to insanity. Those whose diet consists primarily of processed rice are prone to beriberi, which brings on swelling and nerve disorders.

We can understand health as a social issue simply by noting that a host of diseases virtually unknown to members of rich societies are a common experience of life – and death – in poor countries.

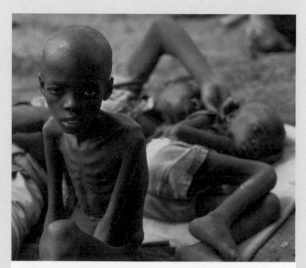

In the Sudan, famine is typically followed by the spread of disease.

Source: Corbis Sygma © W. Campbell

hold, factories were choking the cities with people drawn from the countryside in search of economic opportunity. Unprecedented population concentration spawned serious problems of sanitation and overcrowded housing. Moreover, factories continuously fouled the air with smoke, a health threat unrecognised until well into the twentieth century. Accidents in the workplace were also common.

But as the nineteenth century progressed, health in Western Europe and North America improved. This change was mainly due to a rising standard of living that translated into better nutrition and safer housing for the majority of people. After 1850, medical advances had further promoted health, primarily by controlling infectious diseases. To illustrate, in 1854 John Snow noted the street addresses of London's cholera victims and traced the source of this disease to contaminated drinking water (Rockett, 1994). Soon after, scientists linked cholera to specific bacteria and developed a protective vaccine against the deadly disease. Armed with this knowledge, early environmentalists campaigned against age-old practices such as discharging raw sewage into rivers used for drinking water. As the twentieth century dawned, death rates from infectious diseases had fallen sharply.

As the prevalence of infectious diseases has declined, chronic illnesses, including heart disease and cancer, are left to claim almost two-thirds of the population of Europe, generally in old age. In short, while nothing alters the reality of death, industrial societies manage to delay our demise for decades. Figures 20.4, 20.5 and 20.6 illustrate expectation of life at birth, infant mortality, and mortality by sex and cause for the UK.

The rise of a medical model

Industrialisation facilitated a 'medical model' of health. The majority of the most significant changes in health in industrialised societies occurred as a consequence of changes in society (such as improved sanitation and cleanliness, education and better food). At the same time, the scientific method started to shape thinking about illness in Western societies through the gradual emergence of a medical model. In an ideal type mode, this model claims:

1. Diseases arise from a biological breakdown within the individual.

2. Diseases have specific causes (like viruses) which can be located.

3. The focus of attention is, therefore, upon the body of the ill person, rather than on general well-being.

4. The correct response to illness, therefore, is treatment within a medical environment and/or through pharmaceuticals.

5. Treatment is 'scientifically neutral'; that is, free of value judgements (Hart, 1985).

Such a model is widespread, yet each of the factors outlined above can be challenged. Critics reject the focus on biology, contending that biology plays only one part

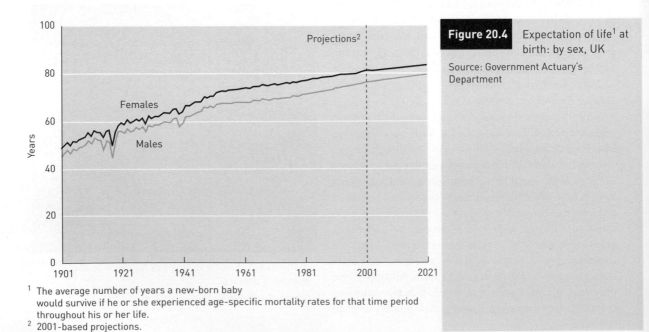

Figure 20.4 Expectation of life[1] at birth: by sex, UK

Source: Government Actuary's Department

[1] The average number of years a new-born baby would survive if he or she experienced age-specific mortality rates for that time period throughout his or her life.

[2] 2001-based projections.

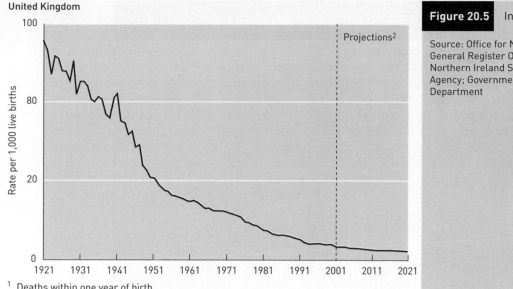

United Kingdom

Figure 20.5 Infant mortality[1],UK

Source: Office for National Statistics; General Register Office for Scotland; Northern Ireland Statistics and Research Agency; Government Actuary's Department

[1] Deaths within one year of birth.
[2] 2001-based projections.

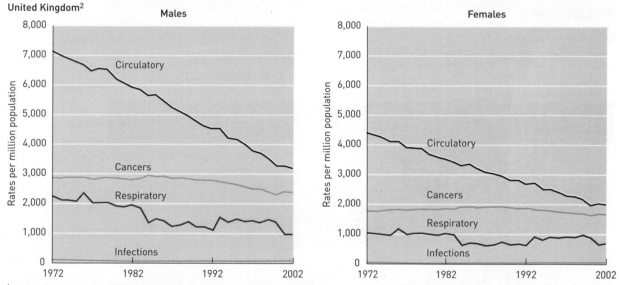

[1] Data are for all ages and have been age standardised using the European standard population.
[2] Data for 2000 are for England and Wales only.

Figure 20.6 Mortality[1]: by sex and major cause, UK

Source: Office for National Statistics

in the total 'health life' of an individual. Social factors, including stress, difficulty coping with a changing social environment or a personal tragedy, can also affect health. Addressing one aspect of the problem may not cure the whole person. Moreover, some would critique the medical establishment for distancing people from their own bodies. They argue that doctors should help people to understand how their bodies work, rather than using baffling jargon and handing down judgements that remove people's control of their own bodies.

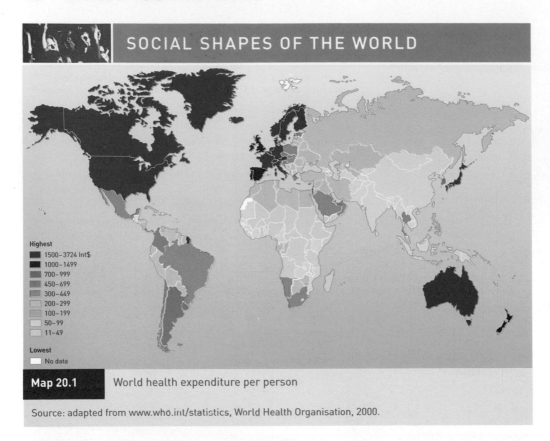

SOCIAL SHAPES OF THE WORLD

Highest
- 1500–3724 Int$
- 1000–1499
- 700–999
- 450–699
- 300–449
- 200–299
- 100–199
- 50–99
- 11–49

Lowest
- No data

Map 20.1   World health expenditure per person

Source: adapted from www.who.int/statistics, World Health Organisation, 2000.

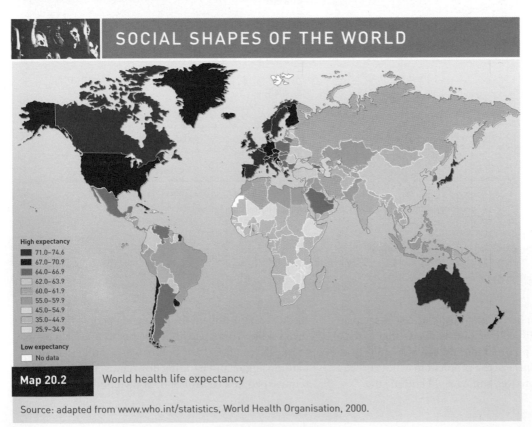

SOCIAL SHAPES OF THE WORLD

High expectancy
- 71.0–74.6
- 67.0–70.9
- 64.0–66.9
- 62.0–63.9
- 60.0–61.9
- 55.0–59.9
- 45.0–54.9
- 35.0–44.9
- 25.9–34.9

Low expectancy
- No data

Map 20.2   World health life expectancy

Source: adapted from www.who.int/statistics, World Health Organisation, 2000.

Some social links to illness

Given these problems with the medical model, sociologists often highlight the many social factors that play a role in producing illness. A UK government report on inequalities and health, the Acheson Report (Acheson, 1998) (discussed below), suggests a full spectrum of factors that need to be identified in understanding the main determinants of health. They are depicted in Figure 20.7 and range through:

- the broadest features of the society – we have already seen how low-income and high-income societies are likely to have different disease patterns

- specific living conditions such as work and housing: poor work conditions and housing can be highly correlated with poor health

- social and community networks of support: isolation and lack of support can trigger or exacerbate health problems

- individual lifestyle factors, such as drinking alcohol heavily or smoking may be linked to health disruption

- age, sex and constitutional factors.

Social epidemiology and inequalities in health

Most people in Europe are healthy by world standards. Some categories of people, however, enjoy far better health and well-being than others. Here we will look at some of the social patterns of health in the UK – which is another way of saying that we will be looking at social inequalities. The patterns in the UK are fairly typical of those in many Western societies. Once again, as we have seen throughout this book, one of the major mechanisms of social organisation is inequality. And just as we have seen that inequalities shape disease and health in low-income societies, so too they shape them in high-income societies.

Social epidemiology is *the study of how health and disease are distributed throughout a society's population.* Just as early social epidemiologists examined the origin and spread of epidemic diseases, researchers today find links between health and physical and social environments. Such analysis rests on comparing the health of different categories of people.

Social class

Lesley Doyal has argued that: 'Class differences in morbidity and mortality . . . provide strong evidence to support the argument that social and economic factors remain extremely important in determining the ways in which people live and die' (Doyal, 1979: 65). In 2002, in England and Wales, the infant mortality among babies born inside marriage whose fathers were in semi-routine occupations was 7.5 per 1,000 live births, almost three times the rate of 2.7 per 1,000 live births of those whose fathers were in higher managerial occupations (*Social Trends*, 2004: 107). Note though that for all groups there have been significant long-term declines in infant

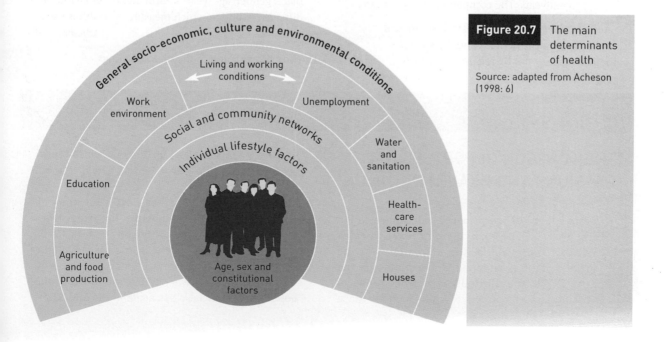

Figure 20.7 The main determinants of health

Source: adapted from Acheson (1998: 6)

mortality. Thus, in 1921 84 children per 1,000 live births died before the age of one, yet by 2002, the rate had dropped to only 4.8. (But as we have seen, this is certainly not true in all parts of the world where infant mortality has remained very high indeed).

The Black Report

The most important study to look at health inequalities in the UK was the Black Report (1980): *The Report of the Working Party on Inequalities in Health* (updated in 1992 as *The Health Divide*). Townsend and Davidson (1982) argued that: (1) inequalities in health are found at birth (as above), in childhood, in adolescence and throughout adult life; (2) some of these inequalities were among the worst in Europe; and (3) inequalities have also been growing. One of its most famous findings was that the child of an unskilled manual worker will die around seven years earlier than a counterpart born to professional parents.

Linked closely to this is inequality in health care. Some research suggests that working-class patients are treated somewhat differently. They may, for example, be given less time and be less well known to their doctors. More than this, there may be an 'inverse care law' – those whose need is less may get more resources, while those in greatest need get less – and the poorest may not get such good treatment from within the NHS (Tudor-Hart, 1971; Hart, 1985).

All in all, the link between class and inequality seems evident. But the question that is then posed concerns why. The Black Report looked at four main arguments which might explain social class differences around health. The four arguments have framed much of the debate in recent years. The competing arguments are:

- *Statistical artefacts*. This suggests there are real problems of measurement and the statistics themselves may not be reliable indicators.

- *Natural-health selection explanations*. This suggests that health status itself may influence positioning in the class structure. The healthy drift upwards, the sick drift downwards. (Note that this has a social Darwinism ring to it.)

- *Materialist explanations*. This suggests that material deprivations – poverty, low incomes, bad housing conditions, pollution at work – shape the experiences of health.

- *Cultural explanations*. This suggests that certain class ways of life – more smoking in working-class groups, poorer diets, less exercise – shape the health experiences.

The Black Report concluded that the last two explanations were the most satisfactory.

The Acheson Report

More recently, the Acheson Report (1998) has drawn together a number of studies to provide a review of the state of health in the UK. It notes that:

> Inequalities in health exist, whether measured in terms of mortality, life expectancy or health status; whether categorised by socioeconomic measures or by ethnic group or gender. Recent efforts to compare the level and nature of health inequalities in international terms indicate that Britain is generally around the middle of comparable western countries. . . . Although in general disadvantage is associated with worse health, the patterns of inequalities vary by place, gender, age, year of birth and other factors, and differ according to which measure of health is used.
>
> (Acheson, 1998)

The box shows some of the major findings.

THE ACHESON REPORT: SOCIAL DIVISIONS AND HEALTH IN THE UK

- *Death rates*. Although death rates have fallen over the last 20 years, the difference in rates between those at the top and bottom of the social scale has widened. For example, in the early 1970s, the mortality rate among men of working age was almost twice as high for those in class V (unskilled) as for those in class I (professional). By the early 1990s, it was almost three times higher.

- *Average life expectancy at birth*. For men in classes I and II combined, life expectancy increased by two years between the late 1970s and the late 1980s. For those in classes IV and V combined, the increase was smaller, 1.4 years. The difference between those at the top and bottom of the social class scale in the late 1980s was five years: 75 years compared with 70 years. For women, the differential was smaller, 80 years compared with 77 years.

- *Life expectancy at age 65*. Again, in the late 1980s, this was considerably higher among those in higher social classes, and the differential increased over the period from the late 1970s to the late 1980s, particularly for women.
- *Infant mortality rates* were lower among babies born to those of higher social classes. In 1994–96, nearly five out of every 1,000 babies born to parents in class I and II died in their first year. For those babies born to families in classes IV and V, the infant mortality rate was over seven per 1,000 babies.
- *Obesity*. Being overweight is a measure of possible ill health, with obesity a risk factor for many chronic diseases. There is a marked social class gradient in obesity which is greater among women than among men. In 1996, 25 per cent of women in class V were classified as obese compared to 14 per cent of women in class I. For men, there was no clear difference in the proportions reported as obese, except that men in class I had lower rates of obesity, 11 per cent, compared to about 18 per cent in other groups. Overall, rates of obesity are rising. For men, 13 per cent were classified as obese in 1993 compared to 16 per cent in 1996. For women, the rise was from 16 per cent to 18 per cent.

- *Raised blood pressure*. There is a clear social class differential among women, with those in higher classes being less likely than those in the manual classes to have hypertension. In 1996, 17 per cent of women in class I and 24 per cent in class V had hypertension. There was no such difference for men where the comparable proportions were 20 per cent and 21 per cent respectively.
- *Major accidents*. Among men, major accidents are more common in the manual classes for those aged under 55. Between 55 and 64, the non-manual classes have higher major accident rates. For women, there are no differences in accident rates until after the age of 75 when those women in the non-manual group have higher rates of major accidents.
- *Mental health*. This also varies markedly by social class. In 1993–94, all neurotic disorders, such as anxiety, depression and phobias, were more common among women in classes IV and V than those in classes I and II – 24 per cent and 15 per cent respectively. This difference was not seen among men. However, there were striking gradients for alcohol and drug dependence among men, but not women. For example, 10 per cent of men in classes IV and V were dependent on alcohol compared to 5 per cent in classes I and II.

Source: Acheson (1998)

Ethnicity

Diseases can also affect ethnic groups significantly differently. In general, people in Black (Caribbean, African and other) groups and Indians have higher rates of limiting long-standing illness than white people. Those of Pakistani or Bangladeshi origin have the highest rates. In contrast, the Chinese and 'other Asians' have rates lower than the white population. The infant mortality rate has been consistently higher for infants born in the New Commonwealth and Pakistan than for those born in the UK.

There are also some diseases which disproportionately affect certain groups: sickle-cell anaemia affects mainly Afro-Caribbeans, while rickets affects mostly Asians. Admission rates for mental illness are also higher for Afro-Caribbeans (with a much greater likelihood of a schizophrenia diagnosis). And there is some evidence that there is a much higher risk of heart disease among

Asians and a much higher risk of a stroke among Afro-Caribbeans (Skellington, 1996: 113–121).

Gender issues

Women generally fare better than men across the life course. At each age, the age-specific mortality rate for boys is higher than for girls, although recently death rates have decreased by 29 per cent for males and by 25 per cent for females, narrowing the differential in death rates slightly. Although the life expectancy gap between males and females is decreasing, this is not the case for healthy life expectancy. Healthy life expectancy of females is only two to three years more than that of males.

Despite women having a longer life expectancy (and this seems to be increasing across the world), they are more likely to be ill. They are more likely to visit doctors than men, and more likely to be admitted to hospitals. (Much of this seems connected to issues of reproduction.) All this is compounded by class. Women tend to be poorer, for example, and this creates a greater potential for ill health. Women are also supposed to put the needs of children (and others) first (Graham, 1993).

Smoking is higher among girls than boys, but in later life the proportions of men and women smoking even out (at 29 and 28 per cent respectively). For both children and adults, males are more likely to drink alcohol heavily than females, but the rate among women is on the increase. Men are more likely to become more aggressive, resulting in higher rates of accidents, violence and suicide. In the European Union (as elsewhere) violent deaths (suicides and accidents) are the single most important cause of death among young men between ages 15 and 24 (Eurostat, 1995b: 228).

In general, perceptions of what it is to be a man (see Chapter 14) create pressures for adult men to be more competitive, to repress their emotions and to engage in hazardous behaviour such as smoking cigarettes and drinking alcohol to excess.

Age

In industrialised countries, death is now rare among young people, with two notable exceptions: a rise in mortality resulting from accidents and, more recently, from acquired immune deficiency syndrome (AIDS). (See Map 20.3 later in this chapter for a global perspective on HIV infection.)

Health-care systems and the medical establishment

Medicine is *a social institution concerned with combating disease and improving health.* Medicine is a vital part of a broader concept of **health care**, which is *any activity intended to improve health.* Through most of human history, health care was the responsibility of individuals and their families. Medicine emerges only as societies become more productive, assigning their members formal, specialised roles. Such medical practitioners recognise the healing properties of certain plants and offer insights into the emotional and spiritual needs of the ill. From our point of view, traditional healers such as acupuncturists and herbalists may seem like unscientific 'witch doctors', but, in truth, they do much to improve human health throughout the world (Ayensu, 1981). As a society industrialises, health care becomes the responsibility of specially schooled and legally licensed healers, from anaesthetists to X-ray technicians.

Comparative health-care systems

Most industrial societies have comprehensive public systems of health care, the major exception being the United States. However, they work in very different ways. Socialised (or nationalised) medical systems are

EUROPEAN EYE

HEALTH CARE IN EUROPE

Taken as a whole, the health of Europe is among the best in the world (only Japan is better) with life expectancy high and increasing, and mortality rates low and declining. The infant mortality rate, for example, was 34.8 per 1,000 live births in 1960, but by 1986 it had dropped to 8.1. The southern European countries have seen the most substantial improvements. But stubborn differences linked to inequalities remain (Abbott and Giarchi, 1997).

In general, there is a growing emphasis upon primary health care (provision focused upon whole communities and their general health status). Health care costs present problems for all countries and the newer technologies are prohibitively expensive. Some countries finance their health systems from collective taxation (the UK, Sweden), some on state-run health insurance funds (Germany, Norway, Denmark, Belgium), some have private schemes (Greece, Austria, The Netherlands) and others have a mixed system of private and state (Ireland, France, Switzerland).

In 1891 Sweden instituted a compulsory, comprehensive system of government medical care. Swedes pay for health care with their taxes, which are among the highest in the world. In most cases, doctors receive salaries from the government rather than fees from patients, and most hospitals are managed by government. Because this medical system resembles that of socialist societies, it is often described as **socialised medicine**, *a health-care system in which the government owns and operates most medical facilities and employs most doctors.*

collective, take inequalities seriously and aim to provide comprehensive coverage for all. They are funded centrally. By contrast, privatised systems tend to work by market forces and allow choices for many while creating a 'health underclass' for whom services are minimal.

Medicine in socialist societies

In societies with predominantly socialist economies, the government provides medical care directly to the people. It is an axiom of socialism that all citizens have the right to basic medical care. To translate this ideal of equity into reality, people do not rely on their private financial resources to pay doctors and hospitals; rather, the government funnels public funds to pay medical costs. The state owns and operates medical facilities and pays salaries to practitioners, who are government employees.

People's Republic of China

A poor, agrarian society that is only beginning to industrialise, the People's Republic of China, faces the daunting task of attending to the health of more than 1 billion people. Traditional healing arts, including acupuncture and the use of medicinal herbs, are still widely practised in China. In addition, a holistic concern for the interplay of mind and body marks the Chinese approach to health (Sidel and Sidel, 1982b). China recently experimented with private medical care, but by 1990 the government had re-established control over this dimension of life. China's famed barefoot doctors, roughly comparable to US paramedics, have brought some modern methods of medical care to millions of peasants in remote rural villages.

Medicine in capitalist societies

People living in nations with predominantly capitalist economies are more likely to provide for their own health care in accordance with financial resources and personal preferences. However, the high costs of medical care – beyond the reach of many people – mean that government programmes underwrite a considerable proportion of health-related expenses.

United Kingdom

In the UK, as a result of the Beveridge recommendations, the National Health Service (NHS) was introduced in 1948 as a tripartite system of hospitals, local health authorities and an 'executive council sector' responsible

for GPs, dentists and the like. Thus all UK citizens are entitled to medical care provided by the National Health Service, but those who can afford to may purchase more extensive care from doctors and hospitals that operate privately. Doyal has suggested this system is more of a nationalised system than a socialised one because it remains full of inequalities: the upper class and wealthy choose the private system, leaving the middle and working classes to be the recipients of the National Health Service.

In 1989 basic changes to the NHS were introduced to make the system more efficient and cost-effective. These changes centred around the 'internal market', another version of Thatcher's emphasis on 'marketisation' (goods and services working on market principles of supply and demand) and privatisation (the transfer of state assets/property from public to private ownership). Hospitals could opt to become self-governing trusts; general practitioners (doctors) could opt to become 'fund-holders'; there was an emphasis on performance indicators; compulsory tendering for contracts was made mandatory; and 'consumer sovereignty' was embodied in a *patients' charter*, part of a consumer-led range of services. The new National Health Service, then, is much more market-driven than the old one, and it works with a much more interventionist style of management derived from the private sector and often linked to total quality control (TQC). Ranade (1994) suggests that it became post-Fordist (see Chapters 6 and 14). There was a shift from mass needs and mass delivery to welfare pluralism as NHS organisations became 'flexible firms'. With the new NHS, there is the growth of information technology, fragmented and pluralistic management, polarisation, flexibility and 'value for money', along with a decline in the numbers of professionals and an increase in the numbers of ancillary workers.

Canada

Canada exemplifies the 'single-payer' model of health care. Like a vast insurance company, the Canadian government pays doctors and hospitals, which operate privately. But the federal government, in consultation with provincial governments and medical associations, sets a schedule of fees for medical services. Thus Canada has government-funded and regulated medical care but, because practitioners operate privately, not true socialised medicine. Moreover, some doctors work entirely outside the government-funded system, charging whatever fees they wish.

Canada's system can boast of providing care for everyone at a lower cost than the (non-universal) medical system in Europe. At the same time, however, the

Canadian system makes less use of state-of-the-art technology and responds slowly to people's needs, often requiring those facing major surgery to wait months or even a year for attention (Grant, 1984; Vayda and Deber, 1984; Rosenthal, 1991).

Japan

Doctors in Japan operate privately, but a combination of government programmes and private insurance pays medical costs. The Japanese approach health care much as the Europeans do, with most medical expenses paid through government.

United States

The United States stands alone among industrialised societies in having no government-sponsored medical system that provides care to every citizen. Called a **direct-fee system**, the US system is *a medical care system in which patients pay directly for the services of doctors and hospitals*. Thus while Europeans look to government to cover about 80 per cent of their medical costs (paid for through taxation), the US government pays less than half its country's medical bills (US Bureau of the Census, 1999).

The mostly private US medical care system allows affluent people to purchase their medical care, yet the poor fare worse than their counterparts in Europe. This disparity can be seen in the relatively high death rates among both infants and adults in the United States compared to many European countries (UNHDP, 1995).

There are nevertheless public insurance programmes. In 1965 Congress created Medicare and Medicaid. Medicare pays a portion of the medical costs of men and women over 65; in 1998 it covered 37 million women and men, about 14 per cent of the population. During the same year, Medicaid, a medical insurance programme for the poor, provided benefits to nearly 34 million people, or about 13 per cent of the population. An additional 25 million veterans (9 per cent of the population) can obtain free care in government-operated hospitals. In all, 36 per cent had some medical care benefits from the government, but most also participate in a private insurance programme.

In all, 85 per cent of the US population has some medical care coverage, either private or public. Yet most plans pay only part of the cost of treating a serious illness, threatening even middle-class people with financial ruin. And most programmes also exclude many medical services, such as dental care and treatment for mental health problems. Most seriously, 44 million people (about 16 per cent of the population) have no

medical insurance at all. Many more people lose their medical coverage temporarily each year due to layoffs or job changes. While some of these people choose to forgo medical coverage (especially young people who simply take their good health for granted), most work part-time or full-time for small businesses that provide no health care benefits. In general, then, the people caught in a medical care bind are those (most commonly women, minorities and their children) with limited incomes who can afford neither to get sick nor to purchase the medical care they need to stay healthy (Health Insurance Association of America, 1991; Hersch and White-Means, 1993; Smith, 1993).

Holistic, alternative or complementary medicine

The scientific model of medicine has recently been tempered by the more traditional notion of **holistic medicine**, *an approach to health care that emphasises prevention of illness and takes account of a person's entire physical and social environment*.

It covers a range of treatments such as herbalism, homeopathy, acupuncture and osteopathy. Saks (1992) suggests that in the UK there are some 11,000 therapists working in alternative medicine and a further 17,000 non-registered practitioners. They are usually 'holistic', that is covering the whole person rather than just a specific illness (Pietroni, 1991). In 1993, the British Medical Association (BMA) recognised both the need and the value of these 'alternatives' while stressing also the need for 'good practice' within them, including sound training, ethical codes, a register of members and an organised structure (British Medical Association, 1993). They are becoming increasingly popular, because biomedicine was distancing itself from its patients and not matching its promise to treat many illnesses effectively. Patients were therefore becoming more and more alienated from doctors.

The following are foundations of holistic health care (Duhl, 1980; Ferguson, 1980; Gordon, 1980):

1. *Patients are people.* Holistic practitioners are concerned not only with symptoms but with how each person's environment and lifestyle affect health. For example, the likelihood of illness increases under stress caused by poverty or intense competition at work. Holistic practitioners extend the bounds of conventional medicine, taking an active role in combating environmental pollution and other dangers to public health.

2. *Responsibility, not dependency*. The complexity of contemporary medicine fosters patients' dependence on doctors. Holistic medicine tries to shift some responsibility for health from doctors to patients themselves by enhancing their abilities to engage in health-promoting behaviour. Holistic medicine favours a more *active* approach to *health*, rather than a *reactive* approach to *illness*.

3. *Personal treatment*. Conventional medicine locates medical care in impersonal surgeries and hospitals, which are disease-centred settings. Holistic practitioners favour, as much as possible, a personal and relaxed environment such as the home. Holistic medicine seeks to re-establish the personal social ties that united healers and patients before the era of specialists.

Clearly, holistic care does not oppose scientific medicine but shifts its emphasis away from narrowly treating disease towards the goal of achieving the highest possible level of well-being for everyone.

Understanding health and medicine

We can, once again, return to each of the major theoretical paradigms in sociology introduced in Chapter 1 to find ways of understanding health and illness sociologically.

The functions of sick roles

The dominant functionalist theorist of the mid-twentieth century, Talcott Parsons (1902–79), viewed medicine as a social system's way of keeping its members healthy. From this point of view, illness is dysfunctional, undermining the performance of social roles and thus impeding the operation of society.

The sick role

The normative response to disease, according to Parsons, is for an individual to assume the **sick role**, *patterns of behaviour defined as appropriate for people who are ill*. As explained by Parsons, the sick role has four characteristics.

1. *Illness suspends routine responsibilities*. Serious illness relaxes or suspends normal social obligations, such as going to work or attending school. To prevent abuse of this licence, however, people do not simply declare themselves ill; they must enlist the support of others,

especially a recognised medical expert, before assuming the sick role.

2. *A person's illness is not deliberate*. We assume that sick people are not responsible for their ailments; illness is something that happens to them. Therefore, the failure of ill people to fulfil routine responsibilities should carry no threat of punishment.

3. *A sick person must want to be well*. We also assume that no one wants to be sick. Thus, people suspected of feigning illness to escape responsibility or to receive special attention have no legitimate claim to the sick role.

4. *An ailing person must seek competent help*. People who are ill have an obligation to seek competent assistance and to cooperate with health-care practitioners. By failing to accept medical help or to follow 'doctor's orders', a person gives up any claim on the sick role's exemption from routine responsibilities (Parsons, 1964; orig. 1951).

The doctor's role

The doctor's role centres on assessing claims of sickness and restoring sick people to normal routines. This responsibility, Parsons explained, rests on specialised knowledge. Doctors expect patients to follow 'doctor's orders', and to provide whatever personal information may reasonably assist their efforts.

Although it is inevitably hierarchical, the doctor–patient relationship varies from society to society. In Japan, for example, tradition provides doctors with great authority over patients. One manifestation of this elevated position is that Japanese doctors routinely withhold information about the seriousness of an illness on the grounds that such knowledge might undermine a patient's fighting spirit (Darnton and Hoshia, 1989). Even three decades ago, doctors in Europe acted in much the same way. But the patients' rights movement embodies the public demand that doctors readily share more medical information and offer patients a choice of treatment options. A more egalitarian relationship between doctor and patient is also developing in European societies and, gradually, in Japan as well.

Critical comment

Parsons' notion of the sick role illuminates how society accommodates illness, as well as some non-illness situations, such as pregnancy (Myers and Grasmick, 1989). In this scheme, the doctor operates as the 'gatekeeper', regulating access to the sick role.

The social construction of health and illness

Both health and medical care can be seen as human constructions that indicate various meanings around illness. Research in the constructionist perspective looks at the doctors' and other health-care professionals' ideologies around different diseases. It examines the 'lay health beliefs' (people's common-sense views of illness), it delves into the construction of medical knowledge and its application, and it analyses the biographical construction of the illness career and the changing sense of self as a sick person. Constructionists investigate a wide range of matters, and we will look at a few of these below (Bury, 1986).

The social construction of illness

How we respond to illness is based on social definitions that may or may not square with medical knowledge. For instance, people with AIDS contend with fear and sometimes outright bigotry that have no basis in medical fact. Students, for example, have been known to ignore signs of illness on the eve of a vacation, yet dutifully march into the Health Centre before a difficult examination and claim their medical certificate. Health, in short, is not an objective fact but a negotiated outcome. Even the 'expert opinions' of medical professionals are influenced by non-medical factors.

Moreover, how people define a medical situation often affects how they actually feel. Medical experts have long marvelled at psychosomatic disorders (a fusion of Greek words meaning 'mind' and 'body'), in which state of mind guides physical sensations (Hamrick *et al.*, 1986).

The social organisation of medical knowledge

Constructionists look at the ways in which medical knowledge is produced and organised: for example, how an illness such as schizophrenia is identified and used by psychiatrists, and the ways in which people come to be classified into routine, normal cases (Scheff, 1967). Social constructionists make problematic the very issues which might appear self-evident in health practice, such as the nature of medical knowledge and medical 'facts'. Far from being obvious, 'scientific' or given, they are found to be bound up with culture. They ask how diagnoses are made and where this knowledge comes from.

To take what may seem an unproblematic example: dentistry. Dentistry has not always been with us, and Sarah Nettleton has shown how 'the dental examination' emerged from nineteenth-century public health

programmes and worked to establish the notion of the 'normal mouth' which could be used as the baseline for comparing all other mouths. Progressively, this led to the development of a new profession which claimed the field and built up its own specialist routines and ideas. Ideas in health do not just happen: they have to be socially (and historically) constructed, and interactionists ask how this happens (Nettleton, 1992, 1995).

The social construction of treatment

In Chapter 7, we used the dramaturgical approach of Erving Goffman to explain how doctors craft their physical surroundings ('the office') and present themselves to others to foster specific impressions of competence and power. Joan Emerson (1970) illustrates this process of reality construction by analysing a situation familiar to women, a gynaecological examination carried out by a male doctor. After observing 75 such examinations, she explains that this setting is especially precarious, because it is so vulnerable to misinterpretation. The man's touching of a woman's genitals – conventionally viewed as a sexual act and possibly even an assault – must, in this case, be defined as impersonal and professional.

To ensure that people construct reality in this way, doctors and nurses remove sexual connotations as completely as possible. They furnish the examination room with nothing but medical equipment; all personnel wear medical uniforms. Staff members act as if such examinations are simply routine, although, from the patient's point of view, they may be quite unusual. Further, rapport between doctor and patient is established before the examination begins. Once under way, the doctor's performance is strictly professional, suggesting to the patient that inspecting the genitals is no different from surveying any other part of the body. A female nurse is usually present during the examination, not only to assist the doctor but to dispel any impression that a man and woman are 'alone in a room'.

Emerson's analysis has practical implications. It suggests that understanding how reality is socially constructed in the examination room is just as crucial as mastering the medical skills required for effective treatment. Aware of this, some medical training now incorporates instructions which get medical students to actually climb on to an examination table and place their feet in the metal stirrups, with their legs spread apart, to gain an appreciation of the patient's point of view. It is claimed that: 'The only way to understand a woman's feelings is to be there.'

The social organisation of illness

Constructionists also look at the ways in which people live their lives through illnesses, at their 'regimes' of health. They are concerned with how people give meaning to their illness, how they organise their days around medications, how they develop various strategies for 'coping' with illness. They have been particularly keen to examine various chronic diseases, such as multiple sclerosis, Parkinson's disease and cancers, all of which have long-term effects. Bury distinguishes three concepts which help us see the different ways in which people respond to their illnesses. *Coping* shows how people (passively) 'put up' with illness; *strategies* show what people do when faced with illness; and *style* refers to the ways in which people actively respond to and present their illnesses (Bury, 1991). And Corbin and Strauss have made a linked set of distinctions. First, there is *illness work*: how people manage their symptoms, medications and illness crises. Second, there is *everyday life work*: how people keep their routine lives going – shopping, eating, cleaning, child-rearing. And third, there is *biographical work*: how people provide narratives and stories of their lives to make sense of their illness and to account for their medical history (Corbin and Strauss, 1985; Kleinman, 1988).

Narratives of illness

Closely linked to this, then, are the stories and narratives that people produce of their illness. Arthur Kleinman's influential book, *The Illness Narratives* (1988), examines life narratives of distressing illnesses – chronic pain, AIDS, dying, colostomy. Distinguishing the bodily disease from the socially located illness, he suggests that doctors hitherto have given too much primacy to the former, neglecting the needs patients have for making sense of their lives and illness, learning from the social narratives of illness that others have provided. Pain on its own needs a sense-making frame, which patients should be encouraged to find. As he says: 'The illness narrative is a story the patient tells, and significant others retell, to give coherence to the distinctive events and long-term course of suffering' (Kleinman, 1988: 49). He provides an opening checklist of the kinds of question that could be asked of a patient:

> What is the cause of the disorder? Why did it have its onset precisely when it did? What does the illness do to my body? What course is it following now, and what course can I expect it to follow in the future? What is the source of improvements, and exacerbations? How can I control the illness, its exacerbations and its consequences? What are the principal effects the illness has had on my (our) life? What do I most fear about this illness? What treatment do I wish to receive? What do I expect of the treatment? . . . Such questions are not asked simply to gain information. They are deeply felt. The facial expression, the tone of voice, posture, body movements, gait, and especially the eyes expose the emotional turmoil that is so much part of the long-term experience of chronic illness.
>
> (Kleinman, 1988: 43–44)

Awareness of illness

Constructionists look not just at the ill but also at all those who surround them. In a classic study, Glaser and Strauss looked at the ways in which friends and families deal with the person who is known to be dying of cancer. In particular, they researched the difficult issues of whether the patient knows – or does not know – they are dying, and how friends and families cope in different ways with this. In some instances families may know the patient is dying while the patient may not; in other cases, it may be the other way around. All of this can lead to different forms of interactions around the death bed: not least to problems of deception and lying (Glaser and Strauss, 1967).

Medical settings

Interactionists also study medical settings – the dentist's surgery, the abortion clinic, the hospital – looking at daily routines and rituals. For instance, in a classic study, tellingly entitled *The Ceremonial Order of the Clinic* (1979), the late British sociologist Phil Strong looked at over 1,000 consultations between children, parents and doctors in outpatient clinics in Scotland. In all the situations, an enduring feature of the ritual was the doctor's ability to control what was happening. But within this control, four standard ritual patterns emerged. In the *bureaucratic ritual*, rules are followed, people are polite to each other and mothers are presumed to be 'technically incompetent'. In the *clinical ritual*, the mothers assume the doctor's 'authority'. In the private ritual, the doctor's competence is accepted because it is 'sold'. And in a fourth *charity pattern*, doctors reveal the mother's inadequacy (Strong, 1979). In such studies, interactionists point to a core feature of medical work: that it is ritualistic and stable.

The medicalisation process

Constructionists often talk about **medicalisation**, *the process by which events and experiences are given medical meaning and turned into medical problems.* They suggest that many behaviours seen as moral or personal concerns at one time have recently become part of the orbit of medical work. Birth is a good example. For centuries, women gave birth without medical help (and in most parts of the world they still do), but in modern industrial societies it is seen almost as a heresy to employ 'natural childbirth methods' away from a medical regime. Likewise, with many forms of so-called deviance. Everything from eating problems ('anorexics', 'bulimics', 'obesity') and school truancy to alcohol use ('alcoholism') and excessive sex ('sex addiction') has been brought into the field of medicine and therapy (Conrad and Schneider, 1990). Here, moral issues become medical ones and medicine becomes a major institution of social control.

Critical comment

One strength of the symbolic-interaction paradigm lies in revealing the relativity of sickness and health. What people view as normal or deviant, healthful or harmful, depends on a host of factors, many of which are not, strictly speaking, medical. This approach also shows that all medical procedures involve a subtle process of reality construction between patient and doctors.

But the approach also raises the problem of objective standards of well-being. Certain physical conditions do indeed cause specific negative changes in human capacities, whether we think so or not. People who lack sufficient nutrition and safe water, for example, suffer from their unhealthy environment, however they define their surroundings. The constructionist position can be overstated to the point when all medical knowledge is seen as suspect. But a more balanced view can incorporate interactionist/constructionist insights into a wider approach.

Inequalities, conflict, and health and illness

Conflict analysis ties health to various dimensions of social inequality, some of which have been discussed above. To take gender as an example, a number of feminist sociologists have analysed the ways in which inequalities can seriously affect women (for example, in creating extra stress) and they have provided case studies of the ways in which medical power may well be exerted over women (for example, in dealing with reproduction). Further, doctors are most frequently men, while health carers are usually women: a hierarchy of inequality around health work is reproduced (Doyal, 1995; Abbott and Wallace, 1996).

Another example would highlight world inequalities. As we have seen in the earlier parts of this chapter, while the industrial world may be enjoying unprecedented 'good health', poorer countries are still experiencing high levels of disease and morbidity.

More broadly, researchers working in a conflict paradigm have focused on three main issues: *access to medical care*, the effects of *the profit motive* on treatment, and the *politics of medicine.*

The access issue

Personal health is the foundation of social life. Yet, from a Marxist-conflict perspective, capitalist societies make health a commodity, so that health follows wealth. This problem is probably more serious in the United States than in other industrialised societies because that country has no universal health-care system. Capitalism may provide excellent health care for the rich; it simply does not provide it very well for the rest of the population.

Indeed, the concentration of wealth in capitalist societies makes the goal of equal medical care impossible to achieve. Only a wholesale redistribution of economic resources, say the Marxists, would allow medical care to be uniformly available (Bodenheimer, 1977; Navarro, 1977).

The profit motive

Beyond the access issue, radical critic John Ehrenreich (1978) argues, the profit motive turns doctors, hospitals and the pharmaceutical industry into multibillion-pound corporate conglomerates. The pharmaceutical industry is the most profitable of all industries (see Figure 20.8). In 2002, their total drug sales reached $430 billion. The quest for ever-increasing profits encourages questionable medical practices, including ordering needless tests, performing unnecessary surgery and overly prescribing drugs (Kaplan *et al.*, 1985). While a third of the world cannot afford essential drugs, the rich West proliferates 'blockbuster drugs', such as the wonder drug Viagra to enhance sexual potency, which can bring in billions of dollars. In the United States, more than 2 million women have undergone silicone breast implant surgery, under the assumption that the plastic packets of silicone were safe. Recently, however, it became clear that these implants are not safe enough, a fact apparently known to some manufacturers for decades!

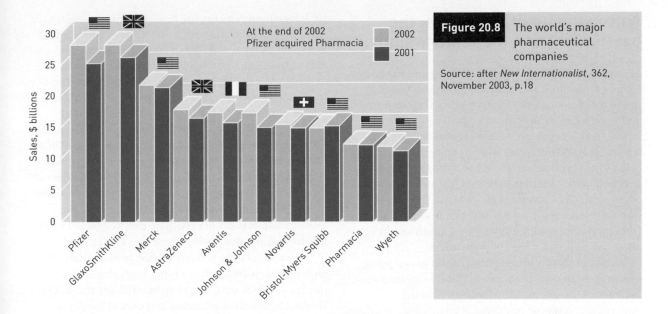

Figure 20.8 The world's major pharmaceutical companies

Source: after *New Internationalist*, 362, November 2003, p.18

The decision to perform surgery often reflects the financial interests of surgeons and hospitals more than the medical needs of patients. And, of course, any drugs or medical procedure prescribed for people subjects them to risks, which harm between 5 and 10 per cent of patients (Illich, 1976; Sidel and Sidel, 1982a; Cowley, 1995).

Sometimes, too, doctors may have a direct financial interest in the tests and procedures they order for their patients (Pear and Eckholm, 1991). In short, conflict theorists conclude, health care should be motivated by a concern for people, not profits.

Medicine as politics

Although medicine declares itself to be politically neutral, scientific medicine frequently takes sides on significant social issues. The history of medicine, critics contend, is replete with racial and sexual discrimination, defended by 'scientific' facts (Leavitt, 1984). Consider the diagnosis of 'hysteria', a term which has its origins in the Greek word *hyster*, meaning 'uterus'. In coining this word, medical professionals apparently suggested that being a woman is synonymous with being sick or crazy. The introduction to this chapter has already looked at the gender politics underlying the practice of clitoridectomy, or female genital mutilation.

Surveying the entire medical field, some critics see political mischief in today's scientific medicine. Scientists explain illness in terms of bacteria and viruses, ignoring the effects of social inequality on health. From the scientific perspective, in other words, poor people get sick because of a lack of sanitation and an unhealthy diet, even though poverty may be the underlying cause of these ills. In this way, critics charge, scientific medicine depoliticises health by reducing complex political issues to matters of simple biology.

Critical comment

Conflict analysis offers another approach to the relationships among health, medicine and our society. According to this view, social inequality is the reason some people have far better health than others; moreover, conflict theorists denounce the profit motive as inconsistent with the interests of patients.

The most common objection to the conflict approach is that it minimises the overall improvement in health through the years and scientific medicine's contribution to the high standard of living in the West today. Even though they could certainly do better, health indicators rose steadily over the course of the twentieth century.

In sum, sociology's three major theoretical paradigms convincingly argue that health and medicine are social issues. Indeed, advancing technology is forcing us to confront the social foundations of this institution. The famous French scientist Louis Pasteur (1822–95) spent much of his life studying how bacteria cause disease. Before his death, he remarked that health depends much less on bacteria than on the social environment in which bacteria operate (Gordon, 1980: 7). Explaining Pasteur's insight is sociology's contribution to human health.

A growing health problem: the overweight and the underweight

In recent years, concerns linked to eating and the body have become more and more identifiable as 'medical problems'. Governments increasingly talk about them and initiate health education programmes, while the World Health Organisation has suggested their global significance (WHO, 2004). Thus at one extreme, 60 per cent of the US population and two-thirds of men and over half of women in the UK are estimated to be overweight. Underweight is also an issue. Found especially among the young, and girls in particular (though it is increasing among boys), underweight issues affect 5–7 per cent of the UK population.

Weight problems bring serious health issues: being overweight can pose problems of diabetes, heart disease, hypertension and some forms of cancer; being underweight can pose problems of emaciation, diarrhoea and, in extreme cases, the symptoms can lead to starvation and a cessation of menstruation. Both can ultimately be life-threatening. The most extreme forms of being underweight are anorexia (a sustained and deliberate restriction of food intake) and bulimia (where food may be consumed in binges but is subsequently ('thrown up'). The most extreme form of being overweight is obesity.

Anorexia and bulimia

Anorexia and bulimia bring an abnormally low body weight. In the UK about 1 per cent of female adolescents have anorexia and about 4 per cent of college-aged women have bulimia. Only about 10 per cent of people with anorexia and bulimia are male. This gender difference may reflect our society's different expectations for men and women. Men are supposed to be strong and powerful. They feel ashamed of skinny bodies and want to be big and powerful.

Many have suggested that these eating disorders are part of a wider preoccupation with the body and 'looking good'. The impact here is especially on younger women and girls, with the need to look attractive and slender (though increasingly younger men are being influenced too). Susan Bordo (1993) sees these women as in some ways protesting against the cultural ideals of femininity.

Obesity

Obesity is defined in terms of the Body Mass Index (BMI). This is a number generated by dividing a person's weight (in kilogrammes) by his/her height (in metres) squared ('Obese' = a BMI of more than 30; 'Overweight' = a BMI of 25–30; 'Normal' = a BMI of 20–25; 'Underweight' = a BMI of less than 20). Obesity is increasingly seen as one of the world's escalating public health problems. The International Obesity Task Force (IOTF) revealed that 1.7 billion of the world's population was overweight or obese. In the UK, obesity levels have trebled in the past 20 years. Currently, about 24 million adults in the UK are overweight or obese and the levels are still rising (Health Survey England, 2001). In Europe, one in four adults will be obese by 2010 (Tackling Obesity in England, National Audit Office, 2001). In the United States, nearly two-thirds of adults (64.5 per cent) are overweight, with three in ten (30.5 per cent) being obese (see Figure 10.9).

Curiously, obesity is not restricted to industrialised or high-income societies. It is a bitter irony that as low-income societies are trying to reduce hunger, the World Health Organisation estimates that over 115 million people in low-income societies suffer from obesity (and 300 million overall). In 1999 a United Nations survey found that in Brazil and Colombia the figure was around 40 per cent – a figure comparable to much of Europe. In China, the consumption of high-fat foods has soared (Figure 20.10). However, this should be no surprise. We have already seen that we have enough food to feed the world; it is just that often it does not get to the right places (see Voices Box). Traditional diets feature grains and vegetables, but as incomes in developing societies rise these now give way to meals high in fat and sugar, which is the main source of the problem (Table 20.1).

Several social factors seem to be shaping the 'crisis of obesity'. First, our culture is increasingly sedentary. Many people sit for long hours at work with a subsequent decline of exercise. Rising affluence has brought the growth of conveniences like cars, computers and televisions, all of which remove activity and generate passivity. Second, we have witnessed the development of fast foods. In 2001, 2 billion meals were eaten at 'quick service' catering outlets in the UK. Sales of snacks and confectionery continue to rise in the UK, outstripping

Table 20.1	Percentage of obese people in the world
Worldwide	8.2%
Least developed countries	1.8%
Developing countries	4.8%
Emerging economies	17.1%
Developed market economies	20.4%

Source: *Newsweek*, 11 August 2003.

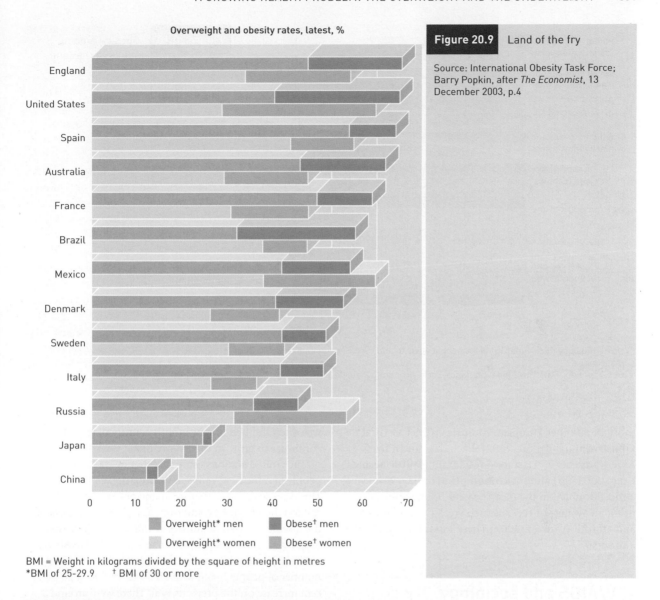

Overweight and obesity rates, latest, %

Figure 20.9 Land of the fry

Source: International Obesity Task Force; Barry Popkin, after *The Economist*, 13 December 2003, p.4

Legend:
- Overweight* men
- Obese† men
- Overweight* women
- Obese† women

BMI = Weight in kilograms divided by the square of height in metres
*BMI of 25–29.9   † BMI of 30 or more

VOICES

WORLD OBESITY

Chen Linnan, aged 57, recalls her days of hard labour. As a farmer, she spent all day rotating soil, plucking green beans and digging potatoes. Life was tough, but 'I was healthy', she says. 'I never had to see a doctor before the age of 45.' In the 1980s, as China began shifting to a market economy, Chen became a factory supervisor. Her rising income, combined with her husband's, allowed the couple to buy modern appliances. Rather than wringing clothes by hand, Chen got a washing machine. A refrigerator cut out the need for her daily walk to the shops. Television and air conditioning meant she spent hours relaxing on the sofa, devouring sunflower seeds. Her farming weight (45 kilos) rose to 84. Today she spends a month each year in the hospital, under observation for diabetes and dangerously high blood pressure (*Newsweek*, 11 August 2003).

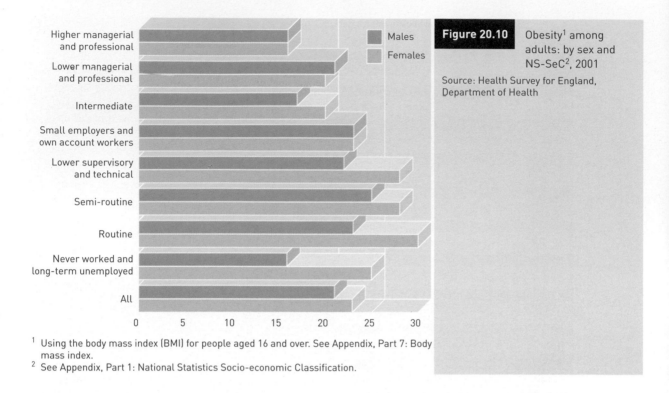

Figure 20.10 Obesity[1] among adults: by sex and NS-SeC[2], 2001

Source: Health Survey for England, Department of Health

[1] Using the body mass index (BMI) for people aged 16 and over. See Appendix, Part 7: Body mass index.

[2] See Appendix, Part 1: National Statistics Socio-economic Classification.

those in all other European countries (Chief Medical Officer, Annual Report, 2002). Each day one in five Americans eats in a fast food restaurant (Millstone and Lang, 2003: 95) and the consumption of fizzy drinks has almost doubled in the past 15 years. Young adults now drink an average of six cans each week (National Diet and Nutrition Survey, 2002).These foods are high in fats and sugar.

HIV/AIDS and sociology

Acquired immuno-deficiency syndrome (AIDS), is an incurable disease in which the body's immune system breaks down. Early symptoms of the disease include heavy night sweats, chronic diarrhea, pneumonia, skin cancers, and a general malfunctioning of the body as its immune system breaks down. The recent historical patterns of disease have suggested a marked shift from contagious diseases (still prominent in low-income countries) to degenerative diseases such as cancers and strokes (common in high-income societies). The arrival of AIDS seemed to change all this, for it had all the hallmarks of a major infectious epidemic not dissimilar to the 'plagues' of much of history. Indeed, for a while it

was often dubbed 'the twentieth-century plague'. It continues to grow in the twenty first.

The United Nations estimated that in 2003 4.8 million people became newly infected with HIV (see Table 20.2). This is more than ever before in any one year. In 2003, 2.9 million died from HIV and over 20 million have died since the disease was first identified in 1981. Also, there were roughly 37.8 million people living with HIV (UNAIDS., 2004: 23). In the UK at the end of 2002, the estimated number of people living with HIV was 49,500, a 20 per cent increase on the previous year. There were around 4,000 deaths (*Social Trends*, 2004: 118).

AIDS/HIV is now present in all countries throughout the world, but its 'shape' – its rates, how it is transmitted and whom it impacts – differ greatly. Map 20.3 shows the global estimates for different continents. The highest rates are to be found in sub-Saharan Africa (with 38 per cent of 15–49 year olds in Swaziland and Botswana being infected). The most rapid expansion seems to be taking place in the People's Republic of China and Eastern Europe. The smallest numbers are to be found in the West, where expensive medications seem to have slowed the infection a little. Each area has its own pattern, but everywhere it is a major health concern (see Table 20.3).

Table 20.2	Total number of adults and children living with HIV at end of 2003	
People newly infected with HIV in 2003	Total	4.8 million
	Adults	4.1 million
	Children < 15 years	630,000
Number of people living with HIV/AIDS	Total	37.8 million
	Adults	35.7 million
	Women	17 million
	Children < 15 years	2.1 million
AIDS deaths in 2003	Total	2.9 million
	Adults	2.4 million
	Children < 15 years	490,000
Total number of AIDS deaths since start of epidemic		38 million

Source: adapted from UNAIDS (2004)

The nature of HIV and AIDS

AIDS was first identified in 1981 among small clusters of gay men in North America and was for a short while called GRID (Gay Related Immune Deficiency). Soon it was recognised to exist in many other groups, including hemophiliacs, heroin users, Haitians, prostitutes and, ultimately, heterosexuals. It was renamed AIDS in 1982.

Its prime cause was identified in the mid-1980s as a virus which breaks down the immune system (HIV – Human Immune Deficiency Virus). The main risk of transmission happens through the exchange of bodily fluids – notably blood, semen, a mother's milk – in which the HIV virus can be found. Wherever the virus may be passed on to others, people are 'at risk'. As a result, some of the major roots of transmission include sexual activities, intravenous drug use and blood contamination (such as blood transfusion). Women with HIV can give it to babies during pregnancy. Once people are infected, they can pass it on to others.

The virus can be tested for through the presence of its antibodies. Although the search is on for some kind of

The NAMES project AIDS Memorial Quilt began in 1987 as a panel of quilts remembering those who had died of AIDS. It was displayed for the first time in Washington DC on October 11th 1987 when it had 1,920 panels and covered a space larger than football field. It has continued to grow, and in October 2004 was composed of 5,683 blocks – making it now almost impossible to display in its entirety. Panels can, however be viewed. It is the largest community art project in the world. See http://www.aidsquilt.org

Source: © The NAMES Project Foundation AIDS Memorial Quilt, Atlanta, GA. Paul Margolies, Photographer

SOCIAL SHAPES OF THE WORLD

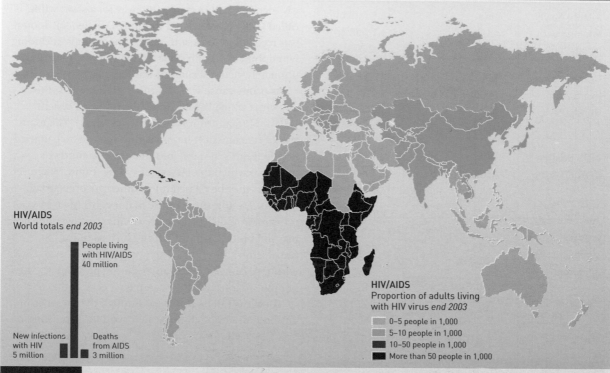

HIV/AIDS
World totals *end 2003*

People living
with HIV/AIDS
40 million

New infections
with HIV
5 million

Deaths
from AIDS
3 million

HIV/AIDS
Proportion of adults living
with HIV virus *end 2003*

- 0–5 people in 1,000
- 5–10 people in 1,000
- 10–50 people in 1,000
- More than 50 people in 1,000

Map 20.3   Worldwide incidence of HIV/AIDS at the end of 2003

About two-thirds of all global HIV cases are recorded in sub-Saharan Africa. This high infection rate reflects the prevalence of other venereal diseases and infrequent use of condoms, factors that promote heterosexual transmission of HIV South and North America each represent another 10 per cent of all cases, and Southeast Asia, where HIV is spreading most rapidly, accounts for another 10 per cent. The incidence of infection is still low in Europe. Least affected are North Africa and the Middle East, Australia and New Zealand.

Source: adapted from Dan Smith, *The State of the World Atlas*, 6th edn, pp. 80–81

preventive vaccine, the main medical advances to date have been through various drug treatments which slow down the progress of the diseases. There are now a whole array of (usually very expensive) drugs, such as AZT, 3TC and Combivir, which can be taken. By the mid-1990s many people with AIDS in high-income countries were living their lives with little disruption and with little fear of imminent death. This was not true of people in lower-income countries, however, where AIDS had become a major killer and where the costs of such treatments were prohibitive.

Sociological implications of AIDS

The social implications of AIDS are so many that it becomes almost a test case for the relevance of sociology

to health. In what follows we briefly suggest just a few of these implications.

First, it raises issues about the social causes of illness and health and the patterns of social epidemiology. There are a number of distinctive social patterns of AIDS distribution. It is quite wrong (and dangerous), for example, to say (as it once was) that AIDS is a feature of younger gay men in the big cities, as this is only one of a range of patterns. In many cities, it may be linked to intraveneous drug use; sometimes it is linked to networks of prostitution; sometimes to casual sex patterns. In some parts of the world, it is clearly linked to heterosexual transmission and often to the refusal of men to wear condoms. In many parts of the world it is linked to infected women passing it to their children. Each epidemic has local features and is changing all the time. There may be one epidemic among sexually active

African men and women in Eastern Africa, another kind of epidemic among drug injectors and their partners in Russia, and a third among men who have sex with men in Rio de Janeiro, and so on. *Sociologists need to study local contexts which shape disease.*

Second, HIV transmission is largely gendered. 'Worldwide, women may be more affected by the consequences of HIV/AIDS, but it is the sexual and drug taking behaviour of men which enables the virus to spread' (Foreman, 1999: vii). Men are at risk; women are vulnerable. Men's behaviour is often influenced by harmful views about 'what it is to be a man', and this in turn is often linked to being powerful in sexual relations. Some suggest that masculinity may well be the prime cause of the epidemic, so much so that in 2001 the theme of the World AIDS Conference was 'Men make a difference' (UNAIDS.org, 24 May 2001). Men refuse to stop passing it on; and women have little choice in getting it. It is bound up with the man's sense of masculinity and the need to establish this through having sex.

Third, it is linked to stigma and prejudice. Many groups have been blamed for the illness: gay men,

Table 20.3	Regional HIV/AIDS statistics and features, end of 2003					
Region	Epidemic started	Adults and children living with HIV/AIDS	Adults and children newly infected with HIV	Adult prevalance rate[1]	Percentage of HIV-positive adults who are women	Main mode(s) of transmission[2] for adults living with HIV/AIDS
Sub-Saharan Africa	late 70s–early 80s	25.0–28.2 million	3.0–3.4 million	7.5–8.5%	55%	Hetero
North Africa and Middle East	late 80s	470,000–730,000	43,000–67,000	0.2–0.4%	40%	Hetero, IDU
South and Southeast Asia	late 80s	4.6–8.2 million	610,000–1.1 million	0.4–0.8%	35%	Hetero, IDU
East Asia and Pacific	late 80s	700,000–1.3 million	150,000–270,000	0.1–0.1%	20%	IDU, hetero, MSM
Latin America	late 70s–early 80s	1.3–1.9 million	120,000–180,000	0.5–0.7%	30%	MSM, IDU, hetero
Caribbean	late 70s–early 80s	350,000–590,000	45,000–80,000	1.9–3.1%	50%	Hetro, MSM
Eastern Europe and Central Asia	early 90s	1.2–1.8 million	180,000–250,000	0.5–0.9%	20%	IDU
Western Europe	late 70s–early 80s	520,000–680,000	30,000–40,000	0.3–0.3%	25%	MSM, IDU
North America	late 70s–early 80s	790,000–1.2 million	36,000–54,000	0.5–0.7%	20%	MSM, IDU, hetero
Australia and New Zealand	late 70s–early 80s	12,000–18,000	700–1000	0.–0.1%	10%	MSM
Total		40 million [34–46 million]	5 million [4.2–5.8 million]	1.2% [0.9–1.3]	48%	

[1] The proportion of adults (15–49 years of age) living with HIV/AIDS in 2003, using 2003 population numbers

[2] Hetero (heterosexual transmission), IDU (transmission through injecting drug use), MSM (sexual transmission among men who have sex with men)

Source: adapted from UNAIDS (2004)

Africans, drug users, sex workers. AIDS is the classic case of a disease being used for racism, sexism and a more general scapegoating.

Fourth, the illness has a major impact on children, especially in low-income countries. Many children contract HIV early in life – it is estimated at 20 per cent in a number of African countries. They die young. But many children also find their parents have died of the disease and they become 'AIDS orphans'. In Uganda alone, there are 1.7 millions AIDS-orphaned children (*New Internationalist*, 2001: 524).

Fifth, it also raises issues over how a disease or illness comes to be represented in various forms of media. AIDS is not only a disease but a discourse. It is represented in health documents, in media images and films, in health campaigns, and it is represented not only in words but in images.

Sixth, AIDS raises measurement problems. To identify people with HIV requires a medical test for antibodies. Figures from organisations such as the United Nations are usually based on this. But there are many ways in which these figures cannot be relied on. People are unwilling to take the test. People may not even begin to recognise they have the early stages of the disease and hence have no reason to be tested. In many countries throughout the world, awareness may be so low, and the facilities for testing so thin on the ground, that estimates become impossible. For instance, it has been suggested that although China officially has a very low rate – about 20,000 registered cases in 2000 – the virus and the

disease may be so under-reported that the figure could escalate to many millions by 2001. Hence one needs to be aware, when reading any AIDS statistics, that they are often very unreliable and need to be approached critically.

Seventh, it raises issues of generation and change. HIV has been around for more than 20 years. A full generation has been brought up with the background awareness of this new disease. Some people have never lived in a world where it did not exist. At the same time, the enormous concern about AIDS which was prevalent in the 1980s (the UK government, for example, leafleted every household in the country about it) has now declined, and with this decline in awareness of AIDS, prevention has declined too. Thus, whereas during much of the 1980s and early 1990s there were clear signs that many gay men changed their sexual practices to 'safer sex', by the late 1990s there was evidence that the sexual behaviour of young gay men had reverted to unsafe sexual practices. AIDS as a disease raises the continuing issue of social change.

Finally, AIDS raises major political and cross-cultural issues. AIDS is a pandemic, that is it is found in virtually all countries across the world. But the focus until recently has been on Western countries, where the numbers, though large, are small by comparison with the poorer countries of the world. For much of its history, the epidemic outside the West has been less well noticed and much less well funded. While in North America and the UK, medications have been found which can control and

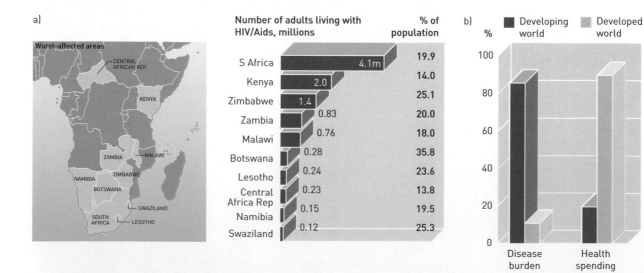

Figure 20.11   (a) AIDS in sub-Saharan Africa; (b) worldwide disease burden index and health spending

Sources: adapted from UNAIDS statistics; (a) adapted from *The Guardian*, 8 July 2000. Copyright Guardian Newspapers Limited 2000; (b) adapted from *The Guardian*, 31 May 2001, from World Bank, 2000. Copyright Guardian Newspapers Limited 2001.

delay AIDS, so that many people with the disease can now function well for long periods, in Africa the medical services were initially far too expensive. They could not be afforded, and the big medical companies did not supply them. The pharmaceutical industry spends roughly 80 per cent of its products on 20 per cent of the world population (*Newsweek*, 19 March 2001), with GlaxoSmithKline (GSK) leading the way (through a merger between Glaxo Wellcome and SmithKline) and claiming that every minute 1,100 people receive a prescription for a GSK product.

In low-income countries, AIDS drugs had long been unaffordable, but in April 2001, after the threat of a South African lawsuit, the global drug companies came under attack and faced a major reputation scare: drugs executives became the 'new villains'. 'Big Pharma' found itself in the firing line. A United Nations initiative led to GSK agreeing to supply a combination drug for $2 a day to low-income countries.

But even with such large reductions, poor countries may not be able to afford such drugs without assistance from high-income countries. Kenya, for example, has an annual health budget of around $9 billion; with 2.2 million AIDS patients, caring for them would cost around $12 billion a year, even with 85 per cent discounts (*Newsweek*, 19 March 2001: 23).

Death, dying and sociology

AIDS has brought the phenomenon of young people dying in the prime of their life to the fore. Throughout most of human history, confronting death has been commonplace. Until recently, no one assumed that a newborn child would live for long, and indeed this situation remains the case in most low-income societies of the world today. For those fortunate enough to survive infancy, illness prompted by poor nutrition, accidents and natural catastrophes such as drought or famine combine to make life uncertain, at best. Indeed, in times of great need, death was (and is) often deliberate, the result of a strategy to protect the majority by sacrificing a group's least productive members. *Infanticide* is the killing of newborn infants; *geronticide*, by contrast, is the killing of the elderly. If death was routine in the past, it was also readily accepted. Medieval Christianity assured Europeans, for example, that death fitted into the divine plan for human existence.

As some societies gradually gained control over many causes of death, death became less of an everyday occurrence. Fewer children died at birth, and accidents

and disease took a smaller toll among adults. Except in times of war or catastrophe, people came to view dying as quite *extra*ordinary, except among the very old. In 1900, about one-third of all deaths in Europe occurred before the age of five, another third occurred before the age of 55, and the remaining one-third of men and women died in what was then defined as old age. By 1995, 85 per cent of our population died *after* the age of 55. Thus death and ageing have become fused in our culture: this has not always been so.

The modern separation of life and death

Sociologists have become increasingly interested in the sociology of death. If social conditions prepared our ancestors to accept their deaths, modern society, with its youth culture and aggressive medical technology, has fostered a desire for immortality, or eternal youth. In this sense, death has become separated from life.

Death is *physically* removed from everyday activities. The clearest evidence of this is that many of us have never seen a person die. While our ancestors typically died at home in the presence of family and friends, most deaths today occur in impersonal settings such as hospitals and nursing homes. Even hospitals commonly relegate dying patients to a special part of the building, and hospital morgues are located well out of sight of patients and visitors alike (Sudnow, 1967; Ariès, 1974).

Death and dying

Two of the first sociologists to study death were Barney Glaser and Anslem Strauss (1967). In the 1960s they conducted fieldwork in a hospital ward full of patients dying from cancer. Among their concerns were:

- *The learning of new roles and statuses as one moved towards death*. There was in fact a dying role with its own expectations.

- *The timing of death*. They examined the sequences around the death process and the stages through which the dying and their families and friends moved.

- *Awareness of dying*. They examined 'who knew what about the death' and this meant looking at a range of devices in which friends or families could sometimes be prevented from knowing about the possibility of death, and sometimes how even the patient could be misled.

- *Anguish*.

The revival of death

Tony Walter (1994, 1998) has looked not just at death and dying, but also the shifts in funeral patterns and bereavement. He asks some interesting questions. How, for example, does a country (say the UK) each year care for half a million dying people, dispose of half a million corpses, manage more than half a million bereaved members and, depending on your point of view, help half a million souls on to the next life, not to mention represent all this in art, television and other media? Societies resolve these problems in very different ways and this is all part of the sociology of death and dying.

One of Walter's claims is that contemporary death is becoming more and more prominent. There was a period

(for much of the twentieth century in the Western world) when death was hidden away from sight, but this is no more. He suggests that there are two strands to this process. One, which he calls a later modern strand, is driven by experts such as Kübler-Ross (1969) and informs people how to cope with death. Thus Kübler-Ross famously takes us through five stages of dying. She claims that individuals initially react with *denial*, then swell with *anger*, try to *negotiate* a divine intervention, gradually fall into *resignation* and finally reach *acceptance*. Those who will grieve the loss of a significant person must also adjust to the approaching death.

According to some researchers, bereavement parallels the stages of dying described by Kübler-Ross. Those close to a dying person, for instance, may initially deny the

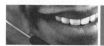

VOICES

DISABILITY THEORY

A voice that has been overlooked in sociology until very recently has been that of the disabled. Increasingly, however, a sociology of disablement has been appearing – often written by those who are themselves disabled.

Disability theory works with what is called a 'social model of disability', which has its roots in the campaigns against discrimination, isolation and enforced dependency that were organised by disabled people themselves. Rejecting the medical and individualised

model of 'personal tragedy', this more sociological account highlights the barriers, disadvantages and inequalities that disabled people face.

Part of this new theory is to understand the ways in which the disabled increasingly confront the 'able bodied society' through political actions and through a rethinking of the ways in which bodies are socially constructed in society. The photograph here shows how wheelchairs can be mobilised for activity rather than being simply passive vehicles.

Source: see Barnes *et al.*, 1999: Chapter 4

Disabled student with tutor, playing drums in secondary school.

Source: © Alamy/Jacky Chapman/Janine Weidel Photography

reality of impending death, reaching the point of acceptance only in time. Many, however, question the validity of any linear 'stage theory', arguing that bereavement may not follow a rigid schedule. But all the experts agree that how family and friends view a death influences the attitudes of the person who is dying. Specifically, acceptance by others of the approaching death helps the dying person do the same. Denial of the impending death may isolate the dying person, who is then unable to share feelings and experiences with others.

One recent development intended to provide emotional and medical support to dying people is the *hospice*. Unlike hospitals, which are designed to cure disease, hospices help people have a 'good death'. These care centres work to minimise pain and suffering – either there or at home – and encourage family members to remain close by. Founded by Dame Cecily Saunders in 1967, there are now over 200 hospices in the UK (Lawton, 2000).

A postmodern strand of thinking about death has also developed. This suggests that dealing with death is increasingly driven by ordinary people, and allows for an enormous array of variety and difference in individual experiences of death. These days, for instance, people are much more likely to plan their own funerals, selecting music and even pre-recording a speech, and people even stipulate that mourners should follow their funerals with parties and even revelry. The traditions of the church funeral are also increasingly breaking down for some groups (Walter, 1994). Some of this started with the arrival of young men dying from AIDS-related illness throughout the 1980s. Here was the (tragic) sight of lots of young (generally gay) men dying. In their youthfulness, the old rituals and ceremonies just did not seem right.

Taking stock and looking ahead: health in the twenty-first century

At the beginning of the twentieth century, deaths from infectious disease were widespread and scientists had yet to develop basic antibiotics such as penicillin. Thus, even common infections represented a deadly threat to health. Today, members of our society take for granted the good health and long life that was the exception, not the rule, a century ago. There is every reason to expect that health will continue to improve in the present century.

Another encouraging trend is public recognition that, to a significant extent, we can take responsibility for our own health (Caplow *et al.*, 1991). Every one of us can live better and longer if we avoid tobacco, eat sensibly and in moderation, and exercise regularly.

The remission society

Part of the future will be the growing number of people who live in states which are neither wholly well nor wholly sick. These are the people living on medications, who function with transplants and prostheses of all kinds. We cannot see they are ill, and in some senses they are not, but they are dependent on technologies for their daily health. Arthur Frank (1995) calls this 'the remission society' and suggests that we are in need of new maps to shape our lives so that we can deal with this. He writes:

> These people are all around, though often invisible. A man standing behind me in the airport security check announces that he has a pacemaker; suddenly his invisible condition becomes an issue. Once past the metal detector, his 'remission' status disappears into the background. (Frank, 1995: 8)

Continuing disease

Yet certain health problems will continue to plague society in the decades to come. Eating problems are fast coming to gain a significant focus. With no ultimate cure in sight, it seems likely that the AIDS epidemic will persist for some time. At this point, the only way to steer clear of contracting HIV is to make a personal decision to avoid any of the risky behaviours noted in this chapter.

The changing social profile of people with AIDS, which increasingly afflicts the poor in Africa and Asia, reminds us that health must be seen as a world issue. Even if Europe falls short in addressing the health of marginalised members of society, it also neglects the much wider devastations to be found in low-income societies. Problems of health are far greater in the poor societies of the world than they are in Europe. The good news is that life expectancy for the world as a whole has been rising – from 48 years in 1950 to 65 years today – and the biggest gains have been in poor countries (Mosley and Cowley, 1991). But in much of Latin America, Asia and especially in Africa, hundreds of millions of adults and children lack adequate food, safe water and need medical attention. Improving health in the world's poorest societies remains a critical challenge in the new century.

CONTROVERSY AND DEBATE

WHEN IS THE TIME TO DIE? THE 'RIGHT TO DIE' DEBATE

Because death struck at any time, often without warning, our ancestors would have found the question 'can people live too long?' to be absurd. But as increasing numbers of people live longer and longer, new questions arise about the best time and ways to die. One issue is the right of the elderly (and terminally ill) to die when they choose – the euthanasia debate. Another issue concerns the medical prolonging of life. While there is widespread support for using technology to prolong life, the high cost of nursing care for the elderly puts impossible burdens on the health service, prompting people to wonder how much old age we can now afford.

Recent decades, with a surge in the elderly population, have thus generated major new ethical debates. The question of how we die – by natural causes, by self-inducement or by physician-assisted death (PAD) – is on the worldwide agenda. And it is an issue that divides philosophers, doctors, ethicists, politicians and religious leaders around the world.

The Netherlands decision

In April 2001, The Netherlands became the first country in the world to legalise euthanasia, recognising a practice that had already been tolerated for over two decades. The Dutch (and some 90 per cent supported the law) believe legalising euthanasia will clear up a confused area of law which left doctors open to being prosecuted for murder. The US state of Oregon allows physician-assisted suicide, and Belgium passed euthanasia legislation in October 2001.

The new Dutch law insists that adult patients must have made a voluntary, well-considered and lasting request to die, that they must face a future of unbearable suffering and that there must be no reasonable alternative. A second doctor must be consulted and life must be ended in a medically appropriate way.

Euthanasia is possibly quite common – if covertly practised – in many other countries, and the Dutch argue that it is better to legislate than to leave it precariously practised 'underground'. There is now the worry, however, of 'death tourism' – people might travel to The Netherlands for help in finding euthana-

sia. In some ways, the Dutch decision is a momentous one. While the new reproductive technologies give us a major control of birth, so now euthanasia has given us a major control over death.

In the same year in the UK, a 47-year-old woman with motor neurone disease received her doctor's assistance in easing her death, prompting a British Medical Association enquiry. Everywhere these issues are arriving on the agenda of public debate. And even though euthanasia is against the law in most countries, there are organisations developing which counsel the terminally ill into a 'peaceful and painless death'. The Swiss organisation Dignitas has seen some 146 people die since its inception in 1998, more than two thirds of them foreigners - giving rise to a fear of what has been called 'death tourism'.

The Hemlock Society

In the United States, Derek Humphrey is a founder and executive director of the Hemlock Society. Since 1980, this organisation has offered support and practical assistance to people who wish to die. Humphrey argues that the time has come for people to have straightforward information about how to end their own lives. Hence he published the book, *Final Exit*, in 1991 – a 'suicide, how to' manual that gives specific instructions for killing (swallowing sleeping pills, self-starvation, suffocation, etc.). It was an immediate and remarkably popular best-seller, especially among the elderly, suggesting that millions of people agree with him. Not surprisingly, when *Final Exit* was published, it sparked controversy. While supporters view the work as a humane effort to assist people who are painfully and terminally ill, critics claim that it encourages suicide by people who are experiencing only temporary depression. Yet the book has been translated into 12 languages, a second edition was released in 1997, and in 2000 a supplement was added to update some of the techniques!

The appearance of *Final Exit* also raises broader questions that are no less disturbing and controversial. Older people are, on the one hand, fearful of not being able to afford the medical care they may need and, on the other, alarmed at the prospect of losing control of their lives to a medical establishment that often seeks to prolong life at any cost. People of all ages worry whether the health-care system can meet the escalating demands of seniors only by short-changing the young.

CONTROVERSY AND DEBATE CONTINUED

Against the spiralling costs of prolonging life, then, we may well have to ask if what is technically possible is necessarily socially desirable. In the new century, warns gerontologist Daniel Callahan (1987), a surging elderly population ready and eager to extend their lives will eventually force us either to 'pull the plug' on old age or to short-change everyone else. Raising this issue highlights the problem of priorities and selectivity in the health service. Callahan makes a bold case for limits. He reasons, first, that to spend more on behalf of the elderly we must spend less on others. With a serious problem of poverty among children, he asks, can we continue to direct more money towards the needs of the oldest members of our society at the expense of those just growing up?

Second, Callahan reminds us, a longer life does not necessarily make for a better life. Costs aside, does stressful heart surgery that may prolong the life of an 84-year-old person by a year or two truly improve quality of life? Costs considered, would those resources yield more 'quality of life' if used, say, to transplant a kidney into a ten-year-old boy? Third, Callahan urges us to reconsider our notion of death. Today many people rage against death as an enemy to be conquered at all costs. Yet, he suggests, a sensible health-care programme for an ageing society must acknowledge death as a natural end to the life course. If we cannot make peace with death for our own well-being, limited financial resources demand that we do so for the benefit of others (Callahan, 1987).

A compelling counterpoint, of course, is that those people who have worked all their lives to make our society what it is should, in their final years, enjoy society's generosity. Moreover, in light of our tradition of personal independence and responsibility, can we ethically deny an ageing individual medical care that this person is able and willing to pay for? What is clear from everyone's point of view is that, in the twenty-first century, we will face questions that few would have imagined even 50 years ago. Is optimum longevity good for everyone? Is it even possible for everyone?

CONTINUE THE DEBATE:

1. Should governments devise legislation to permit euthanasia? If yes, what safeguards need to be incorporated?

2. Evaluate the suggestion that doctors and hospitals should devise a double standard, offering more complete care to younger people but more limited care to society's oldest members.

3. Do you think we have a cultural avoidance of death that drives us to extend life at all costs?

4. Is the idea of rationing medical care really new? Hasn't our society historically done exactly this by allowing some people to amass more wealth than others?

SUMMARY

1. Health is a social as well as a biological issue, and well-being depends on the extent and distribution of a society's resources. Culture shapes both definitions of health and patterns of health care.

2. Through most of human history, health has been poor by today's standards. Health improved dramatically in Western Europe and North America in the nineteenth century, first because industrialisation raised living standards and later as medical advances controlled infectious diseases.

3. Infectious diseases were the major killers at the beginning of the twentieth century. Today most people in Europe die in old age of heart disease, cancer or stroke.

4. Health in low-income countries is undermined by inadequate sanitation and hunger. Average life expectancy is about 20 years less than in Europe; in the poorest nations, half the children do not survive to adulthood.

5. In Europe, more than three-quarters of children born today can expect to live to at least age 65. Throughout the life course, however, people of high social position enjoy better health than the poor.

6. Cigarette smoking increased during the twentieth century to become the greatest preventable cause of death in Europe. Now that the health hazards of smoking are known, social tolerance for consumption of tobacco products is declining.

7. The incidence of sexually transmitted diseases has risen since 1960, an exception to the general decline in infectious disease.

8. Historically a family concern, health care is now the responsibility of trained specialists. The model of scientific medicine underlies the UK medical establishment.

9. Holistic healing encourages people to assume greater responsibility for their own health and well-being and urges professional healers to gain personal knowledge of patients and their environment.

10. Socialist societies define medical care as a right that governments offer equally to everyone. Capitalist societies view medical care as a commodity to be purchased, although most capitalist governments support medical care through socialised medicine or national health insurance.

11. The United States, with a direct-fee system, is the only industrialised society that has no comprehensive medical care programme. Most people in the United States purchase private health insurance, government insurance or membership in a health maintenance organisation. One in six adults in the United States cannot afford to pay for medical care.

12. Functional analysis links health and medicine to other social structures. A concept central to functional analysis is the sick role, by which the ill person is excused from routine social responsibilities.

13. The symbolic-interaction paradigm investigates how health and medical treatments are largely matters of subjective perception and social definition. It researches medicine at work in everyday medical settings.

14. Conflict analysis focuses on the unequal distribution of health and medical care. It criticises the US medical establishment for relying too heavily on drugs and surgery, for giving free rein to the profit motive in medicine and for overemphasising the biological rather than the social causes of illness.

15. Three case studies of health issues and sociology are provided: food and body disorders, AIDS and HIV, and death and dying.

CRITICAL-THINKING QUESTIONS

1. Compare the presentation of health and treatment in any two television programmes, such as *ER* and *Casualty*.

2. In a global context, what are the 'diseases of poverty' that kill people in poor countries? What are the 'diseases of affluence', the leading killers in rich nations? Why are there such different patterns of disease?

3. Do you think the United States should or should not follow the lead of other industrial countries by enacting a government programme of health care for everyone? Why?

4. Think of any health issue that interests you (cancer, multiple sclerosis, depression, disability, etc.) and consider how the issues raised around AIDS and HIV could be applicable to these areas too. Discuss the ways in which matters such as gender, statistics, global politics, epidemiology and social movements may be key issues in the sociological study of health.

Further reading

Introductory textbooks:

Mildred Blaxter, *Health* (2004)

Joan Busfield, *Health and Health Care in Modern Britain* (2000)

Sarah Nettleton, *The Sociology of Health and Illness* (1995)

Graham Scrambler, *Health and Social Change: A Critical Theory* (2002)

Brian Turner, *Medical Power and Social Knowledge* (2nd edn, 1996)

Blaxter's is the best place to start for some stimulating ideas. The other books are more detailed.

On disability:

Colin Barnes, Geoff Mercer and Tom Shakespeare, *Exploring Disability: A Sociological Introduction* (1999) An excellent overview of the sociology of disability.

On death:

Tony Walter, *On Bereavement: The Culture of Grief* (1998)

Tony Walter, *The Revival of Death* (1994)
Two books by Tony Walter which explore recent work on death, funerals and bereavement. The latter is the first book since Lofland in the late 1970s to sociologically analyse the 'death and dying' social movement. In so doing, it breaks new ground in relating recent work on the medical sociology of death to wider sociological debates on modernity and postmodernity.

Gender and health:

Lesley Doyal, *What Makes Women Sick* (1995)

P. Foster, *Women and the Health Care Industry* (1995) Two books that consider women and health.

Susan Bordo, *Unbearable Weight: Feminism, Western Culture and the Body* (1993)

A collection of papers around anorexia, eating disorders and the body, all written from a feminist perspective.

Watch a video/Read a book

- John McTiernan's *Medicine Man* (1992): ecology, medicine and romance in a South American rain forest.
- Peter Bogdanovich's *Mask* (1985): mother, played by Cher, fights for rights of a badly disfigured boy.
- Milos Forman's *One Flew Over the Cuckoo's Nest* (1975): classic on surviving life in a mental hospital. A good accompaniment to Erving Goffman's *Asylums: Essays on the Social Situation of Mental Patients and Other Inmates* (1961).
- Mike Nichol's *Regarding Henry* (1991): tough lawyer is seriously injured and makes a slow recovery.
- Gregg Araki's *The Living End* (1992): take a harrowing road trip with two dying HIV gay men.
- Norman Rene's *Longtime Companion* (1990): though it plays like a soap opera, this warm and compassionate film focuses on a group of friends on Fire Island and the emergence of AIDS in their community.

On disability films, see Martin F. Norden, *The Cinema of Isolation: A History of Physical Disability in the Movies* (1994), and note especially:

- David Lynch's *The Elephant Man* (1980)
- Jim Sheridan's *My Left Foot* (1989)
- Luis Manoki's *Gaby – A True Story* (1987)
- Randa Haines's *Children of a Lesser God* (1986)
- Maria Tosi's *Whose Life is it anyway?* (1981)

On mental illness, read Doris Lessing's classic *The Golden Notebook* (2002).

Connecting up

Connect to other chapters

- Connect world health patterns to global inequalities (Chapter 9), urbanisation (Chapter 23) and environmental change (Chapter 24).
- Link health to social class (Chapter 10).
- Consider AIDS in relation to gender studies (Chapter 12).
- Link interactional health studies to classroom interactional studies (Chapter 19) and symbolic interactionism (Chapter 1).

To the websites

- Department of Health:
  http://www.dh.gov.uk/home/fs/en
- World Health Organisation:
  http://www.who.int/en
- A useful guide to all matters linked to euthanasia can be found at:
  http://www.internationaltaskforce.org/holland.htm

- The major world source for information on AIDS is UNAIDS:
  http://www.unaids.org/en/default.asp
- On the pharmaceutical industry and AIDS, see:
  http://www.icaso.org/
  which is the International Council of AIDS service organisations on drug imports.
- See also a series of activist reports from a leading New York AIDS campaigning organisation, ACT UP:
  www.actupny.org/reports/
- The Eating Disorder Association can be found at:
  http://www.edauk.com/
  the main UK-based website.
- ANRAD:
  http://www.anred.com/stats.html
  This is a very useful website on eating disorders, organised through questions. It is US-based.
- The Food Standards Agency:
  http://www.food.gov.uk
  Useful for details on all foods and diets.

For additional case studies, multiple choice questions, internet exercises, and annotated weblinks specific to this chapter, visit this book's website at www.pearsoned.co.uk/plummer

CHAPTER 21

THE MASS MEDIA

'The Medium is the Message': it is the medium that shapes and controls the scale and form of human association and action.
Marshall McLuhan

KEY THEMES

- Changing patterns of communication
- Sociological approaches to the media
- The major areas for a media analysis
- Shifts in the media in the twenty-first century

SOCIOLOGIST KIRK JOHNSON

has spent some years in the small Indian village of Danawli, studying the impact of television. At the time of his research, some 25 of the 104 households in the village had TV sets. The elders of the village worried a great deal about the arrival of this new medium. One, for example, argued that '*TV is the devil.*

. . . It has only caused us pain and is very bad for us'. Another said: '*Television is ruining our culture. . . . People no longer speak like they used to. They all, especially the young people, talk about the life in the cities or in England and America. They don't know anything about own history or traditions. I have heard some even talk about love marriage.*' Another said: '*Children used to come to hear the stories of olden days. Everyone used to listen to me. The young people today only want to watch television and movies and go to Panchgani until late at night*' (Johnson, 2000: 216 and 192)

But for many the television had broadened their horizons into the modern world. They saw a whole array of new experiences: different kinds of gender and class relations; different kinds of marriage and the 'desire for fewer children'; they saw the shift from success by heredity to achievement by merit and a change

in the perception of caste relations. Television challenged the positions of traditional leaders. '*We have learned*', says one man, '*that our leaders are corrupt, even the national leaders are corrupt. On TV they show us about how corrupt our parliament members are . . .*' (Johnson, 2000: 218).

Television promotes a greater receptiveness to new values and an openness to change. Many families may not have had TV in their home, but they would visit the homes of others to watch TV and it had helped to bring some people together. New kinds of relationship are being formed, and this is particularly noticeable among the young and children.

Danawli reveals a transitional phase in the spread of television in rural India, and Kirk Johnson concludes that 'the one material commodity which has most dramatically influenced social change in rural India has been the television set' (Johnson, 2000: 15). Again, another older man speaks:

> There is no doubt about it. You can ask anyone. TV is the one thing that has most changed the way people live. You see how people watch TV. They are also so into TV that nothing else matters. The house could be burning down and no one would realise it. TV is very powerful. Our young people see things on the TV that we never saw, and this has changed the way they behave. They want everything they see. They are not satisfied any more with working the field and providing for the family.'
> (Johnson, 2000: 213)

(Left) Max Ferguson, 1986 News Vendor. Oil on paper. © Private collection
Source: Bridgeman Art Library

(Above) Cinema-going and TV watching in large groups is very popular in India, as shown in this makeshift outdoor cinema.
Source: Network © Witold Krassowski

The media age

This is the time of the media. Many of us live our lives increasingly in and through the media. To take television as a prime example: watching television is the most common home-based leisure activity for men and women in the UK. Virtually everyone watches it. Ninety-nine per cent of households in the UK own one television; 86 per cent have a video recorder, renting an average of ten films per year. In 2002, 85 per cent of men and women watched television every day.

But television is only one media form. Half the UK population aged over 15 read a national daily newspaper, *The Sun*, *Daily Mirror* and *Daily Mail* being the most popular. Thirty-four million (58 per cent of the population) hold local library tickets. Some 180 million CDs were sold in 1999 (and 80 million singles), making roughly four CDs per head of the population. Three-quarters of the population go to the cinema, and the figures are highest among the young: in 2002, over 50 per cent of 15–24 year olds went to the cinema once a month or more. DVD was launched in the UK in 1998 and has become the fastest-selling electronic format of all time – sales of DVDs doubled between 2001 and 2002, and 169 million VHS or DVDs were sold in 2002 (*Social Trends*, 2004: Chapter 13).

But obviously this is not just a UK phenomenon: it is global. In the United States the figures are even higher: 70 per cent of families own two or more televisions, and these sets are 'on' for an average of more than seven hours' per day. And a 1996 survey of young people in 41 nations found they watched an average of six hours' television per day. The significance of television in society has been extensively studied! (Allen, 1992: 1; Abercrombie, 1996: 2; Herman and McChesney, 1997: 41; *Social Trends*, 2004).

Ownership and watching do not tell the full story. What is important about the mass media is the way in which they have come to play a prominent role in many aspects of our everyday lives. All the institutions discussed in this book have been changed by them. Political elections, for example, are geared up to television and the press; it is hard to imagine elections without the constant 'spin' and 'hype' in all the media. Likewise, religion has its 'televangelical' networks; and business and finance depend upon the new technologies for rapid information as well as a constant stream of advertising. And where would public events – sport or parliament or news – be if they were not relayed in our homes on television? Sports spectacles, from the Olympics to football, depend on the television for their mass audiences.

Even the family has changed dramatically because of television. Many homes give pride of place to the TV set in their living room, draping it with family photos – symbolic of its importance. Television becomes a part of everyday life, marking out family time and routines. It is the intimate machine, giving impressions of talking to you through chat programmes, advice programmes and close-up interviews with all kinds of people. The media become friend and family. Indeed, much of what is shown on the screen actually depicts friends and families – the most popular programmes are the 'soap operas' which are always about this. But then we take to university or work all the details of the soap lives we have seen on TV and start to discuss them with friends. TV characters invade our lives as new friends (Abercrombie, 1996: 17–19 and Chapter 7). And the new taste for 'reality television', such as *Survivor* or *Big Brother*, holds large audiences for events that dissolve the boundaries between television and reality – a feature brought home in films such as *The Truman Show*. Here a man is born on to a massive television set, becomes the focus of a major soap opera, and does not know it. (Till the end of the film, that is, when he breaks out of the programme to find his 'real' life!)

We are media saturated. Indeed, one commentator has tellingly remarked that:

> in one hour's television viewing, each one of us is likely to experience more images than a member of a non-industrial society would in a lifetime. The quantitative difference is so great as to become categorical; we do not just experience more images, but we live with a completely different relationship between the image and other orders of experience.
>
> (Fiske, 1991: 58)

As we have seen earlier, the Spanish sociologist, Manuel Castells, has argued that 'new information technologies are transforming the way we produce, consume, manage, live and die' (Castells, 1989: 15). In this chapter, we will look at how our modern mass media system developed and examine some of the theories that have tried to explain how it works. We will show how media research needs to look at what media messages contain, how media messages are made and how they are understood by the audiences. Finally, we will glimpse their importance in the new century, as the media become increasingly globalised.

Communication and social change

The history of societies can partially be written as the history of media communications. We have seen in Chapter 4 how social life changed between hunting and gathering societies and industrial society and how technology is one guiding feature of social change. Technology can do nothing in itself: it takes people to act on the media to bring about change. But without the media themselves, no change would be possible. What we can see is direct one-to-one, face-to-face communication developing into the **mass media**, *any social or technological devices used for the selection, transmission or reception of information.*

One aspect of that technology is the means of communication. As the means of communication change, so do social lives. The major developments in human culture and consciousness are linked to changes in our modes of communication – the evolution from words and primitive speech through writing to typeface and now modern electronic worlds (Ong, 1982).

Our focus here is not upon the content of the media but on their form. In a famous phrase, US media guru Marshall McLuhan proclaimed that *The Medium is the Message* (McLuhan, 1964). What he meant by this is that

independently of what is being said, it is the kind of 'medium which shapes and controls the scale of human association and action'. McLuhan sees the history of media as falling into three major periods. The first is an oral culture, where the ear is the important sense. Listening to the words is a harmonious, circular way of thought. The second is the writing and printing culture, where 'the ear' is exchanged for 'the eye'. It brings more linear thought. The third is the electronic culture. And here the media bring radical shifts again.

Consider Table 21.1 which outlines the evolution of the main forms of communication in society. We can return to our image of the world's history scaled to a 24-hour clock starting at midnight and continuing till the next midnight, introduced in Chapter 5. Here, speech is invented around 9.30 in the evening. Writing is not invented till about eight minutes before midnight. Electronic devices appear some 11 seconds, and digital electronics 2 seconds, before the clock strikes midnight (Neuman, 1991: 7). Table 21.2 gives some landmarks in media history.

Table 21.1	Stages in the development of human communication
1 The Age of Signs	No speech or writing, only sounds and bodily gestures. Maybe 70 million years ago?
2 The Age of Speech	Oral cultures, pre-literate, start to appear at most 100,000 years ago. Cro-Magnon and other prehistoric cultures. Linguists can identify around 50 prehistoric vocabularies.
3 The Age of Writing	Writing starts to appear around 5,000 years ago. Sumerians, Egyptian civilisation, Turkey, Iraq, Iran. Initially pictographs, hieroglyphics, clay tablets. Later papyrus – a light and portable medium. Alphabets slowly replace images and songs, and this promotes linear, rational and abstract thought. Problems of censorship start to appear. Chirography – or manuscripts – become main form in Middle Ages.
4 The Age of Print	First printing press in West *c.* 1445–56 (printing appeared in China nearly 800 years earlier). Gutenberg publishes Bible. Greatly amplifies reach and impact of alphabet. Media censorship by church. Typography dominates. Printing speeds up with the Industrial Revolution.
5 The Age of Electronics	Electrical and electronic media, from late 19th century. Emergence of photography.
6 The future?	Digital, high tech, computers: The Information Age . . .

Table 21.2	Some modern landmarks in media history
1456	Gutenberg Press: printing of first book (The Bible) in Western world (but evidence of printing in China some 800 years earlier!)
17th century	Press starts to develop
1620–21	Corantos (news sheets) in Holland reporting (with King's authority) on wars
1665	Oxford – court news (later *London Gazette*)
1690	First American newspaper reporting on colonies
1785	*The Times* first published, followed by *The Observer* in 1791
1838	*The Times* of India founded. Morse code invented
1839	First photographs and sales of Daguerrotype camera
19th century	Many of today's newspapers started in mid-19th century: *News of the World* in 1843, *The Daily Telegraph* in 1855 (when stamp duties were abolished). *The Daily Mail* was the first million-selling mass circulation
1876	Alexander Graham Bell initiates the telephone
1877	Edison patents the phonograph; first replayable recordings
1891	Kinematography and 'peep scopes' arrive
1896	First permanent cinema: 400-seater Vuitascope Hall, New Orleans
	In late 1890s and 1900s, short films like *How Bridget served the salad undressed* and in 1903 *The Great Train Robbery*
1910	Nickelodeon – some 10,000 family-orientated exhibition halls exist in the United States
1915	*Birth of a Nation*: first 'major' film
1921	First US radio station: KDKA Pittsburgh
1922	Radio arrives in Britain with the British Broadcasting Company
1926	50 million people per week go to the movies in the United States
1936	Television arrives in Britain at Alexandra Palace, for a small audience; but with the onset of the Second World War was not fully developed until the 1950s. ITV came in 1955; BBC2 in 1962; Channel 4 in 1982; Channel 5 in 1997
1950	UNIVAC (Universal Automatic Computer): first mass-produced computer
1952	First video recorder demonstration in United States
1960s	Emergence of Internet through US Department of Defense; development of global satellite communications
1967	First local BBC; first colour TV in UK
1971	First successful video game reaches United States arcades
Early 1970s	Early development of optical fibre systems of communication
1981	MTV first televised (starts in United States on 1 August 1981). Developed like a radio station, always on the air, appealing to same market niche
1985	First 'multiplex' cinema in the UK (The Point in Milton Keynes)
1992	Internet takes off
1995	'Privatised Cyberspace': Internet becomes commercial when United States government pulls out; first commercial DVDs appear
1999	Rapid increase in usage of DVDs
1990s	Rapid expansion of cell/mobile phones and their development as all-purpose means of communication

Oral cultures

For most of our history, then, societies have been entirely dependent upon face-to-face grunts! Language and speech only started to appear with more sophisticated societies, about 100,000 years ago. These were oral cultures, and culture here depended a great deal upon the ability to remember and to tell stories that were passed on from generation to generation. Without such stories, cultures and knowledge would have died out. Certainly, these were 'slow societies' where not a great deal could be retained. For continuity, memory must have been vital. And stories played a crucial role.

Writing cultures

Significant changes started to happen when the spoken word was written down. This depended upon first, a written language system – an alphabet or code of some kind – and second, upon a means for writing and an object to write upon. Oral cultures depend upon memory. Poetry and stories became very important in trying to pass on from generation to generation a sense of continuing culture. But writing makes it much easier to pass on this history.

And such a form will depend upon an alphabet or other system of writing. In China, some time around 3,000 years ago, a writing system developed with some 50,000 characters! And with this emerged an elite who could master it: the mandarins. Phonetic alphabets, based on sounds, are more recent and mark a major advance in ease of use.

In some ancient civilisations, writing was carved on stone which was not at all easily transportable. Stone drawings are hard to change or revise – this medium therefore makes for relatively unchanging and stable societies. In Egypt, the dominance of stone as a medium gave a monopoly to those who owned it. But once papyrus was introduced, it played a major role in communication becoming more flexible.

The next major change came when the churches started to develop significant manuscript writings. The medieval church had a monopoly over religious and all other information, which was controlled in manuscripts by a special class of priests. Again, these were far from available to most people.

Print cultures

And so we reach a time, just a few hundred years ago, when the method of print was invented. This was truly a revolution. Now the control of the elite church's scribes could be bypassed, because for the first time in history there arose the possibility that large numbers of people could become literate (able to read and write). This brought with it:

- An ability to store and transmit culture much more readily
- The potential to include those people previously excluded from knowledge
- A potentially different way of thinking in which the person 'engages' with a text rather than another person
- The potential for mass culture, mass society and mass education
- The development of new minds in which literate modes of thought become part of our everyday consciousness
- A new sense of 'authorship' and control over the text.

Despite the slow spreading of print, it was really only in the nineteenth century – with the birth of mass newspapers – that whole societies started to become literate. And at the same time, a mass education system was required to equip people for the new social order (see Chapter 19). Again, it was also a means of excluding people. There were constant fears of how this new literacy was 'dangerous'.

Electronic cultures

With the new electronic media, our experiences are no longer limited by where or who we are. Media, and especially television, weaken the strong sense we used to have of being in a place. Limited confines such as the family home, the office or the prison are now invaded by the television, which starts to shift the boundaries of how we experience the world.

In an important study, Joshua Meyrowitz (1986) looks at how the pattern of information flow changes with television. With television we 'eavesdrop' on a host of different worlds. We can gain access to worlds that in the past were not accessible. Thus, for example, children's worlds and adults' worlds, men's worlds and women's worlds could in the past be kept separate. There were things that adults could talk about when children had gone to bed; things that men could talk about when women were not there. But television cuts out these separate spaces. We now inhabit 'no sense of place'. Our sense of place has changed.

Television weakens the traditional distinction between physical place and social situations. Public spheres now enter the living room; public and private get blurred. Television has changed our way of experiencing the world because it has changed what we know about everything. Television parades before us an array of differences: men can learn about women, children about adult worlds, heterosexuals about gays,

RESEARCH IN ACTION

STUDYING MICRO-MEDIA IN THE WORLD OF GOTHS

The methods of contemporary sociology are less and less dependent upon standard interviews and questionnaires. Access to new media forms has changed all that. Recent work on youth styles, for example, has looked at the significance of such new media in the creation of youth and club cultures. While there may be dominant media forms, club cultures and the like develop their own niche media – in the form of music and style magazines – and micro-media. Thornton defines the latter as: 'Flyers, fanzines, flyposters, listings, telephone information lines, pirate radio, e-mailing lists and internet archive sites ... an array of media from the most rudimentary of print forms to the latest in digital interactive technologies are the low circulating narrowly targeted micro-media' (Thornton, 1995: 137).

In his research on Goths, Paul Hodkinson (2002) employs a range of research methods, from interviewing and observation to questionnaires and media analysis. He looks, for instance, at various Goth fanzines, analysing their content but also interviewing the producers and readers about them. Fanzines are local, they are not circulated widely, they have no mass distribution. Instead, they are picked up at concerts and have widely dispersed markets. What they do is help construct the values of the Goth scene, creating shared identities. Fanzines can be very influential. As one interviewee puts it:

> J (female) : It has a big role because it's a central point for all the reviews, gig dates, current interviews, where people discover who they like and who they don't. You have to be careful what you put in because to a certain extent you can influence the gothic community as a whole. ... You're in a position where you have a bit of power I guess.
>
> (Hodkinson, 2002: 168)

In addition, Paul Hodkinson looked at Goth websites. Here there were 'pages and pages of relevant sites' (2002: 176). Many Goths had their own home pages and most pages brought with them a cluster of further links. A key aspect of all this was the availability of the Goth discussion groups. Groups such as the early *alt. gothic* and *uk.people.gothic* not only attracted local Goths but enhanced worldwide participation.

Consider the use of these new media in your own researches.

People often think that the sociological method is about interviewing. But there are many other tools of research – and many new ones in the making. Here are some 'fanzines' that were used in Paul Hodkinson's study of Goths. They tell a great deal about the lifestyles and cultures of Goths.

Source: © S.L. Hodkinson

HISTORY OF TELEVISION IN NORWAY

Every country and culture now has its own media worthy of study. The history of various media provides clues as to a culture's social, economic and political history. Norway came later to television than many other cultures, but the shape of its history is very similar to others. It falls into three waves.

1960–70

After an experimental period which started in 1954, 1960 saw the official opening of TV, a formal opening by the King, the Prime Minister and the Director-General. It was a continuation of the NRK (the Norwegian Broadcasting Corporation) which had been consolidated in 1933 through public radio, and it emerged through a close collaboration between the Norwegian Parliament and the NRK. It was also linked to industrial interests: the Norwegian radio industry was keen to produce television sets. Programming was limited – children's programmes at 6.00 p.m., a break; news at 8.00; then programmes till 10.00. In the early 1960s, education was seen as a major goal of what was effectively public television. Although some 50–60 per cent of programming had to be home grown, there was quite an influx of UK and US programmes, therefore bringing these cultures to the forefront of Norwegian life. There was also a classic debate between liberal values and conservative values. The period is summarised neatly: 'In 1960 a television set was regarded as a symbol of luxury and high social status. Ten years later it was a regular piece of furniture – a necessity for everybody' (Bastiansen and Syversten, 1996: 132).

1970–89

This was 'The Era of High Monopoly'. By the 1970s, television was the central medium in Norway. The one channel was a focus for the whole nation, especially over political debates. Programmes could attract 60 per cent of the nation's population. Throughout this period, the structure of programming was more or less the same. Children's shows at 6.00; three news programmes a day; mainly evening broadcasting. The monopoly was accused of bias – largely by conservatives who felt it was monopolised by the left. (It was not a total monopoly, as since the 1960s access to Swedish television had been possible.) Local and satellite broadcasting started in 1981 but on a limited scale and, as in so many countries, consumption was low initially. But significant changes can be heralded from 1989.

1989–now

By the end of 1990, almost 40 per cent of the population could watch satellite television. The media age had arrived. There was a break-up of the old public monopoly and the arrival of a new commercial era with a proliferation of channels. A second commercial channel opened in 1992.

What is interesting about this short television history is the pattern. Norway came later to television than many countries, but its three-wave history is broadly comparable. What we see is a shift from a dominant 'public' medium of pervasive, but limited, scope to a proliferation of new channels and a commercialisation of the medium. While each European country has its own history, this is the broad pattern.

Source: Bastiansen and Syversten (1996: 127–155).

---

whites about blacks, the poor about the rich, the mass about the elite (Meyrowitz, 1986).

Cybercultures, mediated societies and the future

Many now suggest we are just on the edge of a new stage of media life which may extend the electronic cultures we are currently experiencing. Not only do we spend more and more time talking about and living around various media (television, video, DVD), we are shifting our ways of relating, making the PC, the laptop, the mobile phone and its text messages more and more central to our lives. In this way, we come to live in the media (see the discussion of postmodern media theory on page 587).

Media theories

The classical 'hypodermic' model

The earliest theory of the mass media at the turn of the century – often called the magic bullet theory or the 'hypodermic' model of the media – is the simplest propaganda theory of the media. It assumes that people are passive and the media message has a direct impact upon them. It suggests that:

- media messages are presented to members of a mass society, who receive them more or less uniformly
- these messages are stimuli which influence the individual strongly

- the stimuli lead individuals to respond in a similar, uniform fashion
- the effects of mass communication *are powerful, uniform and direct* (our italics, adapted from Lowery and De Fleur, 1988: 23–24).

Although this theory is still popularly used in everyday discussions (especially among those who see the media as dangerous), such an account has long been discredited. Indeed, each point raised above can be taken as a critical issue of exactly what does not happen with the media! We will now look at some of the theories that have been developed to replace this 'hypodermic syringe' model.

Functionalist theories of the media

Functionalist theories of the media look at the ways in which the media serves to integrate society in different ways, and examine the role of media effects in doing this. Seeing media as working as part of the social system, media can provide information, education, entertainment and diversion. Five functions have been particularly noted:

1. *The surveillance function.* The media provide a continuous flow of data about the world we live in. They can warn us of dangers (from hurricanes to wars to dangerous criminals) and be instrumental in providing information on traffic jams, the stock market as well as all kinds of information linked to personal welfare. (They can also be dysfunctional – stirring up undue anxiety, for example.)

2. *The status conferral function.* Here, the media give status to people, public issues, organisations and social movements. Enhanced status comes to all who feature in the media – they become more known about, for good or bad. Not only do major events such as political elections or famous criminal trials come to attention, but many minor issues can be accorded status. Thus, a child with a life-threatening illness, an old person on her 100th birthday or environmental activists protesting about a local pollution problem can all be accorded 'status'.

3. *The 'enforced application of social norms' function.* This highlights the public announcement of social norms, and publicity serves to close the gap between 'private attitudes and public morality'. The leading media analyst Dennis McQuail sees the media as fostering public communication values, which stress freedom, equality and order. The media can promote values by dramatising deviance of all kinds. By bringing to our attention 'youth crime', 'rape', 'child sex offenders',

'drugs' or 'serial killers', the community's awareness is heightened and moral boundaries are drawn (see Chapter 16). Later in this chapter we describe how this often works as a 'moral panic'.

4. *The transmission of culture function.* The media have become prime modern agents of socialisation (see Chapter 7). From young children's programmes such as *Teletubbies* to teenage chat shows, the media serve a key role in passing on elements of a society's culture and heritage.

5. *The narcotising function.* This is more of a dysfunction than a function and refers to the way in which a flood of information can lead to superficiality (Lazarsfeld and Merton, 1996: 16–18; see also Wright, 1967; McQuail, 1994).

Critical comment

Functionalist theories were popular during the mid-twentieth century but have been much in decline since. The above listing suggests why. In many ways, all functionalist theories do is provide a descriptive listing of how an institution works in the current society. The functions listed here may be important, but it is not always clear that they add much depth of understanding.

Conflict theories of the media

Much European work on the mass media has adopted a conflict (and often Marxist) approach to the media. Within this paradigm, the media are seen to be owned by dominant classes who use them as a mechanism to serve their own interests. The media thus come to play a major role in the transmission of ideologies. Broadly, conflict theories highlight two important matters. The first concerns the economic base of the media, in particular the ways in which they follow a profit motive and the ways in which big business conglomerates come to shape them. The second concerns the ideological structuring of the media, in particular the ways in which certain conflicting interests – often of class, ethnicity, gender – are 'screened out' of the messages.

The political economy of the media

This stresses how the major means of communication in society come to be owned by private economic interests. Increasingly, it can be shown that these interests form giant interlocking directorates and are in the hands of powerful tycoons, such as Rupert Murdoch and Silvio Berlusconi. (Berlusconi – who owns Finevest, with a

Table 21.3	Ownership of press media in the UK	
	Approximate share of market	
News International	35%	*Sun, Times, Sunday Times, News of the World*
Mirror Group	23–27%	*Mirror, Sunday Mirror, People*
United Newspapers	14% (9% for Sundays)	*Daily Express, Daily Star, Sunday Express*
Associated Newspapers	15%	*Daily Mail, Mail on Sunday*
Hollinger	7%	*Daily Telegraph, Sunday Telegraph*

Note: These figures are approximate and meant only to indicate a broad level of concentration of the media in a few large firms

virtual monopoly of Italian commercial television – was elected twice as prime minister after much campaigning on his own television!) It has been true for some time that a country's media have been in the hands of a few powerful economic groups. Table 21.3 shows the approximate concentration in the UK in the mid-1990s. But even in the early 1970s, the top five media firms in the UK accounted for 71 per cent of daily newspaper circulation, 78 per cent of admissions to cinemas, 76 per cent of record sales and 74 per cent of homes with commercial television. But what has been happening since that time has been an increasing concentration of ownership globally. Thus Murdoch's transnational company has holdings in the United States, Latin America, Europe (especially the UK and Germany), Australia and Asia. This is discussed further below.

These powerful economic interests work to consistently exclude 'those voices lacking economic power or resources'. All kinds of minority – from ethnic groups to disabled groups, from 'women' to 'gays' – may not be represented in media coverage. But more, much of the media will find that 'the voices which survive will largely belong to those least likely to criticise the prevailing distribution of power and wealth' (Murdock and Golding, 1977: 39).

The culture industry and ideology

German critical theorists Adorno and Horkheimer saw the development of a 'culture industry' which 'transfers the profit motive naked on to cultural forms'. The multibillion dollar Hollywood empire sells its wares – from *Gladiator* to *Pearl Harbor* – for huge profits. True 'culture' dissolves in the face of this commercial marketplace. And even 'great culture' will be dug up and recycled for new profits. For instance, the work of the eighteenth-century novelist Jane Austen has been repackaged into films, television mini-dramas and reworked books. Often this leads to her work becoming

'just like everything else': flattened for profit. Likewise, almost every novel by Charles Dickens has been turned into a musical (*Oliver!* being just the most famous). And every aspect of the media is saturated with this. There are extremes, as in the hype and promotion of leading rock stars such as Eminem or Madonna 'world concerts'. Everywhere, media products 'are commodities through and through' and 'human beings are once more debased'. 'The colour film demolishes the genial old tavern to a greater extent than bombs ever could: the film exterminates its image.' It is 'mass deception', 'anti-enlightenment', and leads to subservience to blind authority (Adorno, 1991: 85–92).

Ideological state apparatuses

The French Marxist philosopher Louis Althusser (1918–90) saw a number of institutions (the media, but also education, religion, the family) as being independent of the state but functioning to reproduce the dominant ideologies through what he called the **ideological state apparatuses** (or ISAs as some have called them more popularly). These are *social institutions which reproduce the dominant ideology, independent of the state.* (In contrast, repressive apparatuses such as police and army employ more direct power.) Ideologies construct imaginary relations for people to live in, which help obscure the actual things that are going on (Althusser, 1971).

Critical comment

Conflict theories are persuasive in alerting us to media capital and bias. There is a growing world concentration of the mass media in the hands of a few major corporations and the research evidence suggests pervasive biases (especially over what is not allowed to be said in the media). But conflict theories may suffer from exaggeration. People are sometimes such as living too much like passive victims and capital is seen as moving too coherently in favour of one outcome. In fact, media practices are complex and varied.

Symbolic interactionism

Herbert Blumer, the founder of symbolic-interactionist analysis, was one of the first sociologists to conduct audience research on cinema-going. As part of a widespread concern about the impact of films on young people, a series of investigations were set up in the late 1920s and early 1930s (popularly known as the Payne Studies, they were initiated by a pro-film censorship group, the Motion Picture Research Council). Blumer was involved with one of these that looked at young people. Straightforwardly, he asked some 1,500 young people to write 'motion-picture autobiographies', backed up with more selective interviews, group discussions and observations. He argued that to know what impact media had on young people's lives, it is best simply to ask them. Following on from this, much of his ensuing book *Movies and Conduct* is given over to young people's first-hand accounts of the films they have seen – how they provide the basis of imitation, play, daydreams, emotional development and 'schemes of life'. He let the people speak for themselves. One entry, dealing with stereotypes, reads:

> Female, 19, white college senior: – One thing these pictures did was to establish a permanent fear of Chinamen in my mind. To this day I do not see a Chinese person but what I think of him as being mixed up in some evil affair. I always pass them as quickly as possible if I meet them in the street, and refuse to go into a Chinese restaurant or laundry.
>
> (Blumer, 1933: 145)

Quite rightly, others more recently have been critical of his straightforward naiveté of approach. Denzin, for example, has recently been very critical of Blumer, suggesting that while progressive in method, it was shrouded with Blumer's assumptions ('pro-middle class and anti-film', Denzin, 1992: 107). It was also open to being used to crusade against film content and viewed texts unproblematically (Clough, 1992). True, Blumer's initial studies in the 1930s now look somewhat simple: but he was the first to take seriously audience responses.

Norman Denzin has focused on the importance of 'the movies' for understanding social life in the twentieth century. He considers the film and going to the cinema to have been the key mode of narrative in that century. Talking of the 'cinematic society', he suggests that watching films shifted much of that century's experience by encouraging a more visual, looking society – a society which he sees as increasingly voyeuristic. Denzin's method is to look at films, ranging from *Blue Velvet* to *Rear Window*, to see how they display the cultural logic of society (Denzin, 1992, 1995).

The theory of moral panics

Drawing heavily on the symbolic-interactionist tradition, Stanley Cohen investigated an emerging youth phenomenon in the UK in the 1960s: that of the Mods and Rockers (see Chapter 5). These young people appeared on the beaches and around the town centres of several south coast holiday resorts in England (including Clacton) over the Easter holiday of 1964. Although Cohen discovered that the amount of serious violence and vandalism was relatively little, he found that the media 'blew it up out of all proportions'. The media – and other 'moral crusaders' – saw the Mods and Rockers as terrorising the town and being 'hell bent on destruction'. Cohen saw this as a 'moral panic' and defined it in the following way:

> Societies appear to be subject, every now and then, to periods of moral panic. A condition, episode, person or group of persons emerges to become defined as a threat to societal values and interests; its nature is presented in a stylised and stereotypical fashion by the mass media; the moral barricades are manned by editors, bishops, politicians and other right thinking people; socially accredited experts pronounce their diagnoses and solutions; ways of coping are evolved . . .
>
> (Cohen, 2003: 28; orig. 1972)

Like Durkheim (in Chapter 4), Cohen argued that when societies entered times of anxiety and crisis, 'folk devils' were created through moral panics to reassert dominant values. For moral panics to exist, these responses have to be out of all proportion to the actual threat or danger. The media played a central role in stirring up concern, often amplifying the problem. From a small initial issue, major hysteria could be created which often served the interest of specific groups worried about specific social issues, such as teenage crime getting out of control.

Since Cohen's influential study, a great many 'folk devils and moral panics' have been identified. The media have mounted major concerns over drugs, mugging, baby battering, granny battering, child abuse of all forms, dole scroungers and welfare cheats, AIDS, video nasties, rapists and serial killers, paedophiles, Satanism and ritual abuse, religious cults, militant trade unionism, 'blacks', and pornography. In some cases the problems behind such issues have been found to be quite major, but in other cases the hysteria is out of all proportion to the actual problem. Phillip Jenkins has shown, for example, that although there is often massive concern over serial killers, they are in fact very rare indeed, and serial killings have remained at roughly the same low rate for the last 100 years (P. Jenkins, 1992). To understand the workings of a moral panic, it is important to look at the way in which the media – newspapers and TV in particular – come to identify a 'problem' and present it in a particular way, and how this may 'fit' into a particular set of social anxieties or worries. Many moral panics, for example, depict dangerous threats to the traditional moral values of family life. When AIDS first appeared in the early 1980s, the media often handled it in a sensational way, depicting it as a dangerous threat to traditional sexuality (S. Cohen, 2003; orig. 1972; P. Jenkins, 1992).

Postmodern media theory

Over the past decade, a group of newer social theorists have come to highlight the centrality of the media in our lives. In particular, they have suggested that we now live our lives increasingly through the products of the mass media, which have come to have an autonomous existence of their own. We are media consumers. And the media messages, from Madonna's video to the soap opera *EastEnders'* murders, become a new form of reality. We are awhirl and awash in signs.

Baudrillard (1929–) sees modern societies as concerned with the consumption of signs. While in his earlier work he explored media 'codes', in his later work 'simulation' becomes the core of social life. Broadly, whatever is really happening in the world no longer matters because people are coming to live so much in a media-mediated world that reality is bypassed. All we are left with are exploding (imploding) signs and **simulacra**, *worlds of media-generated signs and images*. Just what these signs refer to in the world is no longer clearly distinguished.

One of Baudrillard's most famous (and disturbing) remarks concerned the Gulf War (16 January–28 February 1991). He argued that it was a hyper-real representation on our television screens: the real battlefields were now replaced by media saturation. We can watch the bombings, hear the planning, see the war and all its atrocities from the comfort of our living room. The war is a simulation: we are not there, nor will we ever be there. All we will know is the hyper-reality that media messages convey to us (Baudrillard, 1991).

Once the media tried to provide copies of reality, but now they are their own reality. This is the postmodern world we live in. The masses for Baudrillard are mass media consumers. Everything is now reproduced – be it on video, TV, CDs or film. It comes to us already as a pre-experienced hyper-reality.

Critical evaluation

This is a fashionable view that certainly places a great deal of importance on media images. But in that lies the critique. For Baudrillard is accused of excess. For him, it is often as if the Gulf War did not really happen, or indeed that any reality outside the media really happens. This is a serious problem, not least since large numbers of the world's population are not caught up in the media – millions still have no access to the media. And of those that do, many can clearly distinguish between signs and realities.

Three key questions in media analysis

The pioneering media analyst Harold Laswell once said that the goal of media research is to answer the question: *Who* says *what*, in *which channel*, to *whom* with *what effect* (Laswell, 1948)? Following this, and putting it simply, we can say that media analysis directs our attention to three broad areas: codes, encoding and decoding (see Figure 21.1). **Codes** are *rule-governed systems of signs*, **encoding**

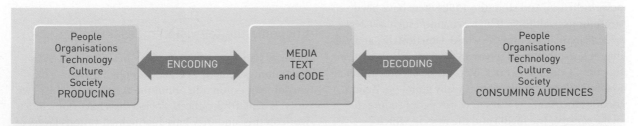

Figure 21.1 A model of media analysis: three questions

involves *putting a message of any kind into a language*, and **decoding** is *the process by which we hear or read and understand a message*.

The first highlights the codes in **media texts**, that is *all media products, such as television programmes, films, CDs, books, newspapers, website pages, etc*. We look for the *logics and rules* that pattern these messages, for they are not usually random. The focus here is on the contents of the media and what organises them. It involves looking at specific contents such as chat shows (on television and radio), film (for example, comedies or musicals) and 'stars' such as Madonna or Eminem. Media texts are analysed for the messages they are trying to get across and their various biases.

A second area concerns the ways in which these media texts are produced. This involves looking at the technologies that emerge to present texts, along with the people who make programmes and their wider social locations. This is called *encoding*, and it enables messages to be put into a language – be they spoken or written, verbal or pictorial. It involves looking at such matters as how journalists produce the news, how specific technologies, such as the Sony Walkman, are manufactured for music production, or the organisation of finance in the ownership of media.

A third question looks at *decoding*. Here the focus is on the audience. This involves looking at such matters as how families watch television, studying soap opera fans, or looking at the way gender may shape how films are viewed (Hall, 1980).

All three act as a feedback loop. In what follows, we will look at some examples of dealing with these questions.

Television news as an example

News is a central media product in modern societies. Not only was the news press the first major means of mass communication in the nineteenth century, but today most TV channels adopt specific mechanisms for the delivery of news. Many radio stations in the UK punctuate their programmes with hourly or half-hourly news bulletins. And since the 1980s there have been continuous 'wall-to-wall' news channels such as CNN, which circulate around the world. Functionalist analysis may suggest that news serves an important information function. Conflict theories, by contrast, see the media as ideological, mystifying what is really going on. Action theories focus on the ways in which people come to make sense of the media and the ways in which audiences read their messages.

The television message as a code

All the programmes and images on TV can be examined for the kinds of values and messages they get across. Take the example of television news: many of us watch it every day. But 'textual sociologists' attempt to see it as a system of codes and values and, if the news does not fit these values, it will not work. Golding and Elliot, in a classic study, suggest that news values include:

- *Featuring of personalities*. Stories need a human angle – people and personalities who have a story to tell. Abstractions and theories are not favoured, but interesting personal stories are.

- *Elites*. The featuring of big or well-known names is better than featuring 'nobodies'.

- *Narrative structures that contain key elements of human drama*. Joy, sorrow, shock, fear, these are the stuff of news.

- *Good visuals and aesthetics*. Since television is a visual medium, news stories without good images become less newsworthy than those with good images. Sometimes news stories may be included simply because there are good images!

- *Entertainment value to attract large audiences*. News must provide materials which are captivating, humorous, titillating, amusing or generally diverting.

- *Importance*. The news item must have significance for large numbers of people in the audience.

- *Proximity*. News stories must be recent and relatively local. Foreign news must have local significance. The news in Norway cannot be the same as the news in Brazil.

- *Brevity*. Nothing can last too long and everything must be packed with information. News is part of what has been called the 'three-minute blip culture'.

- *Negativity*. Bad news is good news. It registers potential threats to social order.

- *Recency*. A premium is put on being first with the news. Once a competitor has the story, it becomes less significant (adapted from Golding and Elliott, 1979: 114–123).

Encoding the television message

Here we start to examine the ways in which television programmes actually get made. Applied to 'news', the encoding question asks about the ways in which a 'news story' is actually produced. Sociologists have done much work on this, and they have highlighted various layers of production.

A first layer looks at the actual *demands of the news programme itself*. Here there is an immediate daily time cycle, a planning structure which creates a routine agenda of predictable stories that provide the background of each day's production requirement (Schlesinger, 1978: 79). Far from being 'news', much of it is planned and routine. Slots need filling: an opening story, a limited number of stories required to fill a 15-minute space, good visuals, all following a regular schedule. Slots must be produced three times a day at the correct time (if there is no news, something has to be found; and if there is too much news, some of it has to be edited out).

A second layer looks at the *day-to-day practices of news journalists*. Here a specific culture of work helps journalists look out for certain kinds of news and not others. It is 'purposive behaviour' (Molotch and Lester, 1974).

A third layer sees the news as being structured by the *organisational demands of a bureaucracy*. We have seen in Chapter 6 how modern organisations tend to be highly ruled-governed agencies: news is produced through such rules. Most noticeable are the rules of news production that are tightly linked to a 'stopwatch culture' (Schlesinger, 1978: 83).

A fourth layer sees the news in the wider context of the *workings of the corporations*. Here such matters as financial structure become important. News that is too offensive or disturbing may lose advertising revenue.

Finally, the news may be linked to wider concerns such as the *community needs and the dominant ideologies*. The Glasgow Media Group (1982) found that wider influences were at work, such that 'impartial news' often reflected a particular mindset of middle-class values.

Decoding the television message

The decoding issue turns to how actual audiences may interpret and watch the news. Here, the task is to get close to actual audiences to see the ways they make sense of the programmes they watch. Often this has a strongly gendered pattern; it may also be shaped by such things as class, age, ethnicity and sexuality. How we 'read' the media is known as audience ethnography (see below).

In one celebrated study, the UK media sociologist David Morley examined the audiences of *Nationwide* (a popular UK 1970s news programme). He works from the premise that the programme can be 'read' or viewed in a number of different ways. The text is *polysemic, open to many interpretations*. He was interested in showing the programme to a range of different groups (university arts students, trade unionists, apprentices, etc.) and getting their feedback. From this, Morley aimed to generate a typology of the 'decodings' made and to analyse their variety.

Broadly, what he found were three main positions in which the 'decoder' stood in relation to the text. For some, the meaning was taken fully within the framework which the message itself suggested (he calls this '*the dominant code*'). For others, the meaning was broadly encoded this way, but through relating it to some specific concrete context which reflected the reader's own position the meaning was modified ('*the negotiated code*'). For still others, they recognised what was trying to be said, but rejected it and imposed a meaning that worked in an opposite way (an '*oppositional reading*') (Morley, 1992: 89).

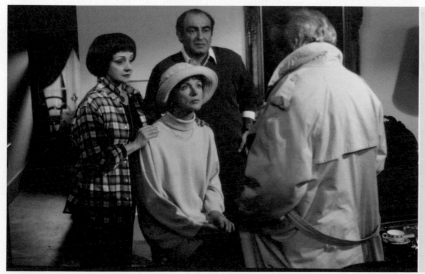

Still from *Une famille formidable*, French soap.
Source: © Pascal Baril/Corbis Kipa

What is important about this approach is the way in which it never sees viewers as passive dummies just soaking up the news. Instead, the news is approached actively and audiences have to work to give it meanings.

Looking at media content

A number of theories have been developed to help us analyse and 'read' the texts and images of the media. We will look at just two: genre theory and semiology. (Others that could be looked at include narrative theory and code analysis.)

Genre theory (from Latin *genus*, meaning 'type') helps us make sense of the seemingly chaotic flux of media programmes by identifying recognisable categories (Table 21.4). Each may then have its own set of rules and codes through which it is turned into a recognisable form.

As an example consider the soap opera – a very popular topic for media analysis. Whether one is a fan of *EastEnders*, *Neighbours*, *Emmerdale*, *Coronation Street*, *Brookside*, *Crossroads* or countless others, certain broad features make them identifiable as a type of programme. (They all, by the way, have their own elaborate websites as well as fanzines and regular features in soap magazines!) Of course, the specific contents, characters and plots will vary. But as a type, soap operas are all likely to have the following.

- *A never-ending story*. Storylines must always carry over to the next episode – there can be no closure as in a one-hour drama.

- *Regular cliff-hangers*. Each episode must come to some sort of climax. Every hour or half-hour, the programme needs to have a crisis which will make the viewer wish to watch the next episode. The programme has to be a 'tease'.

- *Core characters*. The viewers become very familiar with the characters – they come to know a lot about them through watching many episodes. There are a lot of 'regulars' in soaps.

- *Interweaving storylines*. There are never just one or two plots, but a number. There are always several narrative strands proceeding at the same time.

- *The unfolding text*. Narrative progression has to be fairly slow. Often a storyline unfolds over weeks.

- *A woman's genre*. Women are more likely to feature in soaps, and women are more likely to watch them (see Geraghty, 1991; Allen, 1992, 1995)!

Semiology and the study of signs

As we have seen in Chapter 5, semiology is the study of signs. Semiology studies all signs: 'images, gestures, musical sounds, objects and the complex associations of all these, which form the content of ritual, convention or public entertainment' (Barthes, 1967: 9). Signs have no intrinsic or fixed meanings. Instead, their meaning is arbitrary and derived from the way they relate to other words and signs. Language has two components: *langue* (language) and *parole* (speech). The former is the rules and structures of language; the latter is its practice in actual speech and writing. Studying langue would enable the analyst to get at the underlying structures of language. Applied to the media, we become concerned with analysing the content of media as a system of signs, tracing out their relationships to each other – and possibly to an underlying pattern.

Looking at media audiences

One major concern in contemporary approaches to the mass media has been the audience and the impact of media upon them. Modern audiences differ from those of the past. Once – in theatres and stadia – audiences were linked to a specific public setting, planned,

Table 21.4	Television programmes and genre	
TV programmes can be identified by types		
Genre	UK	Global
News, current affairs	BBC News; ITV; *Panorama*	CNN
Documentaries	*Life on Earth*	*National Geographic*
Soap operas	*Coronation Street*; *EastEnders*	*Home and Away* (Australian); *Telenovela* (Latin America exported to the US)
Sitcoms	*The Office*	*Friends* (US)

organised and collectively shared. These days audiences have become much more fragmented and individualised. It is the difference between watching a film in a cinema and watching a video at home. One is public and shared; the other private and personalised.

The main concern of researchers has been to look at the ways in which media impacts audiences. One classic study which looked at the impact of television on children's lives gives a typically cautious conclusion:

> For some children under *some* conditions *some* television is harmful. For *other* children under the *same* conditions, or for the *same* children under *other* conditions, it may be beneficial. For *most* children under *most* conditions, *most* television is neither harmful nor potentially beneficial.
>
> (Schramm, 1961)

Although there has been a long tradition of examining so-called media effects – what the media do to people – it is only fairly recently that researchers have switched the question from what the media do to people to what people do to the media. The classical 'effects literature' has tended to see audiences as fairly passive recipients of media messages. As we have seen above, the most extreme version of this is the hypodermic syringe model – where people are seen to be passively injected with media messages. While no media analyst holds such a view today, it remains popular among public and media moralists. For instance, in the aftermath of the murder of a young child, James Bulger, in the UK in 1993 by two young boys, the video of *Child's Play 3* (in which a similar kind of murder was to be seen) was evoked as a cause of the murder. While it is possible to say that the film may have played a part in the murder – along with many other factors – it cannot be said to have simply caused it.

More recent approaches to the media audience tend to conduct ethnographic research on specific audiences.

Thus, the researcher may enter a 'fan group' and see how they watch their favourite star. Or the researcher may observe and interview women as to how they watch soap operas and what they indeed like about them. In one celebrated study, David Morley entered families and observed the ways in which they watched the media.

Looking at 18 south London working-class families, Morley observed how they used television. One of his key themes is the way such viewing is structured by gender. Among his findings, which have to be seen as very provisional because of the scale of his study, he suggests:

- Adult men have most control over the programme choice, and the video is more likely to be controlled by 'dad'.

- Women are usually engaged in other domestic activities, and watch television more sporadically (except in 'solo' watching by daytime). Husbands seem to watch more than wives.

- Men are more systematic and focused: they watch more attentively.

- Men prefer sport and news, while women prefer drama and fiction features.

- Women are more likely to express guilt over their viewing habits; they also use it as a conversation piece more (Morley, 1986: Chapter 3).

The fragmentation of the mass audience

Although many critics have argued that this is the age of 'mass society', others have argued that what we are seeing is a breakdown of the population into hundreds of very different audiences. To take an example: the world of music used to be divisible into a few broad groupings. There was 'classical music', 'popular music', maybe 'jazz' and a few others. Now, as any browser at a record 'megastore' will find, audiences for music have splintered

Are children affected by video violence? The debate goes on.
Source: Getty Images © Photodisk 1999

in many directions: new age, ethnic, rock, classic rock, show tunes, country and western, punk, reggae, folk. But these are broken down into further categories. Show tunes has its Sondheim aficionados who would not go near an Andrew Lloyd Webber score. And there are those who seek out the most obscure musicals that only ran for one night. And so on. What has happened is the emergence of many media markets – niche markets. At the same time, some 90 per cent of all albums sold in Europe are for rock or light music, while 5–10 per cent are classical (Therborn, 1995: 224).

This may be depicted, as in Figure 21.2, as a move from media having elite audiences, through those having mass audiences to those having more specialised audiences. When a new medium appears it is usually adopted by an educational elite, before spreading out to a wider mass audience. After a while this splinters into a host of specialist groupings. What this means is that much media expansion takes place through increasingly specialised audiences (Figure 21.3).

The globalisation of the media

Throughout the twentieth century, media proliferated and became extended across the world. Indeed, they are one of the central mechanisms through which the processes of globalisation have taken place. Most countries are now connected to film, video, television satellites and cables. And the prognosis is that this will continue to grow in the twenty-first century.

The World Bank says that: 'The global economy is undergoing an Information Revolution that will be as significant in effect as the Industrial Revolution of the

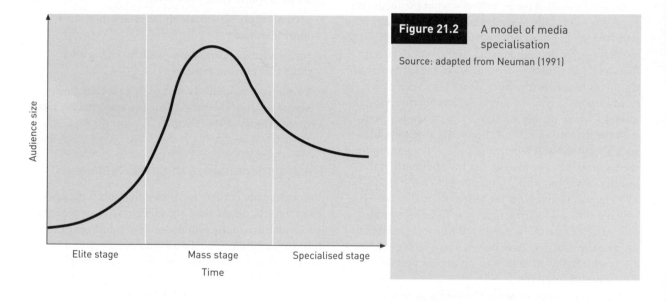

Figure 21.2   A model of media specialisation

Source: adapted from Neuman (1991)

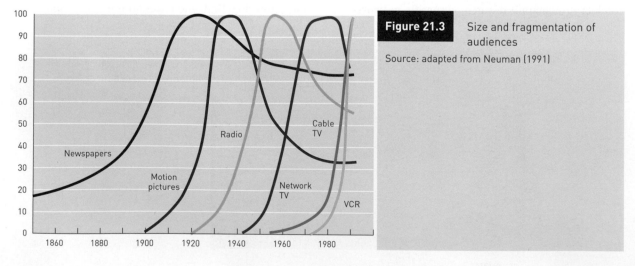

Figure 21.3   Size and fragmentation of audiences

Source: adapted from Neuman (1991)

nineteenth century' (1997: 287). Indeed, worth some £1,000 billion in 1994, the World Bank reckons that the information economy is growing faster than the global economy. Figure 21.4 charts some of the countries participating in the information economy.

Television is at the forefront of the globalisation of the media. While it is still the case that there are hundreds of millions of people who have never seen a television set (especially in Africa which has only 2.5 per cent of the world's televisions), in many of the poorer countries it often assumes pride of place in the home, or is watched by many in communal places. It is estimated that some 2.5 billion people have regular access to television, the dominant growth areas being Africa, Asia and Central

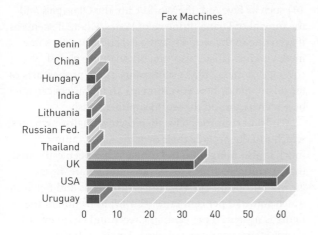

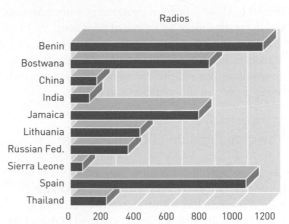

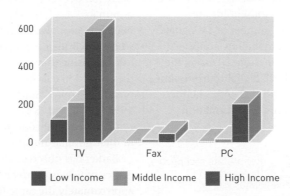

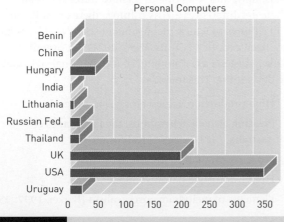

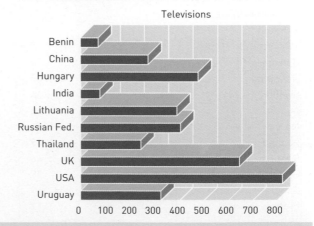

Figure 21.4 Global use of media: some examples

Source: adapted from *World Development Report* by World Bank, The Office of the Publisher. Copyright 1997 by World Bank. Reproduced with permission of World Bank in the format Textbook via Copyright Clearance Center

America (Barker, 1997: 4). Asia has the highest growth. In the People's Republic of China, there was an increase from 18 million in 1975 to 540 million in 1985 to 980 million in 1995. Chinese state television now claims to reach some 84 per cent of the population.

Although the West has had a pronounced influence on the making of television across the world, there seems to be a cycle at work. In globalisation, the West first makes an impact but gradually local programmers become more involved, creating more and more of their own programmes and enhancing national visibility. Eventually local programming becomes dominant, even when based on Western programmes. We can distinguish three key aspects of this globalisation process.

1. The globalisation of media forms

The *means* for such proliferation have grown via new technologies. Many countries initially only had their own local systems, but with the growth of cable and satellite during the 1980s, this has changed (Table 21.5). Cable may not be very significant in the UK, but in The Netherlands some 90 per cent of households are connected. Satellites increase the number of TV signals. ISDN networks (higher bandwidths) allow almost everyone to broadcast their own messages. During the 1990s, there was a massive shift to 'digital transmission' of all kinds of data, and this, combined with satellite, has meant the rapid expansion of the 'information superhighway', with three cores in North America, Europe and East Asia.

2. The globalisation of content

The *content* of programmes has also become increasingly global. There are 'global totemic festivals' (Barker, 1997: 14) such as Live Aid, the World Cup, the Olympics and the funeral of Diana, Princess of Wales, where it seems as if everyone in the world may be experiencing the same media events. This is also true of much live global coverage of many news events: wars, space probes, acts of terrorism, major new governments and disasters can all be screened around the world simultaneously.

While all countries have their own specialist networks which usually provide their own local programming, much is also bought in. In Europe, it has been estimated that around two-thirds of TV programmes are 'home grown' European. The UK, The Netherlands and Belgium watch some 70 per cent European TV; in Denmark the figure is nearer 75 per cent; in Greece and Germany it is nearer 80 per cent. Nevertheless, American films dominate West European markets. Likewise, the music market is strongly American, although this is also an area where the British excel (Therborn, 1995: 223–224). It is not surprising that when people are questioned where they would like to live if they had to live abroad, most prefer the United States, Canada or Australia (Therborn, 1995: 224). And as Therborn (1995: 225) says, 'Europe is not a meaningful concept of current youth culture' (most of their popular music does not come from there).

Barker has observed that there is a tendency for some genres of television to be recycled everywhere in approximately the same forms throughout the world. Thus, news and soap operas seem to travel very well. There *are* differences across cultures: there are still some 150 cultures to which the Australian soap *Neighbours* has not been exported (Crofts, 1995: 102)! But overall, Barker suggests a certain kind of international style may be developing. This includes:

- High production values: glossy and expensive
- Pleasing visual backgrounds: the landscapes of Australia, the beaches of California
- More action than in traditional soaps
- Hollywood-style narrative mode
- Elements of melodrama over realism (Barker, 1997: 95).

Likewise, Barker finds news narration similar. What is news is fairly consistent from country to country, although there are some variations.

Table 21.5	European cable and satellite reception equipment, 1994 (percentage of equipped households)
The Netherlands	98
Belgium	95
Switzerland	75
Germany	70
Denmark	65
Sweden	64
Austria	60
Norway	55
Finland	49
Republic of Ireland	46
United Kingdom	19
Spain	19
France	12

Source: adapted from *Cable and Satellite Europe*, September 1995 (Barker, 1997)

3. The globalisation of ownership and the decline of public television

Traditionally in Europe, radio and television have received *public finance* (via licences and taxes) to provide a *universal service for citizens* by producing programmes which have some form of public *accountability*, some *regulation of content* and some *protection from competition*. The British Broadcasting Corporation is one classic instance of this. It used to account for over half of the viewing time but that proportion is now in serious decline as the new television channels stream online. The BBC World Service, with a long history, is being overtaken by groups such as CNN and MTV. And the story is the same throughout Europe. The Netherlands had 100 per cent public television in 1975, but by 1990 this had been reduced to 58 per cent. In France, the figure was 100 per cent in 1975, reduced to 33 per cent by 1990 (Barker, 1997: 32).

STUDIO ENTERTAINMENT

film production:
- Walt Disney Pictures
- Walt Disney Feature Animation
- Touchstone • Hollywood Pictures
- Caravan Pictures • Miramax Films

television production:
- Walt Disney Network Television
- Walt DisneyTelevision Animation

worldwide film distribution:
- Buena Vista International

recorded music production:
- Buena Vista Music Group

home video release:
- Buena Vista Home Entertainment.

In 2000, Disney won the highest share of the US domestic cinema market for the third year in succession.

Even so, Studio Entertainment's profits nose-dived.

1997 $1,079m
1998 $769m
1999 $116m

Buena Vista Home Entertainment was blamed. Its policy of releasing Disney classics only for limited periods – irritating both small children and harassed parents – has been dumped.

THE BOTTOM LINE
Disney revenue and profit 1995–1999
US$ billion 2000

THEME PARKS AND RESORTS
- 7 theme parks
- 27 hotels
- 2 cruise ships

More punters are going through the turnstiles, and they are spending more. The division is booming, with annual profits increasing by almost 14%. In 2001, new sites were being built in the USA, Japan and France, despite a bumpy introduction for the first Disneyland Paris. Another is planned in Hong Kong.

PUBLISHING

book publishers, including:
- Walt Disney Book Publishing
- Hyperion
- Miramax Books

four magazine publishing groups, including:
- Women's Wear Daily

11 newspapers, including:
- St Louis Daily Record
- Daily Tidings in Orlando
- Oakland Press and Reminder

SPORTS AND THEATRE

Walt Disney Theatrical Productions develops stage musicals, mostly based on Disney cartoon features, such as The Lion King and Beauty and the Beast. Disney also owns

- a National Hockey league team, the Mighty Ducks of Anaheim

- a share in a major league baseball franchise, the Anaheim Angels

- the Walt Disney World Sports Complex, which boasts a golf course, an auto racing track and baseball complex.

BROADCASTING

Although Disney had television and radio interests before 1996, it was the aquisition of ABC that made broadcasting the heartland of the Disney empire. The deal delivered:

- the ABC television network
- 10 TV stations in US regional markets
- radio news networks
- ESPN, a sports radio network
- Radio Disney, a children's radio network
- 42 radio stations
- ABC Television Entertainment Group, a programme maker

HOW THE DISNEY COOKIE CRUMBLES
1999

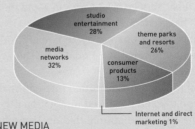

NEW MEDIA

By the end of 1999, Disney had invested US $500 million in Internet activities, despite accumulating losses since 1997. Having bought the search engine Infoseek, Disney then merged it with the rest of its Internet and Direct Marketing division to create the new Disney-oriented portal Go.com. This also provides a domain name around which Disney's other websites are organised. Sites such as disney.go.com, abc.go.com and espn.go.com rank sixth in popularity among US users, attracting 23.1 million visitors in May 2000 alone.

CABLE
- 100% ownership of Disney Channel, Toon Disney and SoapNet
- 80% ownership of sports channel ESPN
- 50% ownership of Lifetime Television
- minority shares in E! Entertainment, A&E and The History Channel

Although Disney's cable business is smaller than its broadcasting business, it is more profitable and it is growing at a faster rate, in line with the general trend in US television, as the networks grapple with declining audience figures and spiralling programme production costs.

Figure 21.5   The wonderful world of Disney's media empire

Source: adapted from *The Global Media Atlas* pp. 64–65 © Myriad Editions Limited, www.MyriadEditions.com

Deregulated television is private and less accountable than public television. Its programmes are more 'market led'. There has been a real shift from a public service idea to a commercialised one with advertising at its core. But it goes further than this: the media is now often owned transnationally.

Although they are constantly merging and buying each other up, the leading media firms in the world are usually said to include Time-Warner (with sales approaching £17 billion in 1997), Disney (£16 billion) (Figure 21.5), Bertelsmann (£10 billion, and the only Europe-based firm), Viacom (£8 billion) and News Corporation (£7 billion). Typically, these firms have media holdings in a wide range of enterprises. For example, *News Corporation*, owned by Rupert Murdoch, has holdings in Twentieth Century Fox (film, television and video and Fox News), 132 newspapers (in Australia, the UK and the United States), 25 magazines, book publishing, Asian Star Television and BSkyB Television satellite. It also has large stakes in Germany's Vox channel, Sky Latin America, Japan Sky Broadcasting, Australian Foxtel Cable, Spanish El Canal Fox, India Sky Broadcasting, Channel V (an Asian music video channel) and Hong Kong Phoenix satellite.

To take another example, *TimeWarner* (with an international labour force of around 340,000) has holdings in 24 magazines (including *Time*), the second largest book publishing business in the world, Warner Bros. films, Warner music group, cinemas, comics, Home Box Office (the largest cable channel in the world), Six Flags theme parks, Warner Bros. retail stores, several global cable channels including CNN, TBS and TNY, Turner Classic movies, The Cartoon Network and CNN-SI all sports news channel, and on, and on (Herman and McChesney, 1997: Chapter 3). In January 2001, it merged with America Online (AOL), making it the world's biggest media company.

Global media are transmitted internationally, received internationally and produced internationally; and they lead to massive international trading. Very often these transnational companies, in putting together the 'media texts', also connect with the equipment manufacturers, combining software and hardware, to make an overall 'synergy'. Barker cites the case of the film *Last Action Hero*: 'This Schwarzenegger 'blockbuster' was made by Columbia Pictures, owned by Sony Corporation. The soundtrack came from CBS, also owned by Sony, and it was screened in cinemas with digital sound systems made by Sony. In addition, Sony produced virtual reality and videogames based on the film.' And, no doubt, these would be played on Sony screens (Barker, 1997: 25).

The growth of Al-Jazeera

One interesting 'global' television service (recently much talked about) is that of *Al-Jazeera* (a term that in Arabic means 'The Peninsula'). Arab television developed from 1996 after the decline of the London-based BBC Arabic network. Based in Qatar (in the Gulf region), it is a state-sponsored Arabic news channel, having (in 2002) a regular audience of 35 million (and is available to some 310 million worldwide). It exists in a region stigmatised for decades and open to huge censorship. After 11 September 2001, this satellite television station became prominent in its coverage of the Afghanistan war, especially exclusive video tapes of Osama bin Laden. Although the United States has tried setting up its own Arab language news channel in the Middle East, it has not proved popular. Al-Jazeera provides the 'other side of the story' (Miladi, 2003: 158), giving global coverage to news that is usually dominated by the English-speaking Western world (especially the United States and the UK) (Miladi, 2003).

The rise of the Internet

Despite the significance of all the media forms discussed in this chapter – from film to television – there is one recent development that is generally considered to bring about the most profound changes of all. This is the emergence of the Internet, a topic that has been raised in earlier chapters (see Chapter 6). This is also coming under the regulation of the media giants, as telecommunication firms merge and join forces with them. But it is also the case that at present it is the form of media which encourages globalisation in a highly individual, fragmented and participatory manner. We discuss this more fully in the next chapter.

Looking ahead: the future of the media

Sociology has come increasingly to recognise that throughout the twentieth century the mass media came to play a growing importance in the lives of societies. This is not just true of the industrial West, but of nearly all cultures. Global 'mediasation' has become a major process in the twenty-first century. The full implications of this have yet to be grasped, but we need to consider at least three questions.

PROFILE

JÜRGEN HABERMAS: THE CHANGING PUBLIC SPHERE

Jürgen Habermas
Source: © Rex features/SIPA

The German sociologist Jürgen Habermas (1929–) is considered one of the world's foremost contemporary social theorists.

Habermas has been concerned with the 'life world' (the immediate environment of the 'social actor'), with knowledge and communication, and how it changes in the modern world. He is concerned with what he calls the changes in the public and private spheres of modern societies. The public sphere is 'a domain of our social life in which such a thing as public opinion can be formed . . . and is open in principle to all citizens' (Habermas, 1989; orig. 1962). The public sphere is an arena where public debate flourishes, and ideas and opinions can grow. Habermas traces its history, suggesting that it was in seventeenth- and eighteenth-century Europe that it developed a clear form. Between the realm of the state (see Chapter 15) and the private sphere of the family, there emerged a new public sphere which allowed people to exercise judgement and to critically engage in public debate. This may have been in the salons and coffee houses of the big European cities.

But nowadays, he worries, such debates have been narrowed by the collapse of this sphere into the mass media. It was originally the newspapers and the mass tabloids that first significantly brought about this change. They developed a much more commercial and consumer-based culture which was linked much more to the privatised worlds of money and commerce rather than a public forum of debate.

He worries about the future of democracy as the media expand and proposes a theory of communicative action. He sees three forms of knowledge at work in society. First is instrumental knowledge which is technical and scientific. Much of this has worked against human progress and has impoverished human lives. Second is hermeneutic knowledge, where the focus is on understanding. But Habermas looks for a third form of knowledge, which could be 'emancipatory'. Believing in progress and modernity, he believes societies can only move forward if people can peel away all the irrationalities partially bestowed on them by media messages and arrive at a 'pure speech' situation in which they can understand clearly each other's ideas. At present this is made impossible because of technology.

First, it seems likely that more and more of our lives – and those of our children – will come to be lived away from the real world and inside a media-created one. Once the full implications of home multimedia start to be realised, will we spend less and less time in public space confronting real events and more and more time in a virtual space? Is the simulacrum arriving?

Second, the media world seems set to become increasingly a commercialised global one dominated by huge transnational corporations. To the extent that this happens, will this mean not only an increasing homogenisation of different cultures, but also a real threat to democracy as more and more of what we see in the world is regulated by high finance?

But third, the top Internet countries are overwhelmingly in the West: 90 per cent of users in 1995 were in North America and Western Europe. At least 80 per cent of the world's countries still lack communications technologies. And overwhelmingly, the typical user of the Net is a North American male looking for entertainment. Although globalisation may be taking place, is this a process that will have serious consequences for the wider inequalities in society?

CONTROVERSY AND DEBATE

ARE THE MEDIA WEAKENING SOCIETY?

Ever since their inception, the mass media have always been attacked as dangerous. They have been at the centre of controversy. In the very earliest days, when books and novels started to be published, there were worries that these could be corrupting. As the earliest popular literature slowly became available to the 'masses', so it was denounced. In 1806, a Samuel P. Jarvis said that 'The evil consequences attendant upon novel reading are much greater than has generally been imagined' (Starker, 1989: 61). Much later, in the 1930s, radio programmes caused great alarm, and Lyman Bryson wrote:

> All great human inventions, even printing, even language itself, have proved to be two-edged swords. They can do as much evil as good. Radio is as great – and as dangerous – as any . . . and it can broadcast injury and discord and ugliness into the farthest reaches of inhabited space. To be lightminded about the radio is to jig along a precipice . . .
>
> Starker (1989: 115)

These days every new media form comes under attack. When Dungeons and Dragons (D&D) was first marketed in 1973 (with 8 million copies sold by 1985), it was accused of 'dabbling in the demonic' by *Christianity Today*. And attempts were made to link teenage suicides and murders to it. In 1992, the issue became 'rap and race' with the song Cop Killer by Ice-T prompting a boycott of Warner Bros. records by parents anxious about lyrics such as:

> I'm 'bout to bust some shots off,
> I'm 'bout to dust some cops off

and a chant:

> Die, Die, Die, Pig, Die.

This may be extreme. But every form of media has had its critics: the early tabloids and newspapers, Hollywood movies from the start of the twentieth century till now, children's comics, the 'plug in drug' of television, 'video nasties', pop music, computers. Over and over again, the media have been posed as a threat and a danger.

Media critics have claimed that the media can have serious effects on its audience. Among the many dangers it poses are the following.

- The fostering of passivity: the 'couch potato' syndrome of inertly watching
- The growth of crime, violence and moral decline: the media shapes low values and provides bad role models
- Trivialisation: we are, in the words of one critic, 'amusing ourselves to death'. Authentic sports, religion and politics get trivialised. Even education becomes 'infotainment'
- The promotion of materialism and commercial values: most media comes with advertising to the forefront and this leads to a 'promotional culture'. Even the weather or the news gets identified with sponsorship
- Brainwashing, manipulation and mass conformity
- The 'simulation' of the world, giving us pseudo-images and false realities: at its most extreme we come to inhabit an unreal media world, cut off from the more authentic experiences.

In short, mass media lead to a degenerating mass culture. As Bernard Rosenberg says: 'At its worst, mass culture threatens not merely to cretinise our taste but to brutalise our sense, while paving the way to totalitarianism' (cited in Starker, 1989: 13).

In contrast, media defenders reject these criticisms and argue that the media can do the following.

- Increase participation and creativity: viewers can be active and critical and use the media – they respond by writing letters, engaging in debates and the like
- Enhance the information a society has and help keep us aware of what is going on
- Increase public debate
- Extend access to all kinds of information and entertainment that previously were restricted to an elite class
- Provide diversity
- Reduce crime and enhance morality through making people more aware of issues.

In short, mass media can enhance a diverse, active and participatory culture.

CONTROVERSY AND DEBATE CONTINUED

Some modern media analysts such as Joli Jensen (1990) see the worry over the media as part of a continuing concern over modernity. The 'dangerous media', they suggest, are repeatedly compared with some mythical golden age in the past and taken to symbolise all the dangers of the modern world – rapid change, differences, a loss of clear authority, etc. They are constantly under attack because they are potent symbols of rapid change and a modern world hurtling into an unknown future. But media are in fact human made, are here to stay and we can shape them in the direction that we wish. They cannot in themselves be blamed for anything.

CONTINUE THE DEBATE:

1. Do you think that watching soap operas – the most popular form of television – can play any useful social role?

2. Do you think 'sport' has been degraded through being turned into a mass media event?

3. Look around you and see what form the attack on the media is currently taking. Dissect this latest example.

4. Weigh up the pros and cons of the new global communications systems.

SUMMARY

1. We live our lives increasingly through the media. Patterns of communication have changed through five main kinds of culture: sign, oral, writing, print and most recently electronic cultures. We now live in a mediated or media-saturated world.

2. Initially sociologists looked at the media through the hypodermic model: this suggests media messages are presented to members of a mass society, who receive them more or less uniformly and are strongly influenced by them. The stimuli lead individuals to respond in a similar, uniform fashion. The effects of mass communication are powerful, uniform and direct. This view has long been discredited and newer theories show the reverse of these assumptions is more or less true.

3. There are many theories of the media. Hypodermic theories of simple media cause and effect are generally discredited. Functionalist theories focus on the ways media perform key functions. Marxist and conflict theory tends to look at the control function of the media and the concentration of media ownership. Interactionist theories focus on meanings and the interpretations of audiences. And postmodern theories tend to focus on the way media assumes a life of its own in the postmodern world, seeing social life as increasingly dominated by simulacra and signs.

4. There are three main areas for a media analysis: media messages, encoding and decoding. Codes are rule-governed systems of signs, encoding involves putting a message of any kind into a language, and decoding is the process by which we hear or read and understand a message.

5. Media texts are analysed through what the media says, how it is produced and how people (audiences) make sense of it.

6. Although there exist public forms of ownership of the media, such as the BBC in the UK, increasingly the media are concentrated in the ownership of a few major companies, such as TimeWarner, Bertelsmann and Viacom.

CRITICAL-THINKING QUESTIONS

1. For the next few days, keep a detailed record of 'you and your media'. Keep a detailed log of just when you engage with the mass media, what the kinds of media were, what messages were sent, and how it impinged on your life. Note all the media you use, from papers and magazines to television and film and CD, PC and mobile. It may surprise you just how much of your life is now 'mediated'.

2. Outline the major 'areas of media' study. Select any one media item, such as a TV programme or a film, and examine the kinds of question you would ask about it.

3. Who owns the media? Using a reference book such as *Who Owns Whom?* examine the ownership of the media and assess the concentration in a few powerful hands.

4. How far do you think mass media has now become globalised? Discuss the implications of this.

GOING FURTHER

Further reading

Introductions to media studies and cultural studies (introduced in Chapter 5):

Fred Inglis, *Media Theory: An Introduction* (1990)

Denis McQuail, *Mass Communication Theory: An Introduction* (4th edn, 2000)
Two classic, comprehensive textbooks.

Paul Marris and Sue Thornham (eds), *Media Studies: A Reader* (1996)
A recent reader which covers the field broadly: there are now a great many of these!

On global media:

Faye Ginsburg, Lila Abu-Lughood and Brian Larkin (eds), *Media Worlds: Anthropology on New Terrain* (2002)
A fascinating series of essays which looks at media in countries as diverse as Tibet, Egypt, Bolivia and northern Nigeria.

Chris Barker, *Global Television: An Introduction* (1997)

Edward S. Herman and Robert W. McChesney, *The Global Media* (2001)
Two comprehensive reviews of the field, though in this rapidly growing field they are both now a little out of date.

Stylianos Papathanassopoulos, *European Television in the Digital Age* (2002)
A guide to the nature of media in Europe.

On the sociology of the audience:

Shaun Moores, *Interpreting Audiences: The Ethnography of Media Consumption* (1993)
Reviews the research on audiences while raising a series of critical problems with them.

General media theory:

Joshua Meyrowitz, *No Sense of Place: The Impact of Electronic Media on Social Behavior* (1986)
A major, and now classic, study which draws upon Goffman (1959) and McLuhan (1964) to show the way in which Television is changing the way we experience the world.

John Thompson, *The Media and Modernity: A Social Theory of Media* (1995)
Examines the rise of media in modern societies.

Norman Denzin, *Images of Postmodern Society: Social Theory and Contemporary Cinema* (1991)
Introduces the idea of the postmodern, discusses the importance of cinema in the twentieth century, and analyses a number of films to show their relevance to modern thinking.

More information

A useful guide to the field is Leah A. Lievrouw and Sonia Livingstone, *Handbook of New Media* (2001). On the media in Europe, see *The Media in Western Europe: The Euromedia Handbook*, edited by Bernt Stubbe Ostergaard and the Euromedia Research Group (2nd edn, 1997). A useful dictionary is James Watson and Anne Hill, *Dictionary of Media and Communication Studies* (5th edn, 2000).

Watch a video

- Orson Welles's *Citizen Kane* (1941): classic 'media mogul' story, based on the life of Randolph Hearst.
- Sydney Lumet's *Network* (1976): Peter Finch and Faye Dunaway in a major media battle – a powerful film.
- Peter Weir's *The Truman Show* (1998) and Gary Ross's *Pleasantville* (1998): two films where 'tele-reality' blurs with reality. Very provocative.
- Robert Redford's *Quiz Show* (1994): media corruption around a 1950s quiz show.

Connecting up

Connect to other chapters

- For links to inequalities, see Chapters 8–13.
- For links to globalisation, see Chapter 2.
- For links to functionalist, conflict and interactionist theories, see Chapter 1.
- For links to theories of culture, see Chapter 5 and for links to societal development, see Chapter 4.

To the websites

- OECD and the Information Economy: http://www.oecd.org/topic/0,2686,en_2649_33757_1_1_1_1_37441,00.html
- UNESCO: http://portal.unesco.org/en
- The Blackwell listing for cultural studies: http://www.blackwellpublishers.co.uk/cultural/
- You may like to dip into the Al-Jazeera website. http://english.aljazeera.net/HomePage

For additional case studies, multiple choice questions, internet exercises, and annotated weblinks specific to this chapter, visit this book's website at www.pearsoned.co.uk/plummer

CHAPTER 22

SCIENCE, CYBERSPACE AND THE RISK SOCIETY

We should be on our guard not to overestimate science and scientific methods when it is a question of human problems; and we should not assume that experts are the only ones who have a right to express themselves on questions affecting the organization of society.

Albert Einstein, cited in Webster (1991: 126)

MICHIO KAKU IS A PHYSICS PROFESSOR and one of those scientists who have a mission to help people see just how much science will change the world. For his best-selling book *Visions: How Science will Revolutionize the 21st Century and Beyond* (1998), he interviewed over 150 scientists over a ten-year period, asking them to predict some of the key changes that were imminent in the world. Some of them we are very familiar with today: telephones, cameras, PCs, faxes, mobile phones, planes, videos, laptops, DVDs. Some we can already see in the making: people walking on the moon; computers that read our voices and talk back to us; children made in test tubes; babies cloned from other babies; smartcards for everything. Ideas that were not on the agenda even 100 years ago, which sounded like pure science fiction, have already happened. But he goes much further than this. He suggests that over the next decades, we will be developing 'smart homes' where our living spaces are fully wired to deal with our every need through hundreds of mini-computers. We will be solving major problems of health through the Human Genome Project's ability to identify major illness linked to genes. Longevity will be radically increased. We will be harnessing the energy from the universe to meet our daily needs. And we will create a 'planetary civilization' capable of regular travel to, living on and communicating with other planets. Reading his book is almost like reading science fiction, yet he claims that this is the scientific future. And if it is, what kind of new society will this bring?

KEY THEMES

- The nature of science in the modern world
- The significance of sociology for science
- Dominant tendencies towards evolutionary thinking
- The relevance of sociology in biotechnology
- The impact of cyberspace on social life

(Left) Galileo showing his telescope to the Doge, Florence, Tribuna di Galileo
Source: Scala, Florence

As we saw in Chapter 1, sociology was born out of a concern with the changing character of this modern, industrial world, with where we have come from and where we are heading. Behind some of these changes was the rapid growth of science as a form of knowledge, and along with it the rise of many new technologies. This chapter looks at the role of knowledge and science in the modern world, and asks about some of the social issues that are raised around them.

Risk and the three scientific revolutions of the twentieth century

Michio Kaku talks of the 'three pillars of science' which he sees as matter, life and mind. Matter leads to the science of the universe, and the *Quantum Revolution*. Life leads to the science of biogenetics and leads to the

This walking robot is a composite image of the M2 robot with the torso of roboticist Dan Paluska. Designed to walk like a human using fluid rather than stiff robotic movement, it follows rules from computer simulations making changes in response to local conditions.

Source: Science Photo Library © Peter Menzel

Biomolecular Revolution. Mind leads to the science of information and the *Computer Revolution*. With these, science in the twentieth century brought three great 'discoveries': the atom, the gene and the computer. Indeed, there has been a move from 'an age of discovery' to 'an age of mastery' (Kaku, 1998: 5).

Science on its own can be 'purely academic'. It may be theoretical and abstract and of little consequence to the daily life of most of the world. Once it starts to be applied through technology, however, each one of its concerns comes to raise vast social and political implications. Thus, for example, the Quantum Revolution may have discovered the atom, but it took technology to harness this enormous energy to put people on the moon *and* to create the atom bombs which dropped on Hiroshima and Nagasaki, killing an estimated 75,000 people. The Biomolecular Revolution may have discovered the gene, but it took people to turn it into a technology called the Human Genome Project which aimed to map out the complete genetic structure of the human being *and* to raise the spectre of cloning, designer babies and racial eugenics. The Information (Computer) Revolution may have discovered digitalisation, but it took people to turn it into modern information technology which has generated unparalleled communication possibilities *and* unleashed a whole array of ethical and political issues, from the 'surveillance society' to the potential for cyborg machines to (eventually) take over from human life. At times, the genre of science-fiction writing seems to come close to reality! We will return to this later in the chapter.

Science, technology and the Risk Society

Recall how in Chapter 2 we introduced the ideas of Ulrich Beck on a *World Risk Society*. We will now start to see in this chapter how the new sciences are generating new technologies which 'manufacture' risks that are different from those found in more traditional societies. These new technologies are humanly produced yet often quite invisible: we just do not know where they may lead us and what dangers they may bring. Scientific 'experts' have the skills and knowledge of science, but the social, ethical and political implications of what they do are a matter not simply for them – 'the experts' – but for everyone in society. In this chapter we shall consider a number of areas, from genetic engineering to computers, which have consequences that we cannot easily predict. In Chapter 24 we shall take this further by considering changes in the environment. Right now, we start our discussion by considering just what science is.

Knowledge and science: traditions of study

Simply put, we know common-sensically what science is through its various manifestations. We do not just see it at work as we use our everyday objects (from mobiles to computers, from cars to planes), but we also grasp it as we look at the world: the infinity of space and its vastness; the random evolutionary mutations that may have brought us human beings about; the existence of DNA. Table 22.1 suggests some of the major developments. Aspects of scientific thought have long existed across civilisations, often as 'natural philosophy', but they were heavily infused with metaphysical and religious assumptions. The so-called *Age of Science* arrives when the belief in our ability to transform the world through 'objective' knowledge becomes a major mode of thought. Human beings become capable of radically transforming, controlling and innovating their worlds. And this is surely one of the keys to industrialisation and social change – the world now looks radically different because of the uses of scientific knowledge.

Sociologists have long been interested not only in seeing whether the study of society could be scientific (see Chapters 2 and 3), but also in studying just what is meant by knowledge and science. Karl Mannheim (1893–1947) is generally seen as the founder of what has come to be known as the **sociology of knowledge**, *that branch of sociology which sees an association between forms of knowledge and society*. Born in Hungary, moving to Germany but leaving there in 1933 for the London School of Economics, he is a key figure in shaping this sociology. He agreed with Marx that belonging to certain groups could shape the kind of beliefs we held. But unlike Marx, he did not always see those groups as class or economic groups. His basic insight was that all knowledge, ideas or 'science' depend upon social structures and situations to shape them.

In what follows, we will start to look at some of the issues that sociologists and others have raised in understanding 'science'.

Paradigms and the philosophy of science

Thomas S. Kuhn (1922–96) suggested that scientists are socialised into scientific communities. These have their own own conventions of knowledge and ways of doing science. They generate their own 'puzzle solving' within an almost unquestioned set of beliefs. Thus, **paradigms** are born: *general ways of seeing the world which suggest what can be seen, done and theorised about in science*. Paradigms

provide 'normal science'. Everyday scientists engage in puzzle solving. There is no objective truth, only a consensus about the truth. As work proceeds, anomalies start to pile up: things that do not fit, or make sense. This leads eventually to a 'paradigmatic crisis' from which a new paradigm may emerge. For Kuhn, there is strictly no clear logical reason why this shift happens: Aristotelian physics was not simply bad Newtonian physics, it was based on a different paradigm, a radically different way of seeing the world.

Many philosophers of science are critical of this view. Karl Popper (1902–94) was one such major critic and Kuhn's major opponent. For Popper, science can never prove the facts of the world: its task is to *falsify* and show what is not or cannot be. One negative case will tell you that a theory or hypothesis is not true. For Popper, scientists should start with a theory and then test it against the world of evidence. They establish very specific hypotheses from which predictions may be made. (For example, Newton's Law of Gravitation suggests specific hypotheses around the movement of bodies.) For Popper, then, 'objective knowledge' could be approached through falsification, not verification, and through deduction, not induction. These are the keys to science, and we discussed some of this in Chapter 3. The debates between Kuhn and Popper are largely philosophical ones but they anticipated the arrival of a tradition of sociological enquiry into science.

The institutional sociology of science

Robert King Merton (1910–2003), a leading functionalist, originally presented his sociology of science in 1942. He saw that science – emerging in the seventeenth century – was analogous to the rise of the Protestant ethic (which is discussed in Chapter 4). Both were opposed to dogma and both fostered forms of hard work. In part, Merton's work was a critique of Soviet and Nazi claims that science was shaped by factors of class or race. He focused especially on the rise of the sciences in the seventeenth century, and suggested that science developed its own 'ethos' (or way of life) with its own distinctive community and culture. Four key norms organised scientific work. These were:

1. *Universalism*. Science should be guided by the search for wider, universal truths and should not be biased by more particular claims linked to, say, class or gender.
2. *Communalism*. Scientists should believe in the earlier findings of science as a common heritage.

Table 22.1	Landmarks of science		
Year* Science		Technology	Society
1600	Kepler – planetary orbits Galileo – mechanics Descartes – mechanical philosophy, analytical geometry Harvey – circulation of blood Classification of plants	Problems of navigation Use of telescope Bacon's view of research	Early colonists in America Persecution of witches Thirty Years' War – religious discord in Europe Growth of early capitalism
1650	Rise of English science Boyle – gas law Alchemical experimentation Huygens – pendulum and wave theory of light Newton – calculus, gravitation, optics	Mercury barometer Improved microscopes Study of pumps and gases	English Civil War Growth of ideas of liberty, toleration and possessive individualism Founding of Royal Society and Académie des Sciences Constitutional monarchy in England Louis XIV in France
1700	Linnaean classification of living things Stagnation in English science	Savery's steam pump Newcomen's steam engine Growth of small-scale manufacture Improved iron and steel making	Establishment of public banks 'Classical' architecture and art English mercantilist colonial policies
1750	Studies in electrostatics Early debates on origin of earth, fossils, flood, etc. Phlogiston theory in chemistry Scientific expeditions Science influenced by nature–philosophy Discovery of chlorine and oxygen Overthrow of phlogiston theory Foundations of modern chemistry	Birth of scientific engineering Agrarian revolution Growth of ideas of technical progress Hot air balloons Improved textile machinery Much-improved steam engines Vaccination	The Enlightenment The Age of Reason British conquest of India Science as liberatory force French *Encyclopédie* American independence Adam Smith's economics French Revolution: 'Liberty, Equality, Fraternity'
1800	Foundations of geology Foundations of electromagnetism Principle of conservation of energy Theory of thermodynamics Theory of biological cells Lead in science shifts from France to Germany	Rapid industrialisation of Britain – factories, machine tools, coal, textiles Growth of transport – canals, roads, railways, shipping Telegraph Growth of gas industry	The Romantic Movement Malthus on population Population increase and shift to cities German university system
1850	Advances in agricultural chemistry Theory of evolution Organic chemistry Periodic table of the elements Cell division, heredity Electromagnetic theory Physical chemistry X-rays, radioactivity, electrons	Industrialisation of the United States and Europe Internal combustion engine Antiseptic surgery, germ theory of disease, public health	Free trade – ethos of competition, survival of the fittest Writings of Marx American Civil War Franco-Prussian War Growth of trade unions Colonial imperialism Growth of monopolies

Table 22.1	Landmarks of science continued		
Year* Science		Technology	Society
1900	Theory of relativity Development of biochemistry Quantum theory Lead in science shifts to the United States Genetics	Introduction of electronics and radio Aeroplanes Poison gas in warfare Car industry, oil US technological dominance	First World War Russian Revolution Depression of 1930s Rise of Fascism and Nazism Second World War
1950	Nuclear physics New tools, e.g. electron microscope, radio telescope, computers Science policy studies Molecular biology – genetic code High-energy physics	Industrialisation of Japan Nuclear weapons, missiles Electronic communications Synthetics, plastics, nylon Artificial fertilisers TV and consumer goods Nuclear power Space technology and exploration High-technology medicine – new drugs, transplants, etc.	Dominance of the United States East–West Cold War Growth of mass entertainment Increased spending on science Growth of military–industrial complex Independence for colonies Widening gap between rich and poor countries
1980	Extensions in cosmology Microelectronics	Computers, information technology Increasing automation	Environmental concerns Energy crisis
1990s –2000	The Human Genome Project Digitalisation	New reproduction technologies Digitalisation Possibility of cloning Mobile phones New medicines for AIDS, Viagra etc.	Postmodernism Globalisation Risk Society Awareness of the environment

* Nearest half-century (approx.)

Source: adapted from Boyle *et al.* (1984: 16, 18, 22)

3. *Disinterestedness*. Scientists should be impartial and should subject their work to rigorous examination by their scientific peers.

4. *Organised scepticism*. Scientists should suspend judgements till the facts are in. 'They should engage in the detached scrutiny of beliefs in terms of empirical and logical criteria' (Merton, 1996).

In some ways, Merton's work created a 'wish list' of what a scientific community should be like, and many subsequent examinations have not found a scientific community where these norms are put into practice. To the contrary, much scientific work proceeds on the basis of idiosyncratic, individualistic and independent beliefs. Much of Merton's work may in fact be prescriptive, as he tried to link 'science' to the bases of liberal democracy.

Science as a social construction: the sociology of scientific knowledge (SSK)

During the 1970s, a growing body of researchers did sociological fieldwork and ethnographies on scientific work as it was conducted in laboratories. They examined just how science was done, both in regular science such as physics and chemistry, but also in irregular or 'deviant' science such as parapsychology, astrology and acupuncture. Their concern was to investigate the content (theories, methods and techniques) of actual scientific work. Scientists were studied like a foreign tribe. The research needed to identify the relevant groups and people, the actors who participate in networks (often global) who work to shape and define a field of enquiry.

(a)

(b)

(c)

(d)

A world of scientists – (a) Galileo, (b) Copernicus, (c) Darwin, (d) Watson & Crick

Source: Science Photo Library (a) © Sheila Terry, (b) © Deltlev van Ravejswaay, (c) © SPL, (d) © A Barrington Brown

These sociologists study what Bruno Latour (1947–) has called 'science in the making' through 'Laboratory Life' (see Latour and Woolgar, 1986). For example, Latour conducted fieldwork in the science laboratories at the Salk Institute in California, observing work on barium peptides. The study looks at how scientists talk about their work, the paperwork they generate, their publications. All these are examples of ways of constructing a scientific fact. Likewise, Harry Collins examined disputes within physics over 'gravitational waves' and showed how accusations mixed technical and non-technical claims. This position leads to what has been called **epistemic relativism**, *knowledge is rooted in a particular time and culture* (Webster, 1991: 15).

Overall, the sociology of science studies adopts one of two approaches. The *interests approach* suggests that science's claims to be true knowledge are actually shaped by certain interests. Sometimes these are political: much research, for example, depends upon sponsorship, especially such things as medical sponsorship. On an even wider level, certain biases may go to the heart of science – it may have a class, race or gender bias. Thus, for example, some feminist scientists have argued that there have been major male biases in science because it is largely a male institution. This is to be found in the kinds of question that science sets itself, in its tools of work, and indeed in a certain kind of male 'clubbiness' among scientists (Fox Keller, 1985). Others have suggested that much science is also shaped by commercial interests, where funding is dependent upon major corporations.

Part of this commercial science may be seen as **Big Science**, which refers to a *particularly strong sense of expertise and its dominance, one that is usually strongly backed by money (capital and industry), supported by governments and given a lot of symbolic prestige*. During the mid-twentieth century this was largely associated with nuclear physics; indeed, it gave rise to both the space race and the nuclear bomb. Both the USSR (Russia) and the United States used these projects as major tools in their symbolic Cold Wars with each other, while at the

same time spending billions on these projects. In more recent times, the science of genetics has become almost as important with its major Human Genome Project (see Controversy and Debate box). Accidents are dismissed as part of the learning curve; critics are silenced as ignorant, uninformed, irrational; the strong march of science equals progress and cannot be halted (De Solla Price, 1963).

An alternative approach to this 'interest' model sees this as inadequate because even its own claims could be open to such arguments. The need, therefore, is for a much more refined *discourse analysis*. Science is now analysed like a text. How do the propositions, claims and ideas of scientists come to take on the status of 'facts'? This kind of study looks at the ways in which science presents itself as a solid and unquestionable body of evidence, whereas in fact the objectivity of science derives from its rhetorical power. Whatever science we are presented with, there is usually a large amount which we have to take on trust and which even the scientists take on trust.

The idea of the *black box* (borrowed from cybernetics) is used here. This is a quick way of suggesting a very complex process that is going on inside (in the 'black box') which nobody need explain and others need not understand. Scientists might claim that it is simply beyond ordinary folk to understand this, yet what is happening may actually be incomprehensible to all, and very messy indeed. But science and scientists develop a rhetoric which justifies itself even when it cannot really explain what it is doing or what is going on. In this view, much science becomes both a rhetorical skill in persuasion as well as an act of faith.

CONTROVERSY AND DEBATE

THE 'SCIENCE WARS'

The 'Science Wars' is the term given to a bitter battle fought between some 'scientists' and some critics of science such as the sociologists of scientific knowledge described in the text. The former claim that their work must have the 'objective status of knowledge'. They suggest that the sociological critics, by focusing on the social situations that produce knowledge, minimise, even trivialise, the importance of science in the advance of humankind. Science puts people on the moon; invents computers that change the world; discovers

causes and cures of major illnesses. This is serious work and serious science. By contrast, the sociologists who say otherwise are not to be taken seriously: they are often frauds, intellectually pretentious and seriously misleading.

But the sociologists and cultural critics of science who do what is known as 'Science and Technology Studies' (STS) claim they are studying how science actually does get done in the laboratory. It is a legitimate social activity to study. They are, however, often very disillusioned with the way in which science – especially physics – has been used, and they become disaffected with it. ▶

CONTROVERSY AND DEBATE CONTINUED

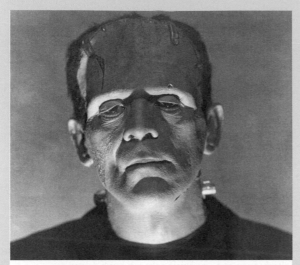

Close-up of Boris Karloff as the monster in a scene from the film *Frankenstein*.
Source: © Corbis

Indeed, it is not just sociologists who worry about this. Many distinguished scientists have also found objections to science, at least in so far as it is to be seen as the saviour of the world, the harbinger of modernity. The 'Scientific Revolution' was a problem. For as science became more and more prominent, it seemed to take on a life of its own – a bit like that mad Frankenstein and his machine. It became divorced from society and politics. We have only to think of the use of the atom bomb.

Steve Fuller (1998) has suggested how the debate is in part based on a series of misunderstandings between the two groups. Table 22.2 suggests how.

Source: extracted from Fuller (1998).

Table 22.2	A map of misreading: how scientists 'socially construct' Science Studies
Where Science Studies says ...	**Scienctists read this as meaning ...**
Science is socially constructed.	Science is whatever enough people think it is.
The validity of scientific claims must be understood in relation to the claimant's perspective.	There is no distinction between reality and how people represent it.
Science Studies has its own aims and methods.	Science Studies willfully ignores the aims and methods of science.
Science is only one possible way of interpreting experience.	Science is merely an interpretation that distorts experience.
Gravity is a concept scientists use to explain why we fall down, not up. There are other explanations.	Gravity exists only in our minds and, if we wanted, we could fall up, not down.
Scientists' accounts of their activities are not necessarily the best explanation for those activities.	Scientists' accounts of their activities can be disregarded when explaining those activities.

Steve Epstein, for example, has studied the claims made around the causes of the disease HIV/AIDS. He suggests that the claim that HIV is the absolute causal agent in AIDS is the guiding assumption behind billions of dollars' worth of research progammes for HIV antibody testing, antiviral drug development and treatment, and vaccine research development around the world. It is the cornerstone of 'what science knows about AIDS' (Epstein, 1998: 26). And yet, he says, there are still controversies of different kinds over the causes and nature of HIV, but they are regarded as heresies and can hardly be heard. Science, then, is socially structured in this way to include core assumptions and exclude rival views. It is not quite as neutral and objective as it is often claimed.

The 'biotechnology revolution': social issues

The biotechnology revolution comes in many forms and in this section we will consider a few of the arguments. At their most general, these biological arguments are not just about science: they have become a mass way of thinking. 'The gene is an icon of our time' (Rothman, 1998: 14). They are seen as the prime movers of life and a cause for almost everything. Whatever the question is, genetics becomes the answer. From the problems of race and war, to rape and cancer, from sexuality to crime, from addictions to disease, almost every issue of our time has been placed within this biological frame. The explanation lies 'in the genes'. Nor is it a new way of thinking: ideas of 'instincts', 'bad seeds', 'good and bad blood', 'nature', etc. have been its precursor and around for a long time. Two core – but interconnected – themes are those which highlight the new disciplines of **sociobiology** (*a theoretical paradigm that explores ways in which our biology affects how humans create culture*) and evolutionary psychology; and those which highlight the

importance of specific DNA codes and gene mapping. We will consider each in turn.

Science, biology and genetic politics

Major recent developments in the biological sciences have focused upon the gene, and these have often been linked theoretically to sociobiology and evolutionary psychology (EP). Edward O. Wilson (1975, 1978) is generally credited as the founder of this field, and optimistically claimed that sociobiology would reveal the biological roots of human culture. Both these theoretical paradigms explore ways in which our biology, and especially our genes, shape how humans become social and how cultures exist (see Chapters 5 and 7). In these arguments, the role of biology is given primacy as a science in explaining the social. Usually such approaches look for distant (distal) causes of our contemporary culture and behaviour thousands of generations ago in our evolutionary pasts. Nowhere is the power of gene analysis clearer than in the development of the Human Genome Project discussed in the box.

CONTROVERSY AND DEBATE

THE HUMAN GENOME PROJECT: DO WE REALLY WANT TO LOOK?

For 13 years, until 2003, teams in Britain, Europe and the United States worked hard to unpack the three-billion-letter DNA alphabet. For many, the Human Genome Project represents perhaps the greatest medical breakthrough of all time: the key to DNA. DNA is the spiralling molecule found in each cell of the human body, the molecule that contains the blueprints of our being and makes each one of us different from every other human. Bit by bit, human beings have been decoded.

And now you can read about it on the Internet. If it were all to be typed single-spaced on A4 paper, the blueprint for a single human being would fill 750,000 pages! Great hopes are held for it in increasing food production, reducing pollution, combating disease and enhancing the quality of life.

In medical terms, the human body is composed of some 100 trillion cells, most of which contain a nucleus of 23 pairs of chromosomes (one of each pair comes from each parent). Each of these chromo-

somes is packed with DNA, segments of which are called genes. Genes guide the production of proteins, the building blocks of the human body.

If genetics sounds complex (and it is), the social implications of understanding genetics are no simpler. Scientists have known about DNA since 1952, but now an aggressive programme is under way to 'map' our genetic landscape. The ambitious goal of the Human Genome Project is nothing less than to understand the operation of each bit of DNA; in essence, the human genome is the collection of all human genes. Researchers argue that knowing them will help us read and understand the computer program that drives our existence. And therein lies the greatest question of all: do we really want to learn the secrets of life itself?

Many scientists offer strong support for the Human Genome Project. They envisage for the future a completely new approach to medicine: rather than treating symptoms, doctors would address the basic causes of illness. Research, they point out, has already identified the genetic abnormalities that cause some forms of cancer, sickle-cell anaemia, muscular dystrophy, Huntington's disease, cystic ▶

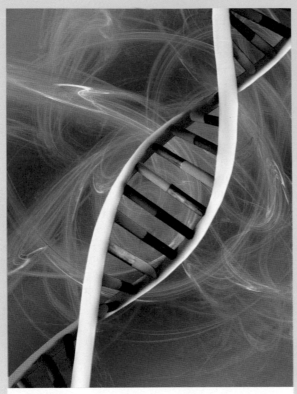

DNA double helix

Source: © Denis Scott/Corbis

At its worst, genetic mapping opens the door to Nazi-like efforts at breeding a super-race.

It seems inevitable that some parents will seek to use genetic testing to evaluate the future health (or even the eye and hair colour) of their unborn child. Should people be permitted to abort a foetus that fails to meet their expectations? Or, further down the road when genetic manipulations become possible, should parents be able to design their own children?

Then there is the issue of 'genetic privacy'. Should a prospective spouse be able to request a genetic evaluation of her fiancé before agreeing to marry? Should life or health insurance companies be allowed to demand genetic testing before writing policies? Should a corporation be permitted to evaluate job applicants in order to weed out those whose future illnesses might drain their health-care funds? Clearly what is scientifically possible is not always morally desirable. Our society is already grappling with questions about how to use the ever-expanding knowledge about human genetics. These ethical dilemmas will only mount as genetic research pinpoints the roots of our make-up in the years to come.

CONTINUE THE DEBATE:

1. Through traditional wedding vows, couples pledge to remain together 'in sickness and in health'. Do you think individuals have a right to know the future health of their potential partner before marrying?

2. What about the desire of some parents to genetically design their children? Would this lead to a class of 'superhumans'?

3. Where do we turn to devise standards for the proper use of genetic information?

Source: www.ornl.gov/hgmis

fibrosis and a host of other crippling and deadly afflictions. In this twenty-first century, with information from the genetic 'crystal ball', screening will allow us to identify people destined to develop serious illnesses, and doctors will be able to manipulate segments of DNA to prevent the onset of diseases before they start.

But many people, both within and outside the scientific community, urge caution in taking such research too far. The problem, they claim, is that no one is sure how genetic information should be used.

The logic of evolution

Both sociobiology and evolutionary psychology rest on the logic of evolution. In his book *On the Origin of Species*, Charles Darwin (1979; orig. 1859) claimed that living organisms change over long periods of time as a result of *natural selection*, a matter of four simple

principles. First, all living things live to reproduce themselves. Second, the blueprint for reproduction lies in the genes, the basic units of life that carry traits of one generation into the next. Genes vary randomly in each species; in effect, this genetic variation allows a species to 'try out' new life patterns in a particular environment. Third, due to genetic variation, some organisms are more

THE 'BIOTECHNOLOGY REVOLUTION': SOCIAL ISSUES

likely than others to survive and to pass on their advantageous genes to their offspring. Fourth, over thousands of generations, specific genetic patterns that promote reproduction survive and become dominant. In this way, as biologists say, a species *adapts* to its environment and dominant traits emerge as the 'nature' of the organism.

Many social traits have been linked back to evolution. Thus, the difference between the sexes, the development of different sexual orientations (for example, homosexuality), the persistence of crime and aggression, the links between race and IQ, the connections between language and the brain, and the universality of rape have all been connected to evolution.

The 'Darwin Wars'

It will not be surprising to learn that many social scientists hotly contest the views of these biologicial evolutionists. The conflict has been called the 'Darwin Wars', whereby new genetics theorists, such as Steven Pinker, Richard Dawkins, Daniel Dennett and Helena Cronin, find themselves disagreeing with both sociologists and some biologists, such as Richard Leowontin, Stephen Jay Gould, Noam Chomsky, and Steven and Hilary Rose, about the role of biology in understanding society.

Now it is not the case that critics are dismissive of Darwin or that they suggest there is no role for biology to play. Quite the contrary, the role of biology has to be taken very seriously and social scientists do misleadingly tend to minimise it. But they suggest that the claims that are made by evolutionary psychologists and sociobiologists often seem too overstated and wide-ranging.

A controversial case: Thornhill and Palmer – the evolutionary role of rape

Take the example of a recent study of rape by US sociobiologists Randy Thornhill and Craig Palmer (2000). Drawing on the evolutionary theory of sex, they claim that rape is a necessary part of the evolutionary process. They see it as completely congruent and compatible with the development of sex differences.

Broadly, and in line with many evolutionary theorists, they suggest that for reproductive potentials to be fulfilled and humans to reproduce themselves satisfactorily, there is an evolutionary necessity for men to have sexual intercourse with as many women as they can. Meanwhile, for women the task is different: it is to find the best man and the best seed. The male is seen as more likely than the female to desire sex with a variety of partners.

All this rests on the argument that the biological significance of a single sperm and a single egg differ dramatically. For healthy men, sperm represents a 'renewable resource' produced by the testes throughout most of the life course. A man releases hundreds of millions of sperm in a single ejaculation – technically, enough to fertilise many millions of women (Barash, 1981: 47)! A newborn female's ovaries, however, contain her entire lifetime allotment of follicles or immature eggs. A woman commonly releases a single mature egg cell from her ovaries each month. So, while a man is biologically capable of fathering thousands of offspring, a woman is able to bear only a relatively small number of children.

Given this biologically based difference, each sex is well served by a distinctive reproductive strategy. From a strictly biological perspective, a man reproduces his genes most efficiently by being promiscuous – that is, readily engaging in sex. This scheme, however, opposes the reproductive interests of a woman, whose relatively few pregnancies demand that she carry the child for nine months, give birth and care for the infant for some time afterwards. Thus, efficient reproduction on the part of the woman depends on carefully selecting a mate whose qualities (beginning with the likelihood that he will simply stay around) will contribute to her child's survival and successful reproduction (Remoff, 1984).

Evolutionary biology suggests that cultural patterns of reproduction, promiscuity, the double standard and indeed rape, like many others, have an underlying bio-logic. Simply put, it has developed around the world because women and men everywhere tend towards distinctive reproductive strategies. Men prefer a higher number of sex partners; women do not.

In this view, rape is seen as universal – across humans and animals. It also goes back a long way in time. Its distant roots in our make-up lie with men competing for women. Rape thus becomes a device in which men can gain reproductive benefits.

This account is well defended by its authors, who have little time for social science, which they see as ideological. But likewise, very few social scientists have taken their work at all seriously. This illustrates very clearly the way in which different scientific communities often speak across each other and do not listen to each other's arguments. What are some of the key issues in these debates?

Key issues

First, critics claim that gene theorists are often too reductionist. This is to say that they reduce the complexity of human life histories, imaginations, influly, bodies, knowledges and selves to a 'seed': to a moment when a sperm joins an egg. Ultimately, they claim, and despite the huge variations of cultures and histories, these seeds contain the potential for all human beings. It is important therefore to ask what is missing from these rather grand claims. Often there is little attempt to look for immediate causes in a culture or a life, but instead to look back to causes that may have appeared thousands of years ago. The tendency is to give priority to distant (or distal) causes rather than more immediate (or proximal) causes.

Critics claim that genetic theorists often ignore time. DNA is called a code, a blueprint, but life unfolds through time and space. Human evolution is a lifelong building project involving history and interactions with many others in the wider social environment. DNA will have its part to play in this lifelong project, of course, but it is surely facile to suggest that it all simply 'unfolds' from a genetic base.

And this leads to the claims that many of these accounts may be too deterministic. While Darwin's evolutionary theory certainly recognised the importance of chance, contingencies and more or less random moments with unpredictable outcomes, many of the newer theories are much more restrictive. The central feature of his theory was that of adaptations constantly taking place. So although there may be broad biological bases, contingency plays an important role too. We need to distinguish here between long-term trends and causes, and enabling adaptations that take place in contexts and local environments. We can speak of long-term evolved human capacities or capabilities without then saying what they cause.

But the key is culture. Even if it is true that men are evolutionary rapists or genetically aggressive, this would not really begin to explain the different levels of aggressiveness and rape across different cultures, ages, classes, ethnicities and times. For rape and violence are not static, fixed things. Likewise, even if some theorists suggest that rape is an evolutionary necessity, this does not begin to explain the variations in rape rates.

On top of all this, there are also ideological concerns. Some critics fear that sociobiology may revive biological arguments, common a century ago, touting the superiority of one race or sex. In general, though, defenders these days counter this by rejecting the past pseudo-science of racial superiority. On the contrary, they contend, new genetic theories may actually unite all of humanity by asserting that all people share a single evolutionary history. With regard to sex, sociobiology does rest on the assumption that men and women differ biologically in some ways that culture cannot overcome –

if, in fact, any society sought to. But, far from asserting that males are somehow more important than females, sociobiology emphasises how both sexes are vital to human reproduction. They claim that science is on their side, and that objections made on moral or political grounds by feminists or anti-racists are just that, and cannot be taken as science.

But critics counterclaim that this raises the problem of the 'authority of the scientist'. Almost everything that these theories touch – from crime to medicine, from gender to race – raises profound ethical and political issues which cannot be ignored. Yet very often the scientist steps over the line of science to become an 'expert' on ethics and morality. The field of bioethics can often become an apologia for the scientist.

Finally, although sociologists are often not in a position to evaluate this, we should note that there is actually a great deal of research from biologists themselves which suggests that many of the claims of the evolutionary psychologists do not match the findings of biological researchers and suffer from being seriously overstated. Thus, Anne Fausto-Sterling finds a much wider range of male and female behaviours than evolutionary psychologists would allow us to believe (Fausto-Sterling, 1992).

Issues of genetic modification

Many of the developments in genetic modification will be available mainly to the wealthy West. With our greater knowledge and mapping of genes, we can already see *gene mapping, profiling, therapy* and *modification* taking place in plants and animals, including human beings.

Thus, *genome profiling* will enable the decoding of the genetic basis of many illnesses, giving medicine more effective mechanisms for diagnosis and treatment. Increasingly, medical practitioners will be able to predict from particular genes the health of an individual. This will lead to more and more knowledge about the pre-born child, as well as a wider range of options for treating disease. But at the same time, this will bring untold risks. For instance, it may lead to higher insurance policies for giving birth to people with suspected 'sick genes'; it may lead to more abortions; it may lead to what Lee Silver suggests may be seen as two human species: a genetically enhanced superior species and a genetically deficient inferior one (Silver, 1998). 'Designer children' may be engineered.

The new genetic discoveries are also open to commercial exploitation. Already companies have claimed to patent certain genes. Commercial companies such as Celera Genomics (under the US scientist Craig Venter, in particular) have raised billions of dollars on the US stock market in an attempt to sell patented genes to industry. (However, international protests followed, and a joint declaration from US President Clinton and UK Prime Minister Blair argued that genetic data should be available to everyone and not commercially patented.) The point is that these new 'sciences' bring many unknown potentials that we may well have to live with in the future.

Genetically modified foods

Modifying the genetic composition of crops and animals through 'selective breeding' has been known as part of agriculture for centuries, but the newer techniques mean that artificial transfers between completely unrelated organisms become a reality. Genetic modification of foods is much more radical than cross-breeding: there is a manipulation of the genetic composition.

GM crops are currently being grown in around 13 countries and being tested in many more. They are being widely grown in China, and America has grown some 3.5 trillion genetically modified plants since 1994. The most prevalent kinds of plant so far have been maize (20 per cent of the US maize crop in 1998) and soya (30 per cent, or 21 million tons). They can give more vitamins and make 'superfoods', such as 'super-rice'.

Since present farming techniques may not be able to deal with the world's starvation problems, developments in biotechnology are sometimes seen as the solution. But they have generated significant conflicts. The United Nations Development Programme, for instance, generally favours their development. They claim that GM crops may give greater yields for farmers and lift people out of poverty. Such crops could help farmers cultivate marginal land prone to draught or salt. They may enhance nutritional qualities of foods, improve their appearance, and be more resistant to general herbicides and plant killers.

Yet, once released into the environment, their impact is hard to predict. There are all kinds of knock-on effect which can produce risks, and these may alter the food production chain. Poor farmers may become locked into technologies that they cannot afford to sustain. In any event, many poorer farmers actually live in countries with food surpluses – the problem is not production of food but its distribution. Direct action has led to many supermarkets banning such foods (*The Economist*, 14 April 2001: 2 1; *The Guardian*, 11 July 2001; Allman, 2000: 556).

Assisted conception and the new reproductive politics

In 1978, in Britain, Louise Brown became the world's first 'test-tube' baby. Now, in the twenty-first century, such techniques have almost become commonplace: more than 200,000 treatment cycles per year are being carried out in Europe – 45,000 in France, 34,000 in Britain and 28,000 in Germany: one birth in 80 in the UK comes from a test tube (*Guardian*, 28 June 2000: 14, based on the European Society of Human Reproduction and Embryology). Tens of thousands of people have been conceived in this way (Table 22.3).

Technically speaking, test-tube babies are the product of *in vitro fertilisation* (IVF), a procedure whereby the male sperm and the female ovum are united 'in glass' rather than in a woman's body. In this complex medical procedure, doctors use drugs to stimulate the woman's ovaries to produce more than one egg during a reproductive cycle. Then they surgically harvest eggs from her ovaries and combine them with sperm in a laboratory dish. The successful fusion of eggs and sperm produces embryos, which surgeons then either implant in the womb of a woman who is to bear the child or freeze for use at a later time.

The immediate benefit of *in vitro* fertilisation is to help couples who cannot conceive normally to have children. Infertile couples – and infertility is on the increase – can hence now have children. Looking further ahead, new

Table 22.3	The 'new reproduction': chronology of key events in the UK
1978	Birth of Louise Brown: the first test-tube baby
1982	Warnock Committee – advises on ethical issues around new reproduction
1985	Surrogacy Arrangements Act – bans commercial surrogacy in the UK
1987	The Pope condemns the new technologies (in his Instruction and Respect for Human Life)
1990s	Growth of stem cell research, infertility research
1990	Human Fertilisation and Embryology Act
1991	Human Fertilisation and Embryology Authority established
1996–97	The Dolly story involving a 'cloned' sheep
2000	President George W. Bush outlaws cloning

Nirmala Devi and her lawyer Navjit Brar leave Chandigarh court on 9 June 1997 after she sought permission from a judge to 'rent her womb'. Devi offered her womb to a childless couple for 50,000 rupees (£1000) to bear a child, after conferring with her bedridden and paralysed husband. Police in the northern Indian city of Chandigarh were threatening to prosecute Devi under the Suppression of Immoral Traffic Act. Devi approached the court to declare her 'renting of womb' as legal and said she had no other source of income and cannot bear the medical expenses of 700 rupees (£15) each month for her ailing husband.

Source: Popperfoto © Rajesh Bhambi/Reuters

birth technologies may eventually reduce the incidence of birth defects. By genetically screening sperm and eggs, medical specialists expect to increase the odds for the birth of a healthy baby (Thompson, 1994).

Ethics and risk

But this is only the most straightforward story. These are only a few of the new developments which have prompted much debate. For assisted conceptions also bring with them the following new phenomena.

1. The rights and choice to reproduce (or not). Problems of infertility and childlessness no longer mean that you cannot have children by other means.

2. Ovary and egg donation, raising issues about who is donating and ultimately who the parents may be.

3. Egg and sperm banks, raising issues of sperm and eggs being frozen for later use; even the foetus can now be brought 'alive' at a later time.

4. Embryo research, where the use of frozen embryos for medical – and maybe other? – research starts to raise concerns about the moral status of the embryo as a research object.

5. Surrogacy, where the issue of someone else's body being used to carry your child is raised.

6. Commercial surrogacy, whereby the selling and buying of babies, embryos, eggs and sperms often by commercial agencies for 'needy' and infertile 'would-be parents' creates new international markets. In some parts of the world (including much of Northern Europe) such markets are generally outlawed; in other countries (for example, the United States) they can be widespread.

7. Much more general issues around the rights to choose exactly the kind of child you want – from choosing the sex of a baby, to avoiding illness and disabilities, to 'age and generation hopping', to cloning for perfection, to gene therapy. In popular language these raise the ethics of 'designer babies', 'cloning' and 'perfect babies'.

All these conflicts raise questions over what it means to give birth and raise children – features that go to the heart of intimacy. But the outcomes of all such decisions have to be seen as unanticipated and risky: we are right on the edge of what Aldous Huxley described in his novel as a *Brave New World*. These new decisions may flow from scientific advances, but they bring in their wake not just a string of medical concerns, but also – once again – many unpredictable risks. Who, for instance, are the children being born this way? What will be their identities? Who are their 'real parents'? And what happens when some of these procedures go wrong?

As doctors, politicians and lawyers decide when to employ or withhold these *new reproductive technologies* (NRTs), they move into a new position to define what constitutes 'families'. In most cases, doctors and hospitals, for instance, have restricted *in vitro* fertilisation to women under 40 years of age who have male partners. Single women, older women and lesbian couples are only slowly gaining access to this technology. In 1991, for example, Arlette Schweitzer, a 42-year-old librarian living in Aberdeen, South Dakota, became the first woman on record to bear her own grandchildren. Because her daughter was unable to have a baby, Schweitzer agreed to have her daughter's fertilised embryos surgically implanted in her own womb. Nine months later, her efforts yielded healthy twins – a boy and girl (Kolata, 1991). Such a case strikingly illustrates how new reproductive technology has created new choices for families and sparked new controversies for society as a whole. The benefits of this rapidly developing technology are exciting, but its use raises daunting ethical questions about the creation and manipulation of life itself. All types of new reproductive technology – from laboratory fertilisation to surrogate motherhood, in which one woman bears a child for another – force us to confront the inadequacy of conventional kinship terms. Is Arlette Schweitzer the mother of the twins she bore? The grandmother? Or both?

Then, too, we need to consider that, when it comes to manipulating life, what is technically possible may not always be morally desirable. While many women and some feminists have welcomed these developments as a way for women to gain more control over their bodies, others are more sceptical. For Andrea Dworkin, this heralds the arrival of a 'farming model' towards women, and one which signals 'the coming *gynocide*'. The new reproductive technologies 'will give conception, gestation and birth over to men – eventually, the whole process of the creation of life will be in their hands' (Dworkin, 1983: 188). Likewise, Gena Corea writes that '[t]he new reproductive technologies represent an escalation of violence against women, a violence camouflaged behind medical terms' (Corea, 1988: 85). British sociologist Diane Richardson has summarised the key objections. She writes:

> the new reproductive technologies are being used to uphold traditional notions of motherhood and femininity, have serious eugenic implications, have a low success rate and are expensive, pose health risks to women and, most importantly, they can be seen as extending control over women's reproductive capacities.
>
> (Richardson, 1994: 87)

Recognising some of these issues, in 1982 the Warnock Committee was set up by the UK government to consider the ethical implications of such new reproductive issues. In its final report, it advocated very close regulation of such activities through a new body, the Human Fertilisation and Embryology Authority (HFEA), with the power, for example, to license IVF clinics. Unlike the system in the United States, the Warnock Committee (1984) was firmly against the commercialisation of such practices – where wombs can be sold (or rented)!

Dolly's story

The story of a baby lamb known as Dolly was introduced to the UK public on 23 February 1997 (though she was actually born on 5 July 1996). Her claim to fame was that she was cloned from a single cell taken from the breast tissue of a single donor. Until this time, as far as we know, all new mammalian life had originated in an embryo through the merger of gametes from a male and female, a mother and a father.

Once the issue of animal cloning has been proved possible, it is but a few steps to the issue of human cloning. Although at present most governments oppose such developments, there have already been maverick scientists who claim to have cloned people. Once again this raises many moral and ethical issues to be considered in the future.

The computer revolution and the information society

At several points in this book, we have noted how the information technology (IT) revolution has refashioned capitalism. 'Globalisation' (Chapter 2), 'postmodernity' and the 'post-industrial society' (Chapter 4), the 'network society' (Chapter 6), the 'information society' (Chapter 14) and the 'media society' (Chapter 21) are all terms that connect to these changes. The Information Revolution is really a shorthand name for all those high-tech machines (such as faxes, satellite dishes, the Internet and mobile phones) which deal with information.

Cees Hamelink (2000) usefully distinguishes four major roles of these new technologies. These are:

1. *Capturing technologies*: those which gather data, such as scanners and remote satellites;

2. *Storing technologies*: those which make data retrievable, such as discs, CD-Roms, and smartcards;

3. *Processing technologies*: those which enable the manipulation of data, such as laptops and gameboys;

4. *Communication technologies*: those which disseminate data, such as broadcasting, mobile phones, faxes and email.

The spread of IT across the world has been an extraordinarily rapid development. In many Western countries it has become part of mainstream life in less than 20 years. Bearing in mind that the World Wide Web was not launched until 1991, already over 180 countries are connected and there are now over 100 million users in the United States alone. A new generation, the Net

Table 22.4	The top 15 'skaters' (countries with an Information Society Index score above 3.500)				
Rank	**Country**	**Rank**	**Country**	**Rank**	**Country**
1	Sweden	6	UK	11	Japan
2	Norway	7	Switzerland	12	Canada
3	Finland	8	Australia	13	Germany
4	US	9	Singapore	14	Austria
5	Denmark	10	Netherlands	15	Hong Kong

Source: *Guardian*, 22 March 2001; International Data Corporation; WorldTimes (www.worldpaper.com), © *The Guardian*

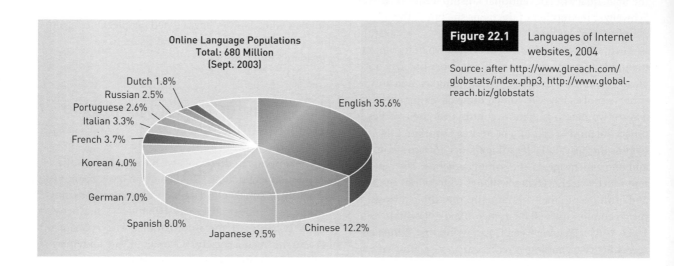

**Online Language Populations
Total: 680 Million
(Sept. 2003)**

Dutch 1.8%
Russian 2.5%
Portuguese 2.6%
Italian 3.3%
French 3.7%
Korean 4.0%
German 7.0%
Spanish 8.0%
Japanese 9.5%
Chinese 12.2%
English 35.6%

| Figure 22.1 | Languages of Internet websites, 2004 |

Source: after http://www.glreach.com/ globstats/index.php3, http://www.global-reach.biz/globstats

Generation, for whom the use of personal computers, information technology and the Net is taken for granted, is growing up. Brought up on Nintendo games and computers, they create a huge generation gap, often reversing adult–child roles as children come to know so much more about these things than either their teachers or their parents. Many 'users' are young, male and relatively wealthy: these are what Douglas Rushkoff (1999) calls the 'Digital Kids'. That said, more and more women are becoming involved; information technology is spreading through the classes and ethnicities; and it is moving through more groups across the world. Table 22.4 shows the countries where it is most in use. Figure 22.1 shows how at present it is dominated by the English language.

The growth of computing

Briefly, we can see the rise of the new information technologies as passing through three phases:

1. *The mainframe phase*. A first phase was dominated by large, mainframe computers pioneered by IBM and others. In 1946 Philadelphia engineers switched on a machine the size of a large room (yet this 'mother of all computers' was no better (that is, could do no more) than today's four-pound, hand-held calculator). Computers were large and expensive, as well as hard to use and different from each other. There were few around and many people were required to operate each one.

2. *The PC phase*. A second phase started in the 1970s when the first PC (ALTO) was built (in 1972). Now the promise of cheaper, smaller and personal computers began. At roughly the same time, the first Internet exchanges started to occur (in November 1969). The Net has its origins in the Pentagon's Advanced Research Projects Agency (ARPA) and gradually spread from the military to the universities. From 1990 private companies came to dominate the space. Between 1998 and 2000 usage in the UK jumped enormously: from 18 to 34 per cent, with

some 45 per cent of adults aged 16 and over saying they had accessed the Internet at some time (*Social Trends*, 2001: 233–234).

3. *Ubiquitous computing.* A third phase is known as 'ubiquitous computing'. Here computers are everywhere and blend into the background of social life. In this stage, most computers are connected to each other, most people have access to computers, and there are many computers per person. Computer usage becomes routinely linked to the Internet. Although we may be in this era already, it may not be till 2020 that it will be in full flower. Computers today are cheap and convenient, most work in similar ways and they can be easily carried around – in laptops, in mobile phones, in watches, in pocket calculators and the like.

Key themes in the 'Digital Age'

Within this information society, there are some clear themes that are emerging. Among the major changes that sociologists note are:

- *Digitalisation.* A common language replacing earlier analogue systems everywhere. It has been called the 'bar coding' of the world – almost every item now comes 'machine readable' with its bar code. It is there at the supermarket checkout, on almost every 'commodity' being produced, and soon it may even be that our body parts become digitalised as, for example, our eyes instead of passports are scanned at airports.

- *Pervasiveness.* IT is to be found everywhere: in the home from kitchen to bathroom, in offices, on the streets, in finance, government, education, health, etc. We carry it with us in smartcards, smart mobiles, smart homes, smart offices, smart weapons. It is present too in the arrival of surveillance (see Chapter 16).

- *Convergence.* Increasingly, all systems start to adopt this new process, and systems start to look more and more alike.

- *Information and ideas.* There is less concern with things and more concern with ideas. It is no longer the factory assembly line but the computer screen which is the dominant image and metaphor of our time.

- *Shift in space and time.* This is a world less bound to physical reality and, as such, we find it shifts our understanding of many classic things that were bound into a material world. Our sense of space and time changes, as we may now move around the global world instantly. Even our sense of a bounded body

may shift as we increasingly engage with ideas in space rather than with embodied people. Virtual realities come to exist.

- *A networking logic.* Finally, as we started to see in Chapter 6, the nature of social groups starts to change. Not only do primary and secondary groups become transformed, more and more we relate to others through 'networks'.

The social impact of information technologies

The changes we have been discussing may well have an impact on almost every topic we have discussed in this book, from health and cities to education to politics. They touch lives in many ways. Indeed, once again we can see the new technologies as part of the Risk Society, for we cannot at this stage in our history begin to really see the consequences of the widespread development of cyberspace. There is more 'manufactured uncertainty'. In many countries throughout the world, the 'dangers' of the information society have indeed been recognised, and the state has placed restraints on its use (Figure 22.2 shows some of this). In what follows we will briefly look at some of the currently identifiable impacts and then consider some of the more negative possibilities.

In Chapter 2, we saw how globalisation itself means a shift in time and space, in part because IT has brought this about. The world has shrunk and become more immediate because of email, websites, mobile phones and the like.

Digital economies

A very central part of this must be the digitalisation of the economy, which has shaped everything from global finance markets and shopping on the Net to 'bar codes' and new forms of work. The global financial economy is absolutely dependent on IT. As Castells (1996: 93) comments:

> Capital is managed around the clock in globally integrated financial markets working in real time for the first time in history: billion dollars-worth of transactions take place in seconds in the electronic circuits throughout the globe.

The Information Revolution is also changing the character of the workplace and even of work itself. Even 20 years ago, Shoshana Zuboff (1982) pointed to four ways in which computers are altering the character of work. She suggested they are:

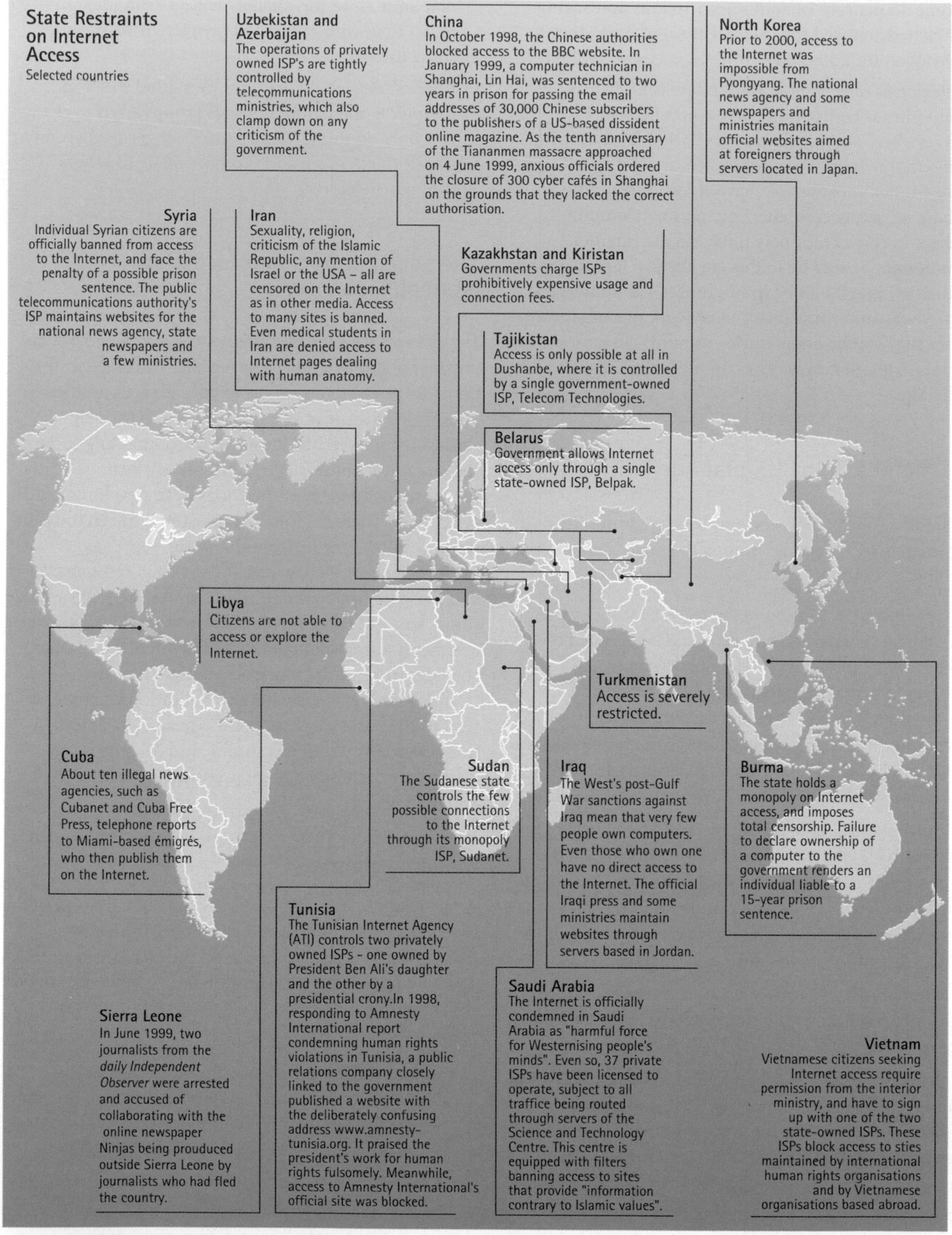

State Restraints on Internet Access
Selected countries

Uzbekistan and Azerbaijan
The operations of privately owned ISP's are tightly controlled by telecommunications ministries, which also clamp down on any criticism of the government.

China
In October 1998, the Chinese authorities blocked access to the BBC website. In January 1999, a computer technician in Shanghai, Lin Hai, was sentenced to two years in prison for passing the email addresses of 30,000 Chinese subscribers to the publishers of a US-based dissident online magazine. As the tenth anniversary of the Tiananmen massacre approached on 4 June 1999, anxious officials ordered the closure of 300 cyber cafés in Shanghai on the grounds that they lacked the correct authorisation.

North Korea
Prior to 2000, access to the Internet was impossible from Pyongyang. The national news agency and some newspapers and ministries maintain official websites aimed at foreigners through servers located in Japan.

Syria
Individual Syrian citizens are officially banned from access to the Internet, and face the penalty of a possible prison sentence. The public telecommunications authority's ISP maintains websites for the national news agency, state newspapers and a few ministries.

Iran
Sexuality, religion, criticism of the Islamic Republic, any mention of Israel or the USA – all are censored on the Internet as in other media. Access to many sites is banned. Even medical students in Iran are denied access to Internet pages dealing with human anatomy.

Kazakhstan and Kiristan
Governments charge ISPs prohibitively expensive usage and connection fees.

Tajikistan
Access is only possible at all in Dushanbe, where it is controlled by a single government-owned ISP, Telecom Technologies.

Belarus
Government allows Internet access only through a single state-owned ISP, Belpak.

Libya
Citizens are not able to access or explore the Internet.

Turkmenistan
Access is severely restricted.

Cuba
About ten illegal news agencies, such as Cubanet and Cuba Free Press, telephone reports to Miami-based émigrés, who then publish them on the Internet.

Sudan
The Sudanese state controls the few possible connections to the Internet through its monopoly ISP, Sudanet.

Iraq
The West's post-Gulf War sanctions against Iraq mean that very few people own computers. Even those who own one have no direct access to the Internet. The official Iraqi press and some ministries maintain websites through servers based in Jordan.

Burma
The state holds a monopoly on Internet access, and imposes total censorship. Failure to declare ownership of a computer to the government renders an individual liable to a 15-year prison sentence.

Tunisia
The Tunisian Internet Agency (ATI) controls two privately owned ISPs - one owned by President Ben Ali's daughter and the other by a presidential crony.In 1998, responding to Amnesty International report condemning human rights violations in Tunisia, a public relations company closely linked to the government published a website with the deliberately confusing address www.amnesty-tunisia.org. It praised the president's work for human rights fulsomely. Meanwhile, access to Amnesty International's official site was blocked.

Saudi Arabia
The Internet is officially condemned in Saudi Arabia as "harmful force for Westernising people's minds". Even so, 37 private ISPs have been licensed to operate, subject to all traffic being routed through servers of the Science and Technology Centre. This centre is equipped with filters banning access to sites that provide "information contrary to Islamic values".

Sierra Leone
In June 1999, two journalists from the *daily Independent Observer* were arrested and accused of collaborating with the online newspaper Ninjas being produuced outside Sierra Leone by journalists who had fled the country.

Vietnam
Vietnamese citizens seeking Internet access require permission from the interior ministry, and have to sign up with one of the two state-owned ISPs. These ISPs block access to sties maintained by international human rights organisations and by Vietnamese organisations based abroad.

Figure 22.2 State restraints on Internet access, selected countries, 2000

Source: adapted from *The Global Media Atlas* p. 87 © Myriad Editions Limited, www.MyriadEditions.com

1. *Deskilling labour*. Just as industrial machinery 'deskilled' the master crafts workers of an earlier era, so computers now threaten to make the skills of managers obsolete. More and more business decisions are based not on executive decision-making but on computer modelling, in which a machine determines whether to buy or sell a product or to approve or reject a loan.

2. *Making work more abstract*. Industrial workers typically have a 'hands on' relationship with their product. Post-industrial workers manipulate words or other symbols in pursuit of more 'user-friendly' software or some other abstract definition of business success.

3. *Limiting workplace interaction*. The Information Revolution forces employees to perform most of their work at computer terminals. This system isolates workers from one another.

4. *Enhancing employers' control of workers*. Computers allow supervisors to monitor each worker's output precisely and continuously, whether employees are working at computer terminals or on an assembly line (see Rule and Brantley, 1992). Technology is not socially neutral; rather, it *shapes* the way we work and alters the balance of power between employers and employees.

Digital democracies

A new shape is also being suggested for politics. In Chapter 15, we suggested how new social movements were partly reshaping politics: such movements as we saw in Seattle, etc., are organised largely in and through networks. We could say that the Web is reshaping the public sphere (see the box featuring Jürgen Habermas on page 597). More and more people can communicate online about matters that are of concern to them through newsgroups, chat rooms, web links, etc.

Digital relationships

As we saw in Chapter 6, new ways of relating start to appear with mobile phones, email and the Internet. One aspect of this is the arrival of online dating. Not only are there highly specialised markets such as CatholicSingles.com and GoodGenes.com, but there are also very large generic sites such as Matchmaker.com, SocialNet.com, and Match.com and Altmatch.com (for gays and lesbians). In China, in 2001, one million (mainly young) people had signed up for Club Yuan, the dating section of the Chinese Sina.com, which is

breaking down centuries-old traditions. 'When you talk to girls on the Internet, what you think and feel is more important than how much money you have, or other status symbols that carry so much weight in the outside world', a Beijing university student who calls himself Supersheng is quoted as saying (*Newsweek*, 'Love Online', 12 March 2001: 46–49).

Creating new cultures and social worlds on the Web

One of the most striking implications for sociologists of the new chat lines, emails, websites and the like is the ways in which they are fashioning networks of new cultures and communications. At the simplest level, a personal homepage becomes a new mode for the presentation of a self (see Chapter 7). People can select, embellish or even radically transform a publicly available sense of who they are through the design and content of their personal page.

Interest groups of all kinds can establish worldwide communications with the like-minded: hobbies, fanzines and all soap operas seem to have their sites (*Star Trek* is suggested to have some 1,200 websites alone: Pullen, 2000). Artists can make their work available on sites – not just their art images and their sales programmes, but also a space for discussion among artists. Vast new sexual communities appear online, creating sites for every imaginable sexual fetish and experience. Major world religions and the thousands of breakaway groups and 'new religious movements' all have their sites, and often they are extremely elaborate and detailed. Indigenous peoples, such as the Cherokee Indians, establish sites to 'strengthen tribal ties while asserting sovereign rights and fostering self determination' (Arnold and Plymire, 2000: 192). Diaspora groups such as Indians can create new digital diasporas that serve to fashion new communities. The Women's Movement can now stretch across the globe – even in poorer and low-income societies – to raise issues and information on the 'cyberfight to stop violence against women', or to discuss and update women's experience at the Beijing Conference on Women's Human Rights. New political organising becomes possible, such as that seen in Seattle or Genoa. It is hard for sociology to ignore the creation of all these new worlds in which self, politics, community are now so intertwined on a global scale (see Gauntlett, 2000, for an expansion of most of these examples and details of websites).

The 'risks' of cyberworlds

As with all technologies, we can ask about how such changes might have produced new social worlds of 'risk' upon us. These are not quite like the worlds of the past where risk may have been even more prominent through natural catastrophe, because these risks are largely unknown and uncertain. To put it simply, as the world of websites, emails and mobile phones has extended rapidly into our lives, what may be the hidden consequences of this quite profound change? More and more people are spending more and more time sitting at and communicating with machines. Might this change their posture, their writing skills, their sense of self, their communities, their communication abilities? We have suggested above that to some extent it already has. Below we consider just four of the more worrying aspects.

Cyberpower, cyberclasses and stratification

One scenario is to see a new world of stratification appearing which is based upon the 'information haves' and the 'information have nots'. This can already be seen in the Western world, where older people without computing skills increasingly find themselves cut off from a new generation that live their everyday lives through these new media and were brought up on 'gameboys'. Although IT may well have touched most countries across the world, it still does not really touch directly most of the world's 6 billion population. There is a global digital divide. Thus, while some commentators believe that cyberspace will enhance democracy and create greater access to power for all (even suggesting that the new virtual hierarchies may well work to undermine offline 'official hierarchies'), critics suggest that cyberspace could generate a world of **cyberclasses**, *a stratification system based on the information 'haves' and 'have nots' linked to the rise in new information technologies.* Political theorist Zillah Eisenstein comments that:

> Cyberspace is accessible to only a small fraction of people outside the west. Eighty-four percent of computer users are found in north america and northern europe. Sixty-nine percent are male, average age thirty-three, with an average household income of $59,000. The top twenty internet-connected computer countries are significantly homogeneous. They are first world, except for singapore. . . . Approximately 80 percent of the world's population still lacks basic telecommunications access. Asia has 1.5 million users, two-thirds of whom are in japan. There are more telephone lines in Manhattan than in all of sub-saharan africa. The united states has thirty-five computers per hundred people; japan has sixteen; taiwan has nine. Ghana, on the other hand, has one computer per thousand people.
>
> (Eisenstein, 1998: 72–73)[1]

It is early days to be clear what the shape of cyberpower will be, but it is interesting to speculate how it may lead to new patterns of social stratification. We may be entering a world where only those with access to information technology have a significant say (and when this is combined with the prospects of the new genetic classes described briefly above becoming a possible future risk, the issues start to multiply).

Information overload

Another scenario looks to the glut of information and how the new society is leading to information overload. We can already see that one consequence of the Web is not simply access to information, but to too much information. A search may be conducted which tells you there are several million pages available for you to browse. A link may be taken which hurls you deeper and deeper into the trivia of the Net. New skills become necessary to manage, sort, handle and select the vast and growing array of data available. We need to be able to distinguish types of information, to be able to assess the validity of information, to be able to streamline, systematise and sort through masses of data to find key materials, otherwise we will be overloaded and incapacitated.

Cybercrimes

Another striking, though not surprising, feature of the new information technologies is the way in which they are generating new worlds of crime. There is already much concern over hacking (entering computer systems without the owner's permission), the unleashing of viruses that can instantly paralyse world communication systems, computer use for the distribution of illegal materials (from drugs and money-laundering to baby-selling and people-selling, and on to a massive world of erotica and pornography). New forms of 'trouble' are starting to appear – cyber-rape, cyber-harassment, cyber-

---

[1] Cyberspace is growing so fast that these figures will be seriously out of date. They are only meant to be indicative of the issues that should be raised. Latest figures are available at http://www.c-i-a.com/. Note too that the lack of capitals for countries is a feature of Eisenstein's writing and not a printing error!

stalking (see the images in films such as *War Games*, *The Net* and *Hackers*). Many of these crimes are 'virtual' because they are much less obviously 'bodily' (they involve digital communications in space) and they seem much harder to control and monitor. (Hackers.com is a major site full of hacking news and resources!)

The dysfunctionality of IT

Some of the changes that come with the new cyberworlds suggest possibilities of deep, social changes within the social organisation of human nature. Writers within this field of study now talk quite cheerily of an era when we become 'cyborgs' and when we enter the 'post-human society'. Human beings are moving beyond their humanness. We are creating new forms of life – finding new forms of time, breaking down classic life rhythms, reordering our sense of time and space, generating a new impersonality. On the Internet, nobody knows you at all, nobody knows who you are, where you are, or even your

age, race or gender. For some it is a way of hiding from others and 'real-time' life, a kind of escape and addiction into a new world.

Looking to the future: technology and the risk society

This chapter has looked briefly at three major revolutions taking place in science technology: the Quantum Revolution, the Biomolecular Revolution and the Computer Revolution. Each of these is bringing major changes to society and, indeed, to the very nature of human life at the start of the twenty-first century. From putting people into space to making babies from test tubes, human life is being reconstructed in novel ways.

The idea of 'Risk Society' starts to alert us to some of the unanticipated dangers that such changes may also bring. In this chapter we have only started to consider some of the issues that this raises.

SUMMARY

1. The 'three pillars of science' are matter, life and mind. Matter leads to the science of the universe and the *Quantum Revolution*. Life leads to the science of biogenetics and the *Biomolecular Revolution*. Mind leads to the science of information and the *Computer Revolution*. With these, science in the twentieth century brought three great 'discoveries': the atom, the gene and the computer. The chapter is roughly structured around these concerns.

2. New technologies bring new risks and are part of the Risk Society.

3. Sociologists study science in a number of ways. Thomas Kuhn introduced the idea of normal science and paradigms. Robert K. Merton saw science as an institution and outlined four key features of it: universalism, communalism, disinterestedness and organised scepticism. More recently, the sociologists of scientific knowledge have seen science as a social construction and examined how science is socially produced in the laboratory by conducting fieldwork studies.

4. The 'Science Wars' indicate the conflicts between those who see science as neutral objective knowledge and those who see it as socially organised and produced.

5. Advances in the new reproductive technologies, *in vitro* fertilisation, aim to help couples who cannot conceive normally to have children, but they raise many new issues of 'risk': from the rights and choice to reproduce (or not); sperm and eggs being frozen for later use; embryo research; surrogacy and commercial surrogacy; cloning for perfection; and the ethics of 'designer babies'.

6. The Information Revolution has developed across the world over the past 20 years. Key themes include its pervasiveness, the importance of digitalisation, the shifts in time and space and the convergence of forms into common networks. It is shifting all aspects of social life and creating digital economies, digital democracies, digital relationships and new cyber-communities. At the same time it brings risks of cyberclasses, cybercrimes, information overload and dysfunctionality.

CRITICAL-THINKING QUESTIONS

1. What problems do you find with the idea that 'technology shapes social life'?

2. Reconsider what you understand by Beck's notion of the 'Risk Society'. Provide illustrations from contemporary science and technology.

3. Examine the Science Wars. How far do you think 'sociology of science studies' undermine scientific work?

4. Examine the ethical issues developed from the Human Genome Project.

GOING FURTHER

Further reading

Introducing the sociology of science:

David J. Hess, *Science Studies: An Advanced Introduction* (1997)
An excellent guide to the sociology of science.

On the 'Risk Society':

Ulrich Beck, *Risk Society* (1992)
The classic and key statement of the emergence of a risk society, though it is far from being an 'easy read'. He has developed his argument further in *World Risk Society* (1999), and it is evaluated from a number of perspectives in Barbara Adam, Ulrich Beck and Joost Van Loon (eds), *The Risk Society and Beyond* (2000).

Popular science:

Michio Kaku, *Visions: How Science will Revolutionize the 21st Century and Beyond* (1998)
Has a major world scientist interviewing 150 other scientists and making major predictions – a good example of an optimistic faith in scientific progress and needs to be read with a sociological eye!

On the new reproductive technologies:

Jeanette Edwards *et al.*, *Technologies of Procreation* (2nd edn, 1999)

Sarah Franklin, *Embodied Progress* (1997)

Gay Becker, *The Elusive Embryo* (2000).
These three books look at the problems of infertility and the solutions to such concerns through the new reproductive technologies. They trace the history, the politics and the experience of NRTs.

Evaluations of sociobiology and the new evolutionary psychology:

Andrew Brown, *The Darwin Wars: The Scientific Battle for the Soul of Man* (1999)

Hilary Rose and Steven Rose, *Alas Poor Darwin: Arguments against Evolutionary Psychology* (2001)

Richard Lewontin, *It Ain't Necessarily So: The Dream of the Human Genome and Other Illusions* (2000)

Barbara Katz Rothman, *Genetic Maps and Human Imaginations: The Limits of Science in Understanding Who We Are* (1998)
These books look at the controversies surrounding the 'biological debates'. Rothman's book is a beautifully written and passionate critique of the worst excesses of science.

On cyberworlds:

Cees Hamelink, *The Ethics of Cyberspace* (2000)

Tim Jordan, *Cyberpower: The Culture and Politics of Cyberspace and the Internet* (1999)

David Gauntlett (ed.), *web.studies* (2000)
Three different entry points to the cyber debates. The first looks at ethical concerns; the second at political and the third is an altogether 'jazzier' account of how the web is impacting our everyday studies and life.

Watch a video/Read a book

Now may be the time to brush up your knowledge on science fiction. Cyberspace can also be found in science fiction, in the work of writers such as William Gibson in his trilogy *Neuromancer* (1984), *Count Zero* (1986) and *Mona Lisa Overdrive* (1988).

Also take a look at:

- James Whale's *Frankenstein* (1931): the classic about a research scientist creating a living monster. There have been many spin offs and remakes of all kinds!
- Fritz Lang's *Metropolis* (1926): futuristic tale is full of striking images and disturbing politics.

On cyberspace, see:

- Brett Leonard's *The LawnMower Man* (1992): the classic for special effects of virtual reality
- Andy Wachowki's *The Matrix* (triology): *The Matrix* (1999), *The Matrix Reloaded* (2003), *The Matrix Revolutions* (2003): many have suggested these are the state-of-the-art 'science' fictions.

Some of the most popular films would include:

- Joseph Sargent's *The Forbin Project* (1969)
- John Carpenter's *Dark Star* (1974)
- Ridley Scott's *Blade Runner* (1982)
- Chris Columbus's *Bicentennial Man* (1999)
- James Cameron's *The Terminator* (1984) and *Terminator II* (1991)
- Jonathan Mostow's *Terminator III: Rise of the machines* (2003)
- Andrei Tarkovsky's *Solaris* (1972).

Connecting up

Connect to other chapters

- Connect theories of science to Chapter 3 and methods.
- Connect reproductive technologies debates to Chapter 17 on families.
- Connect cyberworlds to interaction (Chapter 6), power (Chapter 15), class (Chapters 8–10).

To the websites

- A host of interesting websites relevant to these discussions are included in David Gauntlett's *web.studies* (2000).
- The history of major Muslim/Islamic scientists who antedated the European Renaissance:

  http://www.sullivan-county.com/id2/index.htm
- The Mark Weiser Web page is on:

  http://www.ubiq.com/weiser
- History of space exploration:

  http://www.solarviews.com/eng/history.htm
- The US National Human Genome Research Institute:

  http://www.nhgri.nih.gov/
- The UK National Human Genome Project:

  http://www.hgmp.mrc.ac.uk/
- Human Fertilisation and Embryology Authority:

  http://www.hfea.gov.uk/home

For additional case studies, multiple choice questions, internet exercises, and annotated weblinks specific to this chapter, visit this book's website at **www.pearsoned.co.uk/plummer**

PART FIVE SOCIAL CHANGE

CHAPTER 23

POPULATIONS, CITIES AND THE SHAPE OF THINGS TO COME

The city is a world of strangers

Lynn Loftland

IN 1519 A BAND OF SPANISH conquistadors led by Hernando Cortés reached Tenochtitlán, the capital of the Aztec empire. They were stunned by the beautiful, lake-encircled city, teeming with some 300,000 people – more than lived in any European city at that time. Gazing down broad streets, exploring magnificent stone temples, and examining the golden treasures of the royal palace, Cortés and his soldiers wondered if they were dreaming.

Cortés soon set his mind to looting the city's many priceless treasures. At first, he was repelled by the superior military forces of Montezuma and the Aztecs. But Cortés spent the next two years raising a vast army and finally returned to utterly destroy Tenochtitlán. On the rubble of this ancient urban centre, he constructed a new city in the European fashion – 'Ciudad Imperial de México', Mexico City.

Today Mexico City is once more fighting for its life. Its soaring population had reached over 18 million by the end of the twentieth century – hugely greater than the number that astonished Cortés. A triple burden of rising population, urban sprawl and desperate poverty weighs on Mexico as it does on much of today's world.

KEY THEMES

- The nature of demography and how populations are shaped
- Issues around the 'population explosion'
- The growth of cities – old and new
- The problems that city life raises

(Left) Aerial view of a market in St Paul, Reunion
Source: © Yann Arthus-Bertrand/Corbis

COUNTRY FACT FILE

MEXICO

Population	97,366,000 (1999)
Urban population	73.8%
Per capita GNP	$3,840
Life expectancy	72 years (1998)
Literacy	89% (1995)
Languages	Spanish (official); 1 million people speak indigenous languages
Religions	Mainly Catholic
Main cities	Mexico: 17,500,000;
Guadalajara:	1,650,000; Netzahualcóyotl: 1,250,500; Monterrey: 1,069,000; Puebla: 1,007,200; Ciudad Juárez: 789,500

Source: New Internationalist, *The World Guide*, 2001: 373

SOCIAL SHAPES OF THE WORLD

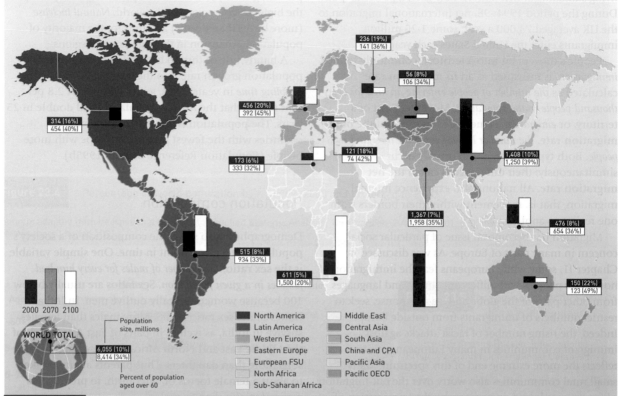

| Map 23.1 | Population growth in global perspective (millions): actual or estimated populations in 2000 and forecasts for 2100 |

North and Latin America are the only two major regions where the population is forecast still to be growing in 2100. In the United States this is largely because of first-generation immigration. Despite war and disease, the population of Africa will grow from 784 million today to around 1.6 billion in 2050. China and its neighbours will start to see their population shrink. India will overtake China as the world's most populous nation by 2020. Europe, including Turkey and the former Soviet Union, will start to see its population fall. By 2100, it is likely that one-third of the world's population will be over age 60.

Source: adapted from International Institute for Applied Systems Analysis; *The Guardian*, 2 August 2001, p. 3 © *The Guardian*.

CONTROVERSY AND DEBATE

APOCALYPSE SOON? WILL PEOPLE OVERWHELM THE EARTH?

Are you worried about the world's increasing population? Think about this: by the time you finish reading this box, the number of people on the planet will rise by more than a thousand. By this time tomorrow, 250,000 more will be born. As Table 23.2 shows, there are about six births for every death on the planet, so that the world's population is marching upward by 90 million annually.

It is no wonder that many population analysts are deeply concerned about the future. The earth has an unprecedented population. Just the 1.6 billion people we have added since 1975 exceeds the planet's total in 1900. Might Thomas Robert Malthus, who pre-

CONTROVERSY AND DEBATE CONTINUED

Table 23.2	How the global population is increasing		
	Births	**Deaths**	**Net increase**
Year	141,000,000	51,000,000	90,000,000
Month	1,750,000	4,250,000	7,500,000
Day	391,000	141,000	250,000
Hour	16,300	5,875	10,425
Minute	270	98	172
Second	4.5	1.6	2.9

dicted that population would outstrip the earth's resources and plunge humanity into war and suffering, be right after all?

Lester Brown, a population and environmental activist, represents the neo-Malthusians who foresee a coming apocalypse if we do not change our ways. Brown concedes that Malthus failed to imagine how much technology (especially fertilisers and plant genetics) could boost the planet's agricultural output. But he maintains that the earth's burgeoning population is rapidly outstripping a host of finite resources. Families in many poor countries can find little firewood; members of rich societies are depleting oil reserves; everyone is draining our reserves of clean water (Brown, et al., 2001).

Just as important, according to the neo-Malthusians, humanity is steadily poisoning the planet with waste. There is a limit to the earth's capacity to absorb pollution, they warn, and as the number of people continues to increase, our quality of life inevitably will decline.

But another camp of analysts sharply disagrees. Julian Simon (1981) points out that two centuries ago, Malthus predicted global catastrophe. Today, however, there are almost six times as many people on the earth and, on average, they live longer, healthier lives than ever before. As Simon sees it, the current state of the planet is cause for great celebration.

Simon argues that the neo-Malthusians err in assuming that the world has finite resources that are spread thinner and thinner as population increases. Rather, the anti-Malthusians counter, people have the capacity to improve their lives. We have yet to determine how many people the earth can support because humans are constantly rewriting the rules, in effect, by deploying new fertilisers, developing new high-yield crops, discovering new forms of energy. Simon points out that today's global economy makes available more resources and products than ever (including energy and a host of consumer goods), and at increasingly low prices. He looks optimistically towards the future, noting that technology, economic investment and, above all, human ingenuity have consistently proven the doomsayers wrong. And he is betting they will continue to do so.

CONTINUE THE DEBATE:

1. Where do you place your bet? Do you think the earth can support 10 or 12 billion people? Why or why not?

2. What are some likely consequences of the fact that almost 90 per cent of current population growth is occurring in poor countries?

3. Does the world population problem only affect people in low-income countries? What must people in rich societies do to ensure our children's future?

History and theory of population growth

Throughout most of human history, societies favoured large families, since human labour was the key to productivity. Additionally, until the development of rubber condoms 150 years ago, controlling birth was uncertain at best. But if birth rates were high, so were death rates, as populations were periodically ravaged by infectious diseases. Thus world population at the dawn of civilisation, about 8000 BCE, hovered well below 100 million.

Figure 23.6 marks a demographic shift which began in about 1800, as the earth's population reached the 1 billion mark. Humans reached the next billion by 1930, barely a century later! The global population reached 3 billion by 1962 – after just 32 years – and 4 billion by 1974, a scant 12 years later. The rate of world population

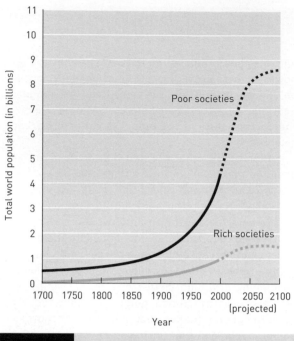

| Figure 23.6 | The increase in world population, 1700–2100 |

increase has recently slowed, but in mid-2000, the world population was estimated at 6.1 billion. In no previous century did the world's population even double. In the twentieth century, it increased *fourfold*.

Currently, global population is increasing by 86 million people each year, with more than 90 per cent of this growth in poor societies. At this rate, the earth's people will probably reach 8.3 billion by 2025 and pass 10 billion within a century from now. Without a change in global consumption and living patterns, this increase will have dramatic social and environmental consequences. For this reason, a number of scholars have reflected on the potential impacts of population growth. This chapter now assesses some of the more influential perspectives.

Malthusian theory

The sudden population growth two centuries ago sparked the development of demography. Thomas Robert Malthus (1766–1834), an English clergyman and economist, noted that the number of people in the world had begun to increase geometrically (that is, doubling each time, 2, 4, 8, 16, 32, etc.). Even though people were improving farming technology and techniques, Malthus feared that the limited range of farmland could only sustain an *arithmetic increase* (as in the series 2, 3, 4, 5, 6)

in the production of food (1926; orig. 1798). He concluded that the world might head towards a period of catastrophic starvation.

Malthus noted that people could slow the tide of population increase through *preventive checks*, such as family planning, sexual abstinence and delayed marriages; however, people objected to birth control on religious grounds, and his common sense told Malthus that people would not abstain from sex or marry very much later. He also predicted that such *positive checks* as famine, disease and war would slow – but not prevent – the progression towards the final catastrophe, a vision that earned him the nickname of 'the dismal parson'.

Critical evaluation

Fortunately for us, Malthus's predictions were flawed. By 1850, the birth rate in Europe began to drop, partly because children were becoming more of an economic liability than an asset and partly because people began to use condoms. Second, Malthus underestimated human ingenuity. Irrigation, fertilisers and pesticides have increased farm production far more than he imagined. Some critics also noted that poor regions suffer deaths from war and famine disproportionately and objected to viewing suffering as a 'law of nature' rather than the product of inequality.

Still, we should not entirely dismiss Malthus's distressing prediction. First, habitable land, clean water and fresh air are certainly finite. Greater industrial productivity has taken a toll on the natural environment. Additionally, as medical advances have lowered death rates, the world population has risen even faster. This planet cannot sustain an indefinite increase in the number of people.

Demographic transition theory

Malthus's rather crude analysis has been superseded by **demographic transition theory**, *a thesis linking population patterns to a society's level of technological development*. Why did world population soar after 1800? Why is population increase much higher in poor countries than in rich nations? Demographic transition theory answers these questions by analysing birth and death rates at four stages of a society's technological development. As shown in Figure 23.7, societies yet to industrialise, those at Stage 1, have high birth rates because of the economic value of children, the absence of effective family planning and the high risk that children will not survive to adulthood. Death rates, too, are high, due to periodic outbreaks of

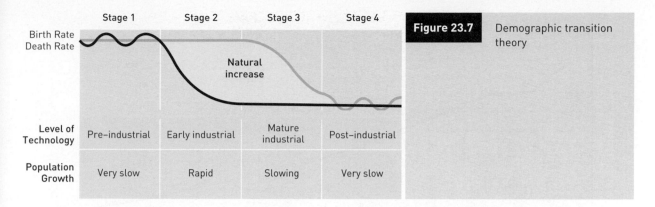

	Stage 1	Stage 2	Stage 3	Stage 4	
Birth Rate / Death Rate			Natural increase		**Figure 23.7** Demographic transition theory
Level of Technology	Pre–industrial	Early industrial	Mature industrial	Post–industrial	
Population Growth	Very slow	Rapid	Slowing	Very slow	

plague or other infectious disease, low living standards and a lack of medical technology. But deaths almost offset births, so population increase is modest.

Stage 2, the onset of industrialisation, brings a demographic transition as population surges upward. Technology expands food supplies and science combats disease. Death rates fall sharply but birth rates remain high, resulting in rapid population growth. It was in an era like this that Malthus formulated his ideas, and that goes a long way towards explaining his pessimism. Most of the world's least economically developed societies today are still in this high-growth stage.

In Stage 3, a mature industrial economy, birth rates drop, finally coming into line with death rates and, once again, curbing population growth. Fertility falls, because most children born do survive to adulthood, and rising living standards make raising children expensive. Affluence, in other words, transforms offspring from economic assets into economic liabilities. Smaller families, also favoured by women working outside the home, are made possible by the widespread availability of family planning. As birth rates follow death rates downward, population growth slows further.

The most recent stage corresponds to a post-industrial economy. The birth rate in such societies continues to fall, in part because dual-income couples gradually become the norm and partly because the costs of raising children continue to rise. This trend, coupled with steady death rates, means that, at best, population grows only very slowly. Recent years have witnessed a natural *decrease* in Europe's population.

Critical evaluation

Demographic transition theory suggests that technology holds the key to demographic shifts. Instead of the runaway population increase Malthus feared, this analysis foresees technology reining in population growth. Demographic transition theory dovetails with

modernisation theory, one approach to global development examined in Chapter 9.

Modernisation theorists are optimistic that industrialisation will also solve the population problems that now are placing strains on poor countries. But critics, notably dependency theorists, counter that current economic arrangements only ensure continued poverty in much of the world. Unless there is a significant redistribution of global resources, they maintain, our planet will become increasingly divided into industrialised 'haves', enjoying low population growth, and non-industrialised 'have-nots', struggling in vain to feed soaring populations.

Global population today

A brief survey of population trends around the world today reveals a growing gap between events in richer and poorer nations. Understanding these trends is the first step to understanding the nature of the population problem.

The low-growth North

When the Industrial Revolution began, growth in Western European and North American populations peaked at 3 per cent annually, doubling the population in little more than one generation. But, since then, growth rates have eased downward throughout the Northern Hemisphere. The natural increase from births over deaths in Europe dropped from 7.7 per thousand in 1960 to 1.00 per thousand in 1990. As Europe entered Stage 4, the birth rate neared the replacement level of 2.1 children per woman, a point demographers designate as **zero population growth**, *the level of reproduction, migration and death that maintains population at a steady state*. Demographers argue that most of Europe will be in steep population decline by the end of the first decade of the new century (Figure 23.8).

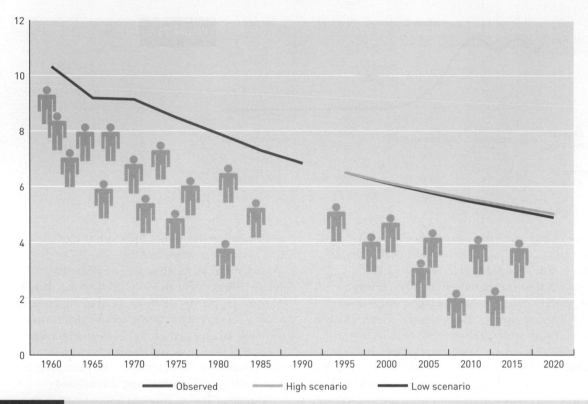

| Figure 23.8 | Population of the EU as a percentage of world population |

Legend: Observed — High scenario — Low scenario

Source: adapted from *Social Trends*, 27 (1992: 139), Social and Regional Statistics Office for National Statistics, Eurostat (1995a)

But at present Europe's population is actually increasing, due to a second key factor, in-migration. In 1993, the migratory balance in the EU worked out at 2.8 per thousand (Germany and Luxembourg had large increases, while Ireland lost almost 2 people per thousand, though Irish outflow had begun to reverse in 1997). In 1992, there were some 16 million 'foreigners' living in Europe – 4.3 per cent of the total population.

The high-growth South

Population growth is a serious and increasing problem in the poor societies of the Southern Hemisphere. Only a few nations lack industrial technology altogether, placing them at demographic transition theory's Stage 1. Most of Latin America, Africa and Asia has moved to Stage 2, still primarily agricultural but with some industry. In these nations, advanced medical technology (much supplied by rich societies) has sharply reduced death rates, but birth rates remain high. A look back at Figure 23.4 shows that poor societies now account for two-thirds of the earth's people, a proportion that continues to rise.

In poor countries, urban families average four to five children; in rural areas, the number is often six to eight

(World Bank, 1991). No one doubts that world population simply cannot keep increasing at anything like its current rate. At a 1994 global population conference in Cairo, delegates from 180 nations not only agreed on the need for vigorous action to contain population growth, but also pointed out the crucial link between population control and the status of women. The box offers a closer look.

In the last decade, the world has made significant progress in lowering fertility. At the same time, however, mortality rates are falling. Although few would oppose medical programmes that save lives, especially those of children, this trend exerts upward pressure on population. In fact, population growth in most low-income regions of the world is due *primarily* to declining death rates. After about 1920, when Europe and North America began to export advances in scientific medicine, nutrition and sanitation around the world, mortality tumbled. Since then, inoculations against infectious diseases and the use of antibiotics and insecticides have pushed down death rates with stunning effectiveness. For example, in Sri Lanka, malaria caused half of all deaths in the 1930s; a decade later, insecticides used to kill malaria-carrying mosquitoes cut the malaria death toll in

CONTROVERSY AND DEBATE

EMPOWERING WOMEN: THE KEY TO CONTROLLING POPULATION GROWTH

Sohad Ahmad lives in a village 50 miles south of Cairo, Egypt's capital city. Her husband is a farmer and her family is poor. At first glance, one might conclude that this woman's situation fits a stereotype all too typical in low-income countries: desperate poverty pushing families to have more and more children to work the fields and earn more income. But this is not the case.

Sohad Ahmad has had only two children, and she and her husband will have no more. Egypt's rising population has already created such a demand for land that her family could not afford more even if they could farm it. More importantly, Sohad Ahmad does not want her life defined only by child-bearing. Thus she has made a personal decision to have no more children.

Women like Sohad Ahmad who are taking control of their fertility and seeking greater opportunities are more and more common across Egypt. Indeed, this country has made great progress in reducing its annual population growth from 3 per cent just ten years ago to 2.3 per cent today. This is why the International Conference on Population and Development selected Cairo for its historic 1994 meeting.

The 1994 Cairo conference was not the first of its kind, but it stands out in several respects. First, it had an unprecedented base of participation, with representatives from 180 nations. Second, delegates from more than 1,200 non-governmental organisations also attended the meeting. Third, the Cairo conference reached virtual consensus on a new path towards effective control of global population, elevating the standing of women.

In the past, population control programmes have been limited to making birth control technology available to women. This is a crucial objective, since only half the world's married women make use of effective birth control. But it has become clear that more than technology is needed to curb population increase. The larger picture shows that, even with available birth control, population continues to grow in societies that define women's primary responsibility as raising children.

Dr Nafis Sadik, an Egyptian woman who headed United Nations efforts at population control for some time, summed up the new approach to lowering birth rates: *give women more choices and they will have fewer children*. In other words, women with access to schooling and jobs, who can decide when and if they wish to marry and who bear children as a matter of choice, will limit their fertility. The door to schooling must be open to older women too, Dr Sadik adds, since they often exercise great influence in local communities.

Evidence from countries around the world is that controlling population and raising the social standing of women are inseparable objectives.

CONTINUE THE DEBATE:

1. Discuss the ways in which a country can control the size of its population.

2. Do you agree that the key to population control is 'empowering women' or is this taking too much responsibility away from men?

3. Is population control really necessary in a world where some countries have such a low birth rate?

Sources: Linden (1994); Ashford (1995); UNFPA (2000)

half. Although we hail such an achievement, this technological advance sent Sri Lanka's population soaring. Similarly, India's infant mortality rate slid from 130 in 1975 to 74 in 1995, a decline that has helped boost that nation's population to 1,000 million.

Improvement in access to family planning in the developing world is clearly necessary, but how it should be introduced and who should direct the change in population is an open question. Many people in less developed countries view family planning initiatives coming from the West as racist, arguing that people in rich nations have little real regard for the welfare of the

world's poor and instead only wish to curb the potential for immigration from the South to the North and the propensity for violence in overcrowded regions from which the North extracts natural resources. Policies of previous governments in India and China that have forced people to limit family size have proved highly unpopular among many groups in each country. Some people in both richer and poorer countries suggest that the best way to control population growth is to distribute the world's resources and wealth more fairly between all countries, and to expand educational and career opportunities for women everywhere.

Urbanisation: the growth of cities

For most of human history, the sights and sounds of great cities such as Hong Kong, Rio de Janeiro, Paris or Los Angeles were completely unknown. The world's people lived in small, nomadic groups, moving as they depleted vegetation or searched for migratory game. Humans survived for tens of thousands of years without permanent settlements. Cities first emerged in the Middle East, then arose on all the continents, but held only a tiny fraction of the earth's people until very recently.

Today, the population of the world's largest five cities exceeds the total planetary population when cities first developed. By 1950, nearly 80 cities had populations in excess of 1 million; by 2000, that number exceeded 250. The United Nations has predicted that within the next ten years, half of the world's population will live in cities. These figures testify to the steady march of **urbanisation**, *the concentration of humanity into cities*. Urbanisation both redistributes the population within a society and transforms many patterns of social life. We will trace these changes in terms of four differing patterns of urban life:

1. The evolution of early cities beginning 12,000 years ago.

2. The rise of industrial cities after 1750.

3. The explosive growth of mega-cities in low-income countries in the late twentieth century.

4. The recent rise of global cities.

The evolution of early cities

Cities are a relatively new development in human history. Only about 12,000 years ago did our ancestors found the earliest permanent settlements, setting the stage for the *first urban revolution*. As glaciers drew back at the end of the last ice age, people congregated in warm regions with fertile soil. At the same time, humans discovered how to domesticate animals and cultivate crops. Whereas hunting and gathering demanded continual movement, raising food could require people to remain in one place. Domesticating animals and plants also yielded a material surplus, which freed some people from concentrating on food production and allowed them to build shelters, make tools, weave clothing and take part in religious rituals. Thus the founding of cities, made possible by favourable ecology and changing technology, was truly revolutionary, enhancing productive specialisation and raising living standards as never before.

The first cities

Historians identify Jericho as one of the first cities. This settlement lies to the north of the Dead Sea in disputed land currently occupied by Israel. About 8000 BCE, Jericho contained about 600 people. By 4000 BCE, numerous cities were flourishing in the Fertile Crescent between the Tigris and Euphrates rivers in present-day Iraq, and urban settlement had begun along the Nile River in Egypt.

Some cities, with populations reaching 50,000, became centres of urban empires. Priest-kings wielded absolute power over lesser nobles, administrators, artisans, soldiers and farmers. Slaves, captured in frequent military campaigns, laboured to build monumental structures such as the pyramids of Egypt (Kenyon, 1957; Hamblin, 1973; Stavrianos, 1983; Lenski *et al.*, 1995).

In at least three other areas of the world, cities developed independently. Several large, complex settlements bordered the Indus River in present-day Pakistan, starting about 2500 BCE. Scholars date Chinese cities from 2000 BCE. And in Latin America, urban centres arose around 1500 BCE (Lamberg-Karlovsky, 1973; Change, 1977; Coe and Diehl, 1980).

Pre-industrial European cities

Urbanisation in Europe began about 1800 BCE on the Mediterranean island of Crete. Cities soon spread throughout Greece, resulting in more than 100 city-states, of which Athens is the most famous. During its Golden Age, lasting barely a century after 500 BCE, Athenians made major contributions to the Western way of life in philosophy, the arts and politics. Yet Athenian society, numbering some 300,000, rested on the labour of slaves, who comprised a third of the population. Their democratic principles notwithstanding, Athenian men also denied the rights of citizenship to women and foreigners (Mumford, 1961; Gouldner, 1965; Stavrianos, 1983).

As Greek civilisation faded, the city of Rome grew to almost 1 million inhabitants and became the centre of a vast empire. By the first century CE, the militaristic Romans had subdued much of northern Africa, Europe and the Middle East. In the process, Rome spread its language, arts and technology. Four centuries later, the Roman Empire fell into disarray, a victim of its gargantuan size, internal corruption and militaristic appetite. Yet, between them, the Greeks and Romans founded cities across Europe from the Atlantic Ocean all the way to Asia, including Vienna, Paris, London and Constantinople.

The fall of the Roman Empire initiated an era of urban decline in Europe lasting 600 years. Cities became smaller as people drew back within defensive walls and competing warlords battled for territory. About the eleventh century, the 'Dark Ages' came to an end as a semblance of peace allowed trade to bring life to cities once again.

Expanding trade prompted medieval cities to tear down their walls. Amsterdam grew considerably from the fourteenth century, as it became more prominent in trade. Beneath towering cathedrals, the narrow and winding streets of London, Brussels and Florence soon teemed with merchants, artisans, priests, peddlers, nobles and servants. Typically, occupational groups such as bakers, key-makers and carpenters clustered together in distinct sections or 'quarters'. Ethnic groups also inhabited their own neighbourhoods, often because people kept them out of other districts. The term ghetto (from the Italian word *borghetto*, meaning 'outside the city walls') first described the segregation of Jews in medieval Venice.

The growth of industrial European cities

Throughout the Middle Ages, steadily increasing commerce enriched a new urban middle class or *bourgeoisie* (from the French, meaning 'of the town'). By the fifteenth century, the power of the bourgeoisie rivalled that of the hereditary nobility. In the 1400s Paris became the largest European city with a population of over a quarter of a million people.

The rise of the modern industrial city

By 1750 industrialisation was well under way, triggering a *second urban revolution*, first in Europe and then in North America. Factories unleashed productive power as never before, causing cities to grow to unprecedented size. London, the largest European city in 1700, with 550,000 people, swelled to 6.5 million by 1900 (Weber, 1963; orig. 1899; Chandler and Fox, 1974). Most of this increase was due to migration from rural areas by people seeking a better standard of living.

Cities not only grew but changed shape as well. The industrial-capitalist city replaced older irregular streets with broad, straight boulevards, which accommodated the increasing flow of commercial traffic. Steam and electric trams, too, criss-crossed the expanding cities. Lewis Mumford (1961) adds that developers divided cities into regular-sized lots, making land a commodity to be bought and sold. Finally, the cathedrals that had guided the life of medieval cities were soon dwarfed by towering, brightly lit and frantic central business districts made up of banks, retail stores and office buildings. Built for business, cities became increasingly crowded and impersonal. Crime rates rose. Especially at the outset, a small number of industrialists lived in grand style, while for most adults and children, factory work proved exhausting and provided bare subsistence.

In 1810, 20 per cent of the British population lived in cities and towns. By 1910 the figure was nearer 80 per cent (Kumar, 1978). Taking Europe as a whole, Therborn (1995: 184) notes that the proportion of European peoples living in cities escalated from a tenth in 1800, to a third by 1900, to two-thirds by 1989. Although European cities have often continued to grow significantly, they have usually had major geographical and political restrictions placed on their development. Consequently, European cities have not tended to reach the proportions of some cities in the newly industrialising world.

The shapes of the twentieth-century city

The twentieth century has seen living spaces changing in a number of directions, from the growth of central cities to expansion beyond suburbs. The pace of urban change has accelerated with time.

The great metropolis: 1860–1950

Following the First World War, waves of people deserted the countryside for cities in hopes of obtaining better jobs. This growth marked the era of the **metropolis** (from Greek words, meaning 'mother city'), *a large city that socially and economically dominates an urban area*. Metropolises soon became the manufacturing, commercial and residential centres. The concentration of industrial technology not only generated expansion of the population, but also changed the physical shape of cities. From the three- or four-storey towns in the United States in 1850, steel girders and mechanical lifts raised structures over ten storeys high in 1880. In 1930, New York's Empire State Building became an urban wonder, a true 'skyscraper' stretching 102 storeys into the clouds.

Decentralisation: commuter towns and the suburbs

The industrial metropolis reached its peak during reconstruction after the Second World War. Since then, something of a turnaround, termed urban decentralisation, has occurred as people have deserted the city centres for outlying suburbs. Many large cities stopped growing, and some lost considerable population, after 1950. During the 1970s the populations of Paris and London dropped by around 20 per cent. Instead of clustering in densely packed central cities, urban populations expanded outwards.

Just as central cities flourished a century ago, we have recently witnessed the expansion of both new towns and **suburbs**, *urban areas beyond the political boundaries of a city*. They began to grow late in the nineteenth century as railways and buses enabled people to work in city centres yet leave behind the centralised congestion when they went home to quieter dormitory communities. The suburban trend caught on more quickly in the United States than in Europe.

Cheaper cars and declining land prices, and the need to move from seriously overcrowded cities such as London, gradually also led to the development of planned new towns, such as Stevenage in Hertfordshire or Basildon in Essex. Here home ownership catered to more prosperous working-class people, and council housing estates catered for the less well-off.

Following the consumers, business, too, began moving to the new towns, and large, often impersonal, shopping centres started to replace the city centre stores of the metropolitan era. Manufacturing companies also decentralised into industrial parks far from the high property taxes, congested streets and the growing crime rates identified with inner cities. The development of the motorway system, with its ring roads encircling central cities, made moving out to the new towns or the suburbs almost irresistible for residents and business people alike.

Suburbanisation also came at the cost of conformity. In the United States one of the most famous suburban sprawls was Levittown, the brainchild of the American developer Abraham Levitt. It was derided by critics as a field of look-alike boxes – a label which aptly suits many of the council estates in Britain as well. Additionally, as businesses have centralised into large chain stores, suburban shopping districts increasingly resemble each other. The main variation often is only the order in which the major department stores and so forth are arranged. But these suburbs also developed a more worrying form of conformity, as communities such as Levittown excluded black, Asian and Hispanic residents (Gans, 1982; orig. 1962). Indeed, racial prejudice against increasing numbers of immigrants and ethnic minorities fuelled the growth of suburbs, prompting many whites to flee to homogeneous, high-prestige enclaves.

Moreover, this rapid growth in suburbs and new towns soon threw older cities into financial problems.

Population decline meant falling tax revenues. The overall result has often been inner-city decay. To many middle-class white people, the deteriorating inner cities became synonymous with slum housing, crime, drugs, unemployment, the poor and minorities. This perception fuelled wave after wave of 'white flight' and urban decline. Suburbs may have their share of poor housing, congestion and crime, but they still appeal to many people because they remain largely white, unlike the inner cities whose populations encompass a greater share of ethnic minorities.

Gentrification

The location of ghettos and centres of urban prosperity, however, do change over time. This change largely results from the process of 'gentrification', whereby areas in decline are transformed into areas of prosperity. Business and politicians periodically cooperate, with businesses providing the money and labour to restore or rebuild facilities, and politicians providing tax and legal incentives to improve the profitability of these 'urban recycling' schemes. The London Docklands, eight and a half square miles of East London, has been transformed from run-down docks and poverty-stricken dwellings to a prosperous business community dotted with luxury flats and trendy boutiques. Gentrification is a process of moving wealth back into the metropolis, but this process carries a heavy price. Urban ghettos are the homes of many poor people, and cheap housing and low-wage jobs do not fit comfortably into high-profit renewal programmes. Often, the poor residents of gentrified areas get pushed aside and are left to relocate themselves in other poor and overcrowded areas (Brownhill, 1990). Like suburbanisation, gentrification in Europe and the United States is a process which more often has worked to the benefit of white people at the expense of ethnic minorities.

Mega-cities and megalopolis: the rise of size

In 1950, only London (with 8 million residents) and New York (with 12.3 million residents) were **mega-cities**, defined as *a city with a population exceeding 8 million* (World Resources Institute, 1996). But by 1990 there were 21 mega-cities, with 16 in the developing world. Some such cities, like Shanghai and Seoul, are compact; others, like Bangkok and Manila, sprawl over a considerable area. The continuing decentralisation of cities has also produced vast urban areas that encompass numerous municipalities. In the early 1960s, the French geographer Jean Gottmann (1961) coined the term **megalopolis** to designate *a vast urban region containing a number of cities and their surrounding suburbs*. Although a megalopolis is composed of hundreds of separate cities and suburbs, from an aeroplane at night one observes what appears to be a single continuous city. These are sometimes also called agglomerations, which link cities to suburbs to smaller cities. Among the major agglomerations are Tokyo, New York, Seoul, Mexico City, Mumbai (Bombay), São Paulo, Cairo, Manila, Shanghai and Lagos (http:/www.citypopulation.de/World). Table 23.3 looks at some projections on the growth of such cities. It is clear that in the 1950s the 'big cities' tended to be both in the West and comparatively small when placed alongside the projections for 2015. Remember these are only estimates: despite attempts to measure city sizes, it is exceedingly difficult (see also Figure 23.9).

Table 23.3	The world's ten largest urban agglomerations in 1950 and 2004, and projected to 2015 (populations in millions)					
1950 est.			**2004 est.**		**2015 est.**	
1. New York, USA	12.3	1. Tokyo, Japan	33.9	1. Tokyo, Japan	36.0
2. London, England	8.7	2. Mexico City, Mexico	18.4	2. Mumbai, India	22.6
3. Tokyo, Japan	6.9	3. New York, USA	21.8	3. Delhi, India	21.0
4. Paris, France	5.4	4. Seoul, S.Korea	21.8	4. Mexico City, Mexico	20.0
5. Moscow, Russia	5.4	5. Sào Paulo, Brazil	19.8	5. São Paulo, Brazil	20.0
6. Shanghai, China	5.3	6. Mumbai, India	19.1	6. New York USA	20.0
7. Essen, Germany	5.3	7. Delhi, India	18.5	7. Dhaka, Bangladesh	18.0
8. Buenos Aires, Argentina	5.0	8. Los Angeles, USA	17.6	8. Jakarta, Indonesia	17.5
9. Chicago, USA	4.9	9. Osaka, Japan	16.7	9. Lagos, Nigeria	17.0
10. Calcutta, India	4.4	10. Jakarta, Indonesia	16.5	10. Calcutta, India	16.7

Source: adapted from United Nations, *World Urbanization Prospects: the 1999 and 2003 revisions UNDESA*

Population, in millions

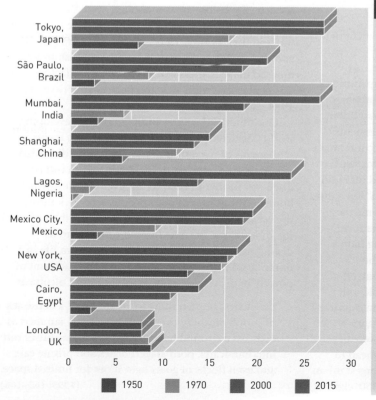

Figure 23.9 Growth of urban agglomerations, 1950–2015

Source: adapted from United Nations, *World Urbanization Prospects: the 1999 revision.* The United Nations is the author of the original material.

Urban tensions

With so many processes in the rise of cities, from the expansion of work with very low wages, low job security and few benefits, to suburbanisation and gentrification, working against the poorest residents, it is small wonder that tensions between city elites and poor people result. Sometimes these tensions arise on a small scale, such as with acts of vandalism and petty crime. Occasionally, they erupt into riots. The UK has experienced a succession of such riots: in Bristol in 1980, in Brixton, Southall, Toxteth and Moss Side in 1981; again in Brixton and Toxteth, as well as in the Broadwater Farm estate (Tottenham) and Handsworth (Birmingham) in 1985; in Bradford and Burnley in 2001. While these riots mainly reflected ethnic grievances, they provided a forum for youths and older poor people from many ethnic groups to vent their frustrations. Like the more internationally famous riots in Los Angeles following the acquittal of white police officers who had beaten the black motorist Rodney King unconscious, these riots generally broke out in response to an act of violence perpetrated against a poor person. Such riots may do little to solve the long-term problems of the poor and have often served to reinforce the stereotypes held by the residents of gentrified city areas and suburbs that the poor constitute a problem which has to be controlled.

Mega-cities in low-income societies

The world has experienced a revolutionary expansion of cities three times in human history. The first urban revolution began around 8000 BCE with the first urban settlements and continued as permanent settlements later appeared on different continents. The second urban revolution took hold about 1750 and lasted for two centuries as the Industrial Revolution touched off rapid growth of cities in Europe and North America. But a third urban revolution started around 1950. This time the change is taking place in the less developed nations.

In 1950, only a quarter of the people living in low-income countries inhabited cities; by 1995, the proportion had risen to 42 per cent. At the time of writing, it exceeds 50 per cent. Moreover, while only seven cities (two of which were in low-income countries) had populations over 5 million in 1950, by 1995 37 cities had passed this mark, and 25 of them were in poor nations. Table 23.3 looks back to 1950 and ahead to 2015, comparing the size of the world's ten largest urban areas (cities and surrounding suburbs). In 1950, eight of the top ten were in industrialised countries. By 2015, however, the majority will be in less economically developed countries.

Not only will these exploding urban areas be the world's largest, but they will encompass unprecedented populations. Relatively rich countries such as Japan may have the resources to provide for cities with upwards of 30 million people, but for poor nations, such as Mexico and Brazil, such supercities will tax resources that are already severely strained. Shanty towns and *favelas* are homes for millions of the world's population.

To understand the third urban revolution, recall that many poor societies are now entering the high-growth stage of demographic transition. Falling death rates continue to fuel population growth in Latin America, Asia and, especially, Africa. For urban areas, the rate of population increase is twice as high because, in addition to natural increase, millions of migrants leave the countryside each year in search of jobs, health care, education and conveniences such as running water and electricity.

Cities often offer more opportunities than rural areas, but they provide no quick fix for the massive problems of escalating population and grinding poverty. In less developed societies many burgeoning cities, including Mexico City described at the beginning of this chapter, are simply unable to meet the basic needs of much of their population. Thousands of rural people stream into Mexico City every day, even though more than 10 per cent of the *current* 25 million residents have no running water in their homes, 15 per cent lack sewerage facilities and the city can process only half the rubbish produced now. To make matters worse, exhaust from factories and cars chokes everyone, rich and poor alike (Friedrich, 1984; Gorman, 1991).

Like other major cities throughout the developing world, Mexico City is surrounded by shanty towns, settlements of makeshift homes built from discarded materials. As explained in Chapter 9 and as will be discussed further in Chapter 24, even city dumps are home to thousands of poor people, who pick through the waste hoping to find enough to ensure their survival for another day. In some cases, it can be hard to distinguish life on the congested streets from life in a dump. Paul Harrison, in a highly readable account of poverty in the city, described rush hour in Calcutta as

> the nearest human thing to an ant heap, a dense sea of people washing over roads hopelessly jammed as taxis swerve round hand-pulled rickshaws, buses run into handcarts, pony stagecoaches and private cars, and even flocks of goats fight it out for limited space.
> (1993: 165–166)

GLOBALISATION AND THE SPREAD OF WORLD CITIES

Aerial view of Mexico City
Source: © Stephanie Maze/Corbis

A few people have found riches in cities of the developing world. In some countries, such as Brazil, members of the urban poor are increasingly returning to the countryside and fighting with well-armed landowners for the right to farm to produce the food, shelter and textiles they need to survive.

Many of these cities can also be seen as 'post-colonial cities'. In them, the rich have lifestyles that are very similar to those of the wealthy in the West, while the urban poor face extremely limited services and incomes.

Globalisation and the spread of world cities

John Friedman (1986) developed the idea of world cities – large, urban regions, highly interconnected, through which finance, economic decision-making and international labour flow. The general idea of world cities is, of course, far from new: people have always travelled to and from major cities, which serve as huge magnets for cosmopolitanism. But from the latter part of the twentieth century onwards – and in large part linked to

the growth of new informational networks and economies – cities started to transform themselves again.

Global cities are cities with much economic power, commanding global investments and the concentration and accumulation of capital. In Europe, only London and Paris can be seen as world cities (see Table 23.3 and Figure 23.10), though other cities, including Frankfurt, Brussels, Amsterdam and Zürich, are also important. London, Tokyo and New York emerged as three leading centres of world finance. While these cities are the homes of stateless corporations and international systems of finance, often housed in spectacular skyscraping buildings, they also have a growing number of poor people – often immigrants – who work for low wages.

For Saskia Sassen, global cities stand out as key command points in the organisation of the world economy, and are the key locations for the marketplaces for the leading industries. They are major sites of production for these industries (Sassen, 2000: 4). Hence, global cities are the prime location of major corporate headquarters of TNCs, international banks, and an international division of labour with privileged foreigners who 'jet set' around the world. They have to be

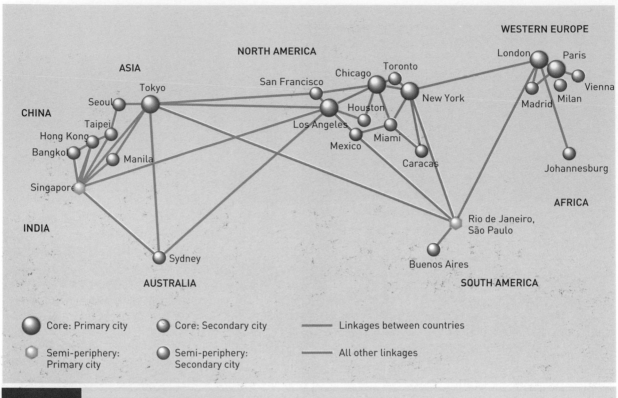

Figure 23.10   Hierarchy of world cities

Source: adapted from *A Geography of the European Union* by Garrat Nagle and Kris Spencer (1996: 101), by permission of Oxford University Press

major centres of communication, and a good air transport system is central. All global cities are connected by air to all other global cities.

These global cities have led to a large number of people now living not in one society but in several simultaneously. Although they are likely to have apartments in a number of cities through the world, their real home is probably the airport and the jet aircraft! These are what novelist Pico Iyer has called 'the global souls' (Iyer, 2000).

Understanding cities?

The Chicago School: Robert Park and Louis Wirth

The first major sociology programme in the United States took root a century ago at the University of Chicago. Chicago, then a new metropolis exploding with population and cultural diversity, became the research focus for generations of sociologists, and the work of these men and women yielded a rich understanding of many dimensions of urban life. Although inspired by European theorists such as Toennies, Durkheim and Simmel, their unique contribution to urban sociology was in making the city itself a laboratory for actual research.

Perhaps the greatest urban sociologist of all was Robert Ezra Park, who for decades provided the leadership that established sociology in the United States. Park is introduced in the Profile box. A second major figure in the Chicago School of urban sociology was Louis Wirth (1897–1952). Wirth's best-known contribution is a brief essay in which he develops a comprehensive theory of urban life (Wirth, 1938).

Wirth began by defining the city as a setting with a large, dense and diverse population. These traits, he argued, combine to form an impersonal, superficial and transitory way of life. Sharing the teeming streets, urbanites surely come into contact with many more people than rural residents do. But, if city people pay any mind to others, they usually know them only in terms of *what they do*: as bus driver, florist or shop assistant, for instance.

PROFILE

ROBERT EZRA PARK: WALKING THE CITY STREETS

I suspect that I have actually covered more ground, tramping about in cities in different parts of the world, than any other living man.

(Park, 1950: viii)

Robert Ezra Park (1864–1944) was a man with a single consuming passion – the city. Walking the streets of the world's great cities, he delighted in observing the full range of human turbulence and triumph. Throughout his 30-year career at the University of Chicago, he led a group of dedicated sociologists in direct, systematic observation of urban life.

Park acknowledged his debt to European sociologists, including Ferdinand Toennies and Georg Simmel (with whom Park studied in Germany). But Park launched urban sociology in the United States by advocating the direct observation of the city rather than what amounted to 'armchair theorising' on the part of his European teachers. At Park's urging, generations of sociologists at the University of Chicago rummaged through practically every part of their city.

From this research, Park came to understand the city as a highly ordered mosaic of distinctive regions, including industrial districts, ethnic communities and vice areas. These so-called 'natural areas' all evolved in relation to one another, forming an urban ecology. To Park, the city operates like a living social organism, a true human kaleidoscope. Urban variety, Park maintained, is the key to the timeless attraction of people to cities:

> The attraction of the metropolis is due in part to the fact that in the long run every individual finds somewhere among the varied manifestations of city life the sort of environment in which he expands and feels at ease; he finds, in short, the moral climate in which his particular nature obtains the stimulations that bring his innate dispositions to full and free expression. It is, I suspect, motives of this kind . . . which drove many, if not most, of the young men and young women from the security of their homes in the country into the big, booming confusion and excitement of city life.
>
> (Park, 1967: 41; orig. 1925)

Park was well aware that many people saw the city as disorganised and even dangerous. Conceding an element of truth in these assertions, Park still found cities intoxicating. Walking the city streets, he became convinced that urban places offer a better way of life – the promise of greater human freedom and opportunity than we can find elsewhere.

Sources: based on Park (1950; 1967, orig. 1925)

Urban relationships are not only specialised and impersonal, Wirth explained, they are also founded on self-interest. For example, shoppers view grocers as the source of goods, while grocers see shoppers as a source of income. Urban people may pleasantly exchange greetings, but friendship is not the reason for their interaction. Finally, limited social involvement coupled with great social diversity also make city dwellers more tolerant than rural villagers. Rural communities often jealously enforce their narrow traditions, but the heterogeneous population of a city rarely shares any single code of moral conduct (Wilson, 1985, 1995).

RESEARCH IN ACTION

ANDERSON: FIELD WORK AND SOCIOLOGY

Elijah Anderson is one of North America's leading black sociologists and he has studied in intense detail the life of young black men in the inner city. His main style of research is fieldwork, or participant observation – he spends a lot of time just hanging around with black youth in the street as well as interviewing them and their relatives.

His most recent book, *Code of the Street* (1999), takes us to another world and grouping, one found in the midst of high-income societies. Many inner cities in North America are ostensibly ravaged by a pervasive violence: many young people come to live tormented lives in the midst of drugs, death and a decaying environment. It is a world also depicted in films such as John Singleton's film *Boyz n' the Hood* (1991). Looking specifically at Germantown Avenue in Philadelphia, he depicts an eight and a half mile long road running through the city from one end to the other where the 'well-to-do, the middle classes, the working poor and the very poor' all live. It is a continuum of lifestyles with a 'code of civility' at one end and a 'street code' at the other. At one end lie the middle classes with busy, employed lives bustling with choices. Restaurants, farmers markets and up-market stores thrive and there is little visible security. People get along and 'virtually every ethnic group is represented' (2000: 18). Although it

is predominantly white, there is a flourishing sense of diversity.

At the opposite extreme the story is really not the same: exterior bars appear on run down shops, discount stores appear, along with grafitti and very run down buildings, many of which are no longer inhabited. It is here that groups of black youths start to appear, hanging around on street corners, outside stores, in the street and at major complexes (2000: 77). Both 'decent' and 'street' families can be found here (and overwhelmingly the former), but the air is thick with danger and potential violence.[1] Street families seem to show a lack of consideration for others, but in effect they have their own 'street code'.

At the heart of the code, Anderson says, 'is the issue of respect – being treated "right". They need to be granted "props" (or proper due) or the deference one deserves.' In the street, this can become something which is 'ever more problematic and uncertain' (2000: 33). If you bother people, you will get disgraced and 'dissed' (disrespected). Often they involve minor issues of demeanour. It is hard to get away from it, even if you are a decent kid struggling to be good. As Anderson puts it:

> In impoverished inner-city black communities ...particularly among young males and perhaps increasingly among females, such flight would be extremely difficult. To run away would likely leave one's self esteem in tatters, while inviting further disrespect.
>
> (Anderson, 1999: 76)

---

[1] The terms 'decent families' and 'street families' are used by the residents themselves (Anderson, 1999: 35).

Urban ecology and the zonal theory of the city

Sociologists (especially members of the Chicago School) also developed **urban ecology**, *the study of the link between the physical and social dimensions of cities.* Chapter 24 spotlights cultural ecology, the study of how cultural patterns are related to the physical environment. Urban ecology is one application of this approach, revealing how the physical and social forms of cities influence one another.

Consider, for example, why cities are located where they are. The first cities emerged in fertile regions where the environment favoured raising crops and, thus, settlement. Pre-industrial societies, concerned with defence, built their cities on mountains (Athens was situated on an outcropping of rock) or surrounded by water (Paris and Mexico City were founded on islands). After the Industrial Revolution, the unparalleled importance of economics led to the founding of cities near rivers and natural harbours that facilitated trade.

Urban ecologists also study the physical design of cities. In 1925 Ernest W. Burgess, a student and colleague of Robert Park, described land use in Chicago in terms of *concentric zones* that look rather like a bull's-eye (Park and Burgess, 1967; orig. 1925) (Figure 23.11). City centres,

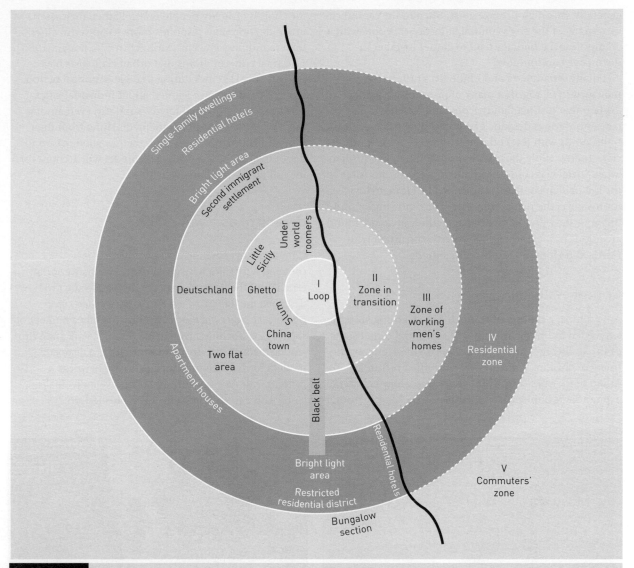

Figure 23.11 The zonal theory of the city: Chicago in the 1920s

Source: adapted from Park, R.E. and Burgess, E. W., 1967 (orig. 1925): 55 *The City* (University of Chicago Press)

Burgess observed, are business districts bordered by a ring of factories, followed by residential rings with housing that becomes more expensive the further it stands from the noise and pollution of the city's centre. Homer Hoyt (1939) refined Burgess's observations by noting that distinctive districts sometimes form *wedge-shaped sectors*. For example, one fashionable area may develop next to another, along a major road, or an industrial district may extend outwards from a city's centre along a railway line.

Chauncey Harris and Edward Ullman (1945) added yet another insight: as cities decentralise, they lose their single-centre form in favour of a *multi-centred model*. As cities grow, residential areas, industrial parks and shopping districts typically push away from one another. Few people wish to live close to industrial areas, for example, so the city becomes a mosaic of distinct districts.

Social area analysis adds another twist to urban ecology by investigating what people in specific residential areas have in common. Three factors seem to explain most of the variation: family patterns, social class and race/ethnicity (Shevky and Bell, 1955; Johnston, 1976). Families with children gravitate to areas offering large flats or single family homes and good schools. The rich generally seek high-prestige areas, often in the central city near many of the city's cultural attractions. People with a common social heritage tend to cluster together in distinctive communities.

Finally, Brian Berry and Philip Rees (1969) have managed to tie together many of these insights. They explain that distinct family types tend to settle in the concentric zones described by Ernest Burgess. Specifically, households with few children tend to cluster towards the city's centre, while those with more children live further away. Social class differences are primarily responsible for the sector-shaped districts described by Homer Hoyt as, for instance, the rich occupy one 'side of the tracks' and the poor the other. And racial and ethnic areas are found at various points throughout the city, consistent with Harris and Ullman's multi-centred model.

Critical evaluation

After almost a century of research, urban ecologists have succeeded in linking the physical and social dimensions of urban life. But, as the researchers themselves concede, their conclusions paint an over-simplified picture of urban life. Critics chime in that urban ecology errs to the extent that it implies that cities take shape simply from

the choices ordinary people make. Rather, they assert, urban development responds more to powerful elites than to ordinary citizens (Molotch, 1976; Feagin, 1983).

A final criticism holds that urban ecologists have studied only US cities during a single historical period. Little of what we have learned about industrial cities applies to pre-industrial towns; similarly, even among industrial cities, socialist settlements differ from their capitalist counterparts. In sum, there is good reason to doubt that any single ecological model will account for the full range of urban diversity.

Urbanism as a way of life

Commentators have increasingly realised that contemporary cities have given rise to distinctive social experience. The Parisian poet Charles Baudelaire (1821–67) described the **flâneur**, *a social type who wanders cities, enjoying the sights and the crowd*. Subsequently a number of sociologists, Toennies, Durkheim, Simmel, Park and Wirth among them, started to analyse the city as a distinctly modern form which brought a pervasive newness, a concern with the transitory and obsessive individualism, along with a new excitement and sophistication.

(a)

(b)

(a) Beverly Hills' bustling Rodeo Drive Shopping Center as seen at dusk. (b) A homeless man stands by a park in Los Angeles in 1983. Starting in the early 1980s, Los Angeles, along with many other American cities, began to experience serious and persistent problems with homelessness.

Source: (a) © David Butow/Corbis Saba (b) © Douglas Kirkland/Corbis

Georg Simmel: the blasé urbanite

We previously encountered the ideas of German sociologist Georg Simmel (1858–1918) when we looked at how size affects the social dynamics of small groups (Chapter 6). Simmel (1950; orig. 1905) also turned his characteristic micro-level focus to the city, probing how urban life shapes people's attitudes and behaviour. From the point of view of the individual, Simmel explained, the city is a crush of people, objects and events. Because the urbanite is easily overwhelmed with stimulation, he continued, a *blasé attitude* emerges as a coping strategy. That is, city people learn to respond selectively by tuning out much of what goes on around them. City dwellers are not without sensitivity and compassion for others, although they sometimes seem 'cold and heartless'. But urban detachment, as Simmel saw it, is better understood as a technique for social survival by which people stand aloof from most others so they can devote their time and energy to those who really matter.

Critical evaluation

What of Wirth's specific claims about urbanism as a way of life? Decades of research have provided support for only some of his conclusions. Wirth correctly maintained that urban settings do sustain a weaker sense of community than do rural areas. But one can easily forget that conflict is found in the countryside as well as the city. Furthermore, while urbanites treat most people impersonally, they typically welcome such privacy and, of course, they do maintain close personal relationships with a select few (Keller, 1968; Cox, 1971; orig. 1965; 1978a; Lee *et al.*, 1984; Wellman, 1999). Where the analysis of Wirth and others falls short, too, is in painting urbanism in broad strokes that overlook the effects of class, race and gender. Herbert Gans (1968) explains that there are many types of urbanites – rich and poor, Asian, black and white, women and men – all leading distinctive lives. In fact, cities often intensify these social differences. That is, we see the extent of social diversity most clearly in cities where different categories of people reside in the largest numbers (Spates and Macionis, 1987).

Modern societies have generally been ambivalent about urban life. As he assumed the US presidency in 1800, Thomas Jefferson repudiated the city as a 'pestilence to the morals, the health and the liberties of man' (quoted in Glaab, 1963: 52). Almost a century later, English author and Nobel prize winner Rudyard Kipling echoed those sentiments after a visit to Chicago: 'Having seen it, I urgently desire never to see it again. It is inhabited by savages' (quoted in Rokove, 1975: 22). Others have disagreed, of course, siding with the Ancient Greeks, who viewed the city as the only place where humanity can expect to find the 'good life'.

Why do cities provoke such spirited and divergent reactions? The answer lies in their ability to encapsulate and intensify human culture. Cities have been the setting for some of the greatest human virtues (from grand architecture to high-tech hospitals) as well as the greatest human failings (from ghettos of extreme poverty to concentrated pollution). Cities offer great economic opportunities, but also generate more extreme forms of social problems, from crime to racial tensions to social alienation. Indeed, a test of the balance between the promise and the failings of city life is emerging most intensely in newly expanding cities in the developing world.

Looking ahead: population and urbanisation in the twenty-first century

The demographic analysis presented in this chapter points to some disturbing trends. We see, first of all, that the earth is gaining unprecedented population because of two parallel shifts: death rates are dropping even as birth rates remain high in much of the world. The numbers lead us to the sobering conclusion that controlling global population in the next century will be a monumental task.

As we have seen, population growth is currently greatest in the least economically developed countries of the world, those that lack productive capacity to support their present populations, much less their future ones. Most of the privileged inhabitants of high-income nations are spared the trauma of poverty. But supporting about 90 million additional people on our planet each year, 80 million of these added to poor societies, will require a global commitment to provide not only food but housing, schools and employment. The well-being of the entire world may ultimately depend on resolving many of the economic and social problems of poor, overly populated countries and bridging the widening gulf between the 'have' and 'have-not' societies.

Great concentrations of people have always had the power to intensify the triumphs and tragedies of human existence. Thus the world's demographic, environmental and social problems are most pronounced in cities, especially in poor nations. In Mexico City, São Paulo (Brazil), Kinshasa (Zaïre), Mumbai (India) and Manila (the Philippines), urban problems now seem to defy solution and the end of remarkable urban growth in the world's low-income countries is nowhere in sight.

Earlier chapters point up two different answers to this problem. One view, linked with modernisation theory, holds that as poor societies industrialise (as Western Europe and North America did a century ago), greater productivity will simultaneously raise living standards and this, in turn, will reduce population growth. A second view, associated with dependency theory, argues that such progress is unlikely as long as poor societies remain economically dependent on rich ones.

Throughout history, the city has improved people's living standards more than any other type of settlement. The question facing humanity now is whether cities in poor countries will be able to meet the needs of vastly larger populations in the coming century. The answer, which rests on issues of international relations, global economic ties and simple justice, will affect us all.

SUMMARY

1. Fertility and mortality, measured as total period fertility rates and crude death rates, are major components of population growth. The overall European population is shrinking slightly. Migration, the third component of population change, has altered the balance between urban and rural populations and has also become the focus of some social tension in the European Union.

2. Demographers use age–sex pyramids to represent the composition of a population graphically and to project population trends. The sex ratio refers to a society's balance of females and males.

3. Historically, world population grew slowly because high birth rates were largely offset by high death rates. About 1750, a demographic transition began as world population rose sharply, mostly due to falling death rates. Thomas Robert Malthus warned that population growth would outpace food production, resulting in social calamity. Demographic transition theorists argue that technological advances gradually prompt a drop in birth rates. Dependency theorists contend that the world's resources must be more evenly distributed to solve population problems equitably.

4. Research shows that lower birth rates and improved economic productivity in poor societies both result from improving the social position of women. World population is expected to reach 8 billion by 2025. Such an increase will probably overwhelm many poor societies, where most of the increase will take place.

5. Closely related to population growth is urbanisation. The first urban revolution began with the appearance of cities some 12,000 years ago. Urbanisation parallels a

dramatic increase in the division of labour, as people assume a wide range of highly specialised, productive roles in society. Pre-industrial cities are characterised by low-rise buildings, narrow winding streets and personal social ties.

6. A second urban revolution began about 1750 as the Industrial Revolution propelled rapid urban growth in Europe. This brought about a change in the physical form of cities. Planners created wide, regular streets to facilitate trade. Their emphasis on commercial life and the increasing size of urban areas rendered city life more anonymous. Since the 1950s, European cities have decentralised. The growth of suburbs is one trait of the post-industrial society.

7. A third urban revolution is now occurring in poor societies of the world, where most of the world's largest cities will soon be found. In addition, we are seeing the development of global cities where large, urban regions become highly interconnected through finance, economic decision-making and international labour flows.

8. At the University of Chicago, Robert Park pioneered the Chicago School of sociology and saw cities as facilitating greater social freedom. Louis Wirth reasoned that large, dense, heterogeneous populations generated a way of life characterised by impersonality, self-interest and tolerance of people's differences. Urban ecology studies the interplay of social and physical dimensions of the city, and mapped out the zonal theory of the city. George Simmel, a European influence on the Chicago School, claimed that the over-stimulation of city life produced a blasé attitude in urbanites.

CRITICAL-THINKING QUESTIONS

1. Do governments have a right to regulate the number of children people choose to have? Are there any moral dilemmas when people in rich countries strive to reduce fertility in poor countries?

2. If the overall population of Europe is shrinking, why are Europeans so worried about immigration from other regions?

3. Over the course of history, how have economic and technological changes transformed the physical shape of cities?

4. According to Ferdinand Toennies, Emile Durkheim, Georg Simmel and Louis Wirth, what characterises urbanism as a way of life? Note several differences in the ideas of these thinkers.

GOING FURTHER

Further reading

On population theory and demography:

Huw Jones, *Population Geography* (2nd edn, 1990)

John R. Weeks, *Population* (6th edn, 1996)
Both offer general introductions to the whole field of demography.

Dorothy Stein, *People Who Count: Population and Politics, Women and Children* (1995)
A lively account of where we've gone wrong! This author sets up a polemic that is a good stimulus to debate.

On cities:

Saskia Sassen, *Cities in a World Economy* (2nd edn, 2000)
An introduction to the ideas of a leading sociologist, but it is not always easy to read.

Mike Savage and Alan Warde, *Urban Sociology, Capitalism and Modernity* (1993)
This provides a good overview of urban sociology.

United Nations, *Urban Agglomerations* (2003a)
This is produced every two years and provides discussion and information on major world cities.

David Smith, *Third World Cities* (2002)
An excellent introductory study, now in its second edition, with case studies from a range of cities including Bangkok, Mexico City and Manila.

More information

There are many sources of statistical data at national, regional and global levels, for example, World Resources Institute, *World Resources 2002–4* (annually, Elsevier) and *Population Trends* (annually, HMSO, London). The most recent figures are likely to be found on the Internet.

David Coleman (ed.), *Europe's Population in the 1990s* (Oxford University Press, 1992) is a series of essays which covers Europe's demography well. David Coleman and John Salt, *The British Population: Patterns, Trends and Processes* (Oxford University Press, 1992), although a little out of date, is a major comprehensive review of the whole field.

Watch a video/Read a book

Many films of the *film noir* genre use the city as a backdrop and create major atmospherics around it.

- Yasujiro Ozu's *Tokyo Story* (1953): examines an elderly couple who move from a small town to their family in a big city, and details the contrasting ways of life.

- John Schlesinger's *Midnight Cowboy* (1969): the anomie and desperation of modern city life in the United States are well revealed in this classic with Dustin Hoffman and Jon Voight.

- Paul Schrader and Martin Scorsese's *Taxi Driver* (1976), and *Falling Down* (1992): the former sees Robert DeNiro in New York in the 1970s, the latter sees Michael

Douglas in Los Angeles in the 1990s, but both films depict the sense of alienation and rage that may come from living in large urban environments.

See also Saul Bellow's *Herzog* (1964) (about Chicago), Edith Wharton's *The Age of Innocence* (1920) (early twentieth-century New York), Tom Wolfe's *The Bonfire of the Vanities* (1988) (set in late twentieth-century New York) and Colm Toibin's *The Story of the Night* (1997) (in Buenos Aires).

Connecting up

Connect to other chapters

- Connect demography to Chapter 24 on the environment.
- Link global cities to globalisation in Chapter 2.
- How does the city, and especially the zonal theory of cities, link to crime, as discussed in Chapter 16?

To the websites

- http://www.un.org/popin/data.html#Global%20Data

  United Nations population statistics. A wealth of tables, discussions and maps for every country in the world.

- http://www.prb.org

  prb stands for Population Reference Bureau and this website contains major files.

For additional case studies, multiple choice questions, internet exercises, and annotated weblinks specific to this chapter, visit this book's website at **www.pearsoned.co.uk/plummer**

CHAPTER 24

SOCIAL CHANGE AND THE ENVIRONMENT

. . . the surface of the earth is truly a living organism. Without the countless and immensely varied forms of life that the earth harbours, our planet would be just another fragment of the universe with a surface as drab as that of the moon and an atmosphere inhospitable to man.

René Dubos (1970; orig. 1959)

SOME 800,000 RESIDENTS awoke coughing, vomiting, eyes burning when the Union Carbide pesticide chemical plant at Bhopal in India exploded around midnight on 3 December 1984. Trying to get away, 'those able to board a bicycle, moped, bullock car. or vehicle of any kind did. But for most of the poor, their feet were the only form of transportation available. Many dropped along the way, gasping for breath and choking on their own vomit. Families were separated; whole groups were wiped out at a time. Those strong enough to keep going ran three, six, up to 12 miles before they stopped. Most ran until they dropped. The explosion may well have killed from 3,000 to 6,000 people instantly. Whole families were wiped out. And a further 200,000 were maimed, brain damaged, deformed and killed by the 40 tonnes of lethal and noxious gases which were emitted into the atmosphere by the explosion and which have taken their toll over many years. Blindness, body deformity, birth defects, mental illness, skin discoloration, cataracts, infant deaths, and spontaneous abortions were just some of the effects. The Union Carbide disaster is commonly agreed to be one of the world's worst environmental accidents (although Chernobyl is a clear 'rival' for this claim).

Yet is it really fair to call all these deaths and continuing mutilations the outcome of 'an accident'. As has been clear for a long time, the 'accident' clearly resulted from corporate negligence and mismanagement. The plant used highly toxic chemicals in its production process, and when water somehow mixed with these, the resulting explosion was catastrophic. Of key importance here is the argument that far fewer people would have died or been injured if the plant had not been located so close to the shantytowns of the poor. The ultimate, terrible impact of the event on the local natural environment and wildlife 20 years on is still not clear. The US owners of the company finally moved out in 1999, leaving behind them a devastated area. They left behind a ruined site along with some 5,000 tonnes of waste, much of which had leaked into the soil. There had been little in the way of a serious clean-up operation and lives are still being ruined.

In 1989, Union Carbide agreed to pay the Indian government $470 million as compensation. This amounts to about $3,000 per family affected. The victims were prevented by law from suing Union Carbide in US courts. Still people go on dying and suffering.

(For details and images of lives ruined by Bhopal, see http://www.bhopal.org/.)

KEY THEMES

- The relevance of sociology to the study of the environment
- The social practices that change the state of the natural environment
- Explanations of these environmental changes
- How social movements and other agencies are responding to this

(Left) Terrified children flee down Route 1 near Trang Ban, South Vietnam in June 1972 after an accidental aerial napalm strike.
Source: Associated Press © 'Nick' Ut

There have been many similar disasters to Bhopal that have gained wider public attention: the slag heap slide at Aberfan in Wales which buried a school in 1966; the spate of oil tanker groundings which have decimated sea life off the shores of Alaska, Britain and Ireland in the 1990s; the nuclear explosion at Chernobyl; and even the scare over 'mad cow disease' (BSE or bovine spongiform encephalopathy) and its links to CJD (Creuzfeldt-Jakob Disease).

These disasters can wreak havok on the environment. For instance, the *Torrey Canyon* oil slick deposited some 117,000 tons of oil in 1967 and killed between 40,000 and 100,000 birds. Significant as this was, it fades when compared to the total annual oil spillage of around 3.6 million tons! Humanity's remaking of the earth during the last two centuries may well exceed changes to our planet from all causes over the last billion years (Milbrath, 1989).

These disasters often arise from the human pursuit of improvements in mining, agriculture, housing, industry and transportation. Many of these changes have benefited some people. A high proportion of people in rich nations now enjoy a level of material comfort that our ancestors scarcely could have imagined. However, as those near to Bhopal learned, such achievements carry both costs and risks. In the modern world, environmental disasters have become common. The way of life that has evolved in rich societies places such great strain on the earth's natural environment that it threatens the future of the entire planet.

Meanwhile, many of the less obviously human-made disasters continue, though, as Figures 24.1, 24.2, 24.3 and 24.4 show, they seem to be increasing. In the 1950s there were 20 great world catastrophes; in the 1970s there were 47; and by the 1990s there were 86 (Brown *et al.*, *State of the World*, 2001: 125). In India, a cyclone in 1998 in Gujarat caused some 10,000 deaths, only to be

followed in 2001 by a major earthquake, taking between 25,000 and 100,000 lives and wreaking property damage valued at some 250 billion rupees (about $5.5 billion) (*The Economist*, 3 February 2001: 73). Meanwhile,

Chernobyl, Ukraine, April 1996: aerial view of the exploded reactor of the Chernobyl nuclear power plant which spread its radioactive clouds across Europe.
Source: Popperfoto © Volodymr Repik/Reuters

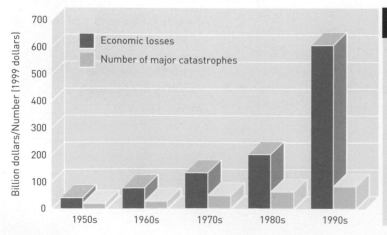

Figure 24.1   Rising tide of major disasters, by decade

Source: adapted from Worldwatch Institute, *State of the World 2001*, copyright 2001, www.worldwatch.org

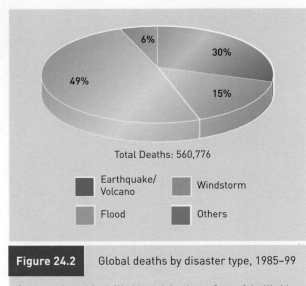

Total Deaths: 560,776

■ Earthquake/ Volcano   ■ Windstorm

■ Flood   ■ Others

Figure 24.2   Global deaths by disaster type, 1985–99

Source: adapted from Worldwatch Institute, *State of the World 2001*, copyright 2001, www.worldwatch.org

landslides in Venezuela killed more than 30,000 people. In 1998–99 alone, over 120,000 people were killed in such natural disasters: floods, earthquakes, fires, cyclones. There are no signs of this trend slowing in the twenty-first century. There were earthquakes in Bhuj, India (2001,

with 20,000 dead), in Afghanistan (2002, with 2,200 dead), in Bam, Iran (2003, with 41,000 dead) and in Al-Hoceima, Morroco (2004, 571 dead). To date in this century, some 60,000 people have died in disasters and almost three-quarters of them have been in earthquakes (*The Economist*, 20 March 2004). Throughout history such disasters have often happened, sometimes wiping out whole societies in one great flood. As these disasters increase, there are major implications for societies, in costs to lives and social organisation. Sociologists study the ways in which different kinds of infrastructure can facilitate or prevent such natural disasters, as well as examining the social responses of people (from victims and their friends and families to help agencies such as the Red Cross).

Another area of growing concern about the environment lies in the spread of modern war. In the award-winning, classic but horrific opening picture to this chapter, we see children running for their lives from the terrible bombing destruction in the My Lai massacre in Vietnam. Throughout history, wars have been responsible for much devastation of the environment. Recently, we find them producing massive hazardous waste, pollution from all kinds of gases, mass destruction of lands, and a littering of large areas with mines waiting to be discovered by the unwary years later. Nuclear weapons pose their own problems of radiation. And the first Gulf War, in which Iraq released some 10 million

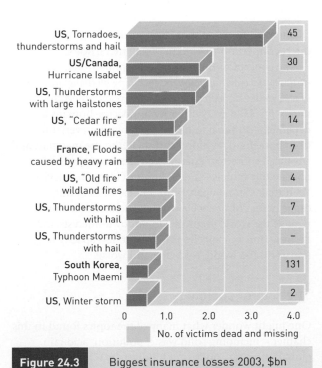

No. of victims dead and missing

Figure 24.3   Biggest insurance losses 2003, $bn

Source: Swiss Re, after *The Economist*, 20 March 2004

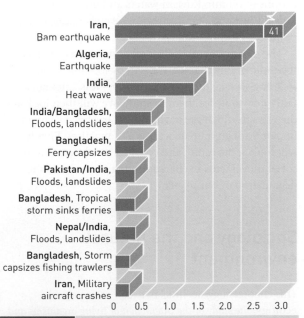

Figure 24.4   Worst human costs – number of victims dead and missing 2003, '000

Source: Swiss Re, after *The Economist*, 20 March 2004

Industrial plant on Tokyo bay
Source: © Michael S. Yamashita/Corbis

gallons of oil into Kuwaiti waters and fired over 700 Kuwaiti oil wells, left that region severely damaged and polluted (Leaning, 2000).

The environment, its degradations and its dangers, is the topic of this chapter. We start by looking at why sociologists take this topic seriously – it is, after all, a fairly new topic for them to study. We will then look at the ways in which the environment has been changing, in part through human actions and practices. Finally, we will look at the future and consider the different roles of social movements in changing what many see as the degradation of our planet.

Sociology and the natural environment

This chapter suggests links between sociology and **ecology**, *the study of the interaction of living organisms and the natural environment*. Researchers from many disciplines have contributed to this latter field, but this chapter will focus on those aspects of ecology that have a direct connection to human social interactions.

The concept of the **natural environment** refers to *the earth's surface and atmosphere, including all living organisms as well as the air, water, soil and other resources necessary to sustain life*. Like every other living species, humans are dependent on the natural environment for everything from basic food, clothing and shelter to the materials and advanced sources of energy needed to construct and operate our vehicles and all kinds of electronic devices. Yet humans stand apart from other species in our capacity for culture; we alone take deliberate action to remake the world according to our own interests and desires. Thus our species is unique in its capacity to transform the world, for better and worse.

The role of sociology

One might wonder what many of the topics found in this chapter – including solid waste, pollution, acid rain, global warming and loss of biodiversity – are doing in a sociology text. Yet, as Leo Marx (1994) points out, all of these problems arise from human, social activities, not the 'natural world' operating on its own. Thus, such ecological issues are also issues for *social* understanding. Sociologists can bring at least four such understandings.

First, and perhaps most important, sociologists can demonstrate how human social patterns have caused mounting stress on the natural environment. That is, sociologists can spotlight how environmental problems are linked to particular global, historical and cultural change. We discuss these below (Cylke, 1993; Redclift and Benton, 1994).

Second, sociologists can show how environmental damages are not equally distributed. Part 3 of this book alerted us to many forms of social divisions, ranging from class and gender to ethnicity and culture. The impact of environmental damage reinforces many of these divisions.

Third, sociologists can conduct research on public opinion towards environmental issues, reporting people's thoughts and fears (whether grounded or not) about these controversies. Moreover, sociologists analyse why certain categories of people fall on one side or another of political debates over an environmental issue.

Finally, sociologists can explore what 'the environment' and 'nature' mean to people of various cultures and social backgrounds. In many pre-industrial societies, and some contemporary cultures such as the Inuit today, nature demands respect and is seen to be alive and nurturing. It is often religious: gods and spirits inhabit the lakes and the skies. Animals may be eaten but they are also seen as part of the order of things. By contrast, modern industrial societies see 'nature' as something to be controlled, shaped, tamed. 'Nature' is something 'we' can regulate through 'science'.

The changing global environment

Environmental degradation is nothing new. But it was really only in the latter years of the twentieth century, as pollution accelerated, that global awareness of the problems grew. It is now apparent that any understanding of the natural environment and its problems must also be global in scope. Regardless of humanity's political divisions into nation states, the planet constitutes a single **ecosystem**, defined as *the system composed of the interaction of all living organisms and their natural environment*. The Greek meaning of *eco* is 'house', which reminds us of the simple fact that our planet is our home.

Even a brief look at the operation of the global ecosystem confirms that all living things and their

natural environment are *interrelated*. Changes to any part of the natural environment ripple through the entire ecosystem, so that what happens in one part of the world inevitably has consequences in another. Advocates of the **Gaia hypothesis** have suggested that *planet earth itself should be seen as a living organism*, inside which humans and other species each have a vital part to play (see Lovelock, 1979).

Consider the effects of our use of chlorofluorocarbons (CFCs) as a propellant in aerosol spray cans and as a gas in refrigerators, freezers and air conditioners. CFCs may have improved our lives in various ways, but as they were released into the atmosphere, they reacted with sunlight to form chlorine atoms, which, in turn, depleted ozone. The ozone layer in the atmosphere serves to limit the amount of harmful ultraviolet radiation reaching the earth from the sun. Thus, there is evidence of a 'hole' in the ozone layer (in the atmosphere over Antarctica) which may produce a rise in human skin cancers and countless other effects on plants and animals (Harrison and Pearce, 2000). While an international agreement has been reached to phase out the use of CFCs, many unscrupulous people continue to prefer to maximise their short-term convenience by continuing to use them. By 1997, the black market global trade in CFCs rivalled the trade in narcotics. Moreover, in spite of global efforts to cut other emissions, some soft drink companies seek to market a new self-cooling can, which will chill warm drinks in two minutes when opened – and release nearly as much pollution as the cars we drive today. Given the complexity of the global ecosystem, many threats to the environment go unrecognised. As the World Watch box explains, the popular, although seemingly innocent, act of eating fast food has significant environmental effects in other parts of the world.

History, change and the environment

How did humanity gain the power to threaten the natural environment? We have already seen the role that population growth may play (see Chapter 23); here we will examine the role of culture and technology. As humans have devised new technologies, so we have gained the ability to make and remake the world as we choose. Table 24.1 suggests some of the historical issues.

Members of societies with simple technology are so directly dependent on nature that their lives are guided by the migration of birds and animals and the rhythm of the seasons. They remain especially vulnerable to natural events, such as fires, floods, droughts and storms. Nevertheless, horticulture (small-scale farming),

WORLD WATCH

THE GLOBAL ECOSYSTEM: THE ENVIRONMENTAL CONSEQUENCES OF EVERYDAY CHOICES

People living in high-income countries, such as most of those in Europe, have the greatest power to affect the earth's ecosystem for the simple reason that they consume so much of the planet's resources. Thus, small, everyday decisions about how to live can add up to large consequences for the planet as a whole.

Consider the commonplace practice of enjoying a burger. McDonald's and dozens of other fast-food chains serve billions of burgers each year to eager customers across the world. This appetite for beef creates a large market for cattle throughout the

COUNTRY FACT FILE	
BRAZIL	
Population	174,610,000 (2002)
Per capita GNP	$3,580 (2000)
Life expectancy	58.5 male; 67.6 female (2000)
Literacy	86% (1996)
Language	Portuguese
Religion	Most baptised – Catholic, but many syncretic Afro-Brazilian cults
Main cities Rio de Janeiro	São Paulo (17,833,757); (5,850,544) (2000)
Human Development Index 2004	72nd

Source: adapted from *World Guide, 2001*; Britannica Almanac, 2004

world. The UK briefly experimented with cheap feeding strategies to reduce the price of beef – only to gain problems with BSE, or 'mad cow disease', as a result. Yet even with the outbreak of the BSE scare in 1995, the European Community as a whole did not apply equally stringent regulations for the slaughter of cattle across member states until July 1997!

Other countries, particularly in Latin America, have responded to the demand for beef by expanding cattle ranching. As consumption of burgers has grown, ranchers in Brazil, Costa Rica and other countries are devoting more and more land to cattle grazing. Latin American cattle graze on grass. This diet produces the lean meat demanded by the fast-food corporations, but it also requires that a great deal of land be dedicated to grazing.

Where is the land to come from? Ranchers in Latin America are solving their land problem by clearing forests at the rate of thousands of square miles each year. These tropical forests, as we shall explain presently, are vital to maintaining the earth's atmosphere. Therefore, forest destruction threatens the well-being of everyone – even the people back in Europe who enjoy burgers without giving a thought to the environment.

Enhancing global consciousness is thus a vital dimension of increasing environmental awareness. Ecologically speaking, our choices and actions ripple throughout the world, even though most of us never realise it. People in Europe are simply looking for a quick burger. Fast-food companies are making a profit by serving meals that people want. Ranchers are trying to earn a living by raising beef cattle. No one intends to harm the planet but, taken together, these actions can have serious consequences for everyone. All people on this planet inhabit a single ecosystem. In a world of countless environmental connections, we need to think critically about the effects of choices we make every day – like what's for lunch!

Source: Based on Myers (1984a).

pastoralism (the herding of animals) and even agriculture (the use of animal-drawn ploughs) started to radically alter the nature of our countrysides and landscapes.

It is, however, with the development of industrial technology that the most dramatic change in humans'

relationship with the natural environment takes place. Industry replaces muscle power with combustion engines that burn fossil fuels, including coal and oil. Such machinery affects the environment in two ways – by consuming natural resources and by releasing pollutants

Table 24.1	A brief history of environment degradation
Pre-1500	Global extinctions of whole species – up to 90 per cent were lost at the end of the Permian and Cretaceous periods; many large mammals lost, some species through overhunting; microbe movements leading to epidemics; long-term natural climate changes
1500–1760	European ecological expansion and capitalist growth starts to lead to rising resource shortage and land degradation; demographic movements and ecological transformation of the Americas
Modern: 1760–1945	Capitalist industrialisation, urbanisation, concentration, ecological expansion and colonialisation; local resource exhaustion, urban air, soil and water pollution, change in rural environments and forest loss; some global extinction of species and some contribution to global warming
Contemporary	Global warming, marine depletion, water in short supply, deforestation, desertification, soil exhaustion, overspills, hazardous waste, acid deposition, nuclear risks, decline of global ecosystem comes with Western growth and consumption. Socialist industrialisation, industrialisation of the South, new risks from technology and warfare

Source: adapted from Harrison and Pearce (2000), Held *et al.* (1999: 391)

into the atmosphere. Humans armed with industrial technology become able to bend nature to their will far more than ever before, tunnelling through mountains, damming rivers, irrigating deserts and drilling for oil on the ocean floor.

The general pattern is clear. High-income, industrial societies place the greatest demands on the planet's ecosystem. While low-income societies use only 14 per cent of the total world energy, high-income societies use 57 per cent (World Bank, 1997: 93). The United States, home to 5 per cent of the world's population, consumes roughly one-third of the world's energy – more than any other country. The typical US adult consumes 100 times more energy annually than the average member of the world's poorest societies. Taking a broader perspective, *the members of all high-income societies represent 20 per cent of humanity, but utilise 80 per cent of all energy* (Connett, 1991; Miller, 1992).

But the environmental impact of industrial technology is not limited to energy consumption. Just as important, industrial societies produce 100 times more goods than agrarian societies do. While these products raise the material standard of living, they greatly escalate the problem of solid waste (because people ultimately throw away most of what they produce) and pollution (because industrial production generates smoke and other toxic substances).

People have been eager to acquire many of the material benefits of industrial technology, but a century after the

dawn of industrial development people began to gauge the long-term consequences of this new technology on the natural environment. Indeed, one defining trait of post-industrial societies is a growing concern for environmental quality. The 'environment' starts to be defined as a social problem by different groups.

From today's vantage point, we draw an ironic and sobering conclusion: as we have reached our greatest technological power, we have placed the natural environment – including ourselves and all other living things – at greatest risk (Voight, cited in Bormann and Kellert, 1991: ix–x). The evidence is mounting that, in our pursuit of material affluence, humanity is running up an **environmental deficit**, *a situation in which our relationship to the environment, while yielding short-term benefits, will have profound, negative long-term consequences* (Bormann, 1990).

The concept of environmental deficit implies three important ideas. First, it stresses that the state of the environment is a *social issue*, reflecting choices people make about how they live. Second, this concept suggests that environmental damage – to the air, land or water – is often *unintended*. By focusing on the short-term benefits of, say, cutting down forests or using easily disposable packaging, we fail to see (or choose to ignore) their long-term environmental effects. Third, in some but not all respects, the environmental deficit is *reversible*. In as much as societies have created environmental problems, in other words, societies can undo most of them.

Growth and its limits

If the world as a whole were suddenly blessed with the material prosperity that people in much of the Western world take for granted, humanity would soon overwhelm the global environment. This conclusion suggests that our planet suffers not just from the problem of economic *under*development in some regions, but also from economic *over*development in others. For just how long can societies continue to grow in this way?

The logic of growth

One of the driving assumptions of modern Western societies is that of progress and material, economic advance. Moreover, we rely on *science*, looking to experts to apply technology to make our lives better. Taken together, such cultural values form the foundation for the *logic of growth*.

This logic of growth looks like an optimistic view of the world, suggesting, first, that people have improved their lives by devising more productive technology and, second, that we shall continue to do so into the future. The logic of growth thus amounts to the assertions that 'people are clever', 'having things is good (having more is better)', and 'life will improve'. A powerful force throughout the history of the Western, capitalist and industrial societies, the logic of growth has driven individuals to sail the seas, clear the land, build towns, railways and roads, and pursue material affluence.

But even optimistic people realise that 'progress' generates unanticipated problems, environmental and otherwise. The logic of growth responds by arguing that people (especially scientists and other technology experts) are inventive and will find a way out of any problems that growth places in our path. If, say, present resources should prove inadequate for our future needs, we will come up with new alternative resources that will do the job just as well.

To illustrate, most people in Europe would probably agree that cars have greatly improved our lives by providing us with a swift and comfortable means of travel. The counterargument, however, highlights some of the hazards car culture raises. Cars have also made us dependent on petrol, and Europe has previously suffered when conflicts in the Middle East have slowed the sale of oil resources. Even if the logic of growth rightly suggests that scientists will develop cars needing an alternative fuel source by the time the planet's oil reserves run dry,

today's millions of cars will make mountains of rubbish in the future.

This is one of many reasons why most environmental scientists criticise the logic of growth. Lester Milbrath (1989) argues that natural resources such as oil, clean air, fresh water and the earth's topsoil – all *finite* – simply cannot be replaced by technologically engineered alternatives. He warns that we can and will exhaust them if we continue to pursue growth at any cost.

And what of our faith in human ingenuity and especially the ability of science to resolve problems of scarcity? While conceding that humans are clever at solving problems, Milbrath adds that human resourcefulness, too, has its limits. Do we dare to assume that we will be able to solve every crisis that confronts us, especially those wreaking serious damage on the life-giving environment? Moreover, the more powerful and complex the technology (nuclear reactors, say, compared to petrol engines), the greater the dangers posed by miscalculation and the more significant the unintended consequences are likely to be. Thus, Milbrath concludes that as we call on the earth to support increasing numbers of people with finite resources, we will almost certainly cause serious injury to the environment and, ultimately, to ourselves.

The limits to growth

If we cannot 'invent' our way out of the problems created by the 'logic of growth', perhaps we have to come up with an alternative way of thinking about the world. Environmentalists, therefore, propose the counterargument that growth must have limits. The *limits to growth thesis*, stated simply, is that humanity must implement policies to control the growth of population, to cut back on production and to use fewer resources in order to avoid environmental collapse.

The Limits to Growth, a controversial book published in 1972 that had a large hand in launching the environmental movement, uses a computer model to calculate the planet's available resources, rates of population growth, amount of land available for cultivation, levels of industrial and food production, and amount of pollutants released into the atmosphere (Meadows *et al.*, 1972). The authors contend that the model reflects changes that have occurred since 1900, then projects forward to the end of the twenty-first century. Long-range predictions using such a complex model are always speculative and some critics think

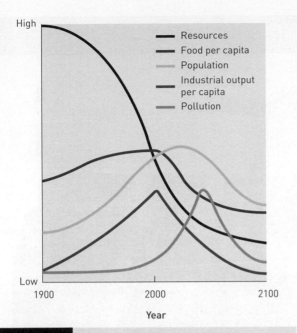

Figure 24.5   The limits to growth: projections

Source: based on Meadows *et al.* (1972)

they are simply wrong (Simon, 1981). But many find the general conclusions of the study, shown in Figure 24.5, convincing.

Following the limits to growth logic, humanity is quickly consuming the earth's finite resources. Supplies of oil, natural gas and other sources of energy will fall sharply, a little faster or slower depending on policies in rich nations and the speed at which other nations industrialise. While food production per person should continue to rise through at least the early part of the new century, the authors calculate, millions will go hungry because existing food supplies are so unequally distributed throughout the world. By mid-century, the model predicts a hunger crisis serious enough that rising mortality rates will first stabilise population and then send it plunging downward. Depletion of resources will eventually cripple industrial output as well. Only then will pollution rates fall.

The lesson of this study is grim: current patterns of life are not sustainable for even another century. This leaves us with the fundamental choice of making deliberate changes in how we live or allowing calamity to force changes upon us.

WORLD WATCH

TURNING THE TIDE: A REPORT FROM EGYPT

Cairo, like many large cities, has become a mess of pollution. No sooner had we left the bus than smoke and stench, the likes of which we had never before encountered, swirled around us. Eyes squinting, handkerchiefs pressed against noses and mouths, we moved slowly uphill along a path ascending mountains of trash and garbage that extended for miles. We had reached the Cairo dump, where the refuse generated by 15 million people in one of the world's largest cities ends up. We walked hunched over and with great care, guided by only a scattering of light from small fires smouldering around us. Up ahead, through clouds of smoke, we saw blazing piles of trash encircled by people seeking warmth and enjoying companionship.

Human beings actually inhabit this inhuman place, creating a surreal scene, like the aftermath of the next global war. As we approached, the fires cast an eerie light on their faces. We stopped some distance from them, separated by a vast chasm of culture and circumstances. But smiles eased the tension and soon we were sharing the comfort of their fires. At that moment, the melodious call to prayer sounded across the city.

The people of the Cairo dump, called the Zebaleen, belong to a religious minority – Coptic Christians – in a predominantly Muslim society. Barred by religious discrimination from many jobs, the Zebaleen use donkey carts and small trucks to pick up the city's refuse and haul it here. For decades, the routine has reached a climax at dawn when hundreds of Zebaleen gather at the dump, swarming over the new piles in search of anything of value.

Upon our visit in 1988, we observed men, women and children picking through Cairo's refuse, filling baskets with anything of value: bits of metal, strips of ribbon, even scraps of discarded food. Every now and then, someone gleefully displayed a 'precious' find that would bring the equivalent of a few dollars in the city. Watching in silence, we became keenly aware of our sturdy shoes and warm clothing and self-conscious that our watches and cameras represented more money than most of the Zebaleen earn in a year.

▶

WORLD WATCH CONTINUED

The Zebaleen people of Cairo have amazed the world with their determination and ingenuity, turning one of the planet's foulest dumps into an efficient recycling centre and providing new apartment units for themselves in the process.

Source: Network © Barry Lewis

Today, the Cairo Zebaleen still work the city's streets collecting trash. But much has changed, as they now represent one of the world's environmental success stories. The Zebaleen now have a legal contract to perform this work and, most important, they have established a large recycling centre near the dump. There, dozens of workers operate large machines that shred discarded cloth into stuffing to fill furniture, car seats and pillows. Others separate plastic and metal into large bins for cleaning and sale. In short, the Zebaleen are big business people. Using start-up loans from the World Bank, not only have the Zebaleen constructed an efficient recycling centre, they also have built for themselves a modern apartment complex, with electricity and running water.

The Zebaleen are still poor by European standards. But they now own the land on which they live and work, and they are prospering. Certainly, they no longer inhabit the bottom rung of Egyptian society. And many international environmental organisations hope their example will inspire others elsewhere. When the 1992 environmental summit meeting convened in Rio de Janeiro, officials presented the Cairo Zebaleen with the United Nations award for environmental protection.

Source: based on Macionis's visits to Egypt, 1988 and 1994

COUNTRY FACT FILE

EGYPT

Population	66,341,000 (2002)
Urban population	42.7% (2001)
Per capita GNP	$1,490 (2000)
Life expectancy	61.3 male; 65.5 female (2000)
Literacy	51% (1995)
Languages	Arabic (official), French and English in business, Nubian and Oromo in daily use
Religions	Sunni Muslim 89%, 10% Coptic minority and other smaller Christian groups
Main cities	Cairo: 10,000,000; Alexandria: 3,382,000; El Giza: 2,144,000
Human Development Index	120th

Source: adapted from the *The World Guide 2001*; Britannica Almanac, 2004

The 'social practices' of degrading the environment

We have reviewed some of the increasing demands on the natural environment. What, then, is the state of the natural environment today? The World Watch box suggests an array of issues. Working from top to bottom, we see how all aspects of our environment – air, life, land, sea – are being degraded. Some of this we may see as an *increase in pollution* (for example, greenhouse gases

in the air); others we may see as a *depletion of major resources* (for example, the loss of water, forests and animal species). In any event, social life is increasingly generating these problems and as such they become areas of major concern for sociologists to understand the social mechanisms which generate environmental degradation. Figure 24.6 compares environmental attitudes in selected industrialising and industrialised countries. In what follows we look at some of the social practices employed by humans – the things we do in our daily lives – that degrade the environment.

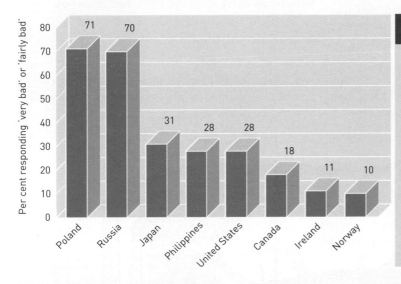

Figure 24.6   **Rating the local environment: a global survey**

Survey question: 'When we say environment, we mean your surroundings – both the natural environment, namely, the air, water land, plants and animals – as well as buildings, streets and the like. Overall, how would you rate the quality of the environment in your local community: very good, fairly good, fairly bad or very bad?'

Source: adapted from Dunlap *et al.* (1992)

WORLD WATCH

THE WORLD AT RISK: A DRAMATICALLY CHANGING ENVIRONMENT

The air: pollution

Fossil fuel burning releases about 6 billion tons of carbon into the air each year, adding about 3 billion tons annually to the 170 billion tons that have settled since the Industrial Revolution. The rate of growth in carbon emissions is around 2 per cent per year. The good news is that there has been a 70 per cent reduction in ozone-producing substances since 1987, showing that change is possible with concerted action. Even so, in 2004 scientists report the ozone hole over Antarctica reaches 26 million square kilometres.

The weather: hotting up?

The nine warmest years in the twentieth century occurred after 1980. The 1990s was the warmest decade of the second millennium. Within the next 40-year period, ocean temperatures could rise by 7°C (enough to melt polar ice caps!) and there are risks of major 'climatic surprises'.

The earth: deforestation and urbanisation

The world is losing 7 million hectares of fertile land a year due to soil degradation, and about 10 million hectares of forest land a year (about the size of South Korea!). While there is less land, more food is needed. The world is becoming increasingly urbanised – 37 per cent in 1970, it is projected to be 61 per cent by 2030. Ten per cent of the world's trees face extinction.

▶

WORLD WATCH CONTINUED

Forests and biodiversity: species decline

The world has lost half of its forests over the past 8,000 years and between 1960 and 1990 about 20 per cent of the world's tropical forest was lost. Between 70 and 95 per cent of the earth's species live in the world's disappearing tropical forest. We are losing 50 species a day; 46 per cent of mammals and 11 per cent of birds are said to be at risk. By 2020, 10 million species are likely to become extinct. In 2003, scientists reported that industrial fishing had killed off 90 per cent of the world's biggest and economically important fish species.

People

While the rate of growth is slowing, world population is still increasing by about 75 million people a year. It will become an ageing population. The current prediction is for a population of 8.9 billion by 2050 (a billion less than was predicted in 1990).

Cars

In 1993, of the world's 607 million cars, one-third were in the United States, and another third were to be found in six other industrialised countries.

Indoor air pollution

In low-income societies, burning wood, animal dung and scraps inside can lead to deadly smoke in confined places. Indoor air pollution may kill between 3 or 4 million people a year.

Illustration: David Eaton

WORLD WATCH CONTINUED

The water: pollution

At present, more than a billion are without access to clean water, and this may reach 2.5 billion by 2025. 2.4 billion lack sanitation services. Freshwater ecosystems are in decline everywhere. Some 35 million people are dying from pollution through contaminated drinking water; deaths from waterborne illnesses are rapidly increasing and may have reached 120 million per year by 2020. Some 58 per cent of the world's reefs and 34 per cent of all fish may be at risk.

Source: Harrison and Pearce (2000); Halweil and Mastny (2004); *Newsweek*, 2 September 2002

Discarding waste in the 'disposable society'

As an interesting exercise, carry a rubbish bag over the course of a single day and collect all the materials you throw away. Most people would be surprised to find out how much waste they generate! Rubbish is a feature of all modern societies, but the most extreme case is the United States – the classic 'disposable society'. In the United States, an average person tosses out close to five pounds of paper, metal, plastic and other disposable materials daily (about 50 tons over a lifetime). For that country as a whole, this amounts to about 1 billion pounds of solid waste produced *each and every day*.

The United States is not the only culprit. In the European Union, legislation designed to facilitate the *safe* transport of goods around the common market and to protect consumer health has led to an escalating use of packaging. Everything (from baked goods to hammers to bicycle helmets) increasingly is sold with excessive packaging – a trend which many manufacturers and retailers have welcomed as packaging can make a product more attractive to the customer (or harder to shoplift).

Consider, too, that manufacturers market soft drinks, beer and fruit juices in aluminium cans, glass jars or plastic containers, which not only consume finite resources but also generate mountains of solid waste.

A GLOSSARY OF ENVIRONMENTAL TERMS

acid rain precipitation that is made acidic by air pollution so that it destroys plant and animal life

cultural ecology a theoretical paradigm that explores the relationship of human culture and the physical environment

ecologically sustainable culture a way of life that meets the needs of the present generation without threatening the environmental legacy of future generations

ecology the study of the interaction of living organisms and the natural environment

ecosystem the system composed of the interaction of all living organisms and their natural environment

environmental deficit the situation in which our relationship to the environment, while yielding short-term benefits, will have profound, negative long-term consequences

environmental racism the pattern by which environmental hazards are greatest in proximity to poor people, especially minorities

global commons resources shared by all members of the international community, such as ocean beds and the atmosphere

greenhouse effect a rise in the earth's average temperature (global warming) due to increasing concentration of carbon dioxide in the atmosphere

natural environment the earth's surface and atmosphere, including various living organisms as well as the air, water, soil and other resources necessary to sustain life

rain forests regions of dense forestation, most of which circle the globe close to the equator

Risk Society society in which risks are of a different magnitude because of technology and globalisation

Then there are countless items intentionally designed to be disposable. A walk through any local supermarket reveals shelves filled with pens, razors, flashlights, batteries and even cameras, intended to be used once and dropped in the nearest bin. Other products – from light bulbs to washing machines – are designed to have a limited useful life, and then become unwanted junk. As Paul H. Connett (1991) points out, even the words we use to describe what we throw away – *waste, litter, rubbish, refuse, garbage* – reveal how little we value what we cannot immediately use and how quickly we push it out of sight and out of mind. Living in a 'disposable society', the average person in the United States consumes 50 times more steel, 170 times more newspaper, 250 times more petrol and 300 times more plastic each year than the typical individual in India (Miller, 1992). An illustration of US garbage disposal is given in Figure 24.7. Comparable high levels of consumption in Europe mean that Western societies not only use a disproportionate share of the planet's natural resources, but also generate most of the world's refuse.

Solid waste that is not burned or recycled never 'goes away'; rather, it ends up in landfills. The practice of using landfills, originally intended to improve sanitation, is now associated with several threats to the natural environment. First, the sheer volume of discarded material is literally filling up landfills. Especially in large cities such as London, there is simply little room left for disposing of rubbish. Second, material placed in landfills contributes to water pollution. Although laws now regulate what can be placed in a landfill, there are dump sites across Europe containing hazardous materials that are polluting water both above and below the ground. Third, what goes into landfills all too often stays there – sometimes for centuries. Tens of millions of tyres, nappies and other items that we bury in landfills each year do not readily decompose, leaving an unwelcome legacy for future generations.

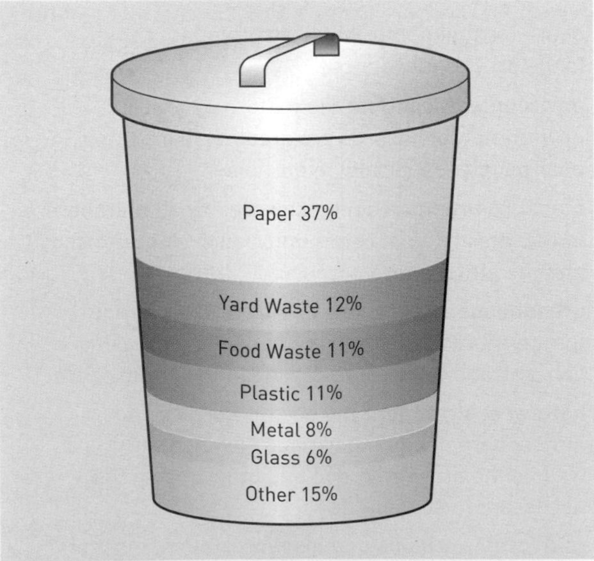

Using transport systems that degrade the environment

Road transport dominates the transportation systems across the world, but air travel is the fastest growing; it has risen from 28 billion passenger kilometres in 1950 to 2.6 trillion passenger kilometres in 1998 (Sheehan, 2001: 106). All this has made rail – the great invention of the nineteenth century – less important. Cars and trucks have helped change the structures of both cities and their surrounding landscapes. Increasingly, people use cars even for very short trips.

The high costs of modern car transportation include the following (Sheehan, 2001: 106):

- Car drivers kill around 1 million people – mainly pedestrians – per year in road accidents
- Cars contribute to local and regional pollution, and in some parts of the world this pollution kills even more people than road accidents
- Cars damage ecosystems through the vast networks of roads created for their use
- Cars make movement in cities difficult, hindering more efficient public transport and persuading those who can afford to fly to take more and more 'to the skies'
- Cars perpetuate social inequalities: people in poorer countries cannot afford cars and spend a disproportionate amount of their time walking long distances for essential trips.

The United States alone uses more than one-third of the world's transport energy and industrial nations overall use some 59 per cent of that energy. Asia and Latin America are becoming the fastest-growing regions.

Figure 24.7 Composition of community rubbish in the United States

Paper 37%
Yard Waste 12%
Food Waste 11%
Plastic 11%
Metal 8%
Glass 6%
Other 15%

Source: adapted from US Environmental Protection Agency, 2002

Making our water dirty

The oceans, lakes and streams supply the lifeblood of the global ecosystem. Throughout human history, people have relied on water for drinking, bathing, cooling, cooking, recreation and a host of other activities. Yet, the oceans have long served as a vast dumping ground for all kinds of waste, including nuclear submarines and human excrement. No one can calculate the precise amount of waste that has been poured into the world's oceans, but the total certainly exceeds millions of tons. The problems caused by disposing of solid waste in this way are crystal clear: polluted water kills fish or makes them dangerous to eat, and also spoils a source of great beauty and pleasure.

Through the process which scientists call the *hydrological cycle*, the earth naturally recycles water and refreshes the land. The process begins as heat from the sun causes the earth's water, 97 per cent of which is in the oceans, to evaporate and form clouds. Next, water returns to earth as rain, which drains into streams and rivers and rushes towards the sea. The hydrological cycle not only renews the supply of water but cleans it as well. Because water evaporates at lower temperatures than most pollutants, the water vapour that rises from the seas is relatively pure and free of contaminants, which are left behind. Although the hydrological cycle generates clean water in the form of rain, it does not destroy pollutants that steadily build up in the oceans, and clean rain can collect pollutants in the air as it falls back to earth. Two key concerns, then, dominate discussions of water and the natural environment. The first is supply; the second is pollution.

Water supply

Talk about a 'drought', along with discussions of the amount of rainfall each month, has become a common concern in European societies, where the weather is relatively kind. But concern over an ample supply of water is hardly new. For thousands of years, since the time of the ancient civilisations of China, Egypt and Rome, water rights have figured prominently in codes of law. Throughout Europe, aqueducts of brick, built by the ancient Romans, stand as testimony to the historical importance of readily available water.

Today some regions of the world, especially the tropics, enjoy a plentiful supply of water, although most of the annual rainfall occurs over a relatively brief season. High demand for water, coupled with more modest reserves, makes water supply a matter of concern in much of Europe and North America as well as most of Asia. In these areas people look to rivers – rather than rainfall – for their water. Especially in the Middle East and parts of Africa, water supply has already reached a critical level. Egypt, for instance, is located in an arid region of the world, where people have long depended on the River Nile for most of their water. But, as the Egyptian

population increases, shortages are becoming commonplace. Egyptians today must make do with a sixth as much water per person from the Nile as they did in 1900, and experts project that the supply will shrink by half again over the next 20 years (Myers, 1984c; Postel, 1993).

Within 30 years, according to current predictions, 1 billion people throughout the Middle East and parts of Africa will lack sufficient water. The world has recently witnessed the tragedy of hunger in the African nations of Ethiopia and Somalia. While we recognise the impact of food shortages there, an even more serious problem for these societies is the lack of adequate water for irrigation and drinking.

Surging population and complex technology – especially in manufacturing and power-generating facilities – have greatly increased our appetite for water. The global demand for water (estimated at about 5 billion cubic feet per year) has tripled since 1950 and is expanding faster than the world's population (Postel, 1993). As a result, even in areas that receive significant rainfall, people are using groundwater faster than it can be naturally replenished. Take the Tamil Nadu region of southern India, for example. There, the rapidly growing population is drawing so much groundwater that the local water table has fallen 100 feet over the last several decades.

In light of such developments, we must face the reality that water is a valuable, finite resource. Greater conservation of water by individuals (who consume, on average, 10 million gallons over a lifetime) is part of the answer. However, households around the world account for no more than 10 per cent of water use. We need to curb water consumption by industry, which currently uses 25 per cent of the global total.

Irrigation channels two-thirds of humanity's water use on to croplands. New irrigation technology may well reduce this demand in the future. But, here again, we see that population increase, as well as economic growth, is placing increasing strains on the ecosystem (Myers, 1984a; Goldfarb, 1991; Falkenmark and Widstrand, 1992; Postel, 1993).

Polluting water

In large cities – from Mexico City to Cairo to Shanghai – many people have little choice but to drink contaminated water. The poor people of the world suffer most as a result of unsafe water. As Chapter 20 noted, infectious diseases such as typhoid, cholera and dysentery, all caused by micro-organisms that contaminate water, run rampant in poor nations. Throughout the low-income regions of the world, then, the source of much illness and death can be traced to microbes thriving in polluted water (Falkenmark and Widstrand, 1992; Harrison and Pearce, 2000).

Thus, besides ensuring ample *supplies* of water, we must recognise that no society has done an exemplary job of protecting the *quality* of its water. In most areas of the world, tap water is not safe for drinking.

Most people living in Europe take for granted that tap water is free from harmful contaminants, and water quality in Europe is generally good by global standards. However, even here the problem of water pollution is growing steadily. The Rhine drainage basin (connecting The Netherlands, Germany, France and Switzerland) contains about 20 per cent of the EU's population, along with its industry. Large quantities of toxic waste – chemicals, heavy metals and sewage – have been found to be entering the river. Although actions have since been taken to reduce the quantities of waste, the possibility of contaminated water remains (Drake, 1994: 218–220). Likewise, the pollution all round the Mediterranean is well known. And in the UK, pollution incidents in rivers have doubled in recent years (Pickering and Owen, 1994).

Polluting the air

Most people in Europe are more aware of air pollution than they are of contaminated water, in part because air serves as our constant and immediate environment. Then, too, many urbanites are familiar with the mix of smoke and fog (the origin of the word 'smog') that hangs over cities.

One of the unanticipated consequences of the development of industrial technology – especially the factory and the motor vehicle – has been a deterioration of air quality. The thick, black smoke belched from factory chimneys, often 24 hours a day, alarmed residents of early industrial cities a century ago. By the end of the Second World War, air pollution was commonplace in most industrial cities. In London, factory discharge, car emissions and smoke from coal fires used to heat households combined to create what was probably the worst urban air quality of the century. In the course of just five days in 1952, an especially thick haze – the infamous 'pea-souper' – that hung over London killed 4,000 people (Harrison and Pearce, 2000).

Recently, improvements have been made in combating air pollution brought on by industry. Laws now mandate the use of low-pollution heating fuels in most cities; the coal fires that choked London a half-century ago, for example, are now forbidden (the Clean

Air Act of 1956 helped to end much of this pollution – though in December 1991, a severe smog did reappear). In addition, scientists have effectively devised new technologies to reduce the noxious output of factory chimneys and, even more important, to lessen the pollution caused by the growing number of cars and lorries. The switch to unleaded petrol, coupled with changes in engine design and exhaust systems, has reduced the car's detrimental environmental impact. Still, with cars accounting for around 80 per cent of all travel in Europe (and 96 per cent in the United States!), the challenge of cleaning the air remains daunting (*Social Trends*, 1997: 202). As the number of cars across the world increase (in 2002, around 41 million passenger vehicles were produced – five times as many as in 1950), so pollution grows. Whereas in 1961, the number of licensed vehicles in Great Britain was just under 9 million; in 1981, there were 19.3 million. By 2002, the figure was 30.6 million. Table 24.2 suggests the damage the emissions from these cars can do (*World Watch*, 2004: *Social Trends*, 2004).

If the rich societies of the world can breathe a bit more easily than they once did, poor societies contend with an increasing problem of air pollution. For one thing, people in low-income countries still rely on wood, coal, peat or other 'dirty' fuels for cooking fires and to heat their homes. Moreover, many nations are so eager to encourage short-term industrial development

Table 24.2	The dangers of cars: what they release into the environment
Pollutant	**Hazard**
Carbon monoxide	Greenhouse gas – slows thought and reflexes
Ozone	Greenhouse gas – irritant on eyes, nose, lungs, etc. Damages trees – with acid rain
Nitrogen oxide	Greenhouse gas One-third of acidity of rainfall
Lead	Impairs mental development in children
Benzene	Cancer and impotence links
Hydrocarbons	Irritate lungs and are potentially cancerous
Carbon dioxide	Most significant greenhouse gas

that they pay little heed to the longer-term dangers of air pollution. As a result, many cities in Latin America, Eastern Europe and Asia are plagued by air pollution that rivals the toxic level found in London 50 years ago. All the major cities – from Bangkok to Mexico City – labour under intense city pollution that makes even breathing difficult!

Acid rain

Acid rain refers to *precipitation that is made acidic by air pollution so that it destroys plant and animal life*. The complex reaction that generates acid rain (or snow) begins as power plants burning fossil fuels (oil and coal) to generate electricity release sulphur and nitrogen oxides into the air. Once the winds sweep these gases into the atmosphere, they react with the air to form sulphuric and nitric acids, which make atmospheric moisture acidic.

One type of pollution often causes another. In this case, air pollution (from chimneys) ends up contaminating water (in lakes and streams that collect acid rain). Notice, too, that acid rain is a global phenomenon because the regions that suffer the effects of acid rain may be thousands of miles from the site of the original pollution. Tall chimneys of British power plants have caused the acid rain that has devastated forests and fish in Norway and Sweden up to 1,000 miles to the northeast (Harrison and Pearce, 2000).

Destroying the land

Rain forests are *regions of dense forestation, most of which circle the globe close to the equator*. The largest tropical rain forests are in South America (notably Brazil), but west-central Africa and Southeast Asia also have sizeable rain forests. In all, the world's rain forests cover an area of some 2 billion acres, which accounts for 7 per cent of the earth's total land surface.

Like the rest of the world's resources, the rain forests are falling victim to the needs and appetites of the surging human population. The demand for beef has sparked more cattle grazing in Latin America; ranchers typically burn forested areas to increase their supply of grazing land. Just as important is the lucrative hardwood trade. High prices are paid for mahogany and other woods by people in rich societies who have, as environmentalist Norman Myers (1984b: 88) puts it, 'a penchant for parquet floors, fine furniture, fancy panelling, weekend yachts, and high-grade coffins'. Under such pressure, the world's rain forests are now just half

their original size, and they continue to shrink by about 1 per cent (65,000 square miles) annually. If this rate of destruction continues unchecked, these forests will vanish before the end of the twenty-first century and, with them, protection for the earth's climate and biodiversity.

Global warming

Natural scientists explain that rain forests play an important part in removing carbon dioxide (CO_2) from the earth's atmosphere. From the time of the Industrial Revolution, the amount of carbon dioxide humanity has produced (most generated by factories and cars) has risen tenfold. Much of this CO_2 is absorbed by the oceans. But plants, which take in carbon dioxide and expel oxygen, also play a major part in maintaining the chemical balance of the atmosphere.

The problem, then, is that production of carbon dioxide is rising while the amount of plant life on earth is shrinking. To make matters worse, rain forests are being destroyed mostly by burning, which releases even more carbon dioxide into the atmosphere. Experts estimate the atmospheric concentration of carbon dioxide is now 10–20 per cent higher than it was 150 years ago. In the atmosphere, carbon dioxide behaves much like the glass roof of a greenhouse, letting heat from the sun pass through to the earth while preventing much of it from radiating back away from the planet. Thus ecologists speculate about a possible **greenhouse effect**, a *rise in the earth's average temperature (global warming) due to increasing concentration of carbon dioxide in the atmosphere* (see Figure 24.8).

Scientists note a small rise in global temperature (about 1°C) over the twentieth century. Some go on to predict that the average temperature of our planet (about 15°C in recent years) will rise by 5–10°C during the twenty-first century. This warming trend would melt much of the polar ice caps, raise sea levels and push the oceans up over low-lying land around the world, flooding Bangladesh, for example, and much of coastal Europe.

Not all scientists share this vision of future global warming. Some point out that global temperature changes have been taking place throughout history, and rain forests have had little or nothing to do with those shifts. Moreover, higher concentrations of carbon dioxide in the atmosphere might actually accelerate plant growth (since plants thrive on this gas), which would serve to correct this imbalance and nudge the earth's temperature downward once again (Silverberg, 1991).

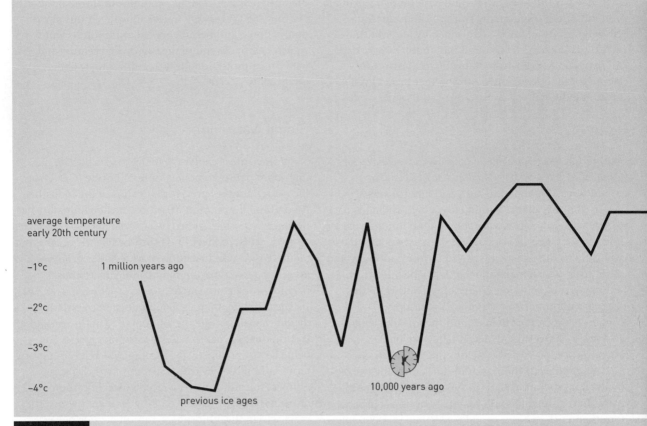

average temperature
early 20th century

–1°c   1 million years ago

–2°c

–3°c

–4°c   10,000 years ago
              previous ice ages

Figure 24.8   'Greenhouse gas' emissions worldwide, and changes in global temperatures
The lower figure shows a baseline of temperature at the start of the twentieth century. Temperatures for

Source: adapted from Dan Smith, *The State of the World Atlas*, 6th edn (1999: 98–99) © Myriad Editions Limited, www.MyriadEditions.com

Declining biodiversity

Whatever the effects on this planet's climate, rain-forest clearance has another undeniable impact. The disappearance of rain forests is a major factor eroding the earth's biodiversity, or, more simply, causing many thousands of species of plant and animal life to disappear forever. While rain forests account for just 7 per cent of the earth's surface, they are home to almost half of this planet's living species. Estimates of the total number of species of animals and plants range from 1.5 million to as high as 30 million. Researchers, in fact, have identified more than 1,000 species of ants alone (Wilson, 1991).

Several dozen unique species of plants and animals cease to exist each day; but, given the vast number of living species on the earth, why should we be concerned with a loss of biodiversity? Environmentalists point to three reasons. First, our planet's biodiversity provides a vast and varied source of human food. Agricultural technology currently 'splices' familiar crops with more exotic plant life to yield crops that are more productive or resistant to insects and disease. In addition, geneticists, looking into the properties of unfamiliar plant and animal life, are working towards generating the quantity and quality of foods necessary to nourish our rapidly increasing population.

Second, the earth's biodiversity is a vital genetic resource. Medical and pharmaceutical industries depend on animal and plant biodiversity in their research to discover compounds that will cure disease and improve our lives. Children in Europe, for example, now have a good chance of surviving leukaemia, a disease that was almost a sure killer two generations ago, because of a compound derived from a pretty tropical flower called the rosy periwinkle. The oral birth control pill used by tens of millions of women is a product of the Mexican forest yam. Scientists have tested tens of thousands of plants for their medical properties, and they have developed hundreds of new medicines each year based on this research.

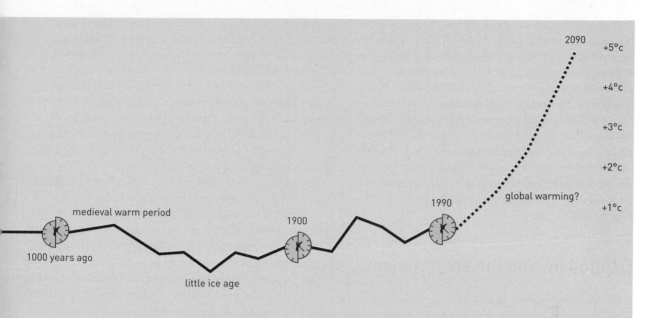

PAST AND FUTURE GLOBAL TEMPERATURES COMPARED WITH AVERAGE TEMPERATURE AT BEGINNING OF CENTURY degrees celsius

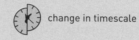 change in timescale

much of history have been well below this, but during the twentieth century they started to rise dramatically.

Members of small, simple societies, such as these people, who thrive in the Philippines, do not have the technological means to greatly affect the natural world. Although we in complex societies like to think of ourselves as superior to such people, the truth is that there is much we can learn from them.

Source: Corbis Sygma P De Vallombreuse

Third, with the loss of any species of life – whether it is one variety of ant, the spotted owl, the magnificent Bengal tiger or the famed Chinese panda – the beauty and complexity of our natural environment is diminished. And there are clear warning signs. Three-quarters of the world's 9,000 species of birds are currently declining in number. Finally, keep in mind that, unlike pollution and other environmental problems, the extinction of species is irreversible and final. As a matter of ethics, then, should those who live today make decisions that will impoverish the world for those who live tomorrow (Myers, 1984b, 1991; Wilson, 1991; Brown *et al.*, 2001)?

Capitalism and the environment

Some sociologists argue that the serious environmental consequences flow from the global disparity of wealth and power. In the hierarchical organisation of societies, a small proportion of our population – what Chapter 15 called the 'power elite' – sets the national and global agenda by controlling the world's economy, law and view of the natural environment. Early capitalists shepherded Europe into the industrial age, hungrily tapping the earth's resources and frantically turning out manufactured goods in pursuit of profits. By and large, it was they who reaped the benefits of the new industrial wealth, while workers toiled in dangerous factories and lived in nearby localities blighted with smoke, racked with noise and shaken by the vibrations of the big machines.

As important: many societies have just ignored the most blatant instances of environmental destruction, even when elite perpetrators run foul of the law. Corporate pollution falls under the category of white-collar crime. Such offences typically escape prosecution. When action is taken, it is usually in the form of fines levied on a company rather than criminal penalties imposed on individuals. Thus, corporate executives who order the burning or burying of toxic waste have been subject to penalties no greater (and sometimes less) than ordinary citizens who throw rubbish from car windows.

Those who embrace a Marxist view of society argue that capitalism itself poses a threat to the environment. The logic of capitalism is the pursuit of profit, and t hat pursuit demands continuous economic growth. What is profitable to capitalists does not necessarily advance the public welfare and is not likely to be good for the natural environment. As noted earlier in this chapter, capitalist industries have long ensured ongoing profits by designing products to have a limited useful life (the concept of 'planned obsolescence'). Such

policies may improve the 'bottom line' in the short term, but they raise the long-term risk of depleting natural resources as well as generating overwhelming amounts of solid waste.

A small share of the earth's population currently consumes most of its energy. Generally, members of rich societies use most of the earth's resources and, in the process, produce the most pollution. By exploiting both the earth and the poor of the less developed countries, these countries have poisoned the air and water in the process. From this point of view, rich nations are actually overdeveloped and consume too much. No one should expect that the majority of the earth's people, who live in poor societies, will be able to match the living standard in these countries; nor, given the current environmental crisis, would that be desirable. Instead, conflict theorists call for a more equitable distribution of resources among all people of the world both as a matter of social justice and as a strategy to preserve the natural environment (Schnaiberg and Gould, 1994; Szasz, 1994).

Environmental racism

An important aspect of this inequality is the worrying growth of **environmental racism**, *the pattern by which environmental hazards are greatest in proximity to poor people, especially minorities*. For example, while many homes in rich countries can consume more than 2,000 litres of good quality water every day, some 500 million people around the globe suffer from an almost total lack of drinking water! The World Health Organisation suggests a basic requirement of 150 litres per day per household. This basic and quite low standard could well be achieved for the whole world if so much water was not squandered by the West (*New Internationalist*, 2001: 23).

Historically, factories that spew pollutants have been built in and near districts inhabited by the poor who often work there. As a result of their low incomes, many could afford housing only in undesirable localities, sometimes in the very shadow of the plants and mills. Although workers in many manufacturing industries have organised in opposition to environmental hazards, they have done so with limited success, largely because the people facing the most serious environmental threats have the least social power to begin with.

Critical comment

This analysis raises important questions of who sets a society's agenda and who benefits (and suffers) most from decisions that affect us all. Environmental problems, from this point of view, are consequences of a global stratification (see Chapter 9). Yet, while it may be true that elites have always dominated industrial society, they have not been able to stem a steady tide towards legal protection of the natural environment.

These protections, in turn, have yielded some significant improvements in our air and water quality. Arguably, however, much of this change has come about because of social movements directed towards environmental action.

CONTROVERSY AND DEBATE

THE ENVIRONMENTAL MOVEMENT: HOW RADICAL SHOULD IT BE?

It isn't much, really, in dispute – only the land we live on, the water we drink, the air we breathe, the food we eat, and the energy that supports us.
(Aaron Wildavsky)

While many people believe that science and technology will improve their lives, environmentalists are not so sure. For them, the world is hurtling towards an ecological disaster. All the evidence described in this chapter must lead one to conclude that our environment is under severe risk, and planet earth could face its own destruction in the not too distant future.

The environmental movement is a major example of a contemporary social movement that aims to have a wide, global impact (see Chapter 15). Born of post-materialist values, the movement itself has changed over time. The 'first wave' of environmentalism was little more than a conservation movement that focused on protecting the natural environment. Its earliest manifestations may have appeared in Britain as long ago as the sixteenth century, with people's concerns for the changing countryside. The movement developed more focus in the nineteenth century through the emergence of groups such as the National Trust (1895) and the Royal Society for the Protection of Birds (created in 1889).

During the 1960s a 'second wave' of environmentalism took root in Europe and became decidedly more radical and critical. In 1962, in the United States, Rachel Carson's book *Silent Spring* explored the dangers of spreading pesticides across the land. Agricultural 'business as usual', Carson warned, was courting disaster. Before long, environmental concerns had become part of the activist culture that marked the decade with people chaining themselves to trees to halt logging and blocking ships armed with nuclear weapons.

By 1970, with the celebration of the first 'Earth Day', the environmental movement had come of age. Its adherents addressed a wide range of issues – including those covered in this chapter – and, increasingly, they directly challenged many of the practices and priorities that had long marked out the Western way of life.

By 1980, around 5 per cent of the population in the UK belonged to one of several thousands of environmental groups. In 1989, a MORI poll revealed that 18 million people regarded themselves as environmentally conscious shoppers; and some 17–35 per cent of people rated the environment as the most important political issue (Garner, 1996: 62–63). At the forefront of these newer groups were *Friends of the Earth* and *Greenpeace*. Greenpeace emerged in the late 1960s and, by 1989, had attracted an estimated 3.5 million members. It has become a major NGO. Friends of the Earth was founded in 1969 in the United States, and by the early 1980s had branches in some 29 countries. Many feminist groups (*eco-feminists*) have also come to identify strongly with environmental change, especially those who argue that women are the sex who reproduce, nurture and care – more than men. As such they have a major responsibility for reproduction and caring for their planet (Garner, 1996: 66).

At the same time, throughout all this, conservative administrations have often adopted a strong pro-business agenda and soon governments and the environmental movement were locking horns over population control, land development and other matters.

Today, the environmental movement falls into three main groupings. One group comprises mainstream lobbyists who usually work in NGOs such as Greenpeace and are often professional and well funded. A second group encompasses popular movements where people lobby for specific issues and work to change things in their own lives, be it picketing the transportation of livestock and concern over 'animal rights' in the UK, marching on railway ▶

CONTROVERSY AND DEBATE CONTINUED

carriages transporting nuclear waste in Germany, or landless peasants marching on Brasilia to address land rights issues. The third, more radical wing of environmentalism draws on Marxism and feminism and takes drastic action to instil a sense of urgency among governments.

Many environmentalists think there is nothing at all radical about their movements. From their point of view, we must learn to live in concert with the environment because, politics aside, humanity cannot survive otherwise. In the end, what these environmentalists are saying is that, in light of the risks we face, making basic changes is common sense. On the surface, at least, the public has come to accept environmentalism. And everywhere one looks, governments are acting to reduce the dangers, under the buzz phrase of 'sustainable development'.

But other environmentalists do not think the problem and solution are so simple. These 'ecological radicals' argue that basic changes are necessary in our way of life if we are to head off disaster down the road. In particular, they believe, we can no longer place economic growth at the heart of culture because this core value is causing an

increasing environmental deficit. The materialist and consumerist vision of the good life can no longer be sustained because it leads to the degradation of the environment. Perhaps society has come to accept the idea that environmentalism is good in principle, but it is far from clear that most people are willing to make the hard choices to achieve a sustainable way of life.

CONTINUE THE DEBATE:

1. Do you think limiting economic growth is necessary in order to secure our environmental future? Would you be willing to accept a lower standard of living to protect the natural environment?

2. What action have you ever taken (signing a petition, participating in a demonstration, modifying your consumption patterns) in support of the environment?

3. Where do you think the major European political parties stand on environmental issues?

Sources: based on Dunlap and Mertig (1992); survey data from Dunlap *et al.* (1992), NORC (1994), and Benton (1997)

So what of the charge that capitalism is particularly hostile to the natural world? There is little doubt that capitalism's logic of growth does indeed place stress on the environment. At the same time, however, capitalist societies have made some strides towards international agreements for environmental protection. And the environmental record of socialist societies is also very poor. For decades, industrialisation was pursued in neglect of environmental concerns, without challenge and with tragic consequences in terms of human health.

Finally, there is little doubt that high-income countries currently place huge demands on the natural environment. However, this pattern is already beginning to shift as global population swells in poor countries. And environmental problems are also likely to grow worse to the extent that poor societies develop economically, using more resources and producing more waste and pollutants in the process. In the long run, all nations of the world share a vital interest in protecting the natural environment. This concern leads us to the final topic of this chapter, the concept of a sustainable environment.

Taking stock and looking ahead: for a sustainable world?

India's great leader Mahatma Gandhi once declared that societies must provide 'enough for people's needs, but not for their greed'. From an environmental point of view, this means that the earth will be able to sustain future generations only if humanity refrains from rapidly and thoughtlessly consuming finite resources such as oil, hardwoods and water. Nor can we persist in polluting the air, water and ground at anything like the current levels. The loss of global forests – through cutting of trees and the destructive effects of acid rain – threatens to undermine the global climate. And we risk the future of the planet by adding people to the world at the rate of 90 million each year.

Today, on every part of the earth inhabited by humanity, the environmental deficit is growing. In effect, our present way of life is borrowing against the well-being of future generations. As we have seen, members of rich societies, who currently consume so much of the earth's resources, are mortgaging the future security of the majority of people who live in the poor countries of the world.

In principle, we could solve the entire range of environmental problems described in this chapter by living in a more environmentally aware manner, one that makes environmental consequences central to our actions. This is the path to a culture that is sustainable, one that does not increase the environmental deficit. An **ecologically sustainable culture**, then, refers to *a way of life that meets the needs of the present generation without threatening the environmental legacy of future generations.* (The concept of 'sustainable development' was popularised through the 1987 UN Commission Report on the Environment – the Brundtland Commission.)

Sustainable living calls for three basic strategies. The first is the *conservation of finite resources*, balancing the desire to satisfy our present wants with the responsibility to preserve what will be needed by future generations. Conservation means using resources more efficiently, seeking alternative resources and learning to live with less. Technology is helping in providing some devices (from light bulbs to boilers) that are far more energy efficient than those available at present. Moreover, alternative energy sources need developing, including harnessing the power of the sun, wind and tides. While relying on help from new technology, a sustainable way of life will ultimately require a rethinking of the pro-consumption attitudes formed during decades of 'cheap electricity' and 'cheap petrol'. The consumer society discussed in Chapter 14 may have to be changed.

EUROPEAN EYE

EUROPEAN ENVIRONMENTAL POLICY

Environmental issues are truly global. Many of the problems, like the releasing of CFCs into the atmosphere, have global effects and require global action. Some problems link to the exploitation of **global commons –** *the resources shared by the international community, such as ocean beds and the atmosphere.* Sometimes small local problems, such as poisonous gases leaking from landfills and water pollution, are multiplied so many times in many local contexts that they become major world hazards. The environment is a global concern requiring global policies.

The UN Conference on the Human Environment in 1972 at Stockholm was the first major international conference on the environment. It led to a Declaration and an Action Plan with 109 recommendations in six broad areas (including human settlements, natural resource management, pollution, educational and social aspects of the environment, development, and international organisations). It led to a programme to manage the 'global commons', and established a UN environment programme. Subsequent world conferences include the Earth Summit held at Rio in 1992 and the Earth Summit 2 in New York in 1997.

Uniquely among international organisations, the European Union has 'the power to agree environmental policies binding on its members' (McCormick, 1991: 128). Since 1957, some 300 pieces of environmental leg-

islation have been passed. Four periods of European policy have been identified:

1957–72 The original Treaty of Rome did not raise environmental issues and there was minimal involvement.
1973–85 In the wake of the *Limits to Growth* report (see discussion in text), the First Environmental Action Programme gave the EU power to act whenever 'real effectiveness' on environmental issues seemed possible. Water quality, air quality and hazardous waste policies (120 directives, 27 decisions and 14 regulations) were implemented.
1986–92 A formal legal framework emerged.
1993–97 In the wake of Maastricht, integration curiously becomes weaker as the EU expands to include new members and as members defend their national self-interest. Nonetheless, the EU continues to promote sustainable environmental policies through such measures as the regulation of fish stocks and funding of sustainable development research.
2001 The Sixth Community Environmental Action Programme lays out a plan for a wider programme of environmental action up to 2010. The World Watch Institute has remarked that: 'The European Union, consisting of some 15 countries and containing 360 million people, provides a model for the rest of the world of an environmentally sustainable food/population balance . . . one seventh of humanity is already there' (Brown *et al.*, 1997: 12–13). For updates, see the European Environmental Agency at http://www.eea.eu.int

The second basic strategy is *reducing waste*. Whenever possible, simply using less is the most effective way to reduce waste. Governments will need to tighten regulations on pollution. They may need to foster this by shifting taxes on to environmental 'bads' such as carbon use or fuel emissions (e.g. fuel taxes). There will be a need to expand recycling programmes. Educational efforts need to enlist widespread support for these initiatives and for legislation requiring the recycling of certain materials.

The third key element in any plan for a sustainable ecosystem is *bringing world population growth under control*. As we have explained, the 2000 global population of over 6 billion is straining the natural environment. Clearly, the higher world population climbs, the more difficult environmental problems will become. Global population is now increasing by about 1.5 per cent each year, a rate that will double the world's people in fewer than 50 years. Few analysts think that the earth can support a population of 10 billion or more; most argue that we must hold the line at about 7 billion. Controlling population growth will require urgent steps in poor regions of the world where growth rates are highest.

Technocentrism and ecocentrism

Although there is some common agreement about the need to *conserve resources, reduce waste and bring population under control*, there are many different positions on how to achieve this. As the Controversy and Debate box on p. 679 discusses, some positions are radical and seek a fundamental change of the world; others believe the existing order just needs a little tinkering. Commonly though, two positions have been identified: a technocentric one and an ecocentric one.

Those holding ecocentric positions (who we might call Radical Greens) see economic growth as at odds with environmental objectives. There must be *limits to growth* (see above) as the valuing of growth in itself will inevitably lead to more and more commodities, goods and waste. They are concerned that adopting technical and scientific solutions to the problems may just increase them: science has always had side-effects and these may well bring yet more damage (we have seen this both in Chapter 22 and in the idea of a Risk Society, discussed above). They suggest that major social and political changes become necessary for environmental change, and they argue that the planet is home not just for humans but for *all* living things. In contrast, technocentric positions put human beings and science at the centre of their arguments. They see the continued

Table 24.3	Models of technocentric and ecocentric solutions to environmental problems
Technocentric	**Ecocentric**
Modified sustainable economic growth	Growth seen as limited and undesirable
Technology can provide solutions	Distrust of science and technological fixes
Solutions within existing policy	Radical social and political change needed
Human-centred – human values	Nature-centred – wider values

Source: adapted from Garner (1996: 30)

need for economic growth, but one in which technical solutions to problems of the environment may be found (see Table 24.3).

As with all such models, they set out polar positions which may help to clarify arguments but which in practice often need some compromise in reality. Sweeping environmental strategies – put in place with the best intentions – will fail without some fundamental changes in the ways in which we come to think about the social and the natural world, and our place in them. By taking a view that sets up our own immediate interests as the standards for how to live, we have obscured several key connections.

First of all, we need to realise that, environmentally speaking, *the present is tied to the future*. Simply put, today's actions shape tomorrow's world. Thus, we must learn to evaluate our short-term choices in terms of their long-range consequences for the natural environment.

Second, rather than viewing humans as 'different' from or 'better' than other forms of life and assuming that we have the right to dominate the planet, we must acknowledge that *all forms of life are interdependent*. Ignoring this truth not only harms other life forms, but it will eventually undermine our own well-being. From the realisation that all life figures in the ecological balance must follow specific programmes that will protect the earth's biodiversity.

Third, and finally, achieving a sustainable ecosystem will require *global cooperation*. The planet's rich and poor nations are currently separated by a vast chasm of divergent interests, cultures and living standards. On the one hand, most countries in the northern half of the world are overdeveloped, using more resources than the earth can sustain over time. On the other hand, most nations in the southern half of the world are underdeveloped, unable to meet the basic needs of many of their people. A sustainable ecosystem depends on bold and unprecedented programmes of international cooperation. And, while the cost of change will certainly be high, it pales before the eventual cost of not responding to the growing environmental deficit.

Along with the transformations just noted, we will reach the goal of a sustainable society only by critically re-evaluating the logic of growth that has dominated our way of life for several centuries.

In closing, we might well consider that the great dinosaurs dominated this planet for some million years and then perished forever. Humanity is far younger, having existed for a mere quarter of a million years. Compared to dinosaurs, our species seems to have the gift of intelligence. But how wisely will we use this ability? What are the chances that our species will continue to flourish on the earth a million years – or even a few hundred years – from now? It may be foolish to assume that our present civilisation is about to collapse, but it is certainly equally foolish to ignore the warning signs. One certainty is that the state of tomorrow's world will depend on choices we make today.

SUMMARY

1. Because the most important factor affecting the state of the natural environment is the way in which human beings organise social life, ecology – the study of how living organisms interact with their environment – is one important focus of sociology.

2. Societies increase the environmental deficit by focusing on short-term benefits and ignoring the long-term consequences brought on by their way of life.

3. Studying the natural environment demands a global perspective. All parts of the ecosystem, including the air, soil and water, are interconnected. Similarly, actions in one part of the globe have an impact on the natural environment elsewhere.

4. The 'logic of growth' argument defends economic development and asserts that people can solve environmental problems as they arise. Countering this view, the 'limits to growth' thesis states that societies have little choice but to curb development to head off eventual environmental collapse.

5. European and other Western countries have transformed into 'disposable societies', generating billions of pounds of solid waste each day. Even though recycling efforts have increased, the majority of waste continues to be dumped in landfills. Water consumption is rapidly increasing throughout the world. Much of the world – notably Africa and the Middle East – is currently approaching a water-supply crisis. The hydrological cycle purifies rainwater, but water pollution from dumping and chemical contamination still poses a serious threat to water quality in Europe. This problem is even more acute in the world's low-income countries. Air quality became steadily worse in Europe and North America after the Industrial Revolution. About 1950, however, a turnaround took place and these societies have made significant progress in curbing air pollution. In low-income countries, particularly in cities, air quality remains at unhealthy levels due to burning of 'dirty' fuels and little regulation of pollution. Acid rain, the product of pollutants entering the atmosphere, often contaminates land and water thousands of miles away. Rain forests play a vital role in removing carbon dioxide from the atmosphere. Under pressure from commercial interests, the world's rain forests are now half their original size and are shrinking by about 1 per cent annually. Global warming refers to predictions that the average temperature of the earth will rise because of increasing levels of carbon dioxide in the atmosphere. Both carbon emissions from factories and cars and the shrinking rain forests, which consume carbon dioxide, aggravate this problem. The elimination of rain forests is also reducing the planet's biodiversity, since these tropical regions are home to about half of all living species. Biodiversity, a source of natural beauty, is also critical to agricultural and medical research.

6. A focus on capitalism highlights the importance of inequality in understanding environmental issues. This perspective blames environmental decay on the self-interest of elites, and notes the pattern of environmental racism whereby the poor, especially minorities, disproportionately suffer from proximity to environmental hazards. It also places responsibility for the declining state of the world's natural environment primarily on rich societies, which consume the most resources.

7. A sustainable environment is one that does not threaten the well-being of future generations. Achieving this goal will require conservation of finite resources, reducing waste and pollution, and controlling the size of the world's population.

CRITICAL-THINKING QUESTIONS

1. What role can sociology play in understanding the natural environment? Can it also help in your own personal ways of dealing with the problems of environmental destruction?

2. In what ways does environmental degradation link to patterns of social division and stratification?

3. What is meant by 'sustainable development' and what evidence supports the contention that humanity is running up an 'environmental deficit'? Is there any evidence suggesting that some environmental problems are subsiding?

4. Discuss the role of social movements in environmental change.

5. Examine the idea of 'the Risk Society' and the problem of environmental degradation.

GOING FURTHER

Further reading

Introduction to Environment issues:

Lester R. Brown *et al.* (eds), *State of the World 2004: The Consumer Society* (2004)
Published annually, this is a collection of essays that focuses on a range of environmental dangers in global perspective.

A. J. McMichael, *Planetary Overload: Global Environment Change and the Health of the Human Species* (1993)
Focuses upon how the major ecological disruptions are posing a threat to the health and very existence of the human species and provides detailed accounts of all the major threats.

On the sociology of the environment:

Robert Garner, *Environmental Politics* (2nd edn, 2001)
Provides a succinct summary of the main issues, splits and groupings around 'environmentalism'.

On 'Risk Society':

Ulrich Beck, *Risk Society* (1992)
The classic key statement of the emergence of a risk society, though it is far from being an 'easy read'. He has developed his argument further in *World Risk Society* (1999).

Classic writings include:

Rachel Carson, *Silent Spring* (1962)
About the dangers of chemical pollution, helped launch the environmental movement in the United States and elsewhere.

Donella H. Meadows *et al.*, *The Limits to Growth: A Report on the Club of Rome's Project on the Predicament of Mankind* (1972)
The classic 1970s study to predict future ecological trends. Its conclusions support the 'limits to growth' thesis.

More information

An elegant visual account of the world's environment can be found in the work of the French photographer Yann Arthus-Bertrand. See his *Earth from the Air* project, book (2002) and website at www.earthfromtheair.com

One of many mappings of the environment crisis can be found in the *AAAS Atlas of Population and Environment* (University of California Press, 2000) edited by Paul Harrison and Fred Pearce. Probably the prime resource for up-to-date information and discussion on ecosystems and the environment is the *World Resources Institute.* They produce a major annual volume (e.g. *World Resources 2000–1, People and Ecosystems – The Fraying Web of Life*, Elsevier Science); and their website is at http://www.wri.org/

Watch a video/Read a book

- Steven Soderbergh's *Erin Brockovich* (2002): Julia Roberts plays a twice-divorced single mother who discovers a suspicious cover-up involving contaminated water in a local community causing devastating illness.
- Mike Nichols' *Silkwood* (1983): Meryl Streep is a whistlebower who speaks out about strange goings on at a factory plant.
- John Wyndham's *The Day of the Triffids* (1951): a powerful story about the sudden blinding of all human beings and the appearance of enormous, mobile predatory plants. A good novel, but Steve Sekely and Freddie Francis's film, *The Day of the Triffids* (1962) was a poorer version of the story.

Connecting up

Connect to other chapters

- Link to cities and demography as an issue in the environment in Chapter 23.
- Link to Risk Society and the environment in Chapter 22.
- Link to global inequalities in Chapter 9.
- Link to social movements in Chapter 15. The environmental movement is a major instance of a new social movement.

To the websites

A major listing of environmental websites can be found at:

http://www.earthsystems.org/All.shtml

Activist resources in the UK include such groupings as:

- Friends of the Earth: http://www.foe.co.uk
- Greenpeace: http://www.greenpeace.org.uk

For additional case studies, multiple choice questions, internet exercises, and annotated weblinks specific to this chapter, visit this book's website at www.pearsoned.co.uk/plummer

CHAPTER 25

FUTURES: THE CHALLENGES FOR SOCIOLOGY IN THE TWENTY-FIRST CENTURY

Postmodernism is concerned with futures, not the future; there is never one future, but a plurality of diverse futures . . . the move from modern to postmodern is not a case of unilinear and universal change, nor a new grand narrative, but an eclectic mixing of old and new elements in a variety of distinct local and global forms. Postmodernity will not have a future but a variety of futures.

John Gibbins and Bo Reimer (1999: 140)

THE FIRELIGHT FLICKERS in the gathering darkness as Chief Kanhonk sits, as he has done at the end of the day for many years, ready to begin an evening of animated talk and storytelling (Simons, 1995). This is the hour when the Kaiapo, a small society in Brazil's lush Amazon region, celebrate their heritage. Because

the Kaiapo are a traditional people with no written language, the elders rely on evenings by the fire to teach their culture and instruct the grandchildren. In the past, evenings like this have been filled with tales of brave Kaiapo warriors fighting off Portuguese traders in pursuit of slaves and gold, but as the minutes pass, only a few villagers assemble for the evening ritual.

'It is the Big Ghost', one man grumbles, explaining the poor turnout. The 'Big Ghost' has indeed descended upon them; its bluish glow spilling from windows of homes throughout the village. The Kaiapo children – and many adults

as well – are watching television. The consequences of installing a satellite dish in the village several years ago have turned out to be greater than anyone imagined. In the end, what their enemies failed to do to the Kaiapo with guns, they may well do to themselves with prime-time programming.

The Kaiapo are among the 230,000 native peoples who inhabit the country we call Brazil. They stand out because of their striking body paint and ornate ceremonial dress. Recently, they have become rich as profits from gold mining and harvesting mahogany trees have flowed into the settlement. Now they must decide if their new-found fortune is a blessing or a curse.

To some, affluence means the opportunity to learn about the outside world through travel and television. Others, like Chief Kanhonk, are not so sure. Sitting by the fire, he thinks aloud, 'I have been saying that people must buy useful things like knives and fishing hooks. Television does not fill the stomach. It only shows our children and grandchildren white people's things.' Bebtopup, the oldest priest, nods in agreement: 'The night is the time the old people teach the young people. Television has stolen the night.'

(Simons, 1995: 471)

(Left) Ron Kitaj: *If Not, Not* (detail). This is one of Kitaj's strongest pictures and integrates modern catastrophes into a classical landscape, reminding us of Italian Renaissance paintings.
Source: Marlborough Fine Art/Scottish Museum of Modern Art

The transformation of the Kaiapo raises profound questions about the causes of change and whether change – even in pursuit of a higher material standard of living – is always for the better. Moreover, the drama of the Kaiapo is being played out around the globe as more and more traditional cultures are being lured away from their heritage by the materialism and affluence of rich societies. This chapter examines social change as a process with both positive and negative consequences. It brings together, by way of a conclusion, a number of key ideas developed in the book. As we have stressed throughout this book, of particular interest are the movements from *modernity*, changes brought about by the Industrial Revolution, towards *postmodernity*, more recent transformations sparked by the Information Revolution and the post-industrial economy.

What is social change?

Almost every chapter of this book has been haunted by the idea of **social change**, *the transformation of culture and social institutions over time*. Recall how in Chapter 1 we argued that sociology was born of three revolutions: the Industrial Revolution, the Political Revolutions associated with democracy, and the Urban Revolution linked in part to the decline in community. But this broad process of social change is ubiquitous in society and has four key characteristics:

1. Social change happens everywhere, although the rate of change varies from place to place. 'Nothing is constant except death and taxes', goes the old saying. Yet social patterns related to death have changed dramatically as life expectancy in the Western world has nearly doubled over the last two centuries. Taxes, meanwhile, unknown through most of human history, emerged only with complex social organisation several thousand years ago. In short, one is hard-pressed to identify anything that is not subject to the twists and turns of change.

   Still, some societies change faster than others. As Chapter 4 explained, hunting and gathering societies tend to change quite slowly. Members of technologically complex societies, on the other hand, can sense significant change even within a single lifetime. Moreover, even in a given society, some cultural elements change more quickly than others. William Ogburn's (1964) theory of *cultural lag* (see Chapter 5) recognises that material culture (that is, things) usually changes faster than non-material culture (ideas and attitudes). For example, medical

techniques that prolong life have developed more rapidly than have ethical standards for deciding when and how to use them.

2. Social change is sometimes intentional but often unplanned. Industrial societies actively promote many kinds of change. For example, scientists seek more efficient forms of energy and advertisers try to convince consumers that life is incomplete without some new gadget. Yet even the experts rarely envisage all the consequences of the changes they promote. Thus, early car manufacturers certainly understood that cars would allow people to travel in a single day distances that had required weeks or months to traverse a century before. But no one foresaw how profoundly the mobility provided by cars would reshape European societies, scattering family members, threatening the environment and reshaping cities and suburbs. In addition, automotive pioneers could hardly have predicted the millions of deaths each year worldwide in car accidents. And as we saw in the last chapter, the car has worked to degrade the environment in many ways. These unplanned outcomes – often very dangerous and quite unpredictable – are what we have seen as the growth of modern society as 'Risk Society'.

3. Social change often generates controversy. As the history of the car demonstrates, most social change yields both positive and negative consequences. Capitalists welcomed the Industrial Revolution because advancing technology increased productivity and swelled profits. Many workers, however, fearing that machines would make their skills obsolete, strongly resisted 'progress'. In the Western world, changing patterns of interaction between black people and white people, between women and men and between gays and heterosexuals give rise to misunderstandings, tensions and, sometimes, outright hostility.

4. Some changes matter more than others. Some social changes have only passing significance, whereas other transformations resonate for generations. At one extreme, clothing fads among the young burst on the scene and dissipate quickly. At the other, we are still adjusting to powerful technological advances such as television half a century after its introduction. Some innovations, such as audio tapes and faxes, seem to have quite short lives; others, such as the car, are much less likely to 'die out' quickly. Looking ahead, who can predict with any certainty how computers will transform the entire world during the twenty-first century? Will the Information Revolution turn out to be as pivotal as the Industrial Revolution? Like the car

and television, computers will have both beneficial and deleterious effects, providing new kinds of job while eliminating old ones, joining people together in ever-expanding electronic networks while threatening personal privacy.

Causes of social change

Throughout the book we have seen many different explanations of widespread social change. There is no reason to champion just one theory: it is much more likely that a number of factors come into play together. These include the following.

Culture and change

Culture is a dynamic system that continually gains new elements and loses others. Chapter 5 identified three important sources of cultural change. First, *invention* produces new objects, ideas and social patterns. Through rocket propulsion research, which began in the 1940s, we have engineered high-tech vehicles for space flight. Today we take such technology for granted; during the present century a significant number of people may well travel in space.

Second, *discovery* occurs when people first take note of certain elements of the world or learn to see them in a new way. Medical advances, for example, offer a growing understanding of the human body. Beyond the direct effects for human health, medical discoveries have also stretched life expectancy, setting in motion 'the greying of the Western world' (see Chapter 13).

Third, *diffusion* creates change as trade, migration and mass communication spread cultural elements throughout the world. Ralph Linton (1937) recognised that many familiar elements of a culture have come to us from other lands. For example, cloth was developed in Asia while coins were devised in Turkey. Generally, material things diffuse more readily than non-material cultural traits. The Kaiapo, described at the beginning of this chapter, have been quick to adopt television but reluctant to embrace the materialism and individualism that sometimes seize those who spend hours watching Western commercial programming.

Through much migration, the Western world has steadily changed in response to cultural diffusion. In recent decades, people from Africa, Asia and other parts of the world have been introducing new cultural patterns, clearly evident in the sights, smells and sounds of cities across European countries. From African music to Thai and Vietnamese food, non-Western cultures diffuse into the West. Conversely, the global power of the Western world ensures that much of Western culture – from the taste of beefburgers to the sounds of Pavarotti – is being diffused to other societies.

Conflict and change

Tension and conflict within a society also produce change. Marx heralded class conflict as the engine that drives societies from one historical era to another. In industrial–capitalist societies the struggle between capitalists and workers propels society towards a socialist system of production. In the century since Marx's death, this model has proven simplistic. Yet, he correctly foresaw that conflicts arising from inequality (now involving race, gender, disability, age and sexuality as well as social class) would force changes in every society, including our own.

Ideas and change

Max Weber, too, contributed to our understanding of social change. While Weber acknowledged the importance of conflict based on material production, he traced the roots of social change to the world of ideas. He illustrated his argument by showing how people who display charisma can convey a message that sometimes changes the world.

Weber also highlighted the importance of ideas by revealing how the world-view of early Protestants prompted them to embrace industrial capitalism. By showing that industrial capitalism developed primarily in areas of Western Europe where the Protestant work ethic was strong, Weber (1958; orig. 1905) concluded that the disciplined rationality of Calvinist Protestants was instrumental in this change.

Ideas also fuel social movements. Chapter 15 looked at social movements and showed how they may emerge from the determination to modify society in some manner (say, to clean up the environment) or from a sense that existing social arrangements are unjust. The international gay rights movement draws strength from the contention that lesbians and gay men should enjoy rights and opportunities equal to those of the heterosexual majority. Opposition to the gay rights movement, moreover, reveals the power of ideas to inhibit as well as to advance social change.

Ideas and conflict

One of the most striking developments since the mid-twentieth century has been the changing nature of war. Since the Second World War, with a few important exceptions, most wars have been waged within countries between rival ethnic groups – major conflicts have continued or resurfaced around ethnicity and religion. But as we saw in Chapter 15, these conflicts are also a major potential source for future world conflict – the concern, for example, of Benjamin Barber (1995) over 'Jihad versus McWorld', or Samuel Huntingon (1996) over the 'clash of civilisations'. When suicide bombers hijacked US passenger planes to crash into the twin towers of the World Trade Center and the Pentagon on 11 September 2001, killing about 6,000 people, the US government identified Islamic fundamentalists from the al-Qaeda terrorist network as those responsible for the attacks and announced a long war to cleanse the world of such terrorism. If this happens, the twenty-first century may well become one of a continual mass global conflict, and old religious wars, which have dominated much of

history, may well return. But, as we write this in October 2004, it is at present far too soon to say where all this may be heading.

Modernity

Throughout this book, we have used many terms that link to modern changes: capitalism, rationality and bureaucracies, nation states, science and technology to name a few. But perhaps the most central concept in the study of social change is **modernity**, *social patterns linked to industrialisation*. In everyday usage, modernity (its Latin root means 'lately') designates the present in relation to the past. Sociologists include within this catch-all concept the many social patterns set in motion by the Industrial Revolution beginning in Western Europe in the mid-eighteenth century. **Modernisation**, then, is *the process of social change initiated by industrialisation*. The time line inside the front cover of the text highlights important events that mark the emergence of modernity.

These images of the Twin Towers of the World Trade Center in New York – before and after the bombing on 11 September 2001 – may well become the defining images of the early part of twenty-first-century life. Conflicts over modernity, ethnicity, religion and capitalism are now reflected on a global stage.

Source: (a) Magnum © Bruno Barbey, (b) Magnum © Susan Meiselas

Key dimensions of modernisation

Peter Berger (1977) notes four major characteristics of modernisation:

1. *The decline of small, traditional communities.* Modernity involves 'the progressive weakening, if not destruction, of the concrete and relatively cohesive communities in which human beings have found solidarity and meaning throughout most of history' (Berger, 1977: 72). For thousands of years, in the camps of hunters and gatherers and in the rural villages of Europe, people lived in small-scale settlements with family and neighbours. Such traditional worlds, based on sentiments and beliefs passed from generation to generation, afford each person a well-defined place. These primary groups limit people's range of experience while conferring a strong sense of identity, belonging and purpose.

   Small, isolated communities still exist in the Western world, of course, but they are now home to only a small percentage of people. Even for rural people, rapid transportation and efficient communication, including television, have brought individuals in touch with the pulse of the larger society and even the entire world.

2. *The expansion of personal choice.* To people in traditional, pre-industrial societies, life is shaped by forces beyond human control – gods, spirits or, simply, fate. Steeped in tradition, members of these societies grant one another a narrow range of personal choices. As the power of tradition erodes, however, people come to see their lives as an unending series of options, a process Berger calls *individualisation*. Many people respond to the alternatives in modern societies by changing their 'lifestyles' over time.

3. *Increasing diversity in beliefs.* In pre-industrial societies, strong family ties and powerful religious beliefs enforce conformity while discouraging diversity and change. Modernisation promotes a more rational, scientific world-view, in which tradition loses its force and morality becomes a matter of individual attitude. The growth of cities, the expansion of impersonal organisations and social interaction among people from various backgrounds combine to foster a diversity of beliefs and behaviour.

4. *Future orientation and growing awareness of time.* People in modern societies think more about the future, while pre-industrial people focus more on the past. Modern people are not only forward-looking but also optimistic that discoveries and new inventions will enhance their lives. In addition, modern people organise daily routines according to precise units of time. With the introduction of clocks in the late Middle Ages, sunlight and seasons faded in importance as measures of time's forward march in favour of hours and minutes. Preoccupied with personal gain, modern people calculate time to the moment and generally believe that 'Time is money!' Berger points out that one key indicator of a society's degree of modernisation is the proportion of people wearing wristwatches.

Finally, recall that modernisation touched off the development of sociology itself. As Chapter 1 explained, the discipline originated in the wake of the Industrial Revolution in Western Europe, precisely where social change was proceeding most rapidly. Early sociologists tried to analyse and explain modernisation and its consequences – both good and bad – for human beings.

The rise of modernity is a complex process involving many dimensions of change, described in previous chapters and summarised in Table 25.1.

The future and change: new kinds of society in the making?

Recently, many sociologists have been conjecturing where future changes in society may take us. We have seen some of these conjectures throughout the book. According to the report *Global Trends 2015* (National Intelligence Council, 2000), which tries to predict where societies may be by the year 2015, there are seven main 'drivers' of change for the future. These are population growth (Chapter 23), environmental damage (Chapter 24), the power of science and technology (Chapter 22), the global economy (Chapters 2 and 14), national and international governance (Chapter 15) and 'future conflicts'. They also stress the role of the United States as a dominant power. We have been discussing most of these issues throughout this book.

Many of the chapters have suggested possible pathways into the future, but they nearly always focus upon some ambivalent characteristics. This is to say that it is not clear where we are going, and that there would seem to be inherent contradictions and tensions in future pathways. For instance, in Chapter 18 on religion we noted a trend (mainly in Europe) towards secularisation, while at the same time noting with Peter Berger that a much broader world-view would see a change towards desecularisation and the increasingly pervasive growth of new religious forms. When we considered McDonaldisation, we saw a trend towards efficiency, predictability, calculability and control in many of our

Table 25.1	Traditional and modern societies: the big picture	
Elements of society	**Traditional societies**	**Modern societies**
Cultural patterns		
Values	Homogeneous; sacred character; few subcultures and countercultures	Heterogeneous; secular character; many subcultures and countercultures
Norms	High moral significance; little tolerance of diversity	Variable moral significance; high tolerance of diversity
Time orientation	Present linked to past	Present linked to future
Technology	Pre-industrial; human and animal energy	Industrial; advanced energy sources
Social structure		
Status and role	Few statuses, most ascribed; few specialised roles	Many statuses, some ascribed and some achieved; many specialised roles
Relationships	Typically primary; little anonymity and privacy	Typically secondary; considerable anonymity and privacy
Communication	Face-to-face	Face-to-face communication supplemented by mass media
Social control	Informal gossip	Formal police and legal system
Social stratification	Rigid patterns of social inequality; little mobility	Fluid patterns of social inequality; considerable mobility
Gender patterns	Pronounced patriarchy; women's lives centred on the home	Declining patriarchy; increasing number of women in the paid labour force
Economy	Based on agriculture; some manufacturing in the home; little white-collar work	Based on industrial mass production; factories become centres of production; increasing white-collar work
State	Small-scale government; little state intervention in society	Large-scale government; considerable state intervention in society
Family	Extended family as the primary means of socialisation and economic production	Nuclear family retains some socialisation functions but is more a unit of consumption than of production
Religion	Religion guides world-view; little religious pluralism	Religion weakens with the rise of science; extensive religious pluralism
Education	Formal schooling limited to elites	Basic schooling becomes universal, with growing proportion receiving advanced education
Health	High birth and death rates; brief life expectancy because of low standard of living and simple medical technology	Low birth and death rates; longer life expectancy because of higher standard of living and sophisticated medical technology
Settlement patterns	Small-scale; population typically small and widely dispersed in rural villages and small towns	Large-scale; population typically large and concentrated in cities
Social change	Slow; change evident over many generations	Rapid; change evident within a single generation

institutions; but as George Ritzer himself advocates, there are also signs that this pattern is being rejected by many (Ritzer, 2000). There is a resistance to McDonaldisation,

And so we could continue. Many trends seem to bring their countertrend and no sociologist can really therefore predict where the future may lie.

Nevertheless, many sociologists at the start of the twenty-first century suggest that we are indeed moving into a different kind of social order. Ulrich Beck talks about the move from a 'first modernity' to a 'second modernity'. The former is what we have been calling modern society and its characteristics are now well known. In general, it involves a nation state (and a welfare state), full employment, collective life and what he says is a 'heedless exploitation of nature'. But the 'second modernity' is different. He writes:

> The collective patterns of life, progress and controllability, full employment and exploitation of nature that were typical of first modernity have now been undermined by five interlinked processes: globalization, individualization, gender revolution, underemployment and global risks. . . . The real theoretical and political challenge of the second modernity is the fact that society must respond to all these challenges simultaneously. . . . There is a pluralization of modernity (which) opens up space for the conceptualization of divergent trajectories of modernity in different parts of the world.
>
> (Beck, 1999: 2–3)

Beck is not alone in his vision. Among the many terms used for the emerging new kind of society we have been encountering in this book are:

- The Postmodern Society
- The Information Society
- The Network Society
- The Desecularised Society
- The Risk Society
- The Cyborg Society
- The Individualised Society
- The Human Rights Society
- The Third Way.

At work behind all these terms are a number of key processes which we have variously identified as 'globalisation', 'mediasation', 'digitalisation', 'disorganised capitalism', 'post-Fordism', 'McDonaldisation', 'desecularisation', 'democratisation' and a 'Third Way'. In part it is also *the world of the post*: post-feminism, post-history, post-identity, post-Marxism, post-colonialism, and of course postmodernism.

But before we get carried away, however, with all this talk of new things, it is important to recognise that in the new century, across the globe, *we all now live simultaneously in traditional, modern and postmodern worlds* (though at different paces and to differing degrees). Elderly folk and most of the 'developing/majority/third-world/low-income' societies may still live overwhelmingly with tradition, whereas many younger folk and richer nations may find the postmodern to be more congenial to the organisation of their lives.

Thus, *traditional societies* are still to be found embedded in intense communities, surrounded by families, neighbours, strong bonding rituals embedded in strongly patriarchal and religious social orders. For most people in the world, traditional worlds remain their core: for many elderly in the West and probably many families outside the West, for example, the prevalence of new forms of societies and intimacies is minimal.

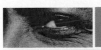

CONTROVERSY AND DEBATE

THE COMMUNITARIAN DEBATE

Shortly after midnight on a crisp March night in 1964, Kitty Genovese pulled into the car park of a New York tower block, locked the doors of her vehicle and headed towards the entrance to her building. Moments from safety, she was accosted by a man wielding a knife. As she screamed, he stabbed her repeatedly. Windows opened above, as curious neighbours searched for the cause of the commotion. But the attack continued – for more than 30 minutes – until Genovese lay dead in the doorway. Subsequent investigation failed to identify the assailant but did confirm a stunning fact: not one of dozens of neighbours who witnessed the attack on Kitty Genovese went to the trouble to come to her aid or even to call the police.

Like the scores of homeless people begging for money on many city streets, the Genovese tragedy forces us to confront the question of what we owe others. Members of modern societies prize their individual rights and personal privacy, sometimes withdrawing from public responsibility to the point that society itself seems to collapse. When a cry for help is met by the silence of indifference, have we pushed our modern conception of personal autonomy too far? In a cultural climate of expanding individual rights, can we sustain a sense of human community? ▶

CONTROVERSY AND DEBATE CONTINUED

These questions point up the tension between traditional and modern social systems, which is evident in the writings of all the sociologists discussed in this chapter. Toennies, Durkheim and others concluded that, in a fundamental respect, traditional community and modern individualism are incompatible. That is, society can unite its members in a moral community only to the extent that it limits their range of personal choices about how to live. In short, while we value both community and autonomy, we cannot have it both ways.

In recent years, sociologist Amitai Etzioni (1993b) has tried to strike a middle ground. The 'communitarian movement', formed in the United States, rests on the simple premise that 'strong rights presume strong responsibilities' or, put otherwise, that an individual's pursuit of self-interest must be balanced by a commitment to the larger community. Etzioni's critique of modernity focuses on the proliferation of individual rights. As he sees it, while people expect the system to provide for them, they are reluctant to support that system. For example, the public is quick to accept government services, but increasingly reluctant to pay taxes.

Specifically, the communitarians advance four proposals designed to balance individual rights with public responsibilities. First, societies should halt the expanding 'culture of rights' by which people have placed their own interests ahead of social responsibility. Second, communitarians argue that all rights involve responsibilities – we cannot simply take from society without giving something back. Third, there are certain responsibilities that no one is free to ignore, such as protecting the natural environment. Fourth, defending some community interests may require limiting individual rights, such as installing security cameras in high streets to photograph human interactions to help identify criminals.

The communitarian movement appeals to many people who, along with Etzioni, seek to balance personal freedom with social responsibility. But critics have attacked this initiative. Some argue that the vague notion of 'social reintegration' falls flat when it comes to addressing problems ranging from voter apathy to street crime. Instead, these critics contend, we need expanded government efforts to enhance equality in modern societies by curbing the political influence of the rich, as well as actively combating racism, sexism and homophobia.

Conservative critics fault Etzioni's proposals as little more than a rerun of the failed leftist ideals of previous decades. Conservatives question whether a free society should engage in the kind of social engineering that Etzioni advocates (such as instituting programmes in schools to foster tolerance and requiring young people to perform a year of national service).

While some believe that Etzioni has identified a moderate, sensible answer to vexing problems, it may well be that people in the diverse European nations will never readily agree about what they owe themselves – and each other.

Continue the debate:

1. Have you ever failed to come to the aid of someone in need or danger? Why?

2. The UK Prime Minister Tony Blair has pushed to reform the British benefit system by requiring young people and single parents to take up training or jobs identified by government agencies – or face losing state support. Do you think this policy fairly addresses the needs of the poor as well as of society at large? Provide some examples to illustrate your view.

3. Do you agree or disagree that your society needs to balance individual rights with more responsibility? Why?

Modern societies have emerged over the past 200 years or so and have become enmeshed in all the features of modernity discussed profusely by social scientists: urbanism, anomie, bureaucratisation, commodification, surveillance, individualisation. As societies become more and more 'modern', so all these features rapidly multiply. However, there is a downside and an upside to all this – a series of traps. On the one hand, our lives in modernity become engaged in a search for authenticity,

meaning, freedom: human relations become individualised in a world of choices. On the other hand, our lives become increasingly trapped within wider bureaucratising and commercialising forces: human relations can become McDonaldised, Disneyfied and subject to brutal exploitation. Lives can be located in contradictory tendencies.

Late-modern (or postmodern) societies incorporate the latter stages of the above with newer possibilities grafted on to the old in a high-tech and global world. We are just 'on the edge' of all this. Some people across the globe are not yet touched a great deal by it. But many are – and increasingly so.

A note on knowledge and change

One further part of all this change has been shifts in the academy and in ways academics think, theorise and research. Moving under various (often contradictory and contested) guises over the past few decades, we have seen a paradigmatic shift, a continuous attack and sustained critique on the orthodoxies of our time. Critical theory, feminism, multiculturalism, discourse theory, social constructionism, standpoint theory, Queer theory, critical realism, post-colonialism, and many others have all made their challenges.

At their hearts, they have made rendered 'knowledge' about social life much more problematic. Again, Beck and Beck-Gernsheim (2003) refers to 'zombie knowledge' from the past, a knowledge which simply hasn't taken on board the rapidly changing times in which we live. And he cites the importance of locating all our old 'knowledge' nowadays in a global frame – we always have to think beyond the local. Our social theorising is embedded in moral and political structures which need to be made much more explicit and part of our work.

Three themes, introduced throughout this book, may help us to do this: globalisation, postmodernism and 'risk'.

Globalisation revisited

As we saw in Chapter 2 and subsequently throughout this book, the concept of globalisation has become an important one in contemporary sociology. We have seen it at work in almost every chapter.

Nowhere is the imagery of globalism more sharply drawn than in the prevalence of worldwide multicultural companies such as Coca-Cola, McDonald's, Nike and Disneyland. They capture the economic, social and cultural impact of this process and simultaneously symbolise what may be good and bad about it. They symbolise, for some, the good life; and yet for others, they are the butt of global social protest (Chapters 9, 14 and 15). Three critical features can be highlighted.

Glocalisation

The first is the relationship between the local and the global. Sociologist Roland Robertson (1992) has usefully coined the term 'glocalisation' as a way of matching the issues of globalisation to local contexts. Glocalisation means that while there are undeniable chains of economic and cultural change crossing the globe, each specific local context picks this up and moulds it uniquely: world processes are taken up through local communities and are transformed into something that clearly shows signs of a global culture while being modified into a unique form that connects to the local culture ('think globally, act locally'). **Glocalisation**, therefore, is the *process by which local communities respond differently to global changes*.

An instance of this is the way in which much food has become globalised: Thai cuisine moves all round the world, but in each local culture it gets modified. London's Thai cuisine is different from Californian Thai or New York Thai, and is clearly different from Bangkok Thai.

Hybridisation

A second and linked concern lies with the relationship between a trend towards homogeneity and a trend towards diversification. While a *McDonaldisation thesis* (see Chapter 6) suggests a certain global uniformity – predictability, calculability, efficiency, standardisation (which may be found not just in McDonald's but also baby stores, package holidays, self-help books, or even university textbooks!), a *hybridisation thesis* suggests a 'global mélange'. **Hybridisation** refers to *the ways in which forms of social life become diversified as they separate from old practices and recombine into new ones* (Pieterse, 1995: 47). The analogy starts with plants that become hybrids. Following Jan Nederveen Pieterse (1995: 45, 62), we can depict these trends as in Table 25.2.

Table 25.2	Globalisation as homogenisation or diversification?
Globalisation as homogenisation	**Globalisation as diversification**
Cultural imperialism	Cultural planetisation
Cultural dependence	Cultural independence
Cultural hegemony	Cultural interpenetration
Autonomy	Synthesis, hybridisation
Modernisation	Modernisations
Westernisation	Global mélange
Cultural synchronisation	Creolisation/crossover
World civilisation	Global ecumene

Source: adapted from Pieterse (2004: 80)

Flows and 'scapes'

The anthropologist Arjun Appadurai (1996) has helpfully captured globalisation as a series of flows across the world. The world is moving and he sees it as a series of shifting 'landscapes' or horizons and perspectives. There are five major 'scapes' which he locates as:

- *Finanscapes*, through which flows of money and capital cross the world

- *Ethnoscapes*, where people constitute the shifting worlds we live in, such as tourists, immigrants, refugees, exiles, guest workers etc., who 'flow' across the globe

- *Mediascapes*, where media messages, information, images, film, satellite communications and digital records flow through spaces across the world

- *Technoscapes*, where technologies of all kinds – from atomic bombs and the Human Genome Project to discmen and computer games – glide through global spaces

- *Ideoscapes*, where ideas, messages and ideologies move through different countries.

Critical comment

We have used the term 'globalisation' a great deal throughout this book, and the argument has been made that this is a major process at work in twenty-first-century societies. But we must stress too that such processes were well under way centuries ago; the world did not function as isolated countries for much of the second millennium, as the histories of wars, travel, exploration, trade and colonialism can attest.

But what we do see in the current era is a major speeding-up of this process (largely through the new technologies) and a greater involvement and awareness of it by more and more people. In this sense, it really does serve as a very important marker of a new world in the making (Giddens, 1999; Held *et al.*, 1999).

Postmodernity revisited

If modernity was the product of the Industrial Revolution, has the Information Revolution propelled us into the postmodern era? A number of scholars answer affirmatively, and use the term **postmodernity** to refer to *social patterns characteristic of post-industrial societies*.

Looking more closely, however, we find disagreement about precisely what constitutes postmodernism. This term – long used in literary, philosophical and even architectural circles – has edged into sociology on a wave of social criticism that has been building since the surge of left-leaning politics in the 1960s. Although there are many variants of postmodern thinking, all share the following five themes (Bernstein, 1992; Borgmann, 1992; Crook *et al.*, 1992; Hall and Neitz, 1993):

1. *In important respects, modernity has failed.* The promise of modernity was a life free from want. As many postmodernist critics see it, however, the twentieth century was unsuccessful in eradicating social problems such as poverty or even in ensuring financial security for many people.

2. *The bright light of 'progress' is fading.* Modern people typically look to the future, expecting that their lives will improve in significant ways. Members (even leaders) of a postmodern society, however, have less confidence about what the future holds. Furthermore, the buoyant optimism that swept society into the modern era more than a century ago has given way to stark pessimism on the part of most adults that life is getting worse.

3. *Science no longer holds all the answers.* The defining trait of the modern era was a scientific outlook and a confident belief that technology would make life better. But postmodern critics contend that science has created more problems (such as degrading the environment) than it has solved. More generally, postmodernist thinkers discredit the foundation of science – the assertion that objective reality and truth exists at all. Reality is socially rather than naturally constructed, they claim; moreover, 'deconstructing' science shows that this system of ideas has been widely used for political purposes, especially by powerful segments of society.

4. *Cultural debates are intensifying.* As we have already explained, modernity came wrapped in the bright promise of enhanced individuality and expanding tolerance. Critics claim, however, that the emerging postmodern society falls short of that promise. Queer theorists assert that heterosexism continues to shape society today. Multiculturalism seeks to empower minorities long pushed to the margins of social life and left to languish there.

5. *Social institutions are changing.* Industrialisation brought sweeping transformation to social institutions; the rise of a post-industrial society is

remaking society once again. We have seen this throughout the book. For example, just as the Industrial Revolution placed material *things* at the centre of productive life, now the Information Revolution has elevated the importance of *ideas*. Similarly, the postmodern family no longer conforms to any singular formula; on the contrary, individuals are devising new and varied ways of relating to one another.

Critical comment

Postmodern critics contend that the Western world has failed in important ways to meet human needs. Yet few would argue that modernity has failed completely; after all, we have seen marked increases in the length and quality of life over the course of the twentieth century. Moreover, even if we were to accept postmodernist criticism that science and traditional notions about progress are bankrupt, what are the alternatives? Then, too, many voices offer strikingly different understandings of recent social trends.

The Risk Society revisited

As Chapters 22, 23 and 24 detailed, contemporary human societies are closely interconnected to science, population and the natural environment: change in one tends to produce change in the others.

Science, technology and change

Three new revolutions will haunt the twenty-first century: those of the atom, the gene and the computer. Each one (as we saw in Chapter 22) brings the potential for major social change. We live in a world where the unleashing of the atom may bring untold destruction in war and terrorism, where cyberworlds may well reshape just what it means to interact with other human beings, and where the new genetics will put within our reach the ability to clone and create designer babies. Notwithstanding any of this, we have already started to put people on the moon.

Such potential changes have also brought with them the need for consideration of ethical issues linked to science and, as the twenty-first century proceeds, we shall probably witness more discussion not simply of science but of the moral role of the scientist.

The natural environment and change

By and large, 'modern' culture has cast nature as a force to be tamed and reshaped to human purposes. From the onset of industrialisation and the rise of capitalism, people have systematically cut down forests to create fields for farming and to make materials for building; they have established towns and cities, extended roads in every direction and dammed rivers as a source of water and energy. Such human construction not only reflects a cultural determination to control the natural environment, it also points up the centrality of the idea of 'growth' in our way of life.

But the consequences of this thinking have placed increasing stress on the natural environment. Western societies confront problems from growing mountains of solid waste, as well as air and water pollution, all the while consuming the lion's share of global resources. A growing awareness that such patterns are not sustainable in the long term is forcing us to confront the need to change our way of life in some basic respects.

Demographic change

World population in 2015 will be over 7 billion, up from 6 billion in 2000. Ninety-five per cent of the increase will be in developing countries, nearly all in rapidly expanding urban areas.

As Chapter 13 explained, many societies are growing older. Soon nearly one in five people in Western countries will be 65 or older. Medical research and health-care services will come to focus more and more on people growing older. There will be increases in health-care and pension costs. The relative size of the working population may fall and new opportunities for later life will have to be found. Common stereotypes about old people may well be undermined as more men and women enter this stage of life. Ways of life may change in countless additional directions as homes and household products are redesigned to meet the needs of growing ranks of older people.

Migration within and among societies is another demographic factor that promotes change. Between 1870 and 1930, millions of rural peoples in Western societies, along with millions of immigrants from poorer countries, swelled the industrial cities. As a result, farm communities declined, metropolises burgeoned and the Western world became for the first time a predominantly urban society. Similar changes are taking place today as people moving between European Union member states interact with new immigrants from Africa and Asia.

The shape of societies to come – A New World Order?

Social change is inherently complex, contradictory and controversial. Thus, in principle, almost everyone in our society supports the idea that individuals should have considerable autonomy in shaping their own lives. Many people will applaud the demise of tradition, viewing this trend as a sign of progress. Yet, as people exercise their freedom of choice, they inevitably challenge social patterns cherished by those who maintain a more traditional way of life. For example, people may choose to live with someone without marrying, or may feel more comfortable in an intimate same-sex partnership. To those who endorse individual choice, such changes symbolise progress; to those who value traditional family patterns, however, these developments signal societal decline.

New technology, too, sparks controversy. More rapid transportation and more efficient communication may improve our lives in some respects. However, complex technology has also eroded traditional attachments to home towns and even to families. Industrial technology has also unleashed an unprecedented threat to the natural environment. In short, we know that change is accelerating over time, but views may differ sharply as to whether any particular change amounts to progress. Table 25.3 marks out some of the contradictory pushes and changes that the move towards a postmodern society brings.

John Gibbins and Bo Reimer, in their book *The Politics of Postmodernity* (1999), distinguished three types of vision of the future among social theorists. One group are the *pessimists* who often see the world as moving towards some kind of final collapse. Another group are the *critics* who see 'crisis' everywhere (often with little chance of real change). A third group are the *optimists* (1999: 142). Although optimists sense that many dangers are imminent (as we do in Table 25.3), they also believe that there are signs of a rise of 'more activist citizens dealing with more responsive political bodies in more areas of life and the globe' (1999: 145). They sense a new kind of politics in the making (which we described in Chapter 15), and a move towards what Giddens calls the democratisation of democracy (Giddens, 1999). So here, there is a positive and political look to the future, but one in which we are also aware of profound problems.

Modernity: global variation

While it is often useful to contrast traditional and modern social patterns, actual societies often fuse the old and the new in unexpected ways. In the People's Republic of China, ancient Confucian principles coexist with contemporary socialist thinking. Similarly, in Mexico and much of Latin America, people engage in centuries-old Christian rituals even as they struggle valiantly to pursue economic development. The description of Brazil's Kaiapo that opened this chapter points to the tensions that typically surround the mixing of traditional and modern social patterns. The broader point is that such combinations are far from unusual – indeed, they are found throughout the world.

Table 25.3	Some antagonisms of the New World Order
The tragic 'dystopian' view	**The romantic 'utopian' view**
Widening inequalities, social divisions	Higher standards of living for large numbers of people
Fragmentation, post-Fordism, disorganisation, Balkanisation	The pluralisation ethos, differences recognised
Impersonality and loss of community	Participation and attatchment in new 'social worlds'
Narcissism, egoism	'Individualism'
McDonaldisation, standardisation, dumbing down	'Choices', reflexivities
Moral decline and incivility	Citizenship, new ethics, moral effervescence
Entrenched hierarchies of exclusion	The democratisation of personhood and relationships
Uncertainty, chaos, a world out of control, risk	Chance for a New World Order, human rights

Towards 'the human rights society'

The twentieth century was not only the century of holocausts and wars, it was also the century when the idea of equality, human rights and the democratic state came into its own. In 1948, the Universal Declaration of Human Rights was adopted, acknowledging rights as a global concern. In its 30 articles, it stresses not only that people should not be held in servitude – 'slavery and the slave trade shall be prohibited in all their forms' – but also that many rights of equality should be upheld: the right to be equal before the law, the right to protection against discrimination, to education, to a standard of living adequate for the health and well-being of oneself and one's family, and the right to freedom of thought, conscience and religion.

Of course, such a document brings many problems. Some argue, for instance, that it is an imposition of Western views on the rest of the world, others argue that it is too idealistic to be fully implemented, and still others suggest that even in countries which have agreed to its principles, abuses of all kinds still occur. Despite this, the United Nations can claim that:

> One of the 20th century's hallmark achievements was its progress in human rights. In 1900 more than half the world's people lived under colonial rule and no country gave all its citizens the right to vote. Today some three quarters of the world lives under democratic regimes. There has also been great progress in eliminating discrimination by race, religion and gender – and in advancing the right to schooling and basic health care.
>
> (UNHDP, 2000: 1)

In conclusion

Back in Chapter 2, we imagined the entire world reduced to a village of 100 people, where 20 residents live in luxury, while 20 struggle to survive. The tragic plight of the world's poor shows that some desperately needed change has not occurred at all. Chapter 9 detailed two competing views of why 1 billion people the world over are extremely poor.

Modernisation theory claimed that in the past the entire world was poor and that technological change, especially the Industrial Revolution, enhanced human productivity and raised living standards. The solution to global poverty was to promote technological development in poor nations.

For reasons suggested earlier, however, global modernisation may be difficult. Recall that David Riesman (Chapter 7) portrayed pre-industrial people as *tradition-directed* and likely to resist change (Riesman, 1950). In response to this cultural brake on development, modernisation theorists call for the world's rich societies to offer assistance to poor countries to encourage productive innovation. Industrial nations can speed development by exporting technology to poor regions, welcoming students from abroad and providing foreign aid to stimulate economic growth.

The review of modernisation theory in Chapter 9 points to some limited success for these policies in Latin America, Taiwan, South Korea, Singapore and Hong Kong. But jump-starting development in the poorest countries of the world poses the greatest challenges. And even where dramatic change has occurred, modernisation entails a trade-off. Traditional people, such as Brazil's Kaiapo, may gain wealth through economic development, but only at the cost of losing their cultural identity and values as they are drawn into the 'global village' of McCulture, based on Western materialism, pop music, trendy clothes and fast food.

One Brazilian anthropologist expressed hope about the future of the Kaiapo: 'At least they quickly understood the consequences of watching television. . . . Now [they] can make a choice' (Simons, 1995: 471). But not everyone thinks that modernisation is really an option. According to a second approach to global stratification, *dependency theory*, today's poor societies have little ability to modernise, even if they wanted to. From this point of view, the major barrier to economic development is not traditionalism but the global domination of rich, capitalist societies. Initially, as Chapter 9 explained, this system took the form of colonialism, whereby European societies seized much of Latin America, Africa and Asia. Trading relationships soon enriched Britain, Spain, Portugal, France and other colonial powers and their colonies simultaneously became dependent and poor. Almost all societies subjected to this form of domination are now politically independent, but colonial-style ties continue in the form of neo-colonialism, with multinational corporations operating throughout the world.

In effect, dependency theory asserts, rich nations achieved their modernisation at the expense of poor ones, which provided valuable natural resources and human labour. Even today, the world's poorest countries remain locked in a disadvantageous economic relationship with rich nations, dependent on wealthy countries to buy their raw materials and in return sell them whatever manufactured products they can afford. Overall, dependency theorists conclude, continuing ties with rich societies will only perpetuate current patterns of global inequality.

CONTROVERSY AND DEBATE

PUTTING IT ALL TOGETHER: SENSING A POSTMODERN FUTURE?

Many sociologists have suggested a rupture is happening within the modern world, and a new social order is starting to appear on a global scale. Postmodernism, late-modernism and post-industrial are all terms used to signify the emergence of this new social order. Jean-François Lyotard (1992: 80) has defined postmodernism as 'an incredulity towards metanarratives'. By this he means that we can no longer believe in one all-encompassing story or truth. We can now see there are many paths, routes, possibilities, truths. Indeed, for another leading French sociologist, Jean Baudrillard, the argument is that the postmodern is: 'the characteristic of a universe where there are no more definitions possible. . . . It has all been done. . . . So all that are left are pieces. All that remains to be done is play with the pieces – that is postmodern' (Baudrillard, 1991: 24).

These controversial theories and ideas have been used throughout this book, and it should be clear that not all sociologists agree with their use. In this chapter, we have suggested five key themes associated with postmodernism. But almost every chapter in this book suggests that something is indeed happening at the start of the twenty-first century which must be seen as a significant change. Thus Chapter 2 ends by suggesting that new ways of approaching society through multiple voices are starting to happen: the old orthodoxies of functionalism, conflict and actions are being challenged. Chapter 3 suggests that new methods are in the making in sociological research. Chapter 4 captures the idea of a new kind of 'post-industrial' society in the making, and Chapter 5 highlights multiculturalism and post-colonialism. Then in Chapter 6, we see a new kind of postmodern

organisation. In Chapter 14 we see a new kind of economy and pattern of work emerging that we call 'post-Fordist'. And so it goes on: new forms of 'post-modern family', new patterns of gender and sexual relations, new modes of consumption, new social movements, new forms of social control and even new religions. We have also seen debates around class which suggest that it may be becoming less important (Chapter 10), while ethnicity (Chapter 11), gender (Chapter 12) and age (Chapter 13) become more important. We have seen the rise of the new computer society – cybersociety – saturated with information and communication (Chapters 21 and 22), and the chapter on the environment (Chapter 24) hurtles us towards a new kind of 'Risk Society'. Even in this final chapter, we have highlighted how sociologists sense ever new forms of society emerging.

Along with all this has been another closely linked theme: globalisation. Here we start to see a major shift in the way the world exists in time and in space. The world becomes smaller and smaller as communications and finances flow around the globe. Hence we start to see global power structures appearing alongside a global media, global cities, and global inequalities. We are moving out of the era of the old nation state and into a new period where countries are profoundly interconnected through global flows.

CONTINUE THE DEBATE:

1. Do you think that societies are really changing as dramatically as this book has been suggesting?

2. If yes, what is making these changes happen?

3. Discuss whether sociology has helped you understand them. What is the future role of sociology?

Whichever approach one finds more convincing, we can no longer isolate the study of the Western world from the rest of the world. At the beginning of the twentieth century, a majority of people in today's high-income countries lived in relatively small settlements with limited awareness of the larger world. Now, at the start of the twenty-first century, people everywhere participate in a far larger human drama. The world seems smaller and the lives of all people are increasingly linked.

We now discuss the relationships among countries in the same way that people a century ago talked about the expanding ties among cities and towns.

The twentieth century witnessed unprecedented human achievement alongside unprecedented human tragedy. As this book has hopefully shown, while the everyday life of many has got better and better, for many more, solutions to some of the problems of human existence – inequalities, poverty, meaninglessness, disease, conflict, war, genocide – have eluded us. To this list of pressing matters new concerns have been added in recent years, such as controlling population growth and establishing a sustainable natural environment. Living in the twenty-first century, we must be prepared to tackle such problems with critical imagination, humanistic compassion and political will. The challenge is great, and sociology will be needed to keep critically alive our developing, wide-ranging understanding of human societies.

SUMMARY

1. Every society changes continuously, intentionally or not, and at varying speeds. Social change often generates controversy.

2. Social change results from invention, discovery and diffusion as well as social conflict.

3. Modernity refers to the social consequences of industrialisation, which, according to Peter Berger, include the erosion of traditional communities, expanding personal choice, increasingly diverse beliefs and a keen awareness of time, especially the future.

4. Social change is too complex and controversial simply to be equated with social progress.

5. In the twenty-first century, sociologists are discussing the current changes in society and many new kinds of society have been suggested. These include 'The postmodern Society', 'The Information Society', 'The Network Society', 'The Risk Society', 'The Cyborg Society', 'The Individualised Society' and 'The Human Rights Society'.

6. At work behind all these terms are a number of key processes which we have variously identified as 'globalisation', 'mediasation', 'digitalisation', 'disorganised capitalism', 'post-Fordism', 'McDonaldisation', 'desecuralisation', 'democratisation' and a 'third way'. All these ideas have been discussed earlier in this book.

7. Globalisation highlights the local and the global, hybridisation and 'scapes'.

8. Postmodernity refers to cultural traits of post-industrial societies. Postmodern criticism of society centres on the failure of modernity, and specifically science, to fulfil its promise of prosperity and well-being.

9. Human societies are closely interconnected to science, population and the natural environment: change in one tends to produce change in others. As changes in these areas becomes more unpredictable in outcomes, we increasingly face a 'Risk Society'.

10. In a global context, modernisation theory links global poverty to the power of tradition. Therefore, some modernisation theorists advocate intentional intervention by rich societies to stimulate the development of poor nations.

11. Dependency theory explains global poverty as the product of the world economic system. The operation of multinational corporations ensures that poor societies will remain economically dependent on rich ones.

12. Looking to the future, sociologists can see both utopian visions based upon human rights and democratisation and dystopian visions based upon growing inequalities and sufferings.

13. The challenge of sociology is to keep alive a critical, wide-ranging understanding of human societies.

CRITICAL-THINKING QUESTIONS

1. Look back over this text and consider whether Durkheim, Weber and Marx accurately predicted the character of the twenty-first-century world. How do their visions of society differ?

2. What is a postmodern society? Are there any postmodern societies in the world today? What do they look like?

3. Examine the tensions and contradictions in Table 25.3, and draw up both a utopia and a dystopia for the future based on some of these ideas.

4. Look back over the book and review the main features of contemporary change suggested in each chapter.

GOING FURTHER

Further reading

Gary Browning, Abigail Halci and Frank Webster (eds), *Understanding Contemporary Society: Theories of the Present* (2000)
A valuable compilation of some 33 short accounts of contemporary society at century's turn.

Will Hutton and Anthony Giddens (eds), *On the Edge: Living with Global Capitalism* (2000)
A set of important essays on global culture.

Amitai Etzioni, *The Spirit of Community: Rights, Responsibilities, and the Communitarian Agenda* (1993b)
The 'handbook of the communitarian movement' and suggests ways to fuse individual rights with collective responsibility.

Peter Berger, Brigitte Berger and Hansfried Kellner, *The Homeless Mind: Modernization and Consciousness* (1974)
Discusses what modernity means.

Steven Connor, *Postmodern Culture: An Introduction to Theories of the Contemporary* (2nd edn, 1997)
A clear, intelligible guide that examines 'culture' with lots of examples.

More information

See also *Global Trends: A Dialogue about the Future with Non-Government Experts*, which can also be found on the website **http://www.cia.gov/cia/reports/globaltrends2015/index.html**

Watch a video

Look at some films which 'play' with the future, such as:

- Robert Zemeckis's *Back to the Future Parts I – III* (1985–90): three films that raise the problem of time in different societies. Fairly lighthearted.

- Wim Wender's *Wings of Desire* (1987): slightly whimsical as angels visit Berlin. Some people connect it to Capra's *It's a Wonderful Life* (see Chapter 1).

- Stanley Kubrick's *2001: A Space Odyssey* (1968): the classic space film.

- Michael Anderson's *1984* (1956) and Michael Radford's *1984* (1984): two films of the classic Orwell novel. 1984 has now long passed but some of the implications of these 'futuristic' scenarios are still open to analysis and discussion.

Connecting up

Connect to other chapters

- Review Marx, Durkheim and Weber on modern societies in Chapter 4.
- Review shifts in identity in Chapter 7.
- Review theories of the global in Chapter 2 and elsewhere.
- Review postmodernity in Chapter 2 and elsewhere.

For additional case studies, multiple choice questions, internet exercises, and annotated weblinks specific to this chapter, visit this book's website at
www.pearsoned.co.uk/plummer

GLOSSARY

A

absolute poverty a lack of resources that is life threatening (often measured as a per capita income equivalent to less than one international dollar a day)

achieved status a social position that someone assumes voluntarily and that reflects personal ability and effort

acid rain precipitation that is made acidic by air pollution and destroys plant and animal life

action perspective a micro-theory that focuses on how actors assemble social meanings

activity theory a high level of activity enhances personal satisfaction in old age

actors people who construct social meanings

Afrocentrism the dominance of African cultural patterns

ageism prejudice and discrimination against the elderly

age–sex pyramid a graphical representation of the age and sex of a population

age stratification the unequal distribution of wealth, power and privileges among people at different stages in the life course

agriculture the technology of large-scale farming using ploughs harnessed to animals or more powerful sources of energy

alienation the experience of isolation resulting from powerlessness

animism the belief that elements of the natural world are conscious life forms that affect humanity

anomie Durkheim's designation of a condition in which society provides little moral guidance to individuals

anticipatory socialisation social learning directed towards gaining a desired position

ascribed status a social position that someone receives at birth or assumes involuntarily later in life

assimilation the process by which minorities gradually adopt patterns of the dominant culture

authoritarianism a political system that denies popular participation in government

authority power that people perceive as legitimate rather than coercive

B

behaviourism specific behaviour patterns are not instinctive but learned

beliefs specific statements that people hold to be true

Big Science a particularly strong sense of expertise and its dominance, one that is usually strongly backed by money, supported by governments and given a lot of symbolic prestige

bilateral descent a system tracing kinship through both men and women

biography person's unique history of thinking, feeling and acting

blue-collar (or manual) occupations lower-prestige work involving mostly manual labour

body projects the process of becoming and transforming a biological entity through social action

bureaucracy an organisational model rationally designed to perform complex tasks efficiently

bureaucratic inertia the tendency of bureaucratic organisations to perpetuate themselves

bureaucratic ritualism a preoccupation with rules and regulations to the point of thwarting an organisation's goals

C

capitalism an economic system in which natural resources and the means of producing goods and services are privately owned

capitalists people who own factories and other productive enterprises

caste system a system of social stratification based on inherited status or ascription

cause and effect a relationship in which change in one variable (the independent variable) causes change in another (the dependent variable)

census is a count of everyone who lives in the country

charisma extraordinary personal qualities that can turn an audience into followers

charismatic authority power legitimised through extraordinary personal abilities that inspire devotion and obedience

church a type of religious organisation well integrated into the larger society

civil religion a quasi-religious loyalty binding individuals in a basically secular society

class conflict antagonism between entire classes over the distribution of wealth and power in society

class consciousness Marx's term for the recognition by workers of their unity as a social class in opposition to capitalists and to capitalism itself

class society a capitalist society with pronounced social stratification

class system a system of social stratification based on individual achievement

code rule-governed system of signs

cohabitation the sharing of a household by an unmarried couple

cohort a category of people with a common characteristic, usually their age

collective behaviour activity involving a large number of people, often spontaneous, and typically in violation of established norms

collectivity a large number of people whose minimal interaction occurs in the absence of well-defined and conventional norms

colonialism the process by which some nations enrich themselves through political and economic control of other countries

communism an economic and political system in which all members of a society are socially equal

concept a mental construct that represents some part of the world, inevitably in a simplified form

conflict perspective a framework for building theory that envisages society as an arena of inequality that generates conflict and change

conglomerates giant corporations composed of many smaller corporations

control holding constant all relevant variables except one in order to observe its effect

conversational analysis a rigorous set of techniques to technically record and then analyse what happens in everyday speech

conversion a personal transformation or religious rebirth

corporation an organisation with a legal existence, including rights and liabilities, apart from those of its members

correlation a relationship by which two (or more) variables change together

cosmogony tale about how the world/universe was created; a theodicy, a tale about how evil and suffering is to be found in the world

counterculture cultural patterns that strongly oppose those widely accepted within a society

credentialism evaluating a person on the basis of educational qualifications

crime the violation of norms a society formally enacts into criminal law

crimes against property (property crimes) crimes that involve theft of property belonging to others

crimes against the person (violent crimes) crimes that direct violence or the threat of violence against others

criminal justice system a societal reaction to alleged violations of the law utilising police, courts and prison officials

criminal recidivism subsequent offences committed by people previously convicted of crimes

critical sociology all knowledge as harbouring political interests and the task of sociology is to critically unmask what is actually going on.

crowd a temporary gathering of people who share a common focus of attention and whose members influence one another

crude birth rate the number of live births in a given year for every thousand people in a population

crude death rate the number of deaths in a given year for every thousand people in a population

cult a religious organisation that is substantially outside a society's cultural traditions

cultural capital a term often used to designate the practices where people can wield power and status because of their educational credentials, general cultural awareness and aesthetic preferences

cultural conflict political opposition, often accompanied by social hostility, rooted in different cultural values

cultural ecology a theoretical paradigm that explores the relationship of human culture and the physical environment

cultural hybridisation refers to the ways in which parts of one culture (language, practices, symbols) get recombined with the cultures of another

cultural integration the close relationship among various elements of a cultural system

cultural lag the fact that cultural elements change at different rates, which may disrupt a cultural system

cultural relativism the practice of judging a culture by its own standards

cultural reproduction the process by which a society transmits dominant knowledge from one generation to another

cultural transmission the process by which one generation passes culture to the next

cultural universals traits that are part of every known culture

culture the beliefs, values, behaviour and material objects that constitute a people's way of life

culture shock personal disorientation that comes from encountering an unfamiliar way of life

cyber widely used prefix for anything connected to computers

cyberclasses a stratification system based on the information 'haves' and 'have-nots' linked to the rise in new information technologies

cybernetics control systems using computers

cyborgs creatures which connect human and biological properties to technological ones.

D

Davis–Moore thesis the assertion that social stratification is a universal pattern because it has beneficial consequences for the operation of a society

decentred a process by which a centre, core or essence is destabilised and weakened

decoding the process by which we hear or read and understand a message

decommodification the degree to which welfare services are free from the market

deductive logical thought reasoning that transforms general ideas into specific hypotheses suitable for scientific testing

degenerate war a deliberate and systematic extension of war against an organised armed enemy to a war against a largely unarmed civilian population

democide mass murders by governments

democracy a political system in which power is exercised by the people as a whole

democratic socialism an economic and political system that combines significant government control of the economy with free elections

demographic transition theory a thesis linking population patterns to a society's level of technological development

demography the study of human population

denomination a church, independent of the state, that accepts religious pluralism

dependency ratio the numbers of dependent children and retired persons relative to productive age groups

dependency theory a model of economic and social development that explains global inequality in terms of the historical exploitation of poor societies by rich ones

dependent variable a variable that is changed by another (independent) variable

descent the system by which members of a society trace kinship over generations

deterrence the attempt to discourage criminality through punishment

deviance the recognised violation of cultural norms

diaspora refers to the dispersal of a population from its 'homeland' into other areas

direct-fee system a medical care system in which patients pay directly for the services of doctors and hospitals

discourses bodies of ideas and language often backed up by institutions

discrimination any action that involves treating various categories of people unequally

disengagement theory the proposition that society enhances its orderly operation by disengaging people from positions of responsibility as they reach old age

Disneyisation the process by which the principle of the Disney theme parks is coming to dominate more and more sectors of American society as well as the rest of the world

displaced peoples are those who often find themselves homeless in their own land

division of labour specialised economic activity

documents of life research documents produced in the natural world by the subjects themselves, such as letters and diaries

dramaturgical analysis Erving Goffman's term for the investigation of social interaction in terms borrowed from theatrical performance

dyad a social group with two members

dysfunction *See* social dysfunction

E

ecclesia a church that is formally allied with the state

ecologically sustainable culture a way of life that meets the needs of the present generation without threatening the environmental legacy of future generations

ecology the study of the interaction of living organisms and the natural environment

economy the social institution that organises the production, distribution and consumption of goods and services

ecosystem the system composed of the interaction of all living organisms and their natural environment

education the social institution guiding the transmission of knowledge, job skills, cultural norms and values

ego Freud's designation of a person's conscious efforts to balance innate, pleasure-seeking drives and the demands of society

electronic tagging a system of home confinement aimed at monitoring, controlling and modifying the behaviour of defendants or offenders

emotional labour the management of feeling to create a publicly observable facial and bodily display

empirical evidence information we can verify with our senses

encoding putting a message of any kind into a language

endogamy marriage between people of the same social category

environmental deficit the situation in which our relationship to the environment, while yielding short-term benefits, will have profound, long-term consequences

environmental racism the pattern by which environmental hazards are greatest in proximity to poor people, especially minorities

epistemic relativism knowledge is rooted in a particular time and culture

epistemology branch of philosophy that investigates the nature of knowledge and truth

essentialism the belief that qualities are inherent in (essential to) specific objects

estate, a system based on a rigidly interlocking hierarchy of rights and obligations

ethnic antagonism hostilities between different ethnic groups

ethnic cleansing *See* genocide

ethnicity a shared cultural heritage

ethnocentrism the practice of judging another culture by the standards of one's own culture

ethnomethodology Harold Garfinkel's term for the study of the way people make sense of their everyday lives

Eurocentrism a view of the world which places Europe at the centre of its thinking

euthanasia (mercy killing) assisting in the death of a person suffering from an incurable disease

exogamy marriage between people of different social categories

experiment a research method for investigating cause and effect under highly controlled conditions

expressive leadership group leadership that emphasises collective well-being

extended family (consanguine family) a family unit including parents and children, but also other kin

F

fad an unconventional social pattern that people embrace briefly but enthusiastically

faith belief anchored in conviction rather than scientific evidence

false consciousness Marx's term for explanations of social problems grounded in the shortcomings of individuals rather than the flaws of society

family a social institution, found in all societies, that unites individuals into cooperative groups that oversee the bearing and raising of children

family of choice people with or without legal or blood ties who feel they belong together and wish to define themselves as a family

family unit a social group of two or more people, related by blood, marriage or adoption, who usually live together

family violence emotional, physical or sexual abuse of one family member by another

fashion a social pattern favoured for a time by a large number of people

feminisation of poverty the trend by which women represent an increasing proportion of the poor

feminism the advocacy of social equality for the sexes, in opposition to patriarchy and sexism

fertility the incidence of child-bearing in a country's population

flâneur a social type who wanders cities, enjoying the sights and the crowd

folkways a society's customs for routine, casual interaction

Fordism an economic system based on mass assembly-line production, mass consumption and standardised commodities

formal organisation a large, secondary group that is organised to achieve its goals efficiently

fourth age an age of eventual dependence

functional illiteracy reading and writing skills insufficient for everyday living

functional paradigm a framework for building theory that envisages society as a complex system whose parts work together to promote solidarity and stability

fundamentalism a conservative religious doctrine that opposes intellectualism and worldly accommodation in favour of restoring a traditional, otherworldly and absolutist spirituality

G

Gaia hypothesis planet earth itself should be seen as a living organism

Gemeinschaft Toennies' term for a type of social organisation by which people have strong social ties and weak self-interest

gender the social aspects of differences and hierarchies between female or male

gender identity the subjective state in which someone comes to say 'I am a man' or 'I am a woman'

gender order the ways in which societies shape notions of masculinity and femininity through power relations

gender performance refers to ways of 'doing gender', the ways in which masculinities and femininities are acted out.

gender regime the gender order as it works through in smaller setttings

gender role refers to learning and performing the socially accepted characteristics for a given sex

gender stratification a society's unequal distribution of wealth, power and privilege between the two sexes

generalised other George Herbert Mead's label for widespread cultural norms and values that we use as references in evaluating ourselves

genocide the systematic annihilation of one category of people by another

genre a species or type of media programme

gerontocracy a form of social organisation in which the elderly have the most wealth, power and prestige

gerontology the study of ageing and the elderly

Gesellschaft Toennies' term for a type of social organisation by which people have weak social ties and considerable self-interest

global commons resources shared by all members of the international community, such as ocean beds and the atmosphere

global economy economic activity spanning many nations of the world with little regard for national borders

global perspective the study of the larger world and our society's place in it

globalisation the increasing interconnectedness of societies

glocalisation process by which local communities respond differently to global changes

governance the exercise of political, economic and administrative authority in the management of a country's affairs at all levels

government formal organisations that direct the political life of a society

greenhouse effect a rise in the earth's average temperature (global warming) due to increasing concentration of carbon dioxide in the atmosphere

gross domestic product (GDP) all the goods and services on record as produced by a country's economy in a given year

gross national product (GNP) all a country's goods and services, as for GDP, with the addition of foreign earnings

groupthink the tendency of group members to conform by adopting a narrow view of some issue

H

hate crime a criminal act against a person or a person's property by an offender motivated by racial or other bias

Hawthorne effect a change in a subject's behaviour caused simply by the awareness of being studied

health a state of complete physical, mental and social well-being

health care any activity intended to improve health

health maintenance organisation (HMO) an organisation that provides comprehensive medical care to subscribers for a fixed fee

hegemonic masculinity the dominant or main ways of being a man in a society

hegemony the means by which a ruling/dominant group wins over a subordinate group through ideas

hermaphrodite a human being with some combination of female and male internal and external genitalia

hidden curriculum subtle presentations of political or cultural ideas in the classroom

high culture cultural patterns that distinguish a society's elite

high-income countries industrial nations in which most people enjoy material abundance

holistic medicine an approach to health care that emphasises prevention of illness and takes account of a person's entire physical and social environment

homogamy marriage between people with the same social characteristics

homophobia the dread of being in close quarters with homosexuals

horticulture technology based on using hand tools to cultivate plants

humanising bureaucracy fostering a more democratic organisational atmosphere that recognises and encourages the contributions of everyone

humanism stance that takes the human subjects seriously and is concerned with their meanings

hunting and gathering simple technology for hunting animals and gathering vegetation

hybridisation ways in which forms of social life become diversified as they separate from old practices and recombine into new ones: a 'global mélange'

hypothesis an unverified statement of a relationship between variables

I

id Freud's designation of the human being's basic drives

ideal culture (as opposed to real culture) social patterns mandated by cultural values and norms

ideal type Weber's term for an abstract statement of the essential characteristics of any social phenomenon

ideal types an abstract statement of the essential, though often exaggerated, characteristic of any social phenomenon

identity *See* social identity

ideological state apparatuses social institutions which reproduce the dominant ideology, independent of the state

ideology cultural beliefs that serve to legitimate key interests and hence justify social stratification

incest taboo a cultural norm forbidding sexual relations or marriage between certain kin

income occupational wages or salaries and earnings from investments

independent variable a variable that causes change in another (dependent) variable

indigenous peoples peoples with ties to the land, water and wildlife of their ancestral domain

inductive logical thought reasoning that transforms specific observations into general theory

industrialism technology that powers sophisticated machinery with advanced sources of energy

industrial reserve army a disadvantaged section of labour that can be supplied cheaply when there is a sudden extra demand

infant mortality rate the number of deaths among infants under one year of age for each thousand live births in a given year

ingroup a social group commanding a member's esteem and loyalty

in-migration rate, calculated as the number of people entering an area for every thousand people in the population

institutional prejudice or discrimination bias in attitudes or action inherent in the operation of society's institutions

instrumental leadership group leadership that emphasises the completion of tasks

interaction order what we do in the immediate presence of others

intergenerational social mobility upward or downward social mobility of children in relation to their parents

interview a series of questions a researcher administers personally to respondents

intragenerational social mobility a change in social position occurring during a person's lifetime

'Islamophobia' – a hatred of all things Muslim

J

juvenile delinquency the violation of legal standards by the young

K

kinship a social bond, based on blood, marriage or adoption, that joins individuals into families

L

labelling theory deviance and conformity result not so much from what people do as from how others respond to those actions; it highlights social responses to crime and deviance

labour unions organisations of workers seeking to improve wages and working conditions through various strategies, including negotiations and strikes

language a system of symbols that allows members of a society to communicate with one another

latent functions consequences of any social pattern that are unrecognised and unintended

liberation theology a fusion of Christian principles with political activism, often Marxist in character

life expectancy the average age to which people in a given society are likely to live

linguistic determinism language shapes the way we think

linguistic relativism distinctions found in one language are not found in another

looking-glass self Cooley's term for the image people have of themselves based on how they believe others perceive them

low-income countries nations with little industrialisation in which severe poverty is the rule

M

macro-level orientation a focus on broad social structures that characterise society as a whole

macro-sociology the study of large-scale society

mainstreaming integrating special students into the overall educational programme

manifest functions the recognised and intended consequences of any social pattern

marginalisation people live on the edge of society and outside the mainstream with little stake in society overall

marketisation an economic system based on the principles of the market, including supply, demand, choice and competition

marriage a legally sanctioned relationship, involving economic cooperation as well as normative sexual activity and child-bearing, that people expect to be enduring

mass media any social or technological devices used for the selection, transmission or reception of information

mass society a society in which industry and expanding bureaucracy have eroded traditional social ties

master status a status that has exceptional importance for social identity, often shaping a person's entire life

material culture the tangible things created by members of a society

matriarchy a form of social organisation in which females dominate males

matrilineal descent a system tracing kinship through women

matrilocality a residential pattern in which a married couple lives with or near the wife's family

McDonaldisation of society a process by which the principles of the fast-food industry come to be applied to more and more features of social life

mean the arithmetic average of a series of numbers

measurement the process of determining the value of a variable in a specific case

mechanical solidarity Durkheim's designation of social bonds, based on shared morality, that unite members of pre-industrial societies

media texts all media products, such as television programmes, films, CDs, books, newspapers, website pages, etc.

median the value that occurs midway in a series of numbers arranged in order of magnitude or, simply, the middle case

medicalisation the process by which events and experiences are given medical meaning and turned into medical problems

medicalisation of deviance the transformation of moral and legal issues into medical matters

medicine a social institution concerned with combating disease and improving health

mega-city a city with a population exceeding 8 million

megalopolis a vast urban region containing a number of cities and their surrounding suburbs

meritocracy a system of social stratification based on personal merit

metropolis a large city that socially and economically dominates an urban area

micro-sociology the study of everyday life in social interactions

middle-class slide a trend towards declining living standards and economic security at the centre of industrial societies

middle-income countries nations characterised by limited industrialisation and moderate personal income

migration the movement of people into and out of a particular territory

military–industrial complex the close association among the national government, the military, and defence industries

minority a category of people, distinguished by physical or cultural traits, who are socially disadvantaged

miscegenation biological reproduction by partners of different racial categories

mob a highly emotional crowd that pursues some violent or destructive goal

mode the value that occurs most often in a series of numbers

mode of production the way a society is organised to produce goods and services

modernisation the process of social change initiated by industrialisation

modernisation theory a model of economic and social development that explains global inequality in terms of differing levels of technological development among societies

modernity social patterns linked to industrialisation

monarchy a political system in which a single family rules from generation to generation

monogamy a form of marriage joining two partners

monopoly domination of a market by a single producer

monotheism belief in a single divine power

moral panic a condition, episode, person or group defined as a threat to social values which is presented in a stylised and stereotypical fashion by the mass media

mores a society's standards of proper moral conduct

mortality the incidence of death in a country's population

multiculturalism an educational programme recognising past and present cultural diversity in society and promoting the equality of all cultural traditions

multiple perspectives takes on many perspectives for looking at social life rather than just one

multinational corporation a large corporation that operates in many different countries

N

nation state a political apparatus over a specific territory with its own citizens backed up by military force and a nationalistic, sovereign creed

natural environment the earth's surface and atmosphere, including all living organisms as well as the air, water, soil and other resources necessary to sustain life

neo-colonialism a new form of global power relationship that involves not direct political control but economic exploitation by multinational corporations

neo-locality a residential pattern in which a married couple lives apart from the parents of both spouses

net migration rate the number of people who enter a territory (in-migration) minus the number of people who leave (out-migration) in a given year

network a web of social ties that links people who identify and interact little with one another

new racism racism based upon cultural, rather than biological, values

newly industrialising countries (NICs) lower-income countries that are fast becoming higher-income countries

non-material culture the intangible world of ideas created by members of a society

non-verbal communication communication using body movements, gestures and facial expressions rather than speech

norms rules and expectations by which a society guides the behaviour of its members

nuclear family (conjugal family) a family unit composed of one or two parents and their children

nuclear proliferation the acquisition of nuclear weapons technology by more and more nations

O

objectivity a state of personal neutrality in conducting research

occupational gender segregation works to concentrate men and women in different types of job

occupational prestige the value that people in a society associate with various occupations

oligarchy the rule of the many by the few

oligopoly domination of a market by a few producers

operationalising a variable specifying exactly what one intends to measure in assigning a value to a variable

oral culture tradition transmission of culture through speech

organic solidarity Durkheim's designation of social bonds, based on specialisation, that unite members of industrial societies

organisational environment a range of factors external to an organisation that affects its operation

other-directedness a receptiveness to the latest trends and fashions, often expressed in the practice of imitating others

outgroup a social group towards which one feels competition or opposition

out-migration rate the number leaving for every thousand people

P

paradigm general ways of seeing the world which suggest what can be seen, done and theorised about in science

parentocracy a system where a child's education is increasingly dependent upon the wealth and wishes of parents, rather than the ability and efforts of pupils

participant observation a research method in which researchers systematically observe people while joining in their routine activities

pastoralism technology based on the domestication of animals

patriarchy a form of social organisation in which men dominate, oppress and exploit women

patrilineal descent a system tracing kinship through men

patrilocality a residential pattern in which a married couple lives with or near the husband's family

peace a state of international relations devoid of violence

peer group a social group whose members have interests, social position and age in common

personal space the surrounding area to which an individual makes some claim to privacy

personality a person's fairly consistent patterns of thinking, feeling and acting

plea bargaining a legal negotiation in which the state reduces the charge against a defendant in exchange for a guilty plea

pluralism a state in which racial and ethnic minorities are distinct but have social parity

pluralist model an analysis of politics that views power as dispersed among many competing interest groups

political action committee (PAC) an organisation formed by a special-interest group, independent of political parties, to pursue political aims by raising and spending money

political revolution the overthrow of one political system in order to establish another

politics the social institution that distributes power, sets a society's agenda and makes decisions

polyandry a form of marriage joining one female with two or more males

polygamy a form of marriage uniting three or more people

polygyny a form of marriage joining one male with two or more females

polysemic open to many interpretations

polytheism belief in many gods

popular culture cultural patterns that are widespread among a society's population

population the people who are the focus of research

positivism a means to understand the world based on science

post-colonialism recognises how many cultures have been made through oppressor–subject relationships and seeks to unpack these, showing how cultures are made

post-colonial theory refers to the wide critiques of (usually 'white') Western cultures that are made from people who have been colonised in the past

post-Fordism an economic system emerging mainly since the 1970s and based on flexibility (rather than standardisation), specialisation and tailor-made goods

post-industrial economy a productive system based on service work and high technology

post-industrialism computer-linked technology that supports an information-based economy

postmodernism ways of thinking which stress a plurality of perspectives as opposed to a unified, single core

postmodernity social patterns characteristic of post-industrial societies

power the ability to achieve desired ends despite resistance from others

power elite model an analysis of politics that views power as concentrated among the rich

practices the practical logics by which we both act and think in a myriad of little encounters of daily life

prediction that is, researchers using what they do know to predict what they don't know

prejudice a rigid and irrational generalisation about an entire category of people

pre-operational stage Piaget's term for the level of human development at which individuals first use language and other symbols

presentation of self an individual's effort to create specific impressions in the minds of others

prestige the value people in a society associate with various occupations

primary group a small social group whose members share personal and enduring relationships

primary labour market occupations that provide extensive benefits to workers

primary sector the part of the economy that generates raw materials directly from the natural environment

primary sex characteristics the genitals, used to reproduce the human species

profane that which is an ordinary element of everyday life

profession a prestigious, white-collar occupation that requires extensive formal education

programmes films, CDs, books, newspapers, website pages, etc.

proletariat people who provide labour necessary to operate factories and other productive enterprises

propaganda information presented with the intention of shaping public opinion

Q

qualitative research investigation by which a researcher gathers impressionistic, not numerical, data

quantitative research investigation by which a researcher collects numerical data

queer theory the view that most sociological theory has a bias towards 'heterosexuality' and that non-heterosexual voices need to be heard

questionnaire a series of written questions a researcher supplies to subjects, requesting their responses

R

race a category composed of people who share biologically transmitted traits that members of a society deem socially significant

racialisation process of ranking people on the basis of their presumed race

racism the belief that one racial category is innately superior or inferior to another

rain forests regions of dense forestation, most of which circle the globe close to the equator

rationalisation of society Weber's term for the historical change from tradition to rationality as the dominant mode of human thought

rationality deliberate, matter-of-fact calculation of the most efficient means to accomplish a particular goal

rational–legal authority (bureaucratic authority) power legitimised by legally enacted rules and regulations

real culture (as opposed to ideal culture) actual social patterns that only approximate cultural expectations

realism scientific method that theorises a 'problematic' in order to see what is really going on

reference group a social group that serves as a point of reference in making evaluations or decisions

refugees people who 'flee their own country for political or economic reasons, or to avoid war and oppression

rehabilitation a programme for reforming an offender to preclude subsequent offences

relative deprivation a perceived disadvantage arising from a specific comparison

relative poverty the deprivation of some people in relation to those who have more

reliability the quality of consistent measurement

religion a social institution involving beliefs and practices based upon a conception of the sacred

religiosity the importance of religion in a person's life

replication repetition of research by others

research method a systematic plan for conducting research

research tool a systematic technique for conducting research

resocialisation radically altering an inmate's personality through deliberate manipulation of the environment

retribution moral vengeance by which society inflicts suffering on an offender comparable to that caused by the offence

retrospective labelling the interpretation of someone's past consistent with present deviance

risk society society where risks are of a different magnitude because of technology and globalisation

ritual formal, ceremonial behaviour

role behaviour expected of someone who holds a particular status

role conflict incompatibility among the roles corresponding to two or more statuses

role set a number of roles attached to a single status

role strain incompatibility among roles corresponding to a single status

routinisation of charisma the transformation of charismatic authority into some combination of traditional and bureaucratic authority

S

sacred that which is extraordinary, inspiring a sense of awe, reverence, and even fear

sample a part of a population researchers select to represent the whole

Sapir–Whorf hypothesis the hypothesis that people perceive the world through the cultural lens of language

scapegoat a person or category of people, typically with little power, whom people unfairly blame for their own troubles

schooling formal instruction under the direction of specially trained teachers

science a logical system that bases knowledge on direct, systematic observation

secondary analysis a research method in which a researcher utilises data collected by others

secondary group a large and impersonal social group whose members pursue a specific interest or activity

secondary labour market jobs that provide minimal benefits to workers

secondary sector the part of the economy that transforms raw materials into manufactured goods

secondary sex characteristics bodily development, apart from the genitals, that distinguishes biologically mature females and males

sect a type of religious organisation that stands apart from the larger society

secularisation the historical decline in the importance of the supernatural and the sacred

segregation the physical and social separation of categories of people

self George Herbert Mead's term for the human capacity to be reflexive and take the role of others

self-employment earning a living without working for a large organisation

self-fulfilling prophecy children defined as low achievers at school learn to become low achievers

semiotics study of symbols and signs

sensorimotor stage Piaget's designation for the level of human development at which individuals experience the world only through sensory contact

sex the biological distinction between females and males

sex ratio the number of males for every hundred females in a given population

sexism the belief that one sex is innately superior to the other

sexual harassment comments, gestures or physical contact of a sexual nature that are deliberate, repeated and unwelcome

sexual orientation an individual's preference in terms of sexual partners: same sex, other sex, either sex, neither sex

sexuality aspects of the body and desire that are linked to the erotic

sexual scripts that help define the who, what, where, when and even why we have sex

sick role patterns of behaviour defined as appropriate for people who are ill

simulacrum a world of media-generated signs and images

slavery a form of stratification in which people are owned by others as property

social change the transformation of culture and social institutions over time

social character personality patterns common to members of a particular society

social class social stratification resulting from the unequal distribution of wealth, power and prestige

social conflict struggle between segments of society over valued resources

social-conflict paradigm a framework for building theory that envisages society as an arena of inequality that generates conflict and change

social construction of reality the process by which people creatively shape reality through social interaction

social control system planned and programmed responses to expected deviance

social democratic a mix of capitalist and socialist/welfare economies and politics

social divisions differences that are rendered socially signifcant (e.g. class, gender, ethnicity)

social dysfunction the undesirable consequences of any social pattern for the operation of society

social epidemiology the study of how health and disease are distributed throughout a society's population

social function the consequences of any social pattern for the operation of society

social group two or more people who identify and interact with one another

social identity our understanding of who we are and who other people are, and, reciprocally, other people's understanding of themselves and others

social institution a major sphere of social life, or societal subsystem, organised to meet a basic human need

social interaction the process by which people act and react in relation to others

social mobility change in people's position in a social hierarchy

social movement organised activity that encourages or discourages social change

social network a web of social ties that links people who identify with one another

social practices *See* practices

social reproduction the maintenance of power and privilege between social classes from one generation to the next

social stratification a system by which society ranks categories of people in a hierarchy

social structure relatively stable patterns of social behaviour

socialisation a lifelong process by which individuals construct their personal biography

socialised medicine a health-care system in which the government owns and operates most medical facilities and employs most doctors

socialism an economic system in which natural resources and the means of producing goods and services are collectively owned

societal protection a means by which society renders an offender incapable of further offences temporarily through incarceration or permanently by execution

society people who interact in a defined territory and share culture

sociobiology a theoretical paradigm that explores ways in which our biology affects how humans create culture

sociocultural evolution the Lenskis' term for the process of change that results from a society's gaining new information, particularly technology

socio-economic status (SES) a composite ranking based on various dimensions of social inequality

sociology the systematic study of human society

sociology of knowledge that branch of sociology which sees an association between forms of knowledge and society

special-interest group a political alliance of people interested in some economic or social issue

spurious correlation an apparent, although false, relationship between two (or more) variables caused by some other variable

standpoint epistemologies all knowledge is grounded in standpoints and standpoint theory enables groups to analyse their situation (problems and oppressions) from within the context of their own experiences

state *See* nation state

state capitalism an economic and political system in which companies are privately owned but cooperate closely with the government

state terrorism the use of violence, generally without the support of law, against individuals or groups by a government or its agents

status a recognised social position that an individual occupies

status frustration the process by which people feel thwarted when they aspire to a certain status

status set all the statuses a person holds at a given time

stereotype a prejudicial, exaggerated description applied to every person in a category of people

stigma a powerfully negative social label that radically changes a person's self-concept and social identity

streaming the assignment of students to different types of educational programme

structural–functional paradigm a framework for building theory that envisages society as a complex system whose parts work together to promote solidarity and stability

structural social mobility a shift in the social position of large numbers of people due more to changes in society itself than to individual efforts

structuration focuses on both action and structure simultaneously. A process whereby action and structure are always two side of the same coin

structured dependency the process by which some people in society receive an unequal share in the results of social production

subculture cultural patterns that set apart some segment of a society's population

suburbs urban areas beyond the political boundaries of a city

superego Freud's designation of the operation of culture within the individual in the form of internalised values and norms

surveillance society society dependent on communication and information technologies for adminstrative and control processes and which result in the close monitoring of everyday life

survey a research method in which subjects respond to a series of items in a questionnaire or an interview

symbol anything that carries a particular meaning recognised by people who share culture

symbolic interaction a theoretical framework that envisages society as the product of the everyday interactions of people doing things together

T

technology knowledge that a society applies to the task of living in a physical environment

terrorism violence or the threat of violence employed by an individual or group as a political strategy

tertiary sector the part of the economy that generates services rather than goods

Thatcherism a system of political beliefs based on free markets and economic individualism

the ethical life how people should behave

theoretical paradigm a basic image of society that guides sociological thinking and research

theoretical perspective can be seen as a basic image that guides thinking and research

theory a statement of how and why specific facts are related

third age a period of life often free from parenting and paid work when a more active, independent life is achieved

Third Way a framework that adapts politics to a changed world, transcending old-style democracy and neo-liberalism

Thomas theorem W. I. Thomas's assertion that situations we define as real become real in their consequences

total institution a setting in which people are isolated from the rest of society and manipulated by an administrative staff

total period fertility rate the average number of children each woman would have in her lifetime if the average number of children born to all women of child-bearing age in any given year remained constant during that woman's child-bearing years

totalitarianism a political system that extensively regulates people's lives

totem an object in the natural world collectively defined as sacred

tracking the assignment of students to different types of educational programmes

trade unions organisations of workers collectively seeking to improve wages and working conditions through various strategies, including negotiations and strikes

tradition sentiments and beliefs passed from generation to generation

traditional authority power legitimised through respect for long-established cultural patterns

tradition-directedness rigid conformity to time-honoured ways of living

transnational corporation a firm which has the power to coordinate and control operations in more than one country, even if it does not own them

transsexuals people who feel they are one sex though biologically they are the other

triad a social group with three members

U

unconscious experiences which become too difficult to confront and so become hidden from the surface workings of life

underclass a group 'under the class structure' which is economically, politically and socially marginalised and excluded

underground economy economic activity generating income that is unreported to the government as required by law

urban ecology the study of the link between the physical and social dimensions of cities

urbanisation the concentration of humanity into cities

V

validity the quality of measuring precisely what one intends to measure

values culturally defined standards by which people assess desirability, goodness and beauty, and which serve as broad guidelines for social living

variable a concept whose value changes from case to case

victimless crimes violations of law in which there are no readily apparent victims

W

war armed conflict among the people of various societies, directed by their governments

wealth the total value of money and other assets, minus outstanding debts

white-collar crime crimes committed by persons of high social position in the course of their occupations

white-collar occupations higher-prestige work involving mostly mental activity

Z

zero population growth the level of reproduction, migration and death that maintains population at a steady state

REFERENCES

A

Abbott, Pamela and George Giacinto Giarchi. 'Health, healthcare and health inequalities', in Tony Spybey (ed.), *Britain in Europe*. London: Routledge, 1997: Chapter 18.

Abbott, Pamela and Claire Wallace. *The Family and the New Right*. London: Pluto Press, 1992.

——. *An Introduction to Sociology: Feminist Perspectives*. London: Routledge, 1996; 2nd edn, 1997; 3rd edn, 2004.

Abercrombie, Nicholas. *Television and Society*. Cambridge: Polity Press, 1996.

——. *Sociology*. Cambridge: Polity Press, 2004.

Aberle, David F. *The Peyote Religion among the Navaho*. Chicago: Aldine, 1966.

Acheson, D. *Independent Inquiry into Inequalities in Health Report*. London: HMSO, 1998.

ACUPA (Archbishop's Commission on Urban Priority Areas). *Faith in the City*. London: Church of England, 1985.

Adam, Barbara, Ulrich Beck and Joost Van Loon (eds). *The Risk Society and Beyond*. London: Sage, 2000.

Adorno, Theodore. *The Culture Industry*. London: Routledge, 1991.

Adorno, Theodore and Max Horkheimer. *Dialectic of Enlightment*. New York: Seabury Press, 1972.

Adorno, Theodore, *et al. The Authoritarian Personality*. New York: Harper & Brothers, 1950.

Agger, B. *Cultural Studies as Critical Theory*. London: Falmer, 1992.

——. *The Virtual Self: A Contemporary Sociology*. Oxford: Blackwell, 2004.

Akeret, R.V. *Photoanalysis*. New York: Wyden, 1973.

Alam, Sultana. 'Women and poverty in Bangladesh'. *Women's Studies International Forum*, Vol. 8, No. 4 (1985): 361–71.

Alba, Richard. *Ethnic Identity: The Transformation of White America*. Chicago: University of Chicago Press, 1985.

Albrow, Martin. *The Global Age*. Cambridge: Polity Press, 1996.

——. *Sociology: The Basics*. London: Routledge, 1999.

Alcock, P. *Understanding Poverty*, 2nd edn. Basingstoke: Macmillan, 1997.

Alexander, Cynthia and Leslie Pal. *Digital Democracy*. Oxford: Oxford University Press, 1998.

Allan, Graham (ed). *The Sociology of the Family: A Reader*. Oxford: Blackwell, 1999.

Allan, Graham and Graham Crow. *Families, Households and Society*. London: Palgrave, 2001.

Allen, Beverley. *Rape Warfare: The Hidden Genocide in Bosnia-Herzegovina and Croatia*. Minneapolis, MN: University of Minnesota Press, 1996.

Allen, R. *Channels of Discourse Reassembled*, 2nd edn. London: Routledge, 1992.

——. *Soap Operas around the World*. London: Routledge, 1995.

Allen, Sheila and Carol Walkowitz. *Homeworking: Myths and Realities*. London: Macmillan, 1987.

Allman, Tim. 'Genetically modified foods', in *The Hutchinson Almanac*. London: Hutchinson, 2000: 561.

Allport, Gordon. *The Use of Personal Documents in Psychological Science*. New York: Social Science Research Council, 1942.

Allsop, Kenneth. *The Bootleggers*. London: Hutchinson, 1961.

Altheide, David L. and Robert P. Snow. *Media Worlds in the Postjournalism Era*. New York: Aldine de Gruyter, 1991.

Althusser, Louis. *Lenin and Philosophy and Other Essays*. London: New Left Books, 1971.

Altman, Dennis. *Aids and the New Puritanism*. London: Pluto Press, 1986.

Amnesty International. *Crimes of Hate, Conspiracy of Silence*. London: Amnesty International, 2001.

Anderson, Benedict. *Imagined Communities*. London: Verso, 1989.

Anderson, Bridget. *Doing the Dirty Work: The Global Politics of Domestic Labour*. London: Zed Books, 2000.

Anderson, Elijah. *Code of the Street*. N.Y: W. Norton, 1999.

Ang, Ian. *Watching Dallas: Soap Opera and the Melodramatic Imagination*. London: Methuen, 1985.

Anthias, Floya and Nira Yuval Davis. *Racialised Boundaries*. London: Routledge, 1993.

Appadurai, Arjun. *Modernity at Large: Cultural Dimensions of Globalization*. London and Minneapolis, MN: University of Minnesota Press, 1996.

Appignanesi, L. and S. Maitland. *The Rushdie File*. London: Fourth Estate, 1989.

Appignanesi, Richard and Chris Garratt. *Postmodernism for Beginners*. Cambridge: Icon Books, 1995.

Arber, Sara and Jay Ginn (eds). *Connecting Gender and Ageing: A Sociological Approach*. Buckingham: Open University Press, 1995.

Archer, Dane and Rosemary Gartner. *Violence and Crime in Cross-National Perspective*. New Haven, CT: Yale University Press, 1987.

Arendt, Hannah. *The Origins of Totalitarianism*. Cleveland, OH: Meridian Books, 1958.

Ariès, Philippe. *Centuries of Childhood: A Social History of Family Life*. New York: Vintage Books, 1965.

——. *Western Attitudes toward Death: From the Middle Ages to the Present*. Patricia M. Ranum, trans. Baltimore, MD: Johns Hopkins University Press, 1974.

Arjomand, Said Amir. *The Turban for the Crown: The Islamic Revolution in Iran*. New York: Oxford University Press, 1988.

Armstrong, Gerry and Richard Giulianotti (eds) *Fear and Loathing in World Football*. Oxford: Berg, 2001.

Arnold, Ellen C. and Darcy C. Plymire. 'The Cherokee Indians and the Internet', in David Gauntlett (ed.), *web.studies*. London: Arnold, 2000: 186–93.

Arthus-Bertrand, Yann. *The Earth from the Air*, revised edn. London: Thames & Hudson, 2002; orig. 1999.

Asante, Molefi Kete. *The Afrocentric Idea*. Philadelphia, PA: Temple University Press, 1987.

——. *Afrocentricity*. Trenton, NJ: Africa World Press, 1988.

Asch, Solomon. *Social Psychology*. Englewood Cliffs, NJ: Prentice-Hall, 1952.

Ashford, Lori S. 'New perspectives on population: lessons from Cairo'. *Population Bulletin*, Vol. 50, No. 1 (March 1995).

Ashworth, Andrew and Edmund Daises. 'Race and criminal justice'. Institute for Study and Treatment of Delinquency, Fact Sheet No. 1, 1997.

Astone, Nan Marie and Sara S. McLanahan. 'Family structure, parental practices and high school completion'. *American Sociological Review*, Vol. 56, No. 3 (June 1991): 309–20.

Atchley, Robert C. *Aging: Continuity and Change*. Belmont, CA: Wadsworth, 1983; 2nd edn, 1987.

Aviad, Janet O'Dea. *Return to Judaism: Religious Renewal in Israel*. Chicago and London: University of Chicago Press, 1983.

Axtell, Roger E. *Gestures: The DOs and TABOOs of Body Language around the World*. New York: Wiley, 1991.

Ayensu, Edward S. 'A worldwide role for the healing powers of plants'. *Smithsonian*, Vol. 12, No. 8 (November 1981): 87–97.

B

Bachrach, Peter and Morton S. Baratz. *Power and Poverty*. New York: Oxford University Press, 1970.

Back, Les. *New Ethnicities and Urban Cultures: Racisms and Multiculture in Young Lives*. London: UCL Press, 1996.

Backman, Carl B. and Murray C. Adams. 'Self-perceived physical attractiveness, self-esteem, race, and gender'. *Sociological Focus*, Vol. 24, No. 4 (October 1991): 283–90.

Bahl, Vinay. 'Caste and class in India'. Paper presented to the Southern Sociological Society, Atlanta, April 1991.

Bailey, Joe (ed.). *Social Europe*. London: Longman, 1992; 2nd edn, 1998.

Bailey, William C. 'Murder, capital punishment and television: execution publicity and homicide rates'. *American Sociological Review*, Vol. 55, No. 5 (October 1990): 628–33.

Bailey, William C. and Ruth D. Peterson. 'Murder and capital punishment: a monthly time-series analysis of execution publicity'. *American Sociological Review*, Vol. 54, No. 5 (October 1989): 722–43.

Baird, Vanessa. 'Currencies of desire'. *New Internationalist*, October 1998.

Bales, Kevin. *Disposable People: New Slavery in the Global Economy*. Berkeley, CA: University of California Press, 2000.

Bales, Robert F. 'The equilibrium problem in small groups', in Talcott Parsons *et al.* (eds), *Working Papers in the Theory of Action*. New York: Free Press, 1953: 111–15.

Bales, Robert F. and Philip E. Slater. 'Role differentiation in small decision-making groups', in Talcott Parsons and Robert F. Bales (eds), *Family, Socialization and Interaction Process*. New York: Free Press, 1955: 259–306.

Ballard, R. and C. Ballard. 'South Asian families', in Rhona Rapport *et al.* (eds), *Families in Britain*. London: Routledge, 1982.

Balnaves, Mark, James Donald and Stephanie Hemelryk. *The Global Media Atlas*. Brighton: British Film Institute and Myriad, 2001.

Baltes, Paul B. and K. Warner Schaie. 'The myth of the twilight years'. *Psychology Today*, Vol. 7, No. 10 (March 1974): 35–9.

Baltzell, E. Digby. *The Protestant Establishment: Aristocracy and Caste in America*. New York: Vintage Books, 1964.

——. 'Introduction to the 1967 edition'. In W. E. B. Du Bois, *The Philadelphia Negro: A Social Study*. New York: Schocken, 1967; orig. 1899.

——. (ed.). *The Search for Community in Modern America*. New York: Harper & Row, 1968.

Banish, R. *City Families. Chicago and London* New York: Pantheon, 1976.

Banks, James A. *Multiethnic Education: Theory and Practice*. Boston, MA: Allyn and Bacon, 1981.

Banks, Olive. *Faces of Feminism*. Oxford: Martin Robertson, 1981.

Barash, David. *The Whispering Within*. New York: Penguin Books, 1981.

Barber, Benjamin. *Jihad vs McWorld*. New York: Ballantine Books, 1995.

Barbour, Phillippe (ed.). *The European Union Handbook*. London: Fitzroy Dearborn, 1996.

Barker, Chris. *Global Television: An Introduction*. Oxford: Blackwell, 1997.

Barker, Eileen. 'Who'd be a Moonie? A comparative study of those who join the Unification Church in Britain', in Bryan Wilson (ed.), *The Social Impact of New Religious Movements*. New York: Rose of Sharon Press, 1981: 59–96.

——. *The Making of a Moonie*. Oxford: Basil Blackwell, 1984.

——. *New Religious Movements: A Practical Introduction*, 4th edn. London: HMSO, 1995.

Barker, Martin. *The New Racism*. London: Junction Books, 1981.

Barnes, Colin, Geoff Mercer and Tom Shakespeare. *Exploring Disability: A Sociological Introduction*. Cambridge: Polity Press, 1999.

Barnett, Bernice McNair. *Sisters in Struggle: Invisible Black Women in the Civil Rights Movement*. London: Routledge, 1997.

Barnett, Hilaire A. *Sourcebook on Feminist Jurisprudence*. London: Cavendish, 1997.

Barrett, Michele. *Women's Oppression Today*. London: Verso, 1980.

Barrow, J. 'West Indian families', in R. Rapoport et al. (eds). *Families in Britain*. London: Routledge, 1982.

Barry, Kathleen. 'Feminist theory: the meaning of women's liberation', in Barbara Haber (ed.), *The Women's Annual 1982–1983*. Boston: G. K. Hall, 1983: 35–78.

Barthes, Roland. *Elements of Semiology*. Annette Lavers and Colin Smith, trans. London: Cape, 1967.

Bartholet, Jeffrey. 'The sounds of silence'. *Newsweek* (19 June 2000).

Bastiansen, Henrik and Trine Syversten. 'Towards a Norwegian television history', in Ib Bondebjerg and Francesco Bono (eds), *Television in Scandinavia*. Luton: John Libby, 1996.

Bateson, Gregory and Margaret Mead. *Balinese Character*. New York: New York Academy of Science, 1942.

Baudrillard, Jean. 'Interview: game with vestiges'. *On the Beach*, Vol 5, Winter (1984): 19-25.

——. *Jean Baudrillard Selected Writings*. Cambridge: Polity Press, 1988.

——. 'The reality gulf'. *Guardian* (11 January 1991): 25.

Bauer, P. T. *Equality, the Third World and Economic Delusion*. Cambridge, MA: Harvard University Press, 1981.

Bauman, Zygmunt. *Modernity and the Holocaust*. Cambridge: Polity Press, 1989.

——. *Modernity and Ambivalence*. Cambridge: Polity Press, 1991.

——. *Globalization: The Human Consequences*. Cambridge: Polity Press, 1998.

——. *Wasted Lives: Modernity and Its Outcasts.* Cambridge: Polity Press, 2004.

Bauman, Zygmunt and Tim May. *Thinking Sociologically*, rev. edn. Oxford: Blackwell, 2001.

Baumeister, Roy. *Identity: Cultural Change and the Struggle for Self*. Oxford: Oxford University Press, 1986.

Baylis, John and Steve Smith (eds). *The Globalization of World Politics*. Oxford: Oxford University Press, 1997; 2nd edn, 2000.

Beasley, Chris. *What is Feminism?* London: Sage, 1999.

Beauvoir, Simone de. *The Woman Destroyed*. Patrick O'Brian, trans. London: Fontana/Collins, 1971.

——. *The Second Sex*. London: Virago, 1997 (orig. 1949 in French; first English edn, 1953).

Beccaria. Cesare. *Essay on Crimes and Punishments*. Indianapolis, IN: Bobbs-Merrill Educational, 1963; orig. 1764.

Bech, Henning. 'Report from a rotten state: marriage and homosexuality in Denmark', in Ken Plummer (ed.), *Modern Homosexualities: Fragments of Lesbian and Gay Experience*. London: Routledge, 1992: 134-47.

Beck, Ulrich. *Risk Society*. London: Sage, 1992.

——. *The Reinvention of Politics*. Cambridge: Polity Press, 1997.

——. *World Risk Society*. Cambridge: Polity Press, 1999.

——. *The Brave New World of Work*. Cambridge: Polity Press, 2000a.

——. *What is Globalization?* Cambridge: Polity Press, 2000b.

Beck, Ulrich and Elisabeth Beck-Gernsheim. *The Normal Chaos of Love*. Cambridge: Polity Press, 1995.

Beck, Ulrich and Elisabeth Beck-Gernsheim. *Individualization*. London: Sage, 2003.

Beck-Gernsheim, Elizabeth. *The Social implications of Bioengineering*. Atlantic Highlands, NJ: Humanities Press, 1991.

——. *Reinventing the Family: In Search of New Lifestyles*. Cambridge: Polity Press, 2002.

Becker, Gay. *The Elusive Embryo*. Berkeley, CA: University of California Press, 2000.

Becker, Howard S. *Outside: Studies in the Sociology of Deviance*. New York: Free Press, 1963; 2nd edn, 1966.

——. *Doing Things Together*. Chicago: Aldine, 1986.

Beckman, Joanna. *Foreign Aid to End Hunger*. Washington, DC: Bread for the World Institute, 2001.

Bedell, George C., Leo Sandon, Jr. and Charles T. Wellborn. *Religion in America*. New York: Macmillan, 1975.

Beeghley, Leonard. *The Structure of Social Stratification in the United States*. Needham Heights, MA: Allyn & Bacon, 1989.

Bekker, Simon. *Ethnicity in Focus: The South African Case*. Durban: Indicator South Africa, 1993.

Bell, Alan P., Martin S. Weinberg and Sue Kiefer-Hammersmith. *Sexual Preference: Its Development in Men and Women*. Bloomington, IN: Indiana University Press, 1981.

Bell, Daniel. *The Coming of Post-Industrial Society: A Venture in Social Forecasting*. New York: Harper Colophon, 1976.

Bell, Judith. *Doing Your Research Project: A Guide for First-Time Researchers in Education and Social Science*, 2nd edn. Buckingham: Open University Press, 1993.

Bellah, Robert N. *The Broken Covenant*. New York: Seabury Press, 1975.

Bellah, Robert N., Richard Madsen, William M. Sullivan, Ann Swidler and Steven M. Tipton. *Habits of the Heart: Individualism and Commitment in American Life*. New York: Harper & Row, 1985.

Belsky, Jay, Richard M. Lerner and Graham B. Spanier. *The Child in the Family*. Reading, MA: Addison-Wesley, 1984.

Benedict, Ruth. 'Continuities and discontinuities in cultural conditioning'. *Psychiatry*, Vol. 1 (May 1938): 161–7.

Benet, Sula. 'Why they live to be 100, or even older, in Abkhasia'. *New York Times Magazine* (26 December 1971): 3, 28–9, 31–4.

Benjamin, Bernard and Chris Wallis. 'The mortality of widowers'. *The Lancet*, Vol. 2 (August 1963): 454–6.

Benjamin, Lois. *The Black Elite: Facing the Color Line in the Twilight of the Twentieth Century*. Chicago: Nelson-Hall, 1991.

Benjamin, Walter. *The Work of Art in the Age of Mechanical Reproduction*. London: Cape, 1970.

Bennett, James. *Oral History and Delinquency*. Chicago: University of Chicago Press, 1981.

Benokraitis, Nijole and Joe Feagin. *Modern Sexism: Blatant, Subtle and Overt Discrimination*, 2nd edn. Englewood Cliffs, NJ: Prentice-Hall, 1995.

Benton, Douglas A. *Applied Human Relations: An Organizational and Skill Development Approach*, 6th edn. Englewood Cliffs, NJ: Prentice-Hall, 1997.

Benton, Ted (ed.). *The Greening of Marxism*. New York: Guilford Press, 1996.

Ben-Ze'ev Aaron. *Love Online: Emotions on the Internet*. Cambridge: Cambridge University Press, 2004

Berger, Alan L. *Children of Job: American Second-Generation Witnesses to the Holocaust*. New York: State University of New York Press, 1997.

Berger, Peter L. *Invitation to Sociology*. New York: Anchor Books, 1963.

——. *The Sacred Canopy: Elements of a Sociological Theory of Religion*. Garden City, NY: Doubleday, 1967; 2nd edn, 1997.

——. *Facing Up to Modernity: Excursions in Society, Politics and Religion*. New York: Basic Books, 1977.

——. *The Capitalist Revolution: Fifty Propositions about Prosperity, Equality and Liberty*. New York: Basic Books, 1986.

——. (ed.). *The Desecularization of the World*. Washington, DC: Ethics and Public Policy, 1999.

Berger, Peter, Brigitte Berger and Hansfried Kellner. *The Homeless Mind: Modernization and Consciousness*. New York: Vintage Books, 1974.

Berger, Peter and Hansfried Kellner. *Sociology Reinterpreted: An Essay on Method and Vocation*. Garden City, NY: Anchor Books, 1981.

Berger, Peter and Thomas Luckmann. *The Social Construction of Reality: A Treatise in the Sociology of Knowledge*. Garden City, NY: Anchor Books, 1967.

Bergesen, Albert (ed.). *Crises in the World-System*. Beverly Hills, CA: Sage, 1983.

Bernard, Jessie. *The Female World*. New York: Free Press, 1981.

——. *The Future of Marriage*. New Haven, CT: Yale University Press, 1982; orig. 1973.

Bernstein, Basil. *Class, Codes and Control* (3 vols). London: Routledge, 1977.

Bernstein, Richard J. *The New Constellation: The Ethical–Political Horizons of Modernity/Postmodernity*. Cambridge, MA: MIT Press, 1992.

Berrill, Kevin T. 'Anti-gay violence and victimization in the United States: an overview', in Gregory M. Herek and Kevin T. Berrill, *Hate Crimes: Confronting Violence against Lesbians and Gay Men*. Newbury Park, CA: Sage, 1992: 19–45.

Berry, Brian L. and Philip H. Rees. 'The factorial ecology of Calcutta'. *American Journal of Sociology*, Vol. 74, No. 5 (March 1969): 445–91.

Best, Joel. *Damned Lies and Statistics*. Berkeley, CA: University of California Press, 2001).

Best, Raphaela. *We've All Got Scars: What Boys and Girls Learn in Elementary School*. Bloomington, IN: Indiana University Press, 1983.

Beveridge, William. *Social Insurance and Allied Services* (The Beveridge Report), Cmd 6404. London: HMSO.

Beynon, Huw. *Working for Ford*. London: Allen Lane, and Harmondsworth: Penguin, 1973.

Beynon, Huw, Ray Hudson and David Sadler. *A Tale of Two Industries: The Contraction of Coal and Steel in the North East of England*. Buckingham: Open University Press, 1991.

Bhadra, Bipul Kumar. *Sociology of C. Wright Mills*. Calcutta, India: Minerva Associates, 1998.

Bhavnani, Kum-Kum. 'Talking racism and the reality of women's studies', in D. Richardson and V. Robinson (eds), *Introducing Womens Studies*. London: Macmillan, 1993.

Biagioli, Mario (ed.). *The Science Studies Reader*. London: Routledge, 1999.

Biblarz, Timothy J. and Adrian E. Raftery. 'The effects of family disruption on social mobility'. *American Sociological Review*, Vol. 58, No. 1 (February 1993): 97–109.

Birren, James *et al. Aging and Biography*. New York: Springer.

Black, Sir Douglas *et al. The Black Report*. London: HMSO, 1980.

Blaikie, Andrew. *Ageing and Popular Culture*. Cambridge: Cambridge University Press, 1999.

Blakemore, Ken and Margaret Boneham. *Age, Race and Ethnicity: A Comparative Approach*. Buckingham: Open University Press, 1993.

Blau, Peter M. *Exchange and Power in Social Life*. New York: Wiley, 1964.

——. *Inequality and Heterogeneity: A Primitive Theory of Social Structure*. New York: Free Press, 1977.

Blau, Peter M., Terry C. Blum and Joseph Schwartz. 'Heterogeneity and intermarriage'. *American Sociological Review*, Vol. 47, No. 1 (February 1982): 45–62.

Blau, Peter M. and Otis Dudley Duncan. *The American Occupational Structure*. New York: Wiley, 1967.

Blaxter, Mildred. *Health*. Cambridge: Polity Press, 2004.

Blumer, Herbert. *Movies and Conduct*. New York: Macmillan, 1933.

Blumer, Herbert G. 'Collective behavior', in Alfred McClung Lee (ed.), *Principles of Sociology*, 3rd edn. New York: Barnes & Noble Books, 1969: 65–121.

Blumstein, Alfred and Joel Wallman (eds). *The Crime Drop in America*. Cambridge: Cambridge University Press, 2000.

Blumstein, Philip and Pepper Schwartz. *American Couples*. New York: William Morrow, 1983.

Bocock, Robert. *Consumption*. London: Routledge, 1993.

Bodenheimer, Thomas S. 'Health care in the United States: who pays?', in Vicente Navarro (ed.), *Health and Medical Care in the US: A Critical Analysis*. Farmingdale, NY: Baywood Publishing, 1977: 61–8.

Boff, Leonardo and Clodovis Boff. *Salvation and Liberation: In Search of a Balance Between Faith and Politics*. Maryknoll, NY: Orbis Books, 1984.

Bogardus, Emory S. 'Comparing racial distance in Ethopia, South Africa, and the United States'. *Sociology and Social Research*, Vol. 52, No. 2 (January 1968): 149–56.

Bohm, Robert M. 'American death penalty opinion, 1936–1986: a critical examination of the Gallup polls', in Robert M. Bohm (ed.), *The Death Penalty in America: Current Research*. Cincinnati, OH: Anderson Publishing, 1991: 113–45.

Bohrmann, Herbert F. and Stephen R. Kellert (eds), *Ecology, Economics and Ethics: The Broken Circle*. New Haven, CT: Yale University Press, 1991: 205–10.

Bondebjerg, Ib and Francesco Bono (eds). *Television in Scandinavia*. Luton: John Libby, 1996: 127–55.

Bonner, Jane. Research presented in 'The Two Brains', Public Broadcasting System telecast, 1984.

Booth, Alan and Lynn White. 'Thinking about divorce'. *Journal of Marriage and the Family*, Vol. 42, No. 3 (August 1980): 605–16.

Booth, Charles. *Life and Labour in London*. London: Macmillan, 17 vols, 1901–02.

Bordo, Susan. *Unbearable Weight: Feminism, Western Culture and the Body*. Berkeley: University of California Press, 1993.

Borgmann, Albert. *Crossing the Postmodern Divide*. Chicago: University of Chicago Press, 1992.

Bormann, F. Herbert. 'The global environmental deficit'. *BioScience*, Vol. 40 (1990): 74.

Bormann, F. Herbert and Stephen R. Kellert. 'The global environmental deficit', in F. Herbert Bormann and Stephen R. Kellert (eds), *Ecology, Economics and Ethics: The Broken Circle*. New Haven, CT: Yale University Press, 1991: ix–xviii.

Bornat, Joanna (ed.). *Reminiscence Reviewed*. Buckingham: Open University Press, 1994.

Bornhoff, Nicholas. *Pink Samurai: An Erotic Exploration of Japanese Society*. London: Grafton Books, 1992.

Bornstein, Kate. *My Gender Workbook*. London: Routledge, 1998.

Boston Women's Health Book Collective. *Our Bodies, Ourselves*. Angela Phillips and Jill Rakusen; eds British edn. Harmondsworth: Penguin, 1978; orig. 1971.

Boswell, Terry E. and William J. Dixon. 'Marx's theory of rebellion: a cross-national analysis of class exploitation, economic development and violent revolt'. *American Sociological Review*, Vol. 58, No. 5 (October 1993): 681–702.

Bott, Elizabeth. *Family and Social Network*. New York: Free Press, 1971; orig. 1957.

Bottoms, Anthony F. 'Some neglected features of modern penal systems', in D. Garland and P. Young (eds), *The Power to Punish*. London: Heinemann, 1988.

Boulding, Elise. *The Underside of History*. Boulder, CO: Westview Press, 1976.

Bourdieu, Pierre. *Distinction*. London: Routledge, 1984.

——. *The Logic of Practice*. Stanford, CA: Stanford University Press, 1990.

Bourdieu, Pierre et al. *The Weight of the World: Social Suffering in Contemporary Society*. Cambridge: Polity Press, 1999.

Bowles, Samuel and Herbert Gintis. *Schooling in Capitalist America: Educational Reform and the Contradictions of Economic Life*. New York: Basic Books, 1976.

Bowley, Graham. 'The last census?' *Prospect*, No. 92 (November 2003): 26–31.

Bowling, Anne et al. 'Adding quality to quantity: older people's views on their quality of life and its enhancement' *Ageing and Mental Health* (November 2002).

Boyle, Charles, Peter Wheale and Brian Sturgess. *People, Science and Technology*. Brighton, Sussex: Wheatsheaf, 1984.

Boyle, Kevin. *Freedom of Religion and Belief: A World Report*. London: Routledge, 1997.

Bradley, Harriet. *Fractured Identities: Changing Patterns of Inequality*. Cambridge: Polity Press, 1996.

Bradshaw, York W. and Michael Wallace. *Global Inequalities*. London: Pine Forge Press, 1996.

Brah, A. & Minhas, R. (1988) 'Structural Racism or Cultural Difference: Schooling for Asian Girls' in M. Woodhead and A. McGrath (1988) *Family, School and Society: A Reader*, London: Hodder and Stoughton.

Braham, Peter and Linda Janes (eds). *Social Differences and Divisions*. Oxford: Blackwell/Open University Press, 2002.

Branegan, Jay. 'Is Singapore a model for the West?' *Time*, Vol. 141, No. 3 (18 January 1993): 36–7.

Branson, Richard. *Losing My Virginity: How I've Survived, Had Fun and Made a Fortune Doing Business My Way*. New York: Times Books, 1998.

Bratlinger, Patrick. *Crusoe's Footprints: Cultural Studies in Britain and America*. New York: Routledge, 1990.

Brecher, Jeremy, Tim Costello and Brendan Smith. *Globalization from Below*. Cambridge, MA: South End Press, 2000.

Breen, Leonard Z. 'The aging individual', in Clark Tibbitts (ed.), *Handbook of Social Gerontology*. Chicago: University of Chicago Press, 1960: 145–62.

Breen, Richard and David B. Rottman. *Class Stratification: A Comparative Perspective*. Hemel Hempstead: Harvester Wheatsheaf, 1994.

Brettell, C.B. *When They Read What We Write: The Politics of Ethnography*. London: Bergin and Garvey, 1993.

Brierley, Peter. 'Religion', in A.H. Halsey with Josephine Webb (eds), *Twentieth Century British Social Trends*. London: Macmillan, 2000.

Brightman, Joan. 'Why Hillary chooses Rodham Clinton'. *American Demographics*, Vol. 16, No. 3 (March 1994): 9–11.

Brinton, Crane. *The Anatomy of Revolution*. New York: Vintage Books, 1965.

Brinton, Mary C. 'The social–institutional cases of gender stratification: Japan as an illustrative case'. *American Journal of Sociology*, Vol. 94, No. 2 (September 1988): 300–34.

British Crime Survey, *2001 Preliminary Report*. London: HMSO, 2001.

British Crime Survey. *2003/04 Preliminary Report*. Home Office Research Series. London: HMSO, 2004.

British Medical Association. *Complementary Medicine: New Approaches to Good Practice*. London: BMA, 1993.

British Social Attitudes. London: Sage, 2004.

Brody, Hugh. *The Other Side of Eden: Hunters, Farmers and the Shaping of the Modern World*. London: Farrar, Straus and Giroux, 2000.

Brown, Andrew. *The Darwin Wars: The Scientific Battle for the Soul of Man*. London: Simon & Schuster, 1999.

Brown, Lester R. et al. (eds). *State of the World 1997*. London: Earthscan, 1997.

——. *State of the World 2001: A Worldwatch Institute Report on Progress toward a Sustainable Society*. London: Earthscan, 2001.

——. *State of the World 2004: The Consumer Society*. London: Earthscan, 2004.

Brown, Mary Ellen (ed.). *Television and Women's Culture: The Politics of the Popular*. Newbury Park, CA: Sage, 1990.

Brown, P. '"The Third Wave": Education and the ideology of "parentocracy"'. *British Journal of Sociology of Education*, Vol. 11 (1990): 65–85.

Brownell, Ginanne. 'Brand It Like Beckham'. *Newsweek* (30 June 2003): 86.

Brownhill, Sue. *Housing London: Issues of Finance and Supply: The Final Report of the Greater London Study*. York: Joseph Rowntree Foundation, 1990.

Browning, Gary, Abigail Halci and Frank Webster (eds). *Understanding Contemporary Society: Theories of the Present*. London: Sage, 2000.

Bruce, Steven. 'The twilight of the gods'. *Sociology Review* (November 1992).

——. *Sociology of Religion*. Oxford: Oxford University Press, 1995.

——. *Religion in the Modern World: From Cathedrals to Cults*. Oxford: Oxford University Press, 1996.

——. *Sociology: A Very Short Introduction*. Oxford: Oxford University Press, 1999.

——. *Fundamentalism*. Oxford: Polity Press, 2000.

——. *Politics and Religion*. Oxford: Polity Press, 2003.

Bruno, Mary. 'Abusing the elderly'. *Newsweek* (23 September 1985): 75–6.

Brundtland, G. (ed). *Our Common Future*. Oxford: Oxford University Press, 1987.

Bryman, Alan. *Disney and His Worlds*. London: Routledge, 1995.

——. *Social Research Methods*, 2nd edn. Oxford: Oxford University Press, 2004.

——. *The Disneyization of Society*, London: Sage, 2004.

Bryson, Bill. 'Of mice and millions'. *Observer Magazine* (28 March 1993): 16–23.

Bryson, Valerie. *Feminist Debates*. London: macmillan, 1999.

Bulmer, Martin and Anthony M. Rees (eds). *Citizenship Today: The Contemporary Relevance of T. H. Marshall*. London: UCL Press, 1996.

Bunting, Madeleine. *Willing Slaves: How the Overwork Culture is Ruling our Lives*. London: Harper Collins, 2004.

Buraway, Michael. 'The Soviet descent into capitalism'. *American Journal of Sociology*, Vol. 102, No. 5 (March 1997): 1420–44.

Burbidge, Mikey and J. Walters (eds). *Breaking the Silence: Gay Teenagers Speak for Themselves*. London: Joint Council of Gay Teenagers, 1981.

Burchard, Tania. 'Social exclusion: concepts and evidence', in David Gordon and Peter Townsend (eds), *Breadline Europe: The Measurement of Poverty*. Bristol: Policy Press, 2000.

Burgess, Robert. *In the Field*. London: Allen & Unwin, 1984.

Burgoyne, Jacqueline, Roger Ormrod and Martin Richards. *Divorce Matters*. Harmondsworth: Penguin, 1987.

Burke, Roger Hopkins. *An Introduction to Criminological Theory*. Cullompton, Devon: Willan Publishing, 2001.

Burke, Tom. 'The future', in Sir Edmund Hillary (ed.), *Ecology 2000: The Changing Face of the Earth*. New York: Beaufort Books, 1984: 227–41.

Bury, M.R. 'Social constructionism and the development of medical sociology'. *Sociology of Health and Illness*, Vol. 8 (1986): 137–68.

——. 'The sociology of chronic illness'. *Sociology of Health and Illness*, Vol. 13, No. 4 (1991): 451–68.

Busby, Linda J. 'Sex role research on the mass media'. *Journal of Communications*, Vol. 25 (Autumn 1975): 107–13.

Busfield, Joan. *Women, Men and Madness*. London: Macmillan, 1997.

——. *Health and Health Care in Modern Britain*. Oxford: Oxford University Press, 2000.

Butler, Judith. *Gender Trouble*. London: Routledge, 1990.

Butler, Robert N. 'The life review'. *Psychiatry*, Vol. 26 (1963): 63–76.

Butler, Robert N. *Why Survive? Being Old in America*. New York: Harper & Row, 1975.

Butterworth, Douglas and John K. Chance. *Latin American Urbanization*. Cambridge: Cambridge University Press, 1981.

Bytheway, Bill. *Ageism*. Buckingham: Open University Press, 1995.

C

Cahnman, Werner J. and Rudolf Heberle. 'Introduction', in *Ferdinand Toennies on Sociology: Pure, Applied, and Empirical*. Chicago: University of Chicago Press, 1971: vii–xxii.

Callahan, Daniel. *Setting Limits: Medical Goals in an Aging Society*. New York: Simon & Schuster, 1987.

Calley, Malcolm J. C. *God's People: West Indian Pentecostal Sects in England*. London: Oxford University Press, 1965.

Calmore, John O. 'National housing policies and black America: trends, issues and implications', in James D. Williams (ed.), *The State of Black America 1986*. New York: National Urban League, 1986: 115–49.

Calvert, Peter and Susan Calvert. *Politics and Society in the Third World*, 2nd edn. London: Longman, 2001.

Cameron, William Bruce. *Modern Social Movements: A Sociological Outline*. New York: Random House, 1966.

Cancian, Francesca M. *Love in America: Gender and Self-Development*. Cambridge: Cambridge University Press, 1987.

Caplan, Lionel. 'Popular conceptions of fundamentalism', in L. Caplan (ed.), *Studies in Religious Fundamentalism*. Albany, NY: State University of New York, 1987: 1–24.

Caplan, Patricia. *Class and Gender in India: Women and Their Organisation in a South Indian City*. New York: Tavistock, 1985.

Caplow, Theodore, Howard M. Bahr, John Modell and Bruce A. Chadwick. *Recent Social Trends in the United States, 1960–1990*. Montreal: McGill-Queen's University Press, 1991.

Carley, Kathleen. 'A theory of group stability'. *American Sociological Review*, Vol. 56, No. 3 (June 1991): 331–54.

Carlson, Norman A. 'Corrections in the United States today: a balance has been struck'. *American Criminal Law Review*, Vol. 13, No. 4 (Spring 1976): 615–47.

Carmichael, Stokely and Charles V. Hamilton. *Black Power: The Politics of Liberation in America*. New York: Vintage Books, 1967.

Carrabine, Eamonn, Paul Iganski, Maggy Lee, Ken Plummer and Nigel South. *Criminology: A Sociological Introduction*. London: Routledge, 2004.

Carrington, Christopher. *No Place Like Home: Relationships and Family Life among Lesbians and Gay Men*. Chicago: University of Chicago Press, 1999.

Carson, Rachel. *Silent Spring*. Boston, MA: Houghton Mifflin, 1962.

Casanova, Jose. *Public Religions in the Modern World*. Chicago: University of Chicago Press, 1994.

Cashmore, Ellis. *Beckham*. Cambridge: Polity Press, 2004.

Cashmore, Ellis and Chris Rojek. *Dictionary of Cultural Theorists*. London: Arnold, 1999.

Castells, Manuel. *The Informational City*. Oxford: Blackwell, 1989.

——. *The Information Age* (3 vols). Oxford: Blackwell. Vol. 1, 1996; Vol. 2, 1997; Vol. 3, 1998.

Castles, Stephen, H. Booth and T. Wallace. *Here for Good: Western Europe's New Ethnic Minorities*. London: Pluto, 1984.

Castles, Stephen and Mark J. Miller. *The Age of Migration: International Population Movements in the Modern World*. London: Macmillan, 1993.

Castro, Janice. 'Disposable workers'. *Time*, Vol. 131, No. 14 (29 March 1993): 43–7.

Central Intelligence Agency. *The World Factbook*, 2000. Washington DC: CIA, 2000 (http://www.cia/gov/publications/factbook)

Chagnon, Napoleon A. *Yanomami: The Fierce People*, 5th edn. New York: Holt, Rinehart & Winston, 1997.

Champion, A. G. *Social and Economic Atlas of the UK*. Oxford: Oxford University Press, 1996.

Chandler, Tertius and Gerald Fox. *3000 Years of Urban History*. New York: Academic Press, 1974.

Change, Kwang-Chih. *The Archaeology of Ancient China*. New Haven, CT: Yale University Press, 1977.

Chaplin, Elizabeth. *Sociology and Visual Representation*. London: Routledge, 1994.

Cherlin, Andrew and Frank F. Furstenberg, Jr. 'The American family in the year 2000'. *The Futurist*, Vol. 17, No. 3 (June 1983): 7–14.

Chisholm, Lynn. 'A crazy quilt: education, training and social change in Europe', in Joe Bailey (ed.), *Social Europe*, 2nd edn. London: Longman, 1998.

Chisholm, Patricia. 'To celebrate our love publicly'. *Maclean's* (28 June 1993): 29.

Chodorow, Nancy. *The Reproduction of Mothering*. Berkeley, CA: University of California Press, 1978.

Chown, Sheila M. 'Morale, careers and personal potentials', in James E. Birren and K. Warner Schaie (eds), *Handbook of the Psychology of Aging*. New York: Van Nostrand Reinhold, 1977: 672–91.

Christie, Kenneth. *The South African Truth Commission*. London: Palgrave, 2000.

Christie, Nils. *Crime Control as Industry: Towards Gulags, Western Style*, 3rd edn. London: Routledge, 2000.

Church, George J. 'Unions arise – with new tricks'. *Time*, Vol. 143, No. 24 (13 June 1994): 56–8.

Clark, Curtis B. 'Geriatric abuse: out of the closet', in *The Tragedy of Elder Abuse: The Problem and the Response*. Hearings before the Select Committee on Aging, House of Representatives (1 July 1986): 49–50.

Clark, Margaret S. (ed.). *Prosocial Behavior*. Newbury Park, CA: Sage, 1991.

Clark, Thomas A. *Blacks in Suburbs*. New Brunswick, NJ: Rutgers University Center for Urban Policy Research, 1979.

Clarke, Adele. 'Modernity, post modernism and human reproductive processes' in Chris Hable Gray (eds.), *The Cyborg Handbook*. New York: Routledge, 1995: 139–55.

Clarke, P. 'Islam in contemporary Europe', in S. Sutherland *et al.* (eds), *The World's Religions*. London: Routledge, 1988.

Clegg, Stuart R. *Modern Organisations: Organisation Studies in the Postmodern World*. London: Sage, 1990.

Clinard, Marshall and Daniel Abbott. *Crime in Developing Countries*. New York: Wiley, 1973.

Clough, Patricia Ticineto. *The Ends of Ethnography: From Realism to Social Criticism*. Newbury Park, CA: Sage, 1992.

Cloward, Richard A. and Lloyd E. Ohlin. *Delinquency and Opportunity: A Theory of Delinquent Gangs*. New York: Free Press, 1966.

Coakley, Jay and Eric Dunning (eds.) *Handbook of Sports Studies*. London: Sage, 2000–2002.

Cochrane, Alan and John Clarke. *Comparing Welfare States: Britain in International Context*. London: Sage, 1993.

Coe, Michael D. and Richard A. Diehl. *In the Land of the Olmec*. Austin, TX: University of Texas Press, 1980.

Coffey, Amanda. *Education and Social Change*. Buckingham: Open University Press, 2001.

Cohen, Albert K. *Delinquent Boys: The Culture of the Gang*. New York: Free Press, 1971; orig. 1955.

Cohen, Joel E. *How Many People Can the Earth Support?* New York: W. W. Norton, 1995.

Cohen, Lloyd R. 'Sexual harassment and the law'. *Society*, Vol. 28, No. 4 (May–June 1991): 8–13.

Cohen, Phil. 'Subculture conflict and working class community', in S. Hall *et al.* (eds), *Culture, Media, Logica*. London: Hutchinson, 1980; orig. 1972.

Cohen, Robin. *Frontiers of Identity: The British and the Others*. Harlow: Longman, 1994.

Cohen, Robin and Paul Kennedy. *Global Sociology*. Basingstoke: Macmillan, 2000.

Cohen, Stanley. *Visions of Social Control*. Cambridge: Polity Press, 1985.

——. *Folk Devils and Moral Panics: The Creation of the Mods and Rockers*, 3rd edn. London: Routledge, 2003; orig. 1972.

Cohen, Stanley and Laurie Taylor. *Escape Attempts: The Theory and Practice of Resistance to Everyday Life*, 2nd edn. London: Routledge, 1995.

Cohen, Stanley and Jock Young (eds). *The Manufacture of News*, 2nd edn. London: Constable, 1981.

Cohn, Richard M. 'Economic development and status change of the aged'. *American Journal of Sociology*, Vol. 87, No. 2 (March 1982): 1150–61.

Coleman, Clive and Jenny Moynihan. *Understanding Crime Data*. Buckingham: Open University Press, 1996.

Coleman, David (ed.). *Europe's Population in the 1990s*. Oxford: Oxford University Press, 1992.

Coleman, David and John Salt. *The British Population: Patterns, Trends and Processes*. Oxford: Oxford University Press, 1992.

Coleman, James S. 'Rational organization'. *Rationality and Society*, Vol. 2 (1990): 94–105.

——. 'The design of organizations and the right to act'. *Sociological Forum*, Vol. 8, No. 4 (December 1993): 527–46.

Coleman, P. *Aging and Reminiscence Processes*. New York: John Wiley, 1986.

Coleman, Richard P. and Lee Rainwater. *Social Standing in America*. New York: Basic Books, 1978.

Collier, Richard. *Masculinities, Crime and Criminology*. London: Sage, 1998.

Collins, Patricia Hill. *Black Feminist Thought*. London: Routledge, 1990.

Collins, Randall. 'A conflict theory of sexual stratification'. *Social Problems*, Vol. 19, No. 1 (Summer 1971): 3–21.

——. *The Credential Society: An Historical Sociology of Education and Stratification*. New York: Academic Press, 1979.

Colloway, N. O. and Paula L. Dollevoet. 'Selected tabular material on aging', in Caleb Finch and Leonard Hayflick (eds), *Handbook of the Biology of Aging*. New York: Van Nostrand Reinhold, 1977: 666–708.

Comte, Auguste. *Auguste Comte and Positivism: The Essential Writings*. Gertrud Lenzer (ed.). New York: Harper Torchbooks, 1975; orig. 1851–54.

Concise Oxford Dictionary of Sociology, The. John Scott (ed.) Oxford: Oxford University Press, 3rd edn, 2005; 2nd edn, 1998 (ed. Gordon Marshall).

Connell, R.W. *Masculinities*. Cambridge: Polity Press, 1995.

——. *Gender*. Cambridge: Polity Press, 2002.

Connett, Paul H. 'The disposable society', in F. Herbert Bormann and Stephen R. Kellert (eds), *Ecology, Economics and Ethics: The Broken Circle*. New Haven, CT: Yale University Press, 1991: 99–122.

Connor, Steven. *Postmodern Culture: An Introduction to Theories of the Contemporary*, 2nd edn. Oxford: Blackwell, 1997.

Conrad, Peter and Joseph Schneider. *Deviance and Medicalization: From Badness to Sickness*, 2nd edn. London: Routledge, 1990 (1st edn, Free Association Press, 1980).

Contreras, Joseph. 'A new day dawns'. *Newsweek* (30 March 1992): 40–1.

Cook, M. *A Brief History of the Human Race*. London: Granta, 2004.

Cooley, Charles Horton. *Human Nature and the Social Order*. New York: Schocken Books, 1964; orig. 1902.

Corbin, J. and Anselm Strauss. 'Managing chronic illness at home'. *Qualitative Sociology*, Vol. 8, No. 3 (1985): 224–47.

Corea, Gena. 'The new reproductive technologies', in Dorchen Leidholdt and Janice C. Raymond (eds), *The Sexual Liberals and the Attack on Feminism*. New York: Pergamon Press, 1988.

Coser, Lewis A. *Masters of Sociological Thought: Ideas in Historical and Social Context*, 2nd edn. New York: Harcourt Brace Jovanovich, 1977.

Cotgrove, Stephen. *Catastrophe or Cornucopia: The Environment, Politics and the Future*. Chichester: Wiley, 1982.

Cottrell, John and the editors of *Time-Life*. *The Great Cities: Mexico City*. Amsterdam: Time-Life, 1979.

Council on Families in America. *Marriage in America: A Report to the Nation*. New York: Institute for American Values, 1995.

Counts, G. S. 'The social status of occupations: a problem in vocational guidance'. *School Review*, Vol. 33 (January 1925): 16–27.

Courtney, Alice E. and Thomas W. Whipple. *Sex Stereotyping in Advertising*. Lexington, MA: D. C. Heath, 1983.

Coveney, Lal *et al. The Sexuality Papers*. London: Hutchinson, 1984.

Cowan, Carolyn Pope. *When Partners Become Parents*. New York: Basic Books, 1992.

Cowgill, Donald and Lowell Holmes. *Aging and Modernization*. New York: Appleton-Century-Crofts, 1972.

Cowley, Geoffrey. 'The prescription that kills'. *Newsweek* (17 July 1995): 54.

Cox, Harvey. *The Secular City*, rev. edn. New York: Macmillan, 1971; orig. 1965.

——. *Turning East: The Promise and Peril of the New Orientalism*. New York: Simon and Schuster, 1977.

——. 'Church and believers: always strangers?', in Thomas Robbins and Dick Anthony, *In Gods We Trust: New Patterns of Religious Pluralism in America*, 2nd edn. New Brunswick, NJ: Transaction, 1990: 449–62.

Coxon, Anthony P. M. *Between the Sheets: The Sexual Diaries of Gay Men*. London: Cassell, 1997.

Craib, Ian. 'Masculinity and male domination'. *Sociological Review*, Vol. 35, No. 4 (November 1987): 721–43.

——. *Modern Social Theory*, 2nd edn. Hemel Hempstead: Harvester Wheatsheaf, 1992.

——. *Classical Social Theory*. Oxford: Oxford University Press, 1997.

Craig, Grace. *Human Development*, 7th edn. Englewood Cliffs, NJ: Prentice-Hall, 1995.

Crewe, Ivor. 'Changing votes and changing voters'. *Electoral Studies* (December 1992).

Crofts, S. 'Global neighbours', in R. Allen (ed.), *Soap Operas around the World*. London: Routledge, 1995.

Crompton, Rosemary. *Class and Stratification*. Cambridge: Polity Press, 1993.

——. *Women and Work in Modern Britain*. Oxford: Oxford University Press, 1997.

Crook, Stephan, Jan Pakulski and Malcolm Waters. *Postmodernity: Change in Advanced Society*. Newbury Park, CA: Sage, 1992.

Crossette, Barbara. 'Female genital mutilation by immigrants is becoming cause for concern in the US'. *New York Times International* (10 December 1995): 11.

Crouch, Colin. *Social Change in Western Europe*. Oxford: Oxford University Press, 1999.

Crystal, David. *English as a Global Language*. Cambridge: Cambridge University Press, 1997.

Cuff, E. C. and G. C. F. Payne (eds). *Perspectives in Sociology*. London: Allen and Unwin, 1979.

Cuff, E. C., Wes Sharrock and D. Francis. *Perspectives in Sociology*, 3rd edn. London: Allen and Unwin, 1990; 4th edn, 1997.

Cumming, Elaine and William E. Henry. *Growing Old: The Process of Disengagement*. New York: Basic Books, 1961.

Curtis, James and Lorne Tepperman (eds). *Haves and Have Nots: An International Reader on Social Inequality*. Englewood Cliffs, NJ: Prentice-Hall, 1994.

Curtiss, Susan. *Genie: A Psycholinguistic Study of a Modern-Day 'Wild Child'*. New York: Academic Press, 1977.

Cutler, David M. and Lawrence F. Katz. 'Rising inequality? Changes in the distribution of income and consumption in the 1980s'. Working Paper No. 3964. Cambridge, MA: National Bureau of Economic Research, 1992.

Cutright, Phillip. 'Occupational inheritance: a cross-national analysis'. *American Journal of Sociology*, Vol. 73, No. 4 (January 1968): 400–16.

Cylke, F. Kurt, Jr. *The Environment*. New York: HarperCollins, 1993.

D

Dahl, Robert A. *Who Governs?* New Haven, CT: Yale University Press, 1961.

——. *Dilemmas of Pluralist Democracy: Autonomy vs. Control*. New Haven, CT: Yale University Press, 1982.

Dahrendorf, Ralf. *Class and Class Conflict in Industrial Society*. Stanford, CA: Stanford University Press, 1959.

Daly, Martin and Margo Wilson. *Homicide*. New York: Aldine, 1988.

Daly, Mary. *Beyond God the Father*. Boston, MA: Beacon Press, 1973.

——. *Gyn Ecology: The Metaethics of Radical Feminism*. Boston, MA: Beacon Press, 1978.

Dandaneau, Steven P. *Taking It Big: Developing Sociological Consciousness in Postmodern Times*. London: Pine Forge Press, 2001

Daniel, W. W. *Racial Discrimination in England* (based on the PEP Report). Harmondsworth: Penguin, 1968.

Dannefer, Dale. 'Adult development and social theory: a reappraisal'. *American Sociological Review*, Vol. 49, No. 1 (February 1984): 100–16.

Darnton, Nina and Yuriko Hoshia. 'Whose life is it, anyway?' *Newsweek*, Vol. 113, No. 4 (13 January 1989): 61.

Darwin, Charles. *The Illustrated Origin of the Species*, abridged by Richard Leakey. London: Faber and Faber, 1979; orig. 1859.

Davidson, Julia O'Connell. *Prostitution, Power and Freedom.* Cambridge: Polity Press, 1998.

Davidson, Julia O'Connell and Derek Layder. *Methods, Sex and Madness.* London: Routledge, 1994a.

Davie, Grace. *Religion in Britain since 1945: Believing without Belonging.* Oxford: Blackwell, 1994b.

——. 'God and Caesar: religion in a rapidly changing Europe', in J. Bailey (ed.), *Social Europe,* 2nd edn. London: Longman, 1998: 231–54.

——. *Religion in Modern Europe: A Memory Mutates.* Oxford: Oxford University Press, 2000.

Davies, Christie. *Ethnic Humor around the World: A Comparative Analysis.* Bloomington, IN: Indiana University Press, 1990.

Davies, James C. 'Toward a theory of revolution'. *American Sociological Review,* Vol. 27, No. 1 (February 1962): 5–19.

Davies, Malcolm, Hazel Croall and Jane Tyrer. *Criminal Justice: An Introduction to the Criminal Justice System in England and Wales.* London: Longman, 1995.

Davies, Mark and Denise B. Kandel. 'Parental and peer influences on adolescents' educational plans: some further evidence'. *American Journal of Sociology,* Vol. 87, No. 2 (September 1981): 363–87.

Davis, Fred. 'Deviance disavowal: the management of strained interaction amongst the visibly handicapped'. *Social Problems,* Vol. 9 (1961): 120–32.

Davis, Kingsley. 'Extreme social isolation of a child'. *American Journal of Sociology,* Vol. 45, No. 4 (January 1940): 554–65.

——. 'Final note on a case of extreme isolation'. *American Journal of Sociology,* Vol. 52, No. 5 (March 1947): 432–7.

Davis, Kingsley and Wilbert Moore. 'Some principles of stratification'. *American Sociological Review,* Vol. 10, No. 2 (April 1945): 242–9.

Davis, Murray. *Smut.* Chicago: University of Chicago Press, 1983.

Dean, Malcolm. *Growing Older in the Twenty-First Century.* European Social Research Council, 2004. Also accessed at: www.shef.ac.uk/uni/projects/gap/Publications.htm.

Deem, Rosemary (ed.). *Schooling for Women's Work.* London: Routledge and Kegan Paul, 1980.

——. 'Governing schools in the 1990s'. *Sociology Review,* Vol. 6, No. 3 (1997): 28–31.

Deem, Rosemary, K. J. Brehony and S. Heath. *Active Citizenship and the Governing of Schools.* Buckingham: Open University Press, 1995.

Delacroix, Jacques and Charles C. Ragin. 'Structural blockage: a crossnational study of economic dependency, state efficacy and underdevelopment'. *American Journal of Sociology,* Vol. 86, No. 6 (May 1981): 1311–47.

Delphy, Christine and Diana Leonard. *Familiar Exploitation: A New Analysis of Marriage in Contemporary Western Societies.* Cambridge: Polity Press, 1992.

Demaine, Jack (ed.). *Sociology of Education Today.* London: Palgrave, 2001.

De Mente, Boye. *Japanese Etiquette and Ethics in Business,* 5th edn. Lincolnwood, IL: NTC Business Books, 1987.

Dennis, Norman and George Erdos. *Families without Fatherhood.* London: IEA Health and Welfare Unit, 1993.

Dennis, Norman, Fernando Henriques and Clifford Slaughter. *Coal is Our Life: An Analysis of a Yorkshire Mining Community.* London: Eyre & Spottiswoode, 1956.

Denzin, Norman K. *Images of Postmodern Society: Social Theory and Contemporary Cinema.* London: Sage, 1991.

——. *Symbolic Interactionism and Cultural Studies: The Politics of Interpretation.* Oxford: Basil Blackwell, 1992.

——. *The Cinematic Society.* London: Sage, 1995.

Denzin, Norman K. and Yvonna S. Lincoln (eds). *Handbook of Qualitative Research.* London: Sage, 1994.

Department of Education and Employment. *Excellence in Schools.* CM 3681. London: HMSO, July 1997.

Der Spiegel. 'Third World metropolises are becoming monsters; rural poverty drives millions to the slums'. *World Press Review* (October 1989).

De Solla Price, D. *Little Science, Big Science.* New York: Columbia University Press, 1963.

Devine, Fiona. *Affluent Workers Revisited.* Edinburgh: Edinburgh University Press, 1992.

——. *Class in Britain and America.* Edinburgh: Edinburgh University Press, 1996.

Devine, Fiona and Sue Heath. *Sociological Research Methods in Context.* London: Macmillan, 1999.

Devine, Fiona and Mary C. Waters. *Social Inequalities in Comparative Perspective.* Oxford: Blackwells, 2004.

DGAA Homelife. *100 at 100: An Interview Study with 100 Centenarians.* London: DGAA Homelife, 1 Dery Street, W8 5HY, 1997.

Dicken, Peter. *Global Shift: Transforming the World Economy,* 3rd edn. London: Sage, 1998 orig. New York: Harper & Row, 1986.

Dickens, Charles. *Oliver Twist.* 1886: 36; orig. 1837–39.

Dobson, Richard B. 'Mobility and stratification in the Soviet Union'. *Annual Review of Sociology,* Vol. 3. Palo Alto, CA: Annual Reviews, 1977: 297–329.

Dollard, John. *Caste and Class in a Southern Town.* New Haven, CT: Yale University Press, 1937 (reprinted in the Sociology of Class series, New York: Routledge, 1998).

Dollard, John, L. Doob, N. Miller, O. Mowrer and R. Sears. *Frustration and Aggression*. New Haven, CT: Yale University Press, 1939.

Domhoff, G. William. *Who Rules America Now? A View of the '80s*. Englewood Cliffs, NJ: Prentice-Hall, 1983.

Donovan, Virginia K. and Ronnie Littenberg. 'Psychology of women: feminist therapy', in Barbara Haber (ed.), *The Women's Annual 1981: The Year in Review*. Boston, MA: G. K. Hall, 1982: 211–35.

Douglas, J. W. B. *The Home and the School*. London: MacGibbon and Kee, 1964.

Douglass, Richard L. 'Domestic neglect and abuse of the elderly: implications for research and service'. *Family Relations*, Vol. 32 (July 1983): 395–402.

Dowd, Nancy E. *In Defense of Single-Parent Families*. New York: New York University Press, 1997.

Downes, David and Paul Rock. *Understanding Deviance*, 2nd edn. Oxford: Clarendon Press, 1988.

Downs, Anthony. *New Visions for Metropolitan America*. Washington, DC: Brookings Institute, 1994.

Doyal, Lesley. *The Political Economy of Health*. London: Pluto, 1979.

——. *What Makes Women Sick*. London: Macmillan, 1995.

Drake, Graham. *Issues in the New Europe*. London: Hodder & Stoughton, 1994.

Du Bois, W. E. B. *Dusk of Dawn*. New York: Harcourt, Brace & World, 1940.

——. *The Philadelphia Negro: A Social Study*. New York: Schocken Books, 1967; orig. 1899.

——. *The Souls of Black Folk*. New York: Penguin Books, 1982; orig. 1903.

Dubos, René. *Mirage of Health: Utopias, Progress and Biological Change*. New York: Harper & Row, 1970; orig. 1959.

——. *Man Adapting*. New Haven, CT: Yale University Press, 1980; orig. 1965.

Du Gay, Paul, Stuart Hall, L. Janes, H. MacKay and K. Negus (eds). *Doing Cultural Studies: The Story of the Sony Walkman*. Buckingham: Open University Press, 1997.

Duhl, Leonard J. 'The social context of health', in Arthur C. Hastings *et al.* (eds), *Health for the Whole Person: The Complete Guide to Holistic Medicine*. Boulder, CO: Westview Press, 1980: 39–48.

Duhring, Simon (ed.). *The Cultural Studies Reader*. London: Routledge, 1993.

Duncombe, Jean and Dennis Marsden. 'Love and intimacy: the gender division of emotion and "emotion work" '. *Sociology*, Vol. 27, No. 2 (1993): 221–41.

Dunlap, Riley E., George H. Gallup, Jr. and Alec M. Gallup. *The Health of the Planet Survey*. Princeton, NJ: The George H. Gallup International Institute, 1992.

Dunlap, Riley E. and Angela G. Mertig. 'The evolution of the US environmental movement from 1970 to 1990: an overview', in Riley E. Dunlap and Angela G. Mertig (eds), *American Evironmentalism: The US Environmental Movement, 1970–1990*. New York: Taylor & Francis, 1992: 1–10.

Dunn, Ashley. 'Ancient Chinese craft shifts building designs in the US'. *The New York Times* (22 September 1994): IA, B4.

Dunphy, Richard. *Sexual Politics: An Introduction*. Edinburgh: Edinburgh University Press, 2000.

Durkheim, Emile. *The Division of Labor in Society*. New York: Free Press, 1964a; orig. 1895.

——. *The Rules of Sociological Method*. New York: Free Press, 1964b; orig. 1893.

——. *The Elementary Forms of Religious Life*. New York: Free Press, 1965; orig. 1915.

——. *Suicide*. New York: Free Press, 1966; orig. 1897.

——. *Selected Writings*. Anthony Giddens, ed., Cambridge: Cambridge University Press, 1972; orig. 1918.

——. *Sociology and Philosophy*. New York: Free Press, 1974; orig. 1924.

Durning, Alan Thein. 'Supporting indigenous peoples', in Lester R. Brown *et al.* (eds), *State of the World 1993: A Worldwatch Institute Report on Progress Toward a Sustainable Society*. New York: W. W. Norton, 1993: 80–100.

Dworkin, Andrea. *Pornography: Men Possessing Women*. New York: Pedigree, 1981.

——. *Right Wing Women*, London: The Women's Press, 1983.

——. *Intercourse*. New York: Free Press, 1987.

E

Ebaugh, Helen Rose Fuchs. *Becoming an EX: The Process of Role Exit*. Chicago: University of Chicago Press, 1988.

——. *Women in the Vanishing Cloister: Organisational Decline in Catholic Religious Orders in the United States*. New Brunswick, NJ: Rutgers University Press, 1993.

Economist, The. 'Japan's missing children'. Vol. 333, No. 7889 (12 November 1994): 46.

——. *Pocket Europe in Figures*. London: Economist Books, 2000.

___. *The World in 2005*. London: Economist Books, 2005.

Eder, Klaus. *The New Politics of Class*. London: Sage, 1993.

Edgell, Steven. *Class*. London: Routledge, 1993.

Edwards, David V. *The American Political Experience*, 3rd edn. Englewood Cliffs, NJ: Prentice-Hall, 1985.

Edwards, Jeanette, *et al. Technologies of Procreation*, 2nd edn. London: Routledge, 1999.

Edwards, Richard. *Contested Terrain: The Transformation of the Workplace in the Twentieth Century*. New York: Basic Books, 1979.

Edye, David and Valerio Lintner (eds), *Contemporary Europe: Economics, Politics and Society*. Hemel Hempstead: Prentice Hall, 1996.

Ehrenreich, Barbara. *Nickel and Dimed: On (Not) Getting by in America*. New York: Henry Holt, 2001.

Ehrenreich, John. 'Introduction', in John Ehrenreich (ed.), *The Cultural Crisis of Modern Medicine*. New York: Monthly Review Press, 1978: 1–35.

Ehrlich, Paul R. *The Population Bomb*. New York: Ballantine Books, 1968.

Eichler, Margrit. *Nonsexist Research Methods: A Practical Guide*. Winchester, MA: Unwin Hyman, 1988.

Eisen, Arnold M. *The Chosen People in America: A Study of Jewish Religious Ideology*. Bloomington, IN: Indiana University Press, 1983.

Eisenstein, Zillah R. (ed.). *Capitalist Patriarchy and the Case for Socialist Feminism*. New York: Monthly Review Press, 1979.

——. *Global Obscenities: Patriarchy, Capitalism and the Lure of Cyberfantasy*. New York: New York University Press, 1998.

Ekman, Paul. 'Biological and cultural contributions to body and facial movements in the expression of emotions', in A. Rorty (ed.), *Explaining Emotions*. Berkeley, CA: University of California Press, 1980a: 73–101.

——. *Face of Man: Universal Expression in a New Guinea Village*. New York: Garland Press, 1980b.

——. *Telling Lies: Clues to Deceit in the Marketplace, Politics, and Marriage*. New York: W. W. Norton, 1985.

Ekman, Paul, Wallace V. Friesen and John Bear. 'The international language of gestures'. *Psychology Today* (May 1984): 64–9.

Elder, Glenn. *Children of the Great Depression*. Chicago: University of Chicago Press, 1974.

——. 'Perspectives on the life course', in Glenn Elder, *Life Course Dynamics*. Ithaca, NY: Cornell University Press, 1985.

Eldridge, John. *C. Wright Mills*. London: Tavistock/Routledge, 1983.

Elias, Norbert. *The Civilizing Process*. Edmund Jephcott, trans. Oxford: Blackwell, 1978a; orig. 1939.

——. *What is Sociology?* Stephen Mennell and Grace Morrissey, trans. London: Hutchinson, 1978b; orig. 1970.

Elkind, David. *The Hurried Child: Growing Up Too Fast Too Soon*. Reading, MA: Addison-Wesley, 1981.

Elliot, Faith Robertson. *Gender, Family and Society*. London: Macmillan, 1996.

Ellison, Christopher G. and Darren E. Sherkat. 'Conservative Protestantism and support for corporal punishment'. *American Sociological Review*, Vol. 58, No. 1 (February 1993): 131–44.

Elmer-DeWitt, Philip. 'First nation in cyberspace'. *Time*, Vol. 142, No. 24 (6 December 1993): 62–4.

——. 'The genetic revolution'. *Time*, Vol. 143, No. 3 (17 January 1994): 46–53.

Ember, Melvin and Carol R. Ember. 'The conditions favoring matrilocal versus patrilocal residence'. *American Anthropologist*, Vol. 73, No. 3 (June 1971): 571–94.

——. *Anthropology*, 6th edn. Englewood Cliffs, NJ: Prentice-Hall, 1991.

Emerson, Joan P. 'Behavior in private places: sustaining definitions of reality in gynecological examinations', in H. P. Dreitzel (ed.), *Recent Sociology*, Vol. 2. New York: Collier, 1970: 74–97.

Encyclopaedia Britannica Almanca. London: Encyclopaedia Britannica, 2004

Endicott, Karen. 'Fathering in an egalitarian society', in Barry S. Hewlett (ed.), *Father–Child Relations: Cultural and Bio-Social Contexts*. New York: Aldine, 1992: 281–96.

Engels, Friedrich. *The Origin of the Family*. Chicago: Charles H. Kerr & Company, 1902; orig. 1884.

Enloe, Cynthia. *Bananas, Beaches, and Bases: Making Feminist Sense of International Politics*. Berkeley, CA: University of California Press, 1990.

Entwistle, Joanne. *The Fashioned Body*. Cambridge: Polity Press, 2000.

Epstein, Steven. *Impure Science: AIDS, Activism and the Politics of Knowledge*. Berkeley, CA: University of California Press, 1998.

Erikson, Erik H. *Childhood and Society*. New York: W. W. Norton, 1963; orig. 1950.

——. *Identity and the Life Cycle*. New York: W. W. Norton, 1980.

Erikson, Kai T. *Wayward Puritans: A Study in the Sociology of Deviance*. New York: Wiley, 1966.

Erikson, Robert and John H. Goldthorpe. *The Constant Flux: A Study of Class Mobility in Industrial Societies*. Oxford: Clarendon Press, 1992.

Esping-Andersen, C. *The Three Worlds of Welfare Capitalism*. Cambridge: Polity Press, 1990.

Esposito, John L. *The Islamic Threat: Myth or Reality*. New York: Oxford University Press, 1992.

Etzioni, Amitai. *A Comparative Analysis of Complex Organization: On Power, Involvement and Their Correlates*, rev. and enlarged edn. New York: Free Press, 1975.

——. 'How to make marriage matter'. *Time*, Vol. 142, No. 10 (6 September 1993a): 76.

——. *The Spirit of Community: Rights, Responsibilities, and the Communitarian Agenda*. New York: Crown Publishers, 1993b.

Etzioni-Halevy, Eva. *Bureaucracy and Democracy: A Political Dilemma*, rev. edn. Boston, MA: Routledge & Kegan Paul, 1985.

European Roma Rights Center. 'Time of the Skinheads: denial and exclusion of Roma in Slovakia'. Country Report Series, No. 3 (January 1997).

Eurostat. *Europe in Figures*, 4th edn. Luxembourg: Office for Official Publications of the European Communities, 1995a.

——. *Women and Men in Europe: A Statistical Portrait*. Luxembourg: Office for Official Publications of the European Communities, 1995b.

——. *Eurostat Yearbook*. Luxembourg: Office for Official Publications of the European Communities, 2000.

——. *Eurostat Yearbook*. Luxembourg: Office for Official Publications of the European Communities, 2001 (also available on website http://europa.eu.int/comm/eurostat/ and CD-Rom).

Evans, M. D. R. 'Immigrant entrepreneurship: effects of ethnic market size and isolated labor pool'. *American Sociological Review*, Vol. 54, No. 6 (December 1989): 950–62.

Evans-Pritchard, E. E. *Kinship and Marriage amongst the Nuer*. Oxford: Clarendon Press, 1951, reprinted 1969.

Evans-Pritchard, John. *Living and Working in Europe*. London: Pitman Publishing, 1997.

F

Fagin, Leonard and Martin Little. *The Forsaken Families: The Effects of Unemployment on Family Life*. Harmondsworth: Penguin, 1984.

Falkenmark, Malin and Carl Widstrand. 'Population and water resources: a delicate balance'. *Population Bulletin*, Vol. 47, No. 3 (November 1992). Washington, DC: Population Reference Bureau.

Family Policy Studies Centre. *Families in Britain*. London: FPSC, 1995.

Fantini, Mario D. *Regaining Excellence in Education*. Columbus, OH: Merrill, 1986.

Farley, Reynolds and William H. Frey. 'Changes in the segregation of whites from blacks during the 1980s: small steps toward a more integrated society'. *American Sociological Review*, Vol. 59, No. 1 (February 1994): 23–45.

Farrell, Michael P. and Stanley D. Rosenberg. *Men at Midlife*. Boston, MA: Auburn House, 1981.

Fausto-Sterling, Anne. *Myths of Gender: Biological Theories about Women and Men*. New York: Basic Books, 1992.

——. *Sexing the Body*. New York: Basic Books, 1999.

Feagin, Joe. *The Urban Real Estate Game*. Englewood Cliffs, NJ: Prentice-Hall, 1983.

——. 'The continuing significance of race: antiblack discrimination in public places'. *American Sociological Review*, Vol. 56, No. 1 (February 1991): 101–16.

Featherman, David L. and Robert M. Hauser. *Opportunity and Change*. New York: Academic Press, 1978.

Featherstone, Mike (ed.). *Global Culture: Nationalism, Globalization and Modernity*. London: Sage, 1990.

——. *Consumer Culture and Postmodernism*. London: Sage, 1991.

Fennell, Graham, Chris Phillipson and Helen Evers. *The Sociology of Old Age*. Buckingham: Open University Press, 1988.

Fennell, Mary C. 'The effects of environmental characteristics on the structure of hospital clusters'. *Administrative Science Quarterly*, Vol. 29, No. 3 (September 1980): 489–510.

Ferguson, Tom. 'Medical self-care: self responsibility for health', in Arthur C. Hastings *et al.* (eds), *Health for the Whole Person: The Complete Guide to Holistic Medicine*. Boulder, CO: Westview Press, 1980: 87–109.

Finch, Janet. *Family Obligations and Social Change*. Cambridge: Polity Press, 1989.

Finch, Janet and Dulcie Groves (eds). *A Labour of Love*. London: Routledge, 1983.

Finch, Janet and Jennifer Mason. *Negotiating Family Responsibilities*. London: Routledge, 1993.

Fine, Michele and Adrian Ash. *Women with Disabilities*. Philadelphia, PA: Temple University Press, 1990.

Finkelstein, Neal W. and Ron Haskins. 'Kindergarten children prefer same-color peers'. *Child Development*, Vol. 54, No. 2 (April 1983): 52–8.

Finkler, Kaja. *Women in Pain: Gender and Morbidity in Mexico*. Philadelphia, PA: University of Pennsylvania Press, 1994.

Finn, Dan. *Training without Jobs: New Deals and Broken Promises: From Raising the School Leaving Age to the Youth Training Scheme*. London: Macmillan, 1987.

Firebaugh, Glenn. 'Growth effects of foreign and domestic investment'. *American Journal of Sociology*, Vol. 98, No. 1 (July 1992): 105–30.

Firebaugh, Glenn and Frank D. Beck. 'Does economic growth benefit the masses? Growth, dependence and welfare in the third world'. *American Sociological Review*, Vol. 59, No. 5 (October 1994): 631–53.

Fischer, Claude S. *The Urban Experience*, 2nd edn. San Diego, CA: Harcourt Brace Jovanovich, 1984.

Fischer, Claude S. *et al. Networks and Places: Social Relations in the Urban Setting*. New York: Free Press, 1977.

Fisher, Elizabeth. *Woman's Creation: Sexual Evolution and the Shaping of Society*. Garden City, NY: Anchor/Doubleday, 1979.

Fisher, Roger and William Ury. 'Getting to YES', in William M. Evan and Stephen Hilgartner (eds), *The Arms Race and Nuclear War*. Englewood Cliffs, NJ: Prentice-Hall, 1988: 261–8.

Fiske, Alan Paige. 'The cultural relativity of selfish individualism: anthropological evidence that humans are inherently sociable', in Margaret S. Clark (ed.), *Prosocial Behavior*. Newbury Park, CA: Sage, 1991: 176–214.

Fiske, John. *Television Culture*. London: Methuen, 1987.

——. 'Postmodernism and culture', in James Curran and Michael Gurevitch (eds), *Mass Media and Society*. London: Methuen, 1991.

Fitzpatrick, Mary Anne. *Between Husbands and Wives: Communication in Marriage*. Newbury Park, CA: Sage, 1988.

Flaherty, Michael G. 'A formal approach to the study of amusement in social interaction'. *Studies in Symbolic Interaction*, Vol. 5. New York: JAI Press, 1984: 71–82.

——. 'Two conceptions of the social situation: some implications of humor'. *The Sociological Quarterly*, Vol. 31, No. 1 (Spring 1990).

Flandrin, Jean-Louis. *Families in Former Times: Kinship, Household and Sexuality*. Richard Southern, trans. Cambridge: Cambridge University Press, 1979.

Flynn, Patricia. 'The disciplinary emergence of bioethics and bioethics committees: moral ordering and its legitimation'. *Sociological Focus*, Vol. 24, No. 2 (May 1991): 145–56.

Foer, Franklin. 'Soccer vs. McWorld'. *Foreign Policy* (January/February 2004): 32.

Foreman, Martin (ed.). *Aids and Men: Taking Risks or Responsibility?* London: Zed Books, 1999.

Fornas, Johan, Ulf Lindeberg and Oue Sernhede. *In Garageland: Rock, Youth and Modernity*. London: Routledge, 1995.

Foster, P. *Women and the Health Care Industry*. Buckingham: Open University Press, 1995.

Foucault, Michel. *Discipline and Punish: The Birth of the Prison*, Alan Sheridan trans. London: Allen Lane, 1977; orig. Paris: Editions Galliand, 1975.

——. *The History of Sexuality*, Vol. 1. London: Allen Lane, 1979 (orig. Paris: Editions Galliand, 1976).

Fox Keller, Evelyn. *Reflections on Gender and Science*. New Haven, CT: Yale University Press, 1985.

Frank, André Gunder. *On Capitalist Underdevelopment*. Bombay: Oxford University Press, 1975.

——. *Crisis: In the World Economy*. New York: Jameson & Meier, 1980.

——. *Reflections on the World Economic Crisis*. New York: Monthly Review Press, 1981.

Frank, Arthur. *The Wounded Storyteller: Body Illness and Ethics*. Chicago: University of Chicago Press, 1995.

Franklin, Sarah. *Embodied Progress*. London: Routledge, 1997.

Frayman, Harold. *Breadline Britain 1990s: The Findings of the Television Series*. London: London Weekend Television, 1991.

Frazier, E. Franklin. *Black Bourgeoisie: The Rise of a New Middle Class*. New York: Free Press, 1965.

——. *The Negro Church in America*. New York: Schocken, 1963.

Fredrickson, George M. *White Supremacy: A Comparative Study in American and South African History*. New York: Oxford University Press, 1981.

Free, Marvin D. 'Religious affiliation, religiosity and impulsive and intentional deviance'. *Sociological Focus*, Vol. 25, No. 1 (February 1992): 77–91.

Freedom House. *Freedom in the World*. New York: Freedom House, 2000.

Freire, Paulo. *Pedagogy of the Oppressed*. London: Sheed and Ward, 1972.

French, Marilyn. *Beyond Power: On Women, Men, and Morals*. New York: Summit Books, 1985.

Freud, Sigismund. *Civilisation and Its Discontents*. Harmondsworth: Penguin, 2004; orig. 1930.

Friedan, Betty. *The Feminine Mystique*. Harmondsworth: Penguin, 1963.

Friedan, Betty. *The Fountain of Age*. New York: Simon & Schuster, 1993.

Friedman, John. 'The world city hypothesis'. *Development and change*, Vol. 17: 69–83.

Friedman, Milton and Rose Friedman. *Free to Choose: A Personal Statement*. London: Secker and Warburg, 1980.

Friedrich, Otto. 'A proud capital's distress'. *Time*, Vol. 124, No. 6 (6 August 1984): 26–30, 33–5.

——. 'United no more'. *Time*, Vol. 129, No. 18 (4 May 1987): 28–37.

Frisby, David. *Georg Simmel*. London: Tavistock, 1984.

Frisby, David and Derek Sayer. *Society*. London: Routledge, 1986.

Fuchs, Victor R. 'Sex differences in economic well-being'. *Science*, Vol. 232 (25 April 1986): 459–64.

Fukuyama, Francis. *The End of History*. Washington, DC: Irving Kristol, 1989 (offprint from *The National Interest*, summer 1989 issue).

——. *Trust: The Social Virtues and the Creation of Prosperity*. London: Hamish Hamilton, 1995.

Fuller, Steve. *Science*. Minneapolis, MN: University of Minnesota Press, 1997.

——. 'Who's afraid of science studies?'. *Independent on Sunday* (28 June 1998).

Funken, Klaus and Penny Cooper (eds). *Old and New Poverty: The Challenge for Reform*. London: Rivers Oram Press, 1995.

Furlong, Andy and Fred Cartmeal. *Young People and Social Change: Individualism and Risk in the Age of High Modernity*. Buckingham: Open University Press, 1997.

Furstenberg, Frank F., Jr. 'The new extended family: the experience of parents and children after remarriage'. Paper presented to the Changing Family Conference XIII: The Blended Family. University of Iowa, 1984.

Furstenberg, Frank F., Jr. and Andrew Cherlin. *Divided Families: What Happens to Children When Parents Part*. Cambridge, MA: Harvard University Press, 1991.

G

Gagliani, Giorgio. 'How many working classes?' *American Journal of Sociology*, Vol. 87, No. 2 (September 1981): 259–85.

Gagnon, J. and W. Simon. *Sexual Conduct*. Chicago: Aldine, 1973.

Galanter, Marc. *Cults: Faith, Healing and Coercion*, 2nd edn. Oxford: Oxford University Press, 1999.

Gallie, D., C. Marsh and C. Vogler. *Social Change and the Experience of Unemployment*. Oxford: Oxford University Press, 1993.

Gallup, George, Jr. *Religion in America*. Princeton, NJ: Princeton Religion Research Center, 1982.

Galster, George. 'Black suburbanization: has it changed the relative location of races?' *Urban Affairs Quarterly*, Vol. 26, No. 4 (June 1991): 621–8.

Gamoran, Adam. 'The variable effects of high-school tracking'. *American Sociological Review*, Vol. 57, No. 6 (December 1992): 812–28.

Gannon, Martin J. *Understanding Global Cultures: Metaphysical Journeys through 23 Nations*. London: Sage, 2nd edn, 2001.

Gans, Herbert J. *People and Plans: Essays on Urban Problems and Solutions*. New York: Basic Books, 1968.

——. *Popular Culture and High Culture*. New York: Basic Books, 1974.

——. *The Urban Villagers: Group and Class in the Life of Italian-Americans*. New York: Free Press, 1982; orig. 1962.

Garfinkel, Harold. 'Conditions of successful degradation ceremonies'. *American Journal of Sociology*, Vol. 61, No. 2 (March 1956): 420–4.

——. *Studies in Ethnomethodology*. Cambridge: Polity Press, 1967.

Garland, David. *Punishment and Modern Society*. Oxford: Clarendon, 1990.

Garner, Robert. *Environmental Politics*. London: Prentice Hall, 1996; 2nd edn, 2001.

Garrity, Patrick J. and Steven A. Maaranen (eds). *Nuclear Weapons in the Changing World: Perspectives from Europe, Asia, and North America*. New York: Plenum Press, 1992.

Gauntlett, David (ed.). *web.studies*. London: Arnold, 2000.

Gay, Peter. *The Enlightment: An Interpretation*. London: Weidenfeld and Nicolson, 1970.

Geertz, Clifford. *The Interpretation of Cultures*. New York: Basic Books, 1973; London: Hutchinson, 1995.

Geertz, Hildred and Clifford Geertz. *Kinship in Bali*. Chicago: University of Chicago Press, 1975.

Gelder, Ken and Sarah Thornton (eds). *The Subcultures Reader*. London: Routledge, 1997.

Gelman, David. 'Who's taking care of our parents?' *Newsweek* (6 May 1985): 61–4, 67–8.

George, Susan. *How the Other Half Dies: The Real Reasons for World Hunger*. Totowa, NJ: Rowman & Allanheld, 1977.

Geraghty, Christine. *Women and Soap Operas*. Cambridge: Polity Press, 1991.

Gergen, David. 'King of the world'. *US News and World Report*, Vol. 132, No. 6 (25 February–4 March 2002): 84.

Gergen, Kenneth J. *The Saturated Self: Dilemmas of Identity in Contemporary Life*. New York: Basic Books, 1991.

Gerlach, Michael L. *The Social Organization of Japanese Business*. Berkeley, CA: University of California Press, 1992.

Gershuny, Jonathan. 'Time for the family'. *Prospect* (January 1997).

Gerstel, Naomi. 'Divorce and stigma'. *Social Problems*, Vol. 43, No. 2 (April 1987): 172–86.

Gerth, H. H. and C. Wright Mills (eds). *From Max Weber: Essays in Sociology*. New York: Oxford University Press, 1946; London: Routledge and Kegan Paul, 1948

Gerzina, G. *Black England*. London: Routledge, 1995.

Geschwender, James A. *Racial Stratification in America*. Dubuque, IA: Wm. C. Brown, 1978.

Gibbins, John and Bo Reimer. *The Politics of Postmodernity*. London: Sage, 1999.

Gibbons, Don C. and Marvin D. Krohn. *Delinquent Behavior*, 4th edn. Englewood Cliffs, NJ: Prentice-Hall, 1986.

Gibbs, Nancy. 'How much should we teach our children about sex?' *Time*, Vol. 141, No. 21 (24 May 1993): 60–6.

Giddens, Anthony. *The Constitution of Society*. Cambridge: Polity Press, 1984.

——. *Sociology: A Brief but Critical Introduction*. New York: Harcourt Brace Jovanovich, 1982; 2nd edn, London: Macmillan, 1986.

——. *The Consequences of Modernity*. Oxford: Polity Press, 1990.

——. *Self Identity and Late Modernity*. Cambridge: Polity Press, 1991.

——. *The Transformation of Intimacy*. Cambridge: Polity Press, 1992.

——. *Beyond Left and Right: The Future of Radical Politics*. Cambridge: Polity Press, 1994.

——. *The Third Way: The Renewal of Social Democracy*. Cambridge: Polity Press, 1998.

——. *Runaway World: How Globalization is Reshaping Our Lives*. London: Profile Books, 1999.

——. (ed.). *The Global Third Way Debate*. Cambridge: Polity Press, 2001.

——. (ed). *The Progressive Manifesto: New Ideas from the Centre-Left*. Cambridge: Polity Press, 2004.

Giddens, Anthony and Jonathan Turner (eds). *Social Theory Today*. Cambridge: Polity Press, 1987.

Giele, Janet Z. 'Gender and sex roles', in Neil J. Smelser (ed.), *Handbook of Sociology*. Newbury Park, CA: Sage, 1988: 291–323.

Gilborn, David. *Racism and Anti-Racism in Real Schools*. Buckingham: Open University Press, 1995.

Gilligan, Carol. *In a Different Voice: Psychological Theory and Women's Development*. Cambridge, MA: Harvard University Press, 1982.

——. *Making Connections: The Relational Worlds of Adolescent Girls at Emma Willard School*. Cambridge, MA: Harvard University Press, 1990.

Gilroy, Paul. *There Ain't No Black in the Union Jack*. London: Hutchinson, 1987.

——. *The Black Atlantic: Modernity and Double Consciousness*. London: Verso, 1994.

Ginsburg, Faye and Rayna Rapp. *Conceiving the New World Order*. Berkeley, CA: University of California Press, 1995.

Ginsburg Faye, Lila Abu-Lughood and Brian Larkin (eds). *Media Worlds: Anthropology on New Terrain*. Berkeley, CA: University of California, 2002.

Giovannini, Maureen. 'Female anthropologist and male informant: gender conflict in a sicilian town', in John J. Macionis and Nijole V. Benokraitis (eds), *Seeing Ourselves: Classic, Contemporary and Cross-Cultural Readings in Sociology*, 2nd edn. Englewood Cliffs, NJ: Prentice-Hall, 1992: 27–32.

Giroux, Henry. *Border Crossings: Cultural Workers and the Politics of Education*. London: Routledge, 1992.

Gittins, Diana. *The Family in Question: Changing Households and Familiar Ideologies*. Basingstoke: Macmillan, 1985; 2nd edn, 1993.

Glaab, Charles N. *The American City: A Documentary History*. Homewood, IL: Dorsey Press, 1963.

Glaser, Barney and Anselm Strauss. *Awareness of Dying*. London: Weidenfeld and Nicolson, 1967.

Glasgow Media Group. *Really Bad News*. London: Writers and Readers, 1982.

Glasner, Angela. 'Gender and Europe: cultural and structural impediments to change', in Joe Banks (ed.), *Social Europe*. London: Longman, 1992.

Glass, Ruth. *Newcomers*. London: Allen & Unwin, 1960.

Glazer, Nathan and Daniel P. Moynihan. *Beyond the Melting Pot*, 2nd edn. Cambridge, MA: MIT Press, 1970.

Glendenning, Caroline and Jane Millar (eds). *Women and Poverty in Britain: The 1990s*. London: Harvester Wheatsheaf, 1987; 2nd edn, 1992.

Glendenning, F. 'What is elder abuse and neglect?', in P. Decalmer and F. Glendenning (eds), *The Mistreatment of Elderly People*. London: Sage, 1993.

Glendon, Mary Ann. *Rights Talk: The Impoverishment of Political Discourse*. New York: Free Press, 1991.

Glenn, Norval D. and Beth Ann Shelton. 'Regional differences in divorce in the United States'. *Journal of Marriage and the Family*, Vol. 47, No. 3 (August 1985): 641–52.

Glock, Charles Y. 'The religious revival in America', in Jane Zahn (ed.), *Religion and the Face of America*. Berkeley, CA: University of California Press, 1959: 25–42.

——. 'On the study of religious commitment'. *Religious Education*, Vol. 62, No. 4 (1962): 98–110.

Gluck, Peter R. and Richard J. Meister. *Cities in Transition*. New York: New Viewpoints, 1979.

Glueck, Sheldon and Eleanor Glueck. *Unraveling Juvenile Delinquency*. New York: Commonwealth Fund, 1950.

Gobineau, J. A. Comte de. *Essay on the Inequality of the Human Races*. New York: Putnam, 1915; orig. 1853.

Goetting, Ann. 'Divorce outcome research'. *Journal of Family Issues*, Vol. 2, No. 3 (September 1981): 350–78.

Goffman, Erving. *The Presentation of Self in Everyday Life*. Garden City, NY: Anchor Books, 1959.

——. *Asylums: Essays on the Social Situation of Mental Patients and Other Inmates*. Garden City, NY: Anchor Books, 1961.

——. *Stigma: Notes on the Management of Spoiled Identity*. Englewood Cliffs, NJ: Prentice-Hall, 1963.

——. *Interactional Ritual: Essays on Face-to-Face Behavior*. Garden City, NY: Anchor Books, 1967.

——. 'The Interaction Order'. *American Sociological Review*, Vol. 48 (1982): 1–17.

Goldberg, Steven. *The Inevitability of Patriarchy*. New York: William Morrow, 1974.

——. *Why Men Rule: A Theory of Male Dominance*. Chicago: Open Court, 1993.

Goldfarb, William. 'Groundwater: the buried life', in F. Herbert Bormann and Stephen R. Kellert (eds), *Ecology, Economics and Ethics: The Broken Circle*. New Haven, CT: Yale University Press, 1991: 123–35.

Golding, Peter and Philip Elliott. *Making the News*. London: Longman, 1979.

Goldman, Robert and Stephen Papson. *Nike Culture*. London: Sage, 1998.

Goldsby, Richard A. *Race and Races*, 2nd edn. New York: Macmillan, 1977.

Goldsmith, H. H. 'Genetic influences on personality from infancy'. *Child Development*, Vol. 54, No. 2 (April 1983): 331–5.

Goldthorpe, John H. (in collaboration with Catriona Llewellyn and Clive Payne). *Social Mobility and Class Structure in Modern Britain*. Oxford: Clarendon Press, 1980.

——. 'On the service class, its formation and future', in A. Giddens and G. Mackenzie (eds), *Social Class and the Division of Labour*. Cambridge: Cambridge University Press, 1982.

——. *Family Life in Western Societies: A Historical Sociology of Family Relationships in Britain and North America*. Cambridge: Cambridge University Press, 1987.

Goldthorpe, John H., David Lockwood, Frank Bechhofer and Jennifer Platt. *The Affluent Worker*. Cambridge: Cambridge University Press, 1968.

Goode, William J. *World Changes in Divorce Patterns*. New Haven, CT: Yale University Press, 1993.

Goodman, Alissa, Paul Johnson and Steven Webb. *Inequality in the UK*. Oxford: Oxford University Press, 1997.

Gordon, David and Peter Townsend (eds). *Breadline Europe: The Measurement of Poverty*. Bristol: Policy Press, 2000.

Gordon, James S. 'The paradigm of holistic medicine', in Arthur C. Hastings *et al.* (eds), *Health for the Whole Person: The Complete Guide to Holistic Medicine*. Boulder, CO: Westview Press, 1980: 3–27.

Goring, Charles Buckman. *The English Convict: A Statistical Study*. Montclair, NJ: Patterson Smith, 1972; orig. 1913.

Gorman, Christine. 'Mexico City's menacing air'. *Time*, Vol. 137, No. 13 (1 April 1991): 61.

Gorssberg, Lawrence, Cary Nelson and Paula Treichler. *Cultural Studies*. London: Routledge, 1992.

Gortz, André. 'Immigrant labour'. *New Left Review* (1961): 28–30.

——. *Farewell to the Working Class: An Essay on Post-industrial Socialism*. London: Pluto Press, 1982; orig. French edition, 1980.

Gottdiener, M. 'Field research and the video tape'. *Sociological Inquiry*, Vol. 49, No. 4 (1980): 59–66.

Gottfredson, Michael R. and Travis Hirschi. 'National crime control policies'. *Society*, Vol. 32, No. 2 (January–February 1995): 30–6.

Gottmann, Jean. *Megalopolis*. New York: Twentieth Century Fund, 1961.

Gould, Stephen J. 'Evolution as fact and theory'. *Discover* (May 1981): 35–7.

Gould, Stephen. J. *Life's Grandeur*, London: Cape, 1996.

Gouldner, Alvin. *Enter Plato*. New York: Free Press, 1965.

——. 'The sociologist as partisan: sociology and the welfare state', in Larry T. Reynolds and Janice M. Reynolds (eds), *The Sociology of Sociology*. New York: Avon Books, 1970a: 218–55.

——. *The Coming Crisis of Western Sociology*. New York: Avon Books, 1970b.

Graham, Hilary. 'The concept of caring in feminist research: the case of domestic service'. *Sociology*, Vol. 25 (1991): 61–78.

——. *Hardship and Health in Women's Lives*. Hemel Hempstead: Harvester Wheatsheaf, 1993.

Gramsci, A. *Selections for the Prison Notebooks*. London: New Left Books, 1971.

Granovetter, Mark. 'The strength of weak ties'. *American Journal of Sociology*, Vol. 78, No. 6 (May 1973): 1360–80.

Grant, Don Sherman II, and Michael Wallace. 'Why do strikes turn violent?' *American Journal of Sociology*, Vol. 96, No. 5 (March 1991): 1117–50.

Grant, Karen R. 'The inverse care law in the context of universal free health insurance in Canada: toward meeting health needs through public policy'. *Sociological Focus*, Vol. 17, No. 2 (April 1984): 137–55.

Gray, Chris Hables (ed.). *The Cyborg Handbook*. London: Routledge, 1995.

Gray, Paul. 'Whose America?' *Time*, Vol. 137, No. 27 (8 July 1991): 12–17.

Gray, Ann. *Research Practice for Cultural Studies*. London: Sage, 2003.

Green, Andy. *Education and State Formation: The Rise of Education Systems in England, France and the USA*, rev. edn. London: Macmillan, 1992.

Green, John C. 'Pat Robertson and the latest crusade: resources and the 1988 presidential campaign'. *Social Sciences Quarterly*, Vol. 74, No. 1 (March 1993): 156–68.

Greenhouse, Linda. 'Justices uphold stiffer sentences for hate crimes'. *New York Times* (12 June 1993): 1, 8.

Gregory, Paul R. and Robert C. Stuart. *Comparative Economic Systems*, 2nd edn. Boston, MA: Houghton Mifflin, 1985.

Griffin, Christine. *Typical Girls*. London: Routledge, 1985.

Grint, Keith. *The Sociology of Work: An Introduction*. Cambridge: Polity Press, 1991; 2nd edn, 1998.

Gruenberg, Barry. 'The happy worker: an analysis of educational and occupational differences in determinants of job satisfaction'. *American Journal of Sociology*, Vol. 86, No. 2 (September 1980): 247–71.

Gubbay, Jon, Chris Middleton and Chet Ballard. *The Student's Companion to Sociology*. Oxford: Blackwell, 1997.

Gubrium, Jaber F. *Speaking of Life: Horizons of Meaning for Nursing Home Residents*. Hawthorne, NY: Aldine de Gruyter, 1993.

Gwartney-Gibbs, Patricia A., Jean Stockard and Susanne Bohmer. 'Learning courtship agression: the influence of parents, peers and personal experiences'. *Family Relations*, Vol. 36, No. 3 (July 1987): 276–82.

H

Habermas, Jürgen. *Towards a Rational Society: Student Protest, Science, and Politics*. Jeremy J. Shapiro, trans. Boston, MA: Beacon Press, 1970; latest edns 1989, paperback 1992; orig. 1962.

Hacker, Helen Mayer. 'Women as a minority group'. *Social Forces*, Vol. 30 (October 1951): 60–9.

——. 'Women as a minority group: 20 years later', in Florence Denmark (ed.), *Who Discriminates Against Women?* Beverly Hills, CA: Sage, 1974: 124–34.

Hackman, J. R. 'The design of work teams', in J. Lorch (ed.), *Handbook of Organizational Behavior*. Englewood Cliffs, NJ: Prentice-Hall, 1988: 315–42.

Hadden, Jeffrey K. and Charles E. Swain. *Prime Time Preachers: The Rising Power of Televangelism*. Reading, MA: Addison-Wesley, 1981.

Hafner, Katie. 'Making sense of the Internet'. *Newsweek* (24 October 1994): 46–8.

Haig, Robin Andrew. *The Anatomy of Humor: Biopsychosocial and Therapeutic Perspectives*. Springfield, IL: Charles C. Thomas, 1988.

Hakken, David and Barbara Andrews. *Computing Myths, Class Realities: An Ethnography of Technology and Working People in Sheffield, England*. Boulder, CO: Westview Press, 1993.

Hall, John H. *Gone from the Promised Land: Jonestown in American Cultural History*. New Brunswick, NJ: Transaction, 1987.

Hall, John R. and Mary Jo Neitz. *Culture: Sociological Perspectives*. Englewood Cliffs, NJ: Prentice-Hall, 1993.

Hall, Stuart. *Policing the Crisis*. London: Macmillan, 1978.

——. 'Encoding and decoding', in Stuart Hall *et al.* (eds), *Culture, Media, Language*. London: Hutchinson, 1980.

——. 'Our mongrel selves'. *New Statesman and Society* (19 June 1992a).

——. 'The question of cultural identity', in Stuart Hall, David Held and Tony McGrew (eds), *Modernity and Its Futures*. Cambridge: Polity Press in association with the Open University, 1992b.

Hall, Stuart, David Held and Tony McGrew (eds). *Modernity and Its Futures*. Cambridge: Polity Press in association with the Open University, 1992.

Hall, Stuart and Martin Jacques. *New Times*. London: Lawrence and Wishart, 1989.

Halliday, Fred. *The World at 2000*. London: Palgrave, 2001.

Hallinan, Maureen T. and Richard A. Williams. 'Interracial friendship choices in secondary schools'. *American Sociological Review*, Vol. 54, No. 1 (February 1989): 67–78.

Halsey, A. H. *Change in British Society*. Oxford: Oxford University Press, 1986.

Halsey, A. H., Jean Floud and C. Arnold Anderson (eds). *Education, Economy, and Society: A Reader in the Sociology of Education*. New York, Free Press; London: Collier-Macmillan, 1961.

Halsey, A. H., Hugh Lauder, Phillip Brown and Amy Stuart Wells. *Education: Culture, Economy and Society*. Oxford: Oxford University Press, 1997.

Halsey, A. H. with Josephine Webb (eds). *Twentieth-Century British Social Trends*. London: Macmillan, 2000.

Halweil, Brian and Lisa Mastney (eds). *The State of the World 2004: The Consumer Society*. London: W. W. Norton & Co, 2004.

Hamblin, Dora Jane. *The First Cities*. New York: Time-Life Books, 1973.

Hamel, Ruth. 'Raging against aging'. *American Demographics*, Vol. 12, No. 3 (March 1990): 42–5.

Hamelink, Cees. *The Ethics of Cyberspace*. London: Sage, 2000.

Hamilton, George. *Religion in the Medieval West*. London: Edward Arnold, 1996.

Hammersley, Martin and Paul Atkinson. *Ethnography: Principles in Practice*, 2nd edn. London: Routledge, 1995.

Hammond, Philip. *The Sacred in a Secular Age*. Berkeley, CA: University of California Press, 1985.

Hamrick, Michael H., David J. Anspaugh and Gene Ezell. *Health*. Columbus, OH: Merrill, 1986.

Hancock, M. Donald. *Politics in Western Europe: An Introduction to the Politics of the United Kingdom, France, Germany, Italy, Sweden, and the European Community*. Basingstoke: Macmillan, 1993.

Hannerz, Ulf. 'Cosmopolitans and locals in world culture', in Mike Featherstone (ed.), *Global Culture: Nationalism, Globalisation, and Modernity*. London: Sage, 1990.

Haraway, Donna. *Simians, Cyborgs and Women: The Reinvention of Nature*. London: Free Association, 1991.

——. *Primate Visions: Gender, Race and Nature in the World of Modern Science*. London: Verso, 1992.

——. '"Cyborgs and Symbiants": living together in the New World Order', in C. G. Hay (ed.), *The Cyborg Handbook*. London: Routledge, 1995: xi–1.

Harding, Sandra. *Whose Science? Whose Knowledge? Thinking from Women's Lives* Milton Keynes: Open University Press, 1991; 2nd edn, 1999.

Hare, Paul A., Edgar F. Borgatta and Robert F. Bales. *Small Groups: Studies in Social Interaction*, rev. edn. New York: Alfred A. Knopf, 1965.

Hareven, Tamara K. 'The life course and aging in historical perspective', in Tamara K. Hareven and Kathleen J. Adams (eds), *Aging and Life Course Transitions: An Interdisciplinary Perspective*. New York: Guilford Press, 1982: 1–26.

Hargreaves, David H. *Interpersonal Relations and Education*. London and Boston, MA: Routledge and Kegan Paul, 1975.

Harlan, William H. 'Social status of the aged in three Indian villages', in Bernice L. Neugarten (ed.), *Middle Age and Aging: A Reader in Social Psychology*. Chicago: University of Chicago Press, 1968: 469–75.

Harlow, Harry F. and Margaret Kuenne Harlow. 'Social deprivation in monkeys'. *Scientific American*, Vol. 207 (November 1962): 137–46.

Harper, Charles L. *Environment and Society: Social Perspectives on Environmental Issues and Problems*. Englewood Cliffs, NJ: Prentice-Hall, 1995.

Harris, Chauncey D. and Edward L. Ullman. 'The nature of cities'. *The Annals*, Vol. 242 (November 1945): 7–17.

Harris, Marvin. *Cultural Anthropology*, 2nd edn. New York: Harper & Row, 1987.

Harrison, Lawrence. 'Promoting cultural change', in L.E. Harrison and S.P. Huntingdon (eds), *Culture Matters*. New York: Basic Books, 296–308.

Harrison, Lawrence E. and Samuel P. Huntington. *Culture Matters: How Values Shape Human Progress*. New York: Basic Books, 2000.

Harrison, Paul. *Inside the Third World: The Anatomy of Poverty*, 2nd edn. New York: Penguin Books, 1984; 3rd edn, 1993.

Harrison, Paul and Fred Pearce. *AAAS Atlas of Population and Environment*. Berkeley: University of California Press, for the American Association for the Advancement of Science, 2000.

Hart, Nicky. *The Sociology of Health and Medicine*. Ormskirk, Lancashire: Causeway Press, 1985.

Hartmann, Betsy and James Boyce. *Needless Hunger: Voices from a Bangladesh Village*. San Francisco: Institute for Food and Development Policy, 1982.

Harvey, David. *The Condition of Postmodernity*. Oxford: Blackwell, 1989.

——. 'Between time and space: reflections on the geographical imagination'. *Annals, Association of American Geographers*, Vol. 80 (1990): 418–34.

Haskey, J. 'Estimated numbers of one-parent families and their prevalence in Great Britain in 1991'. *Population Trends*. London: HMSO, 1992.

Havighurst, Robert J., Bernice L. Neugarten and Sheldon S. Tobin. 'Disengagement and patterns of aging', in Bernice L. Neugarten (ed.), *Middle Age and Aging: A Reader in Social Psychology*. Chicago: University of Chicago Press, 1968: 161–72.

Hawkes, Gail. *A Sociology of Sex and Sexuality*. Buckingham: Open University Press, 1996.

Haxekamp, Jan Laurens and Keith Popple (eds). *Racism in Europe: A Challenge for Youth Policy and Youth Work*. London: UCL Press, 1997.

Hay, Chris Gable (ed.). *The Cyborg Handbook*. London: Routledge, 1995.

Hay, D. *Europe: The Emergence of an Idea*, 2nd edn. Edinburgh: Edinburgh University Press, 1968.

Hayles, N. Katherine. 'The life cycle of cyborgs', in C. G. Hay (ed.), *The Cyborg Handbook*. London: Routledge, 1995: 321–38.

Hazlett, J. *My Generation: Collective Autobiography and Identity Politics*. Madison, WI: University of Wisconsin Press, 1998.

Health Insurance Association of America. *Source Book of Health Insurance Data*. Washington, DC: The Association, 1991.

Heath, Julia A. and W. David Bourne. 'Husbands and housework: parity or parody?' *Social Science Quarterly*, Vol. 76, No. 1 (March 1995): 195–202.

Heelas, Paul. *The New Age Movement*. Oxford, Blackwell, 1996.

Heider, K. G. *Ethnographic Film*. Austin, TX: University of Texas Press, 1976.

Heilbroner, Robert L. *The Making of Economic Society*, 7th edn. Englewood Cliffs, NJ: Prentice-Hall, 1985.

Held, David *et al*. *Global Transformations*. Cambridge: Polity Press, 1999.

Helgesen, Sally. *The Female Advantage: Women's Ways of Leadership*. New York: Doubleday, 1990.

Helmuth, John W. 'World hunger amidst plenty'. *USA Today*, Vol. 117, No. 2526 (March 1989): 48–50.

Hendry, Joy. *Wrapping Culture: Politeness, Presentation and Power in Japan and Other Societies*. Oxford: Clarendon, 1993.

Henley, Nancy, Mykol Hamilton and Barrie Thorne. 'Womanspeak and Manspeak: sex differences in communication, verbal and nonverbal', in John J. Macionis and Nijole V. Benokraitis (eds), *Seeing Ourselves: Classic, Contemporary and Cross-Cultural Readings in Sociology*, 2nd edn. Englewood Cliffs, NJ: Prentice-Hall, 1992: 10–15.

Henry, William A., III. 'Gay parents: under fire and on the rise'. *Time*, Vol. 142, No. 12 (20 September 1993): 66–71.

——. *Guardians of the Flutes: Idioms of Masculinity*. London: McGraw-Hill, 1981.

Herdt, Gilbert (ed.). *Gay and Lesbian Youth*. London: Haworth Press, 1989.

Herek, Gregory M. and Kevin T. Berrill. *Hate Crimes: Confronting Violence against Lesbians and Gay Men*. Newbury Park, CA: Sage, 1992.

Heritage, John. 'Ethnomethodology', in Anthony Giddens and Jonathan Turner (eds), *Social Theory Today*. Oxford: Polity Press, 1987: 224–72.

Herman, Edward S. *Corporate Control, Corporate Power: A Twentieth Century Fund Study*. New York: Cambridge University Press, 1981.

Herman, Edward S. and Robert W. McChesney. *The Global Media*. London: Continuum, 1997.

Herrnstein, Richard J. *IQ and the Meritocracy*. Boston: Little, Brown & Co., 1973.

Herrnstein, Richard J. and Charles Murray. *The Bell Curve: Intelligence and Class Structure in American Life*. New York: Free Press, 1994.

Herrstrom, Staffan. 'Sweden: pro-choice on child care'. *New Perspectives Quarterly*, Vol. 7, No. 1 (Winter 1990): 27–8.

Hersch, Joni and Shelly White-Means. 'Employer-sponsored health and pension benefits and the gender/race wage gap'. *Social Science Quarterly*, Vol. 74, No. 4 (December 1993): 850–66.

Hervieu-Leger, Danièle. *Religion as a Chain of Memory*. Oxford: Polity Press, 2000.

Hess, David J. *Science Studies: An Advanced Introduction*. London: New York University Press, 1997.

Hewitt, John P. *Self and Society*, 8th edn. London: Allyn and Bacon, 1999.

Hewlett, Barry S. 'Husband–wife reciprocity and the father–infant relationship among Aka pygmies', in Barry S. Hewlett (ed.), *Father–Child Relations: Cultural and Bio-Social Contexts*. New York: Aldine, 1992: 153–76.

Hewlett, Sylvia Ann. 'The feminization of the work force'. *New Perspectives Quarterly*, Vol. 7, No. 1 (Winter 1990): 13–15.

Hewson, Claire, Peter Yule, Dianna Laujrent and Carl Vogel. *Internet Research Methods*. London: Sage, 2003.

Hill, Michael. *Understanding Social Policy*, 5th edn. Oxford: Blackwell, 1997.

Hiroshi, Mannari. *The Japanese Business Leaders*. Tokyo: University of Tokyo Press, 1974.

Hirschi, Travis. *Causes of Delinquency*. Berkeley, CA: University of California Press, 1969.

Hirst, Paul and G. Thompson. *Globalization in Question: The International Economy and the Possibilities of Governance*. Cambridge: Polity Press, 1996.

Hobsbawm, Eric. *The Age of Revolution*. London: Weidenfeld and Nicolson, 1962.

——. *The Age of Capital*. London: Weidenfeld and Nicolson, 1975.

——. *The Age of Empire*. London: Weidenfeld and Nicolson, 1987.

——. *Age of Extremes: The Short Twentieth Century, 1914–1991*. London: Michael Joseph, 1994.

Hobson, Dominic. *The National Wealth: Who Gets What in Britain*. London: HarperCollins, 1999.

Hochschild, Arlie. *The Managed Heart*. Berkeley, CA: University of California Press, 1983.

——. *The Second Shift: Working Parents and the Revolution at Home*. London: Judy Piatkus, 1989.

Hodge, Robert W., Donald J. Treiman and Peter H. Rossi. 'A comparative study of occupational prestige', in Reinhard Bendix and Seymour Martin Lipset (eds), *Class, Status and Power: Social Stratification in Comparative Perspective*, 2nd edn. New York: Free Press, 1966: 309–21.

Hodkinson, Paul. *Goth: Identity, Style and Subculture*. Oxford: Berg, 2002.

Hoggart, R. *The Uses of Literacy*. Harmondsworth: Penguin, 1957.

Hohenberg, Paul and Lynne Hollen Lees. *The Making of Urban Europe 1000–1950*. Cambridge, MA: Harvard University Press, 1985.

Holland, Janet, Caroline Ramazanoglu, Sue Sharpe and Rachel Thomson. *The Male in the Head: Young People, Heterosexuality and Power*. London: Tufnell Press, 1998.

Holm, Jean. *The Study of Religions*. New York: Seabury Press, 1977.

Holmes, C. *Anti-Semitism in British Society*. London: Arnold, 1979.

Holmes, Malcolm D., Harmon M. Hosch, Howard C. Daudistel, Dolores Perez and Joseph B. Graves. 'Judges, ethnicity and minority sentencing: evidence among Hispanics'. *Social Science Quarterly*, Vol. 74, No. 3 (September 1993): 496–506.

Holmstrom, David. 'Abuse of elderly, even by adult children, gets more attention and official concern'. *Christian Science Monitor* (28 July 1994): 1.

Homans, George C. *The Human Group*. New Brunswick, NJ: Transaction, 1992; orig. 1950.

Hostetler, John A. *Amish Society*, 3rd edn. Baltimore, MD: Johns Hopkins University Press, 1980.

Hout, Mike, Clem Brooks and Jeff Manza. 'The persistence of classes in post-industrial societies'. *International Sociology*, Vol. 8, No. 3 (September 1993): 259–77.

Howard, M. *et al. Poverty: The Facts*, 4th edn. London: Child Poverty Action Group, 2001.

Howarth, David and Aleta J. Norval (eds). *South Africa in Transition*. London: Palgrave, 1998.

Hoyt, Homer. *The Structure and Growth of Residential Neighborhoods in American Cities*. Washington, DC: Federal Housing Administration, 1939.

Humphrey, Derek. *Final Exit: The Practicalities of Self-Deliverance and Assisted Suicide for the Dying*. Eugene, OR: The Hemlock Society, 1991.

Hunter, Floyd. *Community Power Structure*. Garden City, NY: Doubleday, 1963; orig. 1953.

Hunter, James Davison. *American Evangelicalism: Conservative Religion and the Quandary of Modernity*. New Brunswick, NJ: Rutgers University Press, 1983.

——. 'Conservative Protestantism', in Philip E. Hammond (ed.), *The Sacred in a Secular Age*. Berkeley, CA: University of California Press, 1985: 50–66.

——. *Evangelicalism: The Coming Generation*. Chicago: University of Chicago Press, 1987.

Huntington, Samuel P. *The Clash of Civilizations: Remaking the World Order*. New York: Touchstone, 1996–97.

Hutchinson, James E. 'Science and religion'. *The Herald* (Dade County, FL) (25 December 1994): 1M, 6M.

Hutter, Bridget and Gillian Williams. *Controlling Women*. London: Croom Helm, 1981.

Hutton, Ronald. *The Stations of the Sun: A History of the Ritual Year in Britain*. Oxford: Oxford University Press, 1996.

Hutton, Will. *The State We're In*. London: Cape, 1995.

Hutton, Will and Anthony Giddens (eds). *On the Edge: Living with Global Capitalism*. London: Cape, 2000.

Hyman, Richard. *Strikes*. Basingstoke: Macmillan, 1989a.

——. *The Political Economy of Industrial Relations: Theory and Practice in a Cold Climate*. Basingstoke: Macmillan, 1989b.

I

Iannaccone, Laurence R. 'Why strict churches are strong'. *American Journal of Sociology*, Vol. 99, No. 5 (March 1994): 1180–1211.

Ide, Thomas R. and Arthur J. Cordell. 'Automating work'. *Society*, Vol. 31, No. 6 (September–October 1994): 65–71.

Ignatieff, Michael. *A Just Measure of Pain: The Penitentiary in the Industrial Revolution, 1750–1850*. London: Macmillan, 1978.

Illich, Ivan. *De-Schooling Society*. Harmondsworth: Penguin, 1973.

——. *Medical Nemesis: The Expropriation of Health*. New York: Pantheon Books, 1976.

Inglehart, Ronald. 'Globalization and postmodern values'. *The Washington Quarterly*, Vol. 23, No. 1 (Winter 2000): 215–28.

Inglis, Fred. *Media Theory: An Introduction*. Oxford: Blackwell, 1990.

ISTD Factsheet. 'Race and Criminal Justice'. London: Institute for the Study and Treatment of Delinquency, 1997.

Iyer, Pico. *The Global Soul: Jet Lag, Shopping Malls, and the Search for Home*. London: Bloomsbury, 2000.

J

Jackman, Mary J. *The Velvet Glove: Paternalism and Conflict in Gender, Class, and Race Relations*. Berkeley and Los Angeles, CA: University of California Press, 1994.

Jackson, Brian and Dennis Marsden. *Education and the Working Class*. London: Routledge, 1963.

Jackson, Stevi. *Heterosexuality in Question*. London: Sage, 1999.

Jacob, John E. 'An overview of black America in 1985', in James D. Williams (ed.), *The State of Black America 1986*. New York: National Urban League, 1986: i–xi.

Jacobs, James B. 'Should hate be a crime?' *The Public Interest*, No. 113 (Fall 1993): 3–14.

Jacobs, Jane. *The Economy of Cities*. New York: Vintage Books, 1970.

Jacobson, Jodi L. 'Closing the gender gap in development', in Lester R. Brown *et al.* (eds), *State of the World 1993: A Worldwatch Institute Report on Progress Toward a Sustainable Society*. New York: W. W. Norton, 1993: 61–79.

Jacoby, Russell and Naomi Glauberman (eds). *The Bell Curve Debate*. New York: Random House, 1995.

Jacquet, Constant H. and Alice M. Jones. *Yearbook of American and Canadian Churches 1991*. Nashville, TN: Abingdon Press, 1991.

Jagarowsky, Paul A. and Mary Jo Bane. *Neighborhood Poverty: Basic Questions*. Discussion paper series H-90-3. John F. Kennedy School of Government. Cambridge, MA: Harvard University Press, 1990.

Jagger, Alison. 'Political philosophies of women's liberation', in Laurel Richardson and Verta Taylor (eds), *Feminist Frontiers: Rethinking Sex, Gender, and Society*. Reading, MA: Addison-Wesley, 1983.

Jahoda, M., P. Lazersfeld and H. Zeizel. *Marienthal: Sociology of an Unemployed Community*, 2nd edn. London: Tavistock, 1972; orig. 1933.

James, Adrian L., Keith Bottomley, Alison Liebling and Emma Clare. *Privatising Prisons: Rhetoric and Reality*. London: Sage, 1997.

James, Allison, Chris Jenks and Alan Prout. *Theorizing Childhood*. New York: Teachers' College Press, 1998.

Jameson, Frederick. *Postmodernism or the Logic of Late Capitalism*. London: Verso, 1992.

Jamieson, Anne, Sarah Harper and Christian Victor (eds). *Critical Approaches to Ageing and Later Life*. Buckingham: Open University Press, 1995.

Jamieson, Lynn. *Intimacy: Personal Relationships in Modern Societies*. Oxford: Polity Press, 1998.

Jefferson, Tony. 'Masculinities and crime', in Mike Maguire, Rod Morgan and Rob Reiner (eds), *The Oxford Handbook of Criminology*, 2nd edn. Oxford: Clarendon Press, 1997.

——. 'Masculinities and crime', in Mike Maguire, Rod Morgan, Rob Reiner *et al.* (eds). *The Oxford Handbook of Criminology*. Oxford: Clarendon Press, 1997; 3rd edn, 2003.

Jeffreys, Sheila. *The Sexuality Debates*. New York and London: Routledge & Kegan Paul, 1987.

Jencks, Christopher. 'Genes and crime'. *The New York Review* (12 February 1987): 33–41.

Jencks, Christopher, *et al. Inequality: A Reassessment of the Effect of Family and Schooling in America*. New York: Basic Books, 1972.

Jenkins, Holman, Jr. 'The "poverty" lobby's inflated numbers'. *Wall Street Journal* (14 December 1992): A10.

Jenkins, J. Craig and Charles Perrow. 'Insurgency of the powerless: farm worker movements (1946–1972)'. *American Sociological Review*, Vol. 42, No. 2 (April 1977): 249–68.

Jenkins, Phillip. *Intimate Enemies. Moral Panics in Contemporary Great Britain*. New York: Aldine de Gruyte, 1992.

Jenkins, Richard. *Pierre Bourdieu*. London: Routledge, 1992.

——. *Social Identity*. London: Routledge, 1996.

——. *Rethinking Ethnicity*. London: Sage, 1997.

Jenks, Christopher. *Childhood*. London: Routledge, 1996.

Jensen, Joli. *Redeeming Modernity: Contradictions in Media Criticism*. Newbury Park, CA, and London: Sage, 1990.

Johnson, Cathryn. 'Gender, legitimate authority and leader–subordinate conversations'. *American Sociological Review*, Vol. 59, No. 1 (February 1994): 122–35.

Johnson, Kirk. *Television and Social Change in Rural India*. London: Sage, 2000.

Johnson, Paul. 'The seven deadly sins of terrorism', in Benjamin Netanyahu (ed.), *International Terrorism*. New Brunswick, NJ: Transaction, 1981: 12–22.

——. (ed.). *Twentieth Century Britain: Economic, Social and Cultural Change*. London: Longman, 1994.

Johnston, R. J. 'Residential area characteristics', in D. T. Herbert and R. J. Johnston (eds), *Social Areas in Cities. Vol. 1: Spatial Processes and Form*. New York: Wiley, 1976: 193–235.

Joll, James. *Europe: A Historian's View*. Leeds: Leeds University Press, 1969.

Jones, Huw. *Population Geography*, 2nd edn. London: Paul Chapman, 1990.

Jordan, David C. *Drug Politics: Dirty Money and Democracies*. Norman, OK: University of Oklahoma Press, 1999.

Jordan, Tim. *Cyberpower: The Culture and Politics of Cyberspace and the Internet*. London: Sage, 1999.

Joseph Rowntree Foundation (Income and Wealth Inquiry Group). *Inquiry into Income and Wealth*. York: Joseph Rowntree Foundation, 1995.

——. *Monitoring Poverty and Social Exclusion*. London: Joseph Rowntree Foundation, 1999 (also available through their website: http://www.jrf.org.uk/home.asp).

Joseph Rowntree Foundation. *Progress on Poverty 1997–2003/4: Findings*. York: Joseph Rowntree Foundation, October 2003.

K

Kadushin, Charles. 'Friendship among the French financial elite'. *American Sociological Review*, Vol. 60, No. 2 (April 1995): 202–21.

——. 'A short introduction to social networks'. Working paper for the CERPE Workshop, City University of New York, 21 May 2000.

Kain, Edward L. *The Myth of Family Decline: Understanding Families in a World of Rapid Social Change*. Lexington, MA: Lexington Books, 1990.

Kaku, Michio. *Visions: How Science will Revolutionize the 21st Century and Beyond*. Oxford: Oxford University Press, 1998.

Kaldor, Mary. *New and Old Wars: Organized Violence in a Global Era*. Cambridge: Polity Polity Press, 1999.

Kalish, Richard A. 'The new ageism and the failure models: a polemic'. *The Gerontologist*, Vol. 19, No. 4 (August 1979): 398–402.

Kallen, Evelyn. *Social Inequality and Social Injustice: A Human Rights Perspective*. London: Palgrave, 2004.

Kaminer, Wendy. 'Volunteers: who knows what's in it for them'. *Ms.* (December 1984): 93–4, 96, 126–8.

Kanagy, Conrad L. and Donald B. Kraybille. *The Riddles of Human Society*. London: Pine Forge Press, 1999.

Kanter, Rosabeth Moss. *Men and Women of the Corporation*. New York: Basic Books, 1977.

——. *The Change Masters: Innovation and Entrepreneurship in the American Corporation*. New York: Simon & Schuster, 1983.

——. *When Giants Learn to Dance: Mastering the Challenges of Strategy, Management and Careers in the 1990s*. New York: Simon & Schuster, 1989.

Kanter, Rosabeth Moss and Barry A. Stein. 'The gender pioneers: women in an industrial sales force', in R. M. Kanter and B. A. Stein (eds), *Life in Organizations*. New York: Basic Books, 1979: 134–60.

——. *A Tale of 'O': On Being Different in an Organization*. New York: Harper & Row, 1980.

Kaplan, E. Ann. *Rocking around the Clock: Music, Television, Postmodernism and Consumer Culture*. London: Routledge, 1987.

Kaplan, Eric B., *et al.* 'The usefulness of preoperative laboratory screening'. *Journal of the American Medical Association*, Vol. 253, No. 24 (28 June 1985): 3576–81.

Karatnycky, Adrian. 'Democracies on the rise, democracies at risk'. *Freedom Review*, Vol. 26, No. 1 (January–February 1995): 5–10.

Katz, James E. and Mark Aakhus (eds). *Perpetual Contact: Mobile Communication, Private Talk, Public Performance*. Cambridge: Cambridge University Press, 2002.

Katz, Jonathan. *Gay American History*. New York: Thomas and Cromwell, 1976.

Kaufman, Robert L. and Seymour Spilerman. 'The age structures of occupations and jobs'. *American Journal of Sociology*, Vol. 87, No. 4 (January 1982): 827–51.

Kaufman, Walter. *Religions in Four Dimensions: Existential, Aesthetic, Historical and Comparative*. New York: Reader's Digest Press, 1976.

Keith, Jennie, *et al. The Ageing Experience: Diversity and Commonality across Cultures*. London: Sage, 1994.

Keith, Pat M. and Robert B. Schafer. 'They hate to cook: patterns of distress in an ordinary role'. *Sociological Focus*, Vol. 27, No. 4 (October 1994): 289–301.

Keller, Helen. *The Story of My Life*. New York: Doubleday, 1903.

Keller, Suzanne. *The Urban Neighborhood*. New York: Random House, 1968.

Kellert, Stephen R. and F. Herbert Bormann. 'Closing the circle: weaving strands among ecology, economics and ethics', in Herbert F. Bohrmann and Stephen R. Kellert (eds), *Ecology, Economics and Ethics: The Broken Circle*. New Haven, CT: Yale University Press, 1991: 205–10.

Kelly, Elinor. *Racism in Schools: New Research Evidence*. Stoke-on-Trent: Trentham Books, 1988.

Kelly, Liz. *Surviving Sexual Violence*. Cambridge: Polity Press, 1988.

Kelner, Douglas. *Television and the Crisis of Democracy*

Boulder, CO: Westview Press, 1990.

Kempadoo, Kamal and Jo Doezema. *Global Sex Workers*. London: Routledge, 1998.

Kenyon, G. M. *Restorying Our Lives: Personal Growth through Autobiographical Reflection*. London: Praeger, 1977.

Kenyon, Kathleen. *Digging Up Jericho*. London: Ernest Benn, 1957.

Khazanov, A.M. *Nomads and the Outside World*. Oxford: Oxford University Press.

Kidron, Michael and Ronald Segal. *The New State of the World Atlas*. New York: Simon & Schuster, 1991.

Kilbourne, Brock K. 'The Conway and Siegelman claims against religious cults: an assessment of their data'. *Journal for the Scientific Study of Religion*, Vol. 22, No. 4 (December 1983): 380–5.

Kilgore, Sally B. 'The organizational context of tracking in schools'. *American Sociological Review*, Vol. 56, No. 2 (April 1991): 189–203.

Kimmel, Michael S. *The Gendered Society*. London: Oxford University Press, 2000; 2nd edn, 2004.

King, Anthony, *et al. Britain at the Polls, 1997*. Chatham, NJ: Chatham House, 1997.

King, Martin Luther, Jr. 'The Montgomery bus boycott', in Walt Anderson (ed.), *The Age of Protest*. Pacific Palisades, CA: Goodyear, 1969: 81–91.

Kinkead, Gwen. *Chinatown: A Portrait of a Closed Society*. New York: HarperCollins, 1992.

Kinsey, Alfred. *The Sexual Behaviour of the Human Male*. Philadelphia, PA: Saunders, 1948.

——. *The Sexual Behaviour of the Human Female*. Philadelphia, PA: Saunders, 1953.

Kiser, Edgar and Joachim Schneider. 'Bureaucracy and efficiency: an analysis of taxation in early modern Prussia'. *American Sociological Review*, Vol. 59, No. 2 (April 1994): 187–204.

Kishor, Sunita. ' "May God give sons to all": gender and child mortality in India'. *American Sociological Review*, Vol. 58, No. 2 (April 1993): 247–65.

Kitson, Gay C. and Helen J. Raschke. 'Divorce research: what we know, what we need to know'. *Journal of Divorce*, Vol. 4, No. 3 (Spring 1981): 1–37.

Kittrie, Nicholas N. *The Right To Be Different: Deviance and Enforced Therapy*. Baltimore, MD: Johns Hopkins University Press, 1971.

Kitzinger, Celia. *Feminism and Conversational Analysis*. London: Sage, 2003.

Klein, Naomi. *No Logo*. London: Flamingo, 2000.

Kleinman, Arthur. *The Illness Narratives*. New York: Basic Books, 1988.

Klug, Francesca. *Values for a Godless Age*. Harmondsworth: Penguin, 2000.

Kocsis, Karoly. 'Ethnicity', in David Turnock (ed.), *East Central Europe and the Former Soviet Union*. London: Arnold, 2001: 88–103.

Kohlberg, Lawrence. *The Psychology of Moral Development: The Nature and Validity of Moral Stages*. New York: Harper & Row, 1981.

Kohn, Melvin L. and Carmi Schooler. 'Job conditions and personality: a longitudinal assessment of their reciprocal effects'. *American Journal of Sociology*, Vol. 87, No. 6 (May 1982): 1257–83.

Kolata, Gina. 'When Grandmother is the mother, until birth'. *New York Times* (5 August 1991): 1, 11.

Komarovsky, Mirra. *Blue Collar Marriage*. New York: Vintage Books, 1967.

——. 'Cultural contradictions and sex roles: the masculine case'. *American Journal of Sociology*, Vol. 78, No. 4 (January 1973): 873–84.

——. *Dilemmas of Masculinity: A Study of College Youth*. New York: W. W. Norton, 1976.

Kornhauser, William. *The Politics of Mass Society*. New York: Free Press, 1959.

Kortre, J. N. and E. Hall. *Seasons of Life: The Dramatic Journey from Birth to Death*. Ann Arbor, MI: Ann Arbor Paperback, 1999.

Kotlikoff, Laurence J. and Scott Burns. *The Coming Generational Storm*. London and Cambridge, MA: MIT Press, 2004.

Kozol, Jonathan. *Prisoners of Silence: Breaking the Bonds of Adult Illiteracy in the United States*. New York: Continuum, 1980.

——. 'A nation's wealth'. *Publisher's Weekly* (24 May 1985a): 28–30.

——. *Illiterate America*. Garden City, NY: Doubleday, 1985b.

——. *Savage Inequalities: Children in America's Schools*. New York: Harper Perennial, 1992.

Kramarae, Cheris. *Women and Men Speaking*. Rowley, MA: Newbury House, 1981.

Kraybill, Donald B. *The Riddle of Amish Culture*. Baltimore, MD: Johns Hopkins University Press, 1989.

——. 'The Amish encounter with modernity', in Donald B. Kraybill and Marc A. Olshan (eds), *The Amish Struggle with Modernity*. Hanover, NH: University Press of New England, 1994: 21–33.

Kraybill, Donald B. and Marc A. Olshan (eds). *The Amish Struggle with Modernity*. Hanover, NH: University Press of New England, 1994.

Kriesi, Hanspeter. 'New social movements and the new class in the Netherlands'. *American Journal of Sociology*, Vol. 94, No. 5 (March 1989): 1078–116.

Kriesi, Hanspeter, Ruud Koopmans, Jan Willem Dyvendak and Marco G. Giuni. *New Social Movements in Western Europe*. London: UCL Press, 1995.

Kübler-Ross, Elisabeth. *On Death and Dying*. New York: Macmillan, 1969.

Kuhn, Manford and T. S. McPartland. 'An empirical investigation of self attitudes'. *American Sociological Review*, Vol. 19, No. 4 (1954): 68–76.

Kuhn, Thomas. *The Structure of Scientific Revolutions*, 2nd edn. Chicago: University of Chicago Press, 1970.

Kumar, Krishan. *Prophecy and Progress: The Sociology of Industrial and Post-Industrial Society*. Harmondsworth: Penguin, 1978.

——. *From Post-Industrial to Post-Modern Society: New Theories of the Contemporary World*. Oxford: Blackwell, 1995.

Kurtz, Lester. *Gods in the Global Village: The World's Religions in Sociological Perspective*. London: Pine Forge Press, 1995.

Kushner, Tony and Katherine Knox. *Refugees in an Age of Genocide*. London: Taylor and Francis, 1999.

Kuznets, Simon. *Modern Economic Growth: Rate, Structure and Spread*. New Haven, CT: Yale University Press, 1966.

Kvale, Steiner. *Interviews: An Introduction to Qualitative Research Interviewing*. London: Sage, 1996.

L

Laczo, F. and Colin Phillipson. *Changing Work and Retirement*. Milton Keynes: Open University Press, 1991.

Ladd, John. 'The definition of death and the right to die', in John Ladd (ed.), *Ethical Issues Relating to Life and Death*. New York: Oxford University Press, 1979: 118–45.

Lamberg-Karlovsky, C. C. and Martha Lamberg-Karlovsky. 'An early city in Iran', in *Cities: Their Origin, Growth and Human Impact*. San Francisco: Freeman, 1973: 28–37.

Lambevski, Sasho A. 'Suck my nation: masculinity, ethnicity and the politics of (homo)sex'. *Sexualities*, Vol. 2, No. 4 (November 1999): 397–420.

Lombroso, Cesare. *Crime: Its Causes and Remedies*. Montclair, NJ: Patterson Smith, 1911.

Landers, Rene M. 'Gender, race, and the state courts'. *Radcliffe Quarterly*, Vol. 76, No. 4 (December 1990): 6–9.

Lane, David. 'Social stratification and class', in Erik P. Hoffman and Robbin F. Laird (eds], *The Soviet Polity in the Modern Era*. New York: Aldine, 1984: 563–605.

Lappé, Frances Moore and Joseph Collins. *World Hunger: Twelve Myths*. New York: Grove Press/Food First Books, 1998.

Lappé, Frances Moore, Joseph Collins and David Kinley. *Aid as Obstacle: Twenty Questions about Our Foreign Policy and the Hungry*. San Francisco: Institute for Food and Development Policy, 1981.

Larmer, Brook. 'Dead end kids'. *Newsweek* (25 May 1992): 38–40.

Lash, Scott and John Urry. *The End of Organized Capitalism*. Cambridge: Polity Press, 1987.

Laslett, Peter (ed.). *Household and Family in Past Time: Comparative Studies in the Size and Structure of the Domestic Group over the Last Three Centuries in England, France, Serbia, Japan and Colonial North America, with Further Materials from Western Europe*. Cambridge: Cambridge University Press, 1972.

——. *The World We Have Lost: England before the Industrial Age*, 3rd edn. New York: Charles Scribner's Sons, 1984.

——. *A Fresh Map of Life: The Emergence of the Third Age*. Basingstoke: Macmillan, 1989; 2nd rev. edn, 1996.

Laswell, Harold. 'The structure and function of communication in society', in Lymon Bryson (ed.), *The Communication of Ideas*. New York: Harper & Row, 1948.

Latour, Bruno and Steve Woolgar. *Laboratory Life: The Construction of Scientific Facts*. Princeton, NJ: Princeton University Press, 1986.

Laumann, Edward O., John H. Gagnon, Robert T. Michael and Stuart Michaels. *The Social Organization of Sexuality: Sexual Practices in the United States*. Chicago: University of Chicago Press, 1994.

Lawson, Tony and Joan Garrod. *The Complete A–Z Sociology Handbook*, 3rd edn. London: Hodder & Stoughton, 2003.

Lawton, J. *The Dying Process*. London: Routledge, 2000.

Lazarsfeld, Paul F. and Robert K. Merton. 'Mass communication, popular taste and organized social action', in Paul Marris and Sue Thornham (eds), *Media Studies*. Edinburgh: Edinburgh University Press, 1996.

Lazreg, Marnia. *The Eloquence of Silence: Algerian Women in Question*. New York: Routledge, 1994.

Le Grand, Julien. *The Strategy of Equality*. London: Allen & Unwin, 1982.

Leacock, Eleanor. 'Women's status in egalitarian societies: implications for social evolution'. *Current Anthropology*, Vol. 19, No. 2 (June 1978): 247–75.

Leaning, Jennifer. 'The environmental impact of war'. *Canadian Medical Association Journal*, Vol. 163, No. 9 (2000): 1157–61.

Leavitt, Judith Walzer. 'Women and health in America: an overview', in Judith Walzer Leavitt (ed.), *Women and Health in America*. Madison, WI: University of Wisconsin Press, 1984: 3–7.

Lee, Barrett A., R. S. Oropesa, Barbara J. Metch and Avery M. Guest. 'Testing the decline of community thesis: neighborhood organization in Seattle, 1929 and 1979'. *American Journal of Sociology*, Vol. 89, No. 5 (March 1984): 1161–88.

Lee, David and H. Newby. *The Problem of Sociology*. London: Hutchinson, 1983.

Lee, David and Bryan Turner (eds). *Conflict about Class: Debating Inequality in Late Industrialism*. London: Longman, 1996.

Lee, Nick. *Childhood and Society*. Maidenhead: Open University Press, 2001.

Leerhsen, Charles. 'Unite and conquer'. *Newsweek* (5 February 1990): 50–5.

Lees, Sue. *Sugar and Spice: Sexuality and Adolescent Girls*. Harmondsworth: Penguin, 1993.

Lehne, Gregory. 'Homophobia among men', in D. David and R. Brannon (eds), *The Forty-Nine Per Cent Majority: The Male Sex Role*. London: Addison Wesley, 1976.

Leibfried, Stephan (ed.). *Welfare State Futures*. Cambridge: Cambridge University Press, 2001.

Lemert, Charles (ed.). *Social Theory: The Multicultural and Classic Readings*. Boulder, CO and Oxford: Westview Press, 1993.

Lemert, Edwin M. *Social Pathology*. New York: McGraw-Hill, 1951.

——. *Human Deviance, Social Problems and Social Control*, 2nd edn. Englewood Cliffs, NJ: Prentice- Hall, 1972.

Lengermann, Patricia Madoo and Ruth A. Wallace. *Gender in America: Social Control and Social Change*. Englewood Cliffs, NJ: Prentice-Hall, 1985.

Lennon, Mary Clare and Sarah Rosenfeld. 'Relative fairness and the doctrine of housework: the importance of options'. *American Journal of Sociology*, Vol. 100, No. 2 (September 1994): 506–31.

Lenski, Gerhard. *Power and Privilege: A Theory of Social Stratification*. New York: McGraw-Hill, 1966.

Lenski, Gerhard, Patrick Nolan and Jean Lenski. *Human Societies: An Introduction to Macrosociology*, 9th edn. New York: McGraw-Hill, 2004.

Leonard, Eileen B. *Women, Crime and Society: A Critique of Theoretical Criminology*. New York: Longman, 1982.

Lester, David. *The Death Penalty: Issues and Answers*. Springfield, IL: Charles C. Thomas, 1987.

Lever, Janet. 'Sex differences in the complexity of children's play and games'. *American Sociological Review*, Vol. 43, No. 4 (August 1978): 471–83.

Levi, Michael and Mike Maguire. 'Crime and policing in Europe', in Joe Bailey (ed.), *Social Europe*, 2nd edn. London: Longman, 1998: 177–202.

Levinson, Daniel J., with Charlotte N. Darrow, Edward B. Klein, Maria H. Levinson and Braxton McKee. *The Seasons of a Man's Life*. New York: Alfred A. Knopf, 1978.

Levinson, Daniel, J., with Charlotte N. Darrow, Edward B. Klein, Maria H. Levinson and Braxton McKee. *The Seasons of a Woman's Life*. New York: Knopf, 1996.

Levitas, Ruth. *The Inclusive Society? Social Exclusion and New Labour*. London: Macmillan, 1998.

Levitas, Ruth and Will Guy (eds). *Interpreting Official Statistics*. London: Routledge, 1996.

Levy, Frank. *Dollars and Dreams: The Changing American Income Distribution*. New York: Russell Sage Foundation, 1987.

Lewis, Flora. 'The roots of revolution'. *New York Times Magazine* (11 November 1984): 70–1, 74, 77–8, 82, 84, 86.

Lewis, Gail. 'Discursive histories, the pursuit of multiculturalism and social policy', in Gail Lewis, Sharon Gewirtz and John Clarke, *Rethinking Social Policy*. London: Sage/Open University Press, 2000.

Lewis, Gail, Sharon Gewirtz and John Clarke. *Rethinking Social Policy*. London: Sage/Open University Press, 2000.

Lewis, Jane. 'Gender and the development of welfare regimes'. *European Journal of Social Policy*, Vol. 2, No. 2 (1992): 159–74.

Lewis, Oscar. *Five Families*. New York: Basic Books, 1959.

——. *The Children of Sanchez*. New York: Random House, 1961.

Lewis, Susan, Dafna N. Izraeli and Helen Hootsmans. *Dual-Earner Families: International Perspectives*. Newbury Park, CA: Sage, 1992.

Lewontin, Richard. *It Ain't Necessarily So: The Dream of the Human Genome and Other Illusions*. London: Granta, 2000.

Li, Jiang Hong and Roger A. Wojtkiewicz. 'A new look at the effects of family structure on status attainment'. *Social Science Quarterly*, Vol. 73, No. 3 (September 1992): 581–95.

Lievrouw, Leah A. and Sonia Livingstone. *Handbook of New Media*. London: Sage, 2001.

Light, P. C. *Baby Boomers*. Ontario: Penguin Books, 1988.

Lin, Nan and Wen Xie. 'Occupational prestige in urban China'. *American Journal of Sociology*, Vol. 93, No. 4 (January 1988): 793–832.

Linden, Eugene. 'Can animals think?' *Time*, Vol. 141, No. 12 (22 March 1993): 54–61.

——. 'More power to women, fewer mouths to feed'. *Time*, Vol. 144, No. 13 (26 September 1994): 64–5.

Lindesmith, Alfred R., Anselm L. Strauss and Norman K. Denzin. *Social Psychology*. London: Sage, 8th edn, 1999; orig. 1949.

Linton, Ralph. *The Study of Man*. New York: D. Appleton-Century, 1937.

Lipset, Seymour Martin and Reinhard Bendix. *Social Mobility in Industrial Society*. Berkeley, CA: University of California Press, 1967.

Liska, Allen E. *Perspectives on Deviance*, 3rd edn. Englewood Cliffs, NJ: Prentice-Hall, 1991.

Liska, Allen E. and Barbara D. Warner. 'Functions of crime: a paradoxical process'. *American Journal of Sociology*, Vol. 96, No. 6 (May 1991): 1441–63.

Lo, Clarence Y. H. 'Countermovements and conservative movements in the contemporary US'. *Annual Review of Sociology*, Vol. 8. Palo Alto, CA: Annual Reviews, 1982: 107–34.

Lockwood, David. *Solidarity and Schism: The Problem of Disorder in Durkheimian and Marxist Sociology*. Oxford: Clarendon Press, 1992.

Lockwood, David, John Goldthorpe, Frank Beckhoffer and Jennifer Platt. *The Affluent Worker*. Cambridge: Cambridge University Press, 1967.

Lodge, David. *The Modes of Modern Writing*. London: Arnold, 1977.

Lofland, J. *Doomsday Cult*, 2nd edn. New York: Irvington, 1996; 2nd edn, 1977.

Logan, John R. and Mark Schneider. 'Racial segregation and racial change in American suburbs, 1970–1980'. *American Journal of Sociology*, Vol. 89, No. 4 (January 1984): 874–88.

Lombroso, Cesare. *Crime: Its Causes and Remedies*. Montclair, NJ: Patterson Smith, 1911.

——. *L'Uomo Delinquents*. Turin: Fratelli Books, 1970.

Longino, Charles F., Jr. 'Myths of an aging America'. *American Demographics*, Vol. 16, No. 8 (August 1994): 36–42.

Lopez, Barry. *Arctic Dreams: Imagination and Desire in a Northern Landscape*. London: Picador, 1986.

Lorber, Judith. *Paradoxes of Gender*. New Haven, CT: Yale University Press, 1994.

Lord, Walter. *A Night to Remember*, rev. edn. New York: Holt, Rinehart & Winston, 1976.

Lorenz, Konrad. *On Aggression*. New York: Harcourt, Brace & World, 1966.

Louie, Miriam Ching Yoon. *Sweatshop Warriors*. Cambridge, MA: South End Press, 2001.

Lovelock, James. *Gaia: A New Look at Life on Earth*. Oxford: Oxford University Press, 1979.

Lovenduski, J. 'Feminism and West European politics: an overview', in D. W. Unwin and W. E. Pateson (eds), *Politics in Western Europe Today*. London: Longman, 1990.

Lowery, A. and Melvin L. De Fleur (eds). *Milestones in Mass Communication Research*. London: Longman, 1984; 2nd edn, 1988.

Loy, Pamela Hewitt and Lea P. Stewart. 'The extent and effects of sexual harassment of working women'. *Sociological Focus*, Vol. 17, No. 1 (January 1984): 31–43.

Lubenow, Gerald C. 'A troubling family affair'. *Newsweek* (14 May 1984): 34.

Lull, James. *Media, Communication, Culture: A Global Approach*. Cambridge: Polity Press, 1995.

Lupton, Deborah. *The Emotional Self*. London: Sage, 1998.

Lutra, Mohan. *Britain's Black Population*. London: Arena, 1997.

Lutz, Catherine A. *Unnatural Emotions: Everyday Sentiments on a Micronesia Atoll and Their Challenge to Western Theory*. Chicago: University of Chicago Press, 1988.

Lutz, Catherine A. and Jane L. Collins. *Reading National Geographic*. Chicago: University of Chicago Press, 1993.

Lutz, Catherine A. and Geoffrey M. White. 'The anthropology of emotions', in Bernard J. Siegel, Alan R. Beals and Stephen A. Tyler (eds), *Annual Review of Anthropology*, Vol. 15. Palo Alto, CA: Annual Reviews, 1986: 405–36.

Lynd, Robert S. *Knowledge for What? The Place of Social Science in American Culture*. Princeton, NJ: Princeton University Press, 1967.

Lynd, Robert S. and Helen Merrell Lynd. *Middletown in Transition*. New York: Harcourt, Brace & World, 1937.

Lynott, Patricia Passuth and Barbara J. Logue. 'The "hurried child": the myth of lost childhood on contemporary American society'. *Sociological Forum*, Vol. 8, No. 3 (September 1993): 471–91.

Lyon, David. *Surveillance Society: Monitoring Everyday Life*. Buckingham: Open University Press, 2001.

Lyotard, J. F. *The Postmodern Condition*. Manchester: Manchester University Press, 1992.

M

Ma, Li-Chen. Personal communication to J. J. Macionis, 1987.

Mabry, Marcus. 'New hope for old unions?' *Newsweek* (24 February 1992): 39.

Mac an Ghaill, Mairtin. *The Making of Men: Masculinities, Sexualities and Schooling*. Buckingham: Open University Press, 1994.

McAdam, Doug, John D. McCarthy and Mayer N. Zald. 'Social movements', in Neil J. Smelser (ed.), *Handbook of Sociology*. Newbury Park, CA: Sage, 1988: 695–737.

McCarthy, Jane Ribbens, Rosalind Edwards and Val Gillies. *Parenting and Step-Parenting*. Oxford: Centre for Family and Household Research, Oxford Brookes University, 2000.

McCarthy, John D. and Mayer N. Zald. 'Resource mobilization and social movements: a partial theory'. *American Journal of Sociology*, Vol. 82, No. 6 (May 1977): 1212–41.

McColm, R. Bruce, James Finn, Douglas W. Payne, Joseph E. Ryan, Leonard R. Sussman and George Zarycky. *Freedom in the World: Political Rights and Civil Liberties, 1990–1991*. New York: Freedom House, 1991.

McCormick, John. *British Politics and the Environment*. London: Earthscan, 1991.

McCoy, Clyde B. and James A. Inciardi. *Sex, Drugs and the Continuing Spread of AIDS*. Los Angeles: Roxbury, 1995.

McDonald, Robert. *Youth, the Underclass and Social Exclusion*. London: Routledge, 1997.

McIlroy, John. *Trade Unions in Britain Today*, 2nd edn. Manchester: Manchester University Press, 1995.

Macionis, John J. 'Intimacy: structure and process in interpersonal relationships'. *Alternative Lifestyles*, Vol. 1, No. 1 (February 1978a): 113–30.

——. 'The search for community in modern society: an interpretation'. *Qualitative Sociology*, Vol. 1, No. 2 (September 1978b): 130–43.

Mack, Joanna and Stewart Lansley. *Poor Britain*. London: Allen & Unwin, 1985; 2nd edn, London: Routledge, 1993.

MacKay, Donald G. 'Prescriptive grammar and the pronoun problem', in Barrie Thorne, Cheris Kramarae and Nancy Henley (eds), *Language, Gender and Society*. Rowley, MA: Newbury House, 1983: 38–53.

McKeown, T. *The Role of Medicine: Dream, Mirage and Nemesis*. London: Nuffield Provincial Hospital Trust, 1976.

MacKinnon, Catharine A. *Feminism Unmodified: Discourses on Life and Law*. Cambridge, MA: Harvard University Press, 1987.

Mackinnon, Donald, June Statham and Margaret Hales. *Education in the UK: Facts and Figures*. Buckingham: Open University Press, 1996; 3rd edn, 1999.

Macklin, Eleanor D. 'Nonmarital heterosexual cohabitation: an overview', in Eleanor D. Macklin and Roger H. Rubin (eds), *Contemporary Families and Alternative Lifestyles:*

Handbook on Research and Theory. Beverly Hills, CA: Sage, 1983: 49–74.

McLanahan, Sara. 'Family structure and the reproduction of poverty'. *American Journal of Sociology*, Vol. 90, No. 4 (January 1985): 873–901.

McLaughlin, Eugene and John Muncie (eds). *Sage Dictionary of Criminology*. London: Sage, 2001.

McLean, Gill L. *Facing Death: Conversations with Cancer Patients*. Edinburgh: Churchill Livingstone, 1993.

McLean, Martin. 'The politics of curriculum in European perspective'. *Educational Review*, Vol. 45, No. 2 (1993): 125–35.

McLellan, David. *Karl Marx: Selected Writings 2000*. Oxford: Oxford University Press, 2nd edn 2000.

McLeod, Jane D. and Michael J. Shanahan. 'Poverty, parenting and children's mental health'. *American Sociological Review*, Vol. 58, No. 3 (June 1993): 351–66.

McLuhan, Marshall. *The Medium is the Message*. London: Routledge, 1964.

McMichael, A. J. *Planetary Overload: Global Environment Change and the Health of the Human Species*. Cambridge: Cambridge University Press, 1993.

Macpherson, Sir W. *The Stephen Lawrence Inquiry*. Cm 4262. London: HMSO, 1999.

McQuail, Denis. *Mass Communication Theory*, 3rd edn. London: Sage, 1994; *Mass Communication Theory: An Introduction*, 4th edn, 2000.

McRae, Susan. *Cross-Class Families: A Study of Wives' Occupational Superiority*. New York: Oxford University Press, 1986.

McRobbie, Angela. *Feminism and Youth Culture*. London: Macmillan, 1991.

Maddox, Setma. 'Organizational culture and leadership style: factors affecting self-managed work team performance'. Paper presented at the annual meeting of the Southwest Social Science Association, Dallas, TX, February, 1995.

Madsen, Axel. *Private Power: Multinational Corporations for the Survival of Our Planet*. New York: William Morrow, 1980.

Maguire, Mike, Rod Morgan, Rob Reiner *et al.* (eds). *The Oxford Handbook of Criminology*. Oxford: Clarendon Press, 1997; 3rd edn, 2003.

Majka, Linda C. 'Sexual harassment in the Church'. *Society*, Vol. 28, No. 4 (May–June 1991): 14–21.

Malcolm, Noel. *Bosnia: A Short History*, rev. edn. London: Macmillan, 1996.

Malcolm X (with Alex Haley). *The Autobiography of Malcolm X*. Harmondsworth: Penguin, 1966.

Malthus, Thomas Robert. *First Essay on Population*. London: Macmillan, 1926; orig. 1798.

Mann, Michael. *Encyclopedia of Sociology*. London: Macmillan, 1983.

Manning, Philip. *Erving Goffman and Modern Sociology*. Cambridge: Polity Press, 1992.

Marcuse, Herbert. *One-Dimensional Man*. Boston, MA: Beacon Press, 1964.

Mare, Robert D. 'Five decades of educational assortative mating'. *American Sociological Review*, Vol. 56, No. 1 (February 1991): 15–32.

Margolick, David. 'Rape in marriage is no longer within the law'. *New York Times* (13 December 1984): 6E.

Maris, Paul. Amsterdam: Europe's Drug Capital? *NACRO Bulletin*, No. 25 (1996).

Markham, A.N. *Life Online: Researching Real Experiences in Virtual Space*. London: AltaMira Press, 1998.

Markoff, John. 'Remember Big Brother? Now he's a company man'. *New York Times* (31 March 1991): 7.

Markson, Elizabeth W. 'Moral dilemmas'. *Society*, Vol. 29, No. 5 (July–August 1992): 4–6.

Marris, Paul and Sue Thornham (eds). *Media Studies: A Reader*. Edinburgh: Edinburgh University Press, 1996.

Marris, Robin. *How to Save the Underclass*. Basingstoke: Macmillan, 1996.

Marsden, Peter. 'Core discussion networks of Americans'. *American Sociological Review*, Vol. 52, No. 1 (February 1987): 122–31.

Marshall, Catherine (ed.). *The New Politics of Race and Gender*. Washington, DC, and London: Falmer Press, 1993.

Marshall, Gordon, David Rose, Howard Newby and Carolyn Vogler. *Social Class in Modern Britain*. London: Hutchinson, 1988.

Martell, Luke. *Ecology and Society: An Introduction*. Cambridge: Polity Press, 1994.

Martin, Gus. 'Sea Change: The Modern Terrorist Environment in Perspective', in George Ritzer (ed.), *Handbook of Social Problems*. Thousand Oaks, CA: Sage, 2004: 355–67.

Martin, John M. and Anne T. Romano. *Multinational Crime: Terrorism, Espionage, Drug and Arms Trafficking*. Newbury Park, CA: Sage, 1992.

Martin, Richard C. *Islam: A Cultural Perspective*. Englewood Cliffs, NJ: Prentice-Hall, 1982.

Martin, S. I. *Britain's Slave Trade*. London: Channel 4 Books, 1999.

Martin, William. 'The birth of a media myth'. *The Atlantic*, Vol. 247, No. 6 (June 1981): 7, 10, 11, 16.

Marty, Martin E. and R. Scott Appleby (eds). *Fundamentalisms Comprehended*. Chicago: University of Chicago Press, 1995.

Marullo, Sam. 'The functions and dysfunctions of preparations for fighting nuclear war'. *Sociological Focus*, Vol. 20, No. 2 (April 1987): 135–53.

Marx, Karl. 'Excerpt from "A Contribution to the Critique of Political Economy" ', in Karl Marx and Friedrich Engels, *Marx and Engels: Basic Writings on Politics and Philosophy*. Lewis S. Feurer, ed. Garden City, NY: Anchor Books, 1959: 42–6; 2nd edn, 1977; orig. 1859.

——. *Early Writings*. Tom Bottomore, ed. New York: McGraw-Hill, 1964a.

——. *Karl Marx: Selected Writings in Sociology and Social Philosophy*. T. B. Bottomore, trans. New York: McGraw-Hill, 1964b.

——. *Capital*. Friedrich Engels, ed. New York: International Publishers, 1967; orig. 1867.

——. 'Theses on Feuer', in Robert C. Tucker (ed.), *The Marx–Engels Reader*. New York: W. W. Norton, 1972: 107–9; orig. 1845.

Marx, Karl and Friedrich Engels. 'Manifesto of the Communist Party', in Robert C. Tucker (ed.), *The Marx–Engels Reader*. New York: W. W. Norton, 1972: 331–62; orig. 1848.

——. *The Marx–Engels Reader*. Robert C. Tucker, ed. 2nd edn. New York: W. W. Norton, 1978.

Marx, Leo. 'The environment and the two cultures' divide', in James Rodger Fleming and Henry A. Gemery (eds), *Science, Technology and the Environment: Multidisciplinary Perspectives*. Akron, OH: University of Akron Press, 1994: 3–21.

Mason, David. *Race and Ethnicity in Modern Britain*, 2nd edn. Oxford: Oxford University Press, 2000a.

——. 'Ethnicity', in Geoff Payne (ed.), *Social Divisions*. London: Macmillan, 2000b.

Massey, Douglas S. and Nancy A. Denton. 'Hypersegregation in US metropolitan areas: black and hispanic segregation along five dimensions'. *Demography*, Vol. 26, No. 3 (August 1989): 373–91.

Mathabane, Mark. *African Women: Three Generations*. New York: HarperCollins, 1994.

Matthews, Roger. 'Criminal statistics'. *Criminal Justice Matters*, No. 27 (1977): 14–15.

Matthiessen, Peter. *Indian Country*. New York: Viking Press, 1984.

Matza, David. *Delinquency and Drift*. New York: Wiley, 1964.

Mauss, Armand L. *Social Problems of Social Movements*. Philadelphia, PA: Lippincott, 1975.

Mayhew, Henry. *London's Underworld*. P. Quennel ed. London: Spring Books, 1861.

Mead, George Herbert. *Mind, Self and Society from the Standpoint of a Social Behavourist*. Charles W. Morris, ed. Chicago: University of Chicago Press, 1962; orig. 1934.

Mead, Margaret. *Coming of Age in Samoa*. New York: Dell, 1961; orig. 1928.

——. *Sex and Temperament in Three Primitive Societies*. New York: William Morrow, 1963; orig. 1935.

Meadows, Donella H., Dennis L. Meadows, Jorgan Randers and William W. Behrens, III. *The Limits to Growth: A Report on the Club of Rome's Project on the Predicament of Mankind*. New York: Universe, 1972.

Meltzer, Bernard N. 'Mead's social psychology', in Jerome G. Manis and Bernard N. Meltzer (eds), *Symbolic Interaction: A Reader in Social Psychology*, 3rd edn. Needham Heights, MA: Allyn & Bacon, 1978.

Melucci, Alberto. 'The new social movements: a theoretical approach'. *Social Science Information*, Vol. 19, No. 2 (May 1980): 199–226.

——. *Nomads of the Present: Social Movements and Individual Needs in Contemporary Society*. Philadelphia, PA: Temple University Press, 1989.

Menchú, Rigoberta. *I, Rigoberta Menchú. An Indian Woman in Guatemala*. London: Verso, 1984.

——. *Crossing Borders*. London: Verso, 1998.

Mennell, Stephen. *All Manners of Food: Eating and Taste in England and France from the Middle Ages to the Present*. Oxford: Basil Blackwell, 1985.

Merton, Robert K. 'Social structure and anomie'. *American Sociological Review*, Vol. 3, No. 6 (October 1938): 672–82.

——. *Social Theory and Social Structure*. New York: Free Press, 1968.

——. 'Discrimination and the American creed', in *Sociological Ambivalence and Other Essays*. New York: Free Press, 1976: 189–216.

——. *On Social Structure and Science*. Chicago: University of Chicago Press, 1996.

Messerschmidt, James. *Masculinity and Crime*. Lanham, MD: Rowman and Littlefield, 1993.

——. *Nine Lives: Adolescent Masculinities, the Body and Violence*. London: Sage, 2000.

Meyerhoff, Barbara. *Remembered Lives: The Work of Ritual, Storytelling and Growing Older*. Athens, GA: University of Georgia Press, 1992.

Meyrowitz, Joshua. *No Sense of Place: The Impact of Electronic Media on Social Behavior*. New York and Oxford: Oxford University Press, 1986.

Michels, Robert. *Political Parties*. Glencoe, IL: Free Press, 1949; orig. 1911.

Miladi, Noureddine. 'Mapping the *Al-Jazeera* phenomenon', in D. K. Thussu and D. Freedman (eds), *War and the Media*. London: Sage, 2003: 149–60.

Milbrath, Lester W. *Envisioning a Sustainable Society: Learning Our Way Out*. Albany, NY: State University of New York Press, 1989.

Milgram, Stanley. 'Behavioral study of obedience'. *Journal of Abnormal and Social Psychology*, Vol. 67, No. 4 (1963): 371–8.

——. 'Group pressure and action against a person'. *Journal of Abnormal and Social Psychology*, Vol. 69, No. 2 (August 1964): 137–43.

——. 'Some conditions of obedience and disobedience to authority'. *Human Relations*, Vol. 18 (February 1965): 57–76.

Miliband, Ralph. *The State in Capitalist Society*. London: Weidenfeld and Nicolson, 1969.

Miliband, Ralph and Leo Panitch. *Socialist Register, 1993: Real Problems, False Solutions*. London: Merlin Press, 1993.

Mill, John Stuart and Harriet Taylor Mill. *The Subjection of Women*. Dover publications, 1997, orig. London: Virago, 1983; orig. 1869.

Miller, Arthur G. *The Obedience Experiments: A Case of Controversy in Social Science*. New York: Praeger, 1986.

Miller, Daniel (ed.). *Acknowledging Consumption*. London: Routledge, 1995.

Miller, G. Tyler, Jr. *Living in the Environment: An Introduction to Environmental Science*. Belmont, CA: Wadsworth, 1992.

Miller, Walter B. 'Lower class culture as a generating milieu of gang delinquency', in Marvin E. Wolfgang, Leonard Savitz and Norman Johnston (eds), *The Sociology of Crime and Delinquency*, 2nd edn. New York: Wiley, 1970: 351–63; orig. 1958.

Millet, Kate. *Sexual Politics*. Garden City, NY: Doubleday, 1970.

Mills, C. Wright. *The Power Elite*. New York: Oxford University Press, 1956.

——. *The Sociological Imagination*. New York: Oxford University Press, 1959; 2nd edn, 1967; 3rd edn, 1970.

——. *Power, Politics, and People: The Collected Essays of C. Wright Mills*. London and New York: Oxford University Press, 1967; orig. 1957.

Mink, Barbara. 'How modernization affects women'. *Cornell Alumni News*, Vol. III, No. 3 (April 1989): 10–11.

Mirowsky, John. 'The psycho-economics of feeling underpaid: distributive justice and the earnings of husbands and wives'. *American Journal of Sociology*, Vol. 92, No. 6 (May 1987): 1404–34.

Mirza, Heidi. *Young, Female and Black*. London: Routledge, 1992.

Mirza, Heidi Safia (ed.). *British Black Feminism*. London: Routledge, 1997.

Modood, Tariq. 'Political blackness and British Asians'. *Sociology*, Vol. 28, No. 4 (1994): 859–76.

Modood, Tariq, R. Berthoud, J. Lakey, J. Nazroo, P. Smith, S. Virdee and S. Beishaon. *Ethnic Minorities in Britain*, 4th edn. London: Policy Studies Institute, 1997.

Moen, Phyllis. *Women's Two Roles: A Contemporary Dilemma*. New York and London: Auburn House, 1992.

Molotch, Harvey. 'The city as a growth machine'. *American Journal of Sociology*, Vol. 82, No. 2 (September 1976): 309–33.

Molotch, Harvey and Marilyn Lester. 'News as purposive behaviour'. *American Sociological Review*, Vol. 39 (1974): 101–12.

Montaigue, Fen. 'Russia rising'. *National Geographic*, Vol. 200, No. 5 (September 2001): 2–31.

Mooney, Jayne. *Gender, Violence and the Social Order*. Basingstoke: Macmillan, 2000.

Moore, Gwen. 'Structural determinants of men's and women's personal networks'. *American Sociological Review*, Vol. 55, No. 5 (October 1991): 726–35.

——. 'Gender and informal networks in state government'. *Social Science Quarterly*, Vol. 73, No. 1 (March 1992): 46–61.

Moore, Wilbert E. 'Modernization as rationalization: processes and restraints', in Manning Nash (ed.), *Essays on Economic Development and Cultural Change in Honor of Bert F. Hoselitz*. Chicago: University of Chicago Press, 1977: 29–42.

——. *World Modernization: The Limits of Convergence*. New York: Elsevier, 1979.

Moores, Shaun. *Interpreting Audiences: The Ethnography of Media Consumption*. London: Sage, 1993.

Morgan, David. *Family Connections: An Introduction to Family Studies*. Cambridge: Polity Press, 1996.

——. 'Risk and family practices', in Elizabeth B. Silva and Carol Smart (eds), *The New Family?* London: Sage, 1999.

——. *Farewell to the Family*. London: Institute of Economic Affairs, 1995.

Morgan, Patricia. *Delinquent Fantasies*. London: Temple Smith, 1978.

Morgan, Rod and Tim Newburn. *The Future of Policing*. Oxford: Clarendon Press, 1997.

Morin, S. and E. Garfinkle. 'Male homophobia'. *Journal of Social Issues*, Vol. 34, No. 1 (1978) : 29–47.

Morley, David. *Family Television: Cultural Power and Domestic Leisure*. London: Comedia, 1986.

——. *Television: Audiences and Cultural Studies*. London: Routledge, 1992.

Morley, David and K.-H. Chen (eds). *Stuart Hall: Critical Dialogues in Cultural Studies*. London: Routledge, 1996.

Morris, Lydia. *Dangerous Classes: The Underclass and Social Citizenship*. London: Routledge, 1994.

Morrow, Lance. 'The temping of America'. *Time*, Vol. 131, No. 14 (29 March 1993): 40–1.

Morton, Jackson. 'Census on the Internet'. *American Demographics*, Vol. 17, No. 3 (March 1995): 52–53.

Mosley, W. Henry and Peter Cowley. 'The challenge of world health'. *Population Bulletin*, Vol. 46, No. 4 (December 1991). Washington, DC: Population Reference Bureau.

Mueller, Daniel P. and Philip W. Cooper. 'Children of single-parent families: how do they fare as young adults?' Presentation to the American Sociological Association, San Antonio, TX, 1984.

Muggleton, D. and R. Weinzierl (eds). *The Post-Subcultures Reader*. Oxford: Berg, 2004.

Mumford, Lewis. *The City in History: Its Origins, Its Transformations and Its Prospects*. New York: Harcourt, Brace & World, 1961.

Murdock, George Peter. 'The common denominator of cultures', in Ralph Linton (ed.), *The Science of Man in World Crisis*. New York: Columbia University Press, 1945: 123–42.

——. *Social Structure*. New York: Free Press, 1965; orig. 1949.

Murdock, Graham and P. Golding. 'Capitalism, communication and class relations', in James Curran *et al.*, *Mass Communication and Society*. London: Edward Arnold, 1977.

Murray, Charles. *Losing Ground: American Social Policy 1950–1980*. New York: Basic Books, 1984.

Musello, C. 'Family photography', in J. Wagner (ed.), *Images of Information Still Photography in the Social Sciences*. Beverley Hills, CA: Sage, 1979.

Myers, Norman. 'Humanity's growth', in Sir Edmund Hillary (ed.), *Ecology 2000: The Changing Face of the Earth*. New York: Beaufort Books, 1984a: 16–35.

——. 'The mega-extinction of animals and plants', in Sir Edmund Hillary (ed.), *Ecology 2000: The Changing Face of the Earth*. New York: Beaufort Books, 1984b: 82–107.

——. 'Disappearing cultures', in Sir Edmund Hillary (ed.), *Ecology 2000: The Changing Face of the Earth*. New York: Beaufort Books, 1984c: 162–9.

——. 'Biological diversity and global security', in F. Herbert Bormann and Stephen R. Kellert (eds), *Ecology, Economics and Ethics: The Broken Circle*. New Haven, CT: Yale University Press, 1991: 11–25.

Myers, Sheila and Harold G. Grasmick. 'The social rights and responsibilities of pregnant women: an application of Parsons' sick role model'. Paper presented to Southwestern Sociological Association, Little Rock, AR, March 1989.

N

Nagle, Garrett and Kris Spencer. *A Geography of the European Union*. Oxford: Oxford University Press, 1996.

Naisbitt, John. *Megatrends Asia*. London: Nicholas Brealey, 1997.

Nakx, K. 'The "eclipse" of folk medicine in Western society'. *Sociology of Health and Illness*, Vol. 13, No. 1 (1991): 203.

Narayan, Deepa. *Voices of the Poor: Can Anyone Hear Us?* Oxford: Oxford University Press for the World Bank, 2000.

Nash, J. Madeleine. 'To know your own fate'. *Time*, Vol. 145, No. 14 (3 April 1995): 62.

National Intelligence Council. *Global Trends 2015*. Washington, DC: US Government Printing Office, 2000.

Navarro, Vicente. 'The industrialization of fetishism or the fetishism of industrialization: a critique of Ivan Illich', in Vicente Navarro (ed.), *Health and Medical Care in the US: A Critical Analysis*. Farmingdale, NY: Baywood Publishing, 1977: 38–58.

——. *Crisis, Health and Medicine*. London: Tavistock Institute, 1986.

Nayak, Anoop. *Race, Place and Globalization: Youth Cultures in a Changing World*. Oxford: Berg, 2003.

Nelan, Bruce W. 'Crimes without punishment'. *Time*, Vol. 141, No. 2 (11 January 1993): 21.

Nettle, Daniel and Suzanne Romaine. *Vanishing Voices: The Extinction of the World's Languages*. Oxford: Oxford University Press, 2000.

Nettleton, Sarah. *Power, Pain and Dentistry*. Buckingham: Open University Press, 1992.

——. *The Sociology of Health and Illness*. Cambridge: Polity Press, 1995.

Neugarten, Bernice L. 'Grow old with me. The best is yet to be'. *Psychology Today*, Vol. 5 (December 1971): 45–8, 79, 81.

——. 'Personality and aging', in James E. Birren and K. Warner Schale (eds), *Handbook of the Psychology of Aging*. New York: Van Nostrand Reinhold, 1977: 626–49.

Neuhouser, Kevin. 'The radicalization of the Brazilian Catholic Church in comparative perspective'. *American Sociological Review*, Vol. 54, No. 2 (April 1989): 233–44.

Neuman, W. Russell. *The Future of the Mass Audience*. Cambridge: Cambridge University Press, 1991.

New Internationalist (compiled by Andy Crump and edited by Wayne Ellwood). *The A to Z of World Development*. Oxford: New Internationalist Publications, 1998.

——. *The World Guide 2001–02*. Oxford: New Internationalist Publications, 2001.

Newman, Katherine S. *Declining Fortunes: The Withering of the American Dream*. New York: Basic Books, 1993.

Newman, William M. *American Pluralism: A Study of Minority Groups and Social Theory*. New York: Harper & Row, 1973.

Nielsen, Joyce McCarl (ed.). *Feminist Research Methods: Exemplary Readings in the Social Sciences*. Boulder, CO: Westview Press, 1990.

Nisbet, Robert A. *The Sociological Tradition*. New York: Basic Books, 1966.

——. *The Quest for Community*. New York: Oxford University Press, 1969.

——. 'Sociology as an art form', in *Tradition and Revolt: Historical and Sociological Essays*. New York: Vintage Books, 1970. (Published as *Sociology as an Art Form*. London: Heinemann, 1976.)

——. *A History of the Idea of Progress*. New York: Basic Books, 1989.

Norbeck, Edward. 'Class structure', in *Kodansha Encyclopedia of Japan*. Tokyo: Kodansha, 1983: 322–5.

NORC (National Opinion Research Center). *General Social Surveys, 1972–1991: Cumulative Codebook*. University of Chicago: National Opinion Research Center, 1991.

——. *General Social Surveys, 1972–1994: Cumulative Codebook*. University of Chicago: National Opinion Research Center, 1994.

Norden, Martin F. *The Cinema of Isolation: A History of Physical Disability in the Movies*. New Brunswick, NJ: Rutgers University Press, 1994.

Norris, C. and G. Armstrong. *The Maximum Surveillance Society: The Rise of CCTV*. Oxford: Berg, 1999.

Norris, Pippa (ed.). *Critical Citizens*. Oxford: Oxford University Press, 1999.

O

Oakes, Jeannie. 'Classroom social relationships: exploring the Bowles and Gintis hypothesis'. *Sociology of Education*, Vol. 55, No. 4 (October 1982): 197–212.

——. *Keeping Track: How High Schools Structure Inequality*. New Haven, CT: Yale University Press, 1985.

O'Brien, Jodi and Judith Howard. *Everyday Inequalities: Critical Inquiries*. Oxford: Blackwell, 1998.

O'Donnell, Mike. *Classical and Contemporary Sociology: Theories and Issues*. London: Hodder and Stoughton, 2001.

O'Donnell, Mike and Sue Sharpe. *Uncertain Masculinities: Youth, Ethnicity and Class in Contemporary Britain*. London: Routledge, 2000.

OECD (Organisation for Economic Cooperation and Development), *Education at a Glance*. Paris: OECD, 1997.

——. *Education at a Glance*. Paris: OECD, 2000.

Offe, Claus. 'New social movements: challenging the boundaries of institutional politics'. *Social Research*, Vol. 52 (1985): 817–68.

Ogburn, William F. *On Culture and Social Change*. Chicago: University of Chicago Press, 1964.

Okin, Susan Moller. *Justice, Gender and the Family*. New York: Basic Books, 1989.

Olsen, Marvin E., Dora G. Lodwick and Riley E. Dunlap. *Viewing the World Ecologically*. Boulder, CO: Westview Press, 1992.

Olzak, Susan. 'Labour unrest, immigration and ethnic conflict in urban America'. *American Journal of Sociology*, Vol. 94, No. 6 (1989): 458–74.

Ong, A. *Orality and Literacy*. London: Sage, 1982.

OPCS. *1991 Census Preliminary Report for England and Wales*. London: HMSO, 1991.

Oppenheim, C. *Poverty: The Facts*, 2nd edn. London: Child Poverty Action Group, 1993.

O'Reilly, Karen. *The British on the Costa del Sol*. London: Routledge, 2000.

Orlansky, Michael D. and William L. Heward. *Voices: Interviews with Handicapped People*. Columbus, OH: Merrill, 1981: 85, 92, 133–4, 172.

Orshansky, Mollie. 'How poverty is measured'. *Monthly Labor Review*, Vol. 92, No. 2 (February 1969): 37–41.

Osborne, Richard and Borin Van Loon. *Sociology for Beginners*. Cambridge: Icon Books, 1996.

Ostergaard, Bernt Stubbe and Euromedia Research Group (eds). *The Media in Western Europe: The Euromedia Handbook*, 2nd edn. London: Sage, 1997.

Ouchi, William. *Theory Z: How American Business Can Meet the Japanese Challenge*. Reading, MA: Addison-Wesley, 1981.

P

Pahl, Jan. *Money and Marriage*. Basingstoke: Macmillan Education, 1989.

Pahl, Ray. *Divisions of Labour*. Oxford: Blackwell, 1984.

Pakulski, Jan. 'Mass social movements and social class'. *International Sociology*, Vol. 8, No. 2 (June 1993): 131–58.

Palmore, Erdman. 'Predictors of successful aging'. *The Gerontologist*, Vol. 19, No. 5 (October 1979a): 427–31.

——. 'Advantages of aging'. *The Gerontologist*, Vol. 19, No. 2 (April 1979b): 220–23.

——. 'What can the USA learn from Japan about aging?', in Steven H. Zarit (ed.), *Readings in Aging and Death: Contemporary Perspectives*. New York: Harper & Row, 1982: 166–9.

Papathanassopoulos, Stylianos. *European Television in the Digital Age*. Cambridge: Polity Press, 2002.

Parekh, Bhikhu. 'The Rushdie affair and the British press'. *Social Studies Review* (November 1989): 44.

Park, Robert E. *Race and Culture*. Glencoe, IL: Free Press, 1950.

——. 'The city: suggestions for the investigation of human behavior in the human environment', in Robert E. Park and Ernest W. Burgess, *The City*. Chicago: University of Chicago Press, 1967; orig. 1925: 1–46.

Park, Robert E. and Ernest W. Burgess. *The City*. Chicago: University of Chicago Press, 1967; orig. 1925.

Parker, Richard and Herbert Daniel. *Sexuality, Politics and AIDS in Brazil: In Another World?* Bristol, PA: Taylor & Francis, 1993.

Parkin, Frank. *Class Inequality and Political Order: Social Stratification in Capitalist and Communist Societies*. London: MacGibbon & Kee, 1971.

Parkinson, C. Northcote. *Parkinson's Law and Other Studies in Administration*. New York: Ballantine Books, 1957.

Parrillo, Vincent N. *Diversity in America*. Thousand Oaks, CA: Pine Forge Press, 1996.

Parsons, Talcott. 'Age and sex in the social structure of the United States'. *American Sociological Review*, Vol. 7, No. 4 (August 1942): 604–16.

——. *The Social System*. New York: Free Press, 1964; orig. 1951.

——. *Essays in Sociological Theory*. New York: Free Press, 1964; orig. 1954.

——. *Societies: Evolutionary and Comparative Perspectives*. Englewood Cliffs, NJ: Prentice-Hall, 1966.

Parsons, Talcott and Robert F. Bales (eds). *Family, Socialization and Interaction Process*. New York: Free Press, 1955.

Paul, Ellen Frankel. 'Bared buttocks and federal cases'. *Society*, Vol. 28, No. 4 (1991): 4–7.

Payne, Geoff (ed.). *Social Divisions*. London: Macmillan, 2000, 2nd edn, 2005.

Pear, Robert, with Erik Eckholm. 'When healers are entrepreneurs: a debate over costs and ethics'. *New York Times* (2 June 1991): 1, 17.

Penguin Dictionary of Sociology, The. Nick Abercrombie, Stephen Hill and Bryan Turner (eds). Harmondsworth: Penguin, 4th edn, 2000.

Pessen, Edward. *Riches, Class and Power: America Before the Civil War.* New Brunswick, NJ: Transaction, 1990.

Peter, Laurence J. and Raymond Hull. *The Peter Principle: Why Things Always Go Wrong.* New York: William Morrow, 1969.

Peters Atlas of the World. New York: Harper & Row, 1990.

Peters, Thomas J. and Robert H. Waterman, Jr. *In Search of Excellence: Lessons From America's Best-Run Companies.* New York: Warner Books, 1982.

Phillips, Adam. *On Flirtation.* Cambridge, MA: Harvard University Press, 1994.

Phillipson, Chris. *Capitalism and the Construction of Old Age.* London: Macmillan, 1982.

Phillipson, Chris. *Reconstructing Old Age: New Agendas in Social Theory and Practice.* London: Sage, 1998.

Phizacklea, Annie. *One Way Ticket: Migration and Female Labour.* London: Edward Arnold, 1993.

——. *Unpacking the Fashion Industry: Gender, Racism and Class in Production.* London: Routledge, 1995.

Pickering, K. T. and Lewis A. Owen. *An Introduction to Global Environmental Issues.* London: Routledge, 1994.

Pieterse, Jan Nederveen. 'Globalization as hybridization', in Mike Featherstone *et al.* (eds), *Global Modernities.* London: Sage, 1995.

——. *Globalization and Culture: Global Melange.* Lanham, MD: Rowman & Littlefield, 2004.

Pietroni, P. *Reader's Digest Guide to Alternative Medicine.* London: Reader's Digest Association, 1991.

Pilcher, Jane and Imelda Whelehan. *Fifty Key Concepts in Gender Studies.* London: Sage, 2004.

Pillemer, Karl. 'Maltreatment of the elderly at home and in institutions: extent, risk factors, and policy recommendations', in US Congress. House, Select Committee on Aging, and Senate, Special Committee on Aging, *Legislative Agenda for an Aging Society: 1988 and Beyond.* Washington, DC: US Government Printing Office, 1988.

Pines, Maya. 'The civilization of Genie'. *Psychology Today*, Vol. 15 (September 1981): 28–34.

Pirandello, Luigi. *The Pleasure of Honesty.* 1962.

Pitt, Malcolm. *Introducing Hinduism.* New York: Friendship Press, 1955.

Piven, Frances Fox and Richard A. Cloward. *Regulating the Poor: the Functions of Public Welfare.* London: Tavistock, 1972.

Pizzey, Erin. *Scream Quietly or the Neighbours Will Hear.* Harmondsworth: Penguin, 1974.

Platt, L. *Parallel Lives? Poverty among Ethnic Minority Groups in Britain.* London: Child Poverty Action Group, 2002.

——. 'Poverty', in Geoff Payne (ed.), *Social Divisions.* London: Macmillan, 2000, 3rd edn, 2005.

Plomin, Robert and Terryl T. Foch. 'A twin study of objectively assessed personality in childhood'. *Journal of Personality and Social Psychology*, Vol. 39, No. 4 (October 1980): 680–8.

Plummer, Ken. *Documents of Life: An Introduction to the Problems and Literature of a Humanistic Method.* London: Allen & Unwin, 1983.

——. 'Organising AIDS', in Peter Aggleton and Hilary Homans, (eds), *Social Aspects of AIDS.* London: Falmer Press, 1988.

——. 'Speaking its name: inventing gay and lesbian studies', in Ken Plummer (ed.), *Modern Homosexualities.* London: Routledge, 1992.

——. *Documents of Life 2: An Invitation to a Critical Humanism.* London: Sage, 2001a.

——. 'The square of intimate citizenship'. *Citizenship Studies*, Vol. 5, No. 3 (November 2001b): 237–53.

——. *Intimate Citizenship.* Seattle: University of Washington Press, 2003.

Pogge, Thomas. *World Poverty and Human Rights.* Cambridge: Polity Press, 2002.

Pollak, Otto. *The Criminality of Women.* New York: Basic, 1950; 2nd edn, 1961.

Polsby, Nelson W. 'Three problems in the analysis of community power'. *American Sociological Review*, Vol. 24, No. 6 (December 1959): 796–803.

Popenoe, David 'Family decline in the Swedish welfare state'. *The Public Interest*, No. 102 (Winter 1991): 65–77.

——. 'The controversial truth: two-parent families are better'. *New York Times* (26 December 1992): 21.

——. 'American family decline, 1960–1990: a review and appraisal'. *Journal of Marriage and the Family*, Vol. 55, No. 3 (August 1993): 527–55.

——. 'Scandinavian welfare'. *Society*, Vol. 31, No. 6 (September–October, 1994): 78–81.

Population Reference Bureau. *1995 World Population Data Sheet.* Washington, DC: Population Reference Bureau, 1995a.

——. 'Past and future population doubling times, selected countries'. *Population Today*, Vol. 23, No. 2 (February 1995b): 6.

Population Today. 'Majority of children in poverty live with parents who work'. *Population Today*, Vol. 23, No. 4 (April 1995): 6.

Population Trends, 1997. London: HMSO, 1997.

Population Trends, 2000. London: HMSO, 2001.

Postel, Sandra. 'Facing water scarcity', in Lester R. Brown et al. (eds), *State of the World 1993: A Worldwatch Institute Report on Progress Toward a Sustainable Society*. New York: W. W. Norton, 1993: 22–41.

Postman, Neil. *Amusing Ourselves to Death*. London: Methuen, 1986.

Poulantzas, Nicos. 'The problem of the capitalist state'. *New Left Review*, 1969.

Powell, Chris and George E. C. Paton (eds). *Humour in Society: Resistance and Control*. New York: St Martin's Press, 1988.

Presser, Harriet B. 'The housework gender gap'. *Population Today*, Vol. 21, No. 7/8 (July–August 1993): 5.

Price, Simon. *Human Capital, Hysteresis and Unemployment among Workers with Finite Lives*. London: European Social Research Council on Micro-Social Change, 1991.

Primeggia, Salvatore and Joseph A. Varacalli. 'Southern Italian comedy: Old to New World', in Joseph V. Scelsa, Salvatore J. LaGumina and Lydio Tomasi (eds), *Italian Americans in Transition*. New York: The American Italian Historical Association, 1990: 241–52.

Pryce, Ken. *Endless Pressure*, 2nd edn. Harmondsworth: Penguin, 1986; orig. 1979.

Pullen, Kirsten. 'I-love-Xena.com', in David Gauntlett (ed.), *web.studies*. London: Arnold, 2000: 52–61.

Q

Quinney, Richard. *Class, State and Crime: On the Theory and Practice of Criminal Justice*. New York: David McKay, 1977.

R

Rademacher, Eric W. 'The effect of question wording on college students'. *Pittsburgh Undergraduate Review*, Vol. 8, No. 1 (Spring 1992): 45–81.

Rademaekers, William and Rhea Schoenthal. 'Iceman'. *Time*, Vol. 140, No. 17 (26 October 1992): 62–6.

Ranade, W. *A Future for the NHS? Health Care in the 1990s*, 2nd edn. London: Longman, 1994.

Ransom, David. 'The dictatorship of debt'. *New Internationalist* (May 1999).

Rathje, William and Cullan Murphy. *Rubbish: The Archeology of Garbage*. New York: HarperCollins, 1991.

Redclift, Michael and Ted Benton (eds). *Social Theory and the Global Environment*. London: Routledge, 1994.

Reid, Ivan. *Social Class Differences in Britain*, 3rd edn. London: Fontana, 1989.

——. *Social Class in Britain*. Cambridge: Polity Press, 1998.

Reinharz, Shulamit. *Feminist Methods in Social Research*. New York: Oxford University Press, 1992.

Remoff, Heather Trexler. *Sexual Choice: A Woman's Decision*. New York: Dutton/Lewis, 1984.

Rex, John and Robert Moore. *Race, Community and Conflict*. London: Oxford University Press, 1967.

Richards, Janet. *The Sceptical Feminist: A Philosophical Enquiry*. Harmondsworth: Penguin, 1982.

Richardson, Diane. *Women, Motherhood and Children*. London: Macmillan, 1993.

——. *Women, Motherhood and Childrearing*. London: Macmillan, 1994.

——. *Rethinking Sexuality*, London: Sage, 2000.

Richardson, James T. 'Definitions of cult: from sociological–technical to popular negative'. Paper presented to the American Psychological Association, Boston, MA, August 1990.

Ridgeway, Cecilia L. *The Dynamics of Small Groups*. New York: St Martin's Press, 1983.

Rieff, Philip. 'Introduction', in Charles Horton Cooley, *Social Organization*. New York: Schocken Books, 1962.

Riesman, David. *The Lonely Crowd: A Study of the Changing American Character*. New Haven, CT: Yale University Press, 1970; orig. 1950.

Riley, Matilda White, Anne Foner and Joan Waring. 'Sociology of age', in Neil J. Smelser (ed.), *Handbook of Sociology*. Newbury Park, CA: Sage, 1988: 243–90.

Ritzer, George. *Sociological Theory*. New York: Alfred A. Knopf, 1983: 63–6; 3rd edn, New York: McGraw-Hill, 1992.

——. *The McDonaldization of Society: An Investigation into the Changing Character of Contemporary Social Life*. Thousand Oaks, CA: Pine Forge Press, 1993; 2nd edn, 1996; 3rd edn, 2000.

——. *Expressing America*. London: Sage, 1995.

——. *Enchanting a Disenchanted World*. Thousand Oaks, CA: Pine Forge Press, 1999.

——. (ed.). *The McDonaldization Reader*. Thousand Oaks, CA: Pine Forge Press, London: Sage, 2002.

——. *Cathedrals of Consumption*. Thousand Oaks, CA: Pine Forge Press, 2004a.

——. *Handbook of Social Problems*, Thousand Oaks, CA: Sage, 2004b.

Roberts, Brian. *Biographical Research*. Buckingham: Open University Press, 2002.

Roberts, J. Deotis. *Roots of a Black Future: Family and Church*. Philadelphia, PA: Westminster Press, 1980.

Roberts, Ken. *Class in Modern Britain*. London: Palgrave, 2001.

Robertson, Roland. *Globalization: Social Theory and Global Culture*. London: Sage, 1992.

Robinson, Joyce and Glena Spitze. 'Whistle while you work? The effect of household task performance on women's and men's well-being'. *Social Science Quarterly*, Vol. 73, No. 4 (December 1992): 844–61.

Rockett, Ian R. H. 'Population and health: an introduction to epidemiology'. *Population Bulletin*, Vol. 49, No. 3 (November 1994). Washington, DC: Population Reference Bureau.

Roesch, Roberta. 'Violent families'. *Parents*, Vol. 59, No. 9 (September 1984): 74–6, 150–2.

Roethlisberger, F. J. and William J. Dickson. *Management and the Worker*. Cambridge, MA: Harvard University Press, 1939.

Rojek, Chris. *Stuart Hall*. Cambridge: Polity Press, 2002.

Rokove, Milton L. *Don't Make No Waves, Don't Back No Losers*. Bloomington, IN: Indiana University Press, 1975.

Róna-Tas, Ákos. 'The first shall be last? Entrepreneurship and Communist cadres in the transition from Socialism'. *American Journal of Sociology*, Vol. 100, No. 1 (July 1994): 40–69.

Roof, Wade Clark. *A Generation of Seekers: The Spiritual Journeys of the Baby Boom Generation*. New York: HarperCollins, 1992.

Roof, Wade Clark and William McKinney. *American Mainline Religion: Its Changing Shape and Future*. New Brunswick, NJ: Rutgers University Press, 1987.

Roper, Lyndal. *Oedipus and the Devil: Witchcraft, Sexuality and Religion in Early Modern Europe*. London: Routledge, 1994.

Rose, Hilary and Steven Rose. *Alas, Poor Darwin: Arguments against Evolutionary Psychology*. London: Cape, 2001.

Rose, Jerry D. *Outbreaks*. New York: Free Press, 1982.

Rosen, Ellen Israel. *Bitter Choices: Blue-Collar Women In and Out of Work*. Chicago: University of Chicago Press, 1987.

Rosenbaum, Alan S. (ed.). *The Philosophy of Human Rights: International Perspectives*. London: Aldwych Press, 1980.

Rosenthal, A. *The New Documentary in Action*. Berkeley, CA: University of California Press, 1971.

Rosenthal, Elizabeth. 'Canada's national health plan gives care to all with limits'. *New York Times* (30 April 1991): A1, A1b.

Rossi, Alice S. 'Gender and parenthood', in Alice S. Rossi (ed.), *Gender and the Life Course*. New York: Aldine, 1985: 161–91.

Rostow, Walt W. *The Stages of Economic Growth: A Non-Communist Manifesto*. Cambridge: Cambridge University Press, 1960.

——. *The World Economy: History and Prospect*. Austin, TX: University of Texas Press, 1978.

Rothman, Barbara Katz. *Genetic Maps and Human Imaginations: The Limits of Science in Understanding Who We Are*. New York: W. W. Norton, 1998.

Rothman, M., P. Entzel and B. Dunlop (eds). *Elders, Crime and the Criminal Justice System*. New York: Springer-Verlag, 2000.

Rowbottom, Sheila. *A Century of Women: The History of Women in Britain and the United States*. London: Viking, 1997.

Rowe, David C. amd D. Wayne Osgood. 'Heredity and sociological theories of delinquency: a reconsideration'. *American Sociological Review*, Vol. 49. No. 4 (August 1984): 526–40.

Rowntree, Seebohm. *Poverty: A Study of Town Life*. London: Macmillan, 1902.

Roxborough, Ian. 'War, militarism and national security', in George Ritzer (ed.), *Handbook of Social Problems*. Thousand Oaks, CA: Sage, 2004: 335–54.

Rubin, Beth, A. 'Class struggle American style: unions, strikes and wages'. *American Sociological Review*, Vol. 51, No. 5 (October 1986): 618–31.

Rubin, Gayle. 'Thinking sex', in Carole S. Vance, *Pleasure and Danger*. London: Routledge, 1984.

Rubin, Lillian Breslow. *Worlds of Pain: Life in the Working-Class Family*. New York: Basic Books, 1976.

Ruggiero, Vincento, Mick Ryan and Joe Sim (eds). *Western European Penal Systems: A Critical Anatomy*. London: Sage, 1995.

Rule, James and Peter Brantley. 'Computerized surveillance in the workplace'. *Sociological Forum*, Vol. 7, No. 3 (September 1992): 405–23.

Rummel, R. J. *Death by Government*. New Brunswick, NJ: Transaction, 1996.

Runciman, W. G. 'How many classes are there in society?'. *Sociology*, Vol. 24 (1990): 377–96.

Runnymede Trust. *Multi-ethnic Britain – Facts and Trends*. London: Runnymede Trust, 1994.

——. *Islamophobia – A Challenge for Us All*. London: Runnymede Trust, 1997.

Rushdie, Salman. *Midnight's Children*. London: Picador, 1982.

Rushkoff, Douglas. *Playing the Future: What We Can Learn from Digital Kids*. New York: Riverhead, 1999.

Russell, Cheryl. 'The master trend'. *American Demographics*, Vol. 15, No. 10 (October 1993): 28–37.

Russell, Diana E. H. *Rape in Marriage*. New York: Macmillan, 1982.

Ryan, William. *Blaming the Victim*, rev. edn. New York: Vintage Books, 1976.

Rymer, Russ. *Genie*. New York: HarperPerennial, 1994.

S

Sagan, Carl. *The Dragons of Eden*. New York: Ballantine, 1977.

Said, Edward. *Culture and Imperialism*. London: Chatto, 1993.

Saks, M. *Alternative Medicine*. Oxford: Clarendon Press, 1992.

Sale, Kirkpatrick. *The Conquest of Paradise: Christopher Columbus and the Columbian Legacy*. New York: Alfred A. Knopf, 1990.

Sampson, Anthony. *Who Runs This Place? The Anatomy of Britain in the 21st Century*. London: John Murray, 2004.

Sampson, Robert J. 'Urban black violence: the effects of male joblessness and family disruption'. *American Journal of Sociology*, Vol. 93, No. 2 (September 1987): 348–82.

Sampson, Robert J. and John H. Laub. 'Crime and deviance over the life course: the salience of adult social bonds'. *American Sociological Review*, Vol. 55, No. 5 (October 1990): 609–27.

Samson, Colin. *A Way of Life That Does Not Exist: Canada and the Extinguishment of the Innu*. London: Verso, 2003.

Santoli, Al. 'Fighting child prostitution'. *Freedom Review*, Vol. 25, No. 5 (September–October 1994): 5–8.

Sapir, Edward. 'The status of linguistics as a science'. *Language*, Vol. 5 (1929): 207–14.

——. *Selected Writings of Edward Sapir in Language, Culture and Personality*. David G. Mandelbaum, ed. Berkeley, CA: University of California Press, 1949.

Sargent, Lyman Tower (ed.). *Extremism in America: A Reader*. New York: New York University Press, 1995.

Sassen, Saskia. *The Global City: New York, London, Tokyo*. Princeton, NJ: Princeton University Press, 1991.

——. *Cities in a World Economy*, 2nd edn. London: Sage, 2000.

Sato, Ikuyo. *Kamikaze Biker: Parody and Anomie in Affluent Japan*. Chicago: University of Chicago Press, 1991.

Saunders, Peter. *Social Class and Stratification*. London: Routledge, 1990.

Savage, Mike. *Walter Benjamin and Urban Meaning*. Keele: University of Keele Press, 1993.

Savage, Mike, J. Burlow, P. Dickens and T. Fielding. *Property, Bureaucracy and Culture: Middle-Class Formation in Contemporary Britain*. London: Routledge, 1992.

Savage, Mike and Alan Warde. *Urban Sociology, Capitalism and Modernity*. London: Macmillan, 1993.

Sayers, Janet. *Biological Politics*. London: Tavistock, 1982.

Scaff, Lawrence A. 'Max Weber and Robert Michels'. *American Journal of Sociology*, Vol. 86, No. 6 (May 1981): 1269–86.

Scarman, Leslie George. *The Brixton Disorders, 10–12 April 1981: Report of an Inquiry: Presented to Parliament by the Secretary of State for the Home Department, November 1981*. London: HMSO, 1981.

Schaefer, Richard T. *Sociology*, 7th edn. New York: McGraw-Hill, 2001.

Schaie, I. Warner. 'Intelligence and problem solving', in James E. Birren and R. Bruce Sloane (eds), *Handbook of Mental Health and Aging*. Englewood Cliffs, NJ: Prentice-Hall, 1980: 262–84.

Scharping, Thomas. *Birth Control in China 1978–1994*. New York: Curzon Press, 2000.

Scheff, Thomas J. *Mental Illness and Social Processes*. New York: Harper & Row, 1967.

——. *Being Mentally Ill: A Sociological Theory*, 2nd edn. New York: Aldine, 1984; orig. 1966.

Schellenberg, James A. *Masters of Social Psychology*. New York: Oxford University Press, 1978: 38–62.

Scheper-Hughes, Nancy. *Death Without Weeping: The Violence of Everyday Life in Brazil*. Berkeley, CA: University of California Press, 1992.

——. 'The global traffic in organs'. *Current Anthropology*, Vol. 41, No. 2 (2000): 191–224.

Scheper-Hughes, Nancy and Loic Wacquant (eds). *Commodifying Bodies*. London: Sage, 2002.

Schlesinger, Philip. *Putting 'Reality' Together: BBC News*. London: Constable, 1978.

Schmidt, Roger. *Exploring Religion*. Belmont, CA: Wadsworth, 1980.

Schnaiberg, Allan and Kenneth Alan Gould. *Environment and Society: The Enduring Conflict*. New York: St Martin's Press, 1994.

Schodt, Frederick. *Manga! Manga! The World of Japanese Comics*. London: Kodansha Europe, 1986.

Scholte, Jan Aart. 'The globalisation of world politics', in John Bayles and Steve Smith (eds), *The Globalisation of World Politics*. Oxford: Oxford University Press, 1997.

Schooler, Carmi, Joanne Miller, Karen A. Miller and Carol N. Richtand. 'Work for the household: its nature and consequences for husbands and wives'. *American Journal of Sociology*, Vol. 90, No. 1 (July 1984): 97–124.

Schramm, Wilbur. *TV in the Lives of our Children*. Stanford, CA: Stanford University Press, 1961.

Schulte, Joachim. *Experience and Expression: Wittgenstein's Philosophy of Psychology*. Oxford: Clarendon Press, 1995.

Schumann, Hans Wolfgang. *Buddhism: An Outline of Its Teachings and Schools*. Wheaton, IL: The Theosophical Publishing House/Quest Books, 1974.

Schwartz, Martin D. 'Gender and injury in spousal assault'. *Sociological Focus*, Vol. 20, No. 1 (January 1987): 61–75.

Scott, John. *Who Rules Britain?* Cambridge: Polity Press, 1991.

——. *Poverty and Wealth*. London: Longman, 1994.

——. *Stratification and Power: Structures of Class, Status and Command*. Cambridge: Polity Press, 1996.

——. *Corporate Business and Capitalist Classes*. Oxford: Oxford University Press, 1997.

——. *Social Network Analysis: A Handbook*, 2nd edn. London: Sage, 2000a.

——. 'Class and stratification', in Geoff Payne (ed.), *Social Divisions*. Basingstoke: Macmillan/Palgrave, 2000b; 3rd edn, 2005.

Scott, John and Catherine Griff. *Directors of Industry: The British Corporate Network*, 1904–1976. New York: Blackwell, 1985.

Scott, Peter. *The Meanings of Mass Higher Education*. Buckingham: Open University Press, 1995.

Scott, W. Richard. *Organizations: Rational, Natural and Open Systems*. Englewood Cliffs, NJ: Prentice-Hall, 1981.

Scrambler, Graham. *Health and Social Change: A Critical Theory*. Oxford: Oxford University Press, 2002.

Seabrook, Jeremy. *In the Cities of the South*. London: Verso, 1996; 2nd edn, 2001.

Seager, Joni. *The State of the Women in the World Atlas*. New York: Penguin, 1997.

Sedgwick, Eve Kasofsky. *The Epistemology of the Closet*. Berkeley, CA: University of California Press, 1990.

Segal, Lynne. *Is the Future Female? Troubled Thoughts on Contemporary Feminism*. London: Virago, 1994.

——. *Straight Sex: The Politics of Pleasure*. London: Virago, 1994; 2nd edn, 1997.

——. *Why Feminism*. Cambridge: Polity Press, 1999.

Seidman, Steven (ed.). *Queer Theory/Sociology*. Oxford: Blackwell, 1996.

Sekulic, Dusko, Garth Massey and Randy Hodson. 'Who were the Yugoslavs? Failed sources of common identity in the former Yugoslavia'. *American Sociological Review*, Vol. 59, No. 1 (February 1994): 83–97.

Sellin, Thorsten. *The Penalty of Death*. Beverly Hills, CA: Sage, 1980.

Seltzer, Robert M. *Jewish People, Jewish Thought: The Jewish Experience in History*. New York: Macmillan, 1980.

Sen, Amartya. *Development as Freedom*. New York: Alfred A. Knopf, 1999.

Sen, K. M. *Hinduism*. Baltimore, MD: Penguin Books, 1961.

Sennett, Richard and Jonathan Cobb. *The Hidden Injuries of Class*. New York: Vintage Books, 1973.

Shapiro, Joseph P. and Joannie M. Schrof. 'Honor thy children'. *US News and World Report*, Vol. 118, No. 8 (27 February 1995): 39–49.

Sharma, Ursula. *Caste*. Buckingham: Open University Press, 1999.

Sharpe, Sue. *Just Like a Girl: How Girls Learn to Become Women*, 2nd edn. Harmondsworth: Penguin, 1994.

Shaw, Clifford S. *The Jack Roller*. Chicago: University of Chicago Press, 1966; orig. 1930.

Shaw, Martin. *War and Genocide: Organized Killing in Modern Society*. Cambridge: Polity Press, 2003.

Shawcross, William. *Sideshow: Kissinger, Nixon and the Destruction of Cambodia*. New York: Pocket Books, 1979.

Sheehan, Molly O'Meara. 'Making better transportation choices', in Lester R. Brown *et al.* (eds), *State of the World 2001*. London: Earthscan, 2001: Chapter 6, 103–22.

Sheehan, Tom. 'Senior esteem as a factor in socioeconomic complexity'. *The Gerontologist*, Vol. 16, No. 5 (October 1976): 433–40.

Sheehy, Gail. *Passages: Predictable Crises of Adult Life*. New York: Dutton, 1976.

Sheldon, William H., Emil M. Hartl and Eugene McDermott. *Varieties of Delinquent Youth*. New York: Harper, 1949.

Sheley, James F., Joshua Zhang, Charles J. Brody and James D. Wright. 'Gang organization, gang criminal activity and individual gang members' criminal behavior'. *Social Science Quarterly*, Vol. 76, No. 1 (March 1995): 53–68.

Shenon, Philip. 'A Pacific island nation is stripped of everything'. *New York Times* (10 December 1995): 3.

Sherman, Lawrence W. and Douglas A. Smith. 'Crime, punishment and stake in conformity: legal and informal control of domestic violence'. *American Sociological Review*, Vol. 57, No. 5 (October 1992): 680–90.

Sherman, Sharon R. *Documenting Ourselves: Film, Video, Culture*. Lexington, KY: University of Kentucky Press, 1998.

Sherwin, Susan. *No Longer Patient: Feminist Ethics and Health Care*. Philadelphia, PA: Temple University Press, 1992.

Shevky, Eshref and Wendell Bell. *Social Area Analysis*. Stanford, CA: Stanford University Press, 1955.

Shilling, Chris. *The Body and Social Theory 2nd edn*. London: Sage, 2003.

Shipler, David K. *Russia: Broken Idols, Solemn Dreams*. New York: Penguin Books, 1984.

Shipley, Joseph T. *Dictionary of Word Origins*. Totowa, NJ: Rowman & Allanheld, 1985.

Shupe, Anson, William A. Stacey and Lonnie R. Hazlewood. *Violent Men, Violent Couples: The Dynamics of Domestic Violence*. Lexington, MA: Lexington Books, 1987.

Shweder, R. A. *Welcome to Middle Age (and Other Cultural Fictions)*. Chicago: University of Chicago Press, 1998.

Sidel, Ruth and Victor W. Sidel. *A Healthy State: An International Perspective on the Crisis in United States Medical Care*, rev. edn. New York: Pantheon Books, 1982a.

——. *The Health Care of China*. Boston, MA: Beacon Press, 1982b.

Sills, David L. 'The succession of goals', in Amitai Etzioni (ed.), *A Sociological Reader on Complex Organizations*, 2nd edn. New York: Holt, Rinehart & Winston, 1969: 175–87.

Silva, Elizabeth B. and Carol Smart. *The New Family?* London: Sage, 1999.

Silver, Lee. *Remaking Eden*. London: Phoenix Giant, 1998.

Silverberg, Robert. 'The greenhouse effect: apocalypse now or Chicken Little?' *Omni* (July 1991): 50–4.

Simmel, Georg. *The Sociology of Georg Simmel*. Kurt Wolff, ed. New York: Free Press, 1950: 118–69; orig. 1902.

——. 'The metropolis and mental Life', in Georg Simmel, *The Sociology of Georg Simmel*. Kurt Wolff, ed. New York: Free Press, 1950: 409–24; orig. 1905.

Simon, Julian. *The Ultimate Resource*. Princeton, NJ: Princeton University Press, 1981.

Simons, Carol. 'Japan's Kyoiku mamas', in John J. Macionis and Nijole V. Benokraitis (eds), *Seeing Ourselves: Classic, Contemporary and Cross-Cultural Readings in Sociology*. Englewood Cliffs, NJ: Prentice-Hall, 1989: 281–6.

Simons, Marlise. 'The price of modernization: the case of Brazil's Kaiapo Indians', in John J. Macionis and Nijole V. Benokraitis (eds), *Seeing Ourselves: Classic, Contemporary, and Cross-Cultural Readings in Sociology*, 3rd edn. Englewood Cliffs, NJ: Prentice-Hall, 1995: 470–6.

Simpson, George Eaton and J. Milton Yinger. *Racial and Cultural Minorities: An Analysis of Prejudice and Discrimination*, 4th edn. New York: Harper & Row, 1972.

Sinfield, Adrian. *What Unemployment Means*. Oxford: Martin Robertson, 1981.

Sivard, Ruth Leger. *World Military and Social Expenditures, 1987–88*, 12th edn. Washington, DC: World Priorities, 1988.

Sizer, Theodore R. *Horace's Compromise: The Dilemma of the American High School*. Boston, MA: Houghton Mifflin, 1984.

Skeggs, Beverley. *Formations of Class and Gender: Becoming Respectable*. London: Sage, 1997.

Skellington, R. *'Race' in Britain Today*, 2nd edn. London: Sage, 1996.

Skelton, T. and Gill Valentine (eds). *Cool Places: Geographies of Youth Cultures*. London: Routledge, 1998.

Skocpol, Theda. *States and Social Revolutions: A Comparative Analysis of France, Russia and China*. Cambridge: Cambridge University Press, 1979.

Skolnick, Arlene. *The Psychology of Human Development*. New York: Harcourt Brace Jovanovich, 1986.

Slater, Philip E. 'Contrasting correlates of group size'. *Sociometry*, Vol. 21, No. 2 (June 1958): 129–39.

——. *The Pursuit of Loneliness*. Boston, MA: Beacon Press, 1976.

Smart, Barry. *Michel Foucault*. London: Routledge, 1985.

——. (ed.). *Resisting McDonaldization*. London: Sage, 1999.

Smart, Carol. *Women, Crime and Criminology: A Feminist Critique*. London: Routledge and Kegan Paul, 1977.

——. *The Ties that Bind*. London: Routledge, 1984.

Smart, Carol and Bren Neal. *Family Fragments?* Cambridge: Polity Press, 1999.

Smart, Ninian. *Atlas of World Religions*. Oxford: Oxford University Press, 1999.

Smith, Adam. *An Enquiry into the Nature and Causes of the Wealth of Nations*. New York: The Modern Library, 1937; orig. 1776.

Smith, Anthony and Frank Webster (eds). *The Postmodern University? Contested Voices of Higher Education in Society*. Buckingham: Open University Press, 1997.

Smith, Christian. *The Emergence of Liberation Theology: Radical Religion and Social Movement Theory*. Chicago: Chicago University Press, 1991.

Smith, Dan (ed.). *The State of the World Atlas: New Edition for the 21st Century*. Harmondsworth: Penguin, 1999.

Smith, David. *Third World Cities*, 2nd edn. London: Routledge, 2002.

Smith, David and Shelagh Armstrong. *If the World were a Village*. London: A&C Black Publications, 2003.

Smith, David J. and Sally Tomlinson. *The School Effect: A Study of Multi-racial Comprehensives*. London: Policy Studies Institute, 1989.

Smith, Douglas A. 'Police response to interpersonal violence: defining the parameters of legal control'. *Social Forces*, Vol. 65, No. 3 (March 1987): 767–82.

Smith, Douglas A. and Patrick R. Gartin. 'Specifying specific deterrence: the influence of arrest on future criminal activity'. *American Sociological Review*, Vol. 54, No. 1 (February 1989): 94–105.

Smith, Gordon. *Politics in Western Europe*. Aldershot: Dartmouth, 1990.

Smith, Robert B. 'Health care reform now'. *Society*, Vol. 30, No. 3 (March–April 1993): 56–65.

Smith, Tom W. Research results reported in 'Anti-Semitism decreases but persists'. *Society*, Vol. 33, No. 3 (March/April 1996): 2.

Smith-Lovin, Lynn and Charles Brody. 'Interruptions in group discussions: the effects of gender and group composition'. *American Journal of Sociology*, Vol. 54, No. 3 (June 1989): 424–35.

Smolowe, Jill. 'When violence hits home'. *Time*, Vol. 144, No. 1 (4 July 1994): 18–25.

Snell, Marilyn Berlin. 'The purge of nurture'. *New Perspectives Quarterly*, Vol. 7, No. 1 (Winter 1990): 1–2.

Snodgrass, Jon. *The Jack-Roller at Seventy*. Lexington, MA: DC Heath/Lexington Books, 1982.

Social Trends, 1997. London: HMSO, 1997.

Social Trends, 1999. London: HMSO, 1999.

Social Trends, 2000. London: HMSO, 2000.

Social Trends, 2001. London. HMSO, 2001.

Social Trends, 2002. London: HMSO, 2002.

Social Trends, 2003. London. HMSO, 2003.

Social Trends, 2004. London: HMSO, 2004.

Sorokin, Pitrim and C. Berger. *Time Budgets of Human Behaviour*. Cambridge, MA: Harvard University Press, 1938.

South, Scott J. and Steven F. Messner. 'Structural determinants of intergroup association: interracial marriage and crime'. *American Journal of Sociology*, Vol. 91, No. 6 (May 1986): 1409–30.

Sowell, Thomas. *Ethnic America*. New York: Basic Books, 1981.

——. *Race and Culture*. New York: Basic Books, 1994.

——. 'Ethnicity and IQ', in Steven Fraser (ed.), *The Bell Curve Wars: Race, Intelligence and the Future of America*. New York: Basic Books, 1995: 70–9.

——. *Migrations and Cultures: A World View*. New York: Basic Books, 1996.

Soysal, Yasemin. *Limits of Citizenship: Migrants and Postnational Membership in Europe*. Chicago: University of Chicago Press, 1994.

Spates, James L. 'Counterculture and dominant culture values: a cross-national analysis of the underground press and dominant culture magazines'. *American Sociological Review*, Vol. 41, No. 5 (October 1976): 868–83.

——. 'The sociology of values', in Ralph Turner (ed.), *Annual Review of Sociology*, Vol. 9. Palo Alto, CA: Annual Reviews, 1983: 27–49.

Spates, James L. and John J. Macionis. *The Sociology of Cities*, 2nd edn. Belmont, CA: Wadsworth, 1987.

Spates, James L. and H. Wesley Perkins. 'American and English student values'. *Comparative Social Research*, Vol. 5. Greenwich, CT: JAI Press, 1982: 245–68.

Spector, Leonard S. 'Nuclear proliferation today', in William M. Evan and Stephen Hilgartner (eds), *The Arms Race and Nuclear War*. Englewood Cliffs, NJ: Prentice-Hall, 1988: 25–9.

Speer, James A. 'The new Christian Right and its parent company: a study in political contrasts', in David G. Bromley and Anson Shupe (eds), *New Christian Politics*. Macon, GA: Mercer University Press, 1984: 19–40.

Spender, Dale. *Man Made Language*. London: Routledge and Kegan Paul, 1980.

——. *Women of Ideas and What Men Have Done To Them: From Aphra Behn to Adrienne Rich*. London: Routledge and Kegan Paul, 1982.

Spitzer, Steven. 'Toward a Marxian theory of deviance', in Delos H. Kelly (ed.), *Criminal Behavior: Readings in Criminology*. New York: St Martin's Press, 1980: 175–91.

Spybey, Tony (ed.). *Britain in Europe: An Introduction to Sociology*. London: Routledge, 1997.

Stacey, Judith. *Patriarchy and Socialist Revolution in China*. Berkeley, CA: University of California Press, 1983.

——. *Brave New Families: Stories of Domestic Upheaval in Late Twentieth-Century America*. New York: Basic Books, 1990.

——. 'Good riddance to "the family": a response to David Popenoe'. *Journal of Marriage and the Family*, Vol. 55, No. 3 (August 1993): 545–7.

——. *In the Name of the Family: Rethinking Family Values in the Postmodern Age*. Boston, MA: Beacon Press, 1996: 8.

Stanley, Liz (ed.). *Feminist Praxis: Research, Theory and Epistemology in Feminist Sociology*. London: Routledge and Kegan Paul, 1990.

Stanley, Liz and Sue Wise. *Breaking Out: Feminist Consciousness and Feminist Research*. London: Routledge and Kegan Paul, 1983.

Stanworth, M. D. *Gender and Schooling: A Study of Sexual Divisions in the Classroom*. London: Hutchinson in association with the Explorations in Feminism Collective, 1983.

Stark, Rodney. *Sociology*. Belmont, CA: Wadsworth, 1985.

Stark, Rodney and William Sims Bainbridge. 'Of churches, sects and cults: preliminary concepts for a theory of religious movements'. *Journal for the Scientific Study of Religion*, Vol. 18, No. 2 (June 1979): 117–31.

——. 'Secularization and cult formation in the jazz age'. *Journal for the Scientific Study of Religion*, Vol. 20, No. 4 (December 1981): 360–73.

Starker, Steven. *Evil Influences: Crusades against the Mass Media*. New Brunswick, NJ: Transaction, 1989.

Stavrianos, L. S. *A Global History: The Human Heritage*, 3rd edn. Englewood Cliffs, NJ: Prentice-Hall, 1983.

Steele, Shelby. *The Content of Our Character: A New Vision of Race in America*. New York: St Martin's Press, 1990.

Stein, Dorothy. *People Who Count: Population and Politics, Women and Children*. London: Earthscan, 1995.

Stein, Stuart. *Sociology on the Web: A Student Guide*. Harlow: Pearson, 2003.

Stephens, John D. *The Transition from Capitalism to Socialism*. Urbana, IL: University of Illinois Press, 1986.

Stern, Steve J. *The Secret History of Gender: Women, Men, and Power in Late Colonial Mexico*. Chapel Hill, NC: University of North Carolina Press, 1997.

Stern, Vivien. *Bricks of Shame: Britain's Prisons*, 2nd edn. Harmondsworth: Penguin, 1997.

Sternlieb, George and James W. Hughes. 'The uncertain future of the central city'. *Urban Affairs Quarterly*, Vol. 18, No. 4 (June 1983): 455–72.

Stinchcombe, Arthur L. 'Some empirical consequences of the Davis–Moore theory of stratification', *American Sociological Review*, Vol. 28, No. 5 (October 1963).

Stone, Lawrence. *The Family, Sex and Marriage in England 1500–1800*. New York: Harper & Row, 1977.

Stones, Rob. *Sociological Reasoning: Toward a Past-Modern Society*. London: Macmillan, 1996.

——. *Key Sociological Thinkers*. Basingstoke: Palgrave, 1998.

Storey, John. *Cultural Studies and the Study of Popular Culture*. Edinburgh: Edinburgh University Press, 1996.

Storry, Mike and Peter Childs (eds). *British Cultural Identities*. London: Routledge, 1997.

Storti, Craig. *The Art of Crossing Cultures*. Yarmouth, MN: Intercultural Press, 1990.

Stouffer, Samuel A. *et al. The American Soldier: Adjustment during Army Life*. Princeton, NJ: Princeton University Press, 1949.

Strang, John and Gerry Stimson. *AIDS and Drug Misuse: The Challenge for Policy and Practice in the 1990s*. London: Routledge, 1990.

Straus, Murray A. and Richard J. Gelles. 'Societal change and change in family violence from 1975 to 1985 as revealed by two national surveys'. *Journal of Marriage and the Family*, Vol. 48, No. 4 (August 1986): 465–79.

Streib, Gordon F. 'Are the aged a minority group?', in Bernice L. Neugarten (ed.), *Middle Age and Aging: A Reader in Social Psychology*. Chicago: University of Chicago Press, 1968: 35–46.

Stromquist, Nelly P. (ed.). *Women and Education in Latin America: Knowledge, Power and Change*. Boulder, CO: Lynne Rienner, 1992.

Strong, Philip. *The Ceremonial Order of the Clinic*. London: Routledge, 1979.

Sudnow, David N. *Passing On: The Social Organization of Dying*. Englewood Cliffs, NJ: Prentice-Hall, 1967.

Sumner, William Graham. *Folkways*. New York: Dover, 1959; orig. 1906.

Sutherland, Edwin H. 'White collar criminality'. *American Sociological Review*, Vol. 5, No. 1 (February 1940): 1–12.

Sutherland, Holly, T. Sefton and D. Pichaud. *Poverty in Britain: The Impact of Government Policy since 1997*. York: Joseph Rowntree Foundation, 2003.

Swann, Lord. *Education for All*. Cmmd 9453. London: HMSO, 1985.

Swartz, David. *Culture and Power: The Work of Pierre Bourdieu*. Chicago: University of Chicago Press, 1997.

Szasz, Thomas S. *The Manufacturer of Madness: A Comparative Study of the Inquisition and the Mental Health Movement*. New York: Dell, 1961.

——. *The Myth of Mental Illness: Foundations of a Theory of Personal Conduct*. New York: Harper & Row, 1970; orig. 1961.

——. 'Mental illness is still a myth'. *Society*, Vol. 31, No. 4 (May–June 1994): 34–9.

——. 'Idleness and lawlessness in the therapeutic state'. *Society*, Vol. 32, No. 4 (May/June 1995): 30–5.

T

Taeuber, Karl and Alma Taeuber. *Negroes in Cities*. Chicago: Aldine, 1965.

Tannen, Deborah. *You Just Don't Understand Me: Women and Men in Conversation*. New York: Wm. Morrow, 1990.

——. *Talking from 9 to 5: How Women's and Men's Conversational Styles Affect Who Gets Heard, Who Gets Credit and What Gets Done at Work*. New York: Wm. Morrow, 1994.

Tannenbaum, Frank. *Crime and the Community*. Boston, MA: Ginn & Co., 1938.

Taylor, Ian. *Crime in Context*. Cambridge: Polity Press, 1999.

Taylor, Ian, Paul Walton and Jock Young. *The New Criminology*. London: Routledge, 1973.

Tekçe, Belgin, Linda Oldham and Frederick Shorter. *A Place to Live: Families and Health Care in a Cairo Neighborhood*. Cairo: American University in Cairo, 1994.

Terkel, Studs. *Working*. New York: Pantheon Books, 1974 (UK edn, London: Peregrine, 1977).

Terry, Don. 'In crackdown on bias, a new tool'. *New York Times* (12 June 1993): 8.

Theen, Rolf H. W. 'Party and bureaucracy', in Erik P. Hoffmann and Robbin F. Laird (eds), *The Soviet Polity in the Modern Era*. New York: Aldine, 1984: 131–65.

Therborn, Goran. *European Modernity and Beyond: The Trajectory of European Societies 1945–2000*. London: Sage, 1995.

Thernstrom, Stephan. 'American apartheid? Don't believe it'. *Wall Street Journal* (2 March 1998): A-18.

Thomas, Janet. *The Battle in Seattle*. Colorado: Fulcrum Press, 2000.

Thomas, Piri. *Down These Mean Streets*. New York: Signet, 1967.

Thomas, T. *Sex Crime: Sex Offending and Society*. Cullompton, Devon: Willian Publishing, 2000.

Thomas, W. I. 'The relation of research to the social process', in Morris Janowitz (ed.), *W. I. Thomas on Social Organization and Social Personality*. Chicago: University of Chicago Press, 1966: 289–305; orig. 1931.

Thomas W.I. and D.S. Thomas. *The Child in America*. New York: Knopf, 1928.

Thomas, W. I. and Florian Znaniecki. *The Polish Peasant in Europe and America*. New York: Dover Publications, 1958; orig. 1918.

Thompson, E. P. *The Making of the English Working Class*. Harmondsworth: Penguin, 1963.

Thompson John. *The Media and Modernity: A Social Theory of Media*. Cambridge: Polity Press, 1995.

Thompson, Kenneth (ed.). *Readings from Emile Durkheim*. London: Routledge, 1985.

——. *Key Quotations in Sociology*. London: Routledge, 1996.

Thompson, Larry. 'The breast cancer gene: a woman's dilemma'. *Time*, Vol. 143, No. 3 (17 January 1994): 52.

Thompson, Paul, Catherine Ibsen and Michele Auerldstern. *I Don't Feel Old: The Experience of Later Life*. Oxford: Oxford University Press, 1990.

Thompson, Paul. *Voices of the Past: Oral History*. Oxford: Opus Books, Oxford University Press, 1974; 3rd edn 2000.

Thorne, Burrie and Z. Luria. 'Sexuality and gender in children's daily worlds'. *Social Problems*, Vol. 33, No. 3 (1985): 176–90.

Thornhill, R. and C. Palmer. *A Natural History of Rape: Biological Bases of Sexual Coercion*. Cambridge, MA: MIT Press, 2000.

Thornton, Sarah. *Club Cultures*. Cambridge: Polity Press, 1995.

Tierney, Patrick. *Darkness in El Dorado: How Scientists and Journalists Devastated the Amazon*. New York: W. W. Norton, 2000.

Tilly, Charles. *From Mobilization to Revolution*. Reading, MA: Addison-Wesley, 1978.

——. 'Does modernization breed revolution?', in Jack A. Goldstone (ed.), *Revolutions: Theoretical, Comparative, and Historical Studies*. New York: Harcourt Brace Jovanovich, 1986: 47–57.

Tocqueville, Alexis de. *The Old Regime and the French Revolution*. Stuart Gilbert, trans. Garden City, NY: Anchor/Doubleday Books, 1955; orig. 1856.

——. *Democracy in America*. Garden City, NY: Anchor/Doubleday, 1968; orig. 1834, 1840.

Toennies, Ferdinand. *Community and Society (Gemeinschaft und Gesellschaft)*. New York: Harper & Row, 1963; orig. 1887.

Tolson, A. *The Limits of Masculinity*. London: Tavistock, 1977.

Tolson, Jay. 'The trouble with elites'. *The Wilson Quarterly*, Vol. 19, No. 1 (Winter 1995): 6–8.

Tomlinson, Sally. *A Sociology of Special Education*. London: Routledge, 1982.

Tong, Rosemarie. *Feminist Thought: A More Comprehensive Introduction*. Boulder, CO: Westview Press, 1990.

Totten, Samuel *et al. Century of Genocide*. New York: Garland, 1997.

Towers, Heather. 'From AIDS to Alzheimer's: policy and politics in setting new health agendas', in Joe Bailey (ed.), *Social Europe*. London: Longman, 1992: 190–215.

Townsend, Peter. *The Family Life of Old People*. Harmondsworth: Penguin, 1957.

——. *Poverty in the UK*. Harmondsworth: Penguin, 1979.

——. *Poverty and Labour in London: Interim Report of a Centenary Survey*. London: Low Pay Unit, in conjunction with the Poverty Research (London) Trust, 1987.

Townsend, Peter and Nick Davidson (eds). *Inequalities in Health: The Black Report*. Harmondsworth: Penguin, 1982.

Toynbee, Polly. *Hard Work: Life in Low-Pay Britain*. London: Bloomsbury, 2003.

Treas, Judith. 'Socialist organization and economic development in China: latent consequences for the aged'. *The Gerontologist*, Vol. 19, No. 1 (February 1979): 34–43.

——. 'Older Americans in the 1990s and beyond'. *Population Bulletin*, Vol. 50, No. 2 (May 1995). Washington, DC: Population Reference Bureau.

Trebilcot, Joyce (ed.). *Mothering: Essays in Feminist Theory*. Totowa, NJ: Rowman & Allanheld, 1984.

Treiman, Donald J. 'Industrialization and social stratification', in Edward O. Laumann (ed.), *Social Stratification: Research and Theory for the 1970s*. Indianapolis, IN: Bobbs-Merrill, 1970.

Trenchard, I. and H. Warren. *Something To Tell You: The Experiences and Needs of Young Lesbians and Gay Men in London*. London: Gay Teenage Group, 1984.

Troeltsch, Ernst. *The Social Teaching of the Christian Churches*. New York: Macmillan, 1931.

Truth and Reconciliation Commission of South Africa, Report (5 vols) and CD-Rom. London: Palgrave, 2000.

Tudge, Colin. *The Day Before Yesterday: Five Million Years of Human History*. London: Cape, 1995.

Tudor-Hart, J. 'The inverse care law'. *The Lancet* (27 February 1971): 405–12.

Tumin, Melvin M. 'Some principles of stratification: a critical analysis'. *American Sociological Review*, Vol. 18, No. 4 (August 1953): 387–94.

——. *Social Stratification: The Forms and Functions of Inequality*, 2nd edn. Englewood Cliffs, NJ: Prentice-Hall, 1985.

Tunstall, Jeremy. *Old and Alone: A Sociological Study of Old People*. London: Routledge and Kegan Paul, 1966.

Turkle, Sherry. *Life on the Screen: Identity in the Age of the Internet*. London: Weidenfeld and Nicolson, 1996.

Turner, Brian. *The Body and Society*. Oxford: Blackwell, 1984.

——. *Medical Power and Social Knowledge*. London: Routledge, 1987; 2nd edn, 1996.

Turner, Bryan F. 'Outline of a theory of citizenship'. *Sociology*, Vol. 24, No. 2 (1990): 189–217.

Turner, Charles Hampden and Fons Trompenaars. *The Seven Cultures of Capitalism*. London: Piatkus, 1993.

Turner, G. *British Cultural Studies*. London: Unwin Hyman/Routledge, 1990.

Turner, Ian, Paul Walker and Jack Young. *The New Criminology*. London: Routledge, 1977.

Turner, Jonathan. *Herbert Spencer*. London: Sage, 1985.

Turnock, David (ed.). *East Central Europe and the Former Soviet Union*. London: Arnold, 2001.

Tyree, Andrea, Moshe Semyonov and Robert W. Hodge. 'Gaps and glissandos: inequality, economic development and social mobility in 24 countries'. *American Sociological Review*, Vol. 44, No. 3 (June 1979): 410–24.

U

UNAIDS. *The Impact of AIDS on People and Societies.* New York: UN Publications, 2004.

UNESCO. *Facts and Figures, 2000*. Montreal: Institute for Statistics, 2000. New York: UNESCO, 2000 (and on UNESCO Statistics website: www.unesco.org).

UNFPA (United Nations Population Fund). *Lives Together, Worlds Apart: Men and Women in a Time of Change. The State of the World Population*. New York: UNFPA, 2000 (and on UNFPA website: www.unfpa.org).

Ungerson, Clare. *Policy is Personal: Sex, Gender and Informal Care*. London: Tavistock, 1987.

UNHCR (United Nations High Commission for Refugees). *The State of the World's Refugees: Fifty Years of Humanitarian Action*. Oxford: Oxford University Press, 2000.

UNHDP (United Nations Human Development Programme). *Human Development Report*. New York: Oxford University Press, 1990.

——. *Human Development Report*. New York: Oxford University Press, 1995.

——. *Human Development Report*. New York: Oxford University Press, 1996.

——. *Human Development Report: Human Rights and Development*. New York: Oxford University Press, 2000.

——. *Human Development Report: Making Technologies Work for Human Development*. New York: Oxford University Press, 2001.

——. *Human Development Report. Millenium Development Goals: A Compact amoung Nations to End Poverty*. New York: Oxford University Press, 2003.

——. *Human Development Report: Cultural Liberty in Today's Diverse World*. New York: Oxford University Press, 2004.

UN House of Representatives. *Street Children: A Global Disgrace*. Washington DC: US Goverment Printing Office, 1992.

UNICEF. *The Progress of Nations*. New York: UNICEF, 1996.

——. *Early Marriages, Child Spouses*. New York: UNICEF, March 2001.

United Nations. World Urbanizing Prospects: The 1999 Revision. New York: United Nations, 1999.

——. *The World Population Prospects: The 2002 Revision*. New York: United Nations, 2002.

——. *Urban Agglomerations*. New York: United Nations, 2003a.

——. *World Urbanizing Prospects: The 2003 Revision*. New York: United Nations, 2003b.

—— *Africa's Orphaned Generation*, . New York: UNICEF, 2004a.

——*The Official Summary of the State of the World's Children*. New York: UNICEF, 2004b.

US Bureau of Justice. *Sourcebook of Criminal Justice Statistics 1990*. Timothy J. Flanagan and Kathleen Maguire, eds. Washington, DC: US Government Printing Office, 1991.

——. *Criminal Victimization*. Washington, DC: The Bureau of Justice, 1998.

US Bureau of the Census. Prepublication data on income and wealth provided by the Census Bureau. Washington, DC: Government Publications, 1999, 2001, 2002, 2003.

US Bureau of the Census. *Report on Marriage and Divorce*. Washington DC: US Government Printing Office, 2002.

US Federal Bureau of Investigation. *Crime in the United States, 1998*. Washington DC: The Bureau, 1999.

US Immigration and Naturalization Service. *Legal Immigration, Fiscal Year 2000*. Washington DC: US Immigration and Naturalization Service.

V

Van Biema, David. 'Parents who kill'. *Time*, Vol. 144, No. 20 (14 November 1994): 50–1.

Vance, Carole S. (ed.). *Pleasure and Danger*. London: Routledge, 1984.

Varawa, Joana McIntyre. *Changes in Latitude: An Uncommon Anthropology*. New York: Harper & Row, 1990.

Vattimo, Gianni. *The Transparent Society*. Cambridge: Polity Press, 1992.

Vaughan, Mary Kay. 'Multinational corporations: the world as a company town', in Ahmed Idris-Soven *et al.* (eds), *The World as a Company Town: Multinational Corporations and Social Change*. The Hague: Mouton, 1978: 15–35.

Vayda, Eugene and Raisa B. Deber. 'The Canadian health care system: an overview'. *Social Science and Medicine*, Vol. 18, No. 3 (1984): 191–7.

Veblen, Thorstein. *The Theory of the Leisure Class*. New York: The New American Library, 1953; orig. 1899.

Veum, Jonathan R. 'Accounting for income mobility changes in the United States'. *Social Science Quarterly*, Vol. 73, No. 4 (December 1992): 773–85.

Viguerie, Richard A. *The New Right: We're Ready to Lead*. Falls Church, VA: The Viguerie Company, 1981.

Vincent, John A. *Inequality and Old Age*. London: UCL Press, 1996.

Vines, Gail. 'Whose baby is it anyway?' *New Scientist*, No. 1515 (3 July 1986): 26–7.

Vogel, Ezra F. *The Four Little Dragons: The Spread of Industrialization in East Asia*. Cambridge, MA: Harvard University Press, 1991.

Vogel, Lise. *Marxism and the Oppression of Women: Toward a Unitary Theory*. New Brunswick, NJ: Rutgers University Press, 1983.

Vold, George B. and Thomas J. Bernard. *Theoretical Criminology*, 3rd edn. New York: Oxford University Press, 1986.

von Hirsch, Andrew. *Past or Future Crimes: Deservedness and Dangerousness in the Sentencing of Criminals*. New Brunswick, NJ: Rutgers University Press, 1976.

Vonnegut, Kurt, Jr. 'Harrison Bergeron', in *Welcome to the Monkey House*. New York: Delacorte Press/Seymour Lawrence, 1968: 7–13; orig. 1961.

W

Wadsworth, M.E.J. *The Imprint of Time: Childhood History, and Adult Life*. Oxford: Clarendon Press, 1991.

Walby, Sylvia. *Theorizing Patriarchy*. Cambridge: Polity Press, 1990.

Walker, Alan and Tony Maltby. *Ageing Europe*. Buckingham: Open University Press, 1997.

Walker, Alan and Carol Walker (eds). *Britain Divided*. London: Child Poverty Action Group, 1997.

Walkerdine, Valerie, H. Lucey and J. Melody. *Growing Up Girl: Psychosocial Explorations of Gender and Class*. Basingstoke: Palgrave, 2001.

Walkgate, Sandra. *Gender and Crime: An Introduction*. Cullompton, Devon, Willian Publishing.

Wallerstein, Immanuel. *The Modern World-System: Capitalist Agriculture and the Origins of the European World-Economy in the Sixteenth Century*. New York: Academic Press, 1974.

——. *The Capitalist World-Economy*. New York: Cambridge University Press, 1979.

——. 'Crises: the world economy, the movements and the ideologies', in Albert Bergesen (ed.), *Crises in the World-System*. Beverly Hills, CA: Sage, 1983: 21–36.

——. *The Politics of the World Economy: The States, the Movements and the Civilizations*. Cambridge: Cambridge University Press, 1984.

Wallis, Roy. *The Road to Total Freedom: A Sociological Analysis of Scientology*. London: Heinemann, 1976.

Walmsley, Roy. *World Prison Population List: Findings*, No. 188. London: Home Office, 2003.

Walsh, John P. *Supermarkets Transformed: Understanding Organisational and Technological Innovations*. New Brunswick, NJ: Rutgers University Press, 1993.

Walter, Tony *'The Revival of Death'*. London and New York: Routledge, 1994.

——. *On Bereavement: The Culture of Grief*. Buckingham and Philadelphia, PA: Open University Press, 1998.

Walters, Laurel Shaper. 'World educators compare notes'. *The Christian Science Monitor: Global Report* (7 September 1994): 8.

Walton, John and Charles Ragin. 'Global and national sources of political protest: Third World responses to the debt crisis'. *American Sociological Review*, Vol. 55, No. 6 (December 1990): 876–90.

Warner, R. Stephen. 'Work in progress toward a new paradigm for the sociological study of religion in the United States'. *American Journal of Sociology*, Vol. 98, No. 5 (March 1993): 1044–93.

Warner, W. Lloyd and J. O. Low. *The Social System of the Modern Factory*. Yankee City Series, Vol. 4. New Haven, CT: Yale University Press, 1947.

Warner, W. Lloyd and Paul S. Lunt. *The Social Life of a Modern Community*. New Haven, CT: Yale University Press, 1941.

Warnock Committee. *Report of the Committee of Inquiry into Human Fertilisation and Embryology*. CM9314. London: HMSO, 1984.

Waters, Malcolm. 'Inequality after class', in David Owen (ed.), *Sociology after Postmodernism*. London: Sage, 1997.

Waters, Malcolm. *Globalization*. London: Routledge, 2000.

Watson, James and Anne Hill. *Dictionary of Media and Communication Studies*, 5th edn. London: Arnold, 2000.

Watson, John B. *Behaviorism*, rev. edn. New York: W. W. Norton, 1930.

Waxman, Chaim I. *The Stigma of Poverty: A Critique of Poverty Theories and Policies*, 2nd edn. New York: Pergamon Press, 1983.

Weber, Adna Ferrin. *The Growth of Cities*. New York: Columbia University Press, 1963; orig, 1899.

Weber, Max. *Max Weber on the Methodology of the Social Sciences*. E.A. Shils and H.A. Finch, trans. and eds. Glencoe, IL: Free Press, 1949.

——. *The Protestant Ethic and the Spirit of Capitalism*. New York: Charles Scribner's Sons, 1958; orig. 1905.

——. *Economy and Society*. G. Roth and C. Wittich, eds. Berkeley, CA: University of California Press, 1978; orig. 1921.

Webster, Andrew. *Science, Technology and Society*. Basingstoke: Macmillan, 1991.

Webster, Frank. 'Higher education', in Gary Browning, Abigail Halci and Frank Webster (eds), *Understanding Contemporary Society: Theories of the Present*. London: Sage, 2000: Chapter 22.

Webster, Pamela S., Terri Orbuch and James S. House. 'Effects of childhood family background on adult marital quality and perceived stability'. *American Journal of Sociology*, Vol. 101, No. 2 (September 1995): 404–32.

Weeks, J. *Coming Out: Homosexual Politics in Britain from the Nineteenth Century to the Present*. London: Quartet, 1977.

——. *Sexuality*. London: Routledge, 1986.

Weeks, J., Brian Heaphy and Catherine Donovan. *Same Sex Intimacies: Families of Choice and Other Life Experiments*. London: Routledge, 2001.

Weeks, Jeffrey. *Against Nature: Essays on History, Sexuality and Identity*. London: Rivers Oram Press, 1991.

Weeks, John R. *Population*, 6th edn. Belmont, CA: Wadsworth, 1996.

Weidenbaum, Murray. 'The evolving corporate board'. *Society*, Vol. 32, No. 3 (March–April 1995): 9–20.

Weinberg, George. *Society and the Healthy Homosexual*. New York: Doubleday, 1973.

Weine, Stevan M. *When History is a Nightmare: Lives and Memories of Ethnic Cleansing in Bosnia-Herzegovina*. New Brunswick, NJ: Rutgers University Press, 1999.

Weiner, Gaby and Madeleine Arnot. *Gender and the Politics of Schooling*. London: Hutchinson, 1997.

Weller, Paul. *Religions in the UK: Directory 2001–03*, 3rd edn. Derby: University of Derby, 2003.

Wellings, Kaye *et al. Sexual Behaviour in Britain: The National Survey of Sexual Attitudes and Lifestyles*. Harmondsworth: Penguin, 1994.

Wellman, Barry. 'The community question: intimate networks of East Yorkers'. *American Journal of Sociology*, Vol. 84, No. 5 (March 1979): 1201–31.

——. (ed.). *Networks in the Global Village*. Boulder, CO: Westview Press, 1999.

Wells, Liz (ed). *Photography: A Critical Introduction*. London: Routledge, 2nd edn, 2003.

Wenke, Robert J. *Patterns of Prehistory*. New York: Oxford University Press, 1980.

Wesolowski, Wlodzimierz. 'Transition from authoritarianism to democracy'. *Social Research*, Vol. 57, No. 2 (Summer 1990): 435–61.

West, Candace and Don Zimmerman. 'Doing gender'. *Gender and Society*, Vol. 1, No. 1 (1987): 125–51.

Western, Bruce. 'Postwar unionization in eighteen advanced capitalist countries'. *American Sociological Review*, Vol. 58, No. 2 (April 1993): 266–82.

——. 'A comparative study of working-class disorganization: union decline in eighteen advanced capitalist countries'. *American Sociological Review*, Vol. 60, No. 2 (April 1995): 179–201.

Weston, Kath. *Families We Choose: Lesbians, Gays, Kinship*. New York: Columbia University Press, 1991.

Westwood, Sallie and Parminder Bhachu (eds). *Enterprising Women: Ethnicity, Economy, and Gender Relations*. London: Routledge, 1988.

Wheelis, Allen. *The Quest for Identity*. New York: W. W. Norton, 1958.

White, Merry. *The Material Child: Coming of Age in Japan and America*. New York: Free Press, 1993.

Whittaker, James K. *Caring for Troubled Children: Residential Treatment in a Community*. New York: Aldine de Gruyter, 1997.

Whorf, Benjamin Lee. *Language, Thought and Reality*. Cambridge, MA: MIT Press, 1956; orig. 1941.

Whyte, William H., Jr. *The Organization Man*. Garden City, NY: Anchor Books, 1957.

Wiarda, Howard J. 'Ethnocentrism and Third World development'. *Society*, Vol. 24, No. 6 (September–October 1987): 55–64.

Wichterich, Christa. *The Globalized Woman*. London: Zed Books, 2000.

Wieten, Jan, Graham Murdock and Peter Dahlgren (eds). *Television across Europe*. London: Sage, 2000.

Wiles, P. *Economic Institutions Compared*. New York: Halstead Press, 1977.

Willetts, Peter. 'Transnational actors and international organizations in global politics', in John Baylis and Steve Smith (eds), *The Globalization of World Politics*. Oxford: Oxford University Press, 1997; 2nd edn, 2001.

Williams, Raymond. *Culture and Society: Coleridge to Orwell*. London: Hogarth Press, 1987; orig. 1958.

Williams, Robin M., Jr. *American Society: A Sociological Interpretation*, 3rd edn. New York: Alfred A. Knopf, 1970.

Williams, Simon. *Emotion and Social Theory*. London: Sage, 2001.

Williamson, Jeffrey G. and Peter H. Lindert. *American Inequality: A Macroeconomic History*. New York: Academic Press, 1980.

Willis, Paul. *Learning to Labour*. Farnborough: Saxon House, 1977.

Wilson, Bryan. *Religion in Sociological Perspective*. New York: Oxford University Press, 1982.

Wilson, Edward O. *Sociobiology: The New Synthesis*. Cambridge, MA: Belknap Press of the Harvard University Press, 1975.

——. *On Human Nature*. New York: Bantam Books, 1978.

Wilson, James Q. *Bureaucracy: What Government Agencies Do and Why They Do It*. New York: Basic Books, 1991.

Wilson, James Q. and Richard J. Herrnstein. *Crime and Human Nature*. New York: Simon & Schuster, 1985.

Wilson, Logan. *American Academics Then and Now*. New York: Oxford University Press, 1979.

Wilson, Thomas C. 'Urbanism and tolerance: a test of some hypotheses drawn from Wirth and Stouffer'. *American Sociological Review*, Vol. 50, No. 1 (February 1985): 117–23.

——. 'Urbanism and unconventionality: the case of sexual behavior'. *Social Science Quarterly*, Vol. 76, No. 2 (June 1995): 346–63.

Winkler, Karen J. 'Scholar whose ideas of female psychology stir debate modifies theories, extends studies to young girls'. *Chronicle of Higher Education*, Vol. 36, No. 36 (23 May 1990): A6–A8.

Winn, Marie. *Children without Childhood*. New York: Pantheon Books, 1983.

Wintle, Michael (ed.). *Culture and Identity in Europe*. London: Avebury, 1996.

Wirth, Louis. 'Urbanism as a way of life'. *American Journal of Sociology*, Vol. 44, No. 1 (July 1938): 1–24.

Witte, Rob. *Racist Violence and the State: A Comparative Analysis of Britain, France and the Netherlands*. Harlow: Longman, 1996.

Wolcott, Harry F. *Sneaky Kid and Its Aftermath: Ethics and Intimacy in Fieldwork*. London: Alta Vira Press, 2002.

Wolfe, David B. 'Targeting the mature mind'. *American Demographics*, Vol. 16, No. 3 (March 1994): 32–6.

Wollstonecraft, Mary. *A Vindication of the Rights of Woman*. and so on: Everyman's Library, 1992; orig. 1792.

Wood, Julian. 'Groping towards sexism: boys' sex talk', in A.

McRobbie and M. Nava (eds), *Gender and Generation*. London: Macmillan, 1984.

Woodward, Kenneth L. 'Feminism and the churches'. *Newsweek*, Vol. 13, No. 7 (13 February 1989): 58–61.

Woody, Bette. *Black Women in the Workplace: Impacts of Structural Change in the Economy*. Westport, CT: Greenwood Press, 1992.

Woofitt, Robin and Ian Hutchby. *Conversational Analysis: Principles, Practices and Applications*. Cambridge: Polity Press, 1998.

Wooley, Orland W., Susan C. Wooley and Sue R. Dyrenforth. 'Obesity and women – II: A neglected feminist topic'. *Women's Studies International Quarterly*, Vol. 2 (1979): 81–92.

World Bank. *World Tables 1991*. Baltimore, MD: Johns Hopkins University Press, 1991.

——. *World Development Report 1993*. New York: Oxford University Press, 1993.

——. *Averting the Old Age Crisis: Policies to Protect the Old and Promote Growth*. Oxford: Oxford University Press, 1994.

——. *World Development Report 1995: Workers in an Integrating World*. New York: Oxford University Press, 1995.

——. *World Development Report 1997: Workers in an Integrating World*. New York: Oxford University Press, 1997.

——. *World Development Report 2000: Entering the Twenty-first Century:* New York: Oxford University Press, 2000.

——. *World Development Report 2000/1: Attacking Poverty*. Washington DC: The World Bank, 2001.

——. *World Development Indicators 2003*. Washington DC: The World Bank, 2003.

——. *World Development Report 2003*. Washington DC: The World Bank, 2003.

——. *World Development Report 2004*. Washington DC: The World Bank, 2004.

World Health Organisation. *Constitution of the World Health Organisation*. New York: World Health Organization Interim Commission, 1946.

World Health Report 2000. Health Systems: Improving Performance. New York, NY: WHO, 2000.

——. *Reducing Risks – Promoting Healthy Life*. New York: World Health Organisation, 2002.

——. *Shaping the Future*. New York: World Health Organisation, 2003.

——.*Controlling the Global Obesity Epidemic*. Nutrition reports. http//www.who/int/not/obs.htm, 2004.

World Resources Institute. *World Resources 1996–97*. Oxford: Oxford University Press, 1996.

World Resources Institute. *World Resources 2000–1*. Oxford: Elsevier, 2001.

World Resources Institute. *World Resources 2002-4*. Oxford: Elsevier, 2004.

World Values Survey, 1990–1993. Ann Arbor, MI: Inter-University Consortium for Political and Social Research, 1994.

Worsley, Peter. 'Models of the system', in Mike Featherstone (ed.), *Global Culture: Nationalism, Globalization, and Modernity*. Newbury Park, CA: Sage, 1990.

Wren, Christopher S. 'In Soweto-by-the-Sea, misery lives on as apartheid fades'. *New York Times* (9 June 1991): 1, 7.

Wright, Charles R. *Mass Communications*. New York: Random House, 1967.

Wright, Erik Olin. *Classes*. London: Verso, 1985.

Wright, Erik Olin, Andrew Levine and Elliott Sober. *Reconstructing Marxism: Essays on Explanation and the Theory of History*. London: Verso, 1992.

Wright, Erik Olin and Bill Martin. 'The transformation of the American class structure, 1960–1980'. *American Journal of Sociology*, Vol. 93, No. 1 (July 1987): 1–29.

Wright, Quincy. 'Causes of war in the atomic age', in William M. Evan and Stephen Hilgartner (eds), *The Arms Race and Nuclear War*. Englewood Cliffs, NJ: Prentice-Hall, 1987: 7–10.

Wright, Richard A. *In Defense of Prisons*. Westport, CT: Greenwood Press, 1994.

Y

Yates, John. 'Drug control in Sweden' *NACRO Bulletin*, No. 26 (1996).

Yates, Ronald E. 'Growing old in Japan: they ask gods for a way out'. *Philadelphia Inquirer* (14 August 1986): 3A.

Yeatts, Dale E. 'Self-managed work teams: innovation in progress'. *Business and Economic Quarterly* (Fall–Winter 1991): 2–6.

——. 'Creating the high performance self-managed work team: a review of theoretical perspectives'. Paper presented at the annual meeting of the Social Science Association, Dallas, TX, February 1995.

Yoder, Jan D. and Robert C. Nichols. 'A life perspective: comparison of married and divorced persons'. *Journal of Marriage and the Family*, Vol. 42, No. 2 (May 1980): 413–19.

York, Michael. *The Emerging Network: A Sociology of the New Age and Neo-Pagan Movements*. London: Rowman and Littlefield, 1995.

Yoshizumi, Kyoko. 'Marriage and family: past and present', in Kumiko Fojimura-Famslow and Atsuko Kameda (eds), *Japanese Women: New Feminist Perspectives of the Past,*

Present and Future. New York: The Feminist Press at the City University of New York, 1995.

Young, Gerald. *Adult Development, Therapy, and Culture: A Postmodern Synthesis*. New York and London: Plenum Press, 1997.

Young, Iris Marion. *Justice and the Politics of Difference*. Princeton, NJ: Princeton University Press, 1990.

Young, Jock. *The Exclusive Society*. London: Sage, 2000.

Young, Jock and John Lea. *What Is to be Done about Law and Order?* Harmondsworth: Penguin, 1984.

Young, Michael and Peter Willmott. *Family and Kinship in East London*. Basingstoke: Penguin, 1957.

——. *The Symmetrical Family*. London: Routledge and Kegan Paul, 1973.

Yuan, Gao. *Born Red: A Chronicle of the Cultural Revolution*. Stanford, CA: Stanford University Press, 1987.

Yunker, James A. *Socialism Revised and Modernized: The Case for Pragmatic Market Socialism*. New York: Praeger, 1992.

Z

Zangwill, Israel. *The Melting Pot*. New York: Macmillan, 1921; orig. 1909 (also London: William Heinemann, 1919 and Ayer Company Publishers (USA), 1994).

Zaslavsky, Victor. *The Neo-Stalinist State: Class, Ethnicity and Consensus in Soviet Society*. Armonk, NY: M. E. Sharpe, 1982.

Zeitlin, Irving M. *The Social Condition of Humanity*. New York: Oxford University Press, 1981.

Zellner, William W. *Counter Cultures: A Sociological Analysis*. New York: St Martin's Press, 1994.

Zuboff, Shoshana. 'New worlds of computer-mediated work'. *Harvard Business Review*, Vol. 60, No. 5 (September–October 1982): 142–52.

NAME INDEX

M

SUBJECT INDEX

EUROPE

Europe is the second smallest continent occupying only about 8% of the earth's surface. It has the world's slowest growing populations. The major 'forces' at work in Europe at present are the drives towards Europeanisation through the European Union and the maintenance of a more stable Eastern block in the Post Communist Societies. Europe is often divided into Eastern, Southern, Northern and the the Scandinavian countries.
The Scandinavian countries are amongst the economically most prosperous on earth; the Eastern are amongst some of the poorest.

THE PACIFIC RIM

It may be that for the last five hundred years, the centre of ecomomic, military and political world has been in the North Atlantic, between Europe and the Eastern parts of the USA. But at the start of the twenty first century, major changes are in the making notably around what has be called the 'Pacific Rim'. Japan, the west coast of the USA (California, Seattle etc.), a range of societies linked to ASEAN; and now the growing strength of China.

NORTH AMERICA

ATLANTIC
OCEAN

SOUTH AMERICA

THE AMERICAS

The Americas dominate the western hemisphere extending from the Antarctic to the Arctic and contain the continents of North, South and Central America. It houses some 36 nations and over 500 million people.

LATIN AMERICA

Latin America is the fourth largest of the continents (twice as large as Europe and 13% of the world's land surface, but sparsely populated. It is heavily colonised by Spanish and Portuguese. It houses some of the major cities: Rio de Janeiro, Sao Paulo and Mexico. It also houses various regional groups and there are major political conflicts with some governments being accused of corruption and many civil wars.

POST COMMUNIST/TRANSITIONAL SOCIETIES

The end of the 'cold war' and the break up of the old Soviet Union in the early 1990s led to a proliferation of smaller states in Eastern Europe which are undergoing great economic, political and social difficulties. It has fast become an area of major internal war and conflict, as well as growing crime rates and economic inequalities.

CHINA

China is the largest country in the world with the largest population, the most spoken language (Mandarin) and the seventh major world economy. After centuries of dynastic rule, it became Communist in the early 1950s; today it still retains the authoritarian style of the former second world, being accused of regular, widespread violations of human rights. Partly through its 'one child policy', its GDP is one of the fastest growing of all countries. It is likely to play a major role in the twenty first century. Symbolically, it will host the Olympic Games in 2008.

RUSSIA

P E

CHINA

PACIFIC OCEAN

ARABIA

INDIA

C A

INDONESIA

ASIA

Asia is the largest of the continents, a third of the land surface of the world. Lying in the Eastern hemisphere, it stretches from the Arctic circle to the 10 degrees south of the equator. It has many distinctive regions - even subcontinents. Japan is the most Westernised, with Tokyo being the world's largest city and agglomeration. Two countries, China and India, cover the largest land mass, and have the largest world populations. They have hugely different societies.

INDIA

India was colonized in the nineteenth century by the English, is largely Hindu and rests substantially on a (now outlawed) caste system.

OCEANIA

This is the most sparsely populated region of roughly 30 million including Australia and New Zealand.

AUSTRALIA

LEAGUE OF ARAB STATES

Member states are Egypt, Iraq, Jordan, Lebanon, Saudi Arabia, Syria, N. Yemen, Algeria, Bahrain, Djibouti, Kuwait, Libya, Mauritius, Morocco, Oman, Qatar, Somalia, Tunisia, United Arab Emirates and S. Yemen.

AFRICA

Africa is the second largest of the continents (three times the area of Europe). It falls geographically into strikingly different regions - the Northern Saharan region, the Sub-Saharan regions, as well as the South, East and West. SUB-SAHARAN AFRICA shows very little fertility decline and is the world's hardest hit region for AIDS. There are well over 25 million people living with HIV/AIDS in sub Saharan Africa. It has the lowest levels of life expectancy - 43 for women and 40 for men in Sierra Leone (the poorest country in the world). Sociologist Manuel Castells, speaks of the 'dehumanisation' of Africa. He writes of: 'the collapse of Africa's economics, the disintegration of many of its states, and the breakdown of most of its societies. As a result, famines, epidemics, violence, civil wars, massacres, mass exodus, and social and political chaos are salient features of the land that natured the birth of Lucy, perhaps the shared grandmother of humankind' (Castells, 1996: 83). It is the worst hit of all the continents in terms of accessing the information age. In a striking phrase, he refers to 'vampire states' - many states are entirely patrimonalised by political elites for their own personal profit

SOUTH EAST ASIA

This area has its own economic centre ASEAN (Association of South East Asian Nations) since 1967 and is composed of Indonesia, Malaysia, the Philippines, Singapore, Thailand (and since 1984 Brunei) but since 1992 this has also become part of the Asia-Pacific Economic Co-operation - which includes Australia and New Zealand (APEC).

THE ASIAN TIGERS

Some countries in South East Asia have developed rapidly in recent years, despite occasional setbacks.